Construction Law

SECOND EDITION

Carol J. Patterson, Ross J. Altman,
Stephen A. Hess, and Allen Overcash
Editors

AMERICAN**BAR**ASSOCIATION
Forum on Construction Law

Cover design by ABA Design

The materials contained herein represent the opinions of the authors and/or the editors, and should not be construed to be the views or opinions of the law firms or companies with whom such persons are in partnership with, associated with, or employed by, nor of the American Bar Association or the Forum on Construction Law unless adopted pursuant to the bylaws of the Association.

Nothing contained in this book is to be considered as the rendering of legal advice for specific cases, and readers are responsible for obtaining such advice from their own legal counsel. This book is intended for educational and informational purposes only.

© 2019 American Bar Association. All rights reserved.

No part of this publication may be reproduced, stored in a retrieval system, or transmitted in any form or by any means, electronic, mechanical, photocopying, recording, or otherwise, without the prior written permission of the publisher. For permission contact the ABA Copyrights & Contracts Department, copyright@americanbar.org, or complete the online form at http://www.americanbar.org/utility/reprint.html.

Printed in the United States of America.
23 22 21 20   5 4 3 2

Library of Congress Cataloging-in-Publication Data
Names: Patterson, Carol J., editor. | Altman, Ross J., 1956- editor. | Hess, Stephen A., editor. | Overcash, Allen L., editor. | American Bar Association. Forum on Construction Law, sponsoring body.
Title: Construction law / Carol J. Patterson, Ross J. Altman, Stephen A. Hess, Allen Overcash.
Description: Second edition. | Chicago : American Bar Association, [2019] | Includes bibliographical references and index. | Summary: "The first edition of this book was published ten years ago to create a useful resource for the construction industry by assisting professors in familiarizing students with the principles of construction law. As the editors started work on the second edition, we wanted not only to update the book, but to improve it as well. While the overall organization of the book remains the same, we made some changes that should make the book easier to use. As was the case in the first edition of this book, many of the discussions in the text and the questions at the end of each chapter focus on typical small commercial construction projects and the American Institute of Architects forms of agreement that are widely used on such projects. This is consistent with our intent to familiarize readers with a wide range of issues that arise on most construction projects"—Provided by publisher.
Identifiers: LCCN 2019028435 (print) | LCCN 2019028436 (ebook) | ISBN 9781641054645 (paperback) | ISBN 9781641054652 (epub)
Subjects: LCSH: Construction industry—Law and legislation—United States. | Construction contracts—United States.
Classification: LCC KF1950 .C658 2019 (print) | LCC KF1950 (ebook) | DDC 343.7307/8624—dc23
LC record available at https://lccn.loc.gov/2019028435
LC ebook record available at https://lccn.loc.gov/2019028436

Discounts are available for books ordered in bulk. Special consideration is given to state bars, CLE programs, and other bar-related organizations. Inquire at Book Publishing, ABA Publishing, American Bar Association, 321 N. Clark Street, Chicago, Illinois 60654-7598.

www.ShopABA.org

Contents

About the Editors xxi
About the Authors xxiii
Preface xxix
Acknowledgments xxxi

1 Construction Law: The Historical Perspective   1

1.01 Introduction   1
     A. Construction in the Ancient World   1
     B. Construction's 19th-Century Transformational Events   4
1.02 Construction Dispute Resolution   11
1.03 Construction Law Scholarship   15

2 Participants in the Design and Construction Process   17

2.01 Overview   17
2.02 The Owner   18
2.03 The Design Team   20
     A. The Architect   20
     B. The Engineers and Consultants   21
2.04 The Construction Team   22
     A. The Contractor   22
     B. The Subcontractors   24
2.05 The Typical Supporting Cast   25
     A. Construction Lenders   25
     B. Insurance Companies   27
     C. Sureties   28
     D. Title Insurance   29

	E.	Public Authorities	29
	F.	Others	29
2.06		Assembling the Project Team	30
	A.	Transaction Structure	30
	B.	Why It Matters	32

3 The Owner's Role — 35

3.01		Overview	35
3.02		Providing the Building Site	36
	A.	Access to the Construction Site and Necessary Adjacencies	36
	B.	The Right to Use the Project Site for Its Intended Purpose	38
	C.	Title	38
	D.	Zoning	39
	E.	Availability of Utilities	40
	F.	Archaeological and Historic Sites	41
	G.	Environmental Concerns	42
3.03		Providing Information to the Architect and Contractor	44
	A.	Surveys	44
	B.	Geotechnical Information	44
3.04		The Owner's Implied Warranty to Supply Accurate Information	45
	A.	The *Spearin* Doctrine	45
	B.	Limitations on the Application of *Spearin*	47
		1. Limitations on the *Spearin* Doctrine	49
		2. The *Spearin* Warranty Can Be Disclaimed	51
3.05		The Owner's Program	52
	A.	The Program	52
	B.	The Project Budget and Schedule	53
	C.	Types of Specifications	54
		1. Design Specifications	55
		2. Reference Standard Specifications	55
		3. Performance Specifications	56
		4. Proprietary Specifications	57
3.06		Paying for Construction	57
	A.	Financing the Project	57
	B.	Evidence of Financing	59

4 Project Delivery Systems — 63

- 4.01 Overview — 63
- 4.02 Evolution of Methodologies — 64
- 4.03 Commercial Importance of Project Delivery Systems — 67
- 4.04 Selecting a Project Delivery System — 69
- 4.05 Design-Bid-Build — 70
  - A. Selection Factors — 72
  - B. Risk Factors — 73
  - C. Common Variations — 76
- 4.06 Construction Management — 77
  - A. Agency Construction Management — 78
    1. Selection Factors — 79
    2. Risk Factors — 80
  - B. At-Risk Construction Management — 81
    1. Selection Factors — 81
    2. Risk Factors — 83
- 4.07 Design-Build — 85
  - A. Selection Factors — 86
  - B. Risk Factors — 87
  - C. Common Variations — 90
- 4.08 Innovative Approaches — 91
  - A. Public-Private Partnerships — 92
    1. Selection Factors — 95
    2. Risk Factors — 95
    3. Common Variations — 96
  - B. Integrated Project Delivery — 96
    1. Selection Factors — 97
    2. Risk Factors — 98
    3. Common Variations — 99
  - C. Other Approaches — 99
- 4.09 Methods of Project Delivery System Selection — 100
- 4.10 Selection Constraints — 101
  - A. Method of Construction Procurement — 101
  - B. Compensation Mechanisms — 101
  - C. Owner Capability — 102
  - D. Industry Sector Custom — 103
- 4.11 Legal Importance of Project Delivery Systems — 104
- 4.12 Conclusion — 105

5 Contracting for Construction Projects — 107

- 5.01 Contract Formation — 107
  - A. For Purpose of Design Agreements and Construction Contracts — 107
  - B. Contract Formation Generally — 108
  - C. Commencement of Services or Work Prior to Contract — 109
  - D. Creation of Contracts—Implied Contracts and Quasi-Contracts — 110
- 5.02 How to Select a Contract Form — 112
  - A. Fundamental Issues — 112
  - B. Standard Industry Forms — 112
  - C. Advantages and Disadvantages of Using a Manuscript Document — 113
- 5.03 Overview of Standard Industry Forms — 114
  - A. AIA Documents — 114
  - B. AGC Forms — 118
  - C. EJCDC Forms — 119
  - D. Other Standard Industry Forms — 119
- 5.04 What Is the Contract? — 120
  - A. The Design Agreement (Owner–Architect) — 120
  - B. The Contract Documents (Owner–Contractor) — 120
  - C. The Integration Clause — 121
  - D. Incorporation by Reference versus Enumeration of Documents — 122
- 5.05 Internal Conflicts — 122
- 5.06 Contract Interpretation — 124
  - A. Rules of Contract Construction — 124
  - B. Parol Evidence Rule — 125
  - C. Ambiguity and Intent of Parties — 127
  - D. Reasonable and Logical Interpretation of Entire Contract — 128
  - E. Interpretation against Drafter — 129
  - F. Course of Performance and Prior Dealings — 131
  - G. Custom and Usage — 132
  - H. Terms: Specific over General; Written over Printed — 133
- 5.07 Parties to the Construction Contract — 134
  - A. Owner and Contractor — 134
  - B. Third-Party Beneficiaries — 134
  - C. Collateral Assignment to Lender — 135
  - D. References to Other Parties — 135
- 5.08 Scope of Contract — 136
  - A. Description of Services of Design Professionals — 136

		B.	Description of the Work under a Construction Contract	136
		C.	Owner-Furnished Items	139
		D.	Construction by Owner or by Separate Contractors	140

6 The Design Team's Role and Contracts — 143

6.01 Introduction — 143
  A. Overview of the Contractual Relationship among Parties and General Allocation of Design Function — 144
  B. The Role of the Owner and Owner's Consultants with Respect to Design — 145
  C. The Design Professional Team — 145
   1. Architectural Consultants — 146
   2. Engineering Consultants — 146
   3. The Civil Construction Project (Engineer as Lead Design Professional) — 146

6.02 Statutory Regulation and Licensure of Design Professionals — 147

6.03 Building Codes and the Design Professional — 151
  A. Traditional Building Codes — 154
  B. Socioeconomic "Codes" — 154
   1. Accessibility under ADA — 155
   2. Green Codes — 156
   3. Historic and Landmark Preservation — 158

6.04 Standard of Care Applicable to Design Services — 159
  A. Nature of Standard of Care and Inapplicability of Strict Liability — 159
  B. Common Law Standard of Care — 160
   1. General Statement of Standard of Care — 160
   2. Proof of the Standard of Care and Violation Thereof — 161
   3. Variations from Code and Consequences for Design Professionals — 163
  C. Contractual Standard of Care — 164
  D. Implied Warranties and Design Professionals — 165
   1. Implied Warranties Generally in Construction — 165
   2. Different Treatment of Design Professionals and Implied Warranties — 165

6.05 Performance Specifications versus Design Specifications — 166

6.06 The Design Agreement: Scope of the Design Services — 168
  A. Phases of the Design Process — 169

		1. Schematic Design Phase	170
		2. Design Development Phase	171
		3. Construction Documents Phase	172
		4. Bidding or Negotiation Phase Services	172
		5. Construction Phase Services	173
	B.	Basic Services versus Supplemental or Additional Services	173
6.07	The Design Agreement: The Owner's Responsibilities		174
6.08	The Design Agreement: Ownership of the Design Documents		175
	A.	Applicable Legal Principles	175
	B.	Contractual Provisions	180
6.09	The Design Agreement: The Designer's Obligation to Design to a Budget		181
6.10	The Design Agreement: Other Terms and Conditions		185
	A.	Payment	185
	B.	Insurance	186
	C.	Contractual Limitations of Liability	186
		1. Disclaimers and Exculpatory Provisions	186
		2. Waivers of Consequential Damages and Contractual Limitations of Liability	189
	D.	Termination	193

7 Architect's Contract Administration 197

7.01	Introduction		197
7.02	Nature and Scope of Architect's Role in Contract Administration		198
	A.	Overview of Contract Administration	198
	B.	Overview of Agency Law Principles Relevant to Contract Administration	200
		1. Architect's Authority to Bind the Owner	200
		2. Owner's Liability for the Architect's Acts	201
		3. Architect's Liability for Exceeding Authority or for the Improper Exercise of Authority	201
7.03	Requests for Information, Interpretations, and Clarifications		202
7.04	Quality Control		203
	A.	Review and Approval Procedures	203
	B.	Approving or Objecting to Subcontractors, Manufacturers, and Suppliers	204
	C.	Substitutions, Shop Drawings, and Other Submittals	204

		D.	Decisions on Aesthetic Effect	209
		E.	Site Visits and Inspections	209
	7.05		Coordination	214
	7.06		Approval of Progress Payments	215
	7.07		The Right to Reject Work or to Stop Work	216
	7.08		Issuing Change Orders and Responding to Proposals and Change Order Requests	216
	7.09		Certification of Substantial Completion, Final Completion, and Other Performance	217
	7.10		Architect's Role in Claims Process	218
		A.	Resolving Claims and Disputes	218
		B.	Architect's Role in Contractor Termination	219
	7.11		Architect's Immunity for Performing Quasi-Judicial Functions	221
	7.12		Emerging Contract Administrative Roles	222

8 Contractor Selection 225

	8.01	Introduction	225
	8.02	Private Procurement Generally	226
	8.03	Public Procurement	227
		A. General Considerations	227
		B. Selection of Design Professionals	228
		C. Selection of Contractors	231
		1. Traditional Methodology for Selection of Contractors	231
		2. Contractor Selection Criteria	236

9 Pricing Construction Contracts 255

	9.01	Introduction	255
	9.02	General Pricing Mechanisms for Construction Contracts	256
		A. Stipulated-Sum Contracts	256
		1. Scope Limitations within Contract Price	257
		2. Percentage of Completion Payments and Potential Abuse	259
		B. Cost-Plus Contracts	260
		1. Cost of Work and Limitations Thereon	261
		2. Reasonableness or Necessity of Costs Incurred	265
		3. Contractor's Overhead and Profit	265
		4. Estimates and Cost-Plus Contracts	266
		C. Cost-Plus with Guaranteed Maximum Price	267

	D. Unit-Price Contracts	268
	1. VEQ Clauses	269
	2. Unbalanced Bidding	270
	E. Mixed Pricing Contracts and Change Orders	271
9.03	Specific Price-Related Terms Utilized in Construction Contracts	272
	A. Pricing Mechanisms	272
	1. Index Pricing	272
	2. Time and Material Pricing	273
	3. Default Pricing through Third Party	274
	4. Default Pricing through Dispute Resolution	274
9.04	Contract Terms Related to Pricing	274
	A. Material Price Escalation Clauses	274
	B. Interim Payment Clauses	275
9.05	Comparison of Pricing Terms Based on Pricing Mechanism	276
	A. Scope of Work	276
	B. Changes	277
	C. Sharing of Savings	277
	D. Definition of "Cost of Work"	277
	E. Treatment of Self-Performed Work	278
	F. Allowances	278
	G. Contingencies	278
	H. Builder Rebates/Credits	280
	I. Purpose of Budget	280
	J. Audit Rights	280

10 Subcontractors and Suppliers   283

10.01	Subcontractors and Suppliers	283
	A. Subcontractors versus Suppliers: What Is the Difference and Why Does It Matter?	283
	B. Subcontractors and Suppliers: Telling Them Apart	284
10.02	Selection of Subcontractors and Suppliers	285
	A. Owner Input into Selection Process	285
	B. Formal Restrictions on Choosing Subcontractors and Suppliers	286
	C. Socioeconomic Considerations	287
10.03	Subcontractor Bidding: Who Is Bound by the Bid?	288
	A. The Bidding Process	288
	B. Can the Prime Contractor Enforce the Subcontractor's Bid?	289
	C. Can the Subcontractor Enforce Its Own Bid?	291

10.04	Flow-Down Obligations and Rights	292
	A. Introduction	292
	B. The Nature of Flow-Down and Flow-Up Provisions	293
	C. The Rights and Liabilities of Parties under Flow-Down Provisions	294
	D. Conditional Assignment of Subcontract to the Owner	295
10.05	Coordination of Subcontract Work	296
	A. The Duty of Coordination	296
	B. Duty to Coordinate Subcontract Work	296
	C. Avoiding Coordination Obligations	298
10.06	Subcontractor Indemnity Obligations	299
	A. Judicial Indemnity Authority	299
	B. Subcontractor Indemnity Agreements	299
	C. Anti-Indemnity Statutes	301
10.07	Payment to Subcontractors and Suppliers	302
	A. The Payment Process	302
	B. Bearing the Risk of Owner's Failure to Pay	303
	C. Risk of Payment Provisions	304
	D. Other Methods to Secure Subcontractor Payments	305
10.08	Subcontractor Claims	306
	A. The Problem of Subcontractor Claims	306
	B. Barriers to the Subcontractor Making Its Claim	307
	C. The Pass-Through System and Its Problems	308
	D. Liquidating Agreements	312
10.09	Subcontractors and Suppliers; Collaborative Contracting	313
	A. Attack on the Privity System	313
	B. The Promise of Computerized Communications	314

11 Contract Time and Completion — 319

11.01	Significance of Time for Performance	319
11.02	Construction Scheduling—Critical Path Method Schedules	320
11.03	Schedule Updates	325
11.04	Legal Significance of Construction Schedules	325
11.05	Time of Commencement and Time for Completion	326
11.06	Waiver of Time for Completion	328
11.07	Grounds for Extending the Time for Completion—Compensable and Excusable Delays	334
11.08	Concurrent Delay	341

11.09	Substantial Completion	343
11.10	Final Completion	348
11.11	Proof of Delay Claims through CPM Analysis	350
11.12	Delay Analysis Methods	352
	A. Impacted As-Planned	354
	B. Time Impact Analysis	355
	C. Windows Analysis	356
	D. Collapsed As-Built or "But For" Analysis	356

12 Payment — 361

12.01	Introduction	361
12.02	Basis for Payment	362
12.03	Payment Process	365
	A. Applications for Payment	366
	1. The Contractor's Certification	367
	2. The Architect's Certification	367
	B. Retainage	369
	C. Owner's Payment Obligation	371
	1. Timing	371
	2. Mechanic's Lien	373
	3. Stop Notice/Lien on Funds	374
	4. Lien Waivers	374
	5. Joint Checks	375
	6. Overpayment	377
	D. Changes	379
	E. Interest	379
12.04	Substantial Completion/Substantial Performance	379
12.05	Final Completion/Final Payment	381
	A. Owner's Acceptance of Work/Waiver of Claims	382
	B. Contractor's Acceptance of Payment/Waiver of Claims	383
	C. Liquidated Damages	384
12.06	Specific Payment Issues	385
	A. "Pay If Paid" versus "Pay When Paid"	385
	B. Prompt Pay Act	387
	C. False Claims	388
	D. Lender Liability	389
12.07	Conclusion	390

13 Construction Safety — 393

- 13.01 Introduction — 393
- 13.02 Accident Prevention — 394
  - A. State Legislation — 394
  - B. Occupational Safety and Health Act — 395
  - C. OSHA in Civil Litigation — 397
  - D. Contractual Responsibility for Safety Programs — 402
- 13.03 Recovery of Compensation for Construction Accidents — 403
  - A. Workers' Compensation Laws — 403
  - B. Tort Liability — 404
    1. Active Negligence — 404
    2. Liability Based on Control of the Workplace — 405
  - C. Owners — 405
  - D. Prime Contractors — 409
  - E. Architects and Engineers — 413
- 13.04 Risk Allocation and Transfer — 417
  - A. Risk Allocation and Transfer, Generally — 417
  - B. Insurance — 417
  - C. Indemnity — 418
  - D. Assumption of the Risk and Contributory Negligence by the Injured Party — 421
  - E. Workers' Compensation's Effect on Indemnity and Contribution in Third-Party Actions — 422
- 13.05 Conclusion — 423

14 Changes — 425

- 14.01 The Inevitability of Changes — 425
- 14.02 The Purpose of a Changes Clause — 426
- 14.03 The Change Order Process — 428
- 14.04 Authority to Issue Changes — 432
- 14.05 Notice Requirements for Claims for Changes — 435
- 14.06 Adjustments to Contract Price and Completion Date — 438
- 14.07 Constructive Changes — 441
- 14.08 Duty to Perform the Changed Work — 444
- 14.09 Cardinal Change — 446
- 14.10 Administration of Changes — 448
- 14.11 Releases—Accord and Satisfaction — 450

15 Differing Site Conditions — 457

- 15.01 Introduction — 457
- 15.02 Common Law — 459
  - A. Contracts without a Site Indications or Risk Allocation Clause — 459
  - B. Alternate Legal Theories in the Presence of Representations or Indications — 461
    1. Warranty — 461
    2. Misrepresentation — 462
    3. Superior Knowledge/Concealment — 463
    4. Mutual Mistake — 465
- 15.03 Regulatory and Other Standard Frameworks for Addressing Differing Site Conditions — 465
  - A. Differing Site Conditions—FAR 52.236-2 — 466
  - B. Standard Form Provisions in Commercial Agreements — 468
- 15.04 Elements of a Federal Differing Site Conditions Claim — 469
  - A. Type I—Materially Different Than Indicated — 470
    1. Indications — 470
    2. Reasonableness — 472
    3. Differ Materially — 473
    4. Reasonably Unforeseeable — 473
    5. Causation of Increased Costs — 474
  - B. Type II—Conditions of an Unusual Nature — 475
- 15.05 Limitations on Claims for Differing Site Conditions — 476
  - A. Duty to Investigate — 476
  - B. Disclaimers/Exculpatory Language — 478
  - C. Notice — 479
  - D. Relationship to the Variation in Estimated Quantities Clauses — 480
- 15.06 Differing Site Conditions and Design-Build Contracts — 483
- 15.07 Representative Treatment of Differing Site Conditions in State Courts — 486
  - A. New Jersey — 486
  - B. Virginia — 488
  - C. Illinois — 490
  - D. California — 492
- 15.08 Conclusion — 493

16 Termination of Contract — 497

- 16.01 Introduction — 497
- 16.02 Right to Terminate under the Common Law — 498

16.03	Right to Terminate under Commonly Used Forms	506
	A. Variation from Common Law	506
	B. AIA Forms	507
	1. Termination by Contractor	507
	2. Termination by Owner	509
	C. ConsensusDocs Forms	511
	1. The Order of the Provisions	514
	2. Specified Breach versus Material Breach	514
	3. Right to Cure	514
	4. Survival	515
	D. EJCDC Forms	515
16.04	Post-Termination Issues	516
	A. Post-Termination Responsibilities	516
	B. Damages and Other Relief	516
	C. Role of the Surety	517
	D. Wrongful Termination	518
16.05	Termination for Convenience	521
	A. AIA Treatment	522
	B. ConsensusDocs Treatment	524
	C. Other Forms	525
	D. The Choice	526
16.06	Conclusion	527

17 Mechanic's Liens 529

17.01	Origin of Mechanic's Lien	529
17.02	Statutory Framework	531
17.03	Lien Categories	534
17.04	Requirements for a Lien	535
	A. Contract	535
	B. Improvement	536
	C. Amount of Lien	540
	D. Lien Entitlement	542
17.05	What Is Lienable?	544
17.06	Interests Subject to a Lien	545
17.07	Perfecting the Lien	547
17.08	Priorities	549
17.09	Public Projects	550
17.10	Waiver and Release	552
17.11	Bankruptcy	553

18 Insurance and Bonds   557

18.01	Introduction	557
18.02	The Role of Insurance	557
18.03	Contractual Insurance Requirements	558
18.04	General Liability Insurance Policies	561
18.05	Builders' Risk Insurance Policies	566
18.06	Workers Compensation Insurance	567
18.07	Waivers of Subrogation	567
18.08	Professional Liability Insurance	568
18.09	Surety Bonds—The Tripartite Relationship	568
18.10	Obligations of the Performance Bond Surety	571
18.11	Payment Bonds	578
18.12	Rights and Remedies of Sureties	579
18.13	Letters of Credit	584
18.14	Subcontractor Default Insurance Policies	585

19 Dispute Resolution Processes   587

19.01 Importance to the Construction Industry of Processes for Resolution of Disputes   587
    A. Unique Dispute Resolution Needs of Construction Projects   587
    B. Historical Development of Dispute Resolution in Construction   588

19.02 The Spectrum of Construction Industry Dispute Prevention and Resolution Techniques   589
    A. The Dispute Resolution Step Chart   589
    B. The Four Stages of Dispute Resolution   590
        1. The Dispute Prevention and Cooperation Stage   590
        2. The Dispute Control Stage   591
        3. The Facilitated Non-binding Resolution Stage   591
        4. The Binding Resolution Stage   591

19.03 Individual Construction Dispute Prevention, Control, and Early Resolution Techniques   592
    A. Prevention and Cooperation Techniques   592
        1. Realistic Allocation of Project Risks   592
        2. Incentives to Encourage Cooperation   592
        3. Partnering   593
        4. Open Communications and Notice Provisions   594
    B. Dispute Control and "Real-Time" Early Resolution Techniques   594
        1. Step Negotiations   594

		2.	Geotechnical Baseline Summary Report	595
		3.	Escrow of Bid Documents	595
		4.	Dispute Boards and Standing Neutrals	596
	C.	Other Facilitated Non-binding Resolution of Disputes		600
		1.	Mediation	600
		2.	Independent Decision Maker	600
		3.	Minitrial	601
		4.	Advisory Opinions	601
		5.	Non-binding Summary Advisory Arbitration and Adjudication	602
		6.	Binding Arbitration	602
19.04	Design of Dispute Prevention and Resolution Systems			603
19.05	Principles of Arbitration			604
	A.	Basis in Statute		604
	B.	Contractual Nature of the Remedy		605
	C.	Attacking Arbitration		607
	D.	Modification of Award by Arbitrators		607
	E.	Confirmation or Vacation of Award by Court		608

20 Defective Construction — 611

20.01	Overview of the Legal Analysis of Defects			611
	A.	What Constitutes "Defective" or "Deficient" Construction?		612
		1.	Types of Defects or Deficiencies	612
		2.	Manifestations versus Defects	613
	B.	Responsibility		614
20.02	Owner Claims against Contractors			616
	A.	Contract Claims		616
		1.	Failure to Comply with Drawings and Specifications	616
		2.	Breach of Express Warranty	617
		3.	Breach of Implied Warranty	618
	B.	Tort Claims		619
	C.	Statutory Claims		619
	D.	Notice Requirements		620
20.03	Claims against Design Professionals			620
	A.	Tort and Contract Claims Generally		621
	B.	Defective Drawings and Specifications		622
	C.	Construction Observation		625
	D.	Claims against the Design Professional by Contractors		629

20.04	The *Spearin* Doctrine and Conflicting Warranties	630
	A. The *Spearin* Doctrine	631
	1. Owner's Implied Warranty of Drawings and Specifications	631
	2. Design Specifications	634
	3. Performance Specifications	635
	4. Conflicts between the Contractor's and the Owner's Warranties	636
20.05	Time-Based Defenses to Liability: Statutes of Limitation and Statutes of Repose	638
	A. Statutes of Limitation	639
	B. Statutes of Repose	647

21 The Economic Loss Rule in Construction Law   653

21.01	Introduction	653
21.02	Economic Loss Rule	659
21.03	The Scope and Purpose of the Economic Loss Rule	661
21.04	The Economic Loss Rule's Application Where Parties Are in Privity of Contract	669
	A. Claims of Defective Construction Products/Components (Privity)	669
	B. Claims of Defective Construction Services (Including Poor Workmanship and Improper Furnishing of Materials) (Privity)	674
	C. Claims of Defective Design Professional/Testing Services (Including Insufficient Design and Improper Contract Administration Services) (Privity)	679
21.05	The Economic Loss Rule's Application Where Parties Are Not in Privity of Contract	683
	A. Claims of Defective Construction Products/Components (No Privity)	684
	B. Claims of Defective Construction Services (Including Poor Workmanship and Improper Furnishing of Materials) (No Privity)	696
	C. Claims of Defective Design Professional Services (Including Insufficient Design and Improper Contract Administration Services) (No Privity)	702
21.06	The Economic Loss Rule as Applied to the Tort of Negligent Misrepresentation	709

22 Damages — 717

- 22.01 Introduction — 717
  - A. Overview of Chapter — 717
  - B. "Measures of Damages" versus "Cause of Action" — 718
- 22.02 General Measures of Damages — 719
  - A. Breach of Contract and Related Claims — 719
    1. Expectation Interest (Breach of Contract) — 719
    2. Reliance Interest—Promissory Estoppel — 724
    3. Restitution Interest—Unjust Enrichment — 726
    4. Quantum Meruit — 727
  - B. Tort Claims — 728
- 22.03 Calculation and Proof of Compensatory Damages — 728
  - A. Direct Methods of Proving Actual Damages — 729
    1. Proof of Actual Costs — 729
    2. Methods of Estimating Actual Damages — 734
  - B. Alternate Methods of Proving Damages — 736
    1. Total Cost Method — 736
    2. Modified Total Cost Method — 741
    3. Jury Verdict Method — 742
  - C. Consequential Damages in Construction Contracts — 743
  - D. Punitive Damages — 744
  - E. The Claims Industry and Recordkeeping — 744
- 22.04 Mitigation of Damages — 745
  - A. Duty to Mitigate Damages — 745
  - B. Economic Waste — 745
  - C. Betterment — 746
- 22.05 Contractual and Other Limitations on Liability — 748
  - A. Indemnification Clauses and Limitations on Liability — 748
  - B. Waivers of Consequential/Incidental Damages — 753
  - C. Waiver of Claims for Consequential Damages — 753
  - D. Liquidated Damages for Delay — 753
  - E. No Damages for Delay — 755

23 Public Construction Contracting — 759

- 23.01 Statutory and Regulatory Rules — 761
- 23.02 Criminal Law and Fraud — 763
- 23.03 Sovereign Immunity — 771
- 23.04 Sovereign Acts — 778
- 23.05 The Actual Authority Requirement — 786

23.06	Socioeconomic Requirements	795
23.07	Protests and Disputes	804

24 Technological Advances in Construction: Building Information Modeling (BIM) and Related Tools — 809

24.01	Introduction	809
24.02	What Is BIM?	812
24.03	How BIM Works	813
	A. Difference between CAD and BIM	813
	B. The BIM Life Cycle Process	816
	1. Design Coordination and Analysis	816
	2. 4D (Schedule) and 5D (Cost) Analysis	821
	3. Sustainability Analysis	822
	4. Construction Phase BIM	827
	5. Facility Management BIM	828
	6. Archiving	829
24.04	BIM Contracting	829
	A. BIM Contract Forms	829
	1. AIA Building Information Modeling and Digital Data Exhibit	830
	2. AIA BIM Protocol Attachment	830
	3. C-DOCs Building Information Modeling (BIM) Addendum	832
	B. Assessing Contract Risks	834
24.05	BIM Execution Planning	837
	A. BIM Execution Planning Process	837
	1. Identifying BIM Goals and Uses	838
	2. Designing the BIM Design Execution Process by Creating Process Maps	838
	3. Developing Information Exchanges That Define BIM Deliverables	838
	4. Defining Supporting Infrastructure for BIM Implementation	839
	B. Documentation of BIM Project Execution Plan	839
24.06	Fabrication/3D Printing BIM Applications	840
24.07	Conclusion	843

Table of Cases	845
Index	883

About the Editors

Carol J. Patterson is a senior partner in the New York City office of Zetlin & De Chiara, LLP, where her practice is focused on construction law. She has represented clients in connection with a wide range of commercial, residential, arts, and infrastructure projects. She writes and speaks frequently on construction law issues. She has served as president of the Association of Real Estate Women in New York City, now known as CREW New York. She is a Fellow of the American College of Construction Lawyers and is a member of its Board of Governors. She has served as a member of the Governing Committee of the ABA Forum on the Construction Industry.

Ross J. Altman practices construction law with Laurie & Brennan LLP, based in Chicago. He represents clients in connection with projects located globally, including a wide range of commercial, industrial, and infrastructure projects. He is particularly involved in transactional matters. Mr. Altman also is an adjunct faculty member of the University of Miami School of Law, teaching in the Real Property Development LLM Program. He is a Fellow of the American College of Construction Lawyers, where he has served on the Board of Governors and as the Documents Committee chair. He is on the American Arbitration Association panel of construction industry arbitrators.

Stephen A. Hess developed and teaches a construction law seminar at the University of Denver's Sturm College of Law and practices construction law and litigation with Sherman & Howard, LLC. His writings have appeared in numerous national construction law treatises and construction law journals. Mr. Hess is the author of several books related to litigation, and he has served as editor of *The Construction Lawyer*, which is published by the ABA Forum on the Construction Industry, and *Construction Briefings*, published by Thomson Reuters. He is a Fellow of the American College of Construction Lawyers.

Allen Overcash practices law with Woods & Aitken LLP, in Lincoln, Nebraska. He is a member of the American Arbitration Association's Construction Arbitrator Master Panel, its Panel of Master Mediators, and its ICDR Panel of Arbitrators. He has served as a member of the Board of Governors of the American College of Construction Lawyers and the Governing Committee of the ABA Forum on the Construction Industry, and in 2002 he received the Forum's Cornerstone Award. He is currently an adjunct professor of construction law at the University of Nebraska Law College.

About the Authors

William Allensworth is a retired partner of Allensworth and Porter, LLP, in Austin, Texas. He taught 29 semesters of courses in construction law and construction litigation at the University of Texas School of Law starting in 1999, and he is a Fellow of the American College of Construction Lawyers. He is currently the chair of the Texas Facilities Commission.

Philip L. Bruner is a mediator, arbitrator, and the director of JAMS Global Engineering and Construction Group. Prior to joining JAMS in 2008, he practiced law for 43 years in the construction law field, the last 17 as a senior partner and founding head of the Construction Law Group in the international law firm of Faegre & Benson, LLP. Mr. Bruner is the co-author of *Bruner & O'Connor on Construction Law*.

Carl J. Circo is the Ben J. Altheimer Professor of Legal Advocacy at the University of Arkansas School of Law, where he teaches construction law and other subjects. He previously served on the faculty at the Benjamin N. Cardozo School of Law and also taught law as a visitor at the University of Nebraska and as an adjunct at the University of Missouri–Kansas City. For 20 years, he practiced commercial real estate and construction law in Kansas City.

W. Stephen Dale is a senior vice president and serves as the general counsel for WSP for the United States region. Mr. Dale was formerly a partner with the law firm of Smith Pachter McWhorter, PLC. Mr. Dale has represented contractors and design professionals before federal, state, and regional tribunals in claims, arbitration, and litigation on large, complex infrastructure projects, including rail transit, environmental remediation, and mining, as well as highway, nuclear power, and waterway improvements. He has been a frequent speaker at industry conferences, and is a member of the American Society of

Civil Engineers, having served on the Board of Governors for the Construction Institute and the Committee on Professional Practice. He is a Fellow in the American College of Construction Lawyers.

Eileen M. Diepenbrock is a partner at Diepenbrock Elkin Gleason LP in Sacramento, California, where her practice is focused on construction law and government contracts. She represents owners, contractors, and subcontractors on issues from procurement to contract negotiation to claims and litigation. She is a Fellow of the American College of Construction Lawyers and is active in the ABA Forum on Construction Law. She writes and speaks frequently on construction law issues.

Luke J. Farley, Sr. practices construction and surety law in the Raleigh, North Carolina, office of Ellis & Winters LLP. His practice focuses on contract disputes, state and federal bond claims, and mechanics' liens. He is an active member of the Young Lawyers Division (YLD) of the ABA Forum on Construction Law and serves as YLD liaison to Division 7 (Insurance, Surety & Liens) of the Forum.

Deborah Griffin practices construction law in the Boston office of Holland & Knight, LLP. She is a past chair of the ABA Forum on the Construction Industry and a Fellow of the American College of Construction Lawyers. She has spoken and written extensively on construction, surety, insurance, and bankruptcy topics.

James P. Groton is a retired partner of Sutherland, Asbill & Brennan (now Eversheds Sutherland) where he headed the construction and dispute resolution practices of the firm. He is a Fellow and former president of the American College of construction lawyers, and was the first lawyer to be elected to the National Academy of Construction. He has received many awards for his construction and dispute prevention and resolution work.

A. Holt Gwyn (1949–2017) was a principal in the law firm of Conner Gwyn Schenck, PLLC, in Greensboro and Raleigh, North Carolina. Mr. Gwyn was a former chair of the ABA Forum on Construction Law and a Fellow in the American College of Construction Lawyers. He was the editor in chief of the *Journal of the American College of Construction Lawyers*. He was a frequent author and speaker at the bar and industry groups on construction and environmental law and on alternative dispute resolution issues, and he was instrumental in creating the first edition of this text.

R. Harper Heckman practices in the Greensboro, North Carolina, office of Nexsen Pruet, PLLC, where he chairs the firm's construction practice group. Mr. Heckman is past chair of the ABA's Forum on Construction Law. He is a mediator and arbitrator, an adjunct professor of construction law at the University of North Carolina School of Law, and a Fellow in the American College of Construction Lawyers.

Timothy F. Hegarty is a partner at Zetlin & De Chiara, LLP and has focused his practice in the area of construction law for more than 20 years. He represents owners, developers, institutions, lenders, private equity, architects, engineers, construction managers, and contractors in matters that serve both their transactional and construction dispute resolution needs. He speaks and writes frequently on construction law issues and is an adjunct faculty member of Columbia University where he teaches construction law in the graduate School of Professional Studies.

Kimberly A. Hurtado is the managing shareholder of the Wisconsin law firm Hurtado Zimmerman SC. She has served on the Board of Governors of the American College of Construction Lawyers, on the Governing Committee of the ABA Construction Forum, and is a Founding Fellow of the Construction Lawyers Society of America. She is an adjunct professor at the School of Architecture at Taliesin, and lectures and writes internationally about construction-related technology.

Val S. McWhorter is a founding member of Smith Pachter McWhorter, PLC, and has focused his practice in the area of construction law for 40 years. His practice has included representing contractors in large, complex claims arising under federal, state, and local government contracts, as well as contracts between private parties. He is a frequent speaker on construction-related issues. He is a Fellow in the American College of Construction Lawyers, and a former member of its Board of Governors.

Deborah Mastin mediates and arbitrates large complex and multiparty infrastructure and EPC disputes in the United States and internationally with the American Arbitration Association, International Institute for Conflict Prevention and Resolution, Chartered Institute of Arbitrators, and Trinidad Dispute Resolution Centre. She is a faculty member for the AAA and the ICDR, a tutor for international arbitration at the Chartered Institute of Arbitrators, and teaches at the University of Miami School of Architecture Masters in Construction Management Program. Deborah is a Fellow of American College of

Construction Lawyers, College of Commercial Arbitrators, Chartered Institute of Arbitrators, and the Dispute Board Federation. She graduated from Northeastern University School of Law and MIT School of Architecture and Planning.

Bruce Merwin is a real estate partner in the Houston, Texas, office of Thompson & Knight, LLP, and heads their construction practice. He is the author of numerous articles on construction law and speaks regularly to lawyer groups and construction-related trade associations throughout the state of Texas. He represents developers on design and construction contracts for all types of commercial projects throughout the country. He is the only lawyer in Texas listed in the 2018 edition of *The Best Lawyers in America for Real Estate Law and Construction Law*. He is also a Fellow of the Construction Lawyers Society of America.

Allison Tungate Mikulecky is a Litigation Associate in Sherman & Howard's Litigation Group, focusing her practice on assisting her clients with disputes arising out of commercial contracts, business torts, construction contracts, government contracts, and business and corporate governance issues. She received her JD from the University of Missouri School of Law in 2015. While attending, she served as the lead articles editor for the *Journal of Environmental and Sustainability Law*.

James F. Nagle is of counsel to the firm of Oles Morrison Rinker and Baker in Seattle, Washington. After retiring as a government attorney specializing in federal contracts, he joined Oles as a partner for 25 years. He has written six books and contributed to numerous others on federal contracts. He often teaches and speaks on government contracts.

Andrew D. Ness is now a dispute resolution neutral with JAMS in Washington, DC, following an extended first career as a practicing construction lawyer. Mr. Ness frequently writes and speaks on a range of construction law issues, and, as both advocate and neutral, has resolved major disputes on a wide variety of large construction projects both in the United States and across most of the world. He is a former chair of the ABA Forum on Construction Law and a Fellow of the American College of Construction Lawyers.

Dennis J. Powers is a partner in the Chicago office of the Construction Law Practice Group of DLA Piper, LLP (U.S.). He concentrates his practice in the representation of owners, developers, and contractors in construction disputes of all kinds, including defect and delay claims and extras and payment claims in courts and arbitration across the country.

Matthew C. Ryan is a partner at Allensworth & Porter in Austin, Texas. He has taught as an adjunct professor in construction law and construction litigation since 2006 at the University of Texas at Austin School of Law. He has also served as the chair of the State Bar of Texas Construction Law Section, and holds honorary membership in the Austin Chapter of the American Institute of Architects, where he served on the Board of Directors from 2008 through 2019.

David A. Senter is a member in the Raleigh, North Carolina, office of Nexsen Pruet, PLLC, where he is a member of the firm's Construction Practice Group. David concentrates his practice in the area of construction law. He serves on the Large Complex Case Panel of Construction Arbitrators for the American Arbitration Association and is certified as a mediator by the NC Dispute Resolution Commission. He has authored numerous construction-related materials in bar and trade publications and has spoken on construction-related topics to national audiences. He has served on the Governing Committee of the ABA Forum on the Construction Industry and is an adjunct professor of construction law at the Wake Forest University School of Law.

Nicholas D. Siegfried is a partner in the firm of Siegfried Rivera in Miami, Florida. He is a board certified construction attorney and serves as an adjunct professor at the University of Miami Law School where he teaches a course on Florida's construction lien law. He is the editor of *Florida Construction Lien Law and Florida Construction Law* (Aspen Publishers, 2001).

Stanley P. Sklar is a principal of Dispute Resolution Services, Northbrook, Illinois, concentrating in construction disputes. He serves as a member of the American Arbitration Association Large, Complex Commercial Case Panel. He is a past president and Founding Fellow of the American College of Construction Lawyers and the Society of Illinois Construction Attorneys. He is also a Fellow in the American College of Real Estate Lawyers. Mr. Sklar is an adjunct professor at DePaul University College of Law where also serves as the executive director of Arbitration Studies.

Lorence H. Slutzky retired as a partner in the Chicago office of Robbins, Schwartz, Ltd and after a brief hiatus resumed the practice as the Law Office of Lorence H. Slutzky, Ltd. Mr. Slutzky is a fellow of the American College of

Construction Lawyers, a founder and former president of the Society of Illinois Construction Attorneys, and was for many years an adjunct professor at John Marshall Law School's postgraduate Center for Real Estate Law. He is admitted to practice in Illinois and Florida and is a certified Construction Specialist by the Florida Bar Association.

Richard F. Smith is senior counsel to Smith Pachter McWhorter, PLC, located in Tysons Corner, Virginia. Mr. Smith serves on the mediation and arbitration panels of the American Arbitration Association. He has been a member of the Governing Committee of the ABA Forum on Construction Law and a member of the Board of Governors of the American College of Construction Lawyers. He is also a Fellow in the College of Commercial Arbitrators. He teaches construction law at the University of Virginia Law School.

John H. "Buzz" Tarlow is a founding member of Tarlow Stonecipher Weamer & Kelly, PLLC, in Bozeman, Montana. He practices primarily in the construction field and regularly acts as a mediator and arbitrator in construction disputes. Mr. Tarlow is a member of the National Construction Panel of Arbitrators for the American Arbitration Association, a Fellow of the American College of Construction Lawyers, a member of the ABA Forum on Construction Law, and is an adjunct professor at Montana State University College of Engineering. Mr. Tarlow is also the creator and host of the ABA Forum's podcast "Construction Law Today."

Richard J. Tyler is a senior partner in the New Orleans office of Jones Walker LLP and a former chair of the firm's construction practice. He has been a member of the firm's Business & Commercial Litigation Practice Group since 1982. His practice involves both dispute resolution and transactional work on behalf of owners, contractors, subcontractors, and suppliers on a variety of projects and delivery systems. He serves on the American Arbitration Association roster of neutrals and is a Fellow of the Chartered Institute of Arbitrators (U.K.). He is a frequent author and speaker on construction and dispute resolution topics.

Alan Winkler is an attorney in the firm of Peckar & Abramson, PC. For over 30 years, his practice has been focused on construction law, including construction contracts, counseling clients on issues arising during construction projects, and representing clients in arbitrations and litigations of various disputes. He has handled cases covering a wide variety of projects. He has also lectured and written articles on construction law.

Preface

The first edition of this book was published ten years ago to create a useful resource for the construction industry by assisting professors in familiarizing students with the principles of construction law. It was our goal that the availability of the textbook would encourage law schools and other programs to recognize that construction law is a valuable subject for focused study and to facilitate the development of courses guiding such study. We are pleased that this has been the case. Many professors have found the book useful not only in law schools but also in professional programs for architecture, engineering, and construction management as well. We have also been told that the book is a useful resource not only for many attorneys who are new to the practice of construction law but also for experienced practitioners.

As the editors started work on the second edition, we wanted not only to update the book but to improve it. We reached out to professors who use the book and received very helpful responses, and we want to thank those who took the time to respond to us.

While the overall organization of the book remains the same, we made some changes that should make the book easier to use. As was the case in the first edition of this book, many of the discussions in the text and the questions at the end of each chapter focus on typical small commercial construction projects and the American Institute of Architects forms of agreement that are widely used on such projects. This is consistent with our intent to familiarize readers with a wide range of issues that arise on most construction projects. The initial chapters of the book are still devoted to providing an overview of the construction process, including the roles and responsibilities of the key project participants: owners, designers, contractors, and subcontractors. In this edition, all of the discussions of the roles and responsibilities of the design team on a construction project are presented in Chapters 6 and 7.

The discussion of critical time-related issues, including tools for tracking schedules of work and determining the time of completion, are consolidated in

Chapter 11. The next chapters address specific concerns that arise in the construction process, including payment, changes, differing site conditions, site safety, and contractual provisions for termination of construction contracts. The remainder of the book deals with issues arising out of construction disputes, including mechanic's liens, insurance and bonding, defective construction, damages, the economic loss rule, and, of course, alternative dispute resolution systems.

This edition of the book contains two new chapters that cover material that was not included in the first edition. We recognized that the book did not address the special requirements of one of the most important entities initiating construction projects: the government. A new chapter presents an overview of the legal landscape and specialized requirements for government contracts. We also recognized that one of the most significant changes in the construction industry in the last ten years is the increase in importance of BIM and other electronic tools in the construction process. There is now a chapter on BIM that provides an overview about how BIM can facilitate expedited and improved communication on projects. This is a topic that continues to evolve and it is important for students to have insight into how BIM tools are used on construction projects.

This textbook is published by the Forum on the Construction Industry and is written by industry-leading practitioners, most of whom teach construction law. The selection of topics and the scope of their treatment have been dictated by practical needs in the industry, and the student can assume with confidence that the subject areas presented are those that are most commonly faced in the field. The text presents a core group of subjects with which a well-rounded construction attorney should be familiar on a practical level and provides a sound solid foundation for further study and use in practice.

Acknowledgments

As was true in the last edition, this book is the product of a team effort and we thank the many people who made it possible. We start with each of the authors in this edition and those who contributed to the first edition but were not involved in the book. Their hard work and generous contribution of their time and expertise made this book possible.

This edition benefitted substantially from a complete independent editorial review by Ridgely Jackson, an associate with Laurie & Brennan LLP, whose experience as an editor prior to law school made her especially well qualified for this task. The editors are very grateful for her important contribution to this book. We also extend our thanks to the ABA Forum on Construction Law for its continued strong support of this project. David Scotti, chair of the Publications Committee, provided invaluable, unwavering support as the book progressed. Special thanks also go to recent Forum chairs Wendy Venoit and Thomas Rosenberg for their support of the book. Milca Feliciano and Belinda Lambert made important contributions through their support in connection with the preparation of the manuscript and made the editors' job much easier. We want to extend special thanks to our co-editor on the first edition, William Allensworth. William's input in the first edition is an invaluable contribution to the second. We also want to acknowledge the contribution of the late Holt Gwyn, the author of the chapter on the economic loss rule in the first edition. Holt's work has been revised and updated in this edition, but his voice in the chapter remains strong.

Finally, we thank ABA Publishing and our editor, Sarah Forbes Orwig, and Courtney Coffman, production manager for the book at Lachina, for their contributions to the publications process.

Carol J. Patterson
Ross J. Altman
Stephen A. Hess
Allen A. Overcash

CHAPTER

1

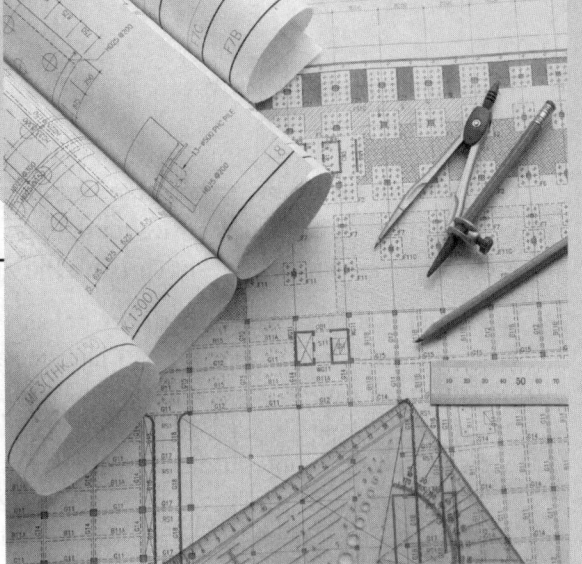

Construction Law: The Historical Perspective

PHILIP L. BRUNER

1.01 INTRODUCTION

A. Construction in the Ancient World

For more than 4,500 years, from primitive Mesopotamian fire-brick and early Egyptian cut-stone construction to the extraordinary structures of the modern-built environment, construction has been a hallmark of the advancement of human civilization.[1] In the oldest story known to humanity written about

---

1. *See* Plutarch, PERICLES (75 AD):

    That which gave most pleasure and ornament to the city of Athens, and the greatest admiration and even astonishment to all strangers, and that which now is Greece's only evidence that the power she boasts of and of her ancient wealth are no romance or idle story, was [Pericles'] construction of the public and sacred buildings.

    See also 1 PHILIP L. BRUNER & PATRICK J. O'CONNOR, BRUNER & O'CONNOR ON CONSTRUCTION LAW § 1:1 (West Group 2002, supplemented annually) [hereinafter BRUNER & O'CONNOR].

2750 BC, a thousand years earlier than Homer's Iliad or the Biblical Old Testament, the author described the Mesopotamian city of Uruk and the life of its historical king named Gilgamesh. Of Uruk the author said:

> This is the wall of Uruk, which no city on earth can equal. See how its ramparts gleam like copper in the sun. Climb the stone staircase, more ancient than the mind can imagine, approach the Eanna Temple, sacred to Ishtar, a temple that no king has equaled in size or beauty, walk on the wall of Uruk, follow its course around the city, inspect its mighty foundations, examine its brickwork, how masterfully it is built, observe the land it encloses: the palm trees, the gardens, the orchards, the glorious palaces and temples, the shops and marketplaces, the houses, the public squares.[2]

Ever since humanity first promulgated rudimentary principles of law have existed to regulate human rights and obligations arising out of societal interaction; they have included principles of law governing the built environment and the construction process. The earliest known principles of construction law were primitive and punitive. Under its "eye for an eye" system of justice, Hammurabi's Code dictated that builders be punished for injuries to others caused by collapse of their buildings. The code provisions pertinent to construction state:

> 229 If a builder build a house for someone, and does not construct it properly, and the house which he built fall in and kill its owner, then the builder shall be put to death.
>
> 230 If it kill the son of the owner, the son of that builder shall be put to death.
>
> 231 If it kill a slave of the owner, then he shall pay slave for slave to the owner of the house.
>
> 232 If it ruin goods, he shall make compensation for all that is ruined, and in as much as he did not construct properly this house which he build and it fell, he shall re-erect the house from his own means.
>
> 233 If a builder build a house for someone, even though he has not yet completed it, if then the walls seem toppling, the builder must make the walls solid from his own means.[3]

As classical antiquity gradually civilized the built environment, so, too, did those times refine the governing law. By the reign of Rome's Caesar Augustus

---

2. *See* STEPHEN MITCHELL, GILGAMESH 198–99 (2004). Twentieth-century archaeological excavations and modern noninvasive exploratory techniques confirm that Uruk, lying near the Euphrates River in southeastern Iraq, was first settled about 7,000 years ago and went on to become the largest city on earth around 3,000 years ago. See Andrew Lawler, *The Everlasting City*, 66(5) ARCHAEOLOGY, Sept./Oct. 2013, at 26–28.

3. THE CODE OF HAMMURABI §§ 229–33 (ca. 1750 BC) (R. W. King trans. 1910).

(27 BCE to AD 14),[4] construction risks inherent in building upon unsuitable soils[5] and building without managerial competence and cost control[6] were widely recognized. Good construction practice under Roman law favored careful contractual articulation of the scope of work and allocation of construction risks.[7]

---

4. When he became Rome's first emperor in 27 BC, Gaius Julius Caesar Octavius (63 BC to AD 14), great nephew of Julius Caesar, was given the name Augustus by the Roman Senate.

5. Jesus of Nazareth, who is said to have practiced carpentry as a boy, employed widely understood metaphors in his sermons, and concluded His Sermon on the Mount with this admonition:

> Everyone then who hears these words of mine and acts on them will be like a *wise man who built his house on a rock*. The rain fell, the floods came, and the winds blew and beat on that house, but it did not fall, because it had been founded on rock. And everyone who hears these words of mine and does not act on them will be like a *foolish man who built his house on sand*. The rain fell, and the floods came, and the winds blew and beat against that house, and it fell—and great was its fall! (Emphasis added.) *Matthew* 7:24–27 (New Revised Standard Edition).

6. *See* MARCUS VITRUVIUS POLLIO, DE ARCHITECTURA, Book X, Introduction (ca. 20 BC) (Morris Hickey Morgan trans., 1914). Known to history as Vitruvius, he was chief engineer to Caesars Julius and Augustus and thus in his time could be called the "chief engineer of the civilized world." Vitruvius wrote a ten-volume treatise for Augustus on Roman construction practices, which survived the ravages of time to influence the architecture of the European Renaissance. Among other things, Vitruvius proposed to Augustus that Rome resurrect an ancient ancestral law of the Greek City of Ephesus (the same place to which Saint Paul almost a hundred years later wrote his Letter to the Ephesians):

> In the famous and important Greek City of Ephesus, there is said to be an ancient ancestral law, the terms of which are severe, but its justice is not inequitable. When an architect accepts the charge of a public work, he has to promise what the cost of it will be. His estimate is handed to the magistrate, and his property is pledged as security until the work is done. When it is finished, if the outlay agrees with his statement, he is complimented by decrees and marks of honor. If no more than a fourth has been added to his estimate, it is furnished by the treasury, and no penalty is inflicted. But when more than one-fourth has been spent in addition on the work, the money required to furnish it is taken from his property.

Roughly two generations after Vitruvius wrote his treatise, Jesus of Nazareth used the same common problem as a metaphor:

> For which of you, intending to build a tower, does not first sit down and estimate the cost, to see whether he has enough to complete it? Otherwise, when he had laid a foundation and is not able to finish, all who see it will begin to ridicule him, saying, "this fellow began to build and was not able to finish." *Luke* 14:28–30 (New Revised Standard Edition).

7. *See* VITRUVIUS, *supra* note 6, Book I, chapter 1. Regarding "construction law," Vitruvius advised the architect—the "master builder" of those days—as follows:

> [A]s for principles of law, [an Architect] should know those which are necessary in the case of buildings having party walls, with regard to water dripping from the eaves, and also the laws about drains, windows, and water supply. And other things

B. Construction's 19th-Century Transformational Events

For 1,900 years following the advent of Augustus's Imperial Rome—through Europe's Dark Ages, Renaissance, and Industrial Revolution—construction law was subsumed by broader and more generalized fields of law and by perceptions of construction as local and parochial and as invoking primarily the "law of the shop," rather than the "law of the courts."[8] Then, beginning in the mid-1800s, American law governing construction was transformed by a series of revolutionary events:

- ❒ In 1857, the founding of the American Institute of Architects, which championed the practice of architecture as a specialized profession distinct from construction contracting, heralded the eclipse of the architect's historic role as "master builder"—the single person in charge of design and construction. Engineering associations thereafter were formed to promote engineering as a profession, separate from both architectural design and construction contracting, which, in turn, spawned a number of professional engineering subspecialties—electrical, mechanical, structural, civil, and geotechnical—to address emerging technical disciplines. Professional specialization accelerated after legislative enactment of state design professional registration laws in

---

of this sort should be known to architects, so that, before they begin upon buildings, they may be careful not to leave disputed items for the householders to settle after the works are finished, and so that in drawing up contracts, the interests of both the employer and the contractor may be wisely safeguarded. For if a contract is skillfully drawn, each may obtain a release from the other without a disadvantage.

Roman builders had good reason to exercise care in contracting because the Roman legal doctrine of *pacta sunt servanda* ("contracts must be honored") imposed strict contractual liability unless nonperformance was excused under the doctrine of *rebus sic stantibus* ("provided the circumstances remain unchanged"). *See also* RESTATEMENT (SECOND) OF CONTRACTS (1982) ch. 11, intro. note "Contract liability is strict liability. It is an accepted maxim that *pacta sunt servanda*, contracts are to be kept."). These ancient principles undergird the modern law of contract and its legal doctrines of sanctity of contract, force majeure, and impracticability. *See* 5 BRUNER & O'CONNOR, *supra* note 1, § 15:22.

8. The earliest treatises on the English common law, which span a 500-year period, make no mention of legal principles of construction law. *See* HENRY OF BRACTON, ON THE LAWS AND CUSTOMS OF ENGLAND (ca. 1230), *available at* http://amesfoundation.law.harvard.edu/Bracton/. WILLIAM BLACKSTONE, COMMENTARIES ON THE LAWS OF ENGLAND (1765-1769), *available at* http://avalon.law.yale.edu/subject_menus/blackstone.asp. In Blackstone's case, the omission is particularly telling because he was trained as an architect prior to going into law and frequently used architectural metaphors in his legal writings. *See* Wilfrid Prest, *Blackstone as Architect: Constructing the Commentaries*, 15 YALE J. L. & HUMAN. 103, 123 (2003).

the United States, beginning with the State of Illinois in 1897. By the mid-20th century, the architectural profession was perceived as having abandoned its age-old role as "master builder."[9]

❑ By 1888, in response to the rigid, express contractual risk allocation imposed by the legal Doctrine of Sanctity of Contract,[10] which allocated almost all construction and completion risks to the contractor, unless the contract expressly stipulated otherwise, the American Institute of Architects and the National Association of Builders (predecessor to the

---

9. *See* Carl M. Sapers, *Ruminations on Architectural Practice*, 25 CONSTR. CONTR. L. REP. ¶ 106 (Apr. 20, 2001) (citations omitted):

> [T]he increasing complexity of construction projects . . . challenged the architect's historic role as the most knowledgeable player at the job site. As Professor Salvadore of Columbia University observed, architects came in the 1970s to know less and less about more and more until the architect is "sometimes said to know nothing about everything." Even if we stop short of Salvadore's caricature, it is clear that the architect was no longer venerated for his or her comprehensive grasp of all aspects of building. . . .
>
> During this same period, whenever the economy tightened, opposing forces claimed greater pieces of the architect's historic domain. Civil engineers claimed the right to design hospitals, office buildings, and court houses, interior designers claimed the right to design 60,000 square foot office build-outs. Mechanical engineers made arguments that, in the end, suggested that the shapely Hancock Tower in Boston was merely a chase for the mechanical system.
>
> Professionals became increasingly targets of the plaintiff's bar; in the 60s and 70s architects were conventionally sued if anything went wrong at the project. The fall of the house of privity made the architect a direct target of unhappy subcontractors and contractors. The rising tide of civil litigation elevated the role of the -insurance industry. The insurance industry not only affected practice by describing conduct that would result in the loss of coverage, it insisted on a place at the table in the AIA Construction Industry documents being drafted. The effect of listening too closely to the cautions of a prudential insurance industry was that the architect further retreated from the dominant role he had once played. . . .

10. *See* Dermott v. Jones, 69 U.S. 1, 2, 7; 17 L. Ed. 762 (1864):

> It is a well settled rule of law that if a party by his contract charges himself with an obligation possible to be performed, he must make it good, unless its performance is rendered impossible by Act of God, the law or the other party. Unforeseen difficulties, however great, will not excuse him. . . . [The rule] rests upon a solid foundation of reason and justice. It regards the sanctity of contracts. It requires parties to do what they have agreed to do. If unexpected impediments lie in the way and a loss must ensue, it leaves the loss where the contract places it. If the parties have made no provision for a dispensation, the rule of law gives none. It does not allow a contract fairly made to be annulled, and it does not permit to be interpolated what the parties themselves have not stipulated.

modern Associated General Contractors of America) negotiated and cosponsored the so-called Uniform Contract—the first national attempt to create a standard construction contract form. Building on that cooperative mutual relationship, the American Institute of Architects, from 1911 to the present, has published 13 editions of its standard construction documents with the endorsement of the Associated General Contractors of America.[11]

❒ By the mid-1800s, states had begun to enact mechanic's lien statutes to protect unpaid subcontractors, laborers, and materialmen who had performed work on private property. The statutes granted such persons defeasible equitable interests in the improved real estate up to the value of their respective contributions. Such statutes, however, were construed to grant no lien rights in public property.[12]

❒ In 1894, troubled by contractor defaults on federal contracts during the financial panic of 1893 and by the absence of mechanic's lien protection on public projects, Congress enacted the Heard Act. The Heard Act required federal contractors, as a condition of contract award, to post surety bonds to protect subcontractors, laborers, and materialmen against the credit risk of nonpayment and to protect the government against the performance risk of default. In 1935, Congress replaced the Heard Act with the more comprehensive Miller Act. All states followed suit by adopting their own "Little Heard" or "Little Miller" acts. These acts fostered the formation of the modern surety industry.[13]

❒ In the late 1800s, the first treatises were published that addressed some of the subjects recognized today as within the ambit of modern "construction law."[14]

❒ The early 1900s witnessed the emergence of a primary judicial vehicle for development of construction law principles—the modern theory of "contextual contract."[15] This vehicle elastically allowed the judiciary to add contractual terms, conditions, and warranties implied by the

---

11. *See* 2 BRUNER & O'CONNOR, *supra* note 1, § 5:2; Justin Sweet, *The American Institute of Architects: Dominant Actor in the Construction Documents Market*, 1991 WIS. L. REV. 317 (1991).

12. *See, e.g.*, Jordan v. Bd. of Educ. of Taylor's Falls, 39 Minn. 298, 39 N.W. 801 (1888) (mechanic's lien could not be foreclosed against public property).

13. *See* 4 A BRUNER & O'CONNOR, *supra* note 1, §§ 12:8–12:9; Willis D. Morgan, *The History and Economics of Suretyship*, 12 CORNELL L.Q. 153 (1926) and 13 CORNELL L.Q. 487 (1927).

14. *See* 1 BRUNER & O'CONNOR, *supra* note 1, § 1:7.

15. *See* Richard Speidel, *An Essay on the Reported Death and Continued Vitality of Contract*, 27 STAN. L. REV. 1149, 1173–74 (1975); 1A BRUNER & O'CONNOR, *supra* note 1, § 3.2 *et seq.*

transaction's surrounding circumstances[16] and complexity,[17] and to interpret express contractual language in conformance with industry usage, custom, and practice.[18] Contextual contract principles led courts to recognize numerous implied conditions in construction contracts as a matter of law: the owner's implied duty of full disclosure, the owner's implied warranty of the adequacy of detailed design, the contractor's implied duty of good workmanship, the contractor's duty of inquiry and clarification, the mutual implied duty of cooperation, and the mutual implied duty of good faith.[19] In addition, the judiciary fashioned contextual contractual principles of unconscionableness, disproportionality, and misrepresentation, and restitutionary principles of promissory estoppel. Moreover, Congress and state legislatures added their own contextual concepts by using the legislative-administrative process to

---

16. *See* Oliver Wendell Holmes, Jr., *The Path of the Law*, 10 Harv. L. Rev. 457, 466 (1897).

> You always can imply a condition in a contract. But why do you imply it? It is because of some belief as to the practice of the community or of a class, or because of some opinion as to policy, or, in short, because of some attitude of yours upon a matter not capable of exact quantitative measurement, and therefore not capable of founding exact logical conclusions. Such matters really are battle grounds . . . where the decision can do no more than embody the preference of a given body in a given time and place. We do not realize how large a part of our law is open to reconsideration upon a slight change in the habit of the public mind.

See also Todd D. Rakoff, *Social Structure, Legal Structure, and Default Rules: A Comment*, 3 S. Cal. Interdisc. L.J. 19, 20 (1999) ("When we look at the world of contracts as a whole, most of the contextualizing comes from having different norms—whether formulated as rules or as standards—for different types of transactions.").

17. *See* Karen Eggleston, Eric A. Posner, & Richard Zeckhauser, *The Design and Interpretation of Contracts: Why Complexity Matters*, 95 Nw. U. L. Rev. 91, 92 (2000) ("We argue that . . . the current tendency of scholars to focus on completeness and neglect complexity has resulted in an inadequate understanding of contracts and contract law.").

18. *See* Oliver Wendell Holmes, Jr., *The Theory of Legal Interpretation*, 12 Harv. L. Rev. 417 (1899); 1A Bruner & O'Connor, *supra* note 1, § 3:33 *et seq.*; David Ratterman, *Codification of Trade Custom and Usage as a Viable Supplement to Construction Contracts*, 11 J. ACCL 1 (Winter 2017).

Rapid evolution and specialization of language continue to cause misunderstandings. Two hundred fifty years ago, Samuel Johnson, in the preface of his Dictionary of the English Language (1755), the first of the great English dictionaries, wrote:

> It must be remembered, that while our language is yet living, invariably by the caprice of everyone that speaks it . . . words are hourly shifting their relations, and can no more be ascertained in a dictionary, than a grove, in the agitation of a storm, can be accurately delineated from its picture in the water.

19. *See* 1A Bruner & O'Connor, *supra* note 1, §§ 3:4–3:32.

preempt areas of law traditionally reserved for private bargainers and the courts.

- By the late 19th century, competitive bidding laws had been enacted in most jurisdictions to prevent chicanery and fraud in the award of public construction and other contracts by requiring public contracts to be awarded to those responsible bidders who submitted the lowest responsive bids. Known today as the "Design-Bid-Build" or "sealed bid" project delivery method, competitive bidding remains the most widely used procurement approach.[20]

- The 19th century's host of new specialized construction trades—electricians, plumbers, iron workers, steamfitters, and others organized to fabricate or install newly invented technologies—necessitated utilization by supervising "general" contractors of improved construction scheduling techniques, and led to the introduction and widespread use of bar charts in the early 1900s and of sophisticated critical path method networks beginning in the 1950s.[21]

- Following the Great San Francisco Earthquake in 1906, municipalities began to take more seriously and to enact comprehensive building and fire codes formulated by regional code organizations. Hundreds of local and regional building codes developed in the 20th century have been replaced by adoption of the new International Building Code introduced in 2003.[22]

- In the 1920s, the science of "soil mechanics" was founded by a young engineer, Carl Terzaghi.[23] This science led to development in the 1940s of the

---

20. *See* 1 BRUNER & O'CONNOR, *supra* note 1, §§ 2:31–2:158; Ralph Nash, Jr. & Michael Love, Jr., *Innovations in Federal Construction Contracting*, 45 GEO. WASH. L. REV. 309, 310–13 (1977).

21. *See* 5 BRUNER & O'CONNOR, *supra* note 1, §§ 15:3–15:6.

22. *See* M. TOBRINER, THE HISTORY OF BUILDING CODES TO THE 1920S (1984); 5 BRUNER & O'CONNOR, *supra* note 1, §§ 16:1–16:2.

23. Interestingly, it was the law that drove Terzaghi to his new calling. After receiving a mechanical engineering degree in Austria in 1904, Terzaghi worked for a design-build firm. He designed a factory building with footings sized in accordance with the empirical formulae of the day, and had the site load tested with a typical two-foot-by-two-foot platform loaded to 150 percent of design load. No settlement occurred within 24 hours, and Terzaghi allowed the construction to proceed. As soon as the building was completed, it began to settle and crack. Terzaghi was sued and lost quite a bit of money; as a result:

> He began to question the reasons for this failure. He was soon impressed with the high standards of engineering design related to concrete construction compared with the guesswork and ignorance associated with the bearing values of soils that support those structures. He decided to devote himself to this most backward, unscientific aspect of civil engineering practice—the study of soils.

Unified Soil Classification System,[24] which created a scientific framework and terminology for precise classification of soils for engineering purposes by geotechnical professionals worldwide.

☐ By the early 20th century, the increasing complexity of the construction process led the industry to promote specialized industry dispute resolution procedures invoking professional decision making and arbitration. By 1905, before any state had authorized enforcement of arbitration agreements or awards, and at a time when the judiciary was hostile to arbitration under a perception that the forum was intended to divest courts of judicial business, the Uniform Contract of the American Institute of Architects and the National Association of Builders called for resolution of disputes by arbitration.[25] Thereafter, the American Institute of Architects' Standard General Conditions of Contract continued to provide for the resolution of disputes by arbitration. By 1925, Congress had enacted the Federal Arbitration Act, followed after 1955 by most states' adoption of the Uniform Arbitration Act. Thereafter, the judiciary openly embraced arbitration as a favored method of alternate dispute resolution.[26]

Hyman Cunin, *Soils Part I: Engineering Aspects and Physical Properties*, THE CONSTRUCTION SPECIFIER 80 (May 1968).

24. *See* ASTM Standard D2487-98, STANDARD CLASSIFICATION OF SOILS FOR ENGINEERING PURPOSES (UNIFIED SOIL CLASSIFICATION SYSTEM).

25. *See* the Uniform Contract art. XII (1905 ed.):

> In case the Owner and Contractor fail to agree in relation to matters of payment, allowance or loss referred to in Arts. III or VIII of this contract, or should either of them dissent from the decision of the Architects referred to in Art. VII of this contract, which dissent shall have been filed in writing with the Architects within ten days of the announcement of such decision, then the matter shall be referred to a Board of Arbitration to consist of one person selected by the Owner, and one person selected by the Contractor, these two to select a third. The decision of any two shall be final and binding on both parties hereto. Each party shall pay one-half of the expense of such reference.

26. *See* Moses H. Cone Memorial Hosp. v. Mercury Constr. Corp., 460 U.S. 1, 24–25, 103 S. Ct. 927, 941–42, 74 L. Ed. 2d 765 (1983) (enunciating pro-arbitration policy). *See also* 7 and 8 BRUNER & O'CONNOR, *supra* note 1. *See also* U.S. Supreme Court Chief Justice Warren E. Burger, *Using Arbitration to Achieve Justice*, 40 ARB. J. 3, 6 (Dec. 1985):

> I cannot emphasize too strongly to those in business and industry—and especially to lawyers—that every private contract of real consequence to the parties ought to be treated as a "candidate" for binding private arbitration. In the drafting of such contracts, lawyers will serve their clients and the public by resorting to tested clauses the American Arbitration Association has developed to fit particular needs. . . .
>
> We must now use the inventiveness, the ingenuity and the resourcefulness of American businessmen and lawyers—the "Yankee Trader" innovativeness—to shape

❐ In the 21st century, the construction industry remains the largest single segment of the production sector of the American economy[27] and probably of the world economy. The industry also remains one of the most technologically complex. The development of modern engineering principles, sophisticated construction practices, and new building and materials technologies produced a host of specialized design disciplines and construction trades to oversee the design and installation of highly specialized modern systems, equipment, and materials unknown prior to the 20th century, that is, electricity, plumbing, heating and ventilating, lighting, telephones, fiber optic cables, elevators and escalators, fire suppression, curtain wall, roofing and insulation, sealants, reinforced concrete, paints and coatings, and high-strength steel and glass. Those disciplines, systems, equipment, and materials fostered an exponential increase in the complexity, size, and scope of the built environment, including skyscraper office towers with deep foundations, large-bore tunnels, massive dams and power plants, subways and interstate highways, wastewater treatment plants, airports, and harbors.

Construction today has acquired a legendary reputation for extraordinary factual and legal complexity,[28] which is not unjustly earned:

---

new tools to meet new needs. In the area of arbitration, the tools and the techniques are ready and waiting for imaginative lawyers to make use of them.

If the courts are to retain public confidence, they cannot let disputes wait two, three and five years or more to be disposed of. The use of private arbitration is one solution, and lawyers should be at the forefront in moving in this direction.

27. *See* U.S. Department of Labor Bureau of Labor Statistics at http://www.BLS.gov/IAG/TGS/IAG23.htm; Thomas Stipanowich, *Restructuring Construction Law: Reality and Reform in a Transactional System*, 1998 Wis. L. Rev. 463, 465 (1998) ("The largest production sector in the United States economy is the construction industry. It accounts for annual expenditures of a half a trillion dollars per year and directly employs one of every 20 workers, represents as much as 13 percent of the gross national product, and touches the lives of every citizen.").

28. The judiciary itself has embellished this legendary reputation. *See, e.g.*, Erlich v. Menezes, 21 Cal. 4th 543, 87 Cal. Rptr. 2d 886, 896, 981 P.2d 978 (1999), in which the Supreme Court of California observed:

[T]he [owners] may have hoped to build their dream home and live happily ever after, but there is a reason that tagline belongs in fairy tales. Building a house may turn out to be a stress-free project; it is much more likely to be the stuff of urban legends—the cause of bankruptcy, marital dissolution, hypertension, and fleeting fantasies ranging from homicide to suicide. Justice Yegan noted below, "No reasonable homeowner can embark on a building project with certainty that the project will be completed to perfection. Indeed, errors are so likely to occur that few if any

Construction is an inherently complex business. Even casual observers of the construction process are struck by the enormous amount of information required to construct a project. Hundreds, even thousands, of detailed drawings are required. Hundreds of thousands of technical specifications, requests for information, and other documents are needed. Complex calculations are used to produce the design. For years, this complexity dictated a labor-intensive, highly redundant methodology for doing the work. Projects were fragmented and broken into many parts. Different entities undertook different parts of a project, both for design and construction. Therefore, the construction industry became exceptionally fragmented. On a project of even average complexity, there may have been from 5 to 15 firms involved in design. From 40 to 100 companies may have been engaged in construction. Many more companies supplied materials, professional services, and other elements necessary for completion of the project. It was effectively impossible to convey the sum of knowledge necessary to construct a facility in a set of plans and specifications. Stated another way, the information technology traditionally used for construction is inadequate.[29]

Construction's complexity has created recognized public safety risks, which, in turn, have led to increased governmental regulation of the construction process through legislative imposition of licensing laws, safety regulations, and building codes.[30] The recognized financial credit risks inherent in the multiparty construction process have led to legislative enactment of an assortment of laws to protect owners and unpaid construction trades against the risks of contract default.

1.02 CONSTRUCTION DISPUTE RESOLUTION

Like other highly complex fields of human endeavor, the construction process has spawned its own unique customs, practices, and technical vocabulary, which, in turn, led courts and legislatures to develop legal principles consistent with industry realities. Construction law has derived much of its uniqueness from industry experience, customs, and perceived foreseeable risks, which

---

homeowners would be justified in resting their peace of mind on [its] timely or correct completion. . . ." The connection between the service sought and the aggravation and distress resulting from incompetence may be somewhat less tenuous than in a malpractice case, but the emotional suffering still derives from an inherently economic concern.

29. See John W. Hinchey, *Visions for the Next Millennium*, in 1 CONSTR. L. HANDBOOK § 2.01[A] (1999).

30. See 5 BRUNER & O'CONNOR, *supra* note 1, § 16:1 *et seq.*

shaped evolving principles of common law and statutory law applicable to the built environment. Oliver Wendell Holmes, Jr. reminds us that:

> The life of the law has not been logic; it has been experience. The felt necessities of the time, the prevalent moral and political theories, intuitions of public policy, avowed or unconscious, even the prejudices which judges share with their fellow-men, have had a good deal more to do than the syllogism in determining the rules by which men should be governed. The law embodies the story of a nation's development through many centuries, and it cannot be dealt with as if it contained only the axioms and corollaries of a book of mathematics. In order to know what it is, we must know what it has been, and what it tends to become.[31]

Under the weight of a century of contextual experience, construction law, indeed, is evolving into a "separate breed of animal."[32] Construction law today is a primordial "soup" in the "melting pot" of the law—a thick broth consisting of centuries-old legal theories fortified by statutory law and seasoned by contextual legal innovations reflecting the broad factual "realities" of the modern construction process. Construction law has been viewed by some academicians incorrectly as mere "advanced contract law"—a misunderstanding that arises from viewing construction law through the prism of a historically narrow academic discipline rather than through the kaleidoscope of complex legal and factual issues inherent in the construction process itself. Construction law is a "capstone" subject that includes the nuances of the "contextual" contract and the towering legal edifice constructed to govern legal relationships among the multitude of parties—design professionals, contractors, subcontractors, material suppliers, sureties, insurers, or tradesmen—typically engaged in varying

---

31. *See* OLIVER WENDELL HOLMES, JR., THE COMMON LAW 1 (1881).

32. Paul Hardeman, Inc. v. Arkansas Power & Light Co., 380 F. Supp. 298, 317 (E.D. Ark. 1974) ("[C]onstruction contracts are a separate breed of animal; and, even if not completely sui generis, still [the] law must be stated in principles reflecting underlying and industry realities. Therefore, it is not safe to broadly generalize. True, general principles of contract law are applied to construction contracts, but they are applied under different operative conditions. Care must be taken, then, not to rely too uncritically on such cases as those arising from the sale of real or personal property. And even within the larger rubric of 'construction contracts,' it is manifest that the law, if sensitive to the underlying realities, will carefully discriminate between, say, a contract to construct a home and a contract to construct a 50-story office building; between a contract to build a private driveway and a contract to construct an interchange on an interstate highway. This is what one would expect a priori; this is, generally, what one finds when he reviews the actual development of the law.").

degrees in construction projects.[33] These legal relationships include (1) multiple express and implied contractual relationships; (2) tort relationships, rights, and obligations where contractual privity does not exist; (3) suretyship relationships invoking equitable principles governing construction bonds; (4) insurance relationships invoking principles applicable to products insuring construction and design risks; (5) agency principles applicable to construction industry participants and their representatives; (6) design professional rights and liabilities created by common law and statutory duties; (7) construction lender relationships and liabilities pertaining to project financing; (8) statutory rights and obligations created by statutes governing mechanic's liens, public contractor bonds, and public contract bidding; (9) statutory rights and obligations arising under the Uniform Commercial Code governing relationships for the purchase of construction materials and equipment; (10) public duties created by building codes, licensing laws, and health and safety laws; (11) problems of proof of causation of loss; (12) damage measurement and computation principles that recognize construction's imperfect world under doctrines such as "substantial performance" and "economic waste"; and (13) issues unique to construction dispute resolution, partnering, and alliancing.

Like other highly complex fields of law, claims and disputes are endemic,[34] and the litigation of construction disputes relies heavily for proof of causation upon the opinion testimony of experts—a fact of life that can be frustrating to

---

33. The American and foreign jurisdictions that certify construction law as a specialized area of legal practice recognize the field to have significant breadth. *See* Amendments to the Rules Regulating the Florida Bar, 875 So.2d 448 (2004), which establish standards by which a Florida lawyer may become a "board certified construction lawyer" and which define "construction law" as follows:

> "Construction law" is the practice of law dealing with matters relating to the design and construction of improvements on private and public projects including, but not limited to, construction dispute resolution, contract negotiation, preparation, award and administration, lobbying and governmental hearings, oversight and document review, construction lending and insurance, construction licensing, and analysis and litigation of problems arising out of the Florida Construction Lien Law, § 255.05, FLORIDA STATUTES, and the federal Miller Act, 40 U.S.C. § 2470.

34. *See, e.g.*, Certified Power Systems, Inc. v. Dominium Energy Brayton Point, LLC, 2012 WL 384600 *18 (Mass. Super. Ct. 2012), in which a pipe fitter foreman with over 32 years of construction experience offered in testimony his perspective on how endemic construction disputes are: "Every job has its problems. I mean, it's construction. It never works right. It's very, very rare that it goes the way it's supposed to go. But there are some that just don't go at all. This [job] was certainly one of them."

courts[35] and mesmerizing to juries[36]—and all too frequently results in detailed factual records of proceedings that appear "formidable" to finders of fact and reviewing appellate judges.[37] Some judges, overburdened by their judicial workloads, have little time for complex construction cases, and contend that construction cases invoke the "law of the shop" rather than a "law of the court" and should be settled by arbitrators or by other alternate dispute resolution devices.[38] Such views over the years have led to wide industry use of

---

35. *See* E. C. Ernst, Inc. v. Manhattan Constr. Co., 387 F. Supp. 1001, 1005–06 (S.D. Ala. 1974), in which a federal judge, during a pretrial conference, advised the parties:

> Being trained in this field, you are in a far better position to adjust your differences than those untrained in these related fields. As an illustration, I, who have no training whatsoever in engineering, have to determine whether or not the emergency generator system proposed to be furnished . . . met the specifications, when experts couldn't agree. This is a strange bit of logic. . . . The object of litigation is to do substantial justice between the parties' litigant, but the parties' litigant should realize that, in most situations, they are by their particular training better able to accomplish this among themselves. . . .

36. The common "lore" in construction litigation is that the more complex cases should not be tried to a jury and should be reserved for trial to the court or to experienced construction arbitrators.

37. *See* Blake Constr. Co., Inc. v. C.G. Coakley Co., Inc., 431 A.2d 569, 575 (D.C. 1981):

> [E]xcept in the middle of a battlefield, nowhere must men coordinate the movement of other men and all materials in the midst of such chaos and with such limited certainty of present facts and future occurrences as in a huge construction project such as the building of this $100 million hospital. Even the most painstaking planning frequently turns out to be mere conjecture and accommodation to changes must necessarily be of the rough, quick, and *ad hoc* sort, analogous to ever-changing commands on the battlefield. Further, it is a difficult task for a court to be able to examine testimony and evidence in the quiet of a courtroom several years later concerning such confusion and then extract from them a determination of precisely when the disorder and constant readjustment, which is to be expected by any subcontractor on the job site [or by any other party for that matter], became so extreme, so debilitating and so unreasonable as to constitute a breach of contract between the contractor and a subcontractor. This was the formidable undertaking faced by the trial judge in the instant case. . . .

38. For example, former U.S. Supreme Court Chief Justice Warren E. Burger expressed this view (believed to be shared by many in the judiciary) as follows:

> The obligation of the legal profession is, or has long been thought to be, to serve as healers of human conflicts. To fulfill that traditional obligation means that there should be mechanisms that can produce an acceptable result in the shortest possible time, with the least possible expense and with a minimum of stress on the participants. That is what justice is all about. . . .
>
> My overview of the work of the courts from a dozen years on the Court of Appeals and now 16 in my present position, added to 20 years of private practice, has given me some new perspectives on the problems of arbitration.

alternative dispute resolution procedures such as arbitration,[39] and innovative dispute review board, mediation, and stepped claims settlement practices.[40]

1.03 CONSTRUCTION LAW SCHOLARSHIP

Although construction is the largest segment of the production sector of the U.S. gross domestic product, and quite likely of the world's gross domestic product, American legal and economic scholars have paid little attention to the industry.[41] The articulated reasons for such academic oversight, although anecdotal, suggest that legal academicians have been unwilling to acquire practical understanding of the complexities of the construction process and, hence, have been unable to develop significant capability to contribute to the development of law undergirding the construction industry.[42] Those few academicians who have mastered construction law suggest that their academic colleagues have

---

> One thing an appellate judge learns very quickly is that a large part of all the litigation in the courts is an exercise in futility and frustration. A large proportion of civil disputes in the courts could be disposed of more satisfactorily in some other way. . . .
>
> My own experience persuades me that in terms of cost, time, and human wear and tear, arbitration is vastly better than conventional litigation for many kinds of cases.
>
> In mentioning these factors, I intend no disparagement of the skills and broad experience of judges. I emphasize this because to find precisely the judge whose talents and experience fit a particular case of great complexity is a fortuitous circumstance. This can be made more likely if two intelligent litigants agree to pick their own private triers of the issues. This is not at all to bypass the lawyers; they are key factors in this process.
>
> The acceptance of this concept has been far too slow in the United States.

Burger, *supra* note 26.

39. Arbitration was mandated by the Uniform Contract as early as 1905 and by subsequent editions of the Conditions of Contract promulgated by the American Institute of Architects. For background, *see* 7 and 8 BRUNER & O'CONNOR, *supra* note 1.

40. *See* James P. Groton, Robert A. Rubin, & Bettina Quintas, *A Comparison of Dispute Review Boards and Adjudication*, 18 INT'L CONSTR. L. REV. 275 (2001); James P. Groton, *The Progressive or "Stepped" Approach to ADR: Designing Systems to Prevent, Control, and Resolve Disputes*, in CONSTRUCTION DISPUTE RESOLUTION FORMBOOK 1–33 (Robert F. Cushman et al. eds., 1997). See Chapter 19 of this book for more detailed discussion of alternative dispute resolution in the construction arena.

41. *See* William A. Klein & Mitu Gulati, *Economic Organization in the Construction Industry: A Case Study of Collaborative Production under High Uncertainty*, 1 BERKELEY BUS. L. J. 138, 139 (2004); *see also* Diane H. Kay, *The Education of the Construction Work Force in the Post-Industrial Era*, 27 AM. PROF. CONSTRUCTOR 25 (Apr. 2003).

42. *See* Stipanowich, *supra* note 27, at 496.

more interest in "public law,"[43] a subject less dependent on custom and practice and less factually intensive. Although occasional cries have been heard within academia over the years for more scholarly study of construction law issues,[44] American academicians continue to contribute little to the teaching and development of construction law.[45]

The American Bar Association Forum on the Construction Industry and the American College of Construction Lawyers, through the writing and publication of this textbook, intend to introduce a generation of fledgling lawyers to the practice of construction law. While it necessarily will be taught primarily by adjunct faculty, it is this author's hope that the book will inspire an interest in the study of construction law, and that some of the students will, in turn, be inspired to teach others.

---

43. Professor Emeritus Justin Sweet of the Boalt Hall School of Law at the University of California, Berkeley, was one of the few 20th-century legal academicians to devote a career to construction law. In his article, *Construction Law: The Need for Empirical Research*, 23 Constr. Litig. Rptr. 3 (Jan. 2002), he offers the following reason for academia's lack of empirical scholarship in the construction law field:

> One is the lack of full-time law teachers with interest in Construction Law. The best and often only empirical work comes out of the law schools. Law teachers can involve statisticians and sociologists in their studies. Money can be found, though I admit not easily. Yet you can count on one hand the number of full-time teachers of Construction Law, maybe not even that many. Law teachers come out of certain schools, clerk for important judges, and are interested mainly in Public Law. This pool does not produce many teachers who want to spend their time in Construction Law.

44. Professor Edward Patterson of Columbia, in his article, *Builder's Measure of Recovery of Breach of Contract*, 31 Col. L. Rev. 1286 (1931) observed:

> The economic importance of the building industry, the frequency of litigation involving this type of contract, and the inadequacy of judicial analyses of the complex problems of [construction] damages warrants academia's attention.

45. In contrast, European law schools have perceived the importance of construction law as a scholarly endeavor. For example, the University of Strathclyde offers an LLM degree in construction law.

CHAPTER 2

Participants in the Design and Construction Process

ROSS J. ALTMAN

2.01 OVERVIEW

The design and construction of a building or other structure is an elaborate process, requiring the talent, execution, and coordination of many different people and organizations. As the size, cost, complexity, or unusual features of a project increase, the number of participants needed to design and construct that project likely increases as well. The financial, technical, business, and regulatory challenges involved in a project, even one of modest size, demand the skill and expertise of a wide range of project participants. Each participant makes a separate contribution to the project. Nonetheless, the activities of one inextricably bear upon the performance of the others.

Like any complex process, ample opportunity exists for difficulty along the way. The reliance of each participant in the design and construction process on the performance of the other participants creates challenges to successful completion. Many participants will not have worked together previously, and each participant may have different policies and methods through which it conducts its operations. International projects may involve language barriers, multiple cultures, and the practical obstacles created by long distances and different time zones. Moreover, every project is tantamount to a custom-made item, presenting its own unique set of problems for the project team to solve.

In order to overcome such challenges, those involved in the production of a project must be well organized and coordinated. This book explores the multitude of legal issues that arise out of a process that has collaboration as its goal but that often fosters disputes and controversy. To consider such legal issues, however, it is first necessary to understand the roles and objectives of each of the typical participants in the design and construction process.

2.02 THE OWNER

The owner furnishes the project site, is responsible for satisfaction of certain regulatory requirements necessary to develop and use the project site, and pays for the development of the project. As the participant that initiates the project, the owner essentially bears responsibility for ensuring that all activities involved in the delivery of the project are performed. Some owners possess skill and prior experience with the design and construction process; those owners, therefore, may assume an active role in the delivery of a project. Other owners may undertake a project only once, and, consequently, participate less directly in project delivery. Regardless, an owner usually delegates various activities to third parties that have the skill, experience, and manpower the owner does not possess.

Each owner differs from all others in some measure. First, issues important to one owner may not be particularly meaningful to another. Cost concerns are paramount to many owners, while other owners may place greater emphasis on time requirements. Second, owners possess a wide range of characteristics. An owner may be a large organization, may be in the private sector, may be well capitalized, may have a complicated internal approval process, or may possess totally different characteristics. The project objectives most important to the owner and traits defining the owner often explain much about the organizational structure of a construction transaction and how a project is delivered.

Public owners, such as federal, state, and local governments, are obligated to procure and manage construction projects pursuant to a statutory and regulatory framework.[1] Public entities are not free to engage in innovative project

---

1. Public entities must comply with a complex set of procurement statutes when awarding a contract, and then only enter into contracts that conform to applicable regulations.

delivery methodologies, absent enabling legislation.[2] Private owners, on the other hand, have significant flexibility in how they procure and conduct the design and construction of a project. Although a private owner may have certain business policies and practices that impose limitations, such restrictions are likely to be less burdensome than those imposed by law on the public owner.

The nature of the owner's interest in the project also can affect the manner in which the project is delivered. If the project is simply an investment vehicle, the owner may focus more on achieving an anticipated rate of return from that investment, rather than on satisfying costly operational preferences of a third-party end user who is purchasing or leasing a portion of the project. An owner who intends to occupy and use the project, however, may treat the project as a long-term capital investment and place greater emphasis on technical and performance aspects of that project.

The manner in which the owner pays for a project may influence the design and construction process. Because late or defective completion of a project adversely affects the ability of a construction lender to recover the loaned amount and anticipated interest, construction lenders commonly require various contractual provisions and project controls aimed at ensuring (1) that the contractor completes the project in conformance with the drawings and specifications, (2) that the payments are made only for work properly completed, and (3) that the loan remains in balance.[3] Owners who undertake projects with their own funds are free from the restrictions and administrative burdens commonly imposed by a construction lender.

Interactions with the owner may depend on the type of business entity in which the owner is organized. Parties that contract with the owner need to know who is authorized to act on behalf of the owner. That determination is relatively easy when dealing with an individual or a partnership. The scope of authority of various persons associated with the owner, however, is less clear when the owner is a limited liability company or corporation. Indeed, larger entities with complex business structures often are unable to act quickly and must establish consensus within their own organization prior to making a decision.

---

2. For example, most public entities enact special legislation prior to proceeding with a public-private partnership for a construction project or other form of procurement that varies from a competitively bid process.

3. In other words, that the undisbursed balance of the loan is greater than the remaining cost to complete the project.

2.03 THE DESIGN TEAM

A. The Architect

Although some owners have in-house design capability, the vast majority of owners retain third-party design professionals to prepare the drawings and specifications from which the project is constructed.[4] For a project in the general building sector, an architect usually leads the design effort.[5] The contractual obligations performed by an architect are usually described as "services."[6] Performance of services typically begins either with the preparation of a program for a project or with the review of a program supplied by the owner.[7] The architect's services are performed in various phases. During each successive phase of design services, the drawings and specifications become more detailed and finalized.[8]

As a practical matter, the drawings and specifications are never really complete. Even if possible, the time and cost to describe every detail of a project in the drawings and specifications would be prohibitive. The construction team must fill in the blanks by constructing what is "reasonably inferable" from the contract documents.[9] Also, certain aspects of the project design may pertain to proprietary products or systems or require particular knowledge unique to such products or systems. Those portions of the design are reserved for the construction team to complete through the shop drawing process.[10]

The architect often assists the owner in procuring the construction contract and administering the construction process. Services provided by an architect during the construction phase are typically limited to performing specified

---

4. For a description of the design process, see Chapter 6.

5. An engineer is more likely to be the lead design professional for projects that don't involve human occupancy (e.g., a bridge or road), or that have a principal purpose other than human occupancy (e.g., a power plant or manufacturing facility).

6. Generally speaking, the parlance of the industry is that design professionals provide "services" and construction contractors perform "work."

7. Schematic design, the first phase of the architect's design services under AIA contract forms, is based on the owner's program. American Institute of Architects, AIA Document B101–2017, Standard Form of Agreement between Owner and Architect §§ 1.1.1 and 3.2.1 (2017) [hereinafter AIA Document B101-2017]. The owner is obligated to provide the architect with certain information, including "a written program which shall set forth the Owner's objectives; schedule; constraints and criteria, including space requirements and relationships; flexibility; expandability; special equipment; systems; and site requirements." *Id.* § 5.1.

8. *See id.* §§ 3.2–3.4.

9. *See* American Institute of Architects, AIA Document A201–2017, *General Conditions of the Contract for Construction* § 1.2.1 (2017) [hereinafter AIA Document A201–2017].

10. The shop drawing process is described in *id.* § 3.12.

activities intended to provide the owner with some level of assurance that the project is being constructed in accordance with the approved drawings and specifications, as well as performing certain administrative functions.[11] Although an architect participates in the construction phase of the project, architects very rarely accept any responsibility for construction means, methods, techniques, sequences, and procedures, or for safety measures and precautions.[12]

B. The Engineers and Consultants

The design services required of the architect commonly include structural, mechanical, and electrical engineering services.[13] Depending on the nature of the project, other specialized engineering or consulting services might be expected. Some architectural firms possess engineering capability, but few perform sophisticated engineering tasks in-house. Instead, an architect commonly enters into sub-consulting agreements with engineers and other specialty design consultants.[14]

Therefore, the architect creates the overall design concept for the project and makes many fundamental design decisions; however, engineers and consultants carry out much of the actual design under sub-consulting agreements with the architect. Even third-party engineers and consultants retained by an architect, however, may need to retain specialists with respect to particular matters. Depending on the scope and complexity of the project, the design team may be composed of multiple tiers of sub-consultants. Notwithstanding the delegation of duties, the architect manages and coordinates the efforts of its entire design team, and remains responsible to the owner for the services rendered by all of the architect's direct and indirect sub-consultants.[15]

Finally, some aspects of the project may require highly specialized design skills or knowledge that an architect neither possesses nor considers itself capable of managing. An architect may be reluctant simply to serve as a conduit

---

11. *See* AIA Document B101–2017, *supra* note 7, § 3.6.

12. Such responsibility is disclaimed routinely. *See* AIA Document B101–2017, *supra* note 7, § 3.6.1.2; AIA Document A201–2017, *supra* note 9, § 4.2.2.

13. *See* AIA Document B101–2017, *supra* note 7, § 3.1.

14. Note that for a larger project, the architect may identify certain subconsultants at the time the owner and architect enter into an agreement. American Institute of Architects, AIA B103–2017, *Standard Form of Agreement between Owner and Architect for a Large or Complex Project*, § 1.1.12 (2017).

15. Although such responsibility is not explicitly stated in AIA documents, the architect delegates the performance of its services to subconsultants. Therefore, the architect generally remains responsible to the owner for such services. *See* 5 Philip L. Bruner & Patrick J. O'Connor, Bruner & O'Connor on Construction Law § 17:71 (West Group 2002).

between the owner and the provider of such specialty services, especially if those services are considered high risk, such as geotechnical or environmental engineering. In such circumstances, the architect typically insists that the owner contract directly with the necessary specialty design professionals.

2.04 THE CONSTRUCTION TEAM

A. The Contractor

Construction companies enter into contracts with the owner to construct a project and, therefore, are known as contractors. When contracting with an owner directly, a contractor is referred to as a prime contractor. Many owners prefer to retain one prime contractor to assume principal responsibility for construction of the project. That prime contractor commonly is referred to as a general contractor.[16] For many reasons, however, some projects require multiple prime contractors. Construction contracts often refer to prime contractors that are not a party to that particular construction contract as separate contractors (i.e., a prime contractor under a separate contract).

The contractual obligations of a contractor are typically referred to as the work.[17] The principal objective of the contractor is to complete construction of the project or the scope of work required under the construction contract. The work involves many other related activities, however, such as reviewing field conditions and construction documents,[18] maintaining labor harmony at the project site,[19] supplying certain materials and other items necessary for the general requirements of construction,[20] obtaining construction permits,[21] preparing shop drawings,[22] maintaining the project site's security,[23] cleaning

---

16. A prime contractor responsible for performing work only in a single trade (e.g., carpentry, concrete) usually would be referred to as a "trade contractor." The term "general contractor" implies responsibility for multiple disciplines or trades.

17. *See* AIA Document A201-2017, *supra* note 9, § 1.1.3, which provides that the "Work means the construction and services required by the Contract Documents . . . and includes all other labor materials, equipment or services provided or to be provided by the Contractor to fulfill the Contractor's obligations.".

18. *See id.* § 3.2.
19. *See id.* § 3.4.3.
20. *See id.* § 3.4.1.
21. *See id.* § 3.7.1.
22. *See id.* § 3.12.5.
23. *See id.* § 10.2.3.

up the project site,[24] testing and start-up of a project,[25] and maintaining safety precautions and programs.[26]

The drawings and specifications prepared by the design team rarely include any instruction to the contractor regarding how the project should be constructed. The contractor exercises its own judgment to determine which construction means, methods, techniques, sequences, and procedures the contractor will employ to construct the project.[27] Such decisions are important, because the manner in which the project is constructed affects the cost and time of the general contractor's performance.

Not all contractors use the same construction means and methods. For example, a contractor may decide to use certain equipment or a methodology that the contractor believes will cost less or save time compared to other approaches favored by its competitors. Owners and architects strive to avoid interfering with how the contractor constructs the project, as such action could adversely affect the contractor's ability to satisfy its contractual obligations. Therefore, owners and architects commonly disclaim any responsibility for the construction means, methods, techniques, sequences, or procedures.[28]

The contractor's approach to constructing a project also is important because the approach bears directly on the safety of construction workers and others who may come into contact with the work. The owner and architect want to avoid, or at least limit, the potential for claims against them arising out of bodily injuries, which can involve significant damages. That concern provides another reason why most construction contracts provide that the contractor, solely, is responsible for construction means, methods, techniques, sequences, and procedures.[29]

---

24. *See id.* § 3.15.

25. Such responsibilities are common to contracts for projects where an engineering process is involved. For example, a power plant or manufacturing facility, or specialized building systems such as elevators. Because such activities are often crucial to confirm the adequacy of the completed project, separate contracts sometimes are required to describe such services and applicable standards, as well as to allocate responsibility. *See* American Institute of Architects, AIA Document B211-2007, *Standard Form of Architect's Services: Commissioning* (2007), regarding the retention of an architect to provide commissioning services.

26. *See* AIA Document A201-2017, *supra* note 9, § 10.2.1.

27. *See id.* § 3.3.1.

28. *See* AIA Document B101-2017, *supra* note 7, § 3.6.1.2; AIA Document A201-2017, *supra* note 9, § 4.2.2.

29. *See* AIA Document A201-2017, *supra* note 9, § 3.3.1.

B. The Subcontractors

Performance of construction work requires a wide range of skill and expertise. Most projects are technically complex, involve multiple trades (e.g., mechanical, electrical, carpentry, concrete), and depend on knowledge of particular products or systems that may be proprietary. Although some general contractors perform construction work with their own forces (i.e., their own employees), such self-performed work is usually limited to a particular trade with which the general contractor is very familiar, such as carpentry or concrete work. It is not efficient for general contractors to maintain a large staff of employees to perform work in each trade. A general contractor would have difficulty keeping a large number of employees busy on a full-time basis, as well as maintaining the level of skill and expertise required of specialized work.

Therefore, most general contractors function as managers of the construction process, and retain other contractors with specialized skill and knowledge for each trade on a project-by-project basis. Such specialized trade contractors, when retained by a prime or general contractor directly, are referred to as subcontractors. On a large project, a general contractor might retain 50 or more subcontractors to perform various portions of the work.[30] Although the work is performed by subcontractors, from a legal standpoint, the general contractor simply delegates its obligations to another party. The general contractor, therefore, remains responsible to the owner for the performance of all work performed through the general contractor's subcontractors.[31]

The scope of work delegated to a subcontractor also may include items that the subcontractor customarily does not perform with its own forces. When a subcontractor retains another contractor to perform such specialized work at the site, that specialized contractor customarily is referred to as a sub-subcontractor.[32] In such an arrangement, the subcontractor retained directly by the general, or prime contractor, might be referred to as a first-tier subcontractor, whereas the sub-subcontractor is sometimes referred to as a second-tier subcontractor. There may be many tiers of subcontractors on a large or complex project.

A subcontractor might also enter into purchase orders or other agreements with suppliers. Unlike subcontractors, suppliers do not perform work at the

---

30. *See* KARL SABBAGH, SKYSCRAPER: THE MAKING OF A BUILDING (Penguin Books 1989) for a description of the development of a large project.
31. *See* AIA Document A201–2017, *supra* note 9, § 3.3.2.
32. *See id.* § 5.1.2.

site, but rather only supply materials or equipment for the project.[33] Sometimes the prime or general contractor may purchase materials and equipment from a supplier directly. Depending on the size or complexity of the scope of work, multiple tiers of suppliers also may be involved in a project.

Even though a subcontractor may delegate a portion of its work to third parties, the subcontractor remains contractually liable to the general contractor for the scope of work that is delegated to such subcontractor, regardless of whether such work is performed by the subcontractor's own forces or through lower-tier subcontractors or suppliers. The subcontractor must supervise and coordinate all such activities.[34]

2.05 THE TYPICAL SUPPORTING CAST

Although the principal players in a project are the owner, the members of the design team, and the members of the construction team, it would not be possible to complete a project without the support of many other entities.

A. Construction Lenders

Few owners have sufficient cash on hand to pay for the design and construction of a project. Even those owners with the assets and liquidity required to fund a project frequently prefer to use such assets to pay for expenses pertaining to their core business or for other investments. Therefore, owners often pay for a construction project through a combination of debt and equity. The debt component may take various forms, such as a traditional construction loan or bond financing.

A lender generally does not make a construction loan unless the owner invests a certain level of equity in the project. Additionally, construction financing is not a long-term loan. Construction lenders expect the loan to be paid off within a short time following completion of the project. That typically is accomplished by the owner obtaining a long-term permanent loan. The proceeds of the permanent loan are used to pay off the construction lender after project completion, and also allow the owner to amortize the costs of construction over

---

33. The American Institute of Architects' AIA form documents do not define the term "supplier." For a more detailed discussion of the distinction between subcontractors and suppliers, see Chapter 10.

34. *See* American Institute of Architects, AIA Document A401–2017, *Standard Form of Agreement between Contractor and Subcontractor* § 4.2 (2017).

a longer period of time. Because of the risk involved in construction activities, the interest rate charged by a construction lender is higher than that charged by a lender providing a loan after project completion.

Sometimes projects are financed through the sale of bonds, which are purchased by investors who expect to be repaid their purchase price plus a stated amount of interest. The bonds might not be retired or paid off until long after project completion occurs, perhaps 10, 20, or even 30 years after the bonds are issued. Bonds are used frequently by public agencies to finance capital improvement projects, although private entities, particularly corporations, may issue bonds to finance construction projects. The interest rate paid under a bond depends on a number of factors, such as project-related risk, credit enhancement techniques, the rating of the bond provided by an outside agency, and tax considerations.[35]

Regardless of the source of construction financing, any entity providing funds or credit enhancement for the project will require that certain measures are taken to ensure repayment of these funds and the agreed-upon interest.

- Without completion of the project, the lender's ability to recover the principal loan amount and anticipated interest is impaired. Although the project will be security for repayment of a construction loan, lenders do not want to take over a partially completed project; that is not a lender's core business and is often a losing proposition. Therefore, as a means of facilitating project completion by the borrower, a construction lender typically requires an allocation of risk in the construction contract that does not overburden its borrower (the owner). To provide additional assurance that the project will be completed, lenders often mandate compliance with various insurance specifications, as well as require a contractor to furnish payment and performance bonds. A lender also may require peer review of particularly important or innovative design elements.
- Construction lenders frequently require procedures to ensure (1) that progress payments are made only for work properly completed and (2) that the balance of the amount remaining to be paid to the general contractor equals or exceeds the value of work not yet performed.[36]

---

35. The interest rate earned on the principal amount of the bond relates directly to the risk that payment will be made by the bond issuer to the bondholder. Higher risk translates into a higher rate of interest.

36. The lender may also want to establish a reserve fund to pay for unexpected costs.

Such procedures often involve use of an architect retained by the construction lender to provide independent advice with respect to the general contractor's applications for payment and completion of the work.

B. Insurance Companies

Each participant in the design and construction process assumes substantial risk. Design errors, worker injuries, and defective construction, just to name a few potential problems, can cause significant damage and loss, and claims and disputes. Quality control efforts and funding of loss reserves may help, but they are not always cost-effective methods to control or manage risk. Few business entities would remain viable for any length of time without implementing some method of risk transfer.

As a result, owners, design professionals, contractors, and others associated with the development or operation of a project routinely procure and maintain insurance.[37] Various types and forms of policies have evolved over time to provide a mosaic-like coverage for the risks most commonly associated with a construction project. As a practical matter, no single insurance policy will provide complete coverage. Therefore, design agreements and construction contracts often specify requirements for a number of insurance policies, most commonly commercial general liability insurance, worker's compensation insurance, employer's liability insurance, motor vehicle liability insurance, professional liability insurance, and environmental liability insurance, as well as other terms and conditions related to procuring and maintaining insurance coverage.

Because insurance is vital to the economic viability of construction projects, insurance companies wield a great deal of influence over the design professions and the construction industry. For example, as a condition of coverage, insurers may require compliance with safety programs or mandate other measures that help ameliorate their exposure to claims and loss payments.[38] Also, insurance companies will accept only certain risks. The participants in a project, therefore, generally attempt to negotiate contract terms that limit their liability to insurable risks. Insurers further manage their risk by entering into agreements, sometimes called treaties, with reinsurers, who provide insurance

---

37. For a more detailed discussion of insurance and its importance to the construction industry, see Chapter 18.

38. This is particularly so with a so-called owner-controlled insurance program (an OCIP) and other similar programs commonly referred to as wrap-ups.

to the primary insurer (i.e., the insurance company that issues the underlying policy to the named insureds). A reinsurer may also reinsure its own risks through another reinsurance company known as a retrocessionaire.

C. Sureties

Payment and performance bonds issued by sureties sometimes are required to provide security for a contractor's performance of its contractual obligations. In essence, the payment bond guarantees payments to certain subcontractors and suppliers, and the performance bond guarantees completion of the construction work and certain obligations that flow out of the work. Generally, only construction work is bondable, not design services. The performance of construction activities can be monitored and evaluated by many metrics, and, therefore, is underwritten routinely by surety companies. The performance of design services, however, is not as easy to assess. Therefore, sureties are reluctant to issue bonds for design activities alone.[39]

Unlike insurance, suretyship is not really a transfer of risk, but more of a form of credit enhancement. An insurer expects to pay losses, and offsets such payments with premiums it receives from its customers and from income generated by investing premiums. In other words, in the event of a valid and covered claim, and subject to the terms of the policy, the insurer will bear the loss.

A surety, on the other hand, charges a fee for conducting a very thorough underwriting process, which may result in the surety issuing a bond to a project owner (also known as an obligee). By issuing the bond, the surety agrees to stand behind and extend its credit on behalf of a contractor (also referred to as the principal). A surety, however, does not intend to bear any loss. Rather, the surety requires the contractor (the principal) to indemnify the surety from all loss, damage, cost, and expense the surety may incur as a result of having issued a bond, and may require collateral or other security through which to satisfy the indemnity obligation.

By law, many public entities require payment and performance bonds on construction projects. Private owners have no such obligation. Many private owners prefer to avoid the expense of a bond or may choose to bond only major subcontractors. Letters of credit sometimes are used as an alternative to a surety bond, particularly on international projects. Insurance products, such as subcontractor default insurance, also provide an alternative to bonds. Such surety bond alternatives, however, are not always permitted on public projects.

---

39. Design services are bonded sometimes in connection with a design-build project.

D. Title Insurance

Title insurance provides protection for defects in title, and for liens and other encumbrances on real property. Policies are available for the benefit of owners and for the benefit of lenders (both construction lenders and permanent lenders). If title insurance is provided during construction, then at the time of each progress payment to the contractor, a "date-down endorsement" is issued to increase the amount of insurance by the amount of progress payment made.

In addition, title insurers often serve as escrow agents for disbursement of funds to contractors, even when not issuing title insurance. When acting as an escrow agent, the title insurer reviews lien waivers, sworn statements, and other documentation to confirm that title is free and clear of claims, liens, and other encumbrances prior to making disbursements of funds or issuing any insurance. If a lien or other encumbrance for which the contractor is responsible is disclosed, an adequate amount of funds may be withheld to satisfy the amount of the encumbrance.

E. Public Authorities

For the health, safety, and general protection of the public, the design professions and construction industry are regulated. Such regulations take many forms and differ somewhat among jurisdictions. Design professionals and some trades in the construction industry must be licensed and registered. Government agencies issue permits to authorize commencement of construction, and issue various certificates to allow occupancy. Government agencies also perform inspections of work in progress and require various tests to demonstrate compliance with minimum safety requirements.

The design and construction process also is subject to many codes. For example, a zoning ordinance will dictate permitted uses of real property as well as various requirements that affect the design of a structure. The design of a project also must comply with applicable building codes, which may be composed of separate codes for structural design, plumbing, electrical, HVAC, and fire protection. Finally, building codes and other laws, such as the Occupational Safety and Health Act, affect the manner in which construction work is performed.

F. Others

The supporting cast just described is simply representative of the type of entities that commonly contribute to the design and construction process. Those with other distinctive skill and expertise also are involved in many projects.

With the emergence of new technologies and methods of delivering a project, the list will only grow.

2.06 ASSEMBLING THE PROJECT TEAM

A. Transaction Structure

As described earlier, the number of participants on any given project extends well beyond the parties most closely associated with the project, that is, the owner, architect, and general contractor. Behind the scenes, a wide range of subcontractors, suppliers, engineers, consultants, and other entities support the design and construction process, or otherwise perform various services or work that contribute to the completion of a project. It is not possible to design and construct a project without the collective efforts of many persons and entities.

Collective efforts, however, do not translate automatically into collaboration. The sheer number of participants in a project gives rise to an almost endless array of interrelationships to consider and coordinate. Each project participant has a contractual relationship with one or more other project participants, but likely also has separate functional relationships with project participants beyond those with whom it has a direct contract.

Consider a relatively straightforward contractual structure for a small project, in which the owner undertakes development of a commercial building for its own use and, perhaps, intends to lease some space to third parties. To accomplish its objectives, the owner retains an architect and a general contractor, enters into lease agreements with a tenant or two, and also endeavors to complete the project as needed to facilitate its own business operations and relationships. Figure 2.1 offers a simplified depiction of some of the contractual relationships that are reasonably certain to occur in connection with such a project.

In reality, Figure 2.1 could highlight many more relationships pertaining to the project; the chart could continue to expand outward to reveal additional tiers of parties further removed from the owner, but who nonetheless affect construction progress or the economics of the overall transaction. Moreover, Figure 2.1 does not depict certain functional relationships, such as the role of public authorities or dealings between parties that may not have a direct contractual relationship. Those relationships would be an overlay on top of the contractual relationships shown in Figure 2.1.

Determining the entities that will participate in a project, and their respective roles, also is affected by the type of project. Construction is not limited to the general building sector. There are many other types of projects and

FIGURE 2.1
Sample Project Contractual Relationships

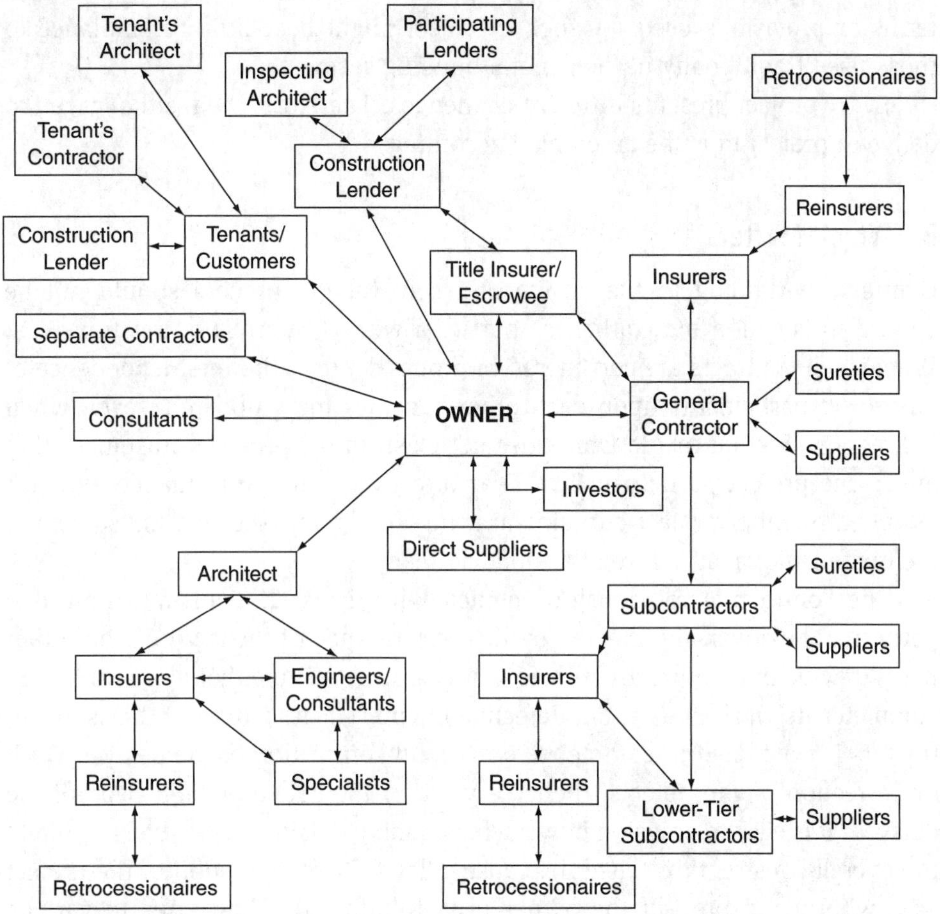

construction industry sectors, each of which has its own customs and practices.[40] The organizational chart in Figure 2.1 might look very different if the project were a highway or a manufacturing facility.

For example, it is unlikely that an architect would lead the design effort for an industrial or infrastructure project. In fact, an architect may not be involved at all (e.g., an engineer might be the appropriate entity to lead the design team for an industrial project). Furthermore, given the importance of certain

---

40. ENGINEERING NEWS-RECORD, a trade publication, periodically publishes a list of the largest contractors and design professionals, often identifying the percentage of business for each listed entity in nine different industry sectors, including general building, manufacturing, power, water supply, sewer/solid waste, industrial process/petroleum, transportation, hazardous waste, and telecommunications.

specialized pieces of equipment to the operation or performance of highly engineered projects, manufacturers and suppliers may have a more prominent role in the organization of the project team. Indeed, many of the contractual terms or provisions used for such a project might bear little resemblance to those used traditionally in the general building sector.

Every project presents different challenges. Therefore, the team engaged to deliver a project must be assembled accordingly.

B. Why It Matters

Contracts pertaining to the design and construction process should not be viewed in isolation but, rather, as part of a web of interrelated relationships. When such contracts are considered in proper context, the interdependence of all project participants upon each other becomes more apparent, even when a direct contractual relationship does not exist. In fact, the circumstances that affect one project participant can bear directly on the performance and risk assumed by other project participants who are several so-called links away in the organizational structure of the project team.

The contractual relationships depicted in Figure 2.1 illustrate how one party may be adversely affected by the performance of those with whom that party may be only indirectly related. For example, assume that a subcontractor completes its work late or in a defective manner. If the work of other subcontractors is scheduled to commence only upon completion of the delayed work or correction of the defects, then the work of the subcontractor also will be delayed. It is easy to envision how such cascading delays might adversely affect the overall construction schedule, cause delay to the completion of the project as a whole, and prevent the owner from fulfilling its obligations to various third parties. As a result, the loss or harm to the owner will have been caused by an entity with whom the owner had no direct contractual relationship.

In sum, whenever stress is placed on any contractual or functional relationship pertaining to a construction project, that stress has the potential to resonate throughout all other project relationships. Those parties more closely linked to the immediate source of the stress are more likely to feel the adverse effects, but that is not always the case. Problems confronted by any one of the project participants easily can reverberate throughout the project team, resulting in defective or delayed performance, and disputes and claims.

Also, in order to fulfill its obligations and avoid undue risk, each project participant attempts to ensure that its obligations and rights with respect to downstream contracting parties align appropriately with its upstream obligations and rights. No project participant wants to assume upstream obligations greater than those it delegates downstream, nor have downstream rights less than those granted upstream. A project participant looks to make its positions within the web of contractual relationships no worse than "back-to-back."

Finally, understanding the interactions among the many project participants is crucially important given the application of the so-called Economic Loss Rule. Discussed in much greater detail in Chapter 21, the Economic Loss Rule is a common law principle that prohibits tort claims for recovery of pure economic loss (e.g., lost profits), with some exceptions depending on jurisdiction. Each state applies some version of the doctrine.

The theory behind the Economic Loss Rule was described by the Supreme Court of Maryland in *Balfour Beatty Infrastructure, Inc. v. Rummel Klepper & Kahl, LLP*,[41] which noted that the reason for requiring privity or its equivalent to impose liability for economic loss "is to limit the defendant's risk of exposure to an actually foreseeable event, thus permitting a defendant to control the risk to which the defendant is exposed."[42] The court further explained that "the complex web of contracts that typically undergirds a public construction project should govern because parties have sufficient opportunity to protect themselves (and anticipate their liability) in negotiating these contracts."[43]

Although the *Balfour Beatty Infrastructure* case involved a public project, the principles of the Economic Loss Rule apply to all construction projects, regardless of ownership or sector. While all persons are expected to conduct themselves in a manner that avoids causing bodily injury or property damage, the failure to act accordingly is addressed by tort law. On the other hand, economic loss arises out of disappointed commercial expectations, the ramifications of which are more appropriately addressed in and determined by the contract between the parties to that specific transaction involved.

Therefore, absent contractual privity, a project participant that suffers economic loss may not have a direct cause of action against the project participant actually responsible for such economic loss. The law may require that such a claim be made against a party with whom the claimant has a direct contract, and then follow the chain of contracts through various third-party actions until it reaches the party ultimately responsible. But, any break in the chain, such as a judgment proof entity or a limitation of liability clause, might prevent that claim from reaching its intended destination. Understanding the web of contractual relationships allows the project participants to evaluate risk, and better allocate responsibility for commercial expectations.

---

41. 451 Md. App. 600, 155 A.3d 445 (Md. 2016).
42. *Id.*, *quoting* Walpert, Smullian & Blumenthal, P.A. v. Katz, 361 Md. 645, 671, 762 A.2d 582 (Md. 2000).
43. *Id.* at 460, 451 Md. at 626.

QUESTIONS

1. If you were counsel to an architect or contractor, what concerns might you have if the owner were a large institutional corporation as opposed to a small partnership?
2. What advantages might an owner have when funding construction out of its own funds as opposed to financing construction through an institutional lender?
3. What advantages and disadvantages might arise for an owner who retains a large architect with in-house engineering capability? What benefits might accrue to an owner who contracts separately with an architect and various engineers?
4. Describe how the failure or default of one project participant might adversely affect others involved in a project. Can any measure be taken to protect against such situations?

CHAPTER 3

The Owner's Role

LORENCE H. SLUTZKY AND DENNIS J. POWERS

3.01 OVERVIEW

To initiate a project, the owner's program or building requirements must be defined, a design professional engaged, and a construction delivery system selected based on rough estimates of construction costs. Once the owner defines the structure's building requirements, appropriate sites are investigated. Site selection must be based on considerations of regulatory restrictions imposed by title, zoning, environmental, and other regulatory restrictions imposed by governmental authorities with jurisdiction as well as political realities. Relevant information is provided to the design professional. Construction documents are prepared. Financing of the project is secured. A contractor is either selected or awarded a construction contract. Building permits, as well as ingress and egress permits are secured. Construction easements and licenses may also be required. The selected contractor commences construction in coordination with the governmental authorities with jurisdiction. Timing of construction in the northern latitudes must be considered in light of the realities of the potential for harsh winters, and in the southern latitudes based upon hurricane season.

3.02 PROVIDING THE BUILDING SITE

Selection and procurement of a building site requires more than just an evaluation of the location for the structure's ultimate use. Indeed, before a decision to purchase the site, a comprehensive analysis of a multitude of factors that may impact design, construction, and ultimate use must be performed. Upon acquisition, the owner typically has a contractual duty to provide the design professional with the legal details pertaining to the property.[1]

Acquisition of a building site requires assessment of many factors, for example, zoning, covenants that follow title restricting what can be built, the existence of easements under or over the property that may impair design or use, and soil bearing capacity and environmental issues that must be considered for their impact on design and construction costs. Similarly, access, location, and sufficiency of utilities must be considered. The zoning, demolition, and the construction permit process are potentially politically charged issues that may be negatively impacted by social conflicts. These conflicts may arise during the acquisition, design, zoning, permitting, staging, construction, or during the ultimate use of the project.

The decision to acquire the building site property includes all of the preceding factors and more. Failure to anticipate these needs is likely to result in delay, additional cost, and possible rejection of the project. Each of these factors must be evaluated as a part of the design and construction equation in making the decision to acquire the proposed building site. Failure to heed these considerations may constitute trespass, resulting in recoverable damage to the property, injunctive relief precluding access to the site, delay and delay damages and related costs, or an inability to commence or complete the project.

A. Access to the Construction Site and Necessary Adjacencies

Prior to the owner issuing a notice to proceed, preferably before the project is bid, access to the construction site as well as necessary easements or licenses to adjacent properties must be secured. Consideration of continuous lateral and subjacent support to adjoining lands must be considered.[2] For example,

---

1. It is the owner's contractual obligation to provide the design professional with a survey of the physical characteristics of the site, legal limitations, a legal description, rights-of-way restrictions, easements, encroachments, deed restrictions, and other critical data. *See, e.g.*, American Institute of Architects, AIA Document B101-2017, Standard Form of Agreement between Owner and Architect § 5.4 (2017) [hereinafter AIA Document B101-2017] and American Institute of Architects, AIA Document B103-2017, Standard Form of Agreement between Owner and Architect for a Large or Complex Project § 5.5 (2017) [hereinafter AIA Document B103-2017].

2. Adjacent Landowner Excavation Protection Act, 765 Ill. Comp. Stat. 140 *et seq.*

underpinning may require access to an adjacent site. A flyover may be required over another jurisdiction's roadway. Construction traffic ingress and egress may require a permit from the state, county, municipality, and/or special district. A temporary easements or license from adjacent private property owners may be required. All necessary temporary construction easements and licenses must be timely secured.

The owner owes to the contractor an implied duty and usually an express obligation to provide unencumbered site access.[3] Prior to the owner issuing the notice to proceed to the contractor, access to the building site must be secured for the type of construction to be undertaken. Unless the responsibility to obtain access to the site is expressly delegated to the contractor, site access remains the owner's responsibility. The obligation to provide site access must remain in effect throughout the course of the contractor's performance, and can be breached even if the owner is not directly responsible for the contractor's inability to gain access to the project site. Access to the site includes permits for construction. Construction permits include the following: building, storm drainage, pollutant discharge, and site roadway construction ingress and egress permits issued by the authority with jurisdiction, for example, the state highway, county highway, or local municipality.

If access to the work area is impeded by work of another contractor, the owner likely will be deemed to have breached its implied or express obligation and, in some jurisdictions, an implied warranty to provide timely and adequate site access to the obstructed contractor.[4]

Ensuring that a contractor has adequate site access may require a construction easement agreement with adjacent landowners that permit the use of the adjacent property for the limited purpose of constructing the building. A failure by an owner to procure the necessary rights of way and easements can lead to liability to the contractor for the delay if the absence of rights of way and easements prevent the contractor from accessing the site. For example, the construction may require an easement to allow the boom of a crane to operate over an adjacent property because title to property in most jurisdictions includes the air rights above the property. In other jurisdictions, a property owner's air rights only may extend to the space used by the adjacent property owner; thus, while such an easement or license is preferred to avoid litigation, it may not be required. Easements over adjoining property also may be needed for access to the construction site. Some jurisdictions provide

---

3. Amp-Rite Electric Co. v. Wheaton Sanitary Dist., 220 Ill. App. 3d 130, 150, 580 N.E.2d 622 (2d Dist. 1991).

4. *See, e.g.*, American Institute of Architects, AIA Document A201–2017, General Conditions of the Contract for Construction § 6.1.4 (2017) [hereinafter AIA Document A201–2017].

a statutory mechanism for an owner to seek court approval to enter adjoining land for construction purposes.[5] Industry form contracts generally require the owner to secure and pay for necessary approvals and easements required for construction.[6]

B. The Right to Use the Project Site for Its Intended Purpose

The owner must possess the unencumbered right to use the property for construction. Restrictions, such as rights of way, leases, easements, utilities, encroachments, or licenses that grant rights to others in the property, may interfere with construction operations. Before beginning construction, the owner must obtain a title report and survey to determine whether these restrictions exist and where they are located on the site. An owner will not be able to unilaterally relocate electric and phone lines or a sewer line that are the subject of enforceable easements. In most standard form agreements between the owner and architect, the owner has the duty to provide a survey to the architect identifying the location of easements and utilities.[7]

The impact of the construction activities and the completed project on adjacent landowners also must be evaluated, as the project cannot adversely impact or damage adjacent property. If a court deems an activity or condition that damages adjoining property is inherently dangerous, which construction work often is, the owner will be liable for that damage even if an independent contractor performing the work caused the damage.[8] Most states have adopted section 839 of the Restatement (Second) of Torts, which governs claims by an adjacent or neighboring landowner for nuisances created by the construction process or the completed structure.[9]

C. Title

Obviously, the owner must hold the necessary unrestricted ownership interest in the project site to permit construction. The title to the property may contain

---

5. *See, e.g.*, Illinois' Entry on Adjoining Land to Accomplish Repair Act, 765 ILL. COMP. STAT. 125/0.01; New York's Access to Adjoining Property to Make Improvements or Repairs Act, N.Y. Real Prop. Actions and Proceedings Law § 881; South Carolina's Petition for License to Enter Adjoining Property to Make Improvements or Repairs, S.C. CODE ANN. § 15-67-270 (Supp. 1999).

6. *See, e.g.*, AIA Document A201–2017, *supra* note 4, §§ 2.3.1, 2.3.4.

7. *See, e.g.*, AIA Document B101–2017, *supra* note 1, § 5.4 and AIA Document B103–2017, *supra* note 1, § 5.5.

8. City of Columbus v. Barngrower, 250 Ga. App. 589, 552 S.E.2d 536 (2001).

9. *See, e.g.*, Willmschen v. Trinity Lakes Improvement, 840 N.E.2d 1275, 1282, 362 Ill. App. 3d 546 (2d Dist. 2005).

restrictions on the use of the property and what may be constructed on the property. Unless the proposed use violates public policy, restrictions on the use of the property and what may be constructed on a piece of property are generally enforceable.[10] These restrictions can include adherence to neighborhood or condominium association rules, which can be very extensive and indeed affect the manner, methods, and means of construction.

Construction may be undertaken by an entity that does not hold the fee simple interest in the property, but merely holds a long-term lease of the property, often referred to as a ground lease. A ground lease grants the lessee use of the property for an extended period of time. Upon expiration of the term, the property, including any improvements constructed by the lessee, often reverts back to the owner of the property. Construction projects also are undertaken by lessees of property, such as tenants of office space that build out their own space. A tenant's construction must comport with the terms of the lease. Moreover, an owner will not be able to perform construction that will interfere with the quiet enjoyment of a valid leasehold interest in the property. A covenant of quiet enjoyment is implied in every lease agreement.

D. Zoning

Virtually all communities limit the type, size, and use of structures based on the location of the structure within the community.[11] Zoning is an outgrowth of the tort of nuisance, that is, you cannot use your land to injure your neighbor. Municipalities, either through enabling legislation (non-home rule units) or the exercise of police power derived from constitutional authority (home rule units), enact plans to control and direct the permitted use and development of property in a municipality by dividing it into geographical districts or zones according to the present and potential use of the property.[12] Zoning may prevent high-rises from being built in single-family residential neighborhoods and the construction of heavy industrial buildings in retail areas.

A municipality has the power to divide the entire community into planned districts of such number, shape, and area, and of such different classes of use as deemed best suited for the growth, lifestyle, and existing uses in

---

10. Bowman v. Walnut Mountain Prop. Owners Ass'n, 251 Ga. App. 91, 553 S.E.2d 389 (2001); Save the Prairie Society v. Greene Development Group, Inc., 323 Ill. App. 3d 862, 256 Ill. Dec. 643, 752 N.E.2d 523 (1st Dist. 2001); Exch. Nat'l Bank of Chi. v. City of Des Plaines, 336 N.E.2d 8, 32 Ill. App. 3d 722 (Ill. App. 1 Dist. 1964).

11. *But see* City of Houston No Zoning Letter dated Jan. 1, 2017, http://www.houstontx.gov/planning/Forms/devregs/2017_no_zoning_letter.pdf.

12. Devaney v. New Haven Bd. of Zoning Appeals, 132 Conn. 537, 45 A.2d 828 (1946).

the community. Zoning districts generally consist of low-density residential, high-density residential, business or retail, light industry, and heavy industry. Zoning restrictions may be cumulative, where any use permitted in a more restrictive district may be permitted in a less restrictive district, or exclusionary, where all uses not explicitly permitted are excluded. Compliance with the applicable zoning law is of critical importance to the owner and the uninterrupted progress of the construction project.

Most municipalities provide a mechanism for an owner to obtain approval to build a project that does not strictly comply with the existing zoning. Thus, an owner may seek a variance from the existing zoning to permit construction of a structure that otherwise would not comply with the specific limitations of the current zoning. Variance request procedures often require public hearings to permit nearby property owners to weigh in on the variance request.

Absent an express contract provision governing who shall be responsible for ensuring compliance with zoning requirements, most jurisdictions impose a duty upon the architect to design a project to conform to zoning requirements. Industry form contracts require the owner to supply to the architect surveys that include zoning information.[13]

E. Availability of Utilities

The availability of utilities and the costs associated with bringing utilities to the site are important considerations in the project budget and schedule. A project in an undeveloped area is often referred to as a greenfield project, and may require substantial economic resources to bring electric, gas, water, storm, and sewer lines perhaps miles to the site. Similarly, although an industrial project may have utilities, they may be inadequate to service the planned building and use of the property and may require extensive upgrades. All of these factors must be considered in the economic evaluation and the scheduling of the project.

Unless the parties agree otherwise, the owner is responsible to provide utilities to the site for the completed building. The parties may contractually allocate responsibility for providing temporary power and heat for use during construction, and many industry form contracts allocate this responsibility to the contractor.[14] The American Institute of Architects (AIA) General Conditions of the Contract for Construction state that unless the contract documents provide otherwise, the contractor shall provide and pay for temporary

---

13. AIA Document B101–2017, *supra* note 1, § 5.4 and AIA Document B103–2007, *supra* note 1, § 5.5.

14. AIA Document A201–2017, *supra* note 4, § 3.4.1.

and permanent water, heat, and utilities necessary for the completion of the work.[15] If the responsibility is allocated to the owner, the owner's failure to timely provide utilities or other services can create owner liability to the contractor if the absence of these utilities or other services impacts construction.[16] Industry form contracts require the owner to supply to the architect and contractor surveys identifying utility locations.[17]

F. Archaeological and Historic Sites

Discovery of Native American artifacts, human skeletal remains, earthworks, or other archaeological and paleontological artifacts on a site can have a significant impact on a project's progress and budget. Most jurisdictions require owners to notify the state archaeologist or historic preservation agency of the discovery of archaeologically significant objects. These jurisdictions also require the owner to cease construction activity to afford the appropriate state agency the opportunity to perform a survey of the site. Express agency approval is often required before resuming construction activities. For example, the state of Illinois reserves to itself the exclusive right to explore, excavate, or collect, through the Illinois Historic Preservation Agency, all archaeological and paleontological resources found on or within any public lands, and prohibits any person from knowingly disturbing any archaeological or paleontological resource[18] or disturb any human skeletal remains.[19] Alaska requires notification of the Department of Natural Resources if historic, prehistoric, or archaeological sites, remains, or objects are discovered during construction. Approval by the Alaska Department of Natural Resources must be obtained before continuing construction.[20] Also, the Federal Antiquities Act provides for criminal penalties for any person who excavates or damages any archaeological resources situated on public lands owned and administered by the United States or Indian lands.[21]

Form industry contracts require the contractor to immediately suspend operations if it encounters human remains or recognizes the existence of burial markers, archaeological sites, or wetlands, and impose upon the owner the

---

15. *Id.*
16. Document A201–2017, *supra* note 4, § 2.3.5.
17. AIA Document B101–2017, *supra* note 1, § 5.4; AIA Document B103–2017, *supra* note 1, § 5.5; AIA Document A201–2017, *supra* note 4, § 2.3.4.
18. 20 Ill. Code Stat. 3435/3.
19. 20 Ill. Code Stat. 3440/4.
20. Alaska Stat. 41.35.070.
21. 16 U.S.C. §§ 470bb(3), 470bb(4), 470ee.

duty to obtain any necessary government authorization to resume construction operations. Form industry contracts further contemplate the contractor seeking adjustments in the project schedule and additional compensation due to the impact of such discoveries upon a project.[22]

The definition of a historic site in some jurisdictions can be quite broad. Historic sites can include any parcel or contiguous grouping of parcels of real estate under common or related ownership or control where any significant improvements are at least 40 years old, or any earthwork, village, burial ground, historic or prehistoric ruin, or other location that is or may be the source of important archaeological data. A construction project deemed a historic site will impose impediments to the owner proceeding with development or alteration of the property.

The National Historic Preservation Act (NHPA) requires that the head of any federal agency having jurisdiction over a federally assisted undertaking takes into account the effect of the undertaking on any site or object included in or eligible for inclusion in the National Register of Historic Places and provide the Advisory Council on Historic Preservation a reasonable opportunity to comment with regard to the undertaking.[23] Further, the National Environmental Policy Act contains provisions for evaluating the degree to which federal projects will adversely affect districts, sites, structures, or objects listed or eligible for listing in the National Register of Historic Places or that may cause loss or destruction of significant scientific, cultural, or historic resources.[24] Preconstruction archaeological studies where appropriate should be considered. The identification of historic resources before construction can trigger mitigation plans to protect the historic resources and avoid unnecessary delay.

G. Environmental Concerns

Construction projects can present a litany of environmental issues that will dramatically impact the expense and progress of a project. Environmental issues arise in a variety of ways. They can range from contaminated soils discovered during new construction to the discovery of asbestos or lead-containing materials in a renovation project. A host of federal statutes and regulations exist dealing with environmental issues, which, together with state regulation, create a great deal of regulation for an owner to negotiate.

Contaminated soils are governed by the Comprehensive Environmental Response Compensation and Liability Act of 1980 (CERCLA) as well as state

---

22. AIA Document A201–2017, *supra* note 4, § 3.7.5.
23. 16 U.S.C. § 470 and 36 C.F.R. § 800.4.
24. 40 C.F.R. § 1508.27(b)(3)(8).

regulation and, in some instances, municipal ordinances.[25] Industry form contracts permit a contractor to cease work if contaminated soils or other hazardous materials are encountered to permit the owner to test the materials and remove them or safely contain them.[26] These contracts also contemplate that the contract time will be extended and the contract sum increased for the contractor's reasonable costs of shutdown, delay, and start-up due to encountering hazardous materials.[27] Such site conditions, if known to the owner, must be disclosed to a contractor to avoid claims by the contractor for additional costs and additional time due to the contaminated nature of the site.

Also, an owner must be cognizant of the Clean Water Act and its wetlands protection provisions.[28] The Environmental Protection Agency (EPA) broadly defines a wetland, thus increasing the likelihood that an owner may be faced with wetlands issues. Special permits are required to work in areas that are deemed wetlands, and special protections exist for wetlands. Further, the Clean Water Act imposes penalties and remedial requirements if construction debris makes its way into protected rivers and streams, and most states and municipalities require the control of sedimentation and its migration onto adjoining properties and into waterways.

Further, construction waste must be disposed of in compliance with federal and state regulations. If the waste is "hazardous," a series of federal regulations, including the Resource Conservation and Recovery Act of 1976 (RCRA), govern its transportation, handling, and disposal.[29] Even if the waste is not hazardous, state statutes may govern the disposal of construction waste due to its unique nature.

If asbestos is encountered on a project, notification to the EPA may be required by federal emissions standards.[30] These standards also govern how the asbestos should be removed. Most states also regulate when and how asbestos is removed. Moreover, the federal Occupational Safety and Health Administration (OSHA), which sets forth safety standards and hazard communication standards for the construction industry, also governs how asbestos must be handled.[31] Failure to adhere to environmental and occupational safety laws governing asbestos can result in parallel administrative, civil, and criminal prosecutions.

---

25. Comprehensive Environmental Response, Compensation and Liability Act of 1980, 42 U.S.C. § 9601 *et seq.*
26. AIA Document A201–2017, *supra* note 4, §§ 10.3.1, 10.3.2.
27. *Id.* § 10.3.2.
28. Clean Water Act, 33 U.S.C. § 1311 *et seq.*
29. 42 U.S.C. § 6901 *et seq.*
30. 40 C.F.R. § 61.140.
31. 29 C.F.R. § 1926.1101, *et seq.*

3.03 PROVIDING INFORMATION TO THE ARCHITECT AND CONTRACTOR

A. Surveys

An owner is generally required by contract to obtain and provide to the architect and contractor engineering information such as a survey of the site that shows the property lines, location of utilities, rights of way, easements, and location of other potential impediments to the construction process. The AIA A201 form, General Conditions of the Contract for Construction, requires the owner to "furnish surveys describing physical characteristics, legal limitations and utility locations for the site of the Project, and a legal description of the site."[32]

Once the owner furnishes such information to the architect or contractor, the architect and contractor have the right to rely on that information. In *Cadral Corp. v. Solomon, Cordwell, Buenz & Assoc., Inc.*,[33] the owner provided the architect with a survey. The architect, by letter to the owner, had defined the requirements of the survey but had not expressly requested the inclusion of "restrictions." After excavation was complete and the caissons and some of the foundations were in place, a subsequent survey (required by the bank financing the construction loan) revealed that the west wall extended beyond the 10-foot building line. The owner filed a breach of contract and malpractice action against the architect, alleging that the architect ignored building-line restrictions. The court determined sufficient evidence existed to support the jury conclusion that the survey provided by the owner, although depicting a line designating a "10 ft. building line," was insufficient to apprise the architects of critical information regarding the building line. Moreover, the AIA A201 form, General Conditions of the Contract for Construction, provides that the contractor shall be entitled to rely on the accuracy of information furnished by the owner.[34]

B. Geotechnical Information

The bearing capacity and nature of the site's soils are important considerations in the design of a building. A frequent source of owner–design professional disputes has been the discovery of unknown soil conditions and responsibility for the unanticipated additional costs for design and construction. Industry

---

32. AIA Document A201–2017, *supra* note 4, § 2.3.4.
33. 147 Ill. App. 3d 466, 497 N.E. 2d 1285, 1287 (1st Dist. 1986).
34. AIA Document A201–2017, *supra* note 4, § 2.3.4.

form design contracts impose the responsibility to secure soil borings and analysis of the bearing capacity of the soils on the owner. The AIA Standard Form of Agreement Between Owner and Architect requires the owner to "furnish services of geotechnical engineers, which may include test borings, test pits, determinations of soil bearing values, percolation tests, evaluations of hazardous materials, seismic evaluation, . . . with written reports and appropriate recommendations."[35]

3.04 THE OWNER'S IMPLIED WARRANTY TO SUPPLY ACCURATE INFORMATION

A. The *Spearin* Doctrine

The owner impliedly warrants the accuracy of the information supplied to a contractor, including the information contained in the drawings and specifications, and sometimes site condition information. On a design-bid-build project in which the owner is responsible to supply the drawings and specifications to the contractor, the owner impliedly warrants to the contractor the adequacy of the drawings and specifications for their intended purpose. This warranty is often referred to as the *Spearin* Doctrine because it arises from the U.S. Supreme Court opinion in United States v. Spearin.[36]

In *Spearin*, the contractor agreed to construct a dry dock for the United States. The work included the relocation of an existing sewer line. Flooding caused by a condition at the site damaged the relocated sewer line constructed by the contractor and the dry-dock worksite, and the United States requested the contractor to reconstruct the damaged sewer line at the contractor's cost. The Supreme Court ruled that the contract documents, which described the character, dimensions, and location of the sewer but did not disclose the existence of the condition that caused the damage, created a warranty by the government that, if so constructed, the sewer would be adequate. Justice Brandeis's opinion states, in part:

> The general rules of law applicable to these facts are well settled. Where one agrees to do, for a fixed sum, a thing possible to be performed, he will not be excused or become entitled to additional compensation, because unforeseen difficulties are encountered. *Day v. United States*, 245 U.S. 159; *Phoenix Bridge Co. v. United States*, 211 U.S. 188. Thus, one who undertakes to erect a structure upon a particular site assumes ordinarily the risk of subsidence of the

---

35. AIA Document B103–2017, *supra* note 1, § 5.6 and AIA Document B101–2017, *supra* note 1, § 5.5.
36. 248 U.S. 132, 39 S. Ct. 59 (1918).

soil. *Simpson v. United States*, 172 U.S. 372; *Dermott v. Jones*, 2 Wall. 1. But if the contractor is bound to build according to plans and specifications prepared by the owner, the contractor will not be responsible for the consequences of defects in the plans and specifications. *MacKnight Flintic Stone Co. v. The Mayor*, 160 N.Y. 72; *Filbert v. Philadelphia*, 181 Pa. St. 530; *Bentley v. State*, 73 Wisconsin, 416. See *Sundstrom v. New York*, 213 N.Y. 68. This responsibility of the owner is not overcome by the usual clauses requiring builders to visit the site, to check the plans, and to inform themselves of the requirements of the work, as is shown by *Christie v. United States*, 237 U.S. 234; *Hollerbach v. United States*, 233 U.S. 165, and *United States v. Utah &c. Stage Co.*, 199 U.S. 414, 424, where it was held that the contractor should be relieved, if he was misled by erroneous statements in the specifications.

. . .

The contention of the Government that the present case is to be distinguished from the *Bentley Case, supra*, and other similar cases, on the ground that the contract with reference to the sewer is purely collateral, is clearly without merit. The risk of the existing system proving adequate might have rested upon *Spearin*, if the contract for the dry-dock had not contained the provision for relocation of the 6-foot sewer. But the insertion of the articles prescribing the character, dimensions and location of the sewer imported a warranty that, if the specifications were complied with, the sewer would be adequate. This implied warranty is not overcome by the general clauses requiring the contractor, to examine the site, to check up the plans, and to assume responsibility for the work until completion and acceptance. The obligation to examine the site did not impose upon him the duty of making a diligent enquiry into the history of the locality with a view to determining, at his peril, whether the sewer specifically prescribed by the Government would prove adequate. The duty to check plans did not impose the obligation to pass upon their adequacy to accomplish the purpose in view. And the provision concerning contractor's responsibility, cannot be construed as abridging rights arising under specific provisions of the contract.[37]

The contractor was not required to repair the defective sewer at its expense because the specifications that dictated the character, dimensions, and location of the sewer constituted a warranty from the government that the sewer was adequate for the existing conditions. The Court also ruled the government's implied warranty superseded contract language that required the contractor to thoroughly check the drawings and examine the worksite, as those requirements do not require a contractor to verify that the improvements as designed by the government are adequate to accomplish their purpose.

---

37. *Spearin*, 248 U.S. at 136, 39 S. Ct. at 169.

Where the contractor performs the work according to the specifications and the work is faulty due to defective specifications, in nearly every jurisdiction the contractor may assert the *Spearin* Doctrine as a defense to a claim by the owner for the cost to remedy the defect (with certain exceptions as discussed later). A contractor is entitled to rely on the drawings and specifications supplied by the owner; a contractor is not liable for defects in construction arising from defective drawings and specification supplied by the owner.[38]

Contractors can use the *Spearin* Doctrine as a shield from claims by the owner and as a basis for a claim by the contractor against the owner if the contractor incurs loss and/or delay due to the deficiency of the drawings and specifications provided to the contractor by the owner.[39] These damages may include the costs incurred by the contractor in attempting to comply with the defective specifications of *Spearin* and the delay in the completion of the project.

B. Limitations on the Application of *Spearin*

The *Spearin* Doctrine, however, can be limited by the contract. If the parties' contract limits the damages and/or remedies that a contractor has, that language may prohibit a *Spearin*-type claim or defense. In *Dugan & Meyer Constr. Co., Inc. v. Ohio Dep't of Admin. Services*,[40] litigation between a contractor and The Ohio State University ensued over delays arising from a $20 million contract for the construction of three buildings at the university. The contractor argued that under *Spearin*, the university breached its implied warranty of sufficiency of the drawings and specifications because the drawings and specifications were improperly prepared, causing the contractor to incur additional costs as a result of the extended duration of the project. The university argued that the contract's prohibition of contractor damages as a result of project delay trumped the contractor's *Spearin* Doctrine claim for inaccurate and incomplete drawings. Although evidence existed of the inadequacy of the drawings and specifications, such as untimely owner responses to 700 requests for information, 250 fieldwork orders, and 85 architectural supplemental instructions, the

---

38. *Spearin*, 248 U.S. at 136, 39 S. Ct. at 61; Penzel Construction Co., Inc. v. Jackson R-2 School Dist., 544 S.W.3d 214 (Mo. App. E.D., 2017); Martin K. Eby Constr. Co., Inc. v. Jacksonville Transp. Auth., 436 F. Supp. 2d 1276, 1308 (M.D. Fla. 2005); Pa. Dep't of Transp. v. Jones D. Morrisey, Inc., 682 A.2d 9 (Pa. Comm. Ct. 1996); Paine v. Spottiswoode, 612 A.2d 235 (Me. 1992); Halcrow, Inc. v. Dist. Ct., 302 P.2d 1148, n.3 (Nev. 2013); Sherman R. Smoot Co. v. Ohio Dep't of Adm. Serv., 136 Ohio App. 3d 166 (2000).

39. 544 S.W.3d 214; Big Chief Drilling Co. v. U.S., 26 Ct. Cl. 1276, 1992 U.S. Cl. Ct. Lexis 454 (1992).

40. 113 Ohio St. 3d 226, 864 N.E.2d 68 (2007).

Ohio Supreme Court held the contractor was not entitled to delay damages but rather was limited to the remedy specified in the contract—an extension of time. In discussing the application of the *Spearin* Doctrine to the contractor's claim, the court stated:

> . . . we decline the opportunity to extend the *Spearin* Doctrine from job-site-conditions cases to cases involving delay due to plan changes.
>
> Moreover, the contract in this case included terms that addressed the contractor's remedy when changes were made to the plans. This court has long recognized that "where a contract is plain and unambiguous, it does not become ambiguous by reason of the fact that in its operation it will work a hardship upon one of the parties thereto and a corresponding advantage to the other, [and] that it is not the province of courts to relieve parties of improvident contracts." *Ohio Crane Co. v. Hicks*, 110 Ohio St. 168, 143, N.E. 388 (1924). In addition, "unless there is fraud or other unlawfulness involved, courts are powerless to save a competent person from the effects of his own voluntary agreement." *Ullmann v. May*, 147 Ohio St. 468, 72 N.E. 63 (1947).
>
> We have previously affirmed these principles in a case involving a competitively bid public construction contract. In *S & M Constructors, Inc. v. Columbus*, 70 Ohio St. 2d 69, 434 N.E. 2d 1349 (1982), the contractor agreed that it would make no claim against the city even if the conditions of the subsurface as reported to contractors before the bidding differed materially from actual subsurface conditions encountered during the project. We held that the "no claim" provision was unambiguous and was enforceable in the absence of a showing of fraud or bad faith on the part of the city. We observed that the *Spearin* Doctrine does not invalidate an express contractual provision: "Where one agrees to do, for a fixed sum, a thing possible to be performed, he will not be excused or become entitled to additional compensation because unforeseen difficulties are encountered." [Citations omitted]
>
> The contract in the case at bar contained several relevant provisions, which were valid under Ohio law when the contract was signed. The parties agreed, "Time is of the essence to the Contract Documents and all obligations thereunder," and the contract provided a specific procedure to be followed in the event of project delay. The contract also contained a no-damages-for-delay clause, which provided that "extension of time granted pursuant to paragraph GC 6.2 shall be the sole remedy which may be provided by the Department" and that the Contractor shall not "be entitled to additional compensation or mitigation of Liquidated Damages for any delay listed in paragraph GC 6.2." The contract provided that the contractor's failure to request, in writing, an extension of time within ten days after the occurrence of a condition necessitating an extension of time "shall

constitute a waiver . . . of any claim for extension or for mitigation of liquidated Damages."[41]

The *Spearin* Doctrine has been adopted by most jurisdictions,[42] but some states, such as Pennsylvania, have refused to apply it. For example, in *Stabler Constr., Inc. v. Comm. of Pennsylvania*,[43] the court stated, "*Spearin* involved a contract with an agency of the federal government, and the *Spearin* court determined the rights and obligations of the parties to that contract by applying federal law. The instant case does not involve or require the application of federal law. Therefore, *Spearin* is not binding on this court."[44]

1. Limitations on the Spearin *Doctrine*

The contractor only will have the benefit of the *Spearin* Doctrine if it performs in accordance with the drawings and specifications furnished by the owner.[45] Thus, if the owner can establish that the contractor failed to follow the owner's drawings and specifications even if they are defective, the owner is insulated from any claims brought by the contractor with respect to the sufficiency of the drawings and specifications.[46]

Under the *Spearin* Doctrine, the owner may escape liability to the contractor for defective drawings and specifications if the design defects are "glaring or obvious," "obviously flawed," or reasonably could have been discovered by the contractor.[47] A contractor has a duty to discover defects in the drawings or specifications that are reasonably discoverable or patent and to warn the owner of the defects.[48] This limitation of the *Spearin* Doctrine applies even where an owner supplies comprehensive design specifications because a contractor is not justified in "blithely proceeding with its work in the face of obvious and recognized errors"; rather, the contractor has a duty either to take

---

41. *Id.* at 73–74.
42. Fidelity and Deposit Co. v. City of Sheboygan Falls, 713 F.2d 1261 (7th Cir. 1983); *Martin K. Eby Constr. Co., Inc.*, 436 F. Supp. 2d at 127.
43. 692 A.2d 1150, 1153 (Pa. 1997).
44. *Id.* at 1153; *see also* Rhone Poulenc Rorer Pharm., Inc. v. Newman Glass Works, 112 F.3d 695 (3d Cir. 1997).
45. Appeal of Conrad Bros., Inc., 1996 WL 675811 (B.C.A. 1996), *aff'd* 135 F.3d 778 (Fed. Cir. 1998).
46. *See* Tyger Constr. Co. v. United States, 31 Fed. Cl. 177 (1994); McConnell v. Corona City Water Co., 149 Cal. 60, 85 P. 929 (1906); Montrose Contracting Co. v. Cnty. of Westchester, 80 F.2d 841 (2d Cir. 1936).
47. PCL Constr. Services., Inc. v. United States, 47 Fed. Cl. 745, 785 (2000); Cent. Ohio Joint Vocational Sch. Bd. Dist. of Educ. v. Peterson Constr. Co., 129 Ohio App. 3d 58 (1998).
48. St. Paul Fire & Marine Ins. Co. v. Pearson Constr. Co., 547 N.E.2d 853, 858 (Ind. 4th Dist. 1989).

appropriate steps to address obvious design defects or demand that the owner take action.[49] A contractor cannot rely on the doctrine if the contractor had knowledge that the plans were obviously flawed and did not inform the owner.

Further, a contractor has a duty to read and understand all of the project documents and to inform itself of the owner's representations concerning the work. Such an inquiry should cause the contractor to discover obvious or potential discrepancies in the contract documents. Discovery of a patent discrepancy triggers a duty on the contractor to inquire,[50] and under federal contracts, a contractor will have patent ambiguities construed against it as a matter of law.[51] In essence, a contractor who is on notice of an incipient problem but neglects to solve it or inquire of the owner as is required by most contracts, cannot rely on the principle that ambiguities in contracts are interpreted against the drafter. The contractor is under an affirmative duty to call attention to the inconsistency. If the contractor fails to call the inconsistency to the attention of the owner, the inconsistency may be construed against the contractor; this often results in an obligation to perform work that was reasonably necessary to complete the project.[52] It is also important to note that industry form contracts often require the contractor to advise the architect or owner of any errors, inconsistencies, or omissions in the contract documents.[53]

For example, in *Caddell Constr. Co., Inc. v. United States*,[54] the contractor argued that the design specifications were so defective as to constitute a breach by the United States of the *Spearin*-implied warranty. For evidence of the defective specifications, the contractor relied primarily on the almost 300 requests for information the contractor was required to send to the government. The Federal Court of Claims rejected this argument, reasoning that design specifications need not be paragons of perfection, but only reasonably accurate, and the fact that the drawings required repeated clarification was not an indication that the drawings were defective. Although the court agreed that

---

49. Allied Contractors, Inc. v. United States, 381 F.2d 995, 999 (Ct. Cl. 1967); *see also* Graham Constr. Co., Inc. v. Earl, 362 Ark. 220, 2005 WL 1041149, at *3 (2005), "A competent and experienced contractor cannot rely upon submitted specifications and plans where he is fully aware, or should have been aware, that the plans and specifications cannot produce the proposed results." (citing Hous. Auth. of the City of Texarkana v. Johnson Constr. Co., 264 Ark. 523, 573 S.W.2d 316 (1978)); *PCL Constr. Services, Inc.*, 47 Fed. Cl. at 794; Mann v. Clowser, 59 S.E.2d 78, 85 (Va. 1950).

50. *See* Gardner-Zenkes Co. v. State, 109 N.E.2d 729, 790 P.2d 1010 (1990).

51. K-Con, Inc. v. Secretary of Army, 908 F.3d 719 (Fed. Cir. 2018).

52. Beacon Constr. Co. v. United States, 314 F.2d 501 (1963).

53. AIA Document A201–2017, *supra* note 4, § 3.2.2.

54. 78 Fed. Cl. 406 (2007).

the drawings contained errors and inconsistencies, it found they were workable and, therefore, not defective. The court in *Caddell Construction* restricted application of the *Spearin* Doctrine to a fundamental design defect that dramatically impacted the project, as opposed to a number of smaller defects, even if cumulatively they dramatically impacted the project. Nor does the existence of a contractual completion date constitute a warranty by the owner that the project can be completed within that time period.[55]

2. The Spearin *Warranty Can Be Disclaimed*

The owner's implied *Spearin* warranty can be disclaimed by a properly drafted specific disclaimer of the adequacy of the drawings and specifications.[56] The courts have differing views of whether a contractor's express warranty will take precedence over the owner's *Spearin* Doctrine implied warranty. In *Rhone Poulenc Rorer Pharmaceuticals Inc. v. Newman Glass Products, Inc.*,[57] the court held that the *Spearin* Doctrine's implied warranty from the owner must yield to the contractor's express warranty that all work will be free from faults and defects and the contractor's express duty to remove and replace any materials the owner or its architect deem defective.[58] There, the court reasoned the parties had contractually allocated to the contractor any risk that the glass specified by the owner would not be appropriate for its application. To the contrary, in *Sherman R. Smoot Co. v. Ohio Dep't of Admin. Services*,[59] the court stated that where the information provided by the government was obviously intended to be used by bidding contractors in formulating their bids, the implied warranty controls over express contract clauses that disclaim any responsibility for the accuracy of information provided to contractors and that require contractors to examine the site and check the plans.

---

55. Am. Ship Bldg. Co. v. United States, 654, F.2d 75 (Ct. Cl. 1981).

56. A contract between the owner and contractor that provides "omissions from the drawings or specifications or the misdescription of details or work which are necessary to carry out the intent of the drawings and specifications shall not relieve the contractor from performing such omitted or misdescribed details of the work, but shall be performed as if fully and correctly set forth and described in the drawings and specifications" may insulate an owner from a contractor's *Spearin* Doctrine claim for defective plans and specifications. Conner Bros. Constr. Co. v. United States, 65 Fed. Cl. 657, 669 (Fed. Cir. 2005); R. B. Wright Constr. Co. Through Rembrant, Inc. v. United States, 919 F.2d 1569 (Fed. Cir. 1990).

57. 112 F.3d 695.

58. However, a contract provision that merely provides that a contractor has inspected the project site is not specific enough to disclaim the owner's *Spearin*-implied warranty. *See* Green Constr. Co. v. Kansas Power & Light Co., 1 F.3d 1005 (10th Cir. 1993).

59. 136 Ohio App. 3d 166 (2000).

3.05 THE OWNER'S PROGRAM

A. The Program

The owner is responsible for preparing what is commonly referred to as a program. The program is a written narrative and graphic document that summarizes major performance and design criteria. The objectives and constraints might include matters such as values and goals to be achieved; institutional purposes; growth objectives; and cultural, technological, temporal, aesthetic, symbolic, economic, environmental, safety, and sustainability preferences. The programmer may assist the owner in defining the level of functionality, efficiency, user comfort, building economics, and visual quality to be achieved by the owner. The program may establish a schedule for programming, design, and construction. The program may establish budget constraints or opportunities, physical and site limitations, space requirements and relationships, functional issues, maintenance and operating requirements, technological concerns (material, equipment and system needs), energy requirements, financing issues, safety issues, and other matters pertinent to the scope of the work to be designed.[60]

Architectural programming is performed prior to preparation of any drawings and specifications. In fact, the program is the basis for the design of the project and, therefore, an extremely important document. The programming process warrants diligence, as the ability to influence the design of a project is greatest during architectural programming. Before ideas are committed to drawings and specifications, the design is nothing more than a collection of concepts and ideas, at best. All aspects of the design are still flexible, and changes can be accomplished with relative ease and efficiency. As the design becomes more developed, however, making any change often becomes challenging to execute. One change may also require other changes, causing additional design fees and schedule delays.

Under most standard industry contract forms, the owner is responsible for furnishing the architect with a written program.[61] The architect, in turn,

---

60. Architectural programming is defined as "a pre-design activity in which the parameters of the project are defined—both quantitatively and qualitatively." It is "the research and decision-making process that defines the problem to be solved by design." THE ARCHITECT'S HANDBOOK OF PROFESSIONAL PRACTICE 664–65, 1133 (15th ed. 2014). *See* AIA Document B202-2009, *Standard Form of Architect's Services: Programming.*

61. AIA Document B101-2017, *supra* note 1, § 5.1, describes the items that are required to be set forth in a written program the owner must provide to the architect, that is, objectives, schedule, constraints, and criteria, including space requirements and relationships, flexibility, expandability, special equipment, systems and site requirements.

reviews the program and provides a preliminary evaluation of the program. Only after the architect has reached an understanding of the project requirements, as embodied in the program, does the architect proceed with the preparation of a preliminary design illustrating the scale and relationship of the project components.[62] The design continues to evolve in greater detail and level of completeness in each successive design phase, but always based on the program. The architect relies on the design objectives set forth in the program, and the architect is entitled to additional compensation if the owner requests a deviation from the direction given in the requirements set forth in the program.[63]

Preparing a program can be a complicated process, depending on the nature of the project. Given the importance of the program in determining the obligations of the architect and the criteria from which the project design is derived, it is somewhat surprising that this task typically is delegated to the owner in agreements between owners and architects. Many owners do not possess the skill to effectively carry out this responsibility on their own. As a consequence, architects often provide programming services as part of so-called additional services, for which additional compensation is received.[64]

B. The Project Budget and Schedule

Two of the more important elements established in the owner's program are the project budget and schedule. Both must be periodically updated to reflect changes in the scope of the project. The AIA owner–architect agreement requires the owner to "establish and periodically update the Owner's budget for the Project, including (1) the budget for the Cost of the Work . . . ; (2) the Owner's other costs; and, (3) reasonable contingencies related to all of these costs."[65] This agreement also requires the owner to notify the architect if the owner significantly increases or decreases the owner's budget for the work, and provides that the owner and architect shall agree to a corresponding change in

---

62. *Id.* §§ 3.2.3 and 3.2.4.

63. *Id.* § 4.2.1.1, which provides, in pertinent part, that the design professional performs compensable "Additional Services" . . . necessitated by an owner's change in the Initial Information, previous instructions or approvals.

64. AIA B101-2017, *supra* note 1, § 4.1.1.1. Programming is expressly deemed a "Supplemental and Additional Service" not within the architect's basic services and compensated in excess of basic compensation.

65. AIA Document B101-2017, *supra* note 1, § 5.2 and AIA Document B103-2017, *supra* note 1, § 5.3.

the project's scope and quality.[66] Modification of the initial information supplied by the owner is likely to be considered a material change in the project resulting in additional services and corresponding additional compensation.[67]

The importance of price and time is relative. For the established manufacturer, getting the production or processing plant operational is of paramount importance to achieve or maintain market share and profit margins. In this situation, price may be secondary. For the economically challenged owner, the cost of the project may be of paramount importance. To the public entity that must issue publicly approved bonds, price is also the primary concern. Accurate estimation of the cost of construction is indispensable to adequately finance the project.

The project schedule is an important and crucial disciplinary tool for the management of the project. If the contract between the owner and contractor establishes that the date of completion of the construction "is of the essence"[68] of the project, then the detailed project schedule, preferably a critical path schedule, will enable the owner to identify slippage and take steps to enforce the schedule and achieve its interim milestones and ultimate completion date. The contractor's failure to adhere to the schedule may result in compensable delay damages.[69] Industry form contracts generally require the contractor to prepare and submit a schedule to the owner and architect consistent with the time limits imposed by the contract. The contractor also is usually required to periodically revise the schedule as required by the project conditions.[70] Because construction rarely proceeds as originally planned, the contractor's duty to periodically update the schedule is important for the success of the project in order to keep all of the parties advised of the current timeline for certain activities. Periodic updates are necessary to coordinate all of the subcontractors' and suppliers' activities.

C. Types of Specifications

After the owner's goals are programmed and conceptualized, and after the owner has approved the design developed, the design professional prepares

---

66. AIA Document B101–2007, *supra* note 1, § 5.2 and AIA Document B103–2007, *supra* note 1, § 5.3.

67. AIA Document B101-2017, *supra* note 1, § 4.2.1.1 and AIA Document B103-2017, *supra* note 1, § 4.2.1.1.

68. AIA Document A201–2017, *supra* note 4, § 8.2.1.

69. *Id.* §§ 3.10.3, 8.3.3.

70. *Id.* § 3.10.1, requires the contractor to revise the schedule and to perform the work in general accordance with the most recent schedules submitted to the owner and architect.

detailed plans and specifications during the construction document phase. The scope of the design professional's duty is ultimately defined and measured by its contract.[71] For public and private entities, where construction is competitively bid, reasonably definite plans and/or specifications are required to permit comparison of equivalents, that is, apples to apples. Without detailed plans and specifications, competing bids cannot be compared because different materials, products, systems, and installation techniques preclude comparison.[72]

Four basic approaches to the preparation of specifications exists: design (prescriptive) specifications, performance specifications, reference specifications, and proprietary specifications.

1. Design Specifications

Design (prescriptive or descriptive) specifications, or the methods system, designate with a great degree of specificity the quantity and quality of materials, and the manner of implementation of the materials, for example, concrete mix of four parts course aggregate and one part cement with 0.5 water/cement ratio. This may imply 3,000 psi, however contractor may not be held responsible for 3,000 psi strict accordance with the specification. The design professional assumes total responsibility for the appropriateness of the materials designated and for the design of the work; the contractor assumes responsibility for performing the work as specified.[73] The contractor, in executing prescriptive specifications, guarantees only its work. The architect, by telling the contractor exactly how to do the job, assumes the responsibility for the result. The contractor is relieved of responsibility for the work to the extent the work complies with the specifications.[74]

2. Reference Standard Specifications

Reference standard specifications use published reference standards that allow the design professional to establish a design concept by designating minimally

---

71. Ferentchak v. Village of Frankfort, 105 Ill. 2d 474, 482–83; 923 N.E.2d 808 (1984); Thompson v. Gordon, 241 Ill. 2d 428, 349 Ill. Dec. 936, 948, 948 N.E.2d 39, 51 (2011) (architect was not to improve critical portion of roadway [Jersey barrier], only to replace it, hence no liability).

72. Robinson's Inc. v. Short, 146 So. 2d 108, 113–14 (Fla. Ct. App. 1962) *cert. denied*, 152 So. 2d 170.

73. S & D Mechanical Contractors v. Enting Water Conditioning Systems, Inc., 71 Ohio App. 3d 228, 593 N.E.2d 354, 358 (1991); Bush v. Jones, 144 F. 942, 943 (3d Cir. 1906).

74. The *Spearin* Doctrine, *infra.*, the contractor has no liability if he performs his work in a workmanlike manner in accordance with the plans and specifications. Georgetown Township High School v. Hardy, 38 Ill. App. 3d 722, 349 N.E.2d 88 (1976). The contractor may rely on the architect's plans and specifications. If the result fails, and the contractor did not deviate from the plans and specifications, the architect is liable. Bush v. Jones, 144 F. 942, 943 (3d Cir. 1906).

acceptable criteria for the contractor's implementation of the work. It is the contractor's obligation to engineer and assemble the components of a structure in accordance with the reference standards.[75] The reference standards typically are published by trade association and government and institutional entities, for example, American Society for Testing and Materials (ASTM), American National Standards Institute (ANSI), American Concrete Institute (ACI), Sheet Metal and Air Conditioning Contractors National Association (SMACNA), and Concrete Reinforcing Steel Institute (CRSI). The design professional's responsibility is limited to the adequacy of the design criteria.[76] This approach is more appropriate where integrated assemblies and composites are utilized[77] to create a systems or standardized building. Reference specifications are uniformly recognized standards of materials and workmanship.

3. Performance Specifications

Performance specifications specify the end result rather than the means to the end, for example, requiring cured concrete strength at a minimum of 3,000 psi.[78] Performance specifications advise the contractor what the final product must be capable of accomplishing.[79] The design professional bears the responsibility to establish the performance result, that is, 3,000 psi. The contractor bears the responsibility to design the assembly to achieve the defined performance requirements, that is, the components and assembly of the cementitious materials to achieve 3,000 psi,[80] as a consequence of which the distinction between design and performance specifications can be critical.[81]

---

75. Berry v. Blackard Constr. Co. 13 Ill. App. 3d 768, 300 N.E.2d 627, 631 (4th Dist. 1973) (Scope of work is to be performed in accordance with the 'Standard Specifications For Water and Sewer Main Construction in Illinois.').

76. Stevens Const. Corp. v. Carolina Corp., 63 Wis. 2d 342, 217 N.W.2d 291 (1974) (The architect scope of work was limited to conceptual designs and layouts. The general contractor was engaged to construct, engineer and install a prestressed concrete system. The design and work was subcontracted to a concrete firm. The concrete firm made an error in design resulting in failure of the system. The general contractor was liable, not the architect).

77. S & D Mechanical Contractors v. Enting Water Conditioning Systems, Inc., 71 Ohio App. 3d 228, 593 N.E.2d 354, 358 (1991).

78. Id.

79. Interwest Constr. v. Brown, 29 F.3d 611, 615 (C.A. Fed. 1994) (Unqualified requirement that chillers provide 900 tons of cooling capacity).

80. Rosell v. Silver Crest Enterprises, 7 Ariz. App. 137, 436 P.2d 915, 916 (1968) ("Where the contractor prepares the plans and specifications, he cannot escape responsibility for defects in the work by contending the defects were in the specifications and not in the work since he is responsible for both.").

81. See, e.g., CGM Constr. v Sydor, No. 521885, 42 N.Y.S.3d 407, 2016 N.Y. Slip Op. 07895, 2016 WL 6883897 (N.Y. App. Div. 2016).

4. Proprietary Specifications

Proprietary specifications are specifications tailored so that a particular manufacturer's model must be used for the contractor to install.[82] In essence, the contract specifications identify an exclusive sole-source product for installation. An equivalent "or equal" product is not authorized. Some states prohibit proprietary specifications by requiring "or equal" products.[83]

Typically, the design professional includes within the plans and specifications design, performance, reference, and proprietary specifications, also known as hybrid or composite specifications.[84]

3.06 PAYING FOR CONSTRUCTION

The owner is responsible for paying for the project, which, in turn, is often governed by the financing the owner can obtain.

A. Financing the Project

A significant percentage of major construction projects utilize a mixture of capital investment and a construction loan. Indeed, the viability of a project often hinges on the owner's ability to secure construction financing. Upon completion of construction, the construction loan is repaid with funds from a permanent loan or other sources available to the owner.

Because many private construction projects are owned by an entity created for the sole purpose of constructing and owning the building, the building often will be the only asset of the borrower. The construction loan agreement will require a security interest in favor of the lender in the project that gives priority to the construction lender over other creditors of the owner. However, such a lender's contractual priority security interest may not ensure priority

---

82. *See* Richard Hoffman Corp. v. Integrated Bldg. Systems, 581 F. Supp. 367 (N.D. Ill. 1984).

83. Even where not prohibited, proprietary specifications can draw criticism. *See, e.g.*, Slippery Rock Area Sch. Dist. v. Tremco, Inc., 2016 WL 3198122, at *6 (W.D. Pa. 2016) ("The proprietary specifications impeded the likelihood of successful bids by otherwise qualified competitors, even though the proprietary specifications would not improve the quality of the roof or reduce the cost. The proprietary bid specifications forced the use of defendants' products and services, and only limited subcontractors could survive the bid approval process. The bidding specifications required products in excess of acceptable industry requirements, in an amount in excess of what was needed, and mandated the use of [manufacturer's] higher priced products as if those products were necessary for a safer roofing system.").

84. *See* Harold J. Rosen, Construction Specifications Writing 39–48 (1974). *See* Christine Beall, *Of Specifications, Liability and the Process of Construction*, Architecture Magazine, Aug. 1989, at 110.

over all other potential claimants due to statutory priorities that may exist. For example, depending on the jurisdiction, a contractor's mechanic's lien rights may have priority over a lender's rights, at least to the extent the contractor has enhanced the value of the property, and taxing bodies such as municipalities may have priority for taxes due. The lender will pay particular attention to attempting to obtain priority over contractors' lien rights.

Some lenders may require an owner to obtain agreements from contractors to subordinate the priority of their lien rights to the lender's mortgage. Such an agreement is not enforceable in all jurisdictions as some jurisdictions by statute prohibit the subordination of a contractor's statutory mechanic's lien rights to a lender's mortgage. Also, a request to a contractor to subordinate its mechanic's lien rights to the lender's mortgage is almost always met with resistance from the contractor, as a contractor's mechanic's lien right is powerful protection. To be effective, such subordination must be permitted in the jurisdiction where the project is located and must be obtained from all of the subcontractors, and in some jurisdictions must be recorded in the county recorder's office.

A lender also will seek to ensure that the construction loan proceeds are used only for their intended purpose—to pay the contractors. Payment made by the owner to the contractor may be conditioned upon receipt of the contractor's payment application, certified by an architect or engineer engaged at the owner's expense to verify that the percentage of construction complete as represented by the contractor is accurate. The lender also may require the certification attest that changes to the contract amount do not cause the balance due to the contractor to exceed the loan balance. If the balance of the loan is exceeded by the current balance owed to the contractor, the owner may be obligated to make up the difference with its funds. The objective is to ensure that the construction loan is always in balance, with the available loan proceeds equal to or more than the amount needed to complete construction.

The construction loan documents also may require that waivers of mechanic's lien rights for a particular payment be tendered by all contractors working on the project and suppliers supplying equipment and materials to the project. To ensure that this procedure is followed, lenders may utilize a title company or other escrowee to collect lien mechanic's waivers before disbursing the loan proceeds.

The lender also may review the proposed construction contract and often will require modifications to the construction contract to protect its interests. As a term of the construction loan, lenders commonly require a collateral assignment of the construction contract from the owner to the lender. Under this assignment, if the lender declares a default of the construction loan and is required to foreclose, or obtains title to the project by agreement with the owner, then under the collateral assignment of the construction contract, the lender will have the option to step into the shoes of the owner to permit the lender to complete construction with the existing contractor.

The construction lender also may require that the contractor provide performance and payment bonds. These bonds reduce the risk that the project will not be completed or that liens will impair title to the project. Akin to insurance, a performance bond gives the lender assurances that should the contractor default, file bankruptcy, or materially breach the contract, a surety will provide funds to complete the project. A payment bond also provides assurances to the lender that a source of funds exists to defend and pay mechanic's lien claimants if the general contractor fails to do so. For a more complete discussion of performance and payment bonds, see Chapter 18.

B. Evidence of Financing

The owner's ability to fund a project is of obvious importance to a contractor. A contractor does not wish to expend resources and assume liabilities to third parties without assurances that it will be paid by the owner. Although a contractor usually has lien rights as security for payment for work performed, such rights may be subordinate to those of others and inadequate to protect the contractor's interests. Prior to commencement of the work, a contractor generally requests evidence that the owner has made financial arrangements to pay for the project, or the construction contract will set forth under what circumstances the contractor is entitled to evidence of adequate funds or financing.[85] If such language exists in the contract, submission of evidence of adequate funds or financing is a condition precedent to the contractor commencing or continuing construction.

Therefore, the need to provide reasonable assurance of the ability to pay is not particularly controversial, at least prior to the commencement of construction. The parties can discuss the concerns of the contractor, and the contractor need not commence work unless it is satisfied. The requirement to provide evidence of financial arrangements after commencement of construction, however, is where most controversies occur. Issues such as under what circumstances the owner must provide evidence beyond that previously furnished,

---

85. AIA Document A201–2017, *supra* note 4, § 2.2.1.

and what constitutes evidence adequate to discharge the owner's obligations can prove to be a source of disagreement.

The AIA form documents attempt to clarify some of those issues by providing that the contractor may demand evidence of financial arrangements after commencement of the work when "the owner has failed to make payments to the Contractor as the Contract Documents require or if a change in the Work materially changes the Contract Sum."[86] Although such language is helpful, it does not resolve all potential disputes on the topic from the perspective of either party and may create additional interpretation issues with respect to good faith payment disputes and standards of materiality. The owner's satisfaction of its obligations to supply such evidence is important, as the contractor often has the right to terminate the contract for cause if such evidence is not promptly forthcoming.[87]

What constitutes reasonable evidence of financial arrangements remains a question of fact that must be evaluated under the circumstances. Acceptable evidence may include a construction loan commitment from the owner's lender, a good credit report, a corporate resolution or government appropriation, or other similar documentation that the owner has the financial ability to pay for the work.[88] Neither party, of course, wishes to argue about the adequacy of evidence of financial arrangements after the project has commenced, but the prospect for such disputes exists unless agreement is reached upfront as to what constitutes acceptable evidence. The owner may have additional concerns regarding the confidentiality of such evidence once it is furnished.

---

86. *Id.* § 2.2.1.
87. *Id.* § 14.1.1.4.
88. *See* 2 PHILIP L. BRUNER & PATRICK J. O'CONNOR, BRUNER & O'CONNOR ON CONSTRUCTION LAW § 5.39 (2002).

QUESTIONS

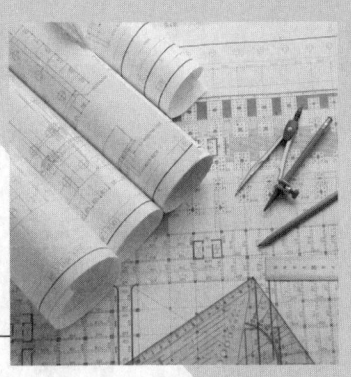

1. A contractor incurs additional costs and delays due to its inability to access the worksite as it had planned because another contractor performing work for the owner has not completed its work. Even if the owner's conduct is not the cause of the second contractor's delay in completing its work, who bears responsibility for the first contractor's additional costs due to its inability to perform the work as it originally planned? How does the analysis change if the contract between the owner and contractor provides that a contractor is not entitled to damages for project delays, but is only entitled to extensions of time?
2. Even though the contractor performs the work in compliance with the design drawings and specifications, the work proves to be faulty, and the owner seeks compensation from the contractor. What defenses does the contractor have to the owner's claim for defective work? What recourse does a contractor have if, due to a series of errors and inadequacies in the drawings and specifications that require numerous clarifications and corrections, a contractor incurs additional costs due to the extended duration of the project? Does the analysis change if the construction contract limits the damages that a contractor may recover or the remedies available to a contactor?
3. What factors and site conditions should be considered and evaluated in selecting a site for construction? Once construction begins, what site conditions must an owner and contractor be cognizant of due to federal, state, and municipal regulation?

CHAPTER 4

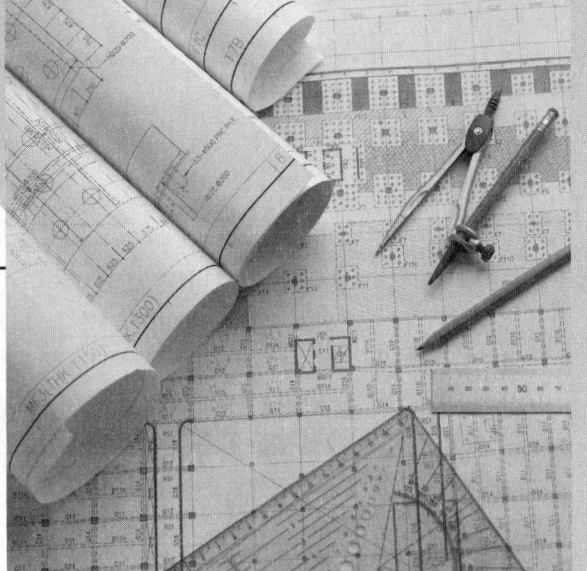

Project Delivery Systems

ROSS J. ALTMAN

4.01 OVERVIEW

A wide range of physical, human, financial, and other resources must be marshaled and coordinated to design, procure, and construct a project. The tasks required to deliver even a simple project often demand multiple design professionals, consultants, specialized contractors, and product and system vendors. As the size and complexity of a project increases, so does the quantity of entities and resources required to deliver that project. Many challenges arise when attempting to orchestrate the efforts among so many project participants and activities. If properly organized and performed, however, the delivery of a project is a collaborative exercise that can achieve the results desired by the project participants.

The owner determines how to structure the process through which the project is delivered. Although consideration must be given to many issues, the methodology used to deliver a project is driven principally by two defining characteristics. First, how the responsibilities for design, procurement, and construction are allocated among the project participants. Second, whether timing for performance of the major activities that comprise design, procurement, and construction is linear or overlapping. Decisions regarding those two matters largely determine the organizational structure of the design, procurement, and construction process, and describe the primary elements of what commonly is referred to as the project delivery system.

4.02 EVOLUTION OF METHODOLOGIES

Prior to the mid-1800s, construction methods and engineering practices were somewhat limited by today's standards. A mason or carpenter, often known as a master builder, was commonly appointed to manage and control the entire project delivery process. Romanesque and Gothic cathedrals of Europe, and many other significant structures that fill the pages of architectural history books, were delivered through such a methodology.[1] Subsequent advances in construction materials and technology, however, required greater design expertise and specialization. Architecture emerged as a separate profession, and the design function was severed from the performance of construction. The Design-Bid-Build project delivery system (described in Section 4.05) was the result, and remained the predominant method of project delivery in the United States throughout most of the 20th century.[2]

Nonetheless, the delivery of every project presents its own unique challenges. Moreover, because the objectives of the owner and applicable market conditions vary from project to project, the Design-Bid-Build system is not an optimal approach for delivery of all projects. Indeed, no single methodology is suitable for all projects. All project delivery systems have advantages and disadvantages. As a result, different methodologies have developed and continue to evolve to address owner preferences, the marketplace, and the almost endless array of challenges that might arise on any given project. Private sector owners have the flexibility to select and adapt any project delivery system desired, but public entities also will consider a range of methodologies if warranted and when properly authorized.[3]

---

1. *See* Frances Gies & Joseph Gies, Cathedral, Forge and Waterwheel (1994); Richard A. Goldthwaite, The Building of Renaissance Florence (1980); and Ross King, Brunelleschi's Dome (2000).

2. The public sector continues to rely heavily upon Design-Bid-Build, due in part to requirements dictated by procurement statutes.

3. Public entities generally may procure design and construction contracts only with project delivery systems that are authorized by the applicable statutory and regulatory regime. Even project delivery systems that are now commonplace, such as forms of Construction Management or Design-Build, can only be used by a public entity if permitted by law. Also see Chapter 23.

The nomenclature used to identify project delivery systems and variations is neither precise nor used consistently. Sometimes multiple terms are used interchangeably to describe the same project delivery system, even when distinctions probably apply to those terms. Such distinctions, however, are often interpreted differently by those employing the terminology.[4] Other terms are used to describe a variety of different project delivery systems.[5] Indeed, the same project delivery system may be known by different labels, depending on who makes the reference.[6] As a result, the terminology used to describe project delivery systems often is confusing and, from time to time, misleading.

Further complicating attempts to standardize terminology, some members of the design professions and construction industry also distinguish between project delivery systems and management techniques. According to those who endorse that distinction, a project delivery system is considered a method to allocate responsibilities with respect to design, procurement, and construction, whereas a device or method used to coordinate the process of design, procurement, and construction is considered a management technique.[7] Although interesting, the terminology commonly used to describe project delivery systems generally does not reflect such nuances. Many arrangements that might be defined more precisely as a management technique are often referred to as a project delivery system.[8]

Because terminology used to describe project delivery systems is not uniform, or at least not uniformly understood, simply referencing a project delivery system by name or descriptive phrase may not adequately explain the methodology. To ensure a mutual understanding of what is contemplated by such references, it often is advisable to describe the defining characteristics

---

4. The terms "Design-Build," "Turnkey," and "Build-to-Suit" often are used interchangeably. Although differences probably are intended by each term, the distinctions identified by those in the design professions and construction industry are not consistent.

5. References to "Construction Management" are ambiguous, as that term applies to a variety of different approaches, all of which fall under the generic category of Construction Management.

6. At-Risk Construction Management is also identified as CM@R, CMAR, CMc, and CM/GC.

7. For example, planning, staffing, budgeting, scheduling, and monitoring programs are all methods used to manage the process of design, procurement, and construction. Such methods might be used in connection with any type of project delivery system.

8. Program management (in many ways a surrogate for the owner's staff, used to analyze facilities, develop programmatic requirements, and monitor overall project development for an owner) and partnering (an effort to promote cooperation among all project participants through education, team-building exercises, and adoption of a "charter" agreement) are examples of management techniques that occasionally are referred to as types of project delivery systems. Agency Construction Management (see Section 4.06.A), which is described routinely as a project delivery system, perhaps more accurately is a management technique applied to the Multiple Prime project delivery system.

of a particular project delivery system. Even that exercise will not remove all doubt, as almost endless ways exist in which to define or distinguish between project delivery systems. Nonetheless, identifying the allocation of principal responsibilities and the timing of performance, as just noted, is a reasonable place to start. Using that approach, most project delivery systems and their permutations can be organized into four basic categories: [9]

- **Design-Bid-Build.** Defining characteristics include (1) three principal participants (owner, architect, and contractor); (2) two separate prime contracts (owner–architect agreement and construction contract); and (3) generally linear sequence of design, procurement, and construction activities.
- **Construction Management.** Defining characteristics include (1) three principal participants (owner, architect, and construction manager); (2) two separate prime contracts (owner-architect agreement, construction management agreement); and (3) potentially overlapping design, procurement, and construction activities.
- **Design-Build.** Defining characteristics include (1) two principal participants (owner and design-build entity); (2) one prime contract between the owner and design-build entity; and (3) generally overlapping design, procurement, and construction activities.
- **Innovative Approaches.** Certain highly customized or novel project delivery systems emerge from time to time. Defining characteristics are not possible to identify in advance with respect to all such approaches that do not fall neatly into any of the other three categories just identified. Many of these methods are viewed by some as management techniques or procurement methods, as opposed to project delivery systems. As a general proposition, innovative approaches that have gained recent publicity usually emphasize some form of collaboration among the principal project participants or a non-conventional allocation of responsibility. Some approaches intend to align interests of contracting parties through a risk share/gain share arrangement.

---

9. A research report by the Construction Industry Institute identifies at least ten principal project delivery system categories, including "traditional Design-Bid-Build, traditional Design-Bid-Build with early procurement, Project Management (agent), Construction Management (agent) with early procurement, Construction Management (at risk), Design-Build or Engineer Procure Construct, multiple Design-Build or Engineer Procure Construct, multiple Prime Contractors, staged Design-Bid-Build, and Turnkey." *Project Delivery and Contract Strategies*, Construction Industry Institute, RR165-11, Dec. 1, 2003. For a general overview of project delivery systems, also see Robert A. Rubin & Linda M. Thomas-Mobley, *Delivery Systems*, Ch. 8, *in* FUNDAMENTALS OF CONSTRUCTION LAW (American Bar Association Forum on the Construction Industry) (2d ed., 2013).

Each of the four general categories of project delivery systems is described and examined in greater detail in Sections 4.05 through 4.08.

4.03 COMMERCIAL IMPORTANCE OF PROJECT DELIVERY SYSTEMS

The project delivery system dictates the overall legal and commercial framework of the transaction. The form of contracts used among the project participants and many contractual terms are a direct consequence of the applicable project delivery system.[10] Indeed, trade groups publish suites of standard form contracts for different project delivery methods.[11]

Different forms are required to address the variety of contractual relationships, but also because each project delivery system provides a transaction structure better suited to achieve certain objectives than others. In other words, different contract forms are needed because the method of project delivery has commercial ramifications.

Although a list of commercial issues that typically concern an owner is extensive, an owner will commonly consider the following matters when deciding which project delivery system might work for its project:

- **Cost.** Most owners hope to complete the project for the lowest price possible. Some owners, however, are willing to pay a higher price if, in exchange for an incremental increase in cost, the owner will receive an appropriate increase in value (e.g., lower cost of operating and maintaining the completed project; or longer useful life of materials, equipment, and systems). Cost predictability is also important. How soon will the owner know the likely final cost to complete the project? How reliable is that price? What is the need for price contingencies to cover the likelihood of unforeseen conditions or cost volatility in the marketplace? Some owners prefer to transfer risk to the other party and pay a premium, if that risk transfer reduces the possibility of future claims for cost adjustments. Other owners are willing to absorb some risk,

---

10. *See* Shively v. Belleville Twp. High Sch. Dist. No. 201, 329 Ill. App. 3d 1156, 769 N.E.2d 1062 (2002). In *Shively*, the parties disagreed as to the type of project delivery system that had been employed on an already completed project. The *Shively* court analyzed the contract between the parties and concluded that many features of the contract were consistent with an Agency Construction Management project delivery system.

11. Form contracts for use in connection with different project delivery systems are published by groups such as the American Institute of Architects, ConsensusDocs, Engineers Joint Contract Documents Committee, the Construction Management Association of America, the Design Build Institute of America, and many other groups, including organizations located overseas.

and the price uncertainty that comes with acceptance of risk, when the trade-off provides a reasonable opportunity to achieve a lower final contract price.

- **Time.** The ability to complete a project on time or ahead of a specified delivery date is generally important to owners. Aside from the owner's desire to obtain beneficial use and occupancy of a project, ongoing construction absorbs an owner's resources. Perhaps more importantly are the cost implications of time. Earlier completion usually translates into reducing debt service for construction financing, accelerating the date upon which the project starts to generate revenue, and replacing less efficient facilities. An owner also may have legal commitments to third parties that can only be fulfilled if the project is completed timely, such as furnishing space to a tenant or supplying goods to a customer. Business cycles also may drive a project. The owner may be in a seasonal business, where failure to open as of a certain date results in significant loss of sales. If a project will be used to produce a product with a limited market advantage or useful life, such as a pharmaceutical plant or computer chip factory, then any delay in completion has extremely adverse consequences.

  For example, certain methods of project delivery are more compatible with the use of so-called fast track construction, in which construction commences before completion of the entire project design. When executed successfully, a fast track or "phased" project is completed earlier than if construction were to commence only after completion of the entire design. With accelerated completion, the owner may achieve the benefits discussed earlier. Fast track construction, however, limits the owner's ability to make design changes, increases the likelihood of design problems, and requires a difficult coordination effort. Fast track construction also creates pricing uncertainty, with a so called guaranteed maximum price sometimes proposed before the design is final. In theory, however, the financial benefits of early completion outweigh any additional cost to complete the project that may arise out of overlapping design, procurement, and construction.

- **Design quality.** Of course, the owner wants an error-free design, with drawings and specifications sufficiently complete to avoid disputes and to produce reliable pricing. The owner also wants its aesthetic and functional objectives satisfied by the design. Technical requirements and performance criteria also should be met. Some owners want the ability to exercise an active role in the design. The owner may intend to develop a distinctive "signature" quality project, in which the visual appearance of the project is identified with, or is an emblem for, the owner or the owner's brand. In such circumstances, aesthetic issues are paramount.[12]

☐ **Reduction in claims.** The design and construction process can be contentious, adversarial, and fraught with claims. Owners are frustrated by such matters, which demand time, drain resources, and affect the project adversely. The owner may want to take measures to diminish the possibility of disputes among the principal project participants. It is important to all owners that construction be completed in conformance with the construction documents and be of high quality. Owners also may be willing to pay for the use of safeguards or procedures that provide greater assurance of construction quality when the trade-off is a reduced probability of warranty issues.

☐ **Other issues.** Some typical concerns of owners might include safety and minimization of job-site accidents and injuries. Other owners may be more concerned with simplifying any administrative burden a project might generate, particularly if the owner does not have in-house construction expertise or if existing resources already are overstretched. Each owner will have other concerns pertaining to its specific circumstances.

4.04 SELECTING A PROJECT DELIVERY SYSTEM

The owner must determine which project objectives are most important, giving consideration to the constraints and market conditions under which the owner operates. Certain project delivery systems are more likely than others to achieve the project objectives with which the owner is most concerned. The likelihood of a project delivery system to achieve the specific objectives of an owner might be described as the "selection factors" for that project delivery system. Not all project objectives can be addressed by any one project delivery system, and prioritizing project objectives involves making some hard choices.

For example, if an owner desires price certainty prior to commencing construction, then a project delivery system in which the design, procurement, and construction activities overlap is usually not an option. Without a complete set

---

12. Although the Transamerica Pyramid in San Francisco, California, is no longer the headquarters of the Transamerica Corporation, the building is depicted in the logo of the company and its distinctive shape remains associated with Transamerica. A more novel example is the headquarters for the former basket maker Longaberger Company in Newark, Ohio, which looks like a seven-story replica of a woven wood basket.

of construction documents, pricing information is less reliable and often subject to various assumptions, clarifications, and exclusions from the contractor. In other words, certain project objectives compete with one another and often are mutually exclusive. Consequently, the owner must prioritize its objectives.

Those choices also may involve a judgment by the owner that the risks created by failing to address certain objectives can be managed effectively or are remote; therefore, those objectives are deemed less important. Project objectives that do not serve as the basis to the project delivery system might be described as "risk factors" because the transaction structure selected is not designed to ameliorate the adverse effects of failing to achieve those objectives. Although a project delivery system can always be fine-tuned and adjusted to lessen the potential adverse effects of a risk factor, it is not possible to eliminate a risk factor entirely. Moreover, removing one risk factor has the potential to create another.

By selecting a project delivery system, the owner attempts (1) to optimize its ability to achieve certain project objectives, (2) to accepting responsibility to manage the risk of other factors, and (3) to set up a transaction structure that incentivizes conduct and performance by the parties to the transaction in a way consistent with project goals. The options and potential permutations are infinite. Every project delivery system has its advocates, each of whom will claim the superiority of the advocate's preferred approach.[13] However, no project delivery system is perfect, nor can any such system or permutation solve all of the challenges an owner confronts. Ultimately, the owner must balance selection factors against risk factors and determine which approach fits best for the project.

4.05 DESIGN-BID-BUILD

Historically, Design-Bid-Build has been the most commonly used method of project delivery in the United States.[14] The method is known by many similar names, such as design-bid-build, design-award-construct, or the so-called traditional approach. Design-Bid-Build is a three-party arrangement, involving two principal contracts. The owner contracts with an architect for the design of the project, and enters into a separate contract with a general contractor for the overall construction of the project. The architect and the general contractor

---

13. Trades groups have formed around various project delivery systems, such as the Construction Management Association of America (the CMAA) and the Design-Build Institute of America (the DBIA).

14. Joint Committee of the American Institute of Architects and the Associated General Contractors of America, *Primer on Project Delivery* 3 (2004).

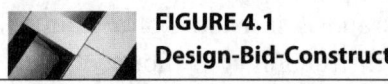

FIGURE 4.1
Design-Bid-Construct

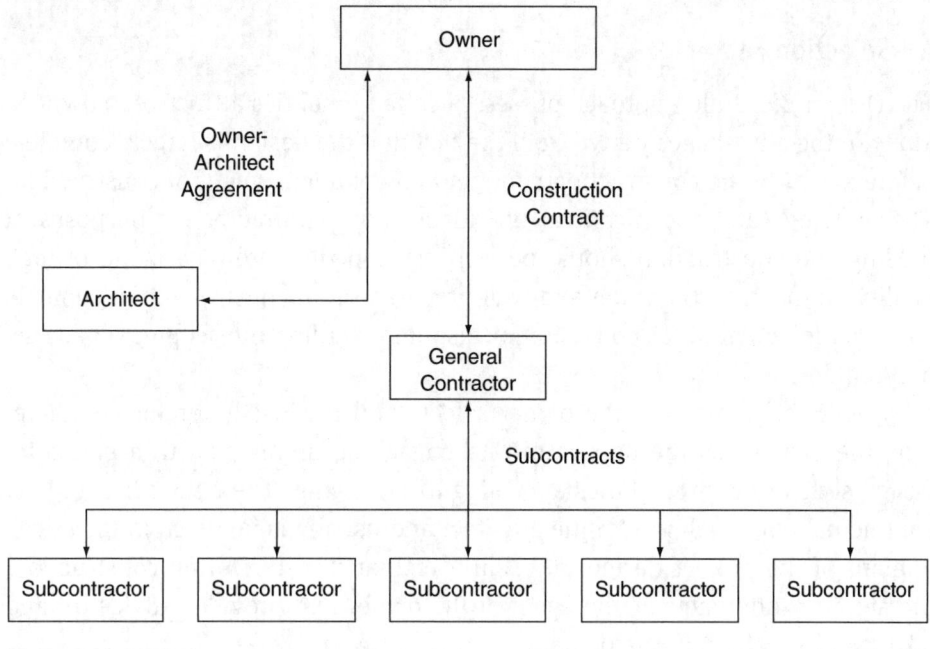

have no direct contractual relationship with each other. Construction usually commences only after (1) the architect completes a final, detailed set of drawings and specifications, and (2) those documents have been published to contractors for competitive bidding or sole-source negotiation. Figure 4.1 provides a diagram of the contractual arrangement in Design-Bid-Build.

The Design-Bid-Build delivery system is intended to capitalize on the separate skill and expertise of design professionals and construction contractors. Design and construction obligations are separated, and delegated to entities with training and expertise in those tasks. The architect is principally responsible for the design of the project,[15] and may retain a team of engineers and other design consultants to assist in that undertaking.[16] A general contractor is principally responsible for the construction of the project described in drawings, specifications, and other documents prepared by the architect and the design

---

15. The principal design professional in civil construction (roads, bridges, processing plants, etc.) is an engineer, but this chapter will refer to the architect for simplicity.

16. *See* American Institute of Architects, AIA Document B101–2007, Standard Form of Agreement between Owner and Architect § 1.1 (2017) [hereinafter AIA Document B101–2017], in which the architect identifies its principal consultants.

team. The general contractor generally retains and is in charge of a team of subcontractors and suppliers to complete the construction obligations.[17]

A. Selection Factors

The Design-Bid-Build approach possesses certain qualities attractive to owners. Many of the advantages derive from the fact that the design is largely complete before award of the construction contract and commencement of construction. The drawings and specifications provided to the contractor for purposes of bidding and construction should be well developed, coordinated, and of high quality. In theory, a thorough and well-prepared set of construction documents reduces the potential for confusion or dispute regarding the scope of construction required.

Under this approach, the owner selects and retains the architect. Therefore, the owner has the opportunity to engage an architect with a particular design style or other attributes appealing to the owner. The owner has a direct contractual relationship with the architect and usually is involved in the development of the project design on a fairly regular basis.[18] During construction, the architect often acts as the agent of the owner and provides advice to, and advocacy on behalf of, the owner.

Because the drawings and specifications are complete when the construction contract is procured, the cost of construction should be more predictable. The Design-Bid-Build approach also lends itself to competitive bidding, which produces a number of residual benefits for the owner. First, the general contractor is not left to guess as to what is included in the work; therefore, a fixed price to complete the work can be provided.[19] Second, subject to contract terms, cost overruns become the risk of the general contractor. Therefore, the

---

17. *See* American Institute of Architects, AIA Document A201–2017, General Conditions of the Contract for Construction § 3.3.2 (2017) [hereinafter AIA Document A201–2017], which provides that "[t]he Contractor shall be responsible to the Owner for acts and omissions of the Contractor's employees, Subcontractors and their agents and employees, and other persons or entities performing portions of the Work for, or on behalf of, the Contractor or any of its Subcontractors."

18. Under the AIA document approach, the design process moves through schematic design, design development, and construction documents phases (see Chapter 7 for a more detailed discussion). The architect is not permitted to commence services in a design phase without approval from the owner of the documents produced in the prior phase. *See* AIA Document B101–2017, *supra* note 16, §§ 3.2.1, 3.2.7, 3.3.1, 3.3.3, 3.4.1, 3.4.5.

19. *See* American Institute of Architects, AIA Document A101–2017, Standard Form of Agreement between Owner and Contractor § 4.1 (2017), which specifies the "Contract Sum" for the performance of the contract.

general contractor assumes the risk of volatility in labor and material pricing. Finally, the pressure of competitive bidding provides the owner with some assurance that the contract sum reflects pricing available in the marketplace.

Because the architect and general contractor have separate contracts with the owner, the Design-Bid-Build methodology has checks and balances built into it. The architect observes construction in progress and acts as the owner's agent to the extent empowered to do so under the agreement between the owner and architect.[20] The architect advocates in construction matters on behalf of the owner, who frequently does not possess meaningful construction knowledge or capability. The general contractor, on the other hand, is motivated to identify deficiencies and errors in the documents prepared by the architect and can serve as a second set of eyes with respect to some aspects of the design.

Members of the design professions and construction industry are very familiar with the Design-Bid-Build process. The roles of the parties are well understood. The owner has a single point of responsibility for design and another single point of responsibility for construction. The administrative burdens of the owner are also easy to identify, and outside assistance is readily available if needed.

B. Risk Factors

The characteristics of the Design-Bid-Build approach, however, are not well suited for all projects and pose certain risks. This approach relies heavily on the architect for the entire design of the project. Little opportunity exists to receive input during the design process from the construction team on matters for which contractors and suppliers often have more expertise than design professionals, such as the following: value engineering, cost estimating, constructability, construction scheduling, labor and material market analysis, equipment availability, design of specialized equipment and proprietary systems, and other similar issues. As a result, the project design might not achieve all objectives of the owner to the fullest extent possible. Although such input may be received after the general contractor is retained, any changes to the design at that point in time will cost more and cause delays in project completion.

---

20. *See* AIA Document B101–2017, *supra* note 16, § 3.6.1.2, which provides that "[t]he Architect shall have the authority to act on behalf of the Owner only to the extent provided in this Agreement." AIA Document A201–2017, *supra* note 17, § 4.2.1, provides that "[t]he Architect will have authority to act on behalf of the Owner only to the extent provided in the Contract Documents."

When using Design-Bid-Build, construction does not start until the design is complete. The process is linear and sequential. As a result, project completion occurs at a date later than if the design, procurement, and construction phases were to overlap. A longer project schedule has disadvantages to the owner. First, delays in locking in price provide a greater opportunity for escalation in construction costs. Second, many projects are intended to generate revenue directly or indirectly, whether through rental income, through sales activities that occur in the completed project, by producing items that are sold, or by furnishing facilities that support revenue generation. But, if the ability to commence the beneficial use and occupancy is delayed, then so is the revenue stream generated by such use and occupancy. Delays in commencement of construction also create the risk of interest rate inflation, and, in turn, significant increases in the cost of debt service over the life of a construction loan.

When a construction contract is subject to a fixed price, the general contractor's entrepreneurial interests may be at odds with the owner's expectations regarding quality of construction and cost control. A general contractor is reluctant to provide any work not called for clearly in the drawings and specifications on which the contractor bid. Performing such work simply is contrary to the economic assumptions upon which the general contractor provided such bid. If questions arise regarding scope or the type of work to be provided, the general contractor will make decisions consistent with its financial interests, not the owner's. Accordingly, the owner may not agree with positions taken by the general contractor. As no set of drawings and specifications is ever 100 percent complete, reasonable inferences must be made from those documents.[21] Expectations regarding what is reasonable to infer from construction documents provides a fertile source of disputes.

The hallmark of Design-Bid-Build, that is, the three-party arrangement, may make claims difficult to sort through. All parties will have a natural tendency to defend their work and services. Architects are inclined to argue that problems result from contractor error. Conversely, contractors are predisposed to contend that the architect's design errors or omissions caused the problems. In many instances, it is difficult to determine fault, and a construction-related dispute not resolved amicably is always expensive to adjudicate. Because neither the architect nor the contractor wishes to be held responsible for the obligations of the other, each will negotiate vigorously for certain exculpatory

---

21. *See* AIA Document A201–2007, *supra* note 17, § 1.2.1, which provides that "performance by the Contractor shall be required only to the extent consistent with the Contract Documents and reasonably inferable from them as being necessary to produce the indicated results."

language in contracts to guard against such risk. Even if the owner (1) is not at fault for problems encountered on a project and (2) possesses legitimate claims through which to recover damages for its losses, the foregoing will be of little consolation when such claims cannot be resolved promptly due to finger-pointing between an architect and a general contractor.

Also, the owner may become the focus of claims between the design team and the construction team. In those states with a more orthodox application of the Economic Loss Rule, the probability of encountering this situation is amplified.[22] For example, if a general contractor believes it has suffered economic loss for which the architect or another member of the design team bears responsibility, the Economic Loss Rule may prohibit the general contractor from bringing a cause of action against any of those parties directly. The general contractor may have no option but to pursue a claim against the party with whom it has a contract—the owner—and place the burden on the owner to bring a third-party action against the architect.

Claims also can be a problem with respect to subcontractors and other lower-tier entities that do not have a direct contract with the owner. The relationship of lower-tier entities to the owner may be very remote, and payment to lower-tier entities for their work or services flows downstream from the owner through other parties prior to receipt by the lower-tier entity. There may be substantial delays between the date the work or service is performed by a lower-tier entity and the date upon which payment for that work or service is received.

As a result, lower-tier entities must absorb a cost to finance their work for the owner. For many lower-tier entities to remain financially viable, that finance cost is included in the contract sum of the lower-tier entity and is passed upstream, eventually reaching the owner, and thereby ultimately increasing total project costs. From a practical standpoint, however, lower-tier entities are often thinly capitalized. The financial stress created by delays in payment to them is often too great. Disputes spring from delays in payment, and sometimes companies fail from such delays.[23]

---

22. See Chapter 21.
23. The Surety Information Office cites a study by BizMiner (a company that analyzes U.S. industries) and concludes that "of the 850,029 building (non-single-family), heavy/highway, industrial buildings/warehouses, hotel/motel and multifamily home construction, and specialty trade contractors operating in 2004, only 649,602 were still in business in 2006—a 23.6% failure rate." *See* Surety Information Office, *Why Do Contractors Fail*, http://suretyinfo.org/?wpfb_dl = 151 (last accessed Jan. 18, 2018).

C. Common Variations

As with all project delivery systems, variations of the Design-Bid-Build approach have been developed. Sometimes modified versions are motivated by a desire to optimize a selection factor or, more likely, an attempt to diminish the potentially adverse effects of a risk factor in the use of Design-Bid-Build. One of the most common variants of Design-Bid-Build is referred to as Multiple Primes. In this method of project delivery, there is no general contractor. Rather, the owner contracts directly with each trade. In essence, the entities referred to as subcontractors under the Design-Bid-Build approach become prime contractors under the Multiple Prime approach. The owner still contracts with the architect separately, and the process of design, procurement, and construction remains linear. Figure 4.2 provides a diagram of the contractual arrangement in the Multiple Prime approach.

In furtherance of various public policy reasons, some states require the use of the Multiple Prime approach under their procurement statutes for public projects.[24] The Multiple Prime approach provides opportunity for participation by a greater number of trade contractors. Because each trade contract is awarded through competitive bidding, the likelihood for exclusionary practices in the award of contracts to the trades is reduced. The use of competitive bidding also provides some assurance of a market price. In practice, however, the Multiple Prime approach may not achieve all of the benefits that the method is designed to attain. Nonetheless, those potential benefits are important considerations to a government agency charged with shepherding public assets.

When the private sector considers the Multiple Prime approach, the reasons are similar but not always identical to those cited by the public sector. Removing a tier of fee or markup from the construction team (the cost of retaining a general contractor) is attractive on some projects. An owner also may like the idea of actively deciding which trade contractors to retain and administering each such contract. The Multiple Prime methodology provides the owner with significant control. Furthermore, eliminating a general contractor from the construction process removes a link in the payment chain, resulting in less financial stress on the trades and those with whom the trades contract. Accordingly, the need for lower-tier entities to build into their price a cost to finance delays in payment is diminished somewhat.

Notwithstanding the advantages of the Multiple Prime method, any change to a project delivery formula may cause new challenges to emerge. Although the owner in a Multiple Prime project may enjoy increased control

---

24. *See* N.Y. State Fin. Law § 135, sometimes referred to as the Wicks Law. Other states have similar legislation, including New Jersey, Ohio, Pennsylvania, and Wisconsin.

**FIGURE 4.2
Multiple Primes**

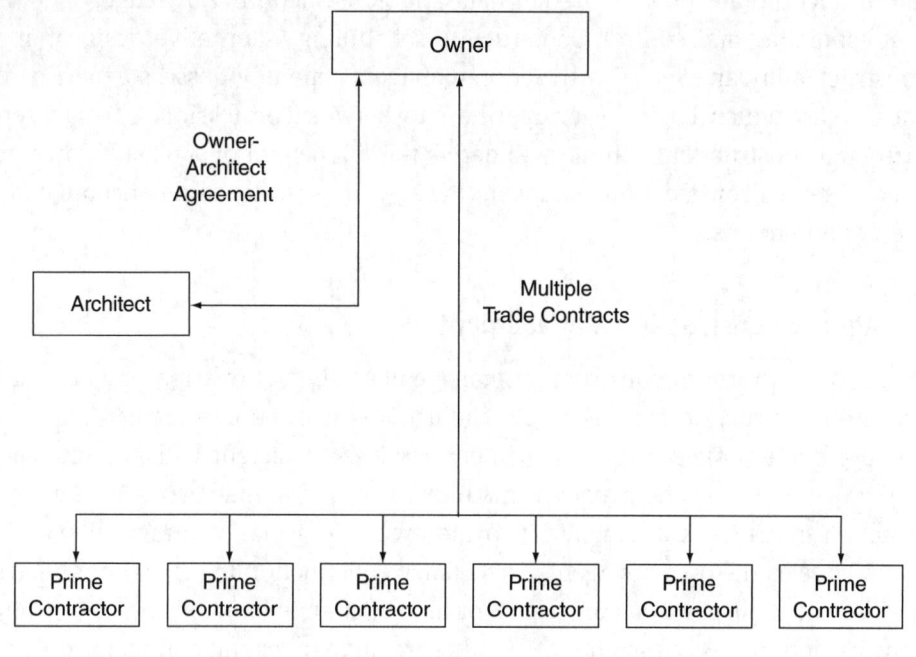

over the trades, with that control comes a heavy coordination and administrative responsibility. Many owners do not have the ability to discharge those obligations successfully. An owner must possess substantial construction skill and experience to act as its own general contractor. Moreover, because a general contractor no longer stands between the owner and the lower-tier contractors, the owner in a Multiple Prime job must deal directly with claims from the numerous trades. Those claims might not be easy to resolve. In addition to customary disagreements between the design team and the construction team, finger-pointing also can be expected among and between the various trade contractors.

4.06 CONSTRUCTION MANAGEMENT

The term "construction management" applies to a variety of project delivery systems. No universal definition exists, and the references to "construction management" are vague, at best, without further clarification. The role of a construction manager may range from an additional consultant to the owner who functions in a purely advisory role to that of a constructor with extensive obligations pertaining to the design and construction of the entire project.

Construction management concepts developed out of increasing dissatisfaction experienced by owners with the inability of the traditional delivery system to incorporate reliable market data and construction knowledge, such as cost estimating and control, construction scheduling, alternative designs, and constructability analysis. Construction managers generally possess expertise in such areas, which basically bridge the gap between professional design services and construction activities. To derive the full benefit of such skill, owners usually retain construction managers during, or prior to commencement of, the design process.

A. Agency Construction Management

One common form of construction management often is referred to as Agency or Pure Construction Management. The agent construction manager is paid a fee to provide professional management services consistent with the interests of the owner. Under the agency version of construction management, the construction manager is a consultant to the owner and may contract with trade contractors as the owner's agent. The agency construction manager coordinates the trades but does not guarantee cost or time of completion, nor does an agency construction manager assume many other traditional general contractor obligations.[25] Figure 4.3 provides a diagram of the contractual arrangement in the Agency Construction Management approach.

In many respects, the Agency Construction Management approach simply takes the Multiple Prime method and augments it with an advisor to the owner. The owner outsources to that advisor the coordination and other responsibilities that the owner retains in a Multiple Prime approach that the owner is not capable of handling itself, due either to lack of necessary skills or available resources. The owner retains the advisor in an effort to ameliorate some of the risk factors inherent in the Multiple Prime approach. Consequently, many in the design professions and construction industry view Agency Construction Management as a management technique applied to the Multiple Prime approach and not as a separate project delivery system. Regardless of that debate, Agency Construction Management has found its way into the parlance

---

25. *See generally* the Construction Management Association of America, *Agency Series Model Contract Documents, available at* http://cmaanet.org (follow CMAA Bookstore link; then follow CMAA Publications); and ConsensusDocs 830, *Owner/Construction Manager as Agent Agreement* (2016); ConsensusDocs 831, *Standard Owner and Construction Manager* (CM Agent does not provide General Conditions Items). (Note: The publisher, ConsensusDocs, is a group comprised of approximately 20 construction associations.)

FIGURE 4.3
Agency Construction Management

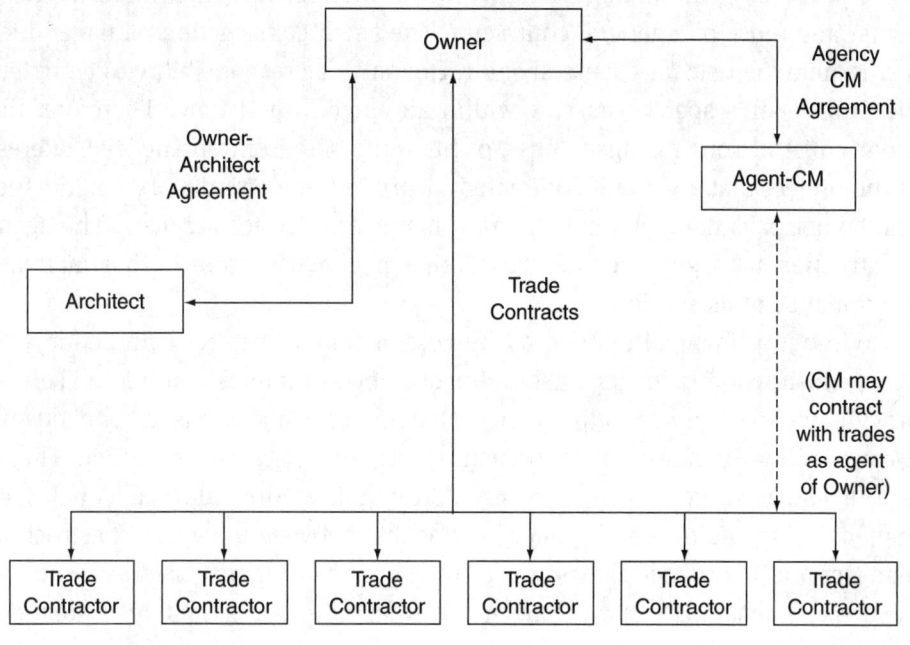

of project delivery systems and is the basis of many contract forms; therefore, the concepts and objectives behind the use of Agency Construction Management warrant understanding.[26]

1. Selection Factors

Essentially a permutation of the Multiple Prime approach, Agency Construction Management possesses many of the same advantages found in the Multiple Prime approach. Adding the agent construction manager to the Multiple Prime arrangement addresses some of its shortcomings. For example, the owner retains the agent construction manager during the design process. As a result, the owner obtains construction-related advice on a timely basis as the drawings and specifications evolve. Also, because of the early participation in the project by a construction advisor, the process lends itself to overlapping the design, procurement, and construction phases of a project. The ability to implement phased, or fast track, construction is one of the most common reasons to engage a construction manager.

---

26. *See supra* note 25.

In addition, Agency Construction Management aligns the interests of the owner with the party principally responsible for managing the construction process, thereby eliminating the inherent conflict between the interests of the owner and those of a general contractor. The agent construction manager does not assume the risks of a general contractor, such as responsibility to complete the project for a specific cost or within an agreed upon time. Therefore, the agent construction manager does not have the same entrepreneurial interest in the project that a general contractor, or prime trade contractor, would have. The owner pays the agent construction manager a fee for services. The agent construction manager does not have other pecuniary interests that motivate performance of its services.

Without a financial interest in the cost or time of project completion, the agent construction manager is less influenced by self-interest and more likely to provide impartial advice to the owner. That advice is a key reason for choosing a construction management approach as the project delivery system. Therefore, it makes sense to use a process that enhances the value and quality of that advice. In addition, the agency relationship between the agent construction manager and the owner allows the agent construction manager to advocate on the owner's behalf. Because the agent construction manager's interests are more aligned with the owner than with the interests of the trades, the agent construction manager can do an effective job of evaluating and defending claims asserted by the trade contractors during construction of the project.

2. Risk Factors

The weaknesses of the Multiple Prime approach not addressed through the retention of the agent construction manager obviously remain present in the Agency Construction Management method. Most notable among them, no single point of responsibility exists for performance and completion of construction. The agent construction manager only coordinates such matters. Although variations are common, the degree to which the agent construction manager retains liability for construction cost, delays in completion, quality of work, safety of the work, and other construction-related matters is usually limited by the contract between the owner and the agent construction manager. Such limitations, more than any other criticisms, are enough to cause reluctance among many owners to consider Agency Construction Management for their projects.

Construction management in all its forms is a relatively new phenomenon, with a short track record compared to other project delivery systems. The obligations and risks assumed by the principal parties, in some respects, still are evolving and do not have a standard industry approach. This leads to some confusion. It also provides the potential for protracted contract negotiations, since each contract tends to be highly customized. Uncertainty also stems from the fact that many see the agent construction manager as providing services that are somewhat professional in nature. Therefore, questions arise as to whether a license is required to provide such services and what kind of insurance is appropriate for the agent construction manager to procure and maintain. Bonding also may be an issue. Finally, the body of law available to define the nature of Agency Construction Management is relatively limited.

B. At-Risk Construction Management

The other project delivery approach most commonly referred to as construction management is a hybrid of Agency Construction Management and Design-Bid-Build. At-Risk Construction Management, as it usually is described, involves retention of a construction manager during or prior to commencement of the design process. The at-risk construction manager provides the same type of pre-construction consulting services provided by an agent construction manager. Cost estimating, construction scheduling, value engineering, and constructability analysis, to name a few, are all of great benefit in optimizing the design of the project.

The at-risk construction manager, however, does not act as the agent of the owner. Trade contractors are retained by the at-risk construction manager directly. The trades, therefore, are subcontractors of the at-risk construction manager. The subcontractors have no contractual privity with the owner and look to the at-risk construction manager for payment. In fact, the at-risk construction manager is often referred to as a "constructor" and is the single point of responsibility for the performance of construction.[27] Figure 4.4 provides a diagram of the contractual arrangement in the At-Risk Construction Management approach.

1. Selection Factors

The At-Risk Construction Management method is an effort to combine the characteristics of Agency Construction Management and Design-Bid-Build that are perceived as more favorable to owners. Unlike the agent construction manager, the at-risk construction manager is responsible for the overall construction of

---

27. American Institute of Architects, AIA Document A133–2009, Standard Form of Agreement between Owner and Construction Manager as Constructor (2009); *see also* AIA Document A201–2017, *supra* note 17, § 1.1.2 (no contractual relationship between the Owner and a Subcontractor); § 5.1.1 (definition of Subcontractor); § 9.6.4 (Owner has no obligation to pay a Subcontractor except as may be required by law).

FIGURE 4.4
At-Risk Construction Management

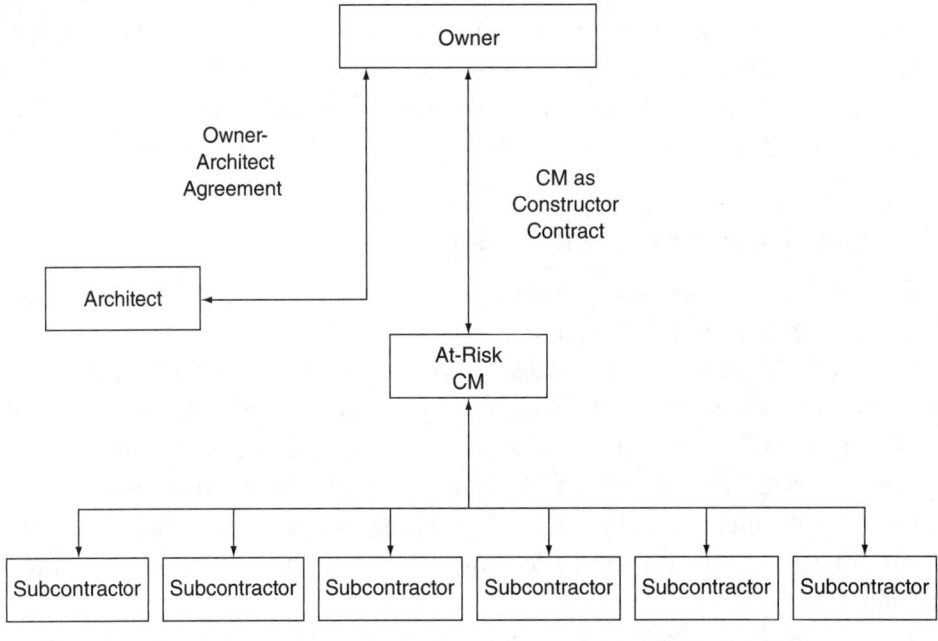

the project. During the construction process, therefore, the at-risk construction manager is very much like a general contractor in the Design-Bid-Build approach. As a constructor, not an agent of the owner, the at-risk construction manager remains obligated for the quality, cost, and timely completion of construction, along with all other responsibilities customarily assumed by a general contractor.

Similar to Agency Construction Management, however, the owner in the At-Risk Construction Management approach also receives the benefit of pre-construction consulting services necessary to optimize the design process. With the benefit of such pre-construction advice, the drawings and specifications produced by the architect should describe a project that presents fewer constructability challenges and is more likely to be completed in accordance with the budget and schedule requirements of the owner. At-Risk Construction Management also facilitates the opportunity to overlap the design, procurement, and construction phases of a project, shortening the duration of a project. Therefore, At-Risk Construction Management is generally associated with fast track construction or some other technique that allows aspects of procurement and construction to commence prior to the completion of the drawings and specifications by the architect.

2. Risk Factors

As a hybrid approach, At-Risk Construction Management has some of the disadvantages of the project delivery systems with which it shares certain characteristics (i.e., Agency Construction Management and Design-Bid-Build). As is the case with Agency Construction Management, no substantial body of law exists from which to gain guidance on legal issues that may arise in connection with At-Risk Construction Management. Further, although the at-risk construction manager has responsibilities very much analogous to those of a general contractor, the pre-construction role of the at-risk construction manager poses questions surrounding licensing, insurance, and bonding.

Many of the risk factors inherent with Design-Bid-Build also remain unsolved by At-Risk Construction Management. Subcontractors and suppliers, particularly those in lower tiers, bear the financial burden of receiving payment long after they provide their work and services. The division of design and construction responsibility during the construction phase of an At-Risk Construction Management project can cause adversarial relationships between the architect and the at-risk construction manager, each assuming that the other is principally responsible for any project problem.

Perhaps the most troublesome risk factor is that the economic incentives of the at-risk construction manager do not entirely align with the interests of the owner. Like a general contractor in a Design-Bid-Build project, the ability of the at-risk construction manager to earn a profit on the project is linked directly to its ability to satisfy certain contractually specified criteria. Consequently, the at-risk construction manager will resist vigorously any condition or circumstance that might cause it to incur unanticipated cost or require additional time to complete construction. Claims are the likely result.

The at-risk construction manager should not be expected to perform work beyond the minimum required by the construction contract. For example, providing items less desirable to the owner or sequencing work in a certain manner may save the at-risk construction manager time and money. Moreover, such measures may be entirely permissible under the terms of a construction contract, which terms typically provide a general contractor or an at-risk construction manager with some latitude in discharging its obligations. Even during pre-construction services, the at-risk construction manager might be inclined to recommend a particular course of action that it believes will facilitate its ability to satisfy contractual obligations, even when better alternatives from the standpoint of the owner might be available.

Issues with respect to ensuring accurate and reliable pricing are common when using an At-Risk Construction Management approach. First, an owner generally retains the at-risk construction manager before design services are complete. Because the drawings and specifications are most likely not well developed at that time, any price furnished by the at-risk construction manager early in the design process represents only an estimate; such a price probably contains a large contingency to protect the at-risk construction manager from costs that might become apparent when the drawings and specifications are better defined.

Usually, the at-risk construction manager does not propose a binding not-to-exceed price, known as a "guaranteed maximum price," until the drawings and specifications achieve a level of completion where the at-risk construction manager is reasonably certain of what will be required to complete the work. That might occur when the drawings and specifications are anywhere from 50 to 90 percent complete, depending on the nature of the work.[28] When the at-risk construction manager is not comfortable with the accuracy and completeness of the drawings and specifications, the guaranteed maximum price will be based on numerous assumptions, clarifications, and exclusions. If the final drawings and specifications are inconsistent with any such qualification, the at-risk construction manager will expect the guaranteed maximum price to be increased.

Finally, At-Risk Construction Management contracts are procured more often through negotiation than through competitive bidding. Because the at-risk construction manager is retained during the design phase, there is no project design to bid.[29] Therefore, the majority of owners retain an at-risk construction manager on the basis of particular skill and expertise, believing that (1) the ability of the at-risk construction manager is of primary importance to the owner, and (2) market pricing will occur through competitive bidding of subcontracts. Some owners will retain a construction manager initially for only pre-construction activities and then seek competitive bids from other at-risk construction managers

---

28. *See* Skidmore, Owings & Merrill v. Intrawest I Ltd. Pshp., NO. 35195-8-I, 1997 Wash. App. LEXIS 1505 (Ct. App. Sept. 8, 1997). The *Skidmore* court found that determining the degree to which drawings and specifications are complete is not an exact science. Various approaches abound. In *Skidmore*, the architect was found to have breached an obligation to furnish 90 percent complete drawings.

29. In such circumstances, some owners seek bids on fee and certain overhead expenses.

when the design is largely complete, but this method is not always an effective way to achieve market pricing for the construction phase. The familiarity of the original at-risk construction manager with the project is usually an advantage that rarely can be overcome by other bidders.

4.07 DESIGN-BUILD

Under the Design-Build approach, an owner contracts with a single entity who undertakes to both design and construct the project. Many owners prefer a single point of responsibility for the entire project and desire to unburden themselves from the day-to-day contract administration responsibilities endemic to running most construction projects. Because Design-Build tends to be a very integrated process among the design and construction teams, the design, procurement, and construction phases almost always overlap. A number of variations of Design-Build are possible, many of which are described in greater detail in Section 4.07.C. Figure 4.5 provides a diagram of the contractual arrangement in the basic approach to Design-Build.

**FIGURE 4.5
Design-Build**

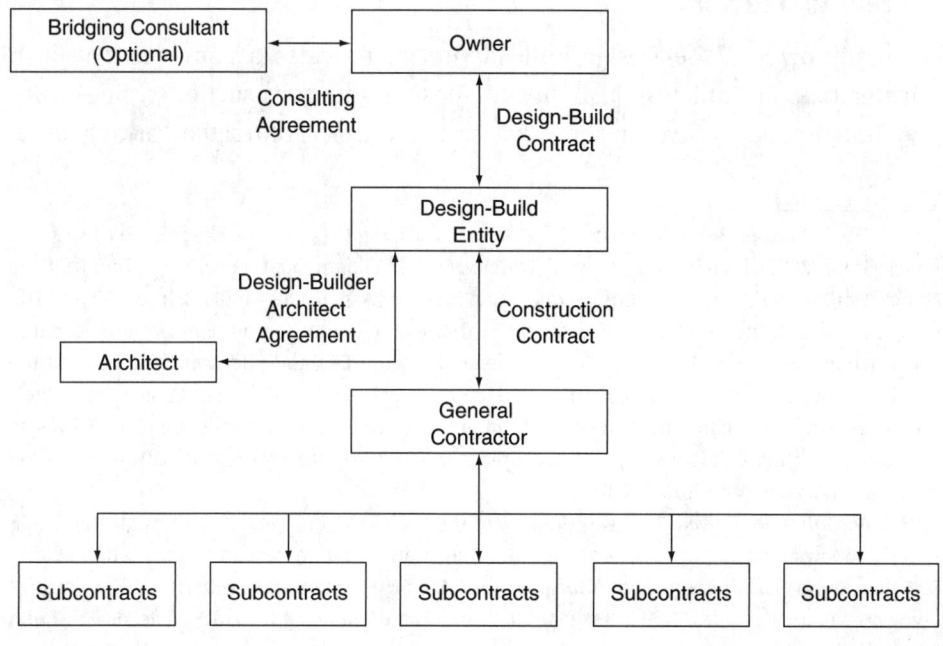

Design-Build is increasingly popular. Some statistical analyses predict that Design-Build eventually will be used more often than any other project delivery system.[30] Although touted primarily by those who promote Design-Build, such projections of future popularity are noteworthy. Indeed, Design-Build is gaining use in the public sector as well, where it had been virtually prohibited under many procurement statutes. Recent surveys reveal that many states have legislation allowing for use of Design-Build to deliver construction projects.[31] The number of states and other government agencies that permit Design-Build is expected to increase.

Design-build entities often are construction contractors who either have in-house design expertise or are comfortable subcontracting with—and assuming responsibility for—an architect to perform such services. Sometimes the design-builder is a joint venture or special-purpose vehicle comprised of entities that collectively possess the requisite skills to accomplish the project, such as a joint venture formed by a contractor and an architect.[32] The joint venture or special-purpose vehicle may self-perform the project, or perform design and construction through subcontracts with its constituent entities or other third parties. Less common is an architect or other design professional to act alone as a design-builder.

A. Selection Factors

For many owners, the Design-Build approach provides a convenient way to transfer risk. Overall responsibility for design and construction resides with the design-build entity. In some ways, the classic contractual arrangement

---

30. *See* 2 PHILIP L. BRUNER & PATRICK J. O'CONNOR, BRUNER & O'CONNOR ON CONSTRUCTION LAW § 6:2 (West Group 2002) [hereinafter BRUNER & O'CONNOR]; G. William Quatman, *Design Build for the Design Professional*, Ch. 1, *in* CONSTRUCTION LAW LIBRARY (Aspen Law and Business 2001). The Design-Build Institute of America and others further estimate that the number of nonresidential construction projects in the United States delivered via the Design-Build approach exceeds the number of such projects delivered using other project delivery systems. *See* Design-Build Project Delivery Market Share and Market Size Report, May 2014,Reed Construction Data/RSMeans Consulting, https://dbia.org/wp-content/uploads/2018/05/Research-RSMeans-2014-DB-Market-Share.pdf (last accessed Apr. 3, 2019).

31. According to the Fed. Highway Admin. of the U.S. Dep't of Transp., as of August 2006, 38 states had laws allowing the use of Design-Build for transportation procurement. Brandon Davis & Nancy Smith, *50-State Survey of Transportation Agency Design-Build Authority* (2009), http://www.nossaman.com/files/22619_8380_4.pdf (last accessed January 18, 2018). The Design-Build Institute of America cites similar statistics for transportation procurement.

32. A design professional–led team and other options are possible, but less common in the general building sector.

in Design-Build is nothing more than the Design-Bid-Build approach pushed down one tier. The risk factors that an owner confronts in the Design-Bid-Build approach still exist, but they now belong to the design-build entity with whom the owner contracts. The design-builder retains the architect and general contractor. The owner is relieved of the challenges that go along with holding those contracts. As a consequence, the owner may devote more of its resources to its core business or other pursuits, as opposed to the project.

Many entities, in addition to the architect, are responsible for the overall design of the project. As discussed in Chapter 2, it is common for architects to delegate aspects of project design to the construction team. For example, product manufacturers and specialty trade contractors generally are far more knowledgeable than architects with respect to building equipment, technology, and systems (e.g., elevators, security systems, and curtain wall systems). Incorporating the knowledge of specialty trade contractors and product manufacturers directly into the initial design process has many benefits. First, such collaboration helps speed the design process and facilitates use by phased or fast track construction. Second, the collaboration produces design documents consistent with current market conditions. Contractors and product manufacturers are more likely to know what building equipment and systems are readily available, how such items are efficiently utilized for a project, and how to best customize them for the particular project being designed. Design-Build facilitates such collaboration. Because the design and construction teams both answer to the entity responsible to deliver the entire project, Design-Build often leads to innovation and creative solutions to an owner's needs.

B. Risk Factors

When an owner transfers risk to the design-builder, the owner also must cede much control over the project. First, in Design-Build, the architect does not answer to the owner directly, but rather reports to the design-builder. Because the owner does not have a direct contractual relationship with the lead design professional, the owner has a limited ability to control the design process. Therefore, if aesthetics are of paramount concern to the owner, the Design-Build approach may not be a good match. Moreover, the owner will not have the independent advice of the architect during the construction phases and, therefore, no check or balance on the performance of the construction team.

The design-builder produces the project design in response to performance criteria or specifications furnished by the owner. The performance criteria specify various "outputs" to which the completed project must conform. For example, structural loads, heating and air conditioning requirements, and other performance criteria are described. It is up to the design-builder, however, to determine how to satisfy the performance criteria. As long as the completed project satisfies the required performance specifications, the design-builder has discharged its design obligations. Accordingly, much depends on the quality of the performance specifications.

Because the Design-Build approach relies on satisfaction of performance criteria, the owner must be certain to specify all appropriate so-called outputs clearly and comprehensively. Those requirements set forth the design obligations of the design-builder. Performance criteria are more effective if they describe requirements that lend themselves to measurement, such as the technical characteristics of building systems and specialty equipment. In the case of an industrial plant, certain performance aspects of the facility and the quality and quantity of items produced are capable of measurement. The easier it is to measure the output, the easier it will be to verify whether the completed project complies with the applicable performance criteria.

The owner, however, may have expectations with respect to the aesthetic and functional qualities of a project. Those characteristics are not easily measured. Therefore, the design-builder has greater latitude with respect to such matters than the owner might like if the design-builder's contractual obligations are governed only by performance specifications. The most direct solution is for the owner to describe aesthetic and functional requirements as completely as possible through design specifications to ensure that the finished product will meet those expectations.[33]

The procurement by an owner of a Design-Build contract also creates numerous challenges. A common approach is for the owner to request proposals from competing design-build entities. The potential design-builders base their proposals on the performance criteria furnished by the owner. Each proposal likely offers a solution that differs from the other proposals. How does the owner compare and choose among proposals that are so-called apples and oranges? Moreover, pricing data provided with a Design-Build proposal is based necessarily on a very rudimentary design and, therefore, lacks reliability.

---

33. Design specifications set forth in precise detail the materials to be used and the manner in which the work is to be performed. The contractor may not deviate from the specifications and is required to follow them as one would a road map. A design specification, also known as a descriptive or prescriptive specification, prescribes the exact materials and procedures of assembly. Performance specifications set forth a standard to be achieved and, unlike a design specification, do not specify specific materials or assembly direction. The contractor is expected to exercise its ingenuity in achieving that objective or standard of performance, selecting the means and assuming a corresponding responsibility for that selection. This permits the contractor to choose a system or construction procedure that is most attractive to the contractor that still fulfills the design criteria. This topic is discussed in greater detail in Chapter 5.

Because many aspects of the design will not be determined by a design-builder until after the proposal is accepted, the design-builder simply may reverse engineer the design in order to meet the budget to which it has committed. Thus, final project quality or features are somewhat variable in order for the design-builder to assure itself of an acceptable return on its investment.

Preparing a proposal is a difficult exercise for a design-builder, even if only basic design information is required as part of its proposal. The design-builder faces a dilemma. The design-builder arguably is best served by developing the design to a point where the design-builder is reasonably confident in its ability to predict all elements needed to produce a final design. If the design-builder is comfortable with the design, reasonable projections are possible for cost, time, performance characteristics, and other matters. The design-builder can reduce contingencies accordingly and submit a more reliable proposal. Such an effort, however, consumes limited resources and is very costly. The design-builder will not recover those costs if another party is awarded the contract or if the owner abandons the project. But, the alternative of putting forth only minimal effort in preparing a proposal is a risky venture. The resulting proposal may not be responsive to the owner's needs and, therefore, a wasted effort. Moreover, the less-developed proposal may put the design-builder at risk. The design-builder has made a wager that it will be able to complete the project for the cost and time proposed, although the design-builder may not have studied the project in detail and as appropriate to make such a judgment.

Another approach to procuring a Design-Build contract is for the owner to negotiate with a preferred provider. This method requires a certain degree of optimism from the owner. Negotiated Design-Build contracts generally come in two parts. During the first phase, the design is developed to a point where a reasonably reliable guaranteed maximum price and related data are submitted to the owner. If the price is too high for the owner or the proposal is otherwise unacceptable, the owner can try to work with the design-builder to arrive at a better proposal, but success is not guaranteed.

Starting over with another design-builder may not be a viable option. First, the owner may not have the ability to invest additional time. Second, the owner also must determine whether it has the right to use the proposal of the current design-builder if the owner proceeds with a different design-build entity. Design-builders sometimes price their design services very competitively, expecting to make their profit during the construction period. Under such circumstances, a design-builder may not be interested in simply turning over its design for exploitation by the owner and another design-builder.

Finally, in large part due to the professional services provided by the design-builder, some jurisdictions may require the design-builder to be licensed. Insurance companies also scrutinize Design-Build projects closely. The line between professional design services and construction work is not always clear in a Design-Build project. Special attention must be exercised to ensure that risks customarily associated with a project are properly insured. Also, sureties sometimes are less willing to issue bonds on such projects or may exclude certain activities from the bond. Sureties are accustomed to defining and underwriting construction risks, but design risks are less measurable.

C. Common Variations

Concentrating all design and construction obligations in the design-builder prevents the owner from selecting an architect with a particular style and from exerting control over the design process that an owner customarily desires. This situation is ameliorated sometimes when the owner uses a so-called bridging technique, in which the owner retains an architect to prepare a preliminary design that subsequently is turned over to a design-builder for completion. A bridging consultant typically prepares an initial design through approximately 35 percent complete design development documents. A lesser or greater level of completion can be performed, but the owner must balance its desire to dictate the project design against depriving the design-builder of design flexibility.[34] Limiting the options available to the design-builder during the design process diminishes the potential for innovation and efficiencies normally achieved through the Design-Build process.

By retaining an architect directly, the owner obtains greater assurance that the completed project will conform to the owner's aesthetic and functional goals. Often, the bridging consultant remains associated with the project, even after the initial design is turned over to the design-builder. The bridging consultant provides the owner with independent advice throughout the completion of the design and during the construction phase. This is helpful to the owner because the architect of record reports to the design-builder. Although the bridging consultant is an additional expense, it may be money well spent by the owner who desires greater influence over the design or who is unsophisticated in construction matters.

Design-Build also is used in connection with many civil and industrial projects. However, structures and facilities, such as bridges, roads, power plants, manufacturing facilities, and waste water treatment plants, are products more of engineering than architecture. In fact, an architect may not be involved on such a project. Civil and industrial projects also frequently require and are dependent on the supply and installation of very large, specialized equipment.

---

34. 2 BRUNER & O'CONNOR, *supra* note 30, § 6.35.

Therefore, the Design-Build approach is adapted for use on civil, industrial, or similar projects. Due to the emphasis on engineering and equipment procurement, the type of Design-Build process used on such projects is generally referred to as Engineer-Procure-Construct, or EPC.

EPC projects are typically very large, complicated, and high-risk propositions. Contracts are heavily negotiated. Most EPC projects contain complex economic terms, which usually include a rigorous completion/acceptance protocol, liquidated damages for delays and failure to achieve numerous performance guarantees, as well as various limitations of liability. Because these projects often involve the installation and assembly of large pieces of specialized equipment, the owner commonly must pay a significant amount of money before anything is delivered to the site.[35] Project financing is typical for an EPC-delivered facility. The lender will rely on revenue generated by the project as security for the construction loan. Because of the limited recourse nature of project finance, an EPC project may involve use of independent engineers and an allocation of risk with a focus on protecting the lender's interests.

Another common variation of Design-Build is referred to occasionally as Turnkey. Although no standard definition of Turnkey exists, it usually describes a project where an owner retains a design-builder to deliver a project, but without payment made by the owner to the design-builder until the project is completed. These projects are often real estate transactions, with a construction component. The design-builder may own the parcel of land on which the project is constructed. Upon completion, a closing will occur where a purchase price is paid to the design-builder and the project is turned over to the owner. The owner need only "turn the key" in order to commence the use and occupancy of the project.

On occasion, the design-builder retains ownership of the project and provides the owner with a long-term lease to use and occupy the project. Those projects are sometimes referred to as Build-to-Suit.

4.08 INNOVATIVE APPROACHES

Project delivery systems continue to evolve as necessary to address new risks and technologies, and to capitalize on opportunities to deliver projects more efficiently. From time to time, that evolutionary process produces project delivery systems that are more than permutations of an established methodology.

---

35. In contrast with an EPC project, an owner in the general building sector typically makes progress payments to the general contractor in relative proportion to the percentage of work installed at the project site. Therefore, under this scenario, the owner will be in a position to take possession (and likely have title) to the work for which it has paid.

Some are truly customized, one-of-a-kind approaches that could not easily be duplicated or adapted for use on other projects. Others have a broader application. Many recent innovations attempt to allocate risk in unconventional ways in order to align interests, and others focus on different techniques intended to increase collaboration among the major project participants.

Because of the time and effort required to craft a novel project delivery system and overcome the natural inclination of project participants to resist a new methodology not well-tested or understood, innovative approaches are more likely to be considered in connection with large, complex, high-profile projects, or perhaps for application to an entire portfolio of projects. In other words, there needs to be a lot at stake or some other compelling reason to go through all the trouble and risk associated with implementing a novel approach to project delivery.

A. Public-Private Partnerships

A Public-Private Partnership, or P3, essentially is a contractual arrangement between a public agency and a private sector project company. In a P3 arrangement, the private sector project company provides a physical improvement or a service that customarily has been provided by the public sector. P3 transactions are not entirely new. By way of example, P3s have been employed for the development of tollways and other infrastructure projects in Spain since the 1960s and France since the 1970s. The United Kingdom became a leading user of the P3 structure in the 1980s, developing an approach referred to as a private finance initiative (PFI). P3s also are popular elsewhere in Europe, and often are used in Latin America and Canada. The approach is particularly attractive in developing countries, where funding obstacles might prevent important projects from proceeding if a P3 approach were not available. The United States, however, is fairly new to adopt this project delivery approach.[36]

A P3 can be structured in many different ways, but most involve some or all of the following traits: (1) the private sector project company is responsible not only to design and construct the project, but generally has some obligation to operate and maintain it for a lengthy period of time, often 30 years or more; (2) the private sector project company contributes equity to the project, and arranges financing for some portion of the project; and (3) the private sector project company receives most of its compensation after completion of

---

36. Many web sites track trends in P3 procurement and P3 projects (potential and actual), such as the National Council for Public-Private Partnerships, http://www.NCPPP.org.

construction, through recovery of tolls, other user fees, or payments from the public agency based on the availability of the project in accordance with certain specified requirements.

In the context of construction, particularly infrastructure projects, a public-private partnership often adopts a methodology similar to (1) a design-build, operate and maintain (DBOM) approach, or (2) a design-build, finance, operate, and maintain (DBFOM) approach. Under those and derivative methods, a public sector entity enters into a concession agreement with a project company from the private sector. In this case, the term "concession" means the public sector entity concedes use of the project to the private sector company for a certain period of time. The project company is responsible for designing and constructing the project as necessary to satisfy specified criteria and then to maintain and operate the project over the life of the concession in compliance with additional specifications. At the end of the concession, possession of the project is returned to the public entity. The project company generally receives no payment, or very limited payment, from the public sector until the project is complete and ready to be put into operation. A simple example of how a P3 project is organized contractually is depicted in Figure 4.6.

The project company is usually a special-purpose entity, often a joint venture enterprise composed of companies that possess the expertise needed to successfully perform the concession agreement. The project company recovers its investment in the project and makes profit (hopefully) from the operating concession. Upon expiration of the concession, the project company generally

FIGURE 4.6
Build-Operate-Transfer

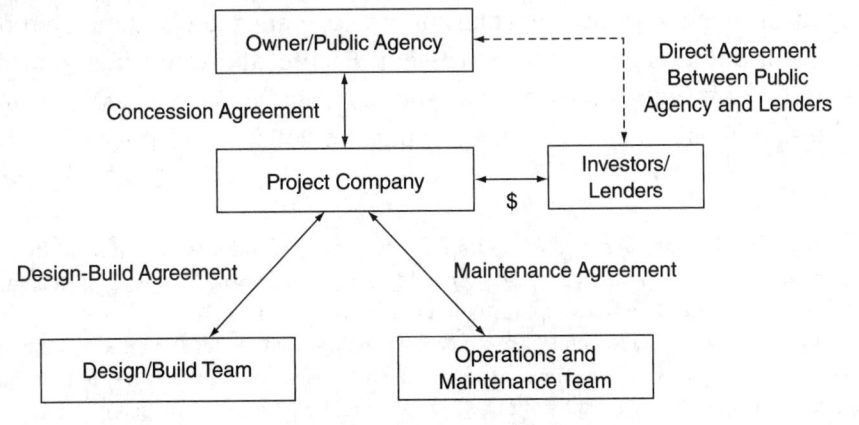

must restore the project to acceptable condition and then turn over the project to the public agency that authorized the project. Either a portion of the revenue generated by the project (e.g., user fees or tolls) is paid to the project company, or payments are made in accordance with predetermined formulae based on specified criteria (e.g., degree of project use, or perhaps simply availability of the improvement with adjustments for key performance indicators). While the return on investment by the project company can be significant, such projects are risky.[37]

The concession agreement is a lengthy and complicated document. Among many issues, it must address the following: performance criteria for the completed project and standards of operation and maintenance; the economics of the transaction; permissible adjustments in fares (for projects such as mass transit systems and toll roads) or other fees and charges; transferability of the concession; and anything else that might come up during the life of the concession. Predicting what the future holds is difficult. From the standpoint of the project company, such projects are more financial transactions than construction projects. The project company must be confident that it will recover its costs and make an appropriate return. It is not enough for the project to be a construction success. The project will not be viable unless it is also a commercial success.

In addition to the concession agreement, the project company enters into several other contracts. Because a project company likely has limited ability to self-perform a concession agreement for an infrastructure project, the project company must flow down its obligations to subcontractors and manage the performance of those subcontractors. A design-build entity is retained by the project company pursuant to engineer, procure, and construct (EPC) or some similar contract. Because the design-build entity's obligations conclude upon the completion of construction, excepting warranty obligations, the project company also must retain a separate entity to operate and maintain the project throughout the duration of the concession. Each of those two major subcontractors, in turn, will enter into lower-tier subcontracts as necessary to fulfill any portion of its respective obligations that are not self-performed.[38]

---

37. Bankruptcies have occurred on P3 projects, for example, the Indiana Toll Road (the project company filed for bankruptcy protection in 2014) and Port of Miami Tunnel (project company restructured due to the voluntary administration of one of its members).

38. Delegating to a single point of responsibility makes it easier for the project company to manage its risk. Nonetheless, commercial conditions may be such that no single entity is willing to accept full responsibility for the entire design, procurement, and construction of a project nor accept joint and several liability exposure in a joint venture of some nature. Under such circumstances, the project company must retain separate design and construction teams. Similarly, the

1. Selection Factors

The P3 model allows public agencies to proceed with projects that otherwise might not be viable due to funding limitations, inadequate resources, or other priorities. As demands on public agencies increase to repair or replace outdated infrastructure and provide other public improvements, the P3 approach and other forms of public-private partnership may become more mainstream. From the standpoint of project delivery systems, the P3 method transfers many traditional owner responsibilities to the project company and aligns the interests of the public agency with the project company.[39]

A public agency typically considers using the P3 methodology only after completing a "value for money" analysis to evaluate if the public will receive benefits that justify the expense of delivering the project via a P3.[40] When the private sector delivers a project on behalf of a public agency, financing likely will be more expensive than if arranged through the public sector, additional legal engineering will be required, and a raft of issues will arise regarding whether control of the completed project by the private sector is in the best interests of the public. Proponents may quickly counter that P3s often allow projects to proceed when funding and other resources are not available, encourage innovation, align interests, transfer risk to the private sector, and possess life cycle and other benefits that outweigh any disadvantage.

2. Risk Factors

The P3 approach is not the right choice for all projects. A common concern is that the private sector may be more willing to participate in projects with the greatest opportunity to earn profit, as opposed to those that address the greatest public need. Similarly, the profit motive may conflict with the public desire for high quality service at a reasonable cost.

P3 transactions take a long time to implement. Because many P3 transactions pertain to major public improvements projects, a lengthy approval process may apply, starting with environmental impact statements and continuing through permits for construction and occupancy certificates. P3 transactions require the support of a large number of stakeholders. An objection by any

---

entities that perform design or construction activities may have no interest in the risks that flow from the operation and maintenance of the completed project during the concession period, and, therefore, a separate agreement will be entered into by the project company with an "operator."

39. For example, the project company will be keenly interested in a well-completed project if it is obligated to operate and maintain the project.

40. *See Guidebook for Value for Money Assessment*, U.S. Dep't of Transp., Fed. Highway Admin. (Dec. 2013), https://www.fhwa.dot.gov/ipd/pdfs/p3/p3_guidebook_vfm_1213.pdf (last accessed Apr. 3, 2019).

single interested party can delay or impair the implementation of a P3 transaction. Even minor disruptions in the planning process can add significant cost to the effort and adversely affect feasibility of the entire transaction.

3. Common Variations

A P3 transaction can be structured to adjust the role of the private sector as desired. Some methods transfer more responsibility and risk to the private sector and provide greater opportunity for a P3 approach. At one end of the spectrum, the public sector retains almost full control and risk. But, other methodologies gradually and incrementally allocate more responsibility and risk to the private sector. Market risk also can be transferred to the private sector, although that often is more a function of the compensation mechanism than the underlying organizational structure of the transaction. The public agency may make partial payments to help defray costs of construction, but often makes no payments until the project is complete and operational.

To date, contracts for P3 projects in the United States have been manuscript documents (contracts prepared uniquely and specifically for each separate transaction, as opposed to form or boilerplate contracts). In part, the necessity of manuscript contracts is the natural consequence of the different legal requirements and varying degrees of experience with the P3 delivery methodology existing in each state or municipality responsible for undertaking a P3 project. Although law firms and advisors that regularly represent public entities engaged in P3 projects have drafted their own template documents, the process of drafting and negotiating contracts for P3 projects in the United States remains time consuming, costly, and somewhat unpredictable. Some guidance can be found in a series of informational guides published by the Federal Highway Administration.[41]

B. Integrated Project Delivery

The design and construction process can be highly confrontational. Project participants often spend significant time and energy attempting to avoid or deflect liability, or dealing with claims. Traditional delivery methods sometimes foster

---

41. The Engineers Joint Contract Documents Committee (EJCDC) published in 2014 a form of Public-Private Partnership Agreement (designated EJCDC P3-508). The EJCDC document principally is a framework document with some proposed model language, but is intended for the parties to complete and incorporate additional terms as needed to properly document the P3 transaction. The form contemplates a project with a revenue stream from user fees, but could be adapted for use with availability payments or interim milestone payments if desired.

separate silos for design and construction activities, which can lead to low productivity and waste. Consequently, some participants in the process have considered how to better align the interests of all parties, and thereby reduce such endemic inefficiencies. The result is a methodology referred to as Integrated Project Delivery (IPD).

An IPD transaction can be structured in different ways, but the general concept involves creating a contractual relationship among members of a core group—often the owner, lead design professional, lead constructor, and sometimes key suppliers or subcontractors. That relationship may be established through several interlocking contracts or a single, multiparty contract. The members of the core group often waive claims against each other (excepting certain matters like third-party claims for bodily injury and property damage), limit liability, and establish a formula to share profits and losses based on metrics tied to how well the completed project complies with pre-determined project goals. In theory, aligning interests and reducing the prospect for claims among the core group members lessens wasteful practices and promotes a focus on the success of the project.

In some forms of IPD, a core group of participants collectively form a team to manage the project. Overall project goals are established and memorialized, often in an appendix to the applicable contracts. Decisions of the management team, for the most part, must be unanimous. Staff may be comingled on the basis of the best person for the job. Every effort is made to align the interests of all the contracting parties. Each member of the core group is reimbursed for its specified costs, with costs verified independently. Everything is open book, often without a cap. To further enhance cooperation, adjudication of disputes between core group parties is not permitted for anything other than the most egregious of accusations, such as fraud.[42]

1. Selection Factors

Integrated Project Delivery is driven out of (1) a desire to maximize the benefits of new information technologies, such as building information modeling, and (2) dissatisfaction with the more traditional project delivery systems viewed as inhibiting innovation, impairing the coordination of design and other major activities, and producing overly adversarial relationships. The philosophy behind Integrated Project Delivery has been defined as:

---

42. *See* AIA Contracts Committee & AIA California Council, *Integrated Project Delivery: A Guide* (2007), https://www.aiacontracts.org/resources/64146-integrated-project-delivery-a-guide (last accessed Jan. 18, 2018).

a project delivery approach that integrates people, systems, business structures and practices into a process that collaboratively harnesses the talents and insights of all participants to optimize project results, increase value to the owner, reduce waste, and maximize efficiency through all phases of design, fabrication and construction.[43]

IPD seems better suited for large, challenging projects where collaborative problem solving is essential for success. Most IPD projects contemplate use of technologies like BIM as well as lean construction techniques.

2. *Risk Factors*

IPD is a paradigm shift from nearly all other project delivery methodologies. IPD demands that the parties put the interests of the project first, ahead of their own individual interests. Not everyone can work in that environment, but the approach is gaining traction, particularly in the health care sector.[44] In addition, not every project fits well with an IPD approach. IPD also requires significant owner involvement and devotion to the process. It will not work if the owner simply intends to delegate responsibility.

Selecting the right parties to participate in an IPD project is obviously crucial. For an IPD project to succeed, each participant must embrace the basic principles of the methodology, which in many ways are contrary to traditional approaches to project delivery. Each core group participant essentially makes a risk-management calculation, and concludes that sharing in the economic

---

43. Id.

44. In May 2008, the AIA published new contract forms for use with the IPD methodology. The AIA offers two approaches to integrated project delivery, both of which mandate the use of building information modeling. The so-called transitional agreements describe an approach that utilizes a familiar AIA style contracting model, and includes (1) American Institute of Architects, AIA Document B195-2008, *Standard Form of Agreement between Owner and Architect for Integrated Project Delivery* (2008) (an owner–architect agreement); (2) American Institute of Architects, AIA Document A195-2008, *Standard Form of Agreement between Owner and Contractor for Integrated Project Delivery* (2008) (an owner–contractor agreement with a guaranteed maximum price amendment); and (3) American Institute of Architects, AIA Document A295-2008, *General Conditions of the Contract for Integrated Project Delivery* (2008) (a "shared" general conditions document). A more complete integration and sharing of risk and reward between the principal project participants is embodied in American Institute of Architects, AIA Document C191-2009, *Standard Form Multi-Party Agreement for Integrated Project Delivery* (2009), and also in American Institute of Architects, AIA Document C195-2008, *Standard Form Single Purpose Entity Agreement for Integrated Project Delivery* (2008) (an agreement for the formation of a special-purpose entity for integrated project delivery). For another approach to integrated project delivery, see ConsensusDocs 300, *Standard Form of Tri-Party Agreement for Collaborative Project Delivery* (2007, revised 2016), and ConsensusDocs 396, *Standard Joining Agreement for Integrated Project* Delivery (2016).

success or failure of the delivery process with other core group members, and reducing the time and resources normally devoted to resolving disputes and claims that plague the design and construction process, will likely produce benefits that outweigh certain losses or damages the participant might suffer as a consequence of participating in an IPD approach.[45]

3. Common Variations

Because IPD is so new, no approach is standard, although the objectives of limiting waste and aligning interests remain paramount. Versions of IPD are sometimes used overseas, and may go by different names. For example, the core concepts of Integrated Project Delivery are visible in a similar approach to project delivery known as an Alliance, which has been pioneered to a great extent in Australia.[46]

C. Other Approaches

Pressure exists to craft delivery systems that produce completed projects more quickly, for less cost, and of higher quality. As a result, new models are always contemplated, as well as variations on existing models. Such efforts also produce new management techniques, such as so-called lean construction.[47] The continuation of the process is more or less guaranteed because no matter how project delivery systems evolve, all systems will have advantages and disadvantages.

---

45. The IPD approach incorporates or complements principles and techniques of so-called lean construction, which is largely derived from manufacturing objectives to produce value, as defined by the customer, without producing waste. By integrating the team that delivers the project, in theory, much of the back-and-forth of the normal project delivery approach can be eliminated. Production becomes more "real time." Lean project delivery also relies on an integrated agreement among the key members to a construction undertaking. Like an alliance, the single, multiparty contract seeks congruence among the interests of the primary project parties, including a sharing of project successes and failures.

46. Project alliances were used to deliver major oil and gas projects in Western Australia, as well as infrastructure projects. *See* Commonwealth of Australia, Department of Infrastructure and Regional Development, *National Alliance Contracting Guidelines* (Sept. 2015), https://www.infrastructure.gov.au/infrastructure/ngpd/files/National_Guide_to_Alliance_Contracting.pdf (last accessed May 7, 2019). Use of alliancing appears more common with respect to projects that are time or quality driven. Such projects have been predominantly industrial or infrastructure projects, although a notable exception is the National Museum of Australia, which opened in Canberra in 2004.

47. Information about lean construction is available through the Lean Construction Institute, at https://www.leanconstruction.org/ (last accessed Jan. 18, 2018).

4.09 METHODS OF PROJECT DELIVERY SYSTEM SELECTION

With a wide variety of options available, how does an owner select a delivery system for a project? As discussed in Section 4.04, the selection process should endeavor to identify a delivery system that improves the potential for the owner to accomplish its project objectives, while reducing the potential for serious project risks. Owners who build infrequently may not know which project delivery system to use and may not care. In that case, owners will rely on their advisors to make such selections, or the choice defaults to the approach used on a prior project. For others, an owner's single overriding concern often drives the choice of project delivery system. Either cost or time considerations, for example, may be so important that all other factors pale in comparison.

For owners who wish to evaluate a variety of project delivery systems, however, a number of different methods exist. All involve consideration of metrics that pertain to particular project goals, such as cost, schedule, quality, and claims avoidance, but operate with different levels of formality and sophistication. After assembling data pertaining to such metrics, the more simple methods employ decision trees or filters to eliminate options deemed less suitable for a project. Other methods are more diagnostic and, through the application of arithmetic formulae and analytical matrices, attempt to identify the optimal delivery system.[48]

Little quantitative analysis exists to determine preference for one project delivery system over another. Few studies have been performed. Some of the most striking data produced, however, reveal that all project delivery systems have a significant number of projects with poor results for each metric under review, even if statistically the overall or median results for a project delivery system are quite favorable.[49] Therefore, no project delivery system is a guarantee of good results. The delivery system must be properly suited for the project, and the project participants must implement the chosen system correctly and execute their responsibilities well, in order for the project to succeed.

---

48. For a more thorough discussion, see Ross J. Altman, Presentation of Paper, *Selection of Project Delivery Systems and Related Implications*, American Bar Association Forum on the Construction Industry, in Toronto, Ontario, Canada, April 29–30, 2005. Examples of analytic methods are described by (1) Georgia State Financing & Investment Commission, *Selecting the Appropriate Project Delivery Option*, 2 Project Delivery Options, Recommended Guidelines (2003), *available at* http://gsfic.georgia.gov/; (2) *Owner's Tool for Project Delivery and Contract Strategy Selection User's Guide*, Construction Industry Institute, IR165-2 (2003).

49. See *Project Delivery Systems: CM at Risk, Design-Build, Design-Bid-Build*, Construction Industry Institute, RR133-11 (Apr. 1, 1998).

4.10 SELECTION CONSTRAINTS

The owner must confirm no major constraints exist that would impair or altogether prevent the implementation of a preferred project delivery system. The analysis might be as simple as acknowledging the corporate culture of the owner, or its past experiences do not allow the proper implementation of a particular project delivery system. In the case of a public entity, rules and regulations governing procurement might prohibit use of a certain project delivery system, no matter how attractive that system might be for a project. Issues commonly vetted in a post-selection analysis are described next.

A. Method of Construction Procurement

The method through which the owner procures construction services affects significantly which project delivery systems are best suited for the project. The most common methods for procurement of construction services include (1) lowest competitive bid, where selection is based solely on cost; (2) best value, where selection is based on a combination of cost and other factors; and (3) qualifications, where selection is based on qualifications and, perhaps, other non-cost factors. Little point exists to use a project delivery system not compatible with the required or desired method of procuring construction services. For example, when use of a lowest competitive bid is the mandated or desired method of procurement, then using a project delivery system that emphasizes overlapping design and construction phases probably is not advisable. If project scope is not well developed at the time of bid submission, the constructor would likely compensate for the lack of information by including a contingency that increases the price; otherwise, the constructor is forced to assume a disproportionate amount of financial risk.

B. Compensation Mechanisms

Several different mechanisms are available to compensate the prime constructor of a project. Compensation mechanisms used most frequently by owners include lump sum (stipulated sum), cost-plus-fee with a guaranteed maximum price, unit price, cost-plus-fee without a guaranteed maximum price, and time and materials.[50] The level of design completion at the time of contract award,

---

50. Different standard industry construction contract forms have been published for various different compensation mechanisms. For example, AIA Document B101–2017 is used when the contractor's compensation is a stipulated sum, but AIA Document A102–2017 is used when the contractor's compensation is based on the cost of work plus a fee (with a guaranteed maximum price). See also Chapter 9 for a discussion of compensation mechanics.

the willingness of the owner to accept a price risk, or some other allocation of risk and reward all play into the approach ultimately selected. As with procurement methods, certain compensation mechanisms are more compatible with particular project delivery systems than others.

For example, a compensation mechanism that limits the owner's budget risk and transfers more financial exposure to the constructor (e.g., lump sum or guaranteed maximum price) requires the owner to yield more project control to the constructor. Therefore, such a compensation mechanism is less compatible with project delivery systems that involve overlapping of design, procurement, and construction phases, unless the owner is comfortable with a performance-based delivery approach (e.g., Design-Build) that permits a range of design solutions as opposed to one based on prescriptive or design specifications where the constructor has less design input.

Depending on factors unique to the project under consideration, different compensation mechanisms may be more appropriate than others. For example, changing from lump sum to a cost reimbursable compensation mechanism increases an owner's ability to change design, but reduces an owner's ability to control costs. If a suitable compensation mechanism cannot be identified for the project delivery system under consideration, then a different project delivery system might be needed.

C. Owner Capability

Each project delivery system requires a different skill set and level of involvement from the owner. A project delivery system that appears optimal based on the criteria of a selection approach is doomed to failure if the owner does not possess the ability to implement properly that project delivery system. To a certain extent, an owner may outsource its role in the project, but that alternative is not always desirable or without risk.

Issues pertaining to the owner's capabilities and expectations include, among others, the following:

- ❐ To what extent does the owner intend or desire to be involved in the production of the design of the project?
- ❐ Does the owner have skilled and available resources to administer the project delivery system?
- ❐ Does the owner have past experience, good or bad, with the project delivery system?
- ❐ Can the owner make timely decisions?
- ❐ Can the owner identify a qualified pool of designers and constructors?

- ❏ Do legal/corporate considerations restrict the owner?
- ❏ Can the owner facilitate project team cooperation and communications?
- ❏ Can the owner administer multiple contracts on the project?
- ❏ Does the owner have the ability or desire to take responsibility for design?
- ❏ What are the funding needs and availability?

Responses to such questions provide guidance as to whether the project delivery system under consideration is suitable.

D. Industry Sector Custom

Within the design professions and construction industry, some industry sectors over time develop their own customs and practices. Many industrial facilities depend on specialized equipment and, consequently, often rely on an EPC form of project delivery. A paper mill project illustrates this point well. The heart and soul of a mill is the paper-making machine. Everything else in the mill is ancillary and exists to support the paper-making machine. The project objectives of the mill owner pertain principally to the speed at which the paper-making machine will run, what periods of downtime are expected, and various characteristics of the product produced by the paper-making machine.

Over the years, manufacturers of paper-making machines have developed proprietary designs, as well as tremendous amounts of know-how regarding the fabrication and method of assembly of those machines. The ability of the original equipment manufacturer to utilize that know-how in the design of a machine generates many efficiencies. Although each paper-making machine involves a varying degree of custom design, many component parts and design features are more or less standard to the original equipment manufacturer. To further ensure economical fabrication and assembly of paper-making machines, original equipment manufacturers make significant investments in machine tools and skilled labor forces.

A mill owner could completely engineer a paper-making machine to the mill owner's own unique specifications, either with its own in-house staff or through outside consultants, and then retain a constructor or vendor to fabricate that particular machine. Procuring a paper-making machine in this manner, however, undoubtedly would require fabrication of component parts and assembly techniques vastly dissimilar from those readily available. The additional cost and time to deliver a paper-making machine in such a fashion would be difficult to justify. Therefore, acquiring the machine through use of an EPC delivery system that capitalizes on the experience and skill of the original equipment manufacturer is the preferred approach.

4.11 LEGAL IMPORTANCE OF PROJECT DELIVERY SYSTEMS

In addition to commercial importance, the project delivery system has legal ramifications beyond determining the allocation and timing of project-related responsibilities. The application of various legal principles and doctrines may depend on which methodology is used for a project. For example, the *Spearin* Doctrine provides that an owner impliedly warrants to a contractor that the drawings and specifications prepared by the design team are accurate and sufficient for the purpose intended.[51] Application of that warranty makes sense in the context of a Design-Bid-Build methodology, where design responsibility is clearly allocated to a design professional retained by the owner, but the same logic may not apply under other project delivery systems where design responsibilities are allocated differently.

Because the regular use of project delivery systems other than Design-Bid-Build is a relatively recent phenomenon, a deep body of law does not always exist through which to examine such methodologies.[52] But, some guidance regarding the application of the *Spearin* Doctrine under different project delivery models was addressed in *Coghlin Electrical Contractors, Inc. v. Gilbane Building Company*,[53] in this case particularly At-Risk Construction Management. After analyzing many of the differences between Design-Bid-Build, At-Risk Construction Management, and Design-Build, the court concluded that the implied warranty still applied to an At-Risk Construction Management approach, but that the scope of its application might be limited.

> Although the owner's implied warranty applies in a public construction management at risk contract, the differences between the responsibilities of a general contractor in a design-bid-build project and those of a CMAR affect the scope of the implied warranty. The general contractor in a design-bid-build project may benefit from the implied warranty where it relied on the plans and specifications in good faith but the CMAR may benefit from the implied warranty only where it has acted in good faith reliance on the design *and* acted reasonably in light of the CMAR's own design responsibilities. The CMAR's level of participation in the design phase of the project and the extent to which the contract delegates design responsibility to the CMAR may affect a fact

---

51. See Chapter 20, Section 4.

52. *See generally* BRUNER & O'CONNOR, *supra* note 30, at 617 ("Because construction management is a newer approach and has not been the subject of as many court decisions, there is less certainty as to interpretation of the contract documents, and less uniformity as to the extent and allocation of responsibilities, and it is more difficult to predict liabilities.").

53. Coghlin Elec. Contractors, Inc. v. Gilbane Bldg. Co., et al., 2015 WL 5123135, (Sept. 2, 2015), 472 Mass. 549 (2015).

finder's determination as to whether the CMAR's reliance was reasonable. The greater the CMAR's design responsibilities in the contract, the greater the CMAR's burden will be to show, when it seeks to establish the owner's liability under the implied warranty, that its reliance on the defective design was both reasonable and in good faith.[54]

Determining the application and scope of the *Spearin* Doctrine and other legal principles with respect to any given project often relates back to the allocation of responsibilities among the project participants.[55] That allocation is a function of the applicable project delivery system. Therefore, a more complete evaluation of the selection factors and risk factors involved in deciding which delivery system to use for a particular project might also include an analysis of how certain legal doctrines and principles apply to the project delivery methodologies under consideration.

4.12 CONCLUSION

No single project delivery system is perfect, and more than one choice can be right for a project. Selecting a project delivery system, however, is not an easy task and involves a certain amount of conjecture. Nonetheless, the process of selection must be undertaken diligently. Industry experience and data, both anecdotal and quantitative, confirm that the choice of a project delivery system is extremely important. The allocation of obligations and their sequence greatly influence the ability of the owner to achieve its project goals. Various tools exist, with different levels of sophistication, to assist the owner in selecting a project delivery system and to remove some of the guesswork from the process.

---

54. *Id.* at 514.
55. See Chapter 3, Section 3.04.

QUESTIONS

1. What project delivery system selection factors might be important to an owner undertaking the development of a manufacturing facility?
2. If an owner wishes to maintain control over the aesthetic and functional design of the project, which project delivery systems would be preferable?
3. If an owner needs a stipulated sum contract, which project delivery systems are less suitable?
4. What features would you consider incorporating into an Alliance or Integrated Project Delivery approach?

CHAPTER 5

Contracting for Construction Projects

BRUCE MERWIN

5.01 CONTRACT FORMATION

A. For Purpose of Design Agreements and Construction Contracts

Construction transactions are complex. They involve multiple parties and are technically complicated. Such transactions require heavily documented financial arrangements, multistep payment procedures, and unique business terms and conditions. Finally, construction transactions also are complex from a legal standpoint. Therefore, it makes sense to prepare well-thought-out contracts to memorialize the agreements among the appropriate parties in connection with the design and construction of a project. The process of preparing and negotiating such contracts often helps the parties arrive at a better meeting of the minds, and thereby diminishes the opportunity for disputes to arise out of frustrated expectations. Furthermore, a contract provides a written record of the deal between the parties to help unravel any disagreement that might occur.

The design and construction process involves reciprocal promises among the many project participants. Owners, architects, and contractors primarily are interested in five considerations affecting their respective contracts. First is the description of the scope of services or work for the project. Second is the time frame within which the project will be completed, often described as the project schedule. Third are the parameters regarding completion of the project within the owner's budget, as amended by change orders. Fourth is the quality of the services and work, and various administrative matters that ensure such quality. Fifth is the interest each party to the contract has in its respective rights and remedies in the event the other party breaches any of its promises. The design agreement and construction contract, in essence, should be a roadmap to successful completion of the project and the establishment of procedures for resolving disputes if problems occur during the design and construction process.

To summarize, design agreements and construction contracts should both recognize that the primary purpose of the contract is to do the following: (1) inform each party what it must do and to what it is entitled, (2) inform each party of its rights when the other party does not perform as promised, and (3) reflect the reality of contract administration and not require one party to agree to procedures that will not likely be followed or will increase significantly the cost of construction. Each party's attempt to protect its own interests should not cause the design services agreement or construction contract to get out of balance to the point that the contract terms themselves become a more significant risk factor than the value and complexity of the services or work.

B. Contract Formation Generally

What constitutes a design agreement or a construction contract? As defined in *Black's Law Dictionary*, a "contract" is "An agreement between two or more parties creating obligations that are enforceable or otherwise recognizable at law."[1] For the contract to exist, there must be an offer, acceptance, and consideration tendered by both parties.[2] If either of the elements of mutual assent or consideration is missing, then no contract exists.[3] Because of the complexity involved in a design agreement or construction contract, such contracts, for the most part, are written agreements executed by both parties.

---

1. BLACK'S LAW DICTIONARY (10th ed. 2014).
2. Harco Energy, Inc. v. Re-Entry People, Inc., 23 S.W.3d 389, 392 (Tex. App. Amarillo 2000, no pet.).
3. Hubbard v. Shankle, 138 S.W.3d 474, 481 (Tex. App. Fort Worth 2004).

An oral contract involving construction can be entered into; the parties are not required to explicitly express their intent in writing. A meeting of the minds can be implied from, and evidenced by, the parties' conduct and course of dealing.[4] The contract, to be enforceable, must be reasonably definite in its terms and must sufficiently describe the essential elements of the agreement. However, oral agreements or contracts may be difficult to establish based solely on conversations between the parties.

C. Commencement of Services or Work Prior to Contract

Although not the preferred approach, owners often commence design and construction activities prior to execution of contracts for design services or construction work. Because of the number of issues that must be addressed in design agreements and construction contracts, great time pressure often exists on owners to commence design services while the balance of the contractual matters are worked out or the economic viability of the project is evaluated. Owners sometimes issue an early start letter or limited authorization to proceed to an architect or other design professional when the advantages of accelerating completion of the design may outweigh the risk of proceeding without having a full contract in place. Recognizing the risk in commencing design without a complete contract, an owner might build various controls into such an early start arrangement by, for example, authorizing performance of only a limited scope of design services with the hope that the deal can be finalized prior to completion of the services for which early commencement has been authorized.

Construction contracts are usually more complex than agreements with design professionals and, on large or particularly difficult transactions, can take months to draft and negotiate. The potentially adverse effects arising out of delays in commencement of construction, therefore, are amplified. For example, many projects require long lead-time items, such as materials, equipment, or systems that must be specially fabricated. A limited window of opportunity may exist to get onto a manufacturer's schedule in order for such items to be delivered to the site and available for incorporation into the work as necessary to conform to the owner's contemplated schedule. Any delay could be costly, and an owner might want to commence the ordering of such items while final terms of a construction contract are negotiated.

Given the volatility in labor and material costs, it may often be critical for the owner to lock in materials prices, reserve the use of equipment or production time of subcontractors, or otherwise start the project prior to finalizing the

---

4. Harrison v. Williams Dental Group, P.C., 140 S.W.3d 912, 916 (Tex. App. Dallas 2004).

terms of a construction contract. Loan agreements and leases entered into by developers often have fixed deadlines, with financial penalties or additional costs if construction is not started by a specific date, requiring commencement prior to the negotiation of a construction contract.

Therefore, early start letters often outline (1) a limited scope of work for a specific price or cost of the work, plus a fee, not to exceed a certain amount, and (2) a specific timetable for performance of such work. If the owner and contractor are not able to reach agreement with respect to the construction contract, then such early start letters provide for the termination of the owner-contractor relationship, final payment of the contractor, and either assignment of subcontracts and purchase orders from the contractor to the owner or termination of such subcontracts and purchase orders. Early start letters also generally provide that they will be superseded by the construction contract entered into between the owner and contractor.

Letters of intent for construction contracts are similar to limited authorizations to proceed, except that most letters of intent are non-binding with respect to the material terms of the construction contract. The purpose of the letter of intent is to express the owner's and contractor's good faith intention to enter into a construction contract once drawings and specifications have been further refined, pricing is further refined, and the contractor has been able to obtain bids from subcontractors and suppliers. Letters of intent, although granting no legal rights, may serve the practical purpose of allowing a contractor to show such letter to subcontractors and suppliers for the purpose of obtaining bids from such subcontractors and suppliers.[5]

D. Creation of Contracts—Implied Contracts and Quasi-Contracts

While express contracts are stated by the parties, implied contracts arise from the actions and conduct of the parties.[6] The facts and circumstances indicate that a mutual intent exists between the parties to a contract.[7] The existence of such a contract becomes a question for the trier of fact.[8]

---

5. Letters of intent may be binding in a limited respect with respect to confidentiality provisions, the obligation to negotiate in good faith for a certain period of time, and also an obligation on the part of the contractor to perform limited work for a specific price. This is similar to early start letters.

6. Haws & Garrett General Contractors, Inc. v. Gorbett Bros. Welding Co., 480 S.W.2d 607, 609 (Tex. 1972).

7. Gillum v. Republic Health Corp., 778 S.W.2d 558, 569 (Tex. App. Dallas 1989).

8. *Haws & Garrett General Contractors, Inc.*, 480 S.W.2d at 610. *See also* Solartech Renewables, LLC v. Techcity Properties, No. 526774, 2018 N.Y. slip op. 08739, 2018 WL 6683171, at *1 (N.Y. App. Div. 2018) (finding that no contract for construction of solar systems existed for want of meeting of minds on specific terms).

In *Haws & Garrett General Contractors, Inc. v. Gorbett Bros. Welding Co.*,[9] a general contractor was engaged in bridge construction, and his superintendent made a telephone order for a crane and an operator. The crane subcontractor prepared a form contract containing a broad, hold harmless provision. However, the contract was not signed until the work was done. The structure was damaged during the work, ostensibly because of the subcontractor's negligence. In response to a lawsuit brought by the general contractor, the subcontractor argued that, since no express agreement existed as to the type of indemnification provision prior to performance of the work, such an agreement should have been an implied condition of the contract.[10]

The Texas Supreme Court, however, rejected this claim of implied agreement on the grounds the subcontractor did not prove that prior contracts between the parties had been preceded by any negotiations regarding the indemnification clause or that any prior agreements with respect to the clause had been made by authorized personnel.[11] Presumably, if the parties' prior course of dealing had evidenced an agreement with respect to this clause, then it could have been an implied term of the bridge contract and would have insulated the subcontractor from negligence liability.

Quasi-contract is generally considered no contract at all, but rather the creation of the court, where appropriate, to correct a substantial injustice and avoid unjust enrichment. For example, with respect to extras, courts seem to be relying on the theory of an implied contract, without indicating whether they are relying on a contract implied in fact, that is, a true contract, or a contract implied in law, that is, a quasi-contract. If the relief granted is based on a theory of an implied-in-fact contract, the remedy is in quantum meruit.

The Latin phrase quantum meruit means "as much as is deserved." The rationale underlying the quantum meruit doctrine is that where one knowingly accepts a benefit from another who is not a volunteer and who does not confer the benefit as a gift, the law may infer a promise by the recipient to pay reasonable compensation.[12] However, if the benefited party is not aware of the work being done at the time the work is performed, then no basis exists for a recovery in quantum meruit. The concept is one of equity, since it would be unjust to allow a party to knowingly receive benefits and/or services without paying for the value of work completed even in the absence of a binding contract.[13]

---

9. *Haws & Garrett General Contractors, Inc.*, 480 S.W.2d at 610.
10. *Id.* at 608–09.
11. *Id.* at 610.
12. Lott v. Brown, 2018 WL 6191301, at *6 (Tex. App. 2018).
13. De Leon v. Saldana, 745 S.W.2d 55, 57 (Tex. App. San Antonio 1987), *writ denied* (July 13, 1988).

5.02 HOW TO SELECT A CONTRACT FORM

A. Fundamental Issues

Although the terms of different agreements for design services may vary significantly, the basic framework of design contracts is similar. Construction contracts, however, come in a variety of shapes and forms. The basic framework of a construction contract is driven predominately by two issues. First, what is the applicable project delivery system? And, second, what is the mechanism used to determine the compensation of the contractor? The terms of a construction contract will be very different depending on the answer to those two questions. Consequently, numerous options exist among construction contract forms in order to provide a starting place document that conforms to the fundamental aspects of the transaction, thereby reducing the need for undue customization in connection with the applicable project.

Once the project delivery system and compensation mechanism are established, the owner and contractor need to determine whether to use a standard industry form or a manuscript (originally drafted) document prepared by one of the parties to the construction contract for use on the project. A number of industry-prepared forms are available for each type of project delivery system and compensation framework, although the American Institute of Architects (AIA) forms are the most commonly used for commercial building construction in the United States.

B. Standard Industry Forms

A number of advantages can be identified for using standard industry forms for most private construction projects, including, without limitation, the following:

- ❑ Many form documents enjoy a reputation of relative fairness to the parties and are accepted by the construction industry as a reasonable starting point for use in writing and administrating construction agreements.
- ❑ The economic realities on any project benefit from the quick conclusion of negotiations on the part of many construction contracts, and standard forms are more likely to be understood and negotiated quickly than manuscript documents. If the parties have to analyze and review each of the risk allocation and other substantive provisions of a manuscript document, the contracting process will take much longer and cost much more than when using AIA and other standard industry forms.

- Most standard forms contemplate related forms with respect to the role of the other parties in the construction process, such as the architect, engineer, and lender.
- Many of the standard industry forms are linked together with forms published by the same trade association; therefore, they fit and accommodate the allocation of risk and responsibility provided in other contractual relationships on the same projects.
- Documents that conform to common law and statutory precepts adopted in the majority of jurisdictions are subject to uniform legal interpretation so as to be predictably enforceable and thus reliable.
- Many form documents contain the expression of unambiguous intentions in language more easily understood by the users and interpreters (lawyers, judges and juries) of the industry forms.

The disadvantages of using standard industry forms are as follows:

- Standard forms may be out of date or fail to reflect current law or customary practices. Standard forms, by their nature, cannot address jurisdictional issues.
- Most standard industry forms contain provisions that have a bias toward the industry group that publishes and promotes the form. To protect against such bias, the other parties to the agreement must know how to modify the key provisions of the standard industry form.
- On specialized projects, a standard industry form may not be appropriate because it does not deal directly with the important issues raised by the specific scope of work. The administrative costs and procedures included in the standard industry form also may be inappropriate. In other words, standard industry forms often describe only the so-called lowest common denominator applicable to a range of projects.
- Forms generally work best for a particular sector of the construction industry. Most AIA forms, for example, contemplate general building projects, and are not well suited for other sectors that involve heavy or complex construction or industrial projects.

C. Advantages and Disadvantages of Using a Manuscript Document

Custom form construction contracts generally are used by large institutional developers continuously involved in construction projects, and by commercial developers and commercial contractors on smaller projects, including design-build projects. Custom form contracts also are used by developers with in-house construction divisions that may or may not be profit centers for the developer. Most owners and contractors developing a custom form start with one of the AIA or other standard industry forms, and modify the form substantially. In some cases, the organizational format of the standard form is retained, which facilitates review by the other party. In other cases, provisions from the AIA form or other standard form are included in the custom form with little or no modification.

The major advantage of custom forms is that they are drafted for a specific project. Since the design and construction process reflects a complex web of different, but interrelated contractual relationships, the custom form can define the precise relationship of the following separate parties in the context of the subject project: owners and developers, architects, contractors, engineers, construction managers, trade subcontractors, suppliers, consulting and testing, design engineers, surety companies, construction lenders, and inspection services. For the owner drafting the custom form, another advantage is the ability to overcome the perceived bias of the standard industry forms towards the architect and contractor.

The disadvantages of using manuscript documents are primarily based on lack of uniformity among, and familiarity with, the terms of such documents. Use of the custom form undoubtedly will raise a host of concerns for the other contracting party, including trying to determine which of the rights and procedures found in the AIA or other standard industry forms have been omitted or substantially modified in the custom form. Almost inevitability, the use of a custom form will cause the other party to the agreement to incur additional expenses due to the time necessary to understand the custom form. Additionally, use of a custom form sometimes will cause the contractor to increase its bid, on general principles, to cover perceived risks or to cover the legal fees incurred in negotiating the form. Finally, the lack of experience with the particular custom form is generally a major stumbling block in reaching a quick conclusion of negotiations with respect to the custom form.

5.03 OVERVIEW OF STANDARD INDUSTRY FORMS

A. AIA Documents

AIA documents are divided into several letter-designated series, and each series pertains to a particular type of form or use. The various forms in each series are drafted carefully to complement documents in each of the other series. Therefore, an AIA form of agreement between owner and architect and an AIA form of agreement between owner and contractor should have consistent terms. The most common series of AIA documents are the A-series, B-series, C-series, and G-series, discussed next in greater detail.

The A-series applies to the owner-contractor relationship. There are two principal types of documents outlining agreements between the owner and contractor, which include:

- *Owner-Contractor Agreements (the 2017 editions of which are numbered A101, A102, A103, and A104 (formerly the A107 and A107-2007 Exhibit A), and A104-2017 Exhibit A and A105.* The owner-contractor agreements set forth the basic economic deal between the parties. Key terms pertaining to time, cost, and other basic parameters of construction are added to the text of the contract form. Different AIA forms of owner-contractor agreements are available for various project delivery systems, with options for different compensation mechanisms commonly employed with each.
- *The General Conditions of the Contract for Construction (A201-2017).* General conditions are an integral part of the contract for construction. They establish the rights, responsibilities, and relationships of the owner, contractor, and architect. The A201 typically is adopted by reference in certain other AIA documents, such as owner-architect agreements, owner-contractor agreements, and contractor-subcontractor agreements. Thus, the A201 often is called the "keystone" document.

Since conditions vary by locality and by project, supplementary conditions often are added to amend or supplement portions of the general conditions as required by the individual project. The A503-2017, Guide for Supplementary Conditions, is not an agreement, but is a guide for creating supplementary conditions for the 2017 edition of the A201.

The B-Series of AIA documents pertains to the relationship between the owner and the architect. The principal forms of agreement between owner and architect include, without limitation, the 2017 editions of the B101-2017, B102-2017, B103-2017, B104-2017, and B105-2017. Different versions of the B-series documents address the different types of projects and applicable role and scope of the architect in providing services for the owner with respect to each type of project.

The C-series documents govern the relationship between the architect and its consultants, such as engineers and other design professionals. They are drafted to "flow down" to such consultants the obligations that the architect has to the owner. Architects want to avoid situations where their obligations to the owner are greater than the obligations that the architect's consultants (i.e., the architect's consulting engineers) have to the architect. For example, the obligations of the architect's consulting engineers (mechanical and structural), as to their respective portion of the design work to the architect, with respect to basic services, additional services, insurance coverage, and indemnification should be consistent with the obligations of the architect to the owner with respect to such issues.

The G-series documents include a number of forms commonly used in the day-to-day administration of the project, such as a certificate for substantial completion, change orders, certificates for payment, applications for payment, schedules of values, and so on.

When using the AIA documents, it makes sense to see them as families of related documents—families that relate to the various delivery approaches that an owner and architect may employ to structure projects. With respect to the AIA documents:

- A number of different B-series forms exist for the owner–architect agreements; selection of the appropriate form is based on the scope of the project and role of the architect.
- The type of contractor compensation employed (stipulated sum, cost-plus-fee) requires different A-series owner–contractor agreement forms.
- The choice of general conditions form tracks the owner–contractor agreement form; a separate form is available for federal work (AIA Document A201 S/C).
- A separate family of design-build documents also exists.
- A number of A-, B-, and G-series documents are designated for use in projects utilizing a construction manager.
- Specific forms are available for interior projects, as well as for projects of abbreviated or limited scope.

The AIA Documents Committee revises the AIA documents periodically, usually about every ten years. There are new 2017 editions for most of the AIA construction contract forms. However, both parties may prefer to continue using the 2007 edition of the construction contracts for two primary reasons. First, they may not like the 2017 revisions because they perceive them as more favorable to the other party. Second, both parties are familiar with the provisions of the 2007 forms and are resistant to change. Refusing to use the updated forms has its risks though. Some of the changes in the 2017 documents are more neutral revisions addressing changes in case law, statutes, and industry practices so that the 2007 documents are no longer outdated. Moreover, parties should not mix versions from different AIA series. A 2007 construction contract will not be entirely consistent with a 2017 architect's agreement, resulting in potential contract administration and enforcement issues. Additionally, the AIA has stated it will discontinue providing electronic format access to the 2007 edition as of October 31, 2018, which should require all parties to use the updated versions. To determine which edition is applicable to a particular project, the drafter of the contract will need to review the Request for Proposal prepared by the owner or architect or the Project Manual prepared by the architect. The bid proposal section of the Project Manual should list the AIA documents applicable to the project.

In the private construction industry, the AIA contract forms have dominated the field for decades. The following reasons probably account for such continued dominance:

- Although the AIA forms are written by a trade association for architects, the AIA seeks input and endorsements from as many industry groups as possible. As a result, the AIA documents enjoy a wide reputation of relative fairness to parties and are accepted by the construction industry as a natural starting point for use in writing, revising, and administrating construction agreements.
- Use of a custom form undoubtedly will raise a host of concerns for the other contracting party, including trying to determine which of the rights and procedures from the AIA forms have been omitted or substantially modified in the custom form. This may result in resentment and additional expense on non-construction matters.
- Most construction projects involve multiple parties, most of whom are familiar with the AIA documents.
- The economic realities of most projects require the quick conclusion of negotiations on the part of many construction participants.
- The AIA forms contain contractual provisions and language that have been frequently interpreted in the courts.
- The experience factor gives the AIA forms a strong edge over competing form contracts or custom contracts of an owner or contractor.
- The AIA provides a wide variety of forms to accommodate the differences of the rules of the road for different types of construction projects, and the AIA forms are linked to fit and accommodate the allocation of risk and responsibility provided in the other AIA forms for other contractual relationships on the same project.
- The history of the AIA forms, their widespread familiarity and use, and the scrutiny and commentary the AIA forms have received from industry groups operate as an inexpensive substitute for legal review and advice in individual transactions. However, it remains important for the parties to the AIA (or other standard task group) forms to retain counsel and make sure that such forms are consistent with the actual intent of the parties. A limited review by counsel would be better than blind reliance that the AIA forms adequately cover all of the important

legal issues relevant to the specific project, without the necessity of revising the AIA forms in some manner. When parties must stop to analyze and allocate each of the risks that they take under a non-AIA form construction contract, the contracting process can take much longer and cost much more than it does when using AIA forms.

- ❐ AIA documents are available in electronic format on a computer disk, so they can be modified in a more efficient manner than striking paragraphs by deletion, interlineations, and/or use of addenda pages or an addendum to the entire form. The electronic system currently in use includes the AIA "additions and deletions report." This alerts the other party to the transaction that the original AIA document has been edited, and avoids misleading the party that the document is an unaltered standard AIA document.

B. AGC Forms

The Associated General Contractors of America (AGC), the nation's oldest and largest construction trade association, is an organization of construction contractors and industry-related companies. The AGC provides a full range of services satisfying the needs and concerns of members, including drafting more than 70 industry-tested contracts and forms. AGC jointly drafts these contracts with owners, contractors, subcontractors, and sureties. The most recently published forms are known as ConsensusDocs, and are also available in electronic format. The stated goal of ConsensusDocs is to better the industry by providing standard contract documents that strive to reflect the consensus for best practices.

ConsensusDocs are organized into seven series:

- ❐ General contracting
- ❐ Collaborative
- ❐ Design-build
- ❐ CM at-risk
- ❐ Subcontracting
- ❐ Program management
- ❐ Public-private partnership

The AGC drafting process purports to craft documents that balance perspectives, and allocate risks and responsibilities fairly. For example, with respect to the design-build series of AGC documents, the drafters contend that those forms reflect industry "best practices" and provide the framework for a cooperative relationship between the parties to the design-build project. Like the AIA series of documents, AGC documents have different forms for the different project delivery systems and compensation mechanisms. All of the AGC forms are interrelated.

C. EJCDC Forms

The Engineers Joint Contract Documents Committee (EJCDC) develops, publishes, and updates standard contract documents for the design and construction of engineered facilities. The EJCDC construction series (C-series) is comprised (as of 2013) of 20 plus documents, including a narrative guide for use in establishing and administrating the contractual relationship between a project owner and a contractor.

The EJCDC documents are drafted with the active participation of representatives of certain owner groups; risk managers; professional liability insurers; surety and insurance experts; construction lawyers; various professional societies, including but not limited to the supporting societies; and construction managers. The EJCDC documents are intended principally for use on projects designed by engineers, including public infrastructure; water and wastewater treatment and conveyance facilities; utility work; solid waste handling and disposal facilities; transportation projects; production and processing facilities; site development work; environmental remediation projects; street, curb and gutter work; tunneling and excavation projects; and similar applications.

D. Other Standard Industry Forms

The Design-Build Institute of America (DBIA), founded in 1993, is an association of leaders in the design and construction industry utilizing design-build and integrated project delivery methods to achieve high-performance projects. The DBIA has published 14 contracts for design-build construction for use by the various participants in the design-build process, including contractors, designers, architects, engineers, owners and managers, and suppliers. The DBIA model contracts cover all project forms of compensation.

The Construction Managers Association of America (CMAA) is a national organization designed to promote the growth and acceptance of construction management as a professional discipline that can add significant value to the entire construction process, from conception to ongoing operation. The CMAA publishes eight principal forms designed to cover the two general approaches to construction management.

5.04 WHAT IS THE CONTRACT?

A. The Design Agreement (Owner–Architect)

The agreement between an owner and architect is composed generally of a single document and exhibits. The exhibits typically might include a timetable for the performance of services, a list of required insurance coverages, an index of key personnel and consultants, a digital data protocol, and other terms or conditions that vary or complete the underlying form of agreement or that are specific to the particular transaction. Some industry forms utilize an exhibit through which the parties identify the business terms unique to their particular transaction, providing an opportunity to keep the form language as intact as possible.

B. The Contract Documents (Owner–Contractor)

The term "contract documents" identifies the documents, in whatever form or medium, that describe the work to be performed by the contractor, and the contractual relationship between the owner and contractor in connection with the performance of such work. The contract documents collectively form the construction contract, and typically include the following instruments:

1. Owner–contractor agreement, which is an agreement between the owner and the contractor containing the essential business elements of the owner–contractor relationship, such as the identity of the parties, a description of the work, the price, the time for commencement and completion, procedures for payment, and a list of the contract documents;
2. General conditions of the contract for construction, which expand upon the information provided in the agreement between the owner and the contractor and provide more complete contract terms governing the parties, such as the owner's obligations to the contractor; the services that the contractor will provide; insurance and bonding requirements; changes in the work; procedures for requesting an extension in time; payment procedures; site safety, suspension, and termination procedures; and, although the architect is not a party to this document, the construction administration services the architect will provide;
3. Supplementary or special conditions of the contract for construction, which modify or supplement the agreement and general conditions of the contracts;

4. Drawings prepared by the design professionals, which are the graphic and pictorial expressions of the work to be performed, and which may be provided in electronic as well as printed media;
5. Specifications prepared by the design professionals, which are the written technical requirements for the materials, equipment, systems, and standards for the work;
6. Addenda modifying or supplementing any of the preceding, which are issued before the construction contract is executed;
7. Other documents/exhibits that describe certain procedures applicable to the work, including governmental requirements, such as special safety requirements; union bidding requirements; affirmative action hiring requirements; minimum wage requirements, and so on; and
8. Modifications or changes to the contract in the form of construction change directives, field orders, change orders, or other modifications that become part of the contract documents after commencement of the work.

Most of the industry-prepared construction contracts include some form of general conditions of the contract for construction, similar to the AIA-A201, as a separate document. These general conditions documents, like the AIA-A201, are incorporated by reference into owner–architect agreements, owner–contractor agreements, contractor–subcontractor agreements, and the architect's subcontracts with consulting engineers. By separating these general conditions contracts from the standard form of agreement between the owner and contractor, the owner and/or contractor can deliver the instrument to a necessary party to the construction project without disclosing the business terms of the owner's agreement with the contractor. Another important benefit of separating the standard form agreement from the general conditions is the ease of dealing with subcontractors and their ability to recognize and understand the relationship between their respective subcontracts and the construction contract.

C. The Integration Clause

Many construction contracts contain a so-called integration clause in which owner and contractor agree that "the Contract represents the entire and integrated agreement between the parties[14] hereto and supersedes prior negotiations, representations or agreements, either written or oral." The provision

---

14. AIA Document A201–2017, General Conditions of the Contact for Construction, § 1.1.2.

then explains how the construction contract may be amended or modified. Practically every well-drafted agreement will have a provision similar to the integration clause contained in the AIA-A201 in order to eliminate oral and written negotiations that have not been included in the contract instrument. This type of clause intends to prevent the invariably lengthy and fluid negotiation process from becoming part of the contract, except to the extent memorialized in the construction contract itself. The integration clause terms expressly provide that the construction contract supersedes all prior negotiations, proposals, bids, representations, or agreements, whether written or oral.

D. Incorporation by Reference versus Enumeration of Documents

The agreement between an owner and contractor usually includes an enumeration of the contract documents to specify which documents comprise the construction contract. Some construction contracts may also incorporate various documents by reference. Regardless of which technique is used, problems arise if it is not clear which documents collectively form the construction contract.[15]

Also, to ensure the owner is not put at risk through the subcontracting process, almost all construction contracts contain a so-called flow-down clause. Such provision requires the contractor to provide in its subcontracts that each subcontractor, to the extent of its work, "be bound to the contractor by terms of the contract documents, and to assume toward the contractor all the obligations and responsibilities, including the responsibility for safety of the subcontractor's work, which the contractor, by these contract documents, assumes toward the owner and architect."[16] In other words, the work of the subcontractor must comply with the same requirements that apply to the contractor. The flow down of these obligations protects the owner by providing assurance that the subcontractor is required to comply with obligations consistent with those of the contractor, and also protects the contractor by ensuring that its obligations to the owner are no greater than the obligations the subcontractor owes to the contractor.

5.05 INTERNAL CONFLICTS

With multiple contract documents collectively forming the construction contract, inconsistent provisions are a possibility. Some drafters attempt to address this issue through creation of a hierarchy of contract documents. A common

---

15. *See* Atlantic Mutual Ins. Co. v. Metron Eng'g and Constr. Co., 83 F.3d 897 (7th Cir.) 1996; Ritchies Food Distrib., Inc. v. Refrigerated Constr. Serv., 2004 WL 957659 (Ohio Ct. App. 2004).
16. AIA Document A201–2017, *supra* note 14, § 5.3.

approach is for modifications and change orders to have the highest degree of priority, followed by the agreement, the supplement to general conditions, the general conditions, the drawings and specifications (which may be equal in priority with differences to be resolved by the architect or, alternatively, the specifications control), and any other ancillary document. The owner, with the architect's assistance, and the contractor should work together to make sure the hierarchy is accurately stated. The contractor will want its bid or proposal to be a contract document and to govern and control over other contract documents in order to protect the basis on which the contractor has agreed to price, times, and other contractual matters.

The construction contract often will have more than one hierarchy to address particular types of conflicts. In addition to the hierarchy that addresses differences or conflicts between the contract documents, a second hierarchy may be included with instructions to resolve a specific type of conflict. For example, many construction contracts provide that in the event of inconsistencies within a particular contract document, contractor shall (1) provide the better quality or greater quantity of work, or (2) comply with the more stringent requirement, either or both in accordance with the owner's interpretation. Other examples include instructions that large-scale drawings govern over small-scale drawings. Contract drafters have devised almost limitless rules to resolve internal conflicts in documents. Regrettably, hierarchies can have unintended results, and multiple hierarchies can themselves conflict, totally nullifying the intended benefit of including a hierarchy provision. Since each project is different, it is critical that the owner and architect work together to make sure the hierarchy is accurately stated.

Many construction contracts do not use a hierarchy of documents to control in the event of inconsistent provisions between or among the contract documents. Instead, contracts may include a general instruction that permits the architect to resolve a conflict, or may use a default mechanism obligating the contractor to comply with the more stringent requirement. Other construction contracts simply provide that the contract documents must be read as a whole. Indeed, the AIA forms provide that:

> The intent of the Contract Documents is to include all items necessary for the proper execution and completion of the Work by the Contractor. The Contract Documents are complementary, and what is required by one shall be as binding as if required by all;[17]

In other words, AIA contract documents are to be read as whole and reconciled accordingly, rather than setting forth a prioritization of documents that

---

17. *Id.* § 1.2.1.

might lead to unpredictable, and undesirable, results. But conflicts can and do occur, so judicial rules of contract interpretation have developed over the years to assist in resolving conflicting requirements, including those not resolved by a document hierarchy.

5.06 CONTRACT INTERPRETATION

A. Rules of Contract Construction

Courts, not juries, determine whether a contract is *ambiguous*.[18] A contract is unambiguous if its language is reasonably susceptible to only one interpretation, and it is ambiguous if it is reasonably susceptible to more than one interpretation.[19] If the court finds that a contract is unambiguous, the court gives the contract the only legal meaning to which the contract is susceptible.[20] The *interpretation* of an ambiguous contract, however, must be determined by the trier of fact.[21]

The three primary rules of contract construction are:

1. Apply the reasonable and logical meaning;
2. Construe the contract in its entirety; and
3. Apply normal and ordinary meaning of a contract's terms.[22]

The language of a contract should be given its plain grammatical meaning, unless it definitely appears that the intention of the parties would be defeated thereby.[23] In *Reilly v. Rangers Management, Inc.*, the Texas Supreme Court stated:

> A court should construe contracts from a utilitarian standpoint bearing in mind the particular business activity sought to be served and need not embrace strained rules of interpretation which would avoid ambiguity at all costs. Courts will avoid where possible and proper a construction which is unreasonable, inequitable, and oppressive.[24]

---

18. Mark V, Inc. v. Mellekas, 845 P.2d 1232, 1235 (N.M. 1993).

19. A. Servidone/B. Anthony Constr. Corp., J.V. v. State, No. 2016-05238, 2019 N.Y. slip op. 00082, 2019 WL 138601 (N.Y. App. Div. 2019) (contract for construction of bridges).

20. R & P Enters. v. LaGuarta, Gavrel & Kirk, Inc., 596 S.W.2d 517, 519 (Tex. 1980); Weekley v. Weekley, 27 S.E.2d 591, 595 (W.Va. 1943).

21. Triangle Constr. Co., Inc. v. Fouche and Associates, Inc., 218 So. 3d 1180 (Miss. App. 2017); *In re*, Nelson Co., 959 F.2d 1260, 1264 (3d Cir. 1992); Reilly v. Rangers Mgmt., Inc., 727 S.W.2d 527, 529 (Tex. 1987).

22. *See, e.g.*, SW. Bell Tel. v. PUC, 467 F.3d 418, 422 (5th Cir. 2006).

23. Wash. Constr. Co. v. Spinella, 84 A.2d 617, 619 (N.J. 1951).

24. *Reilly*, 727 S.W.2d at 530 (citing Neece v. AAA. Realty Co., 322 S.W.2d 597, 602 (1959)); *see also* Hicks v. Smith, 330 S.W.2d 641, 646 (Tex. Civ. App. Fort Worth, 1959, writ ref'd n.r.e.).

If the court finds the contract to be clear after application of the three primary rules stated previously, then the parties cannot resort to secondary rules of construction, such as evidence of custom and usage.[25] If, however, after applying these primary rules of interpretation, a written instrument remains reasonably susceptible to more than one meaning, then extraneous evidence is admissible to determine the true meaning of the instrument.[26]

B. Parol Evidence Rule

Before parties sign an agreement outlining their respective rights and obligations, the parties often engage in preliminary negotiations not intended to establish contracts in and of themselves. When the parties finally sign the written contract, the contract may fail to deal with all issues discussed in preliminary negotiations, or it may deal with such issues differently than in the discussions. The application of the parol evidence rule works to bar these preliminary negotiations from being considered when a dispute arises over a written contract.[27] The rule has been stated in *Corbin on Contracts* as follows:

> When two parties have made a contract and have expressed it in a writing to which they have both assented as the complete and accurate integration of that contract, evidence, whether parol or otherwise, of antecedent understandings and negotiations will not be admitted for the purpose of varying or contradicting the writing.[28]

Although the word "parol" means oral, the parol evidence rule does not limit itself only to prior oral discussions.[29] Any prior writing not incorporated into the final agreement may be excluded as well.[30] Further, and again contrary to its very name, the parol evidence rule is not considered a rule of evidence at all; rather, many courts regard it as a rule of substantive law.[31]

---

25. George v. El Paso Cnty. Water Control & Imp. Dist. No. 1, 332 S.W.2d 144, 148 (Tex. Civ. App. El Paso, 1960, writ ref'd n.r.e.).

26. R & P Enters. v. LaGuarta, Gavrel & Kirk, Inc., 596 S.W.2d 517, 519 (Tex. 1980); Brown v. Royal Maccabees Life Ins. Co., 137 F.3d 1236, 1247 (10th Cir. 1998).

27. The rule also extends to bar consideration of a prior, inconsistent agreement. Southern Green Builders, LP v. Cleveland, 558 S.W.3d 251 (Tex. App. 2018).

28. Corbin on Contracts § 573 (1993).

29. Altrutech, Inc. v. Hooper Holmes, Inc., 6 F. Supp. 2d 1269, 1275 (D. Kan. 1998).

30. *Id. See also* Segari v. Uchello, 44 So. 2d 722, 724 (La. Ct. App. 1950) (stating some narrow exceptions to the general rule).

31. *See, e.g.*, Weber v. Pascarella Mason St., LLC, 930 A.2d 779, 787 (Conn. App. Ct. 2007) (quoting Alstom Power, Inc. v. Balcke-Durr, Inc., 849 A.2d 804, 811 (Conn. 2004)).

The parol evidence rule only applies to prior or collateral communications that vary or contradict the terms of a written contract.[32] Parties always have the power to modify or supplement a written contract after its execution.[33] The added material, however, must satisfy all of the elements of a contract with respect to mutual assent and consideration.[34]

If it appears from the face of the written contract that the contract was intended to be a complete and final expression of the entire agreement (an integration), courts will not permit either party to testify as to prior understandings for the purpose of varying or contradicting the contract as written.[35] The rationale is that one purpose of creating a written agreement is to memorialize the applicable terms and to exclude all other understandings to the contrary.[36] To allow any prior or collateral agreement to vary or contradict the terms of the final written agreement would defeat its purpose.

In determining whether a document is an integration, courts view the surrounding circumstances in which the agreement was reached as well as the actual written words within the contract.[37] Many construction contracts contain a "merger" or "entire agreement" clause. An example of such a clause is found in *Advertising and Policy Committee of the Avis Rent A Car System v. Avis Rent A Car System*:

> The agreement supersedes all prior agreements whether written or oral between the parties hereto [and] contains the entire agreement of the parties, [and] no representations, inducements, promises, or agreements, oral or otherwise, between the parties not embodied herein shall be of any force or effect.[38]

Some cases exist, however, where parol evidence can apply. A party may introduce parol evidence to show that a contract was never formed or that the contract is unenforceable due to fraud, accident, or mutual mistake.[39] Also, if

---

32. *Id.*
33. A.W. Wendell & Sons, Inc. v. Qazi, 626 N.E.2d 280, 287 (Ill. App. Ct. 1993).
34. Hathaway v. Gen. Mills, Inc., 711 S.W.2d 227, 228 (Tex. 1986).
35. Cave Hill Corp. v. Hiers, 570 S.E.2d 790, 794 (Va. 2002).
36. Filippi v. Filippi, 818 A.2d 608, 619 (R.I. 2003).
37. *See* Money v. Fort Hayes State Univ. Endowment Ass'n, 64 P.3d 458, 462 (Kan. App. 2003) ("Kansas law permits the admission of parol evidence to show that even an unambiguous written agreement was not a complete integration. . . .").
38. Adver. & Policy Comm. of the Avis Rent-A-Car Sys. v. Avis Rent-A-Car Sys., 780 S.W.2d 391, 394 (Tex. App. Houston [14th Dist.] 1989, writ granted), *judgment vacated*, 796 S.W.2d 707 (Tex. 1990) (vacating in accordance with terms of settlement agreement).
39. Branstetter v. Cox, 496 P.2d 1345, 1347 (Kan. 1972); Weber v. Pascarella Mason Street, LLC, 930 A.2d 779, 787 (Conn. App. Ct. 2007) (quoting Alstom Power, Inc. v. Balcke-Durr, Inc., 849 A.2d 804, 811 (Conn. 2004)).

a court determines that the writing was not intended to encompass the parties' final agreement, then the writing may be supplemented by proof of other terms and agreements outside of the document.[40] Further, testimony is allowable to place the written word in the context of the specific factual situation surrounding its execution.[41]

C. Ambiguity and Intent of Parties

In construing contracts, the fundamental objective is to ascertain the intent of the parties as expressed by the language of the instrument, regardless of the subjective intent of the parties.[42] "Where the parties reduce an agreement to a writing, which, in view of its completeness and specificity, reasonably appears to be a complete agreement, it is taken to be an integrated agreement unless other evidence can establish that the writing did not constitute a final expression."[43] Courts generally look to the four corners of the instrument to ascertain the intent of the parties.[44] The courts look not to what the parties meant to say, but to the meaning of what they did say.[45]

In the case of *National Union Fire Insurance Co. of Pittsburgh, PA v. CBI Industries, Inc.*, the Texas Supreme Court articulated the law on ambiguity in a contract:

> If a written contract is so worded that it can be given a definite or certain legal meaning, then it is not ambiguous. If, however, the language is subject to two or more reasonable interpretations, then it is ambiguous. Whether a contract is ambiguous is a question of law for the court to decide by looking at the contract as a whole in light of the circumstances present when the contract was entered. Only where a contract is first determined to be ambiguous may the courts consider the parties' interpretation and admit extraneous evidence to determine the true meaning of the instrument.[46]

---

40. *Weber*, 930 A.2d at 787 (quoting Alstom Power, Inc., 849 A.2d at 811).

41. Commercial Union Ins. Co. v. Martinez, 635 S.W.2d 611, 613 (Tex. App. Dallas ,1982, writ ref'd n.r.e.).

42. Missouri *ex rel.* Vincent v. Schneider, 194 S.W.3d 853, 859–60 (Mo. 2006).

43. Restatement (Second) of Contracts § 209(3) (1981).

44. A. Servidone/B. Anthony Constr. Corp., J.V. v. State, No. 2016-05238, 2019 N.Y. slip op. 00082, 2019 WL 138601, at *2 (N.Y. App. Div. 2019); Missler v. Anne Arundel Cnty., 314 A.2d 451, 457 (Md. 1974).

45. *Missler v. Anne Arundel Cnty.*, 314 A.2d at 457 (stating that "[t]he written language embodying the terms of the agreement alone will govern the rights of the parties irrespective of their subjective intent if that language is, on its face, clear and unambiguous").

46. Nat'l Union Fire Ins. Co. of Pittsburgh, PA v. CBI Indus., Inc., 907 S.W.2d 517, 520 (Tex. 1995) (citations omitted); *see also* Columbia Gas Transmission Corp. v. New Ulm Gas, Ltd., 940

Ambiguity does not arise merely because contracting parties disagree as to the correct interpretation of their contract.[47] Only if a contract is found by a court to be ambiguous may the parties differing interpretations be considered.[48] If the disputed provision is plain and unambiguous to a judge, then the parties' construction is immaterial.[49]

In *Standard Constructors, Inc. v. Chevron Chem. Co.*, the Houston appellate court was presented with a dispute concerning claims for overtime charges for use of equipment.[50] In the contract documents, for certain pieces of equipment, "n/a" (agreed to mean "non-applicable") was listed instead of a rate.[51] The court rejected the argument that "n/a" should be construed to mean variable or dependent rates and held that the term "n/a" had one meaning in the contract—"no rate charge."[52] The court stated "[a] contract is not ambiguous merely because a party believes the contract does not mean what it actually says."[53]

D. Reasonable and Logical Interpretation of Entire Contract

A court should view a contract as would a reasonably intelligent third person acquainted with trade usage and surrounding circumstances—all interpretations must be reasonable.[54] Any interpretation that produces illogical results will be rejected. Words, terms, and phrases in the contract are to be given their ordinary and normal meaning unless the parties clearly have given them different interpretations.[55] According to the Restatement of Contracts:

> A. The ordinary meaning of language throughout the country is given to words unless circumstances show that a different meaning is applicable.
>
> B. Technical terms and words of art are given their technical meaning unless the context or a usage which is applicable indicates a different meaning.[56]

S.W.2d 587, 591 (Tex. 1996) (explaining that, in order to determine the parties' agreement, the court needed to examine the entire contract and circumstances surrounding is formulation).

47. *See* McJunkin Corp. v. City of Orangeburg, 238 F.2d 528, 532 (4th Cir. 1956).
48. *Id.*
49. *Id.*
50. Standard Constrs., Inc. v. Chevron Chem. Co., 101 S.W.3d 619, 625 (Tex. App. Houston [1st Dist.] 2003, *petition denied*).
51. *Id.*
52. *Id.*
53. *Id.*
54. Triad Elec. & Controls, Inc. v. Power Sys. Eng'g, Inc., 117 F.3d 180, 191 (5th Cir. 1997).
55. Restatement of Contracts § 235 (1932).
56. *Id.*

Courts continue to apply the reasonable person standard when interpreting contract documents; courts do so while still considering the intent of the parties and the surrounding circumstances at the time of contract formation.[57] Courts presume that the parties to an instrument intend every word in it to have some meaning and purpose; therefore, courts give effect to all parts of an instrument.[58] Where parties to a contract disagree as to the interpretation of a particular provision, the court will not look solely to the disputed provision but will consider all parts of the contract in an effort to determine the meaning of the provision in question.[59]

As the Texas Supreme Court stated:

> When provisions in an agreement appear to be in conflict, the court should examine and consider the entire writing, seeking to harmonize and reconcile the conflicting provisions to the greatest extent possible. In achieving this objective, the court should favor an interpretation that gives effect to all provisions of the contract so that none will be rendered meaningless and the primary purpose of the agreement and intent of the parties will be effectuated.[60]

E. Interpretation against Drafter

An ambiguous agreement is construed most strictly against the party who drafted it under the rule contra proferentem.[61] Therefore, if an instrument is open to more than one reasonable construction, the instrument will be construed most strictly against its author.[62] In many jurisdictions, contra proferentem is a rule of last resort and will be applied only if one party had no choice in the language used, or other canons of interpretation are unavailing.[63]

---

57. Manzo v. Ford, 731 S.W.2d 673, 676 (Tex. App. Houston [14th Dist.] 1987, no writ) (citing Skyland Developers, Inc. v. Sky Harbor Assocs., 586 S.W.2d 564, 570 (Tex. Civ. App. Corpus Christi, 1979, no writ); Stitt v. Royal Park Fashions, Inc., 546 S.W.2d 924, 926 (Tex. Civ. App. Dallas, 1977, writ ref'd n.r.e.).

58. *See, e.g.*, Standard Constrs., Inc. v. Chevron Chem. Co., 101 S.W.3d 619, 625 (Tex. App. Houston [1st Dist.] 2003, petition denied).

59. Manzo v. Ford, 731 S.W.2d 673, 675 (Tex. App. Houston [14th Dist.] 1987, no writ).

60. *Id.* (citing R & P Enters. v. LaGuarta, Gavrel & Kirk, Inc., 596 S.W.2d 517, 519 (Tex. 1980)).

61. CORBIN ON CONTRACTS § 24.27 (1993).

62. Chevron Oil Co. v. E.D. Walton Constr. Co., 517 F.2d 1119, 1122 (5th Cir. 1975); Gulf Constr. Co., v. Self, 676 S.W.2d 624, 628 (Tex. App. Corpus Christi, 1984, writ ref'd n.r.e.); Netherland v. Wittner, 662 S.W.2d 786, 788 (Tex. App. Houston [14th Dist.] 1983, writ ref'd n.r.e.); W.W. Harris v. Phillips Pipe Line Co., 517 S.W.2d 361, 364 (Tex. Civ. App. Austin, 1974, writ ref'd n.r.e.).

63. *See, e.g., In re* Estate of Koch, 912 N.W.2d 205, 215, 322 Mich. App. 383, 401 (Mich. Ct. App. 2017) (claim for breach of indemnity agreement in construction contract).

The applicable principle of law was stated by the Texas Supreme Court in *Temple–Eastex, Inc. v. Addison Bank* as follows:

> In Texas, a writing is generally construed most strictly against its author and in such a manner as to reach a reasonable result consistent with the apparent intent of the parties. If two constructions are possible, a construction rendering the contract possible of performance would be preferred to one that renders its performance impossible or meaningless.[64]

In *Austin Co. v. Vaughn Building Corp.*, when evaluating a breach of warranty claim made by the owner of a building against a general contractor, the Texas Supreme Court interpreted the following warranty clause in the contractor's form agreement:

> Austin guarantees the work against defective workmanship and material for one year from the date of completion of the work as follows: upon written notice of any such defects, Austin will either make necessary repairs or at its option request owner to make such repairs, all at Austin's expense.[65]

The contractor argued that, since written notice of roof leaks was not given until one year and eleven days after completion, the contractor was not obligated under the warranty.[66] The court disagreed, holding that the clause should be construed against the contractor.[67] The court interpreted the provision as providing that the contractor had to repair defects for a period of one year after being notified of them, not one year after completion.[68]

In *Board of Regents of the University of Texas v. S & G Construction Co.*, the owner failed to supply drawings and instructions to be coordinated with existing contractual documents as required by the contract.[69] The owner sought to escape liability for its failure by claiming that oral, day-to-day field directions given by the architect on the project satisfied the contractual requirements.[70] The court accepted the contractor's arguments that the parties had intended that additional instructions be prepared and become part of the contractual documents, and that day-to-day oral directives by the architect could not be

---

64. Temple-Eastex Inc. v. Addison Bank, 672 S.W.2d 793, 798 (Tex. 1984); Borg–Warner Acceptance Corp. v. Tascosa Nat'l Bank, 784 S.W.2d 129 (Tex. App. Amarillo, 1990, writ denied).
65. Austin Co. v. Vaughn Bldg. Corp., 643 S.W.2d 113, 115 (Tex. 1982).
66. *Id.*
67. *Id.*
68. *Id.*
69. Bd. of Regents of the Univ. of Tex. v. S & G Constr. Co., 529 S.W.2d 90, 93 (Tex. Civ. App. Austin, 1975, writ ref'd n.r.e.), *overruled on other grounds by* Federal Sign v. Tex. So. Univ., 951 S.W.2d 401 (Tex. 1997).
70. *Id.* at 94.

considered as such.[71] In reaching this conclusion, the court followed the general rule that any doubt as to the meaning of the contract was to be resolved against the party who prepared the document.[72] This rule particularly applies where an agreement purports to exempt the drafter from liability.[73]

F. Course of Performance and Prior Dealings

Performance of the contract reflects the best evidence of the intentions of the parties to a contract. In the absence of an express term to the contrary, the court will consider evidence of the parties' course of performance, first and foremost, when the court deems a contract ambiguous and allows admission of parol evidence.[74] The Uniform Commercial Code (UCC) defines course of dealing as "a sequence of previous conduct between the parties to a particular transaction which is fairly to be regarded as establishing a common basis of understanding for interpreting their expressions and other conduct."[75] In the context of transactions governed by the UCC, certain statutory language recognizes that the parties have the best understanding of what they mean and that their actions best reflect of the meaning of their agreement. The UCC provides:

> (a) where the contract for sale involves repeated occasions for performance by either party with knowledge of the nature of the performance and opportunity for objection to it by the other, any course of performance accepted or acquiesced in without objection shall be relevant to determine the meaning of the agreement.

> (b) express terms shall control course of performance and course of performance shall control both course of dealing and usage of trade.[76] Actions taken by a contractor or any other party evidencing his or her understanding of the agreement can be considered in determining the intent of an otherwise ambiguous contract.[77]

---

71. *Id.*
72. *Id.*
73. Manzo v. Ford, 731 S.W.2d 673, 676 (Tex. App. Houston [14th Dist.] 1987, no writ); Gen. Corrosion Servs. Corp. v. K Way Equip. Co., 631 S.W.2d 578, 580 (Tex. App. Tyler, 1982, no writ).
74. *See* U.C.C. § 2-202; Nolte v. Hudson Nav. Co., 16 F.2d 182, 184 (2d Cir. 1926) ("[W]hen parties choose such equivocal language, they must be content with the interpretation which they put upon it immediately thereafter, and to which they continuously adhered for nearly 25 years.").
75. U.C.C. § 1-205(1).
76. *See id.* § 1-205.
77. Connelly v. Paul, 731 S.W.2d 657, 660–61 (Tex. App. Houston [1st Dist.] 1987, writ ref'd n.r.e.) ("The conduct of the parties, which indicates a construction that the parties have themselves placed on the contract, and it may be considered in determining the parties' true intent"); *Nolte*, 16 F.2d at 184.

In construing an ambiguous contract, the court also will look at other contracts performed by the parties in the past, or those currently being performed by the parties, which contain the same or similar provisions.[78] A contractor may be found to have impliedly agreed to a certain contractual interpretation by virtue of past performance on other projects.[79] Since course of dealing reflects the prior actions of the specific parties in dispute, the court gives more weight to course of dealing than evidence of the general trade custom and usage.[80]

G. Custom and Usage

Parties are presumed to have entered into a contract governed by the general customs and usages of the particular industry in which they conduct business.[81] When (1) a construction contract is ambiguous, and (2) usage or custom exists in the industry, and (3) the usage or custom is so generally known as to give rise to a presumption the parties knew of it and contracted with reference to it, then the rules of custom and usage can be applied to interpret the contract.[82] For example, the court in *Temple-Eastex, Inc., v. Addison Bank* found as follows:

> Where there is no clear evidence that the parties intended to use a standard or meaning different from customary practice in the industry, courts tend to give a term the meaning it usually has within the industry.[83] This rule is limited by the possibility that, in the construction industry, the owner may require performance in excess of the standard normally accepted, and by the principle that custom and usage will not be used to vary or contradict plain contractual language.[84]

---

78. U.C.C. § 1-205(1).
79. *See* Am. Mach. & Tool v. Strite-Anderson Mfg., 353 N.W.2d 592, 598-99 (Minn. App. 1934).
80. U.C.C. § 1.205(1).
81. *See* Restatement (Second) of Contracts § 220(1); Harrison v. Facade, Inc., 355 S.W.2d 543, 545 (Tex. Civ. App. Dallas, 1962, no writ).
82. *See* Temple-Eastex, Inc., v. Addison Bank, 672 S.W.2d 793, 798 (Tex. 1984) (explaining that custom and usage were used to interpret an ambiguous contract in the banking industry).
83. *See* U.C.C. § 1.205, cmt. 1.
84. George v. El Paso Cnty. Water Control & Imp. Dist. No. 1, 332 S.W.2d 144, 148 (Tex. Civ. App. El Paso, 1960, writ ref'd n.r.e.).

H. Terms: Specific over General; Written over Printed

Another basic rule of contract interpretation provides that a specific or more particular clause must prevail over a general one.[85] For example, a construction contract generally requires that all work meet applicable building codes, but the drawings and specifications may set more stringent performance standards for portions of the work. The specific provisions of the drawings and specifications would be construed to supersede the general provision, and a contractor who simply performed to the standard required by building codes could be in default of the contract.

Parties to a contract should pay close attention to specific terms and be wary of their limiting effect on the whole of the contract. The court, in *Allied Chemical Corp. v. American Independent Oil Co.*, held that "the expression in a contract of one or more things of a class implies the exclusion of all not expressed, even though all could have been implied had none been expressed."[86] For example, if a painting schedule specifically called for some rooms in a school to receive enamel paint, the omission of a room from that list would eliminate the requirement for that specific room, unless the parties' intent to the contrary was affirmatively demonstrated.

Courts will hold that when the printed portions of a contract conflict with handwritten or typewritten portions, the handwritten or typewritten portions will control.[87] This principle has been applied in a number of contexts. For example, in *Montgomery Ward & Co., Inc. v. Dalton*, the court was presented with conflicting warranty provisions.[88] The homeowners relied on the content of the front page of the contract where there appeared a handwritten description of the materials to be used and the work to be performed, also including a handwritten guaranty stating: "20 yr. guarantee 9 yrs. all labor and materials, 11 yrs. prorated 1/240 per mo. transferable."[89] Montgomery Ward relied on the printed contract terms on the back of the document that provided for a more limited warranty.[90] Referring to the handwritten guaranty on the front page

---

85. W. Oil Fields, Inc. v. Pennzoil United, Inc., 421 F.2d 387, 389 (5th Cir. 1970).

86. Allied Chem. Corp. v. Am. Indep. Oil Co., 623 S.W.2d 760, 763 (Tex. App. Houston [1st Dist.] 1981, writ ref'd n.r.e.).

87. *See* Corbin on Contracts § 24.24 (1993).

88. Montgomery Ward & Co., Inc. v. Dalton, 665 S.W.2d 507, 510 (Tex. App. El Paso, 1983, no writ).

89. *Id.*

90. *Id.*

of the agreement, the court stated, "[t]his written guaranty controls over the conflicting printed matter on the back of the instrument. The rule is well established that where the written and printed words and phrases in a contract are in conflict, the written words and phrases control."[91]

5.07 PARTIES TO THE CONSTRUCTION CONTRACT

A. Owner and Contractor

The owner and the contractor are the primary, if not sole, parties to the construction contract. With respect to design-build agreements and construction manager agreements, there may be one additional party to the construction contract.

B. Third-Party Beneficiaries

Most industry contracts include prohibitions against third-party beneficiary rights, even though other parties to the construction process, such as the architect, engineer, subcontractors, and suppliers, are mentioned in various provisions of the construction contract.[92] Generally speaking, neither the owner nor the contractor want the architect to be a third-party beneficiary and be entitled to enforce the provisions of the construction contract against the owner or contractor. Since most construction contracts provide the owner with rights with respect to the contractor's subcontractors and suppliers, the owner may want to be a third-party beneficiary of subcontracts, but will at least want a conditional assignment of such contracts.

The intention of the parties is especially scrutinized by the courts when a third party (someone not a party to the subject contract) claims that amounts are due to him or her as a third-party beneficiary of the contract. Materialmen or suppliers often advance this theory in an effort to obtain funds due from the general contractor to a subcontractor. Some courts consistently have refused to allow claims by materialmen and laborers as third-party beneficiaries to funds retained under construction contracts with others.[93]

---

91. *Id*. at 512.
92. *See* AIA Document A201–2017, *supra* note 14, § 1.1.2.
93. *See, e.g.*, Econ. Forms Corp. v. Williams Bros. Constr. Co., 754 S.W.2d 451, 458–59 (Tex. App. Houston [14th Dist.] 1988, no writ.) (denying recovery for the lessor of certain materials used by a subcontractor and recognizing both that the intention of the parties to the contract controls the issue of whether a third party can enforce a contract provision and the presumption that parties generally contract for themselves and their own benefit); Corpus Christi Bank & Trust v. Smith, 525 S.W.2d 501, 504–05 (Tex. 1975).

A party claiming third-party beneficiary status must establish either that the contracting parties intended to afford some benefit to that third party or that the contracting parties contracted principally for the benefit of that third party.[94] To establish that the contract was directly and primarily entered into for its benefit, the third party must show itself to be either a donee or creditor beneficiary of the contract, as opposed to an incidental beneficiary.[95] A donee beneficiary receives the performance promised under the contract as a pure donation, but a creditor beneficiary receives the performance promised in satisfaction of a legal duty owed to him by the promisee.[96] Courts focus on the intent of the contracting parties in assessing a third party's ability to enforce a contract.[97]

C. Collateral Assignment to Lender

AIA Document A201 and other industry contracts provide for the collateral assignment by the owner to the lender of the owner's rights under the construction contract as additional security for the lender's loan. In most cases, the lender requires a separate consent and assignment instrument to be executed by the owner and contractor that provides the lender with the ability to assume the owner's position under the construction contract or to terminate the construction contract in the event of the owner's default under its loan arrangement with the lender. Considerable negotiations often occur between contractor and lender as to the terms of the collateral assignment relating to the lender's obligation to pay for work under the contract performed prior to lender's assumption of owner's obligations under the contract.

D. References to Other Parties

The references to the architect, engineers, subcontractors, suppliers, and lender are important because each of these other parties plays a significant role with respect to the design, construction, and/or financing of the project, as applicable, and such role should be recognized in the construction contract and should be consistent with the rights of such parties under their separate

---

94. *See generally* SPE GO Holdings, Inc. v. W & O Constr., Inc., 2018 WL 6181645, at *3 (6th Cir. 2018).
95. *See* CORBIN ON CONTRACTS § 774 (1993).
96. *Id.*
97. *See, e.g.,* Chi. R.I. & P. Ry. Co., 75 F.2d at 600. *But see* Hernandez v. Home Depot, U.S.A., No. 05 C 5963, 2007 WL 2298408 (N.D. Ill. Aug. 3, 2007), which gives a somewhat broad interpretation to when a third party is intended to qualify as a beneficiary of a construction contract.

agreements with the owner or contractor. For example, the architect will have certain rights with respect to construction administration and, in the event of a default by the contractor, may need to provide additional design services to correct defective construction. In such event, the contractor should be responsible for the additional design costs incurred by the owner.

5.08 SCOPE OF CONTRACT

A. Description of Services of Design Professionals

Design agreements are challenging documents to prepare. The subject matter of the agreement is yet unknown. A program may exist for the project that describes basic project parameters, but the project itself is just an idea. The agreement between the owner and architect, therefore, sets out the process through which that idea will be developed and documents prepared to depict the project in a combination of two dimensional drawings and written narratives. The scope of a design agreement includes the phases of design services, the deliverables to be furnished as a result of the design services, and construction administration activities that might be provided. All of the foregoing are described in greater detail in chapters that follow.

B. Description of the Work under a Construction Contract

The work to be performed by a contractor has been described as "the construction and services required by the contract documents, whether completed or partially completed, and includes all other labor, materials, equipment, and services provided or to be provided by the contractor to fulfill the contractor's obligations."[98] Owner–contractor agreements typically provide a large blank space to be completed as necessary to describe the work the contractor is obligated to perform. Although this description is, obviously, the essence of any contract, the description often receives only routine consideration when preparing a contract. The parties must not underestimate the difficulty of describing the work accurately and comprehensively, as any failure to ensure an adequate description of the work can frustrate reasonable expectations at a later date. If the owner desires the contractor to perform certain activities that fall outside the scope of the work, an adjustment in both cost and time most likely will be required.

---

98. AIA Document A201–2017, *supra* note 14, § 1.1.3.

Since the work generally will be described by incorporating the drawings and specifications by reference, it is important for the owner's architect, or a third-party architect or engineer retained by the owner (if the project is a design-build project), to review the sufficiency of the drawings and specifications from the standpoint of producing the intended result in compliance with all applicable codes, laws, and regulations.

Additionally, owners generally include a provision in the construction contract requiring the contractor to execute the work described in the contract documents "and reasonably inferable by the contractor as necessary to produce the results "intended" or "indicated" by the contract documents."[99] The "reasonably inferable" language is important because no set of drawings and specifications is perfect.

With respect to the drawings and specifications, who should bear the risk of any inaccuracies or omissions in the drawings and specifications? Contractors undoubtedly will argue that they should be entitled to rely on the accuracy or completeness of the drawings and specifications prepared by the architects and engineers; however, no set of drawings and specifications is perfect, as indicated earlier. Therefore, if, in the course of constructing the improvements, the contractor discovers any error, inconsistency, or omission in the contract documents, the contractor should be obligated to report such item immediately to the architect and/or owner.

Owners may attempt to attribute to the contractor constructive knowledge of a defect if a reasonable and prudent contractor would have caught the mistake. The patent ambiguity rule protects the owner, to wit: the rule requiring the contractor to notify the owner if the contractor is aware of conflicts or defects in the design documents apparent on the face of such documents. Accordingly, the contractor may be charged with knowledge of patent ambiguities so as to preclude the contractor from recovering from such ambiguities. Compulsory disclosure of any conflict or ambiguity of which the contractor has actual knowledge guards against gamesmanship in the bidding process, that is, where a contractor, after being awarded the contract, might use the change process to increase the contract sum to cover the costs resulting from a conflict or ambiguity.

The owner wants to make sure that if the contractor performs any work in conformity with any contract document, while knowing the work to be inconsistent with any other contract document or not in compliance with applicable laws and codes, and does so without first specifically reporting the inconsistency and obtaining from the owner and/or architect written instructions on

---

99. *See id.* § 1.2.1.

how to proceed, then the contractor should be obligated to correct such work, at the owner's direction, without cost to the owner. The contractor also should be required to contact the owner and/or architect without delay upon discovery of problems in the drawings and specifications or compliance with laws. Moreover, the failure to promptly notify the owner of any error or inconsistency, particularly if the contractor knowingly performs work that will need to be re-executed, should be the responsibility of the contractor. A contractor that agrees to this provision is not accepting design responsibility or liability, but only the liability to notify the owner and/or architect of a known potential problem for input from the owner and/or architect prior to execution of the work that is the subject of a potential conflict.

It is also important to the contractor to provide a comprehensive description of the work to be performed by the contractor under the contract documents by reference to and incorporation of the drawings and specifications, as well as by referring to the contractor's qualifications or clarifications (which exhibit, from the contractor's perspective, should have the highest degree of priority). Additionally, references to "good and workmanlike" construction should be avoided. Similarly, the contractor should try to avoid imprecise and general obligations (just as the owner hopes to keep them) that are susceptible to expansive readings, such as (a) subparagraph 1.2.1 of the AIA-A201 language that "the intent of the contract documents is to include all items necessary for the proper execution and completion of the work by the contractor'" (b) language that the contract documents are complementary in what is required and shall be as binding if required by all; and (c) language that the contractor's performance should be required only to the extent consistent with the contract documents and reasonably inferable from them as being necessary to produce the "indicated" results, not "intended" results.

Finally, the reasonably so-called inferable standard itself, from the contractor's viewpoint, is in need of repair to ensure that such a contract clause is not abused. The simplest fix, adopted in some industry contracts, is to limit inferred work to work that is "incidental" to the work shown on the drawings and specifications. A more satisfactory approach is to define more carefully work not shown in the drawings and specifications as "reasonably inferred" or "incidental" to give the parties, and (if necessary) the court, a more thorough set of criteria on which omitted work can be attributed to the contractor.

Several conditions exist that should serve to exclude an addition of work as being cast as part of what is "reasonably inferred" from the drawings and specifications. The most obvious is cost; when omitted work involves material additional cost and is not indicated in the drawings and specifications, the omitted work should not qualify as "reasonably inferred" from drawings and specifications. Second, the design professional's job is to design, not the contractor's. If work requires any meaningful exercise of the design function, the work should not qualify as "reasonably inferred" from the drawings and specifications.

Even when contractors are saddled with some elemental design function, contractors ordinarily are required to prepare submittals to have the design approved. If the omitted work usually would require anything like a submittal, but the omitted work is not specified in the required submittals, then that serves as a very good sign the work is not reasonably inferred from the drawings and specifications. Finally, if the work requires material changes to sequencing or scheduling, the work should not be construed as reasonably inferred.

All these elements ultimately look to the materiality of the change. No doubt, pitched battles can occur as to what is material and what is not. But it is better to fight on those appropriate grounds and get to the heart of the responsibility in an equitable manner than argue over what is "reasonably inferred as necessary," a question that may bear little relationship to the fairness of attributing extra work to the contractor.

C. Owner-Furnished Items

In many commercial projects, the owner will furnish certain materials, equipment, or systems to incorporate into the work. Sometimes, the owner takes advantage of an opportunity to purchase materials (lumber and flooring, as an example) or equipment or fixtures at a discount in advance of the actual need for such items. In addition, the owner may want the contractor to install specialty items obtained from older properties or at auctions. In such events, the owner expects the contractor to install such items, and to remain fully responsible for furnishing the necessary services and other items necessary to install and incorporate such owner-purchased items into the work. The owner will want the contractor's installation of such owner-purchased items to be covered by the contractor's warranties.

In many instances, the contractor will attempt to accept no responsibility for owner-supplied items and will require the owner to contract directly with separate contractors to install owner-supplied items. If, however, the contractor agrees to install owner-supplied items, limited liability, if any, should apply to the contractor for failing to reject non-conforming or defective owner-supplied items. The owner should be required to look directly to the supplier for any non-conforming or defective owner-supplied items, unless the owner-supplied items are damaged by the contractor during installation or during the contractor's performance of the work, or the contractor had actual knowledge of the defects and, nevertheless, installed the owner-supplied items.

D. Construction by Owner or by Separate Contractors

The owner often reserves the right to perform construction on a project with the owner's own forces and/or to award separate contracts in connection with other portions of the project. In such event, the contractor should provide for coordination of the activities of the owner's own forces and each separate contractor with the work of the contractor. Additionally, the owner should be subject to the same obligations and have the same rights apply to the contractor under articles 3, 6, 10, 11, and 12 of the AIA-A201 or other general conditions of the contract. If either party is responsible for delays, improperly timed activities, defective construction, or damage to the work of a separate party, such party shall reimburse the other party for such costs, and promptly remedy the damage wrongfully caused by such responsible party to the completed or partially constructed property of the other party.[100]

---

100. *See id.* §§ 6.1.1, 6.2.3, and 6.2.4.

QUESTIONS

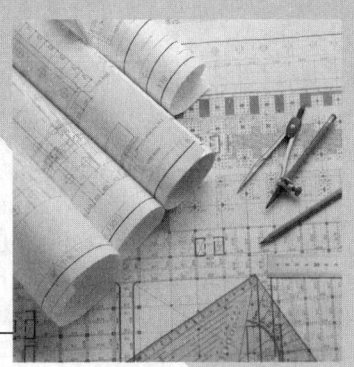

1. What are the primary considerations for entering into early start letters on construction projects?
2. Illustrate two situations where a contractor should be successful in pursuing a quantum meruit claim for work done for another party.
3. Why are industry construction contract forms, like the AIA documents, more frequently used than manuscript forms?
4. Which parties to the industry forms, architects' agreements, and construction contracts generally request more changes and why? What is the primary focus of the requested changes?
5. What circumstances could possibly support the introduction of parol evidence to defend the enforceability of a construction contract, as well as to permit parol evidence to supplement a construction contract?

CHAPTER 6

The Design Team's Role and Contracts

CAROL J. PATTERSON AND TIMOTHY F. HEGARTY

6.01 INTRODUCTION

Early in the development of any project, the owner must engage design professionals to produce the design and construction documents that will become a road map for the execution of the project. This chapter discusses the role and responsibilities of the design team and the legal framework related to the performance of design services. As discussed in prior chapters of this book, there are a number of different contractual relationships and delivery methods for construction projects that have an impact on the role of the design team members and the terms of their respective contracts. This chapter focuses on the typical Design-Bid-Build project, which is the most common delivery method. With this approach, an owner generally retains an architect under one prime contract and retains a contractor under a separate prime contract. While it is not uncommon to draft custom owner–architect agreements tailored to a specific project, for simplicity purposes, references will be made in this chapter to the approach taken to a variety of issues in the widely used owner–architect template, AIA Document B101–2017, Standard Form of Agreement between Owner and Architect (AIA–B101).[1]

This section describes the different kinds of design professionals who contribute to the construction process, the various elements of the design process, and a design professional's traditional role in a Design-Bid-Build project. Section 6.02 provides an overview of the regulation of design professionals, and Section 6.03 discusses the variety of building codes and related regulations that govern construction. Section 6.04 focuses on standards of care in the design professional's practice. Section 6.05 describes the process by which a particular design is implemented through the construction process. The remaining sections, 6.06 through 6.09, describe specific portions of the design professional's agreement with the owner.

A. Overview of the Contractual Relationship among Parties and General Allocation of Design Function

The design team has the primary obligation for performing the necessary design services required for the project. Depending on timing, the owner's related responsibilities vary, but, at a minimum, typically include furnishing the project site and basic information about the project parameters and paying for the design and construction. The contractor's role is essentially to build the project in accordance with the plans and specifications. Accordingly, during the design phase, the contractor's role is generally very limited, unless a portion of the project expressly delineates performance specifications in the contract documents (addressed later in the chapter). This does not mean that the contractor has no role. Indeed, the earlier the contractor is retained, the greater the likelihood that the owner may require the contractor to review and comment on the design documents to advise on practical issues related to feasibility of construction in accordance with the owner's budget and schedule. In addition, the contract documents may require the contractor to provide shop drawings that develop implementation details for certain components of the work.

---

1. As referenced in Chapter 5, the AIA (American Institute of Architects) publishes a wide range of contracts for projects of all types, including owner-architect, owner-contractor, owner-construction management and design-build just to name a few. These are template documents and are carefully drafted to describe the services, rights, and responsibilities of each party to the agreement. These documents are periodically updated to reflect changes in the design and construction industry as well as corresponding developments in the law. However, the parties involved in a particular project often decide that the forms require revision to correctly document their mutual agreement.

B. The Role of the Owner and Owner's Consultants with Respect to Design

Primary responsibilities of the owner include providing necessary information concerning the owner's objectives, including functional and aesthetic requirements, schedule, budget, and site-related constraints necessary to develop a program for the project. On many projects, this may be an ongoing process, because the owner may not have all of this information prior to engaging the architect or engineer. Moreover, it is common for an owner to acquire property with site-related issues before hiring the design team. In those situations, the owner will often directly retain a number of different consultants to address these concerns. These consultants may perform services and provide information related to issues such as zoning, site/civil engineering, environmental, geotechnical, and traffic concerns, all of which involve specialized knowledge outside the capability of most architects. As discussed in more detail later in the chapter, this is a material issue from a liability perspective because those consultants are in contractual privity with the owner, and the owner furnishes their work product to other members of the design team. It is possible the owner may require the architect to retain one or more of these consultants to consolidate responsibility under one agreement.

C. The Design Professional Team

Under traditional Design-Bid-Build procurement, the owner retains the architect under a prime agreement, and the architect, in turn, typically enters into subconsultant agreements with a variety of consultants, including those with engineering and other specialized design disciplines. Many agreements provide that if the architect retains those consultants, the architect is responsible for their services; however, some agreements recognize that the architect's knowledge is limited to its discipline and expressly provide that the architect may rely on the technical expertise of its consultants and will not be responsible for their errors or omissions. This practice varies depending on the geographic location of the project and on the knowledge and expertise of the owner. For example, some more experienced owners prefer to hold all the consultants' contracts directly. Alternatively, the owner may retain the architect under one prime agreement and separately retain all or certain other design consultants pursuant to separate prime agreements. In those situations, the architect is not responsible for the work of these consultants. For example, AIA-B101, section 3.1.2, defines the architect's responsibilities related to the owner's consultants as follows:

The Architect shall coordinate its services with those services provided by the Owner and the Owner's consultants. The Architect shall be entitled to rely on, and shall not be responsible for, the accuracy, completeness, and timeliness of, services and information furnished by the Owner and the Owner's consultants. The Architect shall provide prompt written notice to the Owner if the Architect becomes aware of any error, omission, or inconsistency in such services or information.[2]

A number of design consultants, such as geotechnical engineers, are often retained by the owner to comprise part of the design team. Regardless of who hires the consultants, the architect typically assumes responsibility for coordinating the consultants' services throughout the design process.

1. Architectural Consultants

Many projects require the input of a number of specialized consultants in addition to the architects and engineers. The consultants related to the architectural design of a project may include the following disciplines: landscape, sustainability (green design), lighting, acoustical, code/life safety, elevator and vertical transportation, window, interior design, and kitchen design.

2. Engineering Consultants

It is also common for a project to require input from a number of engineering-based consultants, who are generally required to sign, stamp, and seal their construction documents, including the following disciplines: structural engineering; mechanical (plumbing, heating, ventilation, and air conditioning); fire protection and electrical engineering services; civil engineering; geotechnical engineering and building envelope; and low voltage systems, including telephone, computer, audio-visual, and security systems. It is common for the architect to retain such consultants, although some owners will hire them directly.

3. The Civil Construction Project (Engineer as Lead Design Professional)

Although most building projects, such as office buildings, residential high-rise buildings, hotels, schools, courthouses, warehouses, and commercial retail establishments, are led by architects, certain projects are more appropriately led by engineering design firms. These projects include railways, roads, bridges, dams, tunnels, oil refineries, energy plants, wind farms, and wastewater treatment plants.

---

2. American Institute of Architects, AIA Document B101–2017, Standard Form of Agreement between Owner and Architect § 3.1.2.

While engineer-led projects do not necessarily exclude architects from involvement, the engineer is the lead design professional with overall responsibility for the project design pursuant to the engineer's agreement with the owner. The engineer may retain an architect to perform the architectural services on the project. From a legal perspective, little difference exists between an architect-led and an engineer-led design team. The design agreements between the design professionals and the owner will define the parties' respective obligations. The owner may or may not directly retain certain other consultants. If an engineer is the lead design professional, to the extent the parties desire to use a template document, they may choose to use a form of agreement prepared by the Engineers Joint Contract Documents Committee (EJCDC). In lieu of a template document, it is not uncommon for either the owner or engineer to prepare and negotiate a custom prime agreement tailored to the project.

6.02 STATUTORY REGULATION AND LICENSURE OF DESIGN PROFESSIONALS

Due to public policy concerns, including safeguarding life, health, and property, and promoting the public welfare, persons practicing or offering to practice professional architectural or engineering services must provide evidence that they are qualified to practice and are properly licensed and registered. Architects and engineers receive different degrees in college and each are generally required to pass different professional examinations to become licensed. Architects and engineers are regulated and licensed on an individual state basis.

Services performed by architects and engineers overlap to some extent. Accordingly, many states recognize that registered architects can be the lead designer of a project through the practice of professional architecture, and a registered professional engineer can be the lead designer of a project through the practice of professional engineering. In other words, a degree of commonality exists between the disciplines that allows engineers and architects to assume some similar obligations, but this does not mean that the differences are not important or that licensing laws are not strictly enforced.[3]

---

3. In Rosen v. Bureau of Professional and Occupational Affairs, 763 A.2d 962 (Pa. Commw. Ct. 2000), an engineer and employee of a drafting company, who was retained by a building owner to survey the building and create a set of drawings for a renovation project, appealed from an order of the State Architects Licensure Board, enjoining the engineer from engaging in the practice of architecture without a license and imposing civil penalties. In reversing the board's decision, the Appellate Court held that the services of the engineer were within the practice of engineering and fell squarely within purview of architects licensure law. The appellate court

The consequences of practicing professional design services without a license can be serious. The court addressed this issue in *Sturdza v. United Arab Emirates*, in which an architect sued to recover fees from a foreign government for which she had provided architectural services on a breach of contract or quantum meruit theory.

Sturdza v. United Arab Emirates
11 A.3d 251 (D.C. 2011)[4]

I. Factual and Procedural Background

In 1993, the United Arab Emirates ("UAE") held a competition for the architectural design of a new embassy and chancery building in Washington, D.C. Elena Sturdza, an architect licensed under the laws of Maryland and Texas, but not by the District of Columbia, entered the competition and submitted a design. A jury composed of architects and civil engineers judged the competition entries. At the conclusion of the competition, the UAE informed Sturdza that she had won.

Sturdza and the UAE then entered into contract negotiations. Over the next two years they exchanged multiple contract proposals. During that period, at the UAE's request, Sturdza modified her design and worked with an engineer to address various technical issues. She agreed to defer billing the UAE for her work until the execution of their contract. At last, in early 1996, the UAE sent Sturdza a final draft agreement "incorporating all the changes mandated by the Ambassador." Sturdza informed the UAE that she assented to the changes. Without explanation, however, the UAE then stopped communicating with Sturdza. It never signed a contract with her.

There things stood until late 1997, when Sturdza learned that the UAE had furnished a proposed design for its new embassy to the National Capital Planning Commission. Sturdza obtained a copy of the proposal. She discovered that the UAE had submitted a design prepared by a District of Columbia architect named Angelos Demetriou. This design differed from the one Demetriou had entered in the 1993 competition and, Sturdza believed, it "copied and appropriated many of the design features that had been the hallmark of her design." The UAE eventually contracted with Demetriou to use his revised design in the construction of its embassy.

---

stated that nothing contained in the architect's licensure law shall be construed to prohibit engineers from performing such services included in the practice of architecture as may be incidental to their engineering services.

4. Sturdza v. United Arab Emirates, 11 A.3d 251 (D.C. 2011).

In 1998, Sturdza filed suit against the UAE and Demetriou in the United States District Court for the District of Columbia. Her amended complaint stated several causes of action against one or both defendants. The question that has been certified to us concerns Sturdza's breach of contract and quantum meruit claims against the UAE. Count One of the amended complaint alleged that the UAE had breached its contract with Sturdza by, *inter alia*, failing to memorialize their contract, "concerning which substantial performance had already commenced"; awarding the embassy design contract instead to Demetriou; and failing to pay Sturdza her fee, including her charges for the work she performed after the UAE declared her the winner of the competition. Count Two of the amended complaint sought quantum meruit recovery for Sturdza's preparation of the embassy design and other architectural services. The district court granted summary judgment for the UAE on each of these claims. It concluded that Sturdza is barred from recovering contractual or quasi-contractual damages under District of Columbia law because she was not licensed to practice architecture in the District either when she negotiated and contracted with the UAE or when she performed the services for which she sought compensation.

On appeal, the D.C. Circuit was "inclined to agree" that the District's licensing law precludes Sturdza's contractual and quasi-contractual causes of action. The court noted that Sturdza "went beyond submitting bids and actually performed architectural services—in her own words, 'substantially performed' the contract"—without the required license. For that reason, the court rejected Sturdza's contention that she merely sought to enforce a contract for future services and would have obtained a D.C. license before she actually rendered those services. Nonetheless, the court expressed uncertainty as to "the implications (if any)" of a statutory exception allowing architects licensed in other jurisdictions to agree to provide architectural services in the District if they became licensed under D.C. law before rendering any performance. In addition, the court observed, an unlicensed architect's right to recover in the circumstances of this case raises a question of "extreme public importance" given the special status of the District of Columbia:

> We assume that architects throughout the country (perhaps even around the world) unlicensed to practice in the District often submit bids to perform architectural services in this city of embassies, monuments, and public buildings. Precisely how D.C. law applies to this unique characteristic of Washington, D.C. and its economy is a question best resolved by the D.C. Courts.

Deeming local law to be "genuinely uncertain" on the issue of whether Sturdza's contract and quantum meruit claims were foreclosed in these circumstances, the D.C. Circuit concluded that "the wisest course of action" was to certify the question to the District of Columbia Court of Appeals.

II. The Scope of the Architectural Licensing Requirement

Beginning in 1950 with an amendment of the Architect's Registration Act, and continuing to the present day, the law of the District of Columbia has imposed a licensure requirement on the practice of architecture in this jurisdiction in order "to safeguard life, health, and property, and to promote the public welfare." In its current form, the D.C. Code provides in pertinent part that "[u]nless licensed to practice architecture under this subchapter, no person shall engage, directly or indirectly, in the practice of architecture in the District[. . .]." The same prohibition was in effect at the time of the events giving rise to this case. For licensing purposes, the "practice of architecture" is defined to mean "rendering or offering to render services in connection with the design and construction, enlargement, or alteration of a structure or group of structures that have as their principal purpose human occupancy or habitation [. . .] includ[ing] planning and providing studies, designs, drawings, specifications, and other technical submissions, and the administration of construction contracts." The "practice of architecture" thus encompasses not only the performance of architectural services, but also any negotiations and agreement to provide such services.

Enlarging upon the concern of the D.C. Circuit, Sturdza argues that the District's architectural licensing statute should not be construed to apply to architects who submit plans in the District in international architectural design competitions. According to Sturdza, "it is plain" that the consumer protection concerns underlying the licensure requirement do not apply to such competitions, because the purpose of the law is merely to protect "ordinary local DC consumers against fraudulent practices and representations by persons holding themselves out as experts.". . .

We are not persuaded by Sturdza's argument. It is not "plain" to us that the public welfare rationale for licensing architects is inapplicable to international competitions to design buildings such as the UAE embassy. For the safety and well-being of those who work in and visit such buildings, and of neighboring property owners, we would suppose the District has every reason to insist that the architects who design them and oversee their construction be qualified, and hence licensed, to do so. . . .

But even if we were prepared to agree with Sturdza on these matters, her argument founders on the plain language of the statute. The licensing requirement for the practice of architecture in the District is categorical. It contains no exemption for international design competitions; indeed, it admits of no exception based on the type of client or architectural service rendered. We must apply the statute as it is written and not create *ad hoc* exceptions by judicial decree based on nebulous policy considerations. Sturdza's arguments are addressed more properly to the legislature.

. . .

III. The Bar to Recovery for Unlicensed Practice

The rule is well-established in the District of Columbia "that a contract made in violation of a licensing statute that is designed to protect the public will usually be considered void and unenforceable, and [that] the party violating the statute cannot collect monies due on a quasi-contractual basis" either. Although the operation of this rule may appear to be "harsh and disproportionate" in some cases, we have "uniformly" rejected appeals to deviate from or mitigate it; the "potential unfair applications of the rule at the margins have not persuaded us to sacrifice the benefits of a clear-cut, unmistakable requirement, with equally clear consequences for noncompliance, in this area of consumer protection." Architects who practice without a license are not exempted from the general rule. We have held that one who engages in the "practice of architecture" in this jurisdiction without having secured the necessary District of Columbia license is barred from recovering for his or her services in an action for breach of contract or quantum meruit.

IV. Conclusion

Based on the preceding discussion, we answer the question certified to us by the D.C. Circuit as follows. District of Columbia law does bar an architect from recovering (i) on a contract to perform architectural services in the District or (ii) in quantum meruit for architectural services rendered in the District, if the architect lacked a District of Columbia architect's license when he or she began negotiating the contract, entered into the contract, or performed the architectural services, even if the architect was licensed to practice architecture in another jurisdiction at such times.[5]

6.03 BUILDING CODES AND THE DESIGN PROFESSIONAL

In addition to regulating design professionals so as to protect citizens, state and local governments also provide for the safety of their citizens by regulating construction directly through building codes. Building codes are an exercise of the state's police power to protect the public health, safety, and welfare.

---

5. *Id.* at 253–58 (internal citations and footnotes omitted). In addition to losing the right to compensation for design services, an unlicensed person may be subject to civil or criminal sanctions. *See, e.g.,* Twist Architecture & Design, Inc. v. Or. Bd. of Architect Examiners, 361 Or. 507, 395 P.3d 574, (Or. 2017) (administrative decision); Mich. Comp. Laws. Ann. § 339.601 (practicing a regulated occupation without a license is a crime).

Given this important purpose, designing a project to comply with applicable building codes is essential and a nondelegable duty. In *Johnson v. Salem Title Co.*,[6] a pedestrian on a public sidewalk was injured when a high wind caused a masonry wall to fall on him. The pedestrian sued the architect, landowner, general building contractor, and masonry contractor. After a jury trial, only the architect was found liable.[7] The Supreme Court of Oregon affirmed.[8]

> The plaintiff's only pleading of negligence was that the masonry wall as designed did not comply with a city building ordinance. While there is a conflict in the evidence concerning the velocity of the wind and the conformity of the wall to the city code, all these issues were for the jury unless some reason appears for taking the case from the jury. No such reason has been established.
>
> The architect contends that, whether or not the wall as designed actually met code specifications, it was approved by a city building inspector and the approval of the city's officer is conclusive proof that the wall did meet the requirements of the city ordinance. We are unable to accept such a proposition. If the law requires a certain standard to be met in order to protect the public and that standard is not in fact met, it would make no sense to hold that a building inspector's approval of negligent work could deny relief to injured persons for whose protection the law had been enacted. . . . Whether or not the building inspector's approval might estop the city in litigation between the city and an offending property owner is another question, one that is irrelevant in this case.
>
> Disregarding, therefore, the inspector's approval, we come to the question whether a wall designed contrary to the requirements of a building code can be found by the jury to have been negligently designed. The trial court instructed the jury that if the wall was not designed so as to comply with the city code such a violation would be negligence. The instruction was a substantially correct statement of the law. There was adequate evidence of statutory negligence.
>
> . . .
>
> The question of causation has been presented here in a number of assignments, but the essence of the defense was that the wind which blew on the day in question (October 12, 1962) was of such unprecedented velocity as to amount to a hurricane, or, in these latitudes, an 'act of God.' The jury was instructed accordingly, as requested by the defense, but the jury elected to

---

6. 246 Or. 409, 425 P.2d 519 (1967).

7. That is not to say that *only* design professionals can be found to have nondelegable duties related to building codes. In Marrick Homes LLC v. Rutkowski, 232 Md. App. 689 (Md. Ct. Spec. App. 2017), for example, a contractor was found to have a nondelegable duty to provide certain safety safeguards related to the manner of construction under the applicable building code.

8. Johnson v. Salem Title Co., 246 Or. 409, 425 P.2d 519 (1967).

believe that even in the face of such a wind a properly designed and constructed wall would not have blown down. There was evidence to support the verdict on this issue, and it cannot, therefore, be disturbed.

The final question is the legal effect of the architect's delegation of the design of the wall to an independent consulting engineer. The record does not disclose why the engineer was not made a party defendant, but the evidence is undisputed that the negligent designing of the wall was performed in the engineer's office. The architect, however, relied upon, incorporated into his drawings and specifications, and put his signature upon the work done by the engineer.

The general rule is that the employer of an independent contractor is not liable for the contractor's negligence. . . . However, there are significant exceptions to this rule. If the work to be done is 'inherently dangerous,' the employer is liable for his contractor's negligence. . . . Liability is also imposed in a large class of cases in which it is said as a matter of law that an employer's duty cannot be delegated. . . . Plaintiff contends that the architect was under such a nondelegable duty to design the wall in conformity with the building code.

Nondelegable duties arise in situations in which the law deems a particular duty 'so important and so peremptory that it will be treated as nondelegable * * *. Duties imposed by statute are often found to be of this kind * * *.

This exception to nonliability has been adopted by the American Law institute:

> One who by statute or by administrative regulation is under a duty to provide specified safeguards or precautions for the safety of others is subject to liability to the others for whose protection the duty is imposed for harm caused by the failure of a contractor employed by him to provide such safeguards or precautions.

. . .

The question, therefore, is whether an architect is required to comply with the building-code provisions concerning the structural engineering of walls in designing a building. If he is, then he cannot avoid responsibility by subcontracting that part of his work to others.

. . .

The defendant argues that, as a professional man, the standard of care applicable to him is measured by the practices of the reasonably prudent architect in the same locality. Since it is the custom of architects in Salem to refer engineering work to consulting engineers, he argues, his only obligation was to select a reliable engineering firm. This he did, thereby fulfilling, according to his view, his duty of exercising due care.

Defendant's reliance on local customs among his fellow professionals is misplaced. Selecting a competent engineering firm only indicates that the defendant himself was not negligent. It begs the question of vicarious liability. As Prosser says, "the cases of 'non-delegable duty go further, and hold the employer liable for the negligence of the (independent) contractor, although he has himself done everything that could reasonably be required of him. They are thus cases of vicarious liability."

. . .

In the case at bar the issues of negligence and causation were decided by the jury upon adequate evidence to support the verdict. The issue of vicarious liability was a question of law upon undisputed facts and was correctly resolved against the claim of independent-contractor immunity.[9]

From a contracting perspective, AIA-B101 does not address this issue directly but does include provisions that support the proposition that the architect has assumed responsibility for the work of its engineering consultants. Section 3.1 states that "the Architect's Basic Services consist of those described in this Article 3 and include customary structural mechanical and electrical engineering services."[10] This arguably means that the architect is responsible for these services. Section 3.2.1 also supports this conclusion as it provides in pertinent part:

> The Architect shall review the program and other information furnished by the Owner, and shall review laws, codes, and regulations applicable to the Architect's services.[11]

If an architect intends to avoid assuming responsibility for its consultant's services because the architect is relying on the consultant's professional expertise and is only coordinating their design work, then the architect needs to clearly address this issue in its agreement as discussed in Section 6.01.C.

A. Traditional Building Codes

A plethora of building codes exist that range from those developed by local municipalities, counties, states, and even an international code. The primary building codes in the United States are the International Building Code; the Uniform Building Code; the Standard Building Code; and the National Building Code; however, in each jurisdiction, the design must comply with the applicable requirements adopted by the authorities with jurisdiction over the project.

B. Socioeconomic "Codes"

Not all so-called codes applicable to projects are related to safeguarding life, health, and property. Instead of falling squarely within the category of building

---

9. *Id.* at 411–17, 425 P.2d at 520–22 (internal citations and footnotes omitted).
10. AIA Document B101–2017, *supra* note 2, § 3.1.
11. *Id.* § 3.2.1.

codes, these other codes have come to be known as socioeconomic codes. The following sections identify some of the most important requirements that fall under this category.

1. Accessibility under ADA

Design professionals must consider the requirements of the Americans with Disabilities Act (ADA), which is not a building code but a federal civil rights law enacted in 1990.[12] The primary purposes of the ADA is to eliminate discrimination against individuals with disabilities by ensuring full and equal enjoyment of places of public accommodation, including physical access to such places.

If the project involves multi-unit private housing, then the Fair Housing Act (FHA) may apply. The FHA was adopted in 1968 (and amended by the Fair Housing Amendments Act of 1988)[13] and prohibits discrimination based on race, color, religion, sex, national origin, familial status, and disability, in the operation, leasing, or sale of multi-unit housing.

Not all courts agree as to whether design professionals can be held liable under the ADA or the FHA. Some courts, such as those in Florida and Minnesota, have ruled that architects are responsible for following the mandates of the ADA.[14] Other courts, including those in Maryland, Mississippi, Nevada, Tennessee, Texas, and the U.S. District Court for the District of Columbia, have declined to hold architects responsible under the statute and rejected indemnity claims against architects on the basis that enforcing owners' indemnification claims for an owner's own ADA violations would undermine the goals of the ADA.[15] There has not been a definitive resolution of this question. Similar divergence of judicial opinions have arisen under the FHA.[16]

---

12. 42 U.S.C. § 12181 *et seq*.

13. 42 U.S.C. §§ 3601–3619.

14. United States v. Ellerbe Becket, Inc., 976 F. Supp. 1262 (D. Minn. 1997) (holding architectural firm liable for ADA violations despite fact that it was not the owner, operator, lessor, or lessee of any of the facilities it designed); *accord* Johanson v. Huizenga Holdings, Inc., 963 F. Supp. 1175 (S.D. Fla. 1997).

15. Rolf Jensen & Associates, Inc. v. Eighth Judicial District Ct. of the State of Nevada, 282 P.3d 743 (Nev. 2012); Lonberg v. Sanborn Theaters Inc. 259 F.3d 1029 (9th Cir. 2001); Paralyzed Veterans of Am. v. Ellerbe Becket Architects & Eng'rs, 945 F. Supp. 1 (D.D.C. 1996); and Whitaker v. W. Vill. Ltd. P'ship, No. CIV.A. 3:03-CV-0411P, 2004 WL 1778963, at *3 (N.D. Tex. Aug. 4, 2004).

16. Mont. Fair Hous. v. Am. Capital Dev., 81 F. Supp. 2d 1057 (D. Mont. 1999); Baltimore Neighborhoods, Inc. v. Rommel Builders, Inc., 3 F. Supp. 2d 661 (D. Md. 1998); United States v. The Bryan Co., No. 3:11-CV-302-CWR-LRA, 2012 WL 2051861, at *5 (S.D. Miss. June 6, 2012) (permitting indemnification claims for violations of the ADA or FHA would frustrate, disturb, interfere with, or seriously compromise the purposes of the FHA and ADA); *see also*, Equal Rights

2. Green Codes

Green, or sustainable, building is the practice of designing structures and using processes that are environmentally responsible and resource-efficient from the beginning all the way through to the end of the building's life cycle, that is, initial siting, design, construction, operation, maintenance, renovation, and deconstruction.[17] While the definition is somewhat subjective, green building is recognized as designing and constructing energy efficient projects by utilizing more resource efficient models of construction, renovation, operation, maintenance, and demolition.

As green building has become more popular, some jurisdictions have adopted favorable tax incentives or other economic benefits that favor green building; some jurisdictions require that new construction projects be designed in accordance with various environmental requirements. Like other building codes, no one uniformly accepted green building code exists. LEED, or Leadership in Energy and Environmental Design, is an example of a popular green building rating system that was developed by the U.S. Green Building Council for the design, construction, operation, and maintenance of green buildings.[18] A number of other third-party organizations also offer services to rate or compare green buildings.[19]

Regardless whether a green building is rated, sustainability success, as opposed to aspirations, requires close cooperation and coordination among the owner, contractor, architects, engineers, and the end users at all project stages. The new 2017 AIA documents recognize the growing interest in sustainable design. Section 3.2.5.1 of the AIA-B101 provides in pertinent part:

> The Architect shall consider sustainable design alternatives, such as material choices and building orientation, together with other considerations based on program and aesthetics, in developing a design that is consistent with the Owner's program, schedule and budget for the Cost of the Work.[20]

In addition, to the extent the owner identifies a sustainable objective (such as LEED certification or a goal of achieving some other specific benefit(s) to the environment, including enhancing the health and well-being of the

---

Center v. Archstone Smith Trust, 603 F. Supp. 2d 814, 824 (D. Md. 2009) and United States v. Murphy Dev., LLC, No. 3:08-0960, 2009 WL 3614829, at *2 (M.D. Tenn. Oct. 27, 2009).

17. U.S. Envtl. Prot. Agency, Green Bldg., http://epa.gov/greenbuilding.

18. *See* http://www.usgbc.org.

19. *See, e,g.*, National Green Building Standard, http://www.nahbgreen.org, Green Globes, http://www.greenglobes.com/; the Building Research Establishment Environmental Assessment Method, http://www.breeam.com/; The Well Building Standard, http://www.wellcertified.com/; and The Fitwel certification system, http://fitwel.org/.

20. AIA Document B101-2017, *supra* note 2, § 3.2.5.1.

building occupants; or improving energy efficiency, such as incorporation of performance-based sustainable design or construction elements) in Article 1 of the B101, the form contains a recommendation that the parties complete and incorporate the new AIA-E204™-2017, which is known as the sustainable projects exhibit. The E204–2017 recognizes that multiple parties must participate in achieving these goals, and sets forth the roles and responsibilities for all of the project participants. The intent is that E204–2017 will be incorporated into the owner–architect and owner–contractor agreements, and incorporated as appropriate into each of the other project agreements. No single party can guaranty full compliance with so-called green codes. The design team takes responsibility for producing designs compliant with relevant provisions of the green codes, although the architect or owner may hire a sustainability consultant to assist as well. The construction team must comply with the requirements related to construction, including those applicable to procurement of materials and disposal of waste. The owner will be responsible for proper maintenance and operation of the project to meet these requirements on an ongoing basis. While the E204–2017 was not created as a stand-alone document, it provides a useful overview of the risks, opportunities, responsibilities, and terms unique to projects involving substantial elements of sustainable design and construction. A few of the key terms are set forth here:

§ 1.2 Definitions

§ 1.2.1 Sustainable Objective

The Sustainable Objective is the Owner's goal of incorporating Sustainable Measures into the design, construction, maintenance and operations of the Project to achieve a Sustainability Certification or other benefit to the environment, to enhance the health and well-being of building occupants, or to improve energy efficiency. The Sustainable Objective is identified in the Sustainability Plan.

§ 1.2.2 Sustainable Measure

A Sustainable Measure is a specific design or construction element, or post occupancy use, operation, maintenance or monitoring requirement that must be completed in order to achieve the Sustainable Objective. The Owner, Architect and Contractor shall each have responsibility for the Sustainable Measure(s) allocated to them in the Sustainability Plan.

§ 1.2.3 Sustainability Plan

The Sustainability Plan is a Contract Document that identifies and describes: the Sustainable Objective; the targeted Sustainable Measures; implementation strategies selected to achieve the Sustainable Measures; the Owner's, Architect's and Contractor's roles and responsibilities associated with achieving the Sustainable Measures; the specific details about design reviews, testing or metrics to verify achievement of each Sustainable Measure; and the Sustainability Documentation required for the Project.

§ 1.2.4 Sustainability Certification

The Sustainability Certification is the initial third-party certification of sustainable design, construction, or environmental or energy performance, such as LEED®, Green Globes™, Energy Star or another rating or certification system, that may be designated as the Sustainable Objective or part of the Sustainable Objective for the Project. The term Sustainability Certification shall not apply to any recertification or certification occurring subsequent to the initial certification.

§ 1.2.5 Sustainability Documentation

The Sustainability Documentation includes all documentation related to the Sustainable Objective or to a specific Sustainable Measure that the Owner, Architect or Contractor is required to prepare in accordance with the Contract Documents. Responsibility for preparation of specific portions of the Sustainability Documentation will be allocated among the Owner, Architect and Contractor in the Sustainability Plan and may include documentation required by the Certifying Authority.

§ 6.1 The Owner, Contractor and Architect acknowledge that achieving the Sustainable Objective is dependent on many factors beyond the Contractor's and Architect's control, such as the Owner's use and operation of the Project; the work or services provided by the Owner's other contractors or consultants; or interpretation of credit requirements by a Certifying Authority. Accordingly, neither the Architect nor the Contractor warrant or guarantee that the Project will achieve the Sustainable Objective.

Alternatively, the parties can produce a manuscript agreement to allocate responsibilities for achieving the owner's sustainability goals.

3. *Historic and Landmark Preservation*

Building codes and laws related to historic and landmark preservation affect those properties designated as having historic importance and subject to preservation by the relevant governing body. From the design perspective, preservation means that the protection, repair, alteration, and relocation of such buildings must satisfy certain conditions to meet the authorities' goals. Often the architect has primary design responsibility for such code compliance. In some jurisdictions, where the historic preservation codes are particularly complex, it is common for a specialized historic preservation consultant to be retained by the owner or architect to advise on this aspect of the project. Since historic preservation codes can have an impact on the use, maintenance costs, and property valuation of the designated property, fundamental due process issues may be triggered by a designation for protection. For example, in *New Albany Historic Preservation Com'n v. Bradford Realty, Inc.*,[21] the Court of Appeals of Indiana ruled that historic preservation code requiring approval to replace wood clapboard siding with vinyl siding was valid and, relying upon *Mullane v. Central Hanover Bank & Trust Co.*,[22] held that the property owner's due process rights were not violated by the historic preservation code under the U.S. Constitution's Fourteenth Amendment.[23] In addition, in a ruling that is often cited in support of local authorities' ability to enact preservation laws, the U.S. Supreme Court has upheld the constitutionality of New York City's Landmarks Preservation Law under the U.S. Constitution's Fifth Amendment; the Court held that while the law could affect some property owners more than others, the Landmark Law was not discriminatory and did not, per se, constitute a taking of private property requiring compensation.[24]

6.04 STANDARD OF CARE APPLICABLE TO DESIGN SERVICES

A. Nature of Standard of Care and Inapplicability of Strict Liability

The law does not hold design professionals responsible for all the adverse consequences that may occur in a building, nor does the law expect every design to be flawless in every respect. The law only requires architects and engineers to be able to protect the public against certain dangers and flaws. It is understood that there may be numerous inconsequential errors in any sophisticated set of design documents. In articulating the design professional's liability, the courts do not hold design professionals strictly liable.[25] Instead, the law only

---

21. 965 N.E.2d 79 (2012).
22. 339 U.S. 306, 314, 70 S. Ct. 652, 94 L. Ed. 865 (1950).
23. *See, also* Donovan v. City of Deadwood, 538 N.W.2d 790 (S.D. 1995) (preservation commission could not constitutionally deny permit to demolish building even given viability of preservation code absent procedural due process safeguards).
24. Penn Cent. Transp. Co. v. City of New York, 438 U.S. 104, 98 S. Ct. 2646 (1978); *see also* Dist. Intown Properties Ltd. P'ship v. D.C., 198 F.3d 874 (D.C. Cir. 1999) (Court of Appeals ruled that denial of permits did not amount to total taking in case where owner was denied permits for construction of townhouses on lots which had been subdivided from the lawn of an apartment building, which was designated as historic landmark.).
25. *See, e.g.*, Three Affiliated Tribes of the Fort Berthold Reservation v. Wold Eng'g, P.E., 419 N.W.2d 920 (N.D. 1988); Nelson v. Commw., 368 S.E.2d 239 (N.E. 1988); Chaney Bldg. Co. v. City of Tucson, 716 P.2d 28 (Ariz. 1986); Carter v. Deitz, 556 So. 2d 842 (La. Ct. App. 4th Cir. 1990), *writ denied*, 566 So. 2d 992 (La. 1990) and *writ denied*, 566 So. 2d 993 (La. 1990) and *writ denied*, 566 So.2d 960 (La. 1990) (mere errors of judgment insufficient to establish liability; plaintiff must establish negligence).

imposes liability where there is fault. "Fault" in this sense means deviation from an identifiable standard of care.

The standard of care for an architect (and engineers) is well settled and dates back to at least the 19th century when the Supreme Court of Maine wrote the following in *Coombs v. Beede*:[26]

> The responsibility resting on an architect is essentially the same as that which rests upon the lawyer to his client, or upon the physician to his patient, or which rests upon anyone to another where such person pretends to possess some skill and ability in some special employment, and offers his services to the public on account of his fitness to act in the line of business for which he may be employed. The undertaking of an architect implies that he possesses skill and ability, including taste, sufficient to enable him to perform the required services at least ordinarily and reasonably well; and that he will exercise and apply in the given case his skill and ability, his judgment and taste, reasonably and without neglect. But the undertaking does not imply or warrant a satisfactory result. It will be enough that any failure shall not be by the fault of the architect. There is no implied promise that miscalculations may not occur. An error of judgment is not necessarily evidence of a want of skill or care, for mistakes and miscalculations are incident to all the business of life.[27]

The standard of care does not require a design professional to assume responsibility for the proper performance of products installed in a project as a result of the professional design, so long as the design was consistent with the standard of care. For example, in *Sime v. Tvenge Assocs. Architects & Planners, P.C.*,[28] husband and wife sued architect and engineer, alleging that ventilation system caused injuries to wife from carbon monoxide inhalation. The Supreme Court of North Dakota held that plaintiffs could not recover on strict products liability theory against architects or engineers for allegedly defective design of ventilation system because the policy reasons holding product manufacturers strictly liable did not apply to architectural design of building or ventilation system installed therein.

B. Common Law Standard of Care

1. General Statement of Standard of Care

Most jurisdictions agree that the standard of care for design professions is the standard that would be followed by their peers under similar circumstances.

---

26. Coombs v. Beede, 89 Me. 187, 36 A. 104 (1896).
27. *Id.* at 104.
28. Sime v. Tvenge Assocs. Architects & Planners, P.C., 488 N.W.2d 606 (N.D. 1992).

In a representative decision, the Supreme Court of Minnesota described the general statement of standard of care for architects and engineers as follows:

> The reasoning underlying the general rule as it applies both to architects and other vendors of professional services is relatively straightforward. Architects, doctors, engineers, attorneys, and others deal in somewhat inexact sciences and are continually called upon to exercise their skilled judgment in order to anticipate and provide for random factors which are incapable of precise measurement. The indeterminate nature of these factors makes it impossible for professional service people to gauge them with complete accuracy in every instance. Thus, doctors cannot promise that every operation will be successful; a lawyer can never be certain that a contract he drafts is without latent ambiguity; and an architect cannot be certain that a structural design will interact with natural forces as anticipated. Because of the inescapable possibility of error which inheres in these services, the law has traditionally required, not perfect results, but rather the exercise of that skill and judgment which can be reasonably expected from similarly situated professionals.[29]

2. Proof of the Standard of Care and Violation Thereof

Since architecture and engineering are, in many instances, technical in nature, in order to prove a cause of action for professional negligence against a design professional, expert witness testimony from someone with the requisite experience is generally necessary to establish failure to comply with the standard of care.[30]

In *Garaman, Inc. v. Williams*,[31] the owner retained an architect to design a motel complex. When the owner did not pay the architect the entire amount due the architect for his services, the architect filed a lawsuit against the owner. The owner filed a counterclaim against the architect, claiming that the architect had been negligent in performing his architectural services and that he had breached his contractual duties to the owner. During the bench trial, the architect testified, but the owner failed to present any expert testimony which would establish the standard of care applicable to the architect as a licensed architect or his breach of that standard of care. After losing at the bench trial, the owner appealed. The Supreme Court of Wyoming wrote, in pertinent part, the following:

> The owner did not present any independent expert testimony to establish the standard of care or the architect's breach of that standard. It insists, however, that the architect was an expert and that his testimony established the

---

29. City of Mounds View v. Walijarvi, 263 N.W.2d 420, 424 (Minn. 1978).
30. McKee By & Through McKee v. City of Pleasanton, 242 Kan. 649, 750 P.2d 1007 (1988).
31. Garaman, Inc. v. Williams, 912 P.2d 1121 (Wyo. 1996).

standard of care and his breach of that standard. The owner specifically refers to a segment of the architect's testimony in which he admitted that he had a duty to know the applicable building codes and that, in certain instances, his design of Phase I did not comply with the codes as the Town of Jackson subsequently interpreted them.

We conclude that, under the facts of this case, the architect's testimony was not sufficient to establish the applicable standard of care. The architect's testimony about an architect's duty to comply with the code requirements was simply too general to be considered as establishing an appropriate standard of care. We, therefore, do not need to decide whether, as a general rule, a defendant's testimony may be used to establish the appropriate standard of care.

The architect acknowledged that he had testified previously as an expert witness and that he possessed the degree of care, skill, etc. which a reasonable, careful, and prudent architect would commonly possess. He testified that an architect has a duty to know the applicable codes when he is designing a building. The architect testified that he believed that he had designed the building to meet the applicable code requirements but that, in a few instances, the completed building did not comply with those requirements. He also acknowledged that an architect may, in certain circumstances, be responsible when his design does not comply with building code requirements.

The architect also indicated, however, that code requirements may be difficult to interpret. In the course of designing the project, he had gotten the Town's approval for certain aspects of the design, but, when the building was completed, the Town officials recanted and concluded that the code requirements had not been met.

The owner suggests that, when an architect fails in any way to comply with an applicable code requirement, he is negligent. We do not agree. Much of an architect's work involves the application of his professional judgment, and, as we have stated before, we do not require professionals to warrant perfect results; we only require that they exercise the appropriate degree of care. See *Kemper Architects, P.C.*, 843 P.2d at 1186. The owner failed to question the architect in detail about the standard of care which applies when architects are faced with specific problems associated with interpreting and complying with building code requirements. The owner also did not question the architect about how a reasonably prudent architect would handle a situation in which the town changes its interpretation of the building codes between the time that the project was initially approved and the time that it was presented to the officials for final approval. The owner, therefore, failed to establish the applicable standard of care through appropriate expert testimony.

The owner also argues that it was not required to present expert testimony because the architect's performance was so deficient that laymen could discern the negligence. It is true that under Wyoming law expert testimony is not required when the professional's care was "so obviously wanting in reasonable skill that laymen would discern it." We conclude, however, that this case did not fall within the exception to the expert testimony requirement. A layman simply would not have had sufficient experience to understand architectural concepts such as the interpretation of building codes without being aided by expert testimony. Since the owner failed to present expert testimony about the standard of care, the district court properly granted a judgment as a matter of law in favor of the architect.[32]

3. Variations from Code and Consequences for Design Professionals

Under the common law, an undertaking by an architect or engineer "does not imply or guarantee a perfect plan."[33] One caveat to this general rule is that a design professional's failure to comply with a clear building code requirement is considered to be negligence per se.[34]

Not all failures to comply with applicable codes rise to the level of negligence per se. Some issues of code compliance are subject to alternative interpretations so that compliance is evaluated subject to the governing standard of care as discussed in Section 6.04.A and in Section B. As set forth in *St. Joseph Hospital v. Corbetta Construction Co., Inc.*,[35] architects and engineers represent themselves to be competent in preparation of plans and specifications necessary to construction of suitable structures, including but not limited to knowledge of and compliance with applicable building codes. Thus, when design professionals fail to use reasonable care to produce a satisfactory structure in compliance therewith, they may be sued for breach of implied contract term or for negligence.[36]

Most cases addressing this issue are fact sensitive. For example, in *Simon v. Drake Construction Co.*,[37] the plaintiff construction worker who fell off a ladder at the project site failed to establish a supportable claim that the architect

---

32. *Id.* 912 P.2d at 1124.

33. Bayshore Dev. Co. v. Bonfoey, 75 Fla. 455, 78 So. 507, 510 (1918).

34. Burran v. Dambold, 422 F.2d 133 (1970) (Engineer was guilty of negligence per se for drafting plans and specifications for a building that failed to comply with the applicable building code); St. Joseph Hosp. v. Corbetta Constr. Co., Inc., 316 N.W.2d 51 (Ill. 1974) (architect found liable for owner's costs to replace non-code compliant wall covering); Raymond v. Baehr, 163 N.W.2d 51 (Minn. 1968) (violation of code requiring fireproof materials in vent shafts held negligence per se, despite evidence that building code was not published as strictly required by state law); Kincaid v. Landing Dev. Corp., 344 S.E.2d 869 (S.C. App. 1986) (violation of a statute was negligence per se).

35. St. Joseph Hosp. v. Corbetta Constr. Co., Inc., 21 Ill. App. 3d 925, 316 N.E.2d 51 (1974).

36. Himmel Corp. v. Stade, 52 Ill. App. 3d 294, 367 N.E.2d 411 (1977).

37. Simon v. Drake Constr. Co., 87 Ohio App. 3d 23, 621 N.E.2d 837 (8th Dist. Cuyahoga Cnty. 1993).

who prepared the plans for the construction project committed malpractice. The worker introduced expert testimony that the architect's plans failed to comply with an OSHA regulation requiring ladder wells, but the expert's testimony did not state that this failure violated the applicable standard of care. The court concluded that while the plan's failure to comply with the regulation was some evidence of negligence, it was not negligence per se.

C. Contractual Standard of Care

If the owner and design professional do not wish to leave the standard of care to be decided in accordance with common law, they can agree to a standard in the contract. Section 2.2 of the AIA Document B101 provides a sample standard of care provision as follows:

> The Architect shall perform its services consistent with the professional skill and care ordinarily provided by architects practicing in the same or similar locality under the same or similar circumstances. The Architect shall perform its services as expeditiously as is consistent with such professional skill and care and the orderly progress of the Project.[38]

The Standard Form of Agreement between Owner and Engineer for Professional Services published by the Engineers Joint Contract Documents Committee goes further and expressly disclaims warranties:

> **6.01 Standards of Performance**
>
> *A. Standard of Care.* The standard of care for all professional engineering and related services performed or furnished by Engineer under this Agreement will be the care and skill ordinarily used by members of the subject profession practicing under similar circumstances at the same time and in the same locality. Engineer makes no warranties, express or implied, under this Agreement or otherwise, in connection with Engineer's services.[39]

These examples articulate the standard common law definition. Sometimes the standard of care set forth in the contract will be a heightened standard that goes beyond the common law. Consider the following hypothetical, heightened language:

> Architect/engineer shall perform its services consistent with the *highest* professional skill and care provided by design professionals practicing in the same or similar locality under the same or similar circumstances.

---

38. AIA Document B101–2017, *supra* note 2, § 2.2.

39. Engineers Joint Contract Documents Committee, E-500 (2008), Agreement Between Owner and Engineer for Professional Services.

In other words, design professionals can contractually commit to perform to a standard of care that is higher than the common law standard. By agreeing to perform to a heightened standard of care, the design professional will be held to perform in accordance with the terms of the contract.[40]

D. Implied Warranties and Design Professionals

1. Implied Warranties Generally in Construction

As discussed in Chapter 20, under the *Spearin* Doctrine,[41] an owner impliedly warrants that the plans and specifications, if followed, are sufficient for construction and will result in a properly functioning project. In the absence of an express contract provision disclaiming responsibility for implied warranties, whether a design professional can be held liable to an owner for an implied warranty regarding the suitability of plans and specifications is not as clear.

2. Different Treatment of Design Professionals and Implied Warranties

a. Jurisdictions Imposing Implied Warranties

In *Hill v. Polar Pantries*,[42] the South Carolina Supreme Court ruled against an equipment vendor who was not experienced in design, but provided defective plans. The court stated:

> where 'a person holds himself out as specially qualified to perform work of a particular character, there is an implied warranty that the work which he undertakes shall be of proper workmanship and reasonable fitness for its intended use, and, if a party furnishes specifications and plans for a contractor to follow in a construction job, he thereby impliedly warrants their sufficiency for the purpose in view.[43]

A few other courts have reached similar conclusions.[44]

---

40. CH2M Hill Southeast, Inc. v. Pinellas Cnty., 698 So. 2d 1238 (1997). *See also* Sch. Bd. of Broward Cnty. v. Pierce Goodwin Alexander, 137 So.3d 1059 (2014) (architect was held liable to perform to a higher standard of care delivery of design plans for a building that would be code-compliant, rather than merely requiring plans that would be prepared in accordance with ordinary and reasonable skill).

41. United States v. Spearin, 248 U.S. 132 (1918).

42. Hill v. Polar Pantries, 219 S.C. 263, 64 S.E.2d 885 (1951).

43. *Id.* at 279, 64 S.E. 2d at 888, quoting in part 17 C.J.S. Contracts § 329, at 871.

44. *See also*, Broyles v. Brown Eng'g Co., 275 Ala. 35, 151 So. 2d 767 (1963); Bloomsburg Mills, Inc. v. Sordoni Constr. Co., 401 Pa. 358, 164 A.2d 201 (1960); Beachwalk Villas Condo. Ass'n v. Martin, 305 S.C. 144, 406 S.E.2d 372 (1991) ("[i]f a party furnishes plans and specifications for a contractor to follow in a construction job, he thereby impliedly warrants their sufficiency for the purpose in view."); Tommy L. Griffin Plumbing & Heating Co. v. Jordan, Jones & Goulding, Inc., 320 S.C. 49, 463 S.E.2d 85 (1995) (Engineer of water trunk construction project

b. Refusal to Imply Warranties for Design Professionals

Other courts have refused to imply a warranty by the design professional. In *Allied Properties v. John A. Blume & Assocs.*,[45] the owner sued the engineers retained by the owner to make a feasibility study for a pier for small boats and to design the pier. After a judgment in favor of the engineers, the owner appealed. The Court of Appeal affirmed and followed the well-settled rule in California that where the primary objective of a transaction is to obtain services, the doctrines of implied warranty and strict liability simply do not apply. As originally stated in *Gagne v. Bertram*,[46] the court reiterated:

> The services of experts are sought because of their special skill. They have a duty to exercise the ordinary skill and competence of members of their profession, and a failure to discharge that duty will subject them to liability for negligence. Those who hire such persons are not justified in expecting infallibility, but can expect only reasonable care and competence. They purchase service, not insurance.[47]

Other courts have similarly rejected implied warranties in the owner/architect relationship.[48]

6.05 PERFORMANCE SPECIFICATIONS VERSUS DESIGN SPECIFICATIONS

It is important to note that the design team does not always provide the only set of specifications on a given project. There are two types of specifications: design specifications and performance specifications. A design specification is

---

could be held liable to contractor for breaching implied warranty that plans and specifications furnished to contractor to follow in construction job were sufficient for purpose in view despite fact that no contractual privity existed between engineer and contractor.); and White v. Mitchell, 123 Wash. 630, 213 Pac. 10 (1923) (A contract to construct a new dwelling is one for work, labor and materials. Appellant held itself out as an experienced builder. It furnished the plans for the house. We have no hesitancy in saying, under the circumstances, the trial court was correct in holding that there was an implied warranty that the completed house would be fit for human habitation.).

45. Allied Properties v. John A. Blume & Assocs., 25 Cal. App. 3d 848, 102 Cal. Rptr. 259 (1972).

46. Gagne v. Bertram, 43 Cal. 2d 481, 275 P.2d 15 (1954),

47. *Gagne*, 43 Cal. 2d at 489–90, 275 P.2d at 21.

48. Sienna Court Condo. Ass'n v. Champion Aluminum Corp., 2017 IL App (1st) 143364, 75 N.E.3d 260 (2017), *rev'd on other grounds*, 2018 IL 122022, ___ N.E.3d ___ (2018); Albion Coll. v. Stockade Bldgs. Inc., 2016 WL 2908262, at *8 (Mich. App. 2016); Gravely v. Providence P'ship, 549 F.2d 958 (4th Cir. 1977) (applying Virginia law); Ryan v. Morgan Spear Assoc., Inc., 546 S.W.2d 678 (Texas Civ. App. Corpus Christi 1977), *writ refused n.f.e.*, (June 1, 1977) (implied warranty not recognized in Texas).

prepared by the design team and retained by the owner. To the extent the design team's documents include performance specifications, the contractor is the party that will furnish detailed specifications consistent with the design criteria as specified by the owner's design team. Typically, the contractor will be required to directly retain licensed design professionals to prepare the detailed specifications for execution of the work based on the owner's design team's performance criteria. This issue is explored in more depth in Chapter 3 of this book. At this juncture, it is enough to state that design specifications direct a contractor as to the specific manner in which construction is to be accomplished, and the contractor's responsibility is to ensure that it adheres to the design specifications. A performance specification, on the other hand, describes the overall *results* to be accomplished as measured by performance criteria; the contractor's responsibility is to ensure that the construction satisfies those criteria. As a simple example, a design specification may call out four permissible models of pumps from which the contractor must choose, while a performance specification might specify only the pump capacity for particular placement in a processing plant and leave the selection of the pump to the contractor.

With respect to performance specifications, the contractor, in some sense, bears responsibility for the design of the work so as to ensure compliance with performance criteria. If the contractor's work fails to achieve the stated performance criteria, the contractor generally is liable for the insufficiency or inappropriateness of the design of that portion of the construction. As set forth in *Stuyvesant Dredging Co. v. U.S.*,[49] design specifications define how the work is to be performed and permit no deviations. Contractors have no responsibility for the adequacy of the design specifications. Performance specifications, on the other hand, merely specify the ultimate results to be obtained, and place responsibility on the contractor to determine how to achieve the results specified.[50] Often this requires the contractor to retain licensed design professionals to accomplish this task. Some projects may have both design and performance specifications.[51]

Another key distinction between the two types of specifications, as discussed previously in Section 6.04.C.2, is that design specifications may be deemed to contain an implied warranty that if specifications are followed, an acceptable result will be produced. Performance specifications contain no

---

49. Stuyvesant Dredging Co. v. U.S., 834 F.2d 1576 (1987).
50. *See also* J.L. Simmons Co. v. United States, 412 F.2d 1360, 1362, 188 Ct. Cl. 684 (1969).
51. Blake Constr. Co. v. United States, 987 F.2d 743, 746 (Fed. Cir. 1993) (citing Utility Contractors, Inc. v. United States, 8 Cl. Ct. 42, 50 n.7 (1985); Aleutian Constructors v. United States, 24 Cl. Ct. 372, 379 (1991)).

warranty of accuracy or adequacy.[52] For that reason, most disputes in this area focus on whether the specifications are design or performance specifications. If the plans and specifications are not the functional equivalent of a road map that a contractor would be expected to follow closely, the plans and specifications would be considered performance specifications or some type of hybrid specification. In other words, some degree of ingenuity, thought, and originality is required of the contractor.[53] Examples might include performance specifications for a curtain wall or an HVAC system.

6.06 THE DESIGN AGREEMENT: SCOPE OF THE DESIGN SERVICES

The owner–design professional agreement should clearly set forth the basic tenets of the understanding between the parties. Without a clear set of mutually agreed expectations, increased risk exists that at least one of the parties to the agreement is likely to be disappointed. The negotiation of the contract gives owners and design professionals a chance to reasonably align their expectations. Even if the parties begin with a standard form agreement, more often than not, they should tailor it to the specific needs of the project at hand.

At a minimum, the parties need to define important terms such as compensation, schedule, and scope of services. Equally important is to come to a mutual understanding of the owner's program. This will require the parties to explore the information the parties have to describe the project. Here are just a few of the questions the agreement must answer: Is all necessary information required for the design of the project available? Does the owner have to hire consultants to perform investigation services regarding the site? Has the owner developed a program or will the architect's assistance be necessary to do so? When does the owner expect to occupy the project? How active will be design team be in the project during construction? What are the applicable insurance requirements? Are there any limitations on liability? How do the parties want to resolve disputes? Reference to the AIA Document B101 will be helpful to address many of these issues, but this form is not the only approach the parties may take to define their respective obligations.

---

52. John Massman Contracting Co. v. United States, 23 Cl. Ct. 24 (1991) and Willamette Crushing Co. v. Arizona ex rel. Dep't of Transp. 188 Ariz. 79, 81, 932 P.2d 1350, 1352 (App. 1997).

53. Sterling Millwrights, Inc. v. United States, 26 Cl. Ct. 49, 114 (1992).

A. Phases of the Design Process

For a typical Design-Bid-Build project, the design team begins the complicated design process in a predictable sequence. The standard design phases have been developed over the course of many years and their linear progression runs from conceptual design through construction documents and concludes with construction administration.

Although most AIA documents, including the AIA B101–2017, assume that the project program has been developed by the owner in advance or will be developed with the assistance of the architect as an additional service, this is not always the case, particularly on large, complex projects. On such projects the owner is likely to collaborate with its design team to develop the initial program intended, at a conceptual level, to establish the rough parameters for the size and shape of the project. The owner may have construction advisors who participate in this process as well. At this stage, commonly known as the conceptual design phase, the design team may investigate various conceptual options for the owner to consider. This phase includes critical decisions regarding the overall building type, assumptions about the construction of the project, the scheduling for the project, the general shape and location of the project, and the intended use of the project. These considerations, which should be memorialized in the design agreement, might include:

1. Is the project a new, ground-up building or an addition, renovation, or restoration?
2. What is the design professional's role, for example, design architect (who develops the design concept), architect of record (who prepares the construction documents and provides construction phase services), or engineering consultant? Who retains the other consultants? Was another design professional previously involved?
3. Must any site features or limitations be addressed?
4. What is the owner's project budget? Is funding in place? Is a lender involved?
5. What is the projected footprint for the building? How many square feet? How many floors?
6. Is the project a mixed use building (i.e., commercial, residential, and retail) or a single use building?
7. Will the project include unique and innovative architectural designs or be a simpler architectural structure?
8. Is a building information model required? If so, who prepared and maintains it?

9. Is the owner prepared to invest higher initial capital costs to obtain lower operating costs (such as more sophisticated mechanical and electrical systems); or is the owner prepared to trade lower initial costs for higher operating costs (such as less sophisticated and presumably less efficient mechanical and electrical systems and/or less durable materials)?
10. How critical is the schedule? When does the owner intend to bring the contractor on board?
11. What are the expectations for the design professional to visit the site and perform other services during construction?
12. Does the owner have a sustainability objective, that is, whether to design and construct an environmentally sensitive building that uses, to the extent economically practicable, reusable materials as well as materials currently determined to be environmentally friendly?

The Initial Information Section of the AIA Document B101-2017 addresses many of these issues.

Using the AIA Document B101-2017 as a guide, the following subsections discuss the traditional design phases of a project: schematic design, design development, construction documents, bidding or negotiation, and construction administration.

1. *Schematic Design Phase*

Having conceptually established the type of project the owner wishes to develop, and with a rough sense of a project's size, shape, scope, and the owner's budget, the design team works to flesh out the design of the project contemplated by the owner in accordance with the agreed criteria. The following are pertinent sections from the AIA Document B101-2017:

§ 3.2.1 The Architect shall review the program and other information furnished by the Owner, and shall review laws, codes, and regulations applicable to the Architect's services.

§ 3.2.2 The Architect shall prepare a preliminary evaluation of the Owner's program, schedule, budget for the Cost of the Work, Project site, the proposed procurement and delivery method, and other Initial Information, each in terms of the other, to ascertain the requirements of the Project. The Architect shall notify the Owner of (1) any inconsistencies discovered in the information, and (2) other information or consulting services that may be reasonably needed for the Project.

§ 3.2.3 The Architect shall present its preliminary evaluation to the Owner and shall discuss with the Owner alternative approaches to design and construction of the Project. The Architect shall reach an understanding with the Owner regarding the requirements of the Project.

§ 3.2.4 Based on the Project requirements agreed upon with the Owner, the Architect shall prepare and present, for the Owner's approval, a preliminary design illustrating the scale and relationship of the Project components.

§ 3.2.5 Based on the Owner's approval of the preliminary design, the Architect shall prepare Schematic Design Documents for the Owner's approval. The Schematic Design Documents shall consist of drawings and other documents including a site plan, if appropriate, and preliminary building plans, sections and elevations; and may include some combination of study models, perspective sketches, or digital representations. Preliminary selections of major building systems and construction materials shall be noted on the drawings or described in writing.

§ 3.2.5.1 The Architect shall consider sustainable design alternatives, such as material choices and building orientation, together with other considerations based on program and aesthetics, in developing a design that is consistent with the Owner's program, schedule and budget for the Cost of the Work. The Owner may obtain more advanced sustainable design services as a Supplemental Service under Section 4.1.1.[54]

At this point, the design is still preliminary, but the details are beginning to take shape as the architect presents the schematic design submission for the owner's review and approval.

2. Design Development Phase

Once the schematic design phase is completed and approved by the owner, the design advances into the design development phase. During design development, the scope of features of the project agreed to in the schematic design phase are further developed and refined. All of the major systems for the project are identified and substantially designed and accounted for, although the overall design is not fully completed and coordinated at this time. Section 3.3.1 of the AIA Document B101–2017 provides more detail as follows:

> The Design Development Documents shall illustrate and describe the development of the approved Schematic Design Documents and shall consist of drawings and other documents including plans, sections, elevations, typical construction details, and diagrammatic layouts of building systems to fix and describe the size and character of the Project as to architectural, structural, mechanical and electrical systems, and other appropriate elements. The Design Development Documents shall also include outline specifications that identify major materials and systems and establish, in general, their quality levels.[55]

---

54. AIA Document B101–2017, *supra* note 2.
55. *Id.* § 3.3.1.

The design development phase ends by delivery to the owner of the design development documents for review and approval. Once such approval is obtained, along with any authorization for changes in the project design or other project requirements, the architect proceeds with the construction documents phase.

3. Construction Documents Phase

During the construction documents phase, all design elements of the project are fully designed and all engineering disciplines are coordinated with each other and with the overall design. Section 3.4.1 of the AIA Document B101–2017 provides that:

> The Construction Documents shall illustrate and describe the further development of the approved Design Development Documents and shall consist of Drawings and Specifications setting forth in detail the quality levels and performance criteria of materials and systems and other requirements for the construction of the Work. The Owner and Architect acknowledge that, in order to perform the Work, the Contractor will provide additional information, including Shop Drawings, Product Data, Samples and other similar submittals, which the Architect shall review in accordance with Section 3.6.4.[56]

The construction documents are expected to be sufficiently detailed so that the contractor will be able to construct the project. Many agreements provide that during this phase, the architect will provide construction documents to facilitate obtaining required approvals of the design from the applicable authorities and will assist the owner in connection with confirming that the project is consistent with the owner's budget.

4. Bidding or Negotiation Phase Services

During this phase, the actual cost of the project is determined based on bids on proposals from contractors based on the construction documents. Depending on the complexity of the project and whether the owner has retained preconstruction management services from the contractor team, the design team may or may not be retained to provide bidding or negotiation phase services. To the extent the architect is retained to perform typical functions during this phase, the parties' agreement must describe them. The AIA Document B101 specifies a number of services the architect will perform in connection with the owner's obtaining bids or negotiated proposals from contractors.[57]

---

56. *Id.* § 3.4.1.
57. *Id.* §§ 3.5.1, 3.5.2, 3.5.3.

5. Construction Phase Services

Although this phase is described in greater detail in Chapter 7, it is important to bear in mind that this phase must be addressed in sufficient detail in the contracts between the owner and architect as well as contracts with other members of the design team. Construction phase services typically commence after the contractor or construction manager is brought on board and various trade contractors are hired. During this phase, the subcontractors take the design team's construction documents and augment them through the preparation of shop drawings, which shop drawings contain detailed information required for the execution of the construction. The shop drawings are then sent back through the general contractor or construction manager to the design team to check for general conformance with the intended design. Once the design team signs off on the shop drawings, they are returned to the contractors to commence ordering, fabricating, and erecting or installing the various components of the project.

While the project is under construction, the contractors oversee their various trades, coordinated by either the construction manager or the general contractor on behalf of the owner. Typically, the design team will have some involvement in periodically visiting the project site to determine if, in general, the work is progressing in accordance with their plans and specifications. Members of the design team may also be involved in reviewing the contractor's applications for payment and change orders as described in the applicable contract provisions, such as AIA Document B101 §§ 3.6.3 and 3.6.5. This subject and the shop drawing process are covered in more detail in Chapter 7.[58]

B. Basic Services versus Supplemental or Additional Services

Similar to the contractor who receives a change order from the owner as a result of a change in the work, if the owner requests the design team to perform services that were not part of the original scope of services and the agreed fee for those services (basic services), the design team would receive authorization and compensation to perform supplemental or additional services (collectively, additional services). A myriad of reasons could justify compensation for additional services, but whether a task qualifies as an additional service is typically governed by the contract terms.[59] It would be unfair to burden the architect with obligations not contemplated upon execution of the agreement

---

58. Section 3.6 of the AIA Document B101 provides detailed rights and responsibilities of the parties during the Construction Administration Phase.

59. Article 4 from the AIA Document B101-2017 is dedicated to additional services.

between the owner and architect and to not provide for additional compensation. Also, because the need and scope of additional services cannot be predicted with certainty at the time of contracting, the architect often is paid for additional services on a time and material basis. Such a compensation method may differ from that used for compensation of basic services and may not be subject to the limitations and other price protections that apply to the performance of basic services.

To the extent the owner and design team have clearly identified the parameters of the basic services, defining additional services becomes less complicated. Compensation for additional services can be determined in different ways, such as fixed amount, on an hourly (time and material) basis, or based on a percentage of the cost of the related construction work. Article 4 of AIA Document B101–2017 provides a detailed description of services that are typically considered additional services, such as changes to design documents that previously had been approved by the owner; more extensive services related to LEED certification or other sustainability goals; services necessitated by changes in applicable laws or in the project requirements; services caused by an extension of the agreed duration of the architect's services; services necessitated by unanticipated conditions that arise during construction or by a default of a contractor; or other services outside the agreed scope of the architects services. All of these circumstances require the architect to devote more time and resources to the project than originally contemplated and, as a result, trigger an entitlement to increased compensation.

6.07 THE DESIGN AGREEMENT: THE OWNER'S RESPONSIBILITIES

The conventional roles of the parties are that the architect designs, the contractor builds, and the owner pays. Variations on this theme occur, but this description is still fairly accurate. The owner's typical responsibilities include the following:[60]

- ☐ Providing information regarding requirements for and limitations on the project.
- ☐ Periodically updating the budget for the project, including that portion allocated for the cost of the work.
- ☐ Rendering decisions in a timely manner pertaining to documents submitted by the architect in order to avoid unreasonable delay in the orderly and sequential progress of the architect's services.

---

60. *See, e.g.*, AIA Document B101–2017, *supra* note 2, art. 5.

- ❏ Furnishing the services of certain consultants when specialized services are requested by the architect and reasonably are required by the scope of the project.
- ❏ Furnishing tests, inspections, and reports required by law or the construction contract, such as structural, mechanical, and chemical tests, tests for air and water pollution, and tests for hazardous materials.
- ❏ Furnishing all legal, insurance, and accounting services, including auditing services, that may be reasonably necessary at any time for the project to meet the owner's needs and interests.
- ❏ Providing prompt written notice to the architect if the owner becomes aware of any fault or defect in the project.

This allocation of responsibilities in most agreements between an owner and architect, including the AIA Document B101, reflects a philosophy that (1) the owner contributes the real property to the project and is responsible for its physical condition, as well as the procurement of services needed to evaluate or describe the property, and (2) the owner should obtain from others the design and consulting services that the architect does not customarily perform or manage.[61]

6.08   THE DESIGN AGREEMENT: OWNERSHIP OF THE DESIGN DOCUMENTS

The key work-product produced by the design team is the design documents in various stages of development. Since those documents are of critical importance in enabling the owner to proceed with a project, resolution of issues regarding ownership of these documents is a very important term in a design contract.

A. Applicable Legal Principles

According to federal law, in the absence of a contract provision transferring rights of ownership, the architect retains the copyright to the drawings and specifications that the architect prepares.

The statutory framework that provides such protection to architects and other design professionals was described in *The Yankee Candle Co., Inc. v. New England Candle Co., Inc.*:[62]

---

61. *See, e.g., id.*
62. Yankee Candle Co. v. New England Candle Co., 14 F. Supp. 2d 154 (D. Mass. 1998), *vacated pursuant to settlement*, 29 F. Supp. 2d 44 (Mem) (D. Mass 1998).

The Copyright Act grants a copyright owner exclusive rights in a copyrighted work to authorize reproduction of the work, preparation of derivative works, and public display of the work. 17 U.S.C. §§ 106–20. To establish ownership of a valid copyright, a plaintiff must prove that "the work, when viewed as a whole, is original" and satisfy the required statutory formalities. [Citations Omitted] A work need only exhibit a "minimal degree of creativity" to qualify for copyright protection. [Citations Omitted].

(1) Among the statutory formalities, the Copyright Act requires registration of a work before a plaintiff may file suit. 17 U.S.C. § 411(a). The Copyright Office, after accepting an application, fee, and deposit of a representative copy of the work, see 17 U.S.C.§ 410(c), issues a certificate of registration, which is admissible in an infringement action as "prima facie evidence of the validity of the copyright and of the facts stated in the certificate," §17 U.S.C. 410(c). "In judicial proceedings, a certificate of copyright registration constitutes prima facie evidence of copyrightability and shifts the burden to the defendant to demonstrate why the copyright is not valid." [Citations Omitted]

In passing the Copyright Act of 1976, Congress expressly indicated that architectural plans and drawings deserved copyright protection as "pictorial, graphic and sculptural work" under 17 U.S.C. §101. See H.R.Rep. No. 94-1476, *reprinted* in 1976 U.S.C.C.A.N. 5659, 5668 ("An architect's plans and drawings would, of course, be protected by copyright [law]"). Congress, however, also indicated that architectural structures built from plans possessed only minimal copyright protection.

After the passage of the 1976 Act, courts extended federal copyright protection to architectural plans, but not to buildings constructed from those plans. *See Robert R. Jones Assoc. v. Nino Homes,* 858 F.2d 274, 280 (6th Cir. 1988) ("one may construct a house which is identical to a house depicted in copyrights architectural plans, but one may not directly copy those plans and then use the infringing copy to construct the house"); *Donald Frederick Evans v. Continental Homes, Inc.,* 785 F.2d 897, 901 n. 7 (11th Cir. 1986) ("A builder who constructs a home substantially similar to a dwelling already constructed is not liable for copyright infringement merely based on the substantial similarity if he or she did not engage in an unauthorized copying or use of the copyrighted architectural drawings"); *Demetriades v. Kaufmann,* 680 F.Supp. 658, 665–66 (S.D.N.Y. 1988) (enjoining defendant from copying plaintiff's architectural plans or relying on infringing copies in construction but declining to enjoin construction of defendant's substantially similar house);

In 1990, the Architectural Works Copyright Protection Act ("AWCPA") codified the copyright prophylaxis of architectural plans and architectural works. *See* Pub.L.No. 101-650, Tit. VII, 104 Stat. 5133 (1990) (codified in scattered sections of 17 U.S.C.). The AWCPA makes an "architectural work" an "original work of authorship" eligible for copyright protection. 17 U.S.C. § 102(a)(8). The copyright Act defines an architectural work as "the design of a building as embodied in any tangible medium of expression, including a building, architectural plans, or drawings. The work includes the overall form as well as the arrangement and composition of spaces and elements in the design but does not include individual standard features." 17 U.S.C.§101.

(2) With the passage of the AWCPA, a copyright owner may claim infringement of both the architectural plans and the structure based on such plans. See H.R.Rep. 101-735, reprinted in 1990 U.S.C.C.A.N. 6935, 6950 ("Either or both of these copyrights may be infringed and eligible separately for damages"). Since the passage of the AWCPA, Courts have routinely protected modern architectural structures, such as commercial homes, that possess the minimal amount of originality that copyright law requires, as well as the plans from which owners built them. See *Johnson v. Jones*, 921 F. Supp. 1573, 1583 (E.D. Mich.1996), protecting residential home as architectural work; *Value Group, Inc. v. Mendham Lake Estates, L.P.*, 800 F. Supp. 1228, 1233–35(D.N.J.1992), enjoining construction of house that would infringe on developer's copyrighted single family luxury home.[63]

Often litigation focuses on whether the copyright holder's work is sufficiently original to be entitled to copyright protection. In *Shine v. Childs*, the court analyzed this issue in detail.[64] Plaintiff was a student in the masters of architecture program at the Yale School of Architecture. As part of the required curriculum in his program, he took a studio class on skyscrapers and was required to create a design proposal for a monumental skyscraper. Plaintiff Shine developed a preliminary model that he called Shine '99 and, after putting in more effort, created a more sophisticated model of his design, entitled Olympic Tower. In 1999, Shine presented both designs to a jury of experts invited by the Yale School of Architecture to evaluate and critique its students' work. Defendant Childs was on the panel, and he praised Olympic Tower during the presentation, as did the other luminaries evaluating Shine's work. Shine does not allege that he had any contact with Childs after the December 1999 panel evaluation. However, he does claim that Childs' design for the Freedom Tower, unveiled four years later, infringed Shine '99 and Olympic Tower. Shine thereafter commenced an infringement action against Childs and his firm, alleging infringement of original skyscraper design. Defendants moved to dismiss or for summary judgment and argued the following:

> neither Shine '99 nor Olympic Tower qualifies as an architectural work under the Copyright Act. They argue also that both designs are unoriginal and functional, and therefore unworthy of whatever copyright protection they currently

---

63. *Id.* at 157–58.
64. Shine v. Childs, 382 F. Supp. 2d 602 (S.D.N.Y. 2005).

have. Finally, assuming that plaintiff's copyrights are valid, defendants deny that they copied plaintiff's designs, and assert that there is no substantial similarity between plaintiff's designs and the Freedom Tower. Plaintiff counters that Shine '99 and Olympic Tower are each original, copyrightable designs, that defendants actually copied each work, and that the Freedom Tower is substantially similar to each in different ways.[65]

The court described, in pertinent part, the proof that was required of Shine as follows:

> To prevail, plaintiff must prove (1) ownership of a valid copyright, and (2) copying of constituent elements of the work that are original. To prove copying of original elements of his work, in addition to showing originality, plaintiff must demonstrate both that defendants actually copied his works, and that such copying was illegal because there is substantial similarity between each of his works and the alleged infringing work. . . . [66]

The court's analysis, in pertinent part, was as follows:

> In this analysis, defendants fly high and fast over the large body of Supreme Court and Second Circuit case law on originality and copyright infringement, as well as the text of the AWCPA, which states that "the overall form as well as the arrangement and composition of spaces and elements in the design" of an architectural work may be the subject of a valid copyright. . . . First, defendants fail to acknowledge that plaintiff's "certificates of [copyright] registration constitute prima facie evidence of the validity not only of their copyrights, but also of the originality of [the] works." . . . It is also true, however, that originality is "the sine qua non of copyright," and if a work is not original, then it is not protectable. If a certain element within a work is not original, that element is not protectable "even if other elements, or the work as a whole, warrant protection."
>
> Plaintiff need not clear a high bar in order for his architectural works to qualify as original:
>
>> In the copyright context, originality means the work was independently created by its author, and not copied from someone else's work. The level of originality and creativity that must be shown is minimal, only an "unmistakable dash of originality need be demonstrated, high standards of uniqueness in creativity are dispensed with."

---

65. *Id.* at 607–08.
66. *Id.* at 610 (internal citations omitted).

If the court followed defendants' suggestion and analyzed the elements of plaintiff's works separately, comparing only those elements that are copyrightable to those present in the designs for the Freedom Tower, as our Circuit noted, "we might have to decide that there can be no originality in a painting because all colors of paint have been used somewhere in the past."

Following this analysis, both Shine '99 and Olympic Tower at least arguably are protectable and original. . . . These works each have at least the mere "dash of originality" required for copyrightability, not to mention that they both have been copyrighted, and therefore are prima facie original.

. . .

To prove infringement, [a] plaintiff must first show that his or her work was actually copied. Copying may be established either by direct evidence of copying, or by indirect evidence, including access to the copyrighted work, similarities that are probative of copying between the works, and expert testimony. If actual copying is established, a plaintiff must then show that the copying amounts to an improper appropriation by demonstrating that substantial similarity to protected material exists between the two works.

. . .

"[P]robative," rather than "substantial" similarity is the correct term in referring to the plaintiff's initial burden of proving actual copying by indirect evidence. It is only after actual copying is established that one claiming infringement then proceeds to demonstrate that the copying was improper or unlawful by showing that the second work bears "substantial similarity" to protected expression in the earlier work.)

For the purposes of this motion, defendants concede that Childs had access to both Shine '99 and Olympic Tower when he evaluated them as part of the expert jury . . . all that plaintiff must prove to show actual copying in this action is probative similarity between his works and the Freedom Tower. The court may consider expert testimony when assessing probative similarity. . . . Given the substantial disagreement between plaintiff's expert . . . and defendants' expert . . . on the alleged similarity between Olympic Tower and the Freedom Tower . . . and that these experts' views are, at least to the court's untrained eye, plausible, there is at least an issue of material fact remaining for trial as to the probative similarity between those two works.[67]

While the resolution of such disputes will be inherently fact intensive, as the *Shine* decision demonstrates, the degree of originality required to qualify an architectural work for copyright protection is arguably quite small.

---

67. *Id.* at 610–11 (internal citations omitted).

B. Contractual Provisions

One way to avoid leaving copyright issues to statutory interpretation or common law principles is to expressly address them in the owner–architect agreement. Ownership of the documents is a key issue and is often the source of negotiation in owner–architect agreements. If the architect completes the project, copyright generally is not a major issue from the owner's perspective unless another party seeks to replicate its project contrary to expectations. Design professionals are typically concerned with maintaining the intellectual property rights in their work and with avoiding the liabilities that may arise if those drawings are modified by the owner or others without participation of the design professionals who initially prepared the documents.

If, however, a disagreement arises between the owner and architect that culminates in the termination of the architect prior to completion of the construction documents or construction itself, then the issue of copyright can become critically important. On the one hand, the owner might argue that it needs to have ownership of the documents transferred in the contract so that the owner can retain another design firm to complete the project, without having to resolve its dispute with the architect as a condition precedent. The owner also wants to know that it may use the documents following completion as necessary to maintain, alter, and add to the project in the future. On the other hand, the architect may express concerns, including protecting its architectural design, being paid for its design documents, being released from liability for the design documents after termination, and being indemnified from third-party claims.

These competing concerns should be addressed and reconciled in the contract. Many ways exist to address these issues. Article 7 of the AIA Document B101 provides a relatively common way to deal with ownership issues (1) by declaring that the architect retains all ownership rights to the documents, including copyright, (2) but grants and obligates its consultants to grant the owner a nonexclusive license to use the documents and distribute them to members of the construction team for purposes of constructing, using, maintaining, altering, and adding to the project, and (3) on the condition that owner pays the architect and releases the architect from claims that arise without the architect's participation.[68] In addition, the owner agrees to indemnify and hold harmless architect from claims that may be asserted by third parties as a result of the owner's continued use of the architect's documents without its continued participation.[69]

---

68. *See* AIA Document B101–2017, *supra* note 2, §§ 7.2, 7.3.
69. *Id.* § 7.3.1.

6.09 THE DESIGN AGREEMENT: THE DESIGNER'S OBLIGATION TO DESIGN TO A BUDGET

Most owners have at least three prime goals for their projects: that the projects be built (1) in accordance with the plans and specifications, (2) on time, and (3) within the owner's project budget. From the perspective of the owner, the owner is prepared to commit only so much money to the project. Moreover, on many projects, the owner may be accountable to partners, investors, or lenders. When bids or construction costs exceed the project budget, the owner may not be able to continue with the project solely due to financial reasons. On the other hand, being held accountable to a project budget, without restrictions, can be seem unfair to architects because contractors have many advantages when pricing the work based on completed construction documents, as opposed to estimates calculated by architects during the design process. Consider the following:

- When putting together a bid, the general contractor can rely on the specialized bidding expertise of subcontractors.
- Contractors generally have better access to more recent data on the pricing of labor, materials, and equipment than the architect uses to create cost estimates during the design process.
- Contractors are keenly aware of supply and demand market forces. For example, they take into account how busy the contractor is, a factor that often influences the bid price.

The AIA Document B101 includes a number of provisions that address the architect's responsibilities in connection with producing a design that is consistent with the owner's budget. The architect is expected to not only consider the owner's budget in developing the design but also to prepare a cost estimate and update it in subsequent phases.[70]

It is the owner's responsibility to establish its budget for the project and to include reasonable contingencies in that budget in recognition of the fact that cost estimating is a process fraught with uncertainty.[71] The AIA Document B101 also acknowledges that any evaluations of the owner's budget or cost estimates provided by the architect reflect the architect's judgment as a design professional:

> It is recognized, however, that neither the Architect nor the Owner has control over the cost of labor materials and equipment; the Contractors methods of determining bid prices; or competitive bidding market or negotiating

---

70. Id. §§ 3.2.2, 3.2.5.1, 3.2.5.2, 3.2.6, 3.3.2, 3.3.3, 3.4.1, 3.4.4, 3.4.5.
71. Id. § 5.2.

conditions. Accordingly, the Architect cannot and does not warrant or represent that bids or negotiated prices will not vary from the Owner's budget for the Cost of the Work, or from any estimate of the Cost of the Work, or evaluation, prepared or agreed to by the Architect.[72]

The AIA Document B101 assumes that the architect accepts a degree of responsibility to redesign at its own cost if bids come in over budget, provided that the overage is not due to market conditions it could not reasonably anticipate.[73] Such redesign is the limit of the architect's responsibility for such cost overruns. The architect is not responsible for the owner's out-of-pocket costs, which could be substantial. To balance this allocation of risk, during the design process, the architect was also permitted to mitigate its risk by including contingencies for design, bidding, and price escalation; to determine what materials, equipment, component systems, and types of construction are to be included in the contract documents; to recommend reasonable adjustments to the project program and scope; and to include alternates to reduce costs if necessary to meet the cost agreed limit.[74]

In practice, many sophisticated owners prefer to rely on cost estimates from construction professionals as opposed to the architect. Owners also are reluctant to take on an obligation to involve the architect in the owner's final decisions about changes in the design to reduce costs.[75] Accordingly, owners may hire a construction manager as part of preconstruction services or a cost estimator to review the architect's plans during the design phases. The architect then responds to the estimates by making revisions as necessary to reduce the project costs. If further revisions are required in later phases, the architect is often compensated on an additional services basis.

Project costs in excess of the budget can lead to litigation. The Alabama Supreme Court decision in *Kahn v. Terry*[76] is one example of the many opinions addressing this issue.[77] The pertinent facts follow:

---

72. *Id.* § 6.2.
73. *Id.* § 6.7.
74. *Id.* § 6.3.
75. *See id.* § 6.5.
76. Kahn v. Terry, 628 So. 2d 390 (1993).
77. Other notable cases with some in favor of the architect and some in favor of the owner include: Koontz v. Thomas, 333 S.C. 702, 511 S.E.2d 407 (S.C. App. 1999) (Court affirmed jury verdict holding architect was not liable for bids in excess of estimate.); Hous. Vt. v. Goldsmith & Morris, 165 Vt. 428, 685 A.2d 1086 (1996) (Architect was held responsible for excessive costs as Vermont Supreme Court ruled that "contractual disclaimers of liability for negligence are disfavored."); Kostohryz v. McGuire, 298 Minn. 513, 212 N.W.2d 850 (1973) (The Minnesota Supreme Court affirmed jury verdict finding architect breached his contract by underestimating cost of construction of residence, that expert testimony was not necessary, that architect's duty was to perform the services for which he was engaged in good faith and with reasonable care and

On May 8, 1984, Terry and Kahn Properties, Inc., entered into a design contract. Under the terms of the contract, Terry was to prepare designs for the development of a shopping center . . . that development included the renovation of existing stores and shops in the area and the design and construction of a parking deck. The contract called for an architect's fee of six percent of the construction cost. According to the testimony of Donald R. Kahn, the overall budget for the project was $2,000,000, which included $900,000 for the parking deck.

. . .

Terry and Donald Kahn orally agreed that the design and development of the parking deck would be included in the first phase of the project. They also orally agreed that the parking deck was to consist of 150 parking spaces, at a cost of $6,000 each. On July 13, 1984, Terry mailed design plans and specifications for the parking deck to four general contractors, previously selected by Kahn and Terry, to allow them to bid on the contract. Among the items included in the plans was a "pan and joist" system used to form concrete slabs on the floor of the parking deck. After the bid packages were mailed, several of the contractors contacted Terry and suggested that perhaps a "post-tension" system of concrete slab formation, as opposed to the "pan and joist" system, would be better suited for use in the construction of the parking deck. Terry then issued an addendum to the documents requesting that the contractors submit bids using both systems of concrete formation.

On August 7, 1984, bids were received from the four general contractors, with Cooper and Sayers Construction Company being the lowest bidder, at $1,394,000. Terry negotiated with Cooper and Sayers to lower its bid to conform with the overall budget of $1.2 million for the first phase of the project. Cooper and Sayers lowered its bid to $1,230,000. On August 28, 1984, Terry prepared a construction contract between Kahn and Cooper and Sayers for $1,230,074, but Kahn refused to sign the contract. Kahn terminated Terry's employment on September 14, 1984.

Terry filed a breach of contract action against Donald R. Kahn and Kahn Properties, Inc., seeking compensation for services rendered under the contract. Kahn filed a motion to dismiss, which was denied in August 1985. In October 1985, Kahn filed an answer and counterclaim, alleging, inter alia, that Terry had not performed any services for which compensation was owed, and that the plans and specifications submitted by Terry did not meet the standards specified in the contract. Terry filed a motion for a summary judgment,

---

competence and that the measure of damages was not the excess cost of the structure, but rather was the difference between the total cost of the property and that amount of money which prudent person would pay for the property in its present condition.); and Getzschman v. Miller Chem. Co., Inc., 232 Neb. 885, 443 N.W.2d 260 (1989) (Nebraska Supreme Court affirmed jury verdict in favor of architect who sued clients for breach of contract after client's refusal to pay architect on the ground that the actual construction costs were in excess of client's anticipation.).

which was denied, and the case was tried. The jury awarded Terry $95,693.31 and found against Kahn on the counterclaim.

. . .

Article 3 of the contract governs the construction cost; it provides, in pertinent part:

> No fixed limit of Construction Cost shall be established as a condition of this Agreement by the furnishing, proposal or establishment of a Project budget under Subparagraph 1.1.2 or Paragraph 2.2 or otherwise, unless such fixed limit has been agreed upon in writing and signed by the parties hereto. If such a fixed limit has been established, the Architect shall be permitted to include contingencies for design, bidding and price escalation, to determine what materials, equipment, component systems and types of construction are to be included in the Contract Documents, to make reasonable adjustments in the scope of the Project and to include in the Contract Documents alternate bids to adjust the Construction Cost to the fixed limit. Any such fixed limit shall be increased in the amount of any increase in the Contract Sum occurring after execution of the Contract for Construction.

Although the written contract does not specifically provide for a fixed construction cost, the parties presented conflicting testimony as to whether they had agreed upon a fixed construction cost. Donald Kahn testified that when he met with Terry concerning the contract, he discussed the overall budget of $2 million for the project, as well as the $6,000 cost per parking space. Kahn also testified that he and Terry orally agreed that the construction costs for the first phase of the project were not to exceed $1.2 million. While Kahn argues that they had an oral agreement concerning a fixed limit on construction costs, the written contract provides that such agreements would be in writing and would be signed by the parties. Kahn produced no written evidence of such an agreement.

Terry testified that he and Donald Kahn talked over the general terms and conditions of the contract, rate fees, and other considerations. Terry testified that Kahn told him that the budget for the project was tight and that Kahn mentioned the $1.2 million figure. Terry seems to argue, however, that the figure was mentioned only in terms of the budget and not as a limitation on construction costs for the project.

. . .

Because there was a dispute as to the existence of a fixed limit on construction costs, this matter was correctly submitted to the jury. We conclude that, based on the evidence presented to the jury, it could correctly determine that there was no fixed construction cost limit set in the contract and that Terry was therefore entitled to compensation for his services.[78]

---

78. 628 So. 2d at 392–93.

6.10 THE DESIGN AGREEMENT: OTHER TERMS AND CONDITIONS

A number of other key issues must be addressed in a design agreement. This section addresses a few of the most important: payment, insurance, limitation of liability, and termination.

A. Payment

The parties' agreement must set forth the basis of the design professional's compensation. The AIA Document B101 provides for common alternative methods, which include (1) hourly rates for time devoted to the services, (2) a fixed fee or stipulated sum, (3) a multiple of direct personnel expense based on the designee's actual personnel expense plus a multiplier to cover overhead and profit, and (4) a percentage of construction costs. Each payment mechanism has certain advantages and disadvantages for both parties. From the owner's perspective, a stipulated sum provides the most predictability but may result in overpayment to the architect if the services ultimately require less effort than originally contemplated. From the architect's perspective, a stipulated sum may result in an underpayment if more effort is required than was anticipated when the stipulated sum was established. Hourly rates provide little predictability for the owner, although a cap on hourly fees can be established. Multipliers of direct personnel expense present issues similar to use of hourly rates.

Payments made by the owner to the architect usually fall into three categories: (1) compensation for basic services, (2) compensation for additional services, and (3) reimbursable expenses. Compensation for the performance of basic services typically is calculated using one of the approaches described in the preceding paragraph. Because the commitment of resources for additional services often is unpredictable, and the need for such services often arises unexpectedly, the owner commonly pays the designer on an hourly basis even if a different method of compensation applies to basic services.

In the course of performing its contractual obligations, an architect or other design professional will incur certain routine out-of-pocket expenses that are directly related to the project but are not covered in the compensation for basic or additional services, including costs related to transportation, reproduction of documents, and delivery services.[79] Owners reimburse the designer for such expenses separately, often with some modest multiplier to cover administrative costs and, perhaps, some profit margin for the designer.

---

79. AIA Document B101–2017, *supra* note 2, § 11.8.1.

B. Insurance

Most agreements between owners and architects and other design professionals specify the types and limits of insurance coverage that the designer must maintain (with the owner reimbursing the architect or other professional for the cost of any insurance beyond what the professionals normally maintain). AIA Document B101 section 2.5 identifies typical types of coverage to be maintained by the architect.

Owners may want to require that the professional liability policy be kept in full force and effect for a specified period of time after substantial completion of the project because of the claims-made nature of professional liability insurance policies. Typically, such policies are only in effect for one year and only cover claims made during the policy year. For further discussion regarding insurance, a critical topic in design and construction, see Chapter 18 of this book.

C. Contractual Limitations of Liability

1. *Disclaimers and Exculpatory Provisions*

Most agreements with architects and other design professionals contain a number of disclaimers that limit the obligations of the architect or other design professional.[80] In addition to describing what is included in their services, the agreements also define the professional's obligations by describing what is excluded from these obligations.

Typically, the architect will keep the owner "reasonably informed of the progress and quality"[81] of the completed work. However, the architect generally only determines "in general" if the work observed is being performed in a manner indicating that it will comply with the requirements of the contract documents when fully complete. Moreover, the architect is not required to make exhaustive or continuous on-site inspections but will visit the site only at "intervals appropriate to the stage of the contractor's operations."[82] Finally, most architects insist that their contracts explicitly provide that the architect does not have control over or charge of, and is not responsible for, the construction means, methods, techniques, sequences, or procedures or for safety precautions and programs in connection with the work. Other design professionals request similar limitations on their respective responsibilities.

---

80. A number of disclaimers and exculpatory provisions can be found in AIA Document B101–2017, such as §§ 3.1.2, 3.6.1.2, 3.6.2.1, 3.6.2.2, 6.2, 6.3, 6.4, 6.7, and 7.3.1.
81. AIA Document B101–2017, *supra* note 2, § 2.6.2.1.
82. *Id.*

Such language is the direct result of common law examinations of whether an architect's on-site obligations create any responsibility for the safety of workers on a construction site. A case decided by the Illinois Supreme Court is particularly instructive of how courts have looked at the issue. The plaintiffs in *Miller v. DeWitt*,[83] among other things, alleged that project architects who had a contractual duty to evaluate work in process also had a duty to prevent the contractor from carrying out the work in a faulty manner and, therefore, were responsible to the plaintiffs for the injuries sustained as the result of a roof collapse during construction.

The court in *Miller* affirmed the judgment in favor of the plaintiffs, finding the architect negligent in supervising the work and awarding damages for bodily injuries suffered in a job site accident.[84] Although the *Miller* court based its judgment on the architect's right to stop the work, design professionals had assumed that this right related to the architect's obligations to the owner and was not a basis for third-party claims. As a result of such decisions, design professionals became increasingly concerned with limiting their potential exposure to claims related to the construction process. Standard forms of agreement between an owner and architect (or engineer) now dilute the description of the architect's on-site responsibilities. Architects no longer "supervise" the work, but "observe" the work. Similarly, architects routinely disclaim any responsibility for construction means, methods, techniques, sequences, and procedures, and safety programs and precautions. Their agreements seek to limit other obligations where such control might expose the architect to liability for worker injuries.

The current allocation of responsibilities in most agreements between owners and architects was almost predicted by the dissenting opinion in *Miller v. DeWitt*. The relevant portion of the dissent is set forth here.

> HOUSE, Justice (dissenting).
>
> [The majority opinion] imposes a legal duty on an architect not only to prepare plans and specifications, but to inspect the methods employed by the contractor leading up to completion under the general inspection clause of his contract.
>
> I cannot read into the contract a duty which is not imposed by it. The architect's contract used here is a more or less standard form generally used by architects and engineers. It provides for detailed plans and specifications, obtaining approval of various governmental agencies, issuing certificates of payment and general administration. Supervision is limited. The architect

---

83. Miller v. DeWitt, 37 Ill. 2d 273, 226 N.E.2d 630 (1967).
84. *Id.* at 292, 226 N.E.2d at 643 (Justice House, dissenting).

contracts to attempt prevention of defects but specifically disclaims a guarantee of the performance by the contractor.

. . .

Again, the opinion concedes that architects have no duty to specify the method used to accomplish the finished building, but the belief was stated that the architects "had the right" to insist upon a safe and adequate use of that method. True, but to parlay that "right" into a duty is neither consistent with generally accepted usage nor contemplated by the contract. Obviously, the architect did not contract to be present or represented at all phases of construction and he should not be held responsible for methods used by the contractor which may result in injury. Since there is no contractual obligation, liability is fixed by an expansion of the common law.

I find no support for such a radical departure in either this or any other jurisdiction. The cases cited for comparison are usually between contractor and architect or owner and architect, but not for liability of an architect to an employee of the contractor. The general view is stated in *Garden City Floral Co. v. Hunt* [Citations Omitted]: "To say that he (architect) must supervise the method of doing the work before there is full supervision would place the architect in an entirely different role from that of an architect. . . . As a matter of law the courts recognize that an architect merely supervises the results and does not dictate the methods when not controlled by the specifications."

There are sound reasons for the prevailing view that the architect's primary duty is to provide a sound completed structure in accordance with the owner's requirements, but not to dictate the methods by which the contractor attains that objective. There would be utter chaos if the contractor or his superintendent were to give an order to use his most efficient equipment and personnel, and the architect attempted to countermand and order that the work be done by another method requiring different equipment and skills. When a contractor bids a job he expects to use his equipment and the special talents and experience of his organization. If the threat existed that the details of carrying out his contract be subject to outside interference, contractors naturally would take that into consideration in fixing their bids. If the duty of architects is expanded to require that they be on the job at all times and prescribe methods of construction or be held liable for the negligence of employees of the contractor, . . . they will reflect the added burden in their supervision fees. All of this adds up to an additional and, I think, unnecessary and unwarranted financial burden upon the public without a commensurate benefit. Liability of architects as imposed here is economically unsound.

The huge construction industry in this country had functioned very well without the imposition of liability upon architects and engineers who design, but do not build, structures and other facilities. I see no justification for extending the common law to place liability on architects.[85]

---

85. *Id.* at 292, 226 N.E.2d at 642–43.

2. Waivers of Consequential Damages and Contractual Limitations of Liability

Both parties to the AIA Document B101 waive consequential damages under section 8.1.3. Since, however, the architect is unlikely to suffer consequential damages from the owner's breach of the agreement, but the owner's damages may be almost exclusively consequential, the clause often is heavily negotiated by sophisticated commercial owners.

Options are available to the owner who wishes to retain the right to recover some portion of consequential damages. For example, the owner may reserve this right to the extent of available insurance coverage. The parties might also agree to a limitation on consequential damages, as opposed to an outright waiver. One popular alternative is a contract provision that limits the owner's recovery to the proceeds of the architect's professional liability insurance.

The application of limitations of liability is not restricted to consequential damages. For example, such a provision might apply to all of the architect's liability arising out of the project. This raises questions as to the enforceability of such limitations. Although the law in many jurisdictions restricts the enforceability of certain limitations of liability due to public policy concerns, courts overall recognize parties' rights to negotiate the terms of their contracts, including limitations of liability, as the following decision demonstrates:

Valhal Corp. v. Sullivan Associates, Inc.
44 F.3d 195, 198–204 (3d Cir. 1995)[86]

Before: SIRICA, NYGAARD and McKEE, Circuit Judges.
McKEE, Circuit Judge:
This dispute centers on the enforceability of a limitation of liability clause in a contract between a real estate developer (Valhal Corporation), and an architectural firm (Sullivan Associates). Valhal and Sullivan have both filed appeals from the order of the district court denying Sullivan's motion for partial summary judgment and granting Valhal's motion for partial summary judgment. The district concluded that the disputed clause was part of the contract but that it violated public policy and was therefore unenforceable. We will reverse, and dismiss for lack of jurisdiction.

I. Factual and Procedural Background

Valhal is a New York corporation which specializes in the management and development of real estate. Sullivan Associates, Inc., is a Pennsylvania corporation specializing in architectural, planning and engineering services. In March of 1989,

---

86. Internal citations and footnotes omitted.

Valhal became interested in buying a parcel of real estate located at 401 N. 21st Street in Philadelphia, Pennsylvania, known as the "Channel 57 Property." Valhal planned to build a high-rise residential tower on a portion of that property. In early June of 1989, Valhal and Sullivan discussed the possibility of Sullivan performing certain work in connection with the project, including a feasibility study.

As a result of those discussions, Sullivan forwarded a proposal to Valhal, dated June 7, 1989, detailing the services which Sullivan would perform. A document entitled "Standard Consulting Contract Terms and Conditions" was attached to the proposal and provided in part:

. . .

> The OWNER agrees to limit the Design Professional's liability to the OWNER and to all construction Contractors and Subcontractors on the project, due to the Design Professional's professional negligent acts, errors or omissions, such that the total aggregate liability of each Design Professional shall not exceed $50,000 or the Design Professional's total fee for services rendered on this project.
>
> Should the OWNER find the above terms unacceptable, an equitable surcharge to absorb the Architect's increase in insurance premiums will be negotiated.

. . .

Sullivan's initial proposal provided that its services would be performed in two phases—Phase "A" and Phase "B"—and that Sullivan's total fee would be $5,000. Valhal responded by requesting that a service to be performed under Phase "B" be included under Phase "A" and by requesting that two completely new services be added to Phase "A." Sullivan agreed and a new proposal was submitted to Valhal on June 22, 1989 in which Sullivan increased its fee from $5,000 to $7,000 because of the additional work it was to perform under Phase A. This second proposal once again incorporated the Standard Contract Terms and Conditions, including the limitation of liability provision, and was again signed by Andrew Sullivan.

. . .

Sullivan responded by performing the services outlined in the July 24, 1989 proposal, and thereafter provided a written report to Valhal in which Sullivan concluded that the Channel 57 property was not burdened with any height restrictions and that it was possible to erect the tower on the property without any special governmental approvals.

Valhal thereafter entered into an Agreement of Sale for the purchase of the Channel 57 property. However, after the sale contingencies expired, Valhal learned that the property was subject to a height restriction which would be violated by its building. Nevertheless, Valhal proceeded to closing and paid the purchase price of $10.1 million. . . . Valhal then brought a diversity action against Sullivan pursuant to 28 U.S.C. § 1332 seeking damages in excess of $2,000,000 for breach of contract, negligence, gross negligence and negligent misrepresentation based upon Sullivan's failure to inform it of the height restriction.

Sullivan thereafter moved for partial summary judgment on the grounds that its liability was expressly limited to $50,000 and that the district court therefore lacked diversity jurisdiction. Valhal moved to strike the limitation of liability provision arguing that it was not a part of the contract and that even if it was, it was unenforceable. Valhal also argued that the limitation of liability clause, if enforceable, was limited only to its claim for negligence and did not apply to its breach of contract claim or to its gross negligence claim. The district court treated the parties' motions as cross-motions for summary judgment, denied Sullivan's motion, and granted Valhal's motion. The court ruled that the provision was part of the contract, but that it was against public policy as expressed in 68 PA. STAT. ANN. § 491 (Purdons 1994) (the anti-indemnity statute) and therefore unenforceable. See Memorandum and Order, dated May 17, 1993. . . .

Thereafter, the jury returned a verdict in favor of Valhal on both the contract and negligence claims but awarded damages of $1,000,000 on the contract claim only. The jury also concluded that Sullivan was not liable for gross negligence or negligent misrepresentation. Sullivan's post-verdict motions were denied, and this appeal followed.

II. Discussion

. . .

B. The Limitation of Liability Clause Is Enforceable.

The heart of the instant controversy is Valhal's contention that the limitation of liability clause is unenforceable even if it is part of the contract with Sullivan. Valhal argues that limitation of liability provisions are disfavored in Pennsylvania and that this particular clause violates a specific public policy against an architect limiting his/her liability for damages caused by his/her own negligence.

Pennsylvania Does Not Have a General Policy Against Such Clauses.

The law recognizes different methods by which a party can limit his/her exposure to damages resulting from his/her negligent performance of a contractual obligation. An exculpatory clause immunizes a person from the consequences of his/her negligence. . . . Similarly, an indemnity clause holds the indemnitee harmless from liability by requiring the indemnitor to bear the cost of any damages for which the indemnitee is held liable. . . . The instant clause has no such consequence. The clause before us does not bar any cause of action, nor does it require someone other than Sullivan to ultimately pay for any loss caused by Sullivan's negligence. Sullivan remains liable for its own negligence and continues to be exposed to liability up to a $50,000 ceiling. Thus, the amount of liability is capped, but Sullivan still bears substantial responsibility for its actions.

. . .

Valhal asserts that exculpatory clauses, indemnity clauses and limitation of liability clauses differ only in form as the effect of each is to limit one's liability for one's own negligence. Brief of Valhal Corp. at 24–25. Valhal contends that, thus, limitation of liability clauses are disfavored in Pennsylvania and must meet stringent standards to be enforceable.

There are similarities between these types of clauses. . . . Indeed, the test used to determine the enforceability of exculpatory and indemnity provisions is the same. *Id.* Those clauses are disfavored and must meet certain conditions to be enforceable. First, the clause must not contravene public policy. Second, the contract must relate solely to the private affairs of the contracting parties and not include a matter of public interest. Third, each party must be a free bargaining agent. In addition, an exculpatory or indemnity clause will still not be enforced unless it is clear that the beneficiary of the clause is being relieved of liability only for his/her own acts of negligence. The clause must be construed strictly and the contract must state the intention of the parties with the greatest particularity. Furthermore, any ambiguity must be construed against the party seeking immunity, and that party also has the burden of proving each of the prerequisites to enforcement. . . . The district applied this test to the limitation of liability clause at issue here. . . .

Courts have developed these limitations as reasonable conditions precedent to allowing a party to contract away responsibility for his/her negligence. It is with good reason therefore, that Pennsylvania allows such contractual provisions only where matters of public interest are not involved. One cannot contract away responsibility to the public to exercise reasonable care in performing a contract. . . .

However, Pennsylvania appellate courts recognize that there are differences between a contract which insulates a party from liability and one which merely places a limit upon that liability. . . . The difference between the two clauses "is . . . a real one." . . . Presumably because of that difference, we find no Pennsylvania cases in which a limitation of liability clause has been disfavored or been tested by the same stringent standards developed for exculpatory, hold harmless, and indemnity clauses. Accordingly, we believe that the district court erred in applying those stringent standards to the clause before us. . . .

Limitation of liability clauses are routinely enforced under the Uniform Commercial Code when contained in sales contracts negotiated between sophisticated parties and when no personal injury or property damage is involved. This is true whether the damages are pled in contract or tort.

. . .

We are persuaded that limitation of liability clauses are not disfavored under Pennsylvania law; especially when contained in contracts between informed business entities dealing at arm's length, and there has been no injury to person or property. Furthermore, such clauses are not subjected to the same stringent standards applied to exculpatory and indemnity clauses. Limitation of liability clauses

> are a way of allocating "unknown or undeterminable risks"... and are a fact of everyday business and commercial life. So long as the limitation which is established is reasonable and not so drastic as to remove the incentive to perform with due care, Pennsylvania courts uphold the limitation.
>
> ... Here, Sullivan is exposed to liability which is seven times the amount of the remuneration under its contract with Valhal. Accordingly, the cap does not immunize Sullivan from the consequences for its own actions. It is a reasonable allocation of risk between two sophisticated parties and does not run afoul of the policy disfavoring clauses which effectively immunize parties from liability.

It is not surprising that many participants in the design and construction process attempt to shift project liability risks to other project participants or to an insurer. Many design and construction contracts use exculpatory provisions, indemnification, and hold harmless agreements, as well as a simple contractual allocation of responsibility and liability for particular matters to another party. Such provisions are often the source of protracted negotiations and accomplish the ultimate objective of insulating a person or entity from liability with varying degrees of success. Consequently, there has been an increase in efforts by various parties—in particular, design professionals—to include a specific contractual limitation of liability in their agreements.

Because the owner receives the principal benefit from the design and completion of the project, design professionals contend the owner is the more appropriate party to assume certain liability risks. Design professionals also point out that damages alleged or claimed against them are potentially enormous, whereas they receive a one-time fee that is only a small percentage of the risk assumed. Many owners are concerned that limiting the liability of an architect may remove an incentive for proper performance. As the court in *Valhal* concluded, however, a limitation of liability provision is not necessarily exculpation from responsibility but rather an allocation of risk intended to reflect a proper risk/reward analysis.

D. Termination

Many construction projects do not survive the journey from conception to completion. Sometimes the parties part company because one or the other fails to perform its obligations. The right of the architect to terminate "for cause" is limited from a practical standpoint to failure by the owner to make payment to the architect in accordance with the agreement. At the option of the architect, nonpayment also is cause for suspension of the performance of services.[87] The architect has no liability to the owner for any delay or damage caused as a result of such suspension. This places the owner in a quandary. The architect, however, confronts a similar dilemma. Any suspension of services or termination has drastic financial implications for the owner and, therefore, the architect must consider carefully the possibility that its actions might be considered wrongful.

Sometimes an owner cannot afford what it wants, the owner's needs may change, efforts to obtain financing for the project fail, or business plans change. Many plans have been drafted for buildings and other projects that were never constructed. Many standard form agreements allow the owner to terminate the agreement for convenience and without cause.[88] Termination for convenience addresses such circumstances. Additionally, if the working relationship between the owner and architect breaks down or a change in personnel severely impairs the original expectations of the parties, it may be a prudent business decision simply to terminate the relationship for convenience and move on.

If the agreement between an owner and architect is terminated through no fault of the architect, some contracts provide for payment of termination expenses to the architect. The AIA approach does not include a formula for calculating termination expenses but simply provides that termination expenses are those that are "directly attributable to termination" for which the architect is not otherwise compensated, *plus* the anticipated profit on services not rendered by the architect as a consequence of termination.[89] Since the profit on unperformed work is always imprecise—and, therefore, subject to exaggeration—this portion of the termination clause is often the subject of negotiation.

---

87. AIA Document B101–2017, *supra* note 2, § 9.1.
88. *Id.* § 9.5.
89. *Id.* § 9.7.

QUESTIONS

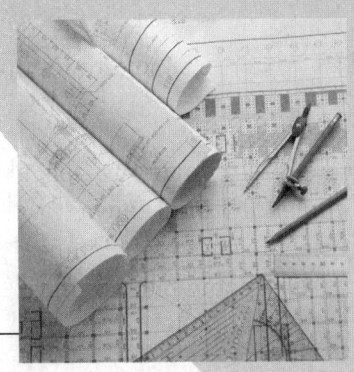

1. During negotiations of an owner–architect agreement, the architect explains to the owner that no set of drawings and specifications is ever 100 percent complete. From prior experience, the owner knows this to be true and doesn't want to pay a premium for the architect to prepare documents that exceed the level of detail customary in the profession. Because of such practical concerns, the architect proposes that the owner maintain a contingency of 5 percent of the construction contract sum to pay for additional costs arising out of errors or omissions in the drawings and specifications. How do you respond if you are counsel to the owner? If you are counsel for the architect, what arguments do you make to support this position?

2. An owner and architect enter into an agreement for the design of a small commercial building, using a typical AIA form of agreement. The agreement includes a project budget. The owner informs the architect that the budget cannot be exceeded by more than 10 percent, as the cost of construction is largely financed and the owner has very little ability to add equity or obtain further financing. The lowest bid from a responsible bidder comes in 30 percent over the budget. After an effort to "design down" to the budget, it becomes clear that the project is not economically viable and will need to be abandoned. What recourse does the owner have against the architect? What could the owner have done during contract negotiations to improve its position in such a circumstance?

3. Shortly after an owner retains an architect to design a commercial project, the parties discuss the program for the project. The architect encourages the owner to consider the use of so-called sustainable architecture and energy efficient elements. The architect contends that such elements will pay for themselves over the useful life of the project and are simply the socially responsible thing to do. The owner likes the idea and can see certain marketing advantages for such a building. The architect's ideas, however, require use of new and untested technologies. Therefore, the architect cautions the owner that the ultimate price of the project is unpredictable and that there likely will be a period of time after completion of construction during which the project will not function properly and will need to be optimized. The owner believes that the architect should bear those risks, as the owner still needs to rely on the architect to implement such ideas. Do you think that the owner is correct? How should an architect respond to the owner's concerns? How should such issues be addressed in the owner–architect agreement?

4. An owner retains an architect who proposes contract language that grants the owner a nonexclusive license to use the design to construct the project. Counsel for the owner rejects the language and tells the architect that the owner must own the design. In response, the architect disagrees and insists that the architect must own the design. Discuss the issues that concern the parties and suggest contract provisions that might resolve such concerns.
5. Why do many owners object to a mutual waiver of consequential damages in an owner–architect agreement? If an architect refuses to delete the waiver in an owner–architect agreement, describe what provisions an owner might try to negotiate to mitigate adverse effect caused by waiving consequential damages by the owner.
6. If the architect would agree to include the services of a geotechnical engineer within the architect's scope of work, would you recommend to the owner that the architect do so? If you were representing the architect, would you recommend against it? Why?
7. An architectural firm you represent has asked you to review language in one of its proposals, which states that the firm "designs to the state of the art" and that its work "is of the highest standard." How might this language affect the standard of care that would be expected of the firm?
8. Would an architect's failure to prepare drawings that complied with the Americans With Disabilities Act be negligence per se?

CHAPTER 7

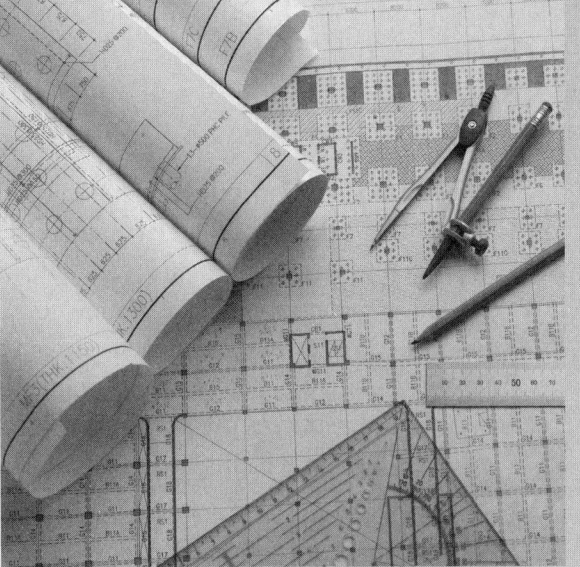

Architect's Contract Administration

CARL J. CIRCO

7.01 INTRODUCTION

Owners often hire design professionals to provide contract administration services in addition to furnishing drawings and specifications for the project. In this context, the term "contract administration" refers to a wide range of activities that assist the owner in its contractual relationship with the general contractor. Those activities may include providing information to the contractor, inspecting the progress of construction, preparing documents in connection with changes to the work, helping to resolve disputes between the owner and the contractor, and many other administrative tasks. Although an owner might hire an architect, an engineer, or some other professional to provide contract administration, for convenience this chapter presumes that an architect is providing those services.

In general, the owner and the architect may agree on whatever contract administration services and procedures they think most appropriate for the project. For many projects, however, the owner retains the same architect who prepares the drawings and specifications to provide a comprehensive array of contract administration services that conform to established industry customs. The 2017 editions of AIA Documents B101[1] (especially section 3.6) and A201[2] (especially sections 4.2 and 15.2) illustrate one of the most common arrangements for contract administration for a commercial project using the Design-Bid-Build project delivery method. For that reason, much of this chapter discusses the architect's contract administration role in a way that reflects the contract administration provisions of these AIA documents. You may want to review these AIA provisions in conjunction with this chapter.

7.02 NATURE AND SCOPE OF ARCHITECT'S ROLE IN CONTRACT ADMINISTRATION

As you will see from the materials in this chapter, contract administration may involve many different activities and may raise several important legal issues. Depending on the owner's needs, the architect may provide such extensive services during the construction phase of a project that the architect occupies a central role throughout the entire construction process. But in other projects, the architect may be involved only in discrete administrative functions once construction begins. For still other projects, the architect may not be involved in any of the administrative aspects of the project at all.

The main purpose of this section is to familiarize you with the general concept of contract administration. Additionally, because agency law provides the underlying legal construct for certain key aspects of contract administration, the concluding subdivision in this section briefly highlights some of the agency law considerations that will be relevant to certain issues presented in later sections of this chapter.

A. Overview of Contract Administration

The contract for design services normally establishes the nature and scope of the architect's role in contract administration.[3] For most projects, nothing in the industry or the law requires the architect to have an ongoing role during construction; however, licensing regulations may require that certain activities relating to the project must be performed only by, or under the supervision of,

---

1. American Institute of Architects, AIA Document B101-2017, Standard Form of Agreement between Owner and Architect (2017) [hereinafter AIA Document B101-2017].

2. American Institute of Architects, AIA Document A201-2017, General Conditions of the Contract for Construction (2017) [hereinafter AIA Document A201-2017].

3. *See* AIA Document B101-2017 *supra* note 1, § 3.6.1.1 (providing that the architect will provide contract administration as contemplated by AIA Document A201-2017).

a properly licensed design professional. Even though some contract administration services are customary for certain segments of the industry, the architect's role may vary greatly based on the experience, sophistication, staffing, and risk tolerance of the owner. For example, an experienced developer of commercial projects might have its own contract administration staff to perform many of the functions that an architect might provide for a less experienced owner. Or a city or other public owner might use an employee, such as the city engineer, to provide most contract administration. Other owners might limit the architect's role to a few administrative functions, such as reviewing the contractor's applications for payment and periodically inspecting the progress of the work. On a residential project, if there is any professional contract administration at all, it may be limited to a walk-through of the house before the owner makes the final payment.

An owner will also sometimes retain an architect to fill a much larger role than normal contract administration, such as serving as a construction manager or project manager. Or the owner may retain an architect to provide continuous on-site representation. The industry sometimes refers to this more intensive on-site position by the term "clerk of the works."[4] But even in these more expansive administrative arrangements, the architect's role in contract administration normally does not give the architect authority over such matters as the means and methods of construction. Indeed, the contract documents customarily reserve these matters to the contractor.[5]

In the course of typical contract administration, the architect may function in three distinct administrative capacities. First, for some purposes, the architect may act as the owner's agent. For example, the contract documents may require that the contractor secure the architect's approval or review of certain construction details, such as a proposed submittal schedule or a list of proposed subcontractors.[6] On these matters, the architect frequently acts on behalf of the owner in an agency capacity. Second, for other purposes, the architect often serves as the owner's representative or consultant. This is commonly the case, for example, when the architect reviews the contractor's

---

4. *See* Bd. of Educ. of Hudson City Sch. Dist. v. Sargent, Webster, Crenshaw & Folley, 539 N.Y.S.2d 814, 818 (N.Y. App. Div. 1989) (in which the court concluded that the evidence at trial was subject to conflicting inferences about whether the individual serving as the clerk of the works was the owner's agent or the project architect's agent). While somewhat outdated, the concept of a clerk of the works remains in vogue in at least a few settings. *See* Camden Nat'l Bank v. Crest Constr., Inc., 952 A.2d 213, 217 (Me. 2008); Fisher v. Coghlan, 778 N.Y.S.2d 812, 814 (N.Y. App. Div. 2004).

5. *See* AIA Document B101-2017, *supra* note 1, § 3.6.1.2.

6. *See* AIA Document A201-2017, *supra* note 2, §§ 3.10.2, 5.2.

periodic applications for payment.[7] The architect generally reviews the applications for payment for the purpose of advising the owner whether to make payment in the full amount requested. Finally, the contract between the owner and the contractor often refers to the architect some or all disagreements, disputes, and claims that arise during construction.[8] When this happens, the architect typically fulfills the role of a neutral mediator or referee between the owner and the contractor.

B. Overview of Agency Law Principles Relevant to Contract Administration

As a preliminary matter in analyzing the legal issues involved in contract administration, it is often important to determine whether, or the extent to which, the architect is serving as the owner's agent. This subsection summarizes certain agency law principles that the reader should keep in mind when the architect acts as the owner's agent. Often, the contract documents give limited express authority to the architect to act for the owner on certain matters, and they also expressly notify the contractor that the architect has no authority to act for the owner on other matters.[9] Additionally, the circumstances may establish apparent agency authority for the architect to bind the owner. Authority may also be implied from provisions of the contract documents or from the circumstances or from a course of dealing between the parties. As already noted, however, for some contract administration purposes, the architect does not serve as the owner's agent at all, but as either a consultant to the owner or as an intermediary or referee between the owner and the contractor. For that reason, before relating the agency law principles summarized here to any particular facet of contract administration, the reader must first determine whether or not the architect is serving as the owner's agent in connection with that facet.

1. Architect's Authority to Bind the Owner

The scope of the architect's agency as established by the relevant contract documents determines generally the extent to which the architect may bind the owner contractually. For example, if the agreement between the owner and the contractor requires the contractor to submit to the architect the names and experience of major subcontractors for a determination of whether the owner

---

7. *See* AIA Document B101–2017, *supra* note 1, § 3.6.3.

8. *See id.*, § 3.6.2.5 (unless otherwise agreed, the architect will make initial decisions on claims as contemplated by Article 15 of AIA Document A201–2017).

9. *See* AIA Document A201–2017, *supra* note 2, § 4.2.1.

or the architect has any objections to the proposed subcontractors, the architect's approval of a subcontractor (or the architect's failure to make a timely or reasonable objection to a proposed subcontractor) probably will have the effect of waiving the owner's right to raise objections to that subcontractor. But an action by the architect falling outside the scope of the agency authority granted to the architect will generally not bind the owner. Thus, if the contract requires that both the owner and the architect must approve change orders that affect the contract price or schedule, the architect normally would not have authority to approve a change order on the owner's behalf.

In *Incorporated Town of Bono v. Universal Tank & Iron Works, Inc.*,[10] the owner's architect told the contractor that a written request for an extension of the time for performance would not be required and that the architect would "take care of the matter." Under the owner–architect agreement, the architect had neither the express nor implied authority to bind the owner to an extension of time. The court held that the architect was not a general agent of the owner but was an agent with limited authority.

2. Owner's Liability for the Architect's Acts

When the architect acts within the scope of the agency, the owner may be liable for the architect's acts and omissions. For example, if the contract documents authorize the architect to direct the contractor to perform additional work, the owner will be liable to pay the contractor for that work, even if the architect, without the contractor's knowledge, violated the owner's instructions by ordering the particular work.[11]

3. Architect's Liability for Exceeding Authority or for the Improper Exercise of Authority

An architect who acts outside the designated scope of authority or whose exercise of that authority is negligent may incur liability to the owner, the contractor, or other third parties adversely affected. This liability may be based on either a contract theory or a tort theory, depending on the jurisdiction's enforcement of the economic loss rule.[12] However, where a contractor knows of the limitations on the design professional's authority, the design professional's actions outside that authority do not bind the owner.[13]

---

10. Inc. Town of Bono v. Universal Tank & Iron Works, Inc., 395 S.W.2d 330 (Ark. 1965).

11. *See, e.g.*, Scribante v. Edwards, 181 P. 75 (Cal. Ct. App. 1919) (contract directed the contractor to lay a concrete floor under the direction of the owner's architect).

12. See Chapter 21.

13. Gen. Constr. Co. v. Pub. Util. Dist. No. 2 of Grant Cnty., 380 P.3d 636, 642, 195 Wash. App. 698, 711 (Wash. Ct. App. 2016) ("The contract restricts which individuals have the authority

7.03 REQUESTS FOR INFORMATION, INTERPRETATIONS, AND CLARIFICATIONS

Many technical matters relating to the drawings and specifications for a project may be referred to the architect during the construction phase through requests for information (RFIs) or may otherwise require interpretations or clarifications by the architect. Sometimes, the contract documents will establish a detailed process for securing the architect's input on these questions.[14] Most commonly, these technical questions come from the contractor or from a subcontractor who submits the inquiry through the contractor. Architects sometimes complain that contractors overuse the process and, in those situations, the architect may have a claim under the owner–architect agreement for additional compensation for providing contract administration services beyond those contemplated by the contract.[15] But contractors often argue that the RFI process is essential to uncover omissions and errors in the design documents and to avoid problems in the field.

Deficient drawings may lead to an unusual number of RFIs and may result in contractor claims for additional compensation. Although the construction contract may require the contractor to review the drawings before undertaking the work and to bring to the owner's attention errors or defects that the contractor discovers, the contractor will have a valid claim if the RFI reveals design defects that lead to delays or additional costs, especially if the defects are latent.[16] Similarly, contractor claims may arise from a failure to respond promptly or properly to RFIs. When information that the architect provides proves to be inaccurate, incomplete, or erroneous, a contractor or other

---

to modify the contract and what situations can constitute waiver of contractual provisions, as well as explicitly defining the authority of the engineer. As the engineer, Mr. Jeske did not have authority under the contract 19 to modify its provisions. His authority extended to direct changes that would not result in additional costs as well as limited authority to direct changes that would cost less than $10,000. He could also require GCC to continue with that changed work pending a decision by PUD on GCC's objection. However, the contract explicitly precluded him from directing work changes that would result in substantially increased costs or from otherwise modifying the contract. ¶41 Accordingly, the trial court properly rejected GCC's claim that PUD had waived the protection of the notice requirements. The engineer simply had no authority to modify the contract and GCC knew that fact.").

14. *See* AIA Document B101–2017, *supra* note 1, § 3.6.4.

15. *See id.*, § 4.2.2.

16. *See* 5 Philip L. Bruner & Patrick J. O'Connor, Jr., Bruner and O'Connor on Construction Law § 15:60 [hereinafter Bruner & O'Connor].

participant in the project who relies on that information may assert that the architect is liable for making a fraudulent or negligent misrepresentation.[17]

Metropolitan Atlanta Rapid Transit Authority v. Green International, Inc.[18] provides an extreme example of a project plagued by requests for information stemming from design deficiencies. There, the court commented that testimony indicated that "the state of the plans created a 'design-as-you-go situation' requiring over 350 written requests for information and clarification or 'RFIs' and over 1,000 revised drawings while the project was already underway."[19] There was also evidence in that case that untimely responses to RFIs contributed to delays in construction.[20] The court upheld $2.8 million in damages that the jury awarded to the contractor on its claim against the owner.

7.04 QUALITY CONTROL

The contract documents may subject a broad array of matters to the architect's review or approval. In acting on these matters, the architect commonly acts as the owner's consultant or representative (or sometimes as the owner's agent), usually for some purpose that serves to ensure the project's quality or its conformance with the drawings and specifications. The subsections that follow briefly discuss some of the most common situations in which the contract documents may call for the architect's involvement during the construction phase for quality control purposes.

A. Review and Approval Procedures

The contract documents may be nearly silent on the process for the architect's review or approval, or they may set out the process in great detail. In either case, disputes or claims are likely to arise if the contractor fails to seek the architect's input on a timely basis or if the architect is negligent or dilatory.

---

17. *See* D.W. Wilburn, Inc. v. K. Norman Berry Associates, Architects, PLLC, 2016 WL 7405774, at *5 (Ky. Ct. App. 2016); *Hudson City*, 539 N.Y.S.2d at 814, 819; U.S. v. Rogers & Rogers, 161 F. Supp. 132 (S.D. Cal. 1958). For further information about liability for negligent misrepresentation, *see* Restatement of Torts (Second) § 552 (1977).

18. 509 S.E.2d 674 (Ga. Ct. App. 1999).

19. *Id.* at 676.

20. *Id.* at 678 (apparently the owner rather than the architect delayed in responding to the RFIs).

B. Approving or Objecting to Subcontractors, Manufacturers, and Suppliers

Absent restrictions stated in the contract between the contractor and the owner, the contractor has the right to assign portions of the work to others without seeking the owner's input or approval. Often, however, the contract documents give the owner or the architect (or both) the opportunity to raise reasonable objections to proposed subcontractors.[21] Additionally, the drawings and specifications or other contract documents may identify manufacturers or suppliers from which the contractor must choose to provide certain equipment and materials. Alternatively, they may require the contractor to submit to the architect information about proposed manufacturers or suppliers for the architect's approval or comment.

C. Substitutions, Shop Drawings, and Other Submittals

Waggoner v. W & W Steel Co.
657 P.2d 147 (Okla. 1982)

BARNES, Vice Chief Justice:

This case presents for resolution on appeal, the following issue:

Is the architect who designed this building responsible for ensuring that the contractor employ safe methods and procedures in performing his work?

During the construction of Presbyterian Hospital in Oklahoma City, Oklahoma, a portion of the steel framework fell, resulting in the death of two workmen and the injury of another. The accident occurred on a Friday, as workers were beginning to secure a portion of the steel in the sixth, seventh, and eighth floors which had been erected that day. The three men were on the structure waiting for other workers to bring up guy lines which were to be used in securing the steel before an approaching thunderstorm rolled in over the construction site. Before the task could be completed, a gust of wind hit the unsecured and unbraced steel, causing it to collapse.

In designing this building, the architects had provided for expansion joints which would allow for expansion and contraction with changing weather conditions. The expansion joint was designed so that a shelf, welded to a column, provided a seat for a beam which was held in place by "keeper angles" welded in on either side of the beam. The opposite end of the beam was secured to another column with large bolts. Unfortunately, at the time of the accident, the "keeper angles" had not been installed and the beams were not secured in any other way.

---

21. *See* AIA Document A201–2017, *supra* note 2, § 5.2.

The erector had built portions of three floors rather than completing all the work on one floor at a time. As a result, the east half of the new sections were without interior columns and cross beams which would have provided lateral bracing for the outside columns. These outer columns bore the weight, not only of the steel beams and trusses which had been erected, but also of large bundles of steel decking which were placed on the beams at each floor level. The outside columns were held upright only by temporary "clip angles" provided by the fabricator to facilitate the alignment and welding of the top columns to the columns below.

After the accident, suit was brought against the owners of the hospital, the fabricator and the architect by the injured worker and representatives of the estates of the deceased workers. The case (three cases were consolidated) went to jury trial with the architect as the sole defendant, the other defendants having been released from the lawsuit by dismissals and summary judgments. After plaintiffs and defendant rested, the trial court directed a verdict for the architect. The Court of Appeals, in reversing the lower court, determined that the architect did owe a duty to the workers, in that the architect "undertook to supervise the construction project." With this, we disagree.

Architects are required to exercise ordinary professional skill and diligence and to conform to accepted architectural standards. Because an architect's undertaking does not imply a guarantee of perfect plans or results, he is liable only for failure to exercise reasonable care and professional skill in preparation and execution of plans *according to their contract*. *Smith v. Goff*, 325 P.2d 1061 (Okla. 1958) (emphasis added). This principal [sic] was reaffirmed in *Wills v. Black & West, Architects*, 344 P.2d 581 (Okla.1959) in which we looked to the contract between the parties to determine the responsibilities of the architect. It is stated in 5 AM. JUR. 2D ARCHITECTS § 5 (1962) that:

> (t)he employment of an architect is ordinarily a matter of contract -between the parties, and the terms of such employment are governed by the terms of the contract into which they entered. The architect's duties may be limited to the preparation of plans and specifications, or they may include, in addition, the supervision of construction.

At common law, privity of contract was required before an action in tort could arise from a breach of duty created by a contract. However, in *Truitt v. Diggs*, 611 P.2d 633 (Okla. 1980), we indicated that in cases involving physical injury to third parties, that restriction has in many cases been eliminated or modified. Therefore, it is possible for an architect to be liable for injuries received by a person with whom he has no privity, but there can be no standard rule. The determination must be made by considering the nature of the architect's undertaking and his conduct pursuant thereto.

To do so in the present case, we must look to the contract which actually consists of several separate documents. Pertinent provisions of the General Conditions of the Contract for Construction are set forth below.

2.2.4 The Architect will make periodic visits to the site to familiarize himself generally with the progress and quality of the Work and to determine in general if the Work is proceeding in accordance with the Contract Documents. On the basis of his on-site observations as an architect, he will keep the Owner informed of the progress of the Work, and will endeavor to guard the Owner against defects and deficiencies in the Work of the Contractor. *The Architect will not be required to make exhaustive or continuous on-site inspections to check the quality or quantity of the Work. The Architect will not be responsible for construction means, methods, techniques, sequences or procedures, or for safety precautions and programs in connection with the Work, and he will not be responsible for the Contractor's failure to carry out the Work in accordance with the Contract Documents* (emphasis added).

4.3 SUPERVISION AND CONSTRUCTION PROCEDURES

4.3.1 The Contractor shall supervise and direct the Work, using his best skill and attention. He shall be solely responsible for all construction means, methods, techniques, and sequences and procedures and for coordinating all portions of the Work under the Contract.

4.13.1 By approving and submitting Shop Drawings and Samples, the Contractor thereby represents that he has determined and verified all field measurements, field construction criteria, materials, catalog numbers and similar data, or will do so, and that he has checked and coordinated each Shop Drawing and Sample with the requirements of the Work and of the Contract Documents.

4.13.5 The Architect will review and approve Shop Drawings and Samples with reasonable promptness so as to cause no delay, but only for conformance with the design concept of the Project and with the information given in the Contract Documents. The Architect's approval of a separate item shall not indicate approval of an assembly in which the item functions.

10.2 SAFETY OF PERSONS AND PROPERTY

10.2.1 The Contractor shall take all reasonable precautions for the safety of, and shall provide all reasonable protection to prevent damage, injury or loss to:

1. all employees on the Work and all other persons who may be affected thereby . . . ;

10.2.2 The Contractor shall comply with all applicable laws, ordinances, rules, regulations and lawful orders of any public authority having jurisdiction for the safety of persons or property or to protect them from damage, injury or loss. He shall erect and maintain, as required by existing conditions and progress of the Work, all reasonable safeguards for safety and protection, including posting danger signs and other warnings against hazards, promulgating safety regulations and notifying owners and users of adjacent utilities.

Appellants maintain that the trial court was in error when he directed a verdict against them because the architect owed a duty to them to exercise ordinary professional skill and diligence in preparing and approving plans for construction, and therefore the question of the alleged violation of that duty should have been submitted to the jury.

We must determine if, under the contractual provisions set out above, the architect had such a duty.

Section 4.3.1 of the General Conditions specifies that the contractor is to supervise the work, being "solely responsible for all construction means, methods, techniques, and sequences and procedures." Although the architect is to periodically visit the construction site, § 2.2.4 provides that he is not required to make "exhaustive or continuous on-site inspections to check the quality or quantity of the work." It goes on to exclude from the architect's responsibilities those which are outlined in 4.3.1 as belonging solely to the contractor. It should also be noted that the owners of the hospital employed an engineer as the project inspector.

Article 10, entitled "Protection of Persons and Property" contains provisions which require the contractor to protect workmen from injury, comply with safety regulations and laws and designate a superintendent whose job it is to prevent accidents. It is to be noted that the responsibilities for all safety precautions and programs are assigned exclusively to the contractor.

Article 4 sets forth the procedure and purpose concerning the shop drawings which appellants contend should have included specifications for temporary bracing and connections. The shop drawings, prepared by a subcontractor, were submitted to the contractor and the architects, as required by the contract. It is the architects' approval of the shop drawings, without provision for temporary connections on the expansion joints, that appellants maintain was negligence.

However, § 4.13.4 provides that the shop drawings are submitted to the *contractor* for determination and verification of "all field measurements, field construction criteria, materials, catalog number and similar data." By approving them, he represents that he has checked each shop drawing with the requirements of the contract. And, as previously noted, § 4.3.1 of the contract makes the contractor "solely responsible for all construction means, methods, techniques, sequences and procedures."

> It is apparent that the shop drawings serve more than one purpose. They are submitted to the contractor for approval regarding aspects of the construction work. But, according to § 4.13.5, *they are submitted to the architects for approval "only for conformance with the design concept of the project and with the information given in the Contract Documents."*
>
> Therefore, it was the duty of the contractor, not the architects, to see that the shop drawings included provisions for temporary connections which fall into the categories of "field construction criteria," "construction means, methods, techniques, sequences and procedures." Since it was not the responsibility of the architects, they obviously would not be negligent in failing to require temporary connections.
>
> Because the contractor, not the architect, was required under the contract to supervise the job and employ all reasonable safety precautions, the architects cannot be held liable for injuries sustained as a result of an unsafe construction procedure. There was no question of fact for the jury. The trial court properly directed a verdict for the architects.
>
> The judgment of the Court of Appeals is vacated and the decision of the trial court is affirmed.
>
> IRWIN, C.J., and LAVENDER, SIMMS, DOOLIN, HARGRAVE, OPALA and WILSON, JJ., concur.

The contract documents commonly require the contractor to submit certain construction details and information for the architect's review.[22] The primary purpose of these requirements is to allow the architect to confirm that the construction will conform to the design concept embodied in the architect's drawings and specifications. For example, because certain fabrication, installation, and construction details require the input of manufacturers, suppliers, and trade contractors, the contract documents may require the contractor to prepare or secure drawings and other information relating to these details. Shop drawings are plans that furnish these special details. Other submittals may include material or product samples, models, and technical information from manufacturers, suppliers, and fabricators.

The architect usually wants to have the opportunity to review these details without taking any responsibility for them because they involve matters that are more properly within the expertise of those who will carry out the work. In other words, the architect's review does not give the architect control over construction means, methods, or techniques; such review merely allows the

---

22. *See* AIA Document B101–2017, *supra* note 1, § 3.6.4.

architect to determine whether these aspects of construction appear to be consistent with the design expressed in the drawings and specifications.[23]

Additionally, the contract documents often permit the contractor to propose for the architect's approval substitutions for equipment or materials specified in the drawings and specifications. This option recognizes that the contractor and its subcontractors and suppliers may have more complete or current information about available products and equipment and may be able to suggest substitutions that meet the quality and functional requirements of the drawings and specifications while offering some advantage over the specified equipment or materials. For example, a substitution may reduce costs, avoid potential delays in delivery schedules, or facilitate the construction process in some other way.

As the *Waggoner* case illustrates, the architect's review and approval of shop drawings or other technical submittals has been a fertile source of litigation, especially when the defect created a safety hazard.[24] In reaction to cases of that nature, project architects and engineers have become exceedingly careful to avoid contractual responsibility for approving or commenting on shop drawings and other submittals, except for the limited purpose of confirming that they conform to the specified design concepts.

D. Decisions on Aesthetic Effect

Architects often retain final authority over decisions that affect project aesthetics. In contrast to how architects usually address shop drawings and submittals, the contract documents normally require the architect's approval of aesthetic details, and they may make the architect's decision on these matters final.[25]

E. Site Visits and Inspections

In many projects, one of the architect's main responsibilities during the construction phase is to visit the site periodically to observe the progress of construction in an effort to guard the owner against defects in the work.[26] The AIA

---

23. See id. § 3.6.4.2.
24. See, e.g., Duncan v. Mo. Bd. for Architects, Prof'l Eng'rs & Land Surveyors, 744 S.W.2d 524 (Mo. Ct. App. 1988) (revocation of licenses of engineers who failed to detect structural error in shop drawings prepared by steel fabricator that resulted in a catastrophic collapse of pedestrian walkways in a hotel lobby); Jaeger v. Henningson, Durham & Richardson, Inc., 714 F.2d 773 (8th Cir. 1983) (architect who failed to recognize that a shop drawing called for lighter gauge steel in a stairway than that required by the construction drawings was liable for a resulting injury).
25. See AIA Document B101–2017, *supra* note 1, § 3.6.2.4.
26. See id. § 3.6.2.

form documents attempt to limit the architect's responsibility for the contractor's failure to perform the work in accordance with the contract documents,[27] but this effort has met with mixed success, as shown in the following case.

Board of Educ. of Hudson City School District v. Sargent, Webster, Crenshaw & Folley
539 N.Y.S.2d 814 (N.Y. App. Div. 1989)

LEVINE, Justice.

In 1966, plaintiff, the Board of Education of the Hudson City School District (hereinafter the School District), entered into an agreement with defendant, Sargent, Webster, Crenshaw & Folley (hereinafter the Architect), on a standard form of agreement of the American Institute of Architects (hereinafter AIA) for the provision of plans and specifications and supervisory architectural services in connection with the construction of a new high school building. Under paragraph 7 (b) of the agreement, the Architect was obligated to make periodic visits to the work site "to determine in general if the work is proceeding in accordance with the Contract Documents." The Architect was also required to "keep [the School District] informed of the progress of the work, will endeavor to guard [it]against defects and deficiencies ... and ... may condemn work as failing to conform to the Contract Documents." The Architect was also to issue certificates of payment, thereby representing that the work was properly performed and authorizing progress and final payments by the School District to the general contractor. Paragraph 7 (b) provided, however, that the Architect was not required to make "exhaustive or continuous on-site inspections to check the quality or quantity of the work and ... will not be responsible for the Contractors' failure to carry out the construction work in accordance with the Contract Documents." The agreement also required the Architect to assemble any written guarantees required of contractors and to make three annual inspections of the building following completion of construction and to advise the School District of any maintenance and remedial measures required.

Third-party defendant, Thompson Construction Corporation (hereinafter Thompson), was engaged as general contractor and construction commenced in the spring of 1969. Thompson contracted with Skyway Roofing Company, Inc. (hereinafter Skyway) to install the roof on the building. The specifications called for a four-ply, built-up, gravel-surfaced roof consisting of four layers of felt and coal tar pitch to assure bonding and waterproofing, with the gravel embedded in the top level of pitch. These layers were to be applied on top of a poured gypsum roof deck. The School District submitted evidence that, for a roof of this type, the layers as applied must be protected from exposure to precipitation during construction, since moisture trapped within the layers has a tendency to vaporize and expand, creating blisters in the plies of felt which may crack and cause leakages. Therefore,

---

27. *Id.* § 3.6.1.2.

the specifications expressly required completion of the application of the plies of roofing in one day or, failing that, the application of a glaze coating of hot bitumen to protect the felts until application of the gravel.

The School District also proved that Skyway failed to comply with the foregoing specifications in that application of the layers was done in phases, leaving the felt plies exposed to rain and snow without protective glazing. In fact, Thompson's daily construction reports indicated that Skyway personnel shoveled snow off the partially completed roof and that this was observed by one of the Architect's representatives on the site. The Architect then engaged an outside roofing expert to inspect Skyway's installation. He concluded that the roof system was seriously out of conformity with the specifications, alluding to the phased construction but, more importantly, to another defect, i.e., the fact that the vapor barrier was not attached to the poured gypsum deck. Based upon that report, the Architect directed Thompson to remove and replace the defective roofing. Thompson refused, insisting that the roof was properly applied. Following various conferences and exchanges of correspondence, the Architect agreed to several less severe remedial measures and, once these were completed, issued certificates of payment for the roofing.

The construction of the high school was completed and a final certificate of payment was issued by the Architect in September 1972. It was much later discovered, however, that the Architect had failed to obtain the two roofing guarantees required by the specifications, i.e., a two-year guarantee from Thompson and Skyway and a manufacturer's 20-year roofing bond. Leaks in the roof developed as early as November or December 1972. Upon initially consulting the Architect about the leaks, the School District's building and grounds superintendent was told by the Architect's representative that the cause of the problem was ice buildup. Each succeeding year, the blistering and the leaks became worse and, by 1979, the School District contemplated replacement of the roof. At this point, it was informed by the Architect that the cause of the problem was the phased installation in violation of the specifications and that the guarantees required by the contract inadvertently had not been obtained.

The School District then brought the instant suit against the Architect and Thompson. Its complaint set forth five causes of action against the Architect, the first two of which were for breach of contract, alleging in the first the Architect's failure to obtain the roofing guarantees and, in the second, the Architect's failure to have informed the School District of the deviation from the specifications in the roof installation and failure to have guarded the School District against the general contractor's defective performance and to have condemned the work as failing to conform to the contract documents.

...

In the foregoing procedural posture, the case proceeded to trial. At the conclusion of all of the evidence, Supreme Court granted the Architect's motion for a directed verdict dismissing all but the first of the School District's causes of action. The court directed a verdict in favor of the School District on its first cause of action (the failure to obtain the roofing guarantees) and assessed damages against the Architect for $6,000, the penal sum of the roofing bond called for by the contract. Finally, the court dismissed the Architect's third-party complaint against Thompson, ruling that the evidence did not establish the Architect's claim for indemnification. These cross appeals ensued.

In our view, the School District's proof regarding its second cause of action was sufficient to withstand the motion for a directed verdict. Hence, the portion of the judgment dismissing the second cause of action should be reversed, that claim reinstated and remitted for retrial. Supreme Court's contrary ruling was based upon the provision of paragraph 7 (b) of the agreement under which the Architect was absolved from responsibility "for the Contractors' failure to carry out the construction work in accordance with the Contract Documents," reading that provision as totally exonerating the Architect from liability for construction defects. While this very clause in the standard AIA architect/owner contract has been given exculpatory effect in this State and other jurisdictions (*see, Jewish Bd. of Guardians v. Grumman Allied Indus.*, 96 AD2d 465, 467, *affd* 62 NY2d 684; *Shepard v. City of Palatka*, 414 So 2d 1077 [Fla]; *Moundsview Ind. School Dist. No. 621 v. Buetow & Assocs.*, 253 NW2d 836 [Minn]), none of the cases involved defects known by the architect during the course of construction, which he failed to apprise the owner of under the contractual duty to "keep the [School District] informed of the progress of the work." We decline to extend the application of the clause in question to an instance such as this, where the trier of facts could find that the architect was aware of the defect and failed to notify the owner of it.

First, in general, exculpatory provisions are disfavored and are narrowly construed (*see Gross v. Sweet*, 49 NY2d 102, 106–107). Second, the underlying rationale for exonerating an architect under the exculpatory clause does not apply to defects known by the architect. The cases reason that an owner who has not contracted and paid for an architect to closely supervise construction should not be able to hold the architect liable for those defects in the contractor's performance which close supervision would have revealed (*see Jewish Bd. of Guardians v. Grumman Allied Indus.*, supra., at 465; *Moundsview Ind. School Dist. No. 621 v. Buetow & Assocs.*, supra., at 839). Clearly, however, the School District did bargain and agree to pay the Architect for periodic inspection and conveyance of information on the progress of the contractor's performance which the Architect acquired as the result of such on-site visits. When, as a result of periodic inspection, an architect discovers defects in the progress of the work which the owner, if notified, could have taken steps to ameliorate, the imposition of liability upon the architect for failure to notify would be based on a breach of his own contractual duty, and not as a guarantor of the contractor's performance (*see Hunt v. Ellisor & Tanner*, 739 SW2d 933, 937 [Tex]).

. . .

Alternatively, the Architect argued before Supreme Court and urges now that the School District's second cause of action failed because of the absence of expert testimony that the Architect's performance fell short of accepted professional standards of architectural practice. Such a deviation by an architect may, it is true, afford the basis of a contract cause of action as well as recovery in tort (*Sears, Roebuck & Co. v. Enco Assocs.*, 43 NY2d 389, 396). At the least, however, the claim in the second cause of action based upon the Architect's failure to notify of the known defective roof installation asserts the breach of a specific contractual undertaking by the Architect, akin to the failure to achieve a particular promised result, which does not require proof of a failure to meet professional standards of care.

...

We also reject the Architect's contention that the School District's proof of damages, i.e., the 1972 costs to correct by replacement of the defectively installed roof, was improper as a measure of damages. The cost to correct and replace defective construction may be a proper measure of damages for a breach of contract by an architect (*Sears, Roebuck & Co. v. Enco Assocs.*, supra.; *Hubert v. Aitken*, 2 NYS 711, 713, *order adhered to on rearg* 5 NYS839, *affd* 123 NY 655; *Schwartz v. Kuhn*, 71 Misc 149, 151; 5 AM JUR 2D, ARCHITECTS, § 24, at 687–688). The testimony of the School District's roofing expert was sufficient to prima facie establish its damages on the foregoing theory.

...

Judgment modified, on the law, without costs, by reversing so much thereof as dismissed plaintiff's second cause of action; said cause of action reinstated and matter remitted to the Supreme Court for a new trial thereon; and, as so modified, affirmed.

WEISS, J.P., and MIKOLL, YESAWICH and HARVEY, JJ., concur.

Suffice it to say that when defective work has been installed by the contractor—especially when the contractor has subsequently become insolvent—the search for culprits often includes the architects who performed site visits. The AIA language is intended to exculpate the architects from this liability, but has met with somewhat inconsistent results, as demonstrated by *Hudson City*[28] and by the *Moundsview*[29] and *Ellisor & Tanner*[30] cases cited in the opinion. Indeed, when the owner's design professional agrees to provide extensive on-site services, some courts have interpreted that obligation to create a duty

---

28. 539 N.Y.S.2d at 814.
29. Moundsview Ind. Sch. Dist. No. 621 v. Buetow & Assocs., 253 N.W.2d 836 (Minn. 1977).
30. Hunt v. Ellisor & Tanner, Inc. 739 S.W.2d 933, 937 (Tex. App. 1987). Both *Moundsview* and *Ellisor & Tanner* are discussed more thoroughly in Chapter 20.

to other project participants who rely on those services, occasionally including, somewhat remarkably, the contractor whose defective work caused the problem.[31]

7.05 COORDINATION

Project architects commonly retain engineering consultants to provide such design services as structural, mechanical, and electrical engineering.[32] Because these consultants work under contracts with the project architect, rather than under contracts with the owner, the architect coordinates the activities and schedules of all of these design components. Also, for some projects, in addition to retaining an architect, the owner may directly retain other design professionals for special purposes, such as interior design or audiovisual design. In those cases, unless the owner has adequate in-house construction administration capability, the owner may arrange for the architect to coordinate these specialized design activities with other project activities to which they relate.[33]

Although an architect may coordinate construction activities for a project, as well as design services, if all or most of the construction will be provided by a single general contractor and that general contractor's subcontractors, it is typically the general contractor, rather than the project architect, that coordinates all of the construction activities. In some projects, however, the major participants are not all under the control or supervision of a single general contractor. For example, an owner may contract directly with multiple prime contractors who will be responsible for distinct aspects of the work.[34] Coordinating the construction activities of separate contractors working on a project

---

31. Magnolia Constr. Co. v. Mississippi Gulf S. Eng'rs, Inc., 518 So. 2d 1194 (Miss. 1988); *Hudson City*, 539 N.Y.S.2d at 814, 818. Jurisdictions that enforce the negligence economic loss rule, discussed in Chapter 21 are less likely to follow these cases.

32. *See* AIA Document B101–2017, *supra* note 1, § 3.1. Note that the AIA standard document contemplates that the architect may provide civil engineering as a supplemental service for which additional compensation will be due. *See id.*, § 4.1.1.8.

33. *See* Metro. Atlanta Rapid Transit Auth. v. Green Int'l, Inc., 509 S.E.2d 674 (1999) (involving inadequate coordination of architectural and structural drawings); Bd. of Educ. v. URS Co., No. 64496, 1994 WL 520862 (Ohio Ct. App. Sept. 22, 1994), *aff'd in part and rev'd in part*, 648 N.E.2d 811 (Ohio 1995) (architect that designed the main classroom building for a school district project also coordinated the design of a planetarium dome for the same project to be designed and built by an expert in dome structures, and the architect served as project manager for the entire project).

34. *See, e.g.*, RPR & Assocs. v. O'Brien/Atkins Assocs., P.A., 921 F. Supp. 1457, 1459–60 (M.D. N.C. 1995) (contractor handling general construction in a multiple prime contractor project sought damages for "items of cost arising from alleged defaults and shortcomings in the administration of the project" by both the owner and the architect).

imposes time demands and liability risks on the architect far in excess of normal contract administration. For those reasons, architects who provide coordination services of this type should carefully assess the additional liability risks involved.[35]

7.06 APPROVAL OF PROGRESS PAYMENTS

Contractually, the architect typically acts as the owner's consultant or representative in reviewing and making recommendations on the contractor's progress payment applications.[36] For a complete discussion of the payment process, see Chapter 12. The architect may be liable to the owner for negligence in approving payment applications. Beyond this, some cases also impose liability on the architect to others when the architect takes improper action on progress payment applications. The architect may be liable to the contractor whose payment application is wrongfully rejected and even to subcontractors, sureties, or construction lenders. Construction lenders and government funding sources frequently arrange for or require a separate or independent inspecting architect to approve progress payments to the contractor.[37]

Under what circumstances should the architect be liable to others for improperly approving a contractor's application for payment? In *Fabe v. WVP Corp.*,[38] an action against the project architect, the court summarily rejected a claim by the state superintendent of insurance, acting as liquidator of the contractor's insolvent surety. The superintendent of insurance alleged that the architect improperly approved the contractor's applications for payment without discovering that the contractor was not paying its subcontractors. The court based its holding on the following contractual provision, which is substantially similar to the language of a standard AIA form:

> The issuance of a Certificate for Payment shall constitute a representation by the Architect to the Owner, based on the Architect's observations at the site . . . and on the data comprising the Contractor's Application for Payment, that the Work has progressed to the point indicated; that, to the best of the Architect's knowledge, information and belief, the quality of the Work is in

---

35. *See generally* Justin Sweet & Marc M. Schneier, Legal Aspects of Architecture, Engineering and the Construction Process § 17.04(C) (9th ed. 2013).
36. *See* AIA Document B101–2017, *supra* note 1, § 3.6.3.
37. *See, e.g.*, Sheetz, Aiken & Aiken, Inc. v. Spann, Hall, Ritchie, Inc., 512 So. 2d 99 (Ala. 1987) (holding that the developer-architect of a subsidized housing project could not recover damages on a contractual third-party beneficiary basis from the architect that the ultimate purchaser of the project hired to review and approve the contractor's payment applications).
38. 760 S.W.2d 490 (Mo. Ct. App. 1988).

accordance with the Contract Documents . . . ; and that the Contractor is entitled to payment in the amount certified. However, *the issuance of a Certificate for Payment shall not be a representation that the Architect has made any examination to ascertain how and for what purpose the Contractor has used the moneys paid on account of the Contract Sum.*[39]

7.07 THE RIGHT TO REJECT WORK OR TO STOP WORK

The contract documents may authorize the architect, commonly as the owner's agent, to reject work that does not comply with the drawings and specifications.[40] They may also authorize the architect to stop construction altogether if serious problems exist. Does the architect's authority to reject work or stop the work impose a legal duty on the architect to act or refrain from acting under any circumstances? If so, to whom is the architect liable for exercising that authority improperly or for failing to exercise it? In one case in which the contract documents gave the project engineer discretion to decide whether or not to shut down the job for adverse winter weather, the owner incurred liability to the contractor because of the engineer's improper failure to exercise the authority.[41] In several cases, the architect's authority to stop the work has been used as a basis to impose liability on the architect for worker injuries or safety violations. In reaction to these cases, design service agreements prepared by or for the protection of architects often take great care to avoid giving the architect any authority to stop the work.[42]

7.08 ISSUING CHANGE ORDERS AND RESPONDING TO PROPOSALS AND CHANGE ORDER REQUESTS

Because Chapter 14 deals extensively with the change order process, here we only briefly consider the architect's role in that process, which is often a dominant role. In one common arrangement, the architect reviews all proposals or requests for changes in the work, prepares written change orders, including new or revised drawings and specifications relating to the changes, and approves all change orders.[43] The architect may have authority to order a change unilaterally if the change involved is consistent with the intent of the agreed drawings, specifications, and other contract documents and does not

---

39. *Id.* at 491 (emphasis original).
40. *See* AIA Document B101-2017, *supra* note 1, § 3.6.2.2.
41. *See* Bignold v. King Cnty., 399 P.2d 611 (Wash. 1965).
42. *See* BRUNER & O'CONNOR, *supra* note 16, §§ 17:52–17:54.
43. *See* AIA Document A201-2017, *supra* note 2, art. 7.

require any adjustment to the price or completion schedule.[44] Ideally, before any significant change is undertaken, the parties will agree on complete drawings and specifications and other details concerning the change involved, as well as on any appropriate adjustments to the price and the completion schedule, in which case the architect will prepare a change order for the parties' signatures that includes all of that information.[45] But practical realities often dictate that work must begin on the basis of a change before a final or complete agreement is reached on any impact the change will have on the price or the schedule. In anticipation of that circumstance, contract documents often establish a procedure for the owner and the architect to order the contractor to undertake the change promptly and for any adjustments in the price or schedule to be resolved later. When that occurs, the architect may have ultimate authority to determine the adjustments, if the owner and the contractor cannot agree.[46]

Because most or all of these activities involve professional design services, the architect may incur liability for design defects, errors, or omissions in change order documentation. Additionally, an architect may be liable for failing to respond properly to proposals and change order requests or for delaying the process.

7.09 CERTIFICATION OF SUBSTANTIAL COMPLETION, FINAL COMPLETION, AND OTHER PERFORMANCE

When the project architect agrees to provide the full range of construction administration services, the architect's final administrative duties normally include determining when the contractor has achieved substantial completion and final completion.[47] Under this arrangement, the dates of substantial completion and final completion are normally established by separate certificates issued by the architect.

As a condition to issuance of the certificate of substantial completion, the contract documents may provide that the architect and the contractor will inspect the project and agree on a list of items that must be corrected or completed (called a punchlist). Any portion of the contract price that the owner has retained from progress payments as security in accordance with the

---

44. *See id.* § 7.4 (denominating such a change a "minor change" and allowing the contractor an opportunity to contest the architect's determination that the proposed change will not affect the price or schedule).
45. *See id.* § 7.2.
46. *See id.* § 7.3.
47. *See* AIA Document B101–2017, *supra* note 1, § 3.6.6.

construction contract may be released to the contractor when the certificate of substantial completion is issued. But the architect may also determine or approve a portion of that balance of the contract price for the owner to continue to withhold until all of the punchlist work is completed. Additionally, at substantial completion, physical possession, and the risk of loss typically transfer to the owner while the contractor continues to remain on site to complete the remaining work and to correct defective work.

At final completion, the architect normally issues a certificate for final payment of the balance due to the contractor. In connection with final completion, the architect also may be responsible, as the owner's consultant, to require and approve final lien waivers, operating manuals, warranty documentation, project start-up procedures and testing, performance tests to establish that the project meets performance standards or guarantees, and other project close-out steps.[48]

7.10 ARCHITECT'S ROLE IN CLAIMS PROCESS

A. Resolving Claims and Disputes

Chapter 19 addresses claims and the dispute resolution process. This chapter is concerned with these matters only with respect to the architect's often significant role in these procedures. Under one common structure, the owner and the contractor either may or must submit all or most claims to the architect for a preliminary determination or recommendation before commencing mediation, arbitration, or litigation.[49] Moreover, the contract documents often provide that the architect's decision becomes final if neither the owner nor the contractor institutes formal dispute resolution procedures.[50] Courts frequently uphold provisions of that nature.[51]

---

48. *See Hudson City*, 539 N.Y.S.2d at 814, 817 (N.Y. App. Div. 1989) (where the owner sued the architect for a variety of negligent administrative actions, including allegedly failing to obtain the appropriate roofing guarantees).

49. The current AIA approach is to submit most claims and disputes to the person named by the owner and the contractor to the role of "initial decision maker." AIA Document A201-2017, *supra* note 2, art. 15. In turn, the AIA documents provide that unless the owner and contractor name someone else, the architect will serve in that role. *Id.* § 15.2.1; AIA Document B101-2017, *supra* note 1, § 3.6.2.5.

50. *See* AIA Document A201-2017, *supra* note 2, § 15.2.5.

51. *See, e.g.*, F.H. Paschen, S.N. Nielsen & Associates, LLC v. Southeastern Commercial Masonry, Inc., 2015 WL 7015389, at *15 (E.D. La. 2015); Elec-Trol, Inc. v. C. J. Kern Contractors, Inc., 284 S.E.2d 119 (N.C. Ct. App. 1981).

Is it a sound idea to designate a design professional retained by the owner to resolve disputes between the owner and the contractor? Because the architect is typically selected and paid solely by the owner, when a contractor challenges a decision by a project architect, courts have used varying standards to subject the architect's decision to at least minimal judicial review, most commonly a standard of good faith or absence of fraud.[52] But even without that added level of judicial scrutiny, a provision giving binding dispute resolution authority to the owner's architect does not necessarily ensure favorable treatment for the owner. As one leading authority noted, architects and other design professionals may be subject to professional rules of conduct that may create a professional duty to act impartially when serving as an arbitrator or mediator.[53]

Several cases uphold provisions in public construction contracts that vest binding dispute resolution authority in a design professional that is also an employee of the owner.[54]

B. Architect's Role in Contractor Termination

Contract documents often provide for the architect to advise the owner if the contractor defaults in performance.[55] The architect's advice may include a recommendation to the owner about whether or not to terminate employment of the contractor. Sometimes, the architect's approval may be a condition precedent to the owner's right to terminate. In what circumstances and under what legal theories may the architect be liable in damages to the contractor for recommending or taking part in a wrongful termination of the contractor?

---

52. *See* BRUNER & O'CONNOR, *supra* note 16, § 17:82.

53. *See id.* § 17:83.

54. *See, e.g.*, Westinghouse Elec. Corp. v. N.Y.C. Transit Auth., 623 N.E.2d 531 (N.Y. 1993); *see generally* Gene Ming Lee, *A Case for Fairness in Public Works Contracting*, 65 FORD. L. REV.1075, 1108 (1996). *But cf.* MCI Constructors, Inc. v. Hazen & Sawyer, P.C. 401 F. Supp. 2d 504, 514 (M.D.N.C. 2005) (applying "an objective standard of reasonableness based upon good faith and fair play" to a decision made in a city's favor pursuant to a construction contract that provided for disputes to be resolved by the city manager, and distinguishing the case from those in which the public employee vested with the authority to resolve disputes was a design professional). It is unclear, however, whether the objective reasonableness standard articulated in the *MCI Constructors* case correctly reflects North Carolina law on the point. *See* 42 E., LLC v. D.R. Horton, Inc., 722 S.E.2d 1, 9–10 (N.C. Ct. App. 2012).

55. *See* AIA Document A201–2017, *supra* note 2, § 14.2.2 (providing that the owner may terminate the contractor under specified circumstances if the architect certifies that cause for termination exists).

In *DiMaria Construction, Inc. v. Interarch*,[56] a New Jersey appellate court, following an arbitration decision holding a termination to be invalid, upheld a judgment against a designer who recommended termination. The judgment was for tortuous interference with the terminated contract. The court refused to overturn a jury verdict against the designer that implicitly determined the designer had acted outside of the scope of its agency and with malice or bad faith. By contrast, in *Dehnert v. Arrow Sprinklers, Inc.*,[57] the Supreme Court of Wyoming reversed a jury verdict against an architect who recommended termination, stating:

> [T]he architect acting in his professional capacity typically is bound by contract to guard the interests of his principal. An architect who acts within the scope of his contractual obligations to the owner will not be liable for advising the owner to terminate a contractor's performance unless the architect acts with malice or in bad faith. Ballou v. Basic Construction Company, 407 F.2d 1137 (4th Cir. 1969); Lundgren v. Freeman, 307 F.2d 104 (9th Cir.1962); Craviolini v. Scholer & Fuller Associated Architects, 89 Ariz. 24, 357 P.2d 611 (1961); Kecko Piping Company, Inc. v. Town of Monroe, 172 Conn. 197, 374 A.2d 179 (1977). In his treaties [sic], LEGAL ASPECTS OF ARCHITECTURE, ENGINEERING AND THE CONSTRUCTION PROCESS, 2d Ed., Justin Sweet explains the concept of an architect's privilege to intervene in the contractual relationship between the owner and the contractor:
>
>> . . . [I]nterference is not wrongful if it is privileged. . . . Privilege can be created by the relationship between owner and design professional. Also, it can be created by contract clauses either giving the design professional the right to terminate or allowing the owner to terminate upon certification by the design professional that adequate cause for termination exists. The privilege is granted to enable the owner to be advised honestly without the risk of the person giving advice being taken to court.
>
> The privilege, whether conferred by law or by contract, must not be abused. If the interference with the contractor's rights were motivated by malice or bad faith, the design professional would be liable for any pecuniary loss caused the contractor. Section 27.10, pp. 536–537.
>
> A showing of malice or bad faith, not negligence, poor judgment or inflexibility, is essential if the contractor is to recover from the architect for contract interference. Ballou v. Basic Construction Company, 407 F.2d at 1141.[58]

---

56. 799 A.2d 555 (N.J. Super. Ct. App. Div. 2001).
57. 705 P.2d 846 (Wyo. 1985).
58. *Id.* at 850–51.

7.11 ARCHITECT'S IMMUNITY FOR PERFORMING QUASI-JUDICIAL FUNCTIONS

Most courts hold that the architect has immunity against liability when serving as a neutral party to resolve construction disputes or to render decisions on other questions presented by the owner or the contractor. When the architect exercises responsibility of this nature, the architect's role is sometimes characterized as a quasi-judicial or arbitral role. But if the architect is serving as the owner's agent or advisor rather than in a quasi-judicial role, the immunity may be lost. Even when the architect is acting in a quasi-judicial role, however, the immunity is not necessarily absolute. This is illustrated by *E. C. Ernst, Inc. v. Manhattan Construction Co. of Texas*[59] where the court held that the architect lost its immunity by the nature of its actions, stating:

> The arbitrator's "quasi-judicial" immunity arises from his resemblance to a judge. The scope of his immunity should be no broader than this resemblance. The arbitrator serves as a private vehicle for the ordering of economic relationships. He is a creature of contract, paid by the parties to perform a duty, and his decision binds the parties because they make a specific, private decision to be bound. His decision is not socially momentous except to those who pay him to decide. The judge, however, is an official governmental instrumentality for resolving societal disputes. The parties submit their disputes to him through the structure of the judicial system, at mostly public expense. His decisions may be glossed with public policy considerations and fraught with the consequences of *stare decisis*. When in discharging his function the arbitrator resembles a judge, we protect the integrity of his decision making by guarding against his fear of being mulcted in damages. Cf. *Broom v. Douglass*, 175 Ala. 268, 57 So. 860 (1912). But he should be immune from liability only to the extent that his action is functionally judge-like.[60]

In *RPR & Assoc. v. O'Brien/Atkins Assoc., P.A.*,[61] an architectural firm and an engineering firm working for a public owner sought to assert sovereign immunity against claims brought by a contractor. The defendants argued that "they are clothed with the State's sovereign immunity because they are acting in the capacity as agents for the State of North Carolina."[62] The court held that the sovereign immunity defense was not available to private parties in that situation, and it also rejected the architectural firm's immunity claim based on its status as an arbiter of disputes between the contractor and the public owner.

---

59. 551 F.2d 1026 (5th Cir. 1977).
60. *Id.* at 1033.
61. 921 F. Supp. 1457 (M.D. N.C. 1995).
62. *Id.* at 1460.

The court concluded that the claims were based on negligence in the performance of professional services. The court held that "when an architect acts not as an arbitrator, but as an architect, the arbitral immunity vanishes and the architect is susceptible to legal action."[63]

7.12 EMERGING CONTRACT ADMINISTRATIVE ROLES

As practices and technologies in the industry evolve, architects are beginning to take on additional administrative roles. These include responsibilities for sustainability objectives, building information modeling protocols, and integrated project delivery procedures.[64]

---

63. *Id.* at 1462.
64. *See* AIA Document B101–2017, *supra* note 1, §§ 1.1.6, 1.3; Carl J. Circo, *A Case Study in Collaborative Technology and the Intentionally Relational Contract: Building Information Modeling and Construction Industry Contracts*, 67 Ark. L. Rev. 873, 921–24 (2014).

QUESTIONS

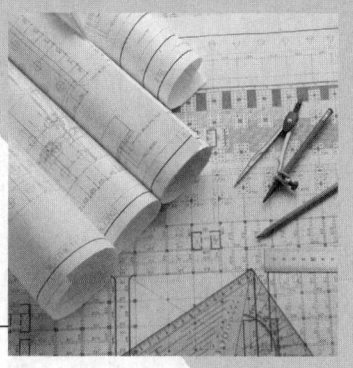

1. You are an attorney for the state department of roads. You are in the process of updating the department's standard bid package for highway construction. Would it be a good idea to include a provision making the department's chief engineer the final arbiter of all claims made by a contractor and all other disputes between a contractor and the department? What are the relevant considerations that you would raise with your client?

2. Contractor Termination

    a. What effect do you think cases such as *DiMaria* and *Arrow Sprinklers* have on a project architect's willingness to advise the owner candidly about the contractor's performance? Can you think of any provisions the architect's counsel might add to the owner–architect agreement to reduce the architect's risk? As counsel to the owner, would you accede to a proposal by the architect's counsel to include a provision in the owner–architect agreement by which the owner agrees to indemnify the architect against the contractor's claims of tortious interference? As counsel to a project architect, would you insist that any protective language be added to the owner–contractor agreement?

    b. Your client is the project architect for a new four-star hotel project. There have been extensive delays. Your client and the owner believe that the contractor caused most of the delays. The contractor blames the owner and your client. The owner, under advice of counsel, is pressing the architect for a recommendation to terminate the contractor for default. The owner–contractor agreement provides for all claims and disputes to be determined initially by the architect, but subject to arbitration if either party is dissatisfied with the architect's decision. The contract also provides that the owner may terminate the contract on account of contractor default if the architect certifies in writing that sufficient cause exists. What is your advice?

CHAPTER 8

Contractor Selection

R. HARPER HECKMAN

8.01 INTRODUCTION

Perhaps the most significant differences between construction in the public and private sectors lie in the area of procurement. Unlike private projects, public procurement is extensively regulated and generally requires that contractors be selected through a competitive, sealed bidding process.[1] In addition to securing for the general public the lowest price for a project, the competitive bidding process is perceived to be the best means for "giv[ing] all qualified contractors the opportunity to compete for government contracts while, at the same time, avoiding favoritism, collusion or fraud."[2] As discussed in the section that follows, private owners enjoy considerably more freedom when procuring design and construction services.

---

1. PHILLIP L. BRUNER & PATRICK J. O'CONNOR, JR., BRUNER AND O'CONNOR ON CONSTRUCTION LAW, § 2:31 (2016).

2. *Id.* § 2:22, n.4 (quoting W. NOEL KEYES, GOVERNMENT CONTRACTS UNDER THE FEDERAL ACQUISITION REGULATION 14.1, at 153 (1986), 48 C.F.R. § 14.1 (2017)) § 2:31.

8.02 PRIVATE PROCUREMENT GENERALLY

Procurement of construction services on private projects typically is characterized by "offer and acceptance" negotiations, which negotiations leave owners free to contract for their project in whatever manner and with whichever contractor they choose. Many private owners elect to contract first for the project's design and then for its construction on a "Design-Bid-Build" basis. However, many means exist by which a private owner may contract for the construction of a project; they include:

- Design-build projects
- Construction management (agency)
- Construction management (at-risk)

A detailed discussion of the various project delivery systems available to the private owner can be found in Chapter 4. A private owner also may elect to construct its project using some or all of the following pricing mechanisms:

- Lump sum, or "fixed price" contracts
- "Cost plus fee" contracts (with or without a guaranteed maximum price)
- "Unit prices"

For more information regarding these pricing mechanisms, please refer to Chapter 9.

Private owners select their contractors in a variety of ways. Indeed, owners hire contractors based upon the same criteria on which they hire lawyers, including the contractor's marketing efforts, reputation, and references. It is not uncommon for a private owner to send a request for proposal to two or more contractors, review their written submissions, and then meet with the finalists before deciding which contractor to engage. While price is an important factor in the owner's decision making, price is not the only criterion.

Even when an owner elects to solicit competitive bids, he or she still is allowed considerable freedom to negotiate privately with each bidder before deciding which bid to accept. For this reason, most competitively bid projects in the private sector are considered "closed bidding" projects, as distinguished from the "open bidding" protocol found in the public sector, in which all bids are opened simultaneously with the contract awarded to the lowest bidder.

Nevertheless, much of the discussion concerning public bidding that follows, particularly those sections having to do with the bid advertisement and package, is applicable to the private sector as well. In reviewing these concepts, however, the reader should be cognizant of the fact that private procurement is significantly less structured than its public counterpart. For example, private contract solicitations and proposals are oftentimes based upon incomplete project design drawings and specifications. Even under the Design-Bid-Build model, private contract negotiations are dynamic processes, where indecisive owners may vacillate on significant issues affecting construction scope, time, and cost. Accordingly, it is imperative that private "bidders" take care to ensure that what they ultimately contract to construct is the same project that they initially bid.

Moreover, since privately procured contracts typically involve a protracted series of verbal and written negotiations, it is important that the contract ultimately executed by the parties contain the final terms and conditions that the parties have agreed upon. In order to avoid claims based upon verbal or written agreements that are not contained in the contract, most construction agreements contain a "merger" or "integration" clause which makes clear that only those provisions contained or incorporated by reference in the contract itself will be binding on the contracting parties. These clauses will generally be enforced so as to bar evidence based upon extrinsic or "parol" agreements not contained in the body of the contract itself.

8.03 PUBLIC PROCUREMENT

A. General Considerations

Before discussing procurement issues in the public sector, we must first answer the question: "What actually is public construction?" Traditionally, the distinction was easy to make. The line between public and private projects has increasingly become blurred, however, in light of recent trends towards privatization of public projects and the advent of private/public partnerships and lease/purchase agreements.[3]

The characterization of a project as a public one generally involves an analysis of the project's: (1) funding, (2) control, and (3) future ownership.[4] Privately funded, publicly created entities normally are exempt from procurement regulations, but significant public funding of otherwise private entities—even in the form of tax relief—can alter the exemption."[5]

Even for projects clearly characterized as public in nature, most procurement codes exempt certain types of projects from their purview. These include:

---

3. Id. § 2:18.
4. Id. § 2:20.
5. Id.

- Small dollar exemptions for projects where the expenditure of public funds is relatively insignificant;[6]
- Emergency work exemptions, where the nature of the work could not withstand the time required for traditional public procurement protocol;
- "Sole source" exemptions where competition is limited to a single bidder with proprietary rights, technology or control over source materials;[7] and
- Professional services exemptions for projects requiring special skills, expertise, and services of a particular person or firm.[8]

B. Selection of Design Professionals

During the design phase of a project, public owners are generally less concerned about cost issues, and more concerned with engaging those professionals who bring particular skills, expertise, leadership, and prestige to the project.[9] Accordingly, the price-based procurement policies utilized for awarding construction contracts may not be well-suited for selecting design professionals.[10] In recognition of this fact, one court has held that

> [i]t is . . . the general rule that contracts for services requiring special skills or training, such as the professions and vocations of . . . architects, . . . engineers, . . . and surveyors, are not required to be let on bids under a statutory or constitutional provision [which requires] that contracts with the state or municipality must not be entered into without first advertising for bids.[11]

Another court has noted that, because an architect requires special taste, skill, technical learning, and ability to perform his job, "it would be bad judgment to advertise and get many bids when the lowest bidder might also be the least capable and most inexperienced."[12] Thus, "the employment of a person who

---

6. *Id.* § 2.40; 48 C.F.R. §§ 13.000, 2.101 (F.A.R. §§ 13.000, 2.101) (setting federal small-dollar exemption at $100,000).
7. Bruner & O'Connor, *supra* note 1, § 2:37.
8. *Id.* § 2:38.
9. *Id.* § 2:38; Fundamentals of Construction Law 54–55 (Carina Y. Enhada et al. eds. 2001).
10. Bruner & O'Connor, *supra* note 1, § 2:30.
11. Parker v. Panama City, 151 So. 2d 469, 472 (Fla. Dist. Ct. App. 1963).
12. Cobb v. Pasadena City Bd. of Ed., 134 Cal. App. 2d 93, 95, 285 P.2d 41, 42 (Cal. Dist. Ct. App. 1955). That is not to say that a no-bid system is beyond suspicions of its own. *See, e.g.,* Schofield v. Gerda, 2017 WL 2180708, at *3 (Tex. Ct. App. 2017) (architecture firm that was given no-bid contract involved in campaign contribution questions).

is highly and technically skilled in his science or profession is one which may properly be made without competitive bidding."[13] In response to these concerns, the federal government and many state governments have created statutes that either exempt or remove design professionals from the competitive bidding process and, instead, attempt to balance the goals of securing the desired design professionals, containing costs, and limiting favoritism or fraud.[14]

"The policy of the Federal Government is to publicly announce all requirements for architectural and engineering services and to negotiate contracts for architectural and engineering services on the basis of demonstrated competence and qualification for the type of professional services required and at fair and reasonable prices."[15] Under this policy, the government encourages design professionals to submit qualification and performance data for the agency's consideration.[16] The agency then "shall conduct discussions with at least [three] firms to consider anticipated concepts and compare alternative methods for furnishing services."[17] From those firms, the agency shall select three or more firms that it deems "most highly qualified to provide the services required,"[18] and then attempt to negotiate a "fair and reasonable" contract with the firm that it considers the most qualified for the job.[19] If those negotiations are unsuccessful, the agency shall then attempt to negotiate a fair and reasonable contract with the "next most qualified of the selected firms," and then the next, until the agency finally reaches an agreement for the design services.[20]

Many states follow the federal practice of advertising or publicly announcing the design project.[21] Similarly, many states require the awarding agency to consider a minimum number of design firms for the project.[22] Other states do

---

13. *Id.* (citations omitted).

14. W.V. Nelson Constr. Co. v. City of Lindstrom, 565 N.W.2d 434, 435–36 (Minn. Ct. App. 1997); CONSTRUCTION LAW ¶ 15.01[1] State Procurement of Construction and A/E Services—An Overview (Steven G.M. Stein ed., 2017).

15. 40 U.S.C.A. § 1101 (formerly 40 U.S.C.A. § 542).

16. *Id.* § 1103(b) (formerly § 543).

17. *Id.* § 1103(c).

18. *Id.* § 1103(d).

19. *Id.* § 1104(a)–(b) (formerly § 544).

20. *Id.* § 1104(b).

21. *See, e.g.*, N.C. GEN. STAT. § 143-64.31(a) (2017); 4 PA. CODE § 64.4 (2017).

22. *See, e.g.*, CAL. GOV. CODE § 4527 (2017) (requiring the consideration of at least three firms); FLA. STAT. § 287.055(4) (2009) (requiring the ranking of at least three firms); MD. STATE FIN. & PROC. CODE § 13-304(b) (2007) (requiring the consideration of at least two firms when the total cost estimate for the design services exceeds $200,000); 4 PA. CODE § 64.8 (2017) (requiring the consideration of at least three design firms); KAN. STAT. ANN. § 75-1253 (2017).

not require that public agencies consider a specific number of firms, but only that they begin negotiations with the "best qualified" firm or firms.[23]

When evaluating design firms, many states specify criteria other than cost. Some states base designer selection solely on the designer's demonstrated "competence and qualifications."[24] Other states consider a larger range of factors, such as the design professional's previous performance, location, workloads, and project complexity.[25]

Some states add enhanced oversight to the design procurement process by requiring the use of third-party decision makers in the bidding process. For example, Pennsylvania, Maryland, and Kansas use independent selection or negotiation committees,[26] while Oklahoma requires that the State Purchasing Director approve all design agreements.[27]

Many states require their constituent agencies to negotiate an agreement with the most qualified designer.[28] If that negotiation is unsuccessful, then they negotiate with the next most qualified firm, and then the next, until they reach an agreement.[29] In many states, the only statutory price limit on these agreements is that they must be "fair and reasonable."[30] Some states, however, have statutorily limited the designer's fee to a fixed percentage of the total project cost.[31]

---

23. *See, e.g.*, N.C. Gen. Stat. § 143-64.31(a) (2014) (allowing an unspecified number of qualified firms); Okla. Stat. tit. 74, § 85.7 (2013) (noting that Oklahoma requires competitive bidding for design services costing more than $25,000 but not specifying how many firms must compete and awarding projects to the "lowest and best, or best value, bidder").

24. *See, e.g.*, La. Rev. Stat. Ann. § 38:2318.1(A) (2016); N.C. Gen. Stat. § 143-64.31(a) (2014); 4 Pa. Code § 64.5 (2017); Cal. Gov. Code § 4526 (2007) (requiring the consideration of "demonstrated competence").

25. *See, e.g.*, Fla. Stat. § 287.055(4) (2017); Kan. Stat. Ann. § 75-1257 (2017).

26. 4 Pa. Code § 64 (2017); Kan. Stat. Ann. §§ 75-1251, 75-1253 (2017).

27. Okla. Stat. tit. 74, § 85.7 (2017).

28. *See, e.g.*, N.C. Gen. Stat. § 143-64.31(a) (2014).

29. *Id.*

30. *See, e.g.*, Cal. Gov. Code §§ 4527–4528 (2017) (requiring selection and ranking of at three firms, followed by negotiations for a "fair and reasonable" agreement). La. Rev. Stat. Ann. § 2318.1(A) (2017) (expressly forbidding the selection of design professional based on price or price-related information but selecting providers of such services "on the basis of competence and qualifications for a fair and reasonable price"); N.C. Gen. Stat. § 143-64.31(a) (2017) (selecting firms without regard to fees and then negotiating for fair and reasonable agreements); Cal. Gov. Code § 4527 (2017) (ranking three firms and then negotiating with best for fair and reasonable deal).

31. Kan. Stat. Ann. §§ 75-125375–1263.

C. Selection of Contractors

Traditionally, public construction procurement has utilized the Design-Bid-Build project delivery system, in which the contract is awarded to the lowest responsive, responsible bidder under a sealed, competitive bid process. Under this so-called open bidding approach, a public owner separates the design and construction phases of the project and obtains a complete project design without any input from the contractor. The owner then has prospective contractors bid on the project as designed and awards the contract to the lowest bidder.

1. Traditional Methodology for Selection of Contractors

a. Advertisement for Bids

Traditional public procurement protocol begins with public owner's advertisement for bids. Advertisements for bids (oftentimes referred to as "solicitations for bids") typically are required to be published in newspapers having general circulation in the geographic area where the project is located. Such advertisements provide prospective bidders with a description of the project sufficiently detailed to allow a reasonable opportunity to consider whether to bid upon it, and instructions on how to obtain the project manual and other relevant documents upon which to base their bids. Other information, such as the required bid security and bonding requirements, how long the bid must be held "firm" (i.e., unrevocable) by the contractor, and any MWBE (Minority and Women Business Enterprises) requirements may be included as well. Most importantly, the announcement should include the date, time, and place for the bid submission and subsequent bid opening.

It is important that the advertisement allow a prospective bidder sufficient time to formulate its bid on the project. Allowing sufficient "lead time" between bid advertisement and bid opening will, in theory, increase the number of contractors and subcontractors submitting bids on the project and decrease bid amounts.[32] More importantly, allowing adequate bid preparation time will prevent unscrupulous public officials from circumventing the requirements of the public procurement laws by giving some bidders a head start by sharing information about an upcoming bid that was not provided to the rest of the contracting community.

b. The Bid Package

In order to ensure that the submissions of all bidders are given equal consideration, the owner must be able to make a fair comparison of the bids submitted.

---

32. BRUNER & O'CONNOR, *supra* note 1, §§ 2:87, 2:58.

Thus, it is essential that the owner standardize the information upon which competing contractors base their bids. This standardized set of owner instructions is generally referred to as the "bid package" or "project manual."

Assuming the project to be bid upon has already been designed, the project plans and specifications will almost certainly be included in the bid package. A copy of the proposed contractual terms, general conditions, and any special or supplementary conditions are also commonly included. Finally, should the owner desire to provide the potential bidders with the results of any geotechnical or other engineering reports made concerning the project site, these will be included in the bid package as well.

Sometimes, an owner has not made its final decision on all items to be constructed by the successful bidder by the time that it puts the project out for bid. Other owners may not know if their construction budget will be sufficient to cover all items on their wish list until the preliminary construction costs are received from the bidders. One mechanism for dealing with this uncertainty is to ask the prospective bidders to submit a base bid package covering those items that an owner clearly intends to construct and also one or more alternates that an owner is free to accept or reject before the final contract price is set. The use of alternates in the competitive bidding process has proven to be fertile ground for bid-related disputes. For example, what if the lowest bidder on the owner's base contract work is no longer the lowest bidder once its bids on the owner's requested alternates are considered?

Another means for allowing an owner flexibility in the bidding process is to ask bidders to include in their bids pricing budgets, or "allowances," for certain items (e.g., floor or wall coverings and plumbing or lighting fixtures). The use of such allowances allows an owner to make its contract award and then later decide on whether it desires to vary the quantity or quality of that item to reduce the final pricing for it.

Sometimes, an owner may desire to correct, clarify, or augment its bid package after it has been distributed to prospective bidders but before their bids are submitted. In order to do so, the owner, typically through its designer, issues "Addenda." These Addenda, like the other materials contained in the bid package, will be binding upon the prospective bidders. Accordingly, an owner will typically require the prospective bidder to formally acknowledge receipt of any addenda issued.

In addition to the advertisement itself, an owner often will conduct a pre-bid conference with the prospective bidders. Such conferences allow the owner to introduce its design and ownership team, solicit questions from the bidders regarding any ambiguities in the bid package, and otherwise generate enthusiasm amongst the prospective contractors and subcontractors who may want to submit bids on the project. Some owners make attendance at these conferences mandatory, while others do not. In either case, it is important that the owner not rely simply on verbal instructions provided to the prospective bidders at these meetings, but instead memorialize these instructions in meeting minutes or, better yet, Addenda. This is particularly important when the instructions have the effect of modifying the express terms of the other materials contained in the bid package.[33]

When construction projects are awarded by virtue of the competitive bidding system, the bid package must be sufficiently correct and complete to allow bids to be submitted without the bidder making exceptions, exclusions, or assumptions with its bid. But most commercial construction projects involve a complex and intertwined system of materials, facilities, and equipment. Project plans may be comprised of hundreds of interrelated drawings, while project specifications may include thousands of pages of technical instructions. Inevitably, these plans and specifications will contain errors, omissions, and inconsistencies that can potentially impact the bidder's construction costs.

What then should a bidder do if it encounters ambiguities in the bid package that may affect its bid? Is a bidder under an obligation to obtain clarification of discrepancies in the materials that comprise the bid package?

Generally speaking, bidders are required to obtain clarification of obvious or "patent" discrepancies in the bid materials but are not held responsible for any hidden or "latent" ambiguities contained therein.[34] Whether a discrepancy is considered latent or patent is dependent upon the size and complexity of the project and bid package, the obviousness of the discrepancy, and the relevant significance of the discrepancy. In the event that a discrepancy is found to be patent, a contractor who without inquiry makes erroneous assumptions concerning that discrepancy is responsible for the extra costs resulting from its assumptions.

The same general considerations regarding a contractor's obligation to discover discrepancies in the bid documents apply to the contractor's obligation to factor site conditions into its bid price. In conducting a pre-bid site investigation, a contractor is held to a standard referred to as the "standard of reasonableness."[35] Generally, a bidder is entitled to rely on the accuracy of information included in the solicitation and is under no obligation to conduct

---

33. BRUNER & O'CONNOR, *supra* note 1, § 2:76 at n.13.
34. BRUNER & O'CONNOR, *supra* note 1, § 2:63.
35. North Slope Tech. Ltd., Inc. v. United States, 14 Cl. Ct. 242, 253 (1988).

his own surveys or go beyond what a simple site viewing might reveal.[36] As the United States District Court for the District of South Carolina has noted:

> Bidding contractors and subcontractors are not held to the knowledge and skill of geologists, geotechnical engineers, or fluid dynamic experts. They are entitled to rely on accurate and reasonably complete information supplied in the bid package and a reasonable site inspection. Beginning with *United States v. Utah, Nevada and California Stage Co.*,[37] a long line of United States Supreme Court decisions has made clear that when the government in its invitation to bid undertakes to specify certain existing conditions material to the performance of the contract, it is bound by these specifications and liable for any increased cost arising from their substantial variation.[38]

But what if the information supplied to bidders, while literally accurate, leaves the bidder with an incomplete or inaccurate picture of the project or project site? In such cases, a claim under the "superior knowledge" doctrine may be made when the government "fails to provide a contractor with vital knowledge in the government's possession which bears upon the cost of the contractor's performance under the contract at issue."[39] In order to recover under a superior knowledge claim, the bidder must demonstrate: (1) the government possessed information that materially affected the contractor's performance costs; (2) the information was not reasonably available to the contractor; (3) any contract specification supplied misled the contractor or did not put it on notice to inquire; and (4) the government failed to provide this information.[40] It is not necessary that the contractor prove that the government's failure was intentional. Even an inadvertent failure can be actionable.[41]

In *North Slope*, for example, the United States Court of Claims held that an owner-provided geotechnical or "soil boring" report is "considered the most reliable reflection of subsurface conditions."[42] Thus, where the government

---

36. Mojave Enters. v. United States, 3 Cl. Ct. 353, 358 (1983); *see* BRUNER & O'CONNOR, *supra* note 1; Helene Curtis Indus., Inc. v. United States, 312 F.2d 774, 160 Ct. Cl. 437 (1963); Burling Builders, Inc. v. CMO, 2017 Ill. App. (1st) 170818-U, ¶ 27, 2017 WL 4340440, at *5 (Ill. Ct. App. 2017) (arbitration clause encompassing owner omissions included owner's failure to discover particular site conditions before letting project out for bid); Magnus Pacific Corp. v. United States, 133 Fed. Cl. 640 (Fed. Cl. 2017).

37. United States v. Utah, Nevada and California Stage Co., 199 U.S. 414, 26 S. Ct. 69, 50 L. Ed. 251 (1905).

38. W.F. Magann v. Diamond Mfg. Co., Inc., 580 F. Supp. 1299, 1313 (D.C.S.C. 1984), *rev'd in part on other grounds*.

39. Hercules, Inc. v. United States, 24 F.3d 188, 196 (Fed. Cir. 1994).

40. *Id.*; J.F. Shea Co. v. United States, 4 Cl. Ct. 46, 53 (1983).

41. *See* Granite Constr. Co. v. United States, 24 Cl. Ct. 735, 750 (1991).

42. 14 Cl. Ct. at 254 (citations omitted).

possesses materials which qualify or expand upon the borings, this information would be "relevant and important to bidders," and the government "should have disclosed the information in the contract documents."[43]

The government discharges its duty to disclose only when its disclosure is communicated effectively to the contractor.[44] Thus, the government does not satisfy its duty of disclosure unless it shows that the disclosure was not only made but also "heard, and understood, actually or apparently."[45] Because "[t]here is no practical way the government can know for sure that someone understands . . . [if the government] has done all it can to get the information out *loudly and clearly*, it has done all it can."[46]

c. Bid Preparation Techniques

To prepare its bid, a contractor is required to estimate both the prices and quantities of a multitude of materials and equipment to be incorporated into the finished project. These include:

1. Material costs
2. Labor costs
3. Equipment costs
4. Subcontractor costs
5. Jobsite overhead or "general conditions" costs (e.g., jobsite trailers, temporary water and electricity, insurance, and office equipment and supplies)
6. Home office overhead expenses (e.g., rent, staff salaries, advertising costs, and professional fees)
7. Profit

On larger projects, accurately estimating the total project costs would be virtually impossible without the input of the many subcontractors and suppliers who desire to contribute to the project. Accordingly, bidders on more complex projects spend a great deal of time in the days and hours leading up to a so-called bid day compiling and analyzing the bids of its potential subcontractors and suppliers and then determining which bids to incorporate into the bidder's own submission to the owner. When a subcontractor or supplier submits a subcontract price that it later cannot honor, a question arises as to whether the general contractor or subcontractor is responsible for the resulting cost overrun. Courts faced with deciding whether the subcontractor is bound

---

43. *Id.*
44. PetroChem Services, Inc. v. United States, 837 F.2d 1076, 1080 (Fed. Cir. 1988).
45. *Id.*
46. *Id.* (emphasis added).

by its proposal to a contractor have tended to adopt one of two distinct positions on the issue, both of which are discussed at length elsewhere.[47]

2. Contractor Selection Criteria

a. The Duty to Award to the Lowest Bidder and Owner's Right to Rebid

On most public projects, an open bidding process is utilized, wherein the various contractor bids are opened publicly at a predetermined time, with the project then awarded to the lowest bidder. Critical to this process is that the owner be required to accept that price without engaging in rebidding or post-bid opening negotiations in an attempt to further drive down project costs.

But what if the owner is not satisfied with the bids received? If the lowest bid submitted is still in excess of the funds available for the project, many states will authorize the public owner to re-advertise the project for bid at a later date. Alternatively, some states authorize the public owner to enter into negotiations with the lowest bidder to reduce the quantity or quality of work in that bidder's scope of work so as to reduce the overall project costs.[48]

Public bidding statutes routinely reserve to the owner the right to reject a bid for other compelling reasons. These statutes also typically allow a public owner to cancel an invitation whenever it is determined to be in its best interests to do so. In so doing, most states will require a showing that the public owner's actions were not undertaken arbitrarily or for purposes of evading public procurement laws.[49]

What if the owner desires to award the project to a bidder other than the one submitting the lowest bid? Generally speaking, an owner is not required to base its award solely on price. To the contrary, a public owner must make its award to the lowest responsive, responsible bidder, taking into consideration factors such as quality, experience, performance, and construction duration. Issues of responsibility and responsiveness will be addressed in the sections that follow.

b. Bid Responsiveness and Waiver of Bidding Irregularities

To achieve the policy objectives underscoring competitive bidding, a bid submitted during the process must be responsive to the requirements stated in the owner's solicitation materials, or the bid will be rejected, even if it is the lowest one received.[50] Responsiveness is required because:

---

47. *See* Chapter 10.
48. N.C. Gen. Stat. § 143-129(b) (2017) (eff. 2015).
49. Bruner & O'Connor, *supra* note 1, §§ 2:151, 2:153.
50. *Id.* § 2:90, at 181.

[a]ny material deviation from the requirements of the invitation or statutory mandates destroys any ability to compare that bid competitively on the basis of price with other bids submitted and, if permitted to be considered, would violate the public policy objectives underlying the competitive bidding procedure of allowing bidders an equal right to compete.[51]

The bid must respond to mandatory requirements in the invitation or statute and should substantially comply with non-mandatory requirements, as well.[52] A material variation is one that would give the bidder "a substantial advantage or benefit not enjoyed by other bidders."[53] Examples of deviations that may be material and unacceptable include bids that are incomplete or late, were "prepared without a mandatory site inspection," propose "alternate work or materials not conforming substantially to specification requirements," or "fail to include required bid security."[54]

A bid that does not conform precisely to the invitation may still be accepted if the deviation is considered to be immaterial.[55] An immaterial deviation is one that has a "negligible effect upon price, quantity, quality, or time of completion of the work to be performed."[56] Examples of non-material (and therefore waivable) bid deviations include failing to initial changes or corrections, submitting a bid with changes initialed by someone other than the person who signed the bid, or failing to acknowledge an amendment to the bid schedule by submitting the bid based on an old schedule.[57] The failure to sign a bid proposal may be material, depending on whether a signature on another document is sufficiently connected to the proposal to make it a binding contract.[58]

---

51. *Id.* § 2:91, at 184.
52. *Id.* § 2:75, at 185.
53. Gostovich v. City of W. Richland, 75 Wash. 2d 583, 587, 452 P.2d 737, 740 (1969) (quoting Duffy v. Vill. of Princeton, 240 Minn. 9, 60 N.W.2d 27, 29 (1953)).
54. BRUNER & O'CONNOR, *supra* note 1, at 185 (listing 13 "deviations that raise issues of 'materiality'").
55. Stephanie Giggetts & Eric Surette, 64 AM. JUR. 2D *Public Works and Contracts* § 65 (Westlaw 2007). *See, e.g.*, Alpha Painting & Constr. Co. Inc. v. Delaware River Port Auth. of Pa. and N.J., 853 F.3d 671, 676 (3d Cir. 2017) (Delaware River Port Authority bid guidelines allow acceptance where deviations are immaterial.).
56. BRUNER & O'CONNOR, *supra* note 1, at 206 (citing 48 C.F.R. § 14.405(d)).
57. *In re Consol. Contracting & Eng'g*, 1996 WL 639911, at *2 (Comp. Gen. Nov. 6, 1996).
58. *Compare* Farmer Constr. Ltd. v. Washington, 98 Wash. 2d 600, 605, 656 P.2d 1086, 1089 (Wash. 1983) (holding that the lack of a signature on the proposal was waivable because the bid proposal and bid bond are connected with each other by internal references, and the bond was signed), *with* S.J. Amoroso Constr. Co. v. United States, 981 F.2d 1073, 1076 (9th Cir. 1992) (holding that the lack of a signature on the required Certificate of Procurement Integrity was a valid reason for determining the bid non-responsive, even though the bidder had signed other documents).

Some awarding bodies lack the statutory discretion to determine whether a requirement is waivable.[59] For the most part, however, public agencies have broad discretion in deciding whether a bid is responsive, and courts will set aside these decisions only if they are arbitrary, capricious, or an abuse of discretion.[60] For example, the Georgia Supreme Court stated that a county school board could waive a requirement, such as providing a list of all subcontractors, if the board decided that the requirement was not material. Similarly, the U.S. District Court for the Ninth Circuit held that rejection of a bid as non-responsive was proper where the required Certificate of Procurement Integrity (CPI) was unsigned when submitted, particularly because the certificate "imposes significant legal obligations on the contractor."[61] The court concluded: "If an agency decides to require a new CPI with such sealed bid, it is not the place of the court to substitute its judgment."[62]

c. Responsible Bidder

In the competitive bidding process, the "lowest responsive bidder" must also qualify as "responsible" before being awarded the contract.[63] In this regard, "[t]he sole question before the agency is whether the low bidder is or is not 'responsible'—*not* whether the bidder is most responsible among all bidders."[64]

As with the issue of responsiveness, the awarding body usually has broad discretion in making decisions regarding bidder responsibility. These subjective decisions may be based on "virtually any evidence reasonably related to the question of whether the contract, if awarded, will be faithfully completed in accordance with its terms—general standards such as integrity, past performance, experience, technical, financial and managerial capability, safety record, [and] licensure."[65] A bidder's "character and reputation," "energy," "fraud or unfairness in previous dealings, honesty, judgment, [and] promptness" may be considered.[66] A bidder's prior legal history and even "social responsibility" also may be valid factors in determining responsibility.[67]

---

59. *See* Hamp's Constr., L.L.C. v. City of New Orleans, 924 So. 2d 104, 110–11 (La. 2006).
60. BRUNER & O'CONNOR, *supra* note 1, § 2:108, at 206.
61. S.J. Amoroso Const. Co. v. U.S., 981 F.2d 1073 (9th Cir. 1992).
62. *Id.*
63. BRUNER & O'CONNOR, *supra* note 1, § 2:112, at 21–14 (discussing "public agency discretion in judging bidder 'responsibility'").
64. *Id.* § 2:110.
65. *Id.* § 2:112, at 214 (internal citations omitted).
66. *Id.* at 215 (quoting Bowen Eng'g Corp. v. W.P.M. Inc., 557 N.E.2d 1358, 1366 (Ind. Ct. App. 1990)).
67. *Id.* § 2:113.

The Wisconsin Court of Appeals, for example, ruled that the rejection of a bidder due to concerns about the bidder's past conduct and "performance of prior contracts" was valid because the awarding body had a rational basis for the decision and the rejection was neither arbitrary or unreasonable.[68] Like judicial review of decisions concerning responsiveness, courts generally set aside decisions regarding responsibility only if they are arbitrary, capricious, or an abuse of discretion.[69]

Determining that the lowest bidder is not responsible is not an abuse of discretion when the lowest bidder fails to submit requested information relevant to the owner's inquiry. In *Kinsey Contracting*, the lowest bidder did not submit the requested audited financial statement, list of pending claims, résumés of supervisors, or the name of the proposed excavation contractor.[70] The second-lowest bidder submitted the required information and was awarded the contract.[71] Although the lowest bidder argued that the term "'lowest responsible bidder' requires only that a contractor with the lowest bid have the proper license for the job, provide the necessary performance and payment bonds, and have adequate financial resources to perform the contract," the North Carolina Court of Appeals held that the award standard, as specified by statute, allowed consideration of other factors.[72] Thus, said the *Kinsey* court, "in the absence of fraud or a palpable abuse of discretion, [courts] have no power to control their action."[73]

Because a determination of responsibility based on standards that were not communicated to the bidders may be overturned as arbitrary and capricious, public agencies often include guidelines or criteria for responsibility in bid invitations.[74] Agencies that waive requirements set forth in established guidelines may still be given deference by courts, as long as the decision is

---

68. D.M.K. Inc. v. Town of Pittsfield, 290 Wis. 2d 474, 478, 483, 711 N.W.2d 672, 674, 677 (Wis. Ct. App. 2006).

69. *See, e.g.*, Synaptek, Inc. v. United States, 141 Fed. Cl. 443 (Fed. Cl. 2018). *See also* Lion Raisins, Inc. v. United States, 51 Fed. Cl. 238, 247 (2001) (holding that suspending a bidder as not responsible was arbitrary and capricious when that bidder was deemed responsible five times in the previous two years).

70. Kinsey Contracting Co., Inc. v. City of Fayetteville, 106 N.C. App. 383, 386, 416 S.E.2d 607, 609 (N.C. Ct. App. 1992).

71. *Id.* at 384, 416 S.E.2d at 608.

72. *Id.* at 385, 416 S.E.2d at 609.

73. *Id.* at 384, 416 S.E.2d at 608 (quoting Mullen v. Town of Louisburg, 225 N.C. 53, 60, 33 S.E.2d 484, 488–89 (1945)).

74. Bruner & O'Connor, *supra* note 1, § 2:112, at 216 (citing Harmony Constr., Inc. v. State Dep't of Transp., 668 A.2d 746 (Del. Ch. 1995)).

"reasonable and rationally based" and the waiver is "not a material deviation from the contract."[75]

Traditionally, responsibility is determined after the bids are reviewed for responsiveness.[76] In recent years, however, prequalification programs have been utilized to allow public agencies to make initial determinations of responsibility before soliciting bids.[77] In some states, however, this initial screening evaluates only some of the attributes (such as financial stability and bonding capacity) used in the later responsibility determinations.[78] In these jurisdictions, while bids are accepted only from bidders who are prequalified, passing this initial screening does not imply that the bidder will be deemed responsible after bids are opened and a final "responsibility" determination is made.[79] Standards of review for prequalification decisions vary; a court may give an agency's decision no deference or substantial deference, depending on whether the agency's reason was "a legal one, a factual one, or one of mixed law and fact."[80]

d. Bid Protests

What if the low bidder on a project believes that it was unfairly rejected for reasons of responsiveness or responsibility? Conversely, what if an unsuccessful bidder believes that the low bidder should be rejected as non-responsive or non-responsible? In both circumstances, a challenge to a public agency's procurement process may be made by undertaking what generally is referred to as a "bid protest."

Certain threshold questions impact a protesting bidder's right to relief. These include:

1. Standing,
2. Waiver resulting from unreasonable delay, and
3. The forum in which the protest is to be made.[81]

---

75. *Id.* at 216–17 (citing Suit-Kote Corp. v. City of Binghamton Bd. of Contract & Supply, 628 N.Y.S.2d 861, 863, 216 A.D.2d 831, 833 (N.Y. App. Div. 1995)).

76. Daniel D. McMillan & Erich R. Luschei, *Prequalification of Contractors by State and Local Agencies: Legal Standard and Procedural Traps*, Constr. Law., Spring 2007.

77. *Id.*

78. *Id.*

79. *Id.* at 25 (citing Crest Constr. Corp. v. Shelby Cnty. Bd. of Educ., 612 So. 2d 425, 430 (Ala. 1992)).

80. *Id.* at 33 (providing examples of courts giving or not giving deference to agencies).

81. Bruner & O'Connor, *supra* note 1, § 2:159.

A party must have standing to protest a bid. At the federal level, a protestor must be an "interested party."[82] An interested party is "an actual or prospective bidder or offeror whose direct economic interest would be affected by the award of the contract or by failure to award the contract,"[83] or as construed in other terms, the protestor must be an actual or prospective bidder (or offeror) who possesses a direct economic interest in the procurement.[84]

For state and local contracts, the 2000 Model Procurement Code for State and Local Governments provides standing to "any actual or prospective bidder, offer or contractor who is aggrieved in connection with the solicitation or award of a contract."[85] Other states, like Nebraska, only allow bid protests to be asserted by a taxpayer or rate payer.[86]

A protestor who challenges any contract award needs to assert its claims in a timely manner.[87] Failure to do so may result in a waiver of the right to protest the award.[88] For federal contracts, different deadlines exist depending on the nature of the protest.[89] State and local contracts also are subject to the statutes and regulations of their jurisdiction, and failure to assert the claim in a timely manner could subject the protest to dismissal.

The forum in which to challenge an improper award is dictated by the type of project involved. Protests involving federal projects can be heard by the awarding agency itself, the General Accounting Office, or the U.S. Court of Federal Claims. In states that have adopted the Model Procurement Code, protests are mandated by statute.[90] In South Carolina, for example, a protest must be made to the chief procurement officer within ten days of the award and must set forth the grounds for the protest and the relief requested.[91]

Some states, such as Florida, Illinois, and New Jersey, have a centralized agency that resolves bid protests.[92] For example, in Maryland, the bid protest must be filed with its board of contract appeals within ten days from receipt of notice that the initial protest was denied by the state procurement office.[93] The

---

82. 28 U.S.C. § 1491(b)(1) (2017) (eff. 2011).
83. 31 U.S.C. § 3551(2)(a) (2017) (eff. 2009).
84. RMGS, Inc. v. United States, 140 Fed. Cl. 728, 736 (Fed. Cl., 2018).
85. 2000 Model Procurement Code for State and Local Governments § 9-101(1).
86. Day v. City of Beatrice, 169 Neb. 858 (1960).
87. Carlson T.V. v. City of Marble, 612 F. Supp. 669 (D. Minn. 1985).
88. 4 C.F.R. § 21.2(b) (2017) (eff. 2008).
89. *See id.* § 21.2.
90. BRUNER & O'CONNOR, *supra* note 1, § 2:162.
91. S.C.L. 1976 § 11-35-4210 (2017).
92. CONSTRUCTION LAW, *supra* note 9 § 2.03 [3].
93. MD. STATE FIN. & PROC. CODE § 15-220 (2017); MD. CODE REGS. 21.10.02.10 (2017).

board reviews the protest, solicits comments from the procurement agency and other interested bidders, and issues a decision.[94] If the bid protestor receives an unfavorable decision from the board, the protestor can appeal to the state court system.[95]

Other states employ a decentralized contracting system in which each agency is responsible for resolving its own protests. For example, Ohio has distinct statutory contract procedures for highway department projects, water improvement projects, and library construction, among many others.[96] In the absence of formal protest procedures at the state or local level, bid protest cases are typically heard in state court.[97]

If the protestor is successful in its protest, its remedies typically are limited to the recovery of its bid preparation costs.[98] Even where the agency has wrongly awarded a contract, it will rarely be required to pay lost profits to the unsuccessful bidder.[99] For this reason, many protestors seek to enjoin the owner from proceeding with its award to the competing bidder.[100] Injunctive relief may be difficult to obtain, however, because the bidder must establish:

1. That it will suffer irreparable injury if defendant is not enjoined, including, but not limited to, absence of an adequate remedy at law;
2. A likelihood of success on the merits;
3. The harm to plaintiff outweighs the harm to defendant; and
4. That it would be in the public interest to enjoin the defendant.[101]

Unsuccessful bidders seeking injunctive relief may also be required to post a bond, which may be forfeited if the challenge is rejected.[102] For this reason, a bid protestor needs to be cautious when filing a claim. If it is later determined that the protest was unlawful, fraudulent, or otherwise inequitable, the "disappointed bidder" who ultimately loses the bid because of it may assert a

---

94. MD. CODE REGS. 21.10.07.03 (2017).

95. CONSTRUCTION LAW, *supra* note 9, § 2.03 [3] State and Local Bid Protests.

96. *Id.*

97. See Eugene McQuillin, The Law of Municipal Corporations, (3d ed. 1949) §§ 29.83, 29.83.05, 29.85, 29.86.

98. *See* Lovering-Johnson, Inc. v. City of Prior Lake, 558 N.W.2d 499, 504 (Minn. Ct. App. 1997).

99. *See* State Mechanical Contractors, Inc. v. Vill. of Pleasant Hill, 132 Ill. App. 3d 1027, 87 Ill. Dec. 532, 477 N.E.2d 509 (Ill. App. 1985); *but see* Clark Constr. Co. v. Pena, 930 F. Supp. 1470, 1478 (M.D. Ala. 1996).

100. *See* H.R. Johnson Constr. Co. v. Bd. of Educ., 16 Ohio Misc. 99, 241 N.E.2d 403 (Ohio Com. Pl. Ct. 1968).

101. *See* ES-KO, Inc. v. United States, 44 Fed. Cl. 429, 432 (Fed. Cl. 1999).

102. *See* NewMech Companies, Inc. v. Independent School Dist. No. 206, 558 N.W.2d 22 (Minn. Ct. App. 1997).

common law claim against the protestor.[103] Nevertheless, in many cases, preliminary injunctions can be effective in preventing an owner from wrongfully awarding the project to a party other than the successful bidder or making payment on a contract that was not in compliance with statutory bid procedures.[104]

e. Bid Security and Mistakes in the Bidding Process

Absent a bid protest, the owner's selection of the lowest, responsible, responsive bidder typically ends the procurement process and results in the execution of a contract with the successful bidder. But what happens if the contractor selected later refuses to execute a contract? Allowing the contractor to withdraw its bid would return the owner to so-called square one in the bidding process. The owner would then face the costs and delay of repeating the bidding process and a potential price increase in the replacement bid.[105] To guard against this possibility, most public construction projects require that all bidders provide some form of bid security (generally a cash deposit or bid bond of at least 5 percent of the total bid price) to ensure that, if selected, the bidder will enter into a contract for the work it bid upon.[106] If the selected contractor refuses to honor its bid, the owner may retain the bid security to offset its resulting loss. This forfeiture encourages a contractor to only submit a bid that it is prepared to honor if selected.

But what if a contractor's bid was made in error? In some cases, a court may allow a contractor to withdraw a mistaken bid without forfeiting its bid bond. To withdraw a bid, the contractor generally must satisfy two conditions.[107] First, the "mistake must be one of 'fact.'" Mistakes in judgment will not suffice.[108] A mistake of fact typically involves a clerical error, such as a numerical miscalculation,[109] typographical mistake,[110] or an omission of a

---

103. Davis & Associates, Inc. v. Midcon, Inc., 127 N.M. 134, 138, 978 P.2d 341, 345 (Ct. App. 1999).

104. *Clark Constr.*, 930 F. Supp. 1470; Pincelli v. Ohio Bridge Corp., 213 N.E.2d 356 (Ohio 1966).

105. FUNDAMENTALS OF CONSTRUCTION LAW, *supra* note 9, at 159.

106. *Id.*

107. *See* James Cape & Sons Co. v. Mulcahy, 285 Wis. 2d 200, 225, 700 N.W.2d 243, 255 (Wis. 2005).

108. BRUNER & O'CONNOR, *supra* note 1, § 2:135.

109. Vintage Constr., Inc. v. State Dep't of Transp., 713 P.2d 1213 (Alaska 1986) (relieving the construction contractor of a bid total for $249,900 more than the actual total of the unit prices listed in the bid document).

110. Kemp v. United States, 38 F. Supp. 568 (D. Md. 1941) (allowing the construction contractor to withdraw its bid of $2,953.85 when it relied on a quote it had received for a machine that stated $2,813 instead of $20,813).

portion of the project advertised for bid.[111] Second, the mistake must be substantial enough to justify depriving the owner of the benefit of its bargain. Some states even require that the mistake be such that the owner would have reason to suspect a mistake by looking at the bid document itself.[112]

f. The *Croson* and *Adarand* Decisions and Hiring Preferences

Because the construction industry has few educational and financial barriers to entry, it has long been a vehicle to effectuate social change. At the same time, the construction sector historically has been dominated by white, male-owned enterprises.

In 1961, President John F. Kennedy used an executive order to introduce affirmative action into the federal procurement process.[113] In 1977, Congress furthered federal efforts to eliminate discrimination by establishing an administrative program that required all contractors to hire Minority Business Enterprises (MBE) for at least 10 percent of all public projects.[114] Three years later, the U.S. Supreme Court upheld this program in *Fullilove v. Klutznick*.[115]

As affirmative action programs gained judicial footing in the construction industry, local governments began implementing so-called set-aside programs to encourage contractors to award subcontracts to minorities by requiring all city construction projects to allocate a set percentage of the project to minority-owned businesses.[116] However, in 1989, in *City of Richmond v. J.A. Croson Co.*, the Supreme Court rejected this use of affirmative action.[117]

The set-aside program in *Croson* "required prime contractors to whom the city awarded construction contracts to subcontract at least 30% of the dollar amount of the contract to one or more MBEs."[118] However, in the project

---

111. James Cape & Sons Co. v. Mulcahy, 285 Wis. 2d 200, 207, 234–35, 700 N.W.2d 243, 246, 260 (allowing the contractor to withdraw a bid but only after forfeiting its bid bond, when the bid did not include a last-minute $130 increase by one of the subcontractors).

112. *See* Arcon Constr. Co. v. State, By and Through Dep't of Transp., 314 N.W.2d 303 (S.D. 1982) (relieving the contractor from its bid on the grounds of unconscionability when the bid recipient "knew of the mistake prior to awarding the contract").

113. Exec. Order No. 10925 (1961) (stating that "[t]he contractor will take affirmative action to ensure that applicants are employed, and that employees are treated during employment, without regard to their race, creed, color, or national origin").

114. 42 U.S.C. § 6705(f)(2) (1977).

115. Fullilove v. Klutznick, 448 U.S. 448, 100 S. Ct. 2758 (1980) (upholding Congress' 10 percent MBE set-aside provision in the Public Works Employment Act of 1977).

116. City of Richmond v. J.A. Croson Co., 488 U.S. 469, 477, 109 S. Ct. 706, 713 (1989).

117. *Id.* at 511, 731.

118. *Id.* at 477–78, 713 ("The 30% set-aside did not apply to city contracts awarded to minority-owned prime contractors.").

at issue, only one MBE subcontractor expressed an interest in the project and even then at prices that were over market rates.[119] The contractor challenged the City's MBE requirements under the Equal Protection Clause of the Fourteenth Amendment.

In striking down Richmond's program, the *Croson* Court invoked a strict scrutiny test for evaluating affirmative action programs in the contractor selection process that asks whether the program is narrowly tailored to serve a compelling government interest and whether there is a "strong basis in evidence for its conclusion that remedial action was necessary."[120] The City of Richmond failed to satisfy this test when it did not present any direct evidentiary support for "the need for remedial action" to the Court. Thus, the Court declared the program unconstitutional.[121]

In 1995, the U.S. Supreme Court, in *Adarand Constructors, Inc. v. Pena*, affirmed its earlier ruling in *Croson* and held that federal affirmative action preference programs must also undergo the strict scrutiny standard of judicial review.[122] In the wake of *Croson* and *Adarand*, the constitutionality of Minority and Women Business Enterprises (MWBE) programs has faced new challenges as the parameters of permissible affirmative action programs are continuously evaluated under the Supreme Court's strict-scrutiny standard.[123] MWBE programs work to remedy "past or present discrimination," an interest courts generally find sufficiently compelling.[124] Therefore, challenges to these programs typically focus on "the adequacy of the evidence" of past discrimination and

---

119. *Id.* at 482–83, 716.

120. *Id.* at 500, 509–10, 725, 730 (quoting Wygant v. Jackson Bd. of Educ., 476 U.S. 267, 277, 106 S. Ct. 1842, 1849 (1986)) (stating, "If the city of Richmond had evidence before it that nonminority contractors were systematically excluding minority businesses from subcontracting opportunities it could take action to end the discriminatory exclusion.").

121. Adarand Constructors v. Slater, 228 F.3d 1147 (10th Cir. 2000). *Adarand* appealed the Tenth Circuit decision, asserting that the Court of Appeals misapplied the strict scrutiny standard and that the federal program was not narrowly tailored. The Supreme Court, after oral argument following its grant of certiorari, dismissed the granting of certiorari as being "improvidently granted." Adarand Constructors, Inc. v. Mineta, 534 U.S. 103, 122 S. Ct. 511 (2001). The case had a nine-year history, beginning with Adarand Constructors v. Skinner, 790 F. Supp. 240 (D. Colo. 1992).

122. Advanced Constructors v. Pena, 115 S. Ct. 2097 (1995).

123. *See* Contractors Ass'n of E. Pa. v. City of Phila., 91 F.3d 586 (3d Cir. 1996); Concrete Gen., Inc. v. Washington Suburban Sanitary Comm'n, 779 F. Supp. 370 (D. Md. 1991); Edinger & Son v. City of Louisville, 802 F.2d 213 (6th Cir. 1986); Eng'g Contractors Ass'n of S. Fla. v. Metro. Dade Co., 122 F.3d 895 (11th Cir. 1997).

124. *Eng'g Contractors*, 122 F.3d at 907 (quoting Ensley Branch, NAACP v. Seibels, 31 F.3d 1548, 1565 (11th Cir. 1994)).

on whether the program at issue is "narrowly tailored."[125] Common targets of challenges include overly broad ordinances or arbitrarily set percentages. The existence of race-neutral remedial alternatives may also be grounds for striking down a program.[126]

In evaluating preference programs, courts consider statistical studies made before and after the program, along with anecdotal evidence.[127] A general claim of societal discrimination, however, is not enough.[128] Strict scrutiny requires a "strong basis in evidence" that reveals patterns of discrimination "persistent in the local construction industry" before and after enactment—census data, statistical disparity studies, local hearings, phone surveys, and questionnaires.[129] Anecdotal evidence from the testimony of minority and non-minority contractors regarding their personal experiences with the local industry also serves to supplement the evidence.[130] While *Croson* did not go as far as to set forth a requirement of negating "all evidence of non-discrimination," it did set forth a more rigorous level of scrutiny.[131] MWBE programs now face a higher standard of proof that requires clear evidence of local discriminatory practices and how the program will counteract the effects.[132]

Numerous MWBE programs have withstood the heightened scrutiny imposed by the *Croson* and *Adarand* Courts. For example, a San Francisco ordinance satisfied the strict scrutiny standard by replacing its previous set-aside

---

125. *Id.* at 906.

126. *Contractors Ass'n*, 91 F.3d at 608–10 (invalidating a program that included subcontractors, not just prime contractors, and that lacked evidence to explain how the city arrived at the percent set or why the city did not instead implement training and financial assistance programs).

127. Derek M. Alphran, *Proving Discrimination after Croson and Adarand: "If It Walks Like a Duck,"* 37 U.S.F. L. Rev. 887, 904, 916, 920 (2003).

128. Croson, 488 U.S. at 470, 109 S. Ct. at 709 ("The city's argument that it is attempting to remedy various forms of past societal discrimination . . . alleged to be responsible for the small number of minority entrepreneurs in the local contracting industry fails, since the city also lists a host of nonracial factors which would seem to face a member of any racial group seeking to establish a new business enterprise, such as deficiencies in working capital, inability to meet bonding requirements, unfamiliarity with bidding procedures, and disability caused by an inadequate track record.").

129. Concrete Works of Colo., Inc. v. City & Co. of Denver, 321 F.3d 950, 990 (10th Cir. 2003), *cert. denied*, 540 U.S. 1028, 124 S. Ct. 556 (2003).

130. *Id.* at 969–70 (noting additional prerequisites, unwarranted bid rejections, slower payment schedules, higher prices for materials, additional obligations, and difficulties joining unions and obtaining lines of credit).

131. *Id.* at 991 (citation omitted).

132. George R. La Noue, *The Impact of Croson on Equal Protection Law and Policy*, 61 Alb. L. Rev. 1, 40 (1997).

provision with "bid preferences."[133] Instead of requiring contractors to hire MWBE for a certain amount of the contract price, the city required a 10 percent bid preference for local MWBE bidders "to be taken into account when the city purchaser calculated the low bid.[134] The set-aside program required by the Illinois Department of Transportation also withstood challenge by allowing each selected contractor to set their own MWBE participation goal for the project that would reflect the availability of MWBEs in the local market.[135] These two programs indicate that jurisdictions can meet the Supreme Court's high standards by designing affirmative action programs with built-in flexibility.

g. Alternative Procurement Methods in the Public Sector

The practice of "competitive bidding" has been widely praised for providing taxpayers with the lowest possible construction costs by fostering competition amongst the bidders and by encouraging each bidder to present its best price. The practice has also been recognized as providing the most effective method of protecting the integrity of the bidding process.

The practice of awarding contracts based on price alone may not always be appropriate, given the complexity of modern construction projects. As a result, private owners have long embraced alternative delivery systems and methods when appropriate for the project at issue. More recently, public owners have begun adopting these approaches, as well.

i. Design-Build Construction in the Public Sector. As the name implies, design-build contracts bundle the project design and project building or construction into one contract. Design-build contracting offers an owner several advantages over the traditional, Design-Bid-Build method, which are discussed in more detail elsewhere in this book. By its very nature, however, design-build construction contracts do not allow an owner to make the sort of apples-to-apples comparisons that are the hallmark of the competitive bidding process. Accordingly, when awarding contracts of a design-build basis, public agencies typically follow procedures similar to those utilized when awarding design-only contracts. Such awards typically identify parameters of the job, advertise those parameters, invite proposals, and evaluate the relative skills of the various bidders.[136] Some public entities do consider the cost of the project, but

---

133. Associated Gen. Contractors of Cal. v. City and Co. of S.F., 748 F. Supp. 1443, 1446 (N.D. Cal. 1990), *aff'd*, 950 F.2d 1401 (9th Cir. 1991).

134. *Id.* at 1445.

135. N. Contracting, Inc. v. Illinois, 2004 WL 422704, *7 (N.D. Ill. Mar. 3, 2004).

136. *See, e.g.*, Cal. Pub. Con. Code § 20209.7 (2007); La. Rev. Stat. Ann. § 48:250.3 (2017) (eff. 2009).

do so by typically assigning weights to the various contractual considerations, such as price, features, functions, time, and life cycle costs. The entities then include those relative weights in their requests for bids, so that the designers-builders can tailor their proposals accordingly.[137] Public procurement policies must either (1) allow the public entity to select the designer-builder based on more subjective measures, or (2) require the use of published criteria, and finally evaluate the potential designer-builder in strict accordance with those criteria.[138]

In an effort to insert some element of competition and owner control into the design-build process, some public procurement laws have introduced the concept of so-called bridging into the design-build process.[139] Under this method, a public owner first contracts for the preparation of a set of preliminary bridging design documents, which typically includes 25 percent to 35 percent of the completed design for the entire project. The bridging design documents are then provided to prospective design-build bidders to review and incorporate into their respective proposals. Through the use of these bridging design documents, the public owner is able to solicit apples-to-apples competitive pricing for use in its deliberations, if it so chooses.

ii. Construction Management in the Public Sector. As discussed in greater detail in Chapter 4, Project Delivery Systems, the construction management project delivery method can take two distinct forms. In one context, a construction manager is used to describe a person or entity who contracts with an owner to manage, as the owner's agent, one or more of the contractors hired directly by the owner to construct the project. Such construction management (agency) engagements, like design contracts, typically are exempted from public procurement laws,[140] but may be subject to the same sort of previously discussed regulations that govern the selection of design professionals.

In its other manifestation, the term "construction management" refers to a contractor who, having entered into a contract with an owner for the construction of some improvement, subcontracts all of the work on the project, reserving for itself only the work of managing the effort. Construction managers under these arrangements are generally considered to be "at-risk construction management," in that they bear financial responsibility in the event the project exceeds the agreed-upon contract sum or duration. Construction

---

137. *See, e.g.*, Cal. Pub. Con. Code § 20209.7 (2007).
138. *See e.g.*, Cal. Pub. Con. Code § 20301.5 (2007); La. Rev. Stat. Ann. § 48:250.3 (2017) (eff. 2009) (noting that "the winning proposal shall be the proposal with the lowest adjusted score").
139. *See, e.g.*, N.C. Gen. Stat. § 143-128.1B.
140. Bruner & O'Connor, *supra* note 1.

management at-risk arrangements generally are not exempt from public procurement laws because they are more akin to a construction contract than a design agreement.

Because construction management at-risk agreements have become increasingly popular with owners, some states have expressly authorized construction management at-risk agreements in the public sector. In North Carolina, for example, construction managers at-risk may be selected under the same state regulations governing the engagement of design professionals. Once selected, the construction manager (at-risk) is required to conduct a traditional open bidding of its first-tier subcontracts, which utilizes certain prequalification criteria, and then awards each subcontract to the lowest responsible, responsive bidder, taking into consideration quality, performance, time, oversight, and other factors that might be deemed appropriate by the owner.[141]

iii. "Best Value" Awards in the Public Sector. Inherent in the competitive bid model is the possibility that the lowest bidder might not be the most qualified builder available. Moreover, the emphasis on construction costs alone ignores other long-term price considerations, such as utility costs, maintenance costs, renovation costs, or life cycle costs. Finally, the owner might not have fully anticipated or articulated its needs during the design phase of the project, and thus the design might need revision after the contract is awarded but before the project is complete.[142]

Value-based contracting in its various forms is an effort to overcome the preceding limitations and allow public bodies some of the same flexibility accorded to private owners. Value-based contracting allows the owner to consider factors other than initial construction costs when awarding the bid.[143] Often those considerations will be the future costs associated with owning the building, namely: "1) excessive renovation costs due to premature obsolescence; 2) excessive repair and renovation costs due to premature deterioration; and 3) excessive operating and maintenance costs due to inadequate design and construction."[144]

---

141. *See* N.C. Gen. Stat. § 143-128.1 (2017) (eff. 2014).

142. ABA at 2. James Schenck, IV & Robert Lee Carson, *Value-Based Procurement—Where Is It, Where Is It Going, and Are Construction Lawyers Ready for It?*, ABA Construction Forum Fall Meeting, October 2003, at p. 14.2.

143. Kiewit Infrastructure West Co. v. United States, 137 Fed. Cl. 689, 696 (Fed. Cl. 2018).

144. *See* Thomson & Kinzer, *Best Value in State Construction Contracting*, 19 Constr. Lawyer 31 (1999) (discussing the federal government's use of "best value" procurement instead of the traditional lowest responsive, responsible bidder model for some projects). *See also* McQuillin, *supra* note 97, § 37.106 (noting that competitive bidding may or may not be required by statute or ordinance).

At least six different types of value-based contracting have been identified:

1. "life cycle costing," which emphasizes the future costs of owning the building;
2. "sustainable design," which emphasizes long-term efficiencies and green technology;
3. "qualifications-based selection," in which the owner selects the designer or builder based on the competence and expertise of such designer or builder;
4. "commissioning," in which the owner documents the building's operational costs and performance and compares that to specified and promised performance;
5. "guaranteed cost savings contracts," where the contractor guarantees a positive return to the owner from the anticipated maintenance and operational savings; and
6. "privatization," in which the contractor assumes the long-term maintenance obligations on the project.[145]

Regardless of the form taken, value-based contracting allows the owner to enjoy greater savings over the life of the project even though the initial construction costs might have been greater than under the lowest-bidder method of contracting.

Value-based contracting is not without its detractors. First, it does little to avoid the appearance of impropriety in awarding bids.[146] Additionally, where owners consider items such as a builder's abilities and previous performance, value-based contracting can create an anti-competitive bias in favor of larger and previously used builders.[147] A few states have attempted to address these issues by requiring that the agencies consider the "equitable distribution" of contracts when they award contracts.[148] Others have attempted to address this by requiring that the awarding body assign specific, published weights to the factors it will consider and then rigidly adhere to those published weights when awarding the project.[149]

Value-based contracting creates new challenges for the construction lawyer, particularly with respect to the long-term accountability of design professionals

---

145. Schenck & Carson, *supra* note 142, at 5-12.
146. *Id.* at 14.
147. *Id.* at 4.
148. Robert S. Barns, Michael J. Schaengold, & Rodney A. Grand, *Best Value in Federal Construction Contracting*, 19 Constr. Lawyer 25, 26 (1999).
149. *See, e.g.*, Fla. Stat. Ann. 287.055(4) (2017); 62 Pa. Cons. Stat. § 905(e) (2017).

and builders.¹⁵⁰ Typically, these professionals have only been held to the standard of ordinary care and skill, have offered very short warranties, and have had their future liability limited by the statute of limitations.¹⁵¹ To hold those professionals accountable in the long term, the owner and builder likely will have to negotiate additional specific, and documented, guarantees.¹⁵² The owner and attorney will then need to keep accurate and detailed building performance records.¹⁵³ The design professionals and builders faced with these additional long-term liabilities will have greater risk exposure and will need longer-term insurance. That added expense will then make the projects more costly and may erode some of the financial benefits that value-based contracting originally offered.

iv. Reverse Online Bidding Techniques. A reverse online auction is an Internet-based method of bidding for the supply of construction services. As in the traditional bidding process, reverse auction bidding calls for an owner to publish a set of plans and specifications for contractors to review and bid upon. Unlike the traditional bidding process, however, where interested bidders submit their bids by hard copy, fax, or e-mail, online bidding takes place live, in real time, via the Internet, with invited bidders bidding against each other. Bidders remain anonymous but receive immediate feedback on the competitiveness of their last bid and have an opportunity to lower their price if they choose. As such, reverse online auctions work something like e-Bay in reverse, with the bidding remaining open until a predetermined deadline that may be extended indefinitely for as long as lower bids continue to be submitted. Once the auction concludes, the auction service provider notifies the owner of the bidding results and then initiates the appropriate follow-up with the winning bidder to complete the formal award of the contract.

Reverse online auctions have become increasingly popular in the private sector. Recently, the federal government has begun to utilize them as well. Proponents of the reverse online auction concept believe that the process is well-suited to determining market price sufficiently and fairly. For this reason, reverse online auctions have become increasingly popular with several nationwide big box retailers and contractors.

Others, particularly contractor groups, are vehemently opposed to the reverse online process.¹⁵⁴ "Critics of the net-based reversed auction bidding

---

150. *See, e.g.*, La. Rev. Stat. Ann. § 48:250.3 (2017) (noting that "the winning proposal shall be the proposal with the lowest adjusted score") (2017) (eff. 2009).
151. ABA at 14–15.
152. ABA at 17–19.
153. ABA at 20.
154. *Id.*

process question whether that process will allow sufficient communication to ferret out incomplete or uncoordinated design documents before such documents negatively impact project scheduling and costs."[155] Additionally, these groups caution that the nature of the auction itself, where a bidder's price is exposed to its competitors and then systematically driven downward, may encourage imprudent bidding. Some even suggest that reverse auctions do not result in any measurable savings to owners, because, unlike with a closed bid, each bidder recognizes that it will have the option to provide successively lower bids as the auction progresses.[156] As a result, a bidder has little incentive to lead with its best price and subsequently may never offer its lowest price. Critics further assert that the use of reverse auctions also may lead to higher costs due to decreased competition in the marketplace. If the contractors opt out of bidding in reverse auctions because of slim profit margins or philosophical or ethical objections, owners may suffer in the long run.

As with any new process or technology, online reverse auction bidding has had its share of technical glitches that have led unsuccessful bidders to mount legal challenges to the procedural fairness of the system. The holdings in these cases highlight the importance of having unambiguous ground rules in reverse auctions.[157]

MTB Group, Inc. v. United States presented the ultimate question of whether a federal government agency is permitted to use an online reverse auction. There, a bidder objected to the Department of Housing and Urban Development's use of an online reverse auction to obtain bids for housing inspection services because it feared that the small pool of bidders would allow other contractors to identify its bid, thereby destroying bidding anonymity.[158] While recognizing that a duty of maintaining bidding anonymity is imposed on all federal officials by law, the Court of Federal Claims nevertheless refused to grant an injunction. In doing so, the court held that the bidders waived their right to anonymity by participating in the auction, thereby consenting to the disclosure of their bids. The refusal of the Court of Federal Claims to strike down the use of online reverse auctions in *MTB Group* appears to indicate that this procurement mechanism will continue to be employed to award public as well as private contracts.

---

155. *See* Associated General Contractors of America, White Paper on Reverse Auctions for Procurement of Construction.
156. *Id.*
157. *See Pacific Island Movers*, B-287643.2 (Comp. Gen. 2001), *Royal Hawaiian Movers*, B-288653 (Comp. Gen. 2001).
158. MTB Group, Inc. v. United States, 65 Fed. Cl. 516, 519 (2005).

QUESTIONS

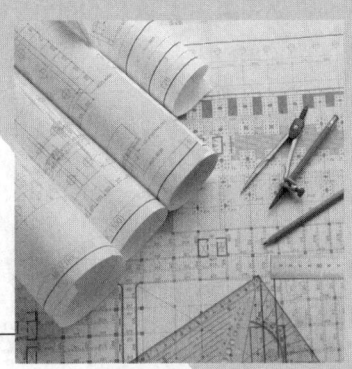

1. What if the lowest bidder on the public owner's base contract work is no longer the lowest bidder once its bids on the owner's requested alternates are considered? Must the owner select the bidder with the lowest base bid? May the owner select whichever bidder it chooses?
2. Would an owner be entitled to reject a bidder as not responsible based on the bidder's litigiousness? What if the bidder believes that it was well within its rights to have sued prior owners? What if it prevailed in those claims? What if the prior litigation involved the same owner awarding the current project?
3. What is the rationale for allowing mistaken bidders to withdraw their bid for clerical errors? Should similar relief be allowed for errors in judgment?

CHAPTER

9

Pricing Construction Contracts

STEPHEN A. HESS

9.01 INTRODUCTION

This chapter discusses the various pricing mechanisms that owners and contractors use to fix the contract price through which a contractor's compensation is determined for performing the work required of the contractor under a prime contract.[1]

Little recitation of case law exists related to this discussion. When the contract price is established by agreement between the parties, interpretation of the contract is governed by the fundamental rules of interpretation that govern all contracts; with few exceptions, those rules apply with equal force and, in many cases, were developed with reference to construction agreements. Instead, this chapter focuses its attention on the typical terms that parties employ in pricing the work to be performed.

---

1. The discussion in this chapter is equally applicable to pricing contracts between general contractors and subcontractors, but the discussion focuses on the owner and contractor for the sake of simplicity.

The pricing of construction contracts goes far beyond fixing the compensation for which a contractor is willing to perform work and the owner is willing to pay for such work. Instead, the specific mechanism that the parties choose has an important role in allocating the economic risks between the owner and the contractor. In addition, many contract clauses vary depending on the type of pricing that is used.

Accordingly, the immediate goal of this chapter is to describe the different pricing mechanisms used by parties to construction contracts. At the same time, and as important, this chapter endeavors to explain the extent to which the selection of a particular pricing mechanism inherently allocates risk between the parties and the manner in which parties mitigate such risks within the agreement itself or in their other commercial relationships. In addition, this chapter identifies and discusses numerous contract terms affected by the selection of the pricing mechanism. In completing this chapter, you should devote as much time to thinking about how the various contract terms are integrated into a cohesive unit as you think about the purpose and meaning of individual terms.

9.02 GENERAL PRICING MECHANISMS FOR CONSTRUCTION CONTRACTS

In the final analysis, pricing mechanisms can be divided into two types: those that fix the price of the work at a stipulated sum (fixed-cost) and those that allow the price to vary depending on the cost incurred by the contractor. This section discusses stipulated-sum contracts in some detail and then turns to an overview of the important considerations related to cost-plus contracts. The section continues by reviewing the manner in which these two basic types of pricing may be combined into one contract and summarizes other variations on these pricing schemes.

A. Stipulated-Sum Contracts

The simplest form of pricing is the stipulated-sum contract under which the contractor agrees to perform all of the work for a fixed figure. A typical contract provision reads:

> The Owner shall pay the Contractor the Contract Sum in current funds for the Contractor's performance of the Contract. The Contract Sum shall be Four Million Five Hundred Thousand and 00/100 Dollars ($4,500,000.00), subject to additions and deductions as provided in the Contract Documents.[2]

---

2. This clause is taken from AIA Document A101–2017, Standard Form of Agreement between Owner and Contractor Where the Basis of Payment Is a Stipulated Sum § 4.1 (2017).

There is nothing remarkable about this language, except perhaps its simplicity. The contractor's obligation is to perform the contract, and for that work the owner is obligated to pay a set figure. The contract price (in AIA terms, the "contract sum") merely fixes the amount of the compensation, and other provisions in the contract deal with such important issues as the payment process and change orders.[3]

1. Scope Limitations within Contract Price

In exchange for the contract sum, the contractor is required to perform all, but no more than, the work identified in the contract. When the owner or circumstances attributable to the owner change in a manner that increases the amount of work the contractor must perform, the contractor generally is entitled to an increase in the contract price. The usual mechanism through which such an increase is added is the contractor's submission (or the owner's proposal and the contractor's acceptance) of a change order. A change order takes its name from the fact that a change is being made in some term(s) of the contract, such as the scope of work, the contract sum, or the schedule.[4]

A fundamental attribute of a stipulated-sum contract is that the contractor bears all the entrepreneurial risk associated with the cost of performance, in exchange for which the contractor is exclusively entitled to reap the benefits of efficient performance. For example, if labor rates increase unpredictably and structural steel supplies experience rapid, unforeseen price spikes, the contractor may find itself in a contract whose performance will actually cost the contractor more money than the contract sum. The fact that unforeseen events cost the contractor its entire profit (and may force the contractor to incur a loss) is irrelevant to the contract sum or the enforceability of the contract. Regardless of actual costs to perform, the contractor is entitled to recover exactly the contract sum and no more.

Of course, the same principles apply if the contractor is able to work very efficiently, and if the construction costs turn out to be less than the contractor anticipated. If a contractor can perform a $4.5 million contract for out-of-pocket costs of $2.7 million, it makes a hefty profit, and the owner cannot object that the contractor is making, in the owner's words, "too much" money. In fact, the owner in a stipulated-sum contract does not usually have any means of finding out, and has no legal rights to know, how much profit the contractor built into its price, and the contractor may have good reason to keep this information from the owner.

---

3. See Chapters 12 and 14, respectively.
4. Changes are discussed in more detail in Chapter 14.

Why are contractors willing to undertake all of this risk? At the outset, the risk for short-term contracts is not generally that great. Although price variations exist in materials and labor, they usually are not so dramatic as to turn a profitable job into a money loser, even if they do shave some amount off the contractor's profit. Second, a contractor that works efficiently has the prospect of making even more than it budgets on a job, and the contractor might want to keep the entire benefit of any savings.[5] Third, a contractor can mitigate the risk of price fluctuations through advance purchases of materials or signing subcontractors to fixed price contracts.

Once the contractor binds itself to a specific stipulated sum for performing work within the scope of the contract, the only method through which it can increase the contract sum is through circumstances giving rise to a change order. For better or worse, this fact inherently gives the contractor substantial motivation to identify any of the work it is required to perform as falling outside the contractual scope of the work, as the contractor will only be entitled to additional compensation if such additional work is out of scope.

For example, civil site plans drawn in haste may fail to show precise boundaries of overlot grading, and the notes to the drawings may leave them tantalizingly ambiguous as to whether the overlot grading only encompasses the immediate building envelope or instead extends an additional 22,500 square feet to the boundaries of the owner's entire property. The contractor has some incentive to read the civil site plans narrowly, in a manner that requires it to perform very little overlot grading outside the footprint of the main building: Any additional work the contractor is required to perform is chargeable to the owner and is not within the original stipulated sum. The owner, on the other hand, will argue vociferously that the 22,500 square feet of alleged "additional" overlot grading is within the original scope of work, and thus within the stipulated sum that the contractor is entitled to be paid.

Two important attributes of stipulated-sum contracts are evidenced by the preceding discussion. First, a pure stipulated sum contract puts all the risk of an increase in actual construction costs on the contractor and gives the contractor the sole benefit of any efficiencies or reductions in the actual costs of performing the work. Second, in stipulated-sum contracts, inherent tension exists in construing the scope of work; that is, a contractor makes money by identifying any necessary work as falling outside the original scope of work in the contract; conversely, the owner saves money by construing as much of the

---

5. The reader may contrast this with a cost-plus contract, which is discussed later, wherein the owner generally gets most of the benefit of a contractor's efficiency in reducing job costs.

work as possible as falling within the original scope of work. This tension may bleed into the relationship between the design professional and the owner.

If the owner believes that it has contracted the entire scope of necessary work through the adoption of the design professional's drawings and specifications, only to find that substantial "extras" are required to get the building the owner envisioned, the owner may try to shift the burden of the additional expense to the design professional. It is not difficult to see in this chain that disputes over scope of work may lead directly to conflicts between the design professional and the contractor.[6]

Both the owner and the contractor want to put themselves in the best financial position they can; thus, many disputes under stipulated-sum contracts involve the proper characterization of the scope of work for which the contractor is entitled to be paid the contract sum.

2. Percentage of Completion Payments and Potential Abuse

The payment process is discussed in more detail in Chapter 12 but the pricing of lump-sum construction contracts has an important function that it is helpful to address at this juncture.

A stipulated-sum contract is usually paid over the course of time in payments known as progress payments, which are often calculated by reference to the method known as percentage of completion. When this method is utilized, the contract provides that the contractor is entitled to be paid each month the total value of the contract, multiplied by the percentage of the work completed through that month (less retention, which is discussed in Chapter 12 on payment). When the only contract pricing is the stipulated sum itself, the determination of the percentage of work completed may be a complex and seemingly arbitrary process for interim payments, but any imprecision in those payments goes away by the end of the project when the entire contract sum is paid upon final completion.[7]

---

6. Although it is beyond the scope of this chapter, the reader may wish to consider how this inherent tension plays out when the architect or design professional is put in the position of being a "neutral" administrator of the contract terms and is given the power, in the first instance, to render decisions concerning disputes between the owner and the contractor. Chapters 2, 6, and 7 discuss the multiple roles of the design professional.

7. Of course, when the percentage of completion method is used to determine payment when a contract is terminated midstream, that imprecision is never corrected. Sabco Corp. v Marquise Const. Corp., No. 13512/10, 2014-00739, 25 N.Y.S.3d 628, 2016 N.Y. slip op. 01313, 2016 WL 716909 (N.Y. App. Div. 2016) (subcontractor's recovery on termination limited to percentage of completion as determined under subcontract).

In order to add some fairness, rationality, and predictability to the percentage of completion method, the contractor may be required to submit with its bid a schedule, referred to as a "schedule of values," that allocates the contract sum among many discrete portions of the work for purposes of more finely assessing the percentage of completion of the work. In substantial projects, the schedule of values may have hundreds of items. In even a modest project, the schedule of values includes many entries.

The use of a schedule of values, however, also offers the contractor the opportunity to take advantage of the payment process in a manner that puts the owner at risk. Assume, for example, that a contractor agrees to build a medical office building for $12,000,000 on a site that requires excavation near the top of the water table, and thus the site must continually be dewatered. When offering its schedule of values, the contractor would do well to allocate $6,000,000 to "building excavation" and $500,000 per month for nine months of continuous "site dewatering." Of course, that would leave just $1,500,000 on the schedule of values for construction of the building itself. From the contractor's perspective, this is all wonderful; by the time the excavation is completed, the contractor will have earned half the contract sum. The owner, on the other hand, has given up substantial security (the unpaid contract sum) and is at substantially greater risk in the event the contractor is unable to complete the work.

As protection against this front-loading of a schedule of values, the payment provisions may void a patently front-loaded schedule of values, or give a third person (such as the architect) the responsibility for approving a schedule of values that will be used in the payment stages. These protections are important, as the failure to pay the contract sum according to the contract's payment terms may give the contractor the right to suspend or to terminate its work, as well as to foreclose a mechanics' lien during which disputes may arise as to the value of work computed under the percentage of completion method.[8]

B. Cost-Plus Contracts

A cost-plus contract is one in which the contract sum is calculated as the sum known as the "cost of work" *plus* some figure for the contractor's overhead and profit. A typical cost-plus contract sets out the contract sum as follows:

---

8. *See, e.g.*, J.D. Construction v. IBEX Int'l Group, 126 Nev. 366 (Nev. 2010) (court in mechanics' lien proceeding could summarily decide issue of value of work performed by contractor under percentage of completion method).

The Owner shall pay the Contractor the Contract Sum in current funds for the Contractor's performance of the Contract. The Contract Sum is the Cost of the Work as defined in Article 7 plus the Contractor's Fee.[9]

Just as we noted the simplicity of the stipulated-sum contract language, the reader will note the apparent simplicity of the language used for the cost-plus contract. But here, the simplicity is deceptive; as the saying goes, the devil lies in the details. And in this case, the precise devil is the definition of the cost of work and, more specifically, what is and what is not included within that "cost" as opposed to being part of the contractor's assumed overhead.

Before we turn to the issue of identifying the cost of work itself, it is helpful to review how the cost-plus contract allocates economic risk. In contrast to the stipulated-sum contract, the cost-plus contract gives the owner all of the risk and all of the benefit of unanticipated changes in material and labor costs, as well as all of the risk and benefit of the contractor's relative efficiency or inefficiency. At the same time, the cost plus contract has the potential of placing a substantially greater burden on the owner to monitor the course of construction from a financial standpoint, as the contractor has less financial risk at stake and less economic motivation to perform that particular work efficiently.

1. Cost of Work and Limitations Thereon

Returning to the issue of identification of costs, the following examples of potentially disputed costs reveal the necessity of a detailed definition of allowable costs that go into calculation of the contract sum as well as the necessity of controls on those costs. These examples are chosen to demonstrate in part that "the cost of work" is not as simple a term as one might imagine, and to allow the reader to understand different mechanisms for handling cost issues.

a. Subcontracted Work

Because the contractor bears the burden of all costs in a stipulated-sum contract, the contractor has a natural incentive to seek out the most cost-effective subcontractor that can perform the work responsibly. In a cost-plus contract, that motivation is absent, and the contractor may choose a more expensive contractor than it might otherwise choose so as to maintain a valuable professional relationship, to avoid the cost and administrative burden of pricing all the subcontract work, to increase its compensation (where it is a percentage of the total cost of work), or for other motivations or considerations that the owner does not share.

---

9. American Institute of Architects, AIA Document A103–2017, Standard Form of Agreement between Owner and Contractor Where the Basis of Payment Is the Cost of Work Plus a Fee without a Guaranteed Maximum Price § 5.1 (2017) [hereinafter AIA Document A103–2017].

The owner may seek protection from overpriced subcontractors in a cost-plus contract. One method for providing protection is to require that the contractor bid the work out just as if it were compiling the cheapest responsible team for a stipulated-sum contract. In the alternative, the owner might retain a construction manager or utilize its design professional for purposes of monitoring the procurement of subcontractors.

This is not to suggest that most contractors are selfish or unscrupulous. One of the biggest motivations for a contractor to keep costs down is that its future in the industry may depend on it. A cost-plus contractor who develops a reputation for overcharging owners is unlikely to flourish.

b. Contractor's Equipment

The cost of work generally includes such costs as rental payments on heavy equipment. When the rental company calculates its rental rates, it assesses the diminution in value that a piece of equipment will experience over its useful rental life; the cost of maintaining, licensing, and insuring the equipment; the cost of operating the equipment when fuels, oil, and other consumables are included in the rental; the taxes it must pay on the equipment; and such incidental items as the rental agency's overhead. These factors, together with some allowance for profit, are divided into the estimated period during which the equipment will be rented, and the result is some periodic rental rate. (As a practical matter, heavy equipment can usually be rented at hourly, daily, weekly, or monthly rates.) Owners usually do not quibble over paying these market rental fees.

On the other hand, some contractors maintain their own fleets of heavy equipment. Should they be entitled to charge the use of such equipment to the owner under a cost-plus contract, or is such equipment usually considered part of the contractor's general overhead for which it receives compensation in the "plus" part of the cost-plus formula?

There really is not much dispute that contractors who use their own equipment are normally entitled to charge for that equipment. A more difficult question is whether the rental rates for contractor-owned equipment should be calculated in a manner that allows the contractor to recover overhead and profit on the equipment itself in addition to the overhead and profit it otherwise recovers under the contract. There is no correct answer to a question like this; instead, what is important is that the parties agree on the method by which the contractor may charge for contractor-owned equipment. A traditional and accepted method is to append a schedule of values to the contract specifying the exact rate a contractor is entitled to bill to the project for its own equipment. In the absence of such a schedule, the attribution of "cost" to contractor-owner equipment can be a contentious and frustrating process for both parties.

c. Small Tool Allowance

The question in the preceding section concerned contractor-owned heavy equipment. A similar issue arises with respect to small tools. Battery-powered portable tools, for example, are not indestructible but instead are consumed over the course of many projects until they must be discarded. Other more durable tools still break, wear down, or otherwise need to be replaced. Are these costs part of the normal cost of work, or are they simply part of the contractor's overhead? Again, there is no correct answer to this question, and, as a practical matter, the answer is not all that important economically in the long run—if contractors never charged separately for small tools, their costs would simply get absorbed as part of their normal overhead, and they would start demanding higher payments for the "plus" portion of cost-plus contracts to recover consumable small tools.

As a practical matter, many cost-plus contracts have chosen to treat small tools as partially consumable items that are included in the compensable cost of the work.[10] That presents the question of how such tools are to be priced for cost purposes. Many contracts simply state a percentage of cost (typically 3 to 6 percent) for a small tool allowance. Others use more precise, but more ungainly mechanisms. For example, the standard AIA contract allows as a portion of the cost of work "the cost or value of the [tool] at the time it is first used on the Project site less the value of the item when it is no longer used at the Project site."[11] From an accounting, valuation, and administration perspective, it should be apparent that a stipulation as to values may cost the owner or contractor more money than it ought to cost, but will be accompanied by a substantial savings in transaction costs, that is, the costs of determining rental value.

d. Self-Performed Work

Some general contractors perform very little of the work they are contractually obligated to complete on a project, and instead delegate all work to subcontractors. Others perform very large portions of work with their own forces. The conceptual issue arises, with respect to such self-performed work, of how the

---

10. Some tools (or parts) are entirely consumed in a single project and can be priced at actual cost (e.g., saw blades, sanding belts).

11. AIA Document A103–2017, *supra* note 9, § 7.5.1. This formulation does not prevent the parties, as an administrative convenience, to value the diminution in value of such tools at 6 percent of their original cost.

work is to be priced.[12] Or, to put it differently, questions arise as to how to allocate the contractor's costs for performing work between the recoverable costs of construction and non-recoverable overhead.

Little problem exists with allowing a contractor to recover the cost of building materials incorporated into the project or the cost of laborers to execute the work. At the same time, the parties must be careful to agree as to the treatment of field personnel. When is a supervisor part of the contractor's unrecoverable overhead, and when is the supervisor appropriately considered a cost that the contractor incurs for which the owner should be billed? The answer is not to be found in any statute or case law—instead, the answer is to be found in the agreement between the parties and, in particular, in the definition of the term "costs" the contractor is allowed to recover.

Is there a typical or standard answer to the question? The AIA treats supervisory and administrative personnel costs as recoverable "when [they are] stationed at the site and performing Work, with the Owner's prior approval."[13]

e. Labor

One more of many issues that arise in determining the cost of the work under a cost-plus contract is the cost of labor. A contractor who pays a roofer $18 per hour in wages actually spends much more than that to keep the roofer on its staff.[14] To employ the roofer and set the roofer out to do work, the contractor usually must pay health insurance, employment taxes, pension benefits, cafeteria plan payments, workers' compensation, insurance, and so on. These additional costs are generally referred to as the labor "burden," and they are not insubstantial; labor burdens generally run 25 to 40 percent of actual wages. Those familiar with the construction industry know that workers' compensation rates for certain categories of labor (e.g., roofers and steelworkers) can be greater than the actual wages paid to such workers!

Three common ways exist of ensuring that the contractor recovers the actual cost of maintaining a labor force. The first allows the contractor to recover the actual costs of the employees by providing certified payroll accounting with the actual cost of the labor burden. This is the most accurate, and most administratively expensive method of pricing labor. A second, similar method specifies the burden as a percentage of the actual payroll the

---

12. A contractor may even be tempted to try to treat work as "self-performed" in order to take advantage of contract compensation when it is really subcontracted work. Westgate Planet Hollywood Las Vegas, LLC v. Tutor-Saliba Corp., 421 P.3d 280 (Nev. 2017) (unpublished).

13. *Id.* § 7.2.2.

14. In addition, in order to maintain a readily accessible workforce, the contractor may pay the roofer wages even when the roofer is idle.

contractor is entitled to recover. This is less precise than the first method, but much easier to administer. A third method schedules labor rates for different classes of workers and allows the contractor these "burdened" rates at the stipulated values.

2. Reasonableness or Necessity of Costs Incurred

Regardless of whether the contract provides a specific mechanism for allowing the owner to participate in regulating the cost through oversight, the contract may contain catchall language to protect the owner to the effect that the cost of work includes only the "reasonable" and "necessary" costs incurred in performing the work. The obvious purpose of such language is to provide some protection against runaway costs where the contractor exhibits no apparent responsibility in its selection of vendors or subcontractors, or otherwise incurs costs at a rate greater than the owner anticipated. In the absence of such a clause, the owner may still have recourse to some general duty of "good faith and fair dealing," although the application of such a general contract standard to the pricing of work under a cost-plus contract can be difficult.

3. Contractor's Overhead and Profit

The "plus" portion of a cost-plus contract is the compensation the contractor receives, both for its profit and for its general so-called home office overhead. As noted previously, questions often arise as to which potential cost items should be recovered separately under the contract, and which items are presumed to be part of the contractor's home office overhead. How are these "plus" figures specified?

a. Fixed Fee

One mechanism for fixing the contractor's fee is to state a flat fee for overhead and profit: "The Contract sum shall be the Cost of the Work (as defined below), plus a fee of $500,000.00 as the exclusive compensation for the Contractor's overhead and profit." When fixed fees are utilized, the contractor often contains a provision to ensure the fixed fee is increased if sufficient changes occur on the project.

b. Percentage of Contract

Another mechanism is to pay the contractor a percentage of the cost of work: "The contract sum shall be the Cost of Work (as defined below) plus 15%, which 15% shall constitute the Contractor's exclusive compensation for overhead and profit."

Some owners are concerned that the payment of a percentage of the cost of work actually encourages a contractor to work less efficiently so as to increase the contractor's own compensation. Such fears are usually unfounded for several reasons. First, most contractors understand the additional money they would earn by working inefficiently is not nearly worth the future business they stand to lose if they develop a reputation as a bad (inefficient) contractor. Second, a contractor busy with other work usually finds it more efficient to generate, to work, and to bill new business rather than to try to live off marginal increases in its compensation under a cost-plus contract. Finally, because an owner always has the ability to challenge the reasonableness of costs incurred, the inefficient contractor faces some risk that it will lose the ability to collect any inefficient costs and will actually lose money on the work to the extent of excessive costs (that is, not only will the contractor lose any profit on such work, but it will not be able to recover the cost of the work itself). That is not to say that no shady practices occur by contractors under cost-plus contracts with percentage of cost compensation schemes, but this concern is usually not substantial enough to justify a party's avoiding these compensation terms where they otherwise fit the parties' expectations.

4. *Estimates and Cost-Plus Contracts*

In deciding whether the owner wishes to use a cost-plus contract or a stipulated-sum contract, the owner may wish to have some idea of the projected cost so as to determine how much risk it is willing to take. The usual source of projected cost information is the design professional, one of whose paid tasks can be the compilation of a formal cost estimate for the work. The design professional's liability for a negligent cost estimate is discussed in Chapter 6.

The contractor may furnish an estimate for the owner's use, as well. Because the contractor and owner have divergent interests and the contractor is not generally paid for a cost estimate, it is not prudent for the owner to place too much reliance on a mere estimate.[15] After all, if the owner wants a fixed cap, the owner has the alternative of entering into a stipulated-sum contract or a cost-plus contract with a guaranteed maximum price, discussed later in this chapter.

At the same time, courts may be concerned that a contractor deliberately provides an artificially low estimate for the purpose of securing the work, with the recognition that the contractor ultimately will not bear the financial burden of this estimate. As a consequence, many government contracts include

---

15. A contractor does well to ensure there is no confusion on this point. *See, e.g.,* Di Sciullo v. Griggs & Co. Homes, Inc., 2015 WL 6393813, at *12 n.4 (E.D.N.C. 2015) (contract expressly provided that estimate was not a limitation on the price or warranty that final price would be no more than estimate).

clauses that cap the allowable costs at those set out in the estimate, absent advanced approval from the government. One court explained:

> The purpose of the [limitation of costs] clause is . . . to . . . protect both the contractor and the government. The ability to obtain government approval of additional costs before incurring them protects the contractor from discovering, after performing the contract at greater cost than anticipated, that its work has been financially disastrous because the government will not pay the additional costs. It also relieves the contractor, if such advance approval is not given, from its obligation to complete the contract or to incur costs in excess of the estimate. The limitation of the government's liability to the estimated cost stated in the contract (unless additional costs are authorized) protects the government from having to pay more than it had anticipated and set aside for the contract if the contractor's costs of performance exceed the estimate. It also gives the government the choice whether to incur additional costs for the contract or to have the contract terminated. It is therefore important that the requirements of the cost limitation provision be followed.[16]

Such clauses do not guarantee that the project will be completed at the cost estimated by the contractor, but it removes some of the incentive the contractor might have for producing a sloppy (or worse, intentionally understated) estimate.

C. Cost-Plus with Guaranteed Maximum Price

In many cases, the owner's greatest concern in a cost-plus contract is the risk of massive cost overruns, and the owner may believe that a cost-plus contract would be acceptable but for that risk. To address this concern, a third type of contract pricing has been created from cost-plus and stipulated-sum contracts that allows an owner to limit its risk, while at the same time allowing the owner to enjoy the benefits of cost-plus contract pricing. This third type of contract uses a hybrid of the two pricing mechanisms described so far and may be called cost-plus with a guaranteed maximum price.

As the name implies, the chief pricing term is a cost-plus term in which (ideally) the allowable and excluded elements of the cost of work are set out in some detail. Such contracts contain a separate cost limitation, however, expressed in language like the following:

> The Contract Sum is guaranteed by the Contractor not to exceed four million five hundred thousand and 00/100 dollars ($4,500,000.00), subject to additions

---

16. Inst. Sci. & Tech. Inst., Inc. v. United States, 53 Fed. Cl. 798, 807 (2002) (quoting Advanced Materials, Inc. v. Perry, 108 F.3d 307, 310 (Fed. Cir. 1997)).

and deductions by Change Order as provided in the Contract Documents. This maximum price is referred to in the Contract Documents as the Guaranteed Maximum Price. Costs which would cause the Guaranteed Maximum Price to be exceeded shall be paid by the Contractor without reimbursement by the Owner.[17]

Under a clause such as this, the owner bears the risk that the cost of work will be as much as the guaranteed maximum price (GMP), and the contractor bears the risk of any excess costs over the GMP.

In light of the risk of excess costs, the contractor under a contract with such a pricing term must take special care to ensure that the GMP is an acceptable figure and must effectively prepare its bid as though it were bidding a stipulated-sum contract. In short, a cost-plus with GMP pricing term operates as a cost-plus contract up to the point that the GMP is reached and a stipulated-sum contract thereafter. The student will appreciate the operation of such contracts in the discussion of specific terms later in this chapter.

D. Unit-Price Contracts

A variation of the stipulated-sum contract is a unit-price contract in which the owner (or the contractor, where the pricing occurs in a subcontract) pays a stated price for each unit of a particular type of construction, but pays for the actual units performed, rather than paying a fixed total. For example, a contract for excavation may provide that the subcontractor will be paid $3 per cubic yard for the excavation and remote disposal of dirt from a building foundation. A unit-price contract, unlike a stipulated-sum contract, puts the risk of variations in estimated quantity on the owner, but gives the owner the benefit of some cost control in the form of a fixed price for each unit of work.

Owner–contractor contracts priced entirely as unit-price contracts are relatively uncommon, but unit-price contracts between general contractors and subcontractors are not unusual, and many owner–contractor agreements contain at least some elements of unit-price contracting. For example, an owner may negotiate for a fixed price (stipulated sum) for the construction of an administration building and key elements of a water treatment plant, but agree, because of uncertainty in measurement (due to the preliminary state of planning, perhaps), to pay unit costs for the excavation and placement of piping that will transport the water to and from the treatment plant. A unit-price

---

17. American Institute of Architects, AIA Document A102–2017, Standard Form of Agreement between Owner and Contractor Where the Basis of Payment Is the Cost of Work Plus a Fee with a Guaranteed Maximum Price § 5.2.1 (2017).

contract requires some stipulation as to who bears responsibility for measuring quantities for payment purposes, as well as how disputes in measurements will be resolved.

1. VEQ Clauses

The use of unit prices generally places the risk of variations in quantities on the owner, but places the risk of variations in cost on the contractor. If excavation and placement of piping is priced as a unit price, the contractor suffers when the cost of pipe increases and benefits when the cost of pipe decreases.

Another element of unit pricing occurs where the cost estimate may vary in a manner in which the parties do not necessarily intend to allocate cost risk to the contractor, and that occurs where the variation in quantities (rather than market conditions) is responsible for the change in cost. If the contract states a unit price, it is often with some assumption by the parties about what the actual quantity will prove to be. A contractor who agrees to build approximately 600 feet of pipeline has very different unit costs from a contractor who agrees to build 60,000 feet of identical pipeline. A contractor who is willing to give a favorable unit price for 1,400 windows may find itself losing money if the design is changed mid-stream and the final building includes 350 windows.

Where the unit price is based on a common assumption or estimate of the expected quantities, the contract may allow revision of the unit price for variations from the estimated quantities on which the parties relied in negotiating the unit price. A "Variations in Estimated Quantities" (VEQ) clause set out in the Federal Acquisition Regulation (FAR) reads as follows:

> If the quantity of a unit-priced item in this contract is an estimated quantity and the actual quantity of the unit-priced item varies more than 15 percent above or below the estimated quantity, an equitable adjustment in the contract price shall be made upon demand of either party. The equitable adjustment shall be based upon any increase or decrease in costs due solely to the variation above 115 percent or below 85 percent of the estimated quantity.[18]

The question has arisen as to whether the variation in estimated quantities outside the 85 to 115 percent range automatically *requires* repricing of the unit price. One court held that it does not, and explained its understanding of the FAR's VEQ clause as follows:

> Contract interpretation begins with the plain language of the agreement. *Gould, Inc. v. United States*, 935 F.2d 1271, 1274 (Fed. Cir. 1991). The VEQ clause requires an equitable adjustment to be based upon any increase or

---

18. 48 C.F.R. § 52.211–18 (2005).

decrease in *costs*. The Government's preferred construction, however, requires the establishment of a new unit price for the overrun amounts by an equitable adjustment of the contractor's unit profit, even where the contractor's unit costs remained constant. This interpretation clearly contravenes the plain meaning of the VEQ clause. The express language of the VEQ clause precludes an equitable adjustment based on anything other than the contractor's costs.[19]

In this context, the use of the term "equitable adjustment" in a government contract is equivalent to a change order altering the contract price of the work that is subject to the VEQ clause. The clause just quoted does not dictate how the repricing is to be accomplished. In private contracts, such repricing is carried out in the same manner as the pricing of any other work for which the contractor or owner is entitled to a change order, and such change order pricing techniques are addressed in Chapter 9.

Although a change in the quantity of goods can be repriced by reference to the actual cost of purchase (and related bulk-quantity discounts), variations in estimated quantities of construction elements apart from goods can have dramatic effects on a contractor's costs. Indeed, such costs can vary with actual quantities even when the cost of materials is constant. For example, a substantial portion of the cost of a discrete type of work may be mobilization and demobilization—getting equipment, materials, and workers to the site and removing equipment and excess materials at the completion of work. When the mobilization and demobilization costs are spread over the installation of 16,000 square feet of concrete masonry unit (CMU) wall, the unit cost for the wall is substantially less than the unit cost of an 800-square-foot wall, the price of which must recover the same mobilization and demobilization costs over many fewer units. Such a reduction in CMU walls would call for an increase in the unit price of the wall, even if the cost of labor and CMU block does not change (per unit).

2. Unbalanced Bidding

When bids for public works are assessed on the basis of unit prices applied to estimated quantities, a contractor's superior knowledge of actual conditions (or its apprehension of an error in the public agency's estimated quantities) can allow the contractor to take advantage of the government through what is referred to as "unbalanced bidding."

Assume, for example, that a solicitation for excavation and installation of a water line estimates 400 linear feet of pipe and 1,200 cubic yards of excavation. Further assume contractors are required to bid the items as unit prices, with

---

19. Foley Co. v. U.S., 11 F.3d 1032, 1034 (Fed. Cir. 1993); *see also* P.R. Constr., Inc. v. United States, 76 Fed. Cl. 621, 636 (2007).

the provision that the low bidder will be the contractor whose total contract price (based on estimated quantities) is the lowest. Now suppose Abercrombie Contractors bids the pipe at $30 per foot and the excavation at $10 per cubic yard, for a total contract bid of $24,000 (400 [×] $30, plus $1,200 [×] $10), and that both unit prices are within the range of reasonableness for that type of work. Barnard Contractors, on the other hand, bids the pipe at $5 per foot (substantially less than the wholesale cost of the pipe) and the dirt work at $18 per yard (at the high end of excavation work). Barnard's total bid is $23,600 (400 [×] $5 per foot, plus 1,200 [×] $18).

The government's estimate of dirt quantities turns out to be grossly short, and the actual quantity is 3,000 cubic yards. Although Barnard won the contract with a lowest total *projected* cost, the *actual* cost to the government of $56,000 (400 [×] $5, plus 3,000 [×] $18) is much higher than the $42,000 Abercrombie would have charged (400 [×] $30, plus 3,000 [×] $10). Given the fact that the unit cost Barnard bid for pipe is just a fraction of the actual cost of the pipe, one might suspect that Barnard submitted a deliberately so-called unbalanced bid to exploit its superior knowledge of the deficiencies in government's estimate of excavation quantities. The government may have a remedy for such unbalanced bidding, which may include rejection of the unbalanced bid[20] or post-award corrective action, including cancellation of the contract.[21]

E. Mixed Pricing Contracts and Change Orders

There is nothing inherently wrong with using some elements of a cost-plus contract in a stipulated-sum contract or vice versa. Ultimately, pricing is a matter of risk allocation, and no reason exists that every risk on a project must be allocated in the same manner. In addition, a change order may be priced in terms very different from those of the underlying contract.

Readers will see, for example, that many stipulated-sum contracts contain clauses that allow the price to change for reasons such as differing site conditions. In such a contract, the contractor may be willing to assume all the cost risks of the project *except* the risks of unanticipated subsurface conditions. In such a case, the stipulated-sum contract is really a stipulated-sum contract with the potential variation in cost based on subsurface conditions. The unexpected construction work required by differing site conditions may itself be priced in a variety of ways. The parties may specify a unit price for particular

---

20. *See, e.g.*, Munilla Constr. Mgmt., LLC v. United States, 130 Fed. Cl. 635, 652 (Fed. Cl., 2017).

21. XPO Logistics Worldwide Gov't Servs, LLC v. United States, 133 Fed. Cl. 162, 176 (Fed. Cl. 2017).

conditions such as excavation or blasting of rock; they may price the additional work on a cost-plus basis; or they may negotiate a flat fee change order.

The careful drafter and contract administrator must ensure that the contract terms are flexible enough to accommodate these various pricing mechanisms. On small change orders, too little may be at issue to justify the expense or administrative burden of adding sophisticated terms to the contract. On the other hand, if a contractor building an office building for a stipulated sum agrees to build an adjacent parking garage, but on a cost-plus basis, both the contractor and the owner take substantial risk by executing a simple change order adding the work for "the actual cost of the work plus 15% overhead and profit" without adding the key elements of a cost-plus contract, such as the definition of the term "costs" that may be charged to the owner.

9.03 SPECIFIC PRICE-RELATED TERMS UTILIZED IN CONSTRUCTION CONTRACTS

A. Pricing Mechanisms

This section identifies and discusses different pricing mechanisms beyond those outlined earlier that contractors, owners, and subcontractors employ in pricing work, especially under change orders. These terms are not presented for detailed analysis, as such an endeavor is beyond the scope of this book, but rather to acquaint readers with some pricing techniques they may encounter in construction contracts. In reviewing the following provisions, it is important to remember how the pricing tool is used to allocate risk of uncertainty in the construction contract.

1. Index Pricing

When the cost of particular materials fluctuates on the open market, the parties may agree that the cost of materials to be charged to the owner will be determined by reference to a published index. The function of such a clause is to allocate the risk of cost to the owner at then-market rates without regard to the actual cost of the materials procured by the contractor. For example, a contractor may have procured a huge quantity of steel for stockpile or through the purchase of futures and may not want to share the cost savings with the owner. After all, when the contractor made the purchase, the owner did not bear the risk that materials would become cheaper in the future. Conversely, the owner may not want to pay elevated prices for materials that the contractor purchased and stockpiled far in advance. The use of an index price to tie costs to present market conditions is one mechanism for dealing with the pricing of materials from a contractor's inventory.

2. Time and Material Pricing

A phrase heard with some frequency in construction circles is the pricing of a change order on a "T&M" basis. This refers to an agreement under which a contractor or subcontractor agrees that the cost of additional work will be based on the time and materials employed to complete the work.[22] T&M work is essentially work performed on a cost-plus basis, where the cost is the cost of the labor, materials, and so on. It may or may not include an express agreement to pay some amount for the contractor's overhead and profit. To remove any ambiguity, many contracts specify that the contractor will be permitted to add a stated percentage (usually in the range of 10 to 20 percent, depending on the type of work being performed) to the T&M portion of work in a change order. T&M pricing invokes the same considerations as cost-plus contracts detailed earlier, but on a smaller scale that may not justify significant drafting efforts. Such clauses are sometime referred to as "NTE" or "not-to-exceed" clauses, where the T&M pricing includes a cap on the expense that the owner will be required to pay.

Time and materials pricing is often utilized as a default mechanism where the parties cannot agree to the pricing of a change order:

> B. The value of any Work covered by a Change Order or of any Claim for an adjustment in the Contract Price will be determined as follows:
>
> 1. where the Work involved is covered by unit prices contained in the Contract Documents, by application of such unit prices . . . , or
> 2. where the Work involved is not covered by unit prices contained in the Contract Documents, by a mutually agreed lump sum (which may include an allowance for overhead and profit not necessarily in accordance with [the calculation of "cost of work"]), or
> 3. where the Work involved is not covered by unit prices contained in the Contract Documents and agreement to a lump sum is not reached . . . , on the basis of the Cost of the Work . . . plus a Contractor's fee for overhead and profit.[23]

---

22. *See, e.g.*, Badger Sheet Metal Works of Green Bay, Inc. v. Process Partners, Inc., 2017 WL 2559982, at *1 (E.D. Wis. 2017), in which the court denied summary judgment where there was a triable issue of fact as to whether a contract was for a fixed price or was a "time and materials" contract where the bid was merely an estimate.

23. EJCDC C-700, Standard General Conditions of the Construction Contract (2007), ¶ 12.01. See also ConsensusDocs 200, Standard Agreement and General Conditions between Owner and Constructor (Lump Sum) (2017), ¶ 8.3.1. (pricing of a change order may be determined by one or more methods, including "unit prices," "a mutually accepted, itemized lump sum," or "cost of the work."); American Institute of Architects, AIA Document A201–2017 General Conditions of the Contract for Construction § 7.3.4 (2017) (in absence of response from or agreement with

3. Default Pricing through Third Party

In the context of directed work[24] performed without a prior agreement as to pricing, the parties may decide in advance that some third party (the architect, for example) will determine the price of work to be performed under a change order if the parties are unable to negotiate a price. Although the use of third-party default pricing may involve some risk of favoritism, or ignorance on the part of the decision maker, or other factors, in many cases the parties are willing to accept such risks as an alternative to the significant transaction costs associated with other pricing mechanisms, such as the dispute resolution techniques described next.

4. Default Pricing through Dispute Resolution

Another method for default pricing—that is, pricing used where the parties cannot agree in advance—is to provide for some interim payment representing a rough value of the work (as determined, for example, by the architect, but only on an interim basis), followed by the parties undertaking some form of dispute resolution to fix the "reasonable" price of the work. The advantage of such a term is that it ensures a neutral third party will determine the "reasonable" price of the work, although not always to the parties' satisfaction, of course. The chief drawback is that imposition of some neutral determination through the contract's dispute resolution provisions may come with substantial transaction costs. For example, a disagreement over $100,000 of value in a change order that adds work to a contract may actually cost $50,000 in attorneys' fees and arbitration expenses to resolve. Such clauses are often effective for a somewhat perverse reason—dispute resolution may not be a particularly effective way to resolve the dispute, and the resulting transaction cost of the dispute resolution mechanism provides the parties with a strong incentive to settle the price.

9.04 CONTRACT TERMS RELATED TO PRICING

A. Material Price Escalation Clauses

As explained previously, in a stipulated-sum contract the contractor bears the burden of price fluctuations in materials and labor. At the same time, the parties may recognize that the only risks the contractor anticipates bearing are

---

contractor to proposed price, architect determines price based on "reasonable expenditures and savings" of contractor, including allowance for overhead and profit).

24. See Chapter 14.

those that are "normal" within the industry, even when these so-called normal risks may have dramatic pricing effects. Thus, at any point in time, some building materials may be unusually expensive, and others may be unusually cheap in light of the many factors that affect pricing.

On the other hand, some unanticipated events may be completely outside the reasonable expectation of the parties, or price increases may far exceed what the parties intended to allocate as part of the risk and benefit that each accepted in the drafting of the agreement. In order to avoid a catastrophic pricing failure, the contractor may seek inclusion of a "material price escalation" clause to deal with such unusual events as worldwide shortages of particular construction materials due to natural disasters (such as 2017 Hurricanes Harvey, Irma, and Maria) or other causes. The necessity of such clauses lies in the fact that the common law of contracts provides little relief from unforeseen—however unfortunate—changes in the cost of an obligor's performance.[25]

In addition, known fluctuations in key construction components may counsel use of variable pricing (such as fuel cost increases) through material price escalation clauses.

B. Interim Payment Clauses

Many contracts allow the owner to direct that the contractor perform additional work even where a dispute exists as to the change order pricing. Such a clause allows the owner to avoid being what may be referred to as "blackmailed" by the contractor on the price by the contractor's refusal to perform work until an outrageous price is accepted. On the other hand, the clause raises the converse problem; what if the owner refuses to agree to a reasonable price with the hope that the contractor will eventually be forced to accept a low price simply to get paid?

The solution to this potentially unfair pressure is the inclusion of an interim payment clause, under the terms of which the owner is obligated to pay some determinable amount for the work pending final contract pricing (and adjustment, if necessary).[26] The interim pricing is often left in the hands of a third person, such as the architect. Through this means, the contractor is paid something for its work until the final contract price is negotiated or otherwise determined.

---

25. Force majeure clauses may also provide some relief to contractors in the face of disasters. Such clauses are outside the scope of this chapter.

26. *See, e.g.*, AIA Document A201–2017, *supra* note 23, § 7.3.4 (in absence of response from or agreement with contractor to proposed price, architect determines price based on "reasonable expenditures and savings" of contractor, including allowance for overhead and profit).

In the absence of an interim payment clause, the contractor (or subcontractor, as the case may be) can face substantial financial distress, because contract clauses requiring the contractor to continue work, even in the face of a pricing dispute, generally are enforceable, and a contractor who suspends work pending resolution of a pricing issue risks being terminated.[27]

9.05 COMPARISON OF PRICING TERMS BASED ON PRICING MECHANISM

This section discusses several attributes and clauses of construction contracts that are affected by—and affect—the pricing mechanism utilized. The function of this section is to give the reader some sense of the important implications of—and assumptions behind—different pricing mechanisms. Each area begins with a brief description of the characteristic of the clause at issue, and summarizes the manner in which the particular clause affects (or is affected by) choice in pricing structure. The first topic—scope of work—is set out in some detail to show the complexity of the concepts presented.

A. Scope of Work

A clause setting out the definition of the work to be performed under a contract usually incorporates detailed drawings and specifications. These drawings and specifications are not simply reference materials—they define the contractor's obligation to perform work under the contract. The scope of the work cannot change except in accordance with the change provisions in the contract. These change provisions, in turn, may include significant pricing, timing, and other terms for changes in the scope of work. At the same time, parties do not always have the luxury of a complete set of drawings and specifications when they want to begin construction.

How might incomplete drawings and specifications affect pricing considerations? Precision in the scope of work under a cost-plus contract is not usually vital to the contractor.[28] After all, the owner will eventually pay for all the work performed, and thus, little economic motivation exists to engage in heated disputes over what is within, and what is outside, the original scope of

---

27. Interim pricing may also be a requirement of a state's "Prompt Pay Act" under which owners and contractors are required to make timely payments, even in the face of disputes about pricing.

28. That is not to say it is unimportant to the owner, as the owner may want a bulletproof set of drawings and specifications to ensure that any cost estimates are reliable.

work. Accordingly, a cost-plus contract may be an appropriate mechanism for pricing work whose design is not complete at the time of contracting.

A stipulated sum, however, is rarely an appropriate pricing mechanism for a project whose design is not complete at the time of contracting. Because the drawings and specifications define the contractor's obligations, a contractor who quotes (and an owner who accepts) a stipulated sum on the basis of incomplete drawings undertakes a substantial risk that disputes will arise concerning whether particular tasks are inside or outside the scope of work, and therefore included (or not included) in the stipulated sum.

At the two extremes—a perfect set of drawings, or a mere design sketch with no details—the contractor can feel comfortable in accepting or rejecting a stipulated sum contract, respectively. The cases that end up in dispute are the borderline cases where a design is nearly complete at the time of contracting.

B. Changes

Contracts usually require change orders to alter the scope of work or contract time. Some contracts have magnificently detailed provisions with Byzantine procedures for effecting changes in the contract. Others have less formal change mechanisms with fewer default remedies, such as default pricing. In negotiating change-order procedures, the level of detail required in change mechanisms, and especially in the management of the change-order process during the course of construction, must take the pricing system into account.

C. Sharing of Savings

A sharing-of-savings clause is intended to give the contractor an incentive to perform efficiently by awarding the contractor a specified financial reward to the extent that the cost of construction comes in below a target amount. These cost-savings provisions are typically expressed in terms of an allocation of the cost savings by percentages to the contractor and to the owner. These clauses ordinarily find employment in cost-plus contacts with a guaranteed maximum price.

D. Definition of "Cost of Work"

As described previously, a clause defining the cost of work to be performed identifies specifically what costs are to be included in any cost of work calculation, as well as what costs are specifically excluded. If you find a "cost of work" definition in a stipulated sum contract, then either the drafter was inattentive, or the pricing mechanism for changes envisions cost-plus pricing.

E. Treatment of Self-Performed Work

The contractor's right to perform work through its own forces and the compensation the contractor will receive for such work can be the subject of specific contract clauses. The discussion of cost of work set out earlier details some of the concerns that arise when a contractor performs work on a project.

F. Allowances

An allowance is a variable pricing term under which a contract price sets out an "allowance," or price of some particular element is included in the contract sum, with the added provision that any variation from the stated allowance will result in a change in the contract price. Allowances are typically utilized for owner-finish items (see the following example), the cost of which cannot be incorporated into the contract until the owner makes decisions as to the exact products to be utilized. At the same time, the owner may want some estimate of the cost of the materials or work, and the contractor thus includes a stated figure in its bid. For example, a contractor building a warehouse with an office may state an "allowance" of $8,000 for floor finishes in office spaces. If the owner chooses expensive carpet, the owner must pay the increased price. If the owner chooses unfinished floors or minimal floor coverings, it saves money.

Allowances can also be utilized as a short-form method of allowing variable pricing for materials whose cost cannot be predicted at the time of contracting. A contractor may, for example, put an allowance in for the log package utilized in a residential construction contract for purposes of finalizing a contract with the owner, but the parties may agree the owner will bear the exact cost of the log package at the time it is purchased.

There is nothing particularly challenging about the use of allowances in a construction contract, except that it is vital to understand that they fulfill very different functions from contingencies.

G. Contingencies

Contractors with substantial experience understand that when they bid on jobs, they can predict with some degree of accuracy the cost of materials, labor, and so forth that go into finishing a project. They also know that most projects will experience some unforeseen occurrences not specifically planned for in the budget. A contractor who projects job costs with no consideration for unplanned expenses undertakes substantial risk.

Over the course of many contracts, a contractor can estimate the amount by which cost overruns exceed the original estimate of identifiable costs, and thereby plan for unplanned expenses in future contracts. For example, a contractor who specializes in the construction of chemical treatment plants may routinely increase its cost estimates by 8 percent of the identifiable costs to account for such unplanned, but nevertheless likely, cost overruns.

Nothing in the use of a contingency as discussed to this point is troublesome. The problems arise, however, when the contractor shares its cost estimate with the owner for the purpose of allowing (for example) the owner to obtain construction financing and for the parties to formulate cost estimates for payment purposes. The owner may see the proposed contingency as a fund from which it can finance alterations in its drawings and specifications. The owner may say, for example, "We forgot to design air-conditioning into the equipment control room—let's take that out of the contingency." Theoretically, a contractor could provide a cost estimate showing no contingency so as to avoid this problem, at which point the owner's lender may impose some contingency with the understanding that no cost estimate is perfect.

As already discussed, contingencies play some role in the estimation of financing of a construction project, and they also play a role in a contractor's formulation of an acceptable stipulated-sum price. From the contractor's perspective, whether a contingency presents any concern depends on how it is employed. In a cost-plus contract where the contingency is just a cost-estimating tool for the owner, it presents no trouble—the owner pays all costs, expected or otherwise, and no dispute should arise over "ownership" of control of such contingency accounts.

When the contractor includes a contingency amount in a stipulated-sum contract, ownership and control over the contingency account should not be disputed—the contractor gets paid all of, and only, the stipulated sum, and whether the contractor internally called an expense part of flooring or part of its internal contingency is irrelevant. The only time trouble arises is when the contractor discloses its contingency to the owner for purposes of interim payments or bank-financing purposes, and the owner misunderstands the function of the contingency. Short of keeping the contingency to itself, the parties' protection against disputes is to make it clear that the owner has no interest in the control of the contingency and that it is disclosed to the owner only as a convenience to the owner.

Finally, a contingency may play a specific role in a cost-plus contract with a GMP. The owner and contractor may agree, for example, that the GMP includes up to $2,000,000 for excavation costs as part of the contractor's contingency, so that if excavation costs come to $3,000,000, the parties know how to treat those costs for purposes of calculating the shortfall or excess in relation to the GMP. Absent some stipulation as to the use of contingencies, for example, the contractor may claim that subsurface conditions entitle it to an increase in the contract sum of $3,000,000 for excavation, while the owner would contest that all excavation costs were included in the GMP.

H. Builder Rebates/Credits

A contractor often negotiates purchase agreements with vendors under the terms of which the contractor will receive a rebate on the value of materials it purchases, a credit to its "house account" for subsequent purchases, or even a price discount for timely payment of invoices. In negotiating the cost terms of a cost-plus contract, the parties should be mindful of these various considerations and agree as to their treatment. If a contractor pays for materials using a credit it received from prior purchases, for example, little doubt exists that the contractor should still be entitled to recoup the cost of the materials from the owner. On the other hand, if the contractor gets a 10 percent rebate in the form of cash or future discounts, should the owner be entitled to participate in the cost savings? These questions have no right answers, but rather are issues that should be addressed in the contract where the cost of work may be at issue.

I. Purpose of Budget

When a contractor creates a budget for work under a cost-plus contract, the budget usually serves as a planning tool only, and rarely is intended (or given effect) as a cap on the contract sum. When a contract is priced as a stipulated-sum contract, on the other hand, the only so-called budget the contractor may wish to reveal is a schedule of values for use in the payment process. A contract should articulate the precise import of any construction budget that is exchanged between the parties so as to ensure they share expectations regarding the use of the budget.

J. Audit Rights

In some contracts, owners are given the right to audit the contractor's books and records to assess the accuracy of the contractor's representations concerning costs. There is nothing unusual about audit rights, and they have their place in the cost-plus contract. However, audit rights rarely appropriate in stipulated-sum contracts. The actual costs incurred by the contractor are irrelevant to the contract sum, and the contractor may have no interest in allowing the owner to audit the contractor's books under such a contract.[29] Similarly, the contractor may choose to limit any audit rights that it grants to those portions of a contract that are priced by reference to costs (as when, for example, the parties agree to T&M pricing for a change order to a stipulated-sum contract).

An issue related to audit rights is the extent to which a contractor can be compelled to reveal its costs in litigation. In a recent California case, for example, the court denied an owner's efforts to obtain information concerning the contractor's costs where the contractor was entitled to be paid on a unit-price basis. As noted previously, a unit price fixes the compensation that the contractor receives, and the only variation is the quantity of work it performs. The court explained:

> With respect to the self-performed sidewalk concrete paving, discovery regarding Underground's costs could have been relevant to this issue if the City were correct that some of Underground's sidewalk concrete paving should have been priced on a cost-plus-markup basis. However, as discussed *ante,* we have determined (as did the trial court) that the City was required to pay for all sidewalk concrete paving at the contractual unit price. Accordingly, Underground's costs for self-performed sidewalk concrete paving were not relevant to the amount Underground was entitled to be paid for sidewalk concrete paving, and the City's brief does not explain how those costs were relevant to any other issue litigated at trial.[30]

---

29. City of Buffalo City Sch. Dist. v. LPCiminelli, No. 1287, 17-00176, 73 N.Y.S.3d 836, 843, 2018 N.Y. slip op. 01832, 2018 WL 1357529, (N.Y. App. Div. 2018) (contractor did not breach contract by refusing to allow owner to audit costs incurred under stipulated sum contract).

30. Underground Construction Co., Inc. v. City of Oakland, 2013 WL 1998909, at *19 (Cal. App. 2013).

QUESTIONS

Two owner representatives call you the same day with the same project; that is, to draft a construction contract for the construction of a new project. They provide the following information:

Owner 1 is a private consortium of well-financed investors who want to get in on the wave of building in Las Vegas, where every new casino is bigger and more spectacular than the last. Speed to market is a major consideration, and like many fast-track projects on The Strip, construction will begin as the project is being designed. The casino will return several times the anticipated cost of the construction, and while the investors are not profligate spenders and will keep an eye on the construction costs, they are more concerned with early completion, because cost variations are not expected to be substantial when compared with the revenue that the project will bring in. The project is being built in an area with ready access to building materials, and little prospect exists of unusual construction problems inherent in the Las Vegas building environment.

Owner 2 is a public wastewater treatment district formed by the property owners in a small community in the heart of the Rocky Mountains in Colorado. The community is growing; leach fields and septic systems are probably not a viable option for projected new housing in the coming decades; and the community will need more comprehensive wastewater treatment options in the future. Contractors will be hired from 200 miles away in Denver or Colorado Springs, and will need to complete the construction on the district's property in the mountains, where civil construction like this has not been attempted. The district has received a grant from the Colorado Department of Public Health and Environment, some federal matching funds may be available, and the district has some (albeit limited) capacity to issue bonds to finance the balance of construction. All of these sources of financing are one-time sources that probably cannot be increased during construction. Although the district is eager to get the project under way, no imminent need exists for the facilities, and construction will not proceed at an unusual pace.

Your first task is to advise the clients with respect to pricing considerations.

1. What would you tell them about the advantages and disadvantages of each of the pricing mechanisms discussed here?
2. What additional information would you solicit from each of them so as to formulate your recommendation?
3. At first blush, which do you think would be best suited to each owner?

CHAPTER 10

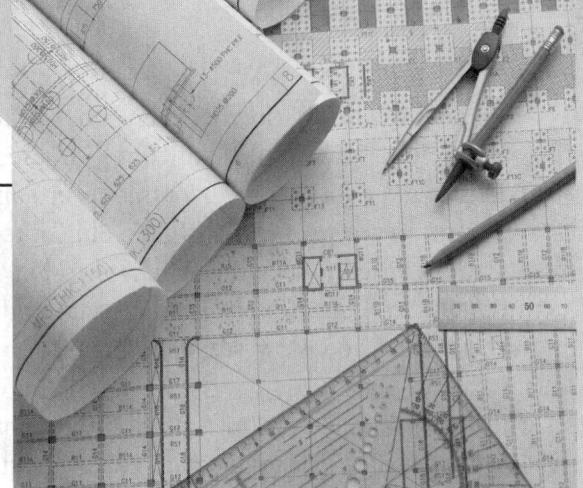

Subcontractors and Suppliers

ALLEN L. OVERCASH

10.01 SUBCONTRACTORS AND SUPPLIERS

A. Subcontractors versus Suppliers: What Is the Difference and Why Does It Matter?

It is common to think of subcontractors as those entities that furnish services, such as the installation of electrical or mechanical systems, to the project at the project site. It is common to think of suppliers as those entities that deliver products or goods to the project, such as electrical or mechanical equipment. The distinction between the two is unclear and becoming fuzzier as traditional subcontractors increasingly furnish and even design products and goods and as more suppliers install their own products.[1]

---

1. The generally accepted distinction between a subcontractor who performs work at the job site and a supplier who does not is not appropriate in federal government contracting, which regards any party furnishing supplies or services for performance of a prime contract or subcontract as a subcontractor. The definition of the party has important implications for the nature of the clauses that are required to be included in its contract. Brian A. Darst, *Subcontract Incorporation by Reference and Flowdown Clauses under Federal Government Construction Projects*, Construction Briefings, Mar. 2005, at 1, 8.

Why does the distinction between subcontractors and suppliers matter and what principles apply to the distinction? This section addresses those issues.

Whether the entity is a subcontractor or supplier may have serious implications for that entity's security rights. Subcontractors and suppliers are sometimes treated differently under mechanic's lien statutes and payment bonds. More importantly, the Uniform Commercial Code (UCC) commonly applies to the furnishing of goods by suppliers but not to the furnishing of services by subcontractors.

The UCC's application to a particular transaction may affect the parties' rights. These include the application of the statute of limitations,[2] the existence of special warranties,[3] the buyer's remedies,[4] buyer's notice requirements,[5] and either party's right to adequate assurance of performance.[6]

B. Subcontractors and Suppliers: Telling Them Apart

All parties are well advised to understand the nature of their transaction—whether the transaction constitutes a subcontractor or supplier relationship. The determination may not be easy since many transactions are mixed; that is, the same party furnishes both services and goods as part of the same agreement.

Some courts have applied a predominant factor test, analyzing "whether the predominant factor . . . is the rendition of service, with goods incidentally involved, or whether they are transactions of sale, with labor incidentally

---

2. The UCC statute of limitations may be of different length than the statute applicable to furnishing services to construction projects. *Compare* Neb. U.C.C. § 2-725(1) (four years) *with* Neb. Rev. Stat. § 25-205 (five years). Further, the ability of the parties by agreement to modify the statutory period may be different. Section 2-725(1) of the Neb. U.C.C. allows the parties to reduce the period of limitation to not less than one year, but they may not extend it. Moreover, when the statute of limitations starts to run may also differ. *Compare* Neb. U.C.C. § 2-725(2) (regardless of knowledge, the cause of action accrues when the breach occurs) *with* Neb. Rev. Stat. § 25-223 (allowing extension of the statutory period if the cause of action is not discovered).

3. The UCC provides for an implied warranty of merchantability (§ 2-314) and an implied warranty of fitness for a particular purpose (§ 2-315), as well as other implied warranties that may also rise from the course of dealing (§ 2-316) and sets forth the method of creating express warranties (§ 2-313). Section 2-316 allows the parties to disclaim and exclude warranties.

4. The UCC provides buyers with certain remedies that they may exercise at various points in any transaction. *See, e.g.*, sections 2-711 (buyer's remedies in general), 2-502 (buyer's right of recovery), 2-712 ("cover"), 2-713 (contract-market damages for non-delivery), 2-714 (breach of warranty), 2-715 (incidental and consequential damages), 2-716 (buyer's right to specific performance or replevin), and 2-717 (deduction of damages from purchase price). The UCC also contains specific provisions allowing parties to limit the buyer's remedies (*see* § 2-719).

5. UCC §§ 2-607(3), 2-608(2).

6. *See* UCC § 2-609.

involved."[7] The fact that the product furnished by the party was fabricated off-site, moved to the project, and simply installed at the project site may be important in determining that the transaction is a supply agreement.[8]

Courts examine the entire transaction to determine its nature. An important question is whether the terms of the parties' contract more closely resemble the standard provisions of a contract for services or for the sale of goods. Therefore, the parties can shape a transaction by the provisions they insert in their contract.[9]

10.02 SELECTION OF SUBCONTRACTORS AND SUPPLIERS

A. Owner Input into Selection Process

The reality of most construction projects is that the prime contractor performs very little of the work on the project. It is generally not practical for prime contractors to maintain a staff of people who are expert in individual trades such as electrical work. Rather, it is more economical for the prime contractor to hire specialized firms that have constant experience in particular trades. The prime contractor's function is to procure and to coordinate the services and supplies furnished to the project by others. Sometimes the owner acquires these items, but more often, the items are furnished by subcontractors and suppliers who contract directly with the prime contractor.

It is logical for the prime contractor to contract with the parties performing the work since the prime contractor is responsible for coordinating the parties' work. However, this arrangement creates some tension, because the satisfactory completion of the owner's project depends largely on the work of legal strangers over whom the owner has no direct control. Although the prime

---

7. Mennonite Deaconess Home and Hosp., Inc. v. Gates Eng'g Co., 219 Neb. 303, 363 N.W.2d 155 (1985).

8. *See* Bonebrake v. Cox, 499 F.2d 951 (8th Cir. 1974).

9. *See* David C. Olsen & Jeffrey S. Rosenstiel, *Predicting When Construction Contracts Are Subject to Article 2 of the UCC*, 21 THE CONST. LAWYER 22 (Winter 2001). According to Olsen and Rosenstiel:

> [T]he contract should address issues that are customarily found in construction contracts, such as: the commencement of the work after a notice to proceed; the compliance with plans and specifications; the need to provide submittals for approval; the need to prosecute the work with adequate workers; the supervision of work by the architect or other professional; the steps that will be taken on the failure to complete the work on time; and the respective rights of the owner and contractor on default by the other.

Id. at 26.

contractor is legally responsible to the owner for the work of subcontractors and suppliers, employees of the prime contractor are not expert in many of the specialty items subcontractors and suppliers furnish. In fact, the owner and/or its designer may perceive that their own expertise in the selection of certain subcontractors and suppliers exceeds that of the prime contractor. Thus, despite the traditional structure of the prime contractor contracting directly with subcontractors and suppliers, the owner still may want a voice in selecting who will perform the work.

The owner's desire to participate in the selection of subcontractors and suppliers is often reflected in the contract with the prime contractor. For example, AIA Document A201–2017, General Conditions of the Contract for Construction, requires the prime contractor to furnish the names of prospective subcontractors and suppliers to the owner.[10] This requirement starts a dialogue between the owner and the prime contractor about who will perform the work. Generally, this standard AIA form gives the owner veto power over the selection process; nevertheless, the provisions in the form recognize the impracticality of allowing the owner to force an unwelcome subcontractor or supplier on the owner's prime contractor.[11]

Cost is one of the prime contractor's primary motives in selecting a subcontractor or supplier. This is particularly true if the prime contractor's contract with the owner involves a fixed price or price incentives. The owner's preferences, which usually are based on concepts of quality, may result in a higher-priced subcontractor or supplier. In such a case, the contractor may have grounds for adjusting the contract price.[12]

B. Formal Restrictions on Choosing Subcontractors and Suppliers

Often, rather than waiting to review the names of subcontractors and suppliers selected by the prime contractor, the owner desires to set the parameters of the selection process. The owner often does this as part of the invitation for bid process so that the bidders are aware of such parameters as they prepare their estimates.

On one extreme, owners actually have named a subcontractor or supplier themselves, and even negotiated the terms of the agreement with such

---

10. American Institute of Architects, AIA Document A201–2017, General Conditions of the Contract for Construction § 5.2.1 (2017) [hereinafter AIA Document A201–2017].

11. *Id.* § 5.2.2 ("The Contractor shall not contract with a proposed person or entity to whom the Owner or Architect has made reasonable and timely objection. The Contractor shall not be required to contract with anyone to whom the Contractor has made reasonable objection.").

12. *Id.* § 5.13.

subcontractor or supplier, with the expectation that the prime contractor is obligated to accept an assignment of that agreement. Another popular specification that a prime contractor must satisfy prescribes a "brand name or equal" product as the only product acceptable for use on the project. This approach has caused a good deal of litigation in the public sector over whether particular products are to be rejected as not "equal" to those specified.[13]

In the case of public bidding, restrictions may apply that limit the number of subcontractors and suppliers a prime contractor chooses. For example, using the restrictions in the area of federal procurement, which is governed by detailed provisions of the Federal Acquisition Regulation (FAR), limits the ability of contracting officers to contract without full and open competition.[14]

C. Socioeconomic Considerations

In the instance of projects constructed for the federal government, a subcontractor or supplier may be subject to the provisions of the Buy American Act[15] that apply to construction materials and products incorporated into a public project.[16] Many federal procurement contracts include preferences for small business concerns. Prime contractors may be required to give such small businesses the "maximum practical opportunity" to participate in the contract.[17]

These programs include preferences for subcontractors that are "small businesses," minority-owned businesses (MBEs), or disadvantaged business enterprises (DBEs).[18] Federal programs administered by the Small Business Administration include so-called 8(a) programs designed to assist small businesses owned and controlled by socially and economically disadvantaged individuals, economically disadvantaged Indian tribes (including Alaska Native corporations), and economically disadvantaged Native Hawaiian organizations; small disadvantaged business programs that involve price preferences to encourage the use of so-called small disadvantaged businesses (SDBs); and the HUBZone program designed to assist small businesses located in "historically underutilized business zones." Goals also exist to award a percentage of subcontracts to women-owned businesses. Generally, companies seeking these

---

13. 1 PHILIP L. BRUNER & PATRICK J. O'CONNOR, JR., BRUNER & O'CONNOR ON CONSTRUCTION LAW § 2:54 (2016) [hereinafter BRUNER & O'CONNOR].

14. STEVEN G.M. STEIN, CONSTRUCTION LAW § 2.02[4] (Matthew Bender 2007) [hereinafter STEIN].

15. 41 U.S.C. §§ 8301–8305.

16. *See generally* John R. Tolle & Jerome H. Gress, *Buy American Act in Construction Contracting: Basic Principles and Guidelines/Edition II*, CONSTRUCTION BRIEFINGS, March 2003, at 1.

17. John R. Tolle, *Small Business Contracting/Edition II—Part I*, CONSTRUCTION BRIEFINGS, April 1999, at 1, 3.

18. BRUNER & O'CONNOR, *supra* note 13, §§ 2:65–2:68.

preferences must qualify for the requisite status by application to the Small Business Administration.[19]

Since the Supreme Court's decision in *Adarand Constructors, Inc. v. Pena*,[20] racial or ethnic classification preference programs will undergo "strict scrutiny" to determine whether such programs serve a compelling governmental interest and are narrowly tailored to further that interest.[21] Since *Adarand*, the absence of "demonstrated need" and "compelling interest" has resulted in rulings that such preferences violate the equal protection clause in the U.S. Constitution.[22]

10.03 SUBCONTRACTOR BIDDING: WHO IS BOUND BY THE BID?

A. The Bidding Process

Since subcontractors perform most of the actual construction work on many projects, the price of their work is a significant factor in the price of the total project. A large part of the cost estimate prepared by the prime contractor for the owner will be the estimate of the amounts the prime contractor will have to pay subcontractors for the work.

Theoretically, the prime contractor could, and in a few cases does, prepare its own estimate of the amount it will pay for subcontract work. But as to major items of work, the prime contractor looks to the subcontractors to tender a bid to the prime as part of the prime contractor's preparation of its overall estimate. This enables the prime contractor to make a more accurate estimate of what the subcontract work will cost. Bids from subcontractors also enable the prime contractor to take advantage of more favorable prices resulting from competition among subcontractors.

The final hours prior to the preparation of a prime contractor's estimate for a project may seem chaotic to the outside observer. Although the subcontractors and the prime contractor have studied the project for some time, final "numbers" are posted minutes before the deadline. Much of the process is verbal, with the prime contractor's final numbers varying significantly as additional subcontractor bids arrive and the manager of the prime contractor maneuvers to be the low bidder.

---

19. John R. Tolle, *Small Business Contracting/Edition II—Part II*, CONSTRUCTION BRIEFINGS, May 1999, at 1, 5.

20. 115 S. Ct. 2097 (1995).

21. Richard O. Duvall, Dorn C. McGrath III, & Craig A. Holman, *Affirmative Action After Adarand*, CONSTRUCTION BRIEFINGS, Sept. 1995, at 1.

22. BRUNER & O'CONNOR, *supra* note 13, § 2:63.

Another complexity in the bidding process is the technical issue of the scope and conditions of the subcontract work. On a complex project with many subcontractors, the specific limits of the scope of each bidder's work may vary among subcontractors vying for the same work or related work. Thus, the exact price of any particular subcontract work may be uncertain unless the record of the parties' negotiations is very precise; in that regard, a risk exists that some of the work the prime contractor is obligated to perform for the owner is omitted from the work contracted to subcontractors (or, alternatively, the relevant terms of the prime contractor's and subcontractor's work differ), creating a so-called scope bust that must be addressed.

B. Can the Prime Contractor Enforce the Subcontractor's Bid?

The prime contractor relies on the subcontractor's estimate for the cost of the subcontract work in framing the prime contractor's own bid. Once awarded the prime contract, the prime contractor then seeks to formalize a written agreement with the subcontractor reflecting the cost estimate that the subcontractor earlier used to prepare its own bid. But what if the subcontractor fails or refuses to honor its earlier bid by entering into a binding agreement?

The parties, as part of the bidding process, might have entered into a binding agreement that provided the subcontractor would be bound to perform its work at the bid price if the prime contractor won the project. Such an agreement would be binding on the subcontractor and could be enforced by the prime contractor.[23]

However, more often than not, no such prior agreement exists. Prime contractors receive bids from a number of competing subcontractors, and subcontractors tender bids to a number of prime contractors competing for the same project. The nature of the project makes it unlikely that the parties formally will bind themselves to each other before the contract is let by the owner.

Absent a binding bilateral agreement, what are the legal rights of the prime contractor who relied on the subcontractor's bid to prepare the prime contractor's bid? If the subcontractor walks away from its offer, does the prime contractor have any legal recourse against the subcontractor? In many jurisdictions, the prime contractor may have rights based on the legal theory of promissory estoppel. While no formal, binding, bilateral agreement exists between the parties, the actions of the prime contractor in reliance on the subcontractor's offer create a binding agreement.

---

23. *See* Bridgeport Restoration Co., Inc. v. A. Petrucci Constr. Co., 211 Conn. 230, 557 A.2d 1263 (1989) (finding an enforceable agreement to enter into subcontract if the project was awarded to the prime).

The common law doctrine of promissory estoppel is summarized in section 90 of the Restatement (Second) of Contracts, and this section has itself become the most often-invoked formulation of the elements of recovery:

> A promise on which the promissory should reasonably expect to induce action or forbearance on the part of the promisee or a third person and which does induce such action or forbearance is binding if injustice can be avoided only by the enforcement of the promise. The remedy granted for breach may be limited as justice requires.[24]

On the basis of this doctrine, many courts have upheld the prime contractor's right to enforce the subcontractor's bid against it.[25] Other courts have disagreed.[26]

Assuming that the court entertains the concept of promissory estoppel as governing subcontractor bidding, what would prevent the court from enforcing the subcontractor's bid? Several facts might interfere with such a result, including the following:

1. The bid was subject to conditions or reservations, including the right to withdraw the bid.[27]
2. The bid was not a clear and definite promise but contained major ambiguities.[28]
3. The prime contractor's reliance on the bid was not reasonable because of an obvious mistake in the bid.[29]

---

24. RESTATEMENT (SECOND) OF CONTRACTS § 90.
25. Drennan v. Star Paving Co., 333 P.2d 757 (Cal. 1958).
26. *See, e.g.*, Virginia Sch. of Arts, Inc. v. Eichelbaum, 493 S.E.2d 510 (Va. 1997).
27. Neal J. Sweeney & Geoffrey Dendy, *Holding Subcontractors To Their Bids/Edition II*, CONSTRUCTION BRIEFINGS, Sept. 1999, at 1, 4; Preload Tech. v. A.B & J. Constr. Co., 696 F.2d 1080 (5th Cir. 1983); Montgomery Indus. Int'l. Inc. v. Thomas Constr. Co., 620 F.2d 91 (5th Cir. 1980), 4 CC ¶ 213; Wargo Builders, Inc. v. Douglas L. Cox Plumbing & Heating, Inc., 268 N.E.2d 597 (Ohio App. 1971); *Drennan*, 333 P.2d at 757.
28. Sweeney & Dendy, *supra* note 27, at 4; Camosy, Inc. v. River Steel, Inc., 624 N.E.2d 894 (Ill. App. 1993).
29. 2 BRUNER & O'CONNOR, *supra* note 13, § 7:42. In the *Drennan* case, the subcontractor refused to honor its bid because the bid contained an error, but the court held that since the prime contractor had no reason to believe the bid was in error, it could justifiably rely upon it and "as between the subcontractor who made the bid and the general contractor who reasonably relied on it, the loss resulting from the mistake should fall on the party who caused it." *Drennan*, 333 P.2d. In the case of Sipco Serv. Marine, Inc. v. Wyatt Field Serv. Co., 857 S.W.2d 602 (Tex. App. 1993), the court upheld the reliance of the contractor as reasonable even though the subcontractor's bid was not the low bid.

4. The prime contractor unreasonably delayed accepting the bid.[30]
5. The prime contractor's acceptance varied the terms of the offer in such a way as to constitute a counteroffer.[31]
6. Rather than accept the bid immediately, the prime contractor engaged in bid shopping or bid chiseling.[32]

C. Can the Subcontractor Enforce Its Own Bid?

As indicated previously, many authorities are loath to side with the prime contractor because such authorities believe it would be one-sided and unfair to allow the prime contractor to enforce an agreement that the subcontractor itself cannot enforce. Absent a binding, pre-bid, bilateral agreement between the parties, what rights does the subcontractor have to force the prime contractor to award the subcontract to the subcontractor on the basis of its original offer?

A subcontractor may view it as unfair that a prime contractor, who used the subcontractor's bid amount in the prime contractor's own calculations of the cost of the project in order for the prime contractor to be awarded the project, may later refuse to enter into an agreement with that subcontractor. Even though the subcontractor itself may be obligated to perform at the prime contractor's election, the subcontractor may not itself be able to enforce its own offer. Yet, this may be the likely result in a court proceeding.[33]

---

30. Sweeney & Dendy, *supra* note 27, at 12; Pavel v. A. S. Johnson, 674 A.2d 521 (Md. App. 1996); *Drennan*, 333 P.2d at 757; BRUNER & O'CONNOR, *supra* note 13, § 7:45.

31. Sweeney & Dendy, *supra* note 27, at 9; F.B. Reynolds v. Texarkana Constr. Co., 374 S.W.2d 818 (Ark. 1964); BRUNER & O'CONNOR, *supra* note 13, § 7:43.

32. See discussion of bid shopping that follows. Some courts use this as a rationale for rejecting the prime contractor's effort to enforce the subcontractor's bid. *See Preload Technology*, 696 F.2d at 1080. The danger of bid shopping is one of the reasons the North Carolina courts will not enforce the subcontractor's bid under a theory of promissory estoppel. As stated in Home Elec. Co. of Lenoir, Inc. v. Hall, etc., 358 S.E.2d 539, 542 (N.C. 1987):

Allowing a cause of action based on promissory estoppel in construction bidding also creates the potential for injustice. It forces the subcontractor to be bound if the general contractor uses his bid, even though the general contractor is not obligated to award the job to that subcontractor. The general contractor is still free to shop around between the time he receives the subcontractor's bid and the time he needs the goods or services, to see if he can obtain them at a lower price.

In *Sipco Serv. Marine, Inc.*, 857 S.W.2d at 602, the court held that the contractor's re-solicitation of bids from all bidders did not constitute bid chiseling or bid shopping as those terms are used in the *Preload* case.

33. *See* Clark Trucking of Hope Mills, Inc. v. Lee, 109 N.C. 71, 426 S.E.2d 288 (N.C. App. 1993) (denying the subcontractor's claim based on a theory of unjust enrichment).

It is not unusual for the prime contractor, having been awarded the construction contract for the project, to negotiate further with prospective subcontractors and suppliers in order to get more favorable terms. Reducing the prices offered by a subcontractor automatically increases the prime contractor's prospective margin on the project, particularly if the prime contractor's price is fixed. Therefore, a strong motivation exists to "shop" the bid of the subcontractor by opening the subcontract work to competitors.

The practice of bid shopping has been a subject of some concern in the construction industry.[34] Many specialty subcontractors and subcontractor organizations view the practice as unfair. In addition, owners are concerned that the practice of reducing subcontract amounts by bid-shopping negotiations may reduce the quality of work on their projects.

In response to concerns over the effects of bid shopping, a number of states have enacted laws aimed at curbing the practice. Generally, these laws provide that prime contractors bidding on public projects must include in their bids a list of the principal subcontractors that will be used on the project. The purpose of these statutes is to control the quality of work and prevent subcontractor bids from being unfairly shopped.[35]

10.04 FLOW-DOWN OBLIGATIONS AND RIGHTS

A. Introduction

While the prime contractor is legally responsible for the project, its subcontractors are largely responsible for carrying out the prime contractor's responsibility. How do you then ensure that all parties will construct the project according to the owner's design? To facilitate this objective, it is normally in the interest of the prime contractor to pass on to each subcontractor the prime contractor's obligations under the prime contractor's contract with the owner.

The prime contractor might assign part of its contract obligations and rights to a subcontractor in order to assure the owner that the subcontractor will perform as the owner requires. But such an assignment would remove the prime contractor from its position of overall responsibility for the project. The

---

34. Thomas P. Lambert, Comment, *Bid Shopping and Peddling in the Subcontract Construction Industry*, 18 UCLA L. Rev. 389, 398 (1970); John B. Gaides, Note, *The "Firm Offer" Problem in Construction Bids and the Need for Promissory Estoppel*, 10 Wm. & Mary L. Rev. 212 (1968).

35. Allen Holt Gwyn, *A Review of Subcontractor-Listing Statutes*, 17 Constr. Lawyer 35 (Jan. 1997). *But see* Klose v. Sequoia Union High Sch. Dist., 258 P.2d 515 (Cal. App. 1953) (holding that subcontractor's inclusion on contractor's statutory list does not create any contractual right on the part of the subcontractor).

objective is to preserve the prime contractor's management responsibility and authority but also to ensure that the project is built as planned.

The answer generally used in the industry is to include the provisions of the contract between the owner and the prime contractor in the contract between the prime contractor and the subcontractor. This is done in one of two ways. One way is to incorporate the provisions of the prime contract into the subcontract. Another way is to include a provision in the subcontract whereby the parties agree to what the industry terms "flow-down" to the subcontractor the prime's responsibilities under the prime contract.

B. The Nature of Flow-Down and Flow-Up Provisions

Incorporation by reference provisions is found in the major forms of subcontracts used in the industry. Article 1.A of AIA Document 401, Standard Form of Agreement between Contractor and Subcontractor, provides that the subcontract documents shall include "the Prime Contract, consisting of the Agreement between the Owner and Contractor and the other Contract Documents enumerated therein."[36]

Not satisfied with the simple incorporation of the prime contract provisions into the subcontract, the popular forms also include provisions causing obligations of the prime contractor to flow down to the subcontractor. For example, article 2 of the AIA subcontract form provides that:

> The Contractor and Subcontractor shall be mutually bound by the terms of this Agreement and, to the extent that the provisions of AIA Document A201–2007 apply to this Agreement pursuant to Section 1.2 and provisions of the Prime Contract apply to the Work of the Subcontractor, the Contractor shall assume toward the Subcontractor all obligations and responsibilities that the Owner, under such documents, assumes toward the Contractor, and the Subcontractor shall assume toward the contractor all obligations and responsibilities which the Contractor, under such documents, assumes toward the Owner and the Architect. The Contractor shall have the benefit of all rights, remedies and redress against the Subcontractor that the Owner, under such documents, has against the Contractor, and the Subcontractor shall have the benefit of all rights, remedies and redress against the Contractor that the Contractor, under such documents, has against the Owner, insofar as applicable to

---

36. *See also* American Institute of Architects, AIA Document A401–2017, Standard Form of Agreement between Contractor and Subcontractor § 15.1.2 (2017). This principle is also reflected in article 2.4 of ConsensusDocs 750 (Standard Agreement between Contractor and Subcontractor). AIA A401–2017 article 1.1 also adds modifications to the prime contract issued prior to the subcontract.

this Subcontract. Where a provision of such documents is inconsistent with a provision of this Agreement, this Agreement shall govern.

Note that the provision confers rights as well as imposing obligations—that is, the subcontractor inherits the rights of the prime contractor as well as the prime's obligations under the prime's contract with the owner. This is sometimes termed a flow-up provision as well as a flow-down provision. Its purpose is to place the prime contractor in a legally neutral position between the subcontractor and the owner.[37] If the owner claims that work performed by the subcontractor does not conform to the owner's requirements, then the prime contractor can turn to the subcontractor for response to that contention.[38] On the other hand, if the subcontractor claims the owner's design information to be faulty, then the subcontractor may have a right to assert that claim against the owner through the prime contractor.[39]

Flow-down provisions are commonly required of the prime contractor by owners. Article 5.3 of AIA Document A201 requires the contractor to include flow-down and flow-up provisions in its subcontracts. This evidences a policy of assuring appropriate performance on the part of all parties working on the project. Prime contractors also commonly follow this policy with their subcontractors. Article 5.3 also provides that the prime contractor may require the subcontractor to enter into similar provisions regarding assumption of rights and responsibilities with sub-subcontractors.

C. The Rights and Liabilities of Parties under Flow-Down Provisions

By their nature, flow-down provisions are general provisions applying broadly to contract terms. When specific issues arise, the applicability of these general provisions to particular issues may be in dispute. A court, for example, may enforce the flow down of a technical requirement as to how the contractor is to build the project, but not enforce a general provision such as the contractor's warranty to the owner or the application of a binding arbitration agreement.

---

37. Note that this is not an assignment. For example, the contractor does not exit its obligations and rights vis-à-vis it and the owner. As a practical matter, the owner and the subcontractor continue to deal with each other through the contractor. (Under section 3.2, the contractor is obligated to make certain information received from the owner available to the subcontractor.) However, section 7.4.1 of AIA Document 401 provides that in the event of termination of the prime contract by the owner for cause, the subcontract is assigned to the owner at the owner's option.

38. Absent a flow-down provision, the prime contractor might be liable to the owner for acts of the subcontractor without adequate recourse against the subcontractor and might not be able to demand the same performance from the subcontractor as the owner demands from them. Darst, *supra* note 1, at 2, 4.

39. See following section on subcontractor pass-through claims.

If the general flow-down provision is regarded as ambiguous, then external evidence, such as conversations between the parties, may be considered to resolve the issue.

The scope of the AIA flow-down provision cited earlier is limited to the extent that the prime contract applies to the subcontractor's portion of the work. This language follows the reasonable conclusions of some judicial authorities that, despite the broad working of a flow-down clause, the flow-down clause alone may not incorporate certain provisions of the underlying prime contract.[40] For example, flow-down provisions have been held not to limit the security rights of the subcontractor unless the limitation is specifically set forth in the subcontract, nor to incorporate specific insurance obligations or dispute remedies.[41]

The best example of the limitations of these clauses is found in federal government contracting, the format of which is largely dictated by the extensive provisions of the Federal Acquisition Regulations. A general flow-down provision may not be enough to incorporate the special requirements of the FARs into the subcontract.[42] It is risky in government contracting to rely only upon a general flow-down clause that may not be construed to apply to all of the provisions of the prime contract and may not be sufficient to incorporate the remedial provisions of the prime contract.[43]

D. Conditional Assignment of Subcontract to the Owner

The importance of subcontractor performance to the owner becomes apparent when the prime contractor defaults on its contract with the owner. In this circumstance, it becomes critical for the owner to preserve the subcontractor's obligation to continue performance of its share of the project.

To protect the owner's rights, it is common to provide for a contingent assignment of the subcontract to the owner in the event of the prime contractor's default at the owner's election.[44] This assures the owner of some continuity in the project's performance even if the prime contractor fails to continue.

---

40. See Jeff Jury, *Everything Flows Downhill—Or Does It? Flow-Down Clauses in Construction Contracts*, CONSTR. BRIEFINGS 1 (June 2007).
41. *Id.*
42. Currently there are more than 50 FAR provisions and more than 35 Department of Defense FAR Supplement flow-down provisions that are considered "mandatory flow-down clauses." Darst, *supra* note 1, at 12.
43. Darst, *supra* note 1, at 11.
44. Article 5.4 of AIA A201–2017.

10.05 COORDINATION OF SUBCONTRACT WORK

A. The Duty of Coordination

The problem of coordination of the work of various construction trades typically arises on a complex project where the owner employs multiple prime contractors to perform the project. Each prime contractor typically desires its work to flow smoothly in an uninterrupted sequence and schedule. This allows the prime contractor to take advantage of repetitious work performed on a "mass production" basis with attendant efficiency and savings in time and money. When a number of separate prime contractors work in close proximity to each other with similarly tight schedules, these desires often conflict.

At any particular time, in any particular location, who has precedence over the others? This conflict is continually addressed in hundreds and even thousands of individual decisions on priority, a process known as coordination. Depending on how the decision process is handled, some prime contractors may suffer delays and inefficiencies and may seek compensation for their unanticipated expenses.

Even in the absence of definitive contract provisions, courts have held that the owner has a duty to coordinate the work of the various prime contractors the owner hires directly. Where an owner awards multiple prime contracts, the owner is responsible for the coordination of the work of all the contractors and, unless otherwise provided in the contract, the owner is liable for delays that one prime contractor causes another.[45]

Aside from the common law, this duty of coordination is imposed by most form construction contracts. For example, article 6.1.3 of the AIA A201 contract form provides: "The Owner shall provide for coordination of the activities of the Owner's own forces and of each separate contractor with the Work of the Contractor, who shall cooperate with them." This provision incorporates the owner's duty of coordination into its contract with the prime contractor.

B. Duty to Coordinate Subcontract Work

Given the strong authority supporting the owner's duty to coordinate the work of multiple prime contractors, it is no surprise that legal authority supports the prime contractor's obligation to coordinate the work of its subcontractors. Courts have found this obligation, also, to be implied by contract.

---

45. BRUNER & O'CONNOR § 15:55 and cases cited.

An example of court enforcement of this obligation is found in the case of *Bat Masonry Co., Inc. v. Pike-Paschen Joint Venture III*.[46] In this case, a masonry subcontractor complained about the manner in which the prime contractor made the subcontractor's work available. The court found that the prime contractor delayed the completion of the slab on grade work that was to precede the masonry, thus shifting the masonry to the winter months. Also, the prime contractor made the subcontractor's work available in small "piecemeal" segments, causing the subcontractor to demobilize. Further, the contractor re-sequenced the work in a manner that obstructed and interfered with the subcontractor's work.

The court in *Bat Masonry* found that these actions violated the coordination duty of the prime contractor to the subcontractor, which the court described as follows: "The contractor's duty is essentially that of reasonable cooperation and support in assisting the subcontractor in the completion of its portion of the work. This duty includes the duty to properly schedule and coordinate the work of subcontractors." Further, the court opined,

> [T]he prime contractor implicitly promises to provide such working conditions as may be necessary to allow its subcontractor to carry out its obligations under contract. . . . If a contractor interferes with the work of its subcontractor, it has breached its obligation and the subcontractor is entitled to recover for the resulting delays. The contractor's implied duty includes the promise not to hinder, delay or interfere with the work of the subcontractor.[47]

Prime contractors generally have been concerned over the implications of this coordination obligation since the prime contractors (1) are responsible for the entire project, and (2) feel they must have the right to direct the schedule and sequence of the work of all subcontractors in order to further complete the project on time. Therefore, even the standard form contracts that govern subcontractor work are relatively ambiguous about the nature of the prime contractor's coordination obligation and give the prime contractor some flexibility over scheduling subcontractor work.

The prime contractor's obligation is referenced in article 3.2.1 of AIA Document A401, Standard Form of Agreement between Contractor and Subcontractor, which provides: "The Contractor shall cooperate with the Subcontractor in scheduling and performing the Contractor's Work to avoid conflicts or interference in the Subcontractor's Work. . . ." However, article 4.2.2 also provides that the subcontractor "shall cooperate with the Contractor in scheduling and

---

46. 842 F. Supp. 174 (D. Maryland 1993).
47. *Id.* at 178.

performing the Subcontractor's Work to avoid conflict, delay in or interference with the Work of the Contractor, other subcontractors, the Owner, or Separate Contractors." And article 4.2.8 provides that "the Subcontractor shall cooperate with the Contractor, other subcontractors, the Owner and Separate Contractors whose work might affect the Subcontractor's Work." Because the clauses variously require the prime contractor to cooperate with the subcontractor and vice versa, a mutual coordination obligation is created.

C. Avoiding Coordination Obligations

The AIA provisions place some coordination burden on the subcontractor. Does this duty insulate the prime contractor from legal coordination responsibility? *Allied Fire & Safety Equipment Co. v. Dick Enterprises, Inc.*[48] dealt with a provision that required the subcontractor to "coordinate its work with the work of other trades." The court held the provision failed to override the prime contractor's implied duty not to interfere with the subcontractor's work. Based on this holding, prime contractors seeking to insulate themselves from liability to subcontractors need to conceive of subcontract language stronger than simply requiring the subcontractor "to coordinate its work with the work of other trades."

The concern of prime contractors over potential liability to subcontractors for the coordination of the work of such subcontractors has fostered a number of even stronger contract provisions than those in the AIA A401 form. These include provisions giving the prime contractor absolute authority to direct the subcontractor's sequence and schedule of work during the project and obligating the subcontractor to follow those directions.

Other approaches have attempted to remove from the subcontractor any right to compensation for delays it encounters in the performance of its work. These provisions face the same hurdles that confront no-damage-for-delay clauses generally. The contract at issue in *Allied Fire* also contained an exculpatory clause under which the prime contractor was not to be held liable for the subcontractor's claims for delay. The court held that this clause was not to be given effect where the contractor "actively delayed and hindered" the performance of the contract.[49]

---

48. 886 F. Supp. 491 (E.D. Pa. 1995).
49. *Id.* at 495.

10.06 SUBCONTRACTOR INDEMNITY OBLIGATIONS

A. Judicial Indemnity Authority

The term "indemnity" has been defined as an obligation designed to prevent another party "from being damnified by the legal consequences of an act . . . of one of the parties or of some third person."[50] The relief from "damnification" may come from a court. Indemnity obligations may be created by common law, obligating an actively negligent party to indemnify a passively negligent party.[51]

It is not unusual for a party to seek a court order requiring one party to indemnify another when the first party's acts make that first party entirely responsible for the second party's potential liability. Some courts have applied a doctrine of "implied indemnity" where a special relationship existed between the parties, and one party ultimately bears responsibility for the loss.[52]

This issue is particularly acute on construction projects, affecting subcontractors who share the project site with other entities, such as other subcontractors, the prime contractor, the owner, and designers. If an accident occurs, a question may arise as to which party bears responsibility, and, in fact, multiple parties may share that responsibility. Therefore, rather than relying on the eventual finding of a court, the parties, through indemnity agreements, commonly seek to apportion liability before an accident happens.

B. Subcontractor Indemnity Agreements

Since subcontractors actively perform work on the project site with a number of employees (and even sub-subcontractors), the prime contractor commonly requests an indemnity agreement from the subcontractors. Such an agreement typically requires the subcontractor to indemnify the prime contractor and other interested parties, such as the owner, from claims arising out of the subcontractor's work. The subcontractor's indemnity obligation consequently would indemnify the prime contractor and others against any secondary liability resulting from the negligent acts of the subcontractor or persons for whom the subcontractor is responsible.

---

50. BLACK'S LAW DICTIONARY (5th ed. 1979).
51. Jeffrey M. Hummel & Z. Taylor Shultz, *Indemnification Principles and Restrictions on Construction Projects*, CONSTR. BRIEFINGS, Aug. 2005, at 1, 2.
52. Id.

A common version of this concept, which is widely accepted, is found in the AIA subcontract form. Article 4.7.1 of AIA Document A401 provides:

> To the fullest extent permitted by law, the Subcontractor shall indemnify and hold harmless the Owner, Contractor, Architect, Architect's consultants, and agents and employees or any of them from and against claims, damages, losses and expenses, including but not limited to attorney's fees, arising out of or resulting from performance of the Subcontractor's Work under this Subcontract, provided that any such claim, damage, loss or expense is attributable to bodily injury, sickness, disease or death, or to injury to or destruction of tangible property (other than the Work itself), but only to the extent caused by the negligent acts or omissions of the Subcontractor, the Subcontractor's Sub-subcontractors, anyone directly or indirectly employed by them or anyone for whose acts they may be liable, regardless of whether or not such claim, damage, loss or expense is caused in part by a party indemnified hereunder.

This provision captures the prime contractor's agreement to indemnify the owner.[53] Note that the AIA subcontract provision (1) applies to losses such as bodily injury and destruction of tangible property commonly covered by insurance policies; (2) is limited to the extent of the subcontractor's negligence; and (3) may be held to be valid even in the face of the negligence of the indemnified party (the "indemnitee"). An additional provision provides that this remedy is not exclusive, thereby recognizing the possibility of judicially imposed indemnity.

The AIA provision is generally regarded as balanced;[54] however, the possibility of abuse in the drafting of such a clause is manifest. Since the prime contractor occupies a strong bargaining position, it might consider expanding the reach of the clause's scope to exonerate the prime contractor completely from any responsibility, even for its own negligence.

Even though a court may uphold a clause agreed to by the parties, the court, nevertheless, may construe the clause very strictly. If, for example, the provision would indemnify the indemnitee against its own negligence, the clause may be limited by statute or the court may require that such intention be expressed in clear and unequivocal terms.[55] Since the courts do not favor such clauses, such

---

53. *See* AIA Document A201–2017, *supra* note 10, § 3.18.1.
54. Hummel & Shultz, *supra* note 51, at 3.
55. *See* Johnson v. Bd. of Cnty. Comm'rs, 913 P.2d 119, 136 (Kan. 1996). *See also* Fretwell v. Prot. Alarm Co., 764 P.2d 149, 152–53 (Okla. 1988) (stating that it "will strictly construe an agreement which would have the result of indemnifying one against his own negligence, but where the intention to do so is unequivocally clear from an examination of the contract, such an agreement is enforceable.").

clauses must be carefully worded in order to be effective.[56] Even so, a reasonable concern exists as to whether the enforcement of an indemnity agreement designed to protect a party from the consequences of its own negligence is good public policy. This concern has prompted a number of legislatures to act on the matter, as discussed in the next section.

C. Anti-Indemnity Statutes

Because of the potential unfairness and adverse social implications of broad indemnity clauses, a number of states have enacted statutes restricting the enforceability of such clauses. Generally, these statutes have fallen into three categories:[57]

1. Sole negligence laws. One type of statute restricts the enforceability of a clause that indemnifies a party against liability for a loss caused by that party's sole negligence.[58]
2. Partial negligence statutes. Certain states have enacted statutes invalidating clauses that provide for indemnification of indemnitees who bear at least partial responsibility through their own actions for the loss.[59]
3. Statutes barring indemnity of design professionals. Some states have enacted laws restricting the enforcement of agreements designed to indemnify design professionals from liability arising from their services.[60]

The interpretation of these anti-indemnity statutes, as well as the indemnity agreements potentially subject to such statutes, has given rise to substantial litigation. Since most of the statutes apply by their terms to construction projects, this may limit the nature of the relationships covered by the statutes.[61] Since the statutes differ a great deal from state to state, the decision as to which state's law to apply may be very important. This decision may be

---

56. In fact, the Kansas Court of Appeals has recommended that drafters explicitly state the indemnitor's obligation to indemnify the indemnitee for the indemnitee's negligence. Zenda Grain & Supply Co. v. Farmland Indus., Inc., 894 P.2d 881, 888 (Kan. App. 1995).

57. Three types of anti-indemnity statutes are described in Allen Holt Gwyn and Paul E. Davis, *Fifty-State Survey of Anti-Indemnity Statutes and Related Case Law*, CONSTR. LAWYER 26 (Summer 2003).

58. *Id.* At the time of their writing, the authors identified 18 states that voided provisions that indemnified losses or damages arising from the indemnitee's sole negligence.

59. *Id.* At the time of their writing, the authors identified 16 states that voided provisions for losses or damages arising from the indemnitee's negligence, whether sole or concurrent.

60. *Id.* at 27. At the time of their writing, the authors identified 19 states that had passed statutes that included prescriptions in this area, some specifically voiding this type of agreement and others having general statutes that included this type of agreement.

61. Smith v. Seaboard Coast Line R.R. Co., 639 F.2d 1235 (5th Cir. 1981).

influenced by the public policy of the states involved.[62] Some statutes exclude from their scope agreements involving the procurement of insurance.[63]

10.07 PAYMENT TO SUBCONTRACTORS AND SUPPLIERS

A. The Payment Process

Generally, payments to subcontractors and suppliers are made from monies received by the prime contractor from the owner of the project. Thus, a third party stands between the owner who pays for the work and the parties who performed the work and expect to receive payment. This three-party relationship has created extensive contract provisions governing the handling of payments, as well as controversy regarding the rights of the parties when payments are delayed or not received at all.

The provisions for passing through payments from the owner to the subcontractor found in the AIA documents illustrate a typical system of handling such payments. Article 11 of AIA Document A401 provides for progress payments to be made by the prime contractor to the subcontractor. Progress payments of the subcontract price are based on an allocation of that price into segments of work to be performed, pursuant to a "schedule of values" (article 11.1.5). The subcontractor submits pay applications each month indicating the percentage of each segment of work completed during the month (article 11.1.6). The prime contractor then includes the amount of the subcontractor's application in its application to the owner (article 11.1.3). Within seven working days after the prime contractor receives payment from the owner (article 11.1.3), the prime contractor is to pay the subcontractor the amount of its application, less amounts retained by the owner applicable to the subcontractor's work and amounts withheld due to the fault of the subcontractor (article 11.1.7.42).

This three-party arrangement, therefore, requires the subcontractor to make formal applications for payment, which are passed on to the owner for approval; the owner then makes payment to the prime contractor for the subcontractor's work based on the amount demonstrated by the subcontractor's application. If the subcontractor's work does not merit payment to the prime

---

62. Hummel & Shultz, *supra* note 51, at 3.

63. Minn. Stat. Ann. § 337.05. In Seward Housing Corp. v. Conroy Bros. Co., 573 N.W.2d 364, 366 n.2, the court explicitly stated section 337.05 allowed enforcement of a provision in a "standard subcontract agreement requiring the subcontractor to purchase liability insurance to cover any negligent acts by the [general contractor]."

contractor, then the owner will not approve the application, and the prime contractor will be justified in not making payment to the subcontractor.

If the prime contractor receives funds from the owner for the subcontractor's work, then the prime contractor is obligated to pass on those funds to the subcontractor. If the subcontractor is not paid, the subcontractor's remedies include stopping its work (article 4.8). Courts have held that the failure of the prime contractor to pay a subcontractor may justify the subcontractor's rescission of the subcontract.[64]

B. Bearing the Risk of Owner's Failure to Pay

If the subcontractor's payment is contingent on the prime contractor's receiving payment from the owner, a serious delay may occur in passing on the amount of retainage applicable to the subcontract work; the delay occurs because the bulk of the prime's retainage will not be released until substantial completion. While a subcontractor may finish its work early in the project, if its retainage payment must await final payment by the owner, that this may delay the payment of retainage for years—something that causes a great deal of controversy in the industry.[65]

The owner may withhold payment from the prime contractor for a variety of reasons, many of which may be unrelated to the subcontractor or its performance.[66] Indeed, a not uncommon occurrence is that disputes between the prime contractor and the owner prompt the owner to withhold payment from the prime contractor; this may occur even though the subcontractor performed its work in an entirely satisfactory manner. In such a case, it is arguably unfair for the prime contractor to fail to pay the subcontractor if the subcontractor is not at fault, even when the prime contractor does not receive payment from the owner.

Disputes between the prime contractor and the owner commonly affect the flow of payments on a project. In turn, this disruption of the payment process causes disputes between the prime contractor and the subcontractor over their respective rights and obligations. This situation has inspired a number of contract provisions relating to these rights and obligations, as well as legal disputes over the interpretation and veracity of such provisions.

---

64. STEIN, *supra* note 14, § 5B.02[4][c].
65. *See id.* § 7.04[11][d].
66. *See* AIA Document A201–2017, *supra* note 10, § 9.5.1.

C. Risk of Payment Provisions

It is increasingly common for prime contractors to insist on including in their subcontracts a provision that the prime contractor's obligation to pay the subcontractor is contingent on the prime contractor's receipt of payment from the owner. The intention of many of these provisions is to pass on to the subcontractor the risk of the owner's failure to make payment for reasons unrelated to the subcontractor's work. Nevertheless, the perception of unfairness of such a clause has created legal difficulties in its enforcement. Courts and commentators often apply the term "pay-when-paid" to denote clauses construed to impose a timing argument; that is, a requirement that the subcontractor's payment is not due until such time as the contractor receives payment. A pay-if-paid clause, on the other hand, attempts to impose not merely a timing constraint, but an absolute condition precedent such that the contractor's obligation to pay the subcontractor does not arise unless an express condition—payment by the owner to the contractor—occurs.

One legal hurdle lies in the interpretation of the clause itself. The courts have construed many clauses to constitute "pay-when-paid clauses" that apply to the timing of payment rather than a condition of payment; as a result, these clauses have not protected the prime contractor from independent liability to the subcontractor.[67] Ambiguities in such clauses are generally construed against the prime contractor seeking to enforce the clause and avoid payment.[68]

Some courts have enforced clearly written pay-if-paid clauses, which make payment by the owner an express condition precedent of the prime's payment obligation to the subcontractor.[69] However, other courts have refused to enforce the clauses. Pay-if-paid clauses are unenforceable in the courts of California since they are inconsistent with the laws regarding subcontractor security.[70] An Iowa court has held the clause enforceable as long as nonpayment was not the fault of the prime contractor.[71]

---

67. *See, e.g.*, Main Elec., Ltd. v. Printz Servs. Corp., 980 P.2d 522 (Colo. 1999); Federal Ins. Co. v. I. Kruger, Inc., 829 So. 2d 732 (Ala. 2002).

68. *See* G.E.I. Recycling, Inc. v. Atl. Envtl., Inc., 821 So. 2d 431 (Fla. Dist. Ct. App. 2002); Lafayette Steel Erectors, Inc. v. Roy Anderson Corp., 71 F. Supp. 582 (S.D. Miss. 1997); Am. Drilling Serv. Co. v. City of Springfield, 614 S.W.2d 266 (Mo. Ct. App. 1981).

69. *See* Gilbane Bldg. Co. v. Brisk Waterproofing Co., 585 A.2d 248 (1991); Berkel & Co. Contractors v. Christman Co., 533 N.W.2d 838 (Mich. Ct. App. 1995).

70. *See* William R. Clarke Corp. v. Safeco Ins. Co. of Am., 938 P.2d 372 (Cal. 1997); Capitol Steel Fabricators, Inc. v. Mega Constr. Co., 68 Cal. Rptr. 2d 672 (Cal. 1998). *See also* WestFair Elec. Contractors v. Aetna Cas. & Surety Co., 661 N.E.2d 967 (N.Y. 1995).

71. Grady v. S. E. Gustafson Constr. Co., 103 N.W.2d 737 (1960).

A majority of the courts refuse to construe a pay-when-paid clause as an absolute defense to nonpayment.[72] The enforceability of such clauses and the reasoning related to enforceability varies a great deal from state to state.[73] In general, courts interpreting such clauses as pay-when-paid clauses impose a judicial interpretation that payment will (absolutely and not conditionally) become due at a reasonable time after the work is performed, regardless of whether the owner pays the contractor.

Other states have legislated against pay-if-paid clauses, even in private contracts,[74] while other states have accepted such clauses but prevented them from interfering with subcontractor lien rights.[75]

Therefore, clauses restricting the right of subcontractors to receive payments due for their work have been faced with substantial legal barriers, and the effectiveness of such clauses is subject to substantial doubt.

D. Other Methods to Secure Subcontractor Payments

To better secure payments to subcontractors and suppliers, a number of states have passed so-called trust fund statutes. These statutes commonly provide that monies paid to a prime contractor for work or materials furnished by subcontractors or suppliers will be held in a trust by the prime contractor for the benefit of those subcontractors and suppliers.[76] The nature and substance of the laws vary from state to state. The laws may have a number of implications for the rights of subcontractors and others depending upon their terms. For example: (1) prime contractors who mishandle the funds may be subject to criminal or civil penalties, and their officials subject to personal liability; (2) the civil remedies of subcontractors and suppliers may include expanded remedies such as attorney's fees and interest; (3) the payments held in trust may be free from the claims of the prime contractor's creditors; and (4) fiduciary responsibilities may be visited upon prime contractors which, among other things, may affect the status of the prime contractor's obligations to the funds under the bankruptcy laws.

Other measures designed to ensure payment to subcontractors include (1) a direct disbursement system (channeling payment through a title company as

---

72. Will M. Hill & Donna M. Evans, *Pay When Paid Provisions: Still a Conundrum*, 18 CONSTR. LAWYER 16 (Apr. 1998).

73. Robert F. Carney & Adam Cizek, *Payment Provisions in Construction Contracts and Construction Trust Fund Statutes: A Fifty-State Survey*, 24 CONSTR. LAWYER 5 (Fall 2004).

74. *See* 6 Del. C. § 3507(e) and WISC. STAT. § 779.135 (West 2003).

75. 770 ILL. COMP. STAT. ANN. 60/21 (West 2003); KAN. STAT. ANN. § 16-1803(c) (Supp. 2005).

76. Carney & Cizek, *supra* note 73.

a disbursing agent), proposed by the American Subcontractors Association; (2) legislation governing federal government contracts that requires the prime contractor to pay subcontractors within a certain period of time or incur interest and possibly repay the funds to the owner; and (3) similar state so-called prompt pay acts.[77]

10.08 SUBCONTRACTOR CLAIMS

A. The Problem of Subcontractor Claims

In the traditional construction contracting format, an owner contracts only with a prime contractor and not with the subcontractors who will perform the work. Commonly, the prime contractor selects the subcontractors and determines the conditions of their employment. The owner regards its contract with the prime contractor as the measure of the prime contractor's responsibility and liability for performance of the project.

As a consequence of the owner's contract with the prime contractor, and the absence of a contractual relationship between the owner and the subcontractors, the owner expects the prime contractor to be responsible for the work of the subcontractors. This includes the administration of the subcontractors' work and the review and approval of any subcontractor claims. Direct dealings between the owner and the subcontractors are inconsistent with this arrangement; can prejudice the legal position of both the owner and the subcontractors; and, in some cases, may constitute a breach of the respective parties' contracts with the general contractor.

On the other hand, the subcontractor is responsible for its scope of work critical to completion of the project. Only the subcontractor thoroughly understands its plan for executing its scope of work and whether and to what extent this plan is impaired by any action or omission of the owner. Particularly, with the highly specialized and technical nature of modern subcontract work, the prime contractor has much less knowledge of problems affecting the subcontract work than does the subcontractor or, perhaps, even the owner.

Subcontractors on construction projects can incur substantial damage from the actions of parties with whom they have no contract. For example, the subcontractor must perform changes made by the project owner or owner's representative. Delays to the prime contractor's work commonly will delay the subcontractor's work as well. Specification and design problems may adversely

---

77. STEIN, *supra* note 14, § 7.05[1][b].

affect the subcontractor's scope of work. Unexpected conditions may cost the subcontractor more time and money than the prime contractor.

Like prime contractors, subcontractors base their bids on the conditions of the project represented to them at the time the subcontractors price their work. When these conditions are changed, the subcontractor likely will incur extra, unanticipated costs not included in the subcontractor's bid price. Subcontractors commonly incur additional costs due to the acts or omissions of the project owner or the designer working with the owner. Naturally, the subcontractors seek compensation for such additional and unanticipated costs when they occur.

Despite the reality that the acts and omissions of owners or their agents may result in extra, unanticipated costs to the subcontractor, the only responsible party with which the subcontractor has an agreement is the prime contractor. When the subcontractor incurs such extra costs, the parties may understand that the prime contractor did not the cause the subcontractor's extra costs for these changed conditions. If the owner or its agent is the party responsible for the change, then the prime and/or the subcontractor may find it logical to pursue the owner to recover the subcontractor's extra costs. In this instance, the subcontractor and/or the prime contractor may wish to pass through the subcontractor's claim to the owner, who is the real party at fault. While the concept may be simple, finding the proper legal ground for these claims is fraught with difficulties.

B. Barriers to the Subcontractor Making Its Claim

Logical support exists for the concept of a direct contest between the subcontractor and the owner as a solution to the problem of subcontractor claims. Several authors suggest that it is at least a good management concept to permit the owner and the subcontractor to meet in the same proceeding and contest their differences.[78] As these authors point out, the primary principle standing in the way of this concept is the idea of privity.[79] No formal contract exists between the subcontractor and the owner; therefore, the subcontractor has no contractual privity with the owner.

The subcontractor's resort to tort theories of recovery against owners traditionally has been thwarted by the Economic Loss Rule, which, in many cases,

---

78. John W. Whelan & George H. Gnoss, *Government Contracts: Subcontractors and Privity*, 10 WILLIAM & MARY L. REV. 80 (1968).

79. *Id.* at 84.

bars the suit.[80] Note that this issue may confuse some courts that deal with the question of whether representations and warranties of the owner to the prime contractor are passed down to the subcontractor.[81]

Given the lack of privity between the subcontractors and the owners, could the parties agree to realign themselves? For example, could the prime contractor assign to its subcontractor the prime contractor's rights against the owner relating to the subcontractor's claim? The decision in *Topco, Inc. v. State of Montana*[82] illustrates the issues raised by the application of the privity concept to situations involving prime contracts and subcontracts that differ in their treatment of the parties' rights. In *Topco*, the prime contractor entered into a contract with the state of Montana to construct a highway. The prime contract amount included a price for the clearing and grubbing work. The prime contractor then subcontracted the clearing and grubbing work at a lower price than that contained in the prime contract. The subcontractor eventually asserted a claim against the state of Montana based on the price of the work specified in the prime contract. Additionally, the prime contractor actually assigned to the subcontractor the prime's rights under the prime contract. Thus, the subcontractor was in the legal position of asserting the prime contractor's rights as its assignee. In *Topco*, the lower court held that the subcontractor's recovery was based on the subcontract price, not on the prime contract price for the clearing and grubbing. This holding was reversed on appeal on the theory that the prime contractor's price would govern the recovery because of the assignment to the subcontractor of the prime's rights under the prime contract. In federal contracting, assignment by the prime contractor of its claim against the government would be illegal.[83]

C. The Pass-Through System and Its Problems

In practice, a system has developed that involves both the prime contractor and the subcontractor in the assertion of the subcontractor's claims against

---

80. *E.g.,* Moorman Mfg. Co. v. Nat'l Tank Co., 435 N.E.2d 443 (Ill. 1982) (holding that while a distant party may recover economic losses from an intentional misrepresentation, the rule would bar any action based on an innocent misrepresentation).

81. *But see* Murphy v. City of Springfield, 738 S.W.2d 521 (Mo. Ct. App. 1987) (allowing a drilling subcontractor to sue the owner directly after incurring economic loss due to the owner's innocent misrepresentation of the subsurface conditions).

82. 912 P.2d 805 (Mont. 1996).

83. Severin v. United States, 99 Ct. Cl. 435 (1943) (disfavoring any assignment by the subcontractor of its claim to the prime contractor, stating: "If the subcontractor did have a claim against the Government, it could not transfer that claim to another person, plaintiffs for example, since assignment of such claims is forbidden by statute." R.S. 3477; 31 U.S.C. 203).

the owner. To pass the subcontractor's claim through to the owner via the prime contractor, the prime contractor will commence a proceeding against the owner "on behalf of" the subcontractor. In this proceeding, the prime contractor will seek to recover the extra costs incurred by the subcontractor that are caused by the owner. Thus, the prime contractor effectively "sponsors" the subcontractor's claim in a proceeding between the prime contractor and the owner to which the subcontractor is not a named party.

This pass-through system is predicated on the concept that the prime contractor is liable to the subcontractor for the subcontractor's claim and, therefore, the prime "passes on" to the owner the prime contractor's liability to its subcontractor. The parties have even argued over who has the burden of proof on this issue. See *Gilbert Pac. Corp. v. Oregon*,[84] in which the owner of the project took the position that the prime contractor should be required to allege that the prime contractor was liable to the subcontractor as part of the prime contractor's pleading. In *Gilbert*, the prime contractor contended this was an affirmative defense that should be alleged by the owner. The court agreed it was a matter of affirmative defense up to the owner to raise.[85]

Prime contractors go to great lengths to protect themselves from liability to subcontractors. They do this through the provisions of the subcontract agreements they draw, as well as the terms of documents they prepare during the project. If these efforts result in a legally binding release of the prime contractor's liability to the subcontractor, how can the prime later pass through any claim of the subcontractor to the owner? This issue was raised in the important case of *Severin v. United States*.[86]

In *Severin*, the plaintiffs, who were the prime contractor, sued the government on behalf of their subcontractor who had incurred damages as a result of the government's action. The court questioned whether the subcontractor had released the prime contractor from liability such that the prime contractor would have no loss allowing it to bring an action. The court stated:

> If we look at plaintiffs as the real party in interest in their own suit, we encounter these facts. Plaintiffs did have a contract with the Government. That contract was breached. That breach might, if the contract had been one between private persons, have given rise to a right to win a suit, and to recover nominal damages, even if no actual damages resulted from the breach. But the futile exercise of suing merely to win a suit was not consented to by the United

---

84. 822 P.2d 729 (Or. Ct. App. 1991).

85. *See also* Kensington Corp. v. State, 253 N.W.2d 781 (Mich. Ct. App. 1997) (placing the burden of proof on the owner to show that the prime contractor was absolved from liability to the subcontractor).

86. 99 Ct. Cl. 435 (1943).

States when it gave its consent to be sued for its breaches of contract. *Nortz v. United States*, 294 U.S. 317, 327; *Great Lakes Construction Co. v. United States*, 95 C. Cls. 479, 502.

Plaintiffs therefore had the burden of proving, not that someone suffered actual damages from the defendant's breach of contract, but that they, plaintiffs, suffered actual damages. If plaintiffs had proved that they, in the performance of their contract with the Government became liable to their subcontractor for the damages which the latter suffered, that liability, though not yet satisfied by payment, might well constitute actual damages to plaintiffs, and sustain their suit. Here, however, the proof shows the opposite. The subcontract, which is in evidence, shows that plaintiffs and the subcontractor agreed with each other as follows:

> 21st. The Contractor or Subcontractor shall not in any event be held responsible for any loss, damate [sic], detention or delay caused by the Owner or any other Subcontractor upon the building; or delays in transportation, fire, strikes, lockouts, civil or military authority, or by insurrection or riot, or by any other cause beyond the control of Contractor or Subcontractor, or in any event for consequential damages.

Thus plaintiffs, effectively so far as we are advised, protected themselves from any damage by way of liability over to the subcontractor for such breaches of contract by the Government as the one which occurred here.

Plaintiffs must, then, so far as their claim includes items of losses suffered by their subcontractor, be merely accommodating another person who was damaged, by letting that other person use, for the purposes of litigation, the name of plaintiffs, who had a contract and could properly have sued if they had been damaged. Orderly administration of justice, as well as the statute against assignment of claims, seem to us to forbid that.

However, dissent in this case by Chief Justice Whaley strongly dissented in this case. He stated:

> There is no legal or equitable assignment involved. This is an action by a contractor to recover damages suffered by himself and his subcontractor, occasioned by the delay of the defendant. It is admitted that defendant's delay caused damages to both the contractor and the subcontractor. The plaintiff failed to prove the amount of his own damages but the damages suffered by the subcontractor were established by clear proof. The majority opinion admits that the subcontractor was damaged in the amount of $737.10 by allowing overhead on this amount to plaintiff.
>
> For fifty years it has been the settled doctrine of this court that a contractor could bring suit for himself and his subcontractor for losses occasioned by delay by the defendant before payment was made to the subcontractor. In innumerable cases from *Stout, Hall & Bangs v. United States*, 27 C. Cls. 385,

to *Consolidated Engineering Company,* No. 43159, decided February 1, 1943 (98 C. Cls. 256), this doctrine has been uniformly followed and never been questioned.

We must bear in mind that general contractors usually sublet specialized work like plumbing and electrical installations to subcontractors. The effect of the majority opinion would be to compel such subcontractors, and they are legion in numbers, to sue in their own names, which they could not do for lack of privity with the United States. This anomalous situation has never been recognized by this court in all its history. And the majority opinion cites no case in the Supreme Court in which subcontractors have been held to be assignors of claims against the United States, merely because they were unfortunate enough to be subcontractors.

The subcontractor of plaintiff agreed in his contract not to hold the contractor for "loss, damage, detention or delay caused by the owner." The contractor is the plaintiff in this action. The subcontractor is not suing the contractor or the defendant. Plaintiff is suing for himself and his subcontractor for an admitted loss. The defendant was not a party to the subcontract. No consideration has been paid by the defendant for the protection given the contractor in the subcontract and without it the defendant cannot avail itself of this defense.

In my judgment it is travesty of justice to allow plaintiff overhead on the losses suffered by his subcontractor and to deny recovery to plaintiff for his subcontractor of the amount admittedly due him from the defendant, which any court of equity would require the contractor to pay over to his subcontractor after payment to him by the defendant.

Following the concept of the majority opinion in *Severin,* what if the prime contractor and the subcontractor had liquidated the amount of the subcontractor's claim? The court, in the case of *John B. Pike & Son, Inc. v. State of New York,*[87] limited the damages recoverable by the prime to the amount that the prime had paid the subcontractor in settlement of a prior lawsuit arising out of a change order for extra work. In *Pike,* the prime had settled a lawsuit with the subcontractor for $75,000 and taken an assignment of all the subcontractor's claims against the owner. The prime's actual recovery was limited to the amount the prime had paid the subcontractor because the prime was to receive all the benefits of the action.

The *Severin* concept has been both criticized[88] and distinguished. In *Owens-Corning Fiberglas Corp. v. United States,*[89] the court dealt with a claim

---

87. 647 N.Y.S.2d 654 (N.Y. Cl. 1996).
88. *See* Whelan & Gnoss, *supra* note 78.
89. 419 F.2d 439, 458, 190 Ct. Cl. 211 (1969).

under the contract provisions rather than a claim for breach of contract. The court felt that these facts distinguished the case from *Severin*. The court stated:

> Plaintiff also argues, and quite correctly, that since this is not a suit for damages for breach of contract as present in the *Severin* cases, but rather a claim for an equitable adjustment by a prime contractor pursuing a remedy redressable under the contract terms, the *Severin* doctrine is not applicable. In *Blount Bros. Constr. v. United States*, 172 Ct. Cl. 1, 348 F.2d 471 (1965), this court held in such circumstances that "we accept the contention of plaintiff that the exculpatory clause did not affect plaintiff's liability to its subcontractor insofar as claims under the prime contract were concerned. Therefore, if the present claims are encompassed by the terms of plaintiff's contract with the Navy, then the *Severin* rule is not a bar." The Boards of Contract Appeals have held the *Severin* doctrine inapplicable to cases where the claim is one for an equitable adjustment redressable under the contract terms. See for example, *A. DuBois & Sons*, 60—2 BCA 2750; *Morrison-Knudsen Co.*, 60—2 BCA 2799, both cited by this court in the *Blount* case, *supra* at 5.

D. Liquidating Agreements

In order to avoid the *Severin* problem prior to the prime contractor's asserting a claim against the owner on behalf of a subcontractor, it is common for the prime contractor and subcontractor to enter into an agreement typically known as a liquidating agreement.[90] This term comes from the fact that, although the subcontractor does not fully release the prime contractor from any liability, the subcontractor "liquidates" the amount of the prime contractor's liability—generally to the amount that the prime contractor can recover from the owner on behalf of the subcontractor.

Following is an excerpt from a typical liquidating agreement:

> Subcontractor hereby agrees to release Prime Contractor from any and all liens and claims, whether arising out of tort, contract or otherwise, or of whatsoever nature, arising out of or under or relating in any way to the Subcontractor Claims, except that Subcontractor does not release Prime Contractor from the payment of any money to be paid or paid and received from or on behalf of Subcontractor Claims. It is agreed that Prime Contractor's liability with regard to the Subcontractor Claims herein reserved is limited solely to the final award and payment on Subcontractor Claims by or on behalf of Owner either through negotiation or arbitration. Upon such payment by Prime Contractor to

---

90. The reasons for liquidating agreements and suggestions for drafting them are discussed by Carl A. Calvert & Carl F. Ingwalson, Jr., *Pass Through Claims & Liquidation Agreements*, 18 CONSTR. LAWYER 29 (Oct. 1998).

Subcontractor of any award made and paid by or on behalf of Owner to Prime Contractor for Subcontractor Claims, if any, Prime Contractor shall be finally and fully released and discharged by Subcontractor with regard to the Subcontractor Claims. If no such award and payment is made by or on behalf of Owner on account of Subcontractor Claims, then Prime Contractor shall have no liability to Subcontractor whatsoever for the Subcontractor Claims.

The Claims Court, in *Folk Construction Co. v. United States*,[91] dealt with a release agreement that required the prime contractor to prosecute the subcontractor's claim against the government. The court held that the release was not "complete and unconditional" because the prime was obligated to cooperate in the presentation of the claim and pay the proceeds over to the subcontractor. Thus, the court held that the *Severin* doctrine did not bar the claim.

In *Bovis Lend Lease LMB, Inc. v. GCT Venture, Inc.*,[92] the court was concerned with a no-damage-for-delay provision in the subcontract agreement. Without questioning the validity of that agreement, the court referred to a later liquidating agreement entered into by the parties. The court held that the subcontractor and the prime contractor had a right to enter into this liquidating agreement without the approval of the owner and; therefore, the prime's assertion of the subcontractor's claim was valid.[93]

10.09 SUBCONTRACTORS AND SUPPLIERS; COLLABORATIVE CONTRACTING

A. Attack on the Privity System

The bulk of authorities in this chapter dealt with parties separated by the barrier of a contract relationship. Classic construction authority recognized that each set of parties "contracted" with each other. The rights and responsibilities of subs and suppliers were based on the terms of their contract with the prime contractor or other parties. Legally, their operations may have been essentially independent of other parties working on the same project. So-called privity of contract was the source and governance of their relationship.

Trends, however, in the construction industry could significantly alter the nature of the rights and responsibilities of subs and suppliers with other parties and eventually may change the entire nature of that relationship. New relationships may transcend the privity barrier. Collaboration with other parties

---

91. 2 Cl. Ct. 681 (1983).
92. 728 N.Y.S.2d 25 (N.Y. App. 2001).
93. *But see* Aetna Bridge Co. v. State Dep't of Transp., 795 A.2d 517 (R.I. 2002).

working on the project may become more important to subs and suppliers than two-party agreements with one other party.

Traditionally, subs and suppliers had to prepare and negotiate a written agreement with another party that prefaced their relationship. This agreement, laboriously negotiated, was the primary governing document between the parties in privity with each other. By its nature, this agreement omitted huge amounts of details regarding the parties' plan for their work as well as other details of the design and construction of the overall project. Information later developed on the project could radically affect the construction of a subcontractor's portion of the project. Current developments may change this picture, however.

B. The Promise of Computerized Communications

One significant trend entering this picture is the use of computerized communications. The mutual use of computers with compatible programs allows the instantaneous exchange of words and data between many parties. Through the use of Building Information Modeling (BIM), a sub-subcontractor can now, in real time, be privy to all the information relating to the design and construction of a project as well as changes in the construction program. More importantly, the sub-sub can itself dictate data for the immediate benefit of all the other parties to the project. Therefore, the sub's ideas regarding the project's design could be included in the design of the project as well as its construction administration.

The construction industry now has available standard forms used to facilitate instant multiparty communication. ConsensusDocs 200.2 Electronic Communications Protocol Addendum has in its standard form room for subcontractors, sub-subcontractors, material suppliers, design professional, design consultants, and others. Each of the parties designates an IT administrator; the IT administrator forms an IT management team that develops the procedures, protocols, and practices for the administration of the electronic communications program.

Building Information Modeling is a most productive application of computerized communications in construction. BIM digitally represents the physical and functional characteristics of a facility. BIM functions as a shared knowledge resource that can include subcontractors and suppliers as well as owners and designers. The computer "model" created through BIM is an electronic, three-dimensional representation of building "elements" representing solid objects with true-to-scale geospatial relationships and dimensions. The model also may include additional information or data and other analyses for the project. Standard industry forms include detailed provisions regarding the use of BIM.[94]

BIM has been described as not just a depiction but a so-called simulation of the facility.[95] The fact that BIM automatically transmits changes in information to the parties prevents the information used by the parties from being inconsistent, and materially adds to the efficiency of the design work.[96] However, some tension exists between the essentially individualistic pattern of privity of contract and the collaborative nature of BIM application.[97] An argument has been made that a need exists to recraft contract relationships to reward "best for project" decisions and equitably allocate responsibility among all construction participants.[98]

BIM itself has certainly provided the parties with a shared knowledge resource to work with. It can be an even more potent force when coupled with a truly cooperative program such as Integrated Project Delivery (IPD). IPD is a project delivery approach that integrates the participants into a process with the purpose of optimizing project results.[99] The participants likely will include

---

94. ConsensusDocs 301 Building Information Modeling Addendum allows time and schedule information to be integrated into the model (4D) and cost data as well (5D). The parties are encouraged to consider the addition of other Project Participants early on which may include subcontractors and suppliers.

AIA Document E203-2013, Building Information Modeling and Digital Data Exhibit, is incorporated into the agreement between the parties for the project. It provides for the establishment of protocols for the implementation of Building Information Modeling on the project. AIA Document G202-2013, Project Building Information Modeling Protocol Form, is distributed to each project participant who has incorporated AIA Document E203-2013, Building Information Modeling and Digital Data Protocol Exhibit, into its agreement for the project. It includes a Model Element Table, which lists hundreds of items in the project and which indicates the Level of Development of each item at each project milestone. Conflicts found by any project participant are to be reported to the manager of the model. Pursuant to AIA Document G201-2013, all project participants are to comply with the digital data formats, transmission methods, and authorized uses set forth in a table included in the document.

95. Howard W. Ashcraft, *Building Information Modeling: A Framework for Collaboration*; Constr. Lawyer 5 (Summer 2008). In this article, Mr. Ashcraft explores in some detail the uses and attributes of BIM describing it not only as a "platform for collaboration" (p. 5) but a "project delivery method, with new risks, rewards, and relationships" (p. 8).

96. *Id.*

97. *Id.* at 11.

98. *Id.* at 18. However, Article 1 of ConsensusDocs 301 states that it is not intended to create privity of contract nor relieve the Design Professional from any design obligations (Firlick 1.1).

99. "Broadly state, the term IPD is used to describe a wide range of project delivery processes and contracting methods that *See*k to infuse the construction industry with a shot of collaborative effort and teamwork." Patrick J. O'Connor, Jr. & Michael B. Bomba, *Integrated Project Delivery Part I: Collaboration through New Contract Forms*, J. Am. Coll. Constr. Lawyers (Summer 2009).

subcontractors and suppliers. As such, IPD brings some basic changes in the structure of the construction relationship of which subcontractors are a part. Much of this relationship is now free of the boundaries of privity.

As in the case of BIM, IPD procedures have been described by a number of industry documents. ConsensusDocs 300 is the Standard Multi-Party Integrated Project Delivery (IPD) Agreement. The parties pledge to a relationship of mutual trust, good faith and fair dealings, including shared risk and reward, collaborative decision making, and open communication. Parties are paid their defined costs and share in the risk pool plan of incentive compensation. AIA Document C195–2008, Standard Form Single Purpose Entity Agreement for Integrated Project Delivery, involves the formation of a separate company for the purpose of furnishing the planning, design, construction, and commissioning of the project through separate agreements with members and non-members of the company. The members are to act as a team to agree on project goals and target cost. The members agree to share the success or failure of the project. AIA Document A295–2008, General Conditions of the Contract for Integrated Project Delivery, is a lengthy (47-page) document providing for the planning, design, and construction of the project in phases. The phases are described as conceptualization, criteria design, detailed design, implementation documents, construction, and closeout.

The key supporting participants on an integrated project include subcontractors.[100] The contractual relationships involved in IPD are "quite different from traditional contract models."[101] Three general forms have emerged: project alliances, relational contracts, and single purpose entities.[102] However, IPD agreements are lengthy and complicated. IPD projects vary because the participants to the project determine how to create the IPD project that suits their needs and comfort levels.[103] While the IPD agreement may require some collaborative effort in its early stages, the risks and rewards for performance of the agreement may revert to the traditional conditions that governed agreements between separate entities, conceivably wasting much of the advantages of the early collaboration.[104]

Therefore, while new concepts and new forms have introduced concepts of mutual collaboration, including subcontractors, suppliers, and other project

---

100. Integrated Project Delivery: A Guide, 4.1.1, at 8.
101. *Id.* at 17.
102. *Id.* at 33.
103. *See* O'Connor & Bomba, *supra* note 99, at 75.
104. Allen L. Overcash, *Will the New Contract Forms for Integrated Project Delivery Make Conflict Obsolete? (Or Are We Still Lost in Our Contract Obsession?)* J. AM. COLL. CONSTR. LAWYERS 33 (Winter 2009).

principles, the new concepts and forms have not uniformly eliminated the risks and rewards that the privity system created. Today, subcontractors and suppliers operate in a complex system that encourages some commitment to collaboration, but continues to require the rights and responsibilities to be based on contracts between entities separated by privity of contract.

QUESTIONS

1. Company A furnishes and installs pre-built kitchen facilities for industrial plants. The principal components of the kitchen facilities are fabricated at the company's plant and then delivered to the site where they are installed by Company A, together with associated mechanical and electrical hook-ups. Will Company A be treated as a subcontractor or supplier, and why might this distinction be important? What if Company A only furnishes the pre-built facilities, which are installed by another entity?
2. A subcontractor tenders a bid to a prime contractor who, in turn, bids on a large construction project. The prime contractor is awarded the project and tenders a formal subcontract agreement to the subcontractor. The subcontractor refuses to execute the subcontract agreement, contending that the scope of its work changed and the general conditions of the agreement are too onerous. Can the prime contractor require the subcontractor to execute and perform an agreement?
3. A subcontractor and prime contractor execute an AIA form of subcontract agreement that contains the normal flow-down provision. The prime contract contains an arbitration clause, but the subcontract does not. When a dispute arises over the scope of the subcontractor's work under the owner's specifications, the prime contractor asserts that the subcontractor must arbitrate rather than sue. Is the prime contractor correct?
4. Using the AIA form of subcontract agreement, the prime contractor requires the subcontractor to work overtime so that its work does not interfere with other subcontractors. Is the subcontractor obligated to follow the prime contractor's requirement? Could the prime contractor pass this cost on to the owner?
5. A subcontractor finishes its work on a project but does not receive final payment since the prime contractor's work will not be completed for some time. Must the subcontractor await payment until the entire project is complete even though its work was satisfactorily completed?
6. Using BIM, a subcontractor participates with the prime contractor and other parties in the design of a new project. At the conclusion of the project, the owner refuses to make final payment based on its contention that the subcontractor's installation was so deficient that it impaired the operation of the project and its value. Is the subcontractor contingently liable for this problem?

CHAPTER 11

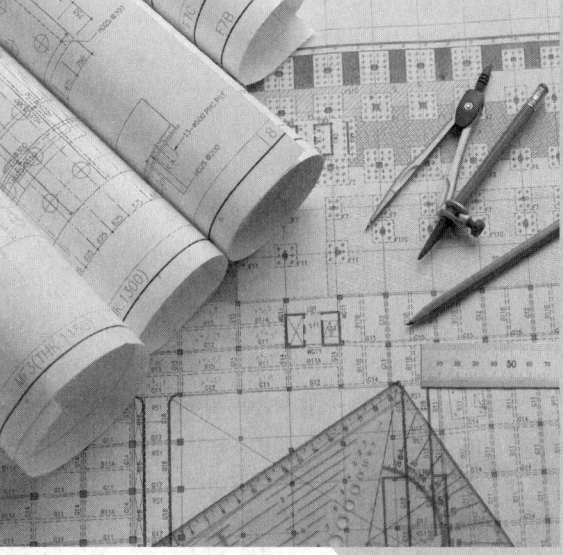

Contract Time and Completion

ANDREW D. NESS

11.01 SIGNIFICANCE OF TIME FOR PERFORMANCE

Whether the contractor completes construction on time is one of the three most critical factors (along with the quality of the work and its price) likely to determine the owner's view of the success of the construction contract. Moreover, disputes between contracting parties concerning the construction process occur more frequently about the timeliness of the contractor's performance than any other single cause. As a result, the legal issues relating to time of performance are a key element of construction law.

Historically, time was not considered such a crucial element of a construction project. The uncertainties of the construction process were considered so great that timely completion was not deemed a material element of a construction contract, unless the contract contained an express agreement to that effect. This rule persisted well into the 20th century. Indeed, the Nebraska Supreme Court reaffirmed the principle as late as 1971.[1] If time of performance

---

1. Kingery Constr. Co. v. Scherbarth Welding, Inc., 185 N.W.2d 857, 859 (Neb. 1971) (finding that time is material only if expressly so stated in the contract, because delays are foreseeable in construction). The rule was also more recently referenced in D&D Underground Utilities Inc. v. Walter Martin Excavating Inc., 2015 WL 13427765 (E.D. Ky. 2015).

is not considered a material element of contract performance, then failure to complete the work by the agreed completion date amounts only to breach of an immaterial performance obligation. Such a non-material breach will support damages for the breach, but is not sufficient to justify contract termination or allow the owner to cease performing its own contract obligations.[2]

This historical common law rule does not comport with the reality of the 21st century. In an era when owners make firm commitments to host a nationally televised football game on a given date, even before ground is broken on the stadium construction, timeliness of performance can often be the most important element of the contractor's performance. No one would seriously argue that the old rule fits today's realities.[3] However, cautious owners nevertheless typically specify in a construction contract that time of performance is considered material, so as to avoid any doubt. A provision that time is considered "of the essence" can be accomplished by a simple statement, such as:

> Time limits stated in the Contract Documents are of the essence of the Contract. By executing the Agreement the Contractor confirms that the Contract Time is a reasonable period for performing the Work.[4]

11.02 CONSTRUCTION SCHEDULING—CRITICAL PATH METHOD SCHEDULES

In addition to the needs of modern life, advances in planning and scheduling techniques have reduced the uncertainties of the construction process previously considered inherent and beyond reasonable control. The key advance in this respect is the development of network analysis systems for construction project scheduling, particularly the critical path method, or CPM. CPM was invented in the 1950s by E.I. DuPont DeNemours & Co., and, enabled by the

---

2. D&D Underground Utilities Inc. v. Walter Martin Excavating Inc., 2015 WL 13427765, at *11 (E.D. Ky. 2015). This case involved an oral subcontract with no agreed completion date and no agreement that time was of the essence, so the subcontractor's obligation was simply to complete within a reasonable time. While the subcontractor breached that obligation, its breach was not a material or "total" breach, and did not relieve the general contractor from its contractual obligations. The general contractor was allowed to recover its delay damages, however, by way of an offset against the amount owed the subcontractor.

3. "Anyone actively involved within the construction process knows that time is of the essence whether such is stated or not. . . . To the vast majority of entities involved in the construction process, time is an absolute implied material feature of every contract." MICHAEL S. SIMON, CONSTRUCTION CLAIMS & LIABILITY § 12.2 (1989).

4. American Institute of Architects, AIA Document A201–2017, General Conditions of the Contract for Construction § 8.2.1 (2017) [hereinafter AIA Document A201–2017].

increasing availability of computers, was widely introduced for construction project scheduling in the 1960s. CPM quickly became the accepted standard. A basic understanding of CPM scheduling principles is critical to assessing and resolving issues relating to time and delays on construction projects.

The first step in preparing a CPM schedule is breaking the project down into the individual activities involved in constructing the project and assigning a planned duration to each activity. Once the activities and their durations have been identified, the next step is to determine the interrelationships between the activities. These relationships are added via logic restraints between activities, such as Activity B cannot start until the completion of Activity A, or Activity C can start when Activity B is 50 percent complete. The activity logic ties determine the sequence of the activities during construction, considering physical, safety, and resource constraints. When adding logic ties, the three basic questions regarding each activity are:

1. What activities must be completed before the activity in question can start?
2. What activities can be performed concurrently?
3. What activities must follow the completion of the activity in question?

The completed schedule is a network of dozens, hundreds, or thousands of activities (depending on the project complexity and level of detail needed for effective management) and all the logic connections among the activities. Once the network is built, the critical path through the network can be determined. The critical path of a network represents the chain of interrelated activities that takes the longest time to complete from the beginning to the end. This longest continuous chain of activities establishes the overall project duration, assuming each activity requires the time allotted to it. The longest path is called the critical path, because if one of the activities along the critical path is delayed by one day, and no other activity along the critical path is changed, the project completion will be delayed one day.

Activities not on the critical path have, to some degree, "float." The amount of float time for an activity represents the number of days by which an activity can be delayed without affecting the existing critical path and the project's forecasted completion date. Float is important because it represents the amount of flexibility that is available for use without delaying the project. This flexibility can be used, for example, to shift resources from a float activity to another task that is critical and taking more time than anticipated. The CPM schedule is a key project management tool that, among other benefits, allows managers to identify the most important activities (those on or close to the critical path), to quickly identify emerging problems that threaten timely completion, and to reallocate resources from non-critical areas to address such problems. A good CPM schedule also enables managers to assess the effect of changed circumstances, such as proposed changes in the work, weather delays, delays in materials delivery, as well as to assess ideas for possible resequencing of activities.

The construction industry did not take long to appreciate that a CPM schedule could also greatly assist in determining financial responsibility for the added costs arising from delayed projects, via proving or defending delay claims. As the following cases illustrate, over time some courts have achieved a sophisticated understanding of the nature and use of CPM schedules in litigation.

Santa Fe Engineers, Inc., ASBCA Nos. 24,578, et al., 94-2 B.C.A. (CCH) ¶ 26,872 (1994)

By Administrative Judge Coldren:

The Critical Path Method (CPM) of Scheduling

The Critical Path Method (CPM) of Scheduling is a planning technique used to determine how long a project will take to complete and to identify the most important items that need to be accomplished in order to meet the project deadline. It is a written description of the manner in which a contractor plans to complete the project on time. It tells the contractor in advance the sequence duration and parameters of dates within which specific work must be performed in order to ensure timely completion of the project. It can be used to monitor progress by measuring actual job accomplishment against the schedule as a baseline.

The CPM is based upon a graphic project model called a network which depicts all activities that must be carried out with their mutual time dependencies as well as durations in a diagram form. An activity is the basic building block of the network and is defined as a single work step that has a recognizable beginning and end, and required times for its accomplishment. Each activity is linked to another through its interdependency or logic. The logic of a network refers to the determined order in which activities are performed with the commencement of some activities logically dependent or a restraint on the completion of others. However, some activities are independent of others and can proceed concurrently. The CPM network literally builds the project on paper, defining the roles and interrelationships of the activities.

Four limiting times for each network activity are calculated. The early start of an activity is the earliest date at which it can possibly start, allowing for the times required to complete the preceding activities. The early finish of an activity is the earliest possible date at which it can be completed, and is determined by adding the activity's duration to its early start date. The late finish of an activity is the very last date at which it can finish and still allow the project to be completed by the designated date. The late start of an activity is the latest possible date that it can be started if the project completion date is to be met. It is calculated by subtracting the activity's duration from its latest finish date.

The "float" of an activity in CPM scheduling is determined by subtracting its early start date from its late start date, although subtracting the early finish from the late finish will yield identical results. The path or paths of activities through the network with zero float is known as the "critical path." Any activity with zero float is a "critical activity" with the result that any delay in its finish dates prolongs project completion by the same amount of time.

The CPM schedule must be revised when work is added and deleted, completed and/or changes in logic are made. It must also be updated monthly to reflect work completed as well as the contractor's plans for completing the remaining work including in particular any significant changes in logic or duration. Each time updating information is entered into the network a new computation must be made because the new information may cause the critical path to shift. A CPM schedule that does not reflect what work is actually being accomplished in the field does not accurately identify the project's critical path and/or activities.

The following case introduces important related concepts, such as negative float, resource leveling, and acceleration.

Utley-James, Inc. GSBCA No. 5370, 85-1 B.C.A. (CCH) ¶ 17,816 (1984)

By Administrative Judge Lieblich:
In critical path scheduling, each task is related to those that logically must precede and follow it. For example, in a building constructed like the McNamara Building, the concrete for the third floor slab cannot be placed until the second floor slab has been poured and the necessary support structure has been completed. The second floor slab and the supports are said to be a "restraint" on the third floor slab. The preparer of the CPM schedule must make sure to take into accounts all such restraints. . . .

In any CPM schedule there are what is called "early start" and "late start" dates. The connotations of these two terms are not the same, and the terms must be used carefully. The early start date is the earliest date by which a given activity logically can start, assuming all preceding activities are on schedule. The late start date is the latest date by which a given activity may start if the contractor is not to fall behind schedule. The terms "early finish" and "late finish" are parallel to "early start" and "late start," but later in time by the number of days the activity is scheduled to take. The number of days between early start and late start (or, what ought to be the same thing, between early finish and late finish) is called "float." If the schedule allows no more time to do the entire job than the entire job requires, there is no float in the job, and at any given place in the schedule there will be at least one job activity with no float. An activity with no float is said to be on the critical path. An accurate CPM schedule is a very powerful management tool for the contractor in its planning of the entire job.

Determining the critical path has an important effect on the Government's management of the contract as well. For example, a delay of fifty days on a job activity with more than fifty day's float should, in theory, have no effect on the completion of the job. The early start and early finish dates for that activity may move fifty days, but they should still be earlier than the late start and late finish dates. In contrast, a job activity on the critical path, for which there is no float, will have the same early start date and late start date (and the same date for both early finish and late finish). One day's delay to that job activity will cost one day in completion of the job unless it is somehow made up.

A job activity that is not originally in the critical path can get on the critical path as a result of a delay that uses up all of its float. If more than the original float is used up by a delay, the activity is not only on the critical path but behind it; unless the completion date for the entire job is extended, the float will become negative, i.e., the early start date will be later than the late start date. This will show that the job activity cannot be started until after it is required to be if the entire project is to adhere to the existing schedule. One of the ways to cure this problem is to change the schedule by extending the completion date for the entire project, thereby putting positive float at the end of the job that can then be distributed among the activities that have developed negative float.

The other cure for negative float is accelerating, i.e., performing activities on the critical path in less time than the schedule allows for. Almost every activity is a direct restraint on others, and the finish date for a given activity is the start date for those it directly restrains. To give a simplified example, we will treat the placing of the concrete for each floor slab as a direct restraint on the placing of the next one. If each slab is scheduled for ten days but can be poured in eight, two days can be made up on each pour. If the floor slabs are on the critical path, a ten-day delay can be made up by pouring five slabs in eight days each instead of ten (assuming that the acceleration of this activity does not put some other, unrestrained activity on the critical path in place of the slabs).

Another concept of importance to CPM scheduling is resource leveling, also called resource loading. Consider, for example, the interior finish work in an office tower like the McNamara Building. The placing of each floor slab is logically restrained by the placing of the slab beneath it, but that is not necessarily true of interior finish work. There is no reason in theory why a carpeting contractor could not come in and carpet every floor of the building on the same day. But there are a variety of reasons why that is not done, and one of the principal reasons is that it makes no sense to supply that much material and that many workers to do all the floors at once when the work can be sequenced with all sorts of other work and handled over a convenient period of time with a suitably sized workforce. To give an accurate indication of the actual planned job schedule, a CPM schedule must take resource leveling into account.

11.03 SCHEDULE UPDATES

Plans naturally evolve and change as events unfold, and certainly this is the case on construction projects of any complexity. A CPM schedule, accordingly, needs periodic updating, most commonly done monthly. The object of updating the schedule is to add physical progress achieved to date (activities completed and status of those in progress), to provide a complete and accurate report of how well the actual construction progress compares with the original or other baseline schedule used as the point of comparison. Updates also provide an opportunity for project management to identify and include any sequence revisions and duration changes needed. The updated schedule should ideally both create an accurate historical record of what was accomplished when, and reflect the contractor's current plans for the activities yet to be undertaken. A construction project is dynamic by nature. Drawings and estimates, no matter how carefully considered, are bound to change as a result of unexpected events. If the project schedule is not regularly updated to reflect these changes, the schedule quickly will become outdated and misleading.

For delay claim purposes, accurate updates are a key element of most methods of forensic schedule analysis. The problem, however, is that the degree of accuracy and thoroughness desired for analysis purposes typically exceeds that needed for month-to-month project management. Schedule updates accordingly often fall short of the accuracy desirable for analysis purposes. A thorough monthly schedule update for a large project is a major undertaking requiring significant time and effort, and project management may be primarily interested in a schedule update that meets their immediate needs, rather than generating something fully accurate for potential later analysis purposes. Moreover, the computer software used for CPM schedules includes numerous shortcuts to enable quick and easy updating, often at the expense of accuracy and transparency. This can lead to misleading results if the updates are later used in a detailed schedule analysis without correction. To combat such problems, contracts sometimes require the owner and contractor to conduct joint monthly updating meetings to force timely engagement on evaluating progress and current plans, and to reach specific agreements on the completion of work activities during the preceding month.

11.04 LEGAL SIGNIFICANCE OF CONSTRUCTION SCHEDULES

The legal application of network analysis—using a forensic CPM schedule analysis as the basis for assessing the effects of particular delay events on the overall project—was quickly recognized. By the latter half of the 1960s, attempts were being made to persuade courts to admit CPM analysis as evidence in support of delay claims. Today, CPM schedule analysis is the predominant means of both proving and disproving claims of delays to the work and resultant time extensions. Some courts have gone so far as to hold that in the absence of a properly prepared and contemporaneously updated CPM schedule, a claim of delay can rarely be proven satisfactorily.[5]

However, this is not to say that courts unanimously accept specific techniques of CPM analysis, or that courts will rely on any CPM analysis that an expert witness cares to present. Judges and arbitrators are increasingly sophisticated at appreciating that (1) CPM schedule analyses can be manipulated to produce the desired result, and, (2) in any event, are only as accurate as the information and schedules on which they are based. Features added to scheduling software in recent years have only eased the task of masking dubious logic and subtle changes in a schedule, making abuses harder to detect.[6] Courts regularly called on to rule on construction delay claims not infrequently discard the views of the scheduling experts presented by one or both sides in reaching their decision.[7] (Specific schedule analysis methods are considered in Sections 11.11 and 11.12.)

11.05 TIME OF COMMENCEMENT AND TIME FOR COMPLETION

Because of the significance of timely performance, establishing the required duration for completion, as well as determining the actual start date and completion date, are all fertile grounds for potential disputes. Accordingly, setting out the time for completion (the "contract time") unambiguously in the contract, as well as establishing clear parameters for determining both the commencement and completion dates, should be key objectives for both owner and contractor.

The starting date, or time of commencement, can be a fixed date specified in the contract or the date the contract is executed. More commonly, however, the contract provides for the owner to issue a "notice to proceed" fixing the time of commencement. In some cases, a specific action establishes the time

---

5. Mega Constr. Co. v. United States, 29 Fed. Cl. 396, 426–35 (Fed. Cl. 1993); Hoffman Constr. Co. of Oregon v. United States, 40 Fed. Cl. 184, 198 (Fed. Cl. 1998), aff'd in part, rev'd in part on other grounds, 178 F.2d 131 (Fed. Cir. 1999).

6. J. Wickwire & S. Ockman, *Use of Critical Path Method on Contract Claims—2000*, 19 CONSTR. LAWYER 12 (Oct. 1999); MICHAEL T. CALLAHAN & H. MURRAY HOHNS, CONSTRUCTION SCHEDULES § 5-5 (3d ed. 2004).

7. *E.g.*, Hensel Phelps Constr. Co., ASBCA No. 49270, 99-2 B.C.A. ¶ 30,531 (1999); Pathman Construction Co., ASBCA No. 23392, 85-2 B.C.A. ¶ 18,096 (1985) (finding that both experts produced unreliable CPM analyses).

of commencement, such as the date the local authority issues the building permit, or the owner's board of directors approves the contract.

The contract time is normally specified in terms of either calendar days, working days, or, much less commonly, by establishing a fixed end date. A typical provision is as follows:

> The Contractor shall achieve Substantial Completion of the entire Work not later than ___ days from the date of commencement, subject to adjustments of this Contract Time as provided in the Contract Documents.[8]

The main benefit of using a notice to proceed and a contract time defined as a number of days is that if there is slippage in the project getting under way (as frequently occurs, due to waiting for construction loan approval or issuance of permits, late completion of precursor work, or any number of other reasons), then the required completion date is automatically extended by a day for each day of delay in issuance of the notice to proceed. This generally works well for relatively brief delays in commencement, but more substantial delays in commencement tend to be more problematic. In a fixed-price environment, the contractor's costs for labor, construction materials, and subcontractor pricing all tend to increase with time. In addition, a substantial delay in commencement can alter the season in which particular work activities will be ongoing, with significant cost effects. For example, the cost of excavation and grading work during a wet season or during the winter typically will be significantly greater than if performed in a drier or more temperate season.

The preferred means of dealing with increased costs due to a substantial commencement delay is to limit the period during which the owner may issue the notice to proceed, and to allow adjustment of the price if that limit is exceeded. Where no such period is specified, the law implies that a notice to proceed must be issued within a reasonable time, determined under the particular circumstances of the contract.[9] Several cases, however, have held that significant delays in issuing a notice to proceed did not entitle the contractor to recover damages, giving the owner wide latitude on the commencement date in the absence of a contractual time limit.[10]

---

8. AIA Document A101–2017, Standard Form of Agreement between Owner and Contractor § 3.3 (2017).

9. Ross Eng'g. Co. v. United States, 92 Ct. Cl. 253, 1940 WL 4077 (Ct. Cl. 1940) (finding that delay in issuing notice to proceed beyond 12 days was unreasonable because it forced the contractor to work in the winter).

10. M. A. Mortenson Co. v. United States, 843 F.2d 1360, 1362 (Fed. Cir. 1988); J. R. Youngdale Constr. Co., Inc. v. United States, 23 Cl. Ct. 460, 1991 WL 130539 (Cl. Ct. 1991), *aff'd*, 956 F.2d 1172 (Fed. Cir. 1992).

The general rule also is that the contractor's execution of the contract constitutes acceptance of the time for completion allowed by the contract. The owner's specification of the time for completion does not give rise to any implied warranty that the work can reasonably be completed within that time period.[11]

11.06 WAIVER OF TIME FOR COMPLETION

Even when a contract unambiguously establishes the time for completion and that "time is of the essence," both requirements can be waived by the conduct of the parties, as illustrated by the following case:

RDP Royal Palm Hotel, L.P., a Florida limited partnership, by and through its general partner, PADC Hospitality Corporation I, Plaintiff, versus Clark Construction Group, Inc., a foreign corporation, Defendant

No. 04-16203, No. 05-11713
UNITED STATES COURT OF APPEALS
FOR THE ELEVENTH CIRCUIT
168 Fed. Appx. 348; 2006 U.S. App. LEXIS 3815
February 17, 2006, Decided
February 17, 2006, Filed
PRIOR HISTORY: Appeals from the United States District Court for the Southern District of Florida. D.C. Docket No. 01-03130 CV-DMM, D.C. Docket No. 01-03130 CV-TEB.
DISPOSITION: AFFIRMED.
JUDGES: Before DUBINA and KRAVITCH, Circuit Judges, and STROM*, District Judge.
* Honorable Lyle E. Strom, United States District Judge for the District of Nebraska, sitting by designation.
OPINION: PER CURIAM:
RDP Royal Palm Hotel, L.P., ("RDP") appeals an adverse judgment in favor of Clark Construction Group, Inc. ("Clark") on RDP's suit for breach of the construction contract between the parties. RDP seeks reversal of the district court's judgment denying its claims against Clark and granting the claims asserted by Clark in its counterclaim. RDP also appeals the district court's order awarding Clark damages, attorney's fees, costs, and litigation expenses. Clark cross-appeals the district court's judgment denying its claim for extended general conditions costs. In addition, Clark appeals the district court's order denying its motion seeking

---

11. Willamette Crushing Co. v. Arizona Dept. of Transp., 932 P.2d 1350, 1354 (Ariz. Ct. App. 1997).

modification of the award of prejudgment interest. After careful review of the record, reading the parties' briefs, and after hearing oral argument, we affirm and remand the district court's judgment.

I. BACKGROUND

These cases arise from a multi-million dollar contract dispute over the construction of the Royal Palms Crowne Plaza Resort ("Resort") on Miami Beach. In May 1998, RDP, the developer and hotel owner, entered into a contract with Clark, the general contractor, for the construction of the Resort. Arquitectonica International, Inc. ("ARQ"), the lead architect, was designated as RDP's authorized agent in the contract and was required to prepare design development and construction documents. According to the contract, Clark agreed to construct the Resort for an amount not to exceed a Guaranteed Maximum Price ("GMP") of approximately $30.4 million. The deadline for substantial completion of the Resort was 518 days from the date of commencement. RDP was permitted to require additional work from Clark within the general scope of the contract by issuing a change order or construction change directive. Under the contract, the GMP and substantial completion deadline were to be adjusted accordingly in light of change orders and construction change directives. Additionally, in the event that Clark failed to complete its work on or before the substantial completion date, RDP had a right to recover liquidated damages.

On September 28, 1998, RDP issued a formal notice to proceed to Clark, establishing the date for substantial completion as February 28, 2000. Clark commenced work but faced many setbacks during the construction. For example, Clark discovered a buried sea wall and contaminated soil which delayed excavation and sheet piling operations; RDP determined that the existing hotel, which was scheduled to be renovated, was too deteriorated for renovation and had to be demolished and reconstructed in its entirety; and dilemmas developed from the construction drawings. Consequently, hundreds of change orders and construction change directives were issued by RDP and ARQ, requiring Clark and its subcontractors to perform additional and different work from that shown on the contract construction documents.

Faced with the construction changes, Clark requested numerous extensions of the substantial completion deadline and increases to the GMP. RDP repeatedly assured Clark that the substantial completion deadline would be extended appropriately. Despite these assurances, RDP and Clark never resolved the extension requests, increased the GMP nor established a new substantial completion deadline.

Eventually, the substantial completion deadline of February 28, 2000, passed and construction continued. RDP and ARQ uninterruptedly issued hundreds of change orders and construction change directives. In turn, Clark continued to construct the Resort in accordance with those modifications, and RDP accepted Clark's continued performance. However, the constant construction modifications disrupted Clark's construction schedule, resulting in coordination problems with various subcontractors, further delays to construction, and increased construction costs. Consequently, on March 1, 2002, Clark filed a mechanic's lien in the amount of $8 million for work performed by four subcontractors.

On March 12, 2002, RDP received a temporary certificate of occupancy, allowing RDP to staff and occupy the Resort in preparation for the opening. Around this time, Clark ceased its work on the Resort because RDP discontinued paying Clark for work completed in the change orders. In turn, RDP hired another contractor to complete the Resort and ultimately opened the Resort for business on May 15, 2002.

In July 2001, RDP sued Clark for breach of contract, intentional misrepresentation/fraud in the inducement, negligent misrepresentation, violation of the Florida Deceptive and Unfair Trade Practices Act, fraudulent and wrongful lien, and tortious interference with a contract. RDP asserted that Clark caused the two year delay in the Resort's completion date. Clark filed a counterclaim against RDP for fraudulent inducement, *quantum meruit* and breach of contract, alleging that RDP caused the delay by providing incomplete and erroneous construction drawings and submitting numerous design changes. Clark also filed a third-party complaint presenting pass-through claims of three subcontractors for damages caused by RDP's breach of contract and construction delays. In another third-party complaint, Clark sued ARQ and Cornerstone Engineering ("Cornerstone"), ARQ's structural engineering consultant, for negligence, indemnity and contribution.

Following a bench trial, the district court[1] entered detailed findings of fact and conclusions of law denying all of RDP's claims against Clark.[2] The district court found that RDP failed to establish a breach of the contract based on untimely performance because it waived the February 28, 2000, substantial completion date by accepting Clark's continued performance. The district court also found that, in the absence of a contractual completion date, RDP was not entitled to recover any damages, liquidated or otherwise, from Clark and failed to prove that Clark's lien was fraudulent. In relation to Clark's counterclaim, the district court found that Clark waived any breach of the contract resulting from the construction drawings, but was entitled to fair and reasonable payment for the construction work completed. The district court awarded Clark the contract balance, damages for the pending change orders, additional general conditions costs, and a 3.75% mark-up on those costs. Notwithstanding these awards, the court denied Clark's requests for extended general conditions costs and extended home office overhead. Moreover, the district court found that Clark was entitled to reasonable subcontractor

---

1. The parties consented to the jurisdiction of the United States Magistrate Judge for all purposes including trial and entry of final judgment pursuant to 28 U.S.C. § 636(c).

2. Prior to trial, the district court dismissed most of RDP's claims; only the breach of contract and fraudulent lien claims survived. On appeal, RDP does not challenge the district court's dismissal of those claims, and therefore, it has abandoned any argument on those claims. *See, e.g.,* Greenbriar, Ltd. v. City of Alabaster, 881 F.2d 1570, 1573 n.6 (11th Cir. 1989).

costs for its pass-through claims against RDP. Further, the district court dismissed Clark's third-party claims against ARQ and Cornerstone.

On August 4, 2004, the district court entered a final judgment denying RDP's claims against Clark in their entirety, denying Clark's claims against ARQ and Cornerstone in their entirety, granting Clark's claims against RDP in the amount of $5.5 million, and granting Clark's pass-through claims against RDP in the amount of $5.9 million.[3] Having reserved jurisdiction for the purpose of awarding interest, attorney's fees, and expenses, the district court subsequently entered an order on November 4, 2004, awarding Clark and its subcontractors over $2.4 million in attorney's fees and $1.5 million in costs and expenses. On November 17, 2004, the district court issued a supplemental judgment awarding Clark a total judgment of approximately $16.7 million with post-judgment interest.

In case number 04-16203, RDP and Clark pursue their respective appeal and cross-appeal of the supplemental judgment. Clark moved for relief from the supplemental judgment under *Fed. R. Civ. P. 60(b)*, seeking modification of the prejudgment interest award. The district court denied Clark's Rule 60(b) motion, and, in case number 05-11713, Clark appeals that denial.

II. DISCUSSION

RDP challenges the district court's findings of fact and conclusions of law, contending that the district court erred in finding that (1) RDP waived its right to liquidated damages; (2) RDP was liable to Clark on the pass-through claims; and, (3) Clark was entitled to recover from RDP an excessive amount of damages. RDP also challenges the district court's order on attorney's fees, costs, and litigation expenses. On cross-appeal, Clark challenges the district court's findings of fact and conclusions of law, arguing that the district court erroneously failed to award damages for extended general conditions costs. In the second appeal, Clark challenges the district court's order denying its Rule 60(b) motion to modify the prejudgment interest award. We address these issues in turn.

Liability and Damages

RDP argues that the district court erroneously found that RDP waived its claim for liquidated damages and asserts that Clark should be held liable for the delays caused by its subcontractors. RDP also argues that the district court erred in awarding Clark and its subcontractors excessive amounts of damages by failing to apportion responsibility for the total delay. RDP further argues that, in calculating damages, the district court failed to apply the contract's provision allowing Clark to recover delay-related damages for reasonable subcontractor costs attributable to RDP more than thirty days after the contractual date for substantial completion. Finally, RDP argues that the district court's finding as to the substantial completion date is incorrect, resulting in an erroneous calculation of prejudgment interest.

---

3. RDP appealed, and Clark cross-appealed, the final judgment. This court dismissed that appeal because the final judgment was not a final appealable order.

We review *de novo* the district court's conclusions of law and its application of the law to the facts. *Merrill Stevens Dry Dock Co. v. M/V Yeocomico II*, 329 F.3d 809, 813 (11th Cir. 2003). However, "we review the district court's factual findings for clear error." *CFTC v. Sidoti*, 178 F.3d 1132, 1135 (11th Cir. 1999). "If the district court's account of the evidence is plausible in light of the record viewed in its entirety, we must uphold the factual findings even if we would have weighed the evidence differently." *Id.* (internal quotations and citation omitted). "The district court's findings need only be plausible." *Id.* (internal quotations and citation omitted).

After reviewing the record, we conclude that the district court was correct in its conclusion that RDP waived its right to enforce the substantial completion date and "time is of the essence" provision of the contract. According to the record, RDP allowed the substantial completion date of February 28, 2000, to pass without setting a new deadline and continued issuing change orders and construction change directives requiring Clark to perform additional work. RDP's conduct in issuing hundreds of change orders and construction change directives after expiration of the substantial completion date of February 28, 2000, constituted waiver of the "time is of the essence" provision of the contract. *See Horovitz v. Levine*, 755 So. 2d 687, 688 (Fla. Dist. Ct. App. 1999) (purported "time is of the essence" proviso in the agreement was waived by the conduct of the parties subsequent to the agreed upon date of completion). In addition, RDP failed to set a new substantial completion date, thus it failed to reserve its right to enforce the liquidated damages provision for any date after February 28, 2000. *See McNeal v. Marco Bay Assocs.*, 492 So. 2d 778, 781 (Fla. Dist. Ct. App. 1986) ("When time has not been made essential to the contract or has been waived, the party entitled to insist on performance must fix a definite date in the future for performance . . . ."). Accordingly, we agree with the district court's conclusion that RDP waived its right to liquidated damages.

In addition, the district court did not err in holding RDP liable for Clark's pass-through claims and awarding damages. The record shows that some delays were caused by Clark's subcontractors, but those delays did not substantially postpone the eventual completion of the Resort. Rather, the substantial delays which severely impacted the Resort's construction (i.e., contaminated soil, incomplete and inaccurate construction documents, multiple design changes by RDP, and delays in plan approvals) were all attributable to RDP and not the fault of Clark's subcontractors. Although RDP asserts that the district court erroneously failed to apportion the total delay among the contributing parties, we find no error because RDP has not established a reasonable basis for such apportionment nor shown that apportionment was required. *See Gesco, Inc. v. Edward L. Nezelek, Inc.*, 414 So. 2d 535, 538 (Fla. Dist. Ct. App. 1982) (evidence must establish a reasonable basis for apportioning responsibility for the total delay); *Tuttle/White Constructors, Inc. v. Montgomery Elevator Co.*, 385 So. 2d 98, 100 (Fla. Dist. Ct. App. 1980) (loss resulting from breach of contract need not be segregated proportionately among the contributing factors causing the injury).

Further, since the district court's factual findings relating to the substantial completion date of March 12, 2002, and thirty-day damages grace period are plausible, we affirm the court's findings. *See Sidoti, 178 F.3d at 1135.*
[Discussion of other issues omitted.]

III. CONCLUSION

For the foregoing reasons, we affirm the district court's judgment but remand the case for the district court to correct the clerical mistakes pointed out in this opinion.
AFFIRMED

Waiver of the completion date by conduct generally precludes the owner both (1) from terminating the contractor for default due to its failure to meet the completion date, and (2) from recovering damages for late completion.[12]

In situations where the owner effectively has waived the established completion date, what then is the contractor's obligation with respect to completing the work? In the absence of any established time for completion, the contractor is responsible only for completing the work within a "reasonable time," to be determined based on the particular circumstances of the contract.[13] An owner only able to hold the contractor to a "reasonable" completion date, which date will be judicially determined only long after the fact, is in an unenviable situation. In most construction projects, the owner needs to make substantial financial commitments based on the expected completion date of the project, whether this involves releasing rights to old facilities in anticipation of new ones, adding personnel to staff a new facility, such as the resort in *Royal Palm Hotel*, or committing to the availability of new space for tenants signing leases. Accordingly, the lack of any firm and enforceable date on which the contractor is obligated to complete its performance is likely to cause substantial practical problems.

However, the owner is not powerless in situations where the original completion date has been waived. The completion date need not remain uncertain for the remainder of contract performance. For instance, the parties can agree

---

12. Star Development Group, LLC v. Constructure Management, Inc., 2018 WL 1525703, at *8 (D. Md. 2018) (waiver of completion date precluded owner from recovering liquidated damages for delay, where contractor completed within a reasonable time); Baker Marine Corp. v. Weatherby Eng'g. Co., 710 S.W.2d 690, 694 (Tex. App. 1986).

13. Drews Co., Inc. v. Ledwith-Wolfe Assocs., 371 S r.E.2d 532, 533 (S.C. 1988); J. J. Brown Co. v. J. L. Simmons Co., 118 N.E.2d 781, 785 (Ill. App. Ct. 1954). The more colorful English phrase used in this situation, to much the same effect, is that time becomes "at large."

on a new completion date in lieu of the original date, which becomes equally enforceable. Even absent such agreement, the owner unilaterally can establish a new completion date, which then will become as material and enforceable a term of the contract as the original completion date. However, the new date must be reasonable under the circumstances, taking into account the performance capabilities of the contractor as of the time notice of the new completion date is given.[14]

11.07 GROUNDS FOR EXTENDING THE TIME FOR COMPLETION—COMPENSABLE AND EXCUSABLE DELAYS

The time for completion as established in the contract is not immutable. Several well-established grounds exist for extending the time for completion, and probably the majority of projects encounter situations whereby the contractor becomes entitled to some amount of time extension.

There are two keys to assessing whether a particular event amounts to a basis for extending the time for completion. First, the event must have actually caused a delay to the work and that delay must have affected the critical path to project completion. An event that does not affect the critical path is not a project delay at all, at least in terms of providing a basis for a time extension (hence the importance of establishing the critical path as well as determining the effect of delays along that path). Second, the owner must have had control over the event, or alternatively, the event must alternatively be one that neither party controls. An extension of the time for completion will be available to the contractor for an action or omission of the owner or other event deemed to be in the owner's control, or neither party's control, but not for an event deemed to be in the contractor's control. Delays within the control of the owner are generally characterized as "compensable" delays because such delays both entitle the contractor to a time extension for the period of delay and to added compensation for the financial effects of that delay. A delay within control of the contractor is generally characterized as an "unexcused" delay, in that no relief from the required completion date or added compensation is available.

The third circumstance allowing extending time for completion occurs when the cause of delay is entirely beyond the control of both owner and contractor. Most commonly, such delays result from events often termed "Acts of God"—fires, floods, hurricanes, earthquakes, and the like. The expense of such delays not caused by either party is generally left where the expense falls,

---

14. DeVito v. United States, 413 F.2d 1147, 1154 (Ct. Cl. 1969).

meaning neither may recover any damages from the other for such delays. Because the contractor will not be liable for damages for its late completion due to such a delay, the effect is that the contractor receives an extension of the time for completion to this extent, but no added compensation. Such delays beyond the control of either party are characterized as "excusable" delays.

These basic principles regarding time extensions for delays, both compensable and excusable, are set out in AIA Document A201–2017 as follows:

> 8.3.1 If the Contractor is delayed at any time in the commencement or progress of the Work by (1) an act or neglect of the Owner or Architect, or of an employee of either, or of a Separate Contractor; (2) by changes ordered in the Work; (3) by labor disputes, fire, unusual delay in deliveries, unavoidable casualties, adverse weather conditions documented in accordance with Section 15.1.6.2, or other causes beyond the Contractor's control; (4) by delay authorized by the Owner pending mediation and binding dispute resolution; or (5) by other causes that the Contractor asserts, and the Architect determines, justify delay, then the Contract Time shall be extended for such reasonable time as the Architect may determine.[15]

Federal government contracts contain a more extensive list of specific types of delays that are considered to be beyond either party's control and, thus, excusable. The following are all causes of delay that in most cases will be considered as arising "from unforeseeable causes beyond the control and without the fault or negligence of the contractor":

1. Acts of God or of the public enemy,
2. Acts of the government in either its sovereign or contractual capacity,
3. Acts of another contractor in the performance of a contract with the government,
4. Fires,
5. Floods,
6. Epidemics,
7. Quarantine restrictions,
8. Strikes,
9. Freight embargoes,
10. Unusually severe weather, or
11. Delays of subcontractors or suppliers at any tier arising from unforeseeable causes beyond the control and without the fault or negligence of both the contractor and the subcontractor or supplier.[16]

---

15. AIA Document A201–2017, *supra* note 3, § 8.3.1.
16. Federal Acquisition Regulation, 48 C.F.R. § 52.249-10.

Under either the AIA documents or federal contracts, the specific examples of excusable delays—fire, strikes, floods, and so on—are just examples and not exhaustive. Other delays similarly qualifying as "beyond the contractor's control" will be considered excusable delays, whether or not mentioned on the list of examples.[17]

The concept of excusable delays, however, involves more than just lack of control over the delay-causing event. There also must be an element of unforeseeability with respect to the event. Accordingly, the particular cause of delay must not be one that the contractor reasonably would foresee under the circumstances of the contract. The reason for requiring this additional element of unforeseeability was well explained by the U.S. Supreme Court in this 1943 decision:

UNITED STATES v. BROOKS-CALLAWAY CO.

No. 366
SUPREME COURT OF THE UNITED STATES
318 U.S. 120; 63 S. Ct. 474; 87 L. Ed. 653; 1943 U.S. LEXIS 1282
January 4, 1943, Argued
February 1, 1943, Decided
JUDGES: Stone, Roberts, Black, Reed, Frankfurter, Douglas, Murphy, Jackson, Rutledge
OPINION: MR. JUSTICE MURPHY delivered the opinion of the Court.

We are asked to decide whether the proviso to Article 9 of the Standard Form of Government Construction Contract[1] which provides that a contractor shall not be charged with liquidated damages because of delays due to unforeseeable causes beyond the control and without the fault of the contractor, including floods,

---

1. In general, Article 9 gives the Government the option of terminating the contractor's right to proceed, or of allowing him to proceed subject to liquidated damages if he fails to proceed with diligence or to complete the work in time. The full text of the proviso is:

> *Provided*, That the right of the contractor to proceed shall not be terminated or the contractor charged with liquidated damages because of any delays in the completion of the work due to unforeseeable causes beyond the control and without the fault or negligence of the contractor, including, but not restricted to, acts of God, or of the public enemy, acts of the Government, fires, floods, epidemics, quarantine restrictions, strikes, freight embargoes, and unusually severe weather or delays of subcontractors due to such causes: ...

---

17. AIA Document A201–2017, *supra* note 4, § 8.3.1; 48 C.F.R. § 52.249-10. 5 PHILIP L. BRUNER & PATRICK J. O'CONNOR, JR., BRUNER & O'CONNOR ON CONSTRUCTION LAW §15:22 (West Group 2002) [hereinafter BRUNER & O'CONNOR].

requires the remission of liquidated damages for delay caused by high water found to have been customary and foreseeable by the contracting officer.

Respondent brought this suit in the Court of Claims to recover the sum of $3,900 which was deducted from the contract price as liquidated damages for delay in the completion of a contract for the construction of levees on the Mississippi River. The contract was not completed until 290 days after the date set, and liquidated damages in the amount of $5,800 (figured at the contract rate of $20 for each day of delay) were originally assessed. Respondent protested, and upon consideration the contracting officer found that respondent had been delayed a total of 278 days by high water, 183 days of which were due to conditions normally to be expected and 95 of which were unforeseeable. He recommended that liquidated damages in the amount of $1,900 (representing 95 days of unforeseeable delay at $20 per day) be remitted and that the balance of $3,900 be retained. Payment was made on this basis.

The Court of Claims held that liquidated damages should not have been assessed for any of the 278 days of delay caused by high water because the high water was a "flood" and under the proviso all floods were unforeseeable *per se*. Accordingly, it gave judgment in respondent's favor in the sum of $3,660.[2] No findings were made as to whether any of the high water was in fact foreseeable. We granted certiorari because the case presents an important question in the interpretation of the Standard Form of Government Construction Contract.

We believe that the construction adopted below is contrary to the purpose and sense of the proviso and may easily produce unreasonable results. The purpose of the proviso is to remove uncertainty and needless litigation by defining with some particularity the otherwise hazy area of unforeseeable events which might excuse nonperformance within the contract period. Thus contractors know they are not to be penalized for unexpected impediments to prompt performance, and, since their bids can be based on foreseeable and probable, rather than possible hindrances, the Government secures the benefit of lower bids and an enlarged selection of bidders.

To avoid a narrow construction of the term, "unforeseeable causes," limiting it perhaps to acts of God, the proviso sets forth some illustrations of unforeseeable interferences. These it describes as "including, but not restricted to, acts of God, or of the public enemy, acts of the Government, fires, floods, epidemics, quarantine restrictions, strikes, freight embargoes, and unusually severe weather, or delays of subcontractors due to such causes." The purpose of the proviso to protect the contractor against the unexpected, and its grammatical sense, both militate against holding that the listed events are always to be regarded as unforeseeable, no matter what the attendant circumstances are. Rather, the adjective "unforeseeable" must modify each event set out in the "including" phrase. Otherwise, absurd results are produced, as was well pointed out by Judge Madden, dissenting below:

---

2. 97 Ct. Cl. 689.

... Not every fire or quarantine or strike or freight embargo should be an excuse for delay under the proviso. The contract might be one to excavate for a building in an area where a coal mine had been on fire for years, well known to everybody, including the contractor, and where a large element of the contract price was attributable to this known difficulty. A quarantine, or freight embargo, may have been in effect for many years as a permanent policy of the controlling government. A strike may be an old and chronic one whose settlement within an early period is not expected. In any of these situations there would be no possible reason why the contractor, who of course anticipated these obstacles in his estimate of time and cost, should have his time extended because of them.

The same is true of high water or "floods." The normally expected high water in a stream over the course of a year, being foreseeable, is not an "unforeseeable" cause of delay. Here plaintiff's vice-president testified that in making its bid plaintiff took into consideration the fact that there would be high water and that when there was, work on the levee would stop. . . .[3]

A logical application of the decision below would even excuse delays from the causes listed although they were within the control, or caused by the fault of the contractor, and this despite the proviso's requirement that the events be "beyond the control and without the fault or negligence of the contractor." If fire is always an excuse, a contractor is free to use inflammable materials in a tinderbox factory and escape any damages for delay due to a resulting fire. Any contractor could shut his eyes to the extremist probability that any of the listed events might occur, submit a low bid, and then take his own good time to finish the work free of the compulsion of mounting damages, thus making the time fixed for completion practically meaningless and depriving the Government of all recompense for the delay.

We intimate no opinion on whether the high water amounted to a "flood" within the meaning of the proviso. Whether high water or flood, the sense of the proviso requires it to be unforeseeable before remission of liquidated damages for delay is warranted. The contracting officer found that 183 days of delay caused by high water were due to conditions normally to be expected. No appeal appears to have been taken from his decision to the head of the department, and it is not clear whether his findings were communicated to respondent so that it might have appealed. The Court of Claims did not determine whether respondent was concluded by the findings of the contracting officer under the second proviso to Article 9[4] and not having made this threshold determination,

---

3. 97 Ct. Cls. 701, 702.
4. The second proviso to Article 9 immediately follows the unforeseeability proviso and states:

Provided further, That the contractor shall within ten days from the beginning of any such delay notify the contracting officer in writing of the causes of delay, who shall ascertain the facts and the extent of the delay, and his findings of

> of course made no findings itself as to foreseeability. We think these matters should be determined in the first instance by the Court of Claims. Accordingly the judgment is reversed and the cause remanded with instructions to determine whether respondent is concluded by the findings of the contracting officer, and, if not, for a finding by the court whether the 183 days of high water or any part of that time were in fact foreseeable.
> **REVERSED.**
>
> ---
>
> facts thereon shall be final and conclusive on the parties thereto, subject only to appeal, within thirty days, by the contractor to the head of the department concerned, whose decision on such appeal as to the facts of delay shall be final and conclusive on the parties hereto.

There also are a number of principles that specifically address which causes of delay will be treated as within a party's control, as opposed to beyond the control of either party. Delays caused by an employee or agent of a party, or by an entity with whom the party has contracted, are considered to be within the control of that party. As such, delays by subcontractors and suppliers are considered to be within the control of the contractor, and thus non-excusable (with the exception noted in the government clause, where the subcontractor's delay is itself entirely excusable in nature, such as a tornado devastating the supplier's plant). Delays by an architect retained by the owner are considered to be within the owner's control, and thus compensable. The rationale for this general rule is that a party has the ability to select those it employs and with whom it contracts. Through control over that selection process and the terms of those contracts, a party has the ability to create legally enforceable obligations and rights against its agents, employees, and contractors.

Financial inability to perform, either by the contractor or its subcontractors or suppliers, is considered within the contractor's control and not an excusable cause of delay. Events such as bankruptcy, in reality, can be caused by factors beyond a company's control, such as an unexpected spike in interest rates or late payments by usually reliable customers. Nevertheless, financial inability to perform is far more in control of the company called upon to perform than in control of the other party, and generally not considered excusable. The exception occurs where a party's financial difficulties are directly caused by actions of the other party, such as failure to make proper and timely payments of substantial amounts legitimately owed.[18]

---

18. Douglas Corp., 58-1 BCA Par. 1727, 1958 WL 266 (ASBCA 1958); United States *ex rel.* Taylor & Polk Constr., Inc. v. Mill Valley Constr., Inc., 29 F.3d 154, 161 (4th Cir. 1994).

Weather is another cause of delay subject to special rules. Every locale has its normal variations in weather over the course of the year, and adverse weather events like heat waves, rain, and snowstorms are certainly foreseeable (in most parts of the country, at least). In planning and pricing its work, the contractor is expected to take into account normal weather variations at the site location during the planned period of performance. However, unusually adverse or "abnormal" weather can be a basis for excusable delay. The difficulty lies in distinguishing abnormal from normal and in measuring the effect of abnormal weather on the critical path activities. Contracts increasingly specify the means for determining if weather conditions are considered abnormal, such as by stating a number of days for each month where precipitation is to be considered "normal," or by specifying a particular methodology for determining if weather conditions are beyond "normal." The most common methodology was developed by the U.S. Army Corps of Engineers, and requires a comparison of the conditions experienced on the project to a ten-year average using the weather records from the nearest National Oceanic and Atmospheric Administration (NOAA) monitoring location.[19] Such a specified methodology avoids the potential for a statistical battle where each party chooses historical data over a period that best supports its position.

Many disputes over the effects of adverse weather involve a determination of the actual delay to the critical path due to the abnormal weather. Different types of weather can affect different types of construction activities in radically different ways, so deciding which construction activity was on the critical path when the unusually adverse conditions occurred can be outcome determinative.[20] Additionally, the contractor remains responsible for mitigating the effects of even unusual adverse weather where practicable and reasonable. For example, heavy rains can be expected to preclude site grading work, and saturated soil conditions that persist after the rain ends may extend the delay period. If, however, the contractor has not taken reasonable steps to provide adequate site drainage and protect disturbed ground from the predictable effects of rainfall, the portion of the delay due to this failing is not excusable.[21]

The contract law doctrine of impossibility or commercial impracticability also is closely related to the concept of excusable delays. Commercial

---

19. Army Corps of Engineers Regulation, Construction Time Extension for Weather, ER 415-1-15 (Oct. 31, 1989).

20. For example, several continuous days of light rain may have little to no effect on many activities, but entirely preclude exterior painting work. The critical path may be affected in such a case only if the painting was on the critical path during the unusual rain.

21. Titan Pac. Constr. Corp. v. United States, 17 Cl. Ct. 630, 639, 1989 WL 78828 (1989), aff'd, 899 F.2d 1227 (Fed. Cir. 1990).

impracticability or "practical impossibility" excuses contract performance where the contract could only be performed at an excessive or unreasonable cost due to circumstances well beyond the contemplation of the parties when they entered into the contract.[22] To the extent performance is excused, the delay caused becomes excusable, and the contractor is entitled to an extension of the time for completion. Because the expense to perform must be wholly out of proportion to what was reasonably expected, and mere hardship does not amount to commercial impracticability, real-world examples of commercial impracticability in construction contracts are few and far between.[23] In some situations the contractor effectively agreed in the contract to perform the near impossible. In that case, the contractor is considered to have assumed the risk of commercial impracticability, thereby making any delay due to impracticability unexcused.[24]

11.08 CONCURRENT DELAY

No discussion of types of delay would be complete without introducing the complex subject of concurrent delays. Delay events on a construction site do not occur neatly and discretely, one at a time. Many times multiple and overlapping delay events occur, with some events the responsibility of the owner and others of the contractor. Sorting out the effects of such multiple delay situations implicates the doctrine of concurrent delay.

There is no generally accepted definition of concurrent delays, but the following comes as close to a consensus as likely exists:

> Where there are two unrelated yet simultaneous delays, one on the part of the owner and one on the part of the contractor, the resulting delay in the construction project is said to be concurrent. Concurrent delays occur "where both parties are responsible for the same period of delay," as opposed to sequential delays where one party and then the other causes different delays *seriatum* or intermittently.[25]

---

22. 5 BRUNER & O'CONNOR, *supra* note 17, § 15:28; Iannuccillo v. Material Sand & Stone Co., 713 A.2d 1234 (R.I. 1998).

23. An illustrative real-world example is Northern Corp. v. Chugach Elec. Ass'n, 518 P.2d 76 (Alaska 1974), where it was held that the use of a haul road across a frozen reservoir in winter was an implicit assumption of the contract, and the unavailability of that road due to unsuitable ice conditions two winters in a row made performance commercially impracticable.

24. Otinger v. Water Works & Sanitary Sewer Bd., 177 So. 2d 320, 323 (Ala. 1965).

25. E. Patrick, et al., eds, THE ANNOTATED CONSTRUCTION LAW GLOSSARY (ABA Forum on the Construction Industry, 2010).

The key word in this definition that draws controversy is "simultaneous." It is the very rare case where two delay events, or the resulting delays they cause, are truly simultaneous. Generally, so long as the two separate delays (1) operate within the same short time period (sometimes taken to mean "within the same schedule update cycle") and (2) overlap at least to some extent, they likely will be treated as concurrent for the period of overlap.

The general rule regarding concurrent delays is that the party claiming damages has the burden of segregating the effects of seemingly concurrent delays. In theory, CPM schedule analysis can in most instances accomplish this by identifying the critical path and distinguishing among the effects of different events on the critical path activities.[26] But where the effects cannot reasonably be segregated, they are considered instead to be inextricably intertwined, with the result that neither party can recover delay damages for the concurrent delay period.

This result follows directly from the reality that neither owner nor contractor can demonstrate that the effect of the other party's delay caused it to incur delay damages. By definition, the delay and the associated delay damages would have been incurred in any event, due to that party's own delay. It is often stated that unsegregated concurrent delays are "the same as" an excusable delay. While this accurately states the bottom-line result, which is that neither party can recover delay damages, this formulation only confuses the issue. Since neither party can demonstrate damages caused solely by the other party, neither is entitled to delay damages, because neither can prove the required element of causation. This result is the *equivalent* of a time extension for the concurrent delay period, just as an excusable delay is a basis for a time extension. However, the underlying rationale is entirely different.

Overall, the subject of concurrent delay quickly becomes very complex as multiple delays by both parties accumulate, and the process of segregating them tends to be intensely fact-specific. Consider, for example, the problem most commonly referred to as "pacing." This classically arises where a significant owner delay occurs, but the owner argues that the delay had little or no critical path effect because the contractor failed to maintain its schedule in other respects (that is, a concurrent contractor delay occurred). The contractor responds that it, indeed, allowed some other activities to slip, on the basis that the owner delay precluded making much overall progress anyway. In other words, the contractor was "pacing" its other activities in light of the overriding

---

26. MW Builders, Inc. v. United States, 134 Fed. Cl. 469, 508 (Fed. Cl. 2017) (although contractor cannot recover for delays unless the government is the sole cause of delay, the contractor can recover where it is able to apportion multiple delays and expenses attributable to each cause).

owner delay. Such case law as exists tends to support this explanation as sufficient when factually supported, and where such pacing does not reduce the otherwise compensable owner delay.[27]

11.09 SUBSTANTIAL COMPLETION

A construction contract typically contains detailed drawings and specifications setting forth both the construction work to be performed and the standard of quality required. The owner is entitled to the benefit of its bargain. Accordingly, the contractor is responsible for full compliance with all requirements of the contract, including all requirements of the drawings and specifications. However, the owner is not generally entitled to 100 percent completion and full compliance with the drawings and specifications by the stated contract completion date. Instead, the state of construction completion that must be reached within the time for completion is, unless otherwise defined by the contract, "substantial completion." The AIA contract definition of substantial completion is typical:

> Substantial Completion is the stage in the progress of the Work when the Work or designated portion thereof is sufficiently complete in accordance with the Contract Documents so that the Owner can occupy or utilize the Work for its intended use.[28]

This rule reflects the reality that a construction project typically involves thousands, if not hundreds of thousands, of details, and, inevitably, finishing touches must be completed well after the point when the owner can utilize the virtually completed project for its intended purpose. Absent this rule, the contractor would remain subject to incurring damages for late completion when the project reached completion but for inconsequential details, such as a missing doorknob or two.

A contract that has been substantially performed may not be terminated for default, and any deficiencies in performance are remedied by an award of damages representing the cost to correct or complete those deficiencies. Similarly, once the point of substantial completion is reached, the contractor has no further liability for delayed completion. In essence, the contractor cannot be considered in material breach if construction has reached substantial completion. Because of the significant consequences of reaching substantial

---

27. When project delays occur and create additional float in the schedule, the contractor is not required to "hurry up and wait" and slavishly follow the original plan of performance. John Driggs Co., Inc., ENGBCA No. 4926, 87-2 B.C.A. (CCH) ¶ 19,833 at 100,388 (1987).

28. AIA Document A201–2017, *supra* note 4, § 9.8.

completion, disputes as to what constitutes substantial completion in the case of a particular project are not uncommon. The following decision illustrates the issues arising in connection with the determination of substantial completion, and how this concept relates to the broader contractual principal of substantial performance.

District Court of Appeal of Florida, Fourth District
J. M. BEESON COMPANY, Appellant, v. Ernesto SARTORI, Appellee

Nos. 87-1953, 87-2415 and 87-2693
Aug. 30, 1989
WARNER, Judge.

This appeal by a general contractor questions an amended final judgment in favor of the owner of a shopping center, awarding liquidated damages for delay and compensatory damages to complete construction.

[Procedural history deleted.]

The appellant and appellee entered into a construction contract in 1983. It provided for the construction of a shopping center including several anchor tenants and out-parcels. The contract provided for liquidated damages of $1,000.00 per day if appellant failed to substantially complete the project within 300 days of commencement. It further provided for a bonus of $1,000.00 per day for each day the project was finished prior to the completion date. Appellant commenced construction and within six months put two anchor tenants into their spaces. The remainder of the retail spaces received their certificates of occupancy within the 300-day period, but an anchor tenant in an outparcel was not given its certificate of occupancy until over a year after commencement. Shortly thereafter, the appellant-contractor left the job because of nonpayment and filed suit. Appellee counterclaimed for breach of contract and for the liquidated damages provided in the contract. After trial, the court awarded judgment in favor of appellee. This appeal ensued.

[Discussion of unrelated issue deleted.]

Secondly, appellant contends that the trial court erred in finding that he did not substantially complete the work. In this case the contract provided that "substantial" completion occurred when "construction is sufficiently complete in accordance with the Contract Documents, so the owner can occupy or utilize the work or designated portion thereof for the use for which it is intended." The "work" under the contract "comprises the completed construction required by the contract documents." Under the contract in this case the work consisted of "construction and completion of a Shopping Center," including all of its component parts such as landscaping and paving.

The contract also provides that the date of substantial completion is to be certified by the supervising architect. On this project, however, there was no supervising architect who approved certificates for payment or certified substantial completion. In fact, the appellee's contract with his architect specifically deleted any responsibilities on behalf of the architect to supervise payments and to certify the date of substantial completion. Thus, we must determine whether or not the trial court applied the correct definition of substantial completion to the facts of this case.

We agree with appellant's contention that the contractual definition of substantial completion in this case is similar to the well-established doctrine of substantial performance, and the terms are interchangeable. *See Ramada Development Co. v. Rauch*, 644 F.2d 1097 (5th Cir. 1981). The doctrine of "substantial performance" as held by this court in *Ocean Ridge Development Corp. v. Quality Plastering, Inc.*, 247 So.2d 72, 75 (Fla. 4th DCA 1971) states:

> Substantial performance is that performance of a contract which, while not full performance, is so nearly equivalent to what was bargained for that it would be unreasonable to deny the promisee the full contract price subject to the promisor's right to recover whatever damages have been occasioned him by the promisee's failure to render full performance. See 3A CORBIN ON CONTRACTS, Section 702 et sequi.

To say that substantial performance is performance which is nearly equivalent to what was bargained for, as the case law defines the term, in essence means that the owner can use the property for the use for which it is intended. Furthermore, in defining substantial performance, one of the tests as enunciated by Corbin is the "degree of frustration of purpose":

> Extremely important factors in solving the present problem [of what is substantial performance] are the character of the performance that the plaintiff promised to render, the purposes and end that it was expected to serve in behalf of the defendant, and the extent to which the nonperformance by the plaintiff has defeated those purposes and ends, or would defeat them if the errors and omissions are corrected. CORBIN ON CONTRACTS, 3A, Section 706.

Thus, substantial completion as defined in the contract is the equivalent of substantial performance under the case law and authorities hereinbefore cited.

In the instant case as of March, 1984, all phases of the shopping center had been completed sufficiently so as to obtain the certificates of occupancy from the city. Thus, the owner was capable of having tenants occupy the spaces and collecting rents thereon, and he was already collecting substantial rents on many of the tenant spaces prior to that date.

Despite the appellee's ability to rent out the shopping center spaces, the trial court found that appellant had not substantially completed the work by relying on an architect who testified that there still may not be substantial performance even though tenants were capable of occupying the premises, if the certificate of substantial completion called for in the contract had not been issued by the supervising architect. But this witness also testified that where there is no architect to give the certification, as there was none in this case, he would rely on the licensing authority and its certificate of occupancy to tell him that all work had been substantially completed under the contract. In this case, that occurred in March, 1984.[1] While this architect also testified that if a portion of the amenities such as landscaping are not fully complete, then there would be no substantial completion according to the contract, such a definition of substantial completion is contrary to both the contract and the case law, and the court erred in placing reliance on it.[2] As even the architect noted, when the owner can put tenants in possession for fixturing and can begin to collect rents, the owner begins to utilize the work for its intended purpose. When the owner was able to occupy and fixture the constructed space, the construction was substantially completed. *Fred Howland, Inc. v. Gore*, 152 Fla. 781, 13 So.2d 303 (1942). At that point, the appellant was entitled to his full contract price, less the cost to complete and the damages due to delay from the contract completion date through the date of substantial completion, and the trial court erred in determining that appellant had not substantially completed the contract.

This decision is also supported by *American Motors Inns of Fla., Inc. v. Bell Elec. Co.*, 260 So.2d 276 (Fla. 4th DCA 1972), where this court held that substantial performance is met if the omission is not so serious that it cannot be remedied by payment from the contract price. In this case, the amount due and owing under the contract was $157,392 at the time the contractor left the job. The amount required to remedy the deficiencies and unperformed work as found by the trial court was $68,939.70. Thus, there were sufficient monies still due the contractor from which the costs of completion could be deducted to satisfy the defects.

[Discussion of unrelated issue deleted.]

Consequently, we reverse the final judgment and remand for a redetermination of the date of substantial completion consistent with the principles set forth in this opinion; to calculate the amount of liquidated damages due to the appellee for failing to substantially complete within the 300-day period; and further to determine the amount due to the contractor on the contract, less the costs to complete. The other point raised for reversal is now moot. We also reverse the awards of attorney's fees and costs and remand for a redetermination after recalculation of the judgment.

REVERSED AND REMANDED.

DOWNEY and DELL, JJ., concur.

---

1. At another place in the testimony the architect conceded that utilization of the buildings may have occurred at an earlier date. Thus, we do not determine, as a matter of law, that substantial completion only occurred at the issuance of the certificate of occupancy in this case.

2. The architect witness also attempted to define substantial completion in terms of the dollar amount left to be done on the project (1/4 of 1% of the contract-price), but that too is contrary to the definition of substantial completion or performance which focuses on the owner's ability to utilize the construction.

As *J.M. Beeson Co.* illustrates, obtaining a certificate of occupancy from the local jurisdiction is often closely related to substantial completion. Most localities require that a certificate of occupancy be obtained before persons other than construction workers can occupy a structure. Factors taken into account in issuing a certificate of occupancy typically include the degree of structural completion and elimination of (or adequate protection against) hazards such as floor openings and lack of permanent handrails. The most important factor, however, is completion of life safety systems such as fire alarms, fire sprinklers, emergency exit signage, and full, unimpeded availability of emergency exits and evacuation routes.

By definition, once a certificate of occupancy is issued, the owner may begin to move in and occupy the premises, so the close relationship to the basic test for substantial completion—that the work be sufficiently completed to be used for its intended purpose—is clear. However, the court in *J.M. Beeson Co.*, consistent with most other courts, declined to hold that obtaining the certificate of occupancy automatically equated to substantial completion.[29] Instead, the general rule is that obtaining a certificate of occupancy is relevant evidence in determining whether the work has reached substantial completion but is not determinative by itself. Nevertheless, the contracting parties may specify obtaining the certificate of occupancy as an objective measure of substantial completion to provide a means of reducing the potential for disputes regarding the achievement of this important milestone.

Consistent with the concept that the project can begin to be used for its intended purpose upon substantial completion, the care, custody, and control of the project customarily transfers from the contractor to the owner upon substantial completion. That is, upon substantial completion, the owner becomes responsible for security, maintenance, heat, utilities, damage to the work (unless caused by the contractor), and insuring the project.[30] The warranty period during which the contractor has continuing responsibility to correct work that does not comply with the contract requirements also normally commences upon substantial completion.[31]

Substantial completion also has a direct financial consequence because most construction contracts provide that the retention amount (amounts withheld by the owner from progress payments made earlier in the project) is to

---

29. *E.g.,* Lawrence v. General Panel Corp., 2019 WL 100382, at *1 (S.C. 2019) (substantial completion under South Carolina's construction defect statute of repose was *not* determined by the issuance of a certificate of occupancy; substantial completion was achieved in March 2007 although the certificate of occupancy was not issued until December 2008).

30. *See* AIA Document A201–2017, *supra* note 4, § 9.8.4.

31. *Id.*

be paid to the contractor upon attaining substantial completion. However, the owner typically will continue to withhold a portion of the contract price representing the estimated value of the relatively minor work remaining as of substantial completion.[32] Because the contractor is no longer subject to termination for default or to the threat of delay damages if completion of remaining work is protracted, many owners hold a multiple of the estimated value of the remaining work as an incentive for the contractor to complete the remaining items promptly.[33] If the contractor fails to complete the outstanding items, the owner can apply the remaining contract funds to finish or correct any uncompleted work.[34]

11.10 FINAL COMPLETION

In construction industry practice, the unfinished details remaining at the point of substantial completion are normally tracked by creation of a "punchlist" that itemizes the unfinished work, area by area. The punchlist for a substantial project may contain thousands of items, although many of them normally will be minor work, such as areas of missing pipe insulation or places where touch-up painting is required.

In addition to unfinished physical work, typically a number of uncompleted paperwork requirements remain after the point of substantial completion. These often include (1) preparing and submitting "as-built" drawings showing any variations between the construction drawings for the work and what was actually installed (for example, the routings of smaller piping lines and electrical cables are often changed in the field to avoid obstacles or constricted areas not anticipated by the construction drawings), (2) submitting to the owner all manufacturers' warranties for equipment supplied for the project, and (3) providing the owner with copies of the operating and maintenance instructions for all equipment supplied.

"Final completion" is the term generally utilized to refer to the point when the work is 100 percent complete, including completion of all punchlist items, and when all non-construction and paperwork requirements of the construction contract, other than warranty responsibilities, have been performed. Final

---

32. *Id.* § 9.8.5.

33. The Engineers Joint Contract Documents Committee (EJCDC) form contract provides that the withholding will be 200 percent of the estimated value of remaining work.

34. Prudential Ins. Co. v. Stratton, 685 S.W.2d 818 (Ark. Ct. App. 1985), *supplemented*, 690 S.W.2d 750 (1985).

completion generally triggers the contractor's right to be paid the full remaining balance of the contract price.

Additionally, construction contracts typically are written to avoid any formal acceptance of the contractor's work by the owner until the point of final completion. For example, section 9.10.1 of AIA Document A201–2017 provides for "final inspection and acceptance" to occur only after the contractor gives notice that all work is complete and ready for such final inspection. The contract frequently will provide that inspections and tests of particular elements of the work at any earlier point by the owner are deemed to be for the owner's convenience and do not constitute acceptance of work not in accordance with the contract requirements. Similarly, progress payments made to the contractor throughout the construction process are deemed not to constitute acceptance of work by the owner if the work does not conform to the contract.[35] Placing the point of formal acceptance at final completion enables the owner to continue to exercise its common law right to reject nonconforming work until the entirety of the work is fully completed. However, considering the reality that most construction work can most efficiently be corrected near the time of its installation, before being covered or blocked by subsequent work, the courts have not given owners free rein to reject work at the end of the contract when the defects were actually discovered, or should have been discovered, at a much earlier stage.[36]

Finally, most construction contracts also tie a waiver of any previously unasserted claims relating to the construction process to final completion and the process of making and accepting final payment. Sections 9.10.4 and 9.10.5 of AIA Document A201–2017 address this as follows:

> 9.10.4 The making of final payment shall constitute a waiver of Claims by the Owner except those arising from:
> 1. liens, Claims, security interests or encumbrances arising out of the Contract and unsettled;
> 2. failure of the Work to comply with the requirements of the Contract Documents;
> 3. terms of special warranties required by the Contract Documents; or

---

35. AIA Document A201–2017, *supra* note 4, § 9.6.6 provides: "A Certificate for Payment, a progress payment, or partial or entire use or occupancy of the Project by the Owner shall not constitute acceptance of Work not in accordance with the Contract Documents."
36. Village of Pawnee v. Azzarelli Constr. Co., 539 N.E.2d 895, 904–07 (Ill App. Ct. 1989); Subsurfco, Inc. v. B-Y Water Dist., 337 N.W.2d 448, 455–56 (S.D. 1983). This topic is more fully treated in Chapter 21.

4. audits performed by the Owner, if permitted by the Contract Documents, after final payment.

9.10.5 Acceptance of final payment by the Contractor, a Subcontractor, or a supplier, shall constitute a waiver of claims by that payee except those previously made in writing and identified by that payee as unsettled at the time of final Application for Payment.[37]

Accordingly, it is important for each party to set forth in writing any claims it may have against the other party prior to final payment.

11.11 PROOF OF DELAY CLAIMS THROUGH CPM ANALYSIS

CPM schedule analyses used in proving or disproving significant delay claims are nearly always presented via expert opinions. Expert testimony in federal courts is governed by Rule 702 of the Federal Rules of Evidence (FRE), and most state courts have similar standards. FRE Rule 702 states:

> If scientific, technical, or other specialized knowledge will assist the trier of fact to understand the evidence or to determine fact in issue, a witness qualified as an expert by knowledge, skill, experience, training, or education may testify thereto in the form of an opinion or otherwise, if (1) the testimony is based upon sufficient facts or data, (2) the testimony is the product of reliable principles and methods, and (3) the witness has applied the principles and methods reliably to the facts of the case.[38]

This rule essentially codifies the standards established by the U.S. Supreme Court in *Daubert v. Merrell Dow Pharm., Inc.*[39] and *Kumho Tire Co. v. Carmichael*.[40] The trial judge acts as the gatekeeper to consider the qualifications of the proposed expert, the sufficiency of the facts and data relied upon, the reliability of the "principles and methods" used by the expert, and the manner that the expert has applied the method used to the facts, before accepting the expert testimony.

With respect to CPM analysis testimony, there are relatively few reported instances where the court simply found the proposed expert to have insufficient qualifications to provide testimony as an expert.[41] Most reported *Daubert* challenges to CPM expert testimony have involved either the sufficiency of

---

37. AIA Document A201–2017, *supra* note 4, §§ 9.10.4–5.
38. Fed. R. Evidence, Rule 702.
39. Daubert v. Merrell Dow Pharm., Inc., 509 U.S. 579 (1993).
40. Kumho Tire Co. v. Carmichael, 526 U.S. 137 (1997).
41. The Sherman R. Smoot Corp., ASBCA No. 52261, 03-1 BCA (CCH) ¶ 32,197 (2003) (expert excluded where his scheduling experience was entirely related to production contracts, not construction projects).

the facts and data utilized, or the way the expert applied his or her analytical method to the facts. However, most decisions on these issues do not arise in the context of a *Daubert* challenge to admissibility of the expert testimony, but rather involve situations where, after hearing the testimony, a particular CPM analysis is rejected for shortcomings in either the data or the method of applying the analysis to the data.

In *Fraya SE*,[42] the contractor challenged the propriety of its termination for default for lack of progress, and offered a CPM analysis through its expert attempting to demonstrate that the contractor could, in fact, have completed the contract on time. The expert's analysis was rejected because (among other reasons) the planned schedule for completing the project relied on by the expert did not take into account the limited building access because of security requirements, and also failed to take into account the extended holidays in December and January observed in Puerto Rico. In other words, the CPM analysis was not soundly grounded in the applicable facts, but instead failed to include two key constraints on the work.

The contractor's CPM analysis was also rejected in *Jimenez, Inc.*[43] The contractor argued that delay resulting from the government's late approval of an air-handling unit was on the critical path, and thus a compensable delay. The installation of the air-handling units, however, was never a critical path activity on any of the contractor's schedules that it submitted during the performance of the project. The CPM expert, however, testified that not only was the delay to the air-handling units on the critical path, but that delay explained the entire delay to the project. The board rejected the expert's opinion, considering the opinion to be a "self-serving analyses, created after project completion which ma[d]e adjustments to attain new and revised projected schedules, depending on theoretical contingencies."[44] In other words, without using the words of FRE Rule 702, the board found that the expert had not reliably applied the principles of CPM analysis to the facts of the case.

A final example is *Fortec Constructors v. United States*,[45] where the court rejected the government's denial of a claim for delays based on extra work, where the denial was premised on evaluation of a CPM schedule that plainly did not reflect reality:

> [I]f the CPM is to be used to evaluate delay on the project, it must be kept current and must reflect delays as they occur.

---

42. Fraya S.E., ASBCA No. 5222, 02-2 BCA (CCH) ¶ 31,975 (2002).
43. Jimenez, Inc., VABCA No. 6351, et al., 02-2 BCA (CCH) ¶ 32019 (2002).
44. 02-2 B.C.A. (CCH) ¶ 32,019 at 158,252.
45. Fortec Constructors v. United States, 8 Cl. Ct. 490, 504–06 (1985).

In the instant case, the CPM was updated only once, in August of 1979. This update did not consider delays in work performed prior to the update, nor, obviously, in work that occurred after the update through the date of acceptance of the project by the [U.S. Army] Corps [of Engineers]. . . .

Reliance upon an incomplete and inaccurate CPM to substantiate denial of time extensions is clearly improper. . . .

It is difficult, if not impossible, for this Court to comprehend how the Corps could have used the CPM to evaluate Fortec's time extension claims without modifying the CPM to reflect the additional work Fortec was directed to perform—the value pit, the frame and grate, the hangar doors, and the roof ventilator. These items were all major components of the hangar project.[46]

Again, the CPM schedule analysis as a technique was not at fault, but it was not applied to a schedule reflecting the actual situation on the project; accordingly, the conclusions reached were properly rejected as invalid.

11.12 DELAY ANALYSIS METHODS

A variety of different methods for conducting a CPM delay analysis for use in litigation developed in essentially trial-and-error fashion over several decades in the hands of individual analysts. Some of these methods have been the subject of one or more judicial decisions passing on their merits, but assessing the legal status of particular methods in many instances is difficult due to differing terminology and sometimes vague judicial descriptions of the competing CPM presentations in a particular case.

In 2005, the trade association AACE International stepped into this confused picture, publishing the first edition of its Recommended Practice for Forensic Schedule Analysis, RP 29R-03. (The most recent edition appeared in 2011.) RP 29R-03 describes its purpose and goals as follows.

1.1 Introduction

The purpose of the AACE International Recommended Practice 29R-03 Forensic Schedule Analysis is to provide a unifying reference of basic technical principles and guidelines for the application of critical path method (CPM) scheduling in forensic schedule analysis. In providing this reference, the RP will foster competent schedule analysis and furnish the industry as whole with the necessary technical information to categorize and evaluate the varying forensic schedule analysis methods. The RP discusses certain methods of schedule delay analysis, irrespective of whether these methods have been deemed acceptable or unacceptable by courts or government boards in various countries around the globe.

---

46. *Id.*

This RP is not intended to establish a standard of practice, nor is it intended to be a prescriptive document applied without exception. Therefore a departure from the recommended protocols should not automatically be treated as an error or deficiency as long as such departure is based on a conscious and sound application of schedule analysis principles. As with any other recommended practice, the RP should be used in conjunction with professional judgment and knowledge of the subject matter. While the recommended protocols contained herein are intended to aid the practitioner in creating a competent work product it may, in some cases, require additional or fewer steps....

Forensic scheduling analysis refers to the study and investigation of events using CPM or other recognized schedule calculation methods. It is recognized that such analyses may potentially be used in a legal proceeding. It is the study of how actual events interacted in the context of a complex model for the purpose of understanding the significance of a specific deviation or series of deviations from some baseline model and their role In determining the sequence of tasks within the complex network.

Forensic schedule analysis, like many other technical fields, is both a science and an art. As such, it relies upon professional judgment and expert opinion and usually requires many subjective decisions. One of the most important of these decisions is what technical approach should be used to measure or quantify delay and identify the effected activities in order to focus on causation. Equally important is how the analyst should apply the chosen method. The desired objective of this RP is to reduce the degree of subjectivity involved in the current state of the art. This is with the full awareness that there are certain types of subjectivity that cannot be minimized, let alone eliminated. Professional judgment and expert opinion ultimately rest on subjectivity, but that subjectivity must be based on diligent factual research and analyses whose procedures can be objectified.

For these reasons, the RP focuses on minimizing procedural subjectivity. It does this by defining terminology, identifying methodologies currently used by forensic scheduling analysts, classifying them, and setting forth recommended procedural protocols for the use of these techniques. By describing uniform procedures that increase the transparency of the analytical method and the analyst's thought process, the guidelines set forth herein will increase both the accountability and the testability of an opinion and minimize the need to contend with "black-box" or "voodoo" analyses....

1.2 Basic Premise and Assumptions

a. Forensic scheduling is a technical field that is associated with, but distinct from, project planning and scheduling. It is not just a subset of planning and scheduling.

b. Procedures that may be sufficient for the purpose of project planning, scheduling and controls may not necessarily be adequate for forensic schedule analysis.

> c. It is assumed that this document will be used by practitioners to foster consistency of practice and be used in a spirit of intellectual honesty.
> d. All methods are subject to manipulation as they all involve judgment calls by the analyst whether in preparation or interpretation.
> e. No forensic schedule analysis method is exact. The level of accuracy in the answers produced by each method is a function of the quality of the data used therein, the accuracy of the assumptions, and the subjective judgments made by the forensic schedule analyst.
> f. Schedules are a project management tool that, in and of themselves, do not demonstrate root causation or responsibility for delays. Legal entitlement to delay damages should be distinct and apart from the forensic schedule analysis methodologies contained in this RP.

The RP additionally identifies and classifies nine separate methods of schedule analysis, and provides protocols for their use.[47] Of the nine methods discussed in the RP, seven involve evaluating the effect of adding delay events to the planned schedule in one manner or another. The other two start with what actually occurred, in the form of an "as-built" schedule, and then attempt to remove the effects of delay events to see what would have happened "but for" those delays. For present purposes, we consider briefly one influential early method mainly of historical interest today, along with the three basic alternatives in primary contemporaneous use.

A. Impacted As-Planned

One of the earliest methods of CPM schedule analysis was to begin with the contractor's plan for the project (a baseline as-planned schedule). Any owner delays encountered were then added to the schedule in the form of additional activities representing the events in question, such as an owner delay in providing adequate construction drawings for a portion of the project.[48] With experience, courts soon began rejecting this approach as overly simplistic,[49] and the method is rarely seen today. By disregarding updates to the schedule and changes in the contractor's plans for the project (including any changes made to mitigate the effects of owner delays), the analysis quickly becomes

---

47. Depending on how one categorizes variations on these methods, a greater or lesser number than nine can easily be derived.

48. RP 29R-03 method 3.1.

49. See Old Dominion Elec. Coop. v. Ragnar Benson, Inc., 2006 U.S Dist. LEXIS 56145 (E. Dist. Va. 2006).

highly theoretical, and not well-grounded in the actual events and actual contractor plan.[50]

B. Time Impact Analysis

Given the inherent flaws of the impacted as-planned method, two alternative approaches have been developed to better tie the delay analysis to the realities on the project when each delay event occurred. One of these, most often referred to as time impact analysis, is essentially forward looking, and thus well adapted to situations where the parties are attempting to reach prompt agreement on a schedule adjustment after a delay event has occurred, but before the delay's full effects have been experienced.

The essence of time impact analysis is to develop a mini-network of activities reflecting the delay event in question. For example, if the owner adds a new equipment item to a process plant project, the mini-network (or "fragnet," short for "fragment of a network") might reflect an added activity for identifying sources of the equipment item; another for placing a purchase order; a third for the expected delivery time needed; a fourth for the time required to install the item, and two more for the associated piping and electrical revisions, respectively, plus the associated logic ties. The second step is then to identify the contractor's reasonable planned schedule just prior to this delay event, which in the classic case is the contractor's most recent schedule update before the delay event occurred. The delay fragnet is then inserted into the schedule in effect just before the delay happened. After rerunning the schedule, the projected effect of the delay event can then be isolated.[51]

Done carefully, this method is well-recognized,[52] but very different results can be reached depending on just where the new activities are added, and sometimes depending even on what order they are added.[53] Where the subsequent updates are available, comparing what was projected to happen to what actually happened can provide something of a check on the reasonableness of the assessment. Time impact analysis, by itself, also does not consider concurrent delays, which significantly limits its usefulness when used retrospectively.

---

50. See RP 29R-03, sections 3.1 L & M.

51. RP 29R-03 methods 3.6 and 3.7 are consistent with this description of time impact analysis. Like "windows analysis," however, the term "time impact analysis" has been applied at times to a far broader range of methods.

52. Cogefar-Impresit, U.S.A., Inc., DOTBCA No. 2721, 97-2 BCA (CCH) ¶ 29,188 (1997).

53. As stated in RP 29R-03, the method is "Extremely sensitive to the order of fragnet and logic insertion." RP 29R-03, sections 3.6 M, 3.7 M.

C. Windows Analysis

The second more advanced alternative is windows analysis, which compares the contractor's plan to actual progress, but within a discrete window of time that may be as short as the duration from one update to the next. As with time impact analysis, the starting point is the status of the project immediately prior to the delay event being analyzed, generally using the most recent schedule update. This starting point is then compared to the schedule current as of the end of the selected window duration, and the amount of time gained or lost on the critical path during the window is determined, along with identifying the activities that caused the gain or loss. The analyst can then focus on the reasons those activities varied from the plan, and form opinions about whether the underlying causes were compensable, excusable, or unexcused. The analysis is retrospective, but based mainly on the forward-looking plans as of the beginning and end of the window, along with the actual progress achieved during the window. Using a series of such windows to analyze discrete time periods is particularly useful on projects where a number of delay events occurred at different stages in the project, as the different delay effects can (in concept at least) be relatively isolated from each other.[54]

Windows analysis is most readily subject to manipulation by selectively choosing the window periods for analysis,[55] and such manipulation can be hard to detect without redoing the analysis utilizing different windows. Like time impact analysis, the method also heavily depends on the accuracy of the schedule updates used, both in terms of how accurately actual progress has been recorded, as well as the reasonableness of the planned schedule going forward.

D. Collapsed As-Built or "But For" Analysis

A collapsed as-built form of analysis starts with the detailed as-built schedule that includes all delays that were encountered on the project for any reason. Then the delays being analyzed are removed from the as-built schedule, and a "collapsed" schedule is generated. The intent is to show what would have

---

54. RP 29R-3, section 3.3 A. Methods 3.3, 3.4 and 3.5 all comport with this generic description of windows analysis. However, RP 23R-03 also notes that most of the nine methods it identifies have been referred to as "windows analysis" at various times.

55. "In a windows analysis, the windows are selected on a subjective basis. One can affect the outcome of the analysis by how one chooses the windows. By selectively choosing the milestones and windows, the results can be controlled." Old Dominion Elec. Coop. v. Ragnar Benson, Inc., 2006 U.S Dist. LEXIS 56145 (E. Dist. Va. 2006), at 117–18.

happened but for the delay events in question.[56] This method is intuitive and easy to understand. It is premised on the actual events as they occurred and avoids reliance on projections and plans.

That said, collapsed as-built analysis has a number of significant problems. The as-built schedule used as the starting point is by definition just a historical record, and does not include the logic relationships and dependencies between activities. When delays are removed, the analyst typically needs to infer those logic relationships in assessing how far activities can be pulled back to earlier dates after removing the delay events. This requires a great many subjective decisions that are subject to both unintended bias and intended manipulation that is difficult to detect. The method is also readily subject to overlooking or masking concurrent delays that would have precluded performing pulled back activities earlier in reality.

In summary, all methods of CPM schedule analysis have limitations and flaws to a greater or lesser degree, and all (as RP 29R-03 recognizes) are subject to manipulation and are inherently inexact.

---

56. RP 23R-03 methods 3.8 and 3.9 are both variants of this method.

QUESTIONS

1. A hospital construction contract specifies that the contractor shall utilize a specific supplier as the "sole source" for laboratory casework. The contractor, accordingly, contracts with that supplier, but that supplier then misses the needed delivery date for the casework by six weeks and causes a critical path delay. Is this delay excusable? See *Edward M. Crough, Inc. v. Dist. of Columbia Dep't of Gen. Servs.*, 572 A.2d 457 (D.C. 1990); *Carter Steel & Fabricating Co. v. Ohio Dep't of Transp.*, 721 N.E.2d 1115 (Ohio Ct. App. 1999).

2. A liquidated damages provision states that liquidated damages for delayed completion will continue to accrue until the work is "fully complete in all respects." Will the contractor's liability for delay liquidated damages nevertheless be interpreted to conclude as of substantial completion, when the owner can use the project for its intended purpose and presumably is no longer incurring significant loss due to delayed completion, or does liquidated damages liability continue to final completion? See *Reliance Ins. Co. v. Utah Dep't of Transp.*, 858 P.2d 1363 (Utah 1993).

3. In many instances, some follow-on activities by others need to take place once construction is complete, before the project is actually put to its intended use. For example, in a shopping center, the completed retail spaces are typically turned over to the prospective tenants for tenant construction, fixturing, and stocking before the retail stores can be opened. In such a case, is work "sufficiently complete to be put to its intended use" when the shopping center is in condition to be opened to the public, or when it is sufficiently complete to allow tenants to begin their pre-opening activities?

4. With respect to the AACE International Forensic Schedule Analysis RP 29R-03, consider the following statements in light of Federal Rule of Evidence 702:

   "This RP is not intended to establish a standard of practice, nor is it intended to be a prescriptive document applied without exception. Therefore a departure from the recommended protocols should not automatically be treated as an error or deficiency as long as such departure is based on a conscious and sound application of schedule analysis principles."

   "Forensic schedule analysis, like many other technical fields, is both a science and an art. As such, it relies upon professional judgment and expert opinion and usually requires many subjective decisions."

"The desired objective of this RP Is to reduce the degree of subjectivity involved in the current state of the art. This is with the full awareness that there are certain types of subjectivity that cannot be minimized, let alone eliminated. Professional judgment and expert opinion ultimately rest on subjectivity."

"All methods are subject to manipulation as they all involve judgment calls by the analyst whether in preparation or interpretation."

"No forensic schedule analysis method is exact."

    A. Is CPM schedule analysis testimony appropriately treated as "scientific," "technical," or "other specialized knowledge" within the meaning of FRE 702?

    B. Assuming the preceding statements from RP 29R-03 are true, how would you argue that a CPM schedule analysis is nevertheless "the product of reliable principles and methods" within the meaning of FRE 702?

    C. What do you think the purpose of the first bulleted statement is, in terms of using RP 29R-03 in court?

5. During the course of the project, the owner took various actions that delayed some of the contractor's activities, and the contractor filed a delay claim. The owner denied the claim on the basis that the delayed activities had substantial float, and that the overall construction schedule was not extended. The contractor admitted that the critical path of its schedule was not extended, but instead argued that the float in its CPM schedule was a valuable resource for the contractor, and that the owner's actions adversely limited its scheduling flexibility. How would a court likely decide this dispute?

CHAPTER 12

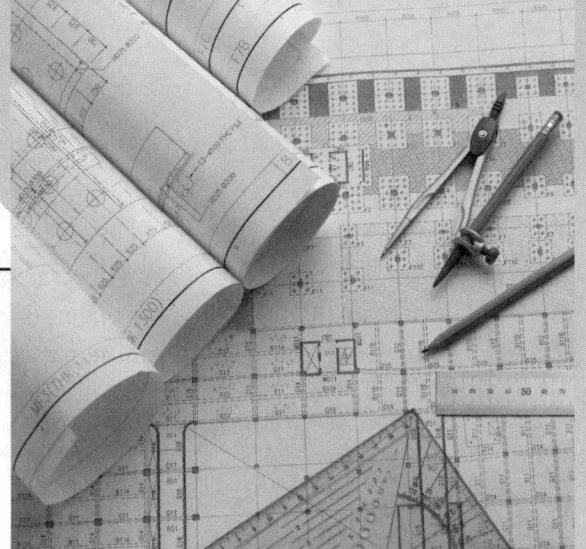

Payment

DAVID A. SENTER

12.01 INTRODUCTION

Payment and cash flow issues are often the most negotiated and litigated issues on construction projects. Construction is all about the flow of funds from the lender to the owner to the contractor to the subcontractors to the suppliers. A contractor typically has to advance certain costs before receiving payment from the owner. For example, a contractor typically will perform work for 30 days before sending its first invoice to the owner. The owner then has 30 days to make payment, and the owner is often entitled to withhold a portion of the payment as retainage. As a result, a contractor may have to wait 60 days or longer before receiving its first payment, which may only represent 90 percent of its billing (where the owner withholds 10 percent retainage). During that 60-day period, however, the contractor must make payment to its employees, subcontractors, and material suppliers. Contractors and subcontractors cannot "be expected to finance the operation to completion without receiving the stipulated payments on account as the work [progresses]. . . . Advance payment is a condition precedent to the contractor's obligation to proceed."[1]

---

1. Guerini Stone Co. v. P.J. Carlin Constr. Co., 248 U.S. 334, 345, 39 S. Ct. 102, 106 (1919).

Subcontractors tend to be smaller, less well capitalized entities than general contractors. Although not always the case, subcontractors may not be as financially strong as either the general contractors for whom they work or the suppliers on whom the they rely for materials. Although subcontractors will not receive payment from the general contractor until a specified portion of the work is completed, subcontractors usually pay their field personnel and tradespeople on a weekly basis and often must pay suppliers in advance for materials received. Placed in this financial squeeze, subcontractors not uncommonly "rob Peter to pay Paul," that is, use payments on one project to pay bills on another.

If payment is delayed at any point in the construction chain, the contractor or subcontractor may run out of money and/or be unable to pay its subcontractors, suppliers, or tradespeople to continue working.[2] The likely result is delayed performance or nonperformance. Thus, a project's success or failure may depend on whether the project participants are paid promptly for their work.

12.02 BASIS FOR PAYMENT

The parties' contract should clearly describe the basis and timing for payment. Many ways exist to structure payment in a construction contract, including stipulated sum (lump sum or fixed price), unit price, "cost plus" (cost of the work, plus the contractor's fee), and others.[3] The traditional pricing mechanism is fixed price. This mechanism arises out of the Design-Bid-Build method of project delivery. Under this method, an owner presents its plans and specifications, prepared by the owner's design professional, either to a contractor to price, or to a group of contractors to bid. Based on those plans and specifications, the owner and the contractor enter into a contract to construct the project for a fixed price, also referred to as a lump sum or stipulated sum.

A unit price contract may be used where the type of work is well defined but the quantity is only estimated. If a contractor must bid a fixed price for an unknown quantity, its price will likely be high so as to include the quantity risk contingency. On the other hand, with a unit-price contract, the quantity contingency is not a significant issue because the contractor receives a specified unit price for each of the units it installs on the project, and the contractor's price likely will be lower.

---

2. Subcontractors, as a whole, file more bankruptcies than any other entity in the construction process. *See* Carina Y. Enhada, Cheri Turnage Gatlin & Fred D. Wilshusen, *Fundamentals of Construction Law*, ABA CONSTRUCTION FORUM 2001 [hereinafter *Fundamentals*].

3. *See id.* at ch. 9 (discussing pricing mechanisms in more detail).

A cost-plus or cost-reimbursement contract provides that the owner will pay or reimburse the contractor for its costs (labor, material, and equipment) and also will pay the contractor a fee, which is usually a percentage of the costs (e.g., cost plus 15 percent). Such contracts should contain a clear definition of "costs," especially as the term relates to the contractor's own personnel, equipment, management, and overhead. The AIA contract documents, for example, deal with "cost" by defining the term to include labor costs; subcontract costs; costs of material and equipment incorporated in the completion of construction; costs of other materials and equipment, temporary facilities, and related items; and miscellaneous costs.[4] Obviously, such an open-ended contract leaves the owner exposed to uncertainties and increased costs. This exposure is often managed by using a cost-plus contract coupled with a Guaranteed Maximum Price, or a GMP. Such a contract involves a typical cost-plus arrangement up to the dollar amount of the GMP. The contractor bears the risk of any costs over the GMP, thereby reducing the owner's risk.

Given the risks involved in cost-plus contracts, AIA Contract Document A102–2017 provides that

> The Contractor accepts the relationship of trust and confidence established by this Agreement and covenants with the Owner to cooperate with the Architect and exercise the Contractor's skill and judgment in furthering the interests of the Owner; to furnish efficient business administration and supervision; to furnish at all times an adequate supply of workers and materials; and to perform the Work in an expeditious and economical manner consistent with the Owner's interests.[5]

Some courts have held that such language creates a fiduciary relationship between the owner and the contractor, thereby increasing the level of the contractor's duty to the owner and providing the basis for a constructive fraud claim.[6] Other courts have held that such language alone does not necessarily create a fiduciary duty.[7]

---

4. AIA Contract Document A102–2017, articles 7 and 8.

5. *Id.* at art. 3.

6. *See* Jones v. J.H. Hiser Constr. Co., 60 Md. App. 671, 484 A.2d 302 (1984). *Compare* Di Sciullo v. Griggs & Co. Homes, Inc., 2015 WL 6393813, at *6 (E.D.N.C. 2015) (contractor did not have fiduciary duty to homeowners with respect to application of deposit toward construction costs).

7. *See* Eastover Ridge, LLC v. Metric Constructors, Inc., 138 N.C. App. 360, 533 S.E.2d 827 (2000) (stating that, notwithstanding Article 3 of the contract, the "architect's constant, close involvement in the project belies any claim that a 'relation of trust and confidence' existed between" owner and contractor); *see generally* Philip L. Bruner & Patrick J. O'Connor, Jr., Construction Law § 6:81 (2002).

Once the price is agreed on, the parties must also agree on how that amount is to be paid. A structure is not built overnight, and the contractor is not expected to finance the project by waiting until the end to receive payment. As a result, the contract should provide for periodic payments as the work progresses, known as "progress payments." Although the parties may contract for any payment period, most progress payments are made on a monthly basis and are determined based on the actual progress of the work.[8] Such progress payments, less retainage, are paid to the contractor at the periods or intervals required by the contract.

The contractor's periodic progress payment is based on the value of the work performed during the period for which payment is made. In order to determine the amount of a given progress payment, the parties typically employ a schedule known as a "schedule of values."[9] This schedule simply sets forth how much various portions of the work are worth, each in the aggregate for the entire project including the contractor's profit for that portion or, in other words, how the total contract price is allocated among various portions of the work.[10] The parties determine and agree on these values at the beginning of the project. During the course of the project, the contractor is paid at regular intervals, usually monthly, with the amount of each payment based on the percentage of the work completed during that payment period as applied against the agreed on schedule of values.

For example, if the footings value in the schedule of values is $50,000, and after one month the contractor has performed 40 percent of this work, then the contractor will be paid $20,000 for its work on that schedule item for that month. In general terms, the total month's payment to the contractor is the sum of the amount due based on percentage of work completed for each item on the schedule of values, less retainage held by the owner and other properly withheld amounts in accordance with the contract.[11]

A contractor's attempt to "front load" is one problem that may arise in connection with the schedule of values. That is, the contractor may attempt to assign a higher value than appropriate in the schedule of values for an item of work performed early in the project, that is, on the front end. The contractor may "skew . . . [its] assigned values in the schedule of values so that work performed early (such as clearing and grubbing, excavation, and foundation work) is valued higher than its cost, while later work (such as painting) is

---

8. *See* AIA Contract Document A101–2017, art. 5.1.1-2; AIA Contract Document A201–2017, art. 9.6; *see also infra* § 14.7.
9. *See* AIA Contract Document A201–2017, art. 9.2 and art. 9.3.1.
10. *See Fundamentals, supra* note 2, at 31.
11. *See* discussion *infra* at § 14.3.1 and § 14.3.2.

undervalued."[12] The result is that the contractor gets paid more than the value of the early work and can collect its profit before the end of the project. If the contractor has been overpaid, the owner has less protection if a problem arises later in the project. Owners and architects should carefully review a contractor's proposed schedule of values to minimize the risk of front loading.[13]

Under a unit price contract, the contractor is paid based on the number of so-called units performed during the relevant period, that is, feet of pipe laid, cubic yards of dirt or rock excavated, and so on.

12.03 PAYMENT PROCESS

Under the Doctrine of Conditions, "[t]he promise by the owner to make any payments is conditioned on the contractor's compliance with the contract documents."[14] A strict application of this doctrine would obviously result in a hardship to the contractor because the contractor would be required to perform the entire contract before it received any payment. A contractor cannot and should not be expected to finance the construction project. In order to alleviate this hardship, contract procedures have developed whereby the contractor can apply for and receive regular payments as the work progresses. As set forth previously, the amount of each payment is based on the value of the work performed during the payment period.

A strict application of this doctrine also can cause hardship at the end of the job. For example, if an owner were entitled to withhold retainage or final payment on a multi-million-dollar project simply because of the need for some paint touch-up work, yet the owner was able to occupy the building, the owner would be unjustly enriched at the expense of the contractor.[15] The loss to the contractor would be disproportionate to the loss to the owner caused by the contractor's nonperformance.[16] To deal with such an issue at the end of the project, the law and certain form contract documents have developed concepts known as "substantial performance" and "substantial completion," discussed later in this chapter.[17]

---

12. See Fundamentals, supra note 2, at 193.
13. See id.
14. JUSTIN SWEET, LEGAL ASPECTS OF ARCHITECTURE, ENGINEERING AND THE CONSTRUCTION PROCESS, 6th ed. 2000, § 22.06A [hereinafter SWEET].
15. See id.
16. See id.
17. See discussion infra at § 14.4.

A. Applications for Payment

To be paid for its work, a contractor must submit what is known as an "application for payment" or a "draw request." The contractor's application for payment sets forth the contractor's representation as to the status of its work, measured against the schedule of values. The application is submitted to the project architect for review. The architect reviews the application, compares it to the work in place, and advises the owner as to whether it is appropriate to make a payment. The architect's written advice is sometimes called a "certificate of payment."[18]

AIA Contract Document A201–2017, article 9.4.2, provides that the architect's level of review is as follows:

> The issuance of a Certificate for Payment will constitute a representation by the Architect to the Owner, based on the Architect's evaluation of the Work and the data in the Application for Payment, that, to the best of the Architect's knowledge, information, and belief, the Work has progressed to the point indicated, the quality of the Work is in accordance with the Contract Documents, and the Contractor is entitled to payment in the amount certified. The foregoing representations are subject to an evaluation of the Work for conformance with the Contract Documents upon Substantial Completion, to results of subsequent tests and inspections, to correction of minor deviations from the Contract Documents prior to completion, and to specific qualifications expressed by the Architect. However, the issuance of a Certificate of Payment will not be a representation that the Architect has (1) made exhaustive or continuous on-site inspections to check the quality or quantity of the Work, (2) reviewed construction means, methods, techniques, sequences, or procedures, (3) reviewed copies of requisitions received from Subcontractors and suppliers and other data requested by the Owner to substantiate the Contractor's right to payment; or (4) made examination to ascertain how or for what purpose the Contractor has used money previously paid on account of the Contract Sum.

The architect may decline to certify payment for myriad reasons—defective work, third-party claims, failure of the contractor to pay its subcontractors, or reasonable evidence that the work cannot be completed for the contract balance or within the contract time, and so on.[19]

---

18. The role of the architect in project administration is discussed in more detail in Chapter 7.
19. *See* AIA Contract Document A201–2017, art. 9.5.1.

1. The Contractor's Certification

A contractor's submission of an application for payment is a representation made by a contractor concerning the completed work. This representation may be considered a warranty. While design professionals such as architects rarely intend to make warranties, contractors routinely make express warranties in writing, express warranties through oral representations, and even implied warranties. A typical contractor warranty clause states that:

> [t]he Contractor warrants to the Owner and Architect that materials and equipment furnished under the Contract will be of good quality and new unless the Contract Documents require or permit otherwise. The Contractor further warrants that the Work will conform to the requirements of the Contract Documents and will be free from defects, except for those inherent in the quality of the Work the Contract Documents require or permit. . . . [20]

The application for payment submitted by a subcontractor to a general contractor constitutes a representation when certified or sworn to by the subcontractor.[21] A general contractor may "rely upon its [subcontractor's] representation that work has been done for which payment is now due."[22] False representations can lead to "liability for fraud, negligent misrepresentation, and representations amounting to an unfair or deceptive trade practice."[23]

2. The Architect's Certification

The architect's certification "constitutes a representation that the contractor is entitled to payment in the amount certified."[24] To ensure that a warranty is not created, or to limit liability, an architect may qualify the certification, stating that the certification does not constitute a representation the architect made "continuous on-site inspections" or "reviewed construction means, methods, techniques," for example. The qualifications may limit what is, and what is not, covered by the representation. These qualification attempts can be seen in article 9.4.2 of AIA A201 quoted earlier.

Although similar to warranties in that both are representations, certifications differ from warranties. Design professionals rarely intend to make express warranties; however, issuing a certification instead of a warranty does

---

20. *See id.* § 3.5.1.
21. Myers & Chapman, Inc. v. Thomas G. Evans, Inc., 323 N.C. 559, 566, 374 S.E.2d 385, 390 (1988).
22. *Id.* 374 S.E.2d at 390.
23. Robert G. Byrd, *Misrepresentation in North Carolina*, 70 N.C. L. Rev. 323, 323 (1992).
24. BRUNER & O'CONNOR, JR., *supra* note 7, at § 8:20.

not preclude all liability. For example, a claim of negligence can be made by an owner against an architect who over-certifies to a lender the amount of work completed because it can be reasonably foreseen that an owner may rely on the accuracy of an architect's certification.[25]

The representation made by an architect in a certification generally is not a warranty concerning the quality of the work, but it should represent an architect's "exercise [of] reasonable care and diligence in the supervision of the work."[26]

Even if an architect does not assume the duty to "supervise" construction, the architect remains bound to exercise reasonable care and diligence in the performance of its professional services, whatever they may be. If a contract between an owner and an architect does not include "any special guarantees or warranties," such warranties and guarantees may be "set out in general terms such that the only implication arising from the terms is that the architect will use reasonable care in preparation of the plans and supervision of the construction of the project."[27]

In summary, inaccurate certifications related to payment, whether intentional or unintentional, may result in additional liability for contractors and architects.

---

25. *See* Browning v. Maurice B. Levien & Co., 262 S.E.2d 355, 358 (N.C. Ct. App. 1980), *disc. rev. denied* 267 S.E.2d 673 (N.C. 1980); *see also* 2 STRONG'S N.C. INDEX 4TH *Architects* § 18 (2007).

26. In Palmer v. Brown, 273 P.2d 306, 317 (Cal. Dist. Ct. App. 1954), a cross-complaint (counterclaim) against the plaintiff architects included a claim "that plaintiffs fraudulently issued certificates to the contractors showing satisfactory completion of work without ascertaining whether the premises were free from liens chargeable to the contractors," and a claim "for plaintiffs' negligence in issuing certificates to the contractors without requiring proof that the premises were free from liens chargeable to the contractors and without carefully examining the work to see that it had been properly done." The appeals court reversed the judgment of the lower court, which had been in favor of the plaintiffs. The appeals court stated that the "architect's certificate as a precondition of payment was for the benefit of defendant," so that the defendant could be assured that the payments did in fact "discharge him and his property for the labor and materials for which he was paying." The plaintiff/architects could be found negligent in not requiring proper receipts, lien releases, or lien waivers from the contractor.

The court also ruled that there was sufficient evidence that the plaintiff/architects had improperly certified payment for work that had not been inspected as required by the contract. Additionally, the court explained that when work certified by an architect is faulty, the architect can be found negligent in terms of its supervision of the construction (if it undertook the duty of supervision in its contract). Although an architect's certification does not make it liable for specific defects, those defects may not have occurred if the architect had exercised reasonable care and diligence in the performance of its contractual obligations during construction.

27. Ryan v. Morgan Spear Assocs., Inc., 546 S.W.2d 678, 682 (Tex. Civ. App. 1977).

B. Retainage

Almost all construction contracts provide that a percentage of payments, usually 5 to 10 percent, shall be retained until some later date, such as substantial completion of the project. The purpose of retainage is to preserve a fund of money that will be available to ensure final completion of the work by the contractor and to correct defects in the work. Typically, the owner holds the full amount of retainage on the entire job until substantial completion, at which time retainage is reduced to an amount estimated to cover only the incomplete or defective items described on a written punchlist. Retainage also gives the owner, lender, and sureties extra security or protection against other issues that might arise, such as defective work, unpaid subcontractors, or liens filed late in or after the construction process.[28]

Most construction contracts provide for 10 percent retainage to be withheld until substantial completion. Another option is to withhold 10 percent until the project is 50 percent complete and, thereafter, withhold no retainage.[29] This effectively reduces retainage to 5 percent at the end of the job. The theory is that, as the contractor completes more and more of the work, the risk diminishes that the project will not be completed or that costs to correct will reach 10 percent. Even if a contract allows for reduction in retainage, the contract also likely will allow the owner to reinstate full retainage in the event of a change of circumstances.

While protecting the owners, retainage can create financial difficulty for contractors by decreasing their short-term cash flow.[30] Contractors, in turn, often respond to this decrease in cash flow by transferring the retainage burden to their subcontractors and, thus, withholding a portion of payments to the subcontractors until the owner eventually pays retainage to the contactor. This practice effectively allows the contractors to secure financing from their subcontractors by delaying some subcontractor payments until the end of the project. This also places a greater burden on subcontractors who perform work earlier in the construction process because those subcontractors must wait longer for project completion when the retained funds are released.

Some jurisdictions have addressed this tension between protecting the owners and financing the contractors by limiting the maximum allowable

---

28. Nat'l Union Indem. Co. v. G. E. Bass & Co., 369 F.2d 75, 77 (5th Cir. 1966); *In re* Lynch III Props. Corp., 125 B.R. 857, 863 (Bkrtcy. E.D.N.Y. 1991); *Fundamentals*, *supra* note 2, at 192–93.

29. *See* AIA Contract Document A101–2017, art. 5.1.7.2.

30. *See* Fireman's Fund Ins. Co. v. United States, 909 F.2d 495, 498 (Fed. Cir. 1988) (noting that "[i]t is true that retainage is an incentive to complete the contract, but it is equally true that contractors may need full progress payments to finance the work").

retainage, which typically ranges from 5 to 10 percent. Some jurisdictions also address this tension by requiring retention of fewer funds as the construction progresses and as adequate performance appears more likely.[31] Other jurisdictions allow contractors to pledge security or establish construction bonds in lieu of retainage.[32] Additional jurisdictions have responded by allowing the retained funds to be placed in escrow and then allowing the contractor to access the interest earned on those funds.[33] Finally, others have addressed the problem of contractors using retainage to secure financing from subcontractors by limiting the percentage held back from subcontractors to no more than the percentage that the owners hold back from the contractors.[34]

The tension between owner security and contractor cash flow is illustrated in *Fireman's Fund Ins. Co. v. United States*,[35] where the government, pursuant to the contract, withheld 10 percent as retainage. The government released that retainage when the project was 85 percent complete, not because the contractor had completed the work, but because the contractor was having severe cash flow problems and appeared not to be paying its subcontractors. Thus, the government was concerned that the contractor would not be able to complete the job. After the government released the retainage, and, thus, the security provided by that retainage, the contractor then abandoned the contract, and the government had to procure another contractor to complete the job without the benefit of any retained funds.[36]

Retainage held by the owner can become the subject of claims by third parties. A performance bond surety who steps in to complete a contract for its principal is protected by the doctrine of equitable subrogation such that the surety is entitled to collect its principal's retainage.[37] In *Pearlman v. Reliance Ins. Co.*,[38] the U.S. Supreme Court held that unpaid contract balances should be paid to a surety who had stepped in to complete the project and thereby was subrogated to the rights of the debtor (its principal), the subcon-

---

31. *See e.g.*, Ark. Code Ann. § 22-9-604 (allowing 5 percent retainage until the project is 50 percent complete, then not allowing any additional retainage to be withheld).

32. *See e.g.*, Ind. Code § 36-1-12-13.1 (requiring the establishment of a constriction bond or, alternatively, retainage); Bruner & O'Connor, Jr., *supra* note 7, at § 8:18, n.5.

33. Tenn. Code. Ann. § 66-11-104 (providing for retainage to be placed in escrow and for the contractor to earn the interest); Bruner & O'Connor, Jr., *supra* note 7, at § 8:18 & n.4.

34. *See e.g.*, N.C. Gen. Stat. § 22C-4.

35. 909 F.2d 495 (Fed. Cir. 1990).

36. As is discussed in Chapter 18, the owner sometimes has the benefit of a performance bond surety to ensure completion. *See also infra* § 14.3.3, regarding overpayment.

37. Prairie State Nat'l Bank v. United States, 164 U.S. 227, 17 S. Ct. 142, 41 L. Ed. 412 (1896); *see generally* Bruner & O'Connor, Jr., *supra* note 7, at § 8:36.

38. 371 U.S. 132, 83 S. Ct. 232, 9 L. Ed. 2d 190 (1962).

tractors, and the owner.[39] In so holding, the court determined that the surety's rights of subrogation were unaffected by bankruptcy, and the contract balance did not even constitute property of the bankruptcy estate. In *Grochal v. Ocean Technical Services Corp. (In re Baltimore Marine Indus., Inc.)*,[40] the Fourth Circuit distinguished *Pearlman* by finding that while in the context of a general contractor's bankruptcy proceeding, a surety who has fully paid all subcontractors has subrogated the general contractor's interest in funds withheld by an owner, an unpaid subcontractor is not subrogated to the general contractor's interest in those funds.

In the non-bankruptcy context, state law drives third-party claims to retainage. For example, in North Carolina, a subcontractor's lien on funds has:

> priority over all other interests or claims theretofore or thereafter created or suffered in the funds by the person against whose interest the lien upon funds is asserted, including, but not limited to, liens arising from garnishment, attachment, levy, judgment, assignments, security interests, and any other type of transfer, whether voluntary or involuntary.[41]

C. Owner's Payment Obligation

1. Timing

The terms of the parties' contract will define the timing of the owner's payment obligation. The owner's failure to make payment of undisputed amounts in a timely manner may be a material breach of the contract; such failure then would support the contractor's decision to stop work.[42] For example, article 9.7 of AIA Contract Document A201–2017 provides as follows:

---

39. *Id.* at 137 and 141, 83 S. Ct. at 235 (stating that "a surety who pays the debt of another is entitled to all the rights of the person he paid" and "the [owner] had a right to use the retained funds to pay laborers and materialmen; the laborers and materialmen had a right to be paid out of that fund; the contractor, had he completed his job and paid his laborers and materialmen, would have become entitled to the fund; and the surety, having paid the laborers and materialmen, is entitled to the benefit of all these rights to the extent necessary to reimburse it").
40. 476 F.3d 238, 242 (4th Cir. 2007).
41. N.C. Gen. Stat. § 44A-22.
42. *See* Guerini Stone Co. v. P.J. Carlin Const. Co., 248 U.S. 334, 39 S. Ct. 102 (1919) (stating that the requirement of progress payments "must be deemed so material that a substantial failure to pay would justify the contractor in declining to proceed"); Silliman Co. v. S. Ippolito & Sons, Inc., 467 A.2d 1249 (Conn. App. Ct. 1983) (holding that a contractor's failure to make progress payments to subcontractor is breach of contract); *see also* Bruner & O'Connor, Jr., *supra* note 7 at § 8:17.

If the Architect does not issue a Certificate for Payment, through no fault of the Contractor, within seven days after receipt of the Contractor's Application for Payment, or if the Owner does not pay the Contractor within seven days after the date established in the Contract Documents, the amount certified by the Architect or awarded by binding dispute resolution, then the Contractor may, upon seven additional days' written notice to the Owner and Architect, stop the Work until payment of the amount owing has been received. The Contract Time shall be extended appropriately and the Contract Sum shall be increased by the amount of the Contractor's reasonable costs of shutdown, delay and start-up, plus interest as provided for in the Contract Documents.

The contractor's decision to stop work must be reasonable and in good faith. Otherwise, the contractor may be in default under the contract despite the other party's withholding of payments.[43] Generally, if the contractor's entitlement to progress payments under the contract is undisputed, then the contractor has the right to stop work until it has been paid.[44] The Restatement (Second) of Contracts contains a good example of this factual scenario:

> A contracts to build a house for B for $50,000, progress payments to be made monthly in an amount equal to 85 percent of the price of the work performed during the preceding month, the balance to be paid on the architect's certificate of satisfactory completion of the house. Without justification B fails to make a $5,000 progress payment. A thereupon stops work on the house and a week goes by. A's failure to continue the work is not a breach and B has no claim against A. B's failure to make the progress payment is an uncured material failure of performance which operates as the non-occurrence of a condition of A's remaining duties of performance under the exchange.[45]

However, the requirement for progress payments "must be deemed so material that a substantial failure to pay would justify the contractor in declining to proceed."[46] Despite the harsh phrasing of this rule, courts almost always find that

---

43. *See* Gramm v. Ins. Unlimited, 378 P.2d 662, 664 (Mont. 1963) (stating that "the particular facts of each case [determine] whether or not non-payment of an installment is a total breach enabling the contractor to cease work, or whether it is merely a partial breach entitling the contractor to sue for the partial breach, but not permitting him to abandon the contract").

44. *See* United States ex rel. Micro-King Co. v. Cmty. Science Tech., Inc., 574 F.2d 1292, 1295 n.3 (5th Cir. 1978); Macri v. U.S. for Use of John H. Maxwell & Co., 353 F.2d 804 (9th Cir. 1965) (noting that "it is well settled that an owner's failure to make progress payments on a building contract may constitute a material breach, justifying the builder's refusal to proceed with the work on the theory that the owner has rendered his performance impossible").

45. Restatement (Second) of Contracts § 237, illus. 1 (1981).

46. Guerini Stone Co., 248 U.S. at 344, 39 S. Ct. at 106.

withholding payment is material.⁴⁷ Nonetheless, the contractor's decision to stop work must be reasonable in order to justify abandonment.⁴⁸ To determine whether the abandonment of work was reasonable, the court generally will analyze the amount of money withheld and the duration of the withholding in light of the contractual language and the factual circumstances.⁴⁹ Additionally, the court will examine the owner's reasons for withholding payment to determine whether cessation of work was reasonable.⁵⁰ Thus, a contractor should examine the language of the contract or payment schedules and the owner's reasons for withholding payment before determining whether to cease work.

In addition to the materiality requirement, a contractor must also be cognizant of whether it has waived its right to cease work when the owner has withheld payments. Waiver may occur when a contractor continues to perform under the contract, despite the owner's nonpayment.⁵¹ If the contractor's right to cease work has been waived and it wrongfully stops work on the construction contract, the contractor may be liable for damages arising from the abandonment.⁵²

2. Mechanic's Lien⁵³

In terms of making payment, the owner must also protect itself from claims of subcontractors and suppliers. Even though subcontractors and suppliers have no direct contract with the owner, they may be entitled to secure their payment from the owner by placing a lien on the real property and/or a lien on any funds the owner owes the general contractor. Lien laws vary widely by state,

---

47. *See* Ernst v. Ohio Dep't of Adm. Serv., 69 Ohio App. 3d 330 (1990); U. S. *ex rel.* E. C. Ernst, Inc. v. Curtis T. Bedwell & Sons, Inc., 506 F. Supp. 1324 (D.C. Pa. 1981); Brady Brick & Supply Co. v. Lotito, 356 N.E.2d 1126 (Ill. App. Ct. 1976).

48. *See* Havens v. Safeway Stores, 678 P.2d 625 (Kan. 1984) (holding that minor delays of six to eight days in making monthly payments did not justify the abandonment of the construction contract).

49. *See id.*; Stewart v. C & C Excavating & Constr. Co., 877 F.2d 711 (8th Cir. 1989) (finding that a debt of $2,385 was an insignificant portion of the contract price and did not justify abandonment); U.S. for Use and Benefit of Aucoin Elec. Supply Co. v. Safeco Ins. Co. of America, 555 F.2d 535, 541 (5th Cir. 1977) (stating that "[e]ven when payment is not made where due, it is not sufficient reason to stop work unless it really prevents work").

50. *See* M. Glosser & Sons, Inc. v. Micco, 309 A.2d 602 (Pa. Commw. Ct. 1973) (finding that withholding payment based on belief that contractor was not paying his subcontractors was improper and constituted breach).

51. *See* Bd. of Regents of Univ. of Texas v. S & G Constr. Co., 529 S.W.2d 90 (Tex. Civ. App. 1975), *overruled on other grounds by* Fed. Sign v. Texas Southern Univ., 951 S.W.2d 401, 121 ED. LAW REP. 394, 40 Tex. Sup. Ct. J. 676 (1997).

52. *See* Providence Washington Ins. Co. v. Beck, 255 N.E.2d 600 (Mass. 1970).

53. *See generally Fundamentals, supra* note 2, at 144 (excerpt).

but they offer significant protections to subcontractors and suppliers and significant risk to owners.[54]

3. Stop Notice/Lien on Funds

In addition to permitting liens that attach to the real property being improved, some states have adopted so-called stop notice statutes.[55] These statutory provisions allow an unpaid party, typically a subcontractor or materialman, to stop, freeze, or trap construction funds prior to disbursement by giving a notice of claim to the person holding these funds, typically the owner or the lender financing the project. Some statutes impose personal liability on the fund holder if it disburses funds in spite of and after having received the stop notice. Strict compliance with timing and service requirements is required in order to enforce a stop notice.

4. Lien Waivers

To manage the contractor or subcontractor nonpayment risk, a prudent owner, prior to making payment, will obtain from the contractor a list of subcontractors and suppliers for the project and obtain lien waivers from the contractor and its subcontractors and suppliers. A lien waiver is a sworn statement from the contractor, subcontractor, or supplier that acknowledges their receipt of payment and waives or releases their claims for work performed through a stated date or up to a stated amount. Lien waivers are routinely required for a contractor or subcontractor to receive each progress payment. Sample lien waiver language is as follows:

> In addition, for and in consideration of the amounts and sums received, the undersigned hereby waives, releases and relinquishes any and all claims, rights, causes of action whatsoever arising out of or in the course of the work performed on the aforementioned project, contract or event transpiring prior to the date hereof, excepting the right to receive payment for work performed and properly completed and retainage, if any, after the date of the above-mentioned payment application or invoice.

Releases and lien waivers "are contractual in nature and their interpretation is governed by the same rules governing interpretation of contracts."[56] "A

---

54. *See* Chapter 17 for a more detailed discussion of liens.
55. For a detailed discussion of the issue by jurisdiction, see *Construction and Effect of Statutes Requiring Construction Fundholder to Withhold Payments upon "Stop Notice" from Subcontractors, Materialman, or Other Person Entitled to Funds*, 4 A.L.R. 5th 772 (1992); *see also, e.g.*, Tex. Prop. Code Ann. § 53.081; N.C. Gen. Stat. § 44A-18.
56. Chemimetals Processing, Inc. v. Schrimsher, 535 S.E.2d 594 (N.C. Ct. App. 2000).

contract plain and unambiguous on its face will be interpreted as a matter of law by the court."[57] Thus, lien waiver agreements entered into after a contract has been signed, and not as a form of consideration for signing of the contract, generally are enforceable.[58]

Some jurisdictions hold that lien waivers do not encompass retainage.[59] Other jurisdictions hold that lien waivers do encompass retainage.[60]

Sometimes owners include in their prime contracts, and contractors include in their subcontracts, a provision requiring the advance or prospective waiver of lien rights, that is, a waiver of lien rights even before execution of the contract or performance of the work. Many states, however, prohibit prospective lien waivers and find them unenforceable.[61]

5. Joint Checks

Typically, payment is made directly from the owner to the contractor. In circumstances where the owner has concerns about the contractor making payment to its subcontractors or suppliers, the owner may insist on issuing a check jointly payable to the contractor and the relevant subcontractor or supplier. In that case, a joint check can only be validly negotiated when endorsed by both payees. If the contractor endorses the check, then the contractor effectively acknowledges payment from the owner. Similarly, the subcontractor's endorsement then acknowledges payment from the contractor for the subcontractor's work. It is left up to the contractor and the subcontractor to agree between themselves as to how the joint check proceeds will be divided. Both of these results enure to the benefit of the owner.

---

57. Dep't of Transp. v. Idol, 440 S.E.2d 863, 864 (N.C. Ct. App. 1994).

58. *See* City of Houston v. R.F. Ball Constr. Co., 570 S.W.2d 75, 78 (Tex. Civ. App. 1978) (stating that "it is the general rule of the law of contracts that when an unambiguous writing has been entered into between the parties, the courts will look to the written instrument as the expression of the parties' intention since it is the parties' objective, not subjective, intent which is significant").

59. *See* Thompson Thrift Construction v. Lynn, 89 N.E.3d 249, 265, 2017 Ohio 1530, ¶ 73 (Ohio Ct. App. 2017) (waiver of lien for "claims" does not waive lien for retainage where claimant did not have "claim" for retainage at time lien waiver was executed); Tharp v. Keeter/Schaefer Investments, L.P., 943 S.W.2d 811 (Mo. Ct. App. 1997) (holding that a lien waiver submitted in connection with progress payments did not apply to retainage as owner knew that the subcontractor expected to recover its retainage at the end of the project).

60. *See* Kern v. City of Lawrenceburg, 625 N.E.2d 1326 (Ind. Ct. App. 1993) (lien waiver that states it applies to all labor and materials furnished through a certain date and applies to unpaid retainage and extra work).

61. *See, e.g.*, FLA. STAT. § 713.20(2) 1999; N.C. GEN. STAT. § 44A-12(f); *but see* TEX. PROP. CODE. ANN. § 53.160(B)(7); *see also Release on Waiver of Mechanic's Lien by General Contractor as Affecting Rights of Subcontractors or Materialmen*, 75 A.L.R.3d 505 (1977).

Many contracts provide that where the owner has a reasonable concern over whether the contractor will make payment to its subcontractors, the owner may issue joint checks. Even absent contractual rights, as a practical matter, the owner can issue joint checks under such circumstances. The alternative would be no payment at all until the owner's concerns are otherwise satisfied.

Oftentimes, the supplier will initiate a joint check. For example, the electrical subcontract on a project may be for $150,000, with $125,000 of that amount representing the electrical materials, including fixtures, conduits, switchgears, controls, and so on. The electrical material supplier to the subcontractor has a significant financial risk and may require a joint check agreement from the general contractor before the material supplier supplies those materials to the electrical subcontractor.

Through a joint check agreement, the general contractor agrees that it will make checks to the subcontractor jointly payable to the supplier. If the contractor makes payments consistent with the joint check agreement, the contractor is protected from claims by the supplier. If, however, the contractor fails to comply and, instead, makes checks payable solely to the subcontractor, the contractor becomes directly liable to the supplier in the event the subcontractor does not pay the supplier. Significantly, the joint check agreement does not make the contractor primarily liable to the supplier. It only requires the contractor to issue joint checks.

Typically, the obligation to issue joint checks is subject to any defenses that the contractor might have pursuant to its contract with the subcontractor. However, the precise wording of the joint check agreement is critical because the agreement rises to the level of an enforceable contract.

A distinction should be drawn between a joint payee and an alternative payee. Payees of checks whose names are separated by "and" are joint payees, while those whose names are separated by "or" are considered alternative payees. A bank can properly cash a joint check only if both parties to the check, that is, the joint payees, have endorsed the check. However, with respect to alternative payees, only the endorsement of one payee is necessary.[62] The joint check rule holds "that a payee by endorsing a check is deemed to have received the full payment regardless whether this indeed is the case."[63]

However beneficial joint checks may be, they are not the panacea one might think. Problems can arise, including the possibility of forged endorsements

---

62. Glen-Gery Corp. v. Warfle Constr. Co., 734 A.2d 926 (Pa. Super. Ct. 1999); *see also* Bituminous Constr., Inc., 816 F.2d 965.

63. BRUNER & O'CONNOR, JR., *supra* note 7, at § 8:53; *see also* Post Bros. Constr. Co. v. Yoder, 569 P.2d 133 (Cal. 1977).

placed on joint checks negotiated with no endorsements. While remedies may exist for such problems, the remedies may be time-consuming and expensive. Thus, construction participants should carefully monitor payment and credit issues.

6. Overpayment

Premature payments and overpayments on a construction project can jeopardize the project itself and have dire consequences for those involved. As discussed earlier, contracting is a cash-flow business. The difference in timing between cash-in and cash-out becomes problematic if the contractor (1) is undercapitalized; (2) is working on a particularly large project; (3) is working on multiple projects; or (4) is faced with a cash flow crisis. When such situations arise, an owner may be persuaded to advance payments to a contractor in an effort to keep the contractor afloat or to keep the project moving. Such payments, however, may have unintended and costly consequences. The consequences are particularly problematic on projects involving payment and performance bonds.[64]

A Surety's Risks and Defenses

The overpayment risks for a surety are significant, because when a surety issues a performance bond, the surety becomes jointly and severally liable to the owner for the timely and satisfactory performance of the contractor's/obligor's responsibilities to the owner/obligee.[65] Courts repeatedly hold that an owner and contractor may not alter, without the surety's consent, a bonded contract that necessarily alters the surety's obligation. As a result, if an owner/obligee makes an unauthorized payment in violation of the underlying bonded contract and without the surety's consent, the surety may be discharged.[66]

An Owner's Risks

An owner has numerous risks associated with overpayment. To begin with, if an overpaid contractor cannot complete the project, then the owner may not have sufficient funds to hire a replacement contractor and complete the project on its own.[67] Moreover, the owner may not be entitled to the protection it expected to receive associated with the performance bond posted by the contractor. For example, a surety may claim that it is discharged due to a material

---

64. Surety bonds are discussed further in Chapter 18.
65. *See* General Motors Acceptance Corp. v. Daniels, 492 A.2d 1306, 1309 (Md. 1985).
66. *See, e.g.*, Argonaut Ins. Co. v. Town of Cloverdale, Ind., 699 F.2d 417, 419 (7th Cir. 1983); Nat'l Union Indem. v. G. E. Bass & Co., 369 F.2d 75, 77 (5th Cir. 1966); McKnight v. Lange Mfg. Co., 155 S.W. 977 (Tex. App. 1913).
67. *See* Fireman's Fund Ins. Co. v. United States, 909 F.2d 495 (Fed. Cir. 1990).

alteration in the underlying contract between the owner and general contractor if the owner has failed to follow the payment provisions recited in the contract. As a general rule, any material alterations of a contract between the principal and the obligee will discharge the surety.[68] Because the owner typically is obligated to inspect the project before rendering payment, a surety also may claim to be discharged if the owner abdicates such inspection responsibilities.[69] In addition, a surety may claim to be discharged from its obligations if the work performed by the contractor and paid for by the owner was defective.

An Architect's Risks

The primary risk to an architect is that, if the architect negligently certified the prepayment or overpayment to the contractor, then the surety may be able to obtain reimbursement from the architect for the surety's loss resulting from the architect's negligence.[70]

A Contractor's Risks

The primary risk to construction companies (and those who own the construction companies) is that the sureties will pursue claims against them for indemnity. With respect to claims for indemnity, sureties will not issue a payment or performance bond on behalf of a contractor unless the contractor, and often the individual owners of the contracting company have executed indemnity agreements. Pursuant to the surety's general agreement of indemnity (GAI), it is granted broad rights of indemnification against the contractor and other indemnitors. Accordingly, if a surety makes payment to an owner, subcontractor, or material supplier as a result of an obligation incurred under a bond, the surety will typically pursue indemnification from the contractor and from the other individual indemnitors that executed the GAI.[71]

---

68. *See* Branch Banking and Trust Co. v. Creasy, 269 S.E.2d 117, 125 (N.C. 1980) (citing Fleming v. Borden, 37 S.E. 219 (N.C. 1900); *but see* First Union Nat'l Bank of North Carolina v. King, 306 S.E.2d 508, 510 (N.C. Ct. App. 1983) (refusing to discharge a surety, despite modification of the contract as between the principal and the creditor because the modification could only benefit the surety).

69. *See* Continental Ins. Co. v. City of Virginia Beach, 908 F. Supp. 341 (E.D. Va. 1995) (holding that where a contract provides for inspection of the construction project before the owner renders payment, and the owner abdicates such inspection responsibilities, the surety will be released to the extent of the harm it suffered).

70. *See* Peerless Ins. Co. v. Cerny & Assoc., Inc., 199 F. Supp. 951 (D. Minn. 1961) (holding that an architect responsible for certifying the contractor's right to an amount of payment has liability to a performance bond surety for negligent certification that results in the obligee's overpayment to the contractor).

71. *See* Prairie State Nat'l Bank v. United States, 164 U.S. 227 (1896) (holding that a surety that completes a government contract upon the contractor's default in performance was entitled to be reimbursed out of the contract funds pursuant to its right of equitable subrogation).

D. Changes

Change is the only constant on a construction project, whether due to owner-directed changes, deficient or incomplete plans and specifications, or unforeseen conditions.[72]

If the contracting parties do not agree that a given event is a change, that issue is resolved through the dispute resolution process. If, however, the parties agree that a change has occurred, then the price of the change is incorporated into the contract by way of a change order. The contract price is then increased in the event of an additional change, or decreased in the event of a deductive change order, and payment for the change is made per the contract requirements.

E. Interest

An owner's failure to make payment in a timely manner represents a material breach of the contract. In addition to an owner's obligation to pay the contract amount due, an owner also may be obligated to pay interest on the past due amount. Typically, construction contracts set forth an interest rate to apply to amounts then due if payments are not timely made. Prejudgment interest is generally allowed in contract cases.[73] Interest on amounts awarded on a contract claim begins to run from the date of breach.[74] Interest will accrue at the legal rate unless a different rate is stated in the contract. Nearly every state has a "legal rate of interest" set by statute.[75]

12.04 SUBSTANTIAL COMPLETION/SUBSTANTIAL PERFORMANCE

Substantial completion is that point in the project where the work "is sufficiently complete in accordance with the Contract Documents so that the Owner can occupy or utilize the Work for its intended use."[76] When it believes the project is substantially complete, the contractor submits to the architect a

---

Compare Berkley Insurance Company v. Hawthorn Bank, 2018 WL 1516885, at *3 (W.D. Mo. 2018) (surety's equitable lien on retainage dates back to date of suretyship agreement, but equitable lien on progress payments does not).

72. See Chapter 14 on Changes.
73. *See, e.g.*, N.C. GEN. STAT. § 24-1; Craftique, Inc. v. Stevens & Co., 364 S.E.2d 129 (N.C. 1988).
74. *See* N.C. GEN. STAT. § 24-5(a).
75. *See* N.C. GEN. STAT. § 24-1 (legal rate of interest is 8 percent).
76. AIA Contract Document A201–2017, art. 9.8.1.

list of items to be completed prior to final payment. The architect then inspects the project and ultimately prepares a list of incomplete or incorrect work items that the contractor must correct and complete to achieve final completion. This list is known in the industry as a punchlist. Once the architect is satisfied that the project, or a designated portion thereof, can be used for its intended purpose, it will issue a certificate of substantial completion.[77]

Substantial completion is a milestone event for several reasons. First, substantial completion triggers the owner's obligation to make payment of retainage; however, such retainage payment is adjusted for the incomplete or incorrect work identified on the punchlist.[78] Second, substantial completion establishes the owner's responsibility for "security, maintenance, heat, utilities, damage to the Work and insurance."[79] Third, substantial completion typically triggers the commencement date of warranties required by the contract.[80] Fourth, substantial completion typically ends the accrual of any liquidated damages provided for by the contract. However, the contract may provide otherwise or may provide for different liquidated damage amounts after substantial completion but before final completion.[81] If the project is late, the owner likely will withhold accrued liquidated damages from the payment of retainage in accordance with the contractor.

When the retainage is to be held until the construction is substantially complete, disputes can arise as to when substantial completion occurs. Often, a final survey or certification(s) will be the event that triggers the obligation to release the funds, but certification(s) alone may not always be dispositive of whether substantial performance has occurred.[82] However, once the owner occupies the premises, substantial completion is hard to deny, whether or not the parties have obtained the necessary certifications.[83]

---

77. *See* AIA Contract Document A201–2017, art. 9.8.2-4.
78. *Id.* at art. 9.8.5.
79. *Id.* at art. 9.8.4.
80. *See id.*
81. *See, e.g.*, W.C. English, Inc. v. Rummel, Klepper & Kahl, LLP, 2017 WL 2123878, at *2 (W.D. Va. 2017) ($3,000 per day in liquidated damages and $5,000 per day in monetary disincentives for failure to meet substantial completion date; $2,000 per day in liquidated damages for failure to meet final completion date).
82. *See* Casa Linda Tile & Marble Installers, Inc. v. Highlands Place 1981, Ltd., 642 So. 2d 766, 768 (Fla. Dist. Ct. App. 1994) (stating that "fail[ure] to secure a contractually required architect's certificate, alone, should not prevent" recovery of funds); Miller v. Bourgoin, 613 A.2d 292, 294–95 (Conn. App. Ct. 1992) (refusing to grant summary judgment for the builder even though a requisite certificate of occupancy had been issued); BRUNER & O'CONNOR, JR., *supra* note 7, at § 8:18 n.1.
83. BRUNER & O'CONNOR, JR., *supra* note 7, at § 8:18 n.1.

In contrast to contracts that provide for a retainage payment to be made when the project achieves substantial completion, courts generally do not support a retainage clause that allows for retention of funds until the contract is fully complete. In *State v. Laconco, Inc.*,[84] a construction contract allowed the funds to be held until "all work" was complete. However, once the project was substantially complete, the court disallowed the withholding of retainage beyond the amount necessary to fund the remaining work.

Other courts typically follow the *Laconco* court's practice, that is, when only a small amount of work remains, such as correcting items identified in a punchlist, those courts require that retainage be reduced to no more than necessary to finance the remaining work.[85] Similarly, once the construction is actually finished, courts typically do not allow withholding retainage to ensure that the contractor performs warranty work.

Finally, issues also exist with respect to whether third parties can enforce retainage rights or access retainage funds. Typically, sureties and third parties who are given express rights in the construction contract can enforce the retainage provisions or access those funds. However, other third parties typically have greater difficulty in enforcing retainage rights or accessing retainage funds.

12.05 FINAL COMPLETION/FINAL PAYMENT

Once the contractor believes it has achieved final completion, the contractor requests a final inspection by the architect and submits its final application for payment. Once the architect conducts its final inspection, and if the architect determines the work has been completed in accordance with the contract, then the architect will issue a certificate of final completion.[86]

By issuing a certificate for payment, the architect represents, among other things, that the contractor has submitted an affidavit and any other required documents, such as a release or lien waiver from subcontractors and suppliers reflecting the contractor's payment of obligations to its subcontractors and suppliers.[87] If a subcontractor or supplier refuses to furnish a release or waiver required by the owner, then the contractor can furnish a bond to indemnify the owner against any potential lien by that subcontractor or supplier. The bond allows the owner to make final payment and still be protected from potential liens.

---

84. 430 So. 2d 1376, 1382 (La. Ct. App. 1983).
85. See *Fundamentals, supra* note 2, at 132.
86. *See generally* AIA Contract Document A201–2017, art. 9.
87. *See* AIA Contract Document A201–2017, art. 9.10.1-2.

The making of final payment by the owner can have an impact in at least two significant ways—acceptance of the work and waiver of claims.

A. Owner's Acceptance of Work/Waiver of Claims

The owner's final payment to its contractor will bar any claims for obvious defects if the payment is considered a clear intention to relinquish those claims.[88] However, most standard contracts make clear that an owner's progress payment for work and final payment do *not* constitute acceptance of defective work.[89]

Absent contractual language specifying whether final payment constitutes acceptance, courts look to the facts surrounding the parties' discussion and the nature of the defective work. If the owner and contractor discuss the defective work, and the contractor promises to repair it, making final payment does not usually constitute a waiver by the owner. For example, in *Khoury Construction Co., Inc. v. Earhart*,[90] the homeowners were able to pursue a claim for defective work despite having made final payment because they pointed out defects to the contractor during construction and continued to complain after taking possession.

If the defects are latent (hidden) and unknown to the owner after conducting a reasonably diligent inspection, then making final payment will not be considered a waiver.[91] If, however, the owner discovers, or should have discovered, a latent defect and fails to request that the contractor fix it, the owner could be deemed to have waived its claim.

If the work is patently (openly and obviously) defective, the owner's acceptance of the project and final payment may implicate the doctrine of waiver. The question is often whether the owner knows of the defect at the time of final payment. For instance, in *Eastover Corp. v. Martin Builders*,[92] the

---

88. *See* Stevens Constr. Corp. v. Carolina Corp., 217 N.W.2d 291 (Wis. 1974).

89. For example, article 9 of AIA Contract Document A201–2017 provides as follows regarding progress payments:

"9.6.6. A Certificate for Payment, a progress payment, or partial or entire use or occupancy of the Project by the Owner shall not constitute acceptance of Work not in accordance with the Contract Documents." (AIA Contract Document A-201–2017, art. 9.6.6).

90. 382 S.E.2d 392 (Ga. Ct. App. 1989).

91. Stevens Constr. Corp. v. Carolina Corp., 217 N.W.2d 291 (Wis. 1974) (citing Milwaukee County v. H. Neidner & Co., 263 N.W. 468 (Wis. 1936)); Fisher v. Simon, 112 N.W.2d 705 (Wis. 1961).

92. 543 So. 2d 1358 (La. Ct. App. 1989).

owner was a general partnership, and the architect was one of the general partners. The architect knew of a patent defect, this knowledge was imputed to the owner, and the claim was barred by the doctrine of waiver.[93] Courts also have held that a defect discoverable through testing and inspection procedures called for by the contract may be considered a patent defect, regardless of the owner's actual knowledge of the defect.[94]

Regardless of whether the defect is latent or patent, any promise by the owner to pay the contractor despite the contractor's deviation from an important aspect of the contract must be supported by consideration.[95] If the owner knows or should know of minor defects and makes payment, such minor defects may be waived.[96]

B. Contractor's Acceptance of Payment/Waiver of Claims

As with the owner's making of payment, the contractor's acceptance of any payment, either progress or final, may constitute a waiver of claims. Again, article 9 of AIA Document A201–2017 deals with the final payment issue as follows:

> 9.10.5 Acceptance of final payment by the Contractor, a Subcontractor, or a supplier, shall constitute a waiver of claims by that payee except those previously made in writing and identified by that payee as unsettled at the time of final Application for Payment.[97]

An issue may arise as to whether or not particular communications are specific enough to constitute a waiver under the terms of the parties' contract, including provisions such as article 9.10.5 of the AIA Document A201–2017 just set forth. If the contractor simply reserves the right to file a claim for additional costs but gives no specifics, the language may be considered insufficient to avoid the final payment bar to all claims.[98]

---

93. *See id.*
94. BRUNER & O'CONNOR, JR., *supra* note 7, at § 8:22; *see* Village of Pawnee v. Azzarelli Constr. Co., 539 N.E.2d 895 (Ill. App. Ct. 1989).
95. SWEET, *supra* note 14, at § 22.06E.
96. *See id.*
97. AIA Contract Document A201–2017, art. 9.10.5.
98. *See* Mingus Constructors, Inc. v. U.S., 812 F.2d 1387, 1389 (Fed. Cir. 1987) (contractor executed release of all claims except those with "amount(s) of which are undetermined at this time," and the court determined this language was insufficient to avoid the final payment bar of all claims).

Usually, the contractor must execute an interim lien waiver in order to receive a progress payment.[99] Oftentimes, these lien waivers will contain an express waiver of all claims through a certain date. In most instances, such a waiver is enforceable.[100]

Absent clear language in a contract, lien waiver, or other project document, the common law doctrines of accord and satisfaction, or compromise and settlement, apply to whether acceptance of payment is a waiver of claims. The central question is whether the owner clearly communicated to the contractor that the payment tendered constitutes full and final payment of all claims. Courts look both to evidence indicating a payment or billing is final, as well as any factors indicating final payment has not yet been made. The specific factual circumstances, as well as the jurisdiction, lead to varied results in these situations. For instance, a court may find that a check offered as final payment under the contract and not as an offer to settle a disputed amount does not result in accord and satisfaction.[101] Alternatively, a court might hold that a situation involving a contractor who knows a check is offered in full settlement and negotiates that check would constitute accord and satisfaction.[102]

C. Liquidated Damages[103]

A liquidated damages provision provides for the assessment of a set sum against the contractor, usually on a per day basis, caused by the contractor's delay. The amount is determined or "liquidated" at the beginning of the job, and enforceable as long as that payment is not viewed as a penalty. A liquidated damages clause may be acceptable to the contractor in those instances where the risk of liquidated damages may be less than the risk of actual damages. Such provisions sometimes include a bonus payment to the contractor if the project is completed ahead of time, also known as an early completion bonus. One could argue that, while these provisions encourage timely completion, they also may tend to result in poor work by forcing or encouraging

---

99. *See* discussion *infra* at § 14.3.3.4.

100. *See id.*; *see also* MW Builders, Inc. v. United States, 136 Fed. Cl. 584 (Fed. Cl. 2018) (contractor could not maintain pass-through claim against government on behalf of subcontractor where subcontractor had executed lien waiver and release that unambiguously waived any claims through period specified in waiver and release); Elec. Supply Co. of Durham, Inc. v. Swain Elec. Co., Inc., 403 S.E.2d 291, 297 (N.C. 1991) (court "note(s) that the use of lien waivers, used other than in anticipation of and in consideration for the awarding of a contract, may also minimize liability by contractors who deal with the owner").

101. *See* Peterson v. Ramsey Cnty., 563 N.W.2d 103 (N.D. 1997).

102. *See* Malarchick v. Pierce, 264 N.W.2d 478 (N.D. 1978).

103. *See Fundamentals*, *supra* note 2, at 129.

contractors to accelerate work efforts to complete their jobs by specified dates in order to avoid the liquidated damages or earn the bonus (as the case may be). In such events, these types of provisions could give rise to claims for defects and damages caused by poor workmanship.

If delay damages appear to be easily calculated, or if the liquidated damage amount is grossly disproportionate to the probable loss the owner will suffer by a delay, the liquidated damages clause may be held to be a penalty and, therefore, unenforceable.[104] Although a court may hold a contractor liable for delay damages even though the delay was caused by other contractors, the owner must prove that the contractor's delay was a substantial factor in the delay of the project.[105] If delays are experienced during the course of a project, the owner may withhold liquidated damages from the contractor's progress payments and final payment. The AIA Contract Documents specifically allow an architect to withhold a certification of payment because of "reasonable evidence that the Work cannot be completed within the Contract Time, and that the unpaid balance would not be adequate to cover actual or liquidated damages for the anticipated delay."[106]

12.06 SPECIFIC PAYMENT ISSUES

A. "Pay If Paid" versus "Pay When Paid"[107]

Pay-if-paid and pay-when-paid clauses are in vogue today, with the most onerous reading as follows:

> Payment of Owner to Contractor for Subcontractor's work is a condition precedent to Contractor's duty to pay Subcontractor under this Subcontract agreement.

When these clauses appear in a subcontract, they should cause a warning bell to go off in a subcontractor's head. Also known as contingent payment clauses, the clauses mean that the general contractor does not have to pay the subcontractor until and unless the owner pays the general contractor. Thus,

---

104. *See, e.g.*, Knutton v. Cofield, 160 S.E.2d 29 (N.C. 1968) (enforcing liquidated damages clause after determining that said clause was not penal); *Contractual Provision for Per Diem Payments for Delay in Performance as One for Liquidated Damages or Penalty*, 12 A.L.R. 4th 891 (1982).

105. *See* Tuttle/White Constructors, Inc. v. Montgomery Elevator Co., 385 So. 2d 98 (Fla. Dist. Ct. App. 1980).

106. AIA Contract Document A201–2017, art. 9.5.1.4.

107. *See Fundamentals, supra* note 2, at 131 (excerpt). Contingent payment clauses are also discussed in Chapter 10.

payment by the owner becomes a condition precedent to the contractor's duty to pay the subcontractor. Such clauses may be construed to shift the credit risk of nonpayment by the owner from the general contractor to the subcontractor, even though the subcontractor had no contract with the owner.

In most states, such a clause must be clear and unambiguous to be enforceable against a subcontractor.[108] If the clause is ambiguous, the general contractor must pay the subcontractor within a reasonable time.[109] However, even when payment is contingent, the general contractor must seek compensation from the owner in good faith and with due diligence, or the provision will be unenforceable.[110] Moreover, in some states, such a clause is unenforceable by statute as a matter of public policy.[111]

Even in states where pay-if-paid provisions are enforceable, courts may craft exceptions to the absolute enforceability of such clauses. First, where the condition precedent (payment by the owner to the general contractor) fails to occur because of the conduct of the general contractor, courts may apply the prevention doctrine.

> The prevention doctrine is a generally recognized principle of contract law according to which if a promissor prevents or hinders fulfillment of a condition to his performance, the condition may be waived or excused. . . . The prevention doctrine does not require proof that the condition would have occurred "but for" the wrongful conduct of the promissor; instead it only requires that the conduct have "contributed materially" to the non-occurrence of the condition.[112]

Thus, if the conduct of the general contractor prevents the owner's payment by the owner to the general contractor, the general contractor cannot successfully defend a claim for payment by its subcontractor by arguing that the condition precedent, payment by the owner, has failed to occur.

---

108. *See, e.g.*, Patriot Contracting, LLC v. Star Ins. Co., 2017 WL 713677, at *3 (E.D. La. 2017) (Louisiana law); Superior Steel, Inc. v. Ascent at Roebling's Bridge, LLC, 540 S.W.3d 770, 786 (Ky. 2017) (resolving enforceability of pay-if-paid clause as matter of first impression); *but see* Moores Bros. Co. v. Brown & Root, Inc., 207 F.3d 717 (4th Cir. 2000) (holding that a surety was not entitled to assert "pay when paid" defense of principal since provision was not incorporated into bond) (applying Virginia law).

109. *See* Bentley, 562 So. 2d at 801 (determining that 90 days was a reasonable time); *Elk & Jacobs Drywall* at 413, 229 S.E.2d at 262 (leaving determination of what constitutes a "reasonable time" up to the jury).

110. *See, e.g.*, Walker v. Chancey, 117 So. 705 (Fla. 1928).

111. *See, e.g.*, N.C. GEN. STAT. § 22C-2.

112. *See* Moore Bros. Co. v. Brown & Root, Inc., 207 F.3d 717 (4th Cir. 2000) (citing RESTATEMENT (SECOND) OF CONTRACTS).

Second, in the surety context, it is unlikely a surety can rely on a so-called pay-if-paid clause in its principal's contract with the owner as a defense to a payment bond claim by a subcontractor unless the surety included an express pay-if-paid condition precedent clause in its surety bond contract.[113] To allow a surety to avoid its obligation under the payment bond simply because the owner did not make payment to the general contractor "defeats the very purpose of a payment bond."[114]

B. Prompt Pay Act

To deal with contractor-to-subcontractor payment abuses, the federal government and many states have enacted legislation to ensure that contractors promptly pay their subcontractors, commonly known as prompt payment acts.[115] These acts usually provide that the contractor will pay the subcontractor within a set number of days from the contractor's receipt of payment from the owner and that the amount of the payment will be the full amount received for the subcontractor's work and materials provided under the subcontract.[116] If a contractor does not timely pay its subcontractors, the contractor shall be liable to the subcontractor for interest on the unpaid amount.[117] Such acts do not, however, blindly require that the contractor make payment to its subcontractors. For instance, a contractor is not required to pay its subcontractor for "unsatisfactory job progress; defective construction not remedied; disputed work; third party claims filed or reasonable evidence that a claim will be filed; failure of subcontractor to make timely payments for labor, equipment, and materials; damage to contractor or another subcontractor; or reasonable evidence that a subcontract cannot be completed for the unpaid balance of the subcontract sum; . . ."[118] The contractor is also permitted to withhold "a

---

113. Moore Bros. Co., 207 F.3d at 723. *See also* United States v. Continental Cas. Co., 2017 WL 3642957, at *11 (D. Md., 2017) (discussing availability *vel non* of defense to surety in depth). *But see* Travelers Cas. & Sur. Co. of America v. Sweet's Contracting, Inc., 450 S.W.3d 229, 237, 2014 Ark. 484, 12 (Ark. 2014) (surety cannot be liable to subcontractor where an enforceable pay-if-paid clause excuses payment by contractor to subcontractor).

114. *Id.* For further discussion with regard to surety bonds, *see* Chapter 18.

115. *See, e.g.*, 31 U.S.C. § 3901 (1998) (Federal Prompt Act) (applicable to those with contracts with the federal government).

116. *See, e.g.*, N.C. Gen. Stat § 22C-3 (requiring payment to be made by contractor within seven days of receipt of payment from the owner).

117. *See, e.g.*, N.C. Gen. Stat § 22C-5 (providing that interest is assessed at the rate of 1 percent per month beginning on the eighth day after contractor receives payment from owner).

118. N.C. Gen. Stat. § 22C-4.

reasonable amount for retainage not to exceed the initial percentage retained by the owner."[119]

C. False Claims

Congress enacted the federal False Claims Act[120] in 1863 primarily to deal with privateering during the Civil War. During recent years, the False Claims Act has been used in connection with the construction industry to combat fraud. While many predicate acts must occur, civil liability arises when one presents a "false or fraudulent claim for payment or approval" to the United States.[121] No specific proof of intent to defraud is required.[122] "Claim" is broadly defined to include "any request or demand, whether under contract or otherwise."[123] Civil damages can include a civil penalty and treble damages.[124] False claims related to payment can arise from a contractor's payment applications, claims for additional compensation, pass-through claims, and damages claims. A handful of states have adopted their own false claims acts, which are modeled after the federal False Claims Act.[125]

A careful review of regular payment applications and claims for additional compensation takes on special meaning on public projects. In *Al Munford Halls, Inc. v. United States*, the contractor sued the government for wrongful termination and submitted a claim for damages arising from that termination.[126] Discovery revealed that the contractor's claim included amounts previously paid by the government and costs not yet incurred by the contractor. By way of a counterclaim, the government thereafter asserted a claim under the False Claims Act, alleging that the contractor's claim was fictitious, inflated, and duplicative. The court agreed and noted as follows:

> The only issue before the court is whether plaintiff knew that its claims to the contracting officer were false or fraudulent as defined by the FCA. To prove a violation of the FCA, the government need not prove that a party intended to deceive the government. *United States v. TDC Management Corp.*, 24 F.3d 292, 298 (D.C.Cir.1994). As stated above, the FCA requires only that the

---

119. *Id.*
120. 31 U.S.C. § 3729 *et seq.* Criminal liability can also arise for false claims. *See* 18 U.S.C. § 287.
121. 31 U.S.C. § 3729(a) (listing predicate acts).
122. *Id.* at § 3729(b).
123. *Id.* at § 3729(b)(2).
124. *Id.* at § 3729(a).
125. *See, e.g.*, CAL GOV'T CODE § 1265 *et seq.*
126. 34 Fed. Cl. 62 (Fed. Cl. 1995), *vacated in part on other grounds*, 86 F.3d 1178 (C.A. Fed. 1996).

government prove that a party knowingly submitted a claim with reckless disregard to the falsity of the information. 31 U.S.C. § 3729(b); *TDC Management Corp.*, 24 F.3d at 298; *Chen-Cheng Wang ex rel. United States v. FMC Corp.*, 975 F.2d 1412, 1420 (9th Cir. 1992). However, innocent mistake or mere negligence is excused. *Chen-Cheng Wang*, 975 F.2d at 1420. For example, a party could not be held liable under the FCA for making an innocent mathematical error in calculating its claim.[127]

D. Lender Liability

As noted earlier, credit is a significant force in the construction industry. That credit begins with the construction loan provided by a financial institution. Given the depth and breadth of the construction loan documents and the level of the lender's risk, the lender often can exercise control with regard to construction payments and other matters. That control itself, however, can lead to significant risk and liability for the lender.

A construction lender's liability related to its duty to conduct inspections during the construction of a project was dealt with in *Lassiter v. Bank of North Carolina*.[128] The plaintiff homeowner/borrower complained that the lender failed to make construction inspections prior to the disbursement of funds. The borrower derived such a duty from the statement of purpose in the loan agreement, which provided that monthly draws on the construction loan "were to be made only on the basis of plaintiffs' draw requests and property inspections by defendant's inspector, 'to ensure that the loan is not drawn down below the point of construction completion.'" During the course of the project, the lender never inspected the construction project and permitted draws on the construction loan. During the construction process, the borrowers learned that the lender had advanced 61 percent of the construction loan but that the project was only 36 percent completed. The court refused to impose an inspection duty on the lender based on the language in the purpose statement contained in the loan agreement:

> The loan agreement between plaintiffs and defendant contained no language obligating defendant to make property inspections before making or allowing a draw. Defendant was to make disbursements based on plaintiffs' request, but these payments were not contingent upon a property inspection. Purpose statements in loan agreements are permissive and do not create an affirmative duty on behalf of the lender . . . even when a loan agreement indicates the

---

127. *Id.*
128. 146 N.C. App. 264, 551 S.E.2d 920 (2001).

lender will only disburse loan proceeds in proportion to the amount of construction completed, it does not require the lender to inspect the construction progress for the borrower's benefit.[129]

Under certain circumstances, the borrower's contractor may claim the benefit of or assert a lien against undisbursed loan proceeds in the hands of the lender. In *Embree Construction Group, Inc. v. Rafcor, Inc.*, the court allowed a general contractor to assert an equitable lien on unadvanced construction loan proceeds still held by the lender.[130] The *Embree* court found that the general contractor had completed construction of the project; that the owner refused to pay the contract balance; and that while receiving the benefit of its security, that is, a completed project, the lender had not advanced all of the construction loan proceeds. The court looked favorably upon the contractor's claim for an equitable lien because the statutory mechanic's lien rights were of no practical value, given that those lien rights were subordinate to the prior recorded deed of trust of the construction lender. The court noted that "when a contractor's lien is subordinate to a construction loan mortgage . . . or to prior encumbrances such as a purchase money mortgage, any lien on the owner's property or its improvements is worthless when the owner is insolvent."[131] The court held that the lender was unjustly enriched by virtue of its refusal to disburse the money remaining in the construction loan account, coupled with the lender's receipt of all of the security for which it bargained in the form of a completed building. Specifically, equitable relief is appropriate where the contractor has completed performance, the entire project itself is completed, and the lender receives a completed project but seeks to retain undisbursed construction loan funds.

12.07 CONCLUSION

Payment is the grease that runs the machine of a construction project. Clearly, many opportunities exist for the process to falter. While contractual provisions must be in place that clearly set forth the parties' obligations to one another, a smooth process begins with parties who mutually respect one another and are committed to complying with their contractual obligations. The parties must maintain that commitment throughout the project.

---

129. 145 N.C. App. at 268, 551 S.E.2d at 923; *see also* Camp v. Leonard, 133 N.C. App. 554, 515 S.E.2d 909 (1999); *but see* Rudolph v. First Southern Fed. Sav. & Loan Assoc., 414 So. 2d 64 (Ala. 1982).

130. 330 N.C. 487, 411 S.E.2d 916 (1992).

131. 330 N.C. at 493, 411 S.E.2d at 921.

QUESTIONS

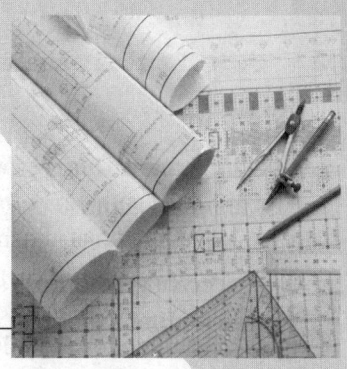

1. Your client, owner, is considering a project to dredge all of the mud, dirt, and debris from a New Orleans canal after Hurricane Katrina. Due to the effects of the hurricane, the amount of mud, dirt, and debris in the canal is unknown. Would you advise owner to use a fixed-price contract or unit-price contract? Why?
2. Owner contracted with contractor to build a new multilevel porch on his home for a fixed price and no progress payments using A101 and A202–2017, AIA Contract Documents. After several days, contractor submitted an application for final payment, stating that the porch was completed. Architect subsequently inspected the porch and signed a certificate of payment. After paying for the work pursuant to the certificate of payment, owner finds that the porch supports are not properly bracketed, causing the porch to be structurally unsound. What are owner's legal rights? Against whom? Under what causes of action? What is the likely outcome?
3. Has owner waived its right to any claims against contractor and architect in question 2?
4. What is the purpose of retainage?
5. After completing a substantial portion of work on a contract to build a house for owner, contractor is entitled to a progress payment of $5,000 pursuant to the terms of the contract. After architect issues a certificate of payment for the progress payment, owner informs contractor that it currently does not have $5,000 and is attempting to obtain a new construction loan. What are contractor's rights at this point? What additional facts would be helpful in determining contractor's rights?
6. Because owner was wary of contractor's reputation for not paying its subcontractors, owner paid contractor and subcontractor with a joint check addressed to both parties. Both contractor and subcontractor endorsed the check, and contractor cashed it at a local bank. Contractor subsequently kept the proceeds from the check and refused to pay subcontractor for work completed. What are subcontractor's rights?
7. Owner contracts with contractor to build a new house for $100,000. The contract provides for retainage of 10 percent, or $10,000. After substantial work, architect submits a certificate of substantial completion and a punchlist consisting of approximately $200 worth of minor fixes. Owner subsequently moves into the house, but refuses to pay the retainage in light of the $200 worth of remaining work. Is owner obligated to pay the retainage?
8. Federal government contracts with contractor to construct a new Supreme Court building in Washington, D.C. The contract contains a liquidated damages

provision of $5,000 per day. Because of a shortage in the labor force, contractor misses the contractual completion date by 180 days. Federal government assesses $900,000 in liquidated damages ($5,000 × 180 days) against contractor. Contractor contends that federal government's actual damages are only $2,500 per day. Can federal government recover its liquidated damages of $5,000 per day even if its actual damages are only $2,500 per day?

9. Using the same facts as question 8, contractor submits a claim for additional compensation to the federal government because of costly changes requested by the federal government during construction. Contractor internally calculates its actual claim, but prior to submitting its claim to the federal government, it increases its claim by 25 percent in order to "leave room for negotiation." If contractor submits its claim to federal government, is contractor submitting a false claim?

CHAPTER 13

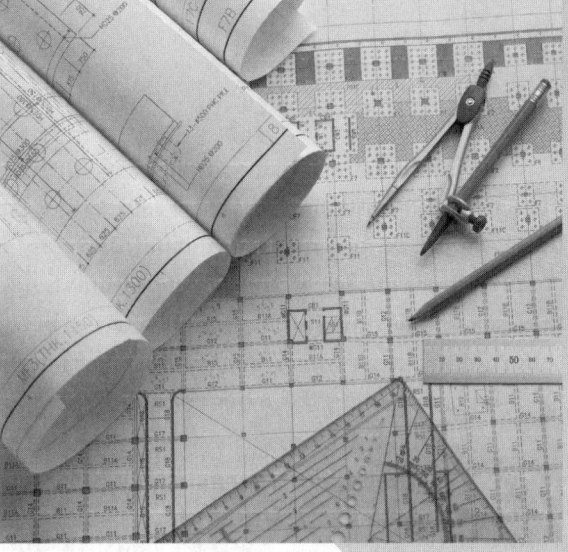

Construction Safety

WILLIAM R. ALLENSWORTH AND MATTHEW C. RYAN

13.01 INTRODUCTION

The construction workplace is one of the most dangerous in the United States, killing thousands of workers each year and disabling many thousands more.[1] The U.S. Bureau of Labor Statistics has cited its "fatal four" leading causes of construction deaths as (1) falls, (2) struck by object, (3) electrocutions, and (4) caught-in/between. The number of on-the-job fatalities for American construction workers reached 5,190 in 2016—effectively 14 deaths per day; and these only represent deaths occurring within the workforce, not the general public.

The prevention of construction accidents, and the allocation of responsibility for property damage and bodily injury arising from such accidents, are the subjects of construction safety law. The law hides in a dense thicket of common law forms, varied and sometimes obtuse regulations, state and federal statutory frameworks, complicated insurance policies, and contractual sophistry, the command of which is the stock-in-trade of a large specialty bar.

---

1. Bureau of Labor Statistics, *Census of Fatal Occupational Injuries (CFOI)—Current and Revised Data* (2016), *available at* http://www.bls.gov/news.release/pdf/cfoi.pdf (last visited Mar. 12, 2018).

This chapter introduces the area of construction safety—more specifically, the safety of workers (and to a lesser extent, that of the general public)—and the roles of the industry's principal players. To structure the discussion, this chapter is divided into three general subdivisions that reflect the most common legal issues arising in construction safety: accident prevention; compensation; and the allocation of responsibility for accidents through tort liability, insurance, statutes, or contract.[2]

13.02 ACCIDENT PREVENTION

The prospect of tort liability for construction accidents encourages employers to implement accident prevention programs, but this section addresses the affirmative duty of accident prevention as either a governmental or contractual requirement.

A. State Legislation

While the prevention of construction accidents has long been a subject of governmental interest, states in the U.S. have enacted safety legislation only since the late 19th century. States legislating safety primarily were those with unionized workforces, and with legislation often developed in piecemeal fashion—frequently in response to notorious accidents, or a series of accidents.[3] Most of these statutes have required general contractors to provide for workplace safety, or for a particular aspect of it, such as protection against falls.[4] Owners traditionally were assumed to have no responsibility, or specifically were exculpated from it.

Traditionally, architects' and engineers' licensing boards have not been heavily involved in accident *prevention*, and, instead, have focused on individual registrants' duties to protect the public's health, safety, and welfare.[5] This has been the lens through which these agencies have looked when eval-

---

2. For more information on the topic of safety in construction law, see Philip L. Bruner & Patrick J. O'Connor, Jr., Bruner & O'Connor on Construction Law §§ 5:1, 7:60, 13:14–13:15, 17:56 (West Group 2002) [hereinafter Bruner & O'Connor].

3. For a well-researched history of this legislation, see Marc M. Schneier, Construction Accident Law: A Comprehensive Guide to Legal Liability and Insurance Claims 48–52 (Forum 1999) [hereinafter Construction Accident Law].

4. The U.S. Bureau of Labor Statistics has cited falls as the runaway leader of construction deaths, capturing 38.7 percent of the total fatalities in 2016. *See supra* note 1.

5. The Texas Occupations Code, for example, includes separate chapters governing the practices of architecture and engineering, but both emphasize the state's interest in protecting the

uating design professionals' conduct on projects involving construction accidents, most notably through a few well-publicized license suspensions or revocations, due to design or contract administration errors on prominent projects.[6] Although state licensing boards may require that a design professional produce a safe *design*, of more significance are state statutes and regulations requiring engineered safety systems during construction—including, in particular, trench safety and highway construction.[7]

B. Occupational Safety and Health Act

In the 1960s, Congress took up the cause of accident prevention, and in the 1970s, then-President Nixon signed into law the Occupational Safety and Health Act (OSHA).[8] The OSHA statute created a safety administration agency and charged the Secretary of Labor with enacting regulations to "assure safe and healthful working conditions for working men and women," and for enforcing those regulations.[9] A number of states adopted OSHA, or portions thereof, as the standards replacing local workplace safety statutes.[10]

These regulations cover virtually every aspect of construction workplace safety in mind-numbing detail, requiring employers to institute safety programs and to ensure their implementation. OSHA, however, is deliberately imprecise in its definition of "employer"; because "employer" status is required for a party to be subject to OSHA, such intentional ambiguity arguably broadens the potential applicability of the act. Over time, this requirement also has led industry participants to create "independent contractor" relationships with individuals, in an effort to (1) escape the effects of the OSHA statute and related regulatory consequences, and (2) build barriers against legal responsibilities for control. The OSHA agency takes the position that the "employer" term includes not only the subcontractors whose employees are workers but also the prime contractors who control the subcontractors, thereby making

---

public's health, safety, and welfare. Tex. Occ. Code § 1001.004(b)(1) (engineers); Tex. Occ. Code § 1051.0015(1) (architects).

6. *See, e.g.*, Duncan v. Missouri Bd. for Architects, Professional Eng'rs and Land Surveyors, 744 S.W.2d 524 (Mo. Ct. App. 1988).

7. *See, e.g.*, Texas Uniform General Conditions in State Construction Contracts, Tex. Gov't Code Ann. § 2166.301 (Vernon 2000).

8. 29 U.S.C. §§ 651–678 (1994).

9. From the preamble to OSHA, 29 U.S.C 651.

10. If a state, with approval from the Secretary of Labor, adopts a comprehensive statutory safety scheme equivalent to OSHA, the enforcement of OSHA is preempted in that state. 29 U.S.C. § 667.

the prime contractors responsible for complying with the OSHA regulations as well.[11]

The theory behind this broad application of OSHA was stated succinctly in *Clarkson Construction Co. v. Occupational Safety and Health Review Comm'n*,[12] in which a subcontractor backed a truck over an employee. In affirming a penalty against the prime contractor who hired the subcontractor, the court reasoned that the prime contractor was an "employer" because:

> [W]e here [are not] dealing with vicarious liability of the employer to third persons in tort. Instead, we are concerned with giving meaning to an Act of Congress, which was designed to require the employer to provide a safe work place for all persons working on the premises. With that in mind, common law definitions ought not to be dispositive in interpreting the Act.
>
> . . .
>
> The Supreme Court has refused to use the traditional approach in defining the term "employee" in the context of other statutes. Moreover, instead of looking at narrow common law definitions, the Supreme Court has looked to the purpose of the Act involved in deciding what the meaning of "employee" should be and also has held it inappropriate to use varying state common law definitions of an employee and employer in construing federal legislation.[13]
>
> The statute with which we are here dealing has a broad remedial purpose, protection of the worker from industrial injury. It has been said that, "[i]n order to accomplish this purpose, it is necessary to look to an employer who controls the working environment. Whether the employer controlling work environment [sic] is also the employer for wage or tort purposes should not be a governing factor."[14]

---

11. *See* OSHA Field Operations Manual, ch. IV, section I(E)(4), Multi-Employer Citation Policy, *available at* https://www.osha.gov/OshDoc/Directive_pdf/CPL_02-00-160.pdf (last accessed Mar. 12, 2018); *see also* ANSI A10.33-1992, ¶¶ 2 (definitions), 5.2 (responsibilities).

12. 531 F.2d 451 (10th Cir. 1976).

13. *Cf.* 29 C.F.R. § 1977.5, which provides that for purposes of section 11(c) of the act (29 U.S.C. § 660(c)) (the antidiscrimination clause) "employee" has a broad definition. The regulation states in part that: "[T]he broad remedial nature of this legislation demonstrates a clear congressional intent that the existence of an employment relationship, for purposes of section 11(c), is to be based upon economic realities rather than upon common law doctrines and concepts."

14. *Clarkson Constr. Co.*, 531 F.2d at 457 (citations omitted).

Design professionals performing contract administration responsibilities consistent with the industry's professional standard of care[15] generally are not regarded as "employers" and, therefore, usually fall outside the scope of OSHA.[16] Construction managers (and design professionals acting as construction managers), however, are much more likely to be viewed by OSHA as "controlling employers" if substantially involved in the day-to-day management or control of the construction site.[17]

C. OSHA in Civil Litigation

OSHA is directly enforced by the agency's own inspectors, who are empowered to levy fines and penalties on employers.[18] The agency's annual budget exceeded half a billion dollars as of 2018.[19] The extent to which OSHA can be used to establish a standard of care for reference in a private cause of action is a much closer question, however, as this Colorado case notes:

---

15. For a detailed treatment of design professionals' liability and the standard of care applicable to them, see Chapter 6.

16. Skidmore, Owings & Merrill, 5 BNA OSHC 1762 (OSHRC 1977) (stating that architect who was not involved in substantial supervision of the construction was not bound by OSHA). *See also* Reich v. Simpson, Gumpertz & Heger, Inc., 3 F.3d 1, 3 (1st Cir.1993) (holding that construction site was not a "place of employment" of the structural engineer for purposes of OSHA, where it had no employees on the site on a daily or even weekly basis, did not have an office or trailer at the site, and did not have any employees at the site on the day in question).

17. Bertrand Goldberg Assoc., 4 BNA OSHC 1587 (OSHRC 1976) (deciding that architect who was also engaged as a construction manager was bound by OSHA in its work directly overseeing the worksite); *see also* CH2M Hill, Inc. v. Herman, 192 F.3d 711, 718–21 (7th Cir. 1999) (holding that (1) OSHA construction standards, including "substantial supervision" test, did not per se exclude professionals working on or as part of a construction project, but (2) firm did not engage in construction work and, thus, was not subject to construction safety standards).

18. Or, if the state has adopted an OSHA-approved version of the act, enforcement is handled by state inspectors. *See, e.g.*, OSHA Instruction Directive No. CSP 01-00-004—State Plan Policies and Procedures Manual (effective Sept. 22, 2015), *available at* https://www.osha.gov/OshDoc/Directive_pdf/CSP_01-00-004.pdf (last accessed Mar. 12, 2018).

19. *See* United States Department of Labor, Occupational Safety & Health Administration, Commonly Used Statistics, *available at* https://www.osha.gov/oshstats/commonstats.html (last accessed Mar. 12, 2018).

Scott v. Matlack, Inc.
39 P.3d 1160 (Col. 2002)[20]

Justice BENDER delivered the Opinion of the Court.

I. Introduction

In this case, we review and reverse the court of appeals' decision. We hold that (1) [precedent] does not preclude the admission of Occupational Safety and Health Act evidence in a negligence suit; [and] (2) it is proper for a trial court to admit Occupational Safety and Health Act regulations as evidence of the standard of care in an industry....

Plaintiffs Randy and Ann Scott sued Defendants Matlack Trucking, Inc. and Conoco Oil Company for negligence, negligence per se, and loss of consortium after Randy Scott fell from the top of a tanker while loading hot asphalt for Matlack at Conoco's Denver facility. After a two-week trial, a jury found the defendants liable on negligence and loss of consortium claims.

[W]e held [previously] that OSH Act regulations do not create a private cause of action and therefore a plaintiff could not establish a negligence per se claim by alleging a defendant violated OSH Act regulations.[1]

In this case, the court of appeals reversed the trial court, holding that this court's [previous] opinion precludes admission of evidence related to the OSH Act in a negligence action.... We reverse and remand this case to the court of appeals for return to the trial court to reinstate the jury award and judgment for the plaintiffs.

....

III. Analysis

....

Negligence vs. Negligence Per Se

As background, we start with an explanation of negligence and negligence per se. To establish a common-law negligence claim, the plaintiff must show that the defendant owed the plaintiff a legal duty to conform to a standard of care, the defendant breached that duty, the plaintiff suffered injury, and there is a causal relationship between the breach and the injury.

The defendant owes a duty to act when it is reasonably foreseeable that the failure to act will create an unreasonable risk of harm to another. A defendant's duty is based on the standard of care owed by a reasonable person in the defendant's position. When the defendant and the plaintiff are part of an industry that conforms to certain well-established safety customs, the jury may consider the

---

20. Internal citations, footnotes, expanded procedural history, and further discussion of negligence as applied to the facts of the case have been omitted.

customs as non-conclusive evidence of reasonable care the defendant should follow in that industry.

In contrast to negligence, negligence *per se* occurs when the defendant violates a statute adopted for the public's safety and the violation proximately causes the plaintiff's injury. To recover, the plaintiff must also demonstrate that the statute was intended to protect against the type of injury she suffered and that she is a member of the group of persons the statute was intended to protect. If the statute applies to the defendant's actions, then the statute conclusively establishes the defendant's standard of care and violation of the statute is a breach of his duty.

2. The OSH Act and Negligence

OSH Act section 653(b)(4) provides that the statute may not be used to enlarge, diminish, or affect an employee's or employer's common-law liability:

> Nothing in this Act shall be construed to supersede or in any manner affect any workmen's compensation law or to enlarge or diminish or affect in any other manner the common law or statutory rights, duties, or liabilities of employers and employees under any law with respect to injuries, diseases, or death of employees arising out of, or in the course of, employment.

[Previously], we followed a majority of courts and ruled a defendant may not be held negligent merely with proof that he violated an OSH Act regulation. We held that OSH Act section 653(b)(4) bars the use of OSH Act regulations to establish a negligence *per se* claim.

. . .

However, [we] did not address whether section 653(b)(4) precludes a plaintiff from using OSH Act regulations in a negligence action as *some* evidence of a defendant's negligence. The Scotts argue that OSH Act evidence may be used to provide non-conclusive, or some, evidence of the industry standard with which a reasonable person in the defendants' industry should comply.

Many jurisdictions that prohibit the use of OSH Act regulations to establish a negligence *per se* claim permit the use of OSH Act regulations in a negligence case as some evidence of the standard of care in the defendant's industry.

The question of whether OSH Act regulations may be admitted as some evidence of the industry standard in a negligence case turns on two issues. The first is whether the OSH Act, as a safety statute, may be borrowed as evidence of the standard of care in the defendants' industry. The second issue is whether the language of section 653(b)(4), "[n]othing in this Act shall . . . enlarge or diminish or affect in any manner the common law or statutory . . . duties, or liabilities of employers and employees" excludes OSH Act regulations from general rules regarding the borrowing of safety statutes.

We turn to the question of whether using, or borrowing, regulations or statutes as some evidence of the standard of care in an industry is permissible. Such use has been permitted in some of our cases. The court of appeals reasoned, "Safety codes and standards are admissible when offered in support of expert testimony and when introduced as objective safety standards generally recognized and accepted as such in the type of industry involved."

In a negligence case in which a plaintiff seeks to borrow a safety statute as some evidence of the standard of care in defendant's industry, we adopt [this] reasoning. Therefore, to be admissible in such a situation, the safety standards must be relevant, offered in support of expert testimony, objective, and recognized and accepted in the industry involved. [Based upon its use in the case by expert witnesses to illuminate a disputed issue of fact, OSH Act regulations, if viewed simply as safety standards] meet the criteria for admissibility as evidence of standard of care in the relevant industry.

However, Matlack and Conoco argue that the usual rules for admitting a safety statute are rendered inapplicable by the express limiting language of section 653(b)(4). The defendants argue that this section restricts OSH Act regulations from being used as evidence, for any reason, in a civil suit. They argue that even borrowing the OSH Act as some evidence of industry standards affects and enlarges an employer's duty.

There is some precedential support for the defendants' position. [T]he Seventh Circuit held that workers' compensation was an injured employee's only remedy and that OSH Act regulations could not be used as evidence of "an expanded standard of care" in a negligence suit.

However, few jurisdictions excluding OSH Act evidence from a negligence suit have done so because section 653(b)(4) absolutely bars use of the OSH Act in civil cases. Instead, those jurisdictions tend to cite controlling statutes or case law particular to their jurisdiction for excluding OSH Act evidence.

Our review of authorities and case law from other jurisdictions reveals three generally accepted conclusions: (1) the OSH Act does not create a federal private cause of action and cannot be used as the sole basis of a negligence or negligence per se claim; (2) the OSH Act cannot be used to establish a state negligence per se claim because of the language in section 653(b)(4); and (3) the OSH Act may be admitted in a negligence action as some evidence of the standard of care required of defendant.

...

[However], the question remains: does borrowing the OSH Act as some evidence of the standard of care enlarge or affect the defendants' duty under the common law in a negligence suit?

In construing this section, we face a logical conundrum. The broad reading of section 653(b)(4) that the defendants urge would require us to conclude that borrowing OSH Act regulations to aid the jury in determining whether a defendant complied with the industry standard, "enlarges" the defendant's liability.

On the other hand, excluding OSH Act regulations might cause an equally impermissible result. If a defendant is permitted to exclude OSH Act regulations based on the defendant's proposed reading of section 653(b)(4), then the jury is left with fewer tools to determine the standard of care with which the defendant should have complied. Restricting the jury in this way would effectively "diminish" the defendant's liability. Moreover, while the language of section 653(b)(4) is expansive, there is no evidence to suggest the Congress intended for evidence of OSH Act regulations to be absolutely barred from civil cases. Also, we note that the Restatement of Torts generally supports borrowing of administrative regulations to inform the industry standard.[2]

. . .

Ultimately, we agree with . . . the Third Circuit, which concluded that "[e]vidence of an OSHA violation, in and of itself, does not 'affect' liability; it is the inferences that the trier of fact draws from the evidence that 'affect' liability." We also agree . . . that borrowing OSH Act regulations in a negligence action is not the same as applying the regulations to the case. This is consistent with Colorado precedent that allows the admission of safety regulations as some evidence of negligence in other contexts.

Thus, we hold that once a trial court determines that a defendant could owe a plaintiff a duty under Colorado law, the jury should be permitted to hear evidence of OSH Act regulations as some indication of the standard of care with which a reasonable person in the defendant's position should comply.

---

1. Canape v. Petersen, 897 P.2d 762 (Colo. 1995).
2. RESTATEMENT (SECOND) OF TORTS § 288B cmt. d (1965), "[T]he requirements of administrative regulations are not adopted by the court as defining a definite standard of conduct in negligence actions, but are accepted as affording relevant evidence."

The court did not directly address whether the plaintiff had to prove that the prime contractor was subject to the regulations as a "controlling employer" in order for the plaintiff to use the regulations to prove the standard of care required of the prime contractor, as opposed to the subcontractor. Since the regulations may be allowed as evidence of a so-called industry standard, then does that standard apply to a prime contractor who is not a "controlling employer" under the OSHA regulations?[21]

---

21. *Cf.* S & H Riggers & Erectors, Inc. v. Occupational Safety & Health Comm'n, 659 F.2d 1273 (5th Cir. 1981) (holding that: (1) absent clear articulation by the Commission of circumstances in which industry practices were not controlling, due process required, in order to establish violations of OSHA regulation governing provision of personal protective equipment to employees in construction industry, showing that employers either (a) failed to provide personal protective equipment customarily required in industry or (b) had actual knowledge that personal protective equipment was required under circumstances of cases, and (2) substantial evidence did not support findings by the Commission that employers, whose practices conformed to industry custom, had actual knowledge that personal protective equipment was necessary to employees under circumstances of cases, as required to establish violations of OSHA regulation governing provision of personal protective equipment to employees in construction industry).

D. Contractual Responsibility for Safety Programs

By statute, most federal construction contracts require the prime contractor to follow OSHA,[22] while the form provisions written by both the AIA and the Engineers Joint Contract Documents Committee (EJCDC) rely on the broader catchall of requiring compliance with all applicable laws, ordinances, rules, and regulations,[23] which presumably includes those promulgated and enforced by OSHA.

The form contracts between owners and prime contractors prepared by the AIA and the EJCDC, of course, tend to be consistent with the following approach to accident prevention: namely, that responsibility is delegated almost exclusively to the prime contractor. The prime contractor is to be "solely responsible for, and have control over, construction means, methods, techniques, sequences, and procedures, and for coordinating all portions of the Work under the Contract,"[24] including the affirmative duty of initiating, maintaining, and supervising all safety precautions and programs, and designating a responsible member of the contractor's organization at the site whose duty shall be the prevention of accidents.[25] Many subcontracts include similar language obligating the subcontractor to fulfill such duties with respect to the subcontractor's portion of the work, and specifically flow down the prime contractor's safety obligations from the prime contract.[26]

---

22. THE CONSTRUCTION CONTRACTS BOOK 319–24 (Daniel S. Brennan, Richard H. Lowe, Jennifer A. Nielsen & John I. Spangler, III, eds., ABA 2004).

23. American Institute of Architects, AIA Document A201-2017, General Conditions of the Contract for Construction § 10.2.2 (2017) [hereinafter AIA Document A201-2017]; Engineers Joint Contract Documents Committee [hereinafter EJCDC], STANDARD GENERAL CONDITIONS OF THE CONSTRUCTION CONTRACT, ¶ 7.13 (2002).

24. AIA Document A201-2017, *supra* note 23 § 3.3.1.

25. AIA Document A201-2017, *supra* note 23, § 10.1 (contractor shall initiate, maintain, and supervise all safety precautions), § 10.2.1 (contractor will take reasonable precautions to prevent injury to employees in the work or other persons on the project), § 10.2.2 (contractor will comply with all laws bearing on the safety of persons), § 10.2.3 (contractor will post warnings and take other reasonable measures), § 10.2.4 (contractor will exercise utmost care when using explosives), 10.2.6 (contractor will appoint a superintendent in charge of safety), and § 10.2.7 (contractor will not permit any part of the construction to be loaded so as to endanger safety).

26. American Institute of Architects, AIA Document A401-2017, Standard Form of Agreement between Contractor and Subcontractor § 4.3.1 (2017).

13.03 RECOVERY OF COMPENSATION FOR CONSTRUCTION ACCIDENTS

The contractual responsibility to provide a safe workplace does not necessarily translate into tort liability to injured workers. The primary basis of compensation for workers' injuries remains statutory workers' compensation schemes, with uncertain resort to tort liability under arcane legal principles. Workers' compensation and tort liability are discussed separately.

A. Workers' Compensation Laws

Until the last century, most construction workers were regarded as independent contractors who, with their widowed spouses and orphans, were solely responsible for their own fortunes. If independent contractors were deemed to be "employees," then their employers had very limited common law responsibility to them, particularly since each of the following allowed a complete defense to liability: the fellow-servant rule, contributory negligence, and assumption of risk. With the maturing of the Industrial Revolution, however—including the enfranchisement of vast numbers of voting employees and the rise of their labor unions—various state legislatures began enacting workers' compensation laws.[27]

Although the laws differ from state to state, they all include some basic tenets: the employer provides workers' compensation insurance, which provides medical and disability insurance benefits paid to the worker, regardless of fault. In return, the employer is insulated from any further liability, except under the most egregious circumstances.[28] The resolution of workers' compensation claims is now largely in the province of administrative law, and the primary issues are the extent and severity of the injury (and, hence, the compensation for the injury) and whether the injury occurred in the "course and scope" of employment.[29]

---

27. For a history of the rise of workers' compensation laws, see Price v. Fishback & Shawn Everett Kantor, *The Adoption of Workers' Compensation in the United States, 1900–1930*, 41 J.L. & Econ. 305 (1998); Paul Raymond Gurtler, *The Workers' Compensation Principle: A Historical Abstract of the Nature of Workers' Compensation*, 9 Hamline J. Pub. L. & Pol'y 285 (1989); Richard A. Epstein, *The Historical Origins and Economic Structure of Workers' Compensation Law*, 16 Ga. L. Rev. 775 (1982).

28. *See, e.g.*, Tex. Labor Code § 408.001(b) (Vernon 2006) (common-law recovery allowed if worker's death was caused by gross negligence or intentional conduct).

29. The simplicity of these issues and the number of claimants ensured huge amounts of legal work for budding litigators. Until very recently, many lions of the civil trial bar had cut their teeth

B. Tort Liability

The workers' compensation system is essentially a Faustian bargain, which generally ensures that the worker will receive less than might be available in an individual claim—but the system also provides a means of more certain and expedited compensation from the employer than the worker might have been able to obtain as an ordinary tort claimant. Only workers' compensation subscribers are insulated from liability, however—that is, those who buy into the system by purchasing the state's statutorily approved insurance coverage. The extent to which the injured worker can recover the remainder of the worker's damages from other members of the construction team, or from the owner, involves questions of duty under tort law. These questions will be examined in detail for each of the major players in any construction: the owner, the prime contractor, and the design professionals.

Generally, the fact patterns in construction accident cases can be divided into two fundamental types, based on the kind of negligence that is involved. Workers' compensation also plays a role in the ability of owners, design professionals, or other contractors who are sued to seek indemnity or contribution from the original employer. The extent to which workers' compensation insulates employers (who purchase insurance) from these types of third-party tort claims is discussed more fully in the indemnity and insurance section of this chapter.

1. Active Negligence

The first type of construction accident case involves a party whose negligence was contemporaneous with the injury (i.e., whose negligent act more or less directly caused the injury). This category, sometimes described as "active negligence," includes negligent acts like knocking a construction worker off a platform with a crane,[30] running over a construction worker with a truck,[31] or dropping tools from scaffolding onto a construction worker's head.[32] Unless the negligent actor is insulated from liability by inclusion by the workers' com-

---

on workers' compensation cases, and the legal lore is full of anecdotes of their trials. Ultimately, the cost of litigation became so expensive, and the results so unjust, that most legislatures have now made the proceedings almost exclusively administrative.

30. Gonnert v. Victor At W. 53, LLC, No. 40690/04, 2006 N.Y. slip op. 50284(U) (N.Y. slip op. Mar. 3, 2006); Nowicki v. Cannon Steel Erection Co., 711 N.E.2d 536 (Ind. Ct. App. 1999); Sulem v. B.T.R. East Greenbush Inc., 589 N.Y.S.2d 969 (N.Y. App. Div. 1992).

31. Scott v. Matlack, Inc., 39 P.3d 1160 (Col. 2002); R. E. Gaddie, Inc. v. Price, 528 S.W.2d 708 (Ky. 1975); Eades v. Capitol Material Co., Inc., 121 F.2d 72 (D.C. 1941).

32. Scully v. Otis Elevator Co., 275 N.E.2d 905 (Ill. App. Ct. 1971); Blair v. Dunham, 134 F.2d 729 (6th Cir. 1943).

pensation bar,[33] such cases are resolved under traditional duty analyses, which focus on the duty of a reasonable person to avoid negligently injuring foreseeable victims.

2. Liability Based on Control of the Workplace

Much more difficult is the group of cases that involves indirect liability for failing to provide a safe workplace for the injured worker, or for failing to remedy dangerous conditions. Generally, these claims are brought by subcontractors' employees against prime contractors or owners, on a theory of premises liability (i.e., property owners or occupiers have a qualified responsibility to protect others from harm caused by defects on the owners' or occupiers' land). The duty analysis in these cases, therefore, is deeply rooted in the law of property and, to a lesser degree, in the law of contracts.

C. Owners

A discussion of the various liabilities that can attach to common players in construction projects should begin with the owner. The archetypal owner is the fee holder who has hired an independent contractor to build or improve a structure on the owner's property. As a general rule, the owner is not responsible for the safety of the independent contractors or for their employees, unless the owner actually hurts them,[34] or retains or exercises control of the contractor's work. This law, founded on the law of property, is enshrined in section 414 of the Restatement of Torts (Second).[35]

Whether the owner has retained sufficient control over the independent contractor to charge the owner with responsibility for the safety of such independent contractor's employees is determined initially by reference to the general contract. Many general contracts, and all AIA and EJCDC form contracts, explicitly state that the prime contractor is solely responsible for the manner, method, and means of construction, and that safety is the obligation of the

---

33. Such determination usually is dependent upon whether the contractor or subcontractor is an "insured" under the local workers' compensation scheme, either statutorily or as an "additional insured."

34. *See* "active negligence" cases at notes 30, 31–32, *supra*.

35. RESTATEMENT (SECOND) OF TORTS § 414 (1977) (Negligence in Exercising Control Retained by Employer: One who entrusts work to an independent contractor, but who retains the control of any part of the work, is subject to liability for physical harm to others for whose safety the employer owes a duty to exercise reasonable care, which is caused by his failure to exercise his control with reasonable care).

prime contractor, not the owner.³⁶ While the general contract may allow the owner some latitude in demanding that the prime contractor execute work safely, or abide by safety programs, these rights generally are insufficient to trigger a duty to the prime contractor's employees. Occasionally, however, the owner may retain so-called actual control of some aspect of the prime contractor's work sufficient to charge the owner with the duty of exercising such control responsibly.

Control of the work, however, is often a close question involving important policy issues, as the following case demonstrates:

Armenteros v. Baptist Hosp. of Miami, Inc.
714 So. 2d 518 (Fla. Dist. Ct. App. 1998)³⁷

Nesbitt, Judge.

Gregorio Armenteros was employed by a subcontractor hired by the general contractor building a structure on Baptist Hospital's grounds. Armenteros claimed that he was injured in a fall from defectively erected scaffolding, and sued the hospital asserting that Baptist had breached its duty of care by allowing an unsafe work condition to remain uncorrected on its premises. Baptist answered and moved for summary judgment on its affirmative defense that it owed no duty to a subcontractor's employee. Armenteros opposed summary judgment asserting that Baptist had retained the right to, and did exercise control over the day-to-day construction operations, hence, Baptist was liable as an owner/contractor. The court granted summary final judgment in Baptist's favor. We affirm.

Armenteros' accident occurred on a construction site at Baptist where a multistory addition was being added above an existing surgery center building.... Throughout the course of the project, Baptist continued to operate its hospital and to provide medical and surgical care to its patients.... To ensure the safety of these patients, the construction schedule had to be sensitive to ongoing hospital activities and the goal of maintaining quality patient care.

To this end, the construction contract stated that construction workers were limited to certain entrances and exits so that the hospital could avoid widespread contamination by construction debris and dirt. Similarly, ... Baptist retained the right to stop work temporarily if the construction was interfering with surgical procedures....

Centex-Rodgers Construction Company was hired to perform a variety of functions, including control of the construction management.... [A] construction contract was signed ... between Baptist Hospital and Centex-Rodgers that specifically identified Baptist as the owner and Centex-Rodgers as the general contractor....

---

36. AIA Document A201–2017, *supra* note 23, § 3.3; EJCDC, Standard General Conditions of the Construction Contract, *supra* note 23, ¶ 7.13.

37. Internal citations and footnotes omitted.

One of the Centex-Rodgers' employees had overall responsibility to oversee all day-to-day construction activities; including overseeing all subcontractors and ensuring that they were doing their work properly and conforming [to] the contract documents and specifications.

Armenteros was injured while in the course of his employment for General Forming Corporation, a subcontractor who was responsible for certain concrete work on the project. General Forming, like all of the successful bidders/subcontractors, had its contract with Centex-Rodgers and not with Baptist.

As a general rule, one who hires an independent contractor is not liable for injuries sustained by that contractor's employees in their work. As the Supreme Court [of Florida] observed:

> [T]he owner may be held liable if he has been actively participating in the construction to the extent that he directly influences the manner in which the work is performed. Conversely, if the owner is a passive nonparticipant, exercising no direct control over the project, he cannot be held liable. To impose liability upon an owner who is not an employer as defined by the statute, one or more specific identifiable acts of negligence, i.e., acts either negligently creating or negligently approving the dangerous condition resulting in the injury or death to the employee, must be established.

Thus, Florida case law has followed the analysis outlined in Restatement (Second) of Torts section 414, which provides:

> One who entrusts work to an independent contractor, but who retains the control of any part of the work, is subject to liability for physical harm to others for whose safety the employer owes a duty to exercise reasonable care, which is caused by his failure to exercise his control with reasonable care.

...

Appellants' contention is that sufficient testimony was given to make it a jury question whether Baptist had exercised enough control to be considered to have actively supervised and directed the project. However the undisputed facts demonstrate that the hospital did no more than purchase materials to utilize its tax free status, inspect the work to ensure the high standards it sought to maintain, and control schedules so as to permit surgeries to go uninterrupted and patients to go unendangered. Such limited acts, even when grouped together, will not constitute the control element necessary for a finding of liability.

Just because an owner has the right to inspect work for conformance with the contract does not change the owner from a passive nonparticipant to an active participant in the construction with the right to supervise or control the work, nor does it destroy the independent status of the contractor and render the owner liable for the contractor's negligence in performing the work by creating a dangerous condition.

> Comment c to RESTATEMENT (SECOND) OF TORTS section 414 supports this analysis and provides:
>
>> c. In order for the rule stated in this Section to apply, the employer must have retained at least some degree of control over the manner in which the work is done. It is not enough that he has merely a general right to order the work stopped or resumed, to inspect its progress or to receive reports, to make suggestions or recommendations, which need not necessarily be followed, or to prescribe alterations and deviations. Such a general right is usually reserved to employers, but it does not mean that the contractor is controlled as to his methods of work, or as to operative detail. There must be such retention of a right of supervision that the contractor is not entirely free to do the work in his own way.
>
> The cases relied on by appellant address scenarios where the owner exercised control over day-to-day work performance. While Baptist admitted interfering with scheduling, there was no evidence that the hospital interfered with the project's actual physical construction. There is no evidence that it was supervising the project. Nor was evidence submitted to refute Baptist's contention that it completely delegated all safety inspection tasks.
>
> Comment c, reproduced above, is directly applicable to the instant question and supports our conclusion that liability should not be imposed merely because Baptist reserved the right to inspect the work, established time schedules, or used its tax exemption status to purchase materials. A hospital/owner should not be exposed to liability merely based on its efforts to insure the safety of its patients.
>
> Reviewing cases across the country considering this issue, the deciding question is who exercised control of the work, and thus was in the position to prevent the harm [that] occurred. . . . [T]he linchpin to a determination of an owner's liability for physical harm to others under the facts alleged is control of the methods of work and operative details. An owner could perform a number of activities and still not expose himself to liability, if the activities were not directed at manner and method of work. . . .
>
> Accordingly, the order under review is affirmed.

The Restatement also cites a number of other conditions under which an injured party may avoid an owner's independent-contractor defense, notably including (among others):

- ❐ Negligent direction ("instruction") of the independent contractor's work;[38]

---

38. RESTATEMENT (SECOND) OF TORTS § 410 (1977).

- Negligence in selecting the contractor;[39]
- Failure to inspect the contractor's work after completion;[40]
- An owner's failure to provide for precautions against "peculiar risks";[41]
- Negligently exercising retained control of the contractor;[42]
- An owner's duty to avoid dangers to those outside the owner's property;[43]
- The duty to supervise contractors and "concessionaires" who attract members of the public onto the property;[44]
- Failure to use care in selecting a contractor when "special hazards" are known to exist;[45]
- Work performed in a public place;[46]
- Maintenance of highways and other public places;[47] and
- Repairs that a lessor has a duty to undertake[48] or gratuitously does undertake.[49]

D. Prime Contractors

At early common law, a prime contractor generally had no responsibility for the safety of its subcontractors' employees.[50] Relying on principles of property law, however, courts imposed liability in egregious cases of prime contractor negligence by creating a legal fiction equating a contractor with an owner.

In this way, the prime contractor could be treated as an "occupier" of property who had a qualified duty under premises liability law to protect others from harm. Prime contractors, therefore, could be liable to the employees of their independent subcontractors if those prime contractors retained control over the work and, by extension, control over the property.[51] Since a prime

---

39. *Id.* § 411.
40. *Id.* § 412.
41. *Id.* § 413.
42. *Id.* § 414.
43. *Id.* § 414A.
44. *Id.* § 415.
45. *Id.* § 416.
46. *Id.* § 417.
47. *Id.* § 418.
48. *Id.* § 419
49. *Id.* § 420.
50. PROSSER AND KEETON ON TORTS § 80 at 569 (W. Page Keeton, Dan B. Dobbs, Robert E. Keeton & David G. Owen eds., West 5th ed. 1984).
51. RESTATEMENT (SECOND) OF TORTS § 414 (1977) (Negligence In Exercising Control Retained By Employer: One who entrusts work to an independent contractor, but who retains the control

contractor is usually much closer to the work than the owner, the amount of control the prime contractor can retain is also much greater. Not surprisingly, close questions of retained control arise more often in actions against prime contractors than in actions against owners.

In resolving the question of control of the work, the starting place is the contract. Curiously, many courts look at this through the prism of the subcontract, rather than the general contract. The subcontract is usually replete with language assigning responsibility for safety to the subcontractor, with the prime contractor retaining the right to insist that the subcontractor perform safely and, in many subcontracts, in accordance with the prime contractor's safety program.

Although these subcontracts attempt to absolve the prime contractor of responsibility for unsafe conditions, the prime contractor can nevertheless be found to have exercised so-called actual control over the jobsite and incur liability for negligence in exercising that actual control. Actual control is a separate inquiry from the contractual right to control, though courts often fuse the two. A Texas case illustrates the interplay of these two intersecting routes in establishing liability.

Lee Lewis Constr., Inc. v. Harrison
70 S.W.3d 778 (Tex. 2001)[52]

Justice HANKINSON delivered the opinion of the Court.

Lubbock's Methodist Hospital hired LLC [Lee Lewis Construction] to remodel the eighth floor of, and add ninth and tenth floors to, its south hospital tower. As the general contractor, LLC then subcontracted the project's interior glass-glazing work to KK Glass. Jimmy Harrison was an employee of KK Glass. Harrison was installing thermal insulation and caulking between the window frames on the tower's tenth floor when he fell and suffered fatal injuries. Although no one witnessed Harrison's fall, the evidence is undisputed that Harrison was not using an independent lifeline that would have stopped his fall.

...

Our review of the evidence concerning negligence begins with duty. The parties agree that the duty in this case is governed by our well-established law concerning a general contractor's duties to a subcontractor's employees. Ordinarily, a

---

of any part of the work, is subject to liability for physical harm to others for whose safety the employer owes a duty to exercise reasonable care, which is caused by his failure to exercise his control with reasonable care); for exhaustive discussion of this topic, see CONSTRUCTION ACCIDENT LAW, *supra* note 3, at 55–217.

52. Internal citations, footnotes, parts of the factual and procedural history, and discussions of proximate cause, gross negligence, and the jury charge have been omitted.

general contractor does not owe a duty to ensure that an independent contractor performs its work in a safe manner. A duty does arise, however, if the general contractor retains some control over the manner in which the independent contractor performs its work. The general contractor's duty of care is commensurate with the control it retains over the independent contractor's work. . . .

A general contractor can retain the right to control so as to give rise to a duty of care in two ways: by contract or by actual exercise of control. We have frequently used the phrases "right of control" or "retained control" interchangeably. The distinction remains important, however, because determining what a contract says is generally a question of law for the court, while determining whether someone exercised actual control is a [sic] generally a question of fact for the jury.

Here, the trial court asked the jury, "Did LLC retain the right to control safety" on the jobsite. . . . LLC argues there is no evidence that it exercised any actual control over KK Glass employees' use of fall-protection equipment. . . . The Harrisons respond that LLC observed and expressly approved of KK Glass employees using faulty fall-protection equipment, including using a bosun's chair without an independent lifeline.

The evidence at trial supports the Harrisons' contention. At trial, Lee Lewis, LLC's owner and president, testified that he assigned to C. L. Lewis, LLC's job superintendent, "the responsibility to routinely inspect the ninth and tenth floor addition to the south tower to see to it that the subcontractors and their employees properly utilized fall protection equipment." Testimony indicated that C. L. Lewis personally witnessed and approved of the specific fall-protections systems KK Glass used. There was testimony that C. L. Lewis "definitely did approve" the lanyard system. There was also testimony that C. L. Lewis knew of and did not object to KK Glass employees using a bosun's chair without an independent lifeline. Although our law makes clear that a general contractor is not an insurer of safety on the jobsite, we agree with the Harrisons that the testimony highlighted above constitutes more than a scintilla of evidence that LLC retained the right to control fall-protection systems on the jobsite. LLC therefore had a duty of care toward Harrison commensurate with that right. Because we conclude that LLC retained the right to control fall-protection systems on the jobsite, we need not address its argument that it did not retain the right to control by contract.

. . . .

Because the evidence of LLC's negligence and gross negligence was legally sufficient to support the jury's verdict, and because any error in the charge submitted was harmless, we affirm the court of appeals' judgment.

Justice JEFFERSON, concurring.

I concur in the Court's judgment. I agree that the evidence supports liability here, but not for the reasons stated by the Court. LLC's approval of the ineffective fall-protection system is not "actual control" as defined by this Court [previously]. [L]iability must be based on more than mere acquiescence or approval. I would affirm the judgment on the ground that LLC had a contractual right to compel compliance with safety standards, actually witnessed repeated and flagrant safety

> violations, and approved those repeated violations even as it enforced its own standards for its own employees.
>
> ...
>
> ... LLC unquestionably retained a contractual right to enforce safety requirements. Although the Court concludes it need not reach the issue of control by contract, I believe the question of LLC's contractual right to control must be addressed.
>
> A general contractor's promulgation and enforcement of basic safety measures should not be sufficient, in itself, to impose liability for injuries to subcontractors' employees. Our tort system should not penalize a general contractor for insisting on compliance with basic safety standards.... Similarly, suggesting, or even requiring, that a subcontractor meet minimal safety requirements should not amount to the sort of "control" sufficient to hold a general contractor liable for injuries to subcontractors' employees.
>
> A different question is presented when the general contractor, who has contractual responsibility for general safety measures, permits its subcontractors to deviate routinely from the most elemental safety precautions. "[A]n employer who is aware that its contractor routinely ignores applicable federal guidelines and standard company policies related to safety may owe a duty to require corrective measures to be taken or to cancel the contract." I would affirm the judgment on this basis.
>
> ...
>
> LLC is liable not merely because it adopted a general safety program or possessed a contractual right to expel subcontractors who routinely flout general safety standards, but also because LLC endorsed KK Glass's repeated use of an obviously hazardous activity.

Lee Lewis is an exceptional case because of the concurring opinion's focus on the general contract. As noted earlier, courts tend to look at the subcontract to determine the extent of the prime contractor's control over the workplace, and to ignore the prime contract even though the AIA and general conditions initially place the responsibility for site safety on the prime contractor.[53] By contrast, the OSHA regulations go so far as to say that the duty for worker safety is a duty that cannot be contracted away:

> (a) The prime contractor and any subcontractors may make their own arrangements with respect to obligations which might be more appropriately treated on a jobsite basis rather than individually. Thus, for example, the prime contractor and his subcontractors may wish to make an express agreement that the prime contractor or one of the subcontractors will provide all required

---

53. AIA Document A201–2017, *supra* note 23, art. 10; EJCDC, STANDARD GENERAL CONDITIONS OF THE CONSTRUCTION CONTRACT, *supra* note 23, ¶ 6.13 (2002 ed.).

first-aid or toilet facilities, thus relieving the subcontractors from the actual, but not any legal, responsibility (or, as the case may be, relieving the other subcontractors from this responsibility). In no case shall the prime contractor be relieved of overall responsibility for compliance with the requirements of this part [of the OSH Act] for all work to be performed under the contract.

(b) By contracting for full performance of a contract subject to section 107 of the Act, the prime contractor assumes all obligations prescribed as employer obligations under the standards contained in this part, whether or not he subcontracts any part of the work.[54]

The terms of the prime contract generally only come into issue when someone other than the worker sues the prime. For example, when a claim is made against an owner or a design professional, the owner or design professional may cross-plead against the prime contractor based on the terms of the prime contract.[55]

E. Architects and Engineers

Occasionally, an accident involving a worker occurs because of a design error. In such a case, liability is premised on claims of professional malpractice, and modern courts have not hesitated to find a duty of care that extends to the worker where the design professional has failed to meet the professional standard of care; has contractually assumed responsibility for temporary safety precautions or for the direction of the work;[56] or has a statutorily imposed duty to ensure worker safety.[57]

The most common type of case, however, seeks to impose a duty on the architect or engineer because of its responsibilities during the contract administration phase of the project. The extent of the architect's or engineer's duty to the workers is usually determined by reference to responsibilities imposed contractually on the architect or engineer. The contracts written by design professional organizations generally disclaim any responsibility on the design professionals' part—usually with some success, as the following case demonstrates.

---

54. 29 C.F.R. § 1926.16(a); *see also* 29 C.F.R. § 1926.20 (establishing that under even minimum standards, the prime or controlling contractor is responsible for ensuring OSHA compliance).

55. *See, e.g.*, Secord v. Willow Ridge Stables, Inc., 690 N.Y.S.2d 375 (N.Y. App. Div. 1999, mem. op.).

56. *See* Miller v. DeWitt, 226 N.E.2d 630, 639 (Ill. 1967).

57. For example, the Illinois Structural Work Act has a broad application to all persons "having charge" of the work, which has been found to include design professionals. *See* Emberton v. State Farm Mut. Auto. Ins. Co., 373 N.E.2d 1348 (Ill. 1978).

Peck v. Horrocks Eng'rs, Inc.
106 F.3d 949 (10th Cir. 1997)[58]

EBEL, Circuit Judge.

Appellant Mary Peck ("Peck") appeals the district court's grant of summary judgment in favor of Appellee Horrocks Engineering ("Horrocks") in a wrongful death case concerning the death of her son, Zachery Peck ("Zachery").... We AFFIRM the judgment of the district court.

Zachery Peck was killed... when a trench wall collapsed on him during the construction of a culinary water system [for] the City of Talmage, Utah.... Zachery was an employee of K & P Plumbing ("K & P"), a contractor that had been selected by the [Water District] to install the pipeline on the project. Horrocks is an engineering firm, which had been hired by the Water District to design and inspect the construction and progress of the project.

.... On the day of the collapse, the trench reached a depth of eight feet to allow the pipe to be laid underneath a steel culvert that crossed the path of the pipeline. An employee of Horrocks was involved in the decision to lay the pipe under the culvert, as opposed to over it. Zachery was laying pipe when the trench collapsed... and he was killed. In violation of OSHA regulations, the trench was neither sloped nor shored [with support beams].

Following the accident, Peck sued Horrocks and the Water District for wrongful death. [The District Court granted summary judgment in favor of Horrocks.] Peck appeals.... We review the grant of summary judgment de novo....

II. ENGINEER LIABILITY

Before Horrocks can be held liable, Peck must establish that Horrocks owed a duty of care to Zachery. Whether a duty of care exists is a question of law.... Only after it has been determined that a duty of care exists can a jury determine whether that duty was breached.

As a general rule, an engineer with construction inspection responsibility owes no duty to an independent contractor's employees. Nonetheless, an engineer may acquire a duty of care toward an independent contractor's employees by contractually assuming a duty to maintain safety, and several courts in other states have also ruled that a duty may be created by the engineer exercising control over worker safety issues at the job site.

...

A. Contractual Assumption of Duty

...

Peck points to two provisions of the Engineering Agreement to support his claim that Horrocks assumed a duty to maintain worker safety. First, Horrocks agreed to "physically oversee... the work... to determine that the work performed [was] in accordance with the plans and specifications." Because the plans and specifications

---

58. Internal citations, footnotes, and discussion of choice-of-law rules have been omitted.

included the requirement that K & P abide by Utah OSHA excavation standards, Peck argues that Horrocks contractually agreed to assume responsibility for the supervision of safety compliance. Second, the Engineering Agreement provides that Horrocks "will comply with and assist the owner to require all contractors . . . [to] comply with all applicable Federal, State and Local laws."

. . .

Horrocks replies that any effort by Peck to infer a duty . . . is foreclosed by Horrocks' express disavowal of any responsibility to maintain safety in both the Engineering Agreement and the Construction Contract. [T]he Engineering Agreement provides that "[Horrocks] shall not be responsible for construction means, methods, techniques, sequences or procedures, or for safety precautions and programs in connection with the work." This same provision is also found in . . . the Construction Contract. Moreover, the Construction Contract expressly allocates responsibility for safety to K & P by providing that "[K & P] will be responsible for initiating, maintaining and supervising all safety precautions and programs in connection with the Work. . . ."

There is a split of authority regarding whether an engineer who contractually assumes responsibility . . . for general supervision of a construction project thereby assumes a duty of care to supervise the safety of employees of the general contractor. . . . The minority rule imposes upon a supervising engineer a duty of care, on the logic that an "[engineer's] contractual duties of supervising work include . . . a duty to ensure that the work was performed safely." The majority rule denies contractual liability, finding that:

[a]n architect, or other design professional, who contracts with an owner of property for the preparation of plans and specifications for the erection of a building and who agrees to be responsible for the general administration of the construction contract between the owner and the general contractor is not contractually responsible for the safety of the workmen on the job site unless such duty is specifically assumed in the contract.

[The Utah Supreme Court follows the majority rule, thus, we determine that, under Utah law, Horrocks' contractual assumption of general supervisory duties did not include an assumption of a duty to maintain safety for K & P's employees.]

B. Implied Assumption of Duty

Several courts in states other than Utah have held that even where an engineer has assumed no contractual liability for safety, the engineer may expand its liability beyond the specific provisions of the employment contract through certain acts of control at the job site. This follows the general rule of torts that "one who undertakes to render services has a duty to exercise reasonable care." That doctrine has no applicability here, even if Utah were to adopt it, because Horrocks expressly declined to undertake responsibility for worker safety on this project and there was no evidence that Horrocks in fact assumed control at the job site over issues of worker safety.

> Peck argues that Horrocks assumed a duty to maintain safety precautions on the day of the accident because it was consulted about whether the trench that collapsed on Zachery should be dug underneath an interfering steel culvert. We disagree. . . . Horrocks played no role in the actual construction of the ditch [and the Utah Supreme Court] makes clear that a supervising engineer's participation in a strategic construction decision does not obligate it to ensure that all safety precautions are complied with in the implementation of that decision. . . .
>
> Peck [also] argues that liability may be predicated upon the simple fact that Horrocks, as an engineer, had actual knowledge of a safety problem and failed to take steps to correct that problem. Although this doctrine has some limited support in other states, we do not believe Utah would impose a duty on an engineer on the basis of knowledge and inaction alone. . . . In any event, the record here is devoid of any evidence that Horrocks knew in advance of the accident that the seven foot deep trench was neither sloped nor shored, or even that a worker would be standing in the bottom of the trench.
>
> . . .
>
> **CONCLUSION**
>
> Because Peck has failed to raise a genuine issue of material fact as to whether Horrocks breached any duty of care owed her son, Zachery, and because the district court did not abuse its discretion in disregarding Radford's affidavit as conclusory, we AFFIRM the district court's dismissal of Peck's claim for wrongful death.

The AIA and EJCDC form contracts provide even more protection for design professionals than the clause interpreted in *Peck v. Horrocks*,[59] and, indeed, the decisions imposing liability on architects or engineers for failing

---

59. AIA Document A201-2017, *supra* note 23, § 4.2.2 ("The Architect, will visit the site at intervals appropriate to the stage of construction . . . [T]he Architect will not be required to make exhaustive or continuous on-site inspections to check the quality or quantity of the work. The Architect will not have control over, charge of, or responsibility for the construction means, methods, techniques, sequences or procedures, or for the safety precautions and programs in connection with the Work, since these are solely the Contractor's rights and responsibilities under the Contract Documents. . . ."); § 4.2.6 ("The Architect has authority to reject Work that does not conform to the Contract Documents. . . . However, neither this authority of the Architect nor a decision made in good faith either to exercise or not to exercise such authority shall give rise to a duty or responsibility of the Architect to the Contractor, Subcontractors, suppliers, their agents or employees, or other persons or entities performing portions of the Work); § 10.1 ("The Contractor shall be responsible for initiating, maintaining, and supervising all safety precautions and programs in connection with the performance of the Contract.").

to protect workers are rare.[60] This does not, however, deter injured claimants' counsel from casting a wide net in their selection of defendants.[61]

13.04 RISK ALLOCATION AND TRANSFER

A. Risk Allocation and Transfer, Generally

Risk allocation, insurance, and indemnity issues, although conceptually separate, are often inseparable in practical application.[62]

Under negligence theories, those participants held to have a duty to the injured worker typically have their liability decided under comparative negligence principles; that is, their negligence is weighed against that of the other participants, including the plaintiff. This effects a rough allocation of the risks, assuming all of the alleged culprits are financially responsible; however, solvency of all parties cannot be assumed. Construction litigation often involves parties that are uninsured, underinsured, on the edge of insolvency, or protected by sovereign immunity, any of which can transfer risk to the other parties, depending on the particular state's comparative negligence and joint liability statutes and jurisprudence.

B. Insurance

Many participants in the construction process are thinly capitalized and lack the financial wherewithal to shoulder the liability for a catastrophic injury. Consequently, many (but not all) purchase liability insurance in varying amounts to defray the risks and pay premiums based on the degree of risk they encounter. Most commercial contracts for construction require the purchase of insurance by all the participants and provide that proof of insurance be furnished prior to commencement of the prime contractor's or subcontractor's work.[63]

Additionally, industry standard contracts often require the other participants to name the owner and higher-level contractors as "additional insureds"

---

60. But such decisions are not unheard of: *see, e.g.*, Carvalho v. Toll Bros. & Developers, 675 A.2d 209 (N.J. 1996).

61. For an examination of whether an architect can be held responsible for personal injuries after a failure to detect *purely construction defects* during contract administration, as well as the potential dangers of including a 2007 AIA form's "endeavor to guard" language, *see* Black + Vernooy Architects v. Smith, 346 S.W.3d 877 (Tex. App.—Austin 2011).

62. They are treated at greater length in Chapter 18. *See also* CONSTRUCTION ACCIDENT LAW, *supra* note 3.

63. AIA Document A201-2017, *supra* note 23, § 11.1.

under the participants' liability policies. When this coverage is provided, the risk is borne by the first-tier and lower-tier subcontractors' insurance carriers, who are forced to build the risk into the rate structure for the contractual liability endorsements of their commercial general liability policies. This effects a transfer of the risk from the sophisticated owner or prime contractor to the subcontractors and their insurance carriers.

C. Indemnity

Recognizing the vagaries of the tort system, including the uncertain results in a retained control dispute, many owners and contractors use their contracts to allocate the risks of liability from construction accidents. This often is done through indemnification clauses, which attempt to transfer to the employer—usually a subcontractor—even the risk of the owner's or contractor's own negligence. The perceived unfairness of these clauses has caused the courts to take a very dim view of them, especially if the language is sophistic and the clause buried in boilerplate language. The following case is typical.

Hagerman Constr. Corp. v. Long Elec. Co.
741 N.E.2d 390 (Ind. Ct. App. 2000)[64]

HOFFMAN, Senior Judge

Third Party Plaintiff-Appellant Hagerman Construction Corp. (Hagerman) appeals the trial court's denial of its motion for summary judgment. We affirm in part and reverse in part.

...

Hagerman was the general contractor on a construction project on the campus of Indiana University-Purdue University in Fort Wayne. Long Electric Company (Long) was a subcontractor on the project, and James Scott (Scott) was an employee of Long. In September 1997, Scott was injured when he was struck on the head by a falling light pole. Scott made a claim for workers' compensation benefits and then filed suit against Hagerman. Hagerman subsequently filed a third party action against Long based upon an indemnity clause contained in the form contract between Hagerman and Long. Hagerman filed a motion for summary judgment requesting the court to find that, pursuant to the parties' contract, Long was required to indemnify Hagerman for any losses Hagerman suffered in the Scott litigation. The trial court denied Hagerman's motion and found that Hagerman was not entitled to indemnification by Long for Hagerman's negligence. This appeal ensued.

...

---

64. Internal citations, discussion of summary judgment standards, and expanded discussion of precedent have been omitted.

Hagerman contends that the trial court erred in denying its motion for summary judgment. Although the parties agree that if Hagerman is solely responsible for Scott's injuries, there should be no indemnification by Long, Hagerman asserts that, based upon the indemnity clause in the parties' contract, Long is required to indemnify Hagerman for Hagerman's own negligence if Long is also at fault. Alternatively, Hagerman claims that even if the contract does not require Long to indemnify Hagerman for Hagerman's negligence, Long is liable to indemnify Hagerman for Long's own negligence.

Absent prohibitive legislation, no public policy prevents parties from contracting as they desire. For instance, in Indiana a party may contract to indemnify another for the other's own negligence. However, this may only be done if the party knowingly and willingly agrees to such indemnification. Such provisions are strictly construed and will not be held to provide indemnification unless it is so stated in clear and unequivocal terms. We disfavor indemnity clauses because we are mindful that to obligate one party to pay for the negligence of another is a harsh burden that a party would not lightly accept.

This Court has followed a two-step analysis to determine whether a party has knowingly and willingly accepted this burden. First, the indemnification clause must expressly state in clear and unequivocal terms that negligence is an area of application where the indemnitor (in this case, Long) has agreed to indemnify the indemnitee (in this case, Hagerman). The second step determines to whom the indemnification clause applies. Again, in clear and unequivocal terms, the clause must state that it applies to indemnification of the indemnitee (in this case, Hagerman) by the indemnitor (in this case, Long) for the indemnitee's own negligence.

In the present case, the indemnification clause used by the parties was taken from a form agreement drafted by the American Institute of Architects and entitled "AIA Document A401, Standard Form of Agreement Between Contractor and Subcontractor, 1987 Edition." The clause provides as follows:

4.6 INDEMNIFICATION

4.6.1 To the fullest extent permitted by law, the Subcontractor shall indemnify and hold harmless the Owner, Contractor, Architect, Architect's consultants, and agents and employees or any of them from and against claims, damages, losses and expenses, including but not limited to attorney's fees, arising out of or resulting from performance of the Subcontractor's Work under this Subcontract, provided that such claim, damage, loss or expense is attributable to bodily injury, sickness, disease or death, or to injury to or destruction of tangible property (other than the Work itself) including loss of use resulting therefrom, but only to the extent caused in whole or in part by negligent acts or omissions of the Subcontractor, the Subcontractor's Sub-subcontractors, anyone directly or indirectly employed by them or anyone for whose acts they may be liable, regardless of whether or not such claim, damage, loss or expense is caused in part by a party indemnified hereunder. Such obligation shall not be construed to negate, abridge, or otherwise reduce other rights or obligations of indemnity which would otherwise exist as to a party or person described in this Paragraph 4.6.

Applying the two-step test set out above, we first note that this indemnification clause expressly defines negligence as an area of application in clear and unequivocal terms. The clause speaks of claims, damages, losses and expenses attributable to bodily injury, sickness, disease or death, and injury to or destruction of property, as well as negligent acts or omissions. These words, taken in this context, are the language of negligence, and, as such, clearly and unequivocally demonstrate that the indemnification clause applies to negligence.

Next, we must determine whether the indemnification clause also expressly states, in clear and unequivocal terms, that it applies to indemnify Hagerman for its own negligence. We conclude that it does not.

...

Similar to our discussion above, ... Long asserts that the phrase "but only to the extent caused in whole or in part by negligent acts or omissions of the Subcontractor..." limits the scope of the liability to only those losses that are caused by the negligence of the sub-contractor or its agents. Hagerman, on the other hand, avers that Long's interpretation of the clause would be inconsistent with other language in the provision that provides for indemnity "to the fullest extent permitted by the law" and "regardless of whether or not such claim, damage, loss or expense is caused in part by a party indemnified hereunder."

We conclude that the indemnification clause does not expressly state, in clear and unequivocal terms, that it applies to indemnify Hagerman for its own negligence. The clause explicitly indemnifies Hagerman for the acts of the sub-contractor, Long, and its sub-subcontractors, employees and anyone for whom it may be liable, but it does not explicitly state that Long must indemnify Hagerman for its own negligent acts. Further, the phrase "but only to the extent" clearly limits Long's obligation to indemnify Hagerman only to the extent that Long, its sub-subcontractors, employees, and anyone for whom it may be liable are negligent. Otherwise, the clause contains no clear statement that would give the contractors notice of the harsh burden that complete indemnification would impose.

...

Based upon the foregoing, we conclude that the trial court properly denied Hagerman's motion for summary judgment as to Long's obligation to indemnify Hagerman for Hagerman's own negligence. However, the trial court erred in denying Hagerman's motion as to Long's obligation to indemnify Hagerman for Long's negligence.

Accordingly, we affirm in part and reverse in part.

As this case shows, the AIA takes a middle-of-the-road approach and attempts to impose comparative indemnity; that is, the indemnitor only agrees to indemnify for its own negligence.[65]

---

65. AIA Document A201–2017, *supra* note 23, § 3.18.

The arbitrary inclusion of the indemnity clauses in adhesion contracts has led to some statutory limits on their use. In some states, architects and engineers may not be allowed to obtain indemnification from their own negligence. In Texas, for example, a design professional cannot seek indemnity from a contractor for defects in the design work.[66] This is a logical extension of Texas laws regarding professional licensure[67] of engineers and the sealing of design documents,[68] which has the stated goal of being able to "fix responsibility for work done or services or acts performed in the practice of engineering."[69]

In other states, the same indemnity prohibition applies to owners and contractors. In New York, it is against public policy for an owner or contractor to bargain for indemnity from its own negligence.[70] Various states' legislatures and courts have chosen to prohibit "risk-shifting" indemnity provisions altogether, or categorize the types or levels of indemnity and condition indemnification on certain notice or disclosure requirements.

D. Assumption of the Risk and Contributory Negligence by the Injured Party

Finally, risk or blame also can be allocated to the injured worker. This is usually argued through the common-law assumption-of-the-risk doctrine,[71] or contributory negligence assigned to the plaintiff, which can function as a form of comparative negligence and, when appropriate, allows for a judgment to

---

66. TEX. CIV. PRAC. & REM. CODE ANN. §§ 130.001 & 130.002 (Vernon 2002) ((a) A covenant or promise, in connection with, or collateral to a construction contract is void and unenforceable if the covenant or promise provides for a contractor who is to perform the work that is the subject of the construction contract to indemnify or hold harmless a registered architect, licensed engineer or an agent, servant, or employee of a registered architect or licensed engineer from liability for damage that: (1) is caused by or results from: (A) defects in plans, designs, or specifications prepared, approved, or used by the architect or engineer; or (B) negligence of the architect or engineer in the rendition or conduct of professional duties called for or arising out of the construction contract and the plans, designs, or specifications that are a part of the construction contract; and (2) arises from: (A) personal injury or death; (B) property injury; or (C) any other expense that arises from personal injury, death, or property injury).

67. TEX. OCCUPATIONS CODE § 1001.301.

68. *Id.* § 1001.401.

69. *Id.* § 1001.004.

70. N.Y. GEN. OBLIG. LAW § 5-322.1 (McKinney 2001). See JUSTIN SWEET AND MARC M. SCHNEIER, LEGAL ASPECTS OF ARCHITECTURE, ENGINEERING AND THE CONSTRUCTION PROCESS § 31.05(D) (Thompson 7th ed. 2004), for a discussion of the historical background of anti-indemnity statutes, generally.

71. For a history of the assumption-of-the-risk doctrine, see CONSTRUCTION ACCIDENT LAW, *supra* note 3, at 17–19, 211–12.

be reduced by the percentage of the plaintiff's fault in the accident.[72] A small group of states, together with the District of Columbia, apply the ruthless pure contributory negligence rule, under which a plaintiff who proximately causes her own injury (or who simply plays any contributory role) is prohibited from recovering any damages whatsoever. A handful of states follow a pure comparative fault system, under which the proportion of the plaintiff's own contributory negligence is the basis for reducing any recovery against the defendants. More than half of the states currently follow a modified comparative fault rule, under which a plaintiff who is 50 percent or 51 percent responsible for the accident in question may not recover any damages whatsoever.[73]

E. Workers' Compensation's Effect on Indemnity and Contribution in Third-Party Actions

If a worker's injury is caused by the combined negligence of his employer and a third party, such as a contractor or design professional, then the worker is entitled to receive workers' compensation benefits from its employer, *and* to pursue tort claims against the third party. Inevitably, the third party will seek to defray its responsibility by shifting the risk back to the employer who may be primarily liable. Under a pure tort standard, this is handled through comparative negligence (as discussed in Section 13.04(A)). Workers' compensation, however, often changes those dynamics; employers' liability is channeled through the workers' compensation system and is removed from the traditional tort claims process.

To protect the integrity of the workers' compensation scheme, many states do not allow an employer who has purchased workers' compensation to be pursued by other negligent parties for common law indemnity or contribution.[74] The general premise is that protection from common law remedies encourages employers to enroll in the workers' compensation system, and that an employer who has insured its workers under the compensation scheme should not have to pay twice. Worth noting, however, is that all the protections

---

72. *See generally* PROSSER AND KEETON ON TORTS § 67 (W. Page Keeton, Dan B. Dobbs, Robert E. Keeton & David G. Owen eds. West 5th ed. 1984).

73. For an excellent state-by-state review of the various contributory negligence standards, see Gary Wickert, *Contributory Negligence/Comparative Fault Laws in All 50 States*, https://www.mwl-law.com/wp-content/uploads/2013/03/contributory-negligence-comparative-fault-laws-in-all-50-states.pdf (last updated Feb. 14, 2018).

74. *See, e.g.*, A & B Constr., Inc. v. Atlas Roofing & Skylight Co., 867 F. Supp. 100 (D.R.I. 1994).

from common-law remedies asserted by third parties discussed in this section may be waived through contract, and often are.[75]

Indeed, this fact counsels parties to be careful in drafting to ensure that they do not bargain away the protection of workers' compensation statutes by agreeing to indemnify a party whose liability is not limited by those laws. In *Jacobs Engineering Group v. Conagra Foods, Inc.*,[76] Jacobs Engineering negotiated an agreement with ConAgra, the owner of a food manufacturing plant, for indemnification for any losses Jacobs suffered arising out of ConAgra's negligence. A catastrophic explosion at ConAgra's plant resulted in the deaths of three of its employees and serious injuries to several others. ConAgra's employees could not sue ConAgra directly in light of Nebraska's workers' compensation laws, but they sued Jacobs and ultimately recovered settlements totaling nearly $109 million. ConAgra argued that its immunity under the workers' compensation statute protected it from liability under the indemnification agreement, but the Nebraska Supreme Court disagreed, holding that the contractual indemnity did not incorporate the statutory immunity. In essence, the indemnity agreement wholly deprived ConAgra of the protection of workers' compensation laws.

13.05 CONCLUSION

The interplay of the law of torts, contract, insurance, procedure, and administrative law is nowhere more interesting or in more frequent collision than with construction safety law. The forceful exercise of political power by the various participants, in varying degrees, has affected the balance of power (and responsibility) among the participants. Modern technology and increasing project complexity leave general contractors facing the daunting challenge of understanding, and possibly controlling, their projects as dozens of specialty subcontractors perform their highly technical work. In the midst of all this, one constant remains: most of the financial risk of catastrophic accidents remains on the worker, who out of all the participants is least able to shoulder it.

---

75. For an in-depth discussion, *see* 2 BRUNER & O'CONNOR, *supra* note 2, § 5:88 (discussing the waiver of workers' compensation protection in standard construction contract forms).

76. 301 Neb. 38, 917 N.W. 2d 435 (Neb. 2018).

QUESTIONS

Plaintiff is an employee of a steel frame erection subcontractor and was fatally injured when the steel frame collapsed during construction. The vertical support beams of the frames were originally supposed to be secured by an "L" brace at the foundation, over which a concrete floor would be poured. Unfortunately, an overly eager concrete subcontractor poured in the concrete floor before all the beams were properly braced. The prime contractor discovered this error soon after it happened. Under time pressure from the owner, the prime contractor proposed to the architect that the unbraced vertical beams be secured by drilling holes in the concrete and hammering in sheared straight bolts (without the horizontal part of the "L"), which would allow the work to proceed without delay. After review, the architect approved the prime contractor's shop drawings; soon after, the sheared bolts were installed and reinforcing concrete was poured around the beams. The next day, as plaintiff climbed a beam secured in this manner, the beam fell. The beam would have held if it had been secured with an "L" brace, or if the concrete had been allowed several days to fully cure before stress was placed on the beam. The prime contractor, architect, and owner all used standard AIA contracts.[77]

1. Does the owner owe any duty to the plaintiff for putting time pressure on the prime contractor? What if the owner had approved the sheared bolt plan rather than the having the architect do it?
2. What determines if the prime contractor owes any duty to the plaintiff?
3. What determines if the architect owes any duty to the plaintiff?
4. What determines if the plaintiff's employer, the steel erection subcontractor, owes a duty to the plaintiff?
5. To what extent can OSHA rules establish the standard of care?
6. If the plaintiff's employer had purchased workers' compensation insurance, what effect would this have on the plaintiff's ability to pursue claims against other parties? What effect would it have on the allocation of liability between the potentially liable parties?
7. If the plaintiff sues the architect, will the architect be entitled to indemnification from the prime contractor, assuming the prime contractor had signed AIA Document A101 and the A201 General Conditions?
8. If the plaintiff had failed to use safety equipment provided on site by the employer, how would that affect the claim?

---

77. The facts in this scenario are based generally on Clemens v. Benzinger, 207 N.Y.S. 539 (1925).

CHAPTER 14

Changes

ALAN WINKLER

14.01 THE INEVITABILITY OF CHANGES

Contract terms dealing with changes to the work are just as important as provisions for critical concerns such as payment and time. This may seem surprising, since a changes clause only comes into play when at least one of the contracting parties contends that a deviation has occurred from the work as originally designed, specified, and contemplated. However, although the owner and the architect/engineer have progressed painstakingly through every phase of the design process—from concept/program development to schematic designs to design development to the issuance of the so-called final construction documents—every project of any significance and many minor projects will require changes to the work. These changes usually require amendments to the price and time of performance. The most common term for the vehicle effecting a mutually agreed amendment is a "change order." A rare project, indeed, would be one built without any change orders. By contrast, it is not unheard of to have dozens or even a hundred change orders issued on a medium-sized project, such as the construction of a school.

Changes can come from a variety of sources. The most obvious is a change in some aspect of the design of the project emanating from the owner's desire to have a finished product differing from that depicted in the drawings and specifications. An owner's desire to change the project, however, is by no means the sole source of changes, however. Changes can also emanate from errors or omissions in the plans, the necessity to deviate from the plans due to field conditions, cost savings suggested by the contractor, or the issuance of new government regulation.

14.02 THE PURPOSE OF A CHANGES CLAUSE

Changes can take three general forms: extra work, additional work, and deleted work. Although courts use the first two changes interchangeably at times, extra work and additional work are conceptually distinct. "Extra work" has been defined as "work arising outside of and independent of the contract; something not required in its performance."[1] An example would be the owner's request to add a room to a building. "Additional work" has been defined as work "necessarily required in the performance of the contract, but the necessity of which arises from unanticipated conditions."[2] An example would be excavating a site to an increased depth from the depth originally required due to the nature of the soil encountered. Despite these differing definitions, both can qualify under the general heading of "changes."[3] "Deleted work," as the name implies, is a diminution in the scope or amount of work required of the contractor.

Absent a changes clause, a claim for the performance of work outside of the requirements of a contract would be treated under the principles of quantum meruit (i.e., an implied contract).[4] A changes clause allows the claim to be treated as a matter of contractual entitlement, with the right of recovery dependent both on the eligibility of the claim under the definition in the provision and on the claimant's compliance with its terms.[5] In addition, because

---

1. Interstate Contracting Corp. v. City of Dallas, Texas, 407 F.3d 708, 712 (5th Cir. 2005).
2. Wisch & Vaughan Constr. Co. v. Melrose Properties, 21 S.W. 3d 36, 40 (Mo. App. S.D. 2000).
3. Courts use the terms "additional work" and "extra work" interchangeably. *See, e.g.*, Dave Kolb Grading, Inc. v. Terra Venture Bridgeton Project Joint Venture, 85 F.3d 351 (8th Cir. 1996); Miller Elevator Co. v. United States, 30 Fed. Cl. 662 (Fed. Cl. 1994). The distinction has also been questioned. *See* Buckley Co. v. City of New York, 505 N.Y.S.2d 140, 143 (N.Y. App. Div. 1986).
4. Fox v. Mountain West Elect., Inc., 52 P.3d 848 (Idaho 2002); Joseph Sternberg, Inc. v. Walber 36th Street Assoc., 594 N.Y.S.2d 144 (N.Y. App. Div. 1993).
5. When an express contract addresses work for which a claimant seeks remuneration, then a quantum meruit claim may be barred as a matter of law. Archon Constr. Co., Inc. v. U.S. Shelter, L.L.C., 78 N.E.3d 1067, 1076, 413 Ill. Dec. 791, 800, 2017 Ill. App (1st) 153409, ¶ 44 (Ill. Ct. App. 2017).

changes are anticipated in every construction contract, a changes clause sets out orderly rules through which an owner can pass changes without having the project held up by a contractor who refuses to consent to an amendment.

As discussed later in this chapter, changes can be either express or constructive. In short, an express change arises when the owner directs the contractor to perform the work in a manner differing from the contract requirements. A constructive change arises when the contractor performs work in a manner differing from the contract requirements without an express directive, but in order to overcome a difficulty that would otherwise impede construction of the project as designed.[6] A well-drafted changes clause regulates both express and constructive changes and defines the owner's right to make an express change. Such a clause also establishes the requirements for the documents memorializing the change. Additionally, it can set the parameters for the pricing of the change and state when billing can be submitted for performance of the change. Likewise, a changes clause can set the notice and documentation requirements for a constructive change claim, as well as the pricing structure for constructive changes.

Perhaps the most unique feature of a changes clause is that a changes clause can authorize one party, namely, the owner, to effect an amendment to a contract unilaterally.[7] Inasmuch as a construction contract is a bilateral agreement, any change in the terms would require the acceptance of both parties to its terms in the absence of a clause permitting unilateral amendment. Given the exigencies of construction, where a change must be implemented promptly in order not to delay the entire project, it is not always practical for the parties to negotiate a mutually acceptable amendment. A changes clause can allow an owner to amend the contract unilaterally by directing the contractor to perform changed work under a pricing formula or under an owner-imposed price, with the right to contest the price preserved.

Another important feature of a changes clause is the provision of a contractual mechanism for deleting work. The deletion of work is more problematic to price than the addition of work because the actual price of the work deleted may be difficult, if not impossible, to prove.[8] Additionally, absent a changes clause allowing for the deletion of work, a contractor could contend that the owner does not have the right to delete work unilaterally, and that any attempt to do so would constitute a breach. The changes clause not only allows

---

6. *See* Section 14.07 in this chapter.
7. *See* 1 Philip L. Bruner & Patrick J. O'Connor, Jr., Bruner & O'Connor on Construction Law § 4:2, at 502 (West 2002).
8. However, the changed work may impact the overall performance of the contract, thus implicating cost considerations beyond the price of the extra or additional work itself.

the owner the flexibility to delete work but also can provide a framework for determining the ensuing reduction in price.

Construction is not a perfect world. Changes are not always independent, since one element frequently has an impact on another. Therefore, changes can and do involve a combination of deleted work and added work. To take a simple example, an owner may decide to upgrade the specified windows. In that event, the owner would be due a credit for the originally specified windows, now deleted from the contract, but would be obligated to pay for the increased cost of the upgraded windows. The change order may have a single price, but it could only be arrived at by subtracting the price for the deduction from the price for the upgrade. Similarly, the change may have a ripple effect on other work, as when the change in windows may change the framing undertaken by the framing subcontractor. Thus a simple change may result in three change orders to document the work—a change order between the owner and the general, a change order between the general contractor and the window supplier, and a change order between the contractor and the framer.

14.03 THE CHANGE ORDER PROCESS

As noted, and in accordance with industry practice, we will call the document memorializing the owner's and the contractor's agreement to an amendment a "change order." Although contracts exists that employ other terms for this document, the term "change order" has become standard in the construction industry, both in the public sector and in the private sector. To give three examples, "change order" is the term utilized in federal contracting[9] and in two of the most commonly used form contracts[10] in the private sector.[11]

Section 7.2.1 of AIA Document A201–2017 defines a change order as follows:

Change Orders

A Change Order is a written instrument prepared by the Architect and signed by the Owner, Contractor and Architect, stating their agreement upon all of the following:

1. The change in the Work;

---

9. *See, e.g.*, Federal Acquisition Regulation (FAR) § 52.243-4 (the changes clause in fixed-price federal construction contracts).

10. *See* American Institute of Architects, AIA Document A201–2017, General Conditions of the Contract for Construction § 7.2 (2007) [hereinafter AIA Document A201–2017] and Associated General Contractors of America (AGC), Document No. 200 ¶ 8.1.

11. There is nothing preventing public entities, such as townships or school districts, from utilizing these form contracts, and some do.

2. The amount of the adjustment, if any, in the Contract Sum; and
3. The extent of the adjustment, if any, in the Contract Time.

Interestingly, although construction contracts (including the AIA forms cited) are typically bilateral agreements between the owner and the contractor, this AIA provision envisions a change order as a trilateral agreement among the owner, the architect, and the contractor.

Section 52.243-4 of the Federal Acquisition Regulation (FAR), on the other hand, envisions the change order as a unilateral directive from the owner (i.e., the government) to the contractor pertaining to the work itself, with the financial consequences to be addressed separately through an equitable adjustment, which modifies the contract price:

CHANGES

(a) The Contracting Officer may, at any time, without notice to the sureties, if any, by written order designated or indicated to be a change order, make changes in the work within the general scope of the contract, including changes—

(1) In the specifications (including drawings and designs);

(2) In the method or manner of performance of the work;

(3) In the Government-furnished facilities, equipment, materials, services, or site; or

(4) Directing acceleration in the performance of the work.

(b) Any other written or oral order (which, as used in this paragraph (b), includes direction, instruction, interpretation, or determination) from the Contracting Officer that causes a change shall be treated as a change order under this clause; provided, that the Contractor gives the Contracting Officer written notice stating—

(1) The date, circumstances, and source of the order; and

(2) That the Contractor regards the order as a change order.

(c) Except as provided in this clause, no order, statement, or conduct of the Contracting Officer shall be treated as a change under this clause or entitle the Contractor to an equitable adjustment.

(d) If any change under this clause causes an increase or decrease in the Contractor's cost of, or the time required for, the performance of any part of the work under this contract, whether or not changed by any such order, the Contracting Officer shall make an equitable adjustment and modify the contract in writing. However, except for an adjustment based on defective specifications, no adjustment for any change under paragraph (b) of this clause shall be made for any costs incurred more than 20 days before the Contractor gives written notice as required. In the case of defective specifications for which the Government is responsible, the equitable adjustment shall include any increased costs reasonably incurred by the Contractor in attempting to comply with the defective specifications.

(e) The Contractor must assert its right to an adjustment under this clause within 30 days after (1) receipt of a written change order under paragraph (a) of this clause, or (2) the furnishing of a written notice under paragraph (b) of this clause, by submitting to the Contracting Officer a written statement describing the general nature and amount of the proposal, unless this period is extended by the Government. The statement or proposal for adjustment may be included in the notice under paragraph (b) of this clause.

(f) No proposal by the Contractor for an equitable adjustment shall be allowed if asserted after final payment under this contract.

Immediately apparent from a comparison of these two changes clauses is that the AIA provision just quoted seemingly does not allow for the contract to be modified unilaterally, while the FAR provision seemingly does not effect a bilateral modification. The reason for this discrepancy is the disparity in philosophy underlying the two clauses.

AIA Document A201–2017, section 7.2, provides for the end product of the change order process: a fully agreed, written, signed modification defining the work, price, and effect on the schedule of the change. FAR section 52.243-4, on the other hand, sets forth how the change order process is initiated by a unilateral directive. Rarely will the government change order process start with an acknowledgment by the owner and the contractor (and possibly the architect) that a change is warranted or required. Rather, as the FAR section provides, the change order process will be initiated by either the owner directing a change or by the contractor claiming that an act or omission of the owner has necessitated the change.

Although the AIA Document A201–2017 contemplates changes to which the parties agree, it also makes provision for either the owner or the contractor to initiate a change even when a certain dispute arises over the change. The procedure under that AIA contract document for the owner to mandate a change unilaterally is through the issuance of a construction change directive.[12] Under that procedure, the architect and the owner issue a construction change directive setting forth how the work is to be changed, and the contractor must implement the change even in the absence of agreement as to the contractor's compensation or extension of time to complete the work.[13] If the parties negotiate and agree to a change order memorializing not only the modification to the scope of the work but also to the price and the time of performance, then the matter is concluded. But even if the parties do not agree as to the terms of the change order, the owner's directive as to the change in *scope* is

---

12. AIA Document A201–2017, *supra* note 10, § 7.3.
13. *Id.* §§ 7.3.1, 7.3.6.

binding, and the construction change directive becomes a unilateral modification awaiting resolution of price and time terms while the work proceeds. Similarly, the owner can issue a proposed change that the owner does not believe warrants a change in the time or price of performance (such as changing the color of paint), and the change becomes binding as a no cost-no time change unless the contractor protests. However, if the contractor protests, the owner can rescind the change or turn it into a change directive; the result of a change directive is that the change still becomes binding, but the contractor preserves its ability to seek additional time and/or compensation.

Another option is for the construction change directive to provide a method for adjusting the price to account for the change, with the architect resolving differences over the method for adjusting the price.[14] Undisputed amounts for the performance of the changed work must be memorialized through a change order.[15] Another way for the owner to initiate a change is for the owner to send a pricing request to the contractor. That way, the owner can decide whether to proceed with the change order based on pricing information from the contractor in advance of the performance of the changed work, rather than becoming committed to paying for the change through the issuance of a construction change directive.

Along similar lines, the AIA sets out conditions parallel to the FAR provision for the contractor to initiate the change in article 15 of AIA Document A201–2017. Under subsection 15.1.5, if the contractor believes that a written interpretation or order by the architect, or other reasonable grounds, will cause the contractor to incur additional costs, the contractor must initiate a claim. The claim will be the assertion of the right to a change order, similar to FAR section 52.243-4(b). If the owner agrees with the contractor's assertion, a change order will be negotiated. If the owner disagrees, the contractor can implement the remaining steps in the claims process to assert the right to a change order.

Many construction projects are performed where neither the FAR nor an AIA form contract is used. However, most construction contracts detail the basic process of the owner initiating a change through either (1) an owner directive requiring the implementation of the change, (2) a pricing request by owner, or (3) where the contractor initiates a claim that changed circumstances warrant the change order.

---

14. *Id.* §§ 7.3.3, 7.3.4.
15. *Id.* § 7.3.10.

14.04 AUTHORITY TO ISSUE CHANGES

Many issues can arise regarding changes. Among them are differences over the scope, the price, and the effect on the schedule of the change. A preliminary issue, however, concerns who directed the change in the first instance. On a medium-sized or large-scale project, dozens of people may be involved in the project in a managerial capacity at the site and in the home offices of the various participants. A general contractor may receive directives from the owner's representative, the project manager for the owner, various corporate officers in the owner's home office, the on-site representative for the architect, and various employees of the architect working on the project off the site. Likewise, a subcontractor may receive directives from the general contractor's project executive, project manager, assistant project manager, project engineer, superintendent, and assistant superintendent, not to mention the president of the general contractor. However, a dichotomy exists between the roles of some of these people with regard to ensuring completion of the project versus their ability to modify the contract. Accordingly, it is important to ascertain whether the person making the directive has the authority to effect a modification.

The first source to examine for a person's authority to direct changes is, of course, the contract. In federal contracts, the person identified as the contracting officer has the right to order changes in the work.[16] In AIA contracts, the owner is obligated to designate a representative with actual authority to bind the owner.[17] Typically, the parties' representatives are identified in the contract, and, unless the scope of the contractually designated representative for the owner is specifically limited, the owner would be hard pressed to maintain that a directive to perform a change issued by its contractually designated representative was unauthorized.[18]

However, not infrequently, someone other than the contractually designated representative issues an informal (or even formal) directive for a change. A dispute over authority usually arises in the context of a contractor's claim against an owner to recover for a claim arising from a constructive change (or a subcontractor's claim against the contractor). The owner may defend the claim on several grounds, including that the person who made the request did not have the authority to direct changes.[19] In that event, resort to the examina-

---

16. FAR §§ 2.101, 52.243-4, 53.301-1402.

17. AIA Document A201–2017, *supra* note 10, § 2.1.1.

18. Fraud or mistake may constitute such grounds. *See* McQuagge v. United States, 197 F. Supp. 460, 468 (W.D. La. 1961).

19. This issue may arise in other contexts, too. For instance, an owner may contend that a contractor's performance of work in a manner differing from the plans and specifications was

tion of doctrines such as implied authority, apparent authority, or ratification must occur in order to determine if the directive is valid.

Authority to direct change is treated differently on public projects than on private construction projects. On federal projects, actual authority is necessary to bind the government. This principle was decided by the Supreme Court in *Federal Crop Ins. Corp. v. Merrill*,[20] where the Court held that the contractor must verify the authority of the agent or employee of the government and cannot rely on the appearance of authority:

> Whatever the form in which the Government functions, anyone entering into an arrangement with the Government takes the risk of having accurately ascertained that he who purports to act for the Government stays within the bounds of his authority. The scope of this authority may be explicitly defined by Congress or be limited by delegated legislation, properly exercised through the rule-making power. And this is so even though, as here, the agent himself may have been unaware of the limitations upon his authority.[21]

The rationale for this principle is that public funds must be zealously protected against improvident expenditures. State and local construction contracts are similarly constrained.[22]

The *Federal Crop Insurance* case precludes the use of apparent authority to validate a directive by someone other than the designated person in the contract to effect a change. However, the reality of public projects is not substantially different from that of private projects: To get the job done, practicality intrudes on the rigid application of the contract. To bridge this gap and to prevent gross inequities, courts have applied the principle of implied authority to government contracts. An implied delegation of actual authority can empower someone other than the contractually designated representative to direct a change. Whether implied authority is found in a project representative depends on the duties that person actually performs. "Implied authority binds the Government where a Government representative without actual authority exercises an integral part of the duties assigned to that Government employee."[23] For example, where the contracting officer delegated the responsibilities for inspection and testing to the resident engineer, implied authority existed on

---

unauthorized and defective, while the contractor may defend that assertion by claiming that it had been directed to install its work in that manner by a representative of the owner.

20. 332 U.S. 380 (1947).
21. *Id.* at 383.
22. *See, e.g.*, Butler v. Bd. of Supervisors for Hinds Cnty., 659 So. 2d 578 (Miss. 1995); Nether Providence Twp. Sch. Auth. v. Thomas M. Durkin & Sons, Inc., 476 A.2d 904 (Pa. 1984); Contra Costa Constr. Corp. v. Daly City, 192 P. 178 (Cal. 1920).
23. *Miller Elevator Co.*, 30 Fed. Cl. at 662, 693.

the part of the resident engineer to direct the contractor to replace materials the engineer considered defective, based on the engineer's interpretation of the specifications.[24]

On private projects, another substitute for actual authority is provided by the principle of apparent authority. Apparent authority is an appearance of authority to act. The person with actual authority must create the appearance of actual authority on the part of another.[25] An owner will be bound by the directive of someone without actual authority where the contractor reasonably believes, on the basis of the owner's acts, that the owner had authorized that person to make the type of directive given.[26]

Like the principle of implied authority, the applicability of the principle of apparent authority depends on a factual inquiry. First, a finding must be made that the owner led the contractor to believe that someone had authority. Second, a finding must be made that the contractor's belief was reasonable, based on the information available and the circumstances of the project. Unlike implied authority, the trigger for application of apparent authority must come from the owner's words or actions, rather than from the nonauthorized person's actual function.[27]

Yet another substitute for actual authority is ratification. Where the owner, after the fact, affirms that an unauthorized directive is valid, the owner is bound by it.[28] Ratification can be relied on even where the contractor knew that the person who issued the directive lacked the authority to do so.[29] Ratification can be based on either the owner's express acts in sanctioning the directive or the owner's conduct impliedly giving approval. An example of the latter is the owner's failure to reject changed work upon learning of its performance.[30]

Ratification applies to public projects as well as to private projects. The principle of ratification is codified in federal contracting through the Federal

---

24. WRB Corp. v. United States, 183 Ct. Cl. 409 (U.S. 1968).

25. Ja Din, Inc. v. L-J, Inc., 898 F. Supp. 894 (E.D. Fla. 1995); Port of Houston Auth. of Harris Cnty. v. Zachry Constr. Corp., 513 S.W.3d 543, 562 (Tex. App.-Hous. (14 Dist.) 2016).

26. Frank Sullivan Co. v. Midwest Sheet Metal Works, 335 F.2d 33 (8th Cir. 1964).

27. In an unusual case, a corporate officer who *falsely* represented that a contractor acted as the corporation's agent for purposes of imposing change orders affecting a subcontractor was subject to a claim by the subcontractors for negligent misrepresentation. Coppola Constr. Co., Inc. v. Hoffman Enterprises Ltd. P'ship, 309 Conn. 342, 71 A.3d 480 (Conn. 2013).

28. Audit Services, Inc. v. Francis Tindall Constr., 600 P.2d 811 (Mont. 1979).

29. Mateyka v. Schroeder, 504 N.E.2d 1289 (Ill. 1987).

30. McDevitt & Street Co. v. Marriott Corp., 713 F. Supp. 906 (E.D. Va. 1989), *aff'd in part and rev'd in part*, 911 F.2d 723 (4th Cir. 1990).

Acquisition Regulation.[31] Where a contracting officer knows of an unauthorized government representative's directive to a contractor, the contracting officer takes no action to repudiate it, and the government receives the benefit of its performance, then the government will be deemed to have ratified that directive.[32]

14.05 NOTICE REQUIREMENTS FOR CLAIMS FOR CHANGES

Most change order clauses contain requirements for the contractor to notify the owner of a claim for extra or additional work. The notification requirements in the AIA Document A201–2017 General Conditions are contained in Article 15 thereof. A contractor asserting a claim for a change must notify the owner in writing within 21 days after the occurrence of the event giving rise to the claim, or within 21 days after the claimant first recognizes the claim, whichever is later.[33] Furthermore, notice must be given prior to performing the work, if a claim for additional costs will be asserted.[34] Under the AIA claims procedure, the architect or another person designated in the contract then has a period of time to review the claim and make an initial decision on it. The initial decision is deemed binding unless, within 30 days of receipt of the initial decision, the aggrieved party requests mediation or pursues the claim through arbitration or the courts, whichever dispute resolution forum is provided for by the contract.[35] In government contracts, section 52.243-4 (1987) of the Federal Acquisition Regulation contains three notification requirements for changes (see Section 14.03).

Other contracts can have more stringent requirements. For instance, a contract could require that (1) a written notice of the claim be provided within five days after the act or omission of the owner occurs; (2) written notice that a directive is being complied with under protest be given within five days after the directive is issued; (3) a verified detailed statement of the damages sustained be submitted within 30 days after the initial notification is provided; (4) time and material tickets signed by representatives of both parties be tendered on a daily basis while the disputed directive is being carried out; and

---

31. FAR § 1.602-3.
32. Williams v. United States, 127 F. Supp. 617 (Ct. Cl. 1955).
33. *See id.* ¶ 15.1.3.1. AIA Document A201–2017 claims procedures regulate all claims, whether by the contractor or the owner and whether for a change or something else. AIA Document A201–2017, *supra* note 10.
34. ¶ 15.1.5.
35. *Id.* ¶ 15.2.5, 15.2.6.1.

(5) the failure to comply strictly with all of the written notification requirements shall effect a waiver of the claim for the change.[36]

Much litigation has arisen over the enforceability of notice provisions, as well as over the question of whether compliance (or substantial compliance) was achieved. Notice provisions can provide an owner with a defense to a claim apart from the substance of whether work performed truly exceeded the scope of the contract.[37] Owners reason that timely notification of a potential claim permits them to explore other less costly solutions for performing the work; to document contemporaneously the costs of the work involved in the claim; to negotiate a prompt resolution of the claim; and to adjust their budget as needed to cover the possibility that the claim will be enforced. Whether or not a notice provision will be upheld so as to bar a claim where the contractor did not comply with its requirements will depend on the wording of the clause and the jurisdiction where the claim is litigated.

In federal contracts, strict compliance with the notification requirements of the changes clause will not always be required. The courts are mindful not to apply the notice requirements in an overly technical manner where the government was aware of the operative facts.[38] The degree of prejudice to the government resulting from the contractor's failure to provide proven notice is a factor employed in determining whether to excuse the insufficient notice.[39] Moreover, the 30-day notice provision in FAR section 52.243-4 (1987) does not apply to constructive changes since the change was not effected through a written change order triggering the start of the 30-day period.[40]

Many jurisdictions enforce contractual notice provisions according to the terms of the provision.[41] To counter the preclusive effect of such clauses, contractors frequently make arguments that the failure to comply with notice provision should be excused through such theories as waiver or estoppel. For

---

36. *See* A.H.A. General Constr., Inc. v. New York City Hous. Auth., 699 N.E.2d 368 (N.Y. Ct. App. 1998).

37. Notice provisions are not unique to construction contracts. Timely notice is required to assert a claim under an insurance policy. *See, e.g.*, Nat'l Am. Ins. Co. v. Certain Underwriters at Lloyd's London, 93 F.3d 529 (9th Cir. 1996).

38. Hoel-Steffen Constr. Co. v. United States, 456 F.2d 760 (Ct. Cl. 1972).

39. Mingus Contractors, Inc. v. United States, 812 F.2d 1387 (Fed. Cir. 1987).

40. Jo-Bar Mfg. Corp. v. United States, 535 F.2d 62 (Ct. Cl. 1976) (holding that the contractor has a "reasonable period of time" to notify the government of the claim for a constructive change).

41. *See* Clark-Fitzpatrick, Inc./Frankl Found. Co. v. Gill, 652 A.2d 440 (R.I. 1994) (holding, however, that formal notice is not required where notice was given and the owner had an opportunity to monitor the costs); Wegroup PC/Architects and Planners v. State, 885 P.2d 709 (Or. 1994); Indian River Constr. Co. v. City of Jacksonville, 390 So. 2d 1139 (Fla. Dist. App. 1977).

instance, where an owner repeatedly issued change orders to a contractor after the changed work had been performed, but without receiving the required contractual notice of the claim, then the owner can be held to have waived strict compliance with the notice provisions.[42] An owner also may be estopped from maintaining that a claim for a change is barred by the failure to provide written notice where the owner's actions caused the contractor to incur the extra cost.[43]

However, some jurisdictions strictly uphold notice requirements. In New York, a contractual provision requiring a contractor to provide the owner with notice and documentation of the claim is considered a condition precedent to the right to recover on the claim.[44] Thus, to avoid the application of the condition precedent, a contractor must show that the owner's actions prevented or hindered compliance with the provision.[45] The failure to comply with a notice provision was held to bar a claim under the law of Mississippi as well.[46] Many of the cases dealing with the issue of whether a claim is barred by the failure to comply with a notice provision emanate from public works contracts. The influence of public works contracts is not surprising since courts can be protective in guarding against the expenditure of public funds. At least one court has gone so far as to hold that notice provisions are treated differently when applied to public contracts (strictly) as opposed to private construction contracts (liberally).[47]

The first step in an analysis of a notice provision is to read the provision. Does the contract state that notice must be strictly provided? Does the provision state that a claim will be waived, absent full compliance? Next, the surrounding circumstances must be examined. Was notice given in some fashion that might allow the contractor to argue it had substantially complied with the provision even absent strict compliance? Did the owner inform the contractor at some point in the project that change orders will not be issued unless there has been full compliance with the contractual procedures? Whether a notice provision will be applied to bar a claim or whether the failure to comply will

---

42. *See, e.g.,* Cardinal Dev. Co. v. Stanley Constr. Co., 497 S.E.2d 847 (Va. 1998); Joseph F. Egan, Inc. v. City of New York, 215 N.E.2d 490 (N.Y. Ct. App. 1966).

43. *See* U.S. *ex rel.* E. & R. Constr. Co. v. Guy H. James Constr. Co., 390 F. Supp. 1193 (M.D. Tenn. 1972), *aff'd*, 489 F.2d 756 (6th Cir. 1974).

44. A.H.A. *General Constr.*, 699 N.E.2d at 368.

45. *Id.*

46. *See* PYCA Indus., Inc. v. Harrison County Waste Water Mgmt. Dist., 177 F.3d 351 (5th Cir. 1999).

47. Barsotti's, Inc. v. Consol. Edison Co. of New York, 680 N.Y.S.2d 88 (N.Y. App. Div. 1998).

be waived is, in many jurisdictions, a nuanced analysis based on a number of factors.

14.06 ADJUSTMENTS TO CONTRACT PRICE AND COMPLETION DATE

A fully executed change order, although technically a contract amendment, looks in some ways as an independent agreement. It will set forth the nature of the transaction (i.e., the scope of the work to be performed); the consideration (i.e., the price of the work); and the additional time, if any, to be allotted for the performance. The change order clauses typically will provide (1) a framework for reaching the goal of a fully agreed, signed change order, and (2) a procedure to be followed in the event that an agreement cannot be reached as to what generally has the potential to be the most contentious aspect: the price. At the same time, change orders are not usually construed as standalone agreements precisely because they are written on the foundation of a detailed contract whose terms govern many aspects of the change order not specifically spelled out.

As previously discussed, under the AIA contractual scheme, a construction change directive is issued to permit the work to proceed in advance of a complete agreement as to the terms of a change order. In AIA Document A201–2017 (General Conditions), section 7.3.3 provides for four methods for determining the price of a change: (1) an agreed lump sum; (2) unit prices; (3) costs to be determined in a manner agreed to by the parties, together with a fee for the contractor; and (4) time and material costs, plus a sum to compensate the contractor for overhead and profit. As envisioned by this provision, the owner and the contractor must, at the least, agree on the construction change directive using one of these four methods for determining the price, if not on the price itself.

An agreed lump sum is nothing more than a mutually agreed, negotiated fixed price. It appears to be unrealistic to mandate in a construction change directive that the price will be based on an agreed lump sum before the owner and the contractor have come to an agreement on that sum, although the owner's proposal of a fixed price at least starts the pricing discussion. But what if the owner and the contractor simply cannot agree on a price? An alternative practice is for a lump sum to be listed in the construction change directive as one of two alternative pricing methods. That way, in case the parties cannot agree on a lump price, the second stipulated method can be employed to resolve the price issue (of course, the owner must specify a time for the contractor to agree to the mechanism before the work is completed, or the contractor will simply complete the work and then choose the most lucrative pricing mechanism).

Unit pricing typically is utilized for repetitive operations where the exact quantity of work cannot be precisely determined at the inception. A classic example is excavation, where the parties may agree that the contractor will be paid X dollars per cubic yard of soil excavated or Y dollars per cubic yard of rock excavated. The contract may already have unit prices that could apply to the changed work, or the parties can agree to unit prices specifically limited to the changed work.

The third and the fourth methods enumerated earlier are similar. Both involve reimbursement for the contractor's actual costs of performing the changed work, plus additional compensation, whether denominated as a "fee" or as "overhead and profit." The third method gives the owner and the contractor some leeway to determine those costs, while the fourth method spells out the reimbursable cost categories. Specifically, those designated cost categories in section 7.34 of AIA Document A201–2017 are:

> Costs of labor, including applicable payroll taxes, fringe benefits required by agreement or custom, workers' compensation insurance, and other employee costs approved by the Architect;

> Costs of materials, supplies and equipment, including costs of transportation, whether incorporated or consumed;

> Rental costs of machinery and equipment, exclusive of hand tools, whether rented from the Contractor or others;

> Costs of premiums for all bonds and insurance; permit fees, and sales, use or similar taxes related to the change; and

> Costs of supervision and field office personnel directly attributable to the change.

These cost categories, known in the industry as "time and materials," or T&M, are designed to cover all of the costs of constructing the changed work. Different contract forms may use different wording for the various time and materials categories, which may affect the eligibility for payment for certain costs. Nevertheless, this general approach of payment for the actual costs for labor, materials, equipment, supplies, insurance, bonds, and supervision is widely recognized in the field. Some owners shun this method, fearing it discourages efficiency, thus prolonging the work and increasing the costs. Some contractors are adverse to this method as well, believing they can achieve greater profitability through a lump sum than through the limited overhead and profit percentage stipulated in the contract. In addition, this method is not always suitable for direct application; a change cannot be priced on a pure time and materials basis, for example, where the change involves both additional work and the deletion of planned work. Impact issues resulting from the change likewise cannot be priced on a time and materials basis. However, T&M is frequently made available as the method of the last resort.

Since construction projects provide fertile grounds for fomenting disputes, especially regarding money, a change provision also may contain a procedure for resolving disagreements as to the eligibility of an item for payment, the amount of labor or quantity of materials necessary for the work, and so on. In section 7.34 of AIA Document A201–2017 (General Conditions), the architect determines the price adjustment on the basis of the designated time and materials categories. However, the architect's determination is not final. The aggrieved party can challenge it through the applicable dispute resolution forum—litigation or arbitration. Nevertheless, the architect's determination may be given deference by requiring that the party challenging the determination show the price adjustment requested was the product of fraud or bad faith, or was palpably erroneous, or a similar higher standard of proof.[48]

Even though inclusion of a price determination mechanism in a changes clause is widely accepted, providing such a mechanism is not universal. As noted in Section 14.03, all the FAR provides in this respect is that "the Contracting Officer shall make an equitable adjustment."[49] The equitable adjustment can be issued before or after performance of the work. If issued before, the price will be based on the contractor's proposal, together with whatever backup documentation can be produced, such as subcontractor and supplier pricing. If issued after, the preferred method is to submit the actual costs incurred in performing the changed work.[50] However, the equitable adjustment will not necessarily be in the amount of the actual costs incurred, plus overhead and profit. The measure for determining the amount of an equitable adjustment is the reasonable cost of the change work.[51] No presumption is made that the contractor's actual costs are reasonable.[52] This addresses the concern that work performed on a time and material basis may not be done efficiently.

---

48. *See In re* Liquidation of Lumbermens Mutual Cas. Co., 2018 IL App (1st) 171613, ¶ 30, 2018 WL 6173580, at *6 (Ill. Ct. App. 2018). J. S. Sweet Co. v. White County Bridge Comm'n, 714 N.E.2d 219 (Ind. Ct. App. 1999); RaDec Constr. Inc. v. Sch. Dist., No. 17 of Douglas County, 535 N.W.2d 408 (Neb. 1995).

49. FAR ¶ 52.243-4.

50. Ace Constructors, Inc. v. United States, 70 Fed. Cl. 253 (2006).

51. Meridian Eng'g Co. v. United States, 130 Fed. Cl. 147 (2016).

52. FAR ¶ 31.201-3(a).

One marked difference between determining costs in federal contracts for changed work as opposed to non-federal contracts lies in the treatment of contractor-owned equipment. For example, assume that the changed work is to dig a foundation deeper, and the contractor uses its own backhoe to perform the work. Since the company owns the backhoe, the cost of the backhoe cannot be determined through actual invoices, as in the same manner for rental equipment. In non-federal contracts, company-owned equipment is priced into change orders (1) by multiplying the time the equipment was on the site while the changed work was performed (2) by a rental rate either included in the contract documents or published in a standard equipment manual.[53] However, in federal contracts, courts avoid using standard published rental rates to price company-owned equipment.[54] For instance, a court utilized a complex calculation based on the acquisition cost, ownership expense, and the time during which the equipment was idle on the site to derive actual costs.[55] However, a published rental rate can be used for valuing company-owned equipment when the government agreed to use the published rate.[56]

Leaving the pricing of a change to be made through an equitable adjustment, without further agreed guidelines, is feasible for federal contracts where both a contracting officer and an administrative process to challenge a contracting officer's determination are in place. Outside the realm of federal contracts, specifying the methods for determining the price gives a measure of certainty to the process of pricing changes.

The same principles discussed earlier with respect to pricing the changed work apply to the additional time associated with the change. If the parties agree, the change order will set forth the additional time by which the completion date is extended as a result of the changed work. Otherwise, the architect will determine the amount of time, to which determination the contractor can take exception and present a challenge in a judicial proceeding.

14.07 CONSTRUCTIVE CHANGES

By contrast to a formal change, where an owner explicitly recognizes in its directive that a change order must be issued, a constructive change covers situations where the owner causes the performance of work beyond the scope of the contract but does not recognize the contractor's entitlement to a change order. A constructive change can arise out of a variety of circumstances, such

---

53. *See* Felhaber Corp. v. State, 410 N.Y.S.2d 920 (N.Y. App. Div. 1978).
54. L. L. Hall Constr. Co. v. United States, 379 F.2d 559 (Ct. Cl. 1966).
55. *Id.*
56. Metric Constr. Co. v. United States, 81 Fed. Cl. 804 (2008).

as overly stringent inspection; improper rejection of work; errors, omissions, or ambiguities in the drawings or specifications; or usurping the contractor's prerogative to select the means and methods of performing the work. Thus, a constructive change arises from either the need to address a condition caused by the owner's wrongful conduct or to comply with an informal directive by the owner.[57] Boiled down to its essence, a constructive change occurs where a contractor is proven right in asserting a dispute or a claim for a change order.

A classic example of a constructive change occurs in a situation where the owner believes that certain work is encompassed by the drawings and specifications, while the contractor contends the work is beyond the scope. For instance, a contract required the contractor to install several thousand new light bulbs "immediately prior to completion." The contractor believed that it could retain the light bulbs installed to provide temporary lighting during construction and replace those that had burned out, while the owner assumed that all of the light bulbs would be replaced at completion. Thus, the owner viewed the scope of the work as requiring the furnishing and installation of all new light bulbs when the building was nearly ready to be turned over to it. The court ruled that the contractor's interpretation was reasonable and consistent with the custom of the industry. Accordingly, the owner's directive to change the light bulbs constituted a constructive change.[58] Thus, in effect, the specifications were found to be ambiguous, and the ambiguity was construed against the owner. While constructive changes often arise out of ambiguous drawings and specifications, the variations are numerous. To give another illustration, where a contract required the contractor to install fume hoods for a science laboratory, but the drawings and specifications did not contain the necessary information to install piping to vent the hoods to the building exterior, the owner's directive to install the piping was held to be a constructive change.[59]

To avoid claims for constructive change orders arising out of ambiguities in the drawings and specifications, owners, especially public owners, sometimes include a contractual provision requiring the contractor to bring ambiguities in the drawings and specifications to the owner's attention prior to bid submission, or waive any claim thereafter.[60] This type of clause is enforceable and operates to prevent the contractor from asserting a claim for a constructive

---

57. Ultimate Concrete, LLC v. United States, 2019 WL 156933 (Fed. Cl., 2019); A.S. McGaughan Co. v. Barram, 113 F.3d 1256 (Fed. Cir. 1997).

58. Metric Constr., Inc. v. Nat'l Aeronautics & Space Admin., 169 F.3d 747 (Fed. Cir. 1999).

59. Julian Speer Co. v. Ohio State Univ., 680 N.E.2d 254 (Ohio Ct. Cl. 1997).

60. As a general rule, contractors are required to bring constructive changes to the attention of the owner or risk losing recovery. RMA Engineering S.A.R.L. v. United States, 140 Fed. Cl. 191 (Fed. Cl. 2018).

change order arising out of a "patent" ambiguity.[61] As a matter of federal contracting law, contractors are liable for any costs arising from patent ambiguities in contract documents, even if they did not discover the patent ambiguities until after work began, contrary to the rule that ambiguities should be construed against the drafter (*contra proferentem*).[62]

The distinction between a patent ambiguity and a latent ambiguity is significant. Under a clause requiring the contractor to advise the owner of ambiguities, the contractor is obligated to bring obvious ambiguities to the owner's attention and ask for a clarification so the contractor could price the work into the bid, if necessary. However, a contractor is not required to review the architect's work and check every detail for completeness and accuracy. Thus, this type of clause would not bar a claim for a constructive change arising out of a latent ambiguity (i.e., an ambiguity not apparent on its face but that could only be reasonably discovered when that aspect of the work is addressed during construction).

A constructive change order arising out of overly stringent inspection arises extrinsically from demands by the owner representative at the project site, rather than intrinsically from the drawings and specifications prepared before the work is performed. A contractor is required to perform the work in conformance with the drawings and specifications to the reasonable satisfaction of the owner, not to the owner's subjective satisfaction. An extreme example arose out of a bridge painting contract. The contract required that loose paint be removed by sandblasting before new paint was applied to the steel. The inspector, however, required the contractor to remove all of the old paint. Moreover, the inspector insisted that the sandblasting continue until no flecks of paint appeared when a piece of tape was stuck on the surface and pulled off. The court upheld the contractor's claim for additional costs by virtue of having been required to perform a different job than was provided for in the contract.[63]

Similarly, improper rejection of work constitutes a constructive change, independent of whether an inspector applies standards above and beyond the contract requirements and the industry norm in reviewing the adequacy of the work. An inspector may reject work as defective by making a mistake in judgment and without applying overly stringent requirements. If adequate work, as measured by the specifications, nonetheless is rejected as defective,

---

61. Newsom v. United States, 676 F.2d 647 (Ct. Cl. 1982); Arnell Constr. Corp. v. Bd. of Educ. of the City of New York, 598 N.Y.S.2d 1 (N.Y. App. Div. 1993).
62. MW Builders, Inc. v. United States, 36 Fed. Cl. 584 (Fed. Cl. 2018).
63. State v. Buckner Constr. Co., 704 S.W.2d 837 (Tex. App. 1985).

a contractor will be able to recover the costs of implementing the unnecessary corrective work as, in effect, a constructive change.[64]

Another scenario in which a constructive change may arise is when the owner improperly dictates the means and methods of work to the contractor, resulting in increased costs. Normally, the contractor has the prerogative of choosing the means and methods of performing the work to achieve the owner's design.[65] Of course, an owner could reserve the right in the contract to approve the contractor's means and methods, or the owner could direct that certain means and methods be utilized. However, owners rarely do so, as it could increase costs and expose the owner to additional liability.[66] Where an owner directs the contractor to perform the work in a particular way, despite not having been accorded such a right in the contract, the contractor will have a claim for a constructive change. One court, for example, examined the ramifications of an owner's direction that the contractor excavate in lifts of one to two feet in order to make it easier for the owner's representatives to inspect the excavation work. Since the contract simply required the contractor to excavate to the required depth for the foundations, the costs for the more expensive "stop and start" operation were recovered by the contractor.[67]

14.08 DUTY TO PERFORM THE CHANGED WORK

As stated at the beginning of this chapter, a unique and essential feature of a changes clause is the ability to effectuate a unilateral change. Therefore, the assumption can be made that a contractor receiving a directive to perform changed work has an obligation to execute the changed work; if the contractor could refuse to proceed, a unilateral modification would not exist. However, the obligation to perform the changed work is not a matter of logic; rather, the obligation is a matter of the contract. Indeed, in the absence of a contract provision allowing the owner to direct changes, the contractor will not be obligated to perform work different from the work specified unless the parties agree to a change order.

---

64. *See* Granite Constr. Co. v. United States, 962 F.2d 998 (Fed. Cir. 1992); *see also* DeAtley Constr., Inc. v. United States, 71 Fed. Cl. 370 (2006) (where aggregate specified proved to be defective and the inspector directed the contractor to replace it with new aggregate, the contractor stated a claim for a constructive change).

65. *See* Burns v. Black & Veatch Architects, Inc., 854 S.W.2d 450 (Mo. Ct. App. 1993).

66. By directing the means and methods of performing the work, an owner may become liable for personal injuries to third parties sustained when an accident occurs from the method directed. *See* Farabaugh v. Penn Turnpike Comm'n, 911 A.2d 1264 (Pa. 2006).

67. Luria Bros. & Co. v. United States, 369 F.2d 701 (Ct. Cl. 1966).

In the AIA Document A201–2017 (General Conditions), the contractor's obligation to perform notwithstanding the absence of a formal change order is stated explicitly in two places. First, the contractor agrees to continue with the performance of the contract pending a final resolution of a claim.[68] Second, the contractor agrees to proceed promptly with the change in the work upon receipt of a construction change directive.[69] The Federal Acquisition Regulation has a similar provision requiring performance pending final resolution of a claim.[70]

Thus, under this type of changes clause obligating a contractor to incur costs performing work without a formal change order, pursuant to a construction change directive or, while the owner contends the work falls within the requirements of the contract despite the contractor's claim to the contrary, then the contractor will have to bear the expenditure without recompense during the claims process. An owner also can abuse this provision when the owner does not have funding to pay for a change or wants to gain leverage in price negotiations. Moreover, if the claims process results in the upholding of the owner's position, then the contractor's recourse is to file a lawsuit or arbitration demand (as the case may be), which can take years to resolve. To refuse outright to perform the work runs the risk of constituting a material breach of the contract, for which the owner could hold the contractor in default.[71]

Since contractors want to avoid performing work without contemporaneous payment, they have sought ways to excuse performance of claimed extra work absent a commitment by the owner to pay for the work. Accordingly, some contractors have attempted to file lawsuits for declaratory judgment absolving them of the responsibility to proceed with performance of the directive. The goal of such a lawsuit is to receive the prompt judicial imprimatur of the contractor's decision not to perform the work and, in that way, to prevent the owner from declaring a default. In one such example, a contractor filed an action for a declaratory judgment asserting that another contractor on the project (not the filing contractor), was responsible for the excavation and installation of concrete pads for underground fuel tanks. The drawings indisputably showed on the work; the issue was which of multiple prime contractors had responsibility to perform that work. Under the contract, the commissioner of the public agency that had entered into the contract could determine whether work was extra, and the contract obligated the contractor to abide by that determination and proceed with the work; however, the contractor had the

---

68. AIA Document A201–2017, *supra* note 10, § 15.1.4.1.
69. *Id.* § 7.3.6.
70. FAR § 52-233.1(i).
71. Stoeckert v. United States, 391 F.2d 639 (Ct. Cl. 1968).

right to assert a claim for compensation. New York's highest court rejected this attempt to avoid performance of the work, holding that "the contractor specifically had undertaken an obligation to perform that work and postpone any claim for additional compensation until after contract completion."[72]

However, an owner's right to require a contractor to proceed with the performance of extra work is not unlimited. If a directive is so irrational and arbitrary, and the consequences of compliance are so onerous and damaging as to constitute an unconscionable result, then a contractor could be justified in refusing to comply with the directive.[73] Also, in the realm of public contracts, if a public official's directive is so preposterous as to suggest collusion, bad faith, or similar circumstances, then the contractor likewise could be justified in refusing to perform the work.[74] These examples are clearly intended to be limited exceptions, and not the rule.

14.09 CARDINAL CHANGE

Another exception exists to the rule that upon the directive of the owner, a contractor must perform work it considers extra, even absent a commitment to compensate the contractor for the work. The exception arises when the extra work constitutes a cardinal change to the contract. The term "cardinal change" is defined as a change to the work that goes so far beyond the scope of the original contact as to constitute a materially different undertaking.[75] The imposition by the owner of a cardinal change upon the contractor amounts to a breach of the contract.[76] A cardinal change (i.e., requiring performance of work outside the contract) differs from a change considered to be within the purview of a changes clause in another respect besides magnitude. A cardinal change can emanate from either one isolated but extremely significant change, or from a series of changes, related or unrelated. While the number of changes alone may be grounds for invoking a cardinal change,[77] the cumulative impact of the changes upon the work as a whole is really more critical to determining the work is a cardinal change.[78]

---

72. Kalisch-Jarcho, Inc. v. City of New York, 533 N.E.2d 258, 261 (N.Y. 1988).
73. Id. at 263.
74. Id. at 262.
75. IES Commercial, Inc. v. Manhattan Torcon A Joint Venture, 2018 WL 4616029, at *5 (D. Md. 2018); Allied Materials & Equip. Co. v. United States, 569 F.2d 562, 563–64 (Ct. Cl. 1978).
76. Edwin R. Marden Corp. v. United States, 442 F.2d 364, 369 (Ct. Cl. 1971).
77. C. Norman Peterson Co. v. Container Corp. of America, 218 Cal. Rptr. 592, 598 (1985).
78. Becho, Inc. v. United States, 47 Fed. Cl. 595, 601 (2000).

In a sense, a case involving a claim of a cardinal change is the closest that construction law comes to a constitutional analysis under the First Amendment. The reason for this analogy is that, like Justice Stewart's conclusion about determining whether something amounts to pornography, the courts examining cardinal change claims have adopted a standard of "I know it when I see it." The Court of Claims, in one of the leading cases on cardinal changes, phrased its parameters as follows:

> There is no exact formula for determining the point at which a single change or series of changes must be considered to be beyond the scope of the contract and necessarily in breach of it. Each case must be analyzed on its own facts and in light of its own circumstances, giving just consideration to the magnitude and quality of the changes ordered and their cumulative effect upon the project as a whole [citation omitted]. The contractor cannot claim a breach of the contract if the project it ultimately constructed is essentially the same as the one it agreed in the contract to erect [citation omitted].[79]

In the final analysis, the critical factors are whether the change or changes are of such a magnitude as to radically alter the nature of the contract itself, whether by the character of the work, the quantity, the method or manner of performance, or the cost,[80] or whether the project constructed remained essentially the project that the contractor had bid for at the outset.[81]

The doctrine of cardinal change originated in the realm of government contracts.[82] Numerous federal decisions have discussed cardinal change, and a number of states recognize this concept as well. Some states explicitly utilize the term "cardinal change,"[83] while others acknowledge the concept by description without using this term specifically.[84] Some states have refused to validate the concept of cardinal change.[85]

Since construction, at its most basic, constitutes a search for the practical solution, an examination is necessary of the consequences of a finding of a cardinal change. A contractor that believes it has encountered a cardinal

---

79. Wunderlich Contracting Co. v. United States, 351 F.2d 956, 966 (Ct. Cl. 1965).

80. *Becho*, 47 Fed. Ct. at 601; Peter Kiewit Sons Co. v. Summit Constr. Co., 422 F.2d 242 (8th Cir. 1969).

81. Aragona Constr. Co. v. United States, 165 Ct. Cl. 382, 390 (1964).

82. *See* Saddler v. United States, 287 F.2d 411 (Ct. Cl. 382, 390 (1961); General Contracting & Constr. Co. v. United States, 84 Ct. Cl. 570 (1937).

83. *See, e.g.*, J. A. Jones Constr. Co. v. Lehrer McGovern Bovis, Inc., 89 P.3d 1009 (Nev. 2004); Hous. Auth. of City of Texarkana v. Johnson Constr. Co., 573 S.W.2d 316 (Ark. 1978).

84. *See, e.g.*, Tufano Contracting Corp. v. State, 269 N.Y.S.2d 564 (N.Y. App. Div. 1966).

85. *See, e.g.*, Gill Constr., Inc. v. 18th & Vine Auth., 157 S.W.3d 699 (Mo. App. 2004); Litton Systems, Inc. v. Frigitemp Corp., 613 F. Supp. 1377 (S.D. Miss. 1985).

change has two choices. The contract may elect to refuse to perform the work and treat the contract as terminated.[86] Alternatively, the contractor can elect to proceed with the work and sue for quantum meruit, thereby possibly exceeding the recovery that could have been had under the contract.[87]

In the final analysis, it is the rare instance where a contractor will declare a termination on the grounds of a cardinal change. If a court ultimately rules the termination unjustified, the consequences would be so severe, both directly to the contractor's business and indirectly through its surety, that a contractor must find itself in such dire circumstances as to have little choice other than to invoke this concept in order to cease performance.

14.10 ADMINISTRATION OF CHANGES

Changes in the absence of a fixed price require administrative attention. Even after a directive, the contractor notifies the owner that the contractor views the work as a change, and the contractor makes the decision to proceed to perform the work, the legal consequences continue. Until payment is made for the changed work, or at least until an agreement is reached regarding the price of the changed work, such work remains an open issue, requiring the attention of both parties.

Both the contractor and the owner have an interest in monitoring the cost of performing the claimed extra work. The contractor needs to know how much the work costs, so that it can submit a claim that will capture all of the expenses associated with the directive. The owner, on the other hand, wants to ensure that the costs the contractor will present to the owner in the claim are accurate and do not include the cost of work already within the contract. In order to advance these interests, someone should keep track of the costs of the claimed extra work.

Many construction contracts provide that extra work is to be paid on a time and materials basis where no agreement as to price is reached or no unit price is stipulated in the contract to cover the particular work operations involved.[88] The costs typically eligible for compensation for extra work performed on a time and materials basis are labor, materials, equipment, supplies, insurance,

---

86. Fuller Co. v. Brown Minneapolis Tank & Fabricating Co., 678 F. Supp. 506, 509 (E.D. Pa. 1987); *but see* Amelco Elec. v. City of Thousand Oaks, 38 P.3d 1120 (Cal. 2002) (holding that a contractor cannot recover against a public owner on the theory of abandonment of the original project).

87. *Peter Kiewit Sons Co.*, 422 F.2d at 242.

88. *See* AIA Document A201-2017, *supra* note 10, § 7.3.4.

and surety bond. A percentage for overhead and profit is then added to these costs to arrive at the final cost.

Some contracts have clauses requiring the contractor to submit time and material tickets for the owner's signature on a daily basis while the contractor performs work that the contractor claims is extra or while the contractor performs acknowledged extra work for which an agreement on price has not been reached in advance. An example of one such clause, in pertinent part, is as follows:

ARTICLE 28. RECORD KEEPING FOR EXTRA OR DISPUTED WORK OR WORK ON A TIME & MATERIALS BASIS

28.1 While the Contractor or any of its Subcontractors is performing Work on a time and material basis or Extra Work on a time and material basis ordered by the Commissioner under Article 25 or where the Contractor believes that it or any of its Subcontractors is performing Extra Work but a final determination by Agency has not been made, or the Contractor or any of its Subcontractors is performing disputed Work (whether on or off the Site), or complying with a determination or order under protest in accordance with Articles 11, 27, and 30, in each such case the Contractor shall furnish the Resident Engineer daily with three (3) copies of written statements signed by the Contractor's representatives at the site showing:

> 28.11. The name, trade, and number of each worker employed on such Work or engaged in complying with such determination or order, the number of hours employed, and the character of the Work each is doing; and

> 28.1.2. The nature and quantity of any materials, plant and equipment furnished or used in connection with the performance of such work or compliance with such determination or order, and from whom purchased or rented.

28.2 A copy of such statement will be countersigned by the Resident Engineer, noting thereon any items not agreed to or questioned, and be returned to the Contractor within two (2) days after submission.

***

28.5 Failure to comply strictly with these requirements shall constitute a waiver of any claim for extra compensation or damages on account of the performance of such Work or compliance with such determination or order.[89]

---

89. This excerpt is from a City of New York form of construction contract.

A contractor's failure to comply with this type of clause by submitting daily time and material tickets may result in the dismissal of the claim.[90]

However, many widely used contracts do not have such a clause. For instance, neither the AIA form contract nor the FAR contains this type of requirement.[91] Nevertheless, even absent such a clause, the contractor should maintain records of the actual costs. The changes clause in the FAR speaks in terms of equitably adjusting the contract price for costs incurred in the performance of the change.[92] An equitable adjustment should be based on the contractor's actual reasonable costs.[93] Should the claim not be resolved, a contractor may find itself precluded from recovery for the change if the contractor cannot establish the actual costs of performing the change. A claim for extra costs on a federal contract was dismissed by the Court of Claims on this very basis:

> The evidence offered consisted of the testimony of a certified public accountant, and was based upon a comparison of the cost of performance under the contract here involved and the cost of performance under a certain other contract. . . . The evident [sic] on this point has been examined with great care. Without questioning the integrity or the technical skill of the witness who presented the testimony upon which plaintiff's claim for extra costs rests, the evidence is unsatisfactory and wholly unconvincing.[94]

State law likewise may bar a recovery for extra work where only estimates of the costs of performance are submitted as proof of damages, so long as the costs of performing the extra work may be segregated from the costs of performing the contract work.[95] Therefore, whether documented in the form of daily time and material records, or in some other segregated format, the actual costs of performing the extra work should be maintained, if at all possible, in the event that a negotiated change order does not result.

14.11 RELEASES—ACCORD AND SATISFACTION

Even if the owner and the contractor agree to and sign a change order, the potential for a dispute regarding the change still exists. Generally, the dispute

---

90. *A.H.A. General Constr., Inc.*, 699 N.E.2d at 368.
91. However, under FAR § 52.243-6, a contracting officer may require the contractor to maintain segregated cost records for a change or series of related changes estimated to exceed $100,000.
92. FAR § 52.243-4(d).
93. Ace Constructors, Inc. v. United States, 70 Fed. Cl. 253 (2006).
94. American Can Co. v. United States, 69 Ct. Cl. 1, 9–10 (1929).
95. Metro. Steel Indus., Inc. v. Perini Corp., 828 N.Y.S.2d 395 (N.Y. App. Div. 2007).

arises over scope or time, or both. A change order is comparable to a contract; a change order is a contract to perform a particular aspect of work not provided for in the parties' original contract. The more details the change order contains as to what it covers, the clearer the terms will be, and disputes will be less likely. Conversely, the more general the language, the greater the chance of an ambiguity (at least in the mind of one of the parties) and the more likely a dispute will occur concerning a matter that should have been settled in the document.

The possibilities for disagreement as to the breadth of a signed change order run the full gamut. A time-related dispute is the easiest to conceptualize. A contractor may claim that the change order only covered the direct costs of performing the additional work, but did not provide compensation for the indirect costs associated with the overall delay to the project due to the change. A scope-related dispute can be extremely technical. For example, a contractor may contend that a change order to substitute cast-in-place concrete walls for hollow masonry block walls (i.e., cinder blocks) accounts only for the cost of the concrete used to construct the walls but not for changes to the structural framework of the building necessitated by the added weight of the concrete over the hollow masonry blocks. In such an instance, the contractor may believe that the structural ramifications of the change are a separate matter and submit only the costs strictly associated with the forming and pouring of the concrete walls. However, the owner may believe that the change order includes all work of any nature whatsoever associated with the change to concrete walls.

In such an instance, the description of the change and what the dollar value of the modification covers would be paramount. However, this sort of factual inquiry could be circumvented by an additional general provision in the change order. Where a change order states that it constitutes payment for "all costs and markups directly or indirectly attributable to the changes," a claim for additional compensation may be barred.[96] Likewise, the recitation in a change order that it "constitutes an accord and satisfaction and represents payment in full (for both time and money) for any and all costs, impact effects, and/or delays arising out of incidental to the work" will preclude a claim for additional compensation relating to the change.[97] Concomitantly, the failure of a change order to recite that it was "in full satisfaction of all claims" resulted in

---

96. King Fisher Marine Serv., Inc. v. United States, 16 Cl. Ct. 231 (1989).
97. Safeco Credit v. United States, 44 Fed. Cl. 406, 419 (1999).

the denial of the government's motion to dismiss the contractor's delay claim for the indirect costs stemming from the changed work.[98]

Aside from barring a further claim on the basis of an accord and satisfaction, a change order may bar a further claim on the basis of release. While an accord and satisfaction constitutes a settlement for a particular claim, a release is broader: release waivers of all claims, known or unknown. In the context of a change order, a release operates to waive all claims, known or unknown, relating and limited to the subject matter of the change order. Whether a further claim arising out of a change order has been released depends, of course, on whether the change order includes language constituting a release.[99] If the change order includes release language, then the change order will operate to bar a further claim concerning the particular change or changes encompassed by the document.[100] Nevertheless, a release could be challenged as being ambiguous and, therefore, not precluding the claim being asserted.[101] Otherwise, a release in a change order would be challenged in the same manner as releases generally (i.e., on such grounds as fraud, unconscionability, or duress). Under the law of most jurisdictions, that is a high hurdle to overcome.[102]

Parties concerned over the possibility of waiving a claim by signing a change order sometimes try to avert such a waiver by including a reservation of rights in the document. The reservation of rights can simply recite, for example, "The Contractor reserves all rights against the Owner for damages and costs incurred due to delays arising out of this change order." Courts have upheld the right of a contractor to assert an additional claim relating to a change order when the change order included a reservation of rights agreed to by both parties.[103] On the other hand, a reservation of rights clause unilaterally inserted into a change order will not be effective to reserve a right to assert a claim otherwise barred by the contract.[104] Thus, a contractor could not recover additional compensation for delays resulting from a change order containing a reservation of rights where the change order stated that it constituted "full and complete compensation" for overhead as provided in the contract's changes

---

98. Westerhold v. United States, 28 Fed. Cl. 172 (1993).
99. Superior Site Work, Inc. v. NASDI, LLC, 2018 WL 3716891, at *20 (E.D.N.Y. 2018).
100. Citadel Corp. v. Sun Chem. Corp., 443 S.E.2d 489 (Ga. Ct. App. 1994).
101. *See id.*
102. *See* Strickland Tower Maintenance, Inc. v. AT&T Communications, Inc., 128 F.3d 1422 (10th Cir. 1997); Vulcan Painters, Inc. v. MCI Contractors, Inc., 41 F.3d 1457 (11th Cir. 1995); *but see* Willms Trucking Co. v. J. W. Constr. Co., 442 S.E.2d 197 (S.C. Ct. App. 1994).
103. Williams & Sons Erectors, Inc. v. South Carolina Steel Corp., 983 F.2d 1176 (2d Cir. 1993); Southland Enterprises, Inc. v. United States, 24 Cl. Ct. 596 (1991).
104. Santa Fe Eng'rs, Inc. v. United States, 801 F.2d 379 (Fed. Cir. 1986); Linda Newman Constr. Co. v. United States, 48 Fed. Cl. 231 (2000).

clause and, in turn, the changes clause contained a limitation on the recovery of overhead.[105]

Nevertheless, a unilateral reservation of rights clause can be effective where the additional claim is neither included in the compensation provided for by the change order, nor barred by the contract.[106] In those jurisdictions that enforce the sovereign immunity doctrine, however, a contractor's insertion of a reservation of rights clause into a change order does not entitle it to obtain compensation not agreed to by the governmental entity in a signed writing.[107]

---

105. *Linda Newman Constr. Co.*, 48 Fed. Cl. at 231.

106. *Id.*; *see also* Mike M. Johnson, Inc. v. Cnty. of Spokane, 78 P.3d 161 (Wash. 2003), noting, *in dictum*, that authority exists to uphold a reservation of rights clause inserted by a contractor into a change order.

107. C.O.B.A.D. Constr. Corp. v. Sch. Bd. of Broward Cnty., 765 So. 2d 844 (Fla. Dist. Ct. App. 2000).

QUESTIONS

Aim to Please Construction Corp. entered into a contract with the federal government to build a veterans hospital. Aim to Please then subcontracted the structural steel work for the project to Not Too Steady Erection Co. The drawings and specifications contained details on the requirements for welding and for attaching certain steel components through mechanical means. However, no bolts were specified or listed on the drawings. The structural engineer made a field visit and noticed that Not Too Steady was letting beams sit on top of columns, without bolting them together. Being alarmed at the implication, the structural engineer directed Not Too Steady's foreman, in the presence of Aim to Please's curtain wall superintendent, to bolt up immediately all the steel that had been erected using galvanized two-inch bolts. Not Too Steady's foreman protested that the forces of gravity and the weight of the steel were sufficient to hold the beams in place until the concrete decks were poured and the curtain wall was installed, but proceeded to comply nonetheless.

In the meantime, Not Too Steady discovered that the drawings and specifications omitted to include cross bracing at certain points where trusses were to be placed, although cross bracing was specifically shown at other locations. After being informed of that by its subcontractor, Aim to Please notified the government that cross bracing would be installed as necessary in locations where they were omitted from the design. While all of this was happening, the government became concerned about the possibility of a power shortage adversely affecting the hospital after the hospital was completed. Accordingly, the government contracting officer directed Aim to Please to build a nuclear power plant at the hospital to serve as a backup source of energy.

Not Too Steady had entered into an AIA subcontract with Aim to Please, which included the A201-2017 General Conditions, without any amendments. The government contract with Aim to Please included a clause providing that all work reasonably necessary for the complete construction of the project was included in the price; Aim to Please's subcontract with Not Too Steady did not contain such a clause. Both the prime contract and the structural steel subcontract contained a patent ambiguity provision.

1. Is Not Too Steady entitled to a change order from Aim to Please for the bolts?
2. What should Not Too Steady do to preserve its rights for furnishing and installing the bolts?
3. Is Aim To Please entitled to a change order from the government for the bolts?
4. What should Aim To Please do to preserve its rights for furnishing and installing the bolts?
5. If the cross bracing is a change, what type of change would the cross bracing be and why?

6. Is Not Too Steady entitled to a change order from Aim To Please for the cross bracing?
7. Is Aim To Please entitled to a change order from the government for the cross bracing?
8. What options does Aim To Please have in regard to the directive to build a nuclear power plant? What are the legal ramifications to Aim To Please's contract?
9. What should Aim To Please's response be if the government issues a change order for the cost of furnishing the bolts?
10. Do any of the individuals who issued these directives have the authority to do so?

CHAPTER 15

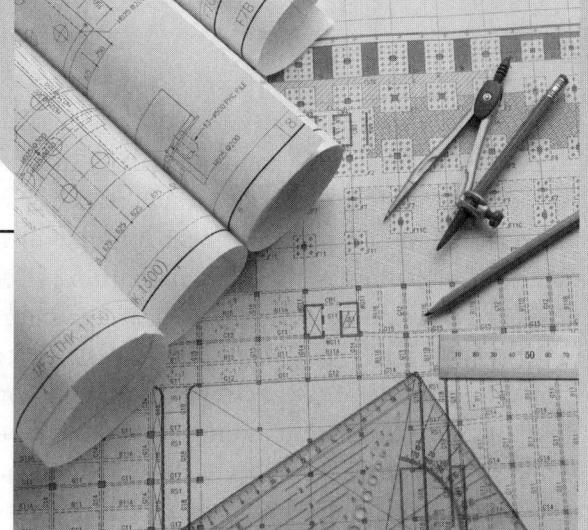

Differing Site Conditions

RICHARD F. SMITH, VAL S. MCWHORTER,
AND W. STEPHEN DALE

15.01 INTRODUCTION

Many construction projects involve work below the visible surface of the earth, or rely in some part on the conditions that exist below ground. Planning and pricing the work from a contractor's perspective requires some determination of what those subsurface conditions entail and how they will impact the work. In many situations, however, neither the owner nor the contractor truly knows the precise subsurface conditions when entering into an agreement. Often the subsurface conditions that would affect the work and, therefore, the cost of the work, do not manifest themselves until after the project has begun. Since the nature of these site conditions can dictate the resources needed to perform the work and, therefore, the price of the contract, both owners and contractors share a keen interest in managing the risk of unknown subsurface conditions.

The phrases "differing site condition" and "changed conditions" are terms of art; the terms refer to unknown physical conditions encountered at the job site that differ materially from the conditions reasonably expected.[1] For

---

The authors wish to thank Julia S. Kopcienski for her valuable assistance in the preparation of this chapter.

1. *See* Federal Acquisition Regulation (FAR) 52.236-2(a) (APR 1984).

example, a differing site condition (DSC) may exist where a contractor unexpectedly encounters rock rather than sand in its excavation, or a geologic formation that should not have been present in the region, or where the soil reflects a moisture content higher than expected. Regardless of whether the unexpected condition is latent or obvious, natural or manmade, the contractual question arises as to how the risk associated with unexpected conditions should be allocated between the parties, and how to resolve disputes between the parties when such conditions are encountered. The DSC clause and other similar provisions help allocate this risk and provide a vehicle for resolving disputes between project owners and contractors relating to these unexpected conditions.

Contractors, owners, and the courts have developed several mechanisms to cope with the lack of perfect information about subsurface conditions. These mechanisms, as discussed in this chapter, typically seek a balance between a variety of competing factors, including (1) the extent of pre-bid investigations that both parties must undertake; (2) the degree of risk each party must bear; (3) the amount a contractor should include as contingency in its bid; and (4) the likelihood of unexpected problems.

As a general rule, in the absence of a specific contract clause addressing subsurface conditions, common law allocates the risk to the contractor and generally places the burden of discovering and/or overcoming unexpected subsurface conditions on the contractor. In practice, however, the bidding process rarely allows time for a contractor to conduct extensive subsurface investigations on its own, and contracts rarely provide a reimbursement tool for expensive investigations by each prospective bidder. This inability to conduct investigations forces contractors to add contingencies to their bids to cover eventualities that may never occur. This practice artificially inflates bid prices to incorporate these contingencies and causes the government or the owner to pay for contingencies, regardless of whether the adverse subsurface problems ever materialize.

To combat the practice of adding these kinds of contingencies into bid prices, standard contract clauses adopted by federal and state governments and trade organizations place a heavier contractual focus on information provided by the government or owner to the contractor. These clauses seek to reduce the contingency included by contractors in their bids by encouraging contractors to rely on information provided by owners and promising an adjustment in the contract price for material deviations from the information provided. This practice allows the government or owner to avoid paying for expensive contingencies that never occur, and allows the contractor protection against unforeseen problems that could impact project cost. In addition, it allows the owner to evaluate bids from contractors on the same pricing basis, rather than on unknown contingencies.

To provide context for the modern clause-based approach to changed subsurface conditions, this chapter first reviews the common law heritage of the Differing Site Conditions clause and the evolution of risk allocation for subsurface conditions. The common law tradition employed general contract principles, including warranty, misrepresentation, mutual mistake, and other conceptual frameworks to allocate responsibility for price increases due to unexpected conditions. After reviewing the various common law approaches, this chapter turns to an overview of governmental and commercial contract clauses designed to address these issues as well as their application in the federal, state, and private context.

15.02 COMMON LAW

A. Contracts without a Site Indications or Risk Allocation Clause

Where fixed-price construction contracts include no special provision for subsurface conditions, the contractor normally bears the risk of unforeseen conditions. In that context, the U.S. Supreme Court summed up the allocation of risk in such circumstances stating: "Where one agrees to do, for a fixed sum, a thing possible to be performed, he will not be excused or become entitled to additional compensation, because unforeseen difficulties are encountered."[2]

This method of contract risk allocation has been echoed in decisions from state and federal courts as well as in the Federal Acquisition Regulation (FAR). The FAR declares that a firm, fixed-price contract without more

> provides for a price that is not subject to any adjustment on the basis of the contractor's cost experience in performing the contract. *This contract type places upon the contractor maximum risk and full responsibility for all costs and resulting profit or loss.* It provides maximum incentive for the contractor to control costs and perform effectively and imposes a minimum administrative burden upon the contracting parties.[3]

This concept of "maximum contractor risk" governed construction contracting until the advent of special risk-allocating clauses and other legal theories that allowed a contractor to recover increased costs due to unexpected subsurface conditions.

---

2. Spearin v. United States, 248 U.S. 132, 136 (1918).
3. Dalton v. Cessna Aircraft Co., 98 F.3d 1298, 1304 (Fed. Cir. 1996), discussing FAR 16.202-1 and firm fixed-price services contracts (emphasis added).

In *Simpson v. United States*,[4] for example, the contractor on a federal project agreed to construct a dry dock at the Brooklyn Navy Yard. The Navy previously had conducted soil testing at the site, but did not include that information in the solicitation or contract documents. In short, the contract documents did not contain any indications of subsurface conditions or any provision that addressed changes in those conditions. During construction, the *Simpson* contractor discovered sandy soil underneath the foundation, which caused unexpected settlement of the dock. The unforeseen soil conditions forced the contractor to incur additional costs to complete the project. The contractor submitted a request to the Navy for additional compensation to cover the costs of working in the sandy soil.

In upholding the Navy's rejection of the contractor's request, the Supreme Court in *Simpson* focused on the absence of any remedy-granting provision addressing the soil conditions, finding that:

> The contract imposed upon the contractors the obligation to construct the dock according to the specifications within a designated time for an agreed price upon a site to be selected by the United States. We look in vain for any statement or agreement or even intimation that any warranty, express or implied, in favor of the contractors was entered into concerning the character of the underlying soil.[5]

Finding no contractual ground by which to release the contractor from its obligations, the Court relied on the plain language of the contract and denied the contractor any increased compensation. *Simpson* represents the trend by which the majority of jurisdictions operated prior to the introduction of the federal Differing Site Conditions clause and other similar clauses,[6] namely that the contractor must bear the risk of encountering adverse conditions.

The same risk allocation scheme persists in private commercial contracting today in the absence of contractual relief. For example, in *American Demolition,*

---

4. 172 U.S. 372 (1899).

5. *Simpson*, 172 U.S. at 380. The *Simpson* contractor also advanced an alternative theory of liability for the subsurface conditions, relying on the government's obligation to make the worksite available for performance of the contract. Under this theory, the contractor contended that making the site available included an implied warranty of subsurface conditions. The Court rejected that argument, holding that making the site "available" did not encompass a broader obligation to warrant the site conditions.

6. The trend continues today in state jurisprudence where contracts lack a remedy granting provision covering unknown subsurface conditions. *See, e.g.*, American Demolition, Inc. v. Hapeville Hotel Ltd., 413 S.E.2d 749 (Ga. App. 1991) (parties expressly removed differing site conditions clause); Abbruzzese v. Miller, 1996 Ohio App. LEXIS 4304 (1996) (denying recovery for unknown subsurface conditions where contract lacked any differing site conditions clause).

Inc. v. Hapeville Hotel Ltd.,[7] the parties relied on standard AIA construction documents. In negotiation, the parties struck out the AIA standard provision allowing a contractor to recover for changed or concealed conditions at the site and did not replace the provision with any other form of relief.[8] The court held that "[t]he contract here contained no changed conditions clause, unequivocally limited the contract payment to a sum certain, and contained an inspection clause. It is clear from these provisions that the contract imposed the risk of uncertainty of subsurface conditions on [the contractor]."[9]

B. Alternate Legal Theories in the Presence of Representations or Indications

The inclusion of contract language or materials that directly address subsurface conditions works a dramatic change in the allocation of risk for subsurface problems. Even in the absence of a specific risk-allocation device, the presence of descriptions or representations in the contract or bid documents as to the nature of the subsurface conditions or to means and methods that would be suitable for addressing the work can relieve the contractor of liability for those conditions. In effecting this shift away from contractor liability, courts have relied on standard contract law devices including warranty, misrepresentation, and mutual mistake, as well as concepts specific to government contracting, such as superior knowledge.

1. Warranty

One of the legal theories on which contractors have successfully relied to recover increased costs associated with adverse conditions is the implied warranty of specifications. This well-established theory rests on the decision of the U.S. Supreme Court in *Spearin v. United States*.[10] In that decision, the Court established the maxim that "if the contractor is bound to build according to plans and specifications prepared by the owner, the contractor will not be responsible for the consequences of defects in the plans and specifications."[11] The *Spearin* Doctrine of implied warranties constitutes the owner's representation to the contractor that the plans and specifications are accurate and suitable for their intended use. Contractors and courts have applied this concept of implied warranty of specifications to changes in subsurface conditions where

---

7. *American Demolition, Inc.*, 413 S.E.2d at 749.
8. *See id.* at 750.
9. *Id.* at 752.
10. *Spearin*, 248 U.S. at 132. *See also* note 2 and accompanying text.
11. *Id.* at 136.

the government-included specifications directed the use of particular equipment, or specific means and methods, or included maps or plans that represented anticipated site conditions. Courts have applied the *Spearin* Doctrine as a basis for finding owner liability for these constructive "representations" of site conditions.[12] The *Spearin* Doctrine is accepted in most states as the basis for an implied warranty of specifications.[13]

2. Misrepresentation

In addition to relying on breach of the implied warranty of specifications, contractors also have relied on the common law theory of misrepresentation to recover increased costs associated with adverse conditions.[14] This common law approach includes both intentional misrepresentation and unintentional or negligent misrepresentation.[15] Under this family of theories, the contractor typically asserts that the government or owner made affirmative representations in the contract documents as to the nature of the work and the subsurface conditions; the contractor relied on these affirmative representations in preparing its bid; and these representations ultimately proved to be false or inaccurate.

---

12. *See, e.g.*, United States v. Atl. Dredging Co., 253 U.S. 1 (1920) (approval of contractor's plan for the work and express contract representations as to methods constituted government plans and specifications for purposes of defective specifications claim).

13. Defective specifications may lead to a compensable claim even in the presence of a differing site conditions clause. Magnus Pacific Corp. v. United States, 133 Fed. Cl. 40, 677 (Fed. Cl. 2017) ("[h]ere, plaintiff's defective plans and specifications claim for cost overruns in embankment fill is grounded in a wide variety of defects in the levee's design documents, not, solely, the solicitations' indications of subsurface conditions at the levee. For that reason, Magnus's defective plans and specifications claim is sufficiently distinct from any claim it might bring under a differing site conditions theory, and thus the defective plans and specifications claim may proceed in this court on its own basis.").

14. *See, e.g.*, Hollerbach v. United States, 233 U.S. 165 (1914) (dam fill material misrepresented in government plans); Christie v. United States, 237 U.S. 234 (1915) (contract borings incorrectly indicated gravel beneath lock and dam structure rather than mixture of material actually found); *Atl. Dredging Co.*, 253 U.S. at 1 (on dredging contract, direction to contractors to conduct site visit does not relieve government of liability for misrepresentations in the plans and specifications); United States v. Smith, 256 U.S. 11 (1921) (where specifications did not reveal presence of limestone, contractor awarded extra costs to work through rock); Levering & Garrigues Co. v. United States, 73 Ct. Cl. 566 (1932) (intentional misrepresentation as grounds to award increased costs).

15. *But see* Souza & McCue Constr. Co., Inc. v. Superior Court of San Benito County, 370 P.2d 338, 340 (Cal. 1962) (proof of an intentional misrepresentation adds little to the recovery since, "[t]his rule is mainly based on the theory that the furnishing of misleading plans and specifications by the public body constitutes a breach of an implied warranty of their correctness. The fact that a breach is fraudulent does not make the rule inapplicable.").

These kinds of claims include allegations akin to negligent misrepresentation,[16] (i.e., that the contract documents misled the contractor), as well as more affirmative misrepresentations evocative of claims for active concealment.[17]

The courts have almost uniformly dismissed the question of good faith or bad faith aspects of misrepresentation. Unlike a tort action, in which additional damages may be available to a victim of intentional or bad faith misrepresentation, the result in a contract action is normally the same regardless of the basis of misrepresentation. In *Levering & Garrigues v. United States*,[18] the claimant contractor entered into a contract to construct an addition at the U.S. Naval Academy. As part of the claim process, the contractor learned that the Navy had long known of the existence and location of certain subsurface conditions but had intentionally failed to disclose that knowledge to bidders. In awarding damages, the Court of Claims ignored the motive and details of the withholding and focused instead on the simple fact that the government misled the contractor.[19] Thus, under this analysis, the court looks only to the nature of the representations, inquiring as to whether that representation amounted to an affirmative statement of site conditions. With that element proven true, the contractor need only demonstrate that the actual conditions differed from that represented by the government.

3. Superior Knowledge/Concealment

A theory akin to misrepresentation is that of superior knowledge. Under this theory, if the government possesses special knowledge vital to the performance of a contract that the contractor does not possess and cannot reasonably acquire, the government must disclose its superior knowledge or compensate the contractor for any increased costs that result from the failure to disclose the information.[20] However, it should be noted that "[W]here the particular

---

16. *See, e.g., Hollerbach*, 233 U.S. at 165 (representations in the plans and specifications "must be taken as true and binding on the Government"); *Christie*, 237 U.S. at 234 (relief for misrepresentations of site conditions may be either intentional or unintentional).

17. *See, e.g., Smith*, 256 U.S. at 11; *Levering & Garrigues Co.*, 73 Ct. Cl. at 566. Accord *Souza & McCue Constr. Co., Inc.*, 370 P.2d at 340.

18. 73 Ct. Cl. at 566.

19. *Id.* at 575.

20. *See* Hardeman-Monier-Hutcherson v. United States, 458 F.2d 1364, 1371–72 (1972) (unusually severe weather ruled not a changed condition, but contractor recovered increased costs based on government's failure to adequately disclose knowledge of weather issues); Helene Curtis Indus., Inc. v. United States, 312 F.2d 774, 778 (Ct. Cl. 1963) (where the government possesses "vital information which it was aware the bidders needed but would not have, [it] could not properly let them flounder on their own. Although it is not a fiduciary toward its contractors,

information is equally available to both parties', it is 'fundamental' that the contractor's relief under a superior knowledge claim is precluded."[21] This legal theory shares some of the traits of misrepresentation, but focuses on concealment rather than affirmative misrepresentations of site conditions. Consequently, in a commercial or private contracting venue, the claim for relief may also proceed under the guise of the tort of concealment.

For example, in *Granite Construction Co., Inc. v. United States*,[22] the Corps of Engineers contracted for a salmon fingerling bypass through a dam on the Columbia River. The Corps, unknown to the contractor, had encountered difficulties performing similar work on another fingerling bypass project using equipment similar to that proposed by the contractor on the current project. When the contractor encountered the same problems as the earlier contractor, it submitted claims to the Corps based on both superior knowledge and the Differing Site Conditions clause. Although the court denied the contractor additional compensation, the court provided a detailed analysis of the factors required to demonstrate superior knowledge in the context of a differing site condition. The analysis yielded the following conclusion:

> Three elements were distilled there to find liability: the Government had information that would be material to performance of the contract; the contractor lacked that knowledge and had no reason to be on notice of it; and the Government either knew or should have known that the plaintiff was in ignorance of the relevant information. The element of misrepresentation, inadvertent or deliberate, is not directly relied upon, but may be implicit in the requirement that the Government know or have reason to know that the contractor is, in effect, stepping into a trap.[23]

The court explained the basis for its decision, stating that "in the absence of affirmative misrepresentations, the Government is not a guarantor against poor judgment with respect to methodologies selected by the contractor."[24] The formula set forth in *Granite Construction Co.* establishes a higher evidentiary burden than that called for by many of the standard contract clauses discussed later in this chapter.

---

the government—where the balance of knowledge is so clearly on its side—can no more betray a contractor into a ruinous course of action by silence than by the written or spoken word.").

21. Tucci & Sons, Inc. v. Dep't of Transp., CBCA No. 4779, 17-1 BCA ¶ 36,599 (2016).

22. 24 Cl. Ct. 735 (1991).

23. *Id.* at 750 (emphasis added). *See also* ASI Constructors, Inc. v. United States, 129 Fed. Cl. 707 (2016).

24. *Granite Constr. Co., Inc.*, 24 Cl. Ct. at 753.

4. Mutual Mistake

Mutual mistake has served as an often attempted, but less often successful, means by which a contractor may recover increased costs for changed conditions. Under the general theory of mutual mistake, where parties to a contract are mistaken at the time of contract formation as to a basic assumption of the contract, and that assumption has a material bearing on the agreed exchange of performances, the adversely affected party may void the contract, unless that party bears the risk of the mistake.[25] In the context of changed conditions, a contractor may argue that both parties were mistaken as to the nature of subsurface conditions. That mistake may arise from mutual assumptions drawn from information in the contract documents regarding the site, or from mutual assumptions based on conditions common to the region. This approach may present a challenge to the claimant in demonstrating that both parties labored under a mutual mistake as opposed to a unilateral mistake.[26] Nevertheless, given the proper factual situation, the claim for mutual mistake continues to exist as a viable theory of recovery.

15.03 REGULATORY AND OTHER STANDARD FRAMEWORKS FOR ADDRESSING DIFFERING SITE CONDITIONS

A contractor faced with bidding work under the common law framework faces three alternatives. First, the contractor could simply not bid the work. Few contractors who choose this option remain in business. Second, the contractor may bid the work based on an optimistic guess about the nature of the subsurface conditions. A poor guess, or an overly optimistic guess in this respect, could result in significant economic losses and, ultimately, in a lawsuit by the contractor for any of the common law claims. Worse still, the contractor may simply absorb the increased costs of performing the actual work. The financial challenges posed by the magnitude of some changed conditions could easily result in default or bankruptcy of the contractor. Third, the contractor could add a contingency to its bid to cover a range of possibilities that might occur once the contractor began work. Under this scenario, the contractor must determine the right contingency, and a poor guess could result in the same problems as option two. Alternatively, an overlarge contingency could make

---

25. *See* Restatement of the Law (Second) of Contracts § 152 (1981) (updated Oct. 2017); Northrop Grumman Corp. v. United States, 47 Fed. Cl. 20, 52 (2000); Nat'l Presto Indus., Inc. v. United States, 338 F.2d 99 (Ct. Cl. 1964). *Accord* FAR 14.407-4(c).

26. *See e.g.*, Flippin Materials Co. v. United States, 160 Ct. Cl. 357 (1963) (court rejected claim for mistake after finding contract documents actually revealed changed conditions and showed no mistake).

the contractor's bid too high and uncompetitive compared to other bids. Moreover, if the contractor does not encounter the problems contemplated by its contingency, the government or owner pays for work not performed, and the contractor receives a windfall.

This functional framework resulting from the common law remedies persisted until 1926, when the federal government began to review the financial and economic impact of these kinds of changes on bidding and performance of public contracts. As part of that review, the federal Board of Contracts and Adjustments determined that bidders on federal contracts more often than not inserted contingencies into their bids in anticipation of problems that might arise in the work due to subsurface conditions. In addition, the government paid these hidden costs regardless of whether the contractor encountered unexpected conditions. Moreover, as later articulated by the Court of Federal Claims:

> Generally, the government is in a better position to provide the contractor with the necessary information about site conditions, given the fact that it has already taken the time to design the project, make its own borings, as well as investigate and evaluate the site prior to submitting the project for bidding.[27]

As a result, the Board of Contracts and Adjustments developed a standard contracting clause to address contingencies in bids, but also provide some protection for the contractor in the event conditions differed from those expected.

A. Differing Site Conditions—FAR 52.236-2

The clause developed by the Board of Contracts and Adjustments was known as the Changed Conditions clause. The concepts and protections that gave rise to the Changed Conditions clause now appear in federal contracts, and many other contracts funded by federal contributions, under the name Differing Site Conditions clause. The federal Differing Site Conditions clause states as follows:

> **Differing Site Conditions (APR 1984)**
> (a) The Contractor shall promptly, and before the conditions are disturbed, give a written notice to the Contracting Officer of—
> (1) Subsurface or latent physical conditions at the site which differ materially from those indicated in this contract; or
> (2) Unknown physical conditions at the site, of an unusual nature, which differ materially from those ordinarily encountered and generally recognized as inhering in work of the character provided for in the contract.

---

27. Youngdale & Sons Constr. Co. v. United States, 27 Fed. Cl. 516, 528 (1993).

(b) The Contracting Officer shall investigate the site conditions promptly after receiving the notice. If the conditions do materially so differ and cause an increase or decrease in the Contractor's cost of, or the time required for, performing any part of the work under this contract, whether or not changed as a result of the conditions, an equitable adjustment shall be made under this clause and the contract modified in writing accordingly.

(c) No request by the Contractor for an equitable adjustment to the contract under this clause shall be allowed, unless the Contractor has given the written notice required; provided, that the time prescribed in paragraph (a) of this clause for giving written notice may be extended by the Contracting Officer.

(d) No request by the Contractor for an equitable adjustment to the contract for differing site conditions shall be allowed if made after final payment under this contract.

The FAR mandates that this clause appear in any "fixed-price construction contract or a fixed-price dismantling, demolition, or removal of improvements contract" that exceeds the simplified acquisition threshold.[28]

In *Foster Construction C.A. & Williams Bros. Co. v. United States*,[29] the U.S. Court of Claims articulated and reinforced the nature and purpose of the federal Differing Site Conditions clause. There, the court described what it termed the "long-standing, deliberately adopted procurement policy" behind the Differing Site Conditions clause, stating:

> The starting point of the policy expressed in the changed conditions clause is the great risk, for bidders on construction projects, of adverse subsurface conditions: "no one can ever know with certainty what will be found during subsurface operations." Whenever dependable information on the subsurface is unavailable, bidders will make their own borings or, more likely, include in their bids a contingency element to cover the risk. Either alternative inflates the costs to the Government. The Government therefore often makes such borings and provides them for the use of the bidders, as part of a contract containing the standard changed conditions clause.
>
> . . .
>
> The purpose of the changed conditions clause is thus to take at least some of the gamble on subsurface conditions out of bidding. Bidders need not weigh the cost and ease of making their own borings against the risk of encountering an adverse subsurface, and they need not consider how large a contingency should be added to the bid to cover the risk. They will have no windfalls and

---

28. FAR 36.502. The "simplified acquisition threshold" is defined in the FAR as the anticipated price threshold below which the federal government may use special procedures for acquiring goods and services.

29. 435 F.2d 873 (Ct. Cl. 1970).

no disasters. The Government benefits from more accurate bidding, without inflation for risks which may not eventuate. It pays for difficult subsurface work only when it is encountered and was not indicated in the logs.[30]

B. Standard Form Provisions in Commercial Agreements

The federal regulatory policy articulated in *Foster* also influenced commercial contracting, as private commercial contracts often include provisions granting relief for unexpected subsurface conditions. Many domestic organizations, including the American Institute of Architects (AIA), the Associated General Contractors of America (AGC), the Engineers' Joint Contract Documents Committee (EJCDC), and the ConsensusDocs,[31] have developed clauses that reflect the same concepts embodied in the federal Differing Site Conditions clause. Each of these individual provisions reflects the different focus of the particular authoring organization.

For example, the AIA General Conditions of the Contract for Construction have long included a variety of changed-conditions clauses. The most current version of that contained in AIA Document A201–2017 includes a clause at section 3.7.4 entitled "Concealed or Unknown Conditions." This provision generally mirrors the purpose and language of the federal Differing Site Conditions clause, but differs primarily with respect to the role of the third-party architect. AIA Document A201–2017 (General Conditions), section 3.7.4 reads:

> 3.7.4 Concealed or Unknown Conditions.
>
> If the Contractor encounters conditions at the site that are (1) subsurface or otherwise concealed physical conditions that differ materially from those indicated in the Contract Documents or (2) unknown physical conditions of an unusual nature that differ materially from those ordinarily found to exist and generally recognized as inherent in construction activities of the character provided for in the Contract Documents, the Contractor shall promptly provide notice to the Owner and the Architect before conditions are disturbed and in no event later than 14 days after first observance of the conditions. The Architect will promptly investigate such conditions and, if the Architect determines that they differ materially and cause an increase or decrease in the Contractor's cost of, or time required for, performance of any part of the Work, will recommend that an equitable adjustment be made in the Contract Sum or Contract Time, or both. If the Architect determines that the conditions at the site are not materially different from those indicated in the Contract

---

30. *Id.* at 887.

31. ConsensusDOCS, 2017 Standard Agreement and General Conditions between Owner and Constructor (Lump Sum), *available at* http://www.consensusdocs.org.

Documents and that no change in the terms of the Contract is justified, the Architect shall promptly notify the Owner and Contractor, stating the reasons. If either party disputes the Architect's determination or recommendation, that party may submit a Claim as provided in Article 15.[32]

In addition to domestic alternatives, the concepts embodied in the federal Differing Site Conditions clause have percolated into the international construction contracting community. Among the alternatives available in that market, the International Federation of Consulting Engineers (FIDIC) has prepared standard construction clauses that appear in various international contracts, both public and private.[33] These standard forms, used by entities such as the World Bank for international development projects, include an Unforeseeable Physical Conditions clause that provides cost and schedule relief for "adverse physical conditions which [the contractor] considers to have been Unforeseeable."

15.04 ELEMENTS OF A FEDERAL DIFFERING SITE CONDITIONS CLAIM

The Differing Site Conditions clause allows for contract adjustments to address two kinds of changed conditions. Those two scenarios, referred to as Type I and Type II differing site conditions, differ primarily by the nature and existence of contract indications. Using the language of the clause itself, a Type I condition involves "Subsurface or latent physical conditions at the site which differ materially from those indicated in this contract."[34] Thus, the Type I claim depends on the difference between the contract indications or representations and the actual conditions encountered. By contrast, a Type II claim involves "[u]nknown physical conditions at the site, of an unusual nature, which differ materially from those ordinarily encountered and generally recognized as

---

32. The 2017 version of this AIA clause requires notice within 14 days, after first observance of the conditions, rather than 21 days, and eliminates the obligation of the architect to provide its decision on a claim in writing, General Conditions of the Contract for Construction § 3.2.1 (2017) [hereinafter AIA Document A201–2017]. As discussed later in the context of the federal framework, the AIA clause carries with it the burden that the contractor perform a reasonable site inspection *See* American Institute of Architects, AIA Document A201–2017, ("Execution of the Contract by the Contractor is a representation that the Contractor has visited the site, become generally familiar with local conditions under which the Work is to be performed, and correlated personal observations with requirements of the Contract Documents.").

33. *See, e.g.*, The World Bank, *Standard Bidding Documents Procurement of Works & User's Guide* ¶ 4.12 (2012) *available at* http://www.worldbank.org/en/projects-operations/products-and-services/brief/procurement-standard-documents-archive (last accessed Jan. 17, 2018).

34. FAR 52.236-2(a)(1) (APR 1984).

inhering in work of the character provided for in the contract."[35] Therefore, a Type II, unlike a Type I, does not depend on the contract indications at all, but instead on the unique and unusual nature of the conditions encountered.

A. Type I—Materially Different Than Indicated

A claim for a Type I differing site condition turns on the difference between the actual conditions encountered by the contractor and those represented in the contract documents. As a result, the nature of the original contract indications, the reasonableness of the contractor's interpretation of those indications, and the contractor's reliance on the indications become critical parts of a claim for a Type I differing site condition. These requirements have resulted in a formal checklist necessary to prevail on a Type I claim. That checklist is as follows:

> (i) The contract documents must have affirmatively indicated or represented the subsurface conditions which form the basis of the plaintiff's claim;
> (ii) The contractor must have acted as a reasonably prudent contractor in interpreting the contract documents;
> (iii) The contractor must have reasonably relied on the indications of subsurface conditions in the contract;
> (iv) The subsurface conditions actually encountered, within the contract site area, must have differed materially from the subsurface conditions indicated in the same contract area;
> (v) The actual subsurface conditions encountered must have been reasonably unforeseeable; and
> (vi) The contractor's claimed excess costs must be shown to be solely attributable to the materially different subsurface conditions within the contract site.[36]

1. Indications

The contract must include affirmative representations, or indications, of the subsurface conditions.[37] The indications may appear anywhere in the contract documents or materials outside the four corners of the contract that are

---

35. FAR 52.236-2(a)(2) (APR 1984).

36. *See* Weeks Dredging & Contracting v. United States, 13 Cl. Ct. 193, 218 (1987), *aff'd*, 861 F.2d 728 (Fed. Cir. 1988). For a five-element version of this test, *see* Ace Constructors, Inc. v. U.S., 70 Fed. Cl. 253, 268–69 (2006).

37. Although most CSC claims arise from subsurface conditions, DSC claims can arise elsewhere. In *Appeal of Parsons Evergreene, LLC*, ASBCA LEXIS 258 (A.S.B.C.A. Sept. 5, 2018), for example, the Board found that the presence of asbestos insulation on pipes was a Type 1 differing site condition where the asbestos insulation was not shown on the plans.

expressly referred to by the contract documents.[38] Indications can be express or implied. Express indications can include practically anything that overtly represents or fairly indicates the subsurface site conditions, such as boring logs, core samples, soil test, soil samples, geotechnical reports, photographs, and field notes. Indications also can be implied from the contract documents, or from omissions in the contract documents, and can include items such as specifications on means and methods, restrictions on blasting or types of equipment, or other indirect information suggestive of certain subsurface conditions. Moreover, any type of contract indication "need not be explicit or specific, but only enough to impress or lull a reasonable bidder" into drawing reasonable conclusions regarding the site conditions.[39] Thus, in the context of subsurface conditions, "all that is required is that there be enough of an indication on the face of the contract documents for a bidder reasonably not to expect subsurface or latent physical conditions at the site differing materially from those indicated in this contract."[40]

Geotechnical reports often are provided by the owner to contractors as part of the contract bid documents. These reports may be extensive and provide details as to what conditions may be encountered at the site. They may include all of the tests performed by or for the owner before the contract is bid. These reports often provide some guidance as to what conditions the contractor may expect at the site and how the conditions will impact the excavation and construction. However, these pre-bid reports may not provide much assistance in determining how the site conditions will influence the excavation and construction. Contractors often hire geotechnical experts to analyze these reports and provide them guidance on what to expect from the reported geotechnical conditions.

The indications, however, must relate to physical conditions at the site. "Physical conditions" within the meaning of the clause do not generally include

---

38. For example, federal construction contracts often include FAR 52.236-4, Physical Data (APR 1984). That provision will be used any time the government decides to provide a contractor with certain types of information including surveys, borings, test pits, tunnels, or other set of data on physical conditions at the site. When so included, the materials articulated under the Physical Data clause will automatically become part of the contract indications.

39. Stock & Grove, Inc. v. United States, 204 Ct. Cl. 103, 133–34 (1974).

40. *Foster Constr. C.A. & Williams Bros. Co.*, 435 F.2d at 875; *see also* Pac. Alaska Contractors, Inc. v. United States, 436 F.2d 461, 469 (Ct. Cl. 1971) (asserting that express representations as to the nature of conditions are not essential to establish entitlement to an equitable adjustment for changed conditions and that all that is necessary are "indications which induced reasonable reliance by the successful bidder that subsurface conditions would be more favorable than those encountered").

weather or acts of God that occur during performance of the project.[41] Physical conditions also do not encompass manmade events such as mob attacks,[42] acts of war,[43] or labor strikes.[44] The term, however, can encompass manmade or artificial conditions at the site that were present at the time of contracting.

Despite including the language "at the site," the clause does not limit the conditions to the physical limits of the worksite. "At the site" can refer to off-site locations required for performance of the work, such as borrow or fill areas, referenced in the contract. Several decisions of federal panels have allowed recovery for differing site conditions that occurred at contract-specified borrow pits that existed outside the worksite parameters.[45]

2. Reasonableness

The law requires that the contractor be reasonable in two respects: first in interpreting the indications, second in relying on them. Reasonable reliance does not impose a duty on the bidder to conduct independent subsurface tests or to have expert knowledge of the subsurface conditions at the site. Often, the contract information will include highly technical facts or analysis. A contractor need only interpret and apply that technical information as a prudent contractor.[46] That scale of prudence will depend in part on the sophistication of the work and the contractor. Thus, a contractor need not predict conditions it

---

41. *See, e.g.*, Turnkey Enterprises Inc. v. United States, 597 F.2d 750, 754 (Ct. Cl. 1979) ("Generally, the government, under the standard Differing Site Conditions Article, does not assume an obligation to compensate a contractor for additional costs or losses it incurs resulting solely from weather conditions, which neither party expected or could anticipate, and not from any act or fault of the government. Weather conditions generally are considered to be acts of God. Neither party is obligated to the other for additional costs or price increases resulting solely from acts of God."). Relief for unusually severe weather, even in the presence of contract provisions that articulate expected weather conditions, arises under different federal clauses. *See, e.g.*, USACE Regulation ER 415-1-15—Time Extensions for Unusually Severe Weather (OCT 89); Fortec Constructors Inc., v. United States, 8 Cl. Ct. 490 (1985), *aff'd*, 804 F.2d 141 (Fed. Cir. 1986).

42. *See* Cross Constr. Co., ENG BCA No. 3676, 79-1 BCA ¶ 13,707 (1979).

43. *See* Keang Nam Enter. Ltd., ASBCA No. 13747, 69-1 BCA ¶ 7,705 (1969).

44. *See* Olympus Corp. v. United States, 98 F.3d 1314 (Fed. Cir. 1996).

45. *See, e.g.*, L. G. Everist, Inc. v. United States, 231 Ct. Cl. 1013 (1982); *Stock & Grove, Inc.*, 204 Ct. Cl. at 103.

46. *See* Peter Kiewit & Sons Co., ENG BCA No. 4861, 4967 and 4973, 85-2 BCA ¶ 18,082 (1985) (subcontractor claim denied where no evidence presented that subcontractor actually relied on contract drawings). The reasonableness analysis does not replace an analysis of actual reliance, or reliance in fact. If the contractor was reasonable in its interpretation of the contract documents, but failed to rely on them in preparing its plans or estimates for the work, it can be precluded from recovery for differing site conditions. *See, e.g.*, Kaiser Indus. Corp. v. United States, 169 Ct. Cl. 310 (1965) (the test remains that of a "prudent contractor" even though "trained geologists might debate interminably about the matter").

could not have reasonably anticipated from an inspection of the contract documents, the contractor's site inspection, or the contractor's general experience.[47] In short, a bidding contractor's reliance on contract indications is reasonable, provided that reliance comports with what a reasonably prudent contractor, experienced in work of the kind called for in the solicitation, would conclude in evaluating the contract indications.[48]

3. Differ Materially

A contractor may satisfy the requirement that the conditions differ materially in many ways. It may demonstrate that the volume of work increased over what the contractor reasonably expected; that the equipment required to perform the work differed from that expected; that the cost of the work increased over what was expected; or any variety of approaches, provided the contractor demonstrates a material difference in the conditions. Proof of increased cost, however, is not a prerequisite for demonstrating a material difference between the expected conditions and the actual conditions.[49] Conversely, increased cost alone is not sufficient to establish a "material difference."

4. Reasonably Unforeseeable

The requirement that the conditions be reasonably unforeseeable works hand-in-hand with the contractor's obligation to interpret and rely on contract indications reasonably. In short, a site condition is reasonably unforeseeable if the condition is not readily discoverable by a reasonable investigation of the contract documents and the site.[50] Recent decisions have expanded the basic

---

47. *See Youngdale & Sons Constr. Co.*, 27 Fed. Cl. at 537–38; Servidone Constr. Corp. v. United States, 19 Cl. Ct. 346, 371 (1990); J. Lawson Jones Constr. Co., Inc., ENG BCA No. 4363, 86-1 BCA ¶ 18,719 at 94,172 (1986); Maverick Diversified, Inc., ASBCA Nos. 19838, 19955, and 20091, 76-2 BCA ¶ 12,104 at 58,150 (1976); Lee R. Smith, ASBCA No. 11135, 66-2 BCA ¶ 5,857 at 27,181 (1966); *Kaiser Indus. Corp.*, 169 Ct. Cl. at 324.

48. *See* Neal & Co. Inc. v. United States, 36 Fed. Cl. 600, 620 (1996) ("a contractor is not to be charged with the technical knowledge or expertise of a geologist, and is therefore 'not required to discover *hidden* subsurface conditions or those beyond the limits of an inspection appropriate to the time available'") (emphasis in original); Kinetic Builders, Inc., ASBCA No. 32627, 88-2 BCA ¶ 20,657 (1988) (no expectation that contractor should become a botanist in order to determine link between tree species and excess water at site).

49. *See, e.g.*, Roscoe-Ajax Constr. Co. Inc. & Knickerbocker Constr. Corp. v. United States, 458 F.2d 55 (Ct. Cl. 1972) (where changed work results in decreased costs, the actual changed site condition may still exist).

50. *See, e.g., Weeks Dredging & Contr.*, 13 Cl. Ct. at 218 (contractor responsible for site inspection and contract documents); Randa/Madison Joint Venture III v. Dahlberg, 239 F.3d 1264, 1272 (Fed. Cir. 2001) (the contractor "bears the risk associated with not examining the information that the contract explicitly referred to and made available for inspection.").

scope of a reasonable inquiry to documents that lie outside the four corners of the contract but are referenced in the documents provided.[51]

5. Causation of Increased Costs

This final element of a claim for Type I differing site conditions calls for the contractor to demonstrate damages and causation. With respect to the quantification portion of damages, the Differing Site Conditions clause relies on the same general cost principles as an equitable adjustment under the Changes clause. The method for determining the quantum of damages for differing site conditions is, therefore, best expressed as follows:

> [T]he amount of the equitable adjustment to which the contractor is entitled as a result of a changed condition is "the difference between what it cost it to do the work and what it would have cost if the unforeseen conditions had not been encountered." Accordingly, expenses which the contractor would have been obliged to incur anyway had no changed condition been encountered are not recoverable as part of the equitable adjustment. The amount of an equitable adjustment for a changed condition is thus not based upon the contractor's original estimate. Similarly, where the contractor could reasonably have handled the changed condition with a less expensive method, the amount of the equitable adjustment will be appropriately adjusted.[52]

When compared to other remedy-granting provisions, however, such as the Variation in Estimated Quantities (VEQ) clause, the Differing Site Conditions clause provides broader relief since it encompasses all cost types affected by the changed conditions.[53]

A contractor must causally link any increased costs or delay in project completion to the changed conditions, and not to other events.[54] The importance of demonstrating causation was highlighted in *Weeks Dredging & Construction v. United States*,[55] where the Claims Court could not distinguish costs attributable to differing site conditions from other contractor-caused problems. The court demanded that the contractor show a "breakdown of how many of the alleged uncompensated days are directly attributable to *each* of the differing site con-

---

51. *See, e.g., Randa/Madison Joint Venture III*, 239 F.3d at 1272.

52. *See, e.g., Roscoe-Ajax Constr. Co.*, 458 F.2d at 60 (*quoting* General Contracting Corp. v. United States, 96 Ct. Cl. 255, 277 (1942)).

53. *See* Section 15.05(D) in this chapter.

54. *Weeks Dredging & Contr. Inc.*, 13 Cl. Ct. at 241 (court chided contractor for being unable to "identify for the court a method whereby we can trace the impact of any *one* alleged differing site condition to the incurrence of any one identifiable excess cost" and asking the court to engage in "rank speculation" as to the causal connection of claimed costs).

55. *Id.* at 193.

ditions, *independent* of the concurrent causes identified by the defendant...."[56] The court opined that absent an ability to segregate increased costs caused by the differing site conditions from those caused by the contractor, the contractor could not recover at all for the differing site conditions.[57] To address this problem on a practical level, contractors may use a variety of accounting methods, such as discrete cost codes or special costs accounts, in an effort to isolate and to capture increased costs attributable to a differing site condition.

B. Type II—Conditions of an Unusual Nature

In contrast to a Type I condition, a Type II Differing Site Condition does not rely on contract indications, but instead arises where no contract indications have been provided.[58] To demonstrate a Type II Differing Site Condition, a contractor must show a combination of two of the following three elements:

1. The physical condition at the site was unknown; or
2. The condition was unusual and could not be reasonably anticipated by the contractor from its study of the contract documents, inspection of the site, and general experience, if any, in the contract area; and
3. The condition encountered was materially different from those ordinarily encountered and generally recognized as inhering in the work of this character.[59]

This test creates a high hurdle for contractors seeking to recover for a Type II condition, and one with fundamentally different requirements from the Type I claim.[60] These situations are highly fact specific and allow presentation of evidence beyond that pertinent to a Type I claim. For example, while a Type I claim focuses exclusively on facts included in or referenced by the contract

---

56. *Id.* at 241.
57. *See id.* at 244.
58. *See generally*, John Cibinic, Jr., Ralph C. Nash, Jr. & James F. Nagle, Administration of Government Contracts 460-64 (5th ed. 2016) [hereinafter Government Contracts].
59. *See Youngdale & Sons Constr. Co.*, 27 Fed. Cl. at 527-28 (quoting *Servidone Constr. Corp.*, 19 Cl. Ct. at 360, *aff'd*, 931 F.2d 860 (Fed. Cir. 1991)).
60. *See* Guy F. Atkinson Co., ENG BCA No. 4693, 87-3 BCA ¶ 19,971 (1987); Soletanche Rodio Nicholson (JV), ENG BCA Nos. 5796 and 5891, 94-1 BCA ¶ 26,472 (1993) ("When asserting a type II, differing site condition claim, the Appellant has a relatively heavy burden"); Charles T. Parker Construction Co. v. United States, 433 F.2d 771, 778 (Ct. Cl. 1970); Shannon J. Briglia & Michael C. Loulakis, *Geotechnical Risk Allocation on Design-Build Construction Projects: The Apple Doesn't Fall Far From the Tree*, 11 No. 2 J. Am. Coll. Constr. Lawyers 4 (2017).

documents, proof of a Type II claim can extend to information discoverable from local inhabitants or other sources of information regarding the area.[61]

15.05 LIMITATIONS ON CLAIMS FOR DIFFERING SITE CONDITIONS

A. Duty to Investigate

In both the federal and commercial context, a contractor bears the duty to conduct a reasonable investigation of the site. While the Differing Site Conditions clause and its like have mitigated the contractor's duty to conduct extensive independent investigations of the site prior to bidding, that mitigation only exists within certain parameters. As set forth in *Foster*, the Differing Site Conditions clause creates a compromise whereby the government does not require the contractor to conduct extensive independent subsurface investigations but, in return, calls for the contractor to make reasonable use of the government-provided data. Such reasonable use of available data includes a realistic visual inspection of the worksite. Thus, in the context of both Type I and Type II claims, the contractor labors under an affirmative obligation to conduct a reasonable site inspection.

Courts and boards commonly seek to balance the requirements of a site investigation against the overarching policy behind the Differing Site Conditions clause. For example, the Court of Claims in *Foster* weighed that balance in favor of the contractor, stating:

> Faithful execution of the policy requires that the promise in the changed conditions clause not be frustrated by an expansive concept of the duty of bidders to investigate the site. That duty, if not carefully limited, could force bidders to rely on their own investigations, lessen their reliance on logs in the contract and reintroduce the practice sought to be eradicated—the computation of bids on the basis of the bidders' own investigations, with contingency elements often substituting for investigation.[62]

The federal government and the commercial contracting industry have developed standard contract clauses to adjust in the owner's favor the struggle between (1) providing accurate information under the Differing Site Conditions clause, and (2) the contractor's obligations to make reasonable use of that information. One means to accomplish that objective lies in site inspection

---

61. *See* Daymar, Inc., DOTBCA No. 77-13, 78-1 BCA ¶ 12,903 (1977) (inquiries to local excavators would have revealed general knowledge of subsurface rock conditions).

62. *Foster Constr. C.A. & Williams Bros. Co.*, 435 F.2d at 887.

provisions such as FAR 52.236-3, Site Investigation and Conditions Affecting the Work (APR 1984).[63] FAR 52.236-3 provides:

> SITE INVESTIGATION AND CONDITIONS AFFECTING THE WORK (APR 1984)
>
> The Contractor acknowledges that it has taken steps reasonably necessary to ascertain the nature and location of the work, and that it has investigated and satisfied itself as to the general and local conditions which can affect the work or its cost, including but not limited to (1) conditions bearing upon transportation, disposal, handling, and storage of materials; (2) the availability of labor, water, electric power, and roads; (3) uncertainties of weather, river stages, tides, or similar physical conditions at the site; (4) the conformation and conditions of the ground; and (5) the character of equipment and facilities needed preliminary to and during work performance. The Contractor also acknowledges that it has satisfied itself as to the character, quality, and quantity of surface and subsurface materials or obstacles to be encountered insofar as this information is reasonably ascertainable from an inspection of the site, including all exploratory work done by the Government, as well as from the drawings and specifications made a part of this contract. Any failure of the Contractor to take the actions described and acknowledged in this paragraph will not relieve the Contractor from responsibility for estimating properly the difficulty and cost of successfully performing the work, or for proceeding to successfully perform the work without additional expense to the Government.
>
> The Government assumes no responsibility for any conclusions or interpretations made by the Contractor based on the information made available by the Government. Nor does the Government assume responsibility for any understanding reached or representation made concerning conditions which can affect the work by any of its officers or agents before the execution of this contract, unless that understanding or representation is expressly stated in this contract. (End of clause)

This provision requires the contractor to confirm it conducted an investigation of the site while also providing a government disclaimer of responsibility for conclusions that the contractor draws from its review of contract data.[64]

In the federal context, the level of investigation required to prevail on a Type I claim differs from that required for a Type II claim. With respect to the

---

63. For a similar provision in the commercial context, see AIA Document A201–2017, *supra* note 32, § 3.2.1.

64. *But see* North Slope Tech. Ltd., Inc. v. United States, 14 Cl. Ct. 242, 253 (1988) (*quoting* Foster Constr. C.A. & Williams Bros. Co., 435 F.2d. at 888) ("[t]he duty to make a pre-bid inspection of the site does not negate the differing site conditions clause 'by putting the contractor at peril to discover hidden subsurface conditions or those beyond the limits of an inspection appropriate to the time available'").

Type I claim, the law charges a contractor with a "relatively simple site viewing" and the knowledge gained from that exercise.[65] By contrast, a contractor seeking recovery for a Type II claim will have to satisfy a higher standard in order to demonstrate that the unknown condition was "materially different from those ordinarily encountered and generally recognized as inhering in the work of this character."[66]

Failure to conduct an adequate investigation, without more, will not preclude recovery for a Differing Site Condition.[67] Where a contractor fails to conduct an adequate inspection, the contractor bears the risk of all conditions that could have been discovered had the inspection been properly performed.[68] Conversely, if a condition would not have been readily apparent from a site inspection, the failure to perform one will not bar recovery.[69] Further, where a site inspection reveals information omitted from the contract materials or in conflict with those materials, a contractor labors under a duty to inquire about the discrepancy.[70]

B. Disclaimers/Exculpatory Language

In addition to site inspection clauses, the government and commercial owners have attempted to insert other exculpatory clauses designed to mitigate the risk allocation scheme embodied in the Differing Site Conditions clause.[71] Those exculpatory provisions range from disclaimers as to the accuracy of the contract data provisions that exclude data accompanying the contract from the formal contract documents and other means of avoiding responsibility for the information provided.[72] In public contracting, courts have met these provisions with healthy skepticism and have placed limits on the scope of exculpatory

---

65. *See generally* GOVERNMENT CONTRACTS, *supra* note 58, at 522; RICHARD J. BEDNAR ET AL., CONSTRUCTION CONTRACTING 600–02 (1991); Briglia & Loulakis, *supra* note 60, at 91–93.

66. Servidone Constr. Corp. v. United States, 19 Cl. Ct. 346, 360 (1990).

67. *See* Vann v. United States, 190 Ct. Cl. 546 (1970).

68. *See, e.g.*, *Weeks Dredging & Contracting*, 13 Cl. Ct. at 193, *aff'd*, 861 F.2d 728 (Fed. Cir. 1988).

69. Coastal Marine Construction, AGBCA No. 89-190-3, 90-2 BCA ¶ 22, 895 (1990).

70. *See generally Fortec Constructors*, 760 F.2d at 1291 (existence of a patent ambiguity in the contract raises the duty of inquiry); Jefferson Constr. Co. v. United States, 176 Ct. Cl. 1363 (1966) (contractor has duty to inquire as to obvious discrepancies in plans).

71. GOVERNMENT CONTRACTS, *supra* note 58, at 530–32; 4 PHILIP L. BRUNER & PATRICK J. O'CONNOR, BRUNER & O'CONNOR ON CONSTRUCTION LAW §14:56 (West Group 2002); *see also*, Owen S. Walker, *Differing Site Condition Claims: What Is Below the Surface of Exculpatory Clauses or Other Disclaimers?*, 48 PROCUREMENT LAWYER 24 (2013).

72. *See, e.g.*, Kaiser Indus. Corp. v. United States, 340 F.2d 322 (Ct. Cl. 1965); Morrison-Knudsen Co. v. United States, 397 F.2d 826, 841 (Ct. Cl. 1968); Briglia & Loulakis, *supra* note 60, at 94.

provisions. In one decision, the former Corps of Engineers Board of Contract Appeals stated:

> A contractor is required to do only what he might reasonably have anticipated from the contract plans and specifications. Where the contract contains a differing site conditions clause, no matter what other clauses the owner puts in the contract, they cannot make him an insurer to perform whatever work he may encounter regardless of its nature. A contract to do a useful job for another is not to be turned into a gambling transaction.[73]

Although generally disfavored, courts may enforce exculpatory provisions that seek not to nullify information provided by the government, but that confirm an absence of information or highlight information specifically not included in the contract documents.[74] These exculpatory provisions, however, will be narrowly construed and must be explicit. In commercial contracting, courts may appear more readily disposed toward exculpatory provisions, giving them greater weight when negotiated between two commercial parties.

C. Notice

Most public and commercial contracts that allow relief for changed or unknown subsurface conditions include a notice provision. In the federal context, the Differing Site Conditions clause requires that "[t]he Contractor shall promptly, and before the conditions are disturbed, give a written notice to the Contracting Officer. . . ." Likewise, the language of the AIA Concealed or Unknown Conditions provision requires that the contractor provide notice "promptly before conditions are disturbed and in no event later than 14 days after first observance of the conditions."[75] Under both provisions, notice operates as a trigger, calling for the government, the owner, or the architect to undertake an investigation of the conditions and to evaluate how the contractor should proceed.

The failure to provide notice and the proper form of notice are frequent sources of debate between contractors and the government or commercial owners. This debate ordinarily revolves around prejudice to the government's or owner's ability to investigate the conditions and make informed decisions about how the contractor should proceed. In the federal context, a contractor's

---

73. S. & M/Traylor Bros. (JV), ENG BCA Nos. 3878, 3904, 3943, 82-1 BCA ¶ 15,484 (1981).

74. *See* P.J. Maffei Bldg. Wrecking Corp. v. United States, 732 F.2d 913 (Fed. Cir. 1984) (where contract drawings were provided for "information only," the absence of data was not considered an indication).

75. AIA Document A201–2017, General Conditions, § 3.7.4.

failure to follow the formal notice requirements does not, of itself, bar a contractor's claim.[76] Where a contractor provides late or otherwise deficient notice of such conditions, a court normally will deny that claim only where the deficient notice prejudices an owner's ability to investigate or mitigate the situation.[77]

Under the AIA provisions, the debate differs somewhat. The AIA Concealed or Unknown Conditions clause requires only that the contractor "promptly provide notice to the Owner and the Architect before conditions are disturbed."[78] Unlike the FAR provision, the AIA provision does not expressly call for the contractor's notice to be written. The courts of Minnesota addressed this issue in *Robert W. Carlstrom Co., Inc. v. German Evangelical Lutheran*,[79] when the contractor provided oral notice to the owner of changed conditions impacting its roofing work. The court held that the plain language of the AIA clause did not include a writing requirement, and opined that the notice requirement in the AIA Concealed or Unknown Conditions clause was "more of an investigation tool rather than a claims provision."[80]

D. Relationship to the Variation in Estimated Quantities Clauses

In federal contracts, as well as some private and state contracts, a contractor may seek recovery for increases in costs resulting from an increase in the estimated quantity of a particular item. Under the framework set forth in FAR 52.211-18, Variation in Estimated Quantity (VEQ), at bid time, a contractor submits a unit price for a certain aspect of the work based on the government's representation that a specific amount of that work will occur. Should the contractor have to perform more or less of that work within certain well-defined limits, the contractor may be entitled to additional compensation, or the government may be entitled to a credit.

---

76. *See, e.g.*, Hoel-Steffen Constr. Co. v. United States, 197 Ct. Cl. 561, 573 (1972) (a "severe and narrow application of the notice requirements . . . would be out of tune with the language and purpose of the notice provisions, as well as with the court's wholesome concern that notice provisions in contract adjustment clauses not be applied too technically and illiberally where the government is quite aware of the operative facts. . . ."); Santa Fe, Inc., VABCA No. 1983, 84-3 BCA ¶ 17,538 (1984) (lack of notice merely places "upon the contractor a heavier burden in proving its case."). Drennon Constr. & Consulting Inc. v. Dep't of the Interior, CBCA No. 2391, 13 BCA ¶ 35,213 (2013).

77. *See, e.g.*, Miller Elevator Co. v. United States, 30 Fed. Cl. 662 (1994).

78. AIA Document A201–2017, General Conditions, § 3.7.4.

79. 662 N.W.2d 168 (Minn. Ct. App. 2003).

80. *Id.* at 173 (*quoting* JUSTIN SWEET, SWEET ON CONTRACTS 398 (1997)).

To demonstrate entitlement to an equitable adjustment under the VEQ, a contractor must show (1) that a unit-priced item varied more than 15 percent above or below an estimated quantity; (2) that the contractor incurred increased costs; and (3) that those increased costs were "due solely to the variation above 115 percent or below 85 percent of the estimated quantity."[81] In determining the value of an equitable adjustment under the VEQ clause, the parties must look to the change in the contractor's costs occasioned "solely" by the quantity variation.[82]

Prior to the introduction of the VEQ clause, contractors often sought relief for material variations in estimated quantities as a differing site condition.[83] In *Perini Corp. v. United States*,[84] the Court of Claims articulated certain limitations on the circumstances under which a contractor could seek an equitable adjustment for quantity variations under the Differing Site Conditions clause as follows:

> The cases that have applied the Changed Conditions article to substantial variations from the quantity estimated in the contract have done so on the basis that such a material deviation was not reasonably foreseeable. They deal with special situations where (1) the contractor could not have verified the estimated quantities from the contract documents and his investigation of the site; (2) he had no opportunity to investigate the conditions at the site or for other reasons had the right to rely on the Government's estimate, or (3) both parties labored under a mutual mistake as to the accuracy of the Government's estimates.[85]

After the introduction of the VEQ clause, courts and boards applied that clause with logic very similar to that found in decisions relating to the Differing Site Conditions clause, focusing on the reasonableness of the contractor's plan.[86]

---

81. FAR 52.211-18 (APR 1984).

82. *See, e.g.*, Foley Co. v. United States, 11 F.3d 1032 (Fed. Cir. 1993) (any adjustment under the VEQ "will be confined in amount to such cost differentials as are directly attributable to a volume deviation greater than 15 percent from stated contract quantities"); Victory Constr. Co. & Paul Krummel (JV) v. United States, 206 Ct. Cl. 274 (Ct. Cl. 1975) (VEQ is not a basis to re-bid unit costs).

83. Such a practice continues today where contractors may effectively plead in the alternative. *See, e.g.*, Gulf Constr. Group, Inc., ENG BCA No. 5958, 93-3 BCA ¶ 26,174 (1993) (After overrun in timber quantities, contractor requested equitable adjustment under both provisions, recovering only under the Differing Site Conditions clause).

84. 180 Ct. Cl. 768 (1967).

85. *Id.* at 780–81.

86. *See, e.g.*, Womack v. United States, 182 Ct. Cl. 399, 412–13 (1968) ("Assuming that the bidder acts reasonably, he is entitled to rely on Government estimates as representing honest and informed conclusions").

Following the introduction of the VEQ clause, courts and boards carved out different spheres of influence for each provision based largely on the same parameters set forth in *Perini*. For example, in *Morrison-Knudsen Co., Inc. v. United States*,[87] the soil quality of government-designated borrow pits resulted in an inability to meet the contract quantity requirements for borrow. As a result, the contracting officer directed the contractor to modify its excavation and hauling methods and to use other borrow pits, actions that resulted in significant changes in the contractor's equipment and costs. The government, in reliance on the quantity variation provision, argued that the changes in borrow material did not result in the degree of quantity change that would allow the contractor any recovery under the clause. The court rejected the government's argument, holding that the limitations imposed by the variations in quantities clause did not provide an exclusive avenue for the contractor. To do otherwise, the court opined:

> [W]ould leave a contractor without administrative recourse against any change in the contract drawings or specifications due to unforeseen field conditions which did not result in the prescribed overrun or underrun in quantities, even though the entire contemplated basis for performance of the contract may have been altered at a substantially increased expense to the contractor.[88]

Moreover, courts have determined that the Differing Site Conditions clause and the Changes clause supersede the VEQ clause where the two clauses directly compete.[89] In these situations, courts have concluded that even though the two provisions may address similar or related topics, each has its own sphere of influence. The VEQ clause addresses simply the narrow universe of cost changes due solely to a change in quantity, whereas the provisions in the broader Changes and Differing Site Conditions clauses cover any circumstance in which a change in the nature of the work results in more complicated or costly work.

---

87. 184 Ct. Cl. 661 (1968).
88. *Id.* at 689.
89. *See, e.g.*, ThermoCor, Inc. v. United States, 35 Fed. Cl. 480, 492 (1996) ("There is no indication that the VEQ clause was to override the Changes clause nor that it was to be the exclusive means for obtaining a changes adjustment."); United Contractors v. United States, 177 Ct. Cl. 151 (1966) ("clauses of this type [VEQ] do not control when the cost of doing the extra work greatly differs from the stated unit-price because of factors not foreseen by either party. In that event, the Changed Conditions clause comes into play and overrides the Special Condition."). *But see* CEMS, Inc. v. United States, 59 Fed. Cl. 168 (2003) (where contractor failed to provide evidence of changed conditions, may be limited to recovery under the VEQ clause only).

15.06 DIFFERING SITE CONDITIONS AND DESIGN-BUILD CONTRACTS

Design-build contracts are frequently becoming the project delivery system of choice. While many advantages exist to the owner and contractor for the design and construction to be a single point of contact and responsibility, design-build contracts create a tension between (1) the owner, which has expectations of full design responsibility with the design-build contractor, and (2) the need for the contractor-designer to have the ability to place reasonable reliance on the contract indicators provided by the owner concerning geotechnical conditions at the site. Owners also may seek to push all the risks on the design-build contractor, while seeking to maintain control of the project and its design.

Differing Site Conditions clauses were introduced into contracts to avoid the contractor inserting large contingencies in the bid, and these standard clauses are often carried into design-build contracts without changes. A body of law is developing as to how the standard differing site conditions clauses should be applied in the design-build environment. How does the existence of a design-build project delivery system impact a contractor's recovery of a differing site condition and the trier of facts' analysis of the standard bases for a DSC claim?

The current cases dealing with Differing Site Conditions claims under design-build contracts can generally be divided into two categories: (1) where the analysis is the same as a typical DSC case as discussed previously, and (2) where a different standard or analysis occurs because of the responsibilities given the designer under a design-build relationship.[90]

For the first group of cases, the analysis of the elements is the same as the typical DSC case, using the lists discussed earlier. What are the indications in the contract documents? Did the contractor rely on such indications in preparing its bid/proposal? Did the contractor perform a reasonable site investigation? Do disclaimers in the contract deny a DSC or shift responsibility to the design-builder? Did the design-builder give timely and adequate notice? Was a materially different condition found at the site?

A growing body of law is developing in this area. Is it possible that the state courts and boards and arbitrators would hold a design-builder to a higher standard of proof for a differing site condition on a Type 1 claim?

In one case, the design-builder was denied its $35 million claim for a Type 1 Differing Site Condition when the design-builder needed to change the design for a pier and seawall once it was able to adequately determine the site conditions. The board denied the claim in part based on the contractor's failure

---

90. Briglia & Loulakis, *supra* note 60, at 102.

to perform an adequate site investigation, failure to adequately study the soils report in the bid documents, and failure to prove the conditions materially differed from the soils report provided by the owner "for information only."[91]

In another design-build DSC claim, the board also denied the claim because of the failure of the design-builder to prove that a materially different condition existed other than as indicated in the bid documents, which condition required a design change by the contractor. The board held the government correct when it required the design-builder to proceed with its design obligations upon rejecting the DSC claim.[92]

In the *Drennon Construction & Consulting, Inc. v. Department of the Interior* case, the design-builder was able to prevail on a DSC claim and a *Spearin* claim.[93] The project involved the widening of a campground road from one to two lanes and elimination of a blind curve. The drawings the owner provided were defective, and Drennon needed to redesign the road and change its location. Drennon then encountered a condition wherein the slopes of a nearby hillside collapsed into the excavation required for the new design, and asserted a DSC claim for the materially different soil conditions from those represented in the solicitation.

The board agreed with the DSC claim and also a defective design claim. The significant movement of the road location was beyond what reasonably could be expected, and the conditions required much more excavation than anticipated. The board rejected a disclaimer to try to shift all design responsibility to the contractor.

With respect to a DSC claim, what is the impact on a design-build contractor when the owner requires a detailed investigation of the site conditions as part of the design preparation? Also, can the owner rely on a broad disclaimer of the geotechnical informat
ion provided in the bidding process to place the total burden of design on the design-build contractor?

The answers to these questions may be found in the *Metcalf Construction* case.[94] In 2002, Metcalf Construction was hired by the federal government to design and build 188 units of housing for the military at the Marine Corps Base Hawaii. One issue involved the existence of "expansive soil," which the government report had characterized as having a "slight expansion potential."

---

91. CCI, Inc., ASBCA No. 57316, 14-1 BCA ¶ 35,546 (2014).
92. Fluor Intercont'l, Inc. v. Dep't of State, CBCA No. 1559, 13 BCA ¶ 35,334 (2013).; *see also*, Nova Group, Inc., ASBCA No. 55408, 10-2 BCA ¶ 34,533 (2010).
93. CBCA No. 2391, 13-1 BCA ¶ 35,213 (2013); Briglia & Loulakis, *supra* note 60, at 106.
94. Metcalf Constr. Co. v. United States, 742 F.3d 984 (Fed. Cir. 2014); Briglia & Loulakis, *supra* note 60, at 109.

Separate issues were the presence of chlordane, disclosed as "acceptable" in the contract documents, and whether this contaminant was acceptable at the levels actually found at the site.

After award of the contract, the contractor was to conduct its own independent soils investigation. This investigation indicated the swelling potential was "moderate to high," not "slight." Metcalf's recommended changes in the construction requirements created a significant delay in the project. The higher levels of chlordane also caused remediation costs and delays.

Among other issues between the parties were (1) the extent of the obligation of a design-build contractor to investigate the site, and (2) the impact of broad disclaimers as to any pre-bid information supplied by the government. Differing site condition claims in design-build contracts based on pre-bid information often are denied based on the obligation to investigate as part of the design process and these disclaimers.

The *Metcalf* decision provides a lengthy discussion of how DSC claims are to be analyzed on federal design-build projects and whether the standard DSC clause will be given the same weight in a design-build relationship as in the Design-Bid-Build relationships. The *Metcalf* appeals court applied the same standard as the normal DSC claim analysis, and held that there should be no difference between design-build and Design-Bid-Build contracts when differing site conditions are encountered and claimed.

In overturning the lower court's opinion, the Court of Appeals for the Federal Circuit held Metcalf could rely on the government's affirmative representations about the soil conditions even in a design-build context.[95] The opinion also affirmed *Foster*, which held the DSC clause takes at least some of the gamble on subsurface conditions out of bidding.[96] The decision also affirmed the duty of the government to have a duty of good faith and fair dealing with its contractors.[97]

The requirement for a site investigation and its impact on design-build contracts is not fully developed in state and private contracts and may need additional cases to determine if the requirement for a site investigation can override a DSC clause.

Another related area of dispute between the owners and design-builders involves the design of foundations for projects. Can the government shift the risk of DSC to design-builders while maintaining control over the final project design?[98] The dispute often turns on whether certain design specifications are

---

95. *Metcalf*, 742 F.3d at 995–96.
96. *Id.* at 996.
97. *Id.* at 991–92.
98. Briglia & Loulakis, *supra* note 60, at 112.

requirements or recommendations and whether an after-bid soil investigation supported a change to the foundation design in the contract.

The issue of mandatory versus recommended design surfaced in *PBS&J Constructors, Inc.*[99] The contractor wanted to use spread footings for part of the construction, and the Corps maintained that deep foundations were required. In the decision, the board analyzed the contract terms dealing with "requirements" as opposed to "recommended" or "recommendations" with regard to the footing design, and whether the contract was ambiguous as claimed by the contractor. The board upheld the Corps actions in disallowing the spread footings, which, in the contract specifications, were stated to not be a viable alternative.

Another case, *Record Steel and Construction v. United States*,[100] revolved around "recommendations" versus "requirements" of a design-build contract, and also whether the contract was ambiguous. In this case, the U.S. Court of Federal Claims held the contract to be latently ambiguous and allowed the claim. The court noted that the designer-of-record should be allowed to exercise its professional judgment in the design and only comply with requirements, not recommendations. In the event of two reasonable interpretations, the court applied the contra proferentem rule against the drafter.

15.07 REPRESENTATIVE TREATMENT OF DIFFERING SITE CONDITIONS IN STATE COURTS

A. New Jersey

The evolution of relief for differing site conditions in New Jersey tracked a process very similar to that experienced on the federal level, forcing the courts to wrestle with construction claims until the introduction of a standard contract clause.[101] During the 1980s, the New Jersey courts tackled the issue of differing

---

99. ASBCA No. 57814, 14-1 BCA ¶ 35,680 (2014).
100. 62 Fed. Cl. 508 (2004).
101. On January 8, 2018, both houses of New Jersey's State Legislature passed N.J. Senate Bill No. 3409, which established a differing site conditions clause for public construction contracts. S.B. 3409, 217th Leg., Second Ann. Sess. (N.J. 2017), *available at* https://legiscan.com/NJ/bill/S3409/2016. The bill instructed New Jersey's Commissioner of Community Affairs to "promulgate rules and regulations . . . necessary to standardize the forms and procedures throughout the State for the new changed conditions process," but these regulations had not been announced as of time of publication of this chapter.

The state of West Virginia has also adopted a Differing Site Conditions Clause very similar to the federal clause, and included it in its Highway contracts. Section 104.9, "Differing Site Conditions," of West Virginia Department of Transportation Division of Highways, *Standard*

site conditions in four major cases. In each, the contract between the state and the contractor lacked a clause specifically addressing changed conditions, but each contained certain representations about the site conditions. In the first three decisions, the New Jersey courts adhered to the traditional common law rules regarding warranty, misrepresentation, and site inspection. In *Sasso Contracting Co. Inc. v. State of New Jersey*[102] and *Golomore Associates v. New Jersey State Highway Auth.*,[103] the New Jersey Appellate Division held essentially that "if the contract supplied the results of tests of soil or other conditions but did not purport to describe actual conditions, or if the contract included disclaimers of responsibility for descriptions, a contractor would not be justified in relying on the results without independent investigation."[104] In the third member of the trio, *Ell-Dorer Contracting Co. v. State of New Jersey*,[105] the Appellate Division reiterated that premise and reinforced a "plain language" approach to risk allocation. In doing so, the court enforced an exculpatory contract provision in which the contractor agreed to submit "no claims against the State, if in carrying out the Project he finds that the actual conditions encountered do not conform to those indicated by said borings, test excavations, and other subsurface investigations."[106]

Shortly after the *Ell-Dorer* decision, however, the New Jersey Supreme Court modified the state's approach in *P.T.&L. Construction Co., Inc. v. State of New Jersey*.[107] In *P.T.&L.*, the state contracted with PT&L to build a highway, which required the excavation and hauling of soil across the worksite, without including a Differing Site Conditions clause in the agreement. After commencement of the work, the contractor claimed that the actual soil conditions differed from those represented in the contract documents and may have been known to the state during bidding. The state denied liability for the additional costs associated with this condition, relying on contract terms, including exculpatory provisions, that called for the contractor to perform its own site inspection.

In its decision, the New Jersey Supreme Court relied on the policy statement set forth by the Federal Court of Claims in *Foster* as the court's touchstone, and balanced that policy against a bidder's obligation to "make his own

---

Specifications Roads and Bridges (2017), *available at* https://transportation.wv.gov/highways/contractadmin/specifications/2017StandSpec/Documents/2017_Standard.pdf.
102. 173 N.J. Super. 486 (App. Div. 1980), *cert. denied*, 85 N.J. 101 (1980).
103. 173 N.J. Super. 55 (App. Div. 1980).
104. *Id.* at 58.
105. 197 N.J. Super. 175, 182 (App. Div. 1984).
106. *Id.*
107. 531 A.2d 1330 (N.J. 1987).

investigations of subsurface conditions prior to submitting his Proposal."[108] The court found that the New Jersey form of contracting (i.e., agreements without a Differing Site Conditions clause) held bidders to a higher standard of care than under the federal framework. If, however, "facts were known or reasonably accessible only to [the government] and were not known to or reasonably discoverable by the [contractor]," then the court would reduce the burden on the contractor.[109] The court tempered its position by holding that any misrepresentations must be overt, and that "[i]nferential conclusions from contract documents, however, shall not be considered a false factual representation in the face of sufficiently clear and unambiguous disclaimers of liability by the State."[110] Thus, while the courts of New Jersey paid homage to the principles embodied in the federal Differing Site Conditions clause, the state ultimately relied on a misrepresentation analysis to provide recovery to a contractor. In response to the decision in *PT&L*, several New Jersey state agencies drafted and implemented clauses that mirror the federal Differing Site Conditions clause.[111]

B. Virginia

Public contracts in Virginia also include standard site investigation and Differing Site Conditions clauses akin to those found in the FAR. These clauses address both subsurface latent conditions as well as above-ground building conditions.[112] Similar to the federal provisions, these clauses require the contractor to conduct a site inspection and provide protection to the contractor for unanticipated differing site conditions.

In *Asphalt Roads & Materials Co. v. Virginia Department of Transportation*,[113] the Supreme Court of Virginia applied federal case law interpreting FAR

---

108. *Id.* at 1339.
109. *Id.* at 1340.
110. *Id.* at 1342.
111. *See, e.g.*, STATE OF NEW JERSEY DEPT. OF TRANSP. STANDARD ROAD AND BRIDGE SPECIFICATIONS (2007) § 104.03.03(3)(a) Differing Site Condition.
112. Section 4.3 of Commonwealth of Virginia Department of Transportation, *General Conditions of Contract between Department and Design-Builder* (Nov. 2016), *available at* http://www.virginiadot.org/business/resources/APD_Docs/APD_Office_Page/2016_VDOT_Design-Build_Standard_Template_Documents_Parts_3,_4_5.pdf (last visited Jan. 17, 2018); Section 104.03 of Commonwealth of Virginia Department of Transportation, *Road and Bridge Specfications* (2016), *available at* http://www.virginiadot.org/business/resources/const/VDOT_2016_RB_Specs.pdf (last visited Jan. 17, 2018); *see also* VIRGINIA CONSTRUCTION LAW DESKBOOK, ¶ 11.301 (Richard F. Smith, Edmund M. Amorosi, Jennifer A. Mahar and Brian J. Vella, eds., 3d ed. 2016).
113. 512 S.E.2d 804 (Va. 1999).

52.236-2 to interpret the Virginia Differing Site Conditions clause. In *Asphalt Roads*, the court addressed the interconnection between differing site conditions and variations in estimated quantities under a highway contract. In performing the work, the contractor discovered a substantially greater amount of unsuitable fill soil than indicated in the contract drawings. When responding to the contractor's request for additional compensation to bring new fill to the site, the Virginia Department of Transportation (VDOT) contended that the Differing Site Conditions clause in the contract only applied to differences in character, not deviations from estimated quantities in the specifications. In awarding relief to the contractor, and consistent with federal case law, the *Asphalt Roads* court found that the purpose of a differing site condition clause ensures the lowest competent bid for basic services such that the owner only pays for differing conditions, including excess quantities as they occur.[114] The court further held that when a contract contains a Differing Site Conditions clause, contractors may rely upon the accuracy of the specifications and need not increase their bids to account for unforeseen conditions or otherwise increase costs by undertaking their own borings and inspections of the project while bidding for a contract.

Virginia has introduced a new concept in its standard design-build program that utilizes a unique "scope validation period" that, on its face, allows the contractor to conduct its own investigation after award of the contract and during the design development phase. Should that investigation discover deficiencies in the information provided by the owner pre-bid, the contractor can seek an adjustment in its contract price to compensate for increased costs that flow from the differing site condition. Specifically, that clause provides:

> 4.2.2 Design-Builder will, after its receipt of Department's Notice to Proceed, undertake such testing, inspections and investigations as may be necessary to perform its obligations under the Contract Documents, including but not limited to additional geotechnical evaluations or Hazardous Materials studies. If Design-Builder intends to conduct additional geotechnical evaluations to supplement or corroborate the information contained in the RFP Documents, it shall do so during the Scope Validation Period. Any Scope Issues that arise from such evaluations shall be treated in the manner set forth in Section 2.2 above . . . ;[115]

---

114. *Id. See also* Cnty. Redevelopment and Hous. Auth. v. W. M. Schlosser Co., Inc., 41 Va. Cir. 118, 126 (1996) (reading contract as a whole, risk-shifting provision could not negate the express provision to compensate the contractor for differing site conditions).

115. *See* Commw. of Va. Dep't of Transp., *General Conditions of Contract between Department and Design-Builder, supra* note 112, at section 4.2.2.

Section 2.2.5 further sets forth some unusual language that calls for the contractor to:

  1. "[Acknowledge] that the Scope Validation Period is a reasonable time to enable Design-Builder to identify Scope Issues that will materially impact Design-Builder's price or time to perform the Work";
  2. "[A]ssume and accept all risks, costs, and responsibilities of any Scope Issue arising from or relating to the Contract Documents, including but not limited to conflicts within or between the RFP Documents and Proposal";
  3. Warrant that the contract documents are "sufficient to enable Design-Builder to complete the design and construction of the Project without any increase in the Contract Price or extension to the Contract Time(s)"; and
  4. "[E]xpressly [disclaim] any responsibility for, and Design-Builder expressly waives its right to seek any increase in the Contract Price or extension to the Contract Time(s) for, any Scope Issue associated with any of the Contract Documents."[116]

To date, VDOT has recognized a number of scope validation claims, including an inaccurate survey on a railroad line and other standard DSC claims.[117]

C. Illinois

In 1999, the Illinois legislature passed the Illinois Public Construction Contract Act (IPCCA), requiring, in part, that all public contracts for improvements in excess of $75,000 contain a Changed Conditions clause.[118] Through this act, the legislature of Illinois ensured that public contracts in Illinois contain a provision very similar to the federal Differing Site Conditions clause.

In addition to the substantive issues of differing site conditions, the courts of Illinois have wrestled with the procedural issues triggered by the Differing Site Conditions clause. For example, in *Kenny Construction Co. of Illinois v. Metro. Sanitary District of Greater Chicago*,[119] a pre-IPCCA decision, the court examined the public owner's duties under the clause and the implications of the owner's behavior after receiving notice of a differing site condition from the contractor. During construction of a sewer tunnel in Chicago, the contractor unexpectedly encountered unfavorable conditions, stopped work, and provided written notification to the district engineer of the problem along with a cost estimate for proceeding with the changed conditions. The district engineer failed to respond to the notice and threatened to default Kenny for failing to

---

116. *See id.* at section 2.2.5.
117. Briglia & Loulakis, *supra* note 60, at 118–19.
118. 30 Ill. Comp. Stat. 557/10 (1999).
119. 288 N.E.2d 1 (Ill. 1971).

perform the work. The contractor then met with the chief engineers for the Sanitary District and received oral instruction from them to proceed with the extra work, but gave no written approval of a change to the contract.[120] The engineer represented that "[i]t would be much easier and more realistic . . . to evaluate the work after it had been completed, and check as to how much more the contractor had expended, than it would be to accept from the contractor before the work began."[121] Later, when the Sanitary District refused to compensate the contractor for its increased cost of complying with the oral direction, the contractor filed suit.[122]

The *Kenny* court found that, under the circumstances, the engineer's statements constituted an undertaking to pay for the extra work, provided the subsurface conditions actually had differed.[123] The court also concluded as follows: notwithstanding the contract's procedural requirements, since the contractor relied to its detriment on the representations of the chief engineer, the district was estopped from avoiding liability; the district avoided liability on the ground that the engineer did not approve the extra work in writing. The court further indicated that the Sanitary District's actions amounted to ratification, having allowed the contractor to perform the work and having accepted the benefits of that work.[124] Thus, relying on various equitable theories, the court in *Kenny Constr. Co.* interpreted the procedural requirements of the Differing Site Conditions clause broadly in order to grant the contractor relief.

Later, in *Fru-Con Corp. and Granite Construction, JV v. Illinois*,[125] the Court of Claims of Illinois reviewed the nature of indications under the Changed Conditions clause found in the Illinois Department of Transportation (IDOT) Standard Specifications for Roads and Bridge Construction. There, a joint venture entered into a contract with IDOT to construct the substructure for a three-lane bridge and a number of piers. After construction began, the joint venture encountered numerous difficulties with river traffic and riverbed erosion. The contractor sought compensation for the work associated with overcoming these difficulties based on various theories, including misrepresentation and changed conditions.

With respect to problems caused by excess river traffic, the *Fru-Con Corp.* court found that the contract documents did not indicate or otherwise warrant that river traffic would be restricted to the navigational clearance during the

---

120. *Id.* at 5.
121. *Id.* at 4.
122. *Id.* at 4.
123. *Id.* at 7.
124. *Id.* at 8–9.
125. 50 Ill. Ct. Cl. 50 (1996).

bridge construction.[126] The court further found that the joint venture's site visit prior to construction should have disclosed the river traffic condition. When turning to the riverbed erosion problems, however, the court emphasized that IDOT knew or should have known of the potential for riverbed erosion.[127] The court focused on the omission of information and found that IDOT's failure to identify the potential erosion hazard qualified as an "indication" that no such condition would be encountered during construction.[128] Thus, the court held that "while it is true the contractor takes certain risks in its bid process, the [owner/government] takes certain risk when it fails to disclose information which affects the execution of the contract, whether that disclosure is intentional or not."[129]

D. California

The Court of Appeals of California first addressed the changed condition issue in *Gogo v. L.A. etc. Flood Control Dist.*,[130] where the court allowed contractor to recover on the theory that:

> [W]here the plans and specifications induce a public contractor reasonably to believe that certain indicated conditions actually exist and may be relied upon in submitting a bid, he is entitled to recover the value of such extra work as was necessitated by the conditions being other than as represented.[131]

Subsequent California decisions expanded on *Gogo* and held that there must be an affirmative misrepresentation or concealment of material facts in the drawings and specifications if the contractor is to recover. The courts indicated that without the affirmative misrepresentation requirement, contractors would be rewarded for inaccurate underbids and encouraged not to act diligently in examining specifications and drawings. For example, in *Wunderlich v. California*,[132] the Supreme Court of California denied recovery to a contractor because there was no positive misrepresentation or concealment of fact. In reaching its decision, the court commented:

> It is obvious that a governmental agency should not be put in the position of encouraging careless bidding by contractors who might anticipate that should

---

126. *Id.* at 77.
127. *Id.* at 91.
128. *Id.*
129. *Id.* at 58.
130. 114 P.2d 65 (Cal. Ct. App. 1941).
131. *Id.* at 69 (citations omitted).
132. 423 P.2d 545 (Cal. 1967).

conditions differ from optimistic expectations reflected in the bidding, the government will bear the costs of the bidder's error. . . . When there is no misrepresentation of factual matters within the state's knowledge or withholding of material information, and when both parties have equal access to information as to the nature of the tests which resulted in the state's findings, the contractor may not claim in the face of a pertinent disclaimer that the presentation of the information, or a reasonable summary thereof, amounts to a warranty of the conditions that will actually be found.[133]

Thereafter, in 1989, the California legislature enacted California Public Contract Code § 7104, which requires public works construction contracts involving excavations in the state to include a Changed Condition clause. The statute requires such contracts to include a contract provision that generally follows the language of the federal Differing Site Conditions clause. In *Condon-Johnson & Assoc., Inc. v. Sacramento Mun. Util. Dist.*,[134] the Court of Appeal of California revisited *Wunderlich* and the effect of disclaimers regarding subsurface conditions in light of Section 7104. The court held that the legislature intended the language found in Section 7104 to assist the contractor in preparing its bid and allowed a contractor to draw reasonable inferences about the actual subsurface conditions from the "indications" in the contract.[135] The court further held that the statute allocated the risk between public entity and contractor and reflected the policy that "it is to a public entities' [*sic*] advantage to provide information upon which the bidder can rely in order to obtain the lowest qualified bid."[136] In that environment, the California Court of Appeal concluded that disclaimers as to the validity of contract indications violated the remedial purpose of Section 7104.[137]

15.08 CONCLUSION

Contractors and owners have addressed the fundamental problem of how to treat changes in subsurface conditions equitably largely through express contract mechanisms. In the absence of those mechanisms, however, courts have looked to common law theories as well as theories created in interpreting the express clauses themselves to determine which party should bear the risk of these events. Administering these mechanisms has generated a body of law that assists in managing a contractor's and an owner's risk of subsurface conditions.

---

133. *Id.* at 550.
134. 149 Cal. App. 4th 1384 (2007).
135. *Id.* at 1394.
136. *Id.* at 1394–95.
137. *Id.* at 1396–98.

QUESTIONS

1. Your client is going to bid on a contract with the federal Differing Site Conditions clause, FAR 52.236-2. He tells you he is somewhat familiar with the property, having played on the site when he was a young boy. He remembers rock around the site, even though the geotechnical report accompanying the contract does not indicate rock is present. He asks if he should go to the site, extensively walk the site, and make a written record of what he observes. He also asks what he should do if he sees rock outcroppings at the site. Should he bid the work based on his observations or the soil conditions reported in the geotechnical report? If the bidding documents provide for questions to the owner, should the contractor submit questions outlining past experience?

2. A Type I Differing Site Conditions is one where "subsurface or latent physical conditions at the site differ materially from those indicated in this contract." Does this mean that a report of some nature should be provided stating the expected subsurface or latent physical conditions, or can the conditions "indicated in this contract" be determined by reading the contract terms as a whole?

3. You have a contract with a Variation in Estimated Quantities clause that allows an adjustment in unit price if the final actual quantity is above or below 115, or 85 percent of the estimated quantity. If rock excavation significantly exceeds the estimated quantity, can you submit a claim for a differing site condition? If so, when should you give written notice to the contracting officer of your claim? How should you determine the amount of your claim? Does it make a difference if you claim a variation in estimated quantities or a differing site condition?

4. Your contract has a Differing Site Conditions clause and an extensive geotechnical report detailing the conditions at the site. The report does not mention the existence of granite, but indicates hard rock may be encountered. A clause in the contract specifically excludes a claim for encountering granite. You encounter extensive amounts of granite at the site the granite requires you to change equipment and expend a significant amount of time excavating the material at great cost. Do you have a claim? What theories might you use to assert a claim?

5. You plan to bid a project with a Differing Site Conditions clause and a geotechnical report. If you do not have the training to understand it, should you find someone in your company who has the training to review it, or should you hire an outside consultant to review the report and provide an analysis for you? How do you demonstrate reasonable reliance on the materials provided? What is the standard for a reasonable investigation? Discuss the difference in the standard for a Type I claim as compared to a Type II differing site conditions claim.

6. Shortly after you are awarded a construction contract, a hurricane causes extensive flooding on the site. Can this be claimed as a differing site condition? What arguments might you make to support your claim?
7. What types of evidence would you use to prove a differing site condition? Outline the methods you would use to document the claim or defend against a claim.
8. Is your failure to investigate the site at all an absolute defense to a differing site conditions claim? What arguments could be advanced on either side of this issue? Does it depend on the nature of the differing site conditions claimed?
9. What should be included in any notice given of a differing site conditions claim? Does the contracting officer's knowledge of the condition waive the need for notice? What arguments could the contracting officer assert to demonstrate prejudice, or other defenses, based on lack of notice?

CHAPTER 16

Termination of Contract

NICHOLAS D. SIEGFRIED AND JOHN H. TARLOW

16.01 INTRODUCTION

A termination of contract occurs when the owner tells the contractor "you're fired," or the contractor tells the owner, "I quit." The issues surrounding termination, however, are rarely that straightforward. Termination of contract is a remedy available for particular causes and defaults. Those causes and defaults may be identified in the contract itself, or may be those causes and defaults for which termination of contract is a remedy under the common law.

Whether a party has the right to terminate a contract is not always clear.

Even when a cause or default supporting termination can be identified, that does not end the inquiry. Construction projects are complicated, and it is unusual for one party to be exclusively responsible for a default or other problems that may occur on a project. How the law responds to such situations cannot often be predicted. Moreover, even when the facts support the *legal* right to terminate a contract, the adverse consequences of doing so may outweigh the *practical* benefit. As a result, termination is a drastic measure, and generally undertaken only under extreme circumstances.

Indeed, reported case law is replete with lengthy discussion and analysis of numerous questions arising from contract terminations, such as the following:

- Did a party have the right to terminate the contract?
- Did the terminating party follow the often complex termination provisions of the contract?
- Should the allegedly non-performing party have the right to fix the problem before termination becomes effective?
- What is the difference between termination for cause and termination for convenience?
- What happens if a party wrongfully terminates a contract?
- If the termination was wrongful, what damages or other remedies are available to the party whose performance was wrongfully terminated?

As discussed in an earlier chapter, a construction project involves a network of many separate contracts. Any one of those contracts might be subject to termination, depending on the pertinent facts. For purposes of illustrating the principal issues involved in contract termination, as well as explaining some of the complicating factors that arise, this chapter considers termination primarily in the context of a construction contract between an owner and prime contractor, and addresses termination by focusing on four key topics.

First, Section 16.02 reviews the basic legal concepts of termination of a contract as established by the common law. Second, Section 16.03 explains the manner in which modern construction contract forms, such as those created by the American Institute of Architects, ConsensusDocs, and the Engineers Joint Contract Documents Committee, establish rules and procedures through which owners and contractors deal with termination. Section 16.04 discusses issues that commonly arise in connection with the termination of construction contracts. Finally, Section 16.05 covers the topic of an owner's termination for convenience.

16.02 RIGHT TO TERMINATE UNDER THE COMMON LAW

Not all breaches of construction contracts are equal. It has been noted that

> any contractually authorized breach by either party for which the contract provides administrative redress cannot constitute a common-law breach of contract . . . such as those addressing changes, suspension of the work, misrepresentation of site conditions, and termination for convenience. . . . [Such contract provisions convert] what otherwise would constitute traditional common-law breaches into a contractual right.[1]

---

1. PHILIP L. BRUNER & PATRICK J. O'CONNOR, JR., BRUNER & O'CONNOR ON CONSTRUCTION LAW § 18:2 (West Group 2002) [hereinafter BRUNER & O'CONNOR].

Under the common law, a party's right to terminate a contract for cause is based on the concept of a "material breach" that is not excused, cured, or waived. A breach of a contract is material only if the breach is substantial enough that it "reasonably compels a clear inference of unwillingness or inability of one party to meet substantially the contractual future performance expectations of the other party, and of the need for the other party to mitigate its damages."[2] Stated differently, "[a] 'material breach' [is] any breach that materially impairs the interest of the non-breaching party in the future performance of a contract."[3] If a party has materially breached the construction contract, the non-breaching party may have grounds to terminate.

A party's failure to perform may arise from a variety of circumstances. An owner's breach may encompass a number of failures, such as not providing the contractor with access to the site, not responding adequately to the contractor's requests for information, or failing to make payments in a timely manner, to name just a few. Breach by the contractor may include, by way of example, not completing the work in accordance with the drawings and specifications, not completing the entire scope of work in accordance with time requirements of the contract, not fulfilling warranty obligations, or not paying subcontractors and suppliers timely.

While all of the events described in the preceding paragraph are examples of breaches of contract, the difficulty and the risk to each party in deciding whether to terminate the contract on the basis of such breaches lies in part in assessing whether the breach is material. For example, if the contractor is one day late in completing some task on the project, is that breach significant enough to warrant a termination of the contract? If the contractor fails to complete a portion of the work in accordance with the drawings and specifications, is the deviation so important as to constitute a material breach of contract? Distinguishing a material breach from an immaterial breach is no easy task, and is especially difficult in the context of a complex construction dispute:

> We note parenthetically and at the outset that, except in the middle of a battlefield, nowhere must men coordinate the movement of other men and all materials in the midst of such chaos and with such limited certainty of present facts and future occurrences as in a huge construction project such as the building of this 100 million dollar hospital. Even the most painstaking planning frequently turns out to be mere conjecture and accommodation to changes must necessarily be of the rough, quick and ad hoc sort, analogous to ever-changing commands on the battlefield. Further, it is a difficult task for a court to be able to examine testimony and evidence in the quiet of a courtroom several years later concerning such confusion and then extract from

---

2. *Id.* § 18:4.
3. *Id.* § 18:1.

them a determination of precisely when the disorder and constant readjustment, which is to be expected by any subcontractor on a job site, become so extreme, so debilitating and so unreasonable as to constitute a breach of contract between a contractor and a subcontractor. This was the formidable undertaking faced by the trial judge in the instant case and which we now review on the record made by the parties before him.[4]

Sometimes the facts or contractual terms provide helpful guidance or instruction in determining if a breach is material enough to warrant termination. For example, if a contractor fails to meet a required completion date, and the contract expressly provides that time is of the essence, then the owner may be better able to justify any termination of the contract. In this context, careful attention to termination language in the contact is vital. For example, a contract may set a maximum amount of liquidated damages for delay that the owner may recover. While the imposition of liquidated damages may provide an adequate remedy for a particular delay, the contract may limit the time during which such damages accrue. If the owner wishes to maintain the option to terminate the contract once liquidated damages are no longer accruing, then the owner should also include a provision in the contract that expressly permits termination once that cap is reached.[5]

A contractor's failure to secure insurance or provide performance security when required by the contract is another example of a breach that often constitutes grounds for termination.[6] Because safety considerations are so important for construction projects, an owner might consider terminating a contractor responsible for repeated safety violations, or violations of the law, such as causing environmental damage, or some type of fraud related to a failure to inspect or test, or falsifying inspection or test results.[7] Other examples of possible material breaches include (depending on the circumstances) the failure to provide warranty coverage, the infringement on a third party's intellectual property rights, a wrongful assignment of a contract, or an attempt to change a major subcontractor or supplier after the contract is awarded.[8]

Payment disputes between owners and contractors, and/or contractors and their subcontractors, may also constitute a material breach. Moreover, when a contract provides that "time is of the essence," the failure to pay timely may

---

4. Blake Constr. Co., Inc. v. C.J. Coakley Co., Inc., 431 A.2d 569, 575 (D.C. 1981).

5. Robert F. Miller, *Putting the Hammer Down: The Owner's Declaration of Default* (Jan. 2003), *available at* https://www.americanbar.org/content/dam/aba/directories/construction_industry_knowledge_base/miller_paper.authcheckdam.pdf.

6. Id.

7. Id.

8. Id.

constitute a material breach. However, unless the contract provides a specific amount of time, a court will determine whether payment was timely under a reasonableness standard. Thus, a contractor or subcontractor considering suspending performance or walking off the job, that is, "abandoning" the project, must be cautious, as not every delay in making a payment constitutes a material breach of the contract.[9]

While the concept of a material breach is easy enough to describe, its application is difficult to assess when considering the facts of a bitterly contested construction dispute, as the following case illustrates.

Mustang Pipeline Company, Inc. v. Driver Pipeline Company, Inc.
134 S.W.3d 195 (Texas 2004)[10]

PER CURIAM

In this breach of contract case, both parties, Mustang Pipeline Co. (Mustang), and Driver Pipeline Co. (Driver), obtained favorable jury findings as to the other's breach of a pipeline construction contract. Mustang initially brought suit against Driver for Driver's failure to complete work in a timely manner. Driver counterclaimed for Mustang's wrongful termination of the contract. It is a fundamental principle of contract law that when one party to a contract commits a material breach of that contract, the other party is discharged or excused from further performance. Furthermore, if it is clear the parties intend that time is of the essence to a contract, timely performance is essential to a party's right to require performance by the other party.

The court of appeals, in affirming the trial court, held that Mustang could not recover damages because Mustang failed to get a jury finding that Driver's breach was material. We hold that an express jury finding on the issue of materiality is not required when "time is of the essence." Because time was of the essence under the contract and Driver failed to timely perform, Mustang was thereafter excused from performance. We reverse in part and render judgment that Driver take nothing.

In January 1997, Mustang entered into a contract under which Driver was to construct the northern 100 miles of a 200 mile pipeline from Mont Belvieu to

---

9. *In re* Fordson Eng'g Corp., 25 B.R. 506, 510 (Bankr. D. Mich. 1982) ("[d]elay in making payment where the amount of work done is disputed or is being negotiated is not on that basis alone a breach of contract."). *See, e.g.*, G4S Tech. LLC v. Mass. Tech. Park Corp., 479 Mass. 721, 723, 99 N.E.3d 728, 732 (Mass. 2018) ("complete and strict performance is still required for all construction contract terms relating to the design and construction itself. We also conclude, however, that ordinary contract principles, including the traditional Massachusetts materiality rule, apply for breaches of other provisions, such as the one at issue governing payment certifications.").

10. Most internal citations have been omitted as have sections discussing issues not related to this chapter.

Longview, Texas. During the bidding process, Mustang stressed that time was of the essence and that the pipeline construction had to be completed no later than April 30, 1997. In response to this time demand, Driver increased its original bid by approximately ten percent, but was still awarded the contract. The parties agreed on a fourteen-week schedule, working eleven hours per day, seven days a week.

Driver contends that extensive rains delayed the project soon after work began. On March 3, 1997, Driver proposed shutting down pipeline construction until the weather improved. On March 5, Driver officially requested a thirty-day extension to the agreed completion date, citing adverse weather and safety concerns as the reason for the delay. At a meeting on March 6, Driver reiterated its intent to shutdown operations and wait for drier weather, and it proposed a new 161-day construction schedule.

Fifty-eight days into the ninety-eight day construction schedule, Driver had completed only fifteen miles of pipeline and suspended operations. The parties dispute whether Driver could have accomplished more during this time by using different equipment or reassigning crews to work on drier areas. The contract includes provisions explaining how the crews and pipeline welds could be protected while working in the rain, suggesting that the parties anticipated working despite at least some inclement weather. By March 17, Driver stated that it was still not ready to resume work on the pipeline, so Mustang's project engineer certified Driver to be in default under the contract. Mustang then contracted with Sunland Corporation to finish Driver's portion of the pipeline, which it completed in September 1997.

Mustang sued Driver for breach of contract to recover the cost of completion, lost profits, and attorney's fees. Driver countersued for breach of contract, alleging that Mustang wrongfully terminated the contract, and sought damages, lost profits and attorney's fees. In their respective answers, both parties raised the other's material breach as an affirmative defense.

The case was tried to a jury. . . .

The jury found that Driver failed to comply with the terms of the contract but also found that Mustang was not justified in terminating the contract. It awarded Mustang $2,104,601 in damages for Driver's breach of contract and awarded Driver $2,515,958 in damages for Mustang's wrongful termination.

Both parties moved for judgment notwithstanding the verdict. Mustang asked the trial court to disregard the jury's finding that Mustang wrongfully terminated the contract and the damages awarded to Driver. Mustang contended that once the jury found that Driver breached the contract, it could not also find that Mustang wrongfully terminated the contract because a breaching party cannot subsequently enforce the contract. The trial court denied Mustang's motion. Driver's motion for judgment notwithstanding the verdict asked the trial court to disregard the jury's finding that Driver breached the contract and the damages awarded to Mustang. Driver argued there was no evidence of probative force to sustain the jury's answers on either the breach of contract or damages questions. The trial court refused to disregard the jury's finding that Driver breached the contract but granted Driver's motion to disregard Mustang's damage award. Thus, the trial court rendered judgment for Driver and awarded Driver actual damages, plus attorney's fees and interest.

Both parties appealed . . . Mustang raised several issues on appeal, arguing that: (1) the trial court erred by refusing to disregard the jury's answer to the wrongful termination question as immaterial; (2) there was legally and factually insufficient evidence to support the jury's wrongful termination finding and the claim was precluded by the contract's termination for convenience provision. . . .

The court of appeals affirmed the trial court's judgment. The court of appeals reasoned that the jury's finding of Driver's breach was relevant to Mustang's liability only if the breach was material. The court of appeals concluded that whether a party's breach is material is a fact question, and, absent an express jury finding, the trial court was not required to treat the breach as material as a matter of law. The court of appeals also concluded there was factually and legally sufficient evidence to support the jury's wrongful termination finding, and the contract's "termination for convenience" clause did not preclude Driver's claim because Mustang did not raise this issue in the trial court. . . .

First, we must consider whether the trial court erred in denying Mustang's motion for judgment notwithstanding the verdict. Mustang argues that the jury's answer regarding Driver's breach rendered the jury's answer regarding Mustang's wrongful termination immaterial, because once a party has breached it cannot later sue on the contract. Accordingly, Mustang contends that the trial court should have disregarded the jury's answer to the second question and granted its motion for judgment notwithstanding the verdict.

The court of appeals was correct in holding that a party is released from further obligation under the contract only if the other party materially breached. However, we disagree with the court's requirement that Mustang obtain an express jury finding that Driver's breach was material. . . . The jury question regarding Driver's breach tracks the Texas Pattern Jury Charge language for the recommended breach of contract question, asking "Did Driver Pipeline Company fail to comply with the contract it had with Mustang Pipeline Company?" ("Did [defendant] fail to comply with the agreement?"). The jury answered yes.

The evidence presented at trial established that Driver's failure to comply was a material breach. The Restatement [(SECOND) OF CONTRACTS § 241 (1981)] . lists five circumstances significant in determining whether a failure to perform is material:

(a) the extent to which the injured party will be deprived of the benefit which he reasonably expected;
(b) the extent to which the injured party can be adequately compensated for the part of that benefit of which he will be deprived;
(c) the extent to which the party failing to perform or to offer to perform will suffer forfeiture;

(d) the likelihood that the party failing to perform or to offer to perform will cure his failure, taking account of the circumstances including any reasonable assurances;

(e) the extent to which the behavior of the party failing to perform or to offer to perform comports with standards of good faith and fair dealing.

The Restatement also articulates circumstances that are significant in determining when a party's duties are discharged under a contract due to the other party's material breach. The relevant factors, in addition to those listed above, are:

(1) the extent to which it reasonably appears to the injured party that delay may prevent or hinder him in making reasonable substitute arrangements.

(2) the extent to which the agreement provides for performance without delay, but a material failure to perform or to offer to perform on a stated day does not of itself discharge the other party's remaining duties unless the circumstances, including the language of the agreement, indicate that performance or an offer to perform by that day is important.

The evidence presented established both that Driver's breach was material and that Mustang was discharged from its duties under the contract based on that breach. Evidence exists to prove, as a matter of law, that time was a material element of the contract. Driver placed an initial bid with Mustang in October 1996, but it increased its bid significantly in January 1997 after learning of the April 30 deadline. The contract specifically stated that "all time limits stated in the Contract are of the essence to the Contract," and the contract called for "100 percent completion of the pipeline system no later than April 30, 1997." In addition to the contract's emphasis on timely completion, it also required that "sufficient forces and equipment . . . be furnished at all times to adequately perform work with ample margin for emergencies and unexpected events, to carry on the work at a sufficient rate of progress to ensure completion within the time specified in the Contract."

In late February 1997, when Mustang realized Driver was behind on the construction schedule, it asked for assurances from Driver that the work would be completed by the deadline. Although Driver had workers, equipment and supervision on the job site, it accomplished only minimal pipeline construction. Mustang also requested a plan from Driver on how it would finish the project by the end of April. It recognized the unseasonably wet conditions, but offered suggestions to Driver about how it might expedite construction. The evidence indicates that Driver never provided a revised plan on how it would attempt to meet the construction schedule. When Mustang terminated the contract, it had approximately forty days before the April 30, 1997 deadline to complete construction on eighty-five miles of pipeline. Even the most ambitious of construction schedules would have great difficulty successfully meeting that deadline. At the point at which

> Mustang terminated the contract, there was virtually no chance that Driver would be able to cure its breach and complete the construction on time.
>
> Based on this evidence, we hold that as a matter of law Driver committed a material breach. Mustang was thereafter discharged from its duties under the contract. Therefore, the trial court should have disregarded the jury's answer to the wrongful termination question and granted Mustang judgment notwithstanding the verdict.
>
> Accordingly, we grant Mustang's petition for review and, without hearing oral argument, affirm the court of appeals' judgment in part, reverse in part, and render judgment that Driver take nothing.

The court made it clear that once a party has materially breached a contract, the other party is excused from further performance and may properly terminate the contract. Moreover, the breaching party will have no further ability to sue on the contract.

The decision to terminate, however, may not always rest entirely with the non-breaching party. For example, if a construction lender is involved in the project, certain actions taken by the contractor may trigger a default under the terms of the loan agreement, thereby providing the lender with various rights and remedies. In order to avoid problems under the loan agreement, an owner will need to consult with its lender to determine the appropriate course of action. The lender may suggest actions to cure the default or may authorize a termination, and indeed the loan documents may require the lender's consent to termination.[11] In either case, the prudent owner will follow the lender's instruction.

As described earlier, whether a breach is deemed material is often fact dependent, and that determination is just the first step in evaluating whether a party has the right to terminate a contract. Generally, a valid termination for cause and recovery of damages must meet the following criteria:

1. A [party] materially breached its contract, based upon an evaluation of the circumstances under the doctrines of substantial performance, economic waste, excusability, waiver, cure mitigation, impracticability, and principles of contract interpretation;

---

11. Miller, *supra* note 5.

2. The material breach was not induced, preceded, or otherwise excused by the terminating party's own supervening material breach of contract;
3. The termination decision resulted from the exercise of independent discretion and good faith motive of those having authority to terminate the contract;
4. The breaching party and its surety [if applicable] were given adequate notice of and an opportunity to cure deficiencies deemed sufficiently material to warrant termination;
5. The terminating party terminated the contract in strict compliance with contractually specified termination procedures;
6. The breaching party's performance bond surety, if any, was allowed to exercise its post-termination performance rights;
7. If there was no performance bond, or if the surety refused to acknowledge its performance obligations, the terminating party's resetting of the contract was both necessary and reasonably accomplished in mitigation of damages; and
8. The terminating party's compensable completion costs were reasonably incurred and properly accounted for.[12]

16.03 RIGHT TO TERMINATE UNDER COMMONLY USED FORMS

Against the backdrop of the basic common law concepts of termination is a world of construction contract forms commonly used in the United States as discussed previously in this book.

A. Variation from Common Law

Before examining how contracts commonly treat termination, a preliminary question should be considered: Why would a contract attempt to vary from, add to, and often complicate the basic concepts of termination of contract that have long been part of the common law, as outlined in Section 16.02? The simple answer is that the common law is not perfectly clear regarding the rules about breach and remedies. First, it is not always easy to discern if a breach is material. Parties to a contract can avoid such guesswork by expressly stating which breaches in their judgment are severe enough to warrant a termination of the contract. Second, the remedies and relief available to the non-breaching

---

12. BRUNER & O'CONNOR, *supra* note 1, § 18:39 (reformatted and citations omitted for clarity).

party also can be specified in the contract, adding clarity to the process and hopefully avoiding or limiting controversy. Third, construction contracts are complex and the parties may want to make their relationship more robust by providing opportunities to cure breaches before the remedy of termination can be invoked.

Although the termination provisions of modern construction contracts have added clarity to some of the questions that arise under the common law, they have not displaced all uncertainty: indeed, they often led to complex legal disputes in which courts devote substantial time and energy attempting to figure out what lengthy termination provisions mean, or how they should be applied in a given case.

B. AIA Forms

The AIA A201 sets forth the reasons and procedures for termination in article 14. One set of rules exists for termination by the contractor (section 14.1), and another governs termination by the owner (sections 14.2 through 14.4).[13]

1. Termination by Contractor

Article 14.1 of AIA A201 provides:

ARTICLE 14 TERMINATION OR SUSPENSION OF THE CONTRACT

14.1 Termination by the Contractor

14.1.1 The Contractor may terminate the Contract if the Work is stopped for a period of 30 consecutive days through no act or fault of the Contractor, a Subcontractor, a Sub-subcontractor, their agents or employees, or any other persons or entities performing portions of the Work, for any of the following reasons:

1. Issuance of an order of a court or other public authority having jurisdiction that requires all Work to be stopped;
2. An act of government, such as a declaration of national emergency, that requires all Work to be stopped;
3. Because the Architect has not issued a Certificate for Payment and has not notified the Contractor of the reason for withholding certification as provided in Section 9.4.1, or because the Owner has not made payment on a Certificate for Payment within the time stated in the Contract Documents; or

---

13. American Institute of Architects, Document A201 (2017) [hereafter, AIA A201-2017], article 14, also includes the rules for suspension of the work by the owner under rules similar to the termination provisions. (AIA A201-2017, section 14.3.).

4. The Owner has failed to furnish to the Contractor reasonable evidence as required by Section 2.2.

14.1.2 The Contractor may terminate the Contact if, through no act or fault of the Contractor, or Subcontractor, a Sub-subcontractor, their agents or employees, or any other persons or entities performing portions of the Work, repeated suspensions, delays, or interruptions of the entire Work by the Owner as described in Section 14.3, constitute in the aggregate more than 100 percent of the total number of days scheduled for completion, or 120 days in any 365-day period, whichever is less.

14.1.3 If one of the reasons described in Section 14.1.1 or 14.1.2 exists, the Contractor may, upon seven days' notice to the Owner and Architect, terminate the Contract and recover from the Owner payment for Work executed, as well as reasonable overhead and profit on Work not executed, and costs incurred by reason of such termination.

14.1.4 If the Work is stopped for a period of 60 consecutive days through no act or fault of the Contractor, a Subcontractor, a Sub-Subcontractor, or their agents or employees, or any other persons or entities performing portions of the Work because the Owner has repeatedly failed to fulfill the Owner's obligations under the Contract Documents with respect to matters important to the progress of the Work, the Contractor may, upon seven additional days' notice to the Owner and the Architect, terminate the Contract and recover from the Owner as provided in Section 14.1.3.

The first question that might be asked here is: How often does a contractor terminate a construction project? It is probably safe to assume that contractors rarely terminate unless they are not being paid.[14] This so-called right to terminate in the event of non-payment is found in section 14.1.1.3, but the owner's failure to pay is also a material breach of any contract for services and, as shown earlier, is recognized by the common law of breach of a contract as a ground for termination. So, does section 14.1 add anything to the rights of a contractor to terminate a contract?

A recent text explains:

Section 14.1 provides for termination by the contractor upon the occurrence of specific events, but there is an unresolved issue as to whether the events listed in Section 14.1 are the only instances in which the contractor can terminate the contract or whether other actions by an owner might constitute a

---

14. AIA A201–2017, section 14.1, explains the basis for contractor's termination of the contract and also sets forth the contractor's compensation under such circumstances. Under section 2.2 of the AIA A201, the contractor has a right to demand from the owner proof that the owner has sufficient funds to pay the contractor.

material breach under common law and permit a contractor to terminate the contract. A majority of commentators agree that Section 14.1 supplements the common law of termination for material breach and establishes specific events that allow a contractor to terminate regardless of whether those events would constitute a material breach under common law. Others view the events specified in Section 14.1 as the only instances in which a contractor may terminate. While there do not appear to be any reported decisions resolving the issue, a contractor likely can still terminate the contract due to a common law material breach because no language in Section 14.1 explicitly limits termination to the vents listed there.[15]

Section 14.1.3 varies the common law by adding as a prerequisite to termination by the contractor an obligation to provide "7 days written notice" of such termination to the owner and the architect. Without such written notice, is the contractor prohibited from terminating the contract? Or perhaps more interestingly, upon receipt of the notice, does the owner have the right to cure the problem, and prevent the contractor from terminating. For example, if the owner fails to pay on a timely basis, and the contractor provides the required written notice, does this mean that the owner can then make payment, and the contractor may not terminate? And could the owner do this multiple times? The AIA A201 does not provide guidance on this issue.

2. Termination by Owner

If contractors terminate a contract primarily for the owner's failure to pay, it seems that owners, at least potentially, might have more types of reasons for termination. For example, the quality and timeliness of the work performed by the contractor might become issues that would lead to termination.

Section 14.2 of the AIA A201 sets forth the rights of the owner to terminate (or suspend)[16] into two broad categories: one for termination *for cause* and one for termination *for convenience*. Termination for cause is discussed in this section and termination for convenience is discussed Section 16.05.

14.2 Termination by the Owner for Cause

14.2.1 The Owner may terminate the Contract if the Contractor:

1. repeatedly refuses or fails to supply enough properly skilled workers or proper materials;

---

15. PEER HAHN, JOSEPH KOVARS, & AMANDA MACVEY, THE 2017 A201 DESKBOOK (American Bar Association 2017).

16. The rules relating to suspension, which are a subset of the rules of termination, are not discussed in this text.

2. fails to make payment to Subcontractors or suppliers in accordance with the respective agreements between the Contractor and the Subcontractors or suppliers;
3. repeatedly disregards applicable laws, statutes, ordinances, codes, rules and regulations, or lawful orders of a public authority; or
4. otherwise is guilty of substantial breach of a provision of the Contract Documents.

14.2.2 When any of the reasons described in Section 14.2.1 exist, the Owner, and upon certification by the Architect that sufficient cause exists to justify such action, the Owner may, without prejudice to any other rights or remedies of the Owner and after giving the Contractor and the Contractor's surety, if any, seven days' notice, terminate the employment of the Contractor and may, subject to any prior rights of the surety:

1. Exclude the Contractor from the site and take possession of all materials, equipment, tools, and construction equipment and machinery thereon owned by the Contractor;
2. Accept assignment of subcontracts pursuant to Section 5.4; and
3. Finish the Work by whatever reasonable method the Owner may deem expedient. Upon written request of the Contractor, the Owner shall furnish to the Contractor a detailed accounting of the costs incurred by the Owner in finishing the Work.

14.2.3 When the Owner terminates the Contract for one of the reasons stated in Section 14.2.1, the Contractor shall not be entitled to receive further payment until the Work is finished.

14.2.4 If the unpaid balance of the Contract Sum exceeds costs of finishing the Work, including compensation for the Architect's services and expenses made necessary thereby, and other damages incurred by the Owner and not expressly waived, such excess shall be paid to the Contractor. If such costs and damages exceed the unpaid balance, the Contractor shall pay the difference to the Owner. The amount to be paid to the Contractor or Owner, as the case may be, shall be certified by the Initial Decision Maker, upon application, and this obligation for payment shall survive termination of the Contract.

a. The "Repeatedly" Requirement

Some of the grounds for termination by the owner require the contractor to have "repeatedly" taken, or failed to take, some action in violation of the contract. It may seem counterintuitive that an owner could be required to tolerate *any* bad act by the contractor (or even more than one) until the act occurs "repeatedly," and perhaps the common law would find one bad act sufficiently material to constitute adequate cause for termination.

If owners, on the basis of prudent management of a construction project and customary circumstances, are naturally reluctant to terminate, why would the AIA make the further requirement of multiple bad acts by the contractor a perquisite of termination? As explained quite eloquently by one court as quoted earlier, construction projects are extremely complex and a demand for absolute perfect, errorless performance is unrealistic. The requirement for "repeated" misconduct is anchored in the sober assessment that a stricter standard is unrealistic, and that the parties' flexibility in anticipating "material" breaches may be served by using such qualifiers. Similarly, the AIA form does *not* use "repeatedly" as a qualifier for such misconduct as might per se be deemed material, such as the contractor's failure to pay subcontractors when due.

b. The Catchall

Section 14.2 provides that the owner may terminate the contract if the contractor is "otherwise guilty of substantial breach of a provision of the Contract Documents." This catchall gives the owner the right to require that the contractor abide by all terms of the deal, or be in jeopardy of termination. In some ways the provision ensures that common law principles are not excluded by express provisions of the contract. Interestingly, the contractor may not have a reciprocal right to terminate the contract where the contact requires continuing performance by the contractor in the face of a dispute.

c. Architect

Another feature found in the termination by owner provision, but not found in the language governing termination by the contractor, is the requirement under section 14.2.2 that the matter be submitted to the architect for certification. Is the use of the architect a protection of the contractor's rights as an extra hurdle for a terminating owner to overcome, or is it a safeguard to prevent unreasonable terminations, perhaps for the benefit of both parties? Or, as has arisen in some cases, is it just another procedural complexity for the parties' lawyers to argue about?

C. ConsensusDocs Forms

ConsensusDocs has created a Standard Agreement and General Conditions between Owner and Constructor (ConsensusDocs 200), last revised in 2018. The pertinent sections regarding termination of the contract for cause are set forth here:

> 11.2 NOTICE TO CURE A DEFAULT If Constructor persistently fails to supply enough qualified workers, proper materials, or equipment to maintain the approved Schedule of the Work, or fails to make prompt payment to its workers, Subcontractors, or Suppliers, disregards a Law or orders of any public authority having jurisdiction, or is otherwise guilty of a material breach of a provision of this Agreement, Constructor may be deemed in default.

11.2.1 After receiving Owner's written notice, if Constructor fails within seven (7) Days after receipt of written notice from Owner to commence and continue satisfactory correction of such default with diligence and promptness, then Owner shall give Constructor a second notice to correct the default within three (3) Business Days after receipt. The second notice to Constructor, and if applicable, the surety, may include, that Owner intends to terminate this Agreement for default absent appropriate corrective action.

11.2.2 If Constructor fails to promptly commence and continue satisfactory correction of the default following receipt of such second notice, Owner without prejudice to any other rights or remedies may: (a) take possession of the Worksite; (b) complete the Work utilizing reasonable means; (c) withhold payment due to Constructor; and (d) as Owner deems necessary, supply workers and materials, equipment, and other facilities for the satisfactory correction of the default, and charge Constructor the costs and expenses, including reasonable Overhead, profit, and attorneys' fees.

11.2.3 In the event of an emergency affecting the safety of persons or property, Owner may immediately commence and continue satisfactory correction of such default without first giving written notice to Constructor, but shall give Constructor prompt written notice.

11.3 OWNER'S RIGHT TO TERMINATE FOR DEFAULT

11.3.1 TERMINATION BY OWNER FOR DEFAULT Upon expiration of the second notice period to cure pursuant to §11.2 and absent appropriate corrective action, Owner may terminate this Agreement by written notice. Termination for default is in addition to any other remedies available to Owner under §11.2. If Owner's costs arising out of Constructor's failure to cure, including the costs of completing the Work and reasonable attorneys' fees, exceed the unpaid Contract Price, Constructor shall be liable to Owner for such excess costs. If Owner's costs are less than the unpaid Contract Price, Owner shall pay the difference to Constructor. If Owner exercises its rights under this section, upon the request of Constructor, Owner shall furnish to Constructor a detailed accounting of the costs incurred by Owner.

11.3.2 USE OF CONSTRUCTOR'S MATERIALS, SUPPLIES, AND EQUIPMENT If Owner or Others perform work under §11.3, Owner shall have the right to take and use any materials and supplies for which Owner has paid and located at the Worksite for the purpose of completing any remaining Work. Owner and others performing work under §11.3 shall also have the right to use construction tools and equipment located on the Worksite and belonging to the Constructor or Subsubcontractors for the purpose of completing the remaining Work, but only after Constructor's written consent. If Owner uses Constructor's construction tools and equipment in accordance with this subsection, then Owner shall indemnify and hold harmless Constructor and applicable Subcontractors and the agents, officers, directors, and employees of each of them, from and against all claims, damages, losses, costs, and expenses, including but not limited to reasonable attorneys' fees, costs, and expenses incurred in connection with Owner's use of Constructor's or applicable subcontractor's construction tools and equipment. Immediately upon completion of the Work, any remaining materials, supplies, or equipment not consumed or incorporated in the Work shall be returned to Constructor in substantially the same condition as when they were taken, reasonable wear and tear excepted.

11.3.3 If Constructor files a petition under the Bankruptcy Code, this Agreement shall terminate if: (a) Constructor or Constructor's trustee rejects the Agreement; (b) a default occurred and Constructor is unable to give adequate assurance of required performance; or (c) Constructor is otherwise unable to comply with the requirements for assuming this Agreement under the applicable provisions of the Bankruptcy Code.

11.3.4 Owner shall make reasonable efforts to mitigate damages arising from Constructor default, and shall promptly invoice Constructor for all amounts due pursuant to §11.2 and §11.3.

[11.4 TERMINATION BY OWNER FOR CONVENIENCE . . . .]

11.5 CONSTRUCTOR'S RIGHT TO TERMINATE

11.5.1 Seven (7) Days' after Owner's receipt of written notice from Constructor, Constructor may terminate this Agreement if the Work has been stopped for a thirty (30) Day period through no fault of Constructor for any of the following reasons:

- (a) under court order or order of other governmental authorities having jurisdiction;
- (b) as a result of the declaration of a national emergency or other governmental act during which, through no act or fault of Constructor, materials are not available; or
- (c) suspension by Owner for convenience pursuant to §11.1.

11.5.2 In addition, upon seven (7) Days' written notice to Owner and an opportunity to cure within three (3) Days, Constructor may terminate this Agreement if Owner:

11.5.2.1 fails to furnish reasonable evidence pursuant to §4.2 that sufficient funds are available and committed for Project financing; or

11.5.2.2. assigns this Agreement over Constructor's reasonable objection; or

11.5.2.3 fails to pay Constructor in accordance with this Agreement and Constructor has stopped Work in compliance with §9.5; or

11.5.2.4 otherwise materially breaches this Agreement.

11.5.3 Upon termination by Constructor in accordance with §0, Constructor is entitled to recover from Owner payment for all Work executed and for any proven loss, cost, or expense in connection with the Work, including all demobilization costs plus reasonable Overhead and profit on Work not performed.

1. The Order of the Provisions

It may be merely coincidence that the ConsensusDocs 200 places the owner termination language before similar language for contractor termination. This is the opposite of the AIA. But does this order suggest some internal thinking by the document's creator? As mentioned earlier, owner termination is probably more likely, and can be based on a wider range of reasons than contractor termination, which is often limited to failure of payment. Despite this difference, notice that most of the reasons for termination of the contract by the owner under the ConsensusDocs form are similar in the AIA form contracts.

2. Specified Breach versus Material Breach

The ConsensusDocs 200, in section 11.2, expressly describes which breaches of the contract by the contractor warrant a termination of the contract by the owner. The general reference to "material breach" is not used. One might question whether the common law basis of termination of contract remains or has been replaced by the specified defaults.

3. Right to Cure

Unlike the AIA A201, the ConsensusDocs 200 does not require an owner to obtain the approval of a third party prior to terminating the contract. But, section 11.2 requires that the owner give the contractor a written statement describing the grounds for default, and then the contractor has two opportunities to cure the problem. As with the requirement that a contractor "repeatedly" or "persistently" fail to perform, it may seem unfair in some sense that the owner must abide the breach even for a short period. On the other hand, all standard industry form agreements recognize the complexity of construction work and are crafted so as to make the owner-contractor relationship sturdy enough that it cannot be disintegrated without sufficient cause and deliberation.

It is still fair to ask: What is the purpose of this right to cure? If the contractor has performed so poorly as to cause the owner to proceed to terminate, should the owner have to continue with the construction contract if, after the notice of termination, the contractor fixes the problem? What if the owner has lost trust in the contractor as a result of the contractor committing the problems that led to the owner's notice of intent to terminate?

4. Survival

Unlike AIA forms, the ConsensusDocs adds a general statement in section 11.6 regarding the survival of obligations and rights under the contract, such as warranties, various certifications, and other matters.

> 11.6 OBLIGATIONS ARISING BEFORE TERMINATION Even after termination, the provisions of this Agreement still apply to any Work performed, payments made, events occurring, costs charged or incurred or obligations arising before the termination date.

D. EJCDC Forms

The Engineers Joint Contracts Documents Committee[17] issues a form contract document entitled "Standard General Conditions of the Construction Contract." It was most recently revised in 2018. For purposes of comparison to the AIA and Consensus Docs forms, the EJCDC provisions regarding termination for cause follow:

> 16.02 *Owner May Terminate for Cause*
>
> > A. The occurrence of any one or more of the following events will constitute a default by Contractor and justify termination for cause:
> >
> > > 1. Contractor's persistent failure to perform the Work in accordance with Contract Documents (including, but not limited to, failure to supply sufficient skilled workers or suitable materials or equipment, or failure to adhere to the Progress Schedule);
> > > 2 Failure of the Contractor to perform or otherwise to comply with a material term of the Contract Documents;
> > > 3. Contractor's disregard of Laws or Regulations of any public body having jurisdiction; or
> > > 4. Contractor's repeated disregard of the authority of the Owner or Engineer.
>
> 16.04 *Contractor May Stop Work or Terminate*
>
> > A. If, through no act or fault of Contractor, (1) the Work is suspended for more than 90 consecutive days by Owner or under an order of court

---

17. The Engineers Joint Contracts Document Committee is a joint venture of three organizations of professional engineers. Its contract documents are typically used in civil construction.

or other public authority, or (2) Engineer fails to act on any Application for Payment within 30 days after it is submitted, or (3) Owner fails for 30 days to pay Contractor any sum finally determined to be due, then Contractor may, upon 7 days' written notice to Owner and Engineer, and provided Owner or Engineer do not remedy such suspension or failure within that time, terminate the contract and recover from Owner payment on the same terms as provided in Paragraph 16.03

16.04 POST-TERMINATION ISSUES

Having examined the concept of material breach under the common law, and termination rights under standard industry form contracts, what are the consequences of a party's decision to terminate the contract? Furthermore, what exactly happens to the rights and responsibilities of the parties once the contract is terminated, and what are the surety's obligations in the event of a termination?

A. Post-Termination Responsibilities

Upon termination of the contract, the owner and contractor have no further obligations to perform the contract. Any terms and conditions that normally would arise after completion of the contract, such as warranty obligations, are also terminated, unless the contract provides otherwise through a "survival clause" like the one set out earlier in the ConsensusDocs 200.

While dependent on the stage of the project, a substitute contractor will not likely take responsibility for the prior work performed by the previous contractor. Accordingly, as to the work performed by the terminated contractor, the owner will not be able to pass through any construction defect claims to the terminated contractor and will be solely responsible for any liability arising out of the work. Surely, parties can anticipate that a construction defect claim against the new contractor will be met with a defense that the cause of the construction defect is due to the work of the prior contractor. To limit this exposure, owners often attempt to keep in place the same subcontractors on the project, as this will assist in mitigating delays on the project and avoid the defense, at least as to those subcontractors, that the defective work was performed by someone else.

B. Damages and Other Relief

Under the common law, the non-breaching party is entitled to damages under a number of different theories. Typically, if the owner terminates, damages are recoverable for any increase in the cost to complete the project, plus other costs arising directly from the termination, such as costs to re-bid and additional fees of design professionals. If the contractor is the non-breaching party, recoverable damages likely include profit that would have been made if the contractor completed the project, plus costs incurred directly from the termination, such as demobilization at the site.

Other damages might be recovered depending on the facts, but determining which damages are recoverable and then proving such damages can be an arduous task. Consequently, many contracts specify the remedies available to the non-breaching party in the event of contract termination. Those remedies certainly will include recovery of specified damages, but may also include non-monetary relief deemed important. For the owner, that may include the right to take over the project site, use equipment, and take assignment of subcontracts in order to reduce disruption. In other words, the owner can take such action as will facilitate the completion of the project.

Because termination for convenience (as more thoroughly discussed in Section 16.05) is a creature of contract, the ramifications of such a termination are determined by the contract. As a general proposition, however, an owner does not recover any damages when terminating the contract for convenience. By definition, such a termination is without cause. The parties are simply ending the relationship, and the contract should spell out any commercial consequences that result from unwinding that relationship.

C. Role of the Surety

As is more thoroughly discussed in a later chapter, the performance of a prime contractor often is secured by a performance bond. Termination of the contract by the owner will trigger various rights and obligations of the surety under the performance bond. In most instances, the owner will have discussed any performance issues with the surety (and may be obligated to do so before terminating the contract), but the obligations of the surety generally will not commence until the owner formally terminates the contract. The failure of the owner to terminate the contract properly and to adhere to any requirements under the performance bond, such as providing appropriate notices to the surety, may impair the ability of the owner to enforce its claims under the terms of the performance bond.

The existence of a performance bond does not alleviate or reduce all of the concerns associated with termination. In fact, any issue concerning default and termination may be magnified once a claim is made against the surety. The surety under the performance bond steps into the shoes of the terminated contractor, and, therefore, is entitled to raise all of the defenses to the termination available to the contractor. Among other things, the surety likely will scrutinize the terms of the contract, investigate the circumstances surrounding the contractor's performance, and evaluate the right of the owner to terminate the contract. The surety will take care to ensure that it only assumes those obligations and liabilities as required under the performance bond and applicable law, and nothing more. In the event the surety accepts responsibility under the bond, it will decide how best to complete the project, which may be a troubling proposition for some owners.[18]

D. Wrongful Termination

The decision to terminate a construction contract is fraught with peril,[19] and a party seeking to terminate the contract should be cognizant of the potential pitfalls and liability that may lie ahead. Even when termination is proper, the practical effect will be delays in completion, likely increases in cost to complete the work, loss of certain rights and remedies, and protracted claims and disputes.

If termination was wrongful, things get even worse. Upon termination of the contract, the terminated party is excused from performance and may immediately sue for damages.[20] The failure of the owner to properly terminate the contractor will excuse the contractor and its surety from any performance obligations.[21] Where a party wrongfully terminates a non-breaching party, such an act itself constitutes a material breach of the contract that entitles the non-breaching party to expectation damages.[22] Accordingly, the non-breaching party should be placed in the position that would have existed had the contract been performed.

When a contractor wrongfully terminates a construction contract, the owner typically may recover (1) its costs of repairing uncured defective

---

18. Miller, *supra* note 5.
19. *See* Walker & Co. v. Harrison, 347 Mich. 630, 81 N.W.2d 352, 355 (1957) (the decision to terminate a contract "is fraught with peril, for should such determination, as viewed by a later court in the calm of its contemplation, be unwarranted, the repudiator himself will have been guilty of material breach and himself have become the aggressor, not an innocent victim"). *See also* American Civil Constr., LLC v. Fort Myer Constr. Corp., 296 F. Supp. 3d 198, 207 (D.D.C. 2018) (whether termination of subcontract was wrongful raised triable issues of fact).
20. Hosp. Mortg. Grp. v. First Prudential Dev. Corp., 411 So. 2d 181 (Fla. 1982).
21. *See* St. Paul Fire & Marine Ins. Co. v. City of Green River, Wyo., 93 F. Supp. 2d 1170 (D. Wyo. 2000), *aff'd*, 6 Fed. Appx. 828 (10th Cir. 2001) (owner's wrongful termination of surety discharged performance bond obligations).
22. For more on damages, see Chapter 22.

work, or, where repair would be wasteful, diminution in value of the unrepaired work; (2) actual or liquidated damages for delay in completion of the contract; plus (3) costs to complete the work within the scope of the terminated contract.[23]

As to a wrongfully terminated contractor, the general rule is that where no payments on account have been made, a contractor who is not in default may recover the total price promised less the cost of performing (in case no work has been done) or of completing performance of the work (where has been partial performance).[24] In fact, damages may extend well beyond the contractor's lost profit on the project in question.[25] Alternatively, the contractor may elect to recover under a reliance theory, thereby allowing the contractor to recover costs incurred in preparing to perform, in performing, or in foregoing opportunities to make other contracts.[26] Finally, the contractor may seek restitution damages work on a quantum meruit basis reflecting the extent to which the owner has been unjustly enriched by the fair value of the contractor's work.[27]

Beyond the issue of damages, the parties must also consider other practical consequences associated with a wrongful termination. For the owner, wrongfully terminating the contractor will leave the owner without recourse to pursue a claim for construction defects or delay.[28] As to the contractor, an imprudent decision to walk off the project will expose the contractor to (1) owner's damages to complete the project, (2) delay damages incurred by the owner, (3) loss of client relationships, (4) intangible damage to reputation, and (5) exposure to possible bad faith extracontractual damages.[29]

Given all the adverse consequences arising out of terminating a contract, both practical and legal, such action should not be taken without careful

---

23. BRUNER & O'CONNOR, *supra* note 1, §18:44.

24. Peru Associates, Inc. v. State, 70 Misc. 2d 775, 777, 334 N.Y.S.2d 772, 776 (Ct. Cl. 1971), *aff'd*, 39 A.D.2d 1018, 335 N.Y.S.2d 373 (1972); Adams v. Dreyfus Interstate Dev. Corp., 352 So. 2d 76 (Fla. 4th Dist. Ct. App. 1977); 24 WILLISTON ON CONTRACTS § 66:14 (4th ed.) STEVEN SIEGFRIED, INTRODUCTION TO CONSTRUCTION LAW 147 (American Law Institute-American Bar Association Committee on Continuing Professional Education, 1987); Brooks v. Holsombach, 525 So. 2d 910 (Fla. 4th Dist. Ct. App. 1988).

25. *See, e.g.*, U.S. Specialty Ins. Co. v. Strategic Planning Associates, LLC, 2019 WL 296864, at *2 n.3 (E.D. La. 2019) ("[claimants] allege a loss of business assets, goodwill, bonding capacity, future business earnings, and the opportunity to seek redress against [another party for that party's] numerous contractual breaches.").

26. RESTATEMENT (SECOND) OF CONTRACTS § 344 (1981).

27. Id.

28. BRUNER & O'CONNOR, *supra* note 1, § 18:3.

29. Id.

thought and evaluation. Moreover, as a termination is likely to produce numerous claims and disputes, some type of formal adjudication is likely. Documentation as to the need to terminate the contract as well as compliance with the contract's termination provisions will be necessary, as the terminating party bears the burden to prove that the termination was justified and properly executed.

The terminating party will need to overcome a number of legal and practical barriers, including (1) the subjective unilateral "self-help" nature of the remedy; (2) the factual complexity of the construction process resulting in an increased likelihood that both parties may be found guilty of some kind of breach of contract; (3) the need to determine which party is guilty of the first uncured material breach; (4) judicial disfavor of termination as a draconian and drastic remedy, constituting a species of forfeiture warranting strict judicial construction and enforcement of the breaching party's pre-termination rights to notice, and an opportunity to cure breaches deemed sufficiently material to warrant contract termination by the non-breaching party; (5) differing judicial views of the evidentiary proof of material breach; (6) the likelihood that the multitude of interdependent subcontractors and suppliers will be damaged by the wrongful termination decision, thus compounding the economic impact of the risk; and (7) the stark reality that rarely can a wrong decision be reversed and only infrequently can judicial second-guessing in subsequent proceedings be avoided.[30]

As a means to avoid the potential pitfalls and consequences of a wrongful termination, owners may include in their contracts a provision that states that any termination for default that is determined by a final non-appealable judgment or arbitration to be wrongful shall be converted into a termination for convenience, more specifically discussed in Section 16.05. Such a provision is common in many public contracts, where numerous circumstances beyond the control of the public entity might render the continued performance of a contract unnecessary or even wasteful.

In the private sector, however, such provisions are intended primarily to limit the owner's potential liability for significant damages in the event a termination for cause proves wrongful. Not surprisingly, contractors dislike such provisions, and view them as essentially protecting the owner from the adverse consequences of making the wrong decision. From the contractor's perspective, a termination for cause has reputational ramifications and may cause other harm to the contractor's ongoing business efforts. Those consequences do not disappear once the termination converts to one for convenience. Therefore, in

---

30. *Id.*

the private sector, contractors argue that an owner should make an election either to terminate for cause or for convenience without a safety net.

16.05 TERMINATION FOR CONVENIENCE

Given the pitfalls of a termination for cause, the industry has sought to find an easier and structured way for the parties to terminate their contractual relationship in what the industry refers to as a "termination for convenience." As implied in the name, this assumes that a termination for convenience is convenient and intended to avoid controversy. Only the owner has the option of terminating the contract for convenience. A termination for convenience clause grants the owner the ability to terminate without committing a breach, even when the contractor has not defaulted. In other words, the owner is given a right to terminate without cause.

The concept of "termination for convenience" originated as a way for the federal government to quickly shut down its wartime efforts when fighting ceased and the accompanying needs decreased. The federal government required a mechanism to quickly adapt to changing circumstances that also protected it from breach of contract claims brought by contractors. Termination for convenience in the public context was practical—if construction was no longer necessary, tax-paying citizens should not have to foot the bill.

Termination for convenience clauses are now also common in private sector construction contracts. A termination for convenience clause allows a private sector owner the flexibility to terminate when, for example, the cost of discontinuing the project is less than the costs to complete. On a similar note, such provisions allow contracting parties to sever a relationship between an owner and a contractor that has turned sour. Essentially, so long as the procedural aspects are followed, the owner can terminate without having a specific reason.

Although a termination for convenience provision is an important right of the owner, an owner should exercise the right prudently. The general rule is that the termination for convenience will be upheld if the exercise was made in good faith and the party exercising the right of termination was not in material breach of the contract at the time of exercise. In fact, it may be prudent for the owner to articulate a good faith basis to terminate the contract for convenience to preclude an argument by the contractor that such termination was made in bad faith.[31] Similarly, the government is required to exercise the termination

---

31. Amanda L. Schermer MacVey, Joseph C. Kovars & Peter W. Hahn, THE 2017 A201 DESKBOOK 236 (American Bar Association, 2017).

for convenience clause in good faith[32] and, in some states, private parties are held to the same standard.[33]

Additionally, courts have found that a notice requirement in a termination for convenience clause provided adequate consideration to the terminated party. For example, a provision allowing the owner to terminate "at any time for any reason by giving at least ten (10) days prior written notice" constituted sufficient consideration and was held enforceable.[34] Conversely, a court may not enforce termination for convenience if the court concludes that the circumstances of the parties' bargain have not materially changed. However, a majority of modern court decisions have rejected the "changed circumstances" test.[35]

Although some arguments exist that a termination for convenience provision makes a contract illusory, such provisions are widely accepted and are found in many of the construction industry standard contract forms, including AIA Document A201-2017,[36] the ConsensusDocs,[37] and the Engineers Joint Construction Documents Committee (EJCDC).

A. AIA Treatment

The A201 provides for termination for convenience, and states as follows:

14.4 Termination by the Owner for Convenience

14.4.1 The Owner may, at any time, terminate the Contract for the Owner's convenience and without cause.

---

32. Krygoski Constr. Co. v. United States, 94 F.3d 1537 (Fed. Cir. 1996) (Only a showing of bad faith or abuse of discretion would defeat the government's right to terminate a contract for convenience.).

33. Questar Builders, Inc. v. CB Flooring, LLC, 978 A.2d 651 (MD. App. 2009) (termination for convenience rights in the private parties' contract were subject to the implied limitation that they be exercised in good faith.).

34. Sylvan Crest Sand & Gravel Co. v. United States, 150 F.2d 642, 643–45 (2d Cir. 1945); Avatar Dev. v. DePani Constr., Inc., 834 So. 2d 873, 875 (Fla. 4th Dist. Ct. App. 2004).

35. Schermer MacVey, Kovars & Hahn, *supra* note 31, at 235.

36. "AIA Contract Documents are the nearly 200 forms and contracts that define the relationships and terms involved in design and construction projects." "Prepared by the AIA with the consensus of owners, contractors, attorneys, architects, engineers, and others, the documents have been finely tuned during their 120-year history." https://www.aiacontracts.org/contract-doc-pages/21536-what-we-do.

37. "ConsensusDocs is a not-for-profit coalition of national associations representing diverse interests in the design and construction industry. ConsensusDocs collaboratively develops and promotes standard form construction contract documents that advance the construction process." https://www.consensusdocs.org/coalition-members/.

14.4.2 Upon receipt of written notice from the Owner of such termination for the Owner's convenience, the Contractor shall

1. cease operations as directed by the Owner in the notice;
2. take actions necessary, or that the Owner may direct, for the protection and preservation of the Work; and
3. except for Work directed to be performed prior to the effective date of termination stated in the notice, terminate all existing subcontracts and purchase orders and enter into no further subcontracts and purchase orders.

14.4.3 In case of such termination for the Owner's convenience, the Owner shall pay the Contractor for Work properly executed; costs incurred by reason the termination, including costs attributable to termination of Subcontracts; and the termination fee, if any, set forth in the Agreement.

Under the AIA A201, termination is effective immediately upon delivery of the written notice of termination. Pursuant to paragraph 14.4.3 of the A201, a contractor terminated for convenience is entitled to payment for work executed; costs incurred by reason of such termination, including costs associated with the termination of subcontracts; and a termination fee, if such terms were agreed to in the contract. Note, however, the A201 does not appear to contemplate partial termination or any continued construction with existing subcontractors and/or replacement contractor.

The negotiated termination fee found in section 14.4.3 of the A201, is a change from the 2007 version of the document, which allowed the contractor to collect reasonable overhead and profit on work not executed. In updating the AIA documents for 2017, the AIA determined that many owners were simply striking this contract provision and, thus, the AIA revisited this issue and provided a fill point to prompt the parties to discuss and insert an appropriate fee in the event of termination.[38]

A negotiated termination fee encourages the parties to address this issue at the time of contract negotiation and seeks to strike a balance between the owner's flexibility in being allowed to terminate the contract for convenience as well as the contractor's expectation of compensation for its acceptance of risk, lost business opportunity, overhead and profit on the unperformed work, and dedication of resources to the project.[39] A termination fee is not designed to provide complete compensation to the contractor and the contractor's down-

---

38. Kenneth W. Cobleigh, American Institute of Architects, Washington, D.C., *The Changes that Matter the Most!* address at ABA Forum on Construction Law, 2017 Fall Meeting (Boston, MA, Oct. 5, 2017).

39. Schermer MacVey et al., *supra* note 31; Kenneth W. Cobleigh, *supra* note 38.

stream parties.[40] However, the fact that the parties now need to negotiate a fee does not make the process any easier. The risk to contractors, as with other "fill in the blank" sections, is that the fee will not be addressed, a blank will be left in the contract, and the contractor will not receive anything in the event of termination for convenience.

Where the fee is negotiated, the parties should consider whether the negotiated termination fee is tied to the stage of the project and, if so, the parties can provide a means to compute the fee as opposed to inserting a specific dollar amount.[41] As with many contractual provisions, when negotiating the termination fee, the parties need to anticipate, as best they can, where they will be financially at different stages of the project to ensure that the negotiated termination fee is fair to both parties no matter when the termination for convenience provision is exercised by the owner.

B. ConsensusDocs Treatment

Section 11.4 of the ConsensusDocs 200 (2017), provides as follows:

11.4 TERMINATION BY OWNER FOR CONVENIENCE

11.4.1 Upon Constructor's receipt of Owner's written notice from Owner, Owner may, without cause, terminate this Agreement. Constructor shall immediately stop the Work, follow Owner's instructions regarding shutdown and termination procedures, and strive to minimize any further costs.

11.4.2 If the Owner terminates this Agreement for convenience, Constructor shall be paid: (a) for the Work performed to date including Overhead and profit; (b) for all demobilization costs and costs incurred resulting from termination, but not including Overhead or profit on Work not performed; (c) reasonable attorneys' fees and costs related to termination; and (d) a premium as follows: [_____].

11.4.3 If the Owner terminates this Agreement, the Constructor shall:

> 11.4.3.1 execute and deliver to Owner all papers and take all action required to assign, transfer, and vest in Owner the rights of Constructor to all materials, supplies, and equipment for which payment has been or will be made in accordance with the Contract Documents and all subcontracts, orders, and commitments which have been made in accordance with the Contract Documents;

---

40. Kenneth W. Cobleigh, *supra* note 38.
41. Kenneth W. Cobleigh, *supra* note 38.

11.4.3.2 exert reasonable effort to reduce to a minimum Owner's liability for subcontracts, orders, and commitments that have not been fulfilled at the time of the termination;

11.4.3.3 cancel any subcontracts, orders, and commitments as Owner directs; and

11.4.3.4 set all prices approved by Owner any materials, supplies, and equipment as Owner directs, with all proceeds paid or credited to Owner.

Note initially that upon termination, much more is required of the contractor in comparison to the AIA A201, that is, the contractor must turn over materials, supplies, and subcontracts to the owner. Also, no notice is required when the prime contract is terminated for convenience. Although this arguably benefits the owner, an owner that fails to reasonably notify the contractor may avail itself to an increase in compensable costs due to the abrupt termination of the project. In regards to payment to the contractor upon termination for convenience, the ConsensusDocs, similar to the negotiated termination fee found in the AIA A201, requires parties to negotiate and insert a premium. The AGC Guidebook[42] states that this premium better balances the owner's and the contractor's respective risks and interests.

Whether the parties are discussing a premium under the ConsensusDocs or a negotiated termination fee under the AIA A201, the contractor should provide a basis for the agreed-upon fee so that is tied to actual anticipated lost profit on the work not performed or other lost business opportunities. This will avoid an argument by the owner that the premium or negotiated termination fee is a penalty and, thus, unenforceable.[43]

C. Other Forms

Similar to the other industry standard form contracts, the EJCDC allows the owner to terminate the contractor for convenience. Paragraph 16.03 of the C-700, Standard General Conditions of the Construction Contract (2018) provides as follows:

A. Upon 7 days' written notice to Contractor and Engineer, Owner may, without cause and without prejudice to any other right or remedy of Owner, terminate the Contract. In such case, Contractor shall be paid for (without duplication of any items):

---

42. https://www.agc.org/sites/default/files/Files/ConsensusDocs/AGC_only_Guidebook_091613_0.pdf.

43. RESTATEMENT (SECOND) OF CONTRACTS § 356 (1981).

1. completed and acceptable Work executed in accordance with the Contract Documents prior to the effective date of termination, including fair and reasonable sums for overhead and profit on such Work;
2. expenses sustained prior to the effective date of termination in performing services and furnishing labor, materials, or equipment as required by the Contract Documents in connection with uncompleted Work, plus fair and reasonable sums for overhead and profit on such expenses; and
3. reasonable expenses directly attributable to termination, including costs incurred to prepare a termination for convenience cost proposal.

B. Contractor shall not be paid for any loss of anticipated profits or revenue, post-termination overhead costs, or other economic loss arising out of or resulting from such termination.

Unlike the AIA and ConsensusDocs forms, the EDCJC form specifically prohibits any payment for lost anticipated profit, revenue, or other economic loss resulting from termination. The EDCJC provisions also differ from the AIA and ConsensusDocs by allowing the contractor compensation *only* for acceptable work that is in accordance with the contract documents. Although owners will certainly approve of this limitation on payment, the EJCDC form does not grant the owner much say in the winding down of the project.

D. The Choice

If an owner faces a defaulting contractor, should the owner then terminate for cause, or should the owner simply terminate the contractor for convenience?

The City of New York thought it would simply be easier to terminate a construction manager for convenience rather than for cause in the case of *Tishman Construction Corp. v. City of New York*.[44] After being terminated for convenience, the construction manager brought suit against the city for payment under various provisions of the contract.[45] The city then counterclaimed for damages to cure the construction manager's defaults under the contract, as well as for overpayment.[46]

The court found that because the city elected to terminate for convenience, the city was precluded from raising its counterclaims under the contract.[47] In

---

44. Tishman Constr. Corp., Inc. v. City of New York, 228 A.D.2d 292, 643 N.Y.S.2d 589 (1st Dep't 1996).
45. Id. at 292.
46. Id. at 293.
47. Id.

the event the city wished to recoup the cost of curing the construction manager's default, it should have terminated under the section of the agreement dealing with termination for cause, which allowed the city to recoup its expenses.[48] The court also rejected the city's argument that it was entitled to proceed with its counterclaim by claiming the city's rights were without limitation under the sections in the contract entitled "All Defenses Reserved" and "No Waivers."[49] The court limited the city's counterclaim to proving that the overpayments were due to fraud or mistake.[50]

16.06 CONCLUSION

A party to a contract may have the right to terminate that contract for a material breach by the other contracting party. Because of the potential difficulty in determining whether a breach is material, and other ramifications resulting from termination, many construction contracts specify causes for termination as well as remedies for the non-breaching party. Even when a termination is justified, many adverse consequences arise from terminating a contract. Costs to complete the contract will almost certainly increase, delays will occur, and protracted disputes may need to be formally adjudicated. And, if the termination is proven wrongful, then things get much, much worse for the terminating party. Because of the consequences and risks that flow from terminating a contract, doing so generally is considered a last resort only to be exercised when circumstances become almost intolerable.

---

48. *Id.*
49. *Id.*
50. *Id.*

QUESTIONS

Shortly before the planned completion of a medical office building, your client, the owner, received a letter from the plumbing subcontractor complaining about the contractor's failure to pay a four-month-old invoice for $7,000 (for which the contractor previously had billed the owner, who had paid it). This, coupled with the contractor's seeming inability to complete the punchlist work, was the "last straw" for the owner, who now wants to terminate the contractor "and finish the work, himself." The owner told the architect to certify the contractor's default and "get someone else in to finish the job." The architect is reluctant to issue the certification, and has asked the owner to reconsider.

1. The owner has now called to ask your advice and for you to outline the potential consequences of the proposed termination. What do you tell the owner?
2. Were the contractor's defaults "material"?
3. What remedies might the contractor have in the event that the termination later was deemed to be "wrongful"?

CHAPTER 17

Mechanic's Liens

EILEEN M. DIEPENBROCK

17.01 ORIGIN OF MECHANIC'S LIEN

A mechanic's lien is a recorded security interest in real property created without the owner's express consent. As such, a mechanic's lien is arguably the most valuable tool available to secure payment services and materials on private works construction projects. A properly perfected mechanic's lien attaches to the property where the services and/or materials were provided; for the amount of the lien is the value of those services or materials provided or the amount by which the property's value has been improved. If payment for the services or materials is not made, then the lien may be foreclosed and the property sold to satisfy the debt. Thus mechanic's liens offer protections beyond simple contract remedies because the value of the work is preserved in the property itself.

The author thanks Conner D. Johnston, an attorney at Diepenbrock Elkin Gleason LP in Sacramento, California for his valuable assistance in the preparation of this chapter.

A properly perfected mechanic's lien clouds the title of the property not only as to the owner at the time the lien is recorded but also as to subsequent purchasers, encumbrancers, and third parties, including, in many states, lenders who record their deeds of trust after the services first began or materials were first provided. In this way, mechanic's liens are similar to a mortgage or deed of trust encumbering a house or building as security for repayment of a loan. The key difference is that mechanic's liens are statutory in origin and may be placed on the owner's property without the owner's consent. Further, the parties entitled to encumber the owner's property with a lien include those who are not in privity of contract with the owner, such as subcontractors.[1]

Mechanic's liens were unknown at common law. Mechanic's liens owe their origins to Thomas Jefferson and James Madison. In 1791, to encourage building the new Capitol building in Washington, D.C., a lien was established by statute and granted to master builders for the erecting and finishing of houses. Maryland passed the new legislation first, followed by Pennsylvania in 1803.[2] Today, each state has its own statutory scheme to protect suppliers of services and materials on private works construction projects by giving the suppliers lien rights, subject to strict compliance with various lien prerequisites and procedures.[3]

The nature and importance of these lien rights can be understood by examining their role in California. In California, lien rights are a creature of the state's constitution, with implementing statutory procedures for enforcing them.[4] In upholding the constitutionality of these lien rights, the California Supreme Court considered the competing interests of the lien claimants versus the property owner who effectively suffers a so-called taking of its property by the imposition of the lien.[5] The court determined that the property owner "suffers only a minor deprivation by reason of the lien since he retains possession and use of the land." As discussed more fully later, the property owner also has protections against improper liens through the various statutory requirements imposed on lien claimants.[6] On the other hand, "the worker whose labor has gone into the property . . . would suffer a major deprivation

---

1. Indus. Asphalt, Inc. v. Garret Corp., 180 Cal. App. 3d 1001 (1986); STEPHEN A. HESS, A MECHANICS' LIEN PRIMER (Construction Briefings, May 2008).

2. BRUCE H. SCHOUMACHER, MECHANICS' LIENS § 19.02 (Construction Law, 2007), citing HAROLD SIEGAN, CASES AND COMMENTS ON MECHANICS' LIENS (1981) and LAWRENCE FRIEDMAN, A HISTORY OF AMERICAN LAW (Simon & Schuster 1973).

3. *See generally* ROBERT F. CUSHMAN & STEPHEN D. BUTLER, FIFTY STATE CONSTRUCTION LIEN AND BOND LAW, 2d ed. (Aspen Law & Business 2000 and 2010 Cumulative Supplement).

4. CAL. CONSTITUTION, Art. XIV, § 3.

5. Connolly Dev. Inc. v. Superior Court, 17 Cal. 3d 803, 807 (1976).

6. *Id.* at 806–07.

by the abolition of the lien" because, without the lien right, "the worker would be left with only an unsecured and potentially uncollectible claim for compensation for labor that has enhanced the value of the property itself."[7] Thus, the California Supreme Court concluded that the balance tips in favor of protection of the lien claimant:

> This protective policy continues to serve the needs of the construction industry. As was pointed out in *Cook v. Carlson* . . . "Labor and material contractors [in the construction industry] are in a particularly vulnerable position. Their credit risks are not as diffused as those of other creditors. They extend a bigger block of credit, they have more riding on one transaction, and they have more people vitally dependent upon eventual payments. They have much more to lose in the event of default. There must be some procedure for the interim protection of contractors in this satiation." Without such interim protection, the improvement may be completed, the loan funds disbursed, and the land sold before the claimant can obtain an adjudication on the merits of his claim. [¶] In summary, we conclude that the recordation of a mechanic's lien . . . inflicts upon the owner only a minimal deprivation of property; that the laborer and materialman have an interest in the specific project subject to the lien since their work and materials have enhanced the value of that property; and that state policy strongly supports the preservation of laws which give the laborer and materialman security for their claim. In measuring these values, we do not deal in cold abstractions: we take into account the social effect of the liens and interests of the workers and materialmen that the liens are designed to protect. We measure these valued interests against the loss, if any caused to the owner. The balance tips in favor of the worker and the materialman. . . .[8]

Against this backdrop, this chapter provides an overview of the key principles and requirements applicable to mechanic's liens.

17.02 STATUTORY FRAMEWORK

Mechanic's liens are a statutory remedy (as opposed to common law remedy) to prevent property owners from being unjustly enriched at the expense of those people whose work improved the property.[9] Because mechanic's liens are created by statute, the laws are strictly construed as to who may claim a lien on what property.[10] However, the remedial provisions of lien laws are

---

7. Id.
8. Id. at 826–28 (quoting Cook v. Carlson, 364 F. Supp. 24, 29 (D.S.D. 1973)).
9. *See generally* Cushman & Butler, *supra* note 3; RICHARD K. ALLEN & STANLEY A. MARTIN, CONSTRUCTION LAW HANDBOOK, 2d ed., § 25.03[A] (Aspen Publishers 2009).
10. *See, e.g.*, FLA. STAT. § 713.37; Mike McGarry & Sons, Inc. v. Construction Resources One, LLC, 107 N.E.3d 91 (Ohio Ct. App. 2018); *see generally* CUSHMAN & BUTLER, *supra* note 3.

construed liberally once a claimant establishes the right to a lien.[11] In addition, the strict statutory requirements imposed by the state's lien laws must be followed for the lien to be enforceable.[12] While the specific requirements vary from state to state, the lien laws typically identify who may assert a lien, what services or materials may be the basis for a lien, the amount for which a lien may be recorded, notice requirements to the property owner and/or lender, the time to record or assert a lien, the content of the lien, the time to enforce the lien, the priority of the lien, and waivers of the lien. Many states also have separate rules for residential construction projects that are stricter, in the sense of providing more protection to residential property owners, than for commercial construction projects.[13]

Mechanic's lien acts also consider all interests at stake, not just those of the lien claimant. This means owners, lenders, and other interested parties should become familiar with the particular lien statutes to protect themselves against lien claims, as well as to understand the defenses that may be available when a lien is asserted. The statutory protections are one of the reasons the California Supreme Court concluded that property owners suffer only a "minor deprivation" in comparison to the risk to the claimant of nonpayment.[14] Thus, for example, some states require a form of notice early in the project to the owner and/or any construction lender of the possibility of liens if payments are not made, as well as what steps can be taken to avoid liens. In California, subtier lien claimants (subcontractors, suppliers, and other parties not under direct contract with the owner) must give the owner and any lender a written notice within 20 days of starting work describing the lien claimant, its involvement in the project, an estimate of the total price of the work to be provided, and an affirmative statement the property is subject to a mechanic's lien if the claimant is not paid in full, even if the prime contractor is paid in full.[15] The function of this pre-construction notice allows an owner to take steps to ensure these subtier parties are paid in due course so as to protect the owner against liens.

In fact, compliance with this requirement is so important in California that failure of a claimant to serve proper notice is grounds for disciplinary action

---

11. Wellons, Inc. v. Eagle Valley Clean Energy, LLC, Civil Action No. 15-cv-01252-RBJ, 2017 U.S. Dist. LEXIS 160889, at *1 (D. Colo. Sept. 29, 2017) (Colo. law).

12. M & G Services, Inc. v. Buffalo Lake Advanced Biofuels, LLC, 895 N.W.2d 277 (Minn. App. 2017); Sutton Siding & Remodeling, Inc. v. Baker, 2017 Ill. App. (4th) 150956-U, ¶ 33, 2017 WL 1065758, at *6 (Ill. Ct. App. 2017).

13. *See generally* Cushman & Butler, *supra* note 3.

14. Connolly Dev. Inc. v. Superior Court, 17 Cal. 3d at 807.

15. Cal. Civ. Code §§ 8200, 8202, 8204.

before the contractor licensing board.[16] Oregon is another state in which—in the context of residential construction—the failure to comply with the notice requirement may subject the lien claimant to disciplinary action before the licensing board.[17] Other states have statutory requirements for notices by sub-tier lien claimants to owners early in the project, although the requirement may be limited to residential construction, and time for such notices varies.[18]

Protection for subtier claimants takes different forms across the country. In Illinois, the protection comes from notice requirements imposed on the contractor, rather than on subtier claimants. Thus, before any payment is made to the contractor, the contractor must provide to the owner a sworn written statement listing the names and addresses of all parties furnishing labor and materials and the amounts due to each.[19] Delaware has a similar statute permitting the owner, from time to time, to request from the contractor a written list of all persons who have furnished labor or materials in connection with the project and who are entitled to assert a lien. If the contractor fails to comply and provide the list within ten days of the request, the contractor is not entitled to any further payments until the contractor furnishes the list.[20] When the owner receives these notices and information, the owner can protect itself by (1) requiring proof of payment from the prime contractor to subcontractors and suppliers, (2) obtaining lien releases from the subtier parties, or (3) issuing joint checks to the contractor and the subtier parties.[21] The owner also may be able to discharge a lien that does not comply strictly with statutory requirements, thereby avoiding an encumbrance on the property.

It is important to understand that lien claims are merely security for payment, and loss of a lien does not usually impair other means of collection. In addition to breach of contract remedies, and potentially stop notices and bond remedies, some states use trust fund statutes as a vehicle to protect unpaid contractors. This relief is a separate and additional remedy from the lien.[22] Under these statutes, money paid for the improvement of real property is held in trust by the receiving party, that is, the upstream contractor or subcontractor. The claims are made against the trust as opposed to a lien against the property. As stated by a New York court analyzing New York's trust law, "a

---

16. Cal. Civ. Code § 8216.
17. Or. Rev. Stat. § 87.093.
18. *See, e.g.*, Ala. Code § 35-11-210; Ariz. Rev. Stat. § 33-992.01; Fla. Stat. § 713.06; Ind. Code §32-28-3-1; Or. Rev. Stat. §§ 87.09, 87.021, 87.023; Wash. Rev. Code § 60.04.13.
19. 770 Ill. Comp. Stat. 60/5.
20. 25 Del. Code § 2705.
21. *See, e.g.*, Ariz. Rev. Stat. §§ 33-992.01, 33-1008.
22. 53 Am. Jur. 2d, Mechanics' Liens § 33.14 (2017).

contractor does not have a sufficient beneficial interest in the moneys, due or to become due from the owner under the contract, to give him a property right in them, except insofar as there is a balance remaining after all subcontractors and other statutory beneficiaries have been paid."[23] If the contractor, who holds the money in trust, pays itself before paying subcontractors and materialmen, the contractor is said to be in breach of trust and faces enhanced damages.

In sum, to be entitled to, and to preserve, the particular remedy of a mechanic's lien, claimants must carefully follow the statutory requirements of the relevant jurisdiction.

17.03 LIEN CATEGORIES

Although it remains important to study each state's particular mechanic's lien statutes, liens are generally divided into two categories: (1) derivative or dependent liens, such as those created under New York statutes, and (2) independent or original liens, such as those created under Pennsylvania statutes.[24] Under the New York statute, subcontractor, laborer, or material supplier liens "depend upon" or are limited by the remaining amount owed by the owner to the prime contractor. Statutes limiting claimants to dependent liens protect owners from paying twice for the same labor and materials.[25] Under the Pennsylvania statue, by comparison, subcontractor, laborer, or material supplier liens are independent of the remaining amount owed to the prime contractor and are considered direct liens as distinguished from derivative, or dependent, liens.[26] These types of statutes in certain states allow subcontractor claims to be brought for an amount independent of what the owner owes to the contractor and may result in double liability.[27]

Since hardships can exist under either lien category, some states have taken, and some commentators have suggested, a hybrid approach, such as following the New York approach for owner-occupied property and the Pennsylvania approach for non-owner-occupied property; alternatively, some suggest following the New York approach for residential property, or following the

---

23. Aquilino v. United States, 10 N.Y. 2d 271, 282 (1961).
24. State v. Tabasso Homes Inc., 42 Del. 110 (1942); AM. JUR., *supra* note 22, § 9.
25. *Id.*; N.D. CENT. CODE § 35-27-02; Price Trucking Corp. v. Norampac Industries, Inc., 748 F.3d 75, 84 (2d Cir. 2014); Graves Lumber Co. v. Croft, 20 N.E.3d 412 (Ohio Ct. App. 9th Dist. Summit County 2014).
26. State v. Tabasso Homes Inc., 42 Del. 110; AM. JUR., *supra* note 22, § 9.
27. Brady Brick & Supply Co. v. Lotito, 43 Ill. App. 3d 69, 72–73 (1976).

Pennsylvania approach when the lien claimant provides certain notices to the owner.[28]

In addition to the two broad categories of liens just described, some states further categorize available liens based on the lien claimant or the type of work. For example, Oklahoma has statutory liens for oil and gas well work, work on mining property, and work on railroads.[29] Texas distinguishes between constitutional liens, available to those who contract directly with the owner, and statutory liens, available to other contractors, material suppliers, and service providers.[30] California has specific statutes applicable to design professional liens and to site improvement liens.[31] While other states also may recognize different categories of liens, such as design professional liens, those states incorporate them into their general lien statutes.[32]

17.04 REQUIREMENTS FOR A LIEN

Several requirements exist that a claimant must satisfy prior to asserting a viable mechanic's lien, although these vary by state. The first requirement is a valid contract, although some states relax this requirement inasmuch as the heart of mechanic's lien law is to avoid unjust enrichment. Second, the work performed must be considered an improvement. Liens only protect work on improvements to real property, and the definition of what constitutes a lienable improvement varies among jurisdictions. Third, the claimant must accurately calculate the amount of the lien. Incorrect lien amounts may render the lien void or open the claimant to penalties if the amount is intentionally overstated. Finally, the claimant must ensure it is statutorily entitled to a lien. Claimants not within the classifications provided by a state's mechanic's lien act are unable to assert a lien.

A. Contract

In states where a valid contract is a prerequisite to assertion of a mechanic's lien, contract requirements for a valid mechanic's lien depend on whether the

---

28. *E.g.*, ALA. CODE § 35-11-210; Carson v. Roediger, 513 N.W.2d 713 (Iowa 1994); Ridge Heating, Air Conditioning & Plumbing, Inc. v. Brennen, 135 Md. App. 247, 762 A.2d 161 (2000), *aff'd* 366 Md. 336, 738 A.2d 691 (2001); AM. JUR., *supra* note 22, § 9.
29. Cushman & Butler, *supra* note 3, § 37.03[A].
30. TEX. CONST., art. 16, § 37; TEX. PROP. CODE § 53.021 *et seq.*
31. *E.g.*, CAL. CIV. CODE §§ 8300–8319, 8402, 8404.
32. Thomas Warner Smith, III, *Mechanic's Lien Priority Rights for Design Professionals*, WASH. & LEE L. REV. (Fall 1989) (including a survey of design professional lien statutes).

party is a direct contractor with the owner or a subcontractor. The requirements are similar for both, but more stringent for subcontractors.

Direct contractors asserting a mechanic's lien must first have a written contract with the owner or somebody "authorized by the landowner to contract for the furnishing of the very labor and materials."[33] Then, the contractor must (1) perform the lienable work, (2) perform the contract provisions that are not waived or excused, (3) provide a contractor's sworn statement or establish that the owner has waived this requirement, (4) timely record a proper claim for lien, and (5) timely file a lawsuit to foreclose the lien. Subcontractors must satisfy the same requirements as contractors in addition to (1) establishing a valid chain of contracts between the contractor and the subcontractor and (2) providing a notice of its subcontractor work.[34]

Contract performance need not be perfect or absolute. Instead, substantial performance by the contractor will still entitle the contractor to a mechanic's lien. Substantial performance is "honest and faithful performance of the contract in its material and substantial parts, with no willful departure from, or omission of, the essential elements of the contract."[35] However, even when the contractor or subcontractor does not substantially perform the contract without fault on its part, the contractor or subcontractor still may claim a lien, but the value of the lien will be limited to the reasonable value of the performance.[36]

B. Improvement

Even if the lien claimant has a valid contract, the lien claimant is not entitled to a mechanic's lien unless the work it performed is "lienable," which term means the work is an "improvement" to the owner's property. Generally, "improvement" is defined as an "addition to property . . . whether permanent or not," especially "one that increases its value or utility or that enhances its appearance."[37] Though state statutes generally track this definition, the precise meaning of improvement is not consistent among the states, with some states specifically describing what qualifies as an "improvement" and other states being more general. For example, Montana's statute states that improvement work must be "for the purpose of producing a change in the physical condition

---

33. McDowell v. Perry, 9 Cal. App. 2d 555, 562 (1935).
34. *Id.*
35. *Id.*; Doornbos Heating & Air Conditioning, Inc. v. James D. Schlenker, M.D., S.C., 403 Ill. App. 3d 468, 483 (2010) (quoting another source).
36. *Id.*; Lewis Elec. Co. v. Miller, 791 N.W.2d 691, 694–95 (Iowa 2010).
37. BLACK'S LAW DICTIONARY (10th ed. 2014).

of the real estate" and includes a list of what is and is not included.[38] New Jersey's statute says an improvement "means any actual or proposed physical changes to real property resulting from the provision of work, services, or material by a contractor, subcontractor, or supplier pursuant to a contract, whether or not such physical change is undertaken" and provides a list of what improvement does and does not include.[39] Alabama's statute is more general, referring to "any building or improvement on land, or for repairing, altering, or beautifying the same."[40]

Whether work performed by a lien claimant constitutes an improvement is a fact-intensive inquiry to be done on a case-by-case basis. Courts may also focus on different factors. In *Christopher B. Burke Engineering, Ltd. v. Heritage Bank of Central Illinois*,[41] a contractor provided engineering services, specifically "creating a plat of subdivision, surveying the property, planning out roads and sewers." The Illinois court analyzed whether there needed to be both a physical improvement and a calculable increase in the property's value. The court first found that a physical improvement is not required because "[i]f a physical improvement is required in order for an engineer to secure a lien for their work, then these professionals would be subject to the whims of the parties with whom they contract, who may decide to complete the project or not. Such an outcome is contrary to the protective purpose of the Act."[42] The court also rejected the need for a calculable increase in property value for similar reasons—the eventual non-construction of the structure does not limit the value of the services rendered for the purpose of improving the property.[43]

New York reached a similar result in *Charles H. Sells, Inc. v. Chance Hills Joint Venture*,[44] where the court examined the meaning of "improvement" in the context of an engineering and surveying firm's lien against the owner of an equestrian development. In that case, the firm provided engineering and surveying services in connection with obtaining municipal approvals for the equestrian development, but no actual physical permanent improvement had taken place. The court first noted the applicable definition of "improvement" requires a "permanent improvement." The court then noted the primary purpose of the lien law is to protect claimants who, at the request or with the consent of the owner, enhance the value of the property. If the owner fails to

---

38. MONT. CODE ANN. § 71-3-522(6).
39. N.J. STAT. ANN. § 2A:44A-2.
40. ALA. CODE § 35-11-210; *see also* AM. JUR., *supra* note 22, §§ 55, 56.
41. 43 N.E. 3d 963 (Ill. 2015).
42. *Id.* at 967.
43. *Id.*
44. 163 Misc. 2d 814, 622 N.Y.S.2d 422 (1995).

complete the project, "the claims for work done to improve the property are no less entitled to the benefits of this statute. By analogy, materials manufactured with the intent of being used to improve a property, but never actually delivered, may provide the basis for a mechanic's lien."[45] Addressing the requirement of a "permanent improvement," the court held the phrase differentiates between labor and materials "consumed by the improvement" as opposed to those that become "a part of the plant and equipment of the contractor. Here, plaintiff provided surveying and engineering work to enable the property to receive municipal approvals as an equestrian facility. This constitutes the permanent improvement intended under [the lien law]."[46] The court distinguished work that "was not strictly speaking either engineering or surveying but rather in the nature of applying for permits and approvals. Such work would indeed not be treated as the basis for a lien."[47]

A Utah court reached a different result in *All Clean, Inc. v. Timberline Properties*,[48] where the court rejected claimed lien rights based on a determination that mitigation work to preserve a property after a flood did not constitute an improvement that was "affixed" to the property. The court noted an amendment to the lien act expanded lienable work under Utah law to landscapers and nurserymen. However, in that case, "improvement" still does not encompass "any work that makes the premises better."[49] Instead, "'improvement' is a legal term that has been "construed to connote physical affixation and enduring change to premises in a manner that adds value."[50] Thus, "the removal of the excess water and the drying, scrubbing, and mold prevention activities within the building" were not improvements because they were not "replacements or changes implicating the structural components of [the owner's] building or its fixtures."[51]

The term "improvement" also must be examined in the context of material suppliers.[52] Lien statutes generally extend their protections to material suppliers.[53] Even if the materials are not "permanently affixed," they still might constitute an improvement to support lien rights if they are consumed in the project. Again, however, this varies from state to state. For example,

---

45. *Id.* at 816.
46. *Id.*
47. *Id.*
48. 264 P.3d 244 (Utah Ct. App. 2011).
49. *Id.* at 248.
50. *Id.* at 248–49.
51. *Id.* at 250.
52. See Section 17.04(D) in this chapter for a discussion of equipment suppliers.
53. Hess, *supra* note 1.

in California, oil for threads of pipe joints, paste for soldering joints, soapstone lubricants for pulling wire through pipes, and lumber used for concrete forms are all examples of materials being consumed in the project for which liens area allowed.[54] In *Bates County Redi-Mix, Inc. v. Windler*,[55] a Missouri court found that the supplier of concrete defectively installed by the subcontractor and subsequently removed was entitled to enforce lien rights. On the other hand, in Indiana, an unpaid supplier of fuel products for use in heavy machinery at the project site is not entitled to assert a mechanic's lien.[56] Ultimately, the challenge for material suppliers becomes proving that materials delivered to the site actually became permanently affixed or were consumed in the project.

As seen in the preceding cases, "improvement" can mean different things under each state's lien act, even if the statutory definitions are similar. Some might require an affixed benefit that adds value to the property whereas others may only require the work to be done for the *purpose* of improving the property. Thus, contractors whose work does not include any physical erection or construction may not be afforded the protection of a mechanic's lien depending on the state's statute and common law. A close inspection of both the definition of "improvement" and its judicial application are important because in every jurisdiction a lienable interest will not exist if the work does not constitute an improvement.

Additionally, it is important to consider whether the improvement is a single improvement or multiple works of improvement. For example, in the context of a planned development, the whole development may be the "improvement," or there may be multiple separate improvements consisting of, for example, common site work, common infrastructure work, site work on individual lots, construction on individual lots, and construction of common areas. Generally, the contract will provide guidance on this topic, but again, the individual state lien laws also must be considered.[57] If the project is considered to consist of multiple separate works of improvements, the statutory lien requirements may apply to each individual improvement. Alternatively,

---

54. Pacific Sash & Door Co. v. Bumiller, 162 Cal. 664 (1912); L.W. Blinn Lumber Co. v. Pioneer Drainage Dist., 50 Cal. App. 364 (1920).

55. 162 S.W.3d 98 (Mo. Ct. App., Western Dist. 2005), *re'hrg denied* 2005.

56. P & P Oil Service Co., Inc. v. Bethlehem Steel Corp., 643 N.E.2d 9 (Ind. Ct. App. 1994). Although the court in this case focused on the fact that the supplier was not in the class of persons entitled to assert a lien, the case also can be seen as illustrative of the different views states take on whether materials supplied are lienable as an improvement.

57. *E.g.*, CAL. CIV. CODE § 8186 (multiple improvements under one contract), § 8446 (conditions for one lien on two or more works of improvement), § 8448 (separate residential units) and § 8554 (site improvements separate from the remainder of the improvement).

states permit the filing of a single lien on multiple works of improvement under certain circumstances, such as when there is a single owner or when the work is contracted for by a single person.[58] Again, a planned development serves as such an example. However, if a lien claimant records a single lien against multiple works of improvement, the lien claimant may be required to segregate the amount due on each individual work of improvement. If the contract is a lump sum payment and does not segregate the amount due for each improvement, the claimant estimates an equitable distribution of the amount due for each based on the proportionate amount of work for each.[59] Importantly, lien claimants must carefully consider whether the improvement is a single improvement or multiple works of improvement so that the lien claimant does not inadvertently compromise its lien rights by not following the correct procedures and requirements.

C. Amount of Lien

Statutory liens are based on principles of unjust enrichment and generally ensure that an owner does not benefit from the value of an improvement at the expenses of a contractor or supplier. Still, the starting point for calculating the amount of a mechanic's lien is the parties' contract. Generally, if the "contribution is made under a contract with the owner and for an agreed price, the lien as against the owner shall be for the sum agreed upon."[60] However, this amount may be decreased for payments already made or increased for extra work performed in conformance with the contract between the parties.[61] In jurisdictions that follow the New York rule discussed earlier, the lien by a subcontractor or other third party also is limited by the contract price in the owner's contract with the contractor, less amounts already paid by the owner.[62]

When the contract is substantially, but not completely, performed, the lien amount may be based on the reasonable value of the services provided, again adjusted for amounts already paid. Similarly, if an explicit agreement between the parties does not exist, then the lien amount will be the reasonable value

---

58. CAL. CIV. CODE § 8446; FLA. STAT. § 713.09; UTAH CODE ANN. § 38-1-8; Schultz v. King, 68 Nev. 207, 228 P.2d 401 (1951).

59. CAL. CIV. CODE § 8446; UTAH CODE ANN. § 38-1-8; Schultz v. King, 68 Nev. 207, 228 P.2d 401 (1951).

60. MINN. STAT. § 514.03.

61. Top line Builders, Inc. v. Bovenkamp, 320 P.3d 130, 140–41 (Wash. Ct. App. 2014).

62. *See, e.g.*, Craft v. Stevenson Lumber Yard, Inc., 179 N.J. 56, 843 A.2d 1076, 1083 (2004).

of the services provided.[63] This amount will be adjusted "for damages, if any, incurred by the owner to finish the general contractor's work."[64]

A claimant also may include certain secondary expenses in the lien amount if payment of the expenses are included in the contract. These can include attorneys' fees, interest, overhead and profits, industrial accident payments, contributions to union health and welfare funds, payroll and Social Security taxes, depreciation of equipment, profit items anticipated by contract, and insurance premiums.[65] These amounts must still be tied to the value of the improvements and the contract price.

In determining the amount of the lien, claimants should take care not to conflate it with their claims for breach of contract. Depending on the jurisdiction, breach of contract remedies may be broader and include such claims that are not properly included in the lien. For example, whether breach of contract damages, such as delay damages, disruption, loss of productivity, or lost profits, can be included in the lien will depend on the particular statute, and, if permitted, likely will have to be based on an argument that these types of damages are part of the reasonable value of the work provided.[66]

Incorrectly calculating the lien amount can have significant consequences. If the lien claimant overstates the amounts, the lien claim may be voided and may subject the claimant to substantial penalties.[67] Generally, if the court finds the overstatement was an innocent mistake or based on honest belief in its correctness, the court may find the lien still valid but reduce the lien to the proper amount.[68] On the other hand, if the overstatement was intentional,

---

63. MINN. STAT. § 514.03; Drilling Serv. Co. v. Baebler, 484 S.W.2d 1 (Mo. 1972); Basic Modular Facilities, Inc. v. Ehsanipour, 70 Cal. App. 4th 1480 (1999) (lien may include reasonable value of services, equipment, and materials based on oral modifications to the contract with the owner if the claimant establishes the owner rescinded, abandoned or breached the contract).

64. Action Concrete Contractors, Inc. v. Chappelear, 745 S.E.2d 77, 80 (S.C. 2013).

65. AM. JUR., *supra* note 22, § 90.

66. CAL. CIV. CODE § 8430(c).

67. *Id.* MEP Construction, LLC v. Truco MP, LLC, 2018 Ill. App. (1st) 180539-U, ¶ 17, 2018 WL 6920124, at *4 (Ill. App. 1 Dist. 2018). MEP Construction, LLC v. Truco MP, LLC, 2018 IL App (1st) 180539-U, ¶ 17, 2018 WL 6920124, at *4 (Ill. App. Ct. 2018) (affirming summary judgment against lien claimant where undisputed evidence showed claim was overstate by more than 100 percent, and noting that even smaller understatements had previously been held to constitute constructive fraud).

68. *E.g.*, Basic Modular Facilities, Inc. v. Ehsanipour, 70 Cal. App. 4th 1482 (1999); E.B. Roberts Constr. Co. v. Concrete Contractors, Inc., 704 P.2d 859, 864 (Colo. 1985); Stricker, P.E. v. H.H. Taylor, 158 Or. App. 608, 975 P.2d 930 (1999); R & L Supply, Ltd. v. Evangelical Lutheran Good Samaritan Society, 462 N.W.2d 515 (S.D. S. Ct. 1990).

made without a reasonable belief of its correctness or otherwise deemed to be fraudulent, the claimant will forfeit its lien rights.[69] But that is not all. In some jurisdictions, an intentional or fraudulent overstatement of lien amounts also will subject the lien claimant to damages and the owner's attorneys' fees. In New York, for example, if a lien is void for willful exaggeration, the owner is entitled to recover

> the amount of any premium for a bond given to obtain the discharge of the lien or the interest on any money deposited for the purpose of discharging the lien, reasonable attorney's fees for services in securing the discharge of the lien, and an amount equal to the difference by which the amount claimed to be due or to become due as stated in the notice of lien exceeded the amount actually due or to become due thereon.[70]

In Texas, a claimant who records a fraudulent lien may be subject to a penalty for the greater of $10,000 or actual damages caused by the violation, plus attorneys' fees, plus punitive damages.[71] Some states even subject a claimant who records a fraudulent lien to criminal liability.[72]

As with the other aspects of lien rights, it is important to understand the individual state laws with respect to what can and cannot be included in the lien amount. Further, lien claimants should take care in being aggressive in setting the lien amount. Absent a good faith belief in an entitlement to the lien amount, as opposed to additional amounts that may be recoverable for breach of contract but may not be included in the lien, the lien claimant risks losing the lien and/or additional, potentially severe penalties.

D. Lien Entitlement

To be entitled to assert a lien, the claimant must be within the class of eligible claimants. Statutory language dictates who is entitled to a lien. Given the variety of people and entities involved with construction projects, especially complex projects, the relevant statutes must be studied carefully to determine who has lien rights. The general categories are mechanics, material suppliers, contractors, subcontractors, and laborers.[73] However, many states expand the

---

69. *E.g.*, Cal. Civ. Code § 8422; Colo. Rev. Stat. § 38-22-128; Fla. Stat. § 713.31; N.D. Stat. § 35-27-16; N.Y. Lien Law § 39; Tex. Civ. Prac. & Rem. Code Ann. § 12.002.

70. N.Y. Lien Law § 39-a.

71. Tex. Civ. Prac. & Rem. Code Ann. § 12.002; *see also* Colo. Rev. Stat. § 38-22-128 (providing for the award of attorneys' fees against a lien claimant for an intentionally overstated lien).

72. Utah Code Ann. § 38-1a-308; *see also* Tex. Pen. Code § 32.49 (failure to release fraudulent lien exposes claimant to criminal penalty).

73. Am. Jur., *supra* note 22, § 59.

list far beyond this to include lessors of equipment, machinists, landscapers, nurserymen, journeymen, and, as discussed previously, architects, engineers, and land surveyors.[74]

Some states do not provide an exclusive list of those eligible to assert mechanic's liens and, instead, claimants encompass "any person" that meets the definition of the type of work covered. This is seen in Washington's lien act, which states: "Any person furnishing labor, professional services, materials, or equipment for the improvement of real property shall have a lien upon the improvement for the contract price."[75]

In many states, second tier material suppliers—or suppliers to materialmen—are not within the class of people entitled to a mechanic's lien.[76] Part of the rationale for not extending lien right to second tier material supplies is the perceived difficulty in tracing the supplied materials to the improvement. In examining this issue, the question arises whether the claimant is, in fact, a second tier supplier or a supplier to a subcontractor. Many states exclude unlicensed contractors from the class of eligible claimants.[77]

A question often arises as to whether equipment suppliers are entitled to lien rights. The answer depends on the wording of the particular lien statute, as well as court decisions. Some states may expressly list equipment suppliers as within the class of eligible lien claimants. Where equipment suppliers are not expressly listed, the states differ in whether the suppliers may be entitled to lien rights, with some states recognizing entitlement on the theory that the lease of equipment falls within the meaning of "furnishing materials" for the construction in question, and other states finding no lien rights.[78] Then, even if an equipment supplier is entitled to a lien right, an examination must be made of whether the supplier actually contributed to the improvement, as discussed in Section 17.04(B). This examination will include such things as whether the equipment was a permanent part of the construction or incorporated into or consumed by the project—which do support lien rights—or simply used in the course of construction—which may not support lien rights.[79] Still further, many

---

74. CAL. CIV. CODE § 8400; IND. CODE § 32-28-3-1; All Clean, Inc. v. Timberline Props., 264 P.3d 244 (Utah Ct. App. 2011); Smith, *supra* note 32.

75. WASH. ANN. § 60.04.021.

76. *E.g.*, Unadilla Silo Co., Inc. v. Hess Bros., Inc., 123 N.J. 268, 586 A.2d 226 (1991) (citing cases from numerous jurisdictions recognizing this rule).

77. *See, e.g.*, CAL. BUS. & PROF. CODE § 7031; FLA. STAT. § 713.02.

78. *E.g.*, Giles & Ransome, Inc. v. First Nat'l Realty Corp., 238 Md. 203, 108 A.2d 582 (1965); Bush Constr. Machinery, Inc. v. Kansas City Factory Outlets, L.L.C., 81 S.W.3d 121 (2002); R.L. Harris, Inc. v. Cincinnati, N.O. & T. P. Ry. Co., 198 Tenn. 339, 280 S.W.2d 800 (1955); Logan Equipment Corp. v. Profile Const. Co., Inc., 585 A.2d 73 (R.I. 1991); AM. JUR., *supra* note 22, § 104.

79. *See* sources cited *supra* note 78.

states will look at whether the equipment supplier also provided an equipment operator. In those jurisdictions, failing to provide an operator results in no lien rights.[80]

Thus, even when a party has fully performed its contract, the party is not entitled to the protections of a mechanic's lien unless the party falls within the statutory definition of an eligible claimant or does not otherwise lose its status by, for example, not maintaining its contractor's license.[81]

17.05 WHAT IS LIENABLE?

As discussed in Section 17.04(B), almost any product used in the improvement of real property can be subject to a mechanic's lien. The lien claimant need only show that the product was delivered to the owner or the owner's agent for the improvement or was delivered to the construction project for the purpose of being used in the project or improvement.

The debate over lienability often turns on whether the property to which the claimant seeks to attach the lien is real or personal property. Real property is subject to mechanic's liens; personal property is not. Often the items supplied constitute "fixtures," which are real property.[82] While the definition of a fixture has some variation among the states, generally personal property is movable, whereas a fixture is permanently attached to the property. Courts typically consider three factors in determining whether the item is a fixture:

1. Actual or constructive annexation of the article to the realty;
2. Adaptation to the use or purpose of that part of the realty with which it is connected, and
3. The intention of the party making the annexation to make the article a permanent accession to the freehold.[83]

For example, the Illinois Appellate Court has held that a $3 million tower for wind energy constitutes a non-lienable "trade fixture" as opposed to an improvement of real property where the tower was movable, albeit at great expense, and the limited permanent construction would not have been difficult to remediate so as to return the property to its prior state as a farm.[84]

---

80. E.g., Giles & Ransome, 238 Md. 203, 108 A.2d 582.
81. Davies Mach. Co. v. Pine Mountain Club, Inc., 39 Cal. App. 3d 18, 24 (1974); *P & P Oil Service Co., Inc. v. Bethlehem Steel Corp.*, 643 N.E.2d 9, 10–11 (1994).
82. Dinsmore v. Lake Elec. Co., Inc., 719 N.E.2d 1282, 1286 (Ind. Ct. App. 1999).
83. *Id.*; *see also* Hess, *supra* note 1.
84. AUI Const. Group, LLC v. Vaessen, 2016 Ill. App. (2d) 160009 (Ill. App. Ct. 2016).

Where the claimant has provided both lienable and non-lienable services or products, care should be taken to include only the former in the lien to avoid the risks discussed previously regarding overstated liens.

17.06 INTERESTS SUBJECT TO A LIEN

Each state's lien law defines the property interest to which the lien may attach. Generally, however, a lien attaches to the work of improvement and to the real property on which the work of improvement is situated, regardless of how the underlying interests are held. Thus, lienable interests are not restricted to just fee-simple ownership but can attach to nearly any interest, including an estate for years and leaseholds.[85] This has been summarized as any transferable, assignable, or conveyable interest in the real estate of the party at whose instance a building, structure, or improvement thereon is erected.[86] Further, a structure must not always be built for the lien rights to attach to the land, for example, in the case of professional service liens when the project does not move forward, as further discussed in Section 17.04(B).

What happens when a party who owns less than a fee simple interest in the property causes the improvements to be made? This question typically arises in the context of leaseholds. States generally allow leasehold estates to be subjected to mechanic's liens, with the lien attaching to the leasehold interest. Claimants, however, often seek to extend the lien to the fee interest of the landlord.[87] States treat this issue in one of several ways. In some states, the landlord is presumed to know the activities of the tenant and can avoid the lien only by giving a specific notice of protection, sometimes called a notice of non-responsibility, protecting the owner's fee interest from the lien. Other states require the contractor to demonstrate that the landlord affirmatively approved the tenant's improvements in order for the lien to attach to the landlord's interest; mere knowledge without affirmative approval of the work will not support the lien. Examples of affirmative approval include a requirement in the lease that the improvements be made and providing an allowance

---

85. Howard S. Wright Constr. Co. v. Superior Court, 106 Cal. App. 4th 314, 321 (2003).

86. AM. JUR., *supra* note 22, § 38. Some states have specific statutes permitting mechanic's liens to attach to items other than real property, such as machinery. *E.g.,* Kent Sand & Gravel, LLC v. Jacksonville Machine & Repair, Inc., 403 Md. 173, 941 A.2d 468 (2008).

87. If the fee interest is non-lienable, the leasehold may be non-lineable as well. *See, e.g.,* George Washington Bridge Bus Station Development Venture, LLC v. Associated Specialty Contracting, No. 150549/16, 3731N, 52 N.Y.S.3d 321, 2017 N.Y. slip op. 02913, 2017 WL 1348160 (N.Y. App. Div. 2017) (developer's leasehold interest could not be liened where property was owned by government).

for them. Still other states permit the landlord to avoid the lien, even when the landlord has actual knowledge of the tenant's improvements, by posting the notice of protection/notice of non-responsibility.[88] Then, even where a notice of protection is permitted, some states find the notice will not avoid the lien when the tenant is required by the lease to make the improvements and can be considered an agent of the owner. This last scenario is known as the Participating Owner doctrine.[89] When a lien does not attach to the landlord's property but only to the leasehold, the recording of a mechanic's lien against the landlord's interest may constitute actionable slander of title.[90]

Leaseholds are not the only way in which a non-contracting owner may find its property subject to a mechanic's lien. California, for example, permits the lien to attach to adjoining property where that property is required for the "convenient use and occupancy" of the work of improvement.[91] The court applied this approach in *Forsgren Associates, Inc. v. Pacific Golf Community Development LLC*,[92] where a developer failed to pay the general contractor for the construction of a golf course and flood channel. The court permitted the lien to attach to a limited portion of the adjacent property where a tee box was located outside the golf course property and where the contractor installed irrigation, provided landscaping, and performed grading and leveling related to the removal of topsoil transported from the golf course. In considering the extent to which the adjacent property was subject to a lien, the court noted that, while the whole of the adjacent property would benefit from the golf course, that was not the proper inquiry. Instead, the inquiry is the extent of the use of the adjacent property for the improvement constructed.[93] In mitigating the unfairness this can cause the adjacent property owner, the courts find that

---

88. *E.g.*, CAL. CIV. CODE § 8442 (notice of non-responsibility); COLO. REV. STAT. § 38-22-105(2) (same); FLA. STAT. § 713.10(2) (lessee must notify contractor if lease exempts landlord's property from liens; landlord protects fee interest from lien if lease containing such protection is recorded); Waterview Site Services, Inc. v. Pay Day, Inc., 125 Conn. App. 561, 11 A.3d 692 (2010) (landlord must consent for its fee interest to be subject to a lien; consent is more than mere knowledge that work is being performed); D & N Electric, Inc. v. Underground Festival, Inc., 202 Ga. App. 435, 414 S.E.2d 891 (1992) (landlord's mere knowledge of tenant improvements insufficient to subject landlord's fee interest to lien, but where lease required the improvements and landlord paid for a portion of the cost through an allowance, the lien would attach); *see also* HESS, *supra* note 1.

89. Howard S. Wright Constr. Co. v. Superior Court, 106 Cal. App. 4th 314, 317 (2003); *see also* Bell v. Tollefsen, 189 Okla. 149 (1989) (lessor's property is subject to lien when the tenant is an agent of the landlord).

90. *See, e.g.*, Cuspide Properties, Ltd. v. Earl Mechanical Servs., 53 N.E.3d 818, 828, 2015 Ohio 5019, ¶ 36 (Ohio Ct. App. 2015).

91. CAL. CIV. CODE § 8440.

92. 182 Cal. App. 4th 135, 105 Cal. Rptr. 654 (2010).

93. *Id.*

the non-contracting adjacent owner can avoid the lien by posting a notice of non-responsibility.[94]

Finally, in addition to public property discussed in Section 17.09, two other categories of real property are exempt from mechanic's liens. First, easements historically have been recognized as exempt from liens. Generally, a mechanic's lien will not attach either to the easement interest or the land on which it sits unless, in the latter case, an independent lien exists over the owner's property.[95] Second, tribal lands normally are protected by sovereign immunity from mechanic's liens unless the tribe by contract or ordinance waives its sovereign immunity rights.[96]

In sum, as with the other aspects of lien law, which interests may or may not be subject to a lien is based on the statutory language and must be analyzed closely prior to filing a lien claim.

17.07 PERFECTING THE LIEN

Creating, or perfecting, a mechanic's lien involves specific steps required by statute. Requirements common to most jurisdictions include (1) giving notice to the owner, (2) recording the lien, and (3) filing a lawsuit to foreclose the lien. However, the specifics of each step in terms of what must be included, applicable time frames, and additional requirements vary.[97] As discussed in Section 17.02, some states require certain potential lien claimants, including subcontractors and suppliers not under direct contract with the owner, to give the owner a written notice within a stated time period of starting work, which notice describes (1) the lien claimant, (2) its involvement in the project, and (3) an estimate of the total price of the work to be provided; the notice of lien also contains an affirmative statement that the property is subject to a mechanic's lien if the claimant is not paid in full, even if the prime contractor is paid in full.[98] Other states require a notice of lien within a stated time of completion of the project. In Illinois, for example, if the lienholder is a subcontractor, the subcontractor must serve a notice on the property owner and lender within 90 days of completing work in the event the subcontractor has not been paid.[99]

---

94. *Id.*
95. McClintic-Marshall Co. v. Ford Motor Co., 236 N.W. 792, 796 (Mich. 1931).
96. *See, e.g.,* Weeks Construction, Inc. v. Oglala Sioux Hous. Auth., 797 F.2d 668 (8th Cir. 1986).
97. *See generally* Cushman & Butler, *supra* note 3.
98. Ala. Code § 35-11-210; Ariz. Rev. Stat. § 33-992.01; Cal. Civ. Code §§ 8200, 8202, 8204; Fla. Stat. § 713.06; Or. Rev. Stat. §§ 87.09, 87.021, 87.023; Wash. Rev. Code § 60.04.13.
99. 770 Ill. Comp. Stat. 60/24 (2006).

Other statutory requirements may include a sworn statement from the general contractor identifying subcontractors and the amount to be paid to each.

All states require the lien to be recorded with the applicable government office, usually the county clerk or recorder of deeds, and all generally require the lien to include the property's information, description of work performed, and amount owed.[100]

After recording the lien, the next step is to file a lawsuit to foreclose the lien. Most states impose strict timelines for bringing a foreclosure lawsuit. Typically, the lawsuit involves a breach of contract claim against the party who owes the unpaid sums and a lien foreclosure claim against the owner. If the claimant is successful, the court will oversee the foreclosure of the property. However, several important nuances must be considered in the foreclosure action.

First, as with other foreclosure actions, all parties with an interest in the property must be joined in order to obtain complete relief; otherwise, the foreclosure may be subject to the interests of unjoined parties, especially those without notice of the claim. Thus, it is highly recommended the lien claimant obtain a title report from a title company with a litigation guaranty ensuring identification of all possible parties with an interest in the property.

Second, many construction contracts include an arbitration clause binding on the lien claimant. In that circumstance, the lien claimant still must timely file its foreclosure lawsuit in court in order to preserve the lien rights. Then, the lawsuit typically is stayed pending the outcome in arbitration. If arbitration results in a successful decision for the lien claimant, the award is presented to the court, which will proceed to oversee the foreclosure. This typical procedure, however, can require a variety of strategic decisions when the underlying dispute does not involve the owner, and the owner is not subject to the arbitration clause. In that case, the owner may agree to the stay of the lawsuit until the lien claimant establishes entitlement to payment in the arbitration. Alternatively, if the owner has defenses to the enforceability of the lien itself, the owner may wish to have those defenses decided by summary judgment or other expedited procedure to avoid the encumbrance on owner's property during the pendency of the arbitration. Similarly, even if the owner is subject to an arbitration clause, the owner may have expedited statutory procedures available to it in court to determine the validity or enforceability of the lien.

---

100. *See generally* CUSHMAN & BUTLER, *supra* note 3.

17.08 PRIORITIES

Understanding the priority of the mechanic's lien over other encumbrances is key to being able to evaluate the lien's actual effectiveness as a remedy. As with other encumbrances, a mechanic's lien still may be subject to any senior interests in the property. While states universally recognize that a properly perfected mechanic's lien has priority over any interest of the owner in the property,[101] whether the mechanic's lien has priority over other types of encumbrances is state-specific. Many states follow the so-called relation back doctrine and provide that mechanic's liens have priority over all encumbrances that attached after commencement of the improvement work, even if the lien is recorded later in time.[102] Thus, the finishing subcontractor's lien is entitled to the same priority as that of the person or supplier that provided the very first work to the improvement. What constitutes "commencement of work," is fact-specific, but generally includes work or labor easily seen. Other states base priority solely on the date the lien is filed.

Regardless of the priority date or the relation back doctrine, some states have special rules for mechanic's lien priority in relation to mortgages. Hawaii, for example, generally follows the relation back doctrine, but provides that a mortgage will have priority (1) if the mortgage is recorded prior to the date of completion; and (2) the mortgage money advanced is used to pay for the improvement, except the interest owed on the principal amount of the debt will not have priority.[103]

As among the lien claimants themselves, some states impose specific priorities based on the class of lien claimant. For example, Idaho ranks the priority of lien claimants as follows: (1) all laborers other than contractors or subcontractors, (2) all materialmen other than contractors or subcontractors, (3) subcontractors, (4) the original contractor, and (5) professional engineers and surveyors.[104] Other states, such as Georgia, rank lien priority among the lien claimants based on the date the lien is filed.[105] All lien claimants within the same class enjoy the same priority. Where states do not have any priority ranking among lien claimants, all lien claimants are on equal footing, with disbursements from the sale of the property shared pro-rata among the claimants.[106]

---

101. Am. Jur., *supra* note 22, § 263; *see generally* CUSHMAN & BUTLER, *supra* note 3.
102. *Id.*; *see, e.g.*, CAL. CIV. CODE § 8450.
103. HAW. REV. STAT. § 507-46; Strouss v. Simmons, 66 Haw. 32, 657 P.2d 1004 (1982).
104. IDAHO CODE § 45-512.
105. GA. CODE ANN. § 44-14-361.1.
106. HESS, *supra* note 1; SCHOUMACHER, *supra* note 2, § 19.08; CUSHMAN & BUTLER, *supra* note 3.

17.09 PUBLIC PROJECTS

It is well-understood that public property—state or federal—may not be encumbered by mechanic's liens absent statutory authority expressly granting such liens.[107] A number of reasons for this exist, including that such a lien would violate public policy by allowing public property to be sold in satisfaction of a private debt.[108] However, unpaid subcontractors or suppliers are not left without remedy. In addition to payment bonds, discussed in Chapter 18, some states permit subcontractors or suppliers who have not been paid to file a lien against funds due to the prime contractor or against the public funds reserved for the project, provided certain statutory prerequisites and procedures are followed.[109]

In modern times, the prohibition against mechanic's liens on public projects has become hazy as more and more projects are hybrid projects with both public and private characteristics. For example, "so-called public private partnerships" may be characterized by franchise or long-term leasing agreements between the government and private developers or service providers. Similarly, the government may enter into a long term lease agreement with a developer providing (1) that the developer will design and construct improvements on land owned by the developer, using bridging and other basic design information provided by the government; (2) that the lease payments will begin upon completion of the construction; and (3) that the government will have an option to purchase the property after a certain period. Another scenario includes the requirement for construction of various infrastructure improvements as a condition of approval of a planned development, with those infrastructure improvements to be dedicated to the local public entity upon completion of the development. In none of these scenarios is the government a party to the construction contract. In at least the last scenario, public funds may not be used to pay for the construction, even on a reimbursement basis. This then leads to the question: What is a public project?

In California, the statutes governing the remedies available on public construction projects specifically state the remedies apply only to works of

---

107. E.g., Four Star Enters. Equip., Inc. v. Emps. Mut. Cas. Co., 451 S.W. 3d 776 (Mo. Ct. App. 2014); City of Westminister v. Brannan Sand & Gravel Co., Inc., 940 P.2d 393 (Colo. 1997). See also George Washington Bridge Bus Station Development Venture, LLC v. Associated Specialty Contracting, No. 150549/16, 3731N, 52 N.Y.S.3d 321, 2017 N.Y. slip op. 02913, 2017 WL 1348160, (N.Y. App. Div. 2017) (tenant's leasehold interest cannot be liened where owner is governmental entity whose property cannot be liened).

108. Am. Jur., *supra* note 22, § 263; Allen & Martin, *supra* note 9, § 25.03[A].

109. E.g., Cal. Civ. Code §§ 9350, 9352, 9354, 9352; Wis. Stats. § 779.15(1); N.Y. Lien Law § 12.

improvement "contracted for" by public entities.[110] Focusing on this language, the court in *Pipeline, Inc. v. Bond Safeguard Ins. Co.*[111] held a developer's agreement with a public entity that required certain subdivision improvements on private property before receipt of a final subdivision map did not create a public project, even though the agreement anticipated dedication of the improvements by the developer to the public entity. This was so, according to the court, because the public entity did not actually contract with the construction contractor for the work of improvement.[112] Under these facts, then, the contractor was entitled to lien the project, and, under the relation-back rules discussed earlier, that lien would take priority over a later dedication of the improvement to the public owner, entitling the contractor to foreclose upon the property even after the dedication.

In another case, a bankruptcy court considered the validity of a design-build contractor's mechanic's lien against a private developer's property interest in a toll road owned by the California Department of Transportation, but constructed and operated by the private developer.[113] Pursuant to special legislation, the Department of Transportation was authorized to enter into franchise agreements with developers to finance, design, construct, and operate lease-back public transportation facilities, including toll roads. The legislation specifically stated that the facilities constructed by the developer are "at all times" owned by the state.[114] In upholding the design-build contractor's mechanic's lien, the court recognized that mechanic's liens are not available against public property.[115] The court, however, also recognized that a governmental franchise "is a special privilege granted to a private enterprise by a duly-empowered governmental entity to use public property to provide vital public services," is considered "a possessory 'estate in real property' similar to a leasehold or an easement," and "is deemed to be *privately* owned with all of the rights attaching to the ownership of the property in general."[116] Coupling this with the fact that mechanic's liens can attach to less than a fee simple estate, such as a

---

110. CAL. CIV. CODE § 9000. *But see* CAL. CIV. CODE § 8038, defining "Public works contract" as having the same meaning as in CAL. PUB. CONT. CODE § 1101, which means "an agreement for the erection, construction, alteration, repair or improvement of any public structure, building, road, or other public improvement of any kind."
111. 223 Cal. App. 4th 438 (2014).
112. *Id.* at 445–47.
113. *In re* South Bay Expressway, L.P. v. Otay River Constructors, 434 B.R. 589 (2010).
114. *Id.* at 593–94.
115. *Id.* at 601.
116. *Id.* at 598, original emphasis.

leasehold, the court found the lien was against the developer's private property interest and, thus, enforceable.[117]

Ultimately, contractors, owners, practitioners, and the courts will need to look beyond mere labels. They will need to examine the actual characteristics of the project, as well as the potential applicability of multiple governing statutes to determine whether a project, especially a hybrid project, is a public or private project and subject to mechanic's liens.[118]

17.10 WAIVER AND RELEASE

As discussed in this chapter, the mechanic's lien laws consider the competing interests of unpaid contractors, laborers, and suppliers, on the one hand, with the interests of owners against improper encumbrances on their property, on the other hand. One of the most common ways for owners to protect themselves is through lien waivers and releases. However, whether a party provides or receives the lien waiver and release, care needs to be taken that the release is effective as intended and only to the extent intended.

Lien waivers and releases often are governed by statute, but also can be simply a matter of contract subject to traditional contract interpretation rules.[119] In either case, the waiver and release must be express, clear, and unambiguous, and must be freely given.[120] In light of the importance of the waiver and release, some states statutorily mandate the exact language to be used for the waiver and release to be effective.[121]

Often two types of lien waivers and releases will be provided—conditional and unconditional. A conditional lien release is given in advance of actual receipt of the funds for the work performed. The release becomes effective once the check clears. An unconditional lien release is effective immediately upon tender of the release and, thus, typically not given unless either the funds are in the lien claimant's hands or the potential lien claimant has other reasons for agreeing to the release before payment.[122] In the normal course of a construction project, an owner can protect itself by requiring that the contrac-

---

117. *Id.* at 601–04.

118. *See* ANNO. 48 ALR 4th 1170 (1986) (various states consider hybrid projects to be public works projects, considering statutory objectives and contexts).

119. Merchs. Envtl. Indus., Inc. v. SLT Realty Ltd. P'ship, 731 N.E. 2d 394 (Ill. App. Ct. 2000).

120. *See, e.g.*, Amfac Dist. Corp. v. J.B. Contractors, Inc., 703 P.2d 566 (Ariz. Ct. App. 1985); First Union Nat'l Bank v. RPB 2, LLC, 674 N.W. 2d 1 (N.D. 2004) (fraudulently obtained waiver and release unenforceable); 770 ILCS 60/21.01 (imposing criminal liability for fraudulently obtained waiver and release).

121. *E.g.*, CAL. CIV. CODE §§ 8120–8138.

122. *Id.*

tor provide conditional lien releases with each progress payment application, with such releases from the contractor itself and from all other lien claimants for the period covered by the pending progress payment, as well as unconditional lien releases for the period covered by the prior progress payment. In that manner, the owner ensures that payment intended for subtier parties has actually reached them.

Sometimes contracts will include an advance waiver of lien rights, or so-called no lien clauses. The enforceability of such clauses again depends on the state. Some states uphold the enforceability of contract clauses providing that the contractor will not assert a mechanic's lien.[123] If the contract is ambiguous, doubts will be resolved against a waiver since, in the absence of clear evidence to the contrary, the presumption is the contractor retains statutory rights.[124] This rule of interpretation becomes even stronger when the contract between the original contractor and the owner contains an advance waiver of lien rights and purports to waive the lien rights of the subcontractors, laborers, or suppliers.[125] Other states find advance waivers of lien rights unlawful outright, regardless of the language, as against public policy, or limit the legality of advance lien rights to certain projects, such as residential construction.[126]

Finally, owners can clear a mechanic's lien from their property by posting, or requiring the prime contractor to post, a lien release bond. In that case, the bond substitutes for the lien, and the lien claimants pursue actions on the bond rather than against the property.

17.11 BANKRUPTCY

An unfortunate part of the construction industry, particularly in economic downtimes, is the risk of bankruptcy. While the mechanic's lien laws are designed to protect lien claimants from the risk of lack of payment, a bankruptcy petition under either Chapter 7 or Chapter 11 of the Bankruptcy Code will impact those lien rights. The filing of a bankruptcy petition immediately triggers the automatic stay on a wide variety of collection activities against the debtor and the bankruptcy estate. Mechanic's liens are within the purview of the automatic stay.[127] This can become particularly problematic in the face

---

123. Jankoviak v. Butcher, 159 N.E.2d 377 (Ill. App. Ct. 1959).
124. Davis v. La Crosse Hospital Ass'n, 121 Wis. 579, 99 N.W. 351 (1904).
125. Kokomo, F. & W. Traction Co. v. Kokomo Trust Co., 193 Ind. 219, 137 N.E. 763 (1923).
126. IND. CODE § 32-28-3-1; MD. REAL PROP. CODE ANN. § 9.113; Nat'l Glass, Inc. v. J.C. Penney Props., Inc., 336 Md. 606, 650 A.2d 246 (1994); ALLEN & MARTIN, *supra* note 9, § 25.03[A].
127. 11 U.S.C. § 362(a)(4).

of a state law setting forth the deadline by which mechanic's liens must be recorded or they will be lost.

California recognizes that a lien still may be recorded if incurred pre-petition, but a post-petition foreclosure action may be barred by the automatic stay. As explained by the court in *Pioneer Constr., Inc. v. Global Inv. Corp.*,[128]

> A mechanic's lien claimant who provided labor and materials prepetition to a debtor in bankruptcy can record a mechanic's lien after the property owner files for bankruptcy without violating the automatic stay. (11 U.S.C. § 362(b)(3).) A mechanic's lienor must file a notice of lien in the debtor's bankruptcy proceedings to inform the debtor and creditors of its intention to enforce the lien. (11 U.S.C. § 546(b)(2); *In re Baldwin Builders* (9th Cir. BAP 1999) 232 B.R. 406, 413.) Once the lien is properly perfected, it is not subject to avoidance by the trustee. (11 U.S.C. § 546(b)). . . . [P]ostpetition lien foreclosure actions (as opposed to the mere recording of a lien) are enforcement actions prohibited by the automatic stay. (*In re Baldwin Builders, supra*, 232 B.R. at pp. 410–411.) Nonetheless, pursuant to 11 United States Code section 108(c), mechanic's lien actions are tolled while the property subject to the lien is property of the estate. (*In re Hunters Run Ltd. Partnership* (9th Cir.1989) 875 F.2d 1425, 1427.).[129]

The rationale for the rule stating a post-petition recording of the lien does not violate the automatic stay is that, in California, the lien relates back to the time of commencement of the work.[130] However, care should be taken to understand the laws of other jurisdictions to make sure the post-petition recording of a lien will not violate the automatic stay.

Whether enforcement of the mechanic's lien through a foreclosure action violates the automatic stay will depend on whether the owner or the general contractor is the debtor. If the debtor is the owner, a foreclosure action will violate the automatic stay. To protect the claimants, though, the owner's bankruptcy will toll the time to file the foreclosure action, although the lien claimant may be required to file a Notice of Continued Perfection in order to preserve the continued enforceability of the lien during the bankruptcy.[131]

Conversely, when the debtor is the prime contractor and not the owner, the bankruptcy does not toll a foreclosure action against the owner, and the

---

128. 202 Cal. App. 4th 161 (2011).

129. *Id.*

130. Showplace Square Loft Co. v. Primecore Mortgage Trust, Inc., 289 B.R. 403 (Bankr. ND Cal. 2003).

131. 11 U.S.C. §§ 362(b)(3), 546(b); *but see In re* Hunters Run Ltd. Partnership, 875 F.2d 1425, 1427 (9th Cir. 1989) (suggesting that under Washington law, a notice of continued perfection is not necessary because the bankruptcy tolls the time for filing the foreclosure action).

foreclosure action against the owner will not violate the automatic stay, unless the contractor is an indispensable party. Again, the states split on whether the contractor is an indispensable party, and the law of the particular jurisdiction must be examined.[132]

A bankruptcy can trigger other concerns and considerations for the lien claimant, such as making a claim in the bankruptcy proceeding and/or seeking relief from the automatic stay to foreclose on its lien. Ultimately, the lien claimant will consult with a bankruptcy attorney to ensure its rights are protected and that it does not violate the automatic stay or other protections afforded the debtor.

---

132. *E.g.*, W.G. Glenney Co. v. Bianco, 27 Conn. App. 199, 604 A.2d 1345 (1992) (contractor not indispensable party in subcontractor's lien foreclosure action); Hamel v. Am. Cont'l Corp., 713 P.2d 1152 (Wyo. 1986) (contractor becomes an indispensable party when the owner insists that the contractor be made a party).

QUESTIONS

One of your long-standing clients, Buck's Construction Labor and Equipment Rental (BCLER), leases temporary skilled and unskilled construction laborers as well as construction equipment to subcontractors and contractors. It operates all across the country and has found success in this field. Although BCLER has gotten burned on a few contracts here and there (which losses it has absorbed into its pricing structure), in recent days the defaults have become more frequent, and a couple have involved fairly large contracts.

Buford, the president of BCLER, tells you that he has become disheartened by this increase in defaults and has decided to see whether the imposition of a lien program can increase his collections. He would like you to produce for him a very concise table that summarizes the lien laws for two states of your choosing whose borders are at least 500 miles apart, after which he will craft and implement a mechanic's lien collection policy with which he can experiment.

Please create this table for Buford. It should include only the following elements, with appropriate statutory or case law citations:

- The name of the two states;
- A general citation to the lien law;
- An indication of whether an employee-leasing company may assert lien rights;
- An indication of whether an equipment lessor may assert lien rights;
- Assuming the company can assert lien rights (even if you conclude that it cannot), circumstances under which the company can lien a landlord's property;
- A statement as to when the lien statement must be recorded;
- A statement as to whether the state has a requirement that the claimant provide the parties advance notice of the intent to file a lien statement; and
- A statement as to the deadline for filing a lawsuit to foreclose the lien.

CHAPTER 18

Insurance and Bonds

DEBORAH GRIFFIN

18.01 INTRODUCTION

This chapter introduces the areas of bonds and insurance, with a particular focus on the difference between the two types of contracts and, in the case of bonds, the fundamental equitable principles that shape the rights and defenses of a surety.

18.02 THE ROLE OF INSURANCE

The role of insurance is to protect oneself against named categories of risk, shifting that risk to the insurer in exchange for payment of a premium. The one purchasing the contract of insurance is called the *insured*, who buys a policy issued by the *insurer*. In the event of a loss covered by the policy, the insurer pays or indemnifies the insured up to the amount of coverage. The insurer has no recourse against the insured except to change the pricing of the policy prospectively or decline to renew the policy when it expires.

The business of insurance is highly regulated. Congress has made a conscious decision to leave the regulation of insurance to the states, a decision manifested in an express exemption from such federal statutes as the antitrust laws.[1] Even the Gramm-Leach-Bliley legislation, which regulates financial services corporations that own insurance companies, leaves the basic regulation of insurance to the states.[2]

In order to issue an insurance policy to an insured in a given state, the insurance company must be registered with that state's insurance commissioner. Information about what companies are registered in a particular jurisdiction is available on most state insurance commissioners' websites.

18.03 CONTRACTUAL INSURANCE REQUIREMENTS

Different types of insurance policies protect against different risks. Construction contracts often require the contractor, the architect, and the owner, respectively, to purchase and maintain in force certain types and levels of coverages. The types of insurance most often required in connection with construction contracts or construction projects are

For owners:	• builders' risk coverage
	• property insurance
	• flood insurance (in flood zones)
	• general liability coverage
For design professionals:	• errors and omissions coverage
For contractors:	• general liability coverage
	• workers' compensation coverage

On some larger projects, the owner can save substantial sums of money by purchasing insurance under an Owner Controlled Insurance Program, or OCIP. With an OCIP, the insurance covers all project participants who enroll in the program (which can include contractors, subcontractors, project managers, design professionals, and the owner) against whatever risks are included. To the extent enrollment in the OCIP satisfies a party's contractual insurance obligation, that party is required to reduce its contract price by the amount of the insurance component of the party's price, passing the savings along to the owner.

Standard insurance requirements for a contractor are set out in various contract forms published by the American Institute of Architects (AIA) or its competitor ConsensusDocs. For example, AIA form A102, Exhibit A–2017, Insurance and Bonds, provides in part:

---

1. McCarran-Ferguson Act, 15 U.S.C. §§ 1011–1015 (2012).
2. Gramm-Leach-Bliley Act, 15 U.S.C. §§ 6801–6809 (2010).

Article 3 Contractor's Insurance and Bonds

3.2 Contractor's Required Insurance Coverage

§ A.3.2.1 The Contractor shall purchase and maintain the following types and limits of insurance from an insurance company or insurance companies lawfully authorized to issue insurance in the jurisdiction where the Project is located. The Contractor shall maintain the required insurance until the expiration of the period for correction of Work as set forth in Section 12.2.2 of the General Conditions....

§ A.3.2.2 Commercial General Liability

§ A.3.2.2.1 Commercial General Liability insurance for the Project written on an occurrence form with policy limits of not less than [blank dollars] each occurrence, [blank dollars] general aggregate, and [blank dollars] aggregate for products-completed operations hazard, providing coverage for claims including

.1 damages because of bodily injury, sickness or disease, including occupational sickness or disease, and death of any person;
.2 personal injury and advertising injury;
.3 damages because of physical damage to or destruction of tangible property, including the loss of use of such property;
.4 bodily injury or property damage arising out of completed operations; and
.5 the Contractor's indemnity obligations under Section 3.18 of the General Conditions.

§ A.3.2.2.2 The Contractor's Commercial General Liability policy under this Section A.3.2.2 shall not contain an exclusion or restriction of coverage for the following:

.1 Claims by one insured against another insured, if the exclusion or restriction is based solely on the fact that the claimant is an insured, and there would otherwise be coverage for the claim.
.2 Claims for property damage to the Contractor's Work arising out of the products-completed operations hazard where the damaged Work or the Work out of which the damage arises was performed by a Subcontractor.
.3 Claims for bodily injury other than to employees of the insured.
.4 Claims for indemnity under Section 3.18 of the General Conditions arising out of injury to employees of the insured.
.5 Claims or loss excluded under a prior work endorsement or other similar exclusionary language.
.6 Claims or loss due to physical damage under a prior injury endorsement or similar exclusionary language.

.7 Claims related to residential, multi-family, or other habitational projects, if the Work is to be performed on such a project.
.8 Claims related to roofing, if the Work involves roofing.
.9 Claims related to exterior insulation finish systems (EIFS), synthetic stucco or similar exterior coatings or surfaces, if the Work involves such coatings or surfaces.
.10 Claims related to earth subsidence or movement, where the Work involves such hazards.
.11 Claims related to explosion, collapse and underground hazards, where the Work involves such hazards.

§ A.2.3 Required Property Insurance

Unless this obligation is placed on the Contractor pursuant to Section A.3.3.2.1, the Owner shall purchase and maintain, from an insurance company or insurance companies lawfully authorized to issue insurance in the jurisdiction where the Project is located, property insurance written on a builder's risk "all-risks" completed value or equivalent policy form and sufficient to cover the total value of the entire Project on a replacement cost basis. The Owner's property insurance coverage shall be no less than the amount of the initial Contract Sum, plus the value of subsequent Modifications and labor performed and materials or equipment supplied by others. The property insurance shall be maintained until Substantial Completion and thereafter as provided in Section A.2.3.1.3, unless otherwise provided in the Contract Documents or otherwise agreed in writing by the parties to this Agreement. This insurance shall include the interests of the Owner, Contractor, Subcontractors, and Sub-subcontractors in the Project as insureds. This insurance shall include the interests of mortgagees as loss payees.

§ A.2.3.1.1 Causes of Loss.

The insurance required by this Section A.2.3.1 shall provide coverage for direct physical loss or damage, and shall not exclude the risks of fire, explosion, theft, vandalism, malicious mischief, collapse, earthquake, flood, or windstorm. The insurance shall also provide coverage for ensuing loss or resulting damage from error, omission, or deficiency in construction methods, design, specifications, workmanship, or materials. ...

AIA's General Conditions document, A201, provides

§ 11.3.1 WAIVERS OF SUBROGATION

The Owner and Contractor waive all rights against (1) each other and any of their subcontractors, sub-subcontractors, agents, and employees, each of the other; (2) the Architect and Architect's consultants; and (3) Separate Contractors, if any, and any of their subcontractors, sub-subcontractors, agents, and employees, for damages caused by fire, or other causes of loss, to the extent those losses are covered by property insurance required by the Agreement or other property insurance applicable to the Project, except such rights as they have to proceeds of such insurance. The Owner or Contractor, as appropriate, shall require similar written waivers in favor of the individuals and entities identified above from the Architect, Architect's consultants, Separate Contractors, subcontractors, and sub-subcontractors. The policies of insurance purchased and maintained by each person or entity agreeing to waive claims pursuant to this section 11.3.1 shall not prohibit this waiver of subrogation. This waiver of subrogation shall be effective as to a person or entity (1) even though that person or entity would otherwise have a duty of indemnification, contractual or otherwise, (2) even though that person or entity did not pay the insurance premium directly or indirectly, or (3) whether or not the person or entity had an insurable interest in the damaged property.

18.04 GENERAL LIABILITY INSURANCE POLICIES

Each insurance company uses its own standard form for each type of insurance it offers. However, organizations such as Insurance Services Office (ISO) and the American Association of Insurance Services develop standardized policy language that many companies adopt.

A typical comprehensive general liability (CGL) insurance policy consists of sections containing the declarations, insuring agreement, exclusions, conditions, and definitions. In the declarations, the policy identifies the insured and any additional insureds, and states the policy period, policy territory, and the dollar limits for each type of coverage under the policy. The insuring agreement section articulates the hazards insured against, using terms as defined in the definitions section. The essence of the grant of coverage is for damage to persons or property caused by an "occurrence," which, in turn, is defined in such a way as to connote an event or result that is unintended and unexpected from the standpoint of the insured. Much litigation has occurred regarding what constitutes an occurrence so as to trigger the coverage under a policy in effect at that time.

The conditions section of the policy imposes burdens on the insured in order to enforce the coverage, such as providing prompt notice of claims and cooperating in the defense of claims.

The Exclusions section of a CGL policy defines limitations on the circumstances in which a risk, otherwise within the scope of an insuring agreement, nonetheless will not be covered. A series of exclusions aims to exclude coverage for the business risks of the insured. For example, a usual provision excludes coverage for the cost of repairing the insured's own work product. Courts have often struggled with the application of these exclusions, as illustrated in the case that follows.

Courts generally place the burden of showing that a claim falls within the scope of a grant of coverage on the insured; the burden of proving the applicability of an exclusion falls on the insurer.

Summit Custom Homes, Inc. v. Great Am. Lloyds Ins. Co., 202 S.W.3d 823 (Tex. Civ. App. 2006)

Opinion By Justice WRIGHT

Summit Custom Homes, Inc. appeals the summary judgment granted in favor of Great American Lloyds Insurance Company . . . and the denial of its summary judgment motion. . . . Summit argues that the trial court erred in granting the summary judgment because (1) the Insurers had a duty to defend, [and] (2) the Insurers had a duty to indemnify. We affirm in part and reverse in part.

Factual and Procedural Background

Summit is a custom home builder. Great American issued Commercial General Liability ("CGL") polices to Summit from January 15, 1996 through January 15, 2000. . . . In 1996, Summit and Stephen and Helen Lazarus signed an agreement for the construction of a residence. Summit completed the Lazaruses' home that same year. In May 2003, the Lazaruses filed suit . . . complaining about construction defects in their home. They asserted claims for negligence, breach of warranty, and breach of contract claiming there were defects in the exterior finishing of the home, referred to as an "Exterior Insulating and Finishing System" or "EIFS." They further argued that the EIFS was defective and sought to have it removed and replaced. Although Summit built the home in 1996, the Lazaruses pleaded the discovery rule because EIFS-related problems were "inherently undiscoverable in that defects in EIFS are latent."

Summit later sued [Great American] seeking a declaration that [it] had breached [its] duties to defend against the suit. Thereafter, Summit filed a motion for partial summary judgment arguing that the underlying pleadings alleged "property damage" from an "occurrence" under the policies at issue. Great American also filed a joint motion for summary judgment arguing that [the plaintiff] failed to allege any facts triggering coverage under the policies. After a hearing, the trial court granted Great American's motion for summary judgment and denied Summit's motion. This appeal followed.

In its first issue, Summit contends the trial court erred in granting the Insurers' joint motion for summary judgment because the Insurers had a duty to defend them against the Lazaruses' claims. The duty to defend arises when a third party sues the insured on allegations that, if taken as true, potentially state a cause of action within the terms of the policy. [Citation omitted.] The duty to defend the lawsuit is determined by the allegations in the underlying pleadings, in light of the policy provisions, and without reference to the truth or falsity of the allegations.

[Citations omitted.] This is sometimes referred to as the "eight corners" rule. [Citation omitted.] In construing the allegations of the underlying suit, the pleadings are strictly construed against the insurer, and any doubt is resolved in favor of coverage. [Citation omitted.] In considering the allegations to determine whether a liability insurer is obligated under its policy to defend, we liberally interpret the meaning of those allegations. [Citation omitted.]

Because the terms of the policy dictate whether the Insurers had a duty to defend, we must first determine which policy is at issue in this case. In *Dorchester Development Corp. v. Safeco Insurance Co.*, the issue before this Court was whether coverage existed for property damage resulting from workmanship performed during the policy period when the property damage did not manifest until after the policy period. *Dorchester Dev. Corp. v. Safeco Ins. Co.*, 737 S.W.2d 380, 383 (Tex. App.-Dallas 1987, no writ). We held that "no liability exists on the part of the insurer unless the property damage manifests itself, or becomes apparent, during the policy period." *Id.* If such damages are not manifested during the policy period, then there is no "occurrence" during the policy period. *Id.*; *see also State Farm & Cas. Co. v. Rodriguez*, 88 S.W.3d 313, 323 (Tex. App.-San Antonio 2002, pet. denied) (relying on *Dorchester* and holding that "property loss occurs when the injury or damages is manifested").

The First District Court of Appeals, however, has rejected the manifestation rule and applied the occurrence rule, expressly refusing to follow this Court's holding in *Dorchester*. *Pilgrim Enter., Inc. v. Maryland Cas. Co.*, 24 S.W.3d 488 (Tex. App.-Houston [1st Dist.] 2000, no pet.). In *Pilgrim*, the court held that an injury did not actually have to be discovered or manifested within the policy period to trigger coverage under the policy. *Id.* at 497.

Here, Summit encourages this Court to revisit its holding in *Dorchester* and apply the occurrence rule to the underlying facts of this case. We decline Summit's invitation.

Great American provided continuous coverage to Summit from 1996 to 2000. Great American's policies did not contain a specific EIFS exclusion. Summit contends that the policy provided by Great American in 1996 required it to provide a defense against the Lazarus suit because the only date alleged for the "occurrence" and "property damage" is 1996. Great American argues that because the Lazaruses pleaded the discovery rule, any property loss manifested later than 1996; therefore, the 1996 policy is inapplicable.

Despite Summit's argument to the contrary, the underlying pleadings do not establish that damage manifested in 1996. The Lazarus petition, filed in May 2003, claimed that during the construction of their home in 1996, EIFS was applied as an exterior veneer system to the home. The Lazaruses further argue that they suffered a reduction in property value, extensive damage to the home, and the need to substantially retrofit or replace the EIFS. The petition also contends that long term water penetration and retention would result in rot damage to the wooden structural elements of the house. However, missing from their factual allegations is any concrete reference to actual damages that occurred in 1996. Summit's counsel stated during oral argument that there were "no specific allegations that damages occurred in 1996, just allegations that since the house was constructed, damages have occurred." In addition to the failure to plead factual allegations of any damage manifesting in 1996, the Lazarus petition specifically invokes the discovery rule for their claims. It states the following: "Each and every claim made by the Plaintiffs herein is subject to the discovery rule because the defects of which Plaintiffs complain were latent and/or otherwise undiscoverable. The defects cause damage within the wall cavity which is not readily apparent to one examining the exterior of the EIFS surface. As a result, the named Plaintiffs would not, in the exercise of reasonable diligence, immediately perceive, or discover the defects complained of herein."

Thus, applying the "eight corners" rule, although the underlying pleadings state Summit constructed the home in 1996, it contains no allegations of actual damage during 1996. However, Great American failed to establish as a matter of law that damages did not manifest sometime in 1996, 1997, 1998, 1999, or 2000. [Citation omitted.] Therefore, summary judgment could only be appropriate regarding Great American's duty to defend if it established as a matter of law that there was no "property damage" caused by an "occurrence," thereby negating any possible coverage under the policies.

We begin by determining whether the Lazaruses' pleadings against Summit allege property damage. "Property damage" is defined in the Great American policy as "physical injury to tangible property, including all resulting loss of use of that property." Physical injury is not defined; however, the plain meaning connotes an alteration in appearance, shape, color, or in other material dimension. *Lennar Corp. v. Great American Ins. Co.*, 2006 WL 406609, *15 (Tex. App.-Houston [14th Dist.] 2006, pet. filed) (citing *Fid. & Deposit Co. of Md. v. Hartford Cas. Ins. Co.*, 215 F. Supp. 2d 1171, 1183 (D. Kan. 2002)).

Although the underlying pleadings do not explicitly describe the damage to the Lazaruses' home, they repeatedly state that the home sustained "extensive damage and additional damage is likely to occur." They further pleaded that use of EIFS causes damage within the wall cavity that is not readily apparent to one examining the exterior of the EIFS surface and that long term water penetration results in rot damage to the wooden structural elements of the house. Therefore, assuming the facts alleged are true, the Lazaruses have sufficiently pleaded physical injury to tangible property resulting in "property damage." [Citation omitted.]

Next, we must determine if the underlying pleadings establish an "occurrence" within the terms of Great American's policies. "Occurrence" means "an accident, including continuous or repeated exposure to substantially the same general harmful conditions." Great American argues that the "business risk doctrine" applies. The principle that a CGL policy does not generally cover the insured's defective construction resulting in damage to its own work is commonly known as the "business risk" doctrine. Here, the Insurers encourage us to be "mindful" of the business risk doctrine because it has vitality in Texas. This argument, as explained by Summit, overlooks the fact that coverage for some business risks is not eliminated when the damaged work, or the work out of which the damage arose, was performed by subcontractors. [Citation omitted.] Although Great American argues that the business risk exclusion precludes an "occurrence" under the policy, the Fourteenth Court of Appeals, in a recent opinion, thoroughly analyzed a similar CGL policy in another EIFS construction case involving Lennar homes and determined there was an "occurrence" under the policy triggering the insurer's duty to defend. *Lennar Corp.*, 2006 WL 406609 at *15.

Recognizing that Texas law is unsettled on whether defective construction constitutes an "occurrence," the Fourteenth Court of Appeals relied on this Court's holding in *Gehan Homes, Ltd.*, as well as other authority, to conclude that "under the standard CGL policy, negligently created, or inadvertent, defective construction resulting in damage to the insured's own work which is unintended and unexpected can constitute an 'occurrence.'" *Id.* at *4; *see also Gehan Homes, Ltd.*, 146 S.W.3d at 843 (holding that an insured builder's negligence resulting in unexpected damage can constitute an "occurrence"). [Footnote omitted.] Therefore, the Insurers' arguments that defective construction can never constitute an "occurrence" is incorrect.

Great American's policies contain business risks exclusions, specifically the "your work" exclusion, which prevents coverage for "property damage" to "your work" arising out of it or any part of it and included in the "products-completed operations hazard." [Footnote omitted] In other words, the "your work" exclusion prevents coverage for "property damage" to the insured's work arising after a construction project is finished and in the owner's possession. *Id.* at *8. If the analysis stopped here, then the business risk exclusion would apply, and there would be no "occurrence." *Id.* at *10 (noting that in the past the "business risk" exclusions operated collectively to preclude coverage for any damage to construction projects).

However, Great American ignores the policy's exception to the business risk exclusion. The exception provides that "[t]his exclusion does not apply if the damaged work or the work out of which the damage arises was performed on your behalf by a subcontractor." In 1986, the insurance industry incorporated the subcontractor exception in the "your work" exclusion of the CGL policy, demonstrating that insurers intended to cover some defective construction resulting in damage to the insured's work. *Id.* at *11. Further, finding no "occurrence" for defective construction that caused damage to the insured's work would render the subcontractor exception superfluous and meaningless. *Id.* Therefore, as the *Lennar* court succinctly stated: "[N]egligently created, or inadvertent, defective construction resulting in damage to the insured's own work that is unintended and unexpected can constitute an 'occurrence.' Nonetheless, the 'your work' or other 'business risk' exclusions may preclude coverage for the damage. However, in some instances, coverage will be restored if the damaged work, or the work out of which the damage arose, was performed by subcontractors." *Id.* at 12.

There is an "occurrence" if an action is intentionally taken, but negligently performed, and the damages are unexpected or unintended. [Citation omitted.] Here, Summit Homes intended to construct the Lazaruses' home using the EIFS system, which was installed and applied by subcontractors. The Lazaruses underlying petition ... assert[s] various negligence causes of action involving the use of EIFS and the supervision of the workers applying the EIFS. Likewise, the Insurers deny that EIFS is defective; therefore, any damages were unintended because defendants believed they were using a superior cladding system that would perform well in residential construction. Therefore, following the analysis in *Lennar Corp.* and our holding in *Gehan Homes, Ltd.*, we conclude that the underlying pleadings assert an "occurrence" within the meaning of Great American's policies.

Because the underlying pleadings establish "property damage" caused by an "occurrence," Great American may have a duty to defend the Lazarus suit against Summit. As noted above, Great American has failed to establish as a matter of law when the alleged damage manifested. Thus, we cannot determine whether the damages occurred "during the policy period." Specifically, we cannot determine whether the 1996, 1997, 1998, 1999, or 2000 Great American policies may apply. Because a genuine issue of material fact exists, the trial court improperly granted Great American's summary judgment. Therefore, we sustain Summit's first issue regarding Great American's duty to defend and reverse and remand to the trial court for further proceedings on this issue.

The ruling of the *Summit* court regarding trigger of coverage was abrogated by subsequent decisions of the Texas Supreme Court.[3] Courts are divided on whether the "actual injury" or "injury-in-fact," versus the "manifestation" rule should apply to trigger insurance coverage; however, courts agree that the analysis starts with the relevant policy language.

18.05 BUILDERS' RISK INSURANCE POLICIES

Builders risk insurance is intended to protect the insureds (usually the owner, general contractor and subcontractors) from the risk of fortuitous property damage to the work under construction and to materials and equipment on the project site. Typical policies permit recovery without a showing of negligence or other fault by any person, so long as the loss was not caused by intentional misconduct or fraud by an insured.

---

3. *See* Don's Bldg. Supply, Inc. v. OneBeacon Ins. Co., 267 S.W.3d 20 (Tex. Sup. Ct. 2008) (rejecting "manifestation" rule and adopting the "actual injury" rule under Texas law; providing extensive multijurisdictional case law survey).

Policies vary as to the covered causes of damage. Some policies only cover explicitly identified risks such as vandalism, earthquake, and fire. Others are broader, insuring against all causes except those explicitly excluded. The latter type of policy would cover such risks as building collapse, design defects, faulty workmanship, and freezing. The causes typically excluded from even the broadest form of builders risk policy are government action, building code violation, and earth movement. Although faulty workmanship is a covered risk, the policy covers damage only to property other than that containing the faulty workmanship; like CGL policies, it will not cover the cost of correcting the faulty workmanship itself.

18.06 WORKERS COMPENSATION INSURANCE

Workers' compensation is a system of insurance designed to provide workers who are injured in the course of their employment with a right to compensation that is awarded without regard to fault and without resort to traditional tort litigation. Most states, by statute, require all employers with a minimum number of employees to provide workers' compensation coverage. Thus, the contractual provision requiring workers' compensation coverage does not usually add a burden that the contractor does not already have by law. Rather, the provision makes clear which contracting party bears the cost of the coverage and gives the other party recourse in the event of a breach—a right not conferred by the workers' compensation statute.

The requirement of providing workers' compensation coverage can be met either by purchasing insurance from a commercial insurer or, if the employer meets certain financial criteria, through a program of self-insurance. The workers' compensation statutory scheme is administered in each state by an administrative agency. These agencies provide an administrative forum for the resolution of disputes about the employee's right to payment, the amount and duration of benefits, and any defenses the employer might have.

18.07 WAIVERS OF SUBROGATION

The standard contractual insurance provision quoted earlier in this chapter included a waiver of subrogation provision. Subrogation is an equitable concept whereby one person who pays for a loss or liability of another becomes entitled to assert the rights of the other against third parties, in an attempt to recoup the loss or liability paid. In the absence of a waiver of such subrogation rights, an insurer that, for example, pays workers' compensation benefits to an injured employee of a subcontractor is subrogated to that employee's rights to sue in tort anyone having tort liability for the conditions that led to the injury. Contract provisions requiring the contracting parties and their insurers to waive subrogation tend to eliminate litigation that would otherwise be instituted to realize such recoveries. The elimination of such recovery opportunities leaves the loss with the insurer that pays the loss in the first instance and, directly or indirectly, increases the insurance premiums for the party insured by that insurance carrier.

18.08 PROFESSIONAL LIABILITY INSURANCE

The insurance a design professional is required to carry differs from that required of contractors. Typically, design professionals must carry coverage for professional errors and perform in accordance with the standard of care to which the courts hold people in that profession (which may or may not be the same as ordinary negligence). Insurers often require a significant deductible on these policies, so that the professional is responsible for the first dollars of loss up to the amount of the deductible before the insurer has to pay for defense or indemnification.

As under CGL policies, E&O policies provide coverage for the cost of defense of covered claims, but differ from CGL policies by having the defense costs erode the policy limits. Such so-called wasting policies may prompt an owner to require that the design professional carry higher limits to counter the risk of erosion of those limits due to defense costs.

Most E&O coverage is written on a "claims made" basis, as compared with CGL policies, which are written on an "occurrence" basis. As a result, the policy for the year in which a party first asserts the claim is the year—and usually the only year—that affords coverage for that claim, regardless of the policy year in which the deficient act or omission occurred or the year in which the damage was sustained. As a consequence, fewer disputes occur over which E&O policy applies than such disputes with CGL policies. However, once a project concludes and the E&O policy year then in effect ends, coverage also ends and is not available for claims arising in subsequent years. For that reason, owners often require in their contracts with design professionals that the design professionals maintain E&O coverage for years after a project's completion, such as for the duration of the likely statute of limitation or statute of repose.

18.09 SURETY BONDS—THE TRIPARTITE RELATIONSHIP

The purpose of a surety bond in the construction context is to provide a party to a construction contract with a guarantee by a commercial surety company that (1) the other party to the contract will perform, and (2) if the party does not, the surety will respond. Put as simply as possible, a party has the status of a *surety* when, by contract, such party agrees to be jointly and severally liable with another for the contractual obligations of the other. The party for whose contractual obligations the surety stands liable is called the *principal*—usually the general contractor or a subcontractor. The party to the contract to whom the surety is bound is called the *obligee*—the owner or, in the case of a bond in which the principal is a subcontractor, the general contractor. These concepts recognize a tripartite relationship with rights and obligations well-recognized and long established under the law.

In the construction context, the most common instruments giving rise to the surety relationship are performance bonds, payment bonds, and lien bonds. Statutes governing public construction projects of any appreciable size require that the general contractor post performance and payment bonds.[4] On private construction, an owner will often require not only a performance bond and a payment bond but also a lien bond, which protects the owner's property against the assertion of mechanics' liens.[5] Payment bonds and lien bonds, and the statutes that govern them, usually grant direct rights on the bond to those who supply labor, materials, and equipment to the bond principal. Persons entitled to make claim under payment bonds are viewed as either additional obligees or as third-party beneficiaries. The diagram in Figure 18.1 may help in understanding the tripartite relationship inherent in a surety bond.

The legal and equitable principles that make up the law of suretyship have been synthesized in the Restatement (Third) of Security, Suretyship and Guaranty ("Restatement"). Among these important principles are:

1. The principal and surety are jointly and severally liable to the obligee (Restatement section 1).
2. The surety is entitled to assert all defenses to liability available to its principal except for the principal's personal lack of capacity (minority, mental incapacity) and its discharge in bankruptcy (Restatement section 34).
3. The dollar amount of the surety's liability is capped by what is referred to as "penal sum" of the bond, provided the surety does not breach its own bond obligations (Restatement section 73 comment b).

---

4. *See, e.g.*, Miller Act; 40 U.S.C. §§ 3131–3134 (2006) (formerly cited as 40 U.S.C. §§ 270a–270f); Mass. G.L. c. 149 §44E(2)(E) (performance bond); Mass. G.L. c. 149 § 29 (payment bond).

5. *See, e.g.*, Mass. G.L. c. 254 § 12.

FIGURE 18.1

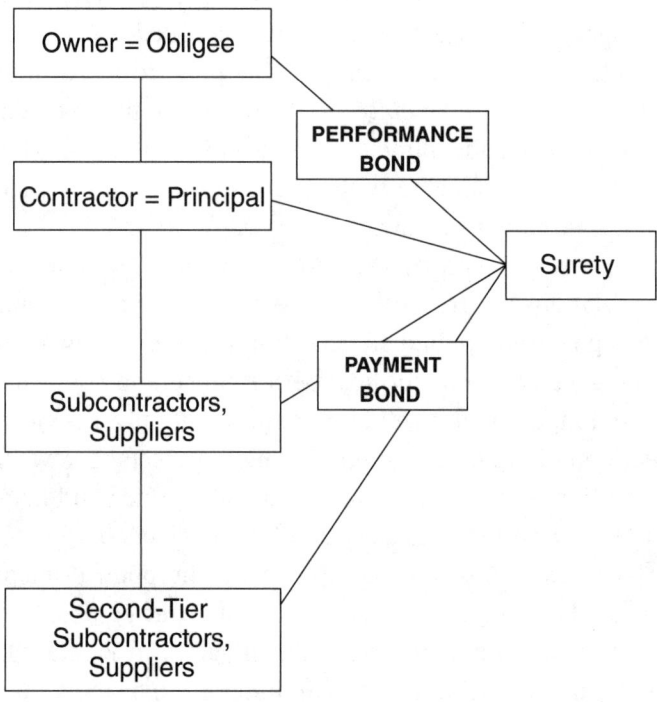

4. The surety's obligation is only to indemnify the obligee for its losses due to the principal's breach of the bonded contract, unless the bond specifies other obligations (Restatement section 32).
5. The surety is entitled to be reimbursed by the principal if the surety has to pay (Restatement sections 18, 21–26).
6. The surety is equitably subrogated to the rights of its principal against others, and to the rights of the obligee and others that the surety pays under the bond (Restatement sections 27–31).
7. The surety may be discharged from its obligations under the bond if the obligee impairs the surety's rights, such as by relinquishing collateral available to the obligee as security for the bonded obligation, substantially modifying the principal's obligations under the bonded contract, or permitting someone other than the principal to perform instead of the principal (Restatement sections 37–44).
8. Surety contracts are subject to the statute of frauds (Restatement section 11).

18.10 OBLIGATIONS OF THE PERFORMANCE BOND SURETY

Sureties commonly meet their obligations under a performance bond in one of four ways: by financing the principal to complete the principal's own obligations, by taking over completion of the work in lieu of the principal, by procuring a contract to complete from a new contractor and tendering the new contract to the obligee, or by cash settlement. Which of these four traditional options is actually available to a surety depends on the wording of the bond. For example, the federal Standard Form 25 Performance Bond does not spell out the surety's options, and federal regulations leave it to the government's contracting officer whether to allow the surety to arrange for completion of the work.[6] Some bond forms require that the surety complete the principal's performance if the obligee so requests (a completion bond). One of the most prevalent forms is Form A312 published by the AIA; it expressly permits the surety to elect any one of the four options.

The literature is replete with advice to sureties about how to assess the relative merits of their options.[7] In general, however, where the reason for default is the contractor principal's poor financial health, the surety may simply *opt* to advance sufficient funds to the contractor principal to enable it to complete the job, thus electing to finance completion by the principal. When the surety arranges for the tender of a new contractor, the surety usually does so either through a bidding process or through negotiation, and requests the new contractor to sign an agreement to complete the contract of the defaulting principal and to supply a new set of performance and payment bonds running in favor of the obligee. The surety then pays sufficient funds to cover the difference between the contract balance on the original contract and the contract amount for the new contractor, up to the penal sum of the original bond. The option of takeover by the surety gives the surety more control over the process of completion, but carries added risk because the surety's liability might not be limited by the penal sum of the bond. The surety will satisfy its obligation through cash settlement alone when the obligee agrees either to arrange for or forego completion and the obligee's damages are readily quantifiable. This option is often used when the principal's work has not begun and other bidders for the original contract remain available, or when the principal's work is nearly complete, with a monetized punch list to quantify the damages.

---

6. *See* 48 C.F.R. § 52.249-10(a) (2006); 48 C.F.R. § 49.402-3(h)–(i) (2006).

7. A leading source of such advice is ABA BOND DEFAULT MANUAL, FOURTH EDITION (Mike F. Pipkin, Carol Z. Smith, Thomas J. Vollbrecht, J. Blake Wilcox, eds., 2015).

Most sophisticated developers and state agencies charged with administering large, complex projects are familiar with the surety's right to elect the option by which the surety will satisfy its obligations. However, owners that undertake only occasional construction projects may have difficulty accepting their lack of control over the process after a contractor's default, with dire results.

St. Paul Fire & Marine Ins. Co. v. City of Green River, 93 F. Supp. 2d 1170 (D. Wyo. 2000)

ORDER GRANTING PLAINTIFF'S MOTION FOR SUMMARY JUDGMENT
BRIMMER, District Judge.

This case is about the extent of a performance bond surety's obligation to finish a construction project within the underlying construction contract's completion deadline after a default by the surety's principal. After reading the briefs, hearing oral arguments, and being fully advised in the premises, the Court FINDS and ORDERS as follows:

BACKGROUND

... Westates Construction Co. ("Westates") entered a contract with the State of Wyoming Joint Powers Water Board (the "Board") for the construction of a water treatment plant in Green River, Wyoming (the "Project"). ... Westates was to achieve substantial completion of the Project on or before December 1, 1998. Significantly, the construction contract provided that time was of the essence and that the Board would be entitled to liquidated damages in the amount of $2,500 per day for delays after the completion deadline....

Prior to construction, St. Paul Fire & Marine Insurance Company ("St. Paul"), as surety, provided a performance bond to the Board, the obligee, to guarantee the principal Westates' performance under the construction contract. Paragraph 4 of the performance bond defines St. Paul's options for performance under the bond in the event of a default by Westates:

When the Owner has satisfied the conditions of Paragraph 3 [requiring, *inter alia*, notice to the Surety, declaration of Contractor default, and Owner's agreement to pay the Surety the balance of the contract price], the Surety shall promptly and at the Surety's expense take one of the following actions:

4.1 Arrange for the Contractor, with consent of the Owner, to perform and complete the Construction Contract; or

4.2 Undertake to perform and complete the construction contract itself, through its agents or through independent contractors; or

4.3 Obtain bids or negotiated proposals from qualified contractors acceptable to the Owner for a contract for performance and completion of the Construction Contract, arrange for a contract to be prepared for execution by the Owner and the contractor selected with the Owner's concurrence, to be secured with performance and payment bonds executed by a qualified surety equivalent to the bonds issued on the Construction Contract, and pay to the Owner the amount of damages as described in Paragraph 6 in excess of the Balance of the Contract Price incurred by the Owner resulting from the Contractor's default; or

4.4 Waive its right to perform and complete, arrange for completion, or obtain a new contractor and with reasonable promptness under the circumstances:

1. After investigation, determine the amount for which it may be liable to the Owner and, as soon as practicable after the amount is determined, tender payment therefor to the Owner; or
2. Deny liability in whole or in part and notify the Owner citing reasons thereof.

... The Project experienced significant delays of which the causes are in dispute. On January 16, 1998, the Board terminated its contract with Westates, filed suit against Westates in state court, and made a claim against the St. Paul performance bond. St. Paul began a due diligence investigation of the Project to ascertain how it should proceed regarding its duties under the performance bond. Simultaneously, negotiations were commenced involving representatives of the Board, Westates, and St. Paul. These negotiations resulted in a compromise proposal, outlined in a term sheet, which provided, among other things, for: (1) a mutual release between the Board, Westates, and St. Paul, with claims preserved against ... the project engineer; ... (3) dismissal of the Board's lawsuit against Westates; (4) rescission of the Board's notice of termination; and (5) completion of the Project by St. Paul. The compromise proposal allowed St. Paul to utilize Westates personnel, though St. Paul would retain management decision making authority. The compromise proposal also called for a May 14, 1999 completion date. ...

... St. Paul made presentations to the Board on February 25, 1998. At the meeting, two letters from Steven Grunsfeld of St. Paul were delivered to the Board. In the first letter, Mr. Grunsfeld indicated St. Paul's willingness to proceed under the compromise proposal, which had not been officially approved by either St. Paul or the Board. In the second letter, Mr. Grunsfeld reported St. Paul's preliminary determination that the Board's termination of Westates was wrongful, but announced St. Paul's election to complete the Project itself under Paragraph 4.2 of the performance bond, albeit under a reservation of rights.

In a February 28, 1998 letter, Dr. Joseph J. Oliver, Chairman of the Board, announced the Board's response to St. Paul's communications. Dr. Oliver wrote:

St. Paul representatives stated [at the February 25, 1998 meeting] that St. Paul would complete the [Project] no sooner than September 24, 1999, despite a contract completion date for the Project of December 1, 1998. Accordingly, the [Board] is justifiably insecure that St. Paul will complete the Project in a timely manner.

In addition, St. Paul representatives have made clear St. Paul's intention to utilize the personnel employed by Westates ... to complete the Project ... even though the [Board] does not consent to Westates or its personnel completing the Project. St. Paul's announced intention to use Westates to finish the Project without consent of the [Board] is an anticipatory breach of the requirements of Section 4.1 of the Performance Bond.

Accordingly, please be advised that the [Board] refuses to allow St. Paul to complete [the Project] under Section 4.2 of the Performance Bond.

On March 3, 1998, St. Paul brought an action in this Court seeking a declaratory judgment that the Board's refusal to permit St. Paul to complete the Project was a material breach of the performance bond, thus exonerating St. Paul from any further obligation under the bond. ... [T]he Board asserted counterclaims against St. Paul for breach of contract, breach of the covenant of good faith and fair dealing, tortious bad faith, and violation of Wyo. Stat. Ann. § 26-15-124(c), which allows for recovery of attorney's fees where an insurance company's refusal to pay the full amount of a claim is unreasonable or without cause. [Both parties] moved for summary judgment ...

ANALYSIS

Central to this dispute is whether St. Paul committed an anticipatory breach of the performance bond when it announced at the February 25, 1998 meeting that it would not complete the Project until September of 1999, well past the completion deadline in the construction contract. The Board contends that St. Paul's actions constituted an anticipatory breach because St. Paul, as surety, stepped into Westates' shoes in the construction contract and was bound by the "time is of the essence" clause contained therein. Thus, according to the Board, St. Paul's announcement that it would not meet the completion deadline constituted a repudiation of the performance bond, thereby justifying the Board's decision to treat the performance bond as repudiated and sue for damages. St. Paul, on the other hand, contends that it was not required to complete the Project within the original completion deadline, and was instead required by Paragraph 5 of the performance bond only to proceed with "reasonable promptness." In St. Paul's view, the Board's action prohibiting St. Paul from completing the Project was a material breach which excused St. Paul from any liability under the bond. Secondarily, the parties dispute whether St. Paul was allowed, under Paragraph 4 of the performance bond, to use Westates personnel without the Board's express consent.

... [G]eneral principles of contract interpretation apply with equal force to surety contracts. ... [A] performance bond should "'be fairly construed with a view to effect the object for which it was given and to accomplish the purpose for which it was designed.'" ...

1. The Board's Claim that St. Paul Committed an Anticipatory Breach

... The Supreme Court of Wyoming outlined the law of anticipatory breach in *J.B. Service Court v. Wharton*:

> An anticipatory breach of contract is one committed before the time has come when there is a present duty of performance, and is the outcome of words or acts evincing an intention to refuse performance in the future. . . . . In ascertaining whether an anticipatory breach of a contract has been committed by a party, it is the intention manifested by his acts and words which controls, and not his secret intention. Moreover, in order to predicate a cause of action upon an anticipatory breach, the words or conduct evidencing the breach must be unequivocal and positive in nature.... In order to justify the adverse party in treating the renunciation as a total breach, the refusal to perform must be of the whole contract or of a promise or obligation going to the whole consideration, and it must be distinct, unequivocal, and absolute.[8] Where a party commits an anticipatory repudiation, the other party is excused from performing under the contract and may sue immediately for damages. [citation omitted.] ...

St. Paul's announcement that it would not meet the December 1, 1998 completion deadline could not constitute an anticipatory repudiation unless St. Paul had an absolute duty to finish the Project by December 1, 1998. Likewise, if St. Paul was within its rights to use Westates personnel, its announced plan to do so would not be an anticipatory breach.

2. St. Paul's Obligation to Finish the Project by the Completion Deadline

Contrary to the Board's contentions, the Court concludes that, while St. Paul was liable for delay damages, it would not be in material breach if it failed to finish the Project by the completion deadline. The Board is certainly correct that, as a general rule, a performance bond surety's liability is coextensive with that of the principal. . . . [T]ime was expressly made of the essence in the underlying construction contract, and Westates was obligated to complete the Project by December 1, 1998, adjusted for extensions. Consequently, St. Paul, as Westates' surety, was likewise bound by the "time is of the essence" clause and completion deadline. [citation omitted.] This means that, upon the principal's default, the surety is liable for damages caused by the principal's delay if the principal was liable for such damages in the underlying contract. [citation omitted.] Here, Paragraph 6.3 of the performance bond explicitly states that St. Paul is liable for liquidated damages caused by Westates' delay. No doubt St. Paul would be in breach of the performance bond if it failed to pay liquidated damages for delays attributable to Westates. In this sense, the Board is correct that St. Paul steps into the shoes of Westates and is bound by the liquidated damages clause.

---

8. 632 P.2d 943, 945 (Wyo. 1981) (*quoting* 17 AM. JUR. 2D CONTRACTS §§ 448, 450 (1964)).

It is a far leap from this conclusion, however, to reach the Board's position that St. Paul would be in material breach of the performance bond if the Project was not completed on the construction deadline. To the contrary, the Court is convinced that the required pace of St. Paul's performance was unambiguously defined by Paragraph 5, which provides that "[i]f the Surety does not proceed with reasonable promptness, the Surety shall be deemed in default on this Bond fifteen days after receipt of an additional written notice from the Owner to the Surety demanding that the Surety perform its obligations under this Bond."...

Because the Court finds that the performance bond unambiguously provides that St. Paul's obligation was only to proceed with reasonable promptness, St. Paul would not have been in default under the bond if the Project was not completed by the completion deadline, so long as St. Paul did in fact proceed with reasonable promptness in completing the Project. [Additional discussion of anticipatory breach omitted.]

Far from categorically disclaiming a duty to perform under the performance bond, St. Paul promptly began a due diligence investigation, took part in negotiations with the Board's counsel, and provided the Board with a schedule for its performance under Paragraph 4.2. . . . St. Paul had a good faith basis to believe that its interpretation of the contract was correct, so that its offer of performance consistent with that interpretation was not an anticipatory breach.

. . . Because St. Paul did not unequivocally renounce its obligations under the performance bond, the Board did not have the right to treat St. Paul's projected completion schedule as an anticipatory breach.

3. Use of Westates Personnel

The Board's second basis for its claim of anticipatory breach is that St. Paul planned to use Westates personnel as part of the team assembled to complete the Project. In the Board's interpretation of the performance bond, St. Paul was allowed to select one, and only one, option for performance under Paragraph 4. Paragraph 4.1, which allows St. Paul to arrange for Westates to complete the Project, requires the Board's consent. St. Paul instead announced its election to complete the project itself pursuant to Paragraph 4.2. The Board claims that, in electing to proceed under Paragraph 4.2, St. Paul was prohibited from using any Westates personnel without the Board's consent. The Board's interpretation is contrary to the unambiguous language of the performance bond, defies common sense, and is unreasonable in light of industry practices.

Turning first to Paragraph 4.2 of the performance bond, the performance option selected by St. Paul, it is clear that there are no limitations on who St. Paul could utilize to complete the Project. In proceeding under Paragraph 4.2, St. Paul assumed primary responsibility to complete the contract, and with that responsibility came the freedom to assemble the project team of its choosing. In contrast, a surety electing to proceed under Paragraph 4.1 does not assume primary responsibility for completing the contract, and the owner is required to maintain an ongoing contractual relationship with the terminated contractor. While it makes sense that the owner would have the right to object to such a "shotgun wedding" to the contractor it just terminated, it does not follow that the Board would have this right when the surety assumes primary contractual responsibility. In fact, the surety performance options contained in the performance bond are standard in the industry, and it is common practice for a surety that elects to perform the project itself to hire the principal's employees under the direction of a consultant, just as St. Paul did here. [Citation omitted.] While the Board accuses St. Paul of trying to "create a hybrid action from the two paragraphs," it is actually the Board that is attempting to graft the owner consent provision contained in Paragraph 4.1 onto the performance option actually selected by St. Paul, Paragraph 4.2. Because St. Paul had the right to utilize Westates personnel as part of its project team, St. Paul's plan to use such personnel could not constitute an anticipatory breach. In sum, neither St. Paul's proposed completion schedule nor its proposed use of Westates personnel constituted an anticipatory breach, and the Board did not have the right to terminate St. Paul, as it did in Dr. Oliver's February 28, 1998 letter.

4. The Board's Material Breach

Having determined that the Board did not have the right to terminate St. Paul, the focus now shifts to the implications of the Board's wrongful termination of St. Paul. If the Board's action constituted a material breach, St. Paul is excused from further performance under the contract. [Citation omitted.] "A material breach occurs where the covenant not performed is of such importance that the contract would not have been made without it." *Id.* Under the performance bond, St. Paul possessed four options for performance in the event of Westates' default. . . . The effect of the Board's termination of St. Paul was to divest St. Paul of its ability to minimize its liability by selecting the lowest cost option and by directing the construction or participating in the contractor selection process. Courts have consistently held that an obligee's action that deprives a surety of its ability to protect itself pursuant to performance options granted under a performance bond constitutes a material breach, which renders the bond null and void. ... St. Paul was likewise prejudiced by the Board's actions. While the Board did properly notify St. Paul of Westates' default, it prohibited St. Paul from exercising its contractual right to perform itself or to participate in the selection of the replacement contractor. Because the Court concludes that St. Paul would not have entered the performance bond in the absence of its performance options under Paragraph 4, the Board's action depriving St. Paul of those options was a material breach, which discharged St. Paul from any further duty of performance under the bond. [Citation omitted.] . . .

For the foregoing reasons, . . . [a]ll of the Joint Powers Water Board's counterclaims against St. Paul are DISMISSED WITH PREJUDICE. ...

18.11 PAYMENT BONDS

Payment bonds ensure that persons who supply labor, materials, and equipment to the principal receive payment for the amount the principal owes them. Payment bonds are almost universally required on public construction because mechanics' liens cannot be imposed on public land. In addition, the assurance of payment by a commercial surety encourages competitive pricing by subcontractors and suppliers, thereby saving money for the public.

Most payment bonds, and the statutes that require them, grant direct rights of action to the suppliers of labor and materials. Such permitted claimants are not limited to those having a direct contractual relationship with the bond principal but extend to lower-tier subcontractors and suppliers as well. Statutes vary as to how remote the relationship may be and still give rights under the bond. However, where such rights exist, the more remote the supplier and the more fungible the materials it supplies, the greater the supplier's burden to show that its materials actually went into the project. Shipping materials directly to the job site, or supplying materials especially fabricated for the project, will usually satisfy this burden.

In addition, most payment bonds, and the statutes that require them, specify a limitation of action period much shorter than that applicable to ordinary contract claims—frequently one year. Lower-tier subcontractors and suppliers often have to give notice of their claims that direct subcontractors need not give. The adequacy and timeliness of notice, and the timeliness of actions on the bond, are a frequent subject of dispute. Under some bonds, the notice and limitation of action periods begin to run from the date the *claimant* last worked or supplied materials or equipment; in other instances, these periods do not begin until the *bond principal* ceases work on the project. Questions often arise as to whether a claimant's return to the project site after substantial completion—such as to perform punch list or warranty work—restarts the notice or limitation-of-action clock.[9]

Payment bond sureties share the same attributes of the suretyship relationship as performance bond sureties. The surety may assert the principal's defenses and is subrogated to the principal's affirmative rights against the subcontractor, at least to the extent of the surety's losses on the bonds for the project at issue. Thus, the surety may assert counterclaims against the

---

9. *See* David J. Oliveri, *Timeliness of Notice to Public Works Contractor on Federal Project, of Indebtedness for Labor or Materials Furnished*, 69 A.L.R. Fed. 600 at § 7 (2011); William E. Aiken, *Construction and Application of Miller Act Provision* (40 U.S.C.A. § 270B(b)); *Limiting Time for Suits on Payment Bond*, 10 A.L.R. Fed. 533 at § 4[c], [d], [e], [f] (2011).

subcontractor that, if successful, could not only reduce or cancel the payment bond claim but also could yield affirmative recovery to mitigate the surety's other losses on the project.[10]

18.12 RIGHTS AND REMEDIES OF SURETIES

An earlier section of this chapter listed various attributes of suretyship status, which included rights of equitable subrogation and the right to be reimbursed, or exonerated, by the principal. The surety's right to pursue claims of the principal against subcontractors, as just discussed, provides a vivid example of the power of the right of equitable subrogation, which will be discussed further later in the chapter.

In addition to these rights that inhere in the suretyship relationship, sureties routinely require a bond principal, and often the principal's shareholders, to execute an agreement of indemnity in the surety's favor, as a condition to establishing a line of bonding credit. The typical indemnity agreement enhances the surety's equitable and common law rights by providing, for example, for an assignment of and security interest in all the principal's assets; the right to an immediate posting of collateral for the amount of reserves posted by the surety, even before the surety pays any claims; and an agreement that an affidavit or copies of vouchers showing payments by a surety will constitute *prima facie* evidence of the fact and amount of the indemnitors' liability under the agreement.

Returning to the right of equitable subrogation, an as previously noted, the surety is equitably subrogated (1) to the rights of its principal against others and (2) to the rights of the obligee and others that the surety pays under the bond. The simplicity of that general principal belies its breadth and importance. Among the rights to which the surety is subrogated are:

- ❒ The principal's right to the unpaid balance of contract funds, including retainage;
- ❒ The obligee's right to make itself whole from the unpaid balance of contract funds, including retainage;

---

10. *See, e.g.*, St. Paul Fire & Marine Ins. Co. v. United States, 370 F.2d 870, 872 (5th Cir. 1967); City of New York v. Aetna Cas. & Surety Co., 1997 WL 379704 at *3, *5 (S.D.N.Y. 1997); Menorah Nursing Home, Inc. v. Zukov, 548 N.Y.S.2d 702, 705 (N.Y. App. Div. 1989); Maryland Cas. Co. v. King, 381 P.2d 153, 158–59 (Okla. 1963); *see also* Am. Ins. Co. v. Ohio Bureau of Workers' Compensation, 577 N.E.2d 756, 758–79 (Ohio App. 1991). A general contractor's surety may also assert a claim against the surety for a subcontractor. *See* Argonaut Ins. Co. v. Commercial Standard Ins. Co., 380 So. 2d 1066 (Fla. App. 1980).

- ☐ The principal's contracts with and claims against third parties arising from the bonded contract, including subcontractors, suppliers, and design professionals;
- ☐ The obligee's rights in collateral posted by the principal;
- ☐ The rights of subcontractors and suppliers whose payment bond claims the surety pays to assert liens against the project property and other rights of direct payment from the owner; and
- ☐ The rights of the obligee, and of subcontractors and suppliers whose payment bond claims the surety pays, to recover damages from the principal on account of the principal's breach of contract.

Not only is the surety subrogated to these rights, but, in the event of a contest with another creditor claiming an interest in the same rights, the surety stands in the shoes of those to whose rights the surety is subrogated for purposes of determining the relative priorities among competing creditors. Under these principles, the rights a surety obtains by equitable subrogation usually defeat the competing claims of a lender holding a perfected security interest in the principal's assets, taxing authorities with statutory tax liens against the principal's assets, and, as shown in the next case, a bankruptcy trustee in the principal's bankruptcy proceeding.

Pearlman v. Reliance Ins. Co., 371 U.S. 132, 83 S.Ct. 232, 9 L.Ed.2d 190 (1962)

Mr. Justice BLACK delivered the opinion of the Court.

This is a dispute between the trustee in bankruptcy of a government contractor and the contractor's payment bond surety over which has the superior right and title to a fund withheld by the Government out of earnings due the contractor.

The petitioner, Pearlman, is trustee of the bankrupt estate of the Dutcher Construction Corporation, which in April 1955 entered into a contract with the United States to do work on the Government's St. Lawrence Seaway project. At the same time the respondent, Reliance Insurance Company [footnote omitted], executed two surety bonds required of the contractor by the Miller Act [then 40 U.S.C. § 270a], one to guarantee performance of the contract, the other to guarantee payment to all persons supplying labor and material for the project. [Footnote omitted.] Under the terms of the contract, which was attached to and made a part of the payment bond, the United States was authorized to retain and hold a percentage of estimated amounts due monthly until final completion and acceptance of all work covered by the contract. Before completion Dutcher had financial trouble and the United States terminated its contract by agreement. Another contractor completed the job, which was finally accepted by the Government. At this time there was left in the Government's withheld fund $87,737.35, which would have been due to be paid to Dutcher had it carried out its obligation to pay its laborers and materialmen. Since it had not met this obligation, its surety had been compelled to pay about $350,000 to discharge debts of the contractor for labor and materials. In this situation the Government was holding over $87,000 which plainly belonged to someone else, and the fund was turned over to the bankrupt's trustee, who held it on the assumption that it had been property of the bankrupt at the time of [bankruptcy] and therefore had vested in the trustee "by operation of law" under § 70 of the Bankruptcy Act. [Footnote omitted.] The surety then filed a petition in the District Court denying that the fund had vested in the trustee, alleging that it, the surety, was "the owner of said sum" of $87,737.35 "free and clear of the claims of the Trustee in Bankruptcy or any other person, firm or corporation," and seeking an order directing the trustee to pay over the fund to the surety forthwith. [Footnote omitted.] The referee in bankruptcy, relying chiefly on this Court's opinion in *United States v. Munsey Trust Co.*, [citation omitted], held that the surety had no superior rights in the fund, refused to direct payment to the surety, and accordingly ordered the surety's claim to be allowed as that of a general creditor only to share on an equality with the general run of unsecured creditors. [Footnote omitted.] The District Court vacated the referee's order and held that cases decided prior to *Munsey* had established the right of a surety under circumstances like this to be accorded priority over general creditors and that *Munsey* had not changed that rule. [Footnote omitted.] The Second Circuit affirmed. [Footnote omitted.] Other federal courts have reached a contrary result [footnote omitted], and as the question is an important and recurring one, we granted *certiorari* to decide it. [Footnote omitted.]

One argument against the surety's claim is that this controversy is governed entirely by the Bankruptcy Act and that § 64 [citation omitted], which prescribes priorities for different classes of creditors, gives no priority to a surety's claim for reimbursement. But the present dispute—who has the property interests in the fund, and how much—is not so simply solved. Ownership of property rights before bankruptcy is one thing; priority of distribution in bankruptcy of property that has passed unencumbered into a bankrupt's estate is quite another. Property interests in a fund not owned by a bankrupt at the time of [bankruptcy], whether complete or partial, legal or equitable, mortgages, liens, or simple priority of rights, are of course not a part of the bankrupt's property and do not vest in the trustee. The Bankruptcy Act simply does not authorize a trustee to distribute other people's property among a bankrupt's creditors. [Footnote omitted.] So here if the surety at the time of adjudication was, as it claimed, either the outright legal or equitable owner of this fund, or had an equitable lien or prior right to it, this property interest of the surety never became a part of the bankruptcy estate to be administered, liquidated, and distributed to general creditors of the bankrupt. ... [O]ur question is not who was entitled to priority in distributions under § 64, but whether the surety had, as it claimed, ownership of, an equitable lien on, or a prior right to this fund before bankruptcy adjudication.

Since there is no statute which expressly declares that a surety does acquire a property interest in a fund like this under the circumstances here, we must seek an answer in prior judicial decisions. Some of the relevant factors in determining the question are beyond dispute. Traditionally sureties compelled to pay debts for their principal have been deemed entitled to reimbursement, even without a contractual promise such as the surety here had.[11] And probably there are few doctrines better established than that a surety who pays the debt of another is entitled to all the rights of the person he paid to enforce his right to be reimbursed.[12] This rule, widely applied in this country[13] and generally known as the right of subrogation, was relied on by the Court of Appeals in this case. It seems rather plain that at least two prior decisions of this Court have held that there is a security interest in a withheld fund like this to which the surety is subrogated, unless, as is argued, the rule laid down in those cases has been changed by passage of the Miller Act or by our holding in the *Munsey* case. Those two cases are *Prairie State Bank v. United States*, [citation omitted], and *Henningsen v. United States Fid. & Guar. Co.*, [citation omitted].

In the *Prairie Bank* case a surety who had been compelled to complete a government contract upon the contractor's default in performance claimed that he was entitled to be reimbursed for his expenditure out of a fund that arose from the Government's retention of 10% of the estimated value of the work done under the terms of the contract between the original contractor and the Government. That contract contained almost the same provisions for retention of the fund as the contract presently before us. The Prairie Bank, contesting the surety's claim, asserted that it had a superior equitable lien arising from moneys advanced by the bank to the contractor before the surety began to complete the work. The Court, in a well-reasoned opinion by Mr. Justice White, held that this fund materially

---

11. "The right of subrogation is not founded on contract. It is a creature of equity; is enforced solely for the purpose of accomplishing the ends of substantial justice; and is independent of any contractual relations between the parties." Memphis & L.R.R. Co. v. Dow, 120 U.S. 287, 301–02, 7 S. Ct. 482, 488, 489, 30 L. Ed. 595 (1887).

12. *See, e.g.*, Hampton v. Phipps, 108 U.S. 260, 263, 2 S. Ct. 622, 27 L. Ed. 719 (1883); Lidderdale's Executors v. Robinson's Executor, 12 Wheat. 594, 6 L. Ed. 740 (1827); Duncan, Fox, & Co. v. North & South Wales Bank, 6 App. Cas. 1 (H.L. 1880). *See generally* Sheldon, Subrogation, § 11 (1882).

13. *See* cases collected in 50 Am. Jur., Subrogation, § 49 (1944).

tended to protect the surety, that its creation raised an equity in the surety's favor, that the United States was entitled to protect itself out of the fund, and that the surety, by asserting the right of subrogation, could protect itself by resort to the same securities and same remedies which had been available to the United States for its protection against the contractor. ... The *Prairie Bank* case thus followed an already established doctrine that a surety who completes a contract has an "equitable right" to indemnification out of a retained fund such as the one claimed by the surety in the present case. The only difference in the two cases is that here the surety incurred his losses by paying debts for the contractor rather than by finishing the contract.

The *Henningsen* case, decided 12 years later in 1908, carried the *Prairie Bank* case still closer to ours. Henningsen had contracts with the United States to construct public buildings. His surety stipulated not only that the contractor would perform and construct the buildings, but also, as stated by the Court, that he would "pay promptly and in full all persons supplying labor and material in the prosecution of the work contracted for." [Footnote omitted.] Henningsen completed the buildings according to contract but failed to pay his laborers and materialmen. The surety paid. This Court applied the equitable principles declared in the *Prairie Bank* case so as to entitle the surety to the same equitable claim to the retained fund that the surety in the *Prairie Bank* case was held to have. Thus the same equitable rules as to subrogation and property interests in a retained fund were held to exist whether a surety completes a contract or whether, though not called upon to complete the contract, it pays the laborers and materialmen. These two cases therefore, together with other cases that have followed them [footnote omitted], establish the surety's right to subrogation in such a fund whether its bond be for performance or payment. Unless this rule has been changed, the surety here has a right to this retained fund. ...

We therefore hold in accord with the established legal principles stated above that the Government had a right to use the retained fund to pay laborers and materialmen; that the laborers and materialmen had a right to be paid out of the fund; that the contractor, had he completed his job and paid his laborers and materialmen, would have become entitled to the fund; and that the surety, having paid the laborers and materialmen, is entitled to the benefit of all these rights to the extent necessary to reimburse it. [Footnote omitted.] Consequently, since the surety in this case has paid out more than the amount of the existing fund, it has a right to all of it. On this basis the judgment of the Court of Appeals is affirmed.

Affirmed.

Mr. Justice WHITE dissents.

Mr. Justice CLARK, with whom Mr. Justice DOUGLAS and Mr. Justice BRENNAN join, concurring in the result. [opinion omitted]

18.13 LETTERS OF CREDIT

On some projects where the owner requires performance security from the contractor, the owner may accept, or even require, an alternative to surety bonds. The most common is a letter of credit. Letters of credit that serve as alternative performance security differ in important respects from the kinds of letters of credit used to achieve a reliable means of payment for such commercial transactions as an international sale of goods. The latter are referred to as commercial letters of credit, whereas letters of credit used as performance security are referred to as standby letters of credit. Both kinds of letters of credit may be governed by the Uniform Commercial Code for domestic transactions in the United States; however, more commonly, especially in international transactions, such letters of credit are governed by the International Standby Practices, published by the Institute of International Banking Law & Practice, Inc., and adopted by the International Chamber of Commerce as Publication No. 590. These instruments may serve either as the sole source of performance security or as collateral for an indemnitor's obligation to a surety that issues performance and payment bonds.

In essence, a standby letter of credit is a commercial instrument issued by a bank under which the bank promises to make payment to the beneficiary of the letter of credit upon demand. The beneficiary is analogous to the performance bond obligee on a surety bond. Sometimes the standby letter of credit requires the beneficiary to make certain representations of fact in order to warrant a payment. The letter will state the street address at which the demand for payment must be received and an expiration date.

The issuing bank will issue a standby letter of credit only after establishing a credit relationship with the person whose performance is being secured, referred to as the "applicant." The applicant can be either the contractor itself or a corporate affiliate, or an individual guarantor. In the documents governing that relationship, the applicant agrees to reimburse the issuing bank if the bank has to make payment to the beneficiary. The issuing bank will often require the deposit of collateral to secure that reimbursement obligation. In these respects, standby letters of credit are quite similar to performance bonds.

The main differences between a standby letter of credit and a performance bond relate to the actions the issuers take after demand is made. When demand is made on a performance bond surety to perform, the surety ordinarily will undertake a detailed investigation of whether the conditions establishing its obligation to make payment have been met. The surety will solicit information from the bond principal, often engage experts, and make an independent assessment of whether or not the principal is in default under the contract. Such investigations can take months to complete, leaving the status of the project stalled and in limbo. If the surety concludes it is obligated to perform its bond obligations, the surety then has the traditional options discussed in Section 18.10.A.

On the other hand, when demand is made on a standby letter of credit, the issuing bank merely looks on the face of the demand and determines whether the words required under the letter of credit appear and that the demand is signed by the appropriate person. If so, the issuing bank does not investigate the accuracy of those words but instead issues payment. Because the issuing bank is usually collateralized against such an eventuality, it makes itself whole, thereby imposing the loss onto the contractor and leaving the contractor to resolve any disputes with the beneficiary about whether or not the contractor was in default. As a result, parties to a standby letter of credit rarely litigate disputes regarding enforcement of the standby letter of credit, whereas the case law abounds with disputes over surety bonds.

18.14 SUBCONTRACTOR DEFAULT INSURANCE POLICIES

Zurich North America was the first insurance company to offer an insurance product called Subguard®, which insures against subcontractor default. In recent years, however, other insurers have entered the subcontractor default insurance market, with XL Catlin offering ConstructAssure®, and Lloyds of London providing subcontractor default insurance through its approved underwriting agency, Cove Program Underwriting Limited. Subcontractor Default Insurance, or SDI, is intended as a substitute for performance and payment bonds on subcontracts and runs in favor of the general contractor. General contractors sometimes prefer SDI over subcontractor bonds because (1) the contractors have more control over procurement of a substitute subcontractor or other means of resolving a subcontractor default, and (2) depending on the terms of the policy, SDI may cover losses upon a subcontractor default, such as:

> completion and correction costs for the subcontract work; investigative and legal costs resulting from the subcontractor's default; and, perhaps, even indirect default costs.

Subcontractor default insurance is a two-party agreement for the benefit of the general contractor. This type of coverage is not available directly to owners and does not protect an owner against a general contractor default.

QUESTIONS

1. What are the eight corners referred to in the "eight corners rule?" What are plausible alternatives to the eight corners rule and what are the pros and cons of each?
2. What business interests of an insurer would lead it to advocate the "manifestation rule" over the "occurrence rule" in determining whether a particular policy is triggered?
3. What business or public interests are reflected in the "business risk doctrine?" What policy provisions attempt to express this doctrine?
4. Reconstruct a plausible debate that would have led the insurance industry to adopt the subcontractor exception to the "your work" exclusion in CGL policies in 1986.
5. What presumptions are used by the court as a basis for ruling against the insurer? Which of them are rebuttable?
6. Why would the parties care which policy was triggered for the following claim?

Plaintiff, an HVAC subcontractor, claims it is owed money by a general contractor on a federal building project. Plaintiff has given the Miller Act surety notice of a claim more than ninety days after completing its punch list but during the one-year warranty period under its subcontract. Sixty days after receipt of the notice of claim, the surety denied the claim as untimely and, because the subcontractor's work was late, exposing the general contractor to liquidated damages. The general contractor did not default on the general contract and has been paid all contract funds, including retainage, by the government.

1. What defenses might the surety have to the above claim?
2. What additional defenses might the surety have if the above claimant was a sub-subcontractor, not having a direct relationship with the bond principal?
3. If the surety is liable to the subcontractor, what recourse might the surety have against other parties to make itself whole? What steps should the surety take upon receipt of notice to protect its rights of recourse?
4. In light of the fact that "suretyship is not insurance," *Pearlman v. Reliance*, 371 U.S. at 140, n.19, does the surety have exposure under state unfair claims settlement practices acts, such as Mass. G.L. c. 176D § 3?

CHAPTER

19

Dispute Resolution Processes

JAMES P. GROTON, DEBORAH BOVARNICK MASTIN
AND STANLEY P. SKLAR

19.01 IMPORTANCE TO THE CONSTRUCTION INDUSTRY OF PROCESSES FOR RESOLUTION OF DISPUTES

A. Unique Dispute Resolution Needs of Construction Projects

The construction industry has used private dispute resolution techniques longer than most industries. This has been a matter of necessity because formal legal remedies often are much too slow and inflexible in the context of a fast-moving activity such as a construction project. Every construction project involves a multitude of players, all with potentially conflicting interests, whose mission is to come together to plan, design, and build a completed structure, on time and within budget. Once the building process has begun, the work cannot be interrupted or delayed without serious cost consequences. In the construction business, "time is money." Accordingly, the construction industry places a premium on coordination and quick solutions to problems.

B. Historical Development of Dispute Resolution in Construction

About 100 years ago, the industry started using a combination of two forms of private dispute resolution that were designed to keep the project moving, reduce conflict, and provide quick and expert resolution of disputes: (1) non-binding decisions by the project architect rendered immediately upon the appearance of a problem, and (2) a prompt, informal ad hoc arbitration convened promptly at the project site to provide a quick decision on any disputed issue involved in the architect's decision that could not be resolved through negotiation. These two techniques complemented each other: the architect's awareness that its decision could quickly and easily be challenged by a prompt arbitration gave the architect an incentive to be scrupulously fair in making decisions. As a result, relatively few architects' decisions needed to be challenged, and those that were challenged were resolved quickly and expertly.

About a generation ago, for reasons that are beyond the scope of this chapter, this system of early, single-issue dispute resolution broke down, and the construction industry went through a tortured period when architects' decisions were frequently ignored, and resolution of individual disputes was deferred. Although mediation provisions began to be incorporated into standard construction contracts, as a matter of practice, parties rarely invoked either mediation or arbitration during the progress of construction, causing the resolution of disputes to be routinely postponed until the end of the construction period.

Unfortunately, when unresolved disputes were allowed to accumulate and fester, their mere existence interfered with the progress and overall success of the project. Unresolved problems held up the payment of money, created uncertainty as to the outcome, impaired relationships and efficiency, and caused delays and disruption. These in turn added costs to the project participants and tended to generate new claims and disputes.

The postponement of dispute resolution to the end of the project also increased the difficulty, expense, delay, and uncertainty of attempting, in a court trial, arbitration, or mediation long after the fact, to reconstruct accurately all of the facts and events that occurred during the lifetime of the project that were relevant to the resolution of the accumulated disputes. This escalated the transaction costs of resolving disputes to the point where the profits of all parties to the dispute, including the nominal "winner," were often wiped out.

Construction industry leaders took a fresh look at the problems of adversarial relationships, disputes, and litigation, and began to invent new techniques to prevent, control, and more quickly resolve disputes. Some of the key steps in the effort to develop new dispute resolution techniques follow.

The Business Roundtable and the Construction Industry Institute investigated the basic root causes of construction problems and pioneered research into realistic risk allocation and the use of incentives, strategic alliances, and long-term "partnering" to foster cooperative relationships. The Army Corps of Engineers experimented with some very successful uses of project-specific partnering. Civil engineers, contractors, and some results-oriented public owners adopted use of "standing neutral" dispute review boards to resolve disputes at the job site level in major tunneling and civil projects.

The main emphasis in these newer devices was on restoring concepts of reasonable dealing and teamwork into the conduct of construction projects, preventing or at least controlling the impact of problems, improving communications, fostering mutual problem solving, encouraging the earliest possible resolution of problems, and assisting disputing parties to reach early resolution of any disputes so that valuable business relationships could be preserved. The effect of these new approaches was to move the dispute resolution process "upstream," closer in time to the sources of the disputes, to deal with root causes and not just the symptoms, of disputes.

This experimental work has matured to the point where there now exist several new, well-developed techniques that have proved to be successful in curbing disputes and getting them resolved during construction.

Nevertheless, given the complexities and uncertainties of the construction process and the conflicting interests of the many participants, many disputes do not get resolved during the course of construction. In these cases, the parties continue to resort to the more traditional dispute resolution techniques of mediation, arbitration, and litigation.

19.02 THE SPECTRUM OF CONSTRUCTION INDUSTRY DISPUTE PREVENTION AND RESOLUTION TECHNIQUES

Today's construction industry members now benefit from a vast array of private dispute prevention and resolution tools that make it entirely possible that a construction project can be concluded without serious disputes ever having to be litigated, arbitrated, or even mediated.

A. The Dispute Resolution Step Chart

These tools form a spectrum or continuum that can be illustrated by the "stair step" sequential model illustrated in Figure 19.1, which depicts dispute prevention and resolution techniques in the order in which they would normally

FIGURE 19.1

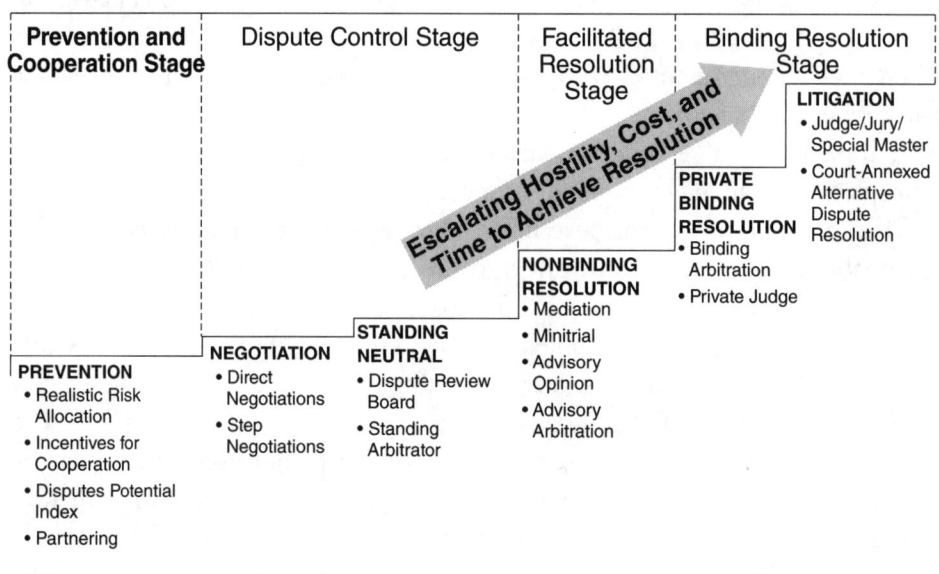

be employed in the life of the dispute, starting first with the techniques that help most in preventing or controlling disputes and offer the greatest potential for saving money and preserving relationships. They are grouped in Figure 19.1 (adapted from materials developed by DART, the Dispute Avoidance and Resolution Task Force) into four successive (and escalating) stages of dispute resolution.

B. The Four Stages of Dispute Resolution

1. *The Dispute Prevention and Cooperation Stage*

The highest and best form of dispute resolution is prevention. One of the best ways to prevent disputes is to establish an atmosphere of cooperation, good faith, and reasonable dealing, both between the parties and among the members of each organization. An important tool in this regard is to make sure that risks are allocated realistically among the parties. Other techniques for encouraging teamwork, such as partnering, incentives for cooperation, and open communications, can help to create such an atmosphere and actually prevent some disputes from arising.

2. The Dispute Control Stage

Dealing promptly and realistically with problems and disagreements at the time they arise and before they can develop into full-fledged disputes can do much to contain and control disputes. Step negotiations, or obtaining "real-time" dispute resolution assistance from a pre-selected dispute review board or standing neutral who is already familiar with the relationship between the parties, can resolve disputes at the source, and the ready availability of these techniques can even help prevent disputes from developing.

3. The Facilitated Non-binding Resolution Stage

If disputes have been allowed to mature to the point where positions have hardened and the parties are at an impasse, the next step is resorting to a more structured and formal facilitated dispute resolution process such as mediation, minitrial, expert's advisory opinion, or non-binding advisory arbitration, with the assistance of one or more neutrals.

It is important to note that if the parties to a construction project are not successful in resolving all disputes during the course of construction, then the transactional costs of dealing with the disputes after the fact rise astronomically. At this point, the complexities and degree of hostility of the dispute begin to increase significantly because it becomes necessary to enlist the assistance of "strangers" to the parties' relationship—such as lawyers, outside experts, and outside neutrals—all of whom have to be educated about the background facts before they can meaningfully address the dispute. Also, with the passage of time and the dispersal of individuals who were involved in the project, the cost of reconstructing the facts becomes significantly more difficult and expensive.

4. The Binding Resolution Stage

If all other efforts at resolution have failed, the last resort is some kind of "back stop" process for final and binding adjudication. If the parties have so agreed, that process will be arbitration; otherwise, the "default" process is court litigation. If the dispute reaches this stage, the parties have essentially lost control of the process and the outcome of the dispute; the transactional costs of processing the dispute escalate even more, and the relationship between the parties has likely been destroyed.

The various specific techniques that can be used to prevent, control, and resolve disputes will be described next in the order in which they would normally be employed in the life of the project or in the course of dealing with a developing dispute.

19.03 INDIVIDUAL CONSTRUCTION DISPUTE PREVENTION, CONTROL, AND EARLY RESOLUTION TECHNIQUES

A. Prevention and Cooperation Techniques

1. Realistic Allocation of Project Risks

Research by the Business Roundtable and the Construction Industry Institute has demonstrated that one of the most powerful ways to prevent and control disputes is to allocate project risks realistically, by assigning each potential risk to the participant in the project who is best able to manage, control, or ensure against the particular risk. It is now well recognized in the construction industry that when lawyers seek to negotiate "the best deal" for their clients, they frequently craft contract provisions that unrealistically and unfairly allocate risks to project participants who are unable to handle the risk, often creating project problems of a far greater magnitude than those the lawyers sought to solve. Realistic allocation of risks improves productivity, lowers costs, and creates better relationships among participants in the project. The result in nearly all cases will be fewer disputes and a greater chance for project success. The standard forms of agreement published by the American Institute of Architects, ConsensusDocs, and the Engineers Joint Contract Documents Committee are an attempt to reflect current industry consensus on sensible risk allocations.

2. Incentives to Encourage Cooperation

The construction industry has developed incentive plans to encourage multiple parties to work together toward a common goal. Such incentives can take many forms. For example, a general contractor or construction manager who needs to coordinate the activities of multiple subcontractors who have the potential of getting into conflict with each other can establish a "bonus pool" that, based on the need for cooperation and the attainment of specific project goals, will be shared among all of the subcontractors. Under such a system, the bonus is payable only if *all* of the subcontractors as a group avoid conflict and meet the assigned goals—the bonus is payable either to everyone or to no one. This technique provides all participants with a common goal, places a premium on teamwork, furnishes a powerful business incentive to work cooperatively, and reduces conflicts that can occur in a common enterprise when every participant might otherwise be motivated solely by its limited perception of its own short-term interests, rather than the success of the enterprise as a whole.

3. Partnering

Partnering is a team-building effort developed by the construction industry in which the participants in a project establish cooperative working relationships through a mutually developed, formal strategy of commitment and communication. It can be used for long-term relationships, or on a project-specific basis.

Partnering on a long-term basis involves the development of a strategic alliance that maximizes the effectiveness of each participant's resources. The relationship is based on trust, dedication to common goals, and understanding each other's individual expectations and values. The expected benefits from such a relationship include improved efficiencies and cost effectiveness, increased opportunity for innovation, and continual improvement of quality products and services.

When used on a project-specific basis, partnering is usually instituted at the beginning of the relationship by holding a retreat among all participants involved in the project who have leadership and management responsibilities, in which the participants, assisted by an independent facilitator, become acquainted with each other's objectives and expectations, recognize common aims, define mutual goals, develop a teamwork approach, initiate open communications, and establish non-adversarial processes for resolving potential problems. The initial retreat is followed up by periodic evaluations and meetings to ensure the communications and teamwork are continuing.

There is sometimes a misperception that partnering changes contract obligations. Partnering is usually extracontractual, establishing a framework for the stakeholders to use for working together in a cooperative and efficient manner. It does not change any of the substantive provisions of the contract, such as requirements for written notices of changes and differing conditions even though the parties are communicating verbally through the partnering process. The U.S. Army Corps of Engineers, which is credited with first using project-specific partnering, claims that it experienced a reduction in construction claims and litigation when a partnering approach was implemented.[1]

Although the partnering process is still generally accepted today as a "best management practice," it is by no means a panacea. Since it requires an "up-front" commitment to hard work and cooperation, it is not always possible to get the level of participation from all of the project stakeholders that is necessary for partnering to work. Sometimes partnering is instituted with the best

---

1. *See generally* https://www.usace.army.mil/Media/News-Archive/Story-Article-View/Article/477787/partnering-equals-teamwork/.

of intentions, but, in practice, parties may simply go through the formalities without seriously using it during the project to facilitate true communication and teamwork. Consequently, partnering is not as popular as it once was.

4. Open Communications and Notice Provisions

The best construction project results are obtained through good communications among project team members, so that incipient problems can be identified, brought out into the open, discussed, and solved, before they become serious. One important aspect of open communications is a contract requirement, consistently followed by all parties, that if any participant in the project needs information from another participant, or perceives that the scope of its work is being increased or impacted by any other participant, it must give prompt written notice to other involved parties. Careful adherence to this fundamental principle of communication, and good faith responses to such notices, will eliminate many potential misunderstandings.

This practice is encouraged by all of the standard construction industry documents. For example, the current edition of the AIA *General Conditions of the Contract for Construction*,[2] contains at least two dozen references to requirements for notices between the parties.

B. Dispute Control and "Real-Time" Early Resolution Techniques

1. Step Negotiations

Negotiation, of course, is the time-honored method by which parties try to resolve disputes through discussions and mutual agreement. There are many different techniques of negotiation. The most successful negotiations are those in which the negotiators conduct their discussions on the basis of the respective *interests* of the parties rather than the traditional approach of focusing on the *positions* of the parties. Negotiation is not only a freestanding dispute resolution technique, but it also can be a useful adjunct to every other dispute resolution technique.

A construction industry improvement on negotiation is the step negotiation procedure, a multi-tiered process that can often be used to break a deadlock. If the individuals from each organization at the lowest project level who are involved in the dispute are not able to resolve a problem promptly at their level, their immediate superiors are asked to confer and try to resolve the problem. If they fail, then the problem is to be passed on to higher management

---

2. American Institute of Architects, AIA Document A201–2017, General Conditions of the Contract for Construction (2017) [hereinafter AIA Document A201–2017].

in both organizations. Because an intermediate manager is not likely to be as closely identified with the problem, the manager's interest in demonstrating to higher management that the manager has the ability to solve problems and to keep messy problems from bothering higher management is a built-in incentive to getting disputes resolved before they ever have to be referred to the highest management level.

However, step negotiation procedures can interfere with a speedy and timely decision. By the time the high-level managers have had an opportunity to confer, several weeks may have elapsed, and the progress on the job has either continued without any decision or has been interrupted at great cost to all involved.[3]

2. Geotechnical Baseline Summary Report

One of the most common sources of disputes on a project is underground conditions, which, by their nature, are never completely known at the time the project is planned, designed, and priced. The Geotechnical Design Summary Report is a document in which the geotechnical conditions on which the designer based its design serves as a baseline by which to identify differing site conditions that are actually experienced in the field during the course of construction. If used in connection with a Differing Site Conditions contract clause in which the owner assumes the risks of unknown subsurface conditions, all competing contractors are able to bid on the same set of assumptions. Use of this device also fosters a more cooperative project climate because it demonstrates openness and candor in communications.

3. Escrow of Bid Documents

The pricing of changes in the scope of work on a project is the source of many disputes. One technique for helping to simplify this pricing process is to specify in the bidding documents that when the successful bidder is identified, that bidder's documents will be kept in an escrow where they will be accessible jointly by the contractor and owner to assist in negotiating price adjustments. Whenever any party believes that references to the original takeoffs, calculations, quotations, and other information that the successful bidder used to arrive at the bid price are relevant to review in a claim, the documents are available to be consulted by representatives of both parties. The availability of these documents is another way to foster a climate of openness and cooperation on a project.

---

3. The implementation of a proactive dispute board or project neutral can motivate the parties to reach a decision about how to address an open issue on the job before the unresolved issue has lingered so long that it impacts the project schedule.

4. Dispute Boards and Standing Neutrals

One of the most innovative and promising developments in controlling disputes between participants in a construction project is the concept of having a pre-selected or "standing" respected neutral expert serve the parties as a dispute resolver throughout the course of the project. This proactive neutral, or a board of three disinterested, knowledgeable experts, called a dispute board (also known as a dispute review board, dispute resolution board, dispute avoidance board, dispute avoidance panel, or a DRB), is jointly selected by the parties at the start of the project relationship, is briefed on the nature of the project, is furnished with the basic construction documents, routinely receives periodic progress reports and is copied on selected project correspondence as the project progresses, and regularly attends job site meetings with the parties to observe and monitor the dynamics and progress of the project relationships.[4] While attending the job site meetings, the dispute board members, or individual member, query the parties about aspects of the ongoing project, such as unanswered requests for information, missing schedule updates, or pending change order requests.

Contracts often provide that conversations held at site visits with a dispute board are confidential settlement discussions, so that project team members can offer potential solutions without impairing formal positions. These regular facilitative interactions with the project team members can build trust between the project team and the dispute board, and create an environment that allows the project team members to come to an accord concerning open issues before any resources have been committed by the project team. This structure can also allow the dispute board to support the project team members by looking forward to the anticipated progress of the work, and to modify future activities on the project, rather than looking back to events that previously transpired and seeking compensation for actions already taken. Some contracts provide that discussion of an issue with the dispute board at a regular site visit meeting is a condition precedent to submission of a formal claim.

In addition to facilitative dispute avoidance and mitigation duties, the dispute board members or individual neutral are also expected to be available on relatively short notice to provide an expert, reasoned, and persuasive written or oral recommendation to the parties as to how to resolve any disputes that the parties are not able to resolve themselves.

---

4. The Dispute Resolution Board Foundation (www.drb.org) offers skills training to prospective and experienced dispute board members as does the Dispute Board Federation (www.dbfederation.org).

When called on to offer a recommendation, dispute boards typically respond quickly, obtaining written position papers from the parties and then conducting a hearing (usually at or near the project site) at which the parties present their positions and respond to questions from the dispute board members. The hearings are usually conducted informally and include decision makers and representatives of the parties with firsthand knowledge of the project and the issues in dispute. Typically, the presenters are not sworn, and no cross-examination is allowed. No contextual background information is usually necessary because the dispute board or neutral has been involved with the progress of the project from its initiation, and the presentations are focused on the unresolved issue at hand. Following the hearing, the dispute board or neutral provides a prompt oral or written recommendation (as requested by the parties), with supporting rationale, intended to persuade the parties to accept the recommendation without further dispute resolution proceedings.

Although in the United States a dispute board or neutral's decisions are typically not binding, experience has shown that parties have almost universally accepted these decisions as the basis for resolving the dispute, without any attempt to seek relief from any other tribunal. This result is enhanced where there is a contractual requirement that in the event of any subsequent arbitration or litigation, the decisions of third parties will be admissible in evidence. When used in accordance with the guidelines recommended by the Dispute Resolution Board Foundation, the ConsensusDocs' DRB Addendum, or the American Arbitration Association's Dispute Review Board Procedures, this technique has been successful according to statistics maintained since 1975 by the Dispute Resolution Board Foundation.[5] Worldwide, over 2,000 projects have used some form of a dispute board.[6]

Dispute boards differ from other dispute resolution structures in that they provide a forum for discussion of future impacts and allow the parties to respond to unanticipated events before any resources have been expended in reaction to the changed circumstance. This allows the parties and their stakeholders to collaborate on a response to the unexpected situation that minimizes the adverse impact and serves the best interests of the project. The evaluative but non-binding nature of the neutral facilitative process can provide a "dose of reality" that encourages parties to be more realistic and objective in their dealings with each other, while also giving the parties an opportunity to

---

5. *See* http://www.drb.org/publications-data/drb-database/.

6. Paula Gerber & Brennan J. Ong, *DRBs Down Under: Ready for Takeoff!*, 16 Dispute Resolution Board Foundation Forum 1 (Feb. 2012).

construct their own solutions to problems, and tends to strengthen the relationship between the parties and create trust and confidence between them. The support of proactive dispute boards enhances the parties' willingness and ability to enter into change orders or agree to project or contractual modifications in an amicable and collaborative manner.

Dispute boards were introduced in the 1970s in public highway tunneling projects. Due to user satisfaction, their use spread to highway and bridge projects and then to other large complex capital projects, including airports, seaports, public transit improvements, university campus facilities, water and waste water projects, energy generation, and distribution projects. Many state Departments of Transportation utilize dispute boards on major projects, and, internationally, they are found in projects financed by the World Bank. The use of dispute boards is now increasingly considered for use in large complex private construction projects.

The expanded use of Building Information Modeling, the utilization of construction managers on construction projects, and the emergence of Integrated Project Delivery systems are examples of other concurrent trends within the design and construction industries towards more collaborative project management structures. Dispute boards and standing neutrals support those management objectives.

The existence of a pre-selected neutral, already familiar with the business relationship between the parties and its progress, avoids many of the initial problems and delays that are involved in selecting and appointing neutrals after a controversy has arisen. The ready availability of the neutral, the speed with which it can render decisions, and particularly the fact that this neutral will hear every dispute that occurs during the life of the relationship, all provide powerful incentives to the parties to deal with each other and the neutral in a timely and frank manner, by discouraging game-playing, dilatory tactics, and the taking of extreme and insupportable positions.

In practice, the nature of this process is such that the mere existence of the neutral usually reduces—and often totally eliminates—the number of disputes that have to be presented to the neutral. In effect, the standing neutral serves not only as a standby dispute *resolution* technique but also as a remarkably successful dispute *prevention or control* device. Even though some expense is involved in the process of selecting, appointing, initially orienting, and periodically keeping the neutral informed about the relationship, the costs are relatively minimal, even in those rare cases where the neutral has to be called on to resolve disputes—especially when compared to the potential costs of resolving a dispute in arbitration or litigation, or even the expense of mediating a dispute after the project is completed.

ConsensusDocs has included a dispute board addendum to its family of documents. The addendum consists of two documents: (1) a template of a contract specification that describes the function of the dispute board, and the selection of dispute board members,[7] and (2) a form engagement contract between the owner, the contractor or construction manager, and each member of the dispute board.[8]

The concept of the standing neutral has also been introduced in the new AIA form of documents. As was the case previously, under the Standard Form of Agreement between Owner and Contractor,[9] claims are to be initially referred to the architect as the "Initial Decision Maker" (IDM). However, the parties may appoint a person other than the architect to be the Initial Decision Maker, who will render decisions on claims.

Lawyers are not typically invited to the regular site visit meetings of dispute boards. Nor are lawyers often selected as members of a dispute board, however lawyers who have significant experience in construction disputes can make valuable contributions to the dispute board panel. When a formal hearing is convened, the nature of dispute board recommendations has tended to keep the formal hearing process relatively non-adversarial, with little active involvement of lawyers in the conduct of hearings. Lawyers who are highly experienced in construction have, however, been used with considerable success as members of dispute board panels, particularly where issues arise that involve contract law and interpretation of complex contracts.

The 2017 editions of the International Federation of Consulting Engineers (FIDIC) Red Book (Construction) and Silver Book (EPC/Turnkey Projects) include specifications for a Dispute Avoidance/Adjudication Board (DAAB).[10] Under the FIDIC structure, the decisions of a DAAB are binding upon the parties for the duration of the project. If neither party timely files a notice of dissatisfaction, the decision is also final. If one party timely files a notice of dissatisfaction, the decision remains binding for the duration of the project, but the dispute is preserved for a subsequent arbitration proceeding after which it becomes final. In the arbitration proceeding, the DAAB decision is admissible, but the arbitration panel is not bound by any prior determination of the DAAB and may review the entire matter before issuing a final award.

---

7. ConsensusDocs Document 200.4 (2013) (www.consensusdocs.org).

8. ConsensusDocs Document 200.5 (2013) (www.consensusdocs.org).

9. American Institute of Architects, AIA Document A101–2017, Standard Form of Agreement between Owner and Contractor (2017) [hereinafter AIA Document A101–2017].

10. CONSTRUCTION CONTRACT 2D ED. (2017 Red Book), *available at* http://fidic.org/books/construction-contract-2nd-ed-2017-red-book; EPC/TURNKEY CONTRACT 2D ED., *available at* http://fidic.org/books/epcturnkey-contract-2nd-ed-2017-silver-book.

C. Other Facilitated Non-binding Resolution of Disputes

1. Mediation

During the past 30 years, construction industry participants who have experienced difficulty in negotiating resolution of disputes have customarily turned to the use of disinterested neutrals to assist them in reaching resolution without having to resort to a binding dispute resolution process. The most common of these techniques is mediation. A neutral mediator can guide the opposing parties in a dispute through facilitated negotiations toward a settlement of their disputes, promptly and constructively. The mediator does not make a binding decision; in a mediation proceeding, the decision-making control remains with the parties involved in the dispute.

In past practice, mediation had rarely been used to resolve disputes during the course of construction. However, the trend in dispute management favors early involvement of a skilled mediator to help the parties shape their exchange of information and to accelerate the resolution of looming disputes. Some project specifications call for a "standing neutral," most often a mediator, who is selected at the inception of a project and is available to meet with the parties on short notice to help the parties enhance their communications and risk assessments. Mediation proceedings and mediation communications are often confidential under state law.[11] If confidential, the parties can expect their mediator to contact them and their lawyer on a confidential basis in advance of a mediation conference. The mediator will attempt to persuade the parties to exchange sufficient documentation so that each party can evaluate new information internally and with its consultants well in advance of the mediation conference. Information revealed for the first time in a mediation conference can be a barrier to successful dispute resolution.

2. Independent Decision Maker

Under AIA Document A201–2017, most claims and disputes between the owner and the contractor must first be referred to an Initial Decision Maker (who is the project architect, or an independent neutral if the parties have so agreed), who must promptly review the claim, seek any needed additional information, and render an initial decision approving or rejecting the claim, or indicating that the IDM is unable to resolve the claim.[12] This initial decision shall be

---

11. *See, e.g.*, FLA. STAT. §§ 44.405, 44.406.

12. The identity of the initial Decision Maker is set forth in the owner–contractor agreement, typically an AIA Document A101 (2017) or AIA Document A102 (2017). The default is that the architect serves as the Initial Decision Maker.

(1) in writing; (2) state the reasons therefor; and (3) specify any change in the contract sum, the contract time, or both. This initial decision "shall be final and binding on the parties but subject to mediation."[13] Mediation may be instituted as follows: Within 30 days from the date of the initial decision, either party may demand in writing that the other party file for mediation within 60 days after the initial decision. If such a demand is made, and the party receiving the demand fails to file for mediation within the time required, then both parties waive their rights to mediate the dispute or to pursue any binding dispute resolution proceeding with respect to the IDM's decision. Thus, this scheme requires that unless a dispute is promptly mediated, the decision of the IDM is final and binding. Anecdotal evidence indicates that the IDM process is rarely chosen by parties as a means to achieve final and binding resolutions to disputes; rather, dispute boards, mediation, and arbitration are the more commonly utilized methods of dispute management.

3. Minitrial

A variant of arbitration is the minitrial, a process in which representatives of both parties present their "best case" arguments to a panel consisting of principal executives of both parties and a disinterested neutral. Following the presentations, the executives confer and try to resolve the dispute in the light of the information they have just received. If the executives are unable to reach an agreement, the neutral steps in to try to facilitate further negotiation and reach an agreed resolution.

4. Advisory Opinions

Occasionally, all that disputing parties need to resolve a technical dispute is a "dose of reality" from a trusted and respected industry professional. If the parties engage an independent neutral expert in the field to meet with the parties, both separately and jointly, obtain information about the issue, and render an objective expert opinion on the subject, the parties often recognize the realities of the situation and reach a negotiated settlement, sometimes without the aid of a mediator. The International Chamber of Commerce offers expert determination services, which can be binding or non-binding.[14]

A typical specification for a dispute board will include the option for parties to seek an oral advisory "guidance" opinion. This opinion is based on a summary presentation by the parties, typically lasting less that one day. The

---

13. AIA Document A201–2017, *supra* note 2, § 15.2.5.
14. *See* expert and neutral services offered by the International Chamber of Commerce, https://iccwbo.org/dispute-resolution-services/experts/.

guidance opinion is often limited to entitlement and is intended to assist the parties in reaching a negotiated or mediated resolution of quantum. If the parties are unable to resolve the dispute on their own, a formal dispute board hearing is available to them to consider the entire matter anew.

5. Non-binding Summary Advisory Arbitration and Adjudication

A somewhat more formal process for providing a "dose of reality" to opposing parties is to engage in an informal summary arbitration in which representatives of the parties present their "best case" arguments to an arbitrator or arbitration panel, which is then asked to issue a non-binding decision or realistic assessment of the issue. Such a ruling often leads to a consensual resolution of the dispute.

Internationally, a popular form for summary dispute resolution is a process known as adjudication. For example, in the United Kingdom, a statute requires construction contracts (are defined) to give parties the right to adjudicate a dispute at any time.[15] An adjudicator is selected at the commencement of a construction project, and disputes regarding interim progress payments and impacts to the project are referred to the adjudicator who determines both entitlement and quantum. Unless extended by the parties, the process is completed within 28 days, and if no party timely challenges the decision of the adjudicator, it becomes final and binding. If an adjudication decision is challenged, it must be implemented by the parties for the duration of the project, and may be subsequently reviewed in an arbitration hearing where a final award is issued.

6. Binding Arbitration

The final step in any private dispute resolution process is binding arbitration pursuant to an express agreement between the parties that they will submit their cases to an independent neutral arbitrator who will issue an award or decision that, if necessary, can be enforced by a court. The arbitration is typically conducted in accordance with an accepted set of rules, such as the American Arbitration Association (AAA) Construction Industry Arbitration Rules, the International Institute for Conflict Prevention & Resolution (CPR) Expedited Rules for Construction Arbitration, or a "fast track" version of those rules. (A detailed discussion of arbitration is contained in Section 19.05.)

---

15. *See* Housing Grants, Construction and Regeneration Act 1996.

19.04 DESIGN OF DISPUTE PREVENTION AND RESOLUTION SYSTEMS

The foregoing description of currently used dispute prevention and resolution techniques has illustrated a progression of tools that can be used to prevent and resolve disputes and avoid litigation. The purpose in developing these techniques has been to move the dispute process "upstream," closer in time to the sources of disputes.

Since no single dispute prevention or resolution technique can serve all dispute resolution needs, the best practice for achieving optimum results is to include in the construction or design contract a well-planned "system" for dispute prevention, control, and final resolution. Dispute resolution system design is simply a process of analyzing the likelihood that a particular relationship or project will have disputes, predicting the kinds of disputes that might arise, and then designing a succession of techniques, filters, screens, and safety nets, using the available tools and techniques, to deal with a succession of different types of problems at different stages in the life of the project, so that problems are likely to be resolved at the earliest possible time.

One of the most important elements in the effectiveness of a dispute resolution system is to institute the system at the beginning of the project and incorporate it into the basic contract documents. Without prior agreement on a process for dealing with problems and disputes, it can be difficult, after a disagreement has developed, to get parties to come to agreement on a method of dispute resolution. A process that is already in place will provide a method for absorbing the impact of a problem; however, without a process, there is no effective way to control the outcome.

A number of contracts provide for a system that has a succession of "steps" that incorporate techniques to deal with various kinds of problems at different stages in the development of a dispute, such as techniques for prevention, techniques for control, a process for non-binding resolution, and finally a "back stop" final resolution process. For example, on a given construction project, the participants may agree to use partnering, accompanied by a number of other devices for preventing and reducing disputes. These techniques might include:

- Specific allocation of time and other resources, early in the project, to foster mutual trust as well as appropriate mutual expectations among the many players;
- Reducing conflicts from disappointed expectations or perceptions of injury;

- ☐ Explicit and realistic allocation of risks among parties;
- ☐ Incentives for cooperation built into payment structures;
- ☐ "Stepped" negotiations when problems occur, implemented immediately;
- ☐ A standing process, such as a proactive dispute board or standing neutral; and
- ☐ Arbitration in the event that none of these techniques work.
- ☐ A well-designed dispute management system should not be so cumbersome that the field personnel avoid using it, and it should provide prompt results in a cost-effective manner.

19.05 PRINCIPLES OF ARBITRATION

A. Basis in Statute

Due to the increasingly complex nature of business, crowded court calendars, and the rising cost of litigation, it became apparent that parties should be entitled to select an alternative method of resolving disputes in a forum of their own choosing.

Perhaps the most compelling reason for arbitration is the need to have triers of fact who are experts in the business matters in dispute. Consequently, the doctrine that arbitration agreements may be revoked by either party has now been superseded by the Federal Arbitration Act (FAA).[16] At the present time, all states enforce agreements to arbitrate existing disputes, and 49 states, the District of Columbia, and the FAA also validate agreements to arbitrate future disputes. Both the federal and state acts make arbitration agreements irrevocable and enforceable and provide a mechanism for compelling arbitration and staying court proceedings until arbitration has been completed.

It has long been recognized that the FAA is a substantive rule that, by virtue of the Supremacy Clause of the Constitution, forecloses any state statute from undercutting the enforceability of arbitration agreements.[17] The deference that is given to arbitration and the federal policy that underlies the FAA thus supports the stay of state litigation pending the outcome of arbitration.[18] Therefore, state statutes that govern arbitration are invalid if they interfere

---

16. 9 U.S.C. § 1.
17. Southland Corp. v. Keating, 465 U.S. 1 (1984).
18. 9 U.S.C. § 3.

with the policy of the FAA.[19] Even though state statutes vary, there is a model Uniform Arbitration Act.[20]

B. Contractual Nature of the Remedy

An arbitration statute, by itself, gives no right to arbitrate. In the absence of a written arbitration agreement, a party may not be required to arbitrate. Not only is it necessary to have an agreement to arbitrate in order to require arbitration, it is also appropriate that the agreement reflect the intention of the parties regarding the nature of the arbitration proceeding. Since arbitration is a creature of contract, the parties have broad leeway to prescribe in their contract agreement the nature and scope of the arbitration proceeding.

Various arbitration organizations prescribe model provisions for the parties to use in framing an arbitration agreement. The American Arbitration Association (AAA) suggests the following model provision for use in construction contracts:

> Any controversy or claim arising out of or relating to this contract, or the breach thereof, shall be settled by arbitration administered by the American Arbitration Association Rules, and judgment on the award rendered by the arbitrator(s) may be entered in any court having jurisdiction thereof.

By inserting this provision in their agreement, the parties have adopted the Construction Industry Arbitration Rules of the AAA, which include extensive provisions for the selection of arbitrators and the administration and hearing of arbitration cases. Parties should understand these rules before incorporating them into their contract.

Beyond the use of standard clauses, parties may wish to agree in advance on a number of aspects of the arbitration proceeding. This includes the manner of selecting the arbitrators, the location of the arbitration hearing, and the choice of the state law to be applied by the arbitrators. Consideration should also be given to the description of the scope of the arbitration delineating the subjects that the arbitrators may consider, as well as the procedures the arbitrators should follow, and the damages or other relief they may award.[21]

---

19. David L. Threlkeld & Co., Inc. v. Metallgesellschaft Ltd. (London), 923 F.2d 245 (2d Cir. 1991).

20. The Uniform Act is presently being revised by the National Conference of Commissioners on Uniform State Laws (NCCUSL). *See* Thomas J. Stipanowich, *What's a NCCUSL? The Uniform Law Commissioners Tackle the Uniform Arbitration Act,* THE CONSTR. LAW., July 1997, at 25.

21. *See* Jonathan D. Shaffer, Carl T. Hahn, & William A. Focht, *Challenges & Pitfalls in Drafting "Arbitration" Clauses,* CONSTRUCTION BRIEFINGS No. 97-4 (1997).

The power of the arbitrator to arbitrate a particular issue is derived from the agreement of the parties. A frequently contested issue is whether a particular controversy is covered by the arbitration agreement. Claims under construction contracts concern such diverse matters as extras, delays, balance due under the contract, deficiencies in performance, liquidated damages, and faulty design. The ability to arbitrate such issues depends upon the language of the agreement.

The broad arbitration clauses of the American Arbitration Association have been held to cover such typical disputes as those involving extras, delays, claims for retainage, deficiencies in performance, and liquidated damages.

The place of arbitration often may be important because of applicable procedural or substantive law bearing upon the enforceability of the arbitration clause or final award. Arbitration locale may be designated in the arbitration clause itself, either expressly or by implication. Agreement of the parties respecting locale will be enforced. The parties may mutually agree on the locale where the arbitration is to be held.

Under common law, arbitrators lack the authority to order discovery. Despite this limitation, there still are several ways to bring about discovery of relevant documents. For example, parties may always agree to voluntarily exchange information. In addition, the rule limiting discovery in aid of arbitration is inapplicable when both parties seek discovery from a third party. The Federal Arbitration Act also permits arbitrators to summon any person to appear before them or to produce any book, record, document, or paper that may be deemed material evidence in the case. When parties refuse to voluntarily exchange information, one party may air the subject before the arbitrator in an effort to use the negative inference that might be drawn by the arbitrator as a weapon to compel discovery. Another practical method used by imaginative counsel is to obtain a subpoena *duces tecum* to compel production of documents or things at the hearing. Many states empower arbitrators to issue subpoenas. In addition, the rules of the AAA permit limited discovery in certain cases.

Arbitrators are entitled to fees for services unless otherwise agreed. Parties to arbitration proceedings are expected to compensate an arbitrator fairly and reasonably for its services. For example, Rule R-52 of the Construction Industry Arbitration Rules of the AAA provides: "Arbitrators shall be compensated a rate consistent with the arbitrator's stated rate of compensation." The Federal Arbitration Act makes no express provision for arbitrators' fees. In contrast, the Uniform Arbitration Act 10 states: "Unless otherwise provided in the agreement to arbitrate, the arbitrators' expenses and fees, together with other expenses, not including counsel fees, incurred in the conduct of the arbitration, shall be paid as provided in the award."

Unlike the 1997 edition of the AIA documents, the 2017 version does not present arbitration as the sole binding method of dispute resolution. In the 2017 version, the parties are to select arbitration, litigation, or another method of resolving disputes following the decision of the Initial Decision Maker.[22] Arbitrations are to be administered under the Construction Industry Arbitration Rules of the American Arbitration Association.[23]

C. Attacking Arbitration

Attacks on the right to arbitrate may be made either before the arbitration commences by petition to stay arbitration or in opposition to a petition to compel arbitration. Such proceedings are generally heard in the manner provided for the hearing of motions.[24] Such an attack may also be made after the arbitration award has been rendered in a proceeding to confirm or vacate such award, provided that objection has been made in the arbitration proceeding. The Uniform Arbitration Act contains a provision similar to that of the Federal Arbitration Act providing only for appeal of an order denying an application to compel arbitration.

As the right to arbitrate arises from the agreement of the parties, that right may be waived, just as any other contractual right may be waived. Since the parties' acts, and particularly court litigation, which is inconsistent with arbitration, may be deemed a waiver of the right to arbitrate, a contractor with a limited statutory period for filing and enforcing its mechanics' lien rights faces a difficult dilemma. Will the filing of the lien claim or suit on the lien waive arbitration? To protect its rights to arbitrate, a contractor who wishes to enforce its rights to a mechanic's lien and also arbitrate its dispute may begin by filing an arbitration demand and afterwards file its lien and complaint to foreclose. In the complaint, the contractor must specifically reserve its right to arbitrate and immediately move for a stay of the litigation pending arbitration.

D. Modification of Award by Arbitrators

In the absence of statute, an arbitrator who has rendered an award ceases to have any authority to modify the award. However, provided that application is timely made (20 days after delivery of award under the Uniform Arbitration Act), arbitrators may modify or correct an award (1) where there is an evident miscalculation of figures or an evident mistake in the description of

---

22. *E.g.*, AIA Document A101–2017, *supra* note 9.
23. *E.g.*, AIA Document A201–2017, *supra* note 2, § 15.4.
24. 9 U.S.C. § 6; Uniform Arbitration Act § 16.

any person, thing, or property referred to in the award; (2) where the award is imperfect in a matter of form not affecting the merits of the controversy; or (3) for the purpose of clarifying the award. As with the case of vacating awards, courts are reluctant to modify awards.[25] Parties who seek modification by the arbitrator and also wish to have the award vacated must be careful to file a motion to vacate the award within the statutory time limit, for the application to the arbitrator for modification does not extend the statutory time limit for a motion to vacate.

E. Confirmation or Vacation of Award by Court

Although the issue is rare, since parties generally seek relief in the state where the award is entered, the question sometimes arises whether an award may be vacated, modified, or confirmed in a state other than the state where the arbitration took place and the award made. In several cases, the courts have held that an arbitration award in one state is legally equivalent to the judgment of a court and may be enforced in another state.

Before the enactment of modern arbitration statutes, it was well established under common law, and remains the rule, that a court will not set aside an award for error in law or fact. Accordingly, a court will not set aside an arbitrator's decision on such grounds as newly discovered evidence or that the matter could not be resolved without a party not involved in the arbitration.

The grounds for vacating an award under the Federal Arbitration Act are very limited. They include when the award is procured by corruption, fraud, or undue means; when there is evident arbitrator partiality or corruption; when the arbitrators refused to postpone the hearing or hear pertinent evidence; or when the arbitrator exceeded its power.[26] State arbitration statutes usually include similar grounds. Certain courts have established some non-statutory grounds for vacating arbitration awards. Some courts have considered vacating awards that involved "manifest disregard of the law" or were contrary to "public policy" or "lack[ed] due process." In general, these grounds have been very narrowly construed, and the burden born by a party seeking to overturn them is very large.[27]

---

25. Prestige Ford v. Ford Dealer Computer Services, 324 F.3d 391 (5th Cir. 2003).
26. 9 U.S.C. § 10.
27. *See* David E. Robbins, *Calling All Arbitrators: Reclaim Control of the Arbitration Process—The Courts Let You*, Dispute Resolution J., Feb.–Apr. 2005.

On March 25, 2008, the U.S. Supreme Court decided the case of *Hall Street Assoc., L.L.C. v. Mattel, Inc.*[28] This case involved the effort of the parties to an arbitration agreement to expand the grounds of court review of the arbitration award. The parties agreed that the award could be vacated, modified, or corrected "(i) where the arbitrator's findings of fact are not supported by substantial evidence, or (ii) where the arbitrator's conclusions of law are erroneous." The court refused to allow a federal court applying the FAA to expand its review of the decision of the arbitrators past the limited statutory grounds found in sections 9, 10, and 11 of the FAA. Therefore, the lower court was not allowed to predicate its review on the standards set forth by the parties in their contract.[29]

The Supreme Court's opinion in *Hall Street Associates* has therefore put to rest the question of whether the parties in their arbitration agreement can expand the grounds of review of a federal court considering an arbitration award under the FAA. Whether there is room under state law for expanded review, either by agreement of the parties or by state statutes, is not clear.

Under the Uniform Arbitration Act 12(c), where a court vacates an award for reasons other than the lack of an arbitration agreement, it may remand the case to the arbitrators for rehearing. A new panel must be appointed where fraud or similar grounds are involved. Otherwise, the remand may be to the old panel, or a new panel, at the court's discretion. A petition for vacating or modifying an award must be filed within certain narrowly prescribed time limits to be considered. Under the Federal Arbitration Act, the limit is three months after the award is filed or delivered.

---

28. 552 U.S. 576, 128 S. Ct. 1396 (2008).

29. The Supreme Court noted that in an earlier decision [Wilko v. Swan, 346 U.S. 427, 74 S. Ct. 182 (1953)] it had used the term "manifest disregard [of the law]" but indicated that that term may have been a collective reference to the grounds set forth in the FAA as well as a new ground for review. In addition, the Supreme Court noted that it did not purport to exclude a "more searching review based on authority outside" the FAA. The Court stated: "The FAA is not the only way into court for parties wanting review of arbitration awards: they may contemplate enforcement under state statutory or common law, for example, where judicial review of different scope is arguable."

QUESTIONS

1. During a partnering session, managers of the contractor and the owner agree to personally discuss any potential changes in the project in order to avoid a "letter-writing war." Later, during the project, in response to claims for extras by the contractor, the owner asserts that the contractor waived its claims by failing to give written notice as required by the contract. Has the contractor waived its claims?

2. Following the conclusion of a project constructed under the 2017 AIA documents, the contractor commences an arbitration provision over a long-standing dispute regarding extra work. The owner responds by arguing that the arbitration proceeding is premature since there has been no initial decision, nor any mediation. The contractor responds that it is clear the parties disagree over this matter and arbitration should proceed. Should it proceed? Who decides?

3. A new state statute allows the state court to vacate an award if the award is in manifest disregard of the law. After the respondent files a petition to vacate in state court, the claimant, who is a citizen of another state, endeavors to remove the action to the federal court and seek an order that the state statute is invalid. Will the claimant prevail?

CHAPTER 20

Defective Construction

RICHARD J. TYLER

Although the phrases "construction defect," "construction deficiency," and "defective construction" are convenient ways to refer to some flaw in a structure that distinguishes the problem from, say, a payment dispute or an OSHA claim, the use of these shorthand phrases belies the complexity of the subject. The mission of this chapter is to bring some analytical order to the broad topic of "construction defects," identifying some of the myriad ways in which construction might be deemed "defective" or "deficient," outlining the specific legal claims under which an owner can recover for defective or deficient construction, examining some defenses that a party charged with defective or deficient construction might assert, and addressing a pair of special issues that arise in dealing with construction defects.

20.01 OVERVIEW OF THE LEGAL ANALYSIS OF DEFECTS

In this section, we provide a rough overview of construction defect analysis by reviewing the types of flaws that may qualify as defective or deficient

---

The author acknowledges the contribution of Michael Drew, a partner in the New Orleans office of Jones Walker LLP, to the original version of this chapter.

construction, and then we provide an overview of the assignment of responsibility for such flaws.

A. What Constitutes "Defective" or "Deficient" Construction?

1. Types of Defects or Deficiencies

There are many ways in which a property owner may be dissatisfied with the results of the design or building process, and the variety of dissatisfaction makes uniform definition of a construction "defect" elusive. One formulation describes a construction defect as work performed that falls below the standard promised or reasonably expected by the purchaser of the work or services. Another formulation looks at whether there is a lessening in the utility and/or value of the project. Yet a third formulation looks to the appropriateness or suitability of the work. However construed, there is general agreement that actionable defects arise out of the construction process itself and that normal wear and tear are not "defects" for purposes of construction claims.[1]

For purposes of this chapter, we will consider completed construction "defective" or "deficient" whenever it fails to satisfy an applicable contractual or legal standard that imposes requirements on the construction. The task of the next few sections will be to describe the standards that apply to construction such that a deviation renders it defective or deficient in some actionable sense.

From a broad perspective, consider the many types of deficiencies that might result in work being deemed defective: (1) materials and equipment furnished are not of the quality required or permitted by the contract (e.g., the pump installed does not work or has insufficient capacity); (2) the work is executed in a defective manner (e.g., paint is applied with inadequate surface preparation, resulting in premature scaling or peeling of the paint and eventual rusting of metal structural members); (3) the work, while executed correctly technically, does not conform to the requirements of the contract (e.g., the contractor applies the wrong color paint);[2] (4) the construction itself

---

1. *See* Richards v. Powercraft Homes, Inc., 678 P.2d 427, 430 (Ariz. 1984). The distinction between wear and tear and defective construction has ramifications in other contexts as well. *See, e.g.,* Walters Beach Condo. Ass'n v. Home-Owners Ins. Co., 2017 WL 5503789, at *3 (Mich. App. 2017) (insurance coverage); Central Parking System of Missouri, LLC v. Tucker Parking Holdings, LLC, 519 S.W.3d 485, 494 (Mo. Ct. App. 2017) (liability for repairs under lease agreement).

2. One treatise suggests that nonconforming work may not be defective where there is no economic consequence to the owner, such as the application of the wrong color paint. *See* 2 PHILIP L. BRUNER & PATRICK J. O'CONNOR, JR., BRUNER & O'CONNOR ON CONSTRUCTION LAW § 7:215 (West Group 2002) [hereinafter BRUNER & O'CONNOR]. *But see* American Institute of Architects, AIA Document A201-2017, General Conditions of the Contract for Construction § 3.5.1 (2007) [hereinafter AIA Document A201-2017] (listing circumstances under which work may be considered defective, including nonconformance with the requirements of the contract documents). We intend the

is perfectly sound but violates building codes in effect at the time of design or construction (e.g., a fire suppression system is functional but undersized); or (5) the work fails to meet professional standards for design at the time drawings were approved (e.g., the roof is designed without taking into account snow loads and the building collapses during a heavy winter storm). Although each of these may constitute a construction "defect" or "deficiency," the legal standards under which an individual claim is prosecuted may be different for each of the causes listed. In assessing claims for construction defects, the first step is to determine the standard that applied to the construction at issue and the manner in which the construction failed to satisfy that standard. The variety and sources of standards are discussed throughout the chapter.

2. Manifestations versus Defects

As the reader approaches construction defects claims, it is vital to note that defects or deficiencies must be distinguished from their manifestations.[3] Although these terms are related—and, often, both must be corrected—a manifestation is to a defect what a symptom is to a disease. The manifestation is the obvious or apparent visible condition that serves as notice of the possibility of a defect.[4] While a defect and its manifestation may be the same thing, oftentimes they are not. For example, a crack in a newly constructed wall is the manifestation of some defect—but what defect? Consider:

1. Is the crack the result of a problem with the material used to construct the wall?
   a. Were the material components defectively manufactured?
   b. Did the design call for improper materials to be used on the wall?
   c. Was the material improperly prepared?
   d. Was the material improperly installed?
2. Is the crack the result of a problem with how the wall is attached to the rest of the structure?
   a. Did the design call for adequate reinforcement?
   b. Was the wall improperly constructed?
   c. Was the material reinforcing the wall defective?

---

phrase "defective or deficient" construction to encompass all failures to satisfy applicable standards of construction as discussed in this chapter.

3. As but one example, statutes of limitations (discussed in Section 20.05) may start to run when a defect causes physical manifestations rather than when the defect itself is discovered. *See, e.g.,* Broomfield Senior Living Owner, LLC v. R.G. Brinkmann Co., 413 P.3d 219 (Colo. App. 2017).

4. *See generally* Bd. of Trustees of Santa Fe Cmty. Coll. v. Caudill Rowlett Scott, Inc., 461 So. 2d 239 (Fla. Dist. Ct. App. 1984). There, the plaintiff discovered leaky pipes shortly after the completion of construction. However, it was not until years after this discovery that plaintiff was able to determine that the defect causing these leaks was the contractor's decision to bury the pipes in clay, causing them to corrode.

3. Is the crack the result of a problem with how the structure's foundation was constructed?
   a. Were the cement or supports improperly manufactured?
   b. Was the foundation improperly designed?
   c. Was the foundation improperly constructed?
4. Is the crack the result of a problem with the ground on which the structure was built?
   a. Will the site not support the building (i.e., unsuitable soils)?
   b. Did the design fail to consider or accommodate the soil type?
   c. Did the geotechnical engineer fail to record the soil type accurately?
   d. Did the contractor know the design was inadequate or the soils unsuitable?
5. Is the crack the result of some problem not connected with the construction (and likely not the responsibility of a party), such as an earthquake of unanticipated magnitude?
6. Is the manifestation of a purported "defect" merely a common, expected, and nonactionable result of natural forces, such as the common cracking that predictably accompanies concrete flatwork in many jurisdictions that experience dramatic climate changes?

This array of potential causes for something as "simple" as a crack in a wall reflects not only the fact that determining causation may be a complex undertaking, but that this complexity also is present in attributing responsibility to the appropriate party or parties, the topic to which we now turn.

B. Responsibility

The fact that a symptom such as a crack may be evidence of many discrete construction deficiencies leads immediately to a second important observation: responsibility for defective or deficient construction may be visited on any number of parties, from the owner's design professional team (including engineering consultants) to the contractor team (including subcontractors or materialmen). Indeed, the symptom under scrutiny may not evidence a *construction* defect at all, but instead may occur in circumstances in which there is no liability for the crack in the wall.

Ascertaining which party is responsible for the defect can be a complicated matter. Depending on the defect that caused the manifestation, any number of different parties may ultimately bear responsibility.[5] For instance, if the crack

---

5. Industry literature on rework—performing the same work more than once in order to correct deficiencies—identifies numerous causes, including construction error from the use of

was due to defective plaster supplied by the manufacturer, then the manufacturer will bear the responsibility for correcting the defect or paying damages to the owner (assuming no contractual limitations of liability). Similarly, if the crack was due to poor soil conditions that the civil engineer failed to identify in its site investigation, the defect will likely be to its account. However, the engineer's liability may be reduced, or even eliminated, if the contractor encountered the soil condition and failed to bring it to the attention of the owner and engineer. Suffice it to say, the assessment of responsibility is a fact-intensive investigation carried out within the framework of the parties' contractual obligations.

A problem such as a severely cracked wall may in fact be caused by an earthquake of unusual magnitude where the owner cannot hold another party liable for the cost of repair. The mere existence of a problem, therefore, does not compel the conclusion either that construction is defective or that someone must be liable to the owner for damages. What distinguishes a cracked wall for which there is a legal remedy from a cracked wall for which no remedy is available? In short, a remedy is available when the crack is the proximate result of some party's failure to conform its work to an applicable legal obligation governing such work. That legal obligation may arise from the voluntary agreement of the parties (such as a construction contract), it may be imposed through common law doctrines (such as warranties of fitness), or it may involve statutory and other governmental requirements (such as building codes).

The next two sections summarize the important sources of standards, the violation of which will render work defective or deficient and give the owner the right to recover from the party responsible for the substandard work. For simplicity of discussion, the standards have been divided between the contractor's construction standards and the design professional's liability. In reality, there are many other parties typically associated with one of those two parties who ultimately may bear responsibility for defective or deficient construction.[6]

---

erroneous construction methods, the omission of some construction activity or task, design error, design omission, design changes, fabrication errors, and fabrication omission. Fayek et al., *Measuring and Classifying Construction Field Rework: A Pilot Study*, a Presentation to Construction Owners Association of Alberta (COAA) Field Rework Committee, May 2003, Table 3.5, *available at* https://www.coaa.ab.ca/COAA-Library/COP-RRT-APD-02-2003-v1%20Measuring%20and%20 Classifying%20Construction%20Rework%20-%20Executive%20Summary.pdf).

6. As but one example, defectively manufactured mortar may leave the manufacturer liable, as well as the subcontractor who used the mortar, as well as the contractor who hired the masonry subcontractor. For purposes of the following discussion, we discuss the legal bases of the contractor's liability to the owner alone, although downstream liability follows similar legal principles.

20.02 OWNER CLAIMS AGAINST CONTRACTORS

Construction law generally recognizes three legal bases from which a defect claim may be asserted against the contractor.

A. Contract Claims

Claims that the contractor has breached the contract for the construction of the work are arguably the most common category of defect claims. Such claims typically focus on whether the contractor complied with the express or implied terms of the contract. A plaintiff claiming breach of contract must prove the existence of (1) a valid contract, (2) a material breach, and (3) damages.[7]

Construction contracts typically contain multiple provisions designed to ensure that the owner receives work that is not defective. Construction contracts usually incorporate by reference the "contract documents," which include the drawings and specifications.[8] The contractor is obligated to perform the work in accordance with the contract documents.[9] The contractor is under an obligation to review the contract documents for the purpose of facilitating construction and to report to the owner and architect any errors or omissions discovered by the contractor.[10] During the performance of the work, the contractor is obligated to correct work that is rejected by the architect or fails to conform to the requirements of the contract documents.[11] Finally, contractors are typically required to repair defective or nonconforming work discovered during the one-year period following substantial completion (commonly referred to as the contractor's "repair warranty").[12]

1. Failure to Comply with Drawings and Specifications

Most Design-Bid-Build construction contracts[13] incorporate specific drawings and specifications that the contractor is obligated to follow in completing its work. A contractor's primary responsibility in completing construction is to adhere to the drawings and specifications, and deviations from the drawings or

---

7. *E.g.*, MODEL JURY INSTRUCTIONS CONSTRUCTION LITIGATION, § 6.02 (ABA 2001).
8. *See, e.g.*, AIA Document A201–2017 *supra* note 2, § 1.1.1.
9. *Id.* § 3.1.2.
10. *Id.* § 3.2.
11. *Id.* § 12.2.1.
12. *Id.* § 12.2.2.
13. Discussed in Chapter 4. *See also* Section 20.04(A).

specifications may render the contractor liable to the owner for such deficiencies or defects.[14]

Drawings and specifications are therefore fertile grounds for finding construction defects. Drawings and specifications generally define three aspects of the construction project: (1) the measurements, (2) the configuration, and (3) the materials to be used in completing the project. These guidelines may be general or may provide detailed instructions on how to execute the work.[15] Each of these aspects may be subject to a separate defect claim, or all three may be part of a single claim.

2. Breach of Express Warranty

A second source of contract-based defect claims can arise out of the express warranties contained in the contract with regard to the quality of the work. Section 3.5.1 of AIA Document A201–2007 is typical:

> The Contractor warrants to the Owner and Architect that materials and equipment furnished under the Contract will be of good quality and new unless the Contract Documents require or permit otherwise. The Contractor further warrants that the Work will conform to the requirements of the Contract Documents and will be free from defects, except for those inherent in the quality of the Work the Contract Documents require or permit. Work, materials or equipment not conforming to these requirements may be considered defective. The Contractor's warranty excludes remedy for damage or defect caused by abuse, alterations to the Work not executed by the Contractor, improper or insufficient maintenance, improper operation, or normal wear and tear and normal usage.

Under this warranty, for example, the contractor assumes an obligation to use new materials, and failure to use new materials will be considered defective, even if the contract drawings did not specify whether or not the materials should be new. A breach of warranty claim, while given special nomenclature, is generally treated in the same fashion as any other breach of contract claim.

---

14. The mere deviation from the drawings and specifications itself constitutes a breach of the contractor's obligations, but inconsequential deviations may not give rise to a claim where there is no cognizable "damage" associated with the breach. *See* note 2, *supra*, discussing application of incorrect paint color.

15. *Compare* J.R. Sinnott Carpentry, Inc. v. Phillips, 443 N.E.2d 597 (Ill. App. Ct. 1982) (contract specification was only a rough drawing made by owner showing location of rooms in proposed house addition) *with* Brewer v. Custom Builders Corp., 356 N.E.2d 565 (Ill. App. Ct. 1976) (professional blueprints were incorporated into contract and showed details such as type of wood to be used in stair construction).

3. Breach of Implied Warranty

In addition to the express warranties stated in the contract, a number of warranties are implied by operation of law without specific agreement of the parties. These warranties can arise from the factual circumstances of the parties' contract, or can be implied as a matter of public policy.[16] There are many implied warranties pertaining to construction contracts, including duties of full disclosure, cooperation, good faith and fair dealing,[17] workmanlike performance, habitability, and design adequacy.[18]

For example, the law implies in many construction contracts a warranty that the work will be performed in a workmanlike manner.[19] The phrase "workmanlike manner" generally means that: (1) the work performed will be performed by one who has the knowledge, training, or experience necessary for the successful practice of the required trade or occupation, and (2) the work performed will be performed in a manner generally considered proficient by those capable of judging such work.[20] This standard is objective. Courts applying the warranty of workmanlike construction will ask whether the work performed would meet the standard of work that one would expect a reasonably skilled and experienced contractor to perform in a similar situation. Expert testimony is typically necessary to prove that a contractor violated this warranty.[21]

Residential housing contracts often carry another implied warranty, known as the implied warranty of habitability.[22] Generally, the elements that must be proved to support an action for breach of the implied warranty of habitability are (1) a sale, (2) by a contractor-vendor, (3) of a residence, (4) with latent defects, (5) that breach the applicable standard of habitability, and (6) cause the purchaser harm.[23] Note that this warranty will only apply to newly constructed homes and will run to the benefit of the original purchaser in many jurisdictions, as it imposes the warranty on the contractor who built the home

---

16. BRUNER & O'CONNOR, *supra* note 2, § 9:63.
17. *Id.* §§ 9:92, 9:99, and 9:103.
18. *Id.* §§ 9:68, 9:71, and 9:78.
19. *See, e.g.*, Netherlands Ins. Co. v. BSHM Architects, Inc., 111 N.E.3d 1229, 1237, 2018 Ohio 3736, ¶ 32 (Ohio Ct. App. 2018); McKinley v. Brandt Constr., Inc., 859 N.E.2d 572, 574 (Ohio Ct. App. 2006) ("Any contract to perform work imposes on the contractor the duty to perform the work in a workmanlike manner. 'Workmanlike manner' has been defined as the way work is customarily done by other contractors in the community.").
20. *See* Young v. Oak Leaf Builders, Inc., 626 S.E.2d 240, 242 (Ga. Ct. App. 2006).
21. BRUNER & O'CONNOR, supra note 2, § 9:68 n.17.
22. BRUNER & O'CONNOR, supra note 2, § 9:72.
23. *See, e.g.*, Sims v. Lewis, 374 So. 2d 298, 303 (Ala. 1979); Theis v. Heuer, 280 N.E.2d 300, 303 (Ind. 1972).

and implies the warranty on first sale. As with the other implied warranties, this warranty is measured against an objective standard. The home need not be perfect. Rather, the test requires an inquiry as to whether a reasonable person faced with such a defect would conclude that the residence was uninhabitable. For example, a contractor's failure to properly insulate a home against cold weather may not breach the implied warranty of habitability if the home is located in Arizona. However, that same defect may constitute a breach of the warranty for a home located in Vermont.

B. Tort Claims

The availability of a tort claim against the builder depends primarily upon the jurisdiction's application of the Economic Loss Rule (also called the Economic Loss Doctrine), discussed in depth in Chapter 21. To the extent that the parties are in privity of contract, many states require that the claim be asserted under contract law, rather than by resort to the law of negligence, at least where the claims arise out of the parties' performance of the contract.

Of course, a contractual remedy is not available for parties not in privity of contract, and therefore an aggrieved party such as the owner may attempt to use a tort theory to state a claim against a material supplier, manufacturer, or subcontractor with whom the owner lacks contractual privity. The availability of these claims is determined by the jurisdiction's application of the Economic Loss Rule, but many—if not most—states require the owner to allege physical damage to property outside the scope of the contract, such as damaged sheetrock from a leaking HVAC unit, which often limits the availability of these claims.

C. Statutory Claims

The final major area under which an owner can bring a claim against a contractor involves statutory rights, which some states confer on owners—particularly homeowners—under the rubric of "deceptive trade practices."

Many of these are derived from consumer protection and trade practice statutes directed at businesses taking unfair advantage of purchasers. These statutes have been invoked in construction cases when an unscrupulous contractor preys on customers through shoddy construction. Mere defective or shoddy construction, standing alone, is usually insufficient to allow the customer to utilize the powerful consumer protection statutes to obtain special relief. Rather, the shoddy construction usually must be accompanied by some egregious misconduct by the builder, such as misleading or fraudulent business practices, conduct that is offensive to established public policy, or conduct that is immoral, unethical, oppressive, or unscrupulous.[24]

The main advantages conferred by these statutes are their broad applicability and the damages remedies available to consumers invoking their provisions. Typically, most deceptive trade practices acts include minimum statutory damages or punitive damage multipliers (such as treble damages), and permit the claimant to recover attorneys' fees that would not otherwise be available. As such, they are attractive vehicles for owners seeking to compel contractors to correct defects or to pay monetary compensation.

D. Notice Requirements

Even when work is defective, the contractor may not be required to answer for the defect or the deficiency unless it has been notified of the defect and, under some circumstances, been given an opportunity to cure the defect. For example, if the project is still under construction, the AIA General Conditions of the Contract for Construction provide that if the contractor fails to carry out the work in accordance with the contract documents, the owner is to give the contractor written notice.[25] If the contractor fails to commence curative work within ten days after receipt of this notice, then the owner may carry out the corrective work itself.[26] The purpose of these notice requirements is to give the contractor an opportunity to cure the defect(s) in the work. Such notice serves several purposes: allowing the contractor the opportunity to avoid termination (if the defect is discovered during the performance of the contract); permitting the contractor to perform the corrective work with his own forces, presumably at lower cost; avoiding similar deficient performance in the future; promoting the informal resolution of disputes; and, assisting the contractor in preserving its claim rights.

20.03 CLAIMS AGAINST DESIGN PROFESSIONALS

One treatise has noted that design professionals generally perform three functions with respect to a traditional Design-Bid-Build construction project: (1) preparation of the drawings and specifications as an independent contractor of the owner; (2) project administration as the agent of the owner; and

---

24. E.g., LSA-R.S. 51:1405A. ("Unfair methods of competition and unfair or deceptive acts or practices in the conduct of any trade or commerce are hereby declared unlawful.").

25. AIA Document A201–2017, *supra* note 2, § 2.4.

26. *Id. See also id.* § 12.2.2 (regarding notice and correction of defective work during the one-year period after substantial completion).

(3) arbiter of disputes between the owner and the contractor.[27] The design professional's failure to adequately perform these functions can adversely affect the contractor's performance of its obligations or impose obligations on the owner. For example, faulty drawings and specifications can lead to delays in the prosecution of the work and expose the owner and contractor to damage claims by each against the other. Likewise, the design professional's role in construction contract administration can create multiple potential problems for the contractor and owner if the design professional fails to perform its duties adequately.

Claims against design professionals are principally based on theories of tort and breach of contract. Contract claims are generally brought by the owner that retained the design professional's services. Although the acts that constitute a breach of contract may also give rise to a tort claim for professional negligence, tort claims against design professionals are typically brought by a contractor who claims to have suffered damage due to the acts or omissions of the design professional.

The contract between the owner and the architect defines the design professional's obligations to the owner and thus is the primary source of liability claims. The typical owner–architect agreement contains express obligations to be performed by the architect (e.g., the timely preparation of drawings and specifications and duties pertaining to the administration of the contract of construction).[28] The failure to carry out express duties constitutes a breach of the contract. Oftentimes, however, the design professional's contractual obligations are stated in subjective terms, in which event the question of contractual breach often will be determined by reference to the tort standard of care; specifically, whether the design professional acted as a reasonable design professional under like circumstances.[29]

A. Tort and Contract Claims Generally

Claims against design professionals most commonly are anchored in tort or in breach of contract. A negligence claim against a design professional is composed of the standard four elements defined in Section 20.03 in connection

---

27. 5 BRUNER & O'CONNOR, *supra* note 2, § 17:4.

28. For example, American Institute of Architects, AIA Document B201-2007, Standard Form of Architect's Services: Design and Construction Contract Administration (2007) [hereinafter AIA Document B201-2007] requires the design professional to make site visits during construction (§ 2.6.2.1), review contractor submittals and shop drawings (§ 2.6.4.2), reject nonconforming work (§ 2.6.2.2), and interpret the contract documents for the contractor (§ 2.6.2.3).

29. 5 BRUNER & O'CONNOR, *supra* note 2, § 17:11.

with claims against contractors. Similarly, breach of contract claims follow the formulation previously set forth. The precise standards that govern design professionals are discussed in more detail in Chapter 6.

B. Defective Drawings and Specifications

How do tort and contract claims typically find their way into construction defect claims against design professionals? One of the design professional's major obligations, if not the principal obligation, is to prepare drawings and specifications that will be used to construct the owner's project. The following case is a fairly typical illustration of the sort of problems that can arise from the breach of that obligation.

St. Joseph Hospital v. Corbetta Constr. Co., Inc.
316 N.E.2d 51 (Ill. App. 1974)

This involves consolidated appeals from two actions in the circuit court of Cook County. Both arose primarily out of problems flowing from the installation of Textolite plastic laminate wall paneling on the walls of the new St. Joseph Hospital during its construction, which paneling proved to have a 'flame spread' rating some 17 times the maximum permitted under the Chicago Building Code and had to be replaced with paneling complying with said Code.

...

The St. Joseph Hospital (the Hospital) in 1958 entered into a contract with architect Belli & Belli of Missouri (Belli) for the erection of a hospital on a new site in Chicago to replace one erected before the Great Chicago Fire of 1871, and the general construction of the hospital was undertaken by the Corbetta Construction Company (Corbetta). In April of 1965, when the building had been substantially completed, the Hospital was advised by the City Collector that its application for a license to operate the Hospital had been disapproved because the wall paneling (General Electric's "Textolite") which covered its rooms and corridors, and had been manufactured and furnished by the General Electric Company (General Electric), did not comply with a Chicago Code requirement that such paneling have a "flame spread" rating of not to exceed 15. Actually it had a rating of 255, 17 times the maximum. The city also threatened criminal action against the Hospital for operating without said license.

At this juncture, the Hospital called upon all of the parties involved to remedy the situation and withheld from Corbetta final payment of some $453,000. Although all of the parties deplored the situation, each took the position that it was not itself at fault and that only others were to blame. At about this time

Corbetta advised the Hospital that it was their intention to file suit for the $453,000 so withheld by the Hospital.

Faced with the threat of two lawsuits and a complete shutdown of its operation, the Hospital, on May 14, 1965, filed a complaint for declaratory judgment against Corbetta, Belli and General Electric, setting forth the above described controversy between the parties, and attaching copies of the various contracts, subcontracts and applicable municipal ordinances. As the result of a petition for immediate relief, an order was entered in this action, permitting the Hospital to take immediate steps to remove the Textolite wall paneling and to replace it with paneling approved by the city of Chicago, all without prejudice to the rights of any of the parties.

...

In Section V of Belli's brief it contends, in substance, that it committed no tort and did not breach its contract with the Hospital to design and supervise the construction of the new hospital, and that it "in the normal course of such supervision ascertained that the General Electric Batten Panel System designated in its change order number G-33 would have to be replaced. This is not any unusual situation."

The evidence in this case establishes that Belli not only was legally required to know but did in fact know that the Chicago Building Code required that paneling installed in such building have a "flame spread" rating of not to exceed 15; that Belli specified General Electric's "Textolite" paneling without making any investigation whatsoever to determine whether or not it met that standard; that during the seven months it took to install the Textolite no one at Belli discovered that said material had a flame spread 17 times the maximum and could not possibly be installed upon the walls of any hospital in Chicago; that Belli therefore made a gross error in specifying it in said change order; and that it was only the insistence of the Building Inspector that a certificate be filed that uncovered the fact that no one had ever bothered to procure the consent of the Building Department to change order G-33 as issued to Corbetta.

According to Belli's brief, this was "commonplace practice" and should somehow be excused because, after the discovery of Belli's error, it refused to issue an architect's certificate certifying that Corbetta had properly completed its work, thus holding up the final payment to Corbetta. No cases are cited in support of this theory.

...

In 12 Vanderbilt Law Review (1959), in an article by Prof. George M. Bell entitled "Professional Negligence of Architects and Engineers," it is said, at pages 715–716, under the subtitle "Liability to the Owner for a Defective Building":

> Architects and engineers hold themselves out as competent to produce work requiring: (a) skill in the preparation of plans, drawings or designs suitable for the particular work to be executed; (b) knowledge of the materials to be used and the proper application for use; (c) knowledge of construction

> methods and procedures. Presumably, if the architect or engineer fails to use reasonable care to produce a satisfactory structure, he may be either sued for a breach of an implied term of his contract or in negligence....
>
> Nor can Belli avoid liability on the ground that, by refusing to issue a final certificate for payment after its error had been discovered, enough money was withheld from Corbetta to cover the loss. As we shall subsequently demonstrate, Corbetta was not itself at fault and payment to it was wrongfully withheld. The error in specifying Textolite was that of Belli; not Corbetta.
>
> We therefore must and do hold that, although others may also be at fault, Belli, which, as architect, specified the Textolite paneling without ascertaining its flame spread rating, and permitted its installation over a period of some seven months, is liable to the Hospital for the damages proximately flowing therefrom. We therefore conclude that the jury's verdict for the Hospital and against Belli as to liability was and is correct and approve that verdict.

This court did not attempt to distinguish between professional liability based on negligence and breach of contract, but other jurisdictions—depending on their interpretation of the economic loss rule, discussed in Chapter 21—might be more inclined to do so. Important issues regarding allocation of comparative responsibility, including comparative negligence, the applicability of tort and contract statutes of limitation, and the assessment of consequential damages can, indeed, be dramatically different under tort and contract theories. In *St. Joseph*, none of these issues apparently was dispositive, but the court did address an interesting "betterment" issue, which often arises in design defect cases:

> The defendants (putting aside for the present their several contentions that they are not liable at all) contend, inter alia, that the Hospital is not entitled to recover the extra cost of the more expensive Micarta paneling and the extra labor costs required by its more difficult installation, and that, insofar as such extra costs are included, the jury's verdict (and the court's judgment thereon) unjustly enriches the Hospital by giving it, free of charge, better and more expensive wall paneling than it had bargained for and thus puts it in a better position than it would have been had the original contracts been fully performed. We are of the considered opinion that this contention is well founded in this case.
>
> ...

... [U]nder the contracts involved, the Hospital was, insofar as wall paneling is concerned, entitled to have Belli use its best professional skill in selecting a wall paneling meeting, among other criteria, the Chicago Building Code's maximum flame spread rating of 15. There is no real doubt that Belli should originally have specified Westinghouse's Micarta asbestos wall paneling which was the only plastic laminate wall paneling which met the flame spread standard set by the Chicago Building Code.

But had Belli so complied with its contract, the Hospital would have had to pay not the relatively modest cost of the Textolite wall paneling material, and the costs of its relatively simple installation, but the greatly increased cost of the Micarta asbestos paneling, plus the greatly increased costs of its more difficult installation. And, as Sister Vincent (the administrator of the hospital during the construction, who signed the order requiring the change from "Novoply" to "Textolite" on behalf of the Hospital) testified, she would have signed a change order specifying a plastic laminate wall covering which cost more "if it was necessary to comply with the Code."

Certainly the Hospital should not receive, without paying more than it originally had agreed to pay for the Textolite, a windfall in the form of the more expensive Micarta paneling and the extra labor costs required by its more difficult installation, merely because its architect initially failed to specify it. The same applies to the door stops, solid core doors and hardware and their installation, which were necessary and were furnished in the reconstruction but were not included in Belli's original plans and specifications.

...

Micarta paneling . . . cost $58,000 in 1963 ($87,000 less 1/3 for paneling not removed.) On this alone the Hospital is ahead $48,000.

The Micarta, being much harder and more expensive to install than the Texto-lite, would have cost $80,000 to install in 1963 (the actual cost of installation of $107,750 was a 30% Increase over 1963). The Textolite cost $33,000 to install in 1963. On this, the Hospital is ahead another $47,000.

To this add door stops $4,298, solid core doors and hardware $8,811 and installation of $8,375 (which were not originally specified or installed but were added at the time the paneling was replaced) for a subtotal of $21,484.

These three items total $116,484, and we therefore will reduce the sum the Hospital is entitled to recover (by retention or otherwise) by this amount.

C. Construction Observation

Another area of significant claim exposure for design professionals arises from the design professional's observation of the contractor and the contractor's activities under the owner–contractor agreement for construction of the project.[30] As noted previously, owner–architect agreements typically impose a variety of duties on the design professional, including making site visits during construction, reviewing contractor submittals and shop drawings, rejecting non-conforming work, and interpreting the contract documents.

These obligations raise an issue as to the design professional's responsibility when a contactor's work is defective. Contractual provisions pertaining to design professional site visits and construction observation have been a fruitful source for owners seeking to expand the liability for construction defects to include not only the contractors who performed defective work but also the design professionals who failed to detect it. The extent and even the existence of this liability are treated differently in different jurisdictions.

Moundsview Indep. Sch. Dist. No. 621 v. Buetow & Assoc., Inc.
253 N.W.2d 836 (Minn. 1977)[31]

In August 1968, Moundsview retained Buetow to prepare plans and specifications for an addition to an elementary school. At the time of the execution of the agreement, Moundsview had the option of requiring Buetow to provide (1) no supervision, (2) general supervision, or (3) continuous on-site inspection of the construction project by a full-time project representative referred to as a "clerk of the works." Moundsview elected to have Buetow provide only a general supervisory function, the specific language of the contract enumerating the requirements as follows:

> The Architect shall make periodic visits to the site to familiarize itself generally with the progress and quality of the Work and to determine in general if the Work is proceeding in accordance with the Contract Documents. On the basis of his on-site observations as an Architect, he shall endeavor to guard the Owner against defects and deficiencies in the Work of the Contractor. The Architect shall not be required to make exhaustive or continuous on-site inspections to check the quality or quantity of the Work. The Architect shall not be responsible for construction means, methods, techniques, sequences or procedures, or for safety precautions and programs in connection with the Work, and he shall not be responsible for the Contractor's failure to carry out the Work in accordance with the Contract Documents.

---

30. This topic is also addressed in Chapter 7.
31. Internal citations omitted.

The contract further provides:

The Architect shall not be responsible for the acts or omissions of the Contractor, or any Subcontractors, or any of the Contractor's or Subcontractors' agents or employees, or any other persons performing any of the Work.

Buetow prepared plans and specifications requiring the placement of wooden plates upon the concrete walls of the building. The plates were to be fastened to the walls by attaching washers and nuts to one-half inch studs secured in cement. During the 79-week construction period, the president of Buetow made 90 visits to the construction site in performance of Buetow's general supervisory obligation.

On May 19, 1975, a severe windstorm blew a portion of the roof off the building causing damage to the addition and to other portions of the school. It was discovered that the roof had not been secured by washers and nuts to the south wall of the school as required by the plans and specifications.

Moundsview brought an action for damages caused by the roof mishap against Buetow, the general contractor, and the roofing subcontractor. In response to an interrogatory from Buetow requesting Moundsview to state all facts upon which it relied to support its allegations against Buetow, Moundsview replied:

. . . Defendant Buetow failed to properly supervise the roof construction, failed to supervise and discover the missing nuts and studs and take proper corrective action.

Thereafter, Buetow made a motion for summary judgment, basing its motion upon the affidavit of one of its officers which stated that Buetow did not observe during any of its construction site visits that the washers and nuts had not been fastened to the studs on the south wall.

. . .

2. Moundsview argues that Buetow breached its duty of architectural supervision by failing to discover that a contractor had failed to fasten one side of the roof to the building with washers and nuts as required by the plans and specifications. It is the general rule that the employment of an architect is a matter of contract, and consequently, he is responsible for all the duties enumerated within the contract of employment. . . . An architect, as a professional, is required to perform his services with reasonable care and competence and will be liable in damages for any failure to do so. . . .

Thus, consideration of whether Buetow breached a duty of supervision requires an initial examination of the contract between the parties to determine the parameters of its supervisory obligation. The argument that Buetow breached its duty to supervise would be more persuasive had Moundsview contracted for full-time project representation rather than mere general supervision. An architect's duty to inspect and supervise the construction site pursuant to a contract requiring only general supervision is not as broad as its duty when a "clerk of the works" is required. The mere fact that Buetow received additional compensation for performing the general supervisory service does not serve to expand its responsibilities to an extent equivalent to the duties of a full-time project representative. Moundsview cannot be allowed to gain the benefit of the more detailed "clerk-of-the-works" inspection service while in fact contracting and paying for only a general supervisory service.

Thus, the question of whether Buetow breached its duty to supervise the construction project is to be determined with reference to the general supervisory obligation enumerated in the contract. The contract provided that the architect " . . . shall not be responsible for the Contractor's failure to carry out the Work in accordance with the Contract Documents." When this section is read in conjunction with the section which provides that "(t)he Architect shall not be responsible for the acts or omissions of the Contractor, or any Subcontractors, or any of the Contractor's or Subcontractors' agents or employees or any other persons performing any of the Work," it is apparent that by the plain language of the contract an architect is exculpated from any liability occasioned by the acts or omissions of a contractor. The language of the contract is unambiguous. The failure of a contractor to follow the plans and specifications caused the roof mishap. By virtue of the aforementioned contractual provisions, Buetow is absolved from any liability, as a matter of law, for a contractor's failure to fasten the roof to the building with washers and nuts.

A very different result was obtained in the case of *Hunt v. Ellisor & Tanner, Inc.*[32] There, the owner brought suit against the architect for breach of contract relative to construction defects, claiming that the architect had breached its obligations to observe "the progress of the Work" and to "endeavor to guard the Owner against defects and deficiencies in the Work of the Contractor." The architect disclaimed liability, citing *Moundsview*. The court rejected the defense as follows:

> We decline to follow *Moundsview*. We conclude that the language said to be exculpatory constitutes nothing other than an agreement that the architect is not the insurer or guarantor of the general contractor's obligation to carry out the work in accordance with the contract documents. We reach this conclusion because the first three sentences of paragraph 2.2.4 of the general conditions impose a nonconstruction responsibility upon the architect; to wit: to visit,

---

32. 739 S.W.2d 933 (Tex. App. 1987).

to familiarize, to determine, to inform and to endeavor to guard. In short, to provide information, not to make improvements upon the job site. Therefore, we reason that the fourth sentence of paragraph 2.2.4 and the paragraph paraphrasing it exist to emphasize the architect's nonconstruction responsibility and to make certain that the architect "will not be responsible for the [general] contractor's failure to carry out the work in accordance with the contract documents." In short, the provider of information to the owner does not insure or guarantee the general contractor's work. It follows, and we so hold, that the contract does not exculpate Ellisor & Tanner from liability for the general contractor's failure to carry out the work in accordance with the contract documents.[33]

D. Claims against the Design Professional by Contractors

To this point, we have focused discussion on the design professional's liability to the owner. While the acts or omissions of design professionals on construction projects can undoubtedly cause damage to the *contractor* as well by making the contractor's performance more expensive and time-consuming. In many jurisdictions the contractor is barred from pursuing claims directly against the design professional by the Economic Loss Doctrine.[34]

As noted elsewhere,[35] however, many states recognize exceptions to the Economic Loss Doctrine and permit claims against design professionals based on concepts such as the professional's knowledge of possible third-party reliance, the reasonable foreseeability that the contractor could be injured by the architect's negligence, negligent and intentional misrepresentation, and an architect/contractor relationship that is the functional equivalent of privity.

---

33. The middle ground between the *Moundsview* and *Hunt* lines of cases has been to find that the architect can be liable to the owner if the design professional fails to learn of the defect due to breach of its contractual obligations to owner; *see, e.g.*, Diocese of Rochester v. R-Monde Contractors, Inc., 562 N.Y.S.2d 593 (N.Y. Sup. Ct. 1989) (failure to make timely and proper inspections); Watson, Watson, Rutland/Architects, Inc. v. Montgomery Cnty. Bd. of Educ., 559 So. 2d 168 (Ala. 1990) (failure of contractor to follow plans and specifications is known to architect during course of construction).

34. *See* 5 Bruner & O'Connor, *supra* note 2, § 17:88 n.20 (state-by-state collection of cases on applicability of economic loss doctrine and recognized exceptions thereto). *Compare* Balfour Beatty Infrastructure, Inc. v. Rummel Klepper & Kahl, LLP, 451 Md. 600 (Md. 2017) (surveying cases addressing the economic loss rule in the context of construction and deciding: "We apply the economic loss doctrine and decline to impose tort liability on Engineer for purely economic injuries alleged by Contractor that was neither in privity nor suffered physical injury or risk of physical injury."

35. *See* Chapter 21.

Forte Bros., Inc. v. Nat'l Amusements, Inc., et al.
525 A.2d 1301 (R.I. 1987)

The issue presented by this case is thus whether a third-party general contractor who may foreseeably be injured or suffer an economic loss proximately caused by the negligent performance of a contractual duty by an architect/site engineer has a cause of action in negligence against the architect/site engineer notwithstanding an absence of privity. The issue is novel to this jurisdiction.

...

A supervising architect, in the performance of its contract with the owner, is required to exercise the ability, skill and care customarily exercised by architects in similar circumstances. This duty of care extends to contractors who share an economic relationship and community of interest with the architect on a construction project. The duty is based on circumstances establishing a direct and reasonable reliance by the contractor on the contractual performance of the architect when the architect knows, or should know, of that reliance. "Altogether too much control over the contractor necessarily rests in the hands of the supervising architect for it not to be placed under a duty imposed by law to perform without negligence his functions as they affect the contractor."

We hold that Forte stated a cause of action in negligence against Allen notwithstanding the trial justice's finding that Allen was acting as agent for National. Viewing the facts in the light most favorable to Forte, as we must, it appears that Forte directly and reasonably relied on Allen's rendering of Allen's contractual duty as supervising architect/site engineer of the construction project to measure Forte's removal of mass boulders, to report the removal to National, and to authorize payment to Forte therefor. Hence, Allen owed Forte a duty to render its services professionally. In so holding, we join "an emerging majority of jurisdictions [which] have taken the position that a contractor can maintain a negligence action against an architect without direct privity of contract between the parties."

20.04 THE *SPEARIN* DOCTRINE AND CONFLICTING WARRANTIES

The taxonomy of claims set out so far should not lead the reader to believe that allocation of responsibility is always a simple matter. Although an identification of all the complexities is beyond the scope of an introductory work such as this, we will discuss two special problems that exemplify the issues that can arise in charging parties with defects.

A. The *Spearin* Doctrine

One of the fundamental doctrines that serves to allocate responsibility for construction defects is the *Spearin* Doctrine.

The most well-known project delivery system is Design-Bid-Build. Under the first step, the owner hires a design professional who transforms the owner's needs and concepts into a set of drawings and specifications for the project. These completed design documents are then presented by the owner to one or more contractors who then furnish a bid for performing the work. After evaluating these bids, the owner negotiates and executes a contract with the contractor to build the work required by the drawings and specifications. This system, however, begs the question of who is responsible when the contractor builds according to the drawings and specifications, but the work nonetheless proves to be defective.

1. Owner's Implied Warranty of Drawings and Specifications

The seminal case on the issue of responsibility for defective drawings and specifications is *United States v. Spearin*.[36] The government contracted with Spearin to build a dry dock at the Brooklyn Navy Yard in accordance with government-furnished drawings and specifications. The job site was intersected by a six-foot brick sewer, and the work required that a section of the sewer be relocated before dry dock construction began. The drawings and specifications prescribed the dimensions, material, and location of the sewer section to be relocated. Spearin fully complied with the contract requirements, and the government accepted the work as satisfactory.

Both before and after its relocation, the sewer connected with a seven-foot sewer line, located outside the project area, that emptied into a tidal basin. About a year after the relocation, a heavy downpour coincided with a high tide, forcing water from the basin up the sewer line. As a result, the relocated sewer broke in several places, and the dry dock was flooded. Upon investigation, it was discovered that the backflow was diverted into the six-foot sewer by a dam in the seven-foot sewer that was not shown on the city's sewer system drawings or on the government's drawings furnished to Spearin.

After the sewer break, Spearin notified the government that he would not resume operations unless the government assumed responsibility for the damage that had already occurred and either made changes in the sewer system or assumed responsibility for future damage. The government insisted that the

---

36. 248 U.S. 132 (1918).

responsibility for remedying existing conditions rested with the contractor. The government ultimately annulled the contract, took possession of the work and materials on the site, and completed the work using other contractors.

Spearin brought suit against the government seeking the balance due for work done under the contract and for damages resulting from the annulment of the contract. The court found in Spearin's favor, and the government appealed to the Supreme Court. The Court held that the government's breach of its implied warranty of the drawings and specifications, followed by the government's repudiation of all responsibility, past and future, justified Spearin's refusal to resume work:

> In the case at bar, the sewer, as well as the other structures, was to be built in accordance with the plans and specifications furnished by the government. The construction of the sewer constituted as much an integral part of the contract as did the construction of any part of the dry dock proper. . . . The risk of the existing system proving adequate might have rested upon Spearin, if the contract for the dry dock had not contained the provision for relocation of the 6-foot sewer. But the insertion of the articles prescribing the character, dimensions and location of the sewer imported a warranty that if the specifications were complied with, the sewer would be adequate. This implied warranty is not overcome by the general clauses requiring the contractor to examine the site, to check up the plans, and to assume responsibility for the work until completion and acceptance. The obligation to examine the site did not impose upon him the duty of making a diligent inquiry into the history of the locality with a view to determining, at his peril, whether the sewer specifically prescribed by the government would prove adequate. The duty to check plans did not impose the obligation to pass upon their adequacy to accomplish the purpose in view. And the provision concerning contractor's responsibility cannot be construed as abridging rights arising under specific provisions of the contract.[37]

Thus, "[w]hen the Government provides specifications directing how a contract is to be performed, the Government warrants that the contractor will be able to perform the contract satisfactorily if it follows the specifications."[38]

The *Spearin* holding, known later as the *Spearin* Doctrine, has been adopted by the majority of the states.[39] Of course, this doctrine presumes that

---

37. *Spearin*, 248 U.S. at 136–37.
38. Hercules, Inc. v. United States, 516 U.S. 417 (1996).
39. A notable exception is the state of Texas, where the jurisprudence has long provided, with some exceptions, that the owner does not impliedly warrant the plans and specifications. Lonergan v. San Antonio Loan & Trust Co., 104 S.W. 1061 (Tex. 1907). In the years that followed the Lonergan decision, some intermediate courts adopted the *Spearin* rationale, but the Texas

a contractor who seeks to invoke the doctrine can demonstrate that it completed construction precisely in accordance with owner-supplied drawings and specifications. That is, in order to establish owner responsibility for defective drawings and specifications, the contractor must show that it reasonably relied on the drawings and specifications (i.e., that the defects were not so patent as to provoke a duty of inquiry on the part of the contractor).[40] In addition, the contractor must also construct the work in strict compliance with the defective drawings and specifications. For example, in *Al Johnson Construction Co. v. U.S.*,[41] the contractor was required to construct a temporary berm to stabilize coffercells on a spillway being constructed in connection with the Tennessee-Tombigbee Waterway project. The berm was not completed when heavy rains caused a rise in the adjacent river, and the berm sloughed away. The contractor sought to recover the extra costs incurred as a result of the failure. The Board of Contract Appeals rejected the contractor's contention that the berm would have failed even if it had been built to the specified height, relying on the testimony of government witnesses who testified that the berm, "if of full height, might or might not have failed." On appeal, the Federal Circuit affirmed, reasoning that the warranty of the drawings and specifications under the *Spearin* Doctrine only applied if the contractor complied with the drawings and specifications:

> In Justice Brandeis' opinion in *Spearin*, it is flatly stated that the implied warranty runs to contractors who have complied with the specifications.
>
> . . .
>
> Of course, this is subject to the exception that contractors can stop performing when the results of actual experience with performance to date reveal that the specifications are defective to the degree they cannot, as a matter of commercial possibility, be complied with. This was the fact situation in the *Spearin* case itself. There was no showing here that the defect of the specifications was of a kind that produced impossibility. Rather, appellant attempted to show the board that the berm would have failed anyway, even if it had met the specification completely.
>
> . . .
>
> There is nothing to show when or how the contractor became disillusioned with respect to the berm. . . . He does not show us when, or even

---

Supreme Court reaffirmed the rule announced in Lonergan in a 2012 decision, El Paso Field Servs. v. MasTec North America, Inc., 389 S.W.3d 802 (Tex. 2012).

40. *See* 3 BRUNER & O'CONNOR, *supra* note 2, § 9:64 (discussing implied duty to seek clarification of obvious design discrepancies). Standard form construction contracts typically place on the contractor the obligation to review the plans and specifications and promptly report any design errors or omissions noted by the contractor. *See, e.g.*, AIA Document A201–2017, *supra* note 2, § 3.2.

41. 854 F.2d 467 (Fed. Cir. 1988).

whether, he became convinced that the berm design was defective. We think the restriction of the implied warranty to those who have fulfilled the specifications, or tried and failed to do so because of the defects themselves, has strong policy behind it that would not be served by allowing the implied warranty to run to one who has not done what he contracted to do and fails to satisfactorily explain why not. Any other exception should therefore be restricted to instances, not now foreseen, of manifest inequity, or to a deviation from the specifications shown to have been entirely irrelevant to the alleged defect.[42]

In *Ralph M. Parsons Co.*,[43] the board explained the reasoning behind the strict compliance requirement as follows:

We have here a threshold evidentiary problem requiring, first, that we inquire into whether or not appellant's design, indeed, was followed in the manner intended by appellant. If it was not, then the Government is hardly in a position to fault appellant's design for its difficulties. . . .

> In actions brought against architects, general rules of evidence have been applied. Where negligence of the architect consists [of] the furnishing of defective plans, specifications, and drawings, it is essential to prove that the builder substantially complied with such plans and specifications and that in consequence of such compliance damages were sustained by plaintiff.

Since this is the Government's claim, it has the burden of showing that its construction contractor "substantially complied" with appellant's plans. Once we are shown this fact, then we can further inquire whether appellant's design was negligently performed and whether for the reason of the Government's compliance therewith it incurred costs or damages.[44]

2. Design Specifications

In addition to the requirement that the contractor demonstrate performance of the work in strict compliance with the drawings and specifications supplied by the owner, the *Spearin* Doctrine by its very nature requires that the drawings and specifications set forth detailed and precise requirements as to materials, equipment, tolerances, or other specific information from which the contractor is not permitted to deviate. Such detailed specifications are known as "design specifications."[45]

---

42. *Id.* at 469–70.
43. ASBCA No. 24347, 85-1 BCA ¶ 17,787; *aff'd on reconsid.*, 85-2 BCA ¶ 18,112.
44. 85-2 BCA at 90,936.
45. *See, e.g.*, J.L. Simmons Co. v. United States, 412 F.2d 1360, 1362 (Ct. Cl. 1969) ("The specifications, which were prepared by the defendant, are a classic example of 'design' specifications.

An example of how the *Spearin* Doctrine can be used by a contractor defensively can be found in the case of *City of Covington v. Heard*.[46] The city sued the contractor that installed sewer pipe, which later failed. The appellate court upheld a summary judgment in favor of the contractor because the undisputed evidence established that the contractor used the specified type of pipe, and installed it in accordance with the drawings and specifications:

> Flextran was an allowable material under the City's own specifications. The City cannot avoid responsibility for its own specifications by allowing the contractor such an option. The law is clear that where specifications call for installation of a material by brand name, and the contractor complies with the specifications by supplying and installing such brand name material, the contractor is immune from defects therein.[47]

3. Performance Specifications

As distinguished from design specifications, performance specifications describe an end result to be achieved by the contractor, such as requiring HVAC equipment capable of delivering a specific volume of air at a certain static pressure, but leave the determination of how to reach the result—what brand or model of equipment—to the contractor.[48] Unlike design specifications, performance specifications do not carry an implied warranty of accuracy or adequacy:

> But not all contract specifications are design specifications—some are merely performance specifications:
>
>> Design specifications explicitly state how the contract is to be performed and permit no deviations. Performance specifications, on the other hand, specify the results to be obtained, and leave it to the contractor to determine how to achieve those results.

. . . In other words, in these specifications, the defendant set forth in precise detail the materials to be employed and the manner in which the work was to be performed, and plaintiff was not privileged to deviate therefrom, but was required to follow them as one would a road map."); GAF Corp. v. United States, 19 Cl. Ct. 490, 500 n.2 (1990) ("Specifications are design when only one material or a certain composition will enable the product to meet the performance standards expressed in the specification."); Aircraft Gear Corp. v. Kaman Aerospace Corp., 856 F. Supp. 446, 452 (N.D. Ill. 1994) (design specifications "set forth precise measurements, tolerances, materials, in process and finished product tests, quality control, inspection requirements, and other specific information.").

46. 428 So. 2d 1135 (La. Ct. App. 1983).
47. *Id.*
48. *See, e.g., J. L. Simmons Co.*, 412 F.2d at 1362; Blake Constr. Co. v. United States, 987 F.2d 743, 745 (Fed. Cir. 1993) (same).

The government does not implicitly warrant performance specifications for complete accuracy or adequacy. "[T]ypical 'performance' type specifications set forth an objective or standard to be achieved, and the successful bidder is expected to exercise his ingenuity in achieving that objective or standard of performance, selecting the means and assuming a corresponding responsibility for that selection."[49]

Specifications can contain provisions that can be characterized as "design," "performance," or a hybrid of the two. To differentiate between design and performance specifications, courts generally examine the level of discretion that the specification at issue affords the contractor. "Discretion serves as the touchstone for assessing the extent of implied warranty and intended liability."[50] A contractor claiming a particular specification is "design" rather than "performance" must establish the specification "do[es] not permit meaningful discretion . . . and the defective specification [is] the cause of [the] injury."[51]

4. Conflicts between the Contractor's and the Owner's Warranties

As previously discussed, construction contracts typically contain an express warranty in favor of the owner that materials and equipment furnished under the contract will be of good quality and new unless otherwise required or permitted by the contract documents, that the work will be free from defects not inherent in the quality required or permitted, and that the work will conform to the requirements of the contract documents.[52] The owner, on the other hand, impliedly warrants the drawings and specifications furnished to the contractor. In most cases, these warranties coexist without difficulty, but the question remains: Who bears responsibility when the materials and equipment that are expressly warranted by the contractor, but supplied under a design specification (impliedly warranted as suitable by the owner), are defective?

Rhone Poulenc Rorer Pharm., Inc. v. Newman Glass Works
112 F.3d 695 (3d Cir. 1997)

Plaintiff Turner Construction Company ("Plaintiff") appeals from an order of the district court granting Defendant Newman Glass Works' ("Defendant") motion for judgment as a matter of law pursuant to Federal Rule of Civil Procedure 50(b).

---

49. George Sollitt Constr. Co. v. United States, 64 Fed. Cl. 229, 296–97 (2005) (citations omitted); *see also* Stuyvesant Dredging Co. v. United States, 834 F.2d 1576 (Fed. Cir. 1987).

50. Conner Bros. Constr. Co., Inc. v. United States, 65 Fed. Cl. 657, 685 (2005).

51. *Id.* For a general discussion of performance specifications, *see* 5 BRUNER & O'CONNOR, *supra* note 2, § 17.76.

52. AIA Document A201-2017, *supra* note 2, § 3.5.1.

. . .

Rhone Poulenc Rorer, Inc. ("Rhone") contracted with Plaintiff to have Plaintiff install opaque spandrel glass in Rhone's headquarters and research facility. In turn, Plaintiff, as the general contractor, entered into two subcontracts with Defendant, which required Defendant to supply and to install the opaque spandrel glass that comprised the structure's curtainwall. The subcontracts, which are identical as relevant here, specify the type of glass Defendant was to install and list the three manufacturers from whom Defendant could purchase the glass. . . . In compliance with the foregoing terms, Defendant set about installing the specified spandrel glass that it had purchased from Spectrum Glass Products, Inc. ("Spectrum"), one of the three listed manufacturers. . . . Before Defendant completed the installation, the opacifier coating began to delaminate from portions of the glass. Plaintiff and its architect noticed the delamination because portions of the installed glass exhibited a mottled appearance. Plaintiff demanded in writing that Defendant replace the defective glass. Defendant refused, and Plaintiff instituted this action for breach of contract.

. . .

We commence our analysis on this appeal by focusing our attention on the warranty provisions of the subcontracts. Section X of the subcontracts requires Defendant to remove and to replace all materials that Plaintiff or its architect "condemn as unsound, defective or improper." In Section 4.5.1 of the general contract, Plaintiff expressly warrants to Rhone that all work will be "free from faults and defects." Defendant, in turn, assumes this warranty toward Plaintiff in the subcontracts. Defendant argues that these express warranties are legally insufficient to support the jury's verdict because these warranties are nullified by Plaintiff's implied warranty that the specified glass was adequate for use in this building. Defendant asserts that under the Supreme Court's 1918 decision in *United States v. Spearin*, 248 U.S. 132 (1918), and its progeny, it cannot be held liable for any defects in the glass because it complied with the specifications in the subcontracts.

. . .

We are presented here with a conflict between the implied and the express warranties. We conclude that the Pennsylvania Supreme Court would find that the express warranties must prevail.

Implied warranties are generally not favored by law and are construed narrowly. This warranty of specification permits a court to allocate the risk of an inadequate specification, quite equitably, to the party that drafted the specification. Here, though, the parties have explicitly allocated to Defendant the risk that the glass would be defective. The parties are free to do so, and there is no indication of overreaching or bad faith by Plaintiff.

Defendant accurately notes that *Spearin* provides that an implied warranty of specification is not overcome by "general clauses" requiring a contractor to visit a site or to review plans. The express warranties in the subcontracts here, however, are not the sort of general clauses about which *Spearin* speaks. Section X of the

> subcontracts very specifically requires Defendant to remove and to replace any materials that Plaintiff or its architect deem defective. Through the incorporation of the general contract's Section 4.5.1 into the subcontracts, Defendant specifically warranted that all work would be "free from faults and defects." These duties far exceed site inspection or plan review.
>
> ...
>
> It is true that here, Defendant had virtually no discretion in carrying out its contractual obligations in light of the exacting specifications in the subcontracts. But it is also true that Defendant entered into subcontracts that require it to remove and to replace any defective materials "at its own cost and expense." We conclude that the implied warranty by Plaintiff based on the specifications of the type and manufacturer of the spandrel glass must yield to Defendant's express warranties against defective materials. In consequence, the district court erred in granting Defendant's motion for judgment as a matter of law.

One might think that the allocation of responsibility to the contractor is unfair when the contractor merely carried out the drawings and specifications. The reader should bear in mind, however, that the contractor is in privity with the supplier (or the subcontractor who in turn purchased the defective materials) and through its own contract chain has the opportunity to shift the ultimate burden of the defective materials to the party responsible for the defect (in this case, presumably, the manufacturer).

20.05 TIME-BASED DEFENSES TO LIABILITY: STATUTES OF LIMITATION AND STATUTES OF REPOSE

Statutes of limitation, statutes of repose, and laches are affirmative defenses to claims, and all three are based on the passage of time. As their names suggest, statutes of limitation and statutes of repose are legislative enactments that impose time limits on a party's ability to commence a legal proceeding concerning a perceived injury. Such statutes are seen as serving a number of public policy interests, including the reduction of uncertainty, minimizing the impact of evidence loss, promoting the prompt enforcement of claims, and reducing the volume of litigation.[53] Laches, on the other hand, is an equitable

---

53. *See, e.g.,* Tyler T. Ochoa & Andrew Wistrich, *The Puzzling Purposes of Statutes of Limitation*, 28 Pac. L.J. 453 (1997), *available at* http://digitalcommons.law.scu.edu/facpubs/81, for a detailed discussion of the public policy interests underlying statutes of limitation.

doctrine that is rooted in the concept that a party who "sleeps" on its rights to the prejudice of another party should be barred from asserting those rights.[54]

A. Statutes of Limitation

Statutes of limitation require that a lawsuit be brought within a specified time after the occurrence of the event giving rise to the claim, commonly referred to as the "accrual" of the cause of action.[55] These statutes serve several important objectives. First, they "protect defendants and the courts from having to deal with cases in which the search for truth may be seriously impaired by the loss of evidence, whether by death or disappearance of witnesses, fading memories, disappearance of documents, or otherwise."[56] Second, public policy dictates that there should come a time when persons will no longer be burdened by the possibility of liability arising from acts occurring in the past. Finally, such statutes promote the goal of certainty and finality in the administration of commercial transactions by terminating liability at a set point in time.[57]

Construction projects are complex, and involve a number of different actors, including owners, design professionals, professional service providers (such as surveyors), contractors, subcontractors, vendors of material and equipment to be incorporated into the work, and lessors of equipment used in prosecuting the work. As a result, claims arising out of a construction project can involve a number of different theories of recovery—breach of contract, breach of express or implied warranty, tort—depending on the identity of the claimant and the identity of receiving party. Virtually every state in the United States has adopted statutes of limitation with respect to different causes of action, such as breach of contract, and the limitations period for a particular cause of action can vary greatly from state to state.[58] Further complicating mat-

---

54. The doctrine of laches is based on the maxim that equity aids the vigilant and not those who slumber on their rights. 1 Story, Commentaries on Equity Jurisprudence 87 (14th ed. 1918). Because most construction defect claims are legal and not equitable, there are few cases applying laches in the context of construction defects and that defense will not be examined in detail here.

. 55. See Garner, Black's Law Dictionary (9th ed.), at 1546. Statute of limitations defined as "[a] law that bars claims after a specified period; specif., a statute establishing a time limit for suing in a civil case, based on the date when the claim accrued (as when the injury occurred or was discovered)."

56. United States v. Kubrick, 444 U.S. 111, 118 (1979) (citations omitted).

57. Sun Valley Water Beds v. Herm Hughes & Son, Inc., 782 P.2d 188 (Utah 1989).

58. For example, the statute of limitations for breach of contract is three years in the District of Columbia (D.C. Code Ann. § 12-301(7)), six years in Georgia (Ga. Code Ann. § 9-3-24), and ten years in Alabama (Ala. Code § 6-2-33(1)). The statute of limitations for torts can also vary widely from state to state, from one year in Louisiana (La. Civ. Code Ann. art. 3492), two years

ters is the fact that most states allow parties to shorten (but not lengthen) the statutory limitations period by contract.[59]

Another complication is the fact that different causes of action, with different limitations periods, may be assertable against the same party. For example, an owner may be able to sue its architect for both breach of the design contract as well as in tort for professional negligence, with each claim carrying a different limitation period. Failure to assert claims timely, or with an adequate articulation of the claim, can result in one or more causes of action being deemed time-barred.

Kroger Co. v. L.G. Barcus & Sons, Inc.
13 So.3d 1232 (La. App. 2d Cir. 6/17/09)

This matter arises out of a lawsuit filed by Kroger against numerous defendants, seeking damages caused by settlement of the foundation and floor of the Kroger store located on Youree Drive in Shreveport, Louisiana. . . .

In its original petition, Kroger alleged . . . that SCA's foundation design and specifications were substandard and inadequate, resulting in the cast piles not being installed to the correct depth. This allegation is referred to as the "design phase" claim. The petition also asserted that after the initial settling of the store, Kroger requested that SCA make recommendations to remedy the settlement problem, but the attempts at remediation had not been successful.

More than three years later, in March 2006, Kroger filed an amended petition reiterating the design phase allegations of the original petition and asserting a "repair phase" claim against SCA and another defendant, Hayward Baker, Inc.

---

in Georgia. In addition, a number of states have adopted specific statutes that apply to injury to property arising out of defective improvements to real property. E.g., VA. CODE ANN. § 8.01-250.

59. *E.g.*, A.J. Tenwood Associates v. Orange Senior Citizens Hous. Co., 491 A.2d 1280 (N.J. App. Div. 1985), *cert denied*, 501 A. 2d 976 (N.J. 1985) (One-year limitation period contained in construction contract enforced: "Although the statutory limitation in this State for actions in contract is six years, such a limitation may be waived by express agreement of the parties. It is fundamental that in the absence of a statute barring such agreements, a contractual stipulation limiting the time for bringing an action upon a contract to a period less than that prescribed by the foregoing statute is valid if the stipulated period is reasonable and does not violate public policy. There is persuasive authority holding that contractual provisions which impose a one year period of limitation on actions are not so unreasonable as to constitute a violation *per se* of public policy." (citations omitted); College of Notre Dame of Maryland, Inc. v. Morabito Consultants, Inc., 752 A.2d 265 (Md. Ct. Spec. App. 2000) (parties may agree to modify the statute of limitations if there is no controlling statute to the contrary, the modification is reasonable, and it is not subject to other defenses such as fraud, duress, or misrepresentation). *See also* Annotation, *Validity of Contractual Time Period, Shorter than Statute of Limitations, For Bringing Suit*, 6 A.L.R. 3d 1197, 1207 (1966 & Electronic Supp. 2007).

> Specifically, in paragraphs 25, 26 and 27 of the amended petition, Kroger alleged that following completion of the original construction, Kroger retained the services of SCA to remedy the settlement problem, but that the engineering services provided by SCA were "ineffective, performed negligently, and their implementation caused additional damages to the Kroger Store."
>
> * * *
>
> Delictual actions are subject to a liberative prescription[60] of one year, running from the day injury or damage is sustained. An action on a contract is governed by the prescriptive period of ten years for personal actions. The nature of the duty breached determines whether an action is in tort or contract. The distinction between damages *ex contractu* and damages *ex delicto* is that the former flow from the breach of a special obligation contractually assumed by the obligor, whereas the latter flow from the violation of a general duty owed to all persons. Even when a tortfeasor and victim are bound by a contract, courts usually apply the delictual prescription to actions that are actually grounded in tort.
>
> The mere fact that the circumstances arose in the context of a contractual relationship does not make the cause of action contractual.
>
> * * *
>
> In its amended petition, Kroger does not allege that a specific contract provision was breached, but that SCA's services were ineffective and negligently performed. Thus, Kroger's petition states a cause of action for breach of a person's general duty to perform repair work in a non-negligent, prudent and skillful manner. Liability for breach of this duty arises *ex delicto*. Accordingly, the district court was correct in finding that Kroger's cause of action was in tort and subject to the one-year liberative prescriptive period of Article 3492.

A contrary result was reached in *Newell Recycling of Atlanta, Inc. v. Jordan Jones and Goulding, Inc.*[61] There, Jordan designed an automobile shredding facility for Newell pursuant to a "Draft Scope of Work," certain letters, and an agreement to prepare a concrete work platform that would control drainage around the shredding facility. More than four years after the facility became operational, Newell sued Jordan for breach of contract and professional malpractice arising from the failure of the concrete platform. The question before the court was whether Newell's claim was timely under the six-year statute

---

60. In Louisiana, "liberative prescription" is "a mode of barring of actions as a result of inaction for a period of time," La. Civ. Code art. 3447, and is the civil law equivalent of "statute of limitations."

61. 703 S.E.2d 323 (Ga. 2010).

of limitations applicable to contracts, or untimely under a four-year statute applicable to professional malpractice. The court applied the six-year limitation period:

> By its plain terms, the four-year statute of limitation . . . does not apply where a contract is evidenced by a sufficient writing. The statute only applies where no sufficiently written contract exists and a cause of action can therefore be based solely on the breach of an express oral or implied promise. Thus, again, based on the Court of Appeals "assuming arguendo that [the relevant documents at issue here were] sufficient to constitute an enforceable, written contract between the parties," the Court of Appeals should have concluded, as the trial court did, that the six-year statute of limitation . . . was applicable to Newell's claims as opposed to the four-year statute of limitations applicable to oral agreements. . . .
>
> In determining which statute of limitation applies, the threshold inquiry is to determine whether a written agreement actually exists between the parties such that any implied duties sued upon would have grown directly out of the existence of the written contract itself.

As the foregoing cases demonstrate, determining the correct limitations period is often a fact-intensive inquiry.

Equally fact-intensive is the determination of the accrual date on which limitations period begins to run. As noted previously, a well-developed body of case law upholds the modification of statutes of limitations by contract, thus the accrual date may be stated in the parties' agreement.[62] The accrual date can also be established by the statute of limitations itself.[63] Where no contractual or statutory provision governs commencement, the accrual date typically depends on the type of claim asserted. A claim for breach of contract typically accrues on the date when the contractual breach occurs, and the statute of limitations will commence to run from that date.[64] A tort claim, on the other

---

62. For example, the 1997 edition of AIA Document A201 provided a set of commencement dates for the running of any "applicable statute of limitations" depending on whether the act or failure to act occurred before Substantial Completion, after Substantial Completion but before the Final Certificate for Payment, or after the Final Certificate for Payment. See American Institute of Architects, AIA Document A201–1997, General Conditions of the Contract for Construction § 13.7. AIA Document A201–2007 replaced this provision with a contractual statute of repose of ten years sunning from Substantial Completion (§ 15.1.2), which provision was carried over into the 2017 A201 Document.

63. E.g., VA. CODE ANN. § 8.01-250 (No action to recover for any injury to property arising out of the defective and unsafe condition of an improvement to real property may be brought more than five years after the performance or furnishing of such services and construction.).

64. If the parties have specified an accrual date, such as substantial completion, the practical effect may be to cause the statute of limitations to commence running before or after it would otherwise run under the law.

hand, accrues when a wrongful act causes some legal injury, even if the fact of injury is not discovered until later, and even if all resulting damages have not yet occurred.[65] As a general rule, the statute of limitations applicable to tort claims is shorter than the limitations period for contract claims.[66]

Under the previously described accrual rules, it is entirely possible for the limitations period to expire before the injured party even knows of the existence of a claim. For example, the defective installation of piping, a breach of the contractor's obligation to perform the work in a workmanlike manner, may not become known for many years after the date of breach, especially if the piping is covered up by other work, such as walls. A fatal design flaw may not manifest itself for a considerable period after the design professional's negligent act. Because of the perceived unfairness of legitimate claims becoming time-barred on a technicality before they are even known to exist, many jurisdictions have adopted the "Discovery Rule," under which the limitations period begins to run only when the non-breaching party first becomes aware (or should have become aware) of the breach of the contract or injury.[67] The following case illustrates policy reasons behind adoption of such a rule:[68]

1000 Virginia Ltd. Partnership v. Vertecs
146 P.3d 423 (Wash. 2006)

¶ 1 In these consolidated cases the trial courts dismissed actions for breach of construction contracts as untimely. The Court of Appeals reversed in each case, holding that the discovery rule applies to determine when a cause of action accrues for breach of a construction contract and that material issues of fact exist as to when the plaintiffs discovered their causes of action. . . . The defendant construction companies challenge the Court of Appeals' holdings that the discovery rule applies. . . . We affirm the Court of Appeals.

¶ 2 1000 Virginia, acting as its own general contractor, built an apartment complex. 1000 Virginia hired subcontractor Vertecs Corporation to do the stucco work. Vertecs was not responsible for caulking, flashings, and weather protection. On December 31, 1992, the certificate of substantial completion was issued. Occasional leaks occurred, and in early 1994 1000 Virginia asked for Vertecs' presence during inspection of windows and vents. Following inspection, Vertecs concluded

---

65. *E.g.*, SV v. RV, 933 S.W.2d 1 (Tex. 1996).

66. For example, in Louisiana, the limitations period for tort claims is one year, LA. CIV. CODE art. 3492, and the limitations period for contract claims is ten years, *id.*, art. 3499.

67. Hilliard & Bartko Joint Venture v. Fedco Sys., Inc., 522 A.2d 961, 969 (Md. 1987) (holding that arbitration was timely where owner found defect within one year and then filed for arbitration within three years where construction contract provided that contractor would correct defects found within one year of completion of contract).

68. In many jurisdictions, the Discovery Rule is imposed by statute rather than by common law.

that caulking had failed in several areas and that some dryer vents were not connected to ductwork. Vertecs said these problems were not within the scope of its work. 1000 Virginia repaired the caulking and ductwork. Leaks continued over the next few years and, after a wet winter in 1996, 1000 Virginia noted increased cracks in the stucco and deterioration in drywall under decks. 1000 Virginia took further corrective action. Despite 1000 Virginia's efforts to resolve the problems, by the end of 1998 1000 Virginia knew substantial repairs were required to correct systemic defects that led to structural damage resulting from water intrusion and fungal problems.

¶ 3   On September 3, 2002, 1000 Virginia brought a breach of contract action against several of its subcontractors, including Vertecs, claiming that defective work led to the water intrusion and resulting damage to the apartment complex.

...

¶ 21   There is little to distinguish a case involving latent defects in a building and a case where a surgical instrument is left in the plaintiff's body during surgery. In both cases the plaintiff may have no way of knowing that a cause of action exists, i.e., no way of knowing the facts that show that the construction contract was breached in the first case or that a duty of care was breached in the latter. Just as a patient may lack the ability to know that a surgical sponge has been left in place which causes serious harm, so too an unsuspecting homeowner may lack the ability to know that an inferior product was used, such as a type of siding, which results in significant damage....

...

¶ 23   Under such circumstances, it is unfair to permit a defendant to escape responsibility for shoddy construction simply because the cause of action is based on contract rather than a tort theory. In addition, it is more equitable to place the burden of loss on the party best able to prevent it, i.e., the contracting party who could avoid breaching the contract. Thus, the same fairness considerations weigh in favor of applying the discovery rule to construction contract actions where latent defects are alleged as weigh in favor of the rule in negligence actions.

¶ 24   Of course, a plaintiff cannot ignore notice of possible defects. The discovery rule requires that "when a plaintiff is placed on notice by some appreciable harm occasioned by another's wrongful conduct, the plaintiff must make further diligent inquiry to ascertain the scope of the actual harm. The plaintiff is charged with what a reasonable inquiry would have discovered." A person who has notice of facts that are sufficient to put him or her upon inquiry notice is deemed to have notice of all facts that reasonable inquiry would disclose. Whether the plaintiff should have been able to detect defects (and presumably demand that they be remedied before the structure is accepted) involves a fact question that may be resolved against the plaintiff. Thus, if a plaintiff in a construction contract case inspects as construction proceeds, voluntarily or as a matter of contractual obligation, or is placed on inquiry notice of harm during construction, these facts will bear on whether the plaintiff should have discovered the cause of action.

¶ 25 Vertecs argues, however, that this court has recognized the need for certainty and predictability in the contract setting and these concerns weigh against applying the discovery rule in cases involving actions on construction contracts. Vertecs argues that the parties to construction contracts rely on statutes of limitations and the rule that a contract action accrues at breach in allocating risks. Vertecs contends that changing accrual rules undermines the certainty and predictability of allocated risks of loss and bargained-for liability exposure. In a similar vein, amicus Associated General Contractors contends that availability and cost of insurance are significant concerns where a discovery rule of accrual applies.

¶ 26 Similar arguments applied and similar concerns were raised when the discovery rule was first applied in the case of negligence actions, but the benefits of applying the rule outweigh the burdens. We believe the same is true in the case of construction contracts. We hold that the discovery rule applies in the case of actions for breach of construction contracts where latent defects are alleged.

. . .

¶ 43 Next, Vertecs challenges the Court of Appeals' holding that there are issues of material fact in 1000 Virginia precluding summary judgment. Vertecs contends that 1000 Virginia knew of its damage in 1994, expressly claimed it was due to Vertecs' conduct, and chose its own repair course over time. Thus, Vertecs says, 1000 Virginia should have discovered its cause of action in 1994 because there was notice of leaks and thus of the breach. However, Vertecs itself contended in 1994 that leaks were due to improper caulking and unconnected ductwork that was not within the scope of its work. Therefore, we do not agree that evidence of the leaks in 1994 is sufficient to support Vertecs' claim that as a matter of law 1000 Virginia discovered or should have discovered its cause of action against Vertecs in 1994.

Application of the Discovery Rule adds another layer of fact investigation to the accrual determination as it necessarily requires inquiry into when the plaintiff discovered its injury, and when plaintiff should have discovered it through the exercise of reasonable diligence. Courts have interpreted the "exercise of reasonable diligence" to mean that the injured party must act promptly when the facts and circumstances would place a reasonable person of common knowledge and experience on notice that a claim might exist.[69]

Finally, the running of the statute of limitations can be suspended or "tolled" by conduct of the breaching party. One such circumstance is "fraudulent concealment" where the defendant is aware of the plaintiff's injury, but by act or statement conceals the injury from the plaintiff. The elements of such a claim are (1) a false statement that concealed the claim from the plaintiff,

---

69. Dean v. Ruscon Corp., 468 S.E.2d (S.C. 1996).

(2) intent, and (3) correct information was not reasonably available through other means.⁷⁰ Tolling of the statute may also occur by equitable estoppel where the defendant engages in conduct that induces the plaintiff to forego a timely suit regarding a cause of action that the plaintiff knew existed, such as through the promise of repairs.⁷¹ The elements of equitable estoppel are (1) a false representation or concealment of material facts; (2) made with knowledge, actual or constructive, of the facts; (3) with the intent that the plaintiff act on the representation of concealment; (4) made to (or hidden from) a plaintiff without knowledge or the means of knowledge of the facts; and (5) detrimental reliance by plaintiff on the representations. While these two tolling doctrines are similar, they are distinguishable: fraudulent concealment involves preventing the plaintiff from knowing the existence of a claim; equitable estoppel involves preventing a plaintiff from asserting a known claim.

Discussion Problem

A commercial strip shopping center constructed in 2005. A subsequent purchaser of the center notices water leaks in late 2007 and contacts the original contractor for assistance with repairs. The contractor makes certain repairs, which are completed in 2008.

The repairs are insufficient, and the owner identifies new leaks in 2010. The owner again contacts the original contractor, who performs additional roof repairs, patches cracks in the stucco walls and unplugs drainage pipes. The contractor assures the owner that, this time, the leaks will stop.

The water leaks return, and in 2013 the homeowner finds leaks at the location of prior repairs. Instead of contacting the original contractor, the owner waits until 2016, and hires a different contractor to begin repairs. Subsequent demolition

---

70. Town Ctr. Office Plaza Ass'n, Inc. v. Carlson Real Estate Ventures, LLC, 2017 WL 1375304, at *7 (Minn. App. 2017) ("To prove fraudulent concealment, tolling any statute of repose or limitations, a party must show (1) the defendant made a statement that concealed plaintiff's potential cause of action, (2) the statement was intentionally false, and (3) the concealment could not have been discovered by reasonable diligence."); *Cf.* Millgard Corp. v. McKee/Mays, 831 F.2d 88 (5th Cir. 1987) (reversing grant of summary judgment on tort claim based on statute of limitations where non-moving party presented unrebutted evidence that the fraudulent concealment was not known until discovery proceedings unearthed incriminating documentary evidence showing that county withheld information concerning unstable soil conditions).

71. Dillon Co. Sch. Dist. Two v. Lewis Sheet Metal, 332 S.E.2d 555 (S.C. Ct. App. 1985) (Court reversed summary judgment finding that defendants' correspondence, employment of an expert, participation in meetings, and the numerous attempts to repair the roof created a jury issue as to whether defendants' conduct lulled a plaintiff into a false sense of security that its roof problems would be corrected and litigation would not be required.).

reveals "extensive" mold damage throughout the building, inadequate or missing foundation elements, and wood rot so extensive that some supporting columns were "partially liquefied" due to moisture infiltration.

In 2017, the owner sues the original contractor for damages resulting from (1) the original faulty construction, (2) faulty remediation work efforts in 2008, and (3) faulty repairs in 2010.

    (1) When did claims relating to the original construction accrue?
    (2) Was accrual of these claims tolled, and, if so, until when?
    (3) When did claims relating to the 2008 repairs accrue?
    (4) Was accrual of these claims tolled, and, if so, until when?
    (5) When did the claims relating to the 2010 repairs accrue?
    (6) Was accrual of these claims tolled, and, if so, until when?

B. Statutes of Repose

Because of exceptions such as the Discovery Rule and tolling doctrines, statutes of limitation may nonetheless result in a participant to a construction project being subject to suit for a considerable time, years or even decades, after project completion. For example, it would be possible for an engineer to be sued 20 years after designing a structure if the defect is not discovered until then. Statutes of repose address the issue of open-ended liability by placing an absolute time limit, from a date certain (usually substantial completion), on the bringing of claims.[72] The repose period commences to run regardless of when the injury occurs, whether the injury has manifested itself, or whether the injured party is even aware of the injury. Once this period of time has passed, the causes of action specified in the statute are extinguished.

Virtually every jurisdiction has adopted a statute of repose for claims arising out of construction projects.[73] These statutes "demonstrate legislative recognition of the protracted and extensive vulnerability to lawsuit of architects and builders by owners and other persons. They represent a response to the inadequacy of the traditional statutes of limitations, whose time period begins upon discovery of the claim or upon occurrence of the injury."[74] Like statutes

---

72. *See* Garner, BLACK'S LAW DICTIONARY (9th ed.), at 1546. Statute of Repose defined as "[a] statute barring any suit that is brought after a specified time since the defendant acted (such as by designing or manufacturing a product), even if this period ends before the plaintiff has suffered a resulting injury."

73. Allen Holt Gwyn, *Legislative Update: Statutes of Repose*, 21:3 THE CONSTR. LAW. 33 (Summer 2001).

74. Sowders v. M.W. Kellogg Co., 663 S.W.2d 644, 647 (Tex. Ct. App. 1983).

of limitation, statutes of repose vary widely from state to state in terms of the parties protected,[75] the date the repose period begins to run,[76] the length of time after which claims are foreclosed,[77] and the types of claims foreclosed.[78]

Initially, statutes of repose were attacked on constitutional grounds, such as the right to "open courts," substantive due process, and equal protection of the law. Such challenges have largely been rejected by the courts.[79]

Discussion Problem

Consultant performed a sewer system evaluation survey in 1977-78, issuing a report in 1978. In 1981, the report was incorporated into a bid package for a unit rate sewer system rehabilitation contract that was issued in 1984. The contract was awarded in August, 1984, and the contractor immediately commenced work. In June, 1985, however, the contractor declared the municipality in material breach and terminated the contract due to there being substantially less work than shown in the survey. The municipality then sent a notice of default to the contractor.

The contractor filed suit against the municipality in July, 1986. The suit sat idle for a number of years. As a trial date was approaching in 1994, the municipality

---

75. *Compare* La. Rev. Stat. Ann. § 9:2772 (protecting "any person performing or furnishing the design, planning, supervision, inspection, or observation of construction or the construction of an improvement to immovable property") *with* Me. Rev. Stat. Ann. tit. 14 § 752-A (covering only "architects and engineers").

76. The date certain on which the repose period commences varies widely from jurisdiction. *See, e.g.*, Ark. Rev. Stat. § 16-56-112 (substantial completion); Fla. Stat. Ann. § 95.11(3)(c) (date of actual possession by owner, date of issuance of certificate of occupancy, date of abandonment of construction, or date of completion or termination of the contract, whichever is later); Idaho Code § 5-241 (final completion); La. Rev. Stat. Ann. § 9:2772 (the date owner's acceptance of the work is filed in the mortgage office, or, if no filing is made, the date owner occupies or takes possession of the improvement, in whole or in part).

77. *Compare* Ark. Rev. Stat. § 16-56-112 (five years) *with* Fla. Stat. Ann. § 95.11(3)(c) (15 years). Some statutes provide for an extension of the repose period if injuries occur in the latter years of the period and under other circumstances. *See, e.g.*, Okla. Stat. Ann. tit. 15, § 110.

78. *Compare* La. Rev. Stat. Ann. § 9:2772 (precluding all actions "whether ex contractu, ex delicto, or otherwise") *with* Mass. Ann. Laws ch. 260, § 2B (precluding only an "[a]ction of tort for damages"). See Gwyn, *supra* note 73 for a table of statutes of repose.

79. Trinity River Auth. v. URS Consultants, 889 S.W.2d 259, 261 n.3 (Tex. 1994) ("Forty-six states have enacted statutes of repose protecting architects and engineers, with the repose period ranging from four to twenty years. Thirty-two of these jurisdictions have upheld their statutes against constitutional attack, while eleven have struck them down on constitutional grounds." (citations omitted). *But see* Perkins v. Northeastern Log Homes, 808 S.W.2d 809 (Ky. 1991) (construction statute of repose violated constitutional provision against special legislation); Turner Constr. Co. v. Scales, 752 P.2d 467 (Alaska 1988) (statute of repose violated equal protection clause of state constitution).

filed a third party demand for indemnity and contribution claims against the design engineer, who, in turn, filed a similar demand against the survey provider.

At the time the survey and design work was performed, a statute of repose was in effect providing that "no action, whether ex contractu, ex delicto, or otherwise" could be brought more than ten years after acceptance of the work by owner; or more than ten years after the improvement has been thus occupied by the owner.

(1) Are the claims against the design engineer and/or survey provider barred by the statute of repose?
(2) Does the fact that the third party demands are for indemnity and contribution affect the result?
(3) Would the answer change if the repose period was shortened to seven years in 1993?
(4) Can a statute of repose be amended retroactively? Why or why not?

The law on statutes of repose is not nearly as well-developed or uniform as the law pertaining to statutes of limitation. For example, it is unclear whether a repose period can be adopted by contract. Some states hold that the repose period cannot be waived,[80] others permit waiver,[81] and others have yet to address the issue. Similarly, a wide disparity of opinion exists on whether a statute of repose can be tolled by fraud,[82] or equitable estoppel.[83]

---

80. Stone & Webster Eng'g Corp. v. Duquesne Light Co., 79 F. Supp. 2d 1, 8–9 (D. Mass. 2000) (making *Erie* guess regarding Pennsylvania law); Trax-Fax, Inc. v. Hobba, 627 S.E.2d 90, 95–96 (Ga. App. 2006) (collecting cases); Cheswold Volunteer Fire Co. v. Lambertson Constr. Co., 489 A.2d 413, 420–21 (Del. 1984) (collecting cases).

81. Harper v. O'Charley's, LLC, 2017 WL 5598815, at *5 (S.D. Ala. 2017) (claim against design professional for negligent design of parking lot, leading to claimant's injuries); ESI Montgomery Cnty., Inc. v. Montenay Int'l Corp., 899 F. Supp. 1061, 1066 (S.D.N.Y. 1995) (upholding an express waiver of period of repose in a federal securities action); First Interstate Bank of Denver v. Central Bank & Trust Co., 937 P.2d 855, 860 (Colo. App. 1997) (upholding written agreement tolling statute of repose pending a final adjudication on federal claims); One North McDowell Assoc. v. McDowell Dev. Co., 389 S.E.2d 834, 836 (N.C. App. 1990) (North Carolina construction statute of repose is subject to an express waiver by written agreement).

82. Northern Montana Hosp. v. Knight, 811 P.2d 1276 (Mont. 1991); Pfeifer v. City of Bellingham, 772 P.2d 1018 (Wash. 1989) (proof of active concealment of dangerous condition could toll statute of repose); Curry v. Thornsberry, 98 S.W.3d 477, 482 (Ark. App. 2003), *aff'd*, 128 S.W.3d 438 (Ark. 2003) (rejecting tolling argument based on fraudulent concealment); KSLA-TV, Inc. v. Radio Corp. of America, 732 F.2d 441 (5th Cir. 1984) (fraudulent concealment would not toll the statute).

83. Sharon Steel Corp. v. Workers Compensation Appeal Bd., 670 A.2d 1194, 1200 (Pa. Commw. 1996) (equitable estoppel may toll operation of workmen's compensation statute of repose); FNB Mortg. Corp. v. Pac. Gen. Grp., 76 Cal. App. 4th 1116 (3d Dist. 1999) (construction

QUESTIONS

1. Subcontractor submits shop drawings for a pre-engineered metal building to contractor who reviews them and submits them to owner. Owner transmits the shop drawings to designer who "reviews them for general compliance with the contract documents" and then requests changes to one of the exterior column lines. Revised shop drawings are submitted, approved by the designer, and used to fabricate the building components. While the building is being erected, it is determined that the foundation slab cannot support the weight of certain columns, which were not load-bearing in the original shop drawings but are shown as load-bearing in the revised shop drawings. Who should bear responsibility for the cost of improving the foundation to support the columns?

2. Design professionals typically claim that imposing liability on them for defective construction effectively makes the design professional the guarantor of the contractor's work. Owners respond by saying that the design professional has the duty to perform with an ordinary and reasonable degree of skill and care, which includes a duty to observe and report deviations from the drawings and specifications that should have been obvious to a skilled construction industry professional. Otherwise, the owners contend, the design professional would not be accountable to anyone for failing to make a reasonably adequate inspection so long as it made inspections, no matter how cursory. Which position is more persuasive? Does your answer change if the defective construction is not readily observable by the design professional?

3. Scholars, practitioners, and lawmakers alike debate the fundamental fairness of a rule that bars meritorious claims even before they are discovered. What policy arguments support the imposition of a statute of repose as applied to construction professionals? Why should a person injured in the collapse of a garage be barred from recovering from the party responsible for the negligent design or construction simply because more than ten years have passed since substantial completion?

---

statute of repose not tolled by promises of, or attempts to repair); Monson v. Paramount Homes, Inc., 515 S.E.2d 445 (N.C. App. 1999) (repairs made by a subcontractor did not toll substantive rights created by statutes of repose; to hold otherwise would subject a defendant to potential open-ended liability for an indefinite period of time, defeating the very purpose for which the statute was enacted).

4. Some states hold that, unlike statutes of limitations, statutes of repose cannot be modified by contract or waived by the parties.[84] But other states permit waiver.[85] Finally, a wide disparity in state law exists on the issue of whether a statute of repose can be equitably tolled by fraud, intentional concealment, or other actions of the putative defendant.[86] Does allowing waiver and equitable tolling defeat the very purpose for which the statute of repose was enacted?

---

84. Stone & Webster Eng'g Corp. v. Duquesne Light Co., 79 F. Supp. 2d 1, 8–9 (D. Mass. 2000) (making *Erie* guess regarding Pennsylvania law); Trax-Fax, Inc. v. Hobba, 627 S.E.2d 90, 95–96 (Ga. Ct. App. 2006) (collecting cases); Cheswold Volunteer Fire Co. v. Lambertson Constr. Co., 489 A.2d 413, 420–21 (Del. 1984) (collecting cases).

85. ESI Montgomery Cnty., Inc. v. Montenay Int'l Corp., 899 F. Supp. 1061, 1066 (S.D.N.Y. 1995) (upholding an express waiver of period of repose in a federal securities action); First Interstate Bank of Denver v. Central Bank & Trust Co., 937 P.2d 855, 860 (Colo. Ct. App. 1997) (upholding written agreement tolling statute of repose pending a final adjudication on federal claims); One North McDowell Assoc. v. McDowell Dev. Co., 389 S.E.2d 834, 836 (N.C. Ct. App. 1990) (North Carolina construction statute of repose is subject to an express waiver by written agreement).

86. Northern Montana Hosp. v. Knight, 811 P.2d 1276 (Mont. 1991) Pfeifer v. City of Bellingham, 772 P.2d 1018 (Wash. 1989) (proof of active concealment of dangerous condition could toll statute of repose); Sharon Steel Corp. v. Workers Comp. Appeal Bd., 670 A.2d 1194, 1200 (Pa. Commw. Ct. 1996) (equitable estoppel may toll operation of workers' compensation statute of repose); Curry v. Thornsberry, 98 S.W.3d 477, 482 (Ark. Ct. App. 2003), *aff'd*, 128 S.W.3d 438 (Ark. 2003) (rejecting tolling argument based on fraudulent concealment); FNB Mortg. Corp. v. Pac. Gen. Grp., 76 Cal. App. 4th 1116 (3d Dist. 1999) (construction statute of repose not tolled by promises of, or attempts to repair); Monson v. Paramount Homes, Inc., 515 S.E.2d 445 (N.C. Ct. App. 1999) (same).

CHAPTER

21

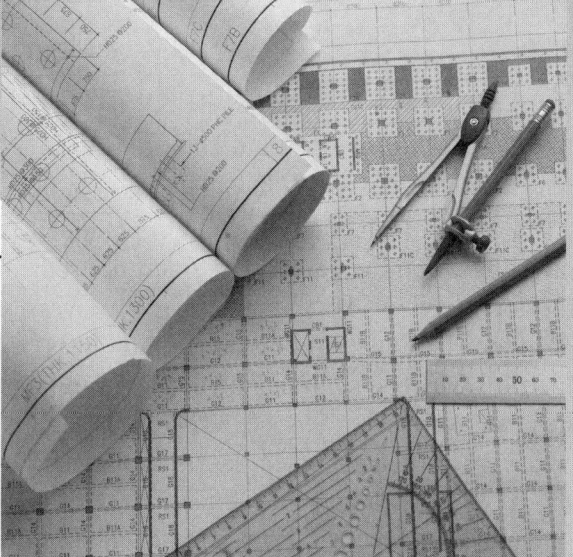

The Economic Loss Rule in Construction Law

A. HOLT GWYN AND LUKE J. FARLEY, SR.

21.01 INTRODUCTION

This chapter addresses the Economic Loss Rule, a common law doctrine that limits the legal theories on which a plaintiff may rely and thus affects the type of damages a plaintiff can recover in tort. More precisely, the Economic Loss Rule is the name given to several related legal limitations on the claims available and the associated relief that parties in commercial and contractual relationships may recover for tort claims such as negligence and strict liability. This chapter focuses on the way different jurisdictions have both formulated and applied the rule in the context of construction disputes. To begin to understand the rule, though, one must first understand its origins and purpose based on the differences between contract law and tort law.

At common law, there were bright-line distinctions between civil actions brought in contract and those brought in tort. Elements of proof were different, as were recoverable damages. Proof of a tort was generally more burdensome—requiring proof of a duty of care, foreseeability, "but for" and proximate causation, rather than simply a contract and a breach. At common law, contracting parties were free to assign various risks between them, and such assignments were generally upheld. If one commercial party was damaged by a contractual partner's act, the remedy was ex contractu. There was no tort recovery. This separateness survives today in article 2 of the Uniform Commercial Code.[1] But in many other areas of commerce, the distinctions and barriers between contract and tort law can be as blurred as the colored glass in a kaleidoscope.

A construction project is a monumental mix of goods and services combined to create a new and functioning edifice. Whether a building, a water-retaining structure, or a system to generate or distribute power, today's projects are complex, requiring coordination among numerous participants who have different expertise. Specialization in the furnishing of construction goods and services permeates the construction industry. Some buildings are still built of bricks and mortar, but increasingly structures consist of sophisticated components installed by specialists using delivery systems with ever more complex relationships and risk allocations. Amenities found in today's starter houses make them complex structures in comparison to the multistory office buildings of the 1930s.

As construction projects become more complex, they cost more. Owners, like all consumers, don't want to pay more.[2] This puts pressure on construction design, especially the design of components. Cost concerns now filter into the design of every construction material. And, because speed of installation is a function of overall cost, price also affects components' means and methods of application. Designers of construction components continually look for ways to make products that cost less, are quicker and easier to install, provide a more desirable appearance, and perform better than last year's models. A quantifiable improvement in any of these characteristics will increase market share. But as construction component design is revisited and revised in the name of cost, performance characteristics are often affected. When the performance criteria of components are materially altered, the performance of major building systems may be compromised. The redundancies of conservative design that were de rigueur for buildings in decades past too often play second fiddle to the latest bells and whistles of convenience.

---

1. For buyers and sellers of goods, Article 2 of the Uniform Commercial Code codifies the rules for contract formation, acceptance, rejection, cover, disclaimers, damages, and consequential and incidental damage waivers.

2. Many off-the-shelf consumer goods decrease in price as availability increases. Consumers of many goods—especially newer technology goods—have become accustomed to getting more for the same price as last year, or even more for a lesser price.

Then, too, the increasing complexity of buildings and components has challenged the architect's role. Architects formerly were the arbiters of component design and selection. This has changed. Product design, and more recently system design, has devolved to component manufacturers. No longer is the architect the project's most knowledgeable leader. As observed by a leading Columbia University professor, by the end of the 1970s, architects came to know less and less about more and more until some were said "to know nothing about everything."[3]

The construction design landscape is evolving, and the designers in the manufacturing sector are on the leading edge. Selection and coordination of building components, long the province of design professionals, are in today's world being usurped by contractors and component manufacturers. Through "value engineering" or outright design delegation,[4] architects defer to component designers. Indeed, contractor-led design-build arrangements often relegate the architect to backroom subcontractor status. The ability to select the component is accompanied by the responsibility to coordinate the chosen products with the building's structure and complementing systems. In this area, design professionals hand off much of their former role, if not all of their responsibility.[5]

Specialization in the construction industry has also transformed the contract process and contractual relationships. Virtually all projects involve dozens of contracts. Specialized equipment must be furnished and installed by ever-more specialized subcontractors and suppliers. The traditional Design-Bid-Build project delivery method is but one of many available contractual schemes.

---

3. MARIO SALVADORE, WHY BUILDINGS STAND UP: THE STRENGTH OF ARCHITECTURE (1980). No longer is the architect capable of the expertise required by the court in Hubert v. Aitken, 2 N.Y.S. 711 (C.P. 1888), aff'd, 25 N.E. 954 (N.Y. 1890) ("he is an expert in carpentry, cements, mortar, in the strength of materials . . . new conveniences . . .").

4. The American Institute of Architects' standard general conditions of the contract between owner and contractor now explicitly allow the delegation of the architect's design responsibility to the contractor and its subcontractors. See American Institute of Architects, AIA A201–2007, General Conditions of the Contract for Construction, § 3.12.10 (2007).

5. Design professionals "of record" retain liability, especially to their clients, for adequate and code-compliant design, whether the design professional performs the work or delegates it to others. JUSTIN SWEET, LEGAL ASPECTS OF ARCHITECTURE, ENGINEERING AND THE CONSTRUCTION PROCESS § 15.10(B) (4th ed. 1989). See also Johnson v. Salem Title Co., 425 P.2d 519 (Or. 1967) (structural engineering requirements were non-delegable, even to a professional engineer). The result is different if the design professional never had the responsibility as part of its scope of services. See Aleutian Constructors v. United States, 24 Cl. Ct. 372 (1991) (specifications required contractor to design and build roof); Mudgett v. Marshall, 574 A.2d 867 (Me. 1990) (error of structural engineer hired by design-build contractor not imputed to owner's design professional not hired to design building).

Owners can choose among construction managers, multi-prime contractors, design-builders, joint ventures, and so on—the ability to customize the construction process grows every year.[6] But there is one industry constant: there are more and more entities providing specialized goods and services. Subcontractors, suppliers, and subconsultants abound, in ever-deepening Dante-esque circles.

The monumental complexity of a construction project has strained the law of contracts. When something goes wrong on a construction site, or when the completed edifice doesn't deliver, there are usually a number of entities with a hand in the cause. Proper installation is the first place to check, but it is often not the entire story. Products that perform well in one setting may, for instance, lack the robustness to weather ambient conditions in another. As product diversification expands, the importance of selecting and coordinating construction components has increased. It is now as significant to select and coordinate as it is to install properly. When problems occur, they can be the fault of the design professional, the installer, the manufacturer, the maintenance team, or all of the above. Getting to the bottom of a construction problem often requires a detailed investigation, and a good deal of finger pointing regrettably ensues. Major responsibility may lie far down, or even outside, the contractual chain.

Contract law has adapted in several areas to market conditions. Warranties from manufacturers of certain goods (typically finished goods, specially designed equipment, and appliances) allow end users and other affected parties legal redress by direct access to the manufacturer—leapfrogging over broken links in the contractual chain.[7] There is also a federal statutory remedy for defective consumer household goods.[8] And some states have promulgated statutory warranties for residential construction that ignore which party contracts

---

6. The American Institute of Architects' Standard Form of Agreement between Owner and Architect, AIA Document B101–2007 (2007) [hereinafter AIA Document B101–2007], provides owners a menu of architectural services from which to choose.

7. *See, e.g.*, Sirrah Enterprises, LLC v. Wunderlich, 399 P.3d 89, 94, 242 Ariz. 542, 547 (Ariz. 2017).

8. The Magnuson-Moss Act, 15 U.S.C.A. § 2301 *et seq.* (2002), provides consumers with statutory remedies for breach of a manufacturer's or vendor's written or implied warranty of a consumer product. The act also provides certain minimum requirements for written warranties. Upon establishing that the warranty was breached, the consumer may elect the remedy of refund, repair, or replacement, and may recover attorney's fees if it prevails. The act applies to personal, family, or household products, but may include "building materials" such as paneling, siding, or storm windows, when purchased in connection with remodeling a home. In one of the leading cases, it was applied to roofing materials. Muchisky v. Frederic Roofing Co., 838 S.W.2d 74 (Mo. Ct. App. 1992) (affirming verdict, and award of attorney's fees, in favor of homeowner on a re-roofing project).

with whom, giving a remedy to end users that an ordinary contract law would not provide.[9] Outside of this sort of intervention, though, common law contract law is still the default remedy for construction disputes.

Under the common law, privity of contract is required to bring a contract action. In the historical construction setting, this worked fairly well. Until the mid-20th century, there would normally be one major construction contract—between owner and master builder, who was often responsible for the design as well as the construction. The contractor would directly employ different types of skilled labor for a job (carpenters, masons, ironworkers, concrete finishers, etc.). Today's builder is different—it separately subcontracts with subcontractors and suppliers, who often then sub-subcontract with other specialty trades. The design professionals are most often hired directly by the owner, under separate contracts. When problems develop, claims may be asserted among multiple business entities, with multiple contractual and subcontractual arrangements. For many of today's construction issues, common law contract causes of action can be cumbersome in the extreme. If a problem takes several years to manifest itself, if contractual responsibilities for the work are not the same up and down the chain of specialization, or if there are gaps in the scope of and responsibilities for the work, damages may occur for which there is no common law contract remedy.[10] This is a fertile field for the seeds of tort law to take root.

In many areas of commerce, tort law has insinuated itself, together with its legally imposed responsibilities and remedies. Beginning with Judge Cardozo's opinion in *MacPherson v. Buick Motor Co.*,[11] courts have imposed the duty to act reasonably as an objective standard of conduct.[12] This duty exists independent of any agreement between parties, and applies to conduct both inside and outside a contractual relationship.[13] Tort law imposes upon all members of society certain minimum standards of behavior—including the obligation to take reasonable steps to protect others from being injured or having their possessions destroyed or damaged. If these standards are violated, tort law compensates without serious regard to risk allocation,[14] so long as the injury is foreseeable and proximately caused by the defendant's or defendants' wrong.

---

9. *See, e.g.*, Fla. Stat. § 712.203 *et seq.* (1992).
10. The Latin phrase is *injuria absque damno, damnum absque injuria*, or *damnum sine injuria*.
11. 111 N.E. 1050 (N.Y. 1916).
12. *Cf.* Beacon Residential Cmty. Assn. v. Skidmore, Owings & Merrill LLP, 59 Cal. 4th 568, 574, 327 P.3d 850, 854 (2014) (noting "the significance of privity [as the sole basis for liability] has greatly eroded over the past century") (citing MacPherson v. Buick Motor Co., 217 N.Y. 382, 111 N.E. 1050 (1916)).
13. *See* Morse/Diesel, Inc. v. Trinity Indus., Inc., 655 F. Supp. 346, 355 (S.D.N.Y. 1987).
14. Joint tortfeasors are subject to joint and several liability.

Tort law is more about compensation and less about risk allocation. This emphasis is reflected in the liberal rules of tort damages. A negligence victim is entitled to recover for both direct and consequential losses proximately caused by a tortfeasor's breach of duty. In contrast, the general rule of contract damages is that consequential damages are not recoverable unless they were within the contemplation of the parties at the time of contracting and became a basis for the parties' bargain.[15]

Particularly invasive into the construction setting have been the torts of negligent construction and negligent misrepresentation.[16] The separate tort of negligent misrepresentation (normally also alleging purely economic damages) may be asserted against owners, design professionals, specialty contractors, and suppliers—any project participant who disseminates information.[17] Although these economic torts have been bemoaned by a number of commentators,[18] they have not been beset upon the construction industry alone. Many states have adopted the Restatement (Second) of Torts, allowing negligence-based causes of action for economic damages in business transactions involving appraisers,[19] building inspectors,[20] construction managers,[21] as well as lawyers,[22] and accountants,[23] despite lack of privity.

But there are certain limitations on tort damages, especially claims for purely economic damages.[24] In the construction industry, this chiefly manifests

---

15. *See* Hadley v. Baxendale, 156 ENG. REP. 145 (Ex. 1854).
16. *Cf. Beacon Residential Cmty. Assn.*, 59 Cal. 4th 568, 574, 327 P.3d 850, 854 (2014) ("declining significance of privity has found its way into construction law").
17. RESTATEMENT (SECOND) OF TORTS § 552 (1977), entitled "Information Negligently Supplied for the Guidance of Others."
18. *See, e.g.*, JUSTIN SWEET, SWEET ON CONSTRUCTION LAW §§ 4.10, 11.13 (ABA 1997); Steven G.M. Stein, Paul Cottrell & Mark Friedlander, *A Blueprint for the Duties and Liabilities of Design Professionals after Moorman*, 60 CHI.-KENT L. REV. 163 (1984).
19. Private Mortgage Inv. Servs., Inc. v. Hotel & Club Assocs., Inc., 296 F.3d 308 (4th Cir. 2002).
20. Thompson v. Waters, 526 S.E.2d 650 (N.C. 2000).
21. EH Constr. LLC v. Delor Design Grp., Inc., No. 1998-CA-001476-NR, 2000 WL 339939 (Ky. Ct. App. Mar. 31, 2000).
22. *See* Rozny v. Marnul, 250 N.E.2d 656 (Ill. 1969); Orshoski v. Krieger, No. OT-01-009, 2001 WL 1388037 (Ohio Ct. App. Nov. 9, 2001), *appeal denied*, 763 N.E.2d 1185 (Ohio 2002) ("The requirement of privity in a legal malpractice action [for negligent misrepresentation] should be put to a well-deserved burial."); Bradford Sec. Processing Services, Inc. v. Plaza Bank & Trust, 653 P.2d 188 (Okla. 1982). *But see* Bovee v. Gravel, No. 2001-347, 2002 WL 1940968 (Vt. Aug. 13, 2002).
23. United States v. Natelli, 527 F.2d 311 (2d Cir. 1975), *cert. denied*, 425 U.S. 934 (1976); Fisher v. Katz, 266 F. Supp. 180 (S.D.N.Y. 1976); Sharp v. Coopers & Lybrand, 83 F.R.D. 343 (E.D. Pa. 1974). *But see* Semida v. Rice, 863 F.2d 1156, 1160 (4th Cir. 1988); Walpert, Smullian & Blumenthal, P.A. v. Katz, 762 A.2d 582 (Md. 2000).
24. Economic damages, in this instance, as opposed to bodily injury or damage to separate property.

itself in the judge-made Economic Loss Rule, prohibiting economic damages, direct or consequential, for tort claims when there is no concurrent physical injury or property damage.[25] In a way, the Economic Loss Rule is a judicial response to what some commentators have characterized as an unfair assault on privity and a cancer-like invasion by torts into the contractual setting.[26] But the economic loss rule has hardly been applied uniformly.[27] Each year, new opinions put a new spin on the rule, making its application and exceptions a matter of locality.

21.02 ECONOMIC LOSS RULE

The Economic Loss Rule first appeared within the context of manufactured products liability.[28] Stated simply, in an action alleging negligence[29] or strict liability,[30] a plaintiff cannot recover its purely economic damages caused by a

---

25. LAN/STV v. Martin K. Eby Constr. Co., Inc., 435 S.W.3d 234, 235 (Tex. 2014) ("In actions for unintentional torts, the common law has long restricted recovery of purely economic damages unaccompanied by injury to the plaintiff or his property.").

26. See, e.g., Murray H. Wright & Edward E. Nicholas, *The Collision of Tort and Contract in the Construction Industry*, 21:3 U. RICH. L. REV. 457 (1987); see also Balfour Beatty Infrastructure, Inc. v. Rummel Klepper & Kahl, LLP, 451 Md. 600, 609–10, 155 A.3d 445, 450 (2017) (Economic Loss Rule "is a principle courts have used to limit the expansion of tort liability absent privity"); Tiara Condo. Ass'n, Inc. v. Marsh & McLennan Companies, Inc., 110 So. 3d 399, 401 (Fla. 2013) (describing the origin of the Economic Loss Rule as a response to "attempts to apply tort remedies to traditional contract law damages"). Several courts and commentators have described the Economic Loss Rule as a "boundary" between tort and contract that preserves the distinctions between these areas of the law. See LAN/STV v. Martin K. Eby Constr. Co., Inc., 435 S.W.3d 234, 240 (Tex. 2014); *Tiara Condo. Ass'n, Inc.* 110 So. 3d at 401; Vincent R. Johnson, *The Boundary-Line Function of the Econ. Loss Rule*, 66 WASH. & LEE L. REV. 523 (2009).

27. Balfour Beatty Infrastructure, Inc. v. Rummel Klepper & Kahl, LLP, 451 Md. 600, 621, 155 A.3d 445, 457–58 (2017) ("Jurisdictions are split over whether to apply the economic loss doctrine in the construction context.") (citing A. Holt Gwyn, *Tort Damages*, in CONSTRUCTION DAMAGES AND REMEDIES 207, 212 (W. Alexander Mosley, ed., 2d ed. 2013).

28. Economic losses in negligence actions were first restricted by the holding in Seely v. White Motor Co., 403 P.2d 145 (Cal. 1965). *See also* East River S.S. Corp. v. Transamerica Delaval, Inc., 476 U.S. 858 (1986). In each of these cases, the product (a truck and a ship's turbines) injured itself, causing repair costs and lost profits, but no bodily injury or physical damage to other property or product.

29. Because many more negligence situations tend to occur in the construction industry—a simple negligence claim may exist against a trade contractor or builder not in privity, when a strict liability (or negligence per se) claim does not—this chapter will focus primarily upon the application of the Economic Loss Rule in negligence-based actions.

30. The Economic Loss Rule is generally also applied in actions alleging strict liability. *See Seely*, 403 P.2d at 145; Stearman v. Centex Homes, 78 Cal. App. 4th 611 (2000) (citing cases); Fieldstone Co. v. Briggs Plumbing Products, Inc., 54 Cal. App. 4th 357, 363–67 (1997) (prematurely rusted sinks damaged only themselves, strict liability claim dismissed), superseded by

defective product that injures only itself. Put another way, the Economic Loss Rule sets out the circumstances under which recovery in tort is prohibited if the only damages the plaintiff has suffered are economic damages.[31] Economic damages represent "inadequate value, costs of repair and replacement of the defective product or consequent loss of profits without any claim of personal injury or damage to other property."[32] Economic loss also includes the "diminution in value of the product because it is inferior in quality and [because it] does not work for the general purpose for which it was manufactured and sold."[33]

The traditional inquiry concerns the type of damage caused by the defective product: Was there injury to a person or other property, or was the damage only to the product? In *Seely v. White Motor Co.*,[34] a consumer's action against a truck manufacturer, the only losses were the cost of repairing the truck and missing income due to the truck's unserviceable state. These damages were not allowed under negligence or strict liability counts, and, because they represented the plaintiff's only damages, the negligence and strict liability causes of action were dismissed.[35] Viewed in this manner, the Economic Loss

---

statute on other grounds, Right to Repair Act, CAL. CIV. CODE § 895 *et seq.*, as recognized in Greystone Homes, Inc. v. Midtec, Inc., 168 Cal. App. 4th 1194, 86 Cal. Rptr. 3d 196 (2008). Strict liability actions under § 402 of the RESTATEMENT OF TORTS generally involve manufactured products. Those supplying services are generally not strictly liable. *See* Murphy v. E.R. Squibb & Sons, Inc., 710 P.2d 247 (Cal. 1985) (strict products liability law does not apply to services); RESTATEMENT (THIRD) OF TORTS: PRODUCTS LIABILITY § 19, subd. (b) ("services, even when provided commercially, are not products" and are governed by the law of negligence).

31. Tiara Condo. Assn, Inc. v. Marsh & McLennan Companies, Inc., 110 So.3d 399, 401 (Fla. 2013); Flagstaff Affordable Hous. Ltd. P'ship v. Design All., Inc., 223 Ariz. 320, 321, 223 P.3d 664, 665 (2010) ("The 'economic loss doctrine' bars plaintiffs, in certain circumstances, from recovering economic damages in tort.").

32. Note, *Economic Loss in Products Liability Jurisprudence*, 66 COLUM. L. REV. 917, 918 (1966) (emphasis added).

33. Comment, *Manufacturers' Liability to Remote Purchasers for "Economic Loss" Damages—Tort or Contract?*, 114 U. PA. L. REV. 539, 541 (1966); *see also* McConnell v. Servinsky Eng'g, PLLC, 22 F. Supp. 3d 610, 614 (W.D. Va. 2014) (describing economic losses as failure to meet a "bargained-for level of quality") *Tiara Condo. Ass'n*, 110 So. 3d 399, 401 (describing economic losses as "disappointed economic expectations" and "the diminution in value of the product because of its inferior quality"); *Flagstaff Affordable Hous.*, 223 Ariz. 320, 323, 223 P.3d 664, 667 (economic loss includes consequential damages such as lost profits).

34. 403 P.2d 145 (Cal. 1965).

35. Importantly, the Supreme Court of California (Traynor, C.J.) upheld the plaintiff's claims for breach of express warranty, sustaining the jury award to the plaintiff of the purchase price of the truck and plaintiff's lost profits. Seely v. White Motor Co., 63 Cal. 2d 9, 403 P.2d 145 (Cal. 1965).

Rule forms a damages restriction only—barring recovery of certain losses from an otherwise viable negligence or strict liability cause of action.[36]

A proper application of the rule occurs when there are *only* economic damages. If a plaintiff has sustained bodily injury[37] or physical harm to "other property," then in both cases it may recover any economic losses, together with those physical damages.[38] All of the plaintiff's damages, of course, must be foreseeable and proximately caused by the defendant's conduct.

The legal and policy considerations that underpin the rule in the products liability context rest upon a manufacturer's responsibility for its goods. Defects that cause physical harm are deemed to be properly chargeable to the manufacturer. Those that affect the product's "level of performance" are not, unless the manufacturer agrees to be so charged (e.g., by giving a warranty).[39] These considerations are said to be based in the different common law concepts dividing tort and contract law. To recover in tort, there must be some showing of harm above and beyond disappointed expectations.[40] When courts attempt to apply the rule outside the products liability context, specifically to damages arising out of the construction of structures by multiple contracting parties, the rule becomes much more difficult to apply, and the scope of the rule broadens to the point it is really multiple rules.

21.03 THE SCOPE AND PURPOSE OF THE ECONOMIC LOSS RULE

The Economic Loss Rule precludes a party's recovery in negligence or strict liability for purely economic damages.[41] The principle of the Economic Loss

---

36. *See* Casey v. Overhead Door Corp., 74 Cal. App. 4th 112, 123 (1999) (plaintiffs were not prejudiced by trial court ruling in limine excluding economic damages—plaintiffs could have introduced other evidence to support negligence count, if plaintiffs had any such evidence).

37. Marrick Homes LLC v. Rutkowski, 232 Md. App. 689, 702, 161 A.3d 53, 61 (2017) (Economic Loss Rule inapplicable where plaintiff suffered "significant physical injury including broken bones and traumatic brain injury").

38. *See* Held v. Mitsubishi Aircraft Int'l, Inc., 672 F. Supp. 369, 376–77 (D. Minn. 1987) (applying Texas law). *But see* 7 World Trade Co. v. Westinghouse Elec. Corp., 682 N.Y.S.2d 385, 387 (1998), fact that two injured workers had negligence claims against product manufacturer does not inure to the project owner's benefit when owner's only losses are replacement of defective product and consequential damages thereto.

39. *Seely*, 403 P.2d at 195.

40. *Id. See* East River S.S. Corp., 476 U.S. at 858, 871; Nat'l Union Fire Ins. Co. v. Pratt & Whitney, 815 P.2d 601, 604 (Nev. 1991). *See also* 1 A.R. FRUMER & M. I. FRIEDMAN, PRODUCTS LIABILITY§ 3.01(2)(f) (1991).

41. *See* Christopher Scott D'Angelo, *The Economic Loss Doctrine: Saving Contract Warranty from Drowning in a Sea of Tort*, 26 U. TOL. REV. 591, 609 (1995) (for a survey of jurisdictions that

Rule is easiest to apply in product liability cases, where the rule originated.[42] In many jurisdictions, the Economic Loss Rule has been extended to claims against all construction service providers, including design professionals, contractors, subcontractors, and suppliers, with or without privity, and whether the claims allege pure negligence, professional negligence, or negligent misrepresentation. A number of courts have held that consumer homeowners are barred from asserting negligence actions against building component manufacturers to recover economic damages—either to repair defective construction or for the diminution in value of their home—unless there is property damage to some other part of the home.[43] A few courts have held that once incorporated into the structure, the entire structure itself becomes the "product."[44]

The willingness of courts and legislatures to restrict recoverable damages is a somewhat recent phenomenon. To the extent such statutes and decisions spring from a desire to correct injustice, it may be that the tenor of a proposed rule or statute is determined by the issue's location on the arc created by the pendulum of public opinion. If public opinion frowns on owners' one-sided, non-negotiated contracts, a legislature may void or a court might limit an onerous clause as against public policy, thereby favoring the designer or

---

have adopted the economic loss rule). *See also* Pulte Home Corp. v. Osmose Wood Preserving, Inc., 60 F.3d 734 (11th Cir. 1995) (builder's claim for defective fire retardant chemical as applied to plywood sheathing barred by rule); Morris v. Osmose Wood Preserving, Inc., 667 A.2d 624 (Md. 1995) (same).

42. Commentators mostly agree that today's Economic Loss Rule was first articulated in Seely v. White Motor Co., 63 Cal. 2d 9, 403 P.2d 145 (Cal. 1965) (*en banc*), which involved the sale, repair, and loss of income from a defective truck. There the court stated: "The distinction that the law has drawn between tort recovery for physical injuries and warranty recovery for economic loss is not arbitrary and does not rest on the 'luck' of one plaintiff in having an accident causing physical injury. The distinction rests, rather, on an understanding of the nature of the responsibility a manufacturer must undertake in distributing his products." *Seely*, 403 P.2d at 151; *see also Tiara Condo. Ass'n*, 110 So. 3d 399, 401 (noting the Economic Loss Rule "appeared initially in both state and federal courts in products liability type cases").

43. While this has long been the position taken by general liability insurers—no property damage to other property, no coverage—recent opinions from the Supreme Courts of California, Nevada, and Alabama prohibit any economic loss claim against construction component suppliers other than a direct contract or warranty claim. These opinions foretell the upcoming battle as to the meaning of property "other than the product itself." *See* Aas v. Superior Court, 12 P.3d 1125 (Cal. 2000) (superseded by the California legislature a year later); Calloway v. City of Reno, 993 P. 2d 1259 (Nev. 2000) (superseded by the Nevada Legislature two years later); Keck v. Dryvit Sys., Inc., 830 So. 2d 1 (Ala. 2002).

44. *See* Wilson v. Dryvit Sys., Inc., 206 F. Supp. 2d 749 (E.D.N.C. 2002); *but see* Jimenez v. Superior Court, 58 P.3d 450 (Cal. 2002), (defective windows considered a distinct product even after installation due to the ease with which they could be removed from one house and installed in another).

contractors. If the body politic believes that damages recovered by "trial lawyers" have run amok,[45] or if a court concludes that asserted losses are not the foreseeable result of a participant's conduct, damages can be limited, legislatively or judicially.

The nuances of the Economic Loss Rule make it a doctrine that is in some jurisdictions riddled with exceptions, and in others honored in the breach.[46] Two decades ago, one court lamented that the concept is "stated with ease, but applied with great difficulty."[47] The same may be said today. Legal commentators and jurists cannot agree upon the reasons courts distinguish between proper and improper applications of the rule.[48] At the end of the 20th century, an astute Florida jurist observed[49] that, in his jurisdiction, there were three distinct, but often overlapping, Economic Loss Rules:

> First, there is the products liability economic loss rule: If the defendant's product physically damages only itself, causing additional economic loss, no recovery is permitted in "tort."

---

45. *See, e.g.,* the present argument presented to state legislatures and Congress in support of personal injury damage caps for pain and suffering—arguments made, cynical commentators note, by insurance companies and special interest groups.

46. *See, e.g.,* Mark C. & Andrea B. Friedlander, *Malpractice and the Moorman Doctrine's "Exception of the Month,"* 86 Ill. B. J. 600 (Nov. 1998); *see also Tiara Condo. Ass'n,* 110 So. 3d 399, 401 (describing the application and parameters of the Economic Loss Rule as "somewhat ill-defined").

47. Sandarac Assoc. v. W.R. Frizzell Architects, 609 So. 2d 1349, 1352 (Fla. Dist. Ct. App. 1992), *overruled by* Moransais v. Heathman, 744 So. 2d 973 (Fla. 1999).

48. Compare the discussion and analyses of the rule within three articles within The Construction Lawyer: (1) Luther P. House, Jr., & Hubert J. Bell, Jr., *The Economic Loss Rule: A Fair Balancing of Interests,* 11:2 The Constr. Law. 1 (1991) (rule is correctly applied in the construction industry based upon the presence or lack of a duty of those sought to be held liable); (2) G. Anthony Smith, *The Continuing Decline of the "Economic Loss Rule" in Construction Litigation,* 10:4 The Constr. Law. 1 (1990) (rule should not be applied in construction setting because of foreseeability of damage to limited class of users); (3) Steven B. Lesser, *Economic Loss Doctrine and Its Impact upon Construction Claims,* 14:3 The Constr. Law. 21–26 (1994) (injured parties too often have no way to affect the hiring or contractual responsibility of, and have no contractual remedy against, project participants. To deny relief to those so harmed violates the protection and the tenets of *Marbury v. Madison*). *Compare also* the analyses of the rule by the court in Casa Clara Condo. Ass'n, Inc. v. Charley Toppino & Sons, Inc., 620 So. 2d 1244 (Fla. 1993) (high salt concrete caused rebar to rust and balconies to crumble—mere economic damage to "product") *with* that by the court in Borough of Lansdowne, Pa. v. Sevenson Envt. Serv., Inc., 2000 WL 1886578 (E.D. Pa. Dec. 12, 2000) (Economic Loss Rule blocks negligence action against construction professional only when parties are in privity).

49. Woodson v. Martin, 663 So. 2d 1327, 1331 (Fla. 2d Dist. Ct. App. 1995) (Attenbernd, Jr. dissenting) *rev'd,* 685 So.2d 1240 (Fla. 1996).

Second, there is the contract economic loss rule: If the parties have entered into a contract, the obligations of the contract cannot be relied upon to establish a cause of action in tort for the recovery of purely economic damages. . . . There must be a separate, "independent tort."

Finally, there is the negligence economic loss rule. Common law negligence generally has not been expanded to protect economic interests in the absence of personal injury or property damage.

Understood this way, the Economic Loss Rule, in reality, is not a single rule but an umbrella term for a collection of closely related doctrines that may be formulated in different ways depending on the jurisdiction.[50] Consequently, the impact of the economic loss limitation is far-ranging. Applied strictly in the construction arena, the rule can eliminate many claims that otherwise might be categorized as property damage.[51] The Economic Loss Rule is seen by some courts as a way to preserve contracting parties' freedom to allocate risks as they choose, and to protect the limited liability bargained for or otherwise afforded to corporations and other business organizations. Because of the concept's draconian effect, however, many courts have struggled with it as applied to realty improved by the construction process.[52] A number of jurisdictions do not honor the economic loss principle in special situations involving defective construction products and services that create realty improvements, but these courts have been less than uniform in their approach. How a jurisdiction will formulate its own version of the rule may depend on how the appellate judiciary of that jurisdiction approaches the "collision" at the intersection of tort and contract law. Courts that seek to "maintain a distinction between contract and tort principles" are likely to agree with the court that held: "Economic losses from a defective building are just as *offensive* to tort law as damages sought for economic losses stemming from a defective product."[53] These jurisdictions prohibit a plaintiff from recovering economic damages—which are

---

50. *See* Vincent R. Johnson, *The Boundary-Line Function of the Econ. Loss Rule*, 66 WASH. & LEE L. REV. 523, 525–26 (2009) (noting the "many variations of the rule").

51. *See* Sidney R. Barrett, *Recovery of Economic Loss in Tort for Construction Defects: A Critical Analysis*, 40 S.C.L. REV. 891 (1989). *See also* Janis K. Cheezem, *Economic Loss in the Construction Setting: Toward an Appropriate Definition of "Other Property,"* 12:2 THE CONSTR. LAW. 21, 22 (1992).

52. *See, e.g.*, discussion between majority and dissenting opinions in Aas v. Superior Court, 24 Cal. 4th 627 (2000).

53. *Calloway*, 993 P.2d at 1259, 1265–66 (Nev. 2000) (emphasis added). *See also East River S.S. Corp.*, 476 U.S. at 858, 866 (setting forth the often-quoted reason for the rule—to protect contract law from "drown[ing] in a sea of tort").

inherently contractual in nature—in actions that sound in tort on the basis that contract law should govern contract-type damages.[54]

In contrast, if the judiciary acknowledges that a "unique relationship" exists among contractors, subcontractors, and design professionals that creates "an interdependence" among project participants, then the court may be more inclined to hold noncontracting parties accountable for economic losses that foreseeably arise from the failure of a project participant to discharge its contractual duties in a non-negligent manner.[55] If the appellate opinion goes on to emphasize that the Economic Loss Rule "may have some genuine, but limited, value in our damages law, . . ." and that "if the doctrine were generally applied to bar all tort claims for economic losses without accompanying personal injury or property damage, the rule would *wreak havoc on the common law of torts*"[56] (emphasis added), one can deduce at least where the court will begin its analysis.

While the Economic Loss Rule is fundamentally about classifying the nature of a loss or the resulting damages, it is helpful to group cases according to whether the litigants were in privity of contract or not. Even grouped this way, decisions from one jurisdiction to the next vary, but sometimes because of different policy considerations. For example, in most construction cases plaintiffs assert claims against the corporate business entities that were the contracting parties on the project (e.g., a general contractor or a subcontractor). In some cases, however, plaintiffs have chosen to also pursue claims against the individual, natural persons who owned or controlled the business entities and actually performed the defective work. Some courts have applied the Economic Loss Rule to bar these types of claims. In these cases the litigants were not, strictly speaking, in privity of contract. For instance, in *Beaufort Builders, Inc.*

---

54. *See* State Ready Mix, Inc. v. Moffatt & Nichol, 232 Cal. App. 4th 1227, 1232, 181 Cal. Rptr. 3d 921, 925 (2015) ("A person may not ordinarily recover in tort for the breach of duties that merely restate contractual obligations."); McConnell v. Servinsky Eng'g, PLLC, 22 F. Supp. 3d 610, 614 (W.D. Va. 2014) ("the law of contracts provides the sole remedy" when "bargained-for level of quality" in a contract is not met); Wyman v. Ayer Properties, LLC, 469 Mass. 64, 70, 11 N.E.3d 1074, 1080 (2014) ("The rule was developed in part to prevent the progression of tort concepts from undermining contract expectations.").

55. *See* Caldwell v. Bechtel, 631 F.2d 989, 1000 (D.C. Cir. 1980); Davidson & Jones, Inc. v. New Hanover Cnty., 255 S.E.2d 580 (N.C. App. 1979); United States *ex rel.* Los Angeles Testing Lab. v. Rogers & Rogers, 161 F. Supp. 132, 135–36 (S.D. Cal. 1958).

56. Moransais v. Heathman, 744 So. 2d 973 (Fla. 1999) (professional engineer's negligent inspection failed to disclose defects which caused economic loss, but which had not caused property damage or personal injury).

v. White Plains Church Ministries, Inc.,[57] a case from 2016, the plaintiff project owner sued the general contractor—a corporation with which it had a written contract—for breach of contract. The owner also sued the president of the corporation who personally performed the defective work for negligence. The president of the corporation asserted the Economic Loss Rule as a defense. The owner responded that, under North Carolina law, where the parties were not in contractual privity, the Economic Loss Rule did not apply. Despite the lack of privity, the state court of appeals determined that the exception was inapplicable because of the close relationship between the corporation and its president and because the work performed by the president was carried out to fulfill the corporation's contract with the owner.[58] Applying the no-privity exception would result in an "impermissible 'end run' around the economic loss rule that [was] inconsistent with the logic underlying that rule."[59] A federal district court reached a similar conclusion in *McConnell v. Servinsky Engineering, PLLC*,[60] where the Economic Loss Rule barred a direct negligence claim against a principal in an engineering firm where the plaintiff had a direct, written contract with the firm. While neither *Beaufort Builders* nor *McConnell* directly address questions of corporate limited liability, the effect of the decisions in those cases was to shield the company's principals from direct liability arising from their own negligent conduct.

While a majority of states have adopted some version of the Economic Loss Rule,[61] it may not be the majority position forever. In 2013 and 2014, the highest courts in Florida, California, and Massachusetts decided several cases that may signal that perhaps the Economic Loss Rule has reached its high water mark. The most significant decision came in 2013 from the Florida Supreme Court in *Tiara Condominium Association, Inc. v. Marsh & McLennan Companies, Inc.*, a case that could signal a general trend of rolling back the rule to its original domain of products liability. In *Tiara*, the Florida Supreme Court, addressing claim of negligence by an insurance broker, pushed backed

---

57. 783 S.E.2d 35 (N.C. Ct. App. 2016).
58. 783 S.E.2d at 42.
59. Id.
60. 22 F. Supp. 3d 610 (W.D. Va. 2014).
61. *See* Wyman v. Ayer Properties, LLC, 469 Mass. 64, 69, 11 N.E.3d 1074, 1079 (2014) (describing the Economic Loss Rule as the "majority" position); *see also* Laura A. Wagner, *The Economic Loss Doctrine: A Recommendation for the Supreme Court of Pennsylvania*, 72 U. Pitt. L. Rev. 825, 832 (2011) for a general survey of the jurisdictions which have adopted the Economic Loss Rule.

against what it termed "a legacy of unprincipled expansion"[62] of the Economic Loss Rule. The court expressed its frustration that the "expansion of the rule beyond its origins [had proven] unwise and unworkable in practice."[63] Based on this frustration, the court limited the application of the Economic Loss Rule to cases involving products liability.[64] The decision is notable in that it overturned precedent stretching back to 1987.[65]

The decisions out of California and Massachusetts, while not as broad, nonetheless limited the reach of the Economic Loss Rule. In 2014, the California Supreme Court decided *Beacon Residential Community Association v. Skidmore, Owings & Merrill LLP*, where the court held, as a matter of first impression, that an architect owed a duty of care to future homeowners in the design of a residential building even if there was no privity of contract between the architect and the subsequent owners.[66] Noting that the "declining significance of privity has found its way into construction law,"[67] the court extended this duty on the basis that the harm to the owners from negligent design was reasonable foreseeable.[68] The decision in *Beacon Residential* is especially significant given that the case was decided by the same court that originated the Economic Loss Rule.[69] Another decision in 2014 from the Supreme Judicial Court of Massachusetts limited the rule based on a consideration of equitable principles. In *Wyman v. Ayer Properties, LLC*,[70] a homeowners' association sued a developer in tort for negligent construction and design of the common elements of the community. As a matter of first impression, the court determined that the HOA could sue in negligence to recover its purely economic losses despite a lack of contractual privity. The court reached its decision after considering the purpose of

---

62. 110 So. 3d at 406.
63. *Id.* at 407.
64. *Id.*; *contra* Balfour Beatty Infrastructure, Inc. v. Rummel Klepper & Kahl, LLP, 451 Md. 600, 609, 155 A.3d 445, 450 (2017) (rejecting argument that the Economic Loss Rule only applies in products liability cases); Flagstaff Affordable Hous. Ltd. P'ship v. Design All., Inc., 223 Ariz. 320, 321, 223 P.3d 664, 665 (2010) (expanding Economic Loss Rule from products liability cases to claims for professional negligence in construction defect cases).
65. *See, e.g.*, AFM Corp. v. S. Bell Tel. & Tel. Co., 515 So. 2d 180 (Fla. 1987).
66. 59 Cal. 4th 568, 327 P.3d 850 (2014).
67. 59 Cal. 4th at 574, 327 P.3d at 854.
68. 59 Cal. 4th at 583–84, 327 P.3d at 861 ("[D]efendants engaged in work on the Project with the knowledge that the finished construction would be sold as condominiums and used as residences.").
69. Seely v. White Motor Co., 403 P.2d 145 (Cal. 1965).
70. 469 Mass. at 64, 11 N.E.3d 1074 (2014).

the Economic Loss Rule. According the supreme judicial court, the Economic Loss Rule was developed to "prevent the progression of tort concepts from undermining contract expectations,"[71] a common theme in Economic Loss Rule jurisprudence. Under this theory, a commercial user is able to protect themselves by seeking "express contractual assurances concerning the product [i.e., warranties, etc.]."[72] But this rationale was inapplicable to the HOA. It did not have a contract with the developer and had no opportunity to bargain for a warranty. The court was particularly troubled by the fact that applying the Economic Loss Rule to the HOA would have left it without a remedy.[73]

Legislatures have also taken up the cause of limiting the Economic Loss Rule—at least in the area of residential construction. In 2002, the California General Assembly passed the Right to Repair Act,[74] which abrogated the Economic Loss Rule in the context of residential construction.[75] The act established a set of minimum standards for residential construction[76] and provided tort liability for general contractors, subcontractors, suppliers, and design professionals for failure to meet the standards.[77] A homeowner can bring a claim for "deficiencies" in the "construction, design, specifications, surveying, planning, testing, or observations of construction"[78] regardless of whether there is privity of contract between the plaintiff and the defendant and regardless of

---

71. 469 Mass. at 68, 11 N.E.3d at 1079.

72. 469 Mass. at 68, 11 N.E.3d at 1079, *quoting* Bay State-Spray & Provincetown S.S., Inc. v. Caterpillar Tractor Co., 404 Mass. 103, 109-10, 533 N.E.2d 1350 (Mass. 1989).

73. 469 Mass. at 71, 11 N.E.3d at 1081.

74. Cal. Civ. Code § 895, *et seq.* (West). In California, the act is also commonly known by its legislative designation, "SB 8000."

75. Greystone Homes, Inc. v. Midtec, Inc., 168 Cal. App. 4th 1194, 1215, 86 Cal. Rptr. 3d 196, 212 (2008) ("While there is generally no duty to prevent economic loss to third parties in negligence actions at common law . . . the Right to Repair Act creates such a duty.").

76. Cal. Civ. Code § 896(a)-(g) (West). The standards cover a broad range of potential defects including "water issues," "structural issues," and "soil issues."

77. Section 942 of the Right to Repair Act provides that "a homeowner need only demonstrate, in accordance with the applicable evidentiary standard, that the home does not meet the applicable standard. . . . No further showing of causation or damages is required to meet the burden of proof regarding a violation of a standard . . . provided that the violation arises out of, pertains to, or is related to, the original construction." *See also Greystone Homes*, 168 Cal. App. 4th at 1210, 86 Cal. Rptr. 3d at 207-08; Beacon Residential Cmty. Assn. v. Skidmore, Owings & Merrill LLP, 59 Cal. 4th 568, 577, 327 P.3d 850, 856 (2014) ("The Right to Repair Act establishes a set of building standards for new residential construction and provides that builders and other entities 'shall . . . be liable for' violation of those standards '[i]n any action seeking recovery of damages arising out of' such construction.").

78. Cal. Civ. Code § 896 (West).

whether there is personal injury or damages to other property.[79] In short, the claims for which privity is not required and economic losses are allowed are quite broad. While the Right to Repair Act was not as sweeping as the recent court decisions, passage of the act indicates concern over the scope of the Economic Loss Rule, especially when it bars claims by innocent consumers.

The current trend in the law seems to be toward reigning in the excesses of the Economic Loss Rule, whether through overturning prior precedent as in *Tiara*, recognizing new claims as in *Wyman* and *Beacon Residential*, or codifying a right to bring a claim as in the Right to Repair Act. Only time will tell whether these cases and legislation will spark a broader movement to roll back the Economic Loss Rule, just as *Seely v. White Motor Co.* inaugurated the rule over 50 years ago.[80]

21.04 THE ECONOMIC LOSS RULE'S APPLICATION WHERE PARTIES ARE IN PRIVITY OF CONTRACT

A. Claims of Defective Construction Products/Components (Privity)

As a descendant of manufactured products liability law, the Economic Loss Rule first was used in the construction context by courts considering allegations of defective construction products or equipment.[81] It follows that out of the many ways a construction project or its participants could be economically harmed, damage due to defective equipment or to a negligently manufactured product stand the closest to the *Seely* model and constitute the scenario where the Economic Loss Rule ought to be most uniformly applied. Such has proved to be the case, especially when the product has injured "only itself."[82]

---

79. *Id.* § 942.
80. 403 P.2d 145 (Cal. 1965).
81. *See* Sunnyslope Grading, Inc. v. Bradford, Miller, & Risberg, Inc., 437 N.W.2d 213 (Wis. 1989) (backhoe's defective parts were covered by manufacturer's warranty, but plaintiff's economic damages of additional repairs, downtime, and lost profits were denied in a tort action where the defective backhoe caused no injury to another person or other property); Sacramento Reg'l Transit Dist. v. Grumman Flexible, 158 Cal. App. 3d 289 (1984) (repair of defective bus parts was not actionable where defect had not caused further damage).
82. William K. Jones, *Product Defects Causing Commercial Loss, The Ascendancy of Contract Over Tort*, 44 U. Miami L. Rev. 731 (1990); *see* Annotation, *Strict Products Liability: Recovery for Damage to Product Alone*, 72 A.L.R. 4th 12 (1985 and Supp. 1995). *See also* Mid Continent Aircraft Corp. v. Curry Cnty. Spraying Serv., Inc., 572 S.W.2d 308, 312 (Tex. 1978) (quoting Dean Page Keeton on the difference between a dangerous condition that harms only the product and a condition that is dangerous to other persons or property).

Wausau Tile, Inc. v. County Concrete Corp.
593 N.W.2d 445 (Wis. 1999)

Justice Crooks delivered the opinion of the Court.

Wausau Tile, Inc. (Wausau Tile) manufactures, sells and distributes "Terra" pavers to entities around the country. Pavers are concrete paving blocks made of cement, aggregate, water, and other materials, for use mainly in exterior walkways.

Wausau Tile contracted with Medusa Corporation (Medusa) to supply the cement for the pavers and arranged for County Concrete Corporation (County Concrete) to supply the aggregate. Wausau Tile's contract with Medusa contained warranties providing that Medusa would remedy or replace cement which did not meet particular specifications.

On April 16, 1996, Wausau Tile filed suit in Marathon County Circuit Court against Medusa, County Concrete, and their insurers, alleging breach of warranty, breach of contract, negligence, and strict liability claims. Wausau Tile claimed that several of the installed pavers had suffered "excessive expansion, deflecting, curling, cracking and/or buckling." Wausau Tile asserted that these problems were caused by alkali-silica gel reactions which resulted from high levels of alkalinity in Medusa's cement and high concentrations of silica in County Concrete's aggregate.

Wausau Tile claimed that the expansion and cracking of the pavers had led to problems and property damages which have given rise to "various claims, demands and suits against Wausau Tile." Wausau Tile alleged that it had "sustained monetary damages in remedying the property damage claims, is facing claims for personal injuries, and has suffered and will continue to suffer lost business and profits." In connection with its tort claims, Wausau Tile sought "actual and consequential damages arising from said problems and defects, including, but not limited to, costs of repair, replacement and remedy of any and all defects, complaints and resulting injuries which have arisen or will arise in the future as a result of the use of said pavers."

We begin by determining whether the circuit court properly dismissed Wausau Tile's negligence and strict liability claims against Medusa as barred by the economic loss doctrine. The economic loss doctrine precludes a purchaser of a product from employing negligence or strict liability theories to recover from the product's manufacturer loss which is solely economic. Economic loss is the loss in a product's value which occurs because the product "is inferior in quality and does not work for the general purposes for which it was manufactured and sold." *Daanen & Janssen, Inc. v. Cedarapids, Inc.*, 405 N.W. 2d 842 (1998).

Economic loss may be either direct or consequential. Direct economic loss is "loss in value of the product itself." All other economic loss caused by the product defect, such as lost profits, is consequential economic loss.

The economic loss doctrine does not preclude a product purchaser's claims of personal injury or damage to property other than the product itself. Similarly, claims which allege economic loss in combination with non-economic loss are not barred by the doctrine. "In short, economic loss is damage to a product itself or monetary loss caused by the defective product, which does not cause personal injury or damage to other property."

In *Daanen,* this court identified three policies supporting the application of the economic loss doctrine to commercial transactions. First, the economic loss doctrine preserves the fundamental distinction between tort law and contract law. Second, application of the doctrine protects the parties' freedom to allocate economic risk by contract. Third, the doctrine encourages the purchaser, which is the party best situated to assess the risk of economic loss, to assume, allocate, or insure against that risk.

The first of these policies recognizes that contract law rests on bargained-for obligations, while tort law is based on legal obligations. In contract law, the parties' duties arise from the terms of their particular agreement; the goal is to hold parties to that agreement so that each receives the benefit of his or her bargain. The aim of tort law, in contrast, is to protect people from misfortunes which are unexpected and overwhelming. The law imposes tort duties upon manufacturers to protect society's interest in safety from the physical harm or personal injury which may result from defective products. Thus, where a product fails in its intended use and injures only itself, thereby causing only economic damages to the purchaser, "the reasons for imposing a tort duty are weak and those for leaving the party to its contractual remedies are strong."

In this case, the damages sought by Wausau Tile can be grouped into three categories: (1) the costs of repairing and replacing cracked, buckled or expanded pavers; (2) the costs of satisfying third parties' claims that the defective pavers either caused personal injury or damaged property adjoining the pavers, such as curbs, mortar beds and walls; and (3) lost profits and business. We consider each of these types of damages in turn.

Repair and replacement costs are typical measures of economic loss. However, it is not the measure of damages which determines whether a claim alleges solely economic loss. Physical harm to property other than the product itself may also be measured by the cost of repair or replacement of the product. Consequently, we must determine whether Wausau Tile has alleged repair or replacement costs as a measure of harm to property other than the defective product.

Wausau Tile argues that the costs of repairing and replacing the pavers do not constitute economic loss because the pavers themselves are property other than the defective product (Medusa's cement). We are not persuaded by that argument.

Damage by a defective component of an integrated system to either the system as a whole or other system components is not damage to "other property" which precludes the application of the economic loss doctrine. Comment e of the RESTATEMENT (THIRD) OF TORTS § 21 acknowledges this "integrated system" rule. It states, in part:

A defective product that causes harm to property other than the defective product itself is governed by the rules of this Restatement. What constitutes harm to other property rather than harm to the product itself may be difficult to determine. A product that nondangerously fails to function due to a product defect has clearly caused harm only to itself. A product that fails to function and causes harm to surrounding property has clearly caused harm to other property. However, when a component part of a machine or a system destroys the rest of the machine or system, the characterization process becomes more difficult. When the product or system is deemed to be an integrated whole, courts treat such damage as harm to the product itself. When so characterized, the damage is excluded from the coverage of this Restatement. A contrary holding would require a finding of property damage in virtually every case in which a product harms itself and would prevent contractual rules from serving their legitimate function in governing commercial transactions.

RESTATEMENT (THIRD) OF TORTS § 21 cmt. e (1997) (emphasis added).

In the instant case, it is undisputed that the pavers were integrated systems comprised of several component materials, including Medusa's cement. The circuit court determined that Medusa's "concrete is an indistinguishable, integral part of the pavers" which "cannot be separately identified from the finished product." We conclude that the crux of Wausau Tile's claim for repair and replacement costs is that the pavers were damaged because one or more of their ingredients was of insufficient quality and did not work for Wausau Tile's intended purpose. This is the essence of a claim for economic loss.

Second, Wausau Tile claims damages in the amount it expended, or anticipates it will expend, in remediation of third party claims of damage to property adjoining the pavers and pedestrians' possible claims of personal injury. Wausau's claims do not allege any personal injury or property damage on Wausau Tile's part. Rather, as Wausau Tile acknowledges in its brief, these claims are an attempt to recoup the commercial costs of settling the claims of third parties which resulted from the product defect. As such, the claims allege consequential economic loss.

Finally, Wausau Tile claims lost business and profits. Wausau Tile's lost business and profits are indirect losses attributable to the inferior quality of the pavers. Accordingly, they constitute economic loss which is not recoverable in tort.

We conclude that Wausau Tile's complaint alleges only economic loss. Therefore, the first policy set forth by this court in *Daanen* supports the application of the economic loss doctrine in this case. Wausau Tile's claims involve failed economic expectations, which are the province of contract law.

The second policy reason for applying the economic loss doctrine is to protect parties' freedom to allocate economic risk via contract. Allowing purchasers to elect recovery under tort theories instead of requiring them to rely on their contractual remedies "rewrites the agreement by allowing a party to recoup a benefit that was not part of the bargain." It strips sellers of the ability to protect themselves from foreseeable risk by negotiating sales agreements.

Wausau Tile and Medusa entered into a contract with a warranty which specifically addressed the suitability of the cement for use in the pavers. Wausau Tile had the opportunity to negotiate a warranty and did so. Presumably, Wausau Tile paid a price commensurate with the warranty it received. If Wausau Tile were permitted to reap the benefits of a broader warranty by recovering its damages in tort, it would receive more than it bargained for (and paid for) and Medusa would receive less than it bargained for (and was paid for). Consequently, the second policy set forth in *Daanen* also supports the application of the economic loss doctrine in this case.

The third policy reason for applying the economic loss doctrine is that the doctrine "encourages the party with the best understanding of the attendant risks of economic loss, the commercial purchaser, to assume, allocate, or insure against the risk of loss caused by a defective product." Purchasers are generally better equipped than sellers to anticipate the economic loss which a defective product could cause their particular businesses. Accordingly, courts have required purchasers to guard against foreseeable economic loss by allocating the risk by contract or by purchasing insurance. The result is a more efficient, more predictable marketplace. If tort recovery were permitted, sellers of products would be "potentially liable for unbargained-for and unexpected risks," leading eventually to higher prices for consumers.

Wausau Tile should reasonably have expected that it might receive defective or unsuitable cement. Because cement is one of the main components of pavers, Wausau Tile should also have foreseen that defective cement might produce defects in the pavers. Evidently, Wausau Tile did foresee this risk because it attempted to allocate the risk contractually with Medusa. Wausau Tile may not now turn to tort law in hopes of obtaining benefits for which it may not have bargained.

We find that the three policy reasons for applying the economic loss doctrine support the application of the doctrine in this case. Because Wausau Tile has alleged purely economic loss, the economic loss doctrine prevents Wausau Tile from maintaining its negligence and strict liability claims against Medusa.

In *Wausau Tile*, the Wisconsin Supreme Court focused on the terms of the parties' contract—the fact that the defective cement had been integrated into the pavers, and that the pavers caused no demonstrable physical injury to any persons or other property. Some courts have, in the products/privity scenario, gone even further. When the rule is considered by a court to be an anti-tort-in-commercial-transactions rule, courts have denied recovery in negligence when the parties are in privity of contract, despite damage to property "other than the product itself." In *Myrtle Beach Pipeline Corp. v. Emerson Elec. Co.*,[83] a specially made pipe leaked, causing a large fuel spill and subsequent clean-up costs. Despite damage to land adjacent to the pipeline project, tort recovery for the clean-up cost was denied on privity grounds.[84]

Beyond the simplest of fact situations, the analytical landscape for injury caused by defective construction products becomes cluttered. During the construction process, products and equipment are incorporated into systems, and many hands are laid upon them. Not all products remain in their as-purchased form once incorporated into a structure. Incorporated products may be identifiable, but to remove or repair them often injures or destroys still other products. Economic losses to the project owner and project participants can also occur when a product is improperly installed.[85] Structures may diminish in value under the stigma of nascent, but unrealized, injury due to defective components, and economic damage can be visited upon the owner or upon various project participants due to improper component-related professional services, including defective design, selection, or coordination of construction components.

B. Claims of Defective Construction Services (Including Poor Workmanship and Improper Furnishing of Materials) (Privity)

Most states agree that when parties are in privity of contract, a tort claim for negligence in the performance of that contract will not lie unless there is bodily injury or damage to property other than that which is the subject matter of the contract itself. Even if economic damages are substantial, they are nonetheless deemed to be sufficiently addressed under the bargained-for rights and responsibilities set forth in the contract between the parties relating to the

---

83. 843 F. Supp. 1027 (D.S.C. 1993).

84. *Id.* at 1048–55. The court discussed the Economic Loss Rule, but was more impressed that these were "sophisticated parties" to a "negotiated" contract. The court added, even if "other property" were damaged, such damage was contemplated by the parties' contract. *Id.* at 1057. *But see* Tourist Vill. Motel, Inc. v. Massachusetts Eng'g Co., 801 F. Supp. 903 (D. N.H. 1992) (fuel drum leak damaged plaintiff's property, Economic Loss Rule not applied).

85. Those providing construction services may be liable in negligence or implied warranty, but are generally not strictly liable for their work or for the components they install. RESTATEMENT (THIRD) OF TORTS: PRODUCTS LIABILITY, § 19, subd. (b) ("services, even when provided commercially, are not products" and are governed by the law of negligence).

subject matter of the damage. This rationale is particularly persuasive in the context of a construction project where there is a "complex web of contracts that allocates risk and liability."[86] The Texas Supreme Court has defended the importance of contractual allocation of risk on a construction project:

> Construction projects operate by agreements among the participants. Typically, those agreements are vertical: the owner contracts with an architect and with a general contractor, the general contractor contracts with subcontractors, a subcontractor may contract with a sub-subcontractor, and so on. The architect does not contract with the general contractor, and the subcontractors do not contract with the architect, the owner, or each other. . . . If the roofing subcontractor could recover from the foundation subcontractor damages for extra costs incurred or business lost due to the latter's negligent delay of construction, the risk of liability to everyone on the project would be magnified and indeterminate . . .[87]
>
> Courts reason that negligent performance of a contract, without more, is a breach of contract only, and should not be confused with a tortious breach of a legal duty, which arises by law independent of the contract. This reasoning is applied to buyers and sellers, whether the contract is for the purchase of a product, the installation of the product, the leasing of equipment, or the furnishing of nonprofessional services in connection with the finished construction of a project.

Recovery in negligence for purely economic damages requires the breach of an independent tort duty, separate from the subject matter of the contract. If the plaintiff is in privity with the defendant, breach of the obligations of the contract ordinarily cannot be relied on to support an action in negligence; the parties have already selected a contractual remedy. Failure to perform one's contract, even carelessly, generally will not support a negligence action for economic damages.[88]

---

86. Balfour Beatty Infrastructure, Inc. v. Rummel Klepper & Kahl, LLP, 451 Md. 600, 629, 155 A.3d 445, 462 (2017).

87. LAN/STV v. Martin K. Eby Const. Co., Inc., 435 S.W.3d 234, 246 (Tex. 2014).

88. *See, e.g.*, Palmetto Linen Serv., Inc. v. U.N.X., Inc., 205 F.3d 126, 129 (4th Cir. 2000), (applying S.C. law) *quoting from* Kennedy v. Columbia Lumber & Mfg. Co., 384 S.E.2d 730, 737 (S.C. 1989) ("the 'economic loss' rule will still apply where duties are created *solely* by contract") (emphasis in original).

Paul M. Spillman v. American Homes of Mocksville, Inc.
422 S.E.2d 740 (N.C. App. 1992)

Chief Justice Hedrick delivered the opinion of the Court.

Plaintiff Paul Spillman instituted this civil action by filing a complaint wherein he alleged negligent breach of contract arising out of plaintiff's purchase of a mobile home from defendant. The claim set forth by plaintiff was based upon the alleged improper construction and installation of the mobile home by defendant. All damage suffered by plaintiff consisted of the cost to repair the defects in the mobile home and to repair the damage to the mobile home resulting from the improper installation.

The jury returned a verdict finding that defendant had negligently performed the contract concerning "the sale and set up of the manufactured home." Defendant appeals from the trial court's denial of its motion for a directed verdict.

Defendant assigns as error the trial court's denial of its motion for a directed verdict. Defendant argues that plaintiff failed to produce evidence sufficient to submit the issue of negligent performance of the contract to the jury.

Plaintiff's claim of negligence is premised upon the allegation that defendant's failure to properly perform the terms of the contract between the parties resulted in damage to the mobile home which is the subject matter of the contract. Such a premise is clearly insufficient. Absent the existence of a public policy exception, as in the case of contracts involving a common carrier, innkeeper or other bailee, *see Ports Authority v. Roofing Co.*, 294 N.C. 73, 82, 240 S.E.2d 345, 350–51 (1978), a tort action does not lie against a party to a contract who simply fails to properly perform the terms of the contract, even if that failure to properly perform was due to the negligent or intentional conduct of that party, when the injury resulting from the breach is damage to the subject matter of the contract. It is the law of contract and not the law of negligence which defines the obligations and remedies of the parties in such a situation.

As the evidence presented by plaintiff does not support a claim of negligence, the trial court's denial of defendant's motion for a directed verdict as to that issue was error. The judgment entered by the District Court is reversed.

F. Craig Stuart v. Coldwell Banker Commercial Group, Inc.
745 P.2d 1284 (Wash. 1987)

UTTER, Justice.

The trial court in this case awarded damages to a homeowners' association against a builder-vendor for construction defects in common and limited common areas of a condominium complex.

Yarrowood is a condominium complex located in Bellevue. One hundred forty-four of the 155 units have private decks. Because of the steep topography and siting, there are 32 entry walkways which traverse from the parking area to provide access to its entrances. Twenty-three of these serve only one apartment each. The bulk of the areas at issue were these private decks and walkways.

In May 1975, when Phase I (67 apartments) was partially constructed, Ferguson, the initial developer, defaulted and Coldwell Banker took over. From that point, Coldwell Banker was the owner, developer, construction contractor and vendor of the apartment units at Yarrowood.

Coldwell Banker turned over management of Yarrowood to the Board of Directors of the Yarrowood Homeowners Association ("the Board") after substantially all of the units were sold. Following a short period in which Coldwell Banker acted as property manager, the Board hired a resident manager to handle complaints from homeowners, and to perform minor maintenance and repairs. The first manager served from early 1978 to 1980. During 1978 and 1979, he received complaints relating to 10 to 15 of the decks at Yarrowood. Some of the decks had damage which was plainly visible from public areas such as the parking lot for one of the buildings. By June 1979, at least one deck had so deteriorated that the homeowner asked the Board about having it rebuilt.

Currently, the state of Washington does not recognize a cause of action for negligent construction on behalf of individual homeowners. Beyond the terms expressed in the contract of sale, the only recognized duty owing from a builder-vendor of a newly completed residence to its first purchaser is that embodied in the implied warranty of habitability, which arises from the sale transaction. Plaintiff homeowners, faced with losses that are not of their own making, present a sympathetic case, and we understand the desire of the trial court to fashion a remedy. We must exercise caution, however, that we do not unduly upset the law upon which expectations are built and business is conducted.

The theory advanced by the trial court is a peculiar combination of tort and contract law, closely related to the tort law of products liability. Dean Prosser characterized the law of products liability as a "hybrid, born of the illicit intercourse of tort and contract, unique in the law." W. Prosser, *Torts* 634 (4th ed. 1971).

Initially, plaintiffs who suffered personal injuries from defective products could only reach the manufacturer under warranty theories. Courts, however, had difficulty meshing the inapposite "intricacies of the law of sale," W. Prosser, *The Assault Upon the Citadel*, 69 Yale L.J. 1099 (1960), such as notice and privity, with the plight presented by injured consumers who did not have a direct contractual relationship with the manufacturer. Accordingly, the doctrine fell prey to logical difficulties inherent in this procrustean approach, which addressed problems of unsafe conduct with a legal theory premised on receiving the benefit of a bargain.

The first cases holding manufacturers liable for injuries caused by their products in the absence of privity of contract used a negligence theory. The landmark decision in this area was *MacPherson v. Buick Motor Co.*, 217 N.Y. 382, 111 N.E. 1050 (1916) (Cardozo, J.). *MacPherson* has been accepted in every jurisdiction in the United States to provide a remedy to plaintiffs injured by manufactured items that are dangerous if negligently made. W. Prosser, *Torts* § 96, at 642–43 (4th ed. 1971). Courts reasoned that privity of contract should not stand as a bar to plaintiff consumers who suffered physical injury from a product negligently made.

As a matter of public policy, it is entirely reasonable to expect manufacturers of goods for sale to the general public to assume responsibility for the safety of their product. In *Seely v. White Motor Co.*, 63 Cal.2d 9, 45 Cal. Rptr. 17, 403 P.2d 145 (1965), Justice Traynor denied recovery to a plaintiff who had pleaded lost profits as the only damages under a negligence theory. Justice Traynor stated at page 18, 45 Cal. Rptr. 17, 403 P.2d 145:

> The distinction that the law has drawn between tort recovery for physical injuries and warranty recovery for economic loss is not arbitrary and does not rest on the "luck" of one plaintiff in having an accident causing physical injury. The distinction rests, rather, on an understanding of the nature of the responsibility a manufacturer must undertake in distributing his products. He can appropriately be held liable for physical injuries caused by defects by requiring his goods to match a standard of safety defined in terms of conditions that create unreasonable risks of harm. He cannot be held for the level of performance of his products in the consumer's business unless he agrees that the product was designed to meet the consumer's demands. A consumer should not be charged at the will of the manufacturer with bearing the risk of physical injury when he buys a product on the market. He can, however, be fairly charged with the risk that the product will not match his economic expectations unless the manufacturer agrees that it will. . . .

Commentators and courts faced with this issue have found it necessary to distinguish economic loss from physical harm or property damage. The distinction is usually drawn depending on the nature of the defect and the manner in which the damage occurred. Defects of quality are evidenced by internal deterioration, and designated as economic loss, while loss stemming from defects that cause accidents involving violence or collision with external objects is treated as physical injury.

> The nature of the defect at Yarrowood was that the decks and walkways were not of the quality desired by the buyers. The "injury" or damage suffered was that the decks themselves deteriorated, not through accident or violent occurrence, but through exposure to the weather.
>
> In cases such as the present one where only the defective product is damaged, the court should identify whether the particular injury amounts to economic loss or physical damage. In drawing the distinction, the determinative factor should not be the items for which damages are sought, such as repair costs. Rather, the line between tort and contract must be drawn by analyzing interrelated factors such as the nature of the defect, the type of risk, and the manner in which the injury arose. These factors bear directly on whether the safety-insurance policy of tort law or the expectation-bargain protection policy of warranty law is most applicable to the claim in question.
>
> Imposition of tort liability upon the builder-vendors would require them to become the guarantors of the complete satisfaction of future purchasers. A builder-vendor could contract to limit liability for defects with the original purchaser and then find themselves liable for the same defects to a future purchaser with whom they had absolutely no contact. The trial court's formulation makes no distinction between subsequent purchasers who may have known nothing of the potential deterioration of the decks, and those buyers who may have been able to see the flaking observable to the naked eye from the exhibits before the court. The latter buyers may well have been able to account for the defects with an adjustment to the purchase price. As to such buyers, any recovery from the court would be a pure windfall. We decline to recognize a cause of action in negligent construction.

In each of these cases, the claimed damage was to the property that was the subject of the contract between the parties. When this is clear, and there is no personal injury or damage to "other property," only a contract action will lie.

C. Claims of Defective Design Professional/Testing Services (Including Insufficient Design and Improper Contract Administration Services) (Privity)

Professional services in the construction context are supplied by architects, engineers, and related consultants.[89] Their negligence creates a conundrum for

---

89. Hydrologists, geotechnical engineers, and geologists are examples of related professional consultants. Licensure or registration with a state governing board normally determines a consultant's status.

the Economic Loss Rule. The relationship between design professionals and their owner clients is unique in the construction industry. It is a professional relationship, one in which trust and confidence are reposed. Design professionals are required to subordinate their interests to those of their clients.[90]

Negligent professional services, including design and construction contract administration services, can economically injure any construction participant, from the owner to a second-tier supplier. The harm can be direct or through principles of indemnification. The foreseeable class of economically damaged plaintiffs with legitimate negligence claims against design professionals is large, greater even perhaps than against a negligent trade contractor. The set of individuals impacted economically by a contractor's faulty work normally is limited to the users of such project. A design professional's negligence, however, can cause economic losses to owners, users, and project participants.

The scope of services undertaken by a design professional directly affects the breadth of the duty required of the professional. Once the obligation is identified, the architect or engineer must meet the standard of care for the services undertaken. To recover in negligence against a design professional, there must be proof of a breach of the standard of care owed. Similarly, most contract-based actions against design professionals also require plaintiffs to demonstrate that the professional breached the professional standard of care for the activity in question, for such is generally also the contract standard.[91] On these points, jurisdictions generally agree. Beyond this legal framework, courts part company. Who may and who may not maintain a negligence action against a design professional for economic loss is a matter as much of local legal history as legal analysis.[92]

It is in the context of construction design professional services that the application of the economic loss rule is most difficult to reconcile. No analytical theme predominates. It is almost as if someone had written the words "privity," "special relationship," "foreseeability," "supervising architect," "no duty," and "covered by another contract" on the six sides of a die cube, and then distributed the cube to the appellate judiciary of various states to assist

---

90. Sweet, *supra* note 18, at § 2.1.

91. AIA Document B101–2007 (the latest draft) provides: "The Architect shall perform its services in accordance with generally accepted professional standards appropriate for the Project at the time services are performed." AIA Document B101–2007, *supra* note 6, § 2.2.

92. The discussion here concerns economic losses sustained by owners, end users, and project participants, rather than instances of bodily injury and physical "property damage." The confusing issue of damage to property "other than the product itself," which pervades the discussion of the Economic Loss Rule in the manufactured product context, is recast in the professional services context, reappearing as whether the damage was contemplated by "a contract."

them in describing the policy considerations that support their interpretation of the scope of the rule. Virtually the only constant in the legal analysis among the states is that economic damages are the subject of the claim.

Still, most courts find that if an owner has reached a bargain with a design professional as to specific limitations to the scope and standard of professional services, the owner must look to that agreement for resolution of economic loss disputes.[93]

City Express, Inc. v. Express Partners
87 Hawaii 466, 959 P.2d 836 (Hawaii 1998)

Nakayama, Justice.

Express Partners filed an appeal of this action after a directed verdict was entered in favor of Architects 2, Inc. We granted certiorari to address the application of the economic loss rule to a negligence action between an owner and an architect who are in privity of contract.

City Express, Inc. entered into a joint venture agreement with developer Thomas Enomoto to construct a new warehouse suited for the purposes of City Express, a warehouse and trucking company. The business entity created by this joint venture agreement is Express Partners.

Express Partners hired Architects 2 to design the warehouse. Architects 2 prepared blueprints, and the warehouse was constructed by Dura/Constructors, Inc. The warehouse was constructed with two levels and a ramp from the first to the second floor. Douglas Sonoda and Lloyd Sako, an architect and engineer respectively employed by Architects 2, testified at trial that it was their understanding, in designing the building, that the second floor would not be utilized by forklifts. Instead, the second floor would be used solely for storage of light objects.

---

93. *See, e.g.*, Flagstaff Affordable Hous. Ltd. P'ship v. Design All., Inc., 223 Ariz. 320, 327, 223 P.3d 664, 671 (2010) (Economic Loss Rule barred professional negligence claim by owner against architect where parties had an express, written contract because "principal function of the economic loss doctrine . . . is to encourage private ordering of economic relationships and to uphold the expectations of the parties by limiting a plaintiff to contractual remedies for loss of the benefit of the bargain"); Terracon Consultants W., Inc. v. Mandalay Resort Grp., 125 Nev. 66, 77–78, 206 P.3d 81, 89 (2009) (where parties had written contract, rule barred professional negligence claim by owner against geotechnical engineer because "contract law is better suited to resolve professional negligence claims"); Brushton-Moira Cent. Sch. Dist. v. Alliance Wall Corp., 600 N.Y.S.2d 511 (1993) (panels selected by architect were inappropriate for school project, held, contract action allowed, tort action dismissed); Key Int'l Mfg. v. Morse/Diesel, Inc., 142 A.D.2d 448 (N.Y. App. 1988) (owner cannot sue architect or prime contractor in negligence for economic loss since the damages sought are of the type remediable in contract).

However, a portion of the blueprints prepared by Architects 2 indicates that the ramp was "for forklift use."

City Express moved into the warehouse upon its completion and began to utilize forklifts on the second floor of the structure. The use of forklifts caused the floor on the second level to crack. In an attempt to correct the problem, an additional five inches of concrete was poured. However, City Express claimed that this did not solve the problem. The additional weight caused structural damage and the floor again began cracking. City Express had to temporarily vacate the building while additional remedial work was done.

The additional remedial work could not correct the structure sufficiently to support the forklifts. Express Partners, the owner of the building, notified City Express that the type of forklifts commonly utilized in the industry could not be operated on the second floor. On March 1, 1985, City Express went out of business. The building was subsequently converted to office use.

On July 31, 1985, City Express filed a complaint against Express Partners. On January 10, 1986, Express Partners filed a third-party complaint against Architects 2. The City Express claim was settled, and Express Partners proceeded to trial against Architects 2 to recoup its damages. The sole issue at trial was the alleged professional negligence of Architects 2.

At the conclusion of Express Partners' case, Architects 2 moved for a directed verdict. The circuit court granted this motion. We granted certiorari to address an important issue of first impression in this jurisdiction, namely, the availability of economic loss damages in a negligence action against a design professional.

The economic loss rule bars recovery in tort for purely economic loss. Where, as in this case, negligent design of a building is claimed, economic loss damages are those that pertain solely to the costs related to the operation and value of the building itself. Excluded are costs for personal injuries caused by the defective design or damage to property other than the building itself. The damages claimed by Express Partners are purely economic—additional costs, lost rent, the cost of remedying the alleged building defects, and the difference between the value of the building as designed and the value it would have had if it had been properly designed.

In the context of construction litigation involving design professionals, sound policy reasons counsel against providing open-ended tort recovery to parties who have negotiated a contractual relationship. If tort and contract remedies were allowed to overlap, certainty and predictability in allocating risk would decrease and impede future business activity. The construction industry in particular would suffer, for it is in this industry that we see most clearly the importance of the precise allocation of risk as secured by contract. *The fees charged by architects, engineers, contractors, developers, vendors, and so on are founded on their expected liability exposure as bargained and provided for in the contract.*

Parties have the freedom to contract. "Construction projects are characterized by detailed and comprehensive contracts that form the foundation of the

> industry's operations. Contracting parties are free to adjust their respective obligations to satisfy their mutual expectations." (citing cases)
>
> Express Partners admits that it was in privity of contract with Architects 2. However, the contract was not presented in evidence and Express Partners proceeded to trial solely on a negligence theory. Because the purely economic damages sought by Express Partners are not recoverable in negligence, the circuit court correctly granted a directed verdict in favor of Architects 2.
>
> In the context of construction litigation, where a party is in privity of contract with a design professional, economic loss damages are limited to contractual remedies, and a negligence action may not be maintained. We believe that this ruling not only encourages the parties to negotiate the limits of liability in a contractual situation, but it holds the parties to the terms of their agreement. Our holding preserves the right of design professionals to limit their exposure to liability through contract. We affirm the ruling of the circuit court.

Notably, the third-party plaintiff in *City Express* failed to enter the architecture contract into evidence, and apparently failed to characterize the claim as one for breach of that contract. As discussed earlier, the professional standard of care to be met by the architect was probably the same regardless of whether the claim was for breach of contract or negligence. One wonders why the developer did not proceed on a claim for breach of contract. Many owners, in order to enhance their construction budget, negotiate a lesser fee with design professionals for a reduced scope of professional services or for a limited cap on the designer's professional liability in the event of a mistake. Perhaps in the *City Express* case, Express Partners made a poor bargain.

21.05 THE ECONOMIC LOSS RULE'S APPLICATION WHERE PARTIES ARE NOT IN PRIVITY OF CONTRACT

When parties are not in privity of contract with one another, the central question under the Economic Loss Rule is whether the lack of privity will bar a tort claim. This analysis takes on added significance in the context of a construction dispute where, in many construction situations, those who suffer economic damages as a result of defective construction work, negligent design services, or a poorly manufactured product are not in privity of contract with (or do not have a contractual remedy against) the provider of the defective work, service, or product. The argument that the parties had the right to negotiate terms is, obviously, not as compelling. Nevertheless, the courts still emphasize the need for a policy that protects the right of construction project participants to allocate risks as they see fit.

A prime example is the buyer of a new residential home in a planned community. In that situation, the home may be sold by a developer who has contracted with both an architect to design the project and a contractor to build it. The homebuyer will have a contract with the developer-vendor but will have no privity of contractor with the architect or the general contractor. Indeed, oftentimes owners or buyers of construction services cannot influence the selection of construction materials, competently judge the quality of a professional's design selection, or evaluate the work of a trade contractor who installs the product. Nor can they bargain for a warranty from any or all of them.[94] Economic losses sustained by owners and participants due to the negligent conduct of others in the process are foreseeable. Under a strict application of the Economic Loss Rule, however, these injuries, even if proved to be proximately caused, are not recoverable in a negligence-based tort action. In the absence of a contractual remedy against the entity causing the loss,[95] or without the ability either to close or to leap gaps in the contractual chain, no recovery will be allowed.[96] The law in some jurisdictions has responded to these concerns by allowing tort claims seeking economic damages in the absence of privity in the context of construction disputes.[97]

A. Claims of Defective Construction Products/Components (No Privity)

Most courts apply the Economic Loss Rule in the manufactured products context whether the parties are in privity of contract or not.[98] Indeed, it is

---

94. *See* Steven B. Lesser, *Economic Loss Doctrine and Its Impact Upon Construction Claims*, 14:3 THE CONSTR. LAW. 21, 22 (1994).

95. Sophisticated parties to the construction process can be very creative in crafting contract clauses that limit contractual liabilities.

96. *See* discussion in Richard E. Speidel, *Warranty Theory, Economic Loss, and the Privity Requirement, Once More into the Void*, 67 B.U. L. REV. 9 (1987), using as a model the outcome of Spring Motors Distrib. v. Ford Motor Co., 489 A.2d 660 (N.J. 1985) (plaintiff allowed Uniform Commercial Code (UCC) statute of limitations to pass before filing suit, negligence and strict liability claims barred by Economic Loss Rule—no recovery). Even in UCC actions, courts may find that the product loses its character as a "good" for UCC warranty purposes once it is applied upon or within a structure. *See, e.g., Keck*, 830 So. 2d at 1, 4; *but see* Johnstone, J. in dissent ("the integration of building materials . . . [as] intended by the manufacturers, suppliers, and sellers in no way detracts from the character of those materials, members, or components as products") 830 So. 2d at 14. *See also* Stoney v. Franklin, 44 UCC Rep. Serv. 2d 1211 (Va. Cir. Ct. 2001) ("goods exist if they 'are movable at the time of identification to the contract of sale'").

97. Beacon Residential Cmty. Assn. v. Skidmore, Owings & Merrill LLP, 59 Cal. 4th 568, 574, 327 P.3d 850, 854 (2014) (noting the "declining significance of privity has found its way into construction law").

98. *See, e.g.*, Sullivan Indus., Inc. v. Double Seal Glass Co., Inc., 480 N.W.2d 623, 628–29 (Mich. App. 1991), citing Consumer Power Co. v. Mississippi Valley Structural Steel Co., 636 F. Supp. 1100, 1106–08 (E.D. Mich. 1986).

quite common for the parties in a products liability case not to be in privity of contract. (Typically they are consumer and manufacturer.) Negligence claims seeking economic damages are dismissed when the parties are in privity on the ground that any liability should be based on the contract terms, as discussed earlier. Negligence claims seeking economic damages are dismissed when the parties are not in privity based on an analysis of whether the damages are "economic damages" or damages arising out of injury to person or other property. Some courts do not directly explain why economic damages may not be recovered by a plaintiff who is not in privity of contract with a manufacturer or supplier, but the existence of negotiated contracts between parties to the sales transactions (even though not between plaintiff and defendant) do seem to underpin the courts' narrow definitions of the types of "other property" damage to which would not be subject to the Economic Loss Rule.[99] In other words, some courts take a very strict approach to what constitutes "other property" as a way ensure contractual agreements and obligations are not circumvented.

Pulte Home Corp. v. Osmose Wood Preserving, Inc.
60 F.3d 734, C.A.11 (Fla.), 1995

TJOFLAT, Chief Judge:

Appellant Pulte Home Corporation ("Pulte"), a nationwide homebuilder, challenges the grant of judgment notwithstanding the verdict in favor of appellee Osmose Wood Preserving, Inc. ("Osmose"), a manufacturer of chemicals that were applied to plywood Pulte used in constructing the roofs of 1876 townhouses. After the townhouses were sold, the chemicals caused the plywood to deteriorate; Pulte subsequently replaced the plywood at a cost exceeding $3,650,000. A jury found that Pulte's loss from replacing the plywood was caused by Osmose's (1) misrepresentation that the plywood would not deteriorate and (2) negligence in failing to warn Pulte that the plywood would deteriorate, and it awarded Pulte $3,750,000 in compensatory damages. Finding that Osmose's misrepresentation was made with fraudulent intent to induce Pulte to purchase Osmose-treated plywood, the jury awarded an additional $2,500,000 in punitive damages.

Following the return of the jury's verdict, but before entering judgment, the district court revisited Osmose's Fed. R. Civ. P. 50(a) motion, which had been made prior to the submission of the case to the jury, and granted Osmose judgment as

---

99. *Palmetto Linen Serv., Inc.*, 205 F.3d at 126, 129 ("sophisticated parties" in privity should have contemplated type of sustained injury, thereby "rendering other property damage inseparable from the defect in the product itself").

a matter of law. The court acted on the theory that Pulte's tort claims were barred by the economic loss rule. We agree with the district court that the economic loss rule barred Pulte's negligence claim, but disagree that the rule precluded its fraud claim. The evidence adduced at trial, however, did not support the fraud claim. We therefore affirm the district court's judgment in full.

Pulte, one of the largest homebuilders in the United States, operates building divisions in several states including Florida and Georgia. Pulte constructs and sells between seven and ten thousand homes each year. These homes include condominiums, single family homes, and multi-family townhouses, which are sold at various prices. The multi-family townhouses consist of a row of single-family housing units that are joined by a common wall and, in part, at the roof.

During the time period relevant to this case, Osmose manufactured a chemical used by lumber suppliers to make plywood fire retardant and specified the procedures that the suppliers had to follow in treating the plywood.

FRT plywood (fire retardant treated) was primarily used as a fire wall and in the common roof areas of multi-family townhouses. Every major building code required the use of noncombustible materials, including, for example, FRT plywood, in the common roof areas of multi-family townhouses. The specific purpose of these code provisions was to ensure that builders designed and constructed multi-family housing in a manner that would prevent the spread of fire between the individual housing units.

Beginning in 1984, Pulte constructed 1876 townhouses with roofs containing FRT plywood treated with Osmose chemicals. When purchasing FRT plywood, Pulte purchasing agents did not specify a particular brand name, such as Osmose, nor did they rely on any of Osmose's promotional materials. Rather, Pulte treated FRT plywood as a "commodity," requiring only that it be cost-effective and contain the code-mandated FRT stamp.

In late 1988, after Pulte had sold the townhouses containing Osmose-treated FRT plywood, Pulte began receiving scattered reports that the plywood in its multi-family townhouses was degrading in service. At the same time, Pulte also became aware of reports in wood industry journals indicating that FRT plywood generally was unfit for use in roof systems because high temperatures and humidity levels in attic environments caused excessive reductions in the strength and structural integrity of the plywood. A normal attic environment in the United States may experience temperatures as high as 170 to 180 degrees. This extreme heat often is accompanied by excessive moisture and humidity. Of course, these temperature and humidity levels vary with the geographic location of the home.

In response to these reports, Pulte immediately notified its homeowners of the situation and warned them to stay off their roofs until Pulte could inspect them. After inspection, Pulte discovered universal degradation in the Osmose-treated FRT plywood, such that, according to Pulte, every roof containing Osmose-treated FRT plywood was "dangerously unpredictable" and unsafe. Tests Osmose conducted confirmed Pulte's findings. The tests, conducted in simulated attic environments, revealed that after 28 days of accelerated aging at 160 degrees, the Osmose-treated FRT plywood lost 72% of its strength. These test results ultimately led Osmose to cease the manufacture and sale of its fire retardant chemicals.

Pulte asked Osmose for assistance in resolving its FRT plywood dilemma, but Osmose refused. Pulte then launched an extensive remedial campaign culminating in the systematic replacement of all of the Osmose-treated FRT plywood. In replacing this plywood, Pulte was also forced to remove and replace other components of its roof systems, including untreated plywood and shingles. In total, Pulte's roof replacement project cost $3,658,200, or $1950 per roof.

On June 2, 1989, Pulte brought this diversity action against Osmose in the United States District Court for the Middle District of Florida. In its five-count complaint, which also named Lowe's Companies and Georgia Pacific Corporation as party defendants, Pulte alleged that Osmose "is engaged in the manufacture and sale of . . . fire retardant chemicals," and that Lowe's and Georgia Pacific sold Pulte the plywood after having treated it with Osmose chemicals. Pulte subsequently reached undisclosed settlement agreements with Lowe's and Georgia Pacific and dismissed its claims against those defendants.

The five counts against Osmose in Pulte's complaint alleged: (1) breach of express and implied warranties; (2) strict liability; (3) negligence; (4) "common law misrepresentation;" and (5) fraud. After the parties joined issue, Pulte voluntarily dismissed its breach of warranty claims. On February 20, 1992, the case proceeded to trial on the claims that remained. At the close of all of the evidence, Osmose moved for judgment as a matter of law pursuant to Fed. R. Civ. P. 50(a). The court denied its motion and submitted the case to the jury on Pulte's claims for strict liability, fraud, and negligence. By special verdict, the jury found in favor of Osmose on Pulte's claim of strict liability, concluding that the chemicals were not defective when they left Osmose's control. The jury also concluded that Osmose had been negligent in failing to warn Pulte that the FRT plywood would deteriorate if incorporated into Pulte's construction of the townhouse roofs (the negligence claim) and that Osmose had fraudulently induced Pulte to purchase the plywood (the misrepresentation and fraud claims). Accordingly, the jury awarded Pulte $3,750,000 in compensatory damages (on both claims) and an additional $2,500,000 in punitive damages (on the misrepresentation and fraud claims). After the jury rendered its verdict, the district court revisited Osmose's Rule 50(a) motion, and, concluding that the economic loss rule barred Pulte's negligence and fraud claims, entered judgment for Osmose. Pulte now appeals.

We conclude that Pulte is not entitled to recover on either its negligence or fraud claims. We find that Pulte's negligence claim is barred by the economic loss rule and does not meet either exception to the rule. Although we disagree with the district court that the economic loss rule, as applied in Florida, bars Pulte's claim for fraud in the inducement, we nonetheless hold that Pulte is not entitled to relief on that claim. In short, Pulte failed to establish essential elements of its claim that Osmose fraudulently induced its purchase of Osmose-treated FRT plywood. Specifically, other than the representations contained in Osmose promotional literature, Pulte presented no evidence from which the jury could conclude that Osmose made any misrepresentations or guarantees to Pulte regarding the strength of the FRT plywood treated with Osmose chemicals. Moreover, to the extent that Osmose's promotional literature misrepresented the properties of plywood treated with its chemicals, Pulte failed to establish that it actually relied on those statements in purchasing the Osmose-treated FRT plywood.

The economic loss rule "prohibits tort recovery when a product damages itself, causing economic loss, but does not cause personal injury or damage to any property other than itself." Economic loss includes "damages for inadequate value, *costs of repair and replacement of the defective product,* or consequent loss of profits— without any claim of personal injury or damage to other property." The rationale underlying the economic loss rule is that parties should protect against the risk of economic loss during contract negotiations through warranty provisions and price adjustments rather than attempt to recover under tort law after the loss occurs.

We first examine Pulte's negligence claim. Pulte alleges that Osmose negligently breached its duty to Pulte by failing to warn Pulte that FRT plywood treated with Osmose chemicals could not be used in attic environments. Stated another way, had Osmose warned Pulte (and other similarly situated purchasers) that FRT plywood treated with its chemicals "[wa]s inferior in quality and [would] not work for the general purposes for which it was manufactured and sold," Pulte would not have bought the product. Pulte's negligence claim presents precisely the type of "disappointed economic expectation" claim that Florida's strict interpretation of the economic loss rule forecloses.

Consequently, we must determine whether Pulte's claim falls within one of the two exceptions to the economic loss rule, which permit a tort claim if personal injury or damage to other property accompanies economic loss. The first exception is readily dismissed: because no individual has been physically injured as a result of the weakened plywood, Pulte's negligence claim does not fall within the personal injury exception to the economic loss rule.

To satisfy the "other property" exception, Pulte must establish damage to property aside from the FRT plywood treated with Osmose chemicals. Pulte incorporated the FRT plywood into its townhouses, such that the deterioration of the plywood destroyed the structural integrity of the roof. As a result, Pulte was forced to remove and replace the FRT plywood. In doing so, Pulte also had to remove and replace other portions of the roof, including untreated plywood and shingles. These other roof components form the basis of Pulte's "other property" argument.

In the present case, Pulte cannot establish that there was damage to other property. The product bargained for and purchased by Pulte was the Osmose-treated FRT plywood. Based on the evidence offered at trial, the FRT plywood itself was

> the only property damaged. Although Pulte did replace roof components other than the FRT plywood, these components were not replaced because they were *damaged*. Rather, replacing the shingles and other materials was *merely a consequence* of replacing the damaged FRT plywood. These costs simply do not trigger the "other property" exception.
>
> Pulte failed to guard against the possibility that the Osmose-treated FRT plywood would not meet its economic expectations. Instead, Pulte chose to assume that the product would meet its specific needs. Pulte did not inquire as to the capabilities of plywood treated with Osmose fire retardant chemicals nor did Pulte demand assurances and warranties from Osmose that the products would meet its expectations. As a result, Pulte suffered a bitter and costly economic loss. Having failed to avail itself of the opportunity to mitigate the risks of potential disappointment at the time of contract negotiation, Pulte cannot now resort to the courts to save it from a bargain improvidently made.
>
> We now turn to Pulte's fraud claim. Although the economic loss rule bars recovery for tort claims arising from breach of a contract, the doctrine does not preclude a claim for damages occasioned by an independent tort, including fraud in the inducement of a contract. Fraud in the inducement and deceit are independent torts for which compensatory and punitive damages may be recovered [citing cases]. Nevertheless, at trial, Pulte failed to prove its claim of fraud in the inducement. The grant of judgment in favor of Osmose is AFFIRMED.

The Eleventh Circuit, applying Florida law in *Pulte*, applied the Economic Loss Rule strictly against the commercial consumer of a manufactured construction product. As there was no contract between Pulte and Osmose, and no manufacturer's warranty of the chemical running to Pulte, as the purchaser, Pulte's only claim was in tort—negligence or fraud.[100] The court was impressed with Pulte's commercial sophistication and the fact that there were contracts between Pulte and the plywood suppliers, and subcontracts between the suppliers and Osmose. The court also noted Pulte had the opportunity to negotiate for warranties or product details prior to purchasing its plywood products. Other consumers of construction products and components might well lack that level of sophistication.

The court also strictly applied the "damage to other property" test. The damage to other property analysis is fairly simple to articulate. Its application

---

100. Note that Pulte's fraud claim would have avoided the Economic Loss Rule if supported by the evidence. *See also* Bradley Woodcraft, Inc. v. Bodden, 795 S.E.2d 253, 258–59 (N.C. Ct. App. 2016) (owner's fraud claim against contractor not barred by the Economic Loss Rule).

is less so. In the construction arena in particular, many if not most times the defective nature of a product can cause "physical damage." Examples include water intrusion from an improperly applied roofing membrane, and cracked marble flooring due to a badly deflecting floor truss. Whether these damages are recoverable in negligence depends on how a particular jurisdiction defines "product" and "other property" which is damaged by the defective product, whether the parties are in privity, and how the jurisdiction frames its desired exceptions to the rule.

If the integrated structure is the "product," the Economic Loss Rule bars recovery for any damaged part of it.[101] A significant number of courts, and the Restatement (Third) of Torts,[102] follow the broad "integrated product" analysis. If the defendant manufacturer of the allegedly defective construction product convinces the court that the product is so integrated into the structure (or a construction system within the structure) that it loses its identity,[103] then the integrated whole becomes the "product." If the structure is the "product," it cannot be "other property" for the purposes of physical damage to avoid the Economic Loss Rule against the manufacturer. On the other hand, a number of

---

101. *See, e.g.*, Calloway v. City of Reno, 993 P.2d 1259, 1267, 116 Nev. 250, 262 (Nev. 2000) (roofing and siding defects causing water damage to interior structural components, held, damage to the "product" only); American Towers Owners v. CCI Mechanical, 930 P.2d 1182 (Utah 1996) (damage to plumbing pipes in the entire complex was damage to the "product" for purposes of the Economic Loss Rule, no recovery); Blagg v. Fred Hunt Co., 612 S.W.2d 321 (Ark. 1981) (house may be a "product" just as is an automobile); Chicago Heights Venture v. Dynamit Nobel of Am., 782 F.2d 723 (7th Cir. 1986) (defective roofing material allowed leaks damaging building, held, building is completed product); Casa Clara Condo. Ass'n, Inc. v. Charley Toppino & Sons, Inc., 620 So. 2d 1244 (Fla. 1993) (concrete with high salt content corroded reinforcing steel in balconies causing balconies to crumble—held, no damage to "other property"); Foxcroft Townhome Owners Ass'n v. Hoffman Rosner Corp., 449 N.E.2d 125 (Ill. 1983) (damages resulting from defective siding not damage to "other property"); Dakota Gasification Co. v. Pascoe Bldg. Sys., 91 F.3d 1094, 1099 (8th Cir. 1996) (applying N.D. law); Detroit Edison Co. v. NABCO, Inc., 35 F.3d 236 (6th Cir. 1994) (applying Mich. law).

102. The RESTATEMENT (THIRD) OF TORTS describes the characterization process (separate or incorporated) when products are incorporated into a system as "difficult." Nonetheless, the RESTATEMENT authors opine: "When the product or system is deemed to be an integrated whole, courts treat such damage as harm to the product itself." RESTATEMENT (THIRD) OF TORTS: PRODUCTS LIABILITY, § 21 cmt. e, 295–96 (1997). But as observed by at least one commentator and several courts, this analysis fails to recognize the duties "that arise independently of the pyramid structure of privity created by the tiers of contracts and subcontracts." Cheezem, *supra* note 51, at 22. *See also* Gilbane Bldg. Co. v. Nemours Found., 606 F. Supp. 995, 1005 (D. Del. 1985) (recognizing the interdependence of construction participants).

103. *See, e.g.*, Nat'l Union Fire Ins. Co. of Pittsburgh, Pa. v. Pratt & Whitney Canada, Inc., 107 Nev. 535 (Nev. 1991) (a defective part in the engine of a factory-assembled airplane damaged the engine and the airplane, held airplane was the integrated whole, and therefore the "product").

courts have not followed the strict "integrated structure as a product" analysis. These judges allow recovery against a remote manufacturer for property damage to "other property" when the defective product damaged another identifiable construction component.[104]

Another issue raised in *Pulte* is whether the demolition of adjacent and otherwise acceptable materials and components in the buildings constituted damage to other property. The court in *Pulte* drew a distinction between direct damage caused to other construction components and "consequential" damage caused by the repair or remediation of defective components.

Some defective products cases (most outside the construction arena) allow recovery of economic damages when the cause of the physical property damage to the product is from an outside source, such as fire.[105] Courts also have made distinctions when damaged property is contained within, but not

---

104. *See, e.g.*, Lamb v. Georgia-Pacific Corp., 392 S.E.2d 307, 308 (Ga. App. 1990) (allegedly defective particle board installed underneath tile floor caused tile to crack, held, costs to repair damaged portion of the tile floor were recoverable as damage to "property other than the product itself," but that other economic damages would be denied); Comptech Int'l. Inc. v. Milam Commerce Park, Ltd., 753 So. 2d 1219 (Fla. 1999) (negligence claim by tenant against landlord in selection of contractor who damaged tenant's electrical systems, warehouse space and computers during renovation, held, existing electrical systems and computers were "other property") overruled by Tiara Condo. Ass'n, Inc. v. Marsh & McLennan Companies, Inc., 110 So. 3d 399, 407 (Fla. 2013); Saratoga Fishing Co. v. J. M. Martinac & Co., 520 U.S. 875, 879 (1997) (ship's defective component damaged equipment added to the ship after the ship's initial purchase, held, added equipment was "other property"); City of La Crosse v. Schubert, Schroeder & Assoc., 240 N.W.2d 124 (Wis. 1976) (remote purchaser's negligence action against manufacturer of a roof that leaked and required replacement, held, damages to other parts of the structure were recoverable); United Air Lines, Inc. v. CEI Indus. of Illinois, Inc., 499 N.E.2d 558 (Ill. App. 1986) (water leaks in defective roof caused collapse of ceiling, held, damage to other property when damage involved "some violence or collision" and not deterioration or internal breakage, held, recovery of economic damages against manufacturer allowed). *See, e.g., Jimenez*, 58 P.3d at 450 (Cal. 2002) (strict liability case against manufacturer—defective windows caused water damage to walls, floors, etc., held, "other property"); Stearman v. Centex Homes, 78 Cal. App. 4th 611 (Cal. Ct. App. 2000) (strict liability case—defective foundation construction and inadequate soil compaction caused slab movement, deformation and cracked walls, held, physical damage to "other property"); Northridge Co. v. W. R. Grace and Co., 471 N.W.2d 179 (Wis. 1991) (asbestos causes physical harm to structure, held, structure is "other property" and outside the Economic Loss Rule).

105. *See, e.g.*, Rocky Mountain Fire & Cas. Co. v. Biddulph Oldsmobile, 640 P.2d 851 (Ariz. 1982) (Winnebago destroyed by fire, held Economic Loss Rule does not apply to property damage, but would apply to claim for lost profits or other commercial losses); Gherna v. Ford Motor Co., 246 Cal. App. 2d 639, 649 (1966) (fire in the engine compartment which destroyed the entire automobile, some economic losses allowed); *but see* Lloyd Wood Coal Co. v. Clark Equip. Co., 543 So. 2d 671 (Ala. 1989) (front end loader's hydraulic hose ruptured causing a fire, but damage only to the product itself, economic losses barred).

integrated into, the structure.[106] In *Scott & Fetzer Co. v. Montgomery Ward & Co.*,[107] fire warning systems malfunctioned in a large warehouse occupied by several tenants. The fire spread throughout the warehouse, causing damage to the structure leased by various tenants and their personal property. The court went so far as to deem the loss of the value of the tenants' leasehold and their personal items to be "not economic" because the damage was for "loss of property other than the defective product."[108]

Courts also struggle with the situation where the product is defective or potentially dangerous, but has not yet injured anyone. The Court of Judicial Appeals of Maryland (Maryland's highest court) carved out an exception to the otherwise accepted Economic Loss Rule (no recovery if the defective product has not caused physical injury) when the defect can lead to a "serious risk of creating a dangerous condition."[109] In *Whiting-Turner*, the defect was both in the product and in the construction installation services of the contractors, not just in a building component, but it does illustrate the problem of potential damage to person or property.

Council of Co-Owners Atlantis Condominium, et al. v. Whiting-Turner Contracting Co., et al.
517 A.2d 336 (Md. 1986).

McAULIFFE, Judge.

The principal issue presented by this appeal is the extent to which tort liability should be imposed upon builders and architects for damages suffered by parties who enjoy no contractual privity with them. We hold that privity is not an absolute prerequisite to the existence of a tort duty in this type of case, and that the duty of

---

106. *See* 2-J Corp. v. Tice, 126 F.3d 539, 544 (3d Cir. 1997) (collapsed metal building caused damage to stored inventory, held, "other property" from defective metal building, manufacturer was liable for economic losses) (applying Pa. law).

107. 493 N.E.2d 1022 (Ill. 1986).

108. *Id.* at 1026. The court also noted that the damage was caused by a "sudden and dangerous conflagration."

109. Council of Co-Owners Atlantis Condo., Inc. v. Whiting-Turner Contracting Co., 517 A.2d 336, 345 (Md. 1986) (electrical utility shafts did not contain required insulation—creating a building code violation and potential hazard). Although the project was multifamily residential, the Maryland court did not create an exception to the Economic Loss Rule strictly for residential properties.

builders and architects to use due care in the design, inspection, and construction of a building extends to those persons foreseeably subjected to the risk of personal injury because of a latent and unreasonably dangerous condition resulting from that negligence. Additionally, we hold that where the dangerous condition is discovered before it results in injury, an action in negligence will lie for the recovery of the reasonable cost of correcting the condition.

The Atlantis Condominium is a twenty-one story building containing 198 separate condominium units and located in Ocean City, Maryland. The council of unit owners as the governing regime of the condominium, and three unit owners who sue in their individual capacity, brought an action in tort against the general contractor, developer, and architects involved in the construction of the building, contending that as a result of their negligence the utility shafts and related electrical work were not constructed and installed in accordance with the plans and specifications and did not comply with the requirements of the applicable building code. They allege that these latent conditions create a fire hazard that "presents a threat to the safety and welfare of the owners and occupants of the Atlantis Condominium and to the personal and real property of [the] owners and occupants."

The specific deficiency alleged is the failure to construct ten vertical utility shafts with materials having a fire resistance rating of two hours. Appellants do not allege negligence in the design of the shafts, but rather a failure to construct the shafts in accordance with the design. They allege negligent construction on the part of Whiting-Turner Contracting Company, the general contractor; negligent inspection, supervision, and acceptance of the work on the part of Meyers & D'Aleo, Inc., the design and supervising architects; and negligent inspection and misrepresentation on the part of Ewing Cole Erdman Rizzio Cherry Parsky, a partnership, and Alexander Ewing, individually, who they allege were the architects employed "to inspect the building and to certify to the Building Inspection Department of Ocean City, Maryland, that the building was constructed pursuant to the approved building permit in accordance with the plans and specifications submitted with the original permit application and that the building was ready for occupancy." Additionally, Appellants allege that Colonial Mortgage Service Company ("Colonial") was a developer of the project and that it knowingly or negligently permitted the shafts to be built at variance with the plans, as well as the requirements of the building code, and negligently obtained an occupancy permit. Appellants also allege that in advertising and selling the units, the developer negligently misrepresented "the building's suitability for occupancy." Appellants seek compensatory and punitive damages from each Appellee.

The builder and the certifying architects filed demurrers, contending that the declaration failed to allege facts sufficient to show a duty owing by them to Appellants. They contended that in the absence of privity no duty could arise. Recognizing, however, that the modern trend was toward the recognition of a duty to third parties under some circumstances, they advanced the alternative argument that a duty should not be recognized in this case because Appellants had suffered only economic loss, and not personal injury or property damage. The developer also demurred, asserting as its sole challenge to the sufficiency of the count against it that there was no allegation of personal injury or property damage, and that it "cannot be liable in tort to plaintiffs for purely economic loss." The trial judge sustained the demurrers without leave to amend, concluding that Maryland law would not recognize a tort duty in the absence of privity under these circumstances, and that in any event a duty would not be recognized where only economic loss was claimed. We restrict our consideration of the sufficiency of the pleadings to those grounds specifically set forth in the demurrer.

It is now the almost universal rule that the contractor is liable to all those who may foreseeably be injured by the structure, not only when he fails to disclose dangerous conditions known to him, *but also when the work is negligently done*. This applies not only to contractors doing original work, but also to those who make repairs, or install parts, as well as supervising architects and engineers. There may be liability for negligent design, as well as for negligent construction. This trend was also reflected by the incorporation of § 385 into the *Restatement (Second) of Torts* (1965). One who on behalf of the possessor of land erects a structure or creates any other condition thereon is subject to liability to others upon or outside of the land for physical harm caused to them by the dangerous character of the structure or condition after his work has been accepted by the possessor, under the same rules as those determining the liability of one who as manufacturer or independent contractor makes a chattel for the use of others.

In following the modern trend, we hold that privity is not an absolute prerequisite to the existence of a tort duty. The duty of the architects and the builders in this case, to use due care in the design, inspection, and construction of this condominium, extended to those persons foreseeably subjected to the risk of personal injury created, as here, by a latent and unreasonably dangerous condition resulting from their negligence.

We turn to the question of whether this type of action may be maintained against a builder or architect where the risk of personal injury exists, but personal injury has not in fact resulted. We conclude that the determination of whether a duty will be imposed in this type of case should depend upon the risk generated by the negligent conduct, rather than upon the fortuitous circumstance of the nature of the resultant damage. Where the risk is of death or personal injury the action will lie for recovery of the reasonable cost of correcting the dangerous condition.

The inquiry of Maryland's highest court, drilling down into the facts, exposed one of the Economic Loss Rule's major weaknesses when applied in the construction context—that a defective product or condition may be potentially dangerous without causing physical (and, therefore, recoverable) damage.[110] Even when a defect creates an inherently dangerous situation, the Economic Loss Rule, strictly applied, bars any recovery (and, therefore, without bodily injury would prevent an action) for the repair or replacement of the defective product.[111] The Maryland court determined that focusing on the "fortuitous circumstance of the nature of the resultant damage" was the wrong approach.[112]

Other cases have reached the opposite result. In an economic loss products case involving potentially dangerous corroding steel wall panels,[113] the U.S. Court of Appeals for the Seventh Circuit strictly applied the Economic Loss Rule to the owner's negligence count. Writing for the court, Judge Posner acknowledged that allowing recovery for bodily injuries caused by a defective product (including economic damages arising from the injuries), but barring recovery for economic damages in the absence of bodily injury caused by the same defective product, was a matter of fortuity. Still, Judge Posner observed, the court "could not recast this case as if one of the corroded wall panels had fallen and broken [the plaintiff's] foot."[114]

---

110. In *Whiting-Turner*, the court observed: "Why should a buyer have to wait for a personal tragedy to occur in order to recover damages to remedy or repair defects?" 517 A.2d at 345.

111. One lower court has opined that only a few jurisdictions allow direct negligence actions for purely economic losses, or have recognized tort-based warranties, against *product manufacturers* of defective construction components not in privity, without a showing of physical harm or the serious risk of harm. *See Wilson*, 206 F. Supp. 2d at 749 (structure as a whole suffered only economic damages even though water intrusion allowed by defective cladding caused structural damage, held, economic loss rule applied to claim v. remote manufacturer) (citing cases). *Compare* the application of the rule to construction service providers.

112. *Id. See also* Kennedy v. Columbia Lumber & Mfg. Co., Inc., 299 S.C. 335 (S.C. 1989), where the court opined: "We find that this legal framework [focusing only upon the type of damage incurred] generates difficulties. This is so because the framework's focus is on consequences, not action. . . . The framework we adopt focuses on activity, not consequence."

113. Miller v. United States Steel Corp., 902 F.2d 573 (7th Cir. 1990).

114. *Id.* at 574. Interestingly, less than two years later, in a somewhat analogous case involving general liability (GL) coverage for "property damage," Judge Posner opined that "The incorporation of a defective product into another product inflicts *physical injury* in the relevant sense [insurance coverage] on the latter [the non-defective product] at the moment of

B. Claims of Defective Construction Services (Including Poor Workmanship and Improper Furnishing of Materials) (No Privity)

Construction involves the delegation and allocation of responsibility and risk by contract.[115] Within the "pyramid" of this process, however, many of the participants are not in privity of contract.[116] Their defective work and products can cause economic damage to other providers, and cause other contractors to be targets of claims involving defective work. Strictly applied, the Economic Loss Rule often prohibits direct negligence actions by construction participants against those principally responsible for construction defects even though the parties to the dispute are not in privity of contract.[117] The theory underlying this strict approach is that the law of contract, not the law of torts should provide the sole remedy[118] since it is preferable to allow parties to allocate economic risks by contract rather than imposing risk allocation as a matter of law.[119]

Naturally, there are exceptions, and different courts emphasize different legal concepts. The issues taken up by the courts to determine the extent of the rule's application where construction services are involved are similar, but differ slightly from those grappled with by courts concerning manufactured

---

incorporation—here, the moment when the defective Qest systems were installed in homes." (emphasis added). *See* Elger Mfg., Inc. v. Liberty Mut. Ins. Co., 972 F.2d 805, 814 (7th Cir. 1992) (declaratory judgment action brought to determine if physical injury occurred for the purposes of property damage triggering GL coverage); *see also* Roger H. Proulx & Co. v. Crest Liners, Inc., 98 Cal. App. 4th 182 (2002) (insurance broker sued in negligence for failure to procure coverage, defended on basis that the underlying claims were barred by economic loss rule, held, claimed damages raised triable issue).

115. Construction providers do not manufacture or supply "products," at least for strict liability purposes. *See* RESTATEMENT (THIRD) OF TORTS: PRODUCTS LIABILITY, §19, subd. (b) ("services, even when provided commercially, are not products" and are therefore governed by the law of negligence).

116. For instance, the mason is a subcontractor to the general contractor, but the mason has no contract with the sitework subcontractor who has left the site a muddy mess, prohibiting the mason from making progress in constructing concrete block walls. *See* LAN/STV v. Martin K. Eby Constr. Co., Inc., 435 S.W.3d 234, 246 (Tex. 2014) for a discussion of nature of the contractual relationships on a typical construction project.

117. As we have seen, privity will trigger the application of the Economic Loss Rule to bar negligence claims for economic losses. *See Wausau Tile*, 593 N.W.2d 445.

118. McConnell v. Servinsky Eng'g, PLLC, 22 F. Supp. 3d 610, 614 (W.D. Va. 2014).

119. LAN/STV v. Martin K. Eby Const. Co., Inc., 435 S.W.3d 234, 235 (Tex. 2014).

products.[120] If the parties to a dispute involving defective construction services are not in privity of contract, courts look to the scope of work and duties the service provider has undertaken contractually, whether damage to "other property" has occurred, whether the defective work can be related to an independent duty, and whether application of the Economic Loss Rule will deprive the plaintiff of remedy.[121] While a few courts have deemed lack of privity an absolute bar to any tort claim for economic losses other than for fraud,[122] most states consider the lack of privity as a starting point to discuss scope of services, damage to "other property," and the presence or absence of an independent duty.[123]

If the plaintiff is not in privity with the provider of defective work, but the damaged work was the subject matter of the provider's contract, the rule will also generally bar recovery based on economic damages to the work, where only the work was injured.[124] On the other hand, a plaintiff may avoid the economic loss rule by demonstrating that regardless of the nature of the damage, the defendant breached a tort duty, independent of (although generally related to) the service provider's contract.[125]

---

120. The agreements of construction service providers are, for instance, generally not governed by the UCC.

121. For a recent decision in which a court considered the equities of allowing the Economic Loss Rule to completely bar a claim *see* Wyman v. Ayer Properties, LLC, 469 Mass. 64, 11 N.E.3d 1074 (2014).

122. *See* Sensenbrenner v. Rust, Orling & Neale Architects, Inc., 374 S.E.2d 55 (Va. 1988) (homeowners' action against pool subcontractor and architect dismissed for lack of privity) abrogated by statute, VA CODE ANN. § 8.01-223 (lack of privity no defense in cases where plaintiff seeks recovery for injury to person or property), as recognized in Nystrom v. Servus Robots, L.L.C., LF-1517-3, 2000 WL 249246, at *3 (Va. Cir. Ct. Mar. 2, 2000).

123. *See, e.g.,* Petrus Family Trust Dated May 1, 1991 v. Kirk, 163 Idaho 490 (Idaho, 2018).

124. Calloway v. City of Reno, 993 P.2d 1259, 1261, 116 Nev. 250, 253 (Nev. 2000) (townhome owners' claims against subcontractors for defective roofing and siding did not state cause of action in negligence for purely economic losses); Jardel Enterprises, Inc. v. Triconsultants, Inc., 770 P.2d 1301 (Colo. App. 1988) (restaurant owner could not bring negligence claim against subcontractor for lost profits resulting from delayed opening of restaurant due to initial construction of the restaurant at the wrong location); Nastri v. Wood Bros. Homes, Inc., 690 P.2d 158, 163–64 (Ariz. App. 1984) (despite latent structural defects, remote purchasers could not recover from builder on negligence theory, but could recover for implied-in-law warranty of habitability).

125. *See* Consol. Hardwoods, Inc. v. Alexander Concrete Constr., Inc., 811 P.2d 440, 443 (Colo. App. 1991) (owner negligence claim allowed against subcontractor because independent duty was breached); Juliano v. Gaston, 455 A.2d 523 (N.J. 1982) (owner may recover against subcontractor in negligence for economic damages).

Town of Alma v. AZCO Constr., Inc.
10 P.3d 1256 (Colo. 2000)

Justice Rice delivered the Opinion of the Court.

The Town of Alma, joined by several individual town residents, filed suit against AZCO Construction, Inc. ("AZCO"), asserting claims for breach of contract, breach of the implied warranty of sound workmanship, and negligence. The trial court dismissed Petitioners' negligence and breach of implied warranty of sound workmanship claims and a jury returned a verdict for AZCO on the breach of contract claim. Petitioners appealed the trial court's dismissal of their negligence and breach of implied warranty of sound workmanship claims and the court of appeals affirmed the dismissal of the claims. We granted Petitioners' petition for writ of certiorari to review the court of appeals' judgment affirming the trial court's dismissal of Petitioners' negligence claim. We now affirm the judgment of the court of appeals.

Petitioners' amended complaint alleged the following facts: On October 28, 1992, the town and AZCO entered into a contract for the construction of improvements to Petitioners' water distribution system. The contract called for AZCO to install new water mains, and to tie those water mains to existing water service lines which served residential properties in the town. The contract contained two separate warranty provisions. Section 29.1 of the contract, titled "GUARANTEE," provided, "[AZCO] shall guarantee all materials and equipment furnished and WORK performed for a period of one (1) year from the date of SUBSTANTIAL COMPLETION. [AZCO] warrants and guarantees . . . that the completed system is free from all defects due to faulty materials or workmanship. . . ." In addition, section 3.3.1 of the "Special Conditions" attached to the contract, titled "MAINTENANCE AND GUARANTY," provided, "[AZCO] hereby guarantees that the entire work constructed by [it] under the contract will fully meet all requirements of the contract as to quality of workmanship and materials. . . . [AZCO] hereby agrees to make at [its] own expense, any repairs or replacement made necessary by defects in materials or workmanship supplied by [it] that become evident within one year after the date of final payment. . . ."

In 1993, AZCO installed 115 flared fittings for the water service line connections. In June 1995, Petitioners discovered leaks in three water service line connections that AZCO installed pursuant to the contract. AZCO repaired those three leaks under the one-year warranty provision of the contract. In November 1995 and June 1996, additional leaks in water service line connections were discovered but AZCO refused to repair these leaks on the basis that the one-year warranty provision had expired. The leaks were repaired at the expense of individual town residents.

Petitioners filed suit against AZCO on November 27, 1996, asserting various claims, including negligence. The trial court granted AZCO's motion to dismiss the negligence claim and the case proceeded to trial on the breach of contract claim only, with the jury returning a verdict for AZCO on this claim.

Petitioners appealed the trial court's dismissal of their negligence claims. In affirming the dismissal of Petitioners' negligence claim, the court of appeals relied on the economic loss rule and stated that "[t]o hold otherwise would permit the non-breaching party to avoid the contractual limitation of remedy." Town of Alma, 985 P.2d at 57. We granted certiorari to review the dismissal of Petitioners' negligence claim.

This case presents an opportunity for us to address the status of the economic loss rule in Colorado. The rule has been applied by our court of appeals in various contexts to bar tort claims. As this is a matter of first impression, our analysis encompasses an examination of the development of the rule in other jurisdictions, as well as a discussion of the principles and rationale underlying the rule.

Limiting tort liability when a contract exists between parties is appropriate because a product's potential nonperformance can be adequately addressed by rational economic actors bargaining at arms length to shape the terms of the contract. For example, a buyer may demand additional warranties on a product while agreeing to pay a higher price, or the same buyer may choose to assume a higher level of risk that a product will not perform properly by accepting a more limited warranty in exchange for a lower product price. Limiting the availability of tort remedies in these situations holds parties to the terms of their bargain. In this way, the law serves to encourage parties to confidently allocate risks and costs during their bargaining without fear that unanticipated liability may arise in the future, effectively negating the parties' efforts to build these cost considerations into the contract. The economic loss rule thus serves to ensure predictability in commercial transactions.

The key to determining the availability of a contract or tort action lies in determining the source of the duty that forms the basis of the action. We find the following discussion by the South Carolina Supreme Court informative:

> The question, thus, is not whether the damages are physical or economic. Rather the question of whether the plaintiff may maintain an action in tort for purely economic loss turns on the determination of the source of the duty [the] plaintiff claims the defendant owed. A breach of a duty which arises under the provisions of a contract between the parties must be redressed under contract, and a tort action will not lie. A breach of a duty *arising independently* of any contract duties between the parties, however, may support a tort action. *Tommy L. Griffin Plumbing & Heating Co. v. Jordan, Jones & Goulding, Inc.*, 320 S.C. 49, 463 S.E.2d 85, 88 (1995) (emphasis added).

Determining when a contract action will lie and when a tort action will lie requires maintaining this distinction in the sources of the respective obligations. The phrase "economic loss rule" necessarily implies that the focus of the inquiry under its analysis is on the type of damages suffered by the aggrieved party. However, the relationship between the type of damages suffered and the availability of a tort action is inexact at best. Examining the type of damages suffered may assist in determining the source of the duty underlying the action (e.g., most actions for lost profits are based on breaches of contractual duties while most actions involving physical injuries to persons are based on common law duties of care). However, some torts are expressly designed to remedy pure economic loss (*e.g.*, professional negligence, fraud, and breach of fiduciary duty). It is here that substantial confusion arises from the use of the term "economic loss rule."

This confusion can be avoided, however, by maintaining the focus on the source of the duty alleged to have been violated. For example, we have recognized that some special relationships by their nature automatically trigger an independent duty of care that supports a tort action even when the parties have entered into a contractual relationship. *See, e.g., Bebo Constr. Co. v. Mattox & O'Brien, P.C.*, 990 P.2d 78, 83 (Colo.1999) (attorney-client relationship creates independent duty of care); *Greenberg v. Perkins*, 845 P.2d 530, 534 (Colo.1993) (physician-patient relationship creates independent duty of care, as does physician's independent medical examination of non-patient); *Farmers Group, Inc. v. Trimble*, 691 P.2d 1138, 1141–42 (Colo.1984) (quasi-fiduciary nature of insurer-insured relationship creates independent duty of care). We have also recognized that certain common law claims that sound in tort and are expressly designed to remedy economic loss may exist independent of a breach of contract claim. *See Brody v. Bock*, 897 P.2d 769, 776 (Colo.1995) (common law fraud claim is based on violation of a duty independent of contract); *Keller v. A. O. Smith Harvestore Prods., Inc.*, 819 P.2d 69, 73 (Colo.1991) (negligent misrepresentation is a tort claim based "not on principles of contractual obligation but on principles of duty and reasonable conduct"). In these situations where we have recognized the existence of a duty *independent* of any contractual obligations, the economic loss rule has no application and does not bar a plaintiff's tort claim because the claim is based on a recognized independent duty of care and thus does not fall within the scope of the rule.

Turning to the facts before us, the contract in the instant case expressly assigned a duty of care to AZCO in the installation of the water system. It was this contractual duty that AZCO allegedly breached. AZCO expressly assumed the duty to guarantee its quality of workmanship and its materials when it undertook to install the water system. As such, Petitioners have failed to demonstrate that AZCO breached any duty independent of its contractual obligations.

Moreover, the town and the individual landowners are only seeking damages for the cost of repair and replacement of the water lines that were the subject of the contract. Damages for the cost of repair and replacement of property that were the subject of the contract constitute economic loss damages that must be supported by an independent duty of care to be recoverable in a negligence action. As there is no independent duty to support Petitioners' negligence claim, the economic loss rule bars this claim.

The court in *Town of Alma* would have allowed recovery in negligence for purely economic damages, specifically defects in the work provided under the contract, provided the plaintiffs could show breach of a tort duty independent of the contract.[126] Conversely, other courts have held that if the plaintiff is in privity with the defendant, or the defendant's contract covers tasks that were defectively performed that caused the complained-of economic damages, the breach of the obligations of the contract ordinarily cannot be relied on to support an action in negligence; the parties (or at least one of the parties) have already selected a contractual remedy. Failure to perform one's contract, even carelessly, generally will not support a negligence action for economic damages to the work.[127]

Emphasizing the duty breached, rather than the nature of the damages resulting from a breach, can also raise questions. In *Town of Alma* the court concluded there was no breach of a duty independent of the contract. Presumably one engaged in any course of conduct, even to carry out a contract, has a duty to exercise reasonable care not to injure others. When a structure is defective in some regard, and the individuals responsible for the structure did not exercise due care, the resulting damages seem to be the result of something very close to negligence. Nevertheless the court concluded the duty owed to the town in *Town of Alma* arose by contract only.

Economic injuries caused by the defective work but visited upon "other property" may be enough to allow a negligence action to proceed.[128] Dam-

---

126. *See also* Olympic Products Co. v. Roof Sys., Inc., 363 S.E.2d 367 (N.C. App. 1988) (manufacturer's failure to properly inspect installation or thereafter to report improper installation deemed independent negligence, economic damages allowed); Raynor Steel Erection v. York Constr. Co., 351 S.E.2d 136 (N.C. 1986) (economic damages allowed in negligence due to general contractor's failure to properly install); Brown v. Fowler, 279 N.W.2d 907 (S.D. 1979) (remote residence purchaser has a negligence claim against builder for economic damages due to breach of separate duty. This was not an implied warranty of habitability case—which under South Dakota law extends only to the initial purchaser).

127. *See, e.g.*, Palmetto Linen Service, Inc. v. U.N.X., Inc., 205 F.3d 126, 129 (4th Cir. 2000) (applying S.C. law), *quoting from Kennedy*, 384 S.E.2d at 737 ("the 'economic loss' rule will still apply where duties are created *solely* by contract") (emphasis in original).

128. *See, e.g.*, Aas v. Superior Court, 12 P.3d 1125, 1130, 101 Cal. Rptr. 2d 718, 723, 24 Cal. 4th 627, 635 (2000) (homeowners' association and individual homeowners could not bring negligence actions against developer, contractor, or subcontractors for construction defects or diminution in value, unless property damage to "other property" could be shown. "Any construction defect can diminish the value of a house. But the difference between price paid and value received, and deviations from standards of quality that have not resulted in property damage or personal injury, are primarily the domain of contract and warranty law or the law of fraud, rather than of negligence") (citing cases).

age to "other property" generally means property unrelated to the service provider's work. Thus, the "incorporation" and "integration" analysis concerning manufactured products also pertains to claims against and between service providers.[129] A number of courts hold that contractors and service providers both owe a tort duty to those not in privity for forseeable losses and damages proximately caused by their negligent acts.[130] These courts made no distinction between the designer and the constructor. Other courts, however, have recognized a distinction, to the benefit of the design professional.

C. Claims of Defective Design Professional Services (Including Insufficient Design and Improper Contract Administration Services) (No Privity)

There are two main varieties of construction disputes involving design professionals where this is no privity of contract between the plaintiff and the defendant. In the first type of case, the plaintiff played no role in the construction of the project but was instead simply a subsequent purchaser, a user of the project, or perhaps an adjacent property owner. This type of case is exemplified by the decision in *2314 Lincoln Park West Condominium Association v. Mann, Gin, Ebel & Frazier, Ltd.* (discussed in the following box) where a homeowners' association sued the designer. The second type of case is one in which the plaintiff was a participant in the construction project, such as the general contractor, who suffered harm as a result of errors or omissions on the part of the designer. Recall that while the general contractor and design professional each have their own contracts with the project owner, they might not have a direct contractual relationship with each other, and, if so, a contractor's only recourse against a designer is in tort. This type of case is exemplified by *Ellis-Don Construction, Inc. v. HKS, Inc.* (also discussed later) where the general contractor sued the designer. The distinctions between types of plaintiff can be helpful in understanding the different ways the Economic Loss Rule has been applied to non-privity claims against design professionals.

---

129. *See* discussion *supra* at notes 101–106 as to the incorporation of products and services to form an "integrated product"—the structure. *But see* Comptech Intern., Inc. v. Milam Commerce Park, Ltd., 753 So. 2d 1219 (Fla. 1999) (tenant sued landlord for negligent selection of contractor, who in renovating tenant space in warehouse, damaged electrical and computer equipment, held, contract was for a service—the renovation—and court suggested that services do not involve "other property." However, to the extent that the warehouse was the object of the contract, the wiring and computers were "other property").

130. *See* McDonough v. Whalen, 313 N.E.2d 435 (Mass. 1974) (both the designer and installer of a defective septic system owed a tort duty to property owners not in privity).

2314 Lincoln Park West Condominium Ass'n v. Mann, Gin, Ebel & Frazier, Ltd.
555 N.E.2d 346 (Ill. 1990)

Justice MILLER delivered the opinion of the court:

The plaintiff, Conservatory Condominium Association, is an association of the owners of the 39 condominium units located at 2314 Lincoln Park West in Chicago. Mann, Gin, Ebel & Frazier, Ltd. (Mann) is the architectural firm that designed the project and certified its completion. The plaintiff brought the present action in Cook County seeking an award of damages for the cost of making certain repairs to the building in which the association members' condominium units are located. Plaintiff seeks recovery on a negligence theory from the architectural firm responsible for the building's design.

The plaintiff alleges that numerous defects in the design and construction of the project had become known to the unit owners by late 1986. According to the complaint, windows and glass doors were loose, the roof leaked, the heating and cooling systems and other utilities were inadequate and did not function properly, and the garage was settling. The plaintiff does not deny that the recovery requested in the present action is for what we have termed economic loss. The plaintiff is seeking an award of damages for the cost of repairing defects in the property, and there is no contention that personal injury or damage to other property has resulted. The plaintiff in the present case seeks compensation for the cost of repairing certain defects allegedly occurring in the construction of the condominium unit owners' residences.

The gravamen of the plaintiff's claim for negligence against Mann is dissatisfaction with the way in which the building was designed and constructed, and the failure of the building to meet the unit owners' expectations. As our prior decisions concerning the construction industry fully illustrate, such a claim concerns the quality, rather than the safety, of the building and thus is a matter more appropriately resolved under contract law.

We decline to impose on Mann a duty in tort to protect the unit owners from the sort of loss asserted. The architect's responsibility originated in its contract with the original owner, and in these circumstances its duties should be measured accordingly. Recovery of the nature requested here essentially seeks damages for a difference in quality. "There is room in the market for goods of varying quality, and if the purchaser buys goods which turn out to be below its expectations, its remedy should be against the person from whom it bought the goods, based upon the contract with that person." [citing cases]

While we do not intend in the present case to determine the future application of *the* economic loss rule in all areas of professional malpractice, we must reject the plaintiff's theory that denial of the negligence claim against the present architect would signal in general the end of malpractice recovery in tort. It may be noted that in suits involving malpractice claims against health care professionals, personal injury will generally be the alleged result, and therefore the rule would not bar recovery in any event. Moreover, we believe that other professional relationships are readily distinguishable from the present case. For example, malpractice actions against attorneys have gone forward, without any suggestion that the form of recovery traditionally recognized in such actions [economic losses] would no longer be allowed. [citing cases] Moreover, those cases recognize an extracontractual duty not only to the client but also to the group of persons the client intended to benefit. Such a duty arises from a consideration of the nature of the undertaking and the lawyer's traditional responsibilities. The same cannot be said with respect to the defendant architect in the present case.

Curiously, Illinois allows nonprivity negligence actions for economic losses against other professionals and nonprofessionals outside the construction process, including accountants,[131] attorneys,[132] and stock market indexing services,[133] but not against architects. The court in *Lincoln Park* sought to distinguish those situations by focusing on different duties and different types of damages.

Ellis-Don Constr., Inc. v. HKS, Inc.
353 F. Supp. 2d 603 (M.D.N.C. 2004)

BULLOCK, District Judge.

This diversity action, filed May 27, 2004, arises out of a hospital construction project in which Ellis-Don Construction, Inc. ("Plaintiff") served as the general contractor and HKS, Inc. ("HKS"), Smith Seckman Reid, Inc. ("SSR"), and Corley Redfoot Zack, Inc. ("CRZ") (together, "Defendants") served as the design team, responsible for overall project design and management. Plaintiff alleges that Defendants performed their duties negligently, resulting in construction delays and cost overruns that forced Plaintiff to incur economic losses in excess of $1,000,000.

The University of North Carolina Hospitals, a state "public body" and owner of the construction project at issue here, contracted with HKS to design and manage

---

131. Congregation of the Passion, Holy Cross Province v. Touche Ross & Co., 636 N.E.2d 503 (1994).

132. Collins v. Reynard, 607 N.E.2d 1185 (Ill. 1992) (an attorney's duty of competence exists "without regard to the terms of any contract of employment").

133. Rosenstein v. Standard & Poor's Corp., 636 N.E.2d 665 (Ill. App. 1993).

the construction of the North Carolina Children's Hospital and North Carolina Women's Hospital. HKS contracted with SSR and CRZ to serve as consultants on the project, with SSR providing services relating to the mechanical, plumbing, electric, and fire protection systems, and CRZ providing architectural services, including planning and design work, administration of the construction process, and inspections. Plaintiff contracted directly with the owner to provide general contractor services for the construction of the hospitals. No contractual privity existed between Plaintiff and any of the Defendants.

In North Carolina, "in the absence of privity of contract an architect may be held liable to a general contractor and his subcontractors for economic loss resulting from breach of a common law duty of care." Such duty of care "flow[s] from the parties' working relationship." Indeed, the courts of North Carolina have stated that the "power of economic life or death" an architect holds over a contractor requires that such a duty of care be recognized, even in the absence of privity of contract.

The Defendants argue that North Carolina's economic loss doctrine has expanded beyond its traditional realm of products liability and sales of goods to preclude Plaintiff's tort claim. The court disagrees. The economic loss doctrine, first articulated by the California Supreme Court in *Seely v. White Motor Co.,* 63 Cal.2d 9, 45 Cal. Rptr. 17, 403 P.2d 145 (1965), and adopted by the United States Supreme Court in *East River S.S. Corp. v. Transamerica Delaval, Inc.,* 476 U.S. 858, 106 S. Ct. 2295, 90 L. Ed. 2d 865 (1986), was conceived of as a means by which to confine products liability in tort to damages for personal injury and injury to property other than the goods sold, and leave to contract law the question of liability for purely economic losses. This approach was, and remains, firmly rooted in traditional concepts of warranty and contract law, and operates to "keep products liability and contract law in separate spheres and to maintain a realistic limitation on damages" in products liability cases. *East River,* 476 U.S. at 871, 106 S. Ct. 2308. In North Carolina, the economic loss doctrine limits the types of damages that a purchaser of a product may recover against the seller or manufacturer of the product through a negligence action. The purchaser cannot use claims of negligence to recover "purely economic losses" caused by the product's failure to meet expectations. Instead, the purchaser must use contract law, including the Uniform Commercial Code (UCC).

The Defendants explore at length the "roots" and "flowering" of North Carolina's economic loss rule in support of their motion to dismiss, but they appear to be harvesting the wrong field in attempting to use the rule as a bar to Plaintiff's tort claim. The economic loss rule poses no obstacle to Plaintiff's claim. As noted, North Carolina's economic loss rule bars claims in tort for purely economic losses in the sale of goods covered by contract law, including the UCC. It does not limit tort actions that arise in the absence of a contract, nor is there any indication that the courts of North Carolina have expanded the rule beyond its traditional role in products liability cases.

As observed in the preceding decisions, a party not in privity with the design professional will be allowed or be precluded from recovering for economic losses based on how the courts of its state apply the Economic Loss Rule. The reported cases go both ways, and the legal bases for the decisions are mixed. A number of courts find that no action for economic losses may be maintained by a third party against a construction design professional, regardless of the scope of its services or the foreseeability of harm. In the majority of these jurisdictions, the Economic Loss Rule (generally the "no duty" or "covered by another contract" analysis rather than the "privity" side) is invoked to reach this result.[134]

These courts do not dismiss actions because the third parties lack privity as such, but instead deduce that plaintiffs not in privity are not owed a duty by the design professional—thereby cutting off all economic damages.[135] To these judges, it is often at least noteworthy that the contract between the contractor and the owner contains provisions (including limitations) relating to foreseeable economic losses.[136] At least one jurisdiction, however, has not employed the Economic Loss Rule (denominated as such) in professional negligence actions, but instead has relied consistently and strictly on privity of contract to delete a third-party cause of action for professional negligence from the state's judicial framework.[137]

---

134. *See, e.g.*, Leis Family Ltd. P'ship v. Silversword Eng'g, 126 Haw. 532, 538, 273 P.3d 1218, 1224 (Ct. App. 2012) (subconsultant designers not in privity with owner did not owe tort duty to avoid economic losses); Fireman's Fund Ins. Co. v. SEC Donohue, Inc., 679 N.E.2d 1197 (Ill. 1997) (economic loss doctrine applies to engineers and architects, barring any recovery for economic losses in tort); Widett v. U.S. Fidelity & Guar. Co., 815 F.2d 885, 886–87 (2d Cir. 1987), (absent privity, architect was not liable for professional negligence to subcontractors that detrimentally relied on erroneous site plans); American Towers Owners Ass'n, Inc. v. CCI Mechanical, Inc., 930 P.2d 1182, 1192 (Utah 1996) (same); Atherton Condo. Apartment-Owners Ass'n Bd. of Directors v. Blume Dev. Co., 799 P.2d 250, 262 (Wash. 1990) (*en banc*) (same); Floor Craft Floor Covering, Inc. v. Parma Cmty. Gen. Hosp. Ass'n, 560 N.E.2d 206 (Ohio 1990) (same); Border Brook Terrace Condo. Ass'n v. Gladstone, 622 A.2d 1248 (N.H. 1993) (economic loss doctrine applied).

135. *See, e.g.*, Rissler & McMurray Co. v. Sheridan Area Water Supply Joint Powers Bd., 929 P.2d 1228 (Wyo. 1996) (engineer's duty under its contract with the water board did not extend to the contractor—either under a design negligence theory or a negligent misrepresentation theory); Fleischer v. Hellmuth, Obata and Kassabaum, Inc., 870 S.W.2d 832 (Mo. App. 1993) (architect had no duty to CM); *but see* Miller v. Big River Concrete, LLC, 14 S.W.3d 129, 134 (Mo. App. 2000) (engineer's negligence in conducting tests was actionable in negligence and negligent misrepresentation despite lack of privity).

136. *See also* Berschauer/Phillips Constr. Co. v. Seattle Sch. Dist. No.1, 881 P.2d 986 (Wash. 1994) (*en banc*) (limiting contractor's recovery of economic damages to remedies provided and disclaimed in owner/contractor construction contract).

137. *See* McConnell v. Servinsky Eng'g, PLLC, 22 F. Supp. 3d 610, 618 (W.D. Va. 2014) ("Virginia law is clear that contracts give rise to professional duties, and privity of contract is a

Other jurisdictions allow third parties to assert professional negligence actions for economic damages.[138] The legal basis cited in these decisions rests in the reasonable foreseeability that harm may result to a particular group from the design professional's negligent conduct.[139] This foreseeability creates a duty to use due professional care.[140]

---

prerequisite to claiming professional negligence."); *see also* Blake Constr. Co. Inc. v. Alley, 353 S.E.2d 724, 727 (Va. 1987) and Bryant Elec. Co. v. City of Fredericksburg, 762 F.2d 1192 (4th Cir. 1985) (there is no cause of action for a contractor to recover against an engineer for economic loss in the absence of privity under Virginia law). Unlike other jurisdictions, Virginia is uniformly strict in its privity requirement, for all professionals. *See, e.g.*, Ward v. Ernst & Young, 435 S.E.2d 628 (Va. 1993) (action against CPA requires privity); Copenhaver v. Rogers, 384 S.E.2d 593 (Va. 1998) (privity required in claim against attorney). Virginia also requires privity for most indemnification actions. *See* Pulte Home Corp. v. Parex, Inc., 579 S.E.2d 188, 2003 WL 1903424 (Va. Apr. 17, 2003). In McConnell v. Servinsky Eng'g, PLLC, 22 F. Supp. 3d 610 (W.D. Va. 2014), the court applied the Economic Loss Rule to bar a negligence claim by a project owner against an individual engineer who was the principal member of the PLLC engaged to do the design work. The court applied the standard Virginia privity analysis to determine that, since the design contract was between the owner and the firm, not the owner and the individual engineer, the lack of privity barred the direct claim against the individual. In an attempt to get around the rule, the plaintiff argued that the engineer assumed legal duties beyond the contract by affixing his professional seal to the plans. The court rejected this argument stating that an "engineer performing a professional service pursuant to a contract does not also assume an independent tort duty." 22 F. Supp. 3d at 616. *Cf.* Beaufort Builders, Inc. v. White Plains Church Ministries, Inc., 783 S.E.2d 35 (N.C. Ct. App. 2016) (Economic Loss Rule barred direct negligence claim by project owner against president of construction company).

138. *See generally* Matthew S. Steffey, *Negligence, Contract, and Architect's Liability for Economic Loss*, 82 KY. L. J. 659, 662 (1993); Frank D. Wagner, Annotation, *Tort Liability of Project Architect for Economic Damages Suffered by Contractor*, 65 A.L.R.3d 249 (1975).

139. *See, e.g.*, Ins. Co. of N. Am. v. Town of Manchester, 17 F. Supp. 2d 81, 84 (D. Conn. 1998) (applying Conn. law) ("foreseeability is key to the determination of a cause of action in negligence").

140. *See* Beacon Residential Cmty. Assn. v. Skidmore, Owings & Merrill LLP, 59 Cal. 4th 568, 327 P.3d 850 (2014) (as matter of first impression, held that an architect who is the principal designer of a residential project, not merely a subconsultant, owed a duty of care to future homeowners in the design of a residential building even if not in privity with owners). The court in *Beacon Residential* determined that an architect could be liable to homeowners in large part because the harm to the owners was foreseeable given that "defendants engaged in work on the Project with the knowledge that the finished construction would be sold as condominiums and used as residences." 59 Cal. 4th at 583–84, 327 P.3d at 861. Moreover, defendants "clearly intended to undertake the responsibility of influencing particular business transactions [i.e., condominium purchases] involving third persons [i.e., prospective homeowners]." 59 Cal. 4th at 584, 327 P.3d at 861. Note, however, that the court was careful to limit its holding to the "*principal architect* on the project—that is, the architect, in providing professional design services, is not subordinate to any other design professional." 59 Cal. 4th at 581, 327 P.3d at 859 (emphasis in original). The limits of the *Beacon* decision were evident in State Ready Mix, Inc. v. Moffatt & Nichol, 232 Cal. App. 4th 1227, 181 Cal. Rptr. 3d 921 (2015), a decision by the California Court

Some courts distinguish between design services that predate the commencement of construction (no duty to third parties for economic losses), and professional services performed during the project (which create a duty). Several of these opinions refer to a "special relationship" between an architect who has contract administration duties and the project participants.[141] This "special relationship" or "intimate nexus" between the designer and other participants in the project can give rise to a "privity equivalent," which permits claims against a designer despite the lack of privity.[142] California was one of the first jurisdictions to recognize that a "supervising architect" who holds the power of the purse against the contractor has power "tantamount to life or

---

of Appeals issued only a year after *Beacon*. In *State Ready Mix*, the court applied the Economic Loss Rule to bar a claim by a materials supplier to the prime contractor against the principal designer on a project. There, the court determined that the supplier's claim against the designer was barred because designer did not have a direct contractual relationship with either the prime contractor or the supplier. 232 Cal. App. 4th at 1232, 181 Cal. Rptr. 3d at 925. Thus, despite being the principal designer as in *Beacon*, the defendant in *State Ready Mix* could not be held liable.

141. *See* Craig v. Everett M. Brooks Co., 222 N.E.2d 752, 755 (Mass. 1967) (engineer was not liable for mistakes in plans, but for professional negligence in improperly placing stakes needed to locate and direct construction); A. R. Moyer, Inc. v. Graham, 285 So. 2d 397 (Fla. 1973) ("supervising architect"); R. H. Macy & Co. v. Williams Tile & Terrazzo, Inc., 585 F. Supp. 175, 180 (N.D. Ga. 1984) (applying Georgia law, architect owes no tort duty to subcontractor if their relationship does not "approach" that of privity or reliance) (citations omitted); *but see* Balfour Beatty Infrastructure, Inc. v. Rummel Klepper & Kahl, LLP, 451 Md. 600, 155 A.3d 445 (2017). In *Balfour*, the Maryland Court of Appeals (court of last resort in Maryland) rejected an argument by a general contractor on a large, public project that the contractor shared an "intimate nexus" with the designer which would justify disregarding the lack of contractual privity and imposing tort duties on the designer. Under Maryland law the "intimate nexus" test is a substitute for privity similar to the "special relationship" test recognized in other jurisdictions. The "intimate nexus test requires the relationship between the parties to be sufficiently close—or intimate—to support finding a tort duty." 451 Md. at, 615, 155 A.3d at 453. But the court was reluctant to essentially impose privity as a matter of law between the contractor and the designer. Instead the court determined contractual agreements were a better way to allocate risk on large, public construction projects. The court noted that "the construction industry is governed by a network of often-complicated contracts, and because the parties have carefully contracted to protect against economic losses, there is no reason to add a tort remedy to the mix for use by parties claiming such losses." 451 Md. At 622, 155 A.3d at 458. Critical to the court's decision in *Balfour* was the fact that the project at issue was a public project, with the court expressing a concern that "[i]mposing a tort duty on design professionals will likely correlate with an increase in project costs and with a corresponding rise in price for government entities." 451 Md. At 626–27, 155 A.3d at 461. Consider whether the court would have reached the same result if the project in *Balfour* had been private instead of public.

142. Balfour Beatty Infrastructure, Inc. v. Rummel Klepper & Kahl, LLP, 451 Md. 600, 621, 155 A.3d 445, 457 (2017) (discussing relationships in the construction industry that give rise to a "privity equivalent").

death."[143] Other jurisdictions decline to distinguish between the date or type of the allegedly negligent professional services[144] and enforce provable economic loss actions against construction design professionals for various sorts of professional conduct.[145]

21.06 THE ECONOMIC LOSS RULE AS APPLIED TO THE TORT OF NEGLIGENT MISREPRESENTATION

The tort of negligent misrepresentation is articulated in section 552 of the Restatement (Second) of Torts. Entitled "Information Negligently Supplied for the Guidance of Others," it states:

> [O]ne who, in the course of his business, profession or employment, or in any other transaction in which he has a pecuniary interest, supplies false information for the guidance of others in business transactions, is subject to liability for pecuniary loss caused to them by their justifiable reliance upon the information, if he fails to exercise reasonable care or competence in obtaining or communicating the information.

---

143. *United States ex rel. Los Angeles Testing Lab.*, 161 F. Supp. at 136.

144. *See* Moransais v. Heathman, 744 So. 2d 973, 983 (Fla. 1999) ("the mere existence of such a contract should not serve per se to bar an action for professional malpractice"); Stone's Throw Condo. Ass'n, Inc. v. Sand Cove Apartments, Inc., 749 So. 2d 520, 522 (Fla App. 1999) (claims based on architect's failure to design to state minimum building code and negligent misrepresentation are not barred by economic loss rule despite lack of privity); Conforti & Eisele, Inc. v. John C. Morris Assoc., 418 A.2d 1290 (N.J. Super. 1980) (contractors may sue architects for professional negligence despite lack of privity); Shoffner Indus., Inc. v. W.B. Lloyd Constr. Co., 257 S.E.2d 50, 55–59 (N.C. App. 1979); Bagwell Coatings, Inc. v. Middle S. Energy, Inc., 797 F.2d 1298 (5th Cir. 1986) (contractor's negligence action allowed against architect who was aware contractor would be harmed if architect did not properly perform its contractual duties to owner); Tommy L. Griffin Plumbing & Heating Co. v. Jordan, Jones & Goulding, Inc., 463 S.E.2d 85 (S.C. 1995) (engineer owed contractor duty not to negligently design or negligently supervise project and was liable to contractor absent privity for economic losses); Pritchard Bros., Inc. v. Grady Co., 428 N.W.2d 391 (Minn. 1988) (contractor may sue architect for professional negligence and for purely economic loss); E.C. Ernst, Inc. v. Manhattan Constr. Co., 551 F.2d 1026, 1031–32 (5th Cir. 1977) (applying Alabama law); Donnelly Constr. Co. v. Oberg/Hunt/Gilleland, 677 P.2d 1292, 1295–97 (Ariz. 1984); Hewett-Kier Constr., Inc. v. Lemuel Ramos and Assoc., Inc., 775 So. 2d 373 (Fla. App. 2002).

145. *See, e.g.,* Dufficy & Sons, Inc. v. BRW, Inc., 74 P.3d 380 (Colo. App. 2002) (citing cases), *rev'd*, 99 P.3d 66 (Colo. 2004) ; Mayor and City Council of Columbus v. Clark-Dietz & Assocs. Eng'rs, Inc., 550 F. Supp. 610, 623 (N.D. Miss. 1982) (architect owes duty to those parties proximately suffering economic losses as a result of architect's negligent design); Magnolia Constr. Co. v. Mississippi Gulf S. Eng'rs, Inc., 518 So. 2d 1194, 1202 (Miss. 1988) (third parties are entitled in Mississippi to rely on a design professional's contractual obligation to the owner and may recover economic losses for architect's negligence).

A separate negligence-based tort of negligent misrepresentation may be asserted against any construction project participant who disseminates information. Owners, construction managers, general and trade contractors, and design professionals may be alleged to have negligently supplied inaccurate information for the guidance of others.[146] The Restatement specifically allows the tort to be maintained whether or not the injured party has a contract with the information-disseminating party.[147] In place of privity, the Restatement inserts foreseeability, requiring that the party providing the information know the class of those intended to receive and use the information,[148] and reasonable reliance by a member of that class upon the information.[149]

A number of jurisdictions are less than comfortable with the breadth of the Restatement's pronouncements. To them, the Restatement's foreseeability standard is a poor substitute for contractual responsibility.[150] As noted by one

---

146. *See* RESTATEMENT (THIRD) OF TORTS § 552.
147. *Id.* § 552, comment g.
148. *Id.* § 552, comment h.
149. To state a claim of negligent misrepresentation, the plaintiff (most often a contractor or subcontractor) must have reasonably relied upon the information provided and been misled by that information. *See, e.g.*, Bilt-Rite Contractors, Inc. v. The Architectural Studio, 581 Pa. 454, 866 A.2d 270 (2005) (adopting RESTATEMENT (SECOND) TORTS § 552) *abrogating Linde* Enterprises, Inc. v. Hazelton City Auth., 412 Pa. Super. 67, 602 A.2d 897 (1992) (in matter of first impression, contractor reasonably relied on plans and specifications drafted by architect in submitting winning bid to school district for construction of school where plans and specifications were made part of bid package supplied to prospective bidders); Sanders Co. Plumbing & Heating, Inc. v. City of Independence, 694 S.W.2d 841 (Mo. Ct. App. 1985) (city provided contractor with inaccurate soil condition data upon which contractor relied in formulating its bid); McDevitt & Street Co. v. Marriott Corp., 713 F. Supp. 906 (E.D. Va. 1989), *aff'd in part, rev'd in part*, 911 F.2d 723 (4th Cir. 1990), *on remand*, 754 F. Supp. 513 (E.D. Va. 1991) (contractor's reliance on owner's soils reports held insufficient to support extra work claim where contractor did not perform pre-bid investigation); D. Federico Co. v. New Bedford Redevelopment Auth., 723 F.2d 122 (1st Cir. 1983); Umpqua River Navigation Co. v. Crescent City Harbor Dist., 618 F.2d 588 (9th Cir. 1980).
150. In LAN/STV v. Martin K. Eby Const. Co., Inc., 435 S.W.3d 234, 246 (Tex. 2014), the Texas Supreme Court determined that a contractor's negligent misrepresentation claim under RESTATEMENT § 552 against an architect was barred by the Economic Loss Rule. In rejecting foreseeability as a basis for recovery, the court observed that the "rule serves to provide a more definite limitation on liability than foreseeability can and reflects a preference for allocating some economic risks by contract rather than by law." 435 S.W.3d at 235. While the contractor cannot recover against the architect, this approach does not leave the contractor without a remedy. As the court noted, the contractor should "look to its agreement with the owner for damages if the project is not as represented." 435 S.W.3d at 248. Another variety of negligent misrepresentation claims—claims against owners for faulty information—were first fully articulated in American jurisprudence by a troika of opinions from the U.S. Supreme Court in the second decade of the 20th century: United States v. Atl. Dredging Co., 253 U.S. 1 (1920); Christie v. United States, 237 U.S. 234 (1915); and Hollerbach v. United States, 233 U.S. 165 (1914). For an excellent description of

court, it is "a standard that sweeps too broadly in a professional or commercial context, portending liability that is socially harmful in its potential scope and uncertainty."[151] In the construction setting in particular, courts have been uneasy assessing tort responsibility for economic damage based on the transmission of inaccurate information related to a contractual undertaking.[152]

A number of courts believe that where there is privity of contract and only economic damages, there is no need for an additional tort of negligent misrepresentation.[153] Other courts have chosen not to allow negligent misrepresentation claims when there is a contract, any contract, that relates to the subject matter of the claimed damages.

Berschauer/Phillips Constr. Co. v. Seattle Sch. Dist. No. 1
881 P.2d 986 (Wash. 1994) (en banc)

GUY, Justice.

We granted review to decide whether a general contractor may recover in tort $3.8 million in economic damages for construction delays against an architect, a structural engineer and a project inspector, none of whom were in privity of contract with the general contractor. Berschauer/Phillips expended more funds than expected and was delayed in its completion of its work, and consequently was damaged monetarily.

---

the effect of these three cases in the development of American construction law, see 4 PHILIP L. BRUNER & PATRICK J. O'CONNOR, JR., BRUNER AND O'CONNOR ON CONSTRUCTION LAW § 14:20 (West Group 2002). Although the facts in these cases involved the government owners' acts of "concealment" and "misrepresentation," accepted American tort law was not sufficiently developed at that time to sanction a separate extracontractual cause of action. And, as the parties were in privity, contract law was sufficient to allow compensatory damages for the misrepresentations. Many states today recognize both contract and tort remedies for similar conduct. Many allegedly injured contractors opt to pursue contract rather than tort claims, especially in jurisdictions slow to accept tort concepts that parallel traditional contract remedies. So long as there are no limiting contract provisions, if the contractor is in privity with the owner, there should be little if any difference in recoverable damages for an owner's negligent misrepresentation under tort or contract theories.

151. Local Joint Executive Bd. v. Stern, 651 P.2d 637, 638 (Nev. 1982).

152. See, e.g., Balfour Beatty Infrastructure, Inc. v. Rummel Klepper & Kahl, LLP, 451 Md. 600, 630, 155 A.3d 445, 462 (2017) (rejecting contractor's claim for negligent misrepresentation against an architect because "complex web of contractual arrangements predominates and injecting a tort duty is not in the public interest").

153. See, e.g., Duquesne Light Co. v. Westinghouse Elec. Corp., 66 F.3d 604 (3d Cir. 1995); City Express, Inc. v. Express Partners, 959 P.2d 836 (Haw. 1998).

> Berschauer/Phillips requests that this court apply the Restatement (Second) of Torts § 552 (1977) to permit a general contractor not in privity of contract to bring a tort cause of action against a design professional for negligent misrepresentations. We acknowledge that § 552 provides support for the recovery of economic damages in the construction industry for negligent misrepresentations. *See* § 552, illustration 9. We also acknowledge that the tort of negligent misrepresentation is recognized in Washington.
>
> We hold that when parties have contracted to protect against potential economic liability, as is the case in the construction industry, contract principles override the tort principles in § 552 and, thus, purely economic damages are not recoverable. There is a beneficial effect to society when contractual agreements are enforced and expectancy interests are not frustrated. In cases involving construction disputes, the contracts entered into among the various parties shall govern their economic expectations. The preservation of the contract represents the most efficient and fair manner in which to limit liability and govern economic expectations in the construction business. Berschauer/Phillips' recovery of economic damages is therefore limited to those damages recovered from the District.

In *Berschauer/Phillips*, the contractor alleged that the design professionals supplied inaccurate information, which caused the contractor to incur extra costs and delay damages in connection with the performance of the construction contract. The fact that the general contractor had a contractual remedy against the owner was dispositive for the court.[154]

Other courts limit the expanse of the Restatement's class of potential plaintiffs by making fine distinctions concerning what constitutes "information in the course of one's business or profession."[155] Illinois, for instance, specifi-

---

154. The fact that there may have been contract provisions in the owner/general contractor agreement that severely limited the general contractor's right to recover foreseeable and substantial delay damages was apparently irrelevant to the Washington court.

155. Restatement (Third) of Torts § 552. For instance, in Excavation Technologies., Inc. v. Columbia Gas Co. of Pa., 604 Pa. 50, 985 A.2d 840 (2009) an excavation contractor sued a utility company on the basis that the utility company had improperly marked utility lines and that the contractor, in performing excavation work, hit the lines and suffered economic damages due to delays in its work. The Pennsylvania Supreme Court determined that the contractor could not maintain a claim under section 552 because the utility company was not in the business of supplying information for pecuniary gain. The utility company was obligated by statute to mark the locations of its lines upon request and to do so without compensation. *But see* Bilt-Rite Contractors, Inc. v. The Architectural Studio, 581 Pa. 454, 866 A.2d 270 (2005) (architect in the business of supplying information).

cally recognizes an exception to the economic loss rule outside the construction context for damages caused by another's negligent misrepresentation as described in the Restatement (Second) of Torts, section 552.[156] When presented with the case of a professional engineer whose plans for a tunnel location were inaccurate by 75 yards, causing additional costs for the contractor and damage to real property owned by others, the Illinois Supreme Court nevertheless held that the engineer was not "in the business of supplying information."[157] In a concluding remark, the court noted that the remedy for inaccurate plans could be expressed "in contract terms."[158]

Courts that allow the tort of negligent misrepresentation in the construction setting also tend to inquire rather deeply into the facts of a contested case, in order to satisfy themselves that those who incurred the economic losses were within the class of recipients whose reliance on the information, and resultant damage for inaccurate information, was foreseeable. Similar to the analysis of the "supervising architect" exception in cases of design professional negligence discussed previously, a number of courts look for a relationship between the parties that is "so close as to be the functional equivalent of contractual privity."[159] If it is found, the Economic Loss Rule's strictness may be avoided.[160]

---

156. *See* Moorman Mfg. Co. v. Nat'l Tank Co., 435 N.E.2d 443, 449 (Ill. 1982), and its progeny. This exception is one of three to the economic loss rule recognized in *Moorman*. The other two are fraud and property damage from a sudden or dangerous occurrence. *Id.* at 450. *See also Rozny*, 250 N.E.2d at 660 (plaintiffs not in privity were allowed to recover economic damages against surveyor for inaccurate information on survey).

157. *SEC Donohue*, 679 N.E.2d at 1201–02 (a design professional's plans and drawings were incidental to the tangible product—the water pipe project). *See also* 2314 Lincoln Park West Condo. Ass'n v. Mann, Gin, Ebel & Frazier, Ltd., 555 N.E.2d 346 (Ill. 1990) (architect's information is incidental to a tangible product, i.e., a structure, and details on plans are normally transformed into the structure (*dicta*)); *but see* Tolan and Son, Inc. v. KLLM Architects, Inc., 719 N.E.2d 288, 298 (Ill App. 1999) (refining the "incidental" analysis to design professionals—project design architects were not "providers of information," but a consulting engineer could be).

158. Fireman's Fund Ins. Co. v. SEC Donohue, Inc., 679 N.E.2d 1197, 1200, 223 Ill. Dec. 424, 427, 176 Ill. 2d 160, 166 (1997). Apparently, this parsing of the RESTATEMENT requirements is limited to the court's anti-tort resentment in the construction sector, and not to other commercial transactions. *See Rosenstein*, 636 N.E.2d at 665 (negligent misrepresentation claim allowed against stock market indexing service by those not in privity). Illinois also allows negligent misrepresentation claims against attorneys and CPAs. This distinction has drawn the criticism of a number of commentators, and three of the state's Supreme Court Justices. *See SEC Donohue*, 679 N.E.2d at 1202 (Heiple, J. in dissent).

159. Ossining Union Free Sch. Dist. v. Anderson LaRocca Anderson, 539 N.E.2d 91 (N.Y. 1989).

160. *Id.* at 92.

Borough of Lansdowne, Pa. v. Sevenson Envtl. Serv., Inc.
2000 WL 1886578 (E.D. Pa. 2000)

Weiner, Judge.

In 1994, the EPA and Army Corps of Engineers designed a project to clean up certain buildings in the Borough that were contaminated by radiation. In 1995, the United States awarded a contract to perform construction work on the site to Sevenson. Sevenson then entered into a subcontract with Terratech to perform excavation and construction of retaining walls. During the construction of a shoring system which was designed to allow the excavation of the site to proceed, large amounts of grout filled and blocked access manholes and sewer lines owned by the Borough near the construction site. The Borough filed its first party complaint to recover damages to its property caused by the grout. During the construction project, Weston was under contract with the United States to prepare plans and review the project design. Terratech's third party complaint alleges that the plans prepared by Weston did not adequately show the location of the Borough's sewer lines which led to the infiltration of the grout.

Weston argues that Terratech fails to state a claim because Weston and Terra-tech lack contractual privity, and that, under Pennsylvania law, neither a general contractor nor a subcontractor has a direct right of action against the owner's architect/designer. We cannot agree. Under Pennsylvania law, which incorporates the Restatement (Second) of Torts § 552, contractual privity is not necessary to maintain a claim for negligent misrepresentation. Pennsylvania has clearly adopted § 552 as the law of negligent misrepresentation. Section 552 has supplanted the need for contractual privity as the device by which liability is limited from the world at large to those whom the actor should reasonably foresee might be harmed by his negligent provision of false information. Rather than focusing upon the existence of a contractual relationship, § 552 limits the liability of the supplier of the information to the "group of persons for whose benefit and guidance he intends to supply the information or knows that the recipient intends to supply it."

Notwithstanding the provisions of § 552, Weston argues that construction design cases are exempt from the reach of § 552 because of the economic loss doctrine; i.e. that Terratech cannot maintain a claim of negligent misrepresentation because there is no privity of contract between them. This argument misconstrues the economic loss doctrine and is not supported by the case law.

A close reading of section 552 itself reveals that the Restatement is concerned with liability in cases where contract remedies are unavailable. Indeed, virtually all the examples provided in [§ 552] involve liability to third parties. The reason is simple: where there is privity in contract between two parties, and where the policies behind tort law are not implicated, there is no need for an additional tort of negligent misrepresentation. On the other hand, privity is not necessary here, because

> liability is limited to the bidders on the project, a potential class of plaintiffs that the engineer is aware may rely on his report.
>
> Design consultants and engineers are within the scope of § 552 and may be held liable for negligent misrepresentation. This court rejects the argument that § 552 does not apply to design consultants and engineers because they are not "in the business of selling information." Design professionals such as architects and engineers are engaged for the very purpose of providing plans and specifications for a construction project. The plans and specifications they provide are an essential component of their work product. Accordingly, we conclude that § 552 has supplanted the need for contractual privity in the circumstances presented.

The Restatement (Second) of Torts, section 552, concern is with foreseeability of damage to the class of recipients of information. Foreseeability supplies consistency in the identity of potential plaintiffs similar to the bargained-for protection of a contract. Foreseeability is vital to courts that uphold a plaintiff's right to sue for negligent misrepresentation regardless of privity and when harmed only economically. Thus, despite the economic loss rule, negligent misrepresentation claims have been maintained against owners,[161] builders and developers,[162] construction managers,[163] design professionals,[164] and construction product manufacturers.[165]

---

161. *See, e.g.,* D. A. Elia Constr. Corp. v. N.Y. State Thruway Auth., 734 N.Y.S.2d 295 (App. Div. 2001); *Sanders Co. Plumbing & Heating, Inc.*, 694 S.W.2d at 841 (city provided contractor with inaccurate soil condition data upon which contractor relied in formulating its bid).

162. Council of Co-Owners Atlantis Condo., Inc. v. Whiting-Turner Contracting Co., 308 Md. 18 (Md. 1986).

163. John Martin Co. v. Morse/Diesel, Inc., 819 S.W.2d 428 (Tenn. 1991) (subcontractor was allowed to maintain negligent misrepresentation claim against CM for improper information directing sub's work).

164. Nota Constr. Corp. v. Keyes Assoc., Inc., 694 N.E.2d 401 (Mass App. 1998) (mistakes and misinformation in architect's plans could give rise to negligent misrepresentation action despite lack of privity); Guardian Constr. v. Tetra Tech, Inc., 583 A.2d 1378 (Del. Super. 1990) (plaintiffs not in privity were allowed to maintain action for negligent misrepresentation against engineer).

165. *See* Village of Cross Keys, Inc. v. U.S. Gypsum Co., 556 A.2d 1126, 1133 (Md. App. 1989) (negligent misrepresentation claim against designer/manufacturer of curtain wall system not barred by Economic Loss Rule, although recovery denied due to failure to follow manufacturer's specifications); *see also* State *ex rel.* Bronster v. United States Steel Corp., 919 P.2d 294, 302 (Haw. 1996) (Economic Loss Rule properly not applied in negligent misrepresentation case against steel manufacturer where no privity; recovery allowed).

QUESTIONS

After following the state competitive bidding process, the Town of Manheister (hereinafter the "Town") entered into a contract with Delta Construction Company (hereinafter "Delta") for a multi-million-dollar construction project known as "Construction of Main Street, Manheister" (the "Main Street Project"). Prior to the execution of the general contract with Delta, the Town had entered into two contracts with Fuss & Budget, an architectural and engineering firm, pursuant to which Fuss & Budget was to provide all the design and engineering services for the Main Street Project. In addition to these services, Fuss & Budget agreed to take responsibility during the Main Street Project for utility coordination, contract administration, bid analysis, schedule monitoring, change order processing, progress payment processing, progress meeting management, and contract document interpretation. Delta claims that Fuss & Budget had to know that Delta's performance of its contract with the Town was dependent in part on Fuss & Budget's proper performance of its role in the project.

Delta claims that the Main Street Project became a "boulevard of broken promises" as a result of Fuss & Budget's negligent performance of its duties. Delta also claims that the dependence of Delta's success and economic well-being on Fuss & Budget's performance of these duties made foreseeable the harm Delta would suffer as a result of Fuss & Budget's failure to exercise such care, and gave rise to a duty of care owed Delta by Fuss & Budget. Delta complains mostly that the architectural and structural drawings and specifications prepared by Fuss & Budget for the project were not coordinated with each other, leading to many discrepancies in location and sizing of various construction components. Sorting through these issues delayed Delta, causing it to stop work while the design issues were resolved, and in some cases to remove work originally installed and replace it after the design issues were resolved by Fuss & Budget. Delta spent more than $500,000 over its contract price in completing the project.

1. What causes of action may Delta bring against Fuss & Budget?
2. What are the elements Delta must prove for each cause of action to establish a prima facie case against Fuss & Budget?
3. What legal arguments would Fuss & Budget use to defend Delta's claims?
4. What documents would Fuss & Budget use to support its legal arguments?
5. Assuming Fuss & Budget was negligent in the performance of its duties in connection with the project, what must Fuss & Budget show the court to avoid liability?
6. Describe the options available to the court as to whether this case should be allowed to go forward, and explain the analyses that a court could use to dismiss the case or allow it to proceed.

CHAPTER 22

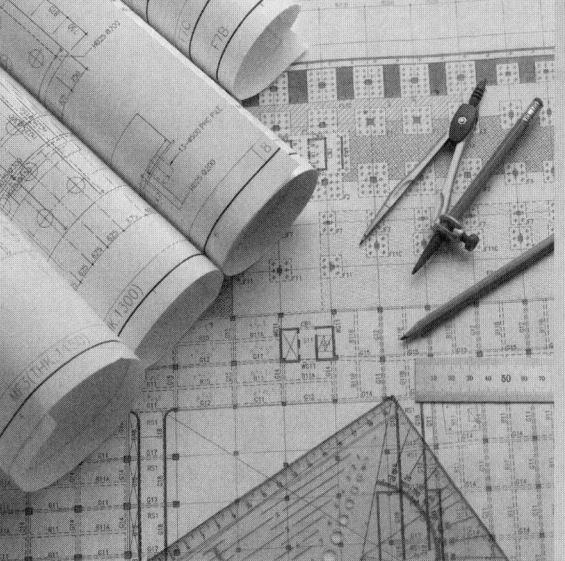

Damages

STEPHEN A. HESS AND ALLISON T. MIKULECKY

22.01 INTRODUCTION

A. Overview of Chapter

The general principles that govern the award of damages in claims involving construction disputes do not differ from those employed in other cases. At the same time, the application of these principles to construction claims provides special considerations that make the assessment of damages a matter of substantial complexity requiring attention to the particular circumstances surrounding construction contracts.

This chapter begins with a brief review of the most important measures of damages utilized in construction cases (Section 22.02). The chapter then sets out the particular application of these rules in the calculation and proof of damages in the construction setting (Section 22.03) and discusses specific legal doctrines that serve to mitigate or bar construction claims (Section 22.04). Finally, the chapter concludes by discussing contractual and other limitations on a party's liability for construction damages (Section 22.05). The function of this chapter is not to provide an exhaustive treatment of all the intricacies of damage doctrines and the calculations of damages—several books from a construction law library would be required to cover those matters in sufficient detail for the working construction lawyer—but rather to introduce the reader to the most important concepts in construction law damages.

B. "Measures of Damages" versus "Cause of Action"

This chapter concerns with the calculation of damages once a claim is proven and does not discuss in detail the various substantive claims that a party may try to establish related to a construction project. Although a specific "cause of action" may be closely intertwined with a related "measure of damages," the distinction between the two concepts is important to understand.[1]

A cause of action is a set of precise elements that a claimant must satisfy to establish its entitlement to relief. Once the claimant proves the cause of action, and the claimant has established its entitlement to relief, the measure of damages defines the *amount* of relief to which the aggrieved party is entitled. As the following discussion suggests, most causes of action are associated with a particular measure of damages.

However, some causes of action leave the claimant with the right to choose among various measures of damage with respect to quantum meruit. Moreover, as the reader will see, courts may modify a presumed measure of damages (or substitute an alternative measure of damages) where the presumed measure of damages would result in injustice to one of the parties, as in the case of economic waste.

Finally, the careful reader will learn that judicial opinions are not always careful to distinguish between causes of action and measures of damages. Any person who delves into the world of "unjust enrichment" or "quantum meruit" will learn quickly that those phrases can be used to refer to causes of action, to measures of damages, or to both at the same time. This is not a matter of sloppy writing or muddled thinking by the courts. Rather, it is a consequence of the very close relationship between causes of action and damages; with a little experience in this arena, an attorney can fluidly move between the analytically distinct concepts.

---

1. *See, e.g.*, Pepi Corp. v. Galliford, 254 S.W.3d 457, 2007 WL 441582 (Tex. Ct. App. 2007), in a dispositive issue related to competing statutes of limitations, the court held that a subcontractor's claim against a property owner was a quantum meruit claim founded on general principles of unjust enrichment, rather than an independent cause of action for unjust enrichment—which cause Texas recognizes.

22.02 GENERAL MEASURES OF DAMAGES

The function of this section is twofold. First, this section brings together a summary of several measures of damages that law students often encounter in different courses. Second, it provides some glimpse into how the common measures of damages play out in the context of construction cases.

A. Breach of Contract and Related Claims

By far the most common claims related to construction projects involve breach of contract.

1. Expectation Interest (Breach of Contract)

Generally, "a party is entitled to have what he contracts for or its equivalent,"[2] which is another way of saying that a party is entitled to the "benefit of his bargain." When a breach by the opposing party deprives the claimant of the benefit of that bargain, a court will endeavor to protect that benefit; in other words, the goal in fashioning a remedy for the breach of most contracts is to put the non-breaching party "in as good a position as he would have been in had the contract been performed."[3] In literature, this is generally referred to as a party's "expectation interest" in the fruit of its contract. Generally, "[s]uch damages are measured as of the date of the breach."[4]

Although this single measure of damages applies to most breach of contract cases, the specific rules that apply toward calculating a party's "benefit of the bargain" may vary, depending on whether the claimant is an owner, a design professional (or construction manager), or a contractor (or subcontractor). The following discussion summarizes the typical damages that each of these parties may seek to recover. At the same time, the reader should bear in mind that the general measure of damages applying to each remains the same—the parties all want to get the benefit of their respective bargains—but the manner of calculating that benefit differs from one party to the next.

a. Owner's Damages

From the perspective of understanding damage claims, the owner of a building or construction project can be understood as contracting for three specific benefits related to the owner's project. First, the owner expects the contract to be completed for the contract price. Second, the owner expects the project to

---

2. Champion Cos. of Wis., Inc. v. Stafford Dev., Ltd. Liab. Co., 794 N.W.2d 916, 918 (Wis. Ct. App. 2010).
3. Shafer Elec. & Constr. v. Mantia, 96 A.3d 989, 995 (Pa. 2014) (home improvement contract).
4. Morgillo v. Empire Paving, Inc., 118 A.3d 760, 770 (Conn. App. Ct. 2015) (paving contract).

be completed within the contract time. Third, the owner wants the project to be of such quality as the owner has contracted for through the contract documents. The frustration of any of these expectations—assuming it amounts to a breach of contract—gives rise to damages. The general measure of damages for such breach, as recited previously, is based on the benefit of the bargain principle, and the fact finder must answer the question: What amount of money would put the owner in the same position it would have found itself if the contractor had finished within the budget, on time, and with a project that was of the description and quality contracted for? In determining how these damages might be calculated, it is helpful to address the three separate dimensions of performance that the owner expects.

First, the owner is entitled to completion of the project for the price specified in the contract.[5] If the contract is for a stipulated sum, this element is easier to measure. The owner is entitled to recover additional expenses when, for example, the owner must complete work that the contractor leaves unfinished, or the owner is forced to cure defective work. Similarly, when the contractor's breach forces the owner to spend more on design professional or construction manager fees, the owner is entitled to recover those additional fees so as to protect the benefit of its bargain. In applying the benefit of the bargain principle to the base cost element of a contract, the court merely compares the actual cost of construction to the promised cost of construction, and the owner is entitled to recover the difference. Imagine, for example, that a hospital contracts for the construction of a cardiac care wing for $14 million. As a direct result of the contractor's poor construction, the owner spends $600,000 in remedial work plus an additional $45,000 in architect fees. The owner bargained for a completed building at $14 million; if the owner was compelled to pay the contractor the full contract price, the owner would have lost $645,000. Accordingly, the court will reduce the owner's obligation to the contractor to $13,355,000 as a means of keeping the owner whole, or protecting the owner's benefit of the bargain. Of course, the owner is not completely excused from paying the contractor. If, at the time of breach, the owner has only paid the contractor $10 million of the contract price, the owner cannot retain the balance of the contract price as a "penalty" for the breach. Instead, the owner would still be obligated to pay the contractor the $3,355,000 balance of the contract price, adjusted to reflect the owner's damages.

Second, the owner is entitled to completion of the project on time. The maxim that "time is money" applies with special force to construction projects for all parties involved. From the owner's perspective, a delay in the

---

5. The different mechanisms of specifying a contract price are discussed further in Chapter 9.

completion of a project has several financial ramifications. A property that produces income—through rentals or through the operation of a business—cannot produce income until the project is completed. The loss of that income is the first impact an owner feels. Moreover, many construction projects are financed through construction loans that convert to permanent financing upon substantial completion; the interest rate the owner will pay or the permanent financing is often markedly less than construction financing rates because of the diminished risk upon completion of the structure. On a $10 million project where the interest rate for the construction loan is two percentage points higher than the permanent loan rate, for example, each month of delay costs the owner more than $16,667.67. In addition, a delayed project may force the owner to incur additional construction management or design professional fees. These are but a few of the damages that an owner may suffer. Even when the contractor completes the project for the contract price, the fact that the project is not completed in time may entitle the owner to some remedy measured by the benefit of the bargain principle.

Third, the owner is entitled to receive a project of the quality promised in the contract documents. When the construction is substandard, two ramifications may arise: (1) the construction may need to be repaired or improved to the quality promised, and (2) the value of the project may be diminished as a consequence of the substandard construction. When construction is substandard, the most common measure of damages to provide the owner with the benefit of its bargain is the cost of reconstruction or repair.[6]

However, where reasonable repairs may leave the project in a condition in which the fair market value is still diminished below that of the promised construction, the court may award an amount of money representing the diminution in value of the property after repair. For example, in *Kelley v. Widener Concrete Constr., LLC*, a homeowner brought an action against the contractor for defectively pouring concrete at the residence. The Missouri Court of Appeals affirmed the trial court's decision to not award homeowners the cost of repair, but rather the diminution in value of the property.[7] In so holding, the Missouri Court of Appeals recognized that

> [t]he preferred measure of damages, as a general rule, in cases of substantial but defective performance by a contractor, is the cost of reconstruction or repair. The "cost rule" measures damages by the cost of repairing the defective work. The "diminished value rule," an exception to the "cost rule," is 'the difference between the value of the property with the defective work and what

---

6. Kelley v. Widener Concrete Constr., LLC, 401 S.W.3d 531, 541 (Mo. Ct. App. 2013).
7. *Kelley*, 401 S.W.3d at 542.

its value would have been if it had been construed according to the terms of the contract. The diminished value rule applies only when the cost of reconstruction or repair would involve "unreasonable economic waste."[8]

Finally, although not invoked very often, an owner may simply have the right to have the offending construction removed and the property restored to the condition in which it was found prior to the construction. For example, if an owner contracts for a sunroom to be added to his house and the construction is defective, the owner may be limited to recovering the cost of the room, plus demolition, plus restoration of the house to the preconstruction condition. As one court explained, "A properly constructed room addition in place of the faulty one would place the plaintiffs in a better position than they previously enjoyed. That is not in accordance with the law which requires merely that the plaintiffs be returned to the position they were in prior to the contract with [contractor]."[9] In this case, the court's concern was to ensure that the owner was not improperly placed in a better position than before, which invoked the doctrine of "betterment," as discussed later.

In all but the last of these cases, the court protects the owner's expectation under a contract, and the measure of damages is designed to ensure that the owner gets the economic value of what it bargained for. In the last case, the court protects the owner's expectation only to the extent of not allowing an owner to be put into a worse position than the owner's pre-contract position. The "cost to restore," however, is really just a form of cancellation of the contract and refund of the price paid; the cost to restore does not go so far as to permit the owner to obtain satisfaction of its expectations.

b. Design Professional's and Construction Manager's Damages

A design professional's or construction manager's "bargain," for purposes of measuring damages, is ordinarily the compensation to which the design professional or construction manager is entitled under the terms of the contract with the owner. When the owner fails to pay the design professional or construction manager, the measure of damages is simply the difference between the contract compensation and the compensation actually paid.

This measure is easiest to apply when the owner simply fails (or is unable) to pay a stated sum under the contract. More often, disputes arise because the design professional or construction manager performs services that arguably

---

8. *Kelley*, 401 S.W.3d at 541. For a discussion of the theoretical underpinnings of these doctrines, see Josh M. Leavitt & Daniel G. Rosenberg, *Toward a Unified Theory of Damages in Construction Cases: Part I—Navigating through the Diminution of Value vs. Cost of Repair Debate in Defect Cases and Allocating Burdens of Proof*, 2 J. AM. COLL. CONSTR. LAWYERS 1.

9. Bourgeois v. Arrow Fence Co., Inc., 592 So. 2d 445, 448 (La. Ct. App. 1991).

fall outside the scope of the original contract, and the measure of damages then becomes that additional compensation to which the design professional or construction manager is entitled for the extra work. Where the contract provides specified rates for such compensation, the damage calculation is readily performed. Where the contract does not specify how compensation is to be determined, courts will typically award "reasonable" compensation. The so-called reasonable compensation is simply the amount a court, a jury, or an arbitrator will decide is reasonable after hearing evidence regarding the additional services and the value thereof. In some cases, the design professional or construction manager may also be entitled to recover interest or attorneys' fees when permitted.

c. Contractor's Damages

A substantial portion of the discussion of damages in the remainder of this chapter concerns the calculation of damages to which a contractor is entitled. As with the previous discussion related to owners, it is helpful to understand the many dimensions of a contractor's expectations when the time comes to assess damages for breach of contract.

From a general perspective, the contractor's ultimate goal is to protect its profit interest in the contract.[10] Such a simplistic statement belies the complexity of determining damages from the contractor's perspective for breach by the owner.[11] In more complex cases, it is helpful to characterize the contractor's general expectation interest (that is, the benefit of the bargain) as the right to complete (1) the contractual scope of work in accordance with plans and specifications; (2) within the time permitted under the contract; (3) without interference from the owner, design professional, or construction manager; and (4) for payment of the negotiated price. The frustration of any of these expectations affects the contractor's bottom line in a manner that ultimately is measured by reference to the original contract price. At the same time, discussing each of these dimensions is instructive.

First, the contractor is entitled to complete the scope of work within the original drawings and specifications. To the extent that the scope of work expands by the addition of other tasks not in the original contract, the contractor is entitled to recover its costs and reasonable overhead and profit associated

---

10. Similarly, when a contractor bids for work that will result in a loss to the contractor even if the owner does not breach, the contractor tries to limit its losses to those that are embodied within the contract price itself, and thus, to avoid excess losses (as opposed to trying to achieve anticipated profit).

11. When the breach is simply a payment default, damages are easy to calculate. This section presumes that the breach arises from interference by the owner, delay, bad plans and specifications, or other causes resulting in more typical damages described later in this chapter.

with the additional work. When work is simply added to the contract, the claim is relatively straightforward. More complicated analysis is required when the drawings and specifications are deficient in some respect, and the resolution of conflicts or deficiencies arguably adds to the work that the contractor is required to perform. From a conceptual standpoint, ultimately, a contractor is required to perform all *but only* the work set out in the original contract—subject to change procedures included in the contract—for the contract price.[12]

Second, the contractor is entitled to complete the contract within the time limits set out in the contract, at least to the extent the contractor's original schedule is reasonable. When the contractor's work is delayed as a consequence of problems attributable to others, the contractor likely will lose money through additional expenditures related to the delay. In protecting the benefit of the contractor's bargain, the court will allow recovery of sufficient damages to compensate the contractor for those additional expenses related to delay in completion of the work.

Third, the contractor is entitled to complete the project without unreasonable interference by the owner, by those acting on behalf of the owner, or by causes for which the owner is contractually responsible even without attribution of fault (such as extreme weather or differing site conditions). Compensable interference may cause delay, of course, for which damages are separately compensable,[13] but such interference can also cost the contractor economically by making the contractor's operations less efficient. This loss of efficiency is often a separately compensable element of damages when the court awards a contractor money to put it in the same position in which the contractor would have found itself but for the interference.

Finally, the contractor expects to be paid its contract price. As set out further in another chapter in this volume, the calculation of the contract price to which the contractor is entitled can be a matter of some sophistication (and ultimately, some contention).

2. Reliance Interest—Promissory Estoppel

The benefit of the bargain measure of damages protects a person's expectation interest in the benefits of the contract that governs the parties' relationship. At

---

12. This presumes that the contract is a lump-sum contract or a cost-plus contract with a guaranteed maximum price. When the contract price is a cost-plus term, the battle will less often be fought over scope of work and instead will focus on the extent to which the contractor's charges for work are reasonable.

13. Not all delays chargeable to the owner are compensable with an increase in the contract price. Unusually severe weather, for example, may only entitle the contractor to additional time to perform even if it causes the contractor to incur more costs to perform than it anticipated.

the same time, situations reoccur in construction disputes in which a contract is never actually formed or is unenforceable, but the aggrieved party is still entitled to relief.

Circumstances may give rise to a claim (a cause of action) for "promissory estoppel" when the following elements can be stopped:

> A promise which the promisor should reasonably expect to induce action or forbearance on the part of the promisee or a third person, and which does induce such action or forbearance, is binding if injustice can be avoided only by enforcement of the promise. The remedy granted for breach may be limited as justice requires.[14]

The language quoted sets out the elements of a cause of action for promissory estoppel and intimates that the measure of damages should be based on "enforcement of that promise . . . limited as justice requires." From a conceptual standpoint, the rule of promissory estoppel protects the promisee's *reliance interest* in the promise. Because promissory estoppel generally arises in the absence of an enforceable contract, it is technically not a party's expectation interest, that is, the party's expectation of receiving the benefit of its bargain, that a court seeks to protect.

The measure of damages for promissory estoppel is somewhat amorphous; promissory estoppel requires that the court award the promisee an amount of money to protect the promisee's reliance on the promise. This reliance interest is typically calculated as the amount of money that the promisee lost in reliance on the promise, and in many cases does not include any element of profit for the promisee. In some cases, an aggrieved party's reliance interest is very much like the calculation of damages as though a contract had been performed. Thus, for example, if a contractor justifiably relies on a steel erector's bid of $250,000 in bidding for the construction of a warehouse, and the steel erector refuses to perform, thereby forcing the contractor to find a replacement at $300,000, the "reliance interest" is $50,000—the difference between the bid and the actual cost. This is precisely the measure that would be used for simple breach of the steel erector's contract had the steel erector not shown up on

---

14. RESTATEMENT (SECOND) OF CONTRACTS § 90 (1981). Promissory estoppel is often pleaded as alternative claim for recovery when the existence of a contract is disputed. *See, e.g.*, W & W Steel, LLC v. BSC Steel, Inc., 944 F. Supp. 2d 1066, 1078 (D. Kan. 2013) ("BSC indicates that it does not dispute that it cannot simultaneously recover under the theories of both breach of contract and promissory estoppel. BSC states that it is asserting the promissory estoppel claim as an alternative to its breach of contract claim because W & W actively disputes BSC's claim of a valid and enforceable contract. BSC contends that, under the doctrine of the election of remedies, it cannot be forced to choose between its alternate theories prior to trial.").

the job.[15] However, this calculation is not always the case, and the measure that protects the promisee's reliance should be distinguished from the remedy for breach of contract. Moreover, as summarized by the Restatement section quoted, courts are at liberty to modify damages "as justice requires."

3. Restitution Interest—Unjust Enrichment

The absence of an enforceable contract between parties does not always bar recovery, as demonstrated by claims based on promissory estoppel. Even in the case of promissory estoppel, however, a court must determine that some conduct by the defendant gives rise to a cause of action by the plaintiff for which a remedy may be granted. Circumstances occur in which a court may fashion a remedy even in the absence of culpable conduct by the defendant.

A common claim for relief found in construction cases—and one pleaded frequently as a hedge against the possibility that the fact finder will determine no enforceable contract existed—is a claim for unjust enrichment. A cause of action for unjust enrichment is established, in most jurisdictions, by proof that the claimant conferred a benefit on the defendant, which benefit the defendant appreciated (or accepted), in circumstances in which the claimant did not intend to act gratuitously, and an injustice would occur to allow the defendant to retain the benefit without having to pay for it.[16]

The value of the benefit conferred is the "reasonable value" of what the benefit would have cost the party to obtain from another person, or the extent to which the party's property has been increased or its other interest advanced.[17] Most courts refer to this remedy as "restitution," as it forces the benefited party to disgorge the value of the benefit, where the value is measured from the perspective of *the enriched party*. Accordingly, unjust enrichment is distinct from both breach of contract and promissory estoppel, which look to the damage suffered by the promisee. Unjust enrichment, instead, looks to the value conferred on the recipient; unjust enrichment is not concerned with adequate compensation of the claiming party so much as it is with making sure the recipient does not benefit unfairly. Thus, for example, if a tenant contracts for the improvement of a building and skips out before paying the bill, the contractor may be able to recover from the owner of the building. However, the measure of damages will not be based on the contract

---

15. Some courts analyze bid defaults under contract principles; others, under principles of promissory estoppel.

16. *See generally* Richard A. Lord, Williston on Contracts § 68:5 (4th ed. 2007). In W & W Steel, LLC v. BSC Steel, Inc., 944 F. Supp. 2d 1066 (D. Kan. 2013), for example, the subcontractor/counterclaimant pleaded alternative claims for breach of contracts, unjust enrichment, and promissory estoppel. This is a common strategy when the existence of a contract is disputed.

17. Restatement (Second) of Contracts § 371 (1981).

price of the improvements or on the cost to the contractor of having relied on the tenant's promise, but rather will be the value of the improvements to the building owner if the contractor can establish entitlement to recovery.

4. Quantum Meruit

As a measure of damages, the term "quantum meruit" means "as much as he deserves" and is usually construed as the fair value of services. Quantum meruit typically is employed to fashion a remedy in the absence of an express, enforceable contract between two parties, but in circumstances in which a court will find that a contract is implied by law. Indeed, assertion of a quantum meruit claim is often deemed inconsistent with a claim for breach of an express contract as explained by one court:

> *Quantum meruit* "operates as an equitable remedy based upon quasi contract or a contract implied in law" which provides "a measure of recovery for the reasonable value of services rendered in order to prevent unjust enrichment." *Quantum meruit* is "not an appropriate remedy when there is an actual agreement between the parties," because "an express contract precludes an implied contract with reference to the same matter."[18]

Many circumstances exist in which quantum meruit is pleaded as a claim. A contractor may be terminated before the completion of its work and (at least in some jurisdictions) may elect to seek the fair value of the services the contractor rendered under a theory of quantum meruit rather than seeking to recover its expectation interest or the benefit of its bargain.[19] In addition, a claim for quantum meruit may be asserted by a *breaching* party to recover some compensation for its work even when the law will not allow it to recover breach of contract damages.[20] Third, a contract may prove to be unenforceable

---

18. Ron Medlin Constr. v. Harris, 704 S.E.2d 486, 489 (N.C. 2010).

19. Mike Bldg. & Constr., Inc. v. Just Homes, LLC, 2010 NY slip op. 20041, ¶ 10, 902 N.Y.S.2d 458, 470 (Sup. Ct.).

20. "Even a party in breach may recover in *quantum meruit* to avoid unjust enrichment so long as the breach was not willful." U.S. for Use and Benefit of Ken's Carpets Unlimited, Inc. v. Interstate Landscaping Co., Inc., 37 F.3d 1500 (6th Cir. 1994) (table). Here again, the phrase "unjust enrichment" is invoked to describe an underlying equitable principle and not a measure of damages. To confuse matters somewhat, in appropriate circumstances courts will limit a breaching party's remedy to restitution measured by principles of unjust enrichment, rather than to quantum meruit where the latter would actually allow a breaching party to benefit from its own malfeasance:

> If a party justifiably refuses to perform on the ground that its remaining duties of performance have been discharged by the other party's breach, the party in breach is entitled to restitution for any benefit that it has conferred by way of part performance or reliance in excess of the loss that it has caused by its own breach.

RESTATEMENT (SECOND) OF CONTRACTS § 374(1) (1981).

due to statutory limitations in circumstances in which the contractor should still be paid something for its work.[21] Other events also may give rise to a claim for quantum meruit, but the foregoing are the most common.

Readers should bear in mind that courts often use quantum meruit to characterize a specific cause of action, the proof of whose elements will entitle the claimant to recover damages measured *in some instances* by the value of services rendered. However, when quantum meruit is used to refer to a specific *cause of action*, rather than to the *measure of damages* tied to the value of services rendered, a court may allow a measure of damages based on something other than the value of services rendered. Accordingly, when the reader encounters a case in which a party on a claim for quantum meruit recovers its out-of-pocket costs, such a case should be understood as invoking quantum meruit as a cause of action and not as a measure of damages. By keeping the difference between a cause of action and a measure of damages in mind, and by understanding that courts may use the term quantum meruit to refer to either, cases discussing quantum meruit are less troubling.

B. Tort Claims

The general measure of compensatory damages for negligence claims is similar to the measure for contract claim, that is, it is that amount of money that will put the injured person in the same position as the injured person would have enjoyed but for the negligence of the defendant. To the extent that a tort claimant can avoid the effect of the Economic Loss Rule[22] in a suit founded on breach of the duty to provide suitable drawings and specifications, or not to design a project negligently, this measure results in calculations similar or identical to those that determine breach of contract damages.[23]

22.03 CALCULATION AND PROOF OF COMPENSATORY DAMAGES

The foregoing discussion set out the common measures of damages that parties encounter in construction disputes. Once the parties establish what measure they will use to determine damages, they must turn their attention to

---

21. Runnells v. Quinn, 890 A.2d 713, 718 (Me. 2006).
22. *See* Chapter 21 in this volume.
23. Some other tort claims have a different measure of damages. For example, the measure of damages for negligent misrepresentation is the difference in value between what the victim would have enjoyed had the facts been as represented and the value of what the victim enjoyed based upon the actual facts. Although this does not always result in a number that is different from the general calculation, it is a different measure in principle.

accumulating proof of losses that support a damage claim calculated by reference to that measure. This section starts by discussing the preferred method of establishing so-called actual damages through direct proof or estimation, outlines several alternative methods that may be employed when proof of actual losses is unavailable; summarizes the limitations on consequential damages in the construction setting as well as limitations on punitive damages; and concludes with some observations concerning the sophistication of the claims process in the construction industry.

A. Direct Methods of Proving Actual Damages

Courts routinely express a strong preference (in some cases, an insistence) that parties who seek remedies for breach of construction contracts provide proof of actual costs in support of their claims. The requirement of proof of actual costs should not be read as requiring precision in such proof. As noted in Section 22.03(A)(2), there are many accepted means of *estimating* losses. In principle, however, courts generally will insist on these direct methods of proof as distinct from the inferential, alternative methods discussed later.

1. Proof of Actual Costs

A few categories of additional costs exist that contractors incur when things do not proceed as planned on a job.

a. In General

Direct costs are typically those costs that can be identified specifically with, and charged in whole or in part to, a particular project and a particular cause within the contract. In those cases where the contractor maintains a detailed and sophisticated cost accounting system, it may be possible to extract direct costs related to particular causes from the cost records. If the engineer changes the specification of pumps mid-project, for example, the additional compensation may be as simple as determining the difference in cost between the pumps specified and the pumps actually utilized.

Many claims are not as straightforward. If the substitution of pumps comes at a time when the pumps are on the project's critical path and there is insufficient lead time to order new pumps without delaying the project, the contractor may be entitled to recover not only the additional costs of the pump but the results of the delay to the work as well. That delay, in turn, may be as simple as three identifiable days of idle labor and equipment. More probably, the calculation of the cost must accommodate the fact that otherwise idle crews or equipment were utilized to accelerate work on different parts of the project, perhaps diminishing the total delay, or at the very least reducing the cost of other work.

In short, the most accurate calculation of damages will always be to trace the direct consequences of a breach by one party, attribute and document a direct cost to every such consequence, and then to award as compensation the sum of those direct costs. On discrete problems in the construction process, a reasonable approximation of direct costs may be had. The accuracy and reliability of direct cost calculations diminishes as the ramifications of a particular breach widen.[24]

b. Price Increases for Labor and Material

It is not unusual for delay or disruption to a project to result in the performance of work during a later period of time at a higher cost than originally anticipated. The escalation in cost may result from scheduled increases in material costs or wage increases in a collective bargaining agreement. Escalated costs may also occur from unknown or unanticipated events (e.g., a natural disaster that increases construction material costs).

A schedule analysis may be necessary to establish that the uncertainty of the length of delay prevented the contractor from obtaining firm material, labor, or subcontract orders and to establish when such orders would have been placed but for the delay.[25] When changes in prices can be documented (both as to binding commitments for prices at the time work should have been performed and at the time work was actually performed), the difference in such prices may be recovered as part of the calculation of damages.

c. Idle Equipment and Related Costs

Where an owner causes delay to a project, and a contractor has committed its construction equipment to the project but has been unable to use it, then the contractor may be entitled to compensation for costs incurred while the equipment is idle. Equipment costs are frequently a substantial element in delay claims, and often disputes occur regarding the rate at which the equipment should be charged.

Different mechanisms exist for valuing idle equipment damages. For contractor-owned equipment, the measure is the contractor's actual cost to own the equipment (and in some cases, an element of profit for its investment in the equipment). Ownership costs include the capital cost of the equipment, depreciation, repairs, storage, taxes, and other direct costs and can be difficult to prove. However, many contracts incorporate equipment schedules for the

---

24. Similarly, proof of direct costs diminishes with incompleteness, inaccuracy, or simplicity of the cost accounting system utilized by the contractor.
25. *See, e.g.,* Fireman's Fund Ins. Co. v. United States, 92 Fed. Cl. 598, 666 (2010); George Sollitt Constr. Co. v. U.S., 64 Fed. Cl. 229, 269 (2005).

purpose of establishing equipment costs for change orders, and these schedules can be equally applied to establish damages for idle equipment. When the contractor rents equipment, the cost attributable to idle equipment is easily established by showing an invoice from a third party and payment thereof. If the contractor's recordkeeping is not sufficiently detailed to determine actual costs, then the contractor may resort to industry-published rates that set forth the average cost of ownership or third-party rental rates.

d. Home Office Overhead

When a contractor maintains a home office for the management of work over several projects, the contractor expects to recover the cost of that home office through its general overhead and profit on the various jobs it performs. Home office overhead includes such things as rent, utilities, salaries of management personnel, phone service, copy machines, and estimators. When a delay on one job precludes the contractor from accepting other work, one effect is that the contractor's home office overhead is spread over fewer jobs, and thereby diminishes the contractor's ability to recover that overhead (in turn, lowering the contractor's overall profitability). Thus, if a contractor expects to bid five jobs for $1 million each and includes an allowance of $40,000 in each contract to pay for home office overhead, it expects to recover $200,000 over those five jobs. If delays on one job preclude the contractor from performing two of those anticipated contracts, however, it effectively loses the ability to recover $80,000 in home office overhead through other work.

Accordingly, home office overhead is recoverable as an element of delay damages when the owner is responsible for the extended performance of a contract.[26] A claimant must establish a prima facie case for recovery of home office overhead, as the general description of the circumstances of home office maintenance is not always accurate. Thus, a contractor must establish that:

1. Performance of the contract was delayed due to inexcusable actions or inaction of the owner;
2. The contractor suffered actual damages as a result of the delay;
3. The nature of the delay made it impractical for the contractor to undertake the performance of other work; or
4. The nature of the delay made it impractical to reduce home office overhead costs.[27]

---

26. *See, e.g.*, K-Con Bldg. Sys. v. United States, 107 Fed. Cl. 571, 597 (2012).
27. *See generally* George Hyman Constr. Co. v. Washington Metro. Transit Auth., 816 F.2d 753 (D.C. Cir. 1987); WILLIAM SCHWARTZKOPF & JOHN MCNAMARA, CALCULATING CONSTRUCTION DAMAGES § 6.07 (3d ed. 2016) (looseleaf).

Once established, the claimant must then determine the proper measure of calculating home office overhead damages. As a result of delay to a project, the contractor does not realize direct billings in the same time period as anticipated. Therefore, the home office overhead is unabsorbed or underabsorbed. Unabsorbed overhead occurs when there is no extra work associated with the extended time against which the contractor can bill its overhead. Underabsorbed overhead typically occurs with disruption or partial delay where the contractor is still realizing some direct billings, but the amount of work has been severely reduced.

Several methods exist for calculating unabsorbed home office overhead. The most frequently used is the *Eichleay* formula. This formula is designed to calculate the daily home office overhead sustained in order to continue day-to-day operations during an owner-caused delay in a project.[28] To determine the amount of unabsorbed home office overhead, the *Eichleay* calculation requires three steps. First, the court must determine the overhead on the delayed contract by multiplying the contractor's total overhead by some ratio between the contractor's billings on the delayed contract and the contractor's total billings for the period of the delayed contract.[29] Second, a daily overhead rate for the delayed contract must be determined by dividing the contract overhead by the total days of contract performance.[30] Third, the total recoverable overhead must be calculated by multiplying the daily overhead rate for the delayed contract by the total length in days of the delay.[31] Although the *Eichleay* formula is the preeminent method of calculating recoverable home office overhead, courts have developed other formulas that incorporate the same concepts.[32] For example, the Hudson formula, which is more prevalent in England and

---

28. *Eichleay Corp.*, ASCBA No. 5183, 60-2 BCA ¶ 2688, 1960 WL 538 (July 29, 1960), *aff'd on reconsider.* 61-1 BCA ¶ 2894, 1960 WL 684 (1960).

John D. Darling, *Delay of Game: One of the Thorniest Issues in Delay and Disruption Litigation Is the Quantification of Actual Damages*, 27 L.A. Law. 31 (2005); *see generally* Jackson Constr. Co. v. United States, 62 Fed. Cl. 84 (2004).

29. Reginald M. Jones, *Recovering Extended Home Office Overhead: What Is the State of Eichleay?*, 40 Procurement Lawyer 8 (2004).

30. *Id.*

31. *Id.*

32. Patrick A. McGeehin & Carleton O. Strouss, *Learning from Eichleay: Unabsorbed Overhead Claims in State and Local Jurisdictions*, 25 Pub. Cont. L.J. 351, 358 (1996). Leading commentators on *Eichleay* have observed that "The *Eichleay* decision, and its ability to quantify the home office expense of individual project delays, has continued to receive both significant praise and abuse." Jon M. Wickwire, Thomas J. Driscoll, Stephen B. Hurlbut & Mark J. Groff, Construction Scheduling: Preparation Liability and Claims 13:14 (3d ed. 2016).

Canada, centers on the percentage of profits and overhead accounted for in the initial bid.[33]

In disputes where contractors have asserted *Eichleay*[34] or similar formulas as a means of home office overhead recovery, owners have asserted a number of defenses that administrative agency decisions have upheld. Among others, the list of defenses and mitigating factors include (1) failure by the contractor to pursue substitute work; (2) offset of the home office overhead claimed by the contractor for additional compensation paid by the owner during the delay period pursuant to change orders; and (3) negation of the claim due to disproportionate recovery by the contractor in active periods following the delay.[35] Although these and other defenses have prevailed in occasional cases, in most situations where a contractor is able to show the existence of the aforementioned elements, *Eichleay* has become the benchmark means for recovery in owner-caused delay cases.[36]

e. Lost Profits

Lost profits are subsumed within the previously discussed damage calculations when the contractor is working under a stipulated sum contract. When the contractor is working under a cost-plus contract, the contractor's lost profit is recoverable as a separate element when establishing the "plus" portion of the contract entitlement.

Design professionals generally do not seek recovery of lost profits per se for *additional* work, but instead seek recovery based on the contractual value of their services, which may include a component for profit. On the other hand, when an owner breaches a contract with a design professional by terminating the contract impermissibly, for example, the design professional is entitled to recover the value of payments promised, less any costs the design professional avoided by not having to perform the work.[37]

Finally, an owner may be entitled to recover its lost profits for delay in completion of a project due to the fault of the general contractor or the design professional or construction manager. The recovery of lost profits for new business has never found much favor in the court inasmuch as lost future profit claims for new businesses can be regarded as speculative. Indeed, the "new business rule" in many courts bars recovery of lost profits for new businesses.

---

33. McGeehin & Strouss, *supra* note 32, at 359.
34. *Eichleay Corp.*, ASBCA 5183, 60-2 BCA ¶ 2688 (1960).
35. McGeehin & Strouss, *supra* note 32, at 364.
36. *Id. at* 359.
37. Other principles, such as the requirement that the design professional mitigate its damages, may alter the calculation in particular circumstances.

The modern trend is not to prohibit the recovery of lost future profits for new businesses outright, but rather to treat the question of such recovery as a matter of evidentiary sufficiency under which the court must assess the extent to which a claim for lost future profits of a new business can survive challenges to the potentially speculative nature of such damage claims.[38] When a business owner can establish with reasonable certainty the fact of its damage and provide sufficient proof as to what its future profits would have been had the building been completed on time, then the business owner may be entitled to recover damages for lost profits.

2. Methods of Estimating Actual Damages

Many cases occur where a contractor cannot identify on a laborer-by-laborer basis all of the additional costs it incurs due to some defect in the owner's performance, but can establish with some reasonable degree of confidence an estimate of the losses that the contractor suffered. In such cases, courts will permit a reasonable estimate to be substituted for proof of the cost of each actual consequence of the affected work.

For the most part, these estimates are utilized when the damages arise in the form of delays or interference with work. A thorough discussion of liability for delays and disruption can be found in Chapter 11. Here, our attention is focused on estimating damages from such delays and disruption.

a. Measured Mile

In a measured mile approach, one compares the productivity achieved on an unaffected portion of the project with the productivity achieved on an affected portion.[39] As an example, if a pipeline contractor is capable of excavating, placing pipe, backfilling, and compacting 600 linear feet of pipe per day during unaffected portions of a construction contract, but can manage only 400 feet per day in harsh winter conditions that arise when its work is improperly delayed, then the contractor's loss of efficiency can be measured directly.

Although such simplistic measurements are rare, productivity is typically based on hours or dollars per unit of work achieved.[40] Such measurement is one of the preferred measures of inefficiency or loss of productivity because it uses actual historical data from the project.[41] It is critical that one prove the

---

38. MICHAEL DODD & J. DUNCAN FINDLAY, 1 STATE-BY-STATE GUIDE TO CONSTRUCTION CONTRACTS AND CLAIMS § 1.05[C][13] at 58 (2006 & Supp. 2007).

39. William Ibbs & Long D. Nguyen, *Using the Classical Measured Mile Approach and Variants to Quantify Cumulative Impact Claims*, 32 CONSTR. LAWYER 18 (Winter 2012). Darling, *supra* note 28, at 36.

40. Ibbs & Nguyen, *id.*

41. *See id.*

affected and unaffected areas compared represent comparable work, where the only material variable is the disruption caused by the breaching party.[42] In addition, the unaffected work must be large enough to be material and to be representative of the type of work on the project as a whole. If the nonbreaching party cannot prove these criteria, then the other party will attack the baseline productivity calculations for being faulty.[43]

By its very nature, the measured mile approach requires that some portion of the project be unaffected by the delay or disruption. As a result, this method may not be available where such delay or disruption has continued throughout the project.[44]

b. Industry Standards and Studies

In certain instances where neither the measured mile approach nor the should-cost estimate are available (the entire project was affected and the contractor had not previously performed comparable work), it may be necessary to rely on industry standards or studies. Such standards and studies have been developed in the industry through the Mechanical Contractors Association of America (MCAA), Business Roundtable, and RSMeans.

These studies attempt to quantify the amount by which interference in a project makes the work performed efficient. The MCAA, for example, estimates that moderately adverse weather conditions can render work 15 percent less efficient than work in normal weather conditions. A contractor can then argue, for example, that its work was rendered 15 percent less efficient when performance of the work was pushed (improperly, of course) into winter conditions and the contractor's workers were not performing as well as they would have performed but for the owner's delay. The argument continues to the effect that the contractor incurred $115,000 in labor and equipment costs to complete work that the contractor could have completed for $100,000 in normal conditions, and this additional cost is an element of damages.

Courts struggle with such methods, and substantial grounds exist on which many of these industry studies may be criticized—among them, the fact that some of the most important studies were never intended to be used to quantify damages.[45] At the same time, the grave suspicion with which these

---

42. Id.

43. Id.

44. For an extensive analysis and criticism of the measured mile approach, *see* Lee Davis, Laura Stipanowich, & Walter Bauer, P.E., *Does the "Measured Mile" Measure Up? When It Has, When It Hasn't, and What May Happen Under Daubert/Kumho*, 2007-04 CONSTRUCTION BRIEFINGS (Apr. 2007).

45. A concise overview of loss of productivity damages can be found in W. Stephen Dale & Robert M. D'Onofrio, *Disruption, Inefficiency & Loss of Productivity on Construction Projects*, 16

studies may be viewed is tempered by the general principle that it is better to award some damages to a party who clearly suffered injury than to award no damages, so long as some reasonable degree of confidence can be established by the evidence.

c. Should-Cost Estimates

When, for whatever reason, the measured mile approach is not available, an estimate of what the cost should have been without disruption may be a reliable substitute. Whereas the measured mile approach compares performance on the same project, performance on other projects for substantially similar work may form the basis for reasonably estimating what performance on a particular project should reasonably have cost, had there been no disruption.[46] Of course, the claimant bears the burden of producing a reputable expert who invokes recognized methods for determining what a project "should" cost to build in the absence of disruption. Like the employment of industry studies, the use of should-cost estimates is viewed with some suspicion.

d. Time and Motion Studies

Where a contractor cannot provide an actual, unaffected performance period for the current job that would allow a measured mile approach, or other contemporaneous jobs that would allow a should-cost estimate, then the contractor may consider using a time-and-motion study. These studies generally are done by experts, and they attempt to measure the loss in both labor and equipment efficiency by approximating an unaffected sequence and comparing it to an affected sequence.[47]

B. Alternate Methods of Proving Damages

1. Total Cost Method

The simplest, but also the most controversial and least accepted method, is the total cost method. The total cost method calculates damages as the difference between the total actual costs incurred, including overhead and profit,

---

CONSTR. BRIEFINGS No. 10 (2016). For an excellent review and critique of the use of a wide variety of industry studies, see Dr. Kathleen M.J. Harmon & Bradley Cole, *Loss of Productivity Studies—Current Uses and Misuses, Part 1*, 2006-8 CONSTR. BRIEFINGS (Aug. 2006) and Dr. Kathleen M.J. Harmon & Bradley Cole, *Loss of Productivity Studies—Current Uses and Misuses, Part 2*, 2006-9 CONSTR. BRIEFINGS (Sept. 2006).

46. DODD & FINDLAY, *supra* note 38, § 1.05[C][6] at 56.
47. *Id.* § 1.05[C][8] at 56.

and the bid amount.[48] For example, imagine that a contractor bids $60 million to complete a hospital complex. The contractor's actual cost to complete is $75 million, and the contractor attributes all of the overrun to the owner as a consequence of design deficiencies, poor administration of the contract by the architect, slow return of submittals on equipment with long lead times for order and delivery, and so on. But for the owner's delays and creation of inefficiencies, the contractor argues, the contractor would have completed the complex within its original bid.

While the simplicity of the method appeals to claimants, courts have criticized the method due to the assumption that all cost overruns are the responsibility of the project owner.[49] As such, courts disfavor use of this method, resulting in criticism and outright rejection in some courts.[50] Courts also have been suspicious of the total cost method because it assumes that the contractor's original bid was reasonable and the work could have been completed for the bid amount, absent breach of the contract. Such method further assumes that all of the cost overruns were caused by the conduct of the breaching party and none were caused by the contractor's own problems or inefficiencies. To protect against the inaccuracies and potential injustice inherent in the total cost method, courts have developed four elements that a claimant must establish before proceeding with the total cost method. The claimant seeking damages through the total cost method must prove:

1. The nature of the particular losses makes it impossible or highly impracticable to determine them with a reasonable degree of accuracy;
2. The contractor's bid or estimate was realistic;
3. The contractors' actual costs were reasonable; and
4. The contractor was not responsible for the cost overrun.[51]

If the claimant can establish each of the four premises, then the claimant may proceed with the calculation of damages under the total cost method.

The following excerpt from a case illustrates the typical discussions that surround these disputed issues. As the reader may imagine, opinions in construction cases tend to be very long and fact-intensive, and only a small portion of the discussion is set out here.

---

48. *See generally* Stephen A. Hess, *The Total Cost Method of Proving Damages*, 2007-2 CONSTR. BRIEFINGS (Feb. 2007).
49. SCHWARTZKOPF & MCNAMARA, *supra* note 27, § 1.03[C] at 14.
50. N. Am. Mech., Inc. v. Walsh Constr. Co. II, LLC, 132 F. Supp. 3d 1064, 1078 (E.D. Wis. 2015).
51. Eagle Supply & Mfg., L.P. v. Bechtel Jacobs Co., LLC, 868 F.3d 423, 432 (6th Cir. 2017).

Baldi Bros. Constructors v. U.S., 50 Fed. Cl. 74 (2001)

MILLER, Judge.

This case is before the court after trial on damages generated by a differing site condition. Plaintiff's claim hinges on the reasonableness of its bid, which is the starting point for the damages claimed.

FACTS

On May 17, 1995, the United States Department of the Navy (the "Navy") awarded Contract No. N62470-95-C-5035 to Baldi Brothers Constructors ("plaintiff"), a small, family-owned corporation of five principals who are brothers or first cousins, based in Beaumont, California. The contract called for construction of a Multi-Purpose Training Range Project at the United States Marine Corps Base, Camp Lejeune, North Carolina.

...

Before deciding to bid on the project, Salvatore Pasquale ("Pat") J. Baldi, a partner and plaintiff's Operations Manager, and Michael ("Mike") V. Baldi, plaintiff's General Manager, visited the site in Jacksonville, North Carolina. ... Based on the information available to Pat Baldi from the contract specifications and his visit to the general area, he created an earthwork estimate assuming that the dirt would be suitable for cutting and filling on-site and that the earthmoving equipment could move rapidly through the area.

...

During the course of construction, plaintiff encountered various subsurface conditions that it did not expect, including saturated peat marsh, super-saturated clays, subsurface water, and other unsuitable soil types. These soils were not the conditions shown on the boring logs incorporated into the contract. ... The unexpected soil conditions required plaintiff to modify its sequence of work, which plaintiff claims increased the costs of construction. Plaintiff had intended to employ "conventional earthmoving scrapers" to perform the cut/fill work. Specifically, scrapers would be used for the excavation and embankment work in a single cut-to-fill operation, but due to the nature of the soil, plaintiff was unable to use scrapers for the earthmoving work. [The Court then found substantial differing site conditions entitling the contractor to relief.]

2. *Damages*

... Plaintiff claims entitlement to an equitable adjustment due to the differing site conditions for the following: 1) increased direct costs of performance; 2) overhead for both the extended field office and home office and equipment stand-by expense as costs of delay; and 3) additional costs incurred by its subcontractor Brey Electric.

1) Total-cost method

"Due to the massive and continuous changes to the earthwork activities on this [p]roject, it was not possible for [plaintiff] to discretely track the actual increased costs of performance incurred. . . ." Pl.'s Br. filed Apr. 12, 2001, at 9. Plaintiff so explains and thereupon invokes the total cost method of calculating damages, or in the alternative, the "modified" total cost method. The total cost method of damages, which provides the difference between the contract price and the actual costs, necessarily assumes that the "original bid was an accurate reflection of a reasonable cost, and that all costs in excess of that had to be attributable to the differing site condition." *Servidone Constr. Corp. v. United States,* 19 Cl. Ct. 346, 384 (1990), *aff'd,* 931 F.2d 860, 863 (Fed. Cir. 1991). Trial courts are advised to use this method with caution because bidding inaccuracies can create an unrealistically low estimate of the contractor's costs, and performance inefficiencies can increase the costs incurred. *Id.,* 931 F.2d at 861–62.

. . .

The designation of a large portion of the construction site as wetlands was the equivalent of the 800-pound gorilla landing on plaintiff's plans for performing the contract. Plaintiff's testimony, largely from Pat Baldi and Debbie J. Saunders, plaintiff's Project Manager who had worked with plaintiff for over 20 years, diminished neither by defendant's cross-examination nor the Navy's unimpressive fact witnesses, detailed how the changed requirements impacted plaintiff's planned operations.

Plaintiff handily satisfies two of the four requirements: the impracticability of proving actual losses directly and plaintiff's lack of responsibility for the added costs. Before plaintiff even began its construction work on the site, it received information requiring it to change its planned operations. The Navy neither timely nor adequately responded to plaintiff's requests for information and direction concerning the soil conditions. Due to the changed site conditions, from the beginning of the project: Work was frequently halted, re-designed, re-designed again when the re-design failed, re-started in a different direction, and re-done (in the instance of a collapsing road); in addition, land required re-drainage, roads were constructed deeper and with more fill material than originally called for, and multiple large vehicles became stuck in the "muck" and "blue goo," as Pat Baldi phrased the conditions, including the off-road dump trucks that plaintiff had rented on the Navy's recommendation. In short, due to the snowball effect of the wetlands on the project plans, it would be easier for plaintiff to identify the items of contract performance that proceeded as planned, rather than the difference in costs between all aspects of the original plan and the work that the deviations occasioned.

With respect to plaintiff's responsibility for any of the additional costs that it incurred, the evidence shows that the wetlands affected the entire project site and that the conditions were exacerbated by natural causes, such as heavy rain.

Plaintiff maintains that the delays and increased costs from rain do not preclude compensation for the differing site conditions. The general rule is that the risk of severe weather in a particular region is not shifted to the Government via the Differing Site Conditions clause. *Hardeman-Monier-Hutcherson, A Joint Venture,* 68-2 BCA ¶ 7,220, 1968 WL 633 (delays to pier construction caused by rough seas did not constitute changed condition). However, when severe weather interacting with an undisclosed property of the construction site delays construction, the Government has been held responsible. *D.H. Dave & Gerben Contracting Co.,* 1962 BCA ¶ 3,493, 1962 WL 939 (excessive rainfall in interaction with drainage area rendering specified performance impossible held changed condition).

2) Increased cost of performance and the reasonableness of plaintiff's bid

Plaintiff claims $819,997.00 in increased performance costs due to the differing site condition. Ms. Saunders is responsible for preparing most bids and testified regarding her preparation of the Camp Lejeune bid. After Pat and Mike Baldi returned from their Camp Lejeune pre-bid area visit and decided that plaintiff would bid on the project, Ms. Saunders sat down with the "estimators" to decide how long they felt the project would take to complete. Ms. Saunders then bid the "general conditions" based on the projected completion time, which was 15 months, or 65 weeks, or 458 days. She prepared the bid using the Lotus spreadsheet program to compile information submitted by various personnel. At trial Ms. Saunders discussed the spreadsheet with the appropriate formulas for time-dependent costs. Project staffing was based on a 65-week project duration, but certain costs were measured by months, weeks, or days. Home office overhead, profit, and bond then were spread among the various line items according to a pro rata formula, whereby a certain percentage of a line item total was derived and added back into the line item. Plaintiff's final bid was $5,629,000.00, the lowest bid that the Navy received.

. . .

Pat Baldi earnestly testified that a production rate of 12,000 CY per day with a 2000-foot haul distance had been achieved in the past and that he had in fact "achieved over 26,000 [cubic] yards a day with . . . five scrapers," because plaintiff grooms its work surfaces meticulously. Although Pat Baldi has been working in this business since he was "old enough to pick up a shovel," and has been doing earthwork estimates since he was 16, his daily production rates for Camp Lejeune were optimistic, to say the least. Pat Baldi chose the 2% curve in determining the per machine production rate of 500 BCY. The Handbook describes the following conditions as warranting the 2% curve: "A hard, smooth, stabilized surfaced roadway without penetration under load, watered, maintained." While hindsight shows that the conditions at Camp Lejeune were a far cry from those warranting a 2% resistance rating, looking at plaintiff's bid prospectively satisfies the court that earnestness does not make up plaintiff's naivete in using such a low resistance rate having never before worked in that region of the country. Indeed, the photographic evidence confirms what Pat and Mike Baldi should have observed as general conditions in the area.

. . .

3) Delay costs and plaintiff's critical path

Plaintiff claims entitlement to $236,030.00, which represents the cost for 191 days of delay for both field and home office overhead. Plaintiff also claims 111 standby days for its scraper spread amounting to $253,497.63, and $24,194.40 for additional earthmoving equipment standby costs. Combined both items, plus profit and bond, total $296,561.00.

After plaintiff was awarded the contract, Ms. Saunders began preparing the schedule of prices and the project schedule. For the latter she used the bid documents and relied on discussions with the project superintendent and the estimator on their plan of action. She then input the information into the Primavera program, which calculated a project end date. The program gave a completion date four months earlier than the original end date. Ms. Saunders was concerned about submitting a schedule with such an early completion date, so she "went back into the program and made some logic changes, added some durations to items, and also took the erosion control and made that the same duration as the original contract days, so we could push the schedule out to show a completion date on the actual completion date on [sic] the contract."

As a result of Ms. Saunders' tinkering with the logic of the schedule and extending erosion control, as well as the duration of other activities, the approved project schedule does not accurately portray the critical path of the project. . . . Regardless of plaintiff's confidence that it would have completed its work well ahead of the contract completion date, the Government should not be liable when plaintiff's predictions are untested. In this case the derailment of the plan of execution occurred from day one. The court finds neither credible documentary nor testimonial evidence to support plaintiff's ambitious schedule. Thus, plaintiff, if it is entitled to any damages for compensable delays, is entitled to no more than 97 compensable delay days.

2. Modified Total Cost Method

The modified total cost method was developed to address some of the inherent flaws in the total cost method. Essentially, the modified total cost method reduces the amount of damages calculated under the total cost method by any errors in the bid, costs attributable to the contractor, and costs attributable to parties other than the owner.[52] The resulting damage is presumed to more accurately reflect the damage directly suffered by the claimant.[53]

In a modified total cost, the contractor scrutinizes carefully its bid and takes responsibility for any errors. The contractor also analyzes its own performance on the project and assumes responsibility for any of its own inefficiencies. This is not to say that the contractor must reduce its claim by all inefficiencies that the contractor experienced, as some normal inefficiencies would be assumed in the contractor's bid. The contractor need only assume responsibility for those problems or inefficiencies outside the norm.

3. Jury Verdict Method

A method of determining damages occasionally invoked by tribunals acting without juries is called the "jury verdict" method. This method is simply a shorthand name to the process by which courts estimate damages in the absence of any other acceptable means where denying any recovery would work an injustice on the aggrieved contractor.[54] The method takes its name from the fact that juries often are presented with marginal damage evidence that—assuming it survives a motion for directed verdict—will be sufficient for the jury to fashion *some* remedy where the fact of the injury is very persuasive and only the quantification of damages is shaky.

As with the total cost method, the jury verdict method is generally disfavored, and where any cognizable means exists of calculating damages through traditional mechanisms—even where the trier of fact cannot be given precise numbers—such methods will be preferred to the jury verdict method. Thus, the jury verdict method may only be invoked in limited circumstances:

> The "jury verdict" method of calculating damages is "designed to produce an approximation of damages based on the entire record." *Raytheon Co. v. White*, 305 F.3d 1354, 1367 (Fed.Cir.2002). Such method is employed when " 'damages cannot be ascertained by any reasonable computation from actual

---

52. *See, e.g.*, Penzel Constr. Co., Inc. v. Jackson R-2 Sch. Dist., 2017 WL 582663 (Mo. App. 2017); Flatiron-Lane v. Case Atlantic Co., 2015 WL 777686 (M.D.N.C. 2015). *But see* Balfour Beatty Rail, Inc. v. Kansas City S. Ry. Co., 173 F. Supp. 3d 363, 422 (N.D. Tex. 2016) (in diversity case, deciding that Texas would not permit use of modified total cost method in case at issue in light of general tendency of courts to allow method only as a last resort).

53. Baldi Bros. Constructors v. United States, 50 Fed. Cl. 74, 79–81 (2001).

54. *See generally* Stephen A. Hess, *The Jury Verdict Method of Proving Damages*, 2007-5 CONSTR. BRIEFINGS (May 2007). The process is generally only applicable to bench trials or to administrative proceedings—in cases before juries, the "jury verdict method" is not a separately cognizable method of calculating damages, as there is an actual jury to decide the damages. *But see* New Pueblo Constructors, Inc. v. State, 144 Ariz. 95, 696 P.2d 185 (1985) (allowing case to go to jury on express "jury verdict" method).

figures,' but it 'is not favored and may be used only when other, more exact, methods cannot be applied.'" CEMS, Inc., 59 Fed.Cl. at 228 (quoting *Dawco Constr., Inc. v. United States*, 930 F.2d 872, 880 (Fed.Cir.1991), *rev'd on other grounds*, *Reflectone, Inc. v. Dalton*, 60 F.3d 1572 (Fed.Cir.1995) (en banc)). Accordingly, as explained by the United States Court of Claims:

> In situations where the court has rejected the 'total cost' method of proving *1032 damages, but where the record nevertheless contains reasonably satisfactory evidence of what the damages are, computed on an acceptable basis, the court has adopted such other evidence; or where such other evidence, although not satisfactory in and of itself upon which to base a judgment, has nevertheless been considered at least sufficient upon which to predicate a 'jury verdict' award, it has rendered a judgment based on such a verdict.

Boyajian v. United States, 423 F.2d 1231, 1244 (Ct.Cl.1970) (internal citations omitted).

As recognized by the Federal Circuit, the primary peril of using the jury verdict method is "the risk that unrealistic assumptions will be adopted and extrapolated, greatly multiplying an award beyond reason, and rewarding preparers of imprecise claims based on undocumented costs with unjustified windfalls." Dawco Constr., 930 F.2d at 882. Accordingly, "[b]efore resorting to the jury verdict method, a court . . . must determine (1) that clear proof of injury exists; (2) that there is no more reliable method for calculating damages;[12] and (3) that the evidence is sufficient to make a fair and reasonable approximation of the damages." *Raytheon Co.*, 305 F.3d at 1367 (*citing WRB Corp. v. United States*, 183 Ct.Cl. 409 (1968)).[55]

The circumstances in which the jury verdict may be invoked are varied,[56] and litigators generally employ the jury verdict method only as a "last resort" or alternative basis for the calculation of damages when the damage case-in-chief bears indicia of fundamental flaws or weaknesses.

C. Consequential Damages in Construction Contracts

Consequential damages or so-called special damages are damages caused by a breach of duty, but whose existence or impact is less readily or directly

---

55. East Coast Repair & Fabrication, LLC v. United States, 199 F. Supp. 3d 1006, 1032 (E.D. Va. 2016).

56. *See generally* JOHN CIBINIC, JR., RALPH C. NASH, JR., & JAMES F. NAGLE, ADMINISTRATION OF GOVERNMENT CONTRACTS 704–09 (4th ed. 2006), reading some cases as utilizing the jury verdict method to adjust for lack of evidence, conflicting evidence, or lack of proof of causation, in addition to its role in approximating quantum of damage.

traceable to the breach than compensatory damages.[57] These damages may include lost rents, lost profits (other than profits anticipated directly from the work), extended financing costs, loss of business, and loss of bonding capacity.[58] Consequential damages may be recoverable in actions based in contract if reasonably foreseeable. Consequential damages generally are not recoverable in actions based on unjust enrichment.

D. Punitive Damages

Punitive damages are intended to punish a malicious wrongdoer and to deter the wrongdoer and others from behaving in a similar fashion in the future. Punitive damages in the construction industry are rare, and most jurisdictions do not allow the recovery of punitive damages for simple breach of contract.[59] Because punitive damages generally are not available in breach of contract actions, in order to recover there must be an independent tort; outrageous or malicious conduct accompanying the breach; or a special relationship between the parties whose protection is important enough that a state's public policy may permit punitive damages. Such relationships, however, rarely involve two parties to a construction contract.

E. The Claims Industry and Recordkeeping

The proof of claims in the construction industry—both with respect to liability and with respect to damages—often involves the review of a substantial volume of different types of construction documents beyond the basic agreement between the parties, such as drawings, specifications, daily logs, requests for information, submittals, payment applications, change orders, invoices, time and material tickets, and weather reports. Most of these documents can be understood only with experience in the construction industry. In addition, the preparation of some aspects of construction claims (especially scheduling) requires very specialized training and tools. The process of understanding what happened on a construction site in hindsight and being able to explain it to a fact finder are skills that require expertise and, in the context of litigation, expert witnesses.

---

57. *See generally* SCHWARTZKOPF & MCNAMARA, *supra* note 27, § 1.03, at 9.
58. *See generally id.* § 1.03, at 9–10.
59. A somewhat dated but otherwise excellent survey of the general rule under which punitive damages may not be awarded for breach of contract (and a taxonomy of exceptions) may be found at Mark Pennington, *Punitive Damages for Breach of Contract: A Core Sample from the Decisions of the Last Ten Years,* 42 ARK. L. REV. 31 (1989).

An entire industry has evolved to provide this expertise. The industry does not merely provide expert witnesses for the purposes of litigation; rather, many claims companies earn their keep through the preparation of change orders, requests for adjustment, and similar claims against owners (or contractors) before the claims ever ripen into litigation.[60]

22.04 MITIGATION OF DAMAGES

A. Duty to Mitigate Damages

Even though victimized by the conduct of another party, an injured party has an affirmative obligation to mitigate its damages. That is, the injured party must take reasonable steps to minimize the damages it will suffer.[61] For instance, where a contractor has been prevented from working on one area of the project, the contractor may have an affirmative obligation to make its best effort to continue to work by moving to another unaffected area of the project, rather than to sit idly by, accumulating additional labor and equipment costs.

When a party does not undertake reasonable steps to mitigate its damages, the party does so at the risk of losing part of its right to recover damages. In particular, a party generally may not recover as part of its damages any money that represents damages the claiming party could have avoided through more prudent conduct.

B. Economic Waste

While the cost of repair is the basic measure of damage for many breaches of construction contracts, this measure may not be applied where the repair cost is exorbitant, taking into account the nature of the damage, the value of the work at issue, the value of the project in general, and the diminution in value of the product in light of the damage. In other terms, where the cost of repair is manifestly excessive in light of the other elements, a court may not award the cost of repair as the measure of damages.[62] "If an injured party's costs of repair are 'clearly excessive' or 'clearly disproportionate' to the actual loss resulting from the breach, then the diminution in market value is the appropriate

---

60. Indeed, construction management itself has advanced to the point that there are dozens of graduate programs across the country that offer master's and even doctorate degrees in construction management or construction science. *See* http://www.gradschools.com (last accessed Oct. 27, 2017).
61. *See, e.g.,* Weill Constr. Co., Inc. v. Thibodeaux, 491 So. 2d 166, 173 (La. Ct. App. 1985).
62. *See generally* Legacy Builders, LLC. v. Andrews, 335 P.3d 1063 (Wy. 2014).

measure of damages."[63] As applied, the value formula consists of the diminution in value of the structure as opposed to the cost actually required to repair the structure.[64]

As an example of economic waste, in *County of Maricopa v. Walsh and Oberg Architects, Inc.*,[65] the county obtained a judgment against its architect for the negligent preparation of drawings and specifications for an underground parking garage that was designed to be waterproof but failed to prevent water from dripping onto cars below. The county alleged that it would cost approximately $498,169 to remove landscaping and cover the top of the underground structure with a waterproof membrane. The Arizona Court of Appeals was persuaded by the fact that it cost the county far less to perform an alternate remedy that would protect the vehicles from water damage and prevent further deterioration. As such, the court of appeals recognized that it would be economic waste to award the county more than a third of a million dollars to merely remove landscaping when an alternate remedy existed.[66]

C. Betterment

The concept of betterment is widely recognized in the construction industry.[67] As a general principle, when a defect in the work or an omission in the drawings exists the owner should not be placed in a better position than if the error had not occurred. This concept is known as "betterment," "added value," or "added first benefit."

The courts have generally held that if the design is incomplete, the owner should pay what the omitted component would have cost if such component had been included in the original design.[68] Logically, the designer should pay any additional costs to the owner, such as any "premium" associated with the change order adding the component to the project. When a design error is not discovered until during or after construction, the owner may be entitled to

---

63. *Id.* at 1068.
64. Storm v. St. Clair Corp., 153 S.W.3d 360, 364 (Mo. Ct. App. 2005).
65. Cnty. of Maricopa v. Walsh & Oberg Architects, Inc., 494 P.2d 44 (Ariz. Ct. App. 1972); *see also* Stovall v. Reliance Ins. Co., 107 P.3d 1219 (Kan. 2005).
66. *Walsh & Oberg Architects*, 494 P.2d at 44; *see also Stovall*, 107 P.3d at 1219.
67. *See* Jerome V. Bales, Shamus O'Meara, & Mark R. Azman, *The "Betterment" or Added Benefit Defense*, 26 Construction Lawyer 14 (2006).
68. *See, e.g.*, City of Westminster v. Centric-Jones Constructors, 100 P.3d 472 (Colo. App. 2003); Sch. Bd. of Broward Cnty. v. Pierce Goodwin, Alexander, & Linville, 137 So. 3d 1059, 1070–71 (Fla. Dist. Ct. App. 2014).

recover the cost of any retrofitting expense, waste, or an intervening increase in the cost of the labor or materials necessary to correct the error.[69]

From the contractor's perspective, its fundamental obligation is to build a project in accordance with the drawings and specifications. However, in some circumstances, contractors and construction managers at risk may also rely on the defense of betterment. For example, if the owner must repair or replace defective work, the courts have generally held that it should not recover the cost of any enhancement exceeding the quality evidenced in the contract documents.[70] When the repairs do not involve any enhancement, the owner's damages may still be reduced to the extent of any extended useful life of the building component.[71]

The doctrine of "betterment" is sometimes easier to state in theory than to apply in principle. A plaintiff owner bears the ultimate burden of proof with respect to damages, and plaintiff's failure to account for betterment may preclude its recovery. As one appellate court observed:

> As to [contractor] MCM's liability for the playground defects, the trial court specifically found that, although the City did not agree to work with MCM to prepare a joint audit of the playground and never provided MCM with an opportunity to cure the deficiencies in the playground, the City suffered damages because the playground did not comply with the safety standards in the contract documents. The trial court, however, found that the City's complete removal and replacement of the playground was excessive, and therefore reduced the damages accordingly.
>
> As to MCM's liability for the subgrade, sod, and landscaping defects, the trial court found that the City was entitled to be reimbursed for the remediation of the defects in the park, and that MCM was partially at fault for failing to recognize that over compacting the soil would cause the grass and landscaping to fail. However, the trial court also found that the City was not entitled to a betterment, which the trial court calculated as the difference between the total amount sought by the City and the entire damage award.
>
> . . .
>
> MCM contends that the trial court's award of damages for the landscaping defects was speculative, and we agree. The City sought approximately $3 million

---

69. *See, e.g.*, Grossman v. Sea Air Towers, Ltd., 513 So. 2d 686 (Fla. App. 1987), *rev. denied*, Grossman v. Sea Air Towers, Ltd., 520 So. 2d 584 (Fla. 1988).

70. *See, e.g.*, City of Plaquemine v. N. Am. Constructors, 832 So. 2d 447, 464–65 (La. App. 2002); St. Joseph Hosp. v. Corbetta Constr. Co., Inc., 316 N.E.2d 51 (Ill. App. 1st Dist. 1974).

71. *See, e.g.*, Mall v. Pawelski, 626 So. 2d 291 (Fla. Dist. Ct. App. 1993); Allied Chem. Corp. v. Van Buren Sch. Dist. No. 42, 575 S.W.2d 445 (Ark. 1979).

in damages against MCM and Hargreaves in connection with the landscaping defects, but the trial court only awarded the City $1,290,037. The trial court stated that the difference between its total award and the amount sought by the City constituted a "betterment," which the trial court defined as aspects of the City's remediation plan which improved upon and differed significantly from the original designs and specifications in the contract documents.

The trial court was correct to exclude betterments from its award, as the measure of damages for breaching a construction contract is "the reasonable cost of construction and completion in accordance with the contract, if this is possible and does not involve unreasonable economic waste." Grossman Holdings Ltd. v. Hourihan, 414 So.2d 1037, 1039 (Fla. 1982) (quoting § 346(1)(a), Restatement (First) of Contracts (1932)) (emphasis added); Kritikos v. Andersen, 125 So.3d 885, 888 (Fla. 4th DCA 2013) (stating that if an owner elects to adopt a more expensive design in the course of making repairs in a construction defect case, then "the recovery should be limited to what would have been the reasonable cost of repair according to the original design") (quoting Temple Beth Sholom & Jewish Ctr., Inc. v. Thyne Constr. Corp., 399 So.2d 525, 526 (Fla. 2d DCA 1981)) (emphasis added).

However, the City has not cited to any evidence and we have found no evidence in the record as to the value of the betterments in the remediation plan, or what it would have cost to restore the City "to the condition [it] would have been in if the contract had been performed." Grossman Holdings Ltd., 414 So.2d at 1039. The only measure of damages provided by the City was the costs associated with the planning, permitting, and construction of a park that is fundamentally different from the one it contracted with MCM to build. Therefore, we find that the trial court speculated as to the value of the betterments in the City's remediation plan and, thus, speculated in its ultimate calculation of the damages owed to the City in connection with the landscaping defects in the park.[72]

22.05 CONTRACTUAL AND OTHER LIMITATIONS ON LIABILITY

A. Indemnification Clauses and Limitations on Liability

Two types of clauses may be found in construction agreements under the terms of which a party seeks to reduce its exposure to liability to the other party. The first type of clause—an indemnification clause—requires that one party (the indemnitor) indemnify the other party (the indemnitee) against any

---

72. Magnum Constr. Mgmt. Corp. v. City of Miami Beach, 209 So. 3d 51, 55–56 (Fla. Ct. App. 2016).

losses the indemnitee may suffer on the construction project. The second type of clause is known as a "hold harmless" or "limitation of liability" clause. Under the terms of such a clause, one party agrees that it will not be permitted to recover damages (or will limit the amount of damages recoverable) from the other party.[73]

Indemnification clauses largely are used to shift the burden of liability onto the party whose ultimate malfeasance results in damages to another defendant. For example, when a subcontractor's deficient construction allows the owner to recover damages from the contractor, the indemnification clause shifts the burden of this loss to the subcontractor (or its insurance carrier). When an indemnification clause functions in this manner, the clause generally is enforceable. Some indemnification clauses, however, attempt to saddle the indemnitor with all losses, even those caused in whole or in part by the indemnitee. Many courts and legislatures find such clauses so unfair that they have declared them unenforceable in many circumstances:[74]

> A provision in a construction contract that requires one party to the contract to indemnify, hold harmless, insure or defend the other party to the contract, including the other party's employees or agents, against liability, claims, damages, losses or expenses, including attorney fees, arising out of bodily injury to persons or damage to property caused by or resulting from, in whole or in part, the negligence, act or omission of the indemnitee, its officers, employees or agents, is void, unenforceable and against the public policy of the state.[75]

A "hold harmless" or "limitation of liability" clause, on the other hand, precludes one party from suing another for particular claims, or limits the amount of damages that a culpable party may be required to pay for its malfeasance. Unless such clauses are oppressive or operate to exclude a party from any meaningful responsibility for its own misconduct, they generally are enforceable. The conceptual difference between limitation of liability clauses and indemnification clauses is such that most states permit enforcement of limitation of liability clauses, even in the face of anti-indemnification statutes.

---

73. Some courts discuss a third type of clause—an "exculpatory clause"—that completely exonerates a party from any liability, and thus operates as an extreme limitation of liability clause. Such clauses are often held unenforceable in personal contracts, although they may be given effect when the parties to a contract are businesses with sufficient bargaining power and their intent to employ an exculpatory clause is clear.

74. *See generally* Allen Holt Gwyn & Paul E. Davis, *Fifty-State Survey of Anti-Indemnity Statutes and Related Cases*, 23 Constr. Law. 26 (2003).

75. N.M. Stat. Ann. § 56-7-1(A).

Fort Knox Self Storage, Inc. v. Western Technologies, Inc.
140 N.M. 233, 142 P.3d 1 (N.M. Ct. App. 2006)

FRY, Judge.

{1} Defendant Western Technologies, Inc. appeals an order awarding Plaintiff Fort Knox Self Storage, Inc. over $110,000 in damages for negligence, over $240,000 in attorney fees, and prejudgment interest. The contract between the parties, in which Western was to provide geotechnical engineering services in evaluating the subsurface conditions of a proposed building site, contained a limitation of liability clause purportedly limiting Western's liability to $50,000. The trial court refused to enforce this clause on the ground that it violated a statute prohibiting any party to a construction contract from agreeing to indemnify any entity for its own negligence. While this is the primary issue on appeal, Western also challenges the award of attorney fees and prejudgment interest.

{2} We reverse the trial court's determination that the limitation of liability clause was void and remand for entry of an order limiting the damages awarded against Western to $50,000. We affirm the award of attorney fees and prejudgment interest.

{3} Fort Knox entered into a contract with Western by which Western agreed to provide geotechnical services in connection with the site where Fort Knox intended to build a self-storage facility. Fort Knox agreed to pay Western $1,750 plus tax for its services. Western performed the agreed services, and, shortly after construction of the facility was completed, Fort Knox employees noticed damage to walls and cracks and fissures in the parking lot. Fort Knox sued, claiming that this damage resulted from the negligence of Western and other parties involved in the construction, or from breach of contract.

{4} During the course of the litigation, Western contended that a provision in its contract with Fort Knox limited its liability, if any, to $50,000. The contract provision stated:

> LIMITATION ON [WESTERN'S] LIABILITY
> NOTWITHSTANDING ANY OTHER PROVISION OF THIS AGREEMENT, [WESTERN'S] TOTAL AGGREGATE LIABILITY IN CONNECTION WITH THIS AGREEMENT AND WORK PERFORMED HEREUNDER SHALL BE STRICTLY LIMITED TO AN AMOUNT EQUAL TO THE GREATER OF $50,000 OR THE TOTAL CONTRACT PRICE PAID TO [WESTERN] UNDER THIS AGREEMENT (LESS DIRECT THIRD-PARTY COSTS), WHETHER SUCH LIABILITY IS ASSERTED FOR BREACH OF REPRESENTATION OR WARRANTY, UNDER ANY INDEMNITY, IN ANY OTHER RESPECT UNDER OR FOR BREACH OF CONTRACT, OR AS A LIABILITY ARISING IN TORT OR BY STATUTE. CLIENT HEREBY WAIVES AND DISCHARGES ALL PRESENT AND FUTURE CLAIMS AGAINST [WESTERN] AND (FOR ACTIONS IN SUCH CAPACITY) ITS SHAREHOLDERS, DIRECTORS, OFFICERS, AGENTS, EMPLOYEES, AND SUBCONTRACTORS, FOR ANY CLAIM OTHER THAN THOSE

DESCRIBED IN THE PRECEDING SENTENCE OR ANY LIABILITY AMOUNT IN EXCESS OF THE AGGREGATE LIMITATION STATED IN THE PRECEDING SENTENCE.

. . .

{11} Fort Knox asserts that the limitation of liability clause is unenforceable because Section 56-7-1 expressly dictates that one cannot seek to avoid responsibility for one's own negligence during the course of construction. It argues that our New Mexico Supreme Court has recognized that the provisions of this statute are broader than those in most states and prohibits agreements that attempt to indemnify in whole or in part against negligent liability. See *Sierra v. Garcia*, 106 N.M. 573, 575, 746 P.2d 1105, 1107 (1987). While we agree with Fort Knox's assessment of the holding in *Sierra*, we do not agree that Section 56-7-1, as interpreted by *Sierra*, applies in this case.

{12} We do not read Section 56-7-1 as prohibiting a limitation of liability based on one's own negligence but as prohibiting the avoidance of all liability for one's own negligence. See *Sierra*, 106 N.M. at 576, 746 P.2d at 1108 (explaining that Section 56-7-1 provides "that liability arising in whole or in part from an indemnitee's negligence . . . may not be contracted away by an indemnity agreement"). The limitation of liability clause in this case does not seek to contract away all liability for Western's negligence but seeks to limit the amount of damages Western must pay for its own negligence. The contract does not indemnify Western against its own negligence. Indeed, it provides that Western may be liable for damages, based on its own negligence, that are twenty-eight times higher than the amount of the contract.

{13} Our view is supported by *Valhal Corp. v. Sullivan Assocs., Inc.*, 44 F.3d 195 (3rd Cir.1995), which involved strikingly similar facts. The contract in *Valhal* contained a limitation of liability clause stating:

> The OWNER agrees to limit the Design Professional's liability to the OWNER and to all construction Contractors and Subcontractors on the project, due to the Design Professional's professional negligent acts, errors or omissions, such that the total aggregate liability of each Design Professional shall not exceed $50,000 or the Design Professional's total fee for services rendered on this project. Should the OWNER find the above terms unacceptable, an equitable surcharge to absorb the Architect's increase in insurance premiums will be negotiated.

Id. at 198 (internal quotation marks omitted). The lower court determined that this provision violated the public policy behind Pennsylvania's anti-indemnification statute. *Id.* at 199 n. 2.

{14} The appellate court reversed, treating the provision as a limitation of liability clause, and rejected the contention that it was unenforceable under Pennsylvania law. The court first distinguished a limitation of liability clause from two other methods of limiting exposure to damages for the negligent performance of a contract. *Id.* at 202. One method is an exculpatory clause, which immunizes a person from the consequences of his or her own negligence. *Id.* Another method is an indemnity clause, which holds the indemnitee harmless by requiring the indemnitor to bear the cost of damages for which the indemnitee may be liable. *Id.* The court then concluded that the clause at issue bore no relation to either of these two methods. The clause did not bar any cause of action or require someone other than the beneficiary of the clause to pay for any loss caused by the beneficiary's negligence. *Id.* The court held that the beneficiary remained liable for its own negligence and was exposed to liability up to a maximum of $50,000. *Id.* The court stated, "Thus, the amount of liability is capped, but [the beneficiary] still bears substantial responsibility for its actions." *Id.; cf. Berlangieri v. Running Elk Corp.,* 2003-nMSC-024, ¶ 1, 134 N.M. 341, 76 P.3d 1098 (holding that an exculpatory release was unenforceable as contrary to public policy).

{15} We recognize, as did the court in *Valhal,* the similarities between exculpatory clauses, indemnity clauses, and limitation of liability clauses. *Valhal,* 44 F.3d at 202. But we also recognize, as did the court in *Valhal,* that there is a significant difference between contracts that insulate a party from any and all liability and those that simply limit liability. *Id.* The *Valhal* court noted that clauses limiting liability "are a fact of everyday business and commercial life" and that such clauses are enforceable as long as they are "reasonable and not so drastic as to remove the incentive to perform with due care." *Id.* at 204. Because the contract exposed the architectural firm in *Valhal* to damages that were seven times the amount of remuneration it would receive under the contract, the court determined that the $50,000 cap did not immunize it from the consequences of its own actions but was a reasonable allocation of risk. *Id.*

{16} Fort Knox argues that the large difference between its total damages (over $1,000,000) and the contract limitation ($50,000) violates public policy. Fort Knox also appears to argue that Western is "immunized" in the manner of an indemnity clause for any damages over $50,000. We are not persuaded, however, that the correct measure of whether a cap is so small as to render the clause unenforceable is the difference between the damages suffered and the cap. The court in *Valhal* was equally unpersuaded by this argument. Although the court recognized that the $50,000 cap could be considered nominal when compared to the more than $2,000,000 in damages being sought, the court rejected this measure of reasonableness. *Id.* at 204. The court stated that the relevant inquiry must be whether the cap is so minimal compared to the expected compensation as to negate or drastically minimize concern for liability for one's actions. *Id.* In this case, the cap of $50,000 is twenty-eight times the amount of remuneration Western received under the contract, which was $1,750 plus tax. Similar to the court's determination in *Valhal,* where the cap was only seven times the expected fee, *id.,* we conclude the cap in this case leaves Western exposed to substantial damages and does not negate Western's liability.

B. Waivers of Consequential/Incidental Damages

When a party breaches an agreement, the opposing party loses the immediate benefit of its bargain, and the breach may cause other, less direct damages such as lost future profits. These less direct damages—proximately caused by the breach but not directly implied by the aggrieved party's benefit of the bargain—are known as "consequential damages." As mentioned in Section 22.03(C), these damages are limited to those reasonably within the contemplation of the parties at the time of their agreement. Many construction contracts—including, notably, the AIA family of documents—contain a contractual waiver of consequential damages:

C. Waiver of Claims for Consequential Damages

The Contractor and Owner waive Claims against each other for consequential damages arising out of or relating to this Contract. This mutual waiver includes

> 1. damages incurred by the Owner for rental expenses, for losses of use, income, profit, financing, business and reputation, and for loss of management or employee productivity or of the services of such persons; and
>
> 2. damages incurred by the Contractor for principal office expenses including the compensation of personnel stationed there, for losses of financing, business and reputation, and for loss of profit, except anticipated profit arising directly from the Work.
>
> This mutual waiver is applicable, without limitation, to all consequential damages due to either party's termination in accordance with Article 14. Nothing contained in this Section 15.1.7 shall be deemed to preclude an assessment of liquidated damages, when applicable, in accordance with the requirements of the Contract Documents.[76]

The intent of the clause is to limit consequential damages, generally, and to eliminate the damages for home office overhead, specifically.[77]

D. Liquidated Damages for Delay

The use of a contract provision providing for the payment to the owner of a liquidated sum for each day of unexcused delay in achieving substantial completion beyond the allowed time for completion has become the norm. Where liquidated delay damages are provided for, they serve as the owner's exclusive

---

76. American Institute of Architects, AIA Document A201–2017, General Conditions of the Contract for Construction § 15.1.7 (2017).

77. *See* discussions of home office overhead [*Eichleay*] damages at Section 22.03(A)(1)(d).

remedy for late completion (presuming the owner has allowed the contractor to complete, rather than terminating the contract), and the owner cannot also recover its actual delay damages even though they exceed the liquidated amount.[78]

Liquidated damages clauses generally are enforceable so long as (1) the liquidated sum chosen by the parties bears a reasonable relationship to the owner's likely actual damages as of the date on which the contract was entered and (2) actual damages are difficult to prove. The limiting principle is that a contractual penalty, meaning an amount intended to punish the contractor for late completion, is unenforceable as a matter of public policy.[79] Within a wide range, however, liquidated damage amounts that can reasonably be seen as a pre-contractual estimate of owner's likely damages for delays will be enforced. Indeed, cases in recent decades finding a liquidated damages amount to be an unenforceable penalty are few and far between.[80]

To maximize the likelihood that they will be enforced, liquidated damages clauses frequently include recitals to the effect that the actual damages in the event of delayed completion would be difficult to ascertain and that the chosen amount is intended as an estimate of actual damages and not as a penalty. Such liquidated damages clauses generally will be enforced when the owner's actual damages are considerably more than the liquidated amount,[81] when they are considerably less,[82] or even when the owner arguably incurred no delay damages at all.[83] The one exception recognized in some jurisdictions is where the contractor has wrongfully abandoned the project. In those cases, the owner has been allowed to elect between recovering liquidated damages or actual damages, on the theory that the liquidated damages provision did not contemplate outright abandonment.[84]

In recent years, incentive/disincentive or "bonus/penalty" provisions have come into more frequent use, which provide for a daily bonus amount payable

---

78. Cnty. of Dauphin v. Fidelity & Deposit Co. of Md., 770 F. Supp. 248, 254 (M.D. Pa. 1991), aff'd, 937 F.2d 596 (3d Cir. 1991).

79. Priebe & Sons v. United States, 332 U.S. 407, 413 (1947).

80. *See, e.g.,* Kingston Constructors, Inc. v. Washington Metro. Area Transit Auth., 930 F. Supp. 651, 656 (D.D.C. 1996) (finding that inclusion in liquidated damages of EPA penalties that clearly would not be assessed made liquidated damage amount a penalty).

81. Saturn Constr. Co. v. Conn. Dep't of Pub. Works, 1994 WL 590604 (Conn. Super. Ct. 1994) (enforcing $1,000 per day liquidated damages despite actual damages of $40,000 per day).

82. C.O. Falter Constr. Corp. v. City of Binghamton, 684 N.Y.S.2d 86 (1999) (finding that majority of $43,000 per day liquidated damages were based on "public inconvenience" if odor control system was not timely completed).

83. United States v. Bethlehem Steel Co., 205 U.S. 105, 121 (1907).

84. City of Elmira v. Larry Walter, Inc., 76 N.Y.2d 912, 563 N.Y.S.2d 45, 564 N.E.2d 655 (1990).

to the contractor for completing the project sooner than the required completion date, and a penalty amount for each day the project is completed late. Although neither the bonus nor the penalty appropriately can be characterized as "damages," such provisions have a great deal of utility in incentivizing early completion, particularly where the daily bonus and penalty amounts are roughly equal, balanced, and not unfair to either party. Accordingly, enforcement of such a balanced incentive/disincentive arrangement should not be repugnant to public policy. At least one decision, however, has invalidated the so-called penalty aspect of such a bonus/penalty arrangement as against public policy.[85]

E. No Damages for Delay

Owners commonly include a clause precluding recovery of damages for delays for which owners are responsible. Such clauses normally will provide that a contractor's sole remedy for delay, regardless of the cause, is for additional time and that no additional compensation will be paid. The allocation of risk for delay in construction contracts (and in the common law rules that define remedies) is of vital importance to contractors, owners, and design professionals. In many cases, delay damages can mount far in excess of other damages.

No-damages-for-delay clauses are generally enforceable. Courts, however, will construe them narrowly and scrutinize them under equitable principles. This has resulted in the development of several exceptions regarding the enforceability of no-damage-for-delay clauses.[86] Such clauses generally may not be enforceable if the cause of the delay is

1. The bad faith of the party seeking to enforce the claim;
2. So long in duration that it amounts to abandonment of the contract;
3. Beyond the contemplation of the parties at the time of contract formation; or
4. The result of active interference of the parties seeking to enforce the clause.[87]

However, the exact articulation of the exceptions varies from state to state. As a consequence, cases construing the application of exceptions to the enforceability of no-damage-of-delay clauses may be of little assistance outside the

---

85. Milton Constr. Co. v. Alabama Highway Dep't, 568 So. 2d 784, 789 (Ala. 1990).
86. *See, e.g.,* Julian Bailey & Stephen A. Hess, *Delay Damages and Site Conditions: Contracts in US and English Law*, 35 CONSTR. LAWYER 6 (Summer 2015); Richard Gary Thomas & Fred Wilshusen, *How to Beat A No-Damages-for-Delay Clause*, 9 CONSTR. LAWYER 17 (1989).
87. John E. Green Plumbing & Heating Co., Inc. v. Turner Constr. Co., 500 F. Supp. 910 (E.D. Mich. 1980), *aff'd,* 742 F.2d 965 (7th Cir. 2004); this topic is more fully explored in Chapter 11.

jurisdiction to which they apply. In addition, the careful reader will observe that the third exception listed—delay damages beyond the contemplation of the parties at the time of contract formation—is quite similar to the test for "consequential" damages that may be beyond the reach of damages, anyway. To state it differently, if delay damages are sufficiently "beyond the contemplation of the parties at the time of contract formation" such that the damages avoid preclusion under a no-damages-for-delay clause, are they recoverable under ordinary contract principles?

QUESTIONS

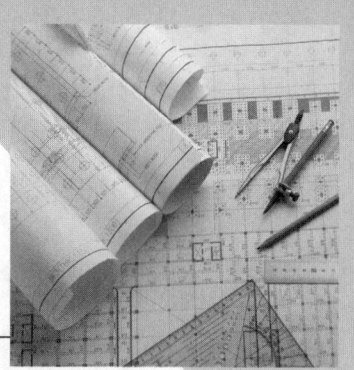

1. If a contractor works in a state that allows an election between quantum meruit and benefit of the bargain as a measure of damages, in what circumstances would the contractor choose to employ quantum meruit?
2. Suppose that you represent the government in the *Baldi* case discussed in this chapter, and are mapping out your litigation strategy. What kind of evidence would you try to discover to fend off use of the total cost method under the facts presented? The *Baldi* court mentioned one indication that the contractor's bid was unreasonably low. What other facts or expert testimony might help your case?

CHAPTER 23

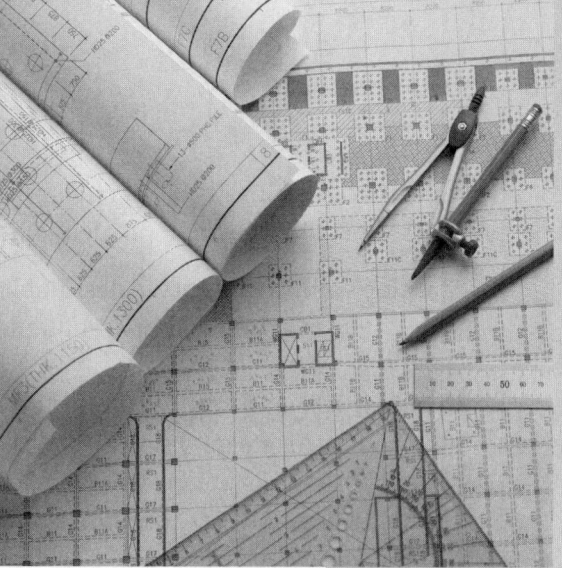

Public Construction Contracting

JAMES F. NAGLE

Public contracting is an important segment of the construction industry. It provides an enormous amount of money for construction activities, either directly via public contracts or indirectly by funding private contracts to which many public contracting rules apply. Moreover, many of the standard practices and clauses that are now endemic to construction projects (changes, differing site conditions, terminations for convenience, etc.) began with public, and especially federal, contracting.

In most of its workings, public contracting is now very similar to private contracting, primarily because so many of the tenets of public contracting have been adopted in private contracting. Indeed, most of this book can be applied to public contracting and many chapters set out rules and doctrines that apply specifically to government contacts. Still, government contracting—and especially federal government contracting—includes unique rules that distinguish it from private contracting and the topic of government contracting deserves special attention. This chapter examines seven of the most important aspects of government contracting that distinguish it from private contracting. They are listed here and described in more detail in the following sections.

1. **Statutory and regulatory rules.** Public contracts are subject to extensive statutory and regulatory requirements and guidance that the contractor ignores at its peril.
2. **Criminal law and fraud.** Contractors who deal with the government deal with a sovereign whose responsibility includes the protection of all its subjects. As a consequence, practices that are commonplace in private contracting can be prohibited—and even criminal—in public contracting.
3. **Sovereign immunity.** The government, unlike a private owner, has sovereign immunity. Specifically, contractors can only sue the public owner to the extent that the public owner has waived its sovereign immunity.
4. **Sovereign acts.** Because the government is a sovereign and any liability affects the public fisc, the government is entitled to special defenses. As one example, there are often matters in which there is no doubt that the public owner, through its agents, has interfered with the contractor's performance. However, if that public agent was acting in its sovereign, as opposed to its contractual, capacity, the government may be entitled to avail itself of what is called the "Sovereign Act" defense.
5. **The actual authority requirement.** In private contracting, an owner may be bound when its representatives act with apparent authority. The federal government, on the other hand, is only bound when its representatives act with actual authority.
6. **Socioeconomic requirements.** Private owners are typically concerned with three items: the price, the quality, and the schedule. In public contracting, there can be a host of other concerns that give rise to special questions not relevant to most private contracts. Has the contractor agreed to pay its workers in accordance with prevailing wage determinations? Has the contractor agreed to use domestic components to comply with the Buy American Act? Is the contractor a member of a socioeconomic class (small business, small disadvantaged business, etc.) or has it agreed to subcontract heavily to members of that class?
7. **Protests and disputes.** Public construction, especially federal, has unique dispute procedures, both for protesting contract awards and for prosecuting contract claims.

23.01 STATUTORY AND REGULATORY RULES[1]

This section focuses on federal contracting as the prime example of a heavily regulated system, but other public entities have similar, though less extensive, regimes.

Federal contracts are normally subject only to federal procurement law, comprised of federal contracting statutes and regulations, as interpreted by the U.S. Court of Appeals for the Federal Circuit, the U.S. Court of Federal Claims, the Boards of Contract Appeals, and the U.S. Comptroller General.[2] Sometimes it will be necessary to review state law, such as those laws regarding warranties under the state's Uniform Commercial Code.

Federal procurement law also includes the regulations set forth in the Federal Acquisition Regulation (FAR) and the agency supplements, both of which are in Title 48 of the Code of Federal Regulations (CFR). For example, chapter 2 of title 48 is the Defense Federal Acquisition Regulatory Supplement (DFARS), and chapter 9 is the Department of Energy Acquisition Regulation (DEAR). Actually, title 48 in its entirety is often referred to as the FARS—the Federal Acquisition Regulatory System. The FAR and its supplements (the size of a large city phone book) implement numerous statutes that apply to federal procurements, such as the Truthful Cost or Pricing Data Act,[3] Competition in Contracting Act,[4] and the Buy American Act.[5]

In the face of this intricate network of regulations, readers should be aware of a doctrine in federal contracting known as the Christian doctrine.[6] The Chris-

---

1. The following section relies heavily on my chapter, *Introduction*, in FEDERAL GOVERNMENT CONSTRUCTION CONTRACTS, 2D ED. (Michael A. Branca, Aaron P. Silberman, John S. Vento, Adrian L. Bastianelli III, Andrew D. Ness & Joseph D. West, eds., ABA Press 2010).

2. *See* James F. Nagle & Bryan A. Kelley, *Exploring the Federal Forums for Government Contracts*, 2 J. AM. C. CONSTR. LAW. 189 (2008), for details on these forums and their predecessors. The clause used in the *Sulzer* case was as follows: Clause I-79 of the Lockheed-Sulzer Bingham subcontract states:

This subcontract shall be governed by and construed in accordance with the law of U.S. Government contracts as set forth by statute and applicable regulations, and decisions by the appropriate courts and Board of Contract Appeals. To the extent that the law referred to in the foregoing sentence is not determinative of an issue arising out of the clauses of this subcontract recourse shall be to the law of the State of California.

3. 10 U.S.C. § 2304.

4. 31 U.S.C. §§ 3551–56; 41 U.S.C. § 3306, 3308, 1708, 1705.

5. 41 U.S.C. §§ 8301–8305.

6. An excellent discussion of the doctrine may be found at K-Con, Inc. v. Secretary of Army, 908 F.3d 719, 724 (Fed. Cir. 2018).

tian doctrine came out of the case *G.L. Christian & Associates v. United States*,[7] in which the government awarded a construction contract but neglected to include a termination for convenience clause even though it was required by the applicable regulation at the time—a forerunner of the FAR. The court ruled that if a clause was required to be in the contract by a regulation having the force and effect of law, it would be incorporated into the contract by operation of law despite its physical omission from the contract. Subsequent decisions have limited the application of the doctrine somewhat by emphasizing the requirement that the omitted clause must represent a fundamental procurement policy before the doctrine will be applied.[8]

The rationale for the *Christian* decision was that since the regulation is publicly published in the Federal Register, contractors are on notice that a contracting officer has no authority on his or her own to ignore the dictates of a regulation having the force and effect of law. When the contractor reviews a solicitation that does not contain a Terminations clause or a Changes clause, it must request proof from the contracting officer that a properly authorized deviation has been granted, allowing the contracting officer not to include a particular clause. Absent such evidence, the contractor must assume that the clause is incorporated into the contract.

The Christian doctrine only applies to clauses that are required to be in the contract. This may also apply to clauses that are "required when applicable" because the "when applicable" is normally determined upon the dollar value of the contract, that is, if a contract is above $100,000 certain clauses must be included. The Christian doctrine never applies to optional clauses because the contractor would not be on notice of any regulatory requirement that this clause be included. FAR 52.301 contains a matrix of all applicable clauses and provisions.

Federal law does not typically apply to subcontracts.[9] Certainly the subcontract itself can identify the applicable body of law that will be used to interpret it. If the prime is a California corporation, the subcontractor is another California corporation, and the contract is formed and performed in California, it would be logical for the parties to agree that the law of California will apply. Frequently, however, the parties will designate "federal procurement law" as

---

7. 160 Ct. Cl. 1, 312 F.2d 418, *reh'g denied*, 160 Ct. Cl. 58, 320 F.2d 345, *cert. denied*, 375 U.S. 954 (1963).

8. Chamberlain Mfg. Corp., ASBCA 18103, 74-1 BCA ¶ 10,368 (1973); General Eng'g & Machine Works v. O'Keefe, 991 F.2d 775, 779 (Fed. Cir. 1993).

9. Some doctrines, such as the "federal enclave" doctrine, may make the choice of law somewhat tricky. Such exceptions are beyond the scope of this chapter.

the body of law to be used in interpreting the subcontract,[10] so that both the prime contract with the government and the subcontract are governed by the same body of law.[11] This does not give a federal court jurisdiction, however, if for example, there is no diversity between the prime and subcontractor.

If the subcontract does not designate what law will apply, a judge may sometimes fill the void by designating federal procurement law as the applicable law.[12] This is done relatively rarely and normally only in those contracts such as national defense or Energy Department contracts for which the judge decides that uniform law across the 50 states must apply.

23.02 CRIMINAL LAW AND FRAUD

Acts that may be accepted and even commonplace in private contracting can subject contractors to civil or even criminal penalties in public contracting.

The Civil False Claims Act,[13] allows the government to sue contractors whom it believes have tried to cheat the government.[14] The statute allows for double and triple damages actually sustained by the government along with a statutory penalty. The court may assess a fine for each false claim submitted to the government. This can include vouchers, invoices, or requests for progress payments. One other unique aspect of the act is the qui tam provision that allows private individuals to bring suits essentially as whistleblowers against entities that may be liable under the False Claims Act.[15] Other statutes include the Criminal False Claims Act[16] and the False Statements Act,[17] which penalize false claims and statements made in the course of securing a government contract. For example, if a contractor knowingly and falsely certifies that it is a small business, that is a false statement. The contract then is improperly entered into and every voucher, invoice, or progress payment request submitted against that improperly awarded contract is a separate false claim.

---

10. *See, e.g.*, Sulzer Bingham Pumps, Inc. v. Lockheed Missiles & Space Co., Inc., 947 F.2d 1362, 1365 (9th Cir. 1991).

11. *See* Nagle, *A Primer on Prime-Subcontractor Disputes under Federal Contracts*, Vol. 29, The Construction Lawyer, at 39 (Winter 2009).

12. *E.g.*, American Pipe & Steel Corp. v. Firestone Co., 292 F.2d 640, 644 (9th Cir. 1961); New SD, Inc. v. Rockwell Inter. Corp., 79 F.3d 953, 955 (9th Cir. 1996).

13. 31 U.S.C. §§ 3721–3733.

14. The False Claims Act also protects individuals from retaliation for trying to prevent the submission of false claims. *See, e.g.*, Meridian Eng'g Co. v. United States, 885 F.3d 1351 (Fed. Cir. 2019) (denying motion for judgment on the pleadings based on alleged retaliation).

15. *See* 31 U.S.C. § 3730(b)(1).

16. 18 U.S.C. § 287.

17. 18 U.S.C. § 1001.

A good example of a contractor who ran afoul of the law and incurred substantial liability for its missteps is set out here:

United States Court of Appeals, Federal Circuit.

DAEWOO ENGINEERING AND CONSTRUCTION CO., LTD., Plaintiff-Appellant,
v.
UNITED STATES, Defendant-Appellee.
No. 2007-5129.
557 F.3d 1332
Feb. 20, 2009.

Rehearing and Rehearing En Banc Denied April 27, 2009.
Before MAYER, FRIEDMAN, and DYK, Circuit Judges.

DYK, Circuit Judge.

Daewoo Engineering and Construction Co., Ltd. ("Daewoo" or "the contractor") brought suit in the Court of Federal Claims, alleging that the United States breached a contract between Daewoo and the United States to build a road in the Republic of Palau. The United States counterclaimed, alleging violations of the False Claims Act, 31 U.S.C. § 3729, and the Contract Disputes Act, 41 U.S.C. § 604,[18] and seeking forfeiture of Daewoo's claims pursuant to 28 U.S.C. § 2514. *Daewoo Eng'g & Const. Co. v. United States,* 73 Fed.Cl. 547, 597 (2006). The Court of Federal Claims held that Daewoo had committed fraud.

The court awarded the government $10,000 for Daewoo's False Claims Act violation and $50,629,855.88 for Daewoo's Contract Disputes Act violation. *Id.* at 597. It also held that Daewoo's claims were forfeited under 28 U.S.C. § 2514. *Id.* We affirm.

BACKGROUND

In 1998, pursuant to a 1994 treaty between the United States and the Republic of Palau, the United States Army Corps of Engineers ("government") solicited bids for the building of a fifty-three-mile road around the island of Babeldaob in the Republic of Palau. The government estimated that the price of constructing the road would be between $100 million and $250 million. Daewoo initially proposed to build the road for $73 million. Daewoo was the lowest bidder by far, with the next lowest bidder proposing $100 million. After the government questioned this price, Daewoo revised its proposal and submitted a final bid of $88.6 million. On March 30, 1999, the government awarded Daewoo the contract for constructing

---

18. Currently cited as 41 U.S.C. §§ 7101–7019.

the road. The contract required completion of the road within 1080 days, a period which began in October 2000.

Construction of the road was subsequently delayed. Daewoo attributed these delays to the humid and rainy weather and moist soils in Palau, and urged the government to reduce the amount of soil compaction required by the contract. After discussing these delays with Daewoo, the government reduced the amount of soil compaction the contract had specified for parts of the road.

On March 29, 2002, Daewoo submitted to the Government a request for equitable adjustment. In this certified claim, Daewoo sought adjustment of the contract price and the time to perform the contract, alleging that the contract used defective specifications, that the government breached its duties to cooperate and to disclose superior knowledge, and that the contract was impossible to perform within the originally specified time period. Daewoo requested $13,348,793.07 in "additional costs as of December 31, 2001" and, in the government's view, also requested $50,629,855.88 in "costs January 1, 2002 [and] [f]orward," a total of $63,978,648.95 ("$64 million"). Daewoo rejected the government's offer of a bilateral time adjustment, and the contracting officer denied Daewoo's claim in August 2002.

Daewoo filed a complaint with the Court of Federal Claims in December 2002, seeking, "with respect to damages suffered through December 31, 2001," an increase in the "compensable and non-compensable contract performance time" of 8 noncompensable and 122 compensable days and "monetary relief in the amount of $13,348,793.07," and "with respect to damages suffered from January 1, 2002, through contract completion," an increase in the "compensable contract performance time" of 776 days and "monetary relief in the amount of $50,629,855.88." Compl. 19-21. The government counterclaimed for damages, seeking $64 million under the Contract Disputes Act and $10,000 under the False Claims Act. The government also entered a special plea in fraud and sought forfeiture of Daewoo's claims under 28 U.S.C. § 2514.

The Court of Federal Claims awarded the government $10,000 under the False Claims Act and $50,629,855.88 ("$50.6 million") under the Contract Disputes Act, and forfeited Daewoo's claims under § 2514. *Daewoo Eng'g,* 73 Fed.Cl. at 597. The Court of Federal Claims concluded that the government "showed by clear and convincing evidence that the contractor knowingly presented a false claim with the intention of being paid for it," thus supporting the $50.6 million penalty under the Contract Disputes Act, the $10,000 award under the False Claims Act, and forfeiture of Daewoo's claims. *Id.* at 584. Alternatively, the Court of Federal Claims analyzed and rejected on the merits Daewoo's claims that the road construction contract had contained a misleading weather-delay clause and defective road design specifications, that the government breached its duty to disclose its superior knowledge of its weather-delay calculation methods, and that the contract was thus impossible to perform. *See id.* at 561-68.

Daewoo timely appealed. We have jurisdiction under 28 U.S.C. § 1295(a)(3).

DISCUSSION

[1] We review legal conclusions of the Court of Federal Claims de novo, and we review its factual findings under a clearly erroneous standard. *See UMC Electronics Co. v. United States,* 249 F.3d 1337, 1339 (Fed.Cir.2001).

[2] Under the antifraud provision of the Contract Disputes Act, 41 U.S.C. § 604,[19] "[i]f a contractor is unable to support any part of his claim and it is determined that such inability is attributable to misrepresentation of fact or fraud on the part of the contractor, he shall be liable to the Government for an amount equal to such unsupported part of the claim." A "misrepresentation of fact" is "a false statement of substantive fact, or any conduct which leads to a belief of a substantive fact material to proper understanding of the matter in hand, made with intent to deceive or mislead." 41 U.S.C. § 601(9).[20] The government must establish this falsity and intent by a preponderance of the evidence. *Commercial Contractors, Inc. v. United States,* 154 F.3d 1357, 1362 (Fed. Cir. 1998).

The Court of Federal Claims held that Daewoo "filed at least $50 million of the [$64 million certified] claim in bad faith" and consequently assessed a $50.6 million penalty against Daewoo under the Contract Disputes Act. *Daewoo Eng'g,* 73 Fed. Cl. at 597. The $50.6 million portion of the claim found to be fraudulent represented the projected costs of completion of the contract.

***

B.

[7] We next address Daewoo's theory that the Court of Federal Claims erred in finding that the $50.6 million portion of the certified claim, the amount of claimed future costs, was fraudulent and in assessing a penalty in that amount. [Footnote 5 omitted]

***

The Court of Federal Claims did not find that Daewoo's theories of the government's breach of the contract—based on alleged defective specifications, failure to disclose superior knowledge, and impossibility—were [themselves] fraudulent (though it ultimately found these theories to be without merit). Rather, the Court of Federal Claims found that Daewoo's $50.6 million projected cost calculation was fraudulent. That calculation assumed that the government was responsible for each day of additional performance beyond the original 1080-day contract period, without even considering whether there was any contractor-caused delay or delay for which the government was not responsible. The calculation then simply assumed that Daewoo's current daily expenditures represented costs for which

---

19. Currently 41 U.S.C. § 7103.
20. Currently *id.* § 7101(9).

the government was responsible.[FN6] Daewoo apparently used no outside experts to make its certified claim calculation, and at trial made no real effort to justify the accuracy of the claim for future costs or even to explain how it was prepared. *See Daewoo Eng'g,* 73 Fed. Cl. at 573, 582. Indeed, Daewoo's damages experts at trial treated the certified claim computation as essentially worthless, did not utilize it, and did not even bother to understand it. *See id.* at 573. The Court of Federal Claims pointed out that Daewoo's claim preparation witnesses inconsistently referred to and interchanged actual, future, estimated, calculated and planned costs. *See id.* at 572, 574–76. The court found that J.W. Kim, who certified the claim, gave false testimony. *Id.* at 569–70, 584 n.63. The court also found that the testimony of Daewoo's witness Mr. Richardson regarding the calculation of Daewoo's certified claim "left no doubt that [Daewoo's] case was unsupportable and was pursued by Daewoo with fraudulent intent." *Id.* at 573 n.45.

The Court of Federal Claims ultimately found that the certified claim was simply a "negotiating ploy," and that Daewoo "did not honestly believe that the Government owed it the various amounts stated when it certified the claim." *Id.* at 588, 590. The court concluded,

> [T]he extra $50 million claim was a means to get the Government's attention, and to show the Government what would happen if it did not approve the new compaction method that plaintiff wanted. Daewoo did not file that part of the claim in good faith; it was not an amount to which plaintiff honestly believed it was entitled. Whether Daewoo wanted the money or wanted the Government's attention, $64 million was not an amount the Government owed plaintiff at the time of certification, and plaintiff knew it.

Id. at 596.[FN7] On appeal Daewoo makes virtually no effort to show that the Court of Federal Claims' findings of fraud are clearly erroneous.

FN6. Daewoo stated that it calculated the $50.6 million in projected costs by using its own weather parameters, rather than those supplied by the government during the bidding period, to re-calculate the number of days needed to complete the contract as 2008 rather than 1080 days. Certified Claim at 32, 54. Daewoo next calculated that 153 of the additional 928 days had occurred before January 1, 2002, and that the remaining 775 were projected to occur after December 31, 2001. *Id.* at 66. Daewoo stated that it averaged "the last three months of costs, October, November and December 2001" and then applied that monthly average to the projected additional 25.5 months (775 days) "as an estimate for costs extending into the future." *Id.*

FN7. The Court of Federal Claims stated that "Daewoo's case against the United States is wholly without merit; its claims are fraudulent," *Daewoo Eng'g,* 73 Fed. Cl. at 550; "[t]he certified claim itself was false or fraudulent and plaintiff knew that it was false or fraudulent," *id.* at 585; "[Daewoo] did not honestly believe that the Government owed it the various amounts stated when it certified the claim," *id.* at 590; "[Daewoo's] claim is fraudulent," *id.* at 595.

Daewoo argues, however, that the findings of the Court of Federal Claims somehow must be set aside, because the court found that the claim was fraudulent in the amount only of $50.6 million rather than $64 million. Daewoo argues that this is so because the government had attempted to prove the fraudulence of both the past and future damages "based on the same theory." Pl.-Appellant's Reply Br. at 10.

Daewoo's premise is incorrect. The Court of Federal Claims found Daewoo's entire $64 million calculation likely was fraudulent,[FN8] but concluded that a penalty of only $50.6 million should be assessed because the remaining $13 million incurred cost claims could have been ultimately supported by alternative methodologies which, while incorrect, would not necessarily have been fraudulent. *Daewoo Eng'g*, 73 Fed.Cl. at 595–96. The court found that the "'part of [the] claim' that is fraudulent without question is $50,629,855.88." *Id.* at 595 (alteration in original). The court's decision to award only $50.6 million as a penalty does not undermine its factual findings.

[8] Finally, Daewoo appears to argue that a claim can be fraudulent only if it rests upon false facts rather than on a baseless calculation. We disagree. Here Daewoo certified, as required by 41 U.S.C. § 605(c)(1),[21] that "the claim is made in good faith; that the supporting data are accurate and complete to the best of my knowledge and belief; that the amount requested accurately reflects the contract adjustment for which the Contractor believes the Government is liable." Certified Claim at 7. By certifying a claim for damages in the amount of $64 million, Daewoo represented that the claim was made "in good faith." It is well established that a baseless certified claim is a fraudulent claim. For instance, the First Circuit has held that if a party knows that its claim that it is entitled to funds under a letter of credit "has no plausible or colorable basis," then the party's "effort to obtain the money is fraudulent." *Itek Corp. v. First Nat'l Bank of Boston*, 730 F.2d 19, 25 (1st Cir.1984); *see also Ward Petroleum Corp. v. Fed. Deposit Ins. Corp.*, 903 F.2d 1297, 1301 (10th Cir.1990).

Congress specifically enacted the fraud provision of the Contract Disputes Act "out of concern that the submission of baseless claims contribute[s] to the so-called horsetrading theory where an amount beyond that which can be legitimately claimed is submitted merely as a negotiating tactic." S.Rep. No. 95-1118, at 20 (1978), *as reprinted in* 1978 U.S.C.C.A.N. 5235, 5254. We have noted that the "purpose of the certification requirement is to trigger[ ] a contractor's potential liability for a fraudulent claim under section 604 of the [Contract Disputes] Act." *Fischbach*

FN8. The Court of Federal Claims held that the government proved that Daewoo "did not believe that the Government owed it $64 million as a matter of right" and that "Daewoo's entire $64 million claim was an attempt to defraud the United States." *Daewoo Eng'g*, 73 Fed.Cl. at 585. The court also stated that "[w]e suspect that Daewoo's entire claim is fraudulent." *Id.* at 595–96.

---

21. Currently *id.* § 7103(b)(1)(A).

& Moore Int'l Corp. v. Christopher, 987 F.2d 759, 763 (Fed. Cir. 1993) (internal quotation marks omitted) (first alteration in original).

[9][10] Daewoo also contends that the $50.6 million penalty was unconstitutional under the Eighth and Fifth Amendments. This assertion is meritless. Under the Eighth Amendment, a penalty is unconstitutional only if it is disproportionate to the possible harm resulting from the conduct. *See United States v. Bajakajian,* 524 U.S. 321, 334, 118 S. Ct. 2028, 141 L.Ed.2d 314 (1998) ("[A] punitive forfeiture violates the Excessive Fines Clause if it is grossly disproportional to the gravity of a defendant's offense."). Here the potential harm was Daewoo's securing a $50.6 million payment from the government; under these circumstances a $50.6 million penalty is not disproportionate. The fact that the fraud may have been unlikely to succeed does not suggest that a penalty is inappropriate. The same standard and result would follow under the Fifth Amendment, if the penalty here were to be treated as equivalent to punitive damages (an issue we do not decide). *See BMW of N. Am., Inc. v. Gore,* 517 U.S. 559, 581, 116 S. Ct. 1589, 134 L.Ed.2d 809 (1996) (noting that in a due process challenge to a punitive damages award, "the proper inquiry is whether there is a reasonable relationship between the punitive damages award and *the harm likely to result* from the defendant's conduct as well as the harm that actually has occurred" (internal quotation marks omitted)).

II

[11] Daewoo also argues that the $10,000 penalty under the False Claims Act was not supported.

Under the False Claims Act, "[a]ny person who . . . knowingly presents" to the government "a false or fraudulent claim for payment or approval" "is liable to the United States Government for a civil penalty of not less than $5,000 and not more than $10,000, plus 3 times the amount of damages which the Government sustains." 31 U.S.C. § 3729(a). "Knowingly" is defined as (1) "actual knowledge," (2) acting "in deliberate ignorance of the truth or falsity" of information, or (3) acting "in reckless disregard of the truth or falsity" of information; "no proof of specific intent to defraud is required." *Id.* § 3729(b). The government must establish a violation of the False Claims Act by a preponderance of the evidence. *Id.* § 3731(c); *Commercial Contractors,* 154 F.3d at 1362.

[12] To support its conclusion that Daewoo violated the False Claims Act, the Court of Federal Claims cited the findings underlying Daewoo's liability under the Contract Disputes Act. *See Daewoo Eng'g,* 73 Fed. Cl. at 585.[FN9] A certified claim may be a source of liability under both the Contract Disputes Act and the False

---

FN9. Daewoo asserts that the Court of Federal Claims improperly applied a negligence standard when holding that Daewoo violated the False Claims Act, but in fact the court recited the correct standard and stated that "[t]he Government proved by any standard that Daewoo's $64 million claim was fraudulent." *Daewoo Eng'g,* 73 Fed. Cl. at 585.

Claims Act. *See UMC Electronics,* 249 F.3d at 1339–40; *Commercial Contractors,* 154 F.3d at 1375. The Court of Federal Claims did not err in concluding that Daewoo violated the False Claims Act. Because the court did not find that the government incurred damages from Daewoo's false claim, the court properly assessed only the statutory penalty.

III

Finally we turn to the contractor's affirmative claims listed in its complaint.

Daewoo's complaint alleged that the government owed it money damages and an increase in the contract's performance time, due to defective specifications in the contract's weather and embankment clauses, breach of the government's duty to disclose its superior knowledge, and the impossibility of performing the contract. *See* Compl. ¶ ¶ 34–76.

[13] Under 28 U.S.C. § 2514, "[a] claim against the United States shall be forfeited to the United States by any person who corruptly practices or attempts to practice any fraud against the United States in the proof, statement, establishment, or allowance thereof." Section 2514 further states that "[i]n such cases the United States Court of Federal Claims shall specifically find such fraud or attempt and render judgment of forfeiture." To prevail under § 2514, the government must "establish by clear and convincing evidence that the contractor knew that its submitted claims were false, and that it intended to defraud the government by submitting those claims." *Commercial Contractors,* 154 F.3d at 1362.

[14] Unlike the antifraud provision of the Contract Disputes Act, 41 U.S.C. § 604,[22] under which a contractor may incur liability only for the unsupported part of a claim, forfeiture under 28 U.S.C. § 2514 requires only part of the claim to be fraudulent. For instance, in *Young-Montenay, Inc. v. United States,* we held that because a contractor had submitted a claim to the government for $153,000 when the contractor knew the government was liable only for $104,000, such a knowingly false claim forfeited the contractor's later damages claim against the government under the contract. 15 F.3d 1040, 1042–43 (Fed. Cir. 1994).

The Court of Federal Claims held that the government "showed by clear and convincing evidence that [Daewoo] knowingly presented a false claim with the intention of being paid for it" and thus that Daewoo's claims against the government were forfeited under § 2514. *Daewoo Eng'g,* 73 Fed. Cl. at 584. Daewoo itself concedes that if the $50.6 million Contract Disputes Act penalty is correct, then the forfeiture of its $13 million is also correct. Since we have upheld the $50.6 million award, we also uphold the forfeiture under § 2514. [Footnote 10 Omitted]

* * *

AFFIRMED.

---

22. Currently *id.* § 7103.

There are numerous practices that are improper in dealing with federal contracts. For example, gratuities are very common in private contracting and not only are permissible but are considered good business in that they show customers, especially long-time customers, that the contractor appreciates their business. Gratuities are prohibited in public contracting. *See* FAR subpart 3.2.

The *Daewoo* case is a comprehensive analysis of some of the major antifraud statutes that the federal government uses. It is by no means, however, a full listing of such statutes, which seem to grow longer with each congressional session. In addition to the statutes reviewed in the case, the False Statements Act, 18 U.S.C. § 1001, has great applicability because contractors will often make statements in the course of a government contract, such as stating they are a small business, that they have already paid their subcontractors, or that the items delivered conform to the contract.

23.03 SOVEREIGN IMMUNITY

Governments possess sovereign immunity and cannot be sued unless the government has waived its sovereign immunity. Typical waivers of sovereign immunity occur in such statutes as the Federal Tort Claims Act[23] and the Contract Disputes Act (CDA).[24]

Dismissal for sovereign immunity can deal with entire substantive claims or it may be for discrete portions of the claim, such as interest, attorneys fees, and so on.[25] The following case applies the principle to a state government.

---

23. 28 U.S.C. § 1346.
24. 41 U.S.C. §§ 7101–7109.
25. *See* England v. Contel Advanced Sys., Inc., 384 F.3d 1372, 1378–79 (2004) (holding that a contractor's claim for interest on contract payments was barred by the doctrine of sovereign immunity); Strand Hunt Constr. v. West, No. 96-1323, 1997 U.S. App. LEXIS 5424 (Fed. Cir. Mar. 21, 1997) (holding that the Court of Appeals did not have subject matter jurisdiction because the contract at issue was not subject to the CDA); Levernier Constr., Inc. v. U.S., 947 F.2d 497, 500–03 (1991) (holding that the prosecution of equitable adjustment claim at issue was not a "civil action" within meaning of the Equal Access to Justice Act (EAJA), and thus the EAJA's waiver of sovereign immunity did not apply).

United States Court of Appeals, Federal Circuit.

STATE CONTRACTING & ENGINEERING CORPORATION and State Paving Corporation, Plaintiffs-Appellants,

v.

State of FLORIDA, Florida Department of Transportation, Recchi America, Inc., The Murphy Construction Company, The Hardaway Company, Hubbard Construction Company, Balfour Beatty Construction, Inc., Community Asphalt Corporation, and Joelson Concrete Pipe Company, Inc., Defendants-Appellees.

No. 00-1434.

258 F.3d 1329

July 20, 2001.

Rehearing and Rehearing En Banc Denied Sept. 6, 2001.

Before RADER, GAJARSA, and DYK, Circuit Judges.

DYK, Circuit Judge.

State Contracting & Engineering Corporation ("State Contracting") and State Paving Corporation ("State Paving") (collectively "plaintiffs") appeal the decision of the United States District Court for the Southern District of Florida granting summary judgment in favor of the defendants. *State Contracting & Eng'g Corp. v. Florida*, No. 97-7014-CIV-DIMITROULEAS (S.D. Fla. Mar. 2, 2000) ("*Final Order*"). We affirm the district court's grant of summary judgment to the State of Florida as to the patent infringement and Lanham Act claims (counts I, II, IV) on grounds of sovereign immunity. We also affirm the district court's grant of summary judgment to the State of Florida as to the takings claim (count V) and the breach of contract claim (count VI). However, we hold that the district court erred in granting summary judgment to the private contractors on the patent infringement claims (counts III and VII), and therefore we vacate and remand as to these claims. Accordingly, we affirm in part, vacate in part, and remand.

BACKGROUND

In 1989, State Paving Corporation, a highway construction company, successfully bid on a State of Florida Department of Transportation ("FDOT" or "State of Florida") project for construction of sound barrier walls. The original agreement was reduced to writing and expressly incorporated the FDOT Standard Specifications for Road and Bridge Construction ("Standard Specifications"). During the course of the construction, State Paving submitted a Value Engineering Change Proposal ("VECP") proposing to use a new design for sound walls that would reduce costs. The new sound wall design described in the VECP allegedly included the use of a post (column) positioned in a cement-filled pile using a new method devised by State Paving which was particularly suitable for use in sandy soil. FDOT accepted the VECP on July 5, 1990, agreeing to change the specifications of the contract to include the use of the sound wall design described in the VECP. The "Supplemental Agreement" signed by the parties stated that the contract adjustment and sum agreed to "constitutes a full and complete settlement" and that State Paving "accepts the terms of this Supplemental Agreement as full compensation for all costs of equipment, manpower, materials, overhead, profit and delay damages and for all their costs, whether direct or indirect, or whether incurred now or in the future, related to the issues set forth in this Agreement." Pursuant to the contract and "Supplemental Agreement," the State of Florida paid State Paving fifty percent of the cost savings realized by the VECP.

On June 29, 1990, State Paving filed a patent application with the United States Patent and Trademark Office for a structure and method using the technology described in the VECP. The application matured into two U.S. patents: (1) Patent No. 5,234,288 (the "'288 patent"), issued on August 10, 1993, directed to an improved method of forming a post by inserting the post into a cement slurry pile which is particularly suitable for use in building structures in sandy soil; and (2) Patent No. 5,429,455 (the "'455 patent"), issued on July 4, 1995, directed to the structure of the post and cement pile.[FN1]

FDOT began using data from the VECP in subsequent requests for bids. State Paving learned about one of these instances in September 1992 and sent a letter to potential bidders, advising them of the pending patent application and seeking a patent royalty. State Paving also sought additional payments under the contract for its use of the VECP data in other contracts to which State Paving was not a party.

The issues were not resolved by negotiation, and in August 1997 State Paving and State Contracting (collectively "State Contracting" or "plaintiffs") brought the present lawsuit against the State of Florida and seven private contractors in the United States District Court for the Southern District of Florida.

The plaintiffs filed a seven-count amended complaint on June 5, 1998, asserting the following claims: (1) direct patent infringement by the State of Florida of the '288 patent directed to the method of forming the improved post and cement pile (count I); (2) direct patent infringement by the State of Florida of the '455 patent directed to the structure of the improved post and cement pile (count II); (3) direct patent infringement by private highway construction contractors which worked for the State of Florida for infringement of both patents (count III); (4) violations of the Lanham Act by the State of Florida for its representation to potential bidders of construction projects that the specified method for sandy soil construction was "unpatented" (count IV); (5) unconstitutional taking by the State of Florida of plaintiffs' proprietary and patent rights in designs and specifications for the construction of sound barrier walls (count V); (6) breach of contract by the State of Florida for failure to compensate plaintiffs under the contract for use of plaintiff's

---

FN1. State Paving assigned its rights under the patents to State Contracting.

proprietary technology on sound barrier construction projects after the original contract with plaintiffs (count VI); and (7) contributory patent infringement by Joelson Concrete Pipe Company based on its manufacture, use and sale of posts specially made as a component of the patented apparatus and method (count VII).

On June 22, 1998, the defendants answered the amended complaint as to all counts except for the Lanham Act claims, which the State of Florida moved to dismiss on grounds of sovereign immunity. In the answer, the defendants counterclaimed for a declaratory judgment of non-infringement and invalidity of the '288 and '455 patents. The district court denied the State of Florida's motion to dismiss the Lanham Act count. That decision was appealed to this court. We remanded the case to the district court to "consider all issues that may be before the court in the first instance" in light of the Supreme Court's decisions in *Florida Prepaid Postsecondary Education Expense Board v. College Savings Bank*, 527 U.S. 627, 119 S. Ct. 2199, 144 L.Ed.2d 575 (1999), and *College Savings Bank v. Florida Prepaid Postsecondary Education Expense Board*, 527 U.S. 666, 119 S. Ct. 2219, 144 L.Ed.2d 605 (1999).[* * * **[Footnote Omitted]** *State Contracting & Eng'g Corp. v. Florida*, No. 99-1236, 1999 WL 717798 (Fed. Cir. Sept. 2, 1999) (nonprecedential order).

On remand, the parties filed cross motions for summary judgment. In the final order of March 2, 2000, the district court dismissed counts I, II, and IV (which stated claims against the State of Florida for patent infringement and violation of the Lanham Act) on grounds of sovereign immunity. The court also granted summary judgment to the State of Florida on count V-the takings claims. The court granted summary judgment on count VI (seeking recovery against the State of Florida under the contract) against State Contracting on the ground that the contract had not been breached. Finally, the court granted summary judgment on counts III and VII (patent infringement) to the private contractors on the ground that the contract with the State created a license to practice the patent. The court failed to expressly address the defendants' counterclaims for a declaratory judgment of non-infringement and invalidity of the '288 and '455 patents in the March 2, 2000, final order. State Contracting appealed to this court.

DISCUSSION

***

III. *Sovereign Immunity*
A. *Patent Infringement and Lanham Act Claims (Counts I, II, and IV)*

***

[6] Under the Court's decisions in *College Savings Bank* and *Florida Prepaid*, [*Florida Prepaid Postsecondary Education Expense Board v. College Savings Bank*, 527 U.S. 627, 119 S. Ct. 2199, 144 L.Ed.2d 575 (1999), and *College Savings Bank v. Florida Prepaid Postsecondary Education Expense Board*, 527 U.S. 666, 119 S. Ct. 2219, 144 L.Ed.2d 605 (1999)] Florida enjoys sovereign immunity with respect to the patent infringement and Lanham Act claims unless Florida has waived sovereign immunity. The district court rejected State Contracting's assertion that Florida has

waived its immunity either generally or specifically by participating in the litigation. On this appeal, plaintiffs contest the district court's waiver decision.

[7][8] We are not persuaded that Florida has generally waived its immunity to suit. The Florida Supreme Court's 1941 decision in *State Road Department of Florida v. Tharp*, 146 Fla. 745, 1 So.2d 868 (1941), held merely that a bill of complaint for an injunction against the State of Florida in state court on a theory of trespass could be maintained because the state had waived immunity by state statute and by the Florida Constitution. The case may also represent a holding that sovereign immunity is waived as to takings claims in state court. The question, however, remains whether Florida has waived sovereign immunity in this particular case as to the patent and Lanham Act claims in the federal district court. It is well-established that an express waiver of sovereign immunity must be unequivocal. *Coll. Sav. Bank*, 527 U.S. at 680, 119 S. Ct. 2219; *Pennhurst State Sch. & Hosp. v. Halderman*, 465 U.S. 89, 99, 104 S. Ct. 900, 79 L.Ed.2d 67 (1984); *Great N. Life Ins. Co. v. Read*, 322 U.S. 47, 54, 64 S. Ct. 873, 88 L.Ed. 1121 (1944). After *College Savings Bank*, it is clear that any waiver of sovereign immunity by a state must be express and voluntary, and cannot be implied or constructive. 527 U.S. at 682, 119 S. Ct. 2219 (expressly overruling *Parden*). The Court also emphasized that the test for finding an express waiver is a stringent one. *Coll. Sav. Bank*, 527 U.S. at 682, 119 S. Ct. 2219. Under this standard we cannot find a general waiver of immunity with respect to Lanham Act and patent claims.

[9] State Contracting also claims that Florida has waived its sovereign immunity by defending this litigation, both on its own behalf and as the representative of the alleged private infringers. It is quite clear that those activities do not amount to a waiver. In *Florida Department of State v. Treasure Salvors, Inc.*, 458 U.S. 670, 683 n.18, 102 S. Ct. 3304, 73 L.Ed.2d 1057 (1982), for example, the Supreme Court held that "[t]he fact that the State appeared and offered defenses on the merits does not foreclose consideration of the Eleventh Amendment issue." *See also Allinder v. Ohio*, 808 F.2d 1180, 1184 (6th Cir. 1987) (holding that the State of Ohio did not waive immunity by generally defending itself when it raised defenses in addition to sovereign immunity).

[10][11] In its answer to the amended complaint, the State of Florida counterclaimed for a declaratory judgment of non-infringement and invalidity of the '288 and '455 patents. State Contracting next asserts that Florida has waived immunity as to the patent claims by filing the counterclaim and by litigating the counterclaim. The question whether the filing of a counterclaim constitutes a waiver of immunity as to the patent claims is substantial, for some courts have suggested that the filing of a counterclaim waives immunity, *see, e.g., Paul N. Howard Co. v. Puerto Rico Aqueduct Sewer Authority*, 744 F.2d 880, 886 (1st Cir. 1984), *Newfield House, Inc. v. Massachusetts Department of Public Welfare*, 651 F.2d 32, 36 n.3 (1st Cir. 1981), and others have made clear that the filing of a patent counterclaim of invalidity is quite a separate matter from asserting affirmative defenses of invalidity, *Cardinal Chem. Co. v. Morton Int'l, Inc.*, 508 U.S. 83, 94, 113 S. Ct. 1967, 124 L.Ed.2d 1

(1993) (discussing differences between filing an answer asserting invalidity and filing a counterclaim for declaratory judgment of invalidity). In *College Savings Bank*, 131 F.3d 353, 366 (3d Cir. 1997), *aff'd*, 527 U.S. 666, 119 S. Ct. 2219, 144 L.Ed.2d 605 (1999), the Third Circuit held that Florida's filing of a Lanham Act counterclaim did not waive its defense of sovereign immunity because it was not until the Supreme Court decision in *Seminole Tribe of Florida v. Florida*, 517 U.S. 44, 116 S. Ct. 1114, 134 L.Ed.2d 252 (1996), that "the successful assertion of an immunity defense became a reasonable possibility." In *Seminole Tribe*, the Supreme Court first held that Congress' authority to abrogate a state's Eleventh Amendment immunity from suit in federal court was confined to the enforcement section of the Fourteenth Amendment. We generally agree with the Third Circuit's approach, with two modifications. We think that the test should be one of "reasonable expectation" rather than "reasonable possibility," thus allowing some greater latitude for the filing of protective counterclaims by the states without waiving immunity, and we conclude that the decision in *Seminole Tribe* did not create a reasonable expectation that the state would prevail on its sovereign immunity claim with respect to the patent infringement counts.

In this case, the patent counterclaim was filed on June 22, 1998. At the time the counterclaim was filed Congress had abrogated the state's patent infringement immunity in the 1994 Patent Remedy Act, and we sustained the abrogation of immunity for patent infringement claims on June 30, 1998, in our *College Savings Bank* decision, 148 F.3d 1343 (Fed.Cir.1998), shortly after the counterclaim was filed. The State of Florida could not have reasonably expected to prevail on its sovereign immunity defense until *Florida Prepaid* was decided by the Supreme Court. Therefore, it was entirely reasonable for the State to file a counterclaim of patent invalidity.[FN3] In short, we agree that the filing of a counterclaim during a period when the State was reasonably unsure about the availability of an immunity defense was not a waiver. The parties agree that Florida took no further action on the counterclaims after the Supreme Court's decision in *Florida Prepaid*. We hold that Florida's mere failure to withdraw the counterclaims after the Supreme Court decision cannot be a waiver of sovereign immunity as to counts I, II, and IV.

B. *Takings Claim (Count V)*

[12] In its complaint, plaintiffs alleged an unconstitutional taking by the State of Florida of their proprietary and patent rights in designs and specifications for the construction of sound barrier walls. The district court held that the takings claim was barred by sovereign immunity because "[a]llowing Plaintiffs' Count V to

---

FN3. The district court noted that "the state of the law at the time Defendants filed their answer, counterclaim and motion to dismiss, was clear that a state *could be sued* for patent infringement under the Patent and Plant Protection Remedy Clarification Act as enacted by Congress." *Final Order*, slip op. at 6-7 (emphasis in original).

proceed would vitiate the Eleventh Amendment analysis in the Supreme Court's *College Savings Bank* opinions by turning every patent infringement case against a state into a Section 1983 takings case for patent profits." *Id.,* slip op. at 9. We affirm the holding of sovereign immunity, but on a different ground. In *Quern v. Jordan,* 440 U.S. 332, 345, 99 S. Ct. 1139, 59 L.Ed.2d 358 (1979), the Supreme Court recognized that 42 U.S.C. § 1983 did not abrogate the states' sovereign immunity for suits in federal court. The Court noted that "[Section] 1983 does not explicitly and by clear language indicate on its face an intent to sweep away the immunity of the States; nor does it have a history which focuses directly on the question of state liability and which shows that Congress considered and firmly decided to abrogate the Eleventh Amendment immunity of the States." *Id.* In light of *Quern,* we affirm the district court's grant of summary judgment in favor of the State of Florida on the takings claim.

C. *Breach of Contract against the State of Florida (Count VI)*

The district court assumed that there was no sovereign immunity as to claims against the State of Florida for breach of contract, and the parties apparently agree, as do we. But the district court also correctly held that the contract claims against Florida were without merit. *Final Order,* slip op. at 9-12.

***

CONCLUSION

Based on the above, we affirm in part, vacate in part, and remand. We hold that the district court did not err in granting summary judgment to the State of Florida on counts I, II, IV, V, and VI, but that the district court erred in granting summary judgment to the private contractors on counts III and VII.

AFFIRMED-IN-PART, VACATED-IN-PART, and REMANDED.

In *State Contracting and Engineering Corp.,* the issue of sovereign immunity focused on the nature of the lawsuit. Another aspect of sovereign immunity deals with who can sue the sovereign. This is especially problematic for the government, because if subcontractors are entitled to sue, then the number of potential litigants has expanded exponentially. For that reason, most waivers of sovereign immunity in the contract area are limited solely to the prime contractor except in the most unique circumstances. In Winter v. FloorPro, Inc., 570 F.3d 1367 (Fed. Cir. 2009), for example, the Federal Circuit rejected a claim by a subcontractor who sought to avoid sovereign immunity by claiming that it was entitled to sue as a third-party beneficiary under the Contract Disputes Act, which grants immunity waivers for contractors in contract disputes with the government.

23.04 SOVEREIGN ACTS

The problem with sovereign acts permeates public contracting. The definition of a protected "sovereign act" is discussed at length in the following case, and generally encompasses a general act of the government that is not aimed specifically and exclusively at one contractor. The clearest example of a sovereign act is when a general act is ordered by a separate federal agency—distinct from the contracting agency. The closer the act gets to the contracting agency, the more likely it is to be a contractual act for which the agency *may* be liable.

The government never waives its right, indeed its duty, to act as a sovereign. So a company may have a contract to construct a new prison with the Federal Bureau of Prisons or the State Department of Prisons, but the state or federal Labor Department may come out with new rules on scaffolding or the Environmental Protective Agency may ban a certain type of paint that the contract allows and the contractor planned to use. All of these may have the impact of increasing or decreasing the costs and time planned for the contract, but neither party has the right under a fixed-priced contract to demand relief.

For a sovereign acts case arising from the September 11, 2001, tragedy, consider the following.

United States Court of Appeals, Federal Circuit.

CONNER BROS. CONSTRUCTION COMPANY, INC., Appellant,

v.

Pete GEREN, Secretary of the Army, Appellee.

No. 2008-1188.

550 F.3d 1368

Dec. 31, 2008.

Before BRYSON, GAJARSA, and DYK, Circuit Judges.

BRYSON, Circuit Judge.

Conner Bros. Construction Company, Inc., a construction contractor doing work for the Army Corps of Engineers, sought delay damages after it was denied access to its construction site on a military base for 41 days following the terrorist attacks of September 11, 2001. The Armed Services Board of Contract Appeals denied Conner's claim on the ground that the sovereign acts doctrine shielded the Army from liability.

* * *

I

On April 21, 2000, Conner contracted with the Corps of Engineers to construct an Army Ranger regimental headquarters facility within the 75th Ranger regimental compound at Fort Benning, Georgia. The Ranger compound is a segregated area within Fort Benning that is under the operational control of the Ranger regimental commander. The contract, which was for the construction of four buildings at two sites within the compound, was administered by a Corps of Engineers project manager.

In response to the terrorist attacks against the United States on September 11, 2001, Fort Benning was placed at force protection condition Delta and shut down to everyone except essential personnel. General (then Colonel) Joseph Votel, the commander of the 75th Ranger regiment, also restricted access to the Ranger compound to mission-essential personnel and ordered his staff to direct Conner to stop work and vacate the compound immediately. Conner's workforce left the compound by 2:00 p.m. on September 11, 2001, at which point its contract work was roughly 70–75% complete. On September 17, 2001, Fort Benning lowered its force protection condition, allowing contractors and other personnel to return to the base. However, the Ranger compound continued to operate under condition Delta and remained subject to General Votel's order restricting access to mission-essential personnel, and Conner continued to be excluded from its worksites within the compound.

In the immediate aftermath of the terrorist attacks, the Rangers prepared for deployment to Afghanistan. They executed a "protracted low-level deployment" whereby they departed in small groups so that their movements would not attract notice. During that period, the Rangers occupied one of the partially constructed buildings on Conner's worksite. General Votel testified that he decided to shut down Conner's construction activities in order to maintain operational security by preventing information leaks while the Rangers prepared to deploy. He explained that because Conner's work was the "biggest thing happening on the installation," Conner's activities put its employees and subcontractors in a unique position to observe sensitive deployment activities.

Conner was excluded from the compound until September 27, 2001, when it was allowed to return to one of its worksites. It was permitted access to its other site on October 15, 2001, and it resumed work there on October 21, 2001. Conner subsequently sought additional time to complete the project and $137,744 in delay damages attributable to 35 of the 41 days during which it was shut down—that is, for the period between September 17, 2001, when other contractors were permitted back on the compound, and October 21, 2001, when Conner returned to work. The contracting officer granted Conner the requested additional time to complete the project but denied the monetary claim. Conner appealed that decision to the Board.

After conducting a three-day hearing, the Board denied Conner's appeal. As an affirmative defense, the Corps of Engineers asserted that the exclusion of Conner from the construction site constituted a sovereign act that precluded Conner from recovering damages for the delay. Conner argued that it was the sole target of the shutdown order, as it was the only contractor ordered to leave the compound. For that reason, Conner argued, the shutdown order was not a "public and general" act, and the government therefore could not invoke the "sovereign acts doctrine" as a defense to liability for breach of contract. The Board, however, found that the exclusion order was a sovereign act because it stemmed from the government's war-making powers, was merely incidental to the accomplishment of a broader governmental objective relating to national security, and was not directed principally at Conner's contract rights. The Board also rejected Conner's arguments that it was entitled to relief under the contract's "Changes" and "Suspension of Work" clauses. Conner now appeals to this court.

II

[1][2] The sovereign acts doctrine provides that "the United States when sued as a contractor cannot be held liable for an obstruction to the performance of the particular contract resulting from its public and general acts as a sovereign." *Horowitz v. United States*, 267 U.S. 458, 461, 45 S. Ct. 344, 69 L.Ed. 736 (1925). The doctrine is an affirmative defense that is an inherent part of every government contract. *Hughes Commc'ns Galaxy, Inc. v. United States*, 998 F.2d 953, 958 (Fed. Cir. 1993). It is based on the government's dual roles as contractor and sovereign, and it is designed to balance "the Government's need for freedom to legislate with its obligation to honor its contracts." *United States v. Winstar Corp.*, 518 U.S. 839, 896, 116 S. Ct. 2432, 135 L.Ed.2d 964 (1996) (principal opinion of Souter, J.).

The doctrine is rooted in three early Court of Claims cases. In *Deming v. United States*, 1 Ct. Cl. 190 (1865), a supplier who had contracted to provide rations to the Marine Corps sued for damages when the enactment of the Legal Tender Act resulted in the imposition of additional duties on some articles making up the rations, thereby raising the contractor's costs. The Court of Claims explained that "[a] contract between the government and a private party cannot be *specially* affected by the enactment of a *general* law" and held that the imposition of the duty constituted a sovereign act that did not form the basis for governmental liability for breach of contract. *Id.* at 191 (emphasis in original). In what has become the iconic statement of the sovereign acts doctrine, the court wrote: "The United States as a contractor are not responsible for the United States as a lawgiver." *Id.*

In *Jones v. United States*, 1 Ct. Cl. 383 (1865), the Court of Claims extended the rule of *Deming* from legislative to executive acts. The court rejected a suit brought by surveyors working for the Commissioner of Indian Affairs when their performance was hindered by the withdrawal of U.S. troops from Indian territories. As in *Deming,* the court emphasized that "the United States as a contractor cannot be held liable directly or indirectly for the public acts of the United States as a sovereign." *Id.* at 385.

Finally, in *Wilson v. United States,* 11 Ct. Cl. 513 (1875), the plaintiff contracted to deliver mules to the Quartermaster-General during the Civil War. When the plaintiff attempted to deliver the mules in Washington, D.C., which was in danger of capture by Confederate forces, the contractor was refused entry to the city under orders from the military governor of Washington barring any person not in the military service from entering the city without signed permission from a commanding general. After the plaintiff was turned away, Confederate soldiers confiscated some of the plaintiff's mules. The plaintiff then sued the United States to obtain compensation for the loss. Reaffirming the principles of *Deming* and *Jones,* the court invoked the sovereign acts doctrine to hold the government free from liability. The court explained that the exclusion order "was general, applying to all persons, and affecting the claimant precisely as though he had contracted with any private corporation." *Id.* at 521.

The Supreme Court addressed the sovereign acts doctrine for the first time in *Horowitz v. United States,* 267 U.S. 458, 45 S. Ct. 344, 69 L.Ed. 736 (1925). In that case, the Court explicitly approved the formulation of the doctrine in the early Court of Claims cases. The plaintiff in *Horowitz* contracted with the Ordnance Department to purchase silk, which he intended to resell at a profit. Although the government had agreed to ship the merchandise within a specified period, its delivery was delayed when the U.S. Railroad Administration embargoed freight shipments of silk. By the time Horowitz received the silk, the price of silk had fallen and Horowitz was forced to sell his silk at a loss. Finding that the embargo was a public and general act, the Court denied Horowitz's claim to recover damages for the delay. *Horowitz,* 267 U.S. at 461, 45 S. Ct. 344. The Court explained:

The two characters which the government possesses as a contractor and as a sovereign cannot be thus fused; nor can the United States while sued in the one character be made liable in damages for their acts done in the other. Whatever acts the government may do, be they legislative or executive, so long as they be public and general, cannot be deemed specially to alter, modify, obstruct or violate the particular contracts into which it enters with private persons.

Id., quoting *Jones,* 1 Ct. Cl. at 384.

In addition to requiring that the governmental act be "public and general," the Court in *Horowitz* explained that private contractors who deal with the United States should not be treated any more favorably than if they had contracted with a private party. Thus, just as private contractors would not recover in the event of an intervening sovereign act that disrupted contract expectations, the Court stated that the same principle would apply to those contracting with the government.

* * *

The Court wrote:

> In this court the United States appear simply as contractors; and they are to be held liable only within the same limits that any other defendant would be in any other court. Though their sovereign acts performed for the general good may work injury to some private contractors, such parties gain nothing by having the United States as their defendants.

Id.; see also Jones, 1 Ct. Cl. at 385 ("If the removal of troops from a district liable to invasion will give the claimant damages for unforeseen expenses, when the other party is a corporate body, then it will when the United States form the other party, but not otherwise."); Richard E. Speidel, *Implied Duties of Cooperation and the Defense of Sovereign Acts in Government Contracts,* 51 Geo. L.J. 516, 539 (1963) (noting policy that "a contractor who deals with the United States in its contractual capacity should occupy no better risk position than if he were dealing with a private party").

In *United States v. Winstar Corp.,* 518 U.S. 839, 116 S. Ct. 2432, 135 L.Ed.2d 964 (1996), the Supreme Court was again presented with a case requiring it to address the meaning of a "public and general act" for purposes of the sovereign acts doctrine. The issue in *Winstar* was whether the government was liable for breach of contract resulting from Congress's enactment of the Financial Institutions Reform, Recovery, and Enforcement Act of 1989 ("FIRREA"). Prior to the Act, the Federal Home Loan Bank Board had induced healthy financial institutions to take over insolvent thrifts by promising favorable accounting treatment for the acquired assets. Subsequently, however, Congress enacted FIRREA, which eliminated those accounting benefits. The Supreme Court held that the legislative elimination of the agreed-upon benefits constituted a breach by the United States of its contractual obligations to the acquiring institutions for which the government was liable.

The Court in *Winstar* rejected the government's argument that the legislation constituted a sovereign act that provided a defense against claims of contract breach. The principal opinion, authored by Justice Souter, explained that in order to place the government on an equal footing with other contractors, "some line has to be drawn" between situations in which the government's act is "relatively free of Government self-interest," and those in which the action is "tainted by a governmental object of self-relief." *Winstar,* 518 U.S. at 896, 116 S. Ct. 2432. The government will not be held liable, Justice Souter explained, "so long as the action's impact upon public contracts is, as in *Horowitz,* merely incidental to the accomplishment of a broader governmental objective." *Id.* at 898, 116 S. Ct. 2432. In contrast, the sovereign acts defense is unavailable "where a substantial part of the impact of the Government's action rendering performance impossible falls on its own contractual obligations." *Id.* The principal opinion concluded that FIRREA was not a public and general act because "[t]he statute not only had the purpose of eliminating the very accounting gimmicks that acquiring thrifts had been promised, but the specific object of abrogating enough of the acquisition contracts as to make that consequence of the legislation a focal point of the congressional debate." *Id.* at 900, 116 S. Ct. 2432.

Although the portion of the principal opinion addressed to the sovereign acts doctrine had the support of only four (and as to some portions, only three) justices, this court has treated that opinion as setting forth the core principles underlying the sovereign acts doctrine. *See Carabetta Enters., Inc. v. United States,* 482 F.3d 1360, 1365 (Fed. Cir. 2007); *Yankee Atomic Elec. Co. v. United States,* 112 F.3d 1569, 1574–77 (Fed. Cir. 1997). That approach probably best approximates the Supreme Court's position with respect to the doctrine. The dissenting justices in *Winstar* would have given the doctrine broader sweep. *Winstar,* 518 U.S. at 933, 116 S. Ct. 2432 (Rehnquist, C.J., dissenting) (a general regulatory action constitutes a "sovereign act" regardless of whether the action was "free of governmental self-interest" or was "tainted" by a governmental objective of "self-relief"). The concurring justices would have construed the doctrine more narrowly, but still would regard it, along with the "unmistakability doctrine," as reversing the normal presumption that a party will be liable for any impossibility that is attributable to its own actions. *Winstar,* 518 U.S. at 920–21, 923–24, 116 S. Ct. 2432 (Scalia, J., concurring in the judgment). In any event, we discern no indication in the separate opinions in *Winstar* that the approach taken by the justices who subscribed to those opinions would lead to a different result on the facts of this case than the result reached by the Board.

[3] In cases following *Winstar,* we have reiterated that the sovereign acts defense is unavailable where the governmental action is specifically directed at nullifying contract rights. *See, e.g., City Line Joint Venture v. United States,* 503 F.3d 1319, 1323 (Fed. Cir. 2007) (legislation abrogating option of low-income apartment owners to prepay mortgages was not a sovereign act because it was "aimed at the contract rights themselves in order to nullify them," quoting *Cienega Gardens v. United States,* 331 F.3d 1319, 1335 (Fed. Cir. 2003)); *Centex Corp. v. United States,* 395 F.3d 1283, 1308 (Fed. Cir. 2005) (legislation breaching agreements entitling financial institutions to take tax deductions for specific losses was not a public and general act because it "was specifically targeted at appropriating the benefits of a government contract"). Even before *Winstar,* our precedent provided that the government could not use the sovereign acts defense as a means to escape from contracts that it subsequently concluded were unwise. *See Everett Plywood Corp. v. United States,* 227 Ct. Cl. 415, 651 F.2d 723, 731–32 (Ct. Cl. 1981).

In addition, when considering whether the alleged sovereign act is exclusively directed to aborting performance of government contracts, courts addressing the sovereign acts doctrine have looked to the extent to which the governmental action was directed to relieving the government of its contractual obligations. As Justice Souter stated in *Winstar,* [*United States v. Winstar Corp.,* 518 U.S. 839, 116 S. Ct. 2432, 135 L.Ed.2d 964 (1996)], "The greater the Government's self-interest, . . . the more suspect becomes the claim that its private contracting partners ought to bear the financial burden of the Government's own improvidence...." *Winstar*, 518 U.S. at 898, 116 S. Ct. 2432 (principal opinion of Souter, J.). The Court of Federal Claims applied that principle in *Casitas Municipal Water District v. United States*, 72 Fed. Cl. 746 (2006), *aff'd in part*, 543 F.3d 1276 (Fed. Cir. 2008). In that case, the United States agreed to construct and operate a water reclamation project in exchange for a commitment from the Casitas Municipal Water District to repay the construction and operation costs. Almost 40 years after construction of the project, the National Marine Fisheries Service listed the West Coast Steelhead Trout as an endangered species and subsequently issued a biological opinion pursuant to the Endangered Species Act requiring Casitas to construct a fish passage facility and adhere to new operating criteria to assist trout migration. When the water district sued the government for breach of contract, the court held that the biological opinion was a sovereign act because "no economic advantage accrued to the United States, as a contracting party, as a result of" its issuance. 72 Fed. Cl. at 755.

[4] Another factor relevant to the "public and general" inquiry is whether the governmental action applies exclusively to the contractor or more broadly to include other parties not in a contractual relationship with the government. In the [*Yankee Atomic Elec. Co. v. United States*, 112 F.3d 1569, 1574–77 (Fed. Cir. 1997)] *Yankee Atomic* case, an electric utility that purchased uranium enrichment services from the government brought suit to recover costs it incurred pursuant to the Energy Policy Act of 1992, which required domestic utilities to pay a pro rata share of costs associated with decontaminating and decommissioning former enrichment facilities. In concluding that the legislation constituted a sovereign act, we emphasized that "the special assessment does not reach only those utility companies that previously contracted with the Government; it also reaches those utilities that purchased the services through the secondary market but had *no* contracts with the Government." 112 F.3d at 1576 (emphasis in original). Thus, any governmental act that obstructs a government contract is more likely to be regarded as incidental when the scope of the governmental act is sufficiently broad to affect parties having no connection to the contract.

In light of these principles, we sustain the Board's decision that the exclusion order that temporarily shut down Conner's performance was a sovereign act and that the government is therefore not liable for delay damages under its contract with Conner. As we explain in detail below, the exclusion order was not directed at relieving the government of its contractual obligations; to the contrary, any effect on Conner was incidental to a broader governmental objective relating to national security.

III

* * *

[9][10] In short, General Votel's order excluding Conner from its worksite fits comfortably within the category of actions that we have consistently upheld as

sovereign acts. In fact, the circumstances of this case closely parallel those in *Wilson*, where the government contractor was refused entry into Washington, D.C., during the Civil War pursuant to an exclusion order issued by the city's military governor. Concluding that the contractor's exclusion was a sovereign act, the court in *Wilson* emphasized that the order was, as here, issued by a military commander rather than a contracting agent and was "limited strictly to the public defense." *Wilson,* 11 Ct. Cl. at 521.[FN1] Like Wilson, Conner suffered losses as a result of the exclusion order. As in *Wilson,* however, the effect on Conner's contract rights was incidental to the achievement of a broader governmental objective relating to national security and therefore did not give rise to governmental liability.

***

IV

[13] As an alternative ground for recovery, Conner contends that the Corps of Engineers breached its implied duty to cooperate by failing to issue a suspension of work order after General Votel issued the exclusion order. As the Board found, however, the contracting officer played no part in the decision to restrict access to the Ranger compound. That decision was a sovereign act involving national security, and it was unrelated to any interests of the government as contractor. The contracting officer was under no obligation to issue a suspension of work order in response to an action taken by the government in its sovereign capacity. *Cf. Urban Plumbing & Heating Co. v. United States,* 187 Ct. Cl. 15, 408 F.2d 382, 392–93 (Ct. Cl. 1969) (finding that contracting officer should have issued a suspension of work order where the government, acting in its contractual capacity and for the convenience of the government as contractor, caused a delay in performance). We therefore uphold the Board's decision that Conner is not entitled to recovery under the "suspension of work" clause of the contract, and we affirm the Board's ruling that Conner's exclusion from the worksite qualified as a sovereign act that relieved the government of liability for delay damages.

AFFIRMED.

FN1. Conner is correct that the fact that the government may have had lawful authority and valid reasons for taking an action is not sufficient to satisfy the "public and general" requirement. Serving the public good is a necessary but insufficient condition for asserting the sovereign acts defense. *See Winstar,* 518 U.S. at 903, 116 S. Ct. 2432 (principal opinion of Souter, J.) (noting that a purpose of advancing the public welfare cannot "serve as a criterion of a 'public and general' sovereign act"). The key issue here-as in all sovereign act cases-is not whether the government had the authority to exclude Conner for national security purposes, but rather who should bear the cost of an action that was admittedly in the public interest: a single contractor or the taxpayers at large. The answer to that question turns on whether the governmental action was public and general, not whether it served the public interest.

23.05 THE ACTUAL AUTHORITY REQUIREMENT

Another unique aspect of contract law in dealing with the government relates to authority to make changes or to bind the government. When dealing with the local, state, or federal government, contractors often interact with people with very official and highly important sounding titles (inspector, resident engineer, project manager, mayor, installation commander, general). The problem is that if all of these individuals had the authority to award or issue changes to an already awarded contract, then the agency would rapidly lose control of its budget. For that reason, public agencies typically designate certain individuals as contracting officers, purchasing agents, or some other title and then specifically designate them as the only ones who have the authority to bind the agency contractually. As a consequence, if a contractor is directed to do something by the resident engineer but not by the contracting officer (who may be blissfully unaware of this development), the agency may have a very good, and sometimes ironclad, basis to reject reimbursement for the extra work that the contractor undoubtedly has incurred and for the benefit that the government has undoubtedly received. The following case is a frightening example of how rigidly this rule can be applied.

United States Court of Appeals, Federal Circuit

Donald C. WINTER, Secretary of the Navy, Appellant

v.

CATH-DR/BALTI JOINT VENTURE, Appellee

No. 2006-1359, August 17, 2007. Rehearing and Rehearing En Banc Denied Nov. 21, 2007.
Before LOURIE, PROST, and MOORE, Circuit Judges.

Opinion for the court filed by Circuit Judge MOORE.
Opinion dissenting-in-part filed by Circuit Judge PROST.

The Secretary of the Navy (Navy) appeals the decision of the Armed Services Board of Contract Appeals (Board) finding in favor of Cath-dr/Balti Joint Venture (Cath) on 13 of 37 claims for an equitable adjustment in contract price. Cath-dr/Balti Joint Venture, ASBCA Nos. 53581, 54239, 05-2 BCA ¶ 33046 (Aug. 17, 2005) (Board Opinion). The Navy asserts that the Board erred in concluding that a Resident Officer in Charge of Contracts[1] (ROICC), who was also the Project Manager (PM) during the performance period, had the authority to commit the government to compensable contract changes. Because the contract explicitly reserved authority to modify the contract to the Contracting Officer (CO), the ROICC did not have actual express or implied authority to direct the contractor to perform compensable contract changes, and we reverse the Board's conclusion as to claims 2, 8, 13, 17, and 26/32. However, we affirm the Board decision on claim 3 because that claim is independently sustainable based on a differing site condition, which the Navy does not appeal. Finally, we remand claims 7, 33, and 37 to the Board to determine whether the ROICC's directives on these claims were ratified.

BACKGROUND

I.

On September 29, 1998, Cath and the Navy entered into a fixed price contract for external renovation of a historic dental research facility at the Great Lakes Naval Training Center in Illinois. The contract incorporates by reference several standard government clauses including Federal Acquisition Regulation (FAR) § 52.243-4 (Aug.1987) (Changes Clause), which provides that the CO may, at any time, make changes in the work within the general scope of the contract by written order designated as a change order. FAR § 52.243-4 also provides that for any change affecting the contractor's cost or time of performance under the contract "whether or not changed by any such order, the [CO] shall make an equitable adjustment and modify the contract in writing." The contract also includes FAR § 52.236-2 Differing Site Conditions (April 1984), which requires that a contractor give written notice to the CO of subsurface, latent, or unknown physical conditions at the site that differ materially from those indicated in the contracting documents. After such notice, the CO "shall" investigate the site conditions and if they do materially differ and cause an increase in the cost of or time required for completion of the contract "an equitable adjustment shall be made under this clause and the contract modified accordingly" by the CO. Additionally, the contract incorporates Naval Facilities Engineering Command (NAVFAC) Clause 5252.201-9300 Contracting Officer Authority (June 1994) and NAVFAC Clause 5252.242-9300 Government Representatives (June 1994). The Contracting Officer Authority clause reserves authority to the CO to bind the government to any "contract, modification, change order, letter or verbal direction to the contractor," and the Government Representatives clause indicates that while the Engineer in Charge (EIC) will be designated by the Contracting Officer as his authorized representative responsible for monitoring performance and technical management, in no event will any modification of the contract by anyone other than the CO bind the government.

II.

Before work under the contract began, a preconstruction conference was held, as required by contract specification section 01110 "Summary of Work," paragraph 1. 10, entitled "Preconstruction Conference." Paragraph 1.10 states that the conference will be held with the CO to "develop a mutual understanding" relative to the administration of the contract. The preconstruction conference attendees included numerous individuals from Cath and the Navy, including both the ROICC PM and

EIC. Although the contract required that the CO attend the preconstruction conference, the CO was not present.

During the preconstruction conference, the Navy set forth its detailed guidelines for contract administration in a presentation that designated the ROICC PM to administer the contract and stated that all correspondence should be addressed to the attention of Lt. Ken Osmun—the active ROICC PM. The presentation directed the contractor to use the Requests for Information (RFI) form routinely and "[i]f necessary, forward RFI to Navy PM for action." The presentation included two slides related to contract modification which state "[m]odifications are written alterations to the contract which may change the work to be performed and/or the contract price and time" and "[n]o work is to be performed beyond the contract requirements without written notification from the ROICC." Another slide related to disputes directed the contractor to submit a request for equitable adjustment to the ROICC if it feels a contract modification is required and "[i]f the ROICC sees no entitlement, or the contractor doesn't agree with the entitlement, the contractor has the right to request a Contracting Officer's Final Decision, using the procedures outlined in the Disputes Clause" but that "[t]he contractor must proceed diligently with the work while awaiting the final decision."

Cath began work under the dental facility contract on January 25, 1999. Soon thereafter, Cath received a letter from the Navy that reassigned the day-to-day administration of the contract to EIC Tim Meland and indicated that all correspondence regarding the contract should be sent to Meland's attention. In response to this letter, Cath submitted a RFI seeking "documentation of assignment of authority" and the "level of authority" of Meland, among others. The Navy responded to this RFI with respect to Meland as follows:

Mr. Tim Meland. Project Manager: Serves as the Government Construction Manager on all assigned projects. Responsible for construction management and contract administration on assigned projects while providing quality assurance and technical engineering construction advice. Provides technical and administrative direction to resolve problems encountered during construction. A project manager analyzes and Interprets contract drawings and specifications to determine the extent of Contractors' responsibility. Prepares and/or coordinates correspondence, submittal reviews, estimates, and contract modifications in support to ensure a satisfactory and timely completion of projects.

During the course of the project, Meland and his successor received numerous RFIs from Cath that requested clarification of the contract requirements and gave notice of site conditions that may require deviation from the contract specifications with a request for a decision. In each case, the ROICC PM signed the response to the RFI. When necessary, the PM asked for the architect/engineer's input, which was also provided to the contractor in the PM's response. Some of these responses included a preprinted statement that the response is a contract requirement, which the PM marked.

III.

After Cath's renovation work under the contract was deemed substantially complete, it submitted a cumulative request for a contract modification and several adjustments to the PM, in accordance with the procedure for equitable adjustment requests set forth in the preconstruction conference presentation. The PM responded, indicating "we will thoroughly review the submitted documentation and will formally respond in writing at a future date." After the ROICC office failed to act on the request for five months, Cath submitted a certified request in December 2000.

A CO issued a 15 page Final Decision on July 27, 2001, detailing each claim and finding entitlement to an equitable adjustment for 12 claims. In this decision, the CO recommended that Cath and the ROICC office negotiate the amount Cath is entitled to for its meritorious claims and asked that Cath's request for a final decision on those claims be "held in abeyance subject to further discussions with the ROICC." Cath attempted on several occasions to meet with the Navy to reach an agreement as to the amount Cath should receive for these claims, but despite the CO's direction in the July 27 decision letter, inexplicably, the Navy refused to meet with Cath.

When this appeal was brought before the Board, it was Cath's position that only an accounting was needed for these twelve claims because of the CO's confirmation that Cath was entitled to recover on those claims. The Board similarly viewed the July 27 decision as a concession to entitlement and issued a Show Cause Order requesting the Navy to explain why entitlement should not be granted to Cath on those twelve claims. The Navy responded that the July 27, 2001 decision was not a determination of entitlement. In a memorandum dated May 6, 2003, the Board indicated that the final decision "clearly concede[s] entitlement on these items, leaving only quantum to be resolved" and stated that the government's interpretation to the contrary was "unreasonable." Shortly thereafter, the Navy issued a second Final Decision two pages in length denying all of Cath's claims, including the twelve claims the CO previously determined had merit. Unlike the first, this second final decision contained no discussion of individual claims, but rather stated that because no additional data had been provided, the claims were denied for lack of entitlement. The Board then considered entitlement and damages for each claim anew.

The Navy argued for the first time on appeal that the CO did not direct the work set forth in the claims for equitable adjustment and that under the contract only the CO has the authority to change the scope of work or authorize compensable changes. In an order dated August 17, 2005, the Board sustained in whole or in part 13 of Cath's 37 claims. Board Opinion, Op. at 81-83. With respect to all but one of the claims that the Navy has appealed to this court, the Board determined that the ROICC PM directed changes that resulted in costs beyond those required by the contract and that these changes were compensable because the delegation of authority clause in the contract gave him responsibility for construction management and contract administration. The Board concluded that Meland, as the PM, had "express actual authority" to resolve minor problems that arose during the project based on the Navy's RFI response, which indicated that he was responsible for construction management and contract administration and that he was authorized to provide "'technical and administrative direction to resolve problems encountered during construction.'" Board Opinion, Op. at 9 (quoting Urban Pathfinders, Inc., ASBCA No. 23134 79-1 BCA ¶ 13,709 at 67,260 (1979)). Additionally, the Board sustained entitlement to recover for claim 3 under the contract's Differing Site Condition clause, FAR § 52.

The Secretary timely appealed the Board's decision. See 41 U.S.C. § 607(g)(1)(B) (2006). This court has jurisdiction under 28 U.S.C. § 1295(a)(10) (2006).

ANALYSIS

The Navy appeals the Board's equitable adjustment of the contract price with respect to claims 2, 7, 8, 13, 17, 26/32, 33, and 37.[2] To demonstrate entitlement to an equitable adjustment, Cath must prove that the contract was modified by someone with actual authority. Where a party contracts with the government, apparent authority of the government's agent to modify the contract is not sufficient; an agent must have actual authority to bind the government. See Trauma Serv. Group v. United States, 104 F.3d 1321, 1325 (Fed.Cir.1997). Such actual authority may be express or implied from the authority granted to that agent. We must determine whether Meland had express or implied authority to bind the government to contract modifications he approved, or whether these changes were ratified by the CO.

I. Express Authority

With respect to contracts for supplies and services, the federal government has given the authority to enter into and modify contracts to only a limited class of government employees: contracting officers. See 48 C.F.R. § 1.601(a) (vesting agency heads with authority to contract for supplies and services and mandating that "[c]ontracts may be entered into and signed on behalf of the Government only by contracting officers"); 48 C.F.R. § 43.102 ("Only contracting officers acting within the scope of their authority are empowered to execute contract modifications on behalf of the Government."). In addition to possessing authority to enter into a contract on behalf of the government, contracting officers have the authority to, among other things, administer the contract and ensure the contractor's compliance with the contract terms. See 48 C.F.R. §§ 1.602-1, -2.

When authorized, the contracting officer may delegate some of its authority to certain designated representatives, who act on behalf of the government during contract administration.   See John Cibinic, Jr., Ralph C. Nash, Jr., & James F. Nagle, Administration of Government Contracts 39 (4th ed.2006). In this case, a limited delegation of authority occurred. The contract entered into by the Navy and Cath contains a clause that states that the contracting officer may designate a "contracting officer's representative (COR)" to perform "specific technical or administrative functions." See 48 C.F.R. § 252.201-7000. It also contains a clause entitled "GOVERNMENT REPRESENTATIVES (JUN 1994)," which states that "[t]he contract will be administered by an authorized representative of the Contracting Officer." That clause goes on to state that "the project Engineer In Charge" is an "authorized representative of the Contracting Officer" and "is responsible for monitoring performance and the technical management of the effort required hereunder, and should be contacted regarding questions or problems of a technical nature."

It is very clear, however, that the contracting officer's limited delegation of authority to the EIC did not include the authority to make contract modifications, nor could it have. For one thing, such a delegation was prohibited by a Department of Defense regulation, which states that "[a] contracting officer's representative (COR), [m]ay not be delegated authority to make any commitments or changes that affect price, quality, quantity, delivery, or other terms and conditions of the contract." 48 C.F.R. § 201.602-2 (1998).[3] Indeed, this express limitation on the COR's authority was incorporated into a clause of the contract itself, which, likewise, states that "[t]he COR is not authorized to make any commitments or changes that will affect price, quality, quantity, delivery, or any other term or condition of the contract." See 48 C.F.R. § 252.201-7000.

Moreover two other clauses in the contract made it clear to Cath that the contracting officer was the only person with the authority to make changes to the contract. The same clause that designates the EIC as an authorized representative of the contracting officer provides that:

[i]n no event, however, will any understanding or agreement, modification, change order, or other matter deviating from the terms of the contract between the contractor and any person other than the Contracting Officer be effective or binding upon the Government, unless formalized by proper contractual documents executed by the Contracting Officer prior to completion of this contract.

And yet another clause of the contract, entitled "CONTRACTING OFFICER AUTHORITY (JUN 1994)," states (emphasis added):

In no event shall any understanding or agreement between the Contractor and any Government employee other than the Contracting Officer on any contract, modification, change order, letter or verbal direction to the Contractor be effective or binding upon the Government. All such actions must be formalized by a proper contractual document executed by an appointed Contracting Officer. The Contractor is hereby put on notice that in the event a Government employee other than the Contracting Officer directs a change in the work to be performed or increases the scope of the work to be performed, it is the Contractor's responsibility to make inquiry of the Contracting Officer before making the deviation. Payments will not be made without being authorized by an appointed Contracting Officer with the legal authority to bind the Government.

The contract is clear, only the CO had the authority to make modifications. Meland did not have the express authority to bind the government to contract modifications.

II. Implied Authority

The issue of implied authority is a much closer case. The government is not without blame for the confusion surrounding the contract in this case. For example, the contract required the CO to attend the preconstruction conference during which the Navy explained contract administration procedures. The CO did not attend. At that meeting the Navy presentation included a slide that stated
Contract Modifications
Modifications are written alterations to the contract which may change the work to be performed and/or the contract price and time. Oral modifications will not be used.

- ☐ Bilateral modification—the contractor and the ROICC have agreed upon an adjustment to the contract
- ☐ Unilateral modification—the ROICC can direct the contractor to take some action under the contract

No work is to be performed beyond the contract requirements without written notification from the ROICC.[4]

Cath dutifully complied with the Navy's directions for day-to-day contract administration presented in the preconstruction conference through the entire process. The problem is that these Navy directives contradicted the clear language of the contract and it is the contract which governs. The law and the unambiguous contract terms compel the result that we reach.

Authority to bind the government may be implied when it is an integral part of the duties assigned to the particular government employee. See H. Landau & Co. v. United States, 886 F.2d 322, 324 (Fed.Cir.1989) (internal citations omitted). In Landau, we held that a government employee possessing both the authority to ensure that a contractor acquired the raw materials needed to fulfill a contract and the authority to draw checks on the government bank account may have also had the "implicit authority" to guarantee payment to the contractor's supplier of raw materials. Id. Landau, however, is inapposite to this case. Here, the ROICC could not have had the implicit authority to authorize contract modifications because the contract language and the government regulation it incorporates by reference explicitly state that only the contracting officer had the authority to modify the contract. Modifying the contract could not be "considered to be an integral part of [the ROICC project manager's] duties" when the contract explicitly and exclusively assigns this duty to the CO. Id. We cannot conclude that Meland had implied authority to direct changes in the contract in contravention of the unambiguous contract language.

III. Ratification

Cath argues that even if Meland did not have actual authority to bind the Navy to contract modifications, the changes directed by Meland were ultimately ratified and were therefore binding. Specifically, Cath argues that the July 27, 2001 Decision on Cath's certified claims, which was issued by the Head of the Contracting Office, reflects the fact that a person with actual authority and sufficient knowledge of the material facts endorsed the actions of Meland and found entitlement for Cath with respect to claims 3, 7, 10, 14, 15, 29, 30, 31, 33, 35, 36, and 37 (only claims 3, 7, 33, and 37 are before this court on appeal). The Navy argues that the CO's July 27 Decision did not amount to ratification because it was not made with full knowledge of the material facts and because it was not a final decision by the CO. The Board did not address ratification since it found that Meland had actual authority to order contract modifications.

Ratification requires knowledge of material facts involving the unauthorized act and approval of the activity by one with authority. Harbert/Lummus Agrifuels Projects v. United States, 142 F.3d 1429, 1433-34 (Fed.Cir.1998). Whether a contract has been ratified involves questions of fact, which has not been addressed by the Board in the first instance. See United States v. Beebe, 180 U.S. 343, 354, 21 S.Ct. 371, 45 L.Ed. 563 (1901); Brainard v. Am. Skandia Life Assurance Corp., 432 F.3d 655, 661 (6th Cir.2005). For example, the parties dispute whether the CO had full knowledge of all material facts at the time he issued the July 27, 2001 Final Decision finding entitlement. While it appears from the detailed fifteen-page decision that the CO did have full knowledge, the government contends he did not. Given the dispute over knowledge and the lack of Board findings on this point, we remand to the Board to consider this issue in the first instance.

The dissent raises two points as to why ratification has not occurred in this case,[5] neither of which was argued by the government. The dissent's points further reinforce that there are questions of fact that should be resolved by the fact finder in the first instance. First, the dissent suggests that the CO's July 27, 2001 Final Decision does not "demonstrate[] the CO's adoption of the Project Manager's unauthorized change orders." But the decision itself suggests otherwise. With respect to claims 7, 33, and 37, it appears that the July 27 Decision constitutes acceptance of Meland's actions and that Cath is entitled to an equitable adjustment.[6] The July 27 Decision states: "In conclusion, our analysis indicates that entitlement is due the contractor for items . 7 . 33 . and 37." The Decision left unsettled only the amount for each adjustment, which it returned "to the Resident Officer in

Charge of Construction for negotiation of an equitable adjustment." The Board similarly viewed the July 27, 2001 Final Decision as a concession to entitlement and issued a Show Cause Order requesting the Navy to explain why entitlement should not be granted. In its May 6, 2003 Memorandum, the Board stated that the Final Decision "clearly concede[s] entitlement on these items, leaving only quantum to be resolved." Whether the statements in the July 27, 2001 Final Decision constitute approval of the contract modification made by the ROICC involves questions of fact, which we believe the Board ought to resolve in the first instance.

The dissent also suggests that the contract requires ratification to occur prior to the completion of the contract, another argument not raised by the government or addressed by either party. The provision cited by the dissent is the Government Representatives Clause and provides the means by which an authorized change can be made during performance of the contract. It does not address, much less preclude, the CO from ratifying an unauthorized change after completion. The dissent itself does not conclude, nor could it based on a dearth of fact finding on this point, that this clause definitively prohibits a finding of ratification in this case. See Dissenting Opinion, at 1350 (stating "the alleged ratification does not appear to have met either of these requirements").

Given the detailed factual nature of the ratification determination, we remand to the Board to consider in the first instance whether the CO's July 27, 2001 Decision constitutes ratification of ROICC Meland's directed changes with respect to appealed claims 7, 33, and 37.[7]

IV. Claim 3

***

CONCLUSION

For the foregoing reasons, the decision of the Board is
AFFIRMED IN PART, REVERSED IN PART, AND VACATED AND REMANDED IN PART.
COSTS

***

FOOTNOTES

1. Resident Officer in Charge of Construction and Resident Officer in Charge Contracts are used interchangeably in the record.

2. The Navy also appeals the Board's conclusion that Cath is entitled to an equitable adjustment with respect to claim 3. Because the Board's rationale on that claim is different than the remaining claims, we separately address claim 3.

3. A more recent version of this regulation similarly states that "[a] COR. [h]as no authority to make any commitments or changes that affect price, quality, quantity, delivery, or other terms and conditions of the contract." 48 C.F.R. § 602-2(2) (2006).

4. It further defined modifications as changes in work, time extensions for certain delays, reimbursement for work suspension, and differing site conditions. These are exactly the types of modifications that were approved by Meland.

> 5. The dissent raises a third point, arguing that we are not bound by the CO's determinations of entitlement. We agree. We are not suggesting that because the CO found entitlement in his July 27, 2001 letter that we are bound to agree. Rather we conclude that the CO's finding of entitlement may be a ratification of the ROICC's contract modification and as such would bind the government to this change.
> 6. With respect to claim 7, the Decision stated "Since the contract drawings did not indicate all the work that needed to be accomplished for this item, the Government agreed that this was a changed condition. An equitable adjustment will be negotiated with the ROICC." With respect to claim 33, the Decision stated that "the Resident Office In Charge of Construction agreed that this is a changed condition. I believe some entitlement is due." With respect to claim 37, the CO stated "[t]he Resident Office In Charge of Construction agreed that there is some entitlement on this item. I recommend further negotiations with the Resident Office In Charge of Construction to negotiate a fair and reasonable cost for this item".
> 7. Although the July 27 Decision also found that Cath was entitled to an equitable adjustment for claim 3, we affirm the Board's decision with respect to claim 3 on other grounds. Thus, the Board need not consider on remand whether ratification occurred with respect to claim 3.

When confronted with the situation, as in the preceding case, what should the contractor have done and what documentation should the contractor have demanded?

Actually, the authority issue is very often wrapped into several other issues. First, is the contracting officer even aware of this unauthorized directive? I say directive, but very often there will be a dispute as to whether the government inspector, for example, merely made a suggestion to the contractor which the contractor is supposedly free to accept or reject as opposed to a "you must do this" requirement.

Second, did the contracting authority ratify the actions of the representative?

Third, did the contracting officer acquiesce? For example, if the contractor properly puts the contracting officer on notice of the unauthorized directive and asks what the contractor should do. The contracting officer has a duty to respond, but fails to do so. At some time, the contractor must take action to move on with the case.

23.06 SOCIOECONOMIC REQUIREMENTS

A public entity will often decide a contract award on reasons that a private owner will rarely consider. Such socioeconomic requirements may stem from the government's desire to ensure that workers are paid a decent wage, that unemployment in particular areas is alleviated, that domestic products are used on the project, or that small businesses, especially those owned by members of a disadvantaged class, are benefitted to the maximum extent possible.

The government has a variety of socioeconomic programs, primarily covered under FAR Parts 19–26. These break down into three general categories: (1) small business programs, (2) domestic preference statutes, and (3) prevailing wage issues.

1. Small business programs are covered under FAR part 19. There are various types of small business programs. The federal government will recognize companies as small if they fit below certain thresholds in the North American Industry Classification System (NAICS) for either a certain dollar value or number of employees. Some programs will look only at size. Others will depend on who owns the small business, whether it is a women-owned small business, disadvantaged class ownership, veteran-owned, service disabled veteran-owned. A third subcategory is where the small business is located. If it is located in an area of high unemployment, traditionally called an historically underutilized business zone (HUBZone), such companies are also entitled to benefits.

    The government favors such small businesses by one of three methods. First, some procurements are set aside only for small businesses or specific category small businesses. Larger businesses or businesses not fitting within that category (for example, a small business cannot necessarily qualify for a women-owned small business set aside) cannot compete. Second, even if it is not a small business set-aside, certain small businesses may be given a preference in the evaluation for award. Third, the government has an extensive small business subcontracting program. See FAR subpart 19.7.

    Similar programs also exist on the state level, often called WMBE programs for women, minority business enterprises. While there have been constitutional challenges to these programs in the past,[26] and there has been some tweaking to them, the programs still exist and are widespread.

2. The second category is domestic preference statutes, the primary one being the Buy American Act (41 U.S.C. § 10a–d), covered under FAR part 25, where the government wants a certification from the contractor that the materials it will be using on the project are domestic supplies or come from a country which is a signatory to a treaty such as

---

26. *See* City of Richmond v. J. A. Croson Constr. Co., 488 U.S. 469 (1989); Adarand Constructors, Inc. v. Pena, 515 U.S. 200 (1995).

the Trade Agreements Act, which grants them equal status to domestic products.
3. The third area is for prevailing wages which are common both on federal and local public projects. The main statute in federal projects is the Davis Bacon Act, (40 U.S.C. §§ 3141–3148) implemented in FAR part 22, which requires the government to ensure that contractors pay their workers a decent wage. Decent wage is defined as the wage at a minimum set by the Department of Labor. Another act that often will intersect with construction projects is the McNamara-O'Hara Service Contract Act of 1965 (41 U.S.C. §§ 6701–6707), which essentially does for services workers what the Davis Bacon Act did for construction workers, that is, it ensured they were paid a decent wage in accordance with the Prevailing Wage Determination by the Labor Department.[27]

This next case does not involve a construction company, but the same principles apply regardless of the type of work being procured.

COMPTROLLER GENERAL

Matter of:
MCS
Portable
Restroom
Service
March 28, 2007
B- 299291, 2007 CPD P 55, 2007 WL 926295 (Comp.Gen.)

***

DECISION
MCS Portable Restroom Service (MCS), a service-disabled veteran-owned small business concern (SDVOSBC), protests the Air Force's decision not to set aside a requirement for SDVOSBCs or, alternatively, to make a sole-source award to an SDVOSBC, for portable chemical toilet services at the United States Air Force Academy and Farish Memorial Park in Colorado, and to instead obtain these services as a small business set-aside under invitation for bids (IFB) No. FA7000–07–B–0002.

We sustain the protest.

The IFB, issued as a 100–percent small business set-aside, sought a contractor to provide all management, tools, supplies, equipment and labor necessary for the

---

27. For more information regarding these socioeconomic issues, see Chapter 12, Angela R. Stevens, Tim Matheny and Lori Ann Lange, *Socio-Economic Issues in Government Contracting*, in FEDERAL GOVERNMENT CONSTRUCTION CONTRACTS, 3d ed. (Michael A. Branca, William E. Franczek, Paul A. Varela, and Barbara G. Werther, eds., ABA Press 2017).

portable chemical toilet services. The IFB provided for an 8–month base period, with 4 option years.

As part of the market research for this acquisition, the contracting officer searched the Central Contractor Registration (CCR) database under North American Industry Classification System code 562991 (Septic Tank and Related Services), and located 28 SDVOSBCs, 29 section 8(a) concerns, 10 Historically Underutilized Business Zone (HUBZone) concerns, and 28 other small business concerns that potentially could perform the work. Agency Report (AR), Tab 6D, Market Research Summary, at 4. On February 14, 2006, the agency sent e-mails to all of these firms and received responses from two SDVOSBCs (MCS and a Florida company that expressed interest in developing a joint venture to perform this work), one HUBZone concern, and four small businesses. On April 18, the agency posted a "sources sought" notice on FedBizOpps and three companies responded: one small business, one women-owned small business, and MCS. Contracting Officer's (CO) Statement at 1.

After considering this market research, the contracting officer determined that she did not have a reasonable expectation of receiving two or more bids from HUBZone or SDVOSBC concerns. AR, Tab 6D, Market Research Summary, at 6. Based on this determination and after receiving approval from the Air Force small business specialist to set aside the procurement for small businesses, AR, Tab 6C, Small Business Coordination Record, the agency, on August 8, posted a synopsis on FedBizOpps of the proposed solicitation for these services as a small business set-aside, that is, not one reserved for a subset of small businesses—either HUBZone or SDVOSBC concerns.

MCS then filed an agency-level protest of this determination. MCS contended that the IFB should have been set aside for SDVOSBCs or, in the alternative, a sole-source award should have been made to MCS because it is an SDVOSBC.

After receiving the protest, the contracting officer searched the CCR for all SDVOSBCs in Colorado and nationwide "to ensure that the market had not changed since the time the initial market research was conducted." CO Statement at 2. This search revealed the existence of 2 SDVOSBCs in Colorado and 20 SDVOSBCs nationwide that could potentially perform the work. AR, Tab 6B, Letter from Air Force to MCS Denying Protest, Sept. 22, 2006, at 2. While it is not clear from the record whether the second CCR search identified firms that were previously identified in the initial CCR search, no efforts were made to contact any of these companies at that time. The agency determined that a sole-source SDVOSBC award was, for reasons explained later in this decision, prohibited by the Federal Acquisition Regulation (FAR). The agency then affirmed its decision to set aside the procurement for small businesses and denied MCS's agency-level protest.

No actual solicitation for the services was issued until December 5, when the IFB was posted on FedBizOpps as a small business set-aside. MCS then timely protested to our Office, reasserting the grounds raised in its agency-level protest.

SDVOSBC SET–ASIDE REQUIREMENTS

MCS first asserts that the agency should have set aside the acquisition for SDVOSBC participation. It complains that the agency's market research was inadequate and does not support the determination to issue the IFB as a small business, rather than as an SDVOSBC, set-aside.

The Small Business Act was amended by section 36 of the Veterans Benefits Act of 2003, Pub. L. No. 108–183, 117 Stat. 2651, 2662 (2003), 15 U.S.C. sect. 657f (Supp. IV 2004), to establish the SDVOSBC procurement program. This amendment provided for procurements with competition restricted to SDVOSBCs as follows:

> In accordance with this section, a contracting officer may award contracts on the basis of competition restricted to [SDVOSBCs] if the contracting officer has a reasonable expectation that not less than 2 [SDVOSBCs] will submit offers and that the award can be made at a fair market price.

15 U.S.C. sect. 657f(b).

This program is implemented in FAR Subpart 19.14, which in part provides:

(a) The contracting officer may set aside acquisitions exceeding the micro-purchase threshold for competition restricted to [SDVOSBCs] when the requirements of paragraph (b) of this section can be satisfied. The contracting officer shall consider [SDVOSBC] set-asides before considering [SDVOSBC] sole source awards. ...

(b) To set-aside an acquisition for competition restricted to [SDVOSBCs], the contracting officer must have a reasonable expectation that—

(1) Offers will be received from two or more [SDVOSBCs]; and

(2) Award will be made at a fair market price.

FAR sect. 19.1405(a), (b).

SBA regulations also provide that:

> the contracting officer should consider setting aside the requirement for 8(a), HUBZone, or [SDVOSBC] participation before considering setting aside the requirement as a small business set-aside.

13 C.F.R. sect. 125.19.

Generally, a procurement set-aside determination is a matter of business judgment within the contracting officer's discretion, which our Office will not disturb absent a showing that it was unreasonable. *See Neal R. Gross & Co., Inc.,* B-2940924.2, Jan. 17, 1991, 91–1 CPD para. 53 at 2. Although the use of any particular method of assessing the availability of firms for a set-aside is not required, measures such as prior procurement history, market surveys, and advice from the agency's small business specialist may all constitute adequate grounds for a contracting officer's decision to set aside, or not to set aside, a procurement. *See American Imaging Servs., Inc.,* B-246124.2, Feb. 13, 1992, 92–1 CPD para. 188 at 3. The assessment must be based on sufficient evidence so as to establish its reasonableness. *See Rochester Optical Mfg. Co.*, B–292247, B–292247.2, Aug. 6, 2003, 2003 CPD para. 138 at 5.

The agency here asserts that it properly determined not to set aside the requirement for SDVOSBCs because, based on its market research, it did not have a reasonable expectation that two or more SDVOSBCs were interested in the procurement. It notes that only one other firm besides MCS responded to the February 2006 e-mail survey, and that the agency reasonably concluded that this firm was no longer interested when the firm did not respond to the "sources sought" notice issued in April 2006.

We solicited and obtained the views of the Small Business Administration (SBA) regarding the propriety of the Air Force's decisions to not set aside this acquisition for SDVOSBCs or make a sole-source award to an SDVOSBC. The SBA disagrees with the contracting officer's actions here. We accord substantial weight to the fact that the contracting officer's determination has been reviewed by the SBA and found not to be reasonable. *See USA Fabrics, Inc.*, B–295737, B–295737.2, Apr. 19, 2005, 2005 CPD para. 82 at 6; *SWR, Inc., supra*, at 5 n.4. In its response, the SBA recognizes that only MCS, an SDVOSBC and the incumbent contractor, and the Florida SDVOSBC, which expressed interest in forming a joint venture, responded to the February 2006 e-mail survey; however, the SBA further asserts that the agency's disregard of the Florida SDVOSBC's expression of interest (which was based upon the assumption that the firm was no longer interested because it did not also respond to the "sources sought" notice) was unreasonable. As the SBA points out, the firm's lack of response to the "sources sought" notice may not evidence a lack of interest—the firm may not have seen the notice or it may have believed a response was unnecessary given that it had already expressed interest. SBA Report (Jan. 26, 2007) at 4. Under these circumstances, the SBA argues, and we agree, that the agency should have followed up with the firm to clarify the firm's interest in the procurement to ascertain whether there was sufficient SDVOSBC interest to allow for a set-aside. *See SWR, Inc.*, B–294266, Oct. 6, 2004, 2004 CPD para. 219 at 6 (agency's two unanswered telephone calls to a HUBZone small business that had previously expressed interest in the procurement was not adequate evidence to support an agency's determination that the firm was no longer interested in the procurement).[FN1]

FN1. The SBA also points out that the agency failed to seek the advice of an SBA representative on whether to set aside the procurement for SDVOSBCs, consulting only with the Air Force small business specialist. Furthermore, as evidence that this procurement may have been appropriate for an SDVOSBC set-aside, the SBA notes that another Air Force base in Colorado has successfully issued a solicitation as an SDVOSBC set-aside for the same or similar services.

Under the circumstances, we conclude that the Air Force failed to make reasonable efforts to ascertain whether this acquisition was suitable for an SDVOSBC set-aside. We acknowledge that, unlike the HUBZone and small business set-aside programs, which generally require set-asides if two or more HUBZone concerns or small business concerns are interested in submitting offers and award is expected to be made at a fair market price, see FAR sections 19.502–1, 19.1305, the decision to make an SDVOSBC set-aside is discretionary with the contracting officer. In this regard, the contracting officer "may," but is not required, to set aside the acquisition for SDVOSBCs, even where it is found that two or more SDVOSBCs are interested in submitting bids and award is anticipated to be made at a fair market price. However, as indicated above, applicable SBA regulations provide that a contracting officer should consider the propriety of setting aside an acquisition for SDVOSBCs before proceeding with a small business set-aside and it is implicit in this regulation that such consideration be reasonable. Consequently, we conclude that the Air Force should perform further market research from which it can reasonably determine whether this acquisition is appropriate for an SDVOSBC set-aside.

SDVOSBC SOLE–SOURCE AWARD

MCS also complains that, even if the agency were correct that there was insufficient interest from two or more SDVOSBCs to set aside the procurement for SDVOSBCs, the agency should have made a sole-source award to MCS.

The agency asserts that FAR sect. 19.1406(a) precludes a sole-source award to an SDVOSBC where more than one SDVOSBC exists that can satisfy the requirement. FAR sect. 19.1406(a) states in pertinent part:

A contracting officer may award contracts to [SDVOSBCs] on a sole source basis . . . , provided—

(1) Only one [SDVOSBC] can satisfy the requirement . . .

In this regard, and as discussed above, after MCS protested that a sole-source SDVOSBC award should be made, the agency reviewed the CCR and found more than one SDVOSBC potentially capable of performing this work (even though they were not contacted and did not express interest in submitting bids). CO Statement at 4. The Air Force's essential argument is that FAR sect. 19.1406(a) precludes making a sole-source award to an SDVOSBC if, as its later CCR review established, more than one SDVOSBC exists that can potentially perform the work.

The protester and the SBA assert that the Air Force misinterprets FAR sect. 19.1406(a). The SBA argues that the FAR should be interpreted "logically and consistently" with the Small Business Act and the implementing SBA regulations, which provide that a contracting officer may consider making a sole-source award to an SDVOSBC unless more than one SDVOSBC is expected to submit a bid under the acquisition. SBA Report (Jan. 26, 2007) at 3.

Our analysis here begins with the Veterans Benefit Act of 2003, which provides for sole-source contract awards to SDVOSBCs and states in pertinent part:

(a) **Sole source contracts**—In accordance with this section, a contracting officer may award a sole-source contract to any [SDVOSBC] if—

(1) such concern is determined to be a responsible contractor with respect to performance of such contract opportunity and the contracting officer does not have a reasonable expectation that 2 or more [SDVOSBCs] will submit offers for the contracting opportunity; . . .

15 U.S.C. sect. 657f.[FN2]

The implementing SBA regulation similarly provides as follows:

A contracting officer may award a sole-source contract to [an SDVOSBC] only when the contracting officer determines that:

(a) None of the provisions of . . . 13 C.F.R. sect. 125.19 apply.

13 C.F.R. sect. 125.20[28].

As relevant here, 13 C.F.R. sect. 125.19[29] provides that an acquisition may be set-aside for SDVOSBCs if there is "a reasonable expectation that at least two responsible SDVOSBCs will submit offers." Thus, both the Act and the implementing SBA regulations provide contracting officers with the discretion to make sole-source awards to SDVOSBCs where the prerequisites that would allow for an SDVOSBC set-aside have not been met.

While the Air Force's position here would seem to be consistent with a literal reading of FAR sect. 19.1406(a), "a regulation must be interpreted so as to harmonize with and further and not conflict with the objective of the statute it implements." *Trustees Of Indiana University v. United States*, 618 F.2d 736, 739 (Ct. Cl. 1980). The "plain meaning" and intent of the Veterans Benefit Act of 2003 is that a sole-source award to an SDVOSBC is permitted if the contracting officer does not have a reasonable expectation that two or more SDVOSBCs would submit bids. We think the FAR should be read consistent with the SBA statutory and regulatory language. To adopt the more restrictive interpretation of the FAR advocated by the Air Force here—that no sole-source award can be made where another SDVOSBC exists that could conceivably perform the contract, even where the firm has expressed no interest in the work—would, in our view, frustrate the intent of the Act itself by limiting sole-source SDVOSBC awards beyond what the statute clearly authorizes and contemplates.

In fact, it is clear that the FAR was not intended to impose restrictions on awarding sole-source SDVOSBC contracts beyond the restrictions included in the Veterans Benefit Act of 2003. The Federal Register notice announcing the final FAR regulation responded to various comments on the draft regulation and discussed

---

FN2. The remaining statutory requirements for making a sole-source award to an SDVOSBC are not relevant here.

---

28. Currently 13 C.F.R. § 125.23.
29. Currently *id.* § 125.22.

the relation between the SDVOSBC set-aside requirements of FAR sect. 19.1405 and those pertaining to sole-source SDVOSBC awards under FAR sect. 19.1406. The FAR Council stated that the regulation was intended to be "consistent with [15 U.S.C. sect. 657f]," and further stated as follows:

If market research indicates that there is only one SDVOSBC source capable of satisfying the requirement at a fair and reasonable price, the contracting officer may award on a sole-source basis. If market research indicates two or more SDVOSBCs are capable of fulfilling the requirement, the contracting officer may set aside the requirement. In the event where only one acceptable SDVOSBC offer is received in response to the set-aside, the contracting officer may make award to that offeror.

70 Fed. Reg. 14949 (Mar. 23, 2005).

This language supports FAR sect. 19.1406(a) being interpreted, consistent with the Veterans Benefit Act of 2003 and SBA's implementing regulations, as allowing a sole-source award to an SDVOSBC when the requirements for setting aside the procurement for SDVOSBCs have not been met. Moreover, in reviewing the FAR case file on this regulation, we find nothing in the comments or in the FAR Council's responses that would suggest that the Council intended an inconsistent or more restrictive rule than was provided for in the Act and the corresponding SBA regulation.[FN3]

Thus, the Air Force did not reasonably exercise its discretion in determining whether this acquisition was appropriate for award on a sole-source basis to an SDVOSBC because it erroneously believed that the FAR precluded such an award.

RECOMMENDATION

We recommend that the contracting officer conduct additional market research to ascertain the interest and capability of SDVOSBCs for this effort and determine whether this acquisition should be set aside for SDVOSBCs. In the event the agency determines that there is not a reasonable expectation of receiving bids from two or more SDVOSBCs, then the agency should consider whether to issue a sole-source SDVOSBC award. We also recommend that MCS be reimbursed the reasonable costs of filing and pursuing the protest, including reasonable attorneys' fees. Bid Protest Regulations, 4 C.F.R. sect. 21.8(d)(1) (2006). MCS's claim for costs, detailing the time expended and costs incurred, must be submitted to the agency within 60 days of receiving this decision. 4 C.F.R. sect. 21.8(f)(1).

The protest is sustained.

Gary L. Kepplinger
General Counsel

FN3. However, we do recognize that the plain wording of FAR sect. 19.1406 is potentially at odds with that of the Act and the SBA regulations. By letter dated today, we are advising the FAR Council of the possible inconsistency in language with the applicable statute so that the Council may review the matter.

For a recent U.S. Supreme Court ruling on the priority of socio-economic rules, see Kingdomware Technologies, Inc., 136 S. Ct. 1969 (2016).

23.07 PROTESTS AND DISPUTES

Because public contracting involves the expenditure of public funds, public contracting will typically provide for some type of protest system by which a disappointed offeror can protest the solicitation or award to a forum that can determine whether the solicitation or award is proper under the procurement statutes and regulations.

Typically solicitations will identify how the protest is to be prepared, the time limits, and to whom the protest must be submitted. Timeliness rules in a protest are much stricter than those in government contract dispute litigation. Protests are normally resolved in a matter of days. The protest must be filed extremely quickly and it will be resolved extremely quickly. Some agencies will require that the matter first go to an administrative tribunal before the offeror can proceed to court.

As always, the federal government provides a model of how to do that. Protests are discussed in FAR subpart 33.1. An offeror can protest to the agency but is not obligated to do so. It can go directly to the Government Accountability Office (GAO) or to the U.S. Court of Federal Claims. If it protests to the agency first, that is not an election of remedies. If it loses at the agency, it can then go to the GAO or to the Court of Federal Claims for a de novo review.[30]

No matter how well written the contract, no matter how reasonable the parties, there are often matters upon which reasonable people will differ. So claims and disputes invariably arise that will still not be resolved by the best intentioned efforts of alternate dispute resolution methods. In such cases, the parties must undergo whichever disputes process is available.

In federal contracts, the Contract Disputes Act, 41 U.S.C. §§ 7101–7109, and as set forth in FAR subparts 33.2 and 33.3, mandates a very formal dispute process, and adherence to the CDA is vital as its requirements are viewed as jurisdictional.[31] Either party may initiate a claim. The contractor may have a claim for an equitable adjustment for damages resulting from alleged government delays.[32] The government may have a claim for excess re-procurement costs or breach of warranty damages. The claim is submitted to the contracting officer for a final decision. Once the final decision is issued, the contractor

---

30. For a detailed review of this, see Nagle and Lasky, *Federal Government Construction Contracts*, in Federal Bid Protests (Michael A. Branca et al. eds., 2010).

31. Meridian Eng'g Co. v. United States, 885 F.3d 1351 (Fed. Cir. 2018).

32. *See, e.g.*, Ultimate Concrete, LLC v. United States, 2019 WL 156933 (Fed. Cl. 2019).

must decide what to do. For example, if its claim is for $1 million but the contracting officer only allows $300,000, the contractor must decide whether it will accept that amount and forego the rest or it can decide to go further. If it decides to go further, the only two forums to which it can go to are the Board of Contract Appeals or the U.S. Court of Federal Claims. It has 90 days to go to the Board of Contract Appeals or one year to the Court of Federal Claims.[33]

The Federal Dispute clause (FAR 52.233-1, sets forth the requirements).

Disputes (MAY 2014)

(a) This contract is subject to 41 U.S.C. chapter 71, Contract Disputes.

(b) Except as provided in 41 U.S.C. chapter 71, all disputes arising under or relating to this contract shall be resolved under this clause.

(c) Claim, as used in this clause, means a written demand or written assertion by one of the contracting parties seeking, as a matter of right, the payment of money in a sum certain, the adjustment or interpretation of contract terms, or other relief arising under or relating to this contract. However, a written demand or written assertion by the Contractor seeking the payment of money exceeding $100,000 is not a claim under 41 U.S.C. chapter 71 until certified. A voucher, invoice, or other routine request for payment that is not in dispute when submitted is not a claim under 41 U.S.C. chapter 71. The submission may be converted to a claim under 41 U.S.C. chapter 71, by complying with the submission and certification requirements of this clause, if it is disputed either as to liability or amount or is not acted upon in a reasonable time.

(d)(1) A claim by the Contractor shall be made in writing and, unless otherwise stated in this contract, submitted within 6 years after accrual of the claim to the Contracting Officer for a written decision. A claim by the Government against the Contractor shall be subject to a written decision by the Contracting Officer.

(d)(2)(i) The Contractor shall provide the certification specified in paragraph (d)(2)(iii) of this clause when submitting any claim exceeding $100,000.

(ii) The certification requirement does not apply to issues in controversy that have not been submitted as all or part of a claim.

(iii) The certification shall state as follows: "I certify that the claim is made in good faith; that the supporting data are accurate and complete to the best of my knowledge and belief; that the amount requested accurately reflects the

---

33. For a detailed discussion of this, see Laurence Schor & Aaron P. Silberman, Chapter 15, *Equitable Adjustments and Claims,* & Paul A. Varela, Michael M. Suga, and Brian R. Dugdale, Chapter 16, *Litigating with the Federal Government, in* FEDERAL GOVERNMENT CONSTRUCTION CONTRACTS, 3d ed. op cit.

contract adjustment for which the Contractor believes the Government is liable; and that I am authorized to certify the claim on behalf of the Contractor."

(3) The certification may be executed by any person authorized to bind the Contractor with respect to the claim.

(e) For Contractor claims of $100,000 or less, the Contracting Officer must, if requested in writing by the Contractor, render a decision within 60 days of the request. For Contractor-certified claims over $100,000, the Contracting Officer must, within 60 days, decide the claim or notify the Contractor of the date by which the decision will be made.

(f) The Contracting Officer's decision shall be final unless the Contractor appeals or files a suit as provided in 41 U.S.C. chapter 71.

(g) If the claim by the Contractor is submitted to the Contracting Officer or a claim by the Government is presented to the Contractor, the parties, by mutual consent, may agree to use alternative dispute resolution (ADR). If the Contractor refuses an offer for ADR, the Contractor shall inform the Contracting Officer, in writing, of the Contractor's specific reasons for rejecting the offer.

(h) The Government shall pay interest on the amount found due and unpaid from (1) the date that the Contracting Officer receives the claim (certified, if required); or (2) the date that payment otherwise would be due, if that date is later, until the date of payment. With regard to claims having defective certifications, as defined in (FAR) 48 CFR 33.201, interest shall be paid from the date that the Contracting Officer initially receives the claim. Simple interest on claims shall be paid at the rate, fixed by the Secretary of the Treasury as provided in the Act, which is applicable to the period during which the Contracting Officer receives the claim and then at the rate applicable for each 6–month period as fixed by the Treasury Secretary during the pendency of the claim.

(i) The Contractor shall proceed diligently with performance of this contract, pending final resolution of any request for relief, claim, appeal, or action arising under the contract, and comply with any decision of the Contracting Officer.

QUESTIONS

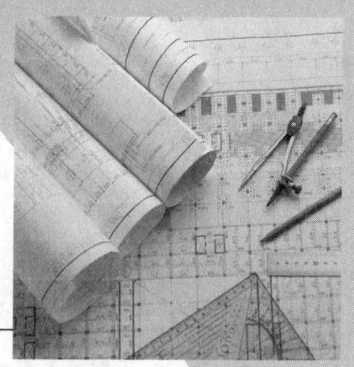

1. A contractor is negotiating with a public contracting officer for a modification on an already awarded contract. The contracting officer is getting ready to retire. The contractor feels that it needs an experienced public official on its staff. Can the contractor open negotiations with the contracting officer while the negotiations on the modification are still pending, and, if so, how? See FAR 3.104.
2. A contractor was terminated for default by a public entity. It is now appealing that termination, but the construction company owner is distraught over the damage to its reputation and wishes to include in the lawsuit a claim for intentional infliction of emotional harm. What problems do you see regarding success of such a claim against a public entity?
3. A contractor is doing dredging work on a lake pursuant to a federal contract with the Army Corps of Engineers. One day the local sheriff arrives at the job trailer and orders a stop to the work. A boat was found drifting on the lake, and they are going to be looking for bodies. Is this a sovereign act? If so, can the contractor claim any relief from the federal government?
4. A contractor is bidding on a federal project to which the Buy American Act will apply. In pricing the steel that will be needed to perform the contract, the contractor discovers that domestic steel cannot be purchased in time to meet the required delivery schedule. Does that justify an exemption to the Buy American Act? Similarly, if the domestic steel was approximately 15 percent more expensive than foreign steel, would that be a justification for waiving the Buy American Act? See FAR 25.204 and regulations cited therein.

CHAPTER 24

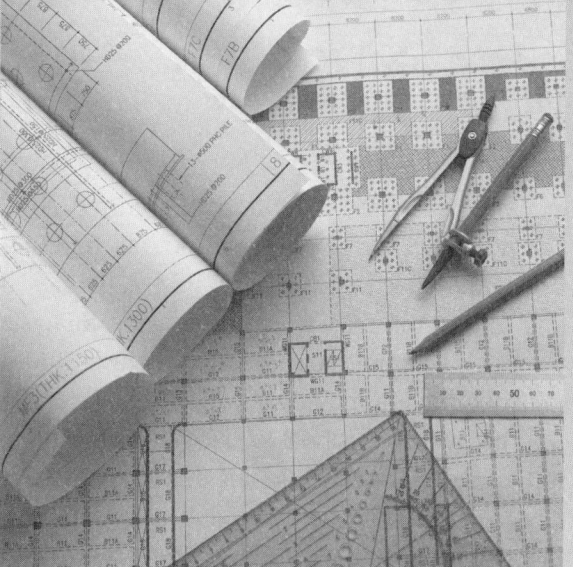

Technological Advances in Construction: Building Information Modeling (BIM) and Related Tools

KIMBERLY A. HURTADO

24.01 INTRODUCTION

A century ago, designs for a construction project were prepared by hand inking onto linen or by using a drafting pencil to mark large sheets of paper using a scaled ruler. Blueprints arrived in the late 1800s. Using lightsensitive sheets to reproduce hand drawn lines on a blue-colored negative plan page, the blueprints alleviated the need for creating multiple copies of plans by hand. In turn, these blueprints were largely replaced in the 1940s by sepia-colored diazo chemical prints. As reproduction technology continued to evolve, xerographic photocopies became common in the 1960s. In the mid-1970s, software for computer-assisted design (CAD) was created, generating electronic two-dimensional (2D) designs that could be read on a computer and then printed onto paper. Designs created with CAD software swiftly supplanted hand drawing of plans, particularly on large commercial projects.

Most recently, a shift has occurred to the use of more sophisticated computer design software known as building information modeling (BIM). Given the speed with which BIM generates three-dimensional (3D) images, and allows for easy visualization and analysis from initial conceptualization through decommissioning of a structure, BIM has rapidly gained popularity in the construction industry.

BIM permits robust collaboration as the project team develops models. Initially, design professionals can share data with their design consultants as design models are prepared and analyzed, comparable to 2D design development. BIM also allows model review between designers and constructors (typically, contractors, subcontractors, and, increasingly, vendors/manufacturers) to coordinate design models electronically with shop and fabrication modeling, rather than manually overlaying 2D plan sheets to make these comparisons. The resulting coordinated models are then shared by designers or constructors with their specialty consultants for sustainability, cost, schedule, civil, and other analyses of models during design development and construction phases. This kind of analysis is difficult, if not impossible, to accomplish without 3D model data. Since these collaborations can occur before construction-ready designs are fully completed, some have raised concerns that legal responsibilities for designs might be impacted, imposing greater risks of liability on parties participating in these collaborative activities than traditional 2D design development.

We looked at the *Spearin* doctrine earlier in this book, which is an owner's implied warranty that plans and specifications prepared by an architect hired by the owner and thereafter delivered to a contractor will be fit for construction. Under this doctrine, the owner (rather than the contractor) bears the risk of the designer's errors or omissions that impair constructability or yield a project that does not perform as intended. This common law rule reflected what, at the time, were well-established roles in a design-bid-build construction process: the owner hired a designer, the designer completed the designs, and the constructor then built the project from those designs. In that process, the contractor had little or no input in the design process. Although the contractor bore some design-related obligations, such as pointing out observed design mistakes and preparing shop drawings, the designer remained responsible for making sure project designs conformed to code requirements and that the plans and specifications were sufficient for the work to be constructed from them.

As other methods of project delivery have evolved, such as design-build and integrated project delivery (IPD), they have softened the strict application of the *Spearin* Doctrine in some jurisdictions on the basis that they permit constructor input during design phase. As a result of these cases, concerns have been raised that the interactive design process possible with BIM might further erode *Spearin*'s comparatively bright-line design responsibilities. For example, given the greater interaction of constructors during model design development, concerns have been raised that designs might be modified without informed consent of the authoring designer.

With BIM, constructors can be given the opportunity to participate actively with designers to resolve conflicts between design and shop model data in joint resolution sessions early in the design process. This can include contractors suggesting design refinements that designers then must determine whether to incorporate into their model. This collaborative process is new enough that the scope of interactive BIM activities can vary widely from project to project. Industry contract forms about BIM describing these collaborations have only recently become commercially available; even more recently, courts have begun issuing common law rulings related to BIM use.[1] As a result of these factors, standards of care for BIM activities have been slow to emerge. Nevertheless, since BIM software offers an unparalleled ability to track model changes, design modifications are difficult to make unbeknownst to the original authoring party. In addition, during resolution of conflicts between design and shop model contributions, authoring designers still control the final content of their own designs and must agree on the solutions implemented to resolve conflicts between the models of others and the authoring designer's own model data. And, most important, upon completion of a design model, the authoring designer still remains responsible to confirm code compliance and design integrity of their entire model before sealing their design for permitting purposes. Given these considerations, although designers can more easily collaborate with constructors using this 3D design medium, each party's responsibilities for the final content of their own model data may not be altered significantly. Architects and engineers will remain responsible for the content of their design models, while subcontractors and suppliers will be responsible for shop, fabrication, and design-build or design-assist systems modeling.

Lawyers likely will be called on to help resolve these issues as BIM use evolves over the next decade or so. As a result, a competent construction lawyer will want a working knowledge of BIM technology. Thus, this chapter provides an overview of basic BIM software and processes, and examines some of the emerging contractual and other legal issues related to BIM use.

---

1. *See* N. Am. Mech., Inc. v. Walsh Constr. Co. II, LLC, 132 F. Supp. 3d 1064 (E.D. Wis. 2015); 3D Imaging Services, LLC v. McLaren, Inc., No. 333100, 2017 WL 3397478 (Mich. Ct. App. Aug. 8, 2017).

24.02 WHAT IS BIM?

BIM is a searchable and easily navigated 3D electronic depiction of a structure or topographic area.[2] The term "BIM" can be used to describe the software that creates a model, the modeling process itself, and also the completed design models that are the end deliverables generated by BIM software.

The National Building Information Model Standard Project Committee of the National Institute of Building Sciences' buildingSMARTalliance®, defines BIM as:

> a digital representation of physical and functional characteristics of a facility. A BIM is a shared knowledge resource for information about a facility forming a reliable basis for decisions during its life-cycle; defined as existing from earliest conception to demolition.
>
> A basic premise of BIM is collaboration by different stakeholders at different phases of the life cycle of a facility to insert, extract, update or modify information in the BIM to support and reflect the roles of that stakeholder.[3]

As a practical matter, BIM represents many things depending on one's perspective:

- Applied to a project, BIM represents information management—data contributed to and shared by all project participants. The goal is to provide right information to the right person at the right time.
- To project participants, BIM represents an interoperable process for project delivery—defining how individual teams work and how many teams work together to conceive, design, build and operate a facility.
- To the design team, BIM represents integrated design—leveraging technology solutions, encouraging creativity, and providing more interdisciplinary feedback to empower a project team.[4]

By comparison, ConsensusDocs® 301 (2016), *Building Information Modeling (BIM) Addendum*, section 2.6, defines BIM as

> the collaborative development of a three-dimensional digital representation that is Intelligent and Parametric, depicting the physical and functional characteristics of a structure or site for use as a shared knowledge resource; it may also include generation of Geometric and non-graphic information, and related

---

2. Civil and topographical models are sometimes referred to as civil information modeling, or CIM.

3. National BIM Standard–United States® (2017); *Frequently Asked Questions About the National BIM Standard–United States*™, https://www.nationalbimstandard.org/faqs#faq1 (last visited Apr. 11, 2019).

4. *Id.*

processes, analysis, and deliverables for use over the lifecycle of the structure or site depicted.[5]

Given the different stakeholders' uses of BIM, definitions of BIM likely will continue to be refined before a consistent, industrywide definition becomes adopted.

Similarly, model development processes are only beginning to be standardized in the construction industry. As a result, while the following discussion explores some of the most common BIM processes and end uses, readers are cautioned that this is a swiftly evolving area of construction technology. They should expect that new processes and software will expand or modify the general articulation of BIM technology presented here. Asking about the BIM software and end uses anticipated to be used on a specific project will be a prudent starting point for a lawyer in order to provide transactional or dispute resolution advice related to BIM.

24.03 HOW BIM WORKS

A. Difference between CAD and BIM

Both CAD and BIM use computer software to depict an electronic, virtual image of a structure or site. With CAD, a designer plots lines that create the shape of a structure and the component systems within it (Figure 24.1). The designer typically prepares 2D plan views (as if looking from above at a cross section of the building), elevations (looking at a vertical face of a building), and details (looking at a smaller part of the building in great detail, often in cross section). CAD can be used to draw an image that appears to be a 3D shape; however, such an image is typically viewable from a single angle or perspective, and is not true 3D BIM, which can be viewed from any vantage point around or inside the virtually created structure.[6]

---

5. ConsensusDocs' definition focuses on three qualities that distinguish BIM objects (which this form contract calls Elements) from those depicted in CAD: First, the model depictions created using BIM software are *Geometric* or using "rectilinear or curvilinear points, lines, and surfaces developed using BIM" as opposed to non-solid geometric modeling—a cube in BIM is a three-dimensional solid object, and not a mere line drawing. They also are *Intelligent*, which means "the imbedded specifications, sizes, material definitions, characteristics, manufacturer properties, identification numbers, and other data describing the attributes and configuration of an Element that are readable directly within the Model," and finally, that they are *Parametric*, that is, "attributes of construction materials, equipment, and assemblies are linked and consistently coordinated and maintained in all Model views and schedules such that a change to a Model Element or other data in any view or schedule is automatically similarly modified in all views and schedules where it appears in the Model." ConsensusDocs® 301 Building Information Modeling (BIM) Addendum, sections 2.25, 2.29, 2.38.

6. ARCHINOVA d.o.o. BIM, Building Information Modeling, http://www.cadtobim.com/what-is-bim.html, (last visited Apr. 11, 2019 5:14 PM).

FIGURE 24.1
CAD and BIM Workflow Comparison[7]

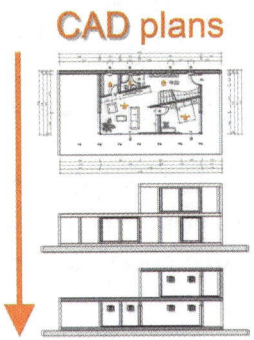
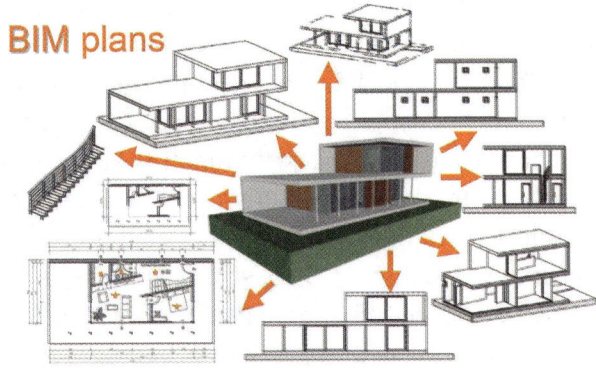

CAD software does not link design data internally. Accordingly, if a building component is modified in one design depiction, such as an elevation, then that same component must be altered manually in every other elevation, plan view, detail, or schedule in the CAD plan set where that same component appears. In addition, analysis of 2D CAD designs prepared by different designers ordinarily has been a manual process—comparing the designs by overlaying two or more paper pages of designs prepared by different designers (for example, comparing architectural and structural engineering for the same area of a structure) on a light table to look for conflicts in the design measurements and layout of building components of each plan.

BIM differs from CAD in three important ways: the 3D models BIM generates are described as being (1) object oriented, (2) intelligent, and (3) parametric. This chapter explores further what these terms mean and the impact of these three unique capabilities.

First, BIM is object oriented. Instead of manually drawing lines to create the shapes of every single feature of a building, BIM uses pre-designed, modifiable classes or families of objects that can be used to quickly populate a 3D model of a structure. These component object families correspond directly to classes of building components found in a typical building, such as walls, windows, doors, columns, roofs, and so on. These template objects are customizable, and the size, quantity, and features of an object can be adapted either by modifying the drawing of the object inserted into a model, or by modifying the accompanying description of the object in a narrative menu.[8] In

---

7. *Id.*

8. It will be interesting to see how BIM software evolves regarding object customization. At present, the ease of populating a model with standard-sized and -configured objects using BIM

addition, many manufacturers provide highly accurate object models for their proprietary software that can be imported into a model to add great accuracy of information about those specific objects.

A second difference between BIM and CAD is that the objects in BIM are intelligent, meaning that they are backed by a database of information about their physical and functional characteristics.[9] Objects in BIM function based on imbedded software rules that control how the objects can behave, as well as providing related information that can be read within the model about the depicted object. For example, a BIM program can have a rule that alerts the user that a door object is being inserted into a model without sufficient clearance for it to swing into a room due to other design elements being in too close a physical proximity to it, with the software automatically generating a warning or requesting an adaptation of the model to address the problem. Each object also can have customized specifications imbedded into its depiction. This can include documentation about decisions made to modify the object as the design develops, and about construction phase requests for information (RFIs) and RFI answers, as well as change requests, change orders, and other important decisions about the object and its configuration in the model design. To access the information, the person using the software simply scrolls over the object in the 3D model, and narrative text box displays will open to further identify the size, shape, configuration, warranty, part number, and other specifications pertinent to that object. Some BIM programs also will allow the user to access relevant contract terms directly, as well as RFI, change order, schedule, and cost documentation related to using hyperlink access to the contracts and other project records simply by scrolling over the object in the model. Effective use of these options requires advance team planning, coordination, and cooperation during project BIM planning and execution.

The third significant difference between BIM and CAD is that many BIM model objects are automatically linked parametrically. This means that when a change is made to such an object in a model, BIM modifies that object and all the components to which the object is connected or related. Such modifications include making an automatic, identical change to the object in each model view, plan, elevation, or schedule in which the object appears. The details of the change also may be recorded within the model's parametric specifications, and typically include the name of the party who makes the

---

software might actually deter aesthetic or substantive design development, or lead to design code compliance concerns where standardized software objects lack features or scaling needed to meet unique local code requirements.

9. *See* ConsensusDocs® 301, sections 2.6, 2.38.

change, date and time of modification, and, if desired, an explanation of the reason for the change. This allows for multiple variations of a design to be generated quickly and cost effectively to evaluate best value[10] options and to visualize aesthetic options for refining the configuration of a structure early in the design process.

B. The BIM Life Cycle Process

BIM is a tool that can be meaningfully used throughout the life cycle of a project. Such use starts with initial concept depictions to implement and evaluate designs. Uses continue during the construction phase and aid in commissioning of the completed structure, then in operating and maintaining the building, all the way through final decommissioning and recycling of a structure's component materials. At each of these phases, BIM has a range of different possible uses rapidly increasing in number and complexity as this technology evolves. For the lawyer seeking to advise a client in using this tool, the goal typically is not to undertake as many BIM activities as possible in each phase, but to assist in selecting the most useful combination of BIM models and analyses to enhance the life cycle goals of the specific project. To do this effectively, a lawyer needs to understand typical BIM uses in each of these life cycle phases.

1. Design Coordination and Analysis

A primary use of 3D BIM is for design conceptualization, preparation, coordination, and analysis.

Very often the BIM tools used for initial design visualization of a structure will have limited scaling abilities (i.e., they are not the equivalent of 2D drawings drawn to accurate scaled dimensions). Instead, these tools quickly develop 3D images designed to help explore overall configuration, material choices, and to provide visual images—for example, to assist in securing funding for or early marketing of a project.[11]

---

10. In a best value analysis, the design is reviewed to select the most useful features and systems possibly to be acquired given the total project budget available. This analysis can be undertaken considering only initial construction cost, but increasingly with BIM, it is broadened to consider the life cycle cost of various options that might be incorporated into the design. In other words, the cost of operation and maintenance of various components are measured along with construction cost to select features best for the project.

11. SketchUp®, www.sketchup.com, and RhinoBIM®, www.rhinoBIM.com, are two types of BIM software that quickly generate visualizations of design ideas but typically do not produce detailed, scalable designs that are dimensionally accurate such that construction could occur using them.

Typically, design model development starts with preparation of a conceptual or massing model. Massing models look a lot like stacks of children's building blocks and are used to depict the overall configuration of the 3D structure (Figure 24.2). Non-scaled BIM conceptualizing tools[12] are again typically used for this visualization and permit exploration of proof of concept analysis (i.e., a demonstration that a design concept is feasible). This kind of massing model also can be used to make early sustainability analysis of the structure, particularly modeling wind and thermal loading conditions resulting from overall configuration of the structure.

Figure 24.2
Example of SketchUp® Massing Model[13]

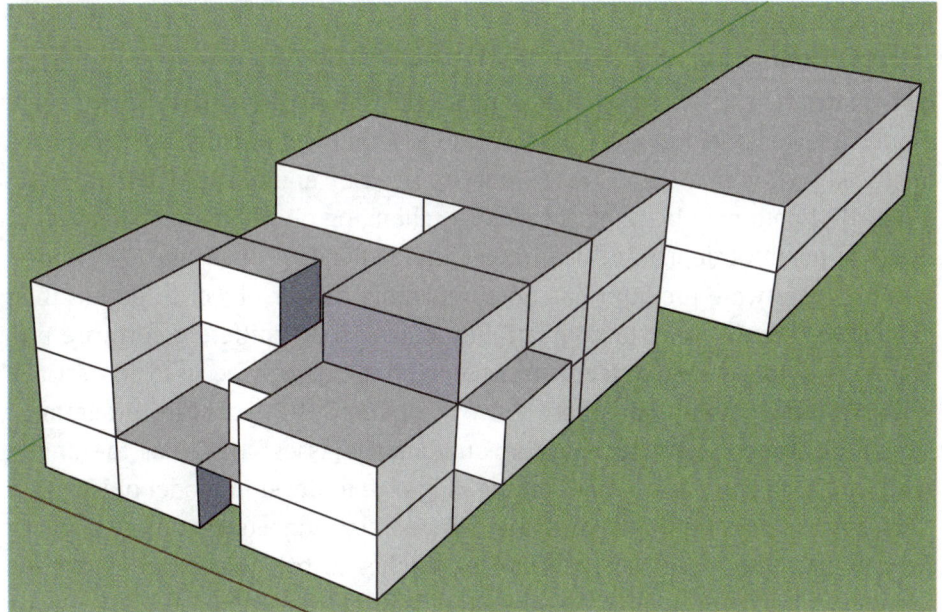

---

12. Design graphical algorithm editors like Grasshopper, www.grasshopper3d.com, Dreamweaver, www.adobe.com/Dreamweaver, and Dynamo, www.dynamobim.org, aid in editing BIM geometry intuitively and efficiently to optimize preliminary visualization and development of the structure.

13. Chris Dizon, *Making Your Models More Useful with Trelligence Affinity*, SKETCHUP BLOG (Dec. 8, 2011), https://blog.sketchup.com/sketchupdate/making-your-models-more-useful-trelligence-affinity.

Some massing model data can be uploaded directly, or otherwise is recreated, using scaled BIM software to prepare an initial architectural design model.[14] The resulting schematic or design development level architectural model and its associated data then may be used by other design disciplines, such as structural, civil, mechanical, electrical, plumbing, and fire protection engineering, as well as interior, security, landscape, or other specialty designers, to develop their specific discipline's companion design models. This is an interactive feedback process unlike the more linear 2D CAD design process where each design discipline completes its own drawings separately and exchanges them when completed. A preliminary architectural design model might include architectural design at 20 percent complete, structural design at 30 percent, and mechanical design at a 10 percent level of development, depending on the variables that need to be analyzed to make evaluations of the structure to refine the designs.

Most BIM software is proprietary, and each software company creates its own underlying software coding to make the software function. As a result, model data generated in one BIM software program will not always be depicted identically when that data is read in or modified by another BIM software program. BIM data may be repurposed (e.g., changing object shapes, finishes, or levels of detail of depiction) or dropped altogether (e.g., missing components because a software program has no comparable tool or object to permit their depiction) due to a lack of compatibility between two different software programs. To address this concern, translator programs can be used to assist in bridging programming gaps between two or more BIM software programs.[15] Designers also can use Information Foundation Classes® (IFCs) as the underlying common computer programming language to develop model objects.[16] A third alternative, often used on larger commercial projects that merit the cost investment, is to write custom software patches to bridge gaps in expression between software programs. These methods all help to enhance BIM software interoperability (i.e., the ability for data from one BIM software program to be accessed and modified more accurately by other BIM software programs when models are combined for analysis or conflict resolution).

---

14. For an excellent overview of BIM architectural modeling process, *see* Chuck Eastman, et al., *BIM Handbook: A Guide to Building Information Modeling for Owners, Managers, Designers, Engineers and Contractors* (2d ed. 2011).

15. Hummingbird® OpenText, https:\\opentext.com, is an example of a translator program that will help to depict an object so it is accurately read by multiple BIM software programs used together on a single project.

16. For further explanation of ifcXML object formatting, see http://www.buildingsmart-tech.org/specifications/ifc-overview.

Once individual design models from various design disciplines are completed, the design models can be joined together. The purpose is to make federated models to coordinate and analyze design information before creating the final construction model from which the structure will be built.[17] Instead of comparison of design features in a manual light table overlay analysis, many BIM software programs will provide the means to undertake automated coordination review and interference resolution—identifying hard clashes, where two objects have been designed in the same physical space, and soft clashes, where objects are not physically impinging on each other but violate code requirements or other spatial needs (like having enough space in front of a vent so air can be drawn efficiently through it). This kind of design coordination to eliminate conflicts among design discipline models is considered the low hanging fruit of BIM and is the most typical type of analysis of completed models using this 3D imaging tool.

Where designers' contract terms regarding intellectual property rights and the scope of permitted reliance on model data permit the exchange, design models can be joined for analysis with trade contractor shop models—models created to depict how the contractor will complete its work consistent with the full design model and specifications. If sufficient scalable detail is depicted in early design models, this detail also can be used by manufacturers to develop fabrication models depicting production specifications for building components, such as steel beams, windows, or stair railings. Legal counsel can assist at the beginning of a project to create appropriate contract licensing and scalability requirements for each stage of model development by articulating when accurate dimensioning should be included in design model data. This, in turn, can result in shop and fabrication models being reliably generated from design model data without re-depicting architectural or structural model data from scratch, and avoid concerns that design models without sufficient scaled detail are inappropriately used for shop and fabrication modeling.

Another issue that must be considered in planning for or contracting about BIM use is the granularity, or level of scaled detail, of a particular model at various points in the design process. A very high level of detail can be included in a full design model, making the model quite unwieldy to share or modify due to the large size of the software files and huge amount of data that must be exchanged. To address the need for models to be of a size reasonably

---

17. Examples of federation software include, for example, Autodesk Navisworks, www.autodesk.com/products/navisworks; Bentley Navigator, www.bentley.com/en/products/brands/navigator; Autodesk BIM 360 Glue, https://knowledge.autodesk.com/support/bim-360-glue; and Trimble Tekla BIMsight, www.teklabimsight.com.

functional for updating as designs evolve, design model data can be segmented into a series of separate smaller models.

In addition, detail models are often created that depict discrete areas of a structure, such as a wall section, roof penetration of a chimney, window assembly, or other parts of the 3D design with even greater granularity than the design model. For example, the work of multiple trade contractors related to a single building area can be depicted by color coding various aspects of the model so coordination of trades and their work sequence can be planned virtually before actual construction on site begins.

Data also can be copied from a BIM model and used to generate 2D CAD drawings. This is typically undertaken because many jurisdictions currently do not allow BIM to be submitted for governmental design approvals or building permits. Lawyers should anticipate that they may be asked to negotiate with government officials to allow BIM data to be substituted for CAD or hard copy plan sets, helping their clients demonstrate that model data includes all of the information typically found in 2D plan depictions and more. Where that is not yet possible, care should be taken in contract documents to identify whether the 3D model or the 2D plans control during construction, in case of conflict or missing data between the two.

Code check programs[18] also can be used to analyze two or more models joined or federated together, undertaking code analysis to review model data prior to finalizing a construction model from which the structure will be built. By incorporating code analysis into the model development process, errors can be uncovered early, allowing for more flexible and cost-effective corrective adaptation during the design phase, rather than the more limited options available when code conflicts are discovered in the field after construction has commenced. For example, if the code requirements for increased size of an HVAC conduit are discovered only after the structural steel beams have been erected on the project site, very limited and costly solutions are available to correct this issue. If identified in a virtual code check analysis, a wider array of options for cost efficiently addressing the problem may be possible.

The BIM data of federated models also can be merged to further examine the attributes of the virtual structure, providing cost, schedule, and environmental/sustainability analysis as the model is being developed.

---

18. Solibri Model Checker®, https:\\solibri.com, among other software programs, can evaluate a model design for code compliance, such as confirming slab thickness, door, window, fire rated wall assembly, and other code requirements.

2. 4D (Schedule) and 5D (Cost) Analysis

Once a 3D model is developed, the two most common types of analyses undertaken using model graphic information are 4D modeling, creating a construction schedule from the model data, and 5D modeling, providing quantity analysis or cost estimating of model components. This 4D and 5D data can be generated starting at initial design concept modeling (though limitations exist on accuracy if using BIM software that produces non-scaled 3D depictions). Once scaled modeling has been commenced to produce dimensionally accurate modeling, these 4D and 5D programs may be used throughout design, construction, and operation phases to assist in confirming budget, as-built schedule development, and cost compliance, including operation and maintenance costing and refurbishment scheduling of the completed structure.

Sequencing construction activities, a major element of construction planning, can be enhanced with BIM data. Typical project scheduling in the United States currently uses a critical path method (CPM) schedule to create a time line for the various aspects of work necessary to construct the project. CPM scheduling depicts dependencies between critical construction activities (for example, the foundation must be constructed before walls can be erected, and walls must be in place before the roof can be installed); however, CPM does not provide a link between space and time. 4D modeling, by comparison, can generate a version of the model that depicts the entire construction sequence, or any component portion, visually—like watching the building built in slow motion.[19] From this BIM sequencing analysis, refinements in the arrangement of work activities can be determined, resulting in potentially significant cost and time savings to the project.

5D BIM analysis can be as simple as identifying quantities of materials, such as the number of a specific manufacturer's double hung windows of a certain size in the building on a narrative schedule. This 5D analysis is increasingly available as a part of the software that generates the model itself or can be derived from data extrapolated from the model and exported to a separate software program, such as an accounting spreadsheet.[20] More complex linked 5D software can provide a detailed cost estimate of all the building components depicted in a model that will be parametrically modified as the structure

---

19. Examples of 4D modelers for BIM-based scheduling include, for example, Synchro PRO, www.synchroltd.com; Trimble Vico, www.vicosoftware.com/5D-BIM-Workflow-in-Vico-Office; Kalloc Fuzor, www.kalloctech.com; Bentley Navigator, www.bentley.com/en/products/brands/navigator.

20. Microsoft Excel®, https://products.office.com/en-us/excel, is the most commonly used external spreadsheet for 5D analysis in the U.S. construction industry.

evolves, for example, delete a window from the model, and the associated window schedule will automatically adjust to show one less in total quantity; similarly, the extrapolated construction budget spreadsheet will be reduced by the cost of the unit price for that window.

3. *Sustainability Analysis*

One of the most highly useful tools for refining a BIM model is software that analyzes the virtual structure to explore sustainability or environmental goals (Figures 24.3 and 24.4). Sustainability analysis can examine buildings as a whole or their component systems (typically, the performance of HVAC, electrical, plumbing, and building envelope). These tools help reduce the modeled structure's negative impact to the natural environment (reducing air pollution, eliminating or reducing waste, and avoiding contaminating water, for example) and the unnecessary depletion of natural resources (such as using passive energy sources, using more efficient fixtures and equipment, reuse of recycled materials, and minimizing material waste) to support long-term ecological benefits. The goal of this sustainability analysis is to limit negative cost and environmental impacts that construction and the built structure may have and to improve the health of the occupants using the structure.

Figure 24.3
Environmental and Heat-Loss Analysis[21]

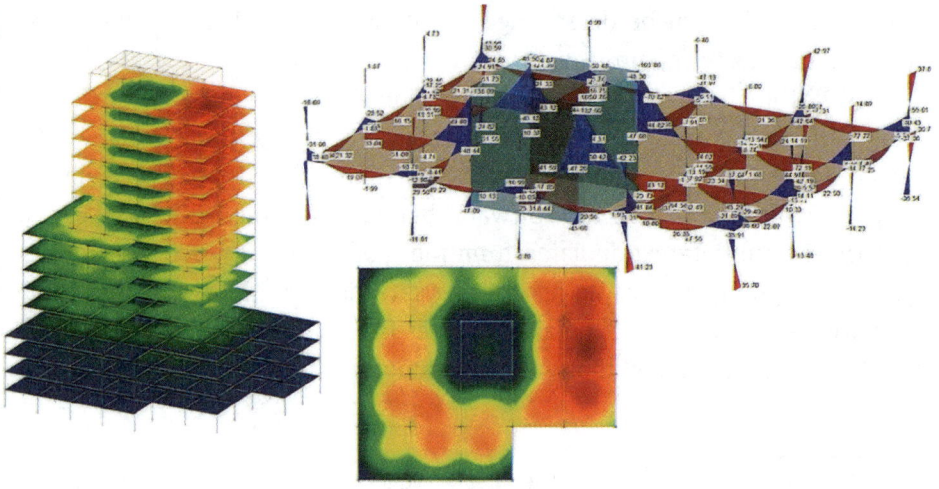

---

21. Aionix Integrated Technology Solutions, https://www.aionix.org/copy-of-bim-coordination.

**Figure 24.4
Solar Analysis**[22]

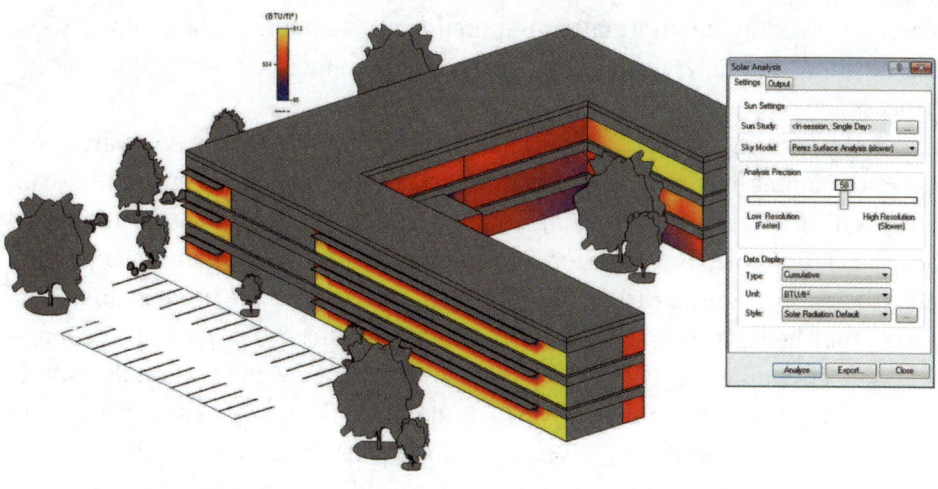

A sustainable construction project can have higher up-front installation and equipment costs than a non-sustainable construction project, but typically has lower operation costs; therefore, the life cycle cost for a sustainable project is often lower overall, supporting use of sustainable design analysis. BIM can assist in evaluating sustainability options for the project and can aid in reducing up-front costs associated with a sustainability analysis through an integrative design process. This process enables the owner, designers, constructors, and other key players to identify and eliminate overlapping relationships, services, and design or operation redundancies that have an impact on the sustainability of the structure. This, in turn, can increase construction and operation efficiencies and reduce overall cost as a result.

The most effective decisions related to sustainable design of a building facility are often made in the early conceptual and schematic design stages. Before the advent of BIM, energy and performance analysis had to be conducted after construction documents were produced. This lack of integration early in the design process led to an inefficient process of retroactively modifying the designs to meet sustainable performance criteria.[23] BIM can collect all

---

22. Autodesk Expands Software Portfolio for Designing High Performance Buildings and Infrastructure, http://inthefold.autodesk.com/in_the_fold/2014/10/autodesk-expands-software-portfolio-for-designing-high-performance-buildings-and-infrastructure.html.

23. A. Schueter & F. Thessling, *Building Information Model Based Energy/Exergy Performance Assessment in Early Design Stages*, 18(2) Automation in Construction 153–63 (2009).

the data provided by designers and constructors into a single federated model. This allows sustainability analysis to be performed throughout the design process, starting at the massing model phase. In turn, this facilitates a reduction in costs by "making the information required for sustainable design, analysis and certification routinely available simply as a byproduct of the standard design process."[24]

A fast-growing group of proprietary sustainability analysis software products are coming into the construction market. Still others are created by construction industry groups seeking to support sustainable goals on a national scale. For example, Building for Environmental and Economic Sustainability (BEES) is a program assisting designers, constructors, and product manufacturers that helps in the selection of building products that are both economical and environmentally preferred. BEES was built by the National Institute of Standards and Technology (NIST) Building and Fire Research Laboratory with support from the U.S. EPA Environmentally Preferable Purchasing Program. Using this software, "[a]ll stages in the life of a product are analyzed: raw material acquisition, manufacture, transportation, installation, use, and recycling and waste management."[25] This creates the ability for true life cycle analysis of a model.

Sustainability assessment tools also exist to provide green building guidance and assessment of environmental performance for new and existing buildings.[26] These online question- or inspection-based assessment tools have environmental ratings or point systems measuring a variety of factors that impact the overall sustainability of a project, including project management, site utilization, energy and water consumption, recycled materials and resources, air quality and indoor environment, and other sustainability factors. The certification of a building using these tools often starts with an initial analysis of construction model data before design is finalized and construction commences (Figure 24.5).

---

24. Autodesk Inc., *Building Information Modeling for Sustainable Design* (2005), http://images.autodesk.com/latin_am_main/files/bim_for_sustainable_design_oct08.pdf.

25. The National Institute of Standards and Technology, BEES Online, https://ws680.nist.gov/Bees/(A(zWnm_7Qn1QEkAAAAMmUwOTE1NzEtYTAwYS00MTUxLWE2OTMtMjNjZmZmZTY1MDBlxZwmGB1Ao7CFQCs5U09F9gxn_c41))/default.aspx.

26. *See, e.g.*, Green Building Initiative Green Globes® Design™, www.thegbi.org; US Green Building Council's *LEED* Certification program, https://new.usgbc.org/leed; and International Living Future Institute Living Building Challenge Certificate, https://living-future.org/lbc/certification.

Figure 24.5
An Example of a Sustainability Certification Process: Green Globes®

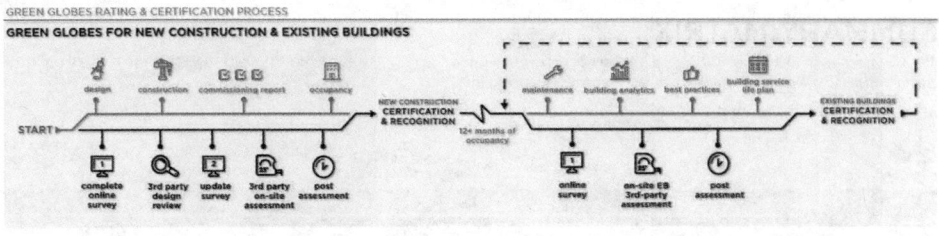

Beyond specifying energy saving appliances and adding individual green building features to a building, some projects use BIM to achieve net zero energy usage; these buildings generate on site all the energy they need for their operation. Even more advanced is regenerative building design. Regenerative buildings integrate into their natural environment and improve the surrounding environment by actively contributing to restoring surrounding plant habitats and wildlife. One example of regenerative certification is the International Living Future Institute's℠ Living Building Challenge (LBC) (Figure 24.6).[27] LBC focuses on reducing a building's energy and water footprint such that the building generates a net positive production. In other words, to achieve this certification, a building's onsite energy and clean water production must exceed the building's usage. The certification program is comprised of seven performance areas, called Petals, which are subdivided into Imperatives. LBC certification requires fulfillment of all Imperatives associated with the project type. The certification process requires a 12-month performance analysis, under which the project will undergo a preliminary and final audit prior to certification, to prove compliance with certification requirements. BIM is a critical tool throughout this and other certification processes, evaluating building performance to refine sustainable performance of the structure during design phase, and then again, to confirm that building performance meets or exceeds planned goals during operation of the completed structure.

Lawyers may be asked to assist in preparing certification applications, as well as handling appeals to certifying agencies, like LBC and the U.S. Green Building Council, to challenge denial of certification or failure to achieve specific performance levels. Use of BIM modeling can help to illustrate planned sustainability goals or compliance with certification requirements in such instances.

---

27. The Living Building Challenge, https://living-future.org/lbc/basics/.

**Figure 24.6
LBC Petal Matrix**

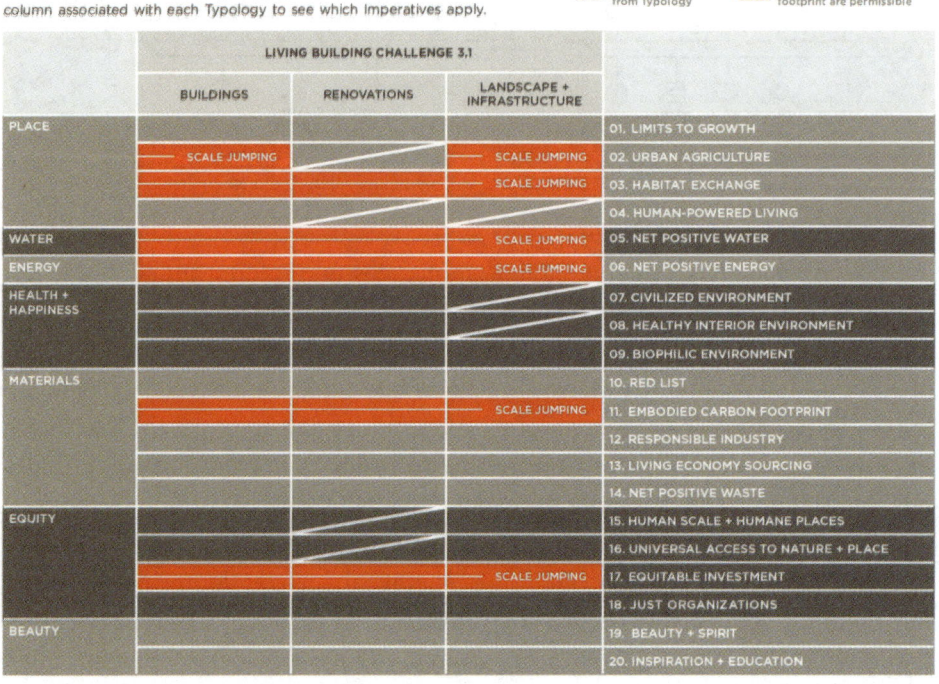

Still other available environmental analysis can be undertaken using proprietary software designed to quickly convert conceptual design models into richly analytical energy models, thus permitting integrated whole building energy analysis.[28] These software tools make it possible to continuously conduct energy and carbon sampling and to compare performance of design alternatives, allowing for more informed decisions early in design development when changes are least expensive. Typical energy analysis software may include web-based climate and solar data, energy and carbon production analysis, and provide building performance simulations (testing virtually how the building will perform based on historical data for local seismic, wind, and weather conditions). These same programs can be used again during operation of the structure to compare planned versus actual energy performance of a designed building, and allow for adjustment of building systems to meet sustainability goals.

---

28. *See, e.g., Autodesk® Revit® Architecture* and *Autodesk® Revit® MEP.*

Designers also can use BIM data to create designs that mitigate risks caused by changing environmental conditions. The goal of such resilient design is to create "an individual building or an entire community to outlast whatever may come, be it floods, fires, wind or a drastic economic downturn."[29] In order to attain this, resilient model design incorporates the surrounding community or geological data into the overall design, acknowledging the interdependencies between a building and its surrounding community.[30] Resilient design modeling also can be used to create structures better responsive to periodic weather changes.[31]

4. Construction Phase BIM

BIM continues to be useful during the construction phase of a project in the following ways, to name just a few uses: as a training tool to demonstrate work sequence and quality requirements; to confirm compliance with project schedules, including providing real-time sequencing correction to them; and to continue monitoring project costs as they are being incurred, adjusting project budget data as changes are made to the project.

For example, construction details derived from model data can be extracted from full design models during the construction phase to develop sequenced training simulations. These static detail models can depict quality control requirements, break up work assignments by color-coding model objects by trade, and then be run through an animation scheduler to depict a virtual building of the detail work. This (1) permits assignment of responsibility for various aspects of the work, and (2) communicates to trade contractors a preferred order for sequencing work activities.

Safety planning can also be developed from 4D applications that group model data into discrete work sequences. Such planning includes using BIM for ingress/egress site logistics, construction site waste management, and material RFID/smart tagging to permit just-in-time delivery of materials to work areas.

---

29. Aline Althen, *Durable Design*, USGBC+, http://plus.usgbc.org/durable-design (last visited Apr. 12, 2019 6:38 AM).

30. For instance, the Swenson Civil Engineering building at the University of Minnesota at Duluth was designed expressly taking into consideration its ecological surroundings by incorporating storm water management because the site drained directly into a protected trout stream. The design included "wooden scuppers that direct rainwater into French drains and an underground storage system and permeable paving and vegetated roofs [that] retain 90 percent of its stormwater." KJ Fields, *The 2012 Evergreen Awards: James I. Swenson Civil Engineering Building*, Architect, Architect Magazine (Oct. 17, 2012), https://www.architectmagazine.com/awards/the-2012-evergreen-awards-james-i-swenson-civil-engineering-building-1_o.

31. A building in San Francisco, 181 Fremont Tower, for example, was designed "to contend with possible seismic activity" and to allow for immediate re-entry after an earthquake. *Id.*

In addition to permitting cost-effective production of shop models, and if BIM is sufficiently detailed, a manufacturer can produce fabrication designs and 3D printing templates for building components directly from model data. This can generate significant cost savings for a project when modeling is adequately sequenced and scaled to permit this use.[32]

5. *Facility Management BIM*

Undertaking facility operation and management of the completed construction (FM) from an as-built 3D model is sometimes called 6D BIM.[33] The information needed for operation and maintenance of building equipment and systems, and their related warranties, all can be imbedded in the 3D model—rather than creating shelves of three-ring binders containing the same information in paper form. Scroll over an object in a model to which this data has been added (for example, a water heater) and an information text box can identify maintenance requirements, confirm quantities of attic stock for repair, and provide warranty terms and other data useful in the day-to-day operation of the equipment.

These FM programs can provide alerts that are static; at a fixed interval, they send an e-mail message advising about maintenance needed. Model data also can be tied to physical sensors in the building's equipment and systems to provide active monitoring alerts. When an event triggering a sensor occurs, an alert is sent in the 3D model system. For example, a BIM FM model can report a sensored plumbing pipe is leaking; a painted surface has deteriorated to a minimal thickness that requires repainting; an HVAC unit is not functioning to achieve planned energy savings; or a secure door has been accessed by someone who lacks an authorization code for its use. BIM data also can be imported into furniture, fixture, and equipment asset spreadsheets in electronic management systems such as Construction-Operations Building Information Exchange, or COBie,[34] as well as tools that list building components of the structure itself and its built-in equipment, like specifications of electrical, mechanical, plumbing, fire protection, and security systems.

---

32. *See, e.g.*, American Steel Institute software, www.autodesk.com/products/advance-steel/overview.

33. The 6D concept is a term used most frequently in Europe. *See, e.g.*, RIBA, www.architecture.com. Examples of facility management platforms include, for example, FM Systems, fmsystems.com; Autodesk 360 OPS, www.autodesk.com/products/bim-360-ops; Ecodomus FM, ecodomus.com; and Trimble® Manhattan™.

34. *See* Bill East, *Construction-Operations Building Information Exchange (COBIE)*, WBDG (last updated Oct. 6, 2016), https://www.wbdg.org/resources/construction-operations-building-information-exchange-cobie.

6. Archiving

Models of an entire multistory structure can result in huge computer files, particularly when highly scaled, and even when segmented by building, floor, section details or other subdivisions of the building. Preservation of records of models at various points of design development and construction, and the ability to read those files later after the building is in active operation, are both necessary. Thus, an important aspect of BIM modeling is the periodic archiving of models (1) during their development, (2) at completion of construction to document the "as-built" structure, and (3) as remodeling and modification of the completed structure occur later during the life of the building. Prudent counsel will help their clients include contract terms that assign BIM archiving responsibilities during critical points during design development, as well as after turnover of the completed structure to the project owner at completion of construction. This may include model hand-off from designers to constructors during the construction phase, and again from constructors to project owner during operation and maintenance of the completed facility.

24.04 BIM CONTRACTING

One of the keys to successful BIM implementation is that everyone who will deliver model content or use BIM on the project needs to agree on shared terms relating to its use. As a result, BIM contract provisions are very often prepared in the form of an exhibit or addendum that can be attached to each of the contracts for parties that contribute to or use BIM at any point in the life cycle of the structure. At a minimum, designers that produce models; consultants that develop 4D, 5D, sustainability, or other analyses; contractors that create shop models or construction analyses of the completed construction model; and owner/end users, all should have terms in their contracts regarding their obligations about BIM. Currently, the terms of a BIM addendum often are developed by the lead designer and owner, or general contractor/CM and owner, and everyone else on the project team inherits that same addendum when they later are retained to work on the project.

A. BIM Contract Forms

Several construction industry contract forms are available as a starting point for developing contract terms related to 3D modeling requirements and deliverables.

1. AIA Building Information Modeling and Digital Data Exhibit

The American Institute of Architects (AIA) E203™–2013, Building Information Modeling and Digital Data Exhibit ("Exhibit"), is an agreement that establishes requirements for the development, use, transmission, and exchange of digital data for a project. This Exhibit allows experienced BIM users to articulate unique protocols and procedures for BIM data use. Further details consistent with the Exhibit then are delineated in the AIA G202–2013, Project Building Information Modeling Protocol form (the "AIA BIM Protocol Attachment").

2. AIA BIM Protocol Attachment

The AIA BIM Protocol Attachment is one of a group of addenda developed by AIA related to electronic conveyance of project information. The fill-in-the-blank terms of the BIM Protocol Attachment presume the contracting parties already have knowledge about and can meaningfully articulate how the models developed with BIM will be used, including articulating the processing sequence by which project models will be created for a particular project.

The AIA Attachment form includes a highly useful BIM Protocol Model Element Table. The Model Element Table provides detailed assignment of modeling responsibilities among project team members, defines milestones in design development, and delineates deliverables from specific project team members. It assigns responsibility for every Model Element by designating a Model Element Author (MEA) and articulates the various stages in the design and construction process by Level of Development (LOD).[35] Prudent legal counsel should have a working understanding of all of these modeling concepts when assisting clients to complete this contract form.

First, each Model Element is classified using CSI UniFormat® classifications, breaking down the component parts of the structure into portions assigned to various designers and engineers.[36] This classification serves as a consistent reference tool for analysis, evaluation, and monitoring during the feasibility, planning, and design stages of buildings. UniFormat® classifications are organized

---

35. For AIA, LODs are equivalent to CAD-related design levels: Massing/Programmatic Concept (Level 100), Schematic (Level 200), Design Development (Level 300), Construction Documents (Level 400) and As Built designs (Level 500). As BIM process becomes more standardized, these levels have been seen by some as being somewhat artificial, so parties sometimes sculpt new phases of design by articulating partial Levels, like Level 350 for the process of comparing the full design model with constructor shop modeling.

36. UniFormat™ (2010), which is published by Construction Specifications Institute and Construction Specifications Canada, https://www.csiresources.org/practice/standards/uniformat, is one of several industry nomenclature tools that help to uniformly name models and their component elements.

around the physical parts of a facility (called systems), and assemblies (known as functional elements). The classifications are organized into five categories of construction information separated by their special functions. These functions include nine categories in five hierarchical levels. UniFormat® is divided into eight main categories, including A: substructure; B: shell; C: interiors; D: services; E: equipment and furnishings; F: special construction and demolition; G: building site work; and Z: general.

The LOD identified for each Model Element in the Attachment is based on completeness and scalability needs of model data at each phase of model development. Currently, LODs are organized in the AIA G202 into five model progression phases. They include:

- 100 Conceptual Design
- 200 Generic Placeholders
- 300 Specific Assemblies
- 400 Detailed Assemblies
- 500 As Built

LOD 100 includes overall building massing indicative of area, height, volume, location, and orientation. LOD 100 may be modeled in three dimensions or represented by other narrative data. At the LOD 100 stage, initial analysis may be conducted pertaining to the whole building, such as volume, building orientation, and estimated cost per square foot.

LOD 200 is roughly comparable to the 2D schematic design phase. The model includes generalized systems or assemblies with approximate quantities, size, shape, location, and orientation. Analysis in LOD 200 may include more detailed information of selected systems and can also include generalized performance criteria.

LOD 300 models specific assemblies that are accurate in terms of quantity, size, shape, location, and orientation. Construction documents and shop modeling may be created from LOD 300 model data, and analysis at this level may include simulations of specific building elements and anticipated systems performance.[37]

LOD 400 models provide further design detail of specific assemblies that are accurate in terms of size, shape, location, quantity, and orientation, with complete fabrication, assembly, and scaled detailing information. LOD 400 is considered suitable for fabrication modeling and construction assembly in the field. LOD 400 is roughly equivalent to construction-ready 2D CAD, but may

---

37. BIMForum, *Level of Development Specification Guide* (2017), http://bimforum.org/wp-content/uploads/2017/11/LOD-Spec-2017-Guide_2017-11-06-1.pdf.

include particularly detailed information to allow fabrication, or pre-fabricated components, to be created directly from model data.

LOD 500 is the final LOD level, representing the as-built conditions of the constructed project. Analysis of LOD 500 model data is typically undertaken for maintenance and operations of the constructed project and for demonstration of compliance with energy modeling or other sustainability goals set for the project.

Although some disagreement exists in the industry about the need or utility of doing so, BIM planning can include variants on the core five levels, assigning them names such as LOD 350, for example. This extension of AIA's LOD 300 was created by BIM Forum to describe a phase of coordination of the design model(s) with shop modeling prepared by contractors and subcontractors to resolve conflicts among them virtually, an activity not part of the archetypal 2D CAD Design-Bid-Build process.

The Model Element Table is further subdivided by Milestones—creating flexibility for different design disciplines to be at different LODs at the time of a specific Milestone where their models may be federated for review and analysis.

3. C-DOCs Building Information Modeling (BIM) Addendum

The ConsensusDocs® (C-DOCs) 301 BIM Addendum[38] is another construction industry form available for those preparing contract documents to address BIM rights and obligations. This form covers six main areas of BIM activities: how the BIM Addendum relates to other contract documents; definitions unique to modeling; the selection and scope of duties of the BIM Manager[39]; development of a BIM Execution Plan,[40] including BIM uses and deliverables by life cycle phase; risk allocation and insurance requirements related to BIM development; and intellectual property rights related to Model[41] development and use.

---

38. ConsensusDocs® 301 Building Information Modeling (BIM) Addendum, https://www.consensusdocs.org/.

39. A BIM Manager is "the Project Participant or parties responsible for the information management program for the Project." ConsensusDocs® 301 section 2.8.

40. A BIM Execution Plans is "a plan that enumerates the goals, implementation processes, metrics, and deliverables that will be used to develop BIM for the Project, which also may be referred to as a PxP or project execution plan." ConsensusDocs® 301 section 2.7.

41. A Model is "an electronic, three-dimensional representation of building Elements representing solid objects with true-to-scale Geospatial relationships and dimensions, which may include additional attribute information, or data, and 4D, 5D, sustainability, or other analyses." ConsensusDocs® 301 section 2.35.

The detailed information in the C-DOCs BIM Addendum form is intended to function, in part, as a tool to help educate project owners about BIM activities that may possibly benefit them, providing lists of possible BIM services and activities that may be selected. Much of the BIM execution planning revolves around identifying those particular activities that will generate enhanced value to the specific project.

Article 3 of the *Addendum* describes the role of the BIM Manager, including oversight and day-to-day management of BIM development, which, in turn, includes development of protocols for the exchange of electronic model data. This typically includes coordinating necessary training, system access, security, and archiving activities. The BIM Manager typically also helps the project team determine how to address any interoperability challenges identified as a result of multiple disciplines using different software programs to generate their respective model data.

The heart of the BIM Addendum is Article 4, which explains an overall process and modeling content that will be included in the parties' BIM Execution Plan. The four-step process described in this article is intended to foster use of BIM as a full life cycle tool, from initial conceptualization through design, construction, commissioning and turnover operation and maintenance, and in eventual decommissioning of a structure at the end of its useful life.[42] The associated charts included with this Addendum focus in considerable detail on as-built model uses for operation and maintenance of the completed structure using BIM.

Once end uses are determined, and a process for completing desired modeling and analyses is completed, Article 4 addresses a thorough list of technology considerations to confirm the necessary infrastructure to support BIM development and subsequent as-built uses.[43]

Finally, as the insurance industry comes to appreciate the risks unique to modeling projects, new forms of insurance protection for BIM activities are being offered. These BIM coverages are reflected in Article 5 of the Addendum.[44] This is another area where lawyers can expect rapid evolution of available coverages, so research at the time of contract development for the specific project as to options for BIM insurance coverages will be important.

---

42. ConsensusDocs® 301 Building Information Modeling (BIM) Addendum, section 4.4.
43. *Id.* section 4.6.
44. *Id.* section 5.8.

B. Assessing Contract Risks

When assessing the risks of employing BIM and developing appropriate contract language for its use, answers to the following six crucial questions are key to developing BIM contract terms.

1. What are the end purposes the model(s) will serve?

Determining the end use(s) of virtual modeling is instrumental to assessing project risk, as well as to assigning contract rights and responsibilities. BIM can consist of simple 3D visualization depictions or be sufficiently detailed to permit multiple, extremely complex design analyses. Modeling can be used as a simple cross-check to detect design conflicts in 2D drawings, or modeling can be used comprehensively in a life cycle analysis tool that includes reliance on model data before and after completion of construction to address ongoing operation, maintenance, and environmental sustainability issues. BIM intended for fabrication, costing, and scheduling purposes will require considerable modeling detail, whereas a model intended solely for production of architectural designs will necessitate quite another, less complex level of completeness.

More than merely determining the scope of the model and its deliverables, the careful contract writer also will use this inquiry to confirm the level of reliance that can be placed on model data by the parties using the model at various intervals, and ask the parties to set LODs for each phase of model development. Where the model is not highly detailed or scalable, provisions for separately reconfirming quantity takeoff from the model and similar considerations should be incorporated into the parties' contract obligations.

2. What is the schedule for deliverables from the model?

As important as scheduling the actual construction itself, it is critical to develop a schedule for model deliverables from the virtual design work. Time-sensitive design analysis dependent on early model completion, with adequate content for subsequent activities such as fabrication directly from model data, can maximize the cost-saving benefits of this technology. To gain these benefits, contracts need to clearly establish who is responsible to coordinate the various stages of model development and to incorporate other data into a main model, as well as when specific design deliverables from the model must be produced, incorporated into the model, exchanged, and reviewed.

3. How and to what extent will data from one model be transferred or incorporated into other models?

At the core of the issue of model data transfer is recognizing the reality that virtual modeling software is technologically just emerging from its infancy.

Given the current state of the art, one software program may not "play nicely" with others, where both are used jointly to fully design a project. This may result in the corruption or destruction of model data generated by one software program when read by a second program. One option is to assign contractual responsibility to the parties creating each design to confirm that their own modeling can be interoperable, that is, read and interpreted by other model programs involved in the design process. Alternatively, control of the model and transfer of modeling data from other programs into the main model can be strictly regulated to avoid this data degradation or loss.

In addition, if construction trades add to the project model simultaneously with architectural, structural, and other designers, then traditional issues of design control, ownership, and liability may change. These concerns are not insurmountable; however, they must be addressed on a project-specific basis, driven by the model deliverables. The parties must control the process and have veto rights established for each point in development of the designs. Given the prospect of significantly greater efficiencies through more fully integrated processes, however, it behooves the industry to maximize this interaction among the various parties that contribute to the modeling process as a whole.

4. How is the modeling process to be managed?

Virtual building requires attention to process, just as with actual construction. Protocols with respect to model security, access, archiving, transmitting, and the like, should be articulated in the parties' BIM Addendum. Minimum standards also should be developed with respect to software interoperability, model content, level of detail, establishing conventions and coordinate systems, and other such processes. Often the parties will designate a person or party to develop and/or manage the modeling process—the model manager or model master—whose duties and powers should be articulated in the project contracts as well.[45]

5. What is the level of reliance that can be placed on model information?

Reliance on model data is a key issue that cannot be separated from purpose. A model intended solely for visualization should not be relied on for accurate or complete construction material quantity takeoff, for example. The relevant scaled data will be missing from such a conceptual model. As a consequence, care should be used to spell out levels of permitted reliance on model data by project phase in the parties' contracts after the complete purposes for the models have been decided.

---

45. *See, e.g.,* ConsensusDocs® 301 Building Information Modeling (BIM) Addendum, art. 3, for a list of typical duties of a BIM Manager.

From a contract perspective, and given the current level of sophistication of BIM software, the reliance issue is really one of articulating what design information will be contained in the model versus 2D detail drawings or other construction documents (such as written specifications or analysis narratives). Under traditional construction contracting paradigms, the construction trades have commonly worked from 2D drawings and specifications. Increasingly, however, BIM is making its way into the field, with handheld personal computer devices used by workers; the devices contain the construction model, rather than workers having to rely on paper copies of the designs.

If the contract documents are defined to include both 2D drawings and 3D models, consider how the two will be coordinated and which of the two will be relied on to control in the event of conflict? If the contract documents are defined only to include 3D models, what is the consequence of providing 2D drawings to public authorities or contractors for permitting and other purposes? Are the 2D drawings merely a product produced by the BIM model (e.g., a printed section depiction generated from the model) or will the drawings separately illustrate finer, scaled details of the project not found in the 3D model at all? If the parties follow the models to be used to build the project, then, at a minimum, these "construction models" should be identified as part of the contract documents; however, the contracts will need to reflect the interaction depending on the source of the 2D drawings.

The push for use of the model as a contract document binding on the parties to the same extent as drawings or specifications is increasing as the granularity and level of detail that can be illustrated with this 3D technology grows. Still, prudent legal counsel will want to assess current permitting requirements and articulate contract terms regarding reliability of model data consistent with those requirements.

6. Will the model be used after construction is completed?

A number of public owners, General Services Administration and Army Corps of Engineers[46] being the most prominent in the United States, believe that BIM can greatly enhance facility management. Accordingly, public owners are contractually mandating that they own the completed model so they may use it for ongoing operation of the building through the end of its life cycle. These

---

46. The U.S. General Services Administration and U.S. Army Corps of Engineers have developed BIM planning processes and are rigorously using BIM as a life cycle tool to increase quality, cost-effectiveness, and as a means to attain sustainability goals. See GSA BIM Guidelines (https://www.gsa.gov/real-estate/design-construction/3d4d-building-information-modeling/bim-guidelines-for-revit/gsa-bim-guidelines-for-revit) and the USACE's CAB/BIM Technology Center (https://cadbimcenter.erdc.dren.mil/Default.aspx).

long-term deliverables may include not just operations activities but also include the decommissioning and recycling of building components at the end of the useful life of the structure.

Such a deliverable raises a number of as-yet unanswered legal issues. What responsibility do model creators have for model data degradation errors that develop over time? Is the completed model a product, subject to the laws that govern goods, such as the doctrines of implied warranty and strict liability? For now, depending on the parties' intent, attorneys may be prudent to include contract provisions that provide the equivalent of express warranty obligations or disclaim, waive, or limit such obligations.

24.05 BIM EXECUTION PLANNING

A. BIM Execution Planning Process

The BIM Project Execution Plan (PxP)[47] is the central contract document describing how BIM will be implemented on a project. This plan is typically authored by the key parties using BIM collectively. A mechanism should be created contractually for team members joining the project after development of the initial plan so that those team members will be made aware of, and be bound by, the adopted BIM PxP requirements. The PxP outlines the overall activities, along with implementation details, for the team to follow throughout the project. It should be developed early in the contracting for a project, and may need to be refined or amended as additional participants are added to the project. It is not a static document, and should be monitored, updated, and revised as needed throughout the delivery of project construction and commissioning handover. "The Plan should define the scope of BIM implementation on the project, identify the process flow for BIM tasks, define the information exchanges between parties, and describe the required project and company infrastructure needed to support the implementation."[48]

When incorporating BIM into a construction project, expect that some parties who may use the modeling tools or view models will not have had extensive experience using a particular BIM software or processes. As a result, those involved in managing the project should be cognizant that BIM may require

---

47. Some construction industry groups call this document a BIM Execution Plan or BxP. *See, e.g.*, BIM Forum BxP Task Force, https://bimforum.org/bxp/.

48. The Computer Integrated Constr. Research Program at The Pennsylvania State Univ. *BIM Project Execution Planning Guide*, https://www.bim.psu.edu/ (last visited Apr. 12, 2019 7:23 AM); *see* BIMForum's *2018 BIM Project Execution Plan Guide* (2018), https://www.pankowfoundation.org/wp-content/uploads/BIMForum_BxP_Guide_V0-00_Public-Comment-Draft_2018-09-26.pdf.

organizational changes, the successful implementation of which will require a higher caliber of ongoing managerial support. As a result, creation and proper implementation of the PxP should be treated as integral to the project's success, and provide a structured process to manage modeling development for the project.

The steps of a typical BIM PxP include:

1. Identifying BIM goals and model end uses,
2. Designing the BIM design execution activities and process maps,
3. Developing information exchanges and formatting for BIM deliverables,
4. Defining supporting computer and related infrastructure for BIM implementation, and
5. Establishing staffing and scheduling deadlines.

1. Identifying BIM Goals and Uses

The developers of the PxP should include "the owner, designers, contractors, engineers, major specialty contractors, facility manager, and project owner."[49] As stated previously, the PxP should be developed early in the life of the project and should be a collaborative process. The developers must strategize to formulate project goals that are specific, measurable, evaluative, and include how to achieve the goals using BIM.

When identifying goals and uses, each end goal must be objectively identified to properly formulate the PxP. The owner must identify the needs and objectives for the project, and this drives goals and end uses for BIM. For instance, a project goal may be to create an ecologically friendly building or create a building with life cycle and facilities management tools embedded in as-built models.

2. Designing the BIM Design Execution Process by Creating Process Maps

The second PxP step is to design an implementation process for each BIM use, such as creating architectural and structural design models and then joining them to develop the federated project designs for construction. An overview process map often is created at this stage to identify each of the different ways in which BIM will be used in the project, including a time line that details the sequential interactions of BIM development.

3. Developing Information Exchanges That Define BIM Deliverables

An information exchange workflow diagram between the project participants should be created next in PxP development. This document lists the

---

49. *Id.* at 16.

relationship between each deliverable, interdependencies that affect the deliverables at each of the phases of the project, and responsible parties for production of the information needed to be exchanged.

4. *Defining Supporting Infrastructure for BIM Implementation*

The PxP also should define the technology infrastructure required to execute the PxP successfully. This technology infrastructure includes requirements for hardware, software programs, software licensing needs, computer and web networks, and modeling formats or nomenclature for the project. When choosing the infrastructure, project-specific BIM uses, processes, and information needs must be considered, as not all software is alike.[50]

B. Documentation of BIM Project Execution Plan

A PxP documents the BIM processes and deliverables that will be used on a project. Specific BIM PxP content requirements will vary depending on the end uses for the modeling and for how much of the life cycle the BIM data will be used.

There are four essential BIM uses described in section 4.4 of ConsensusDocs® 301 Building Information Modeling (BIM) Addendum: (1) conceptual planning; (2) design authoring and analysis; (3) construction administration; (4) commissioning and turnover. Project conditions may justify other enhanced BIM uses, as described in section 4.2.3, or owner-related uses, as described in section 4.2.4, as well.

A written BIM Project Execution Plan is the final output of the BIM execution planning process.[51] The written plan becomes an Exhibit to the BIM Addendum, by amendment or by incorporation by reference. Care should be taken to make sure this Exhibit is made a part of the contracts of each project party involved with model development and use.

It is important to identify the priority of the various models that will be created (if not already established in other contract documents existing between

---

50. Common software platforms include Autodesk® Revit® Architecture; Tekla BIM®; Trimble Vico®; Graphisoft BIM®; Bentley Architecture V8i®; and VectorWorks Architect®, to name but a few.

51. Based on a grant from the U.S. Government, Penn State University has created several manuals designed to standardize PxP process and deliverables. The BIM Planning Guide for Facility Owners, v. 2.0 (http://bim.psu.edu/Owner/default.aspx) provides a thorough "aid [to] facility owners as they develop strategic, implementation and procurement plans for BIM integrating in their organizations." Software that aids in assembling a BIM Execution Plan also is becoming commercially available, such as the Smart.Lean.BIM™ process developed by LODPlanner, https://www.lodplanner.com/.

the parties). This also should include prioritizing any auxiliary documents or other deliverables in the event they contain information conflicting with models. While the order of hierarchy may depend on the organizational structure and vary from one owner to another, it is important to include BIM models (and often, different versions of them) in the hierarchy. For example, information in a BIM model may take priority over 2D drawings; information in a BIM detail model may take priority over an architectural model; and model data in a fully completed, interference-resolved federated construction model will take precedence over earlier federated models or LOD 100 or 200 individual design models. Reliance on CAD drawings also possibly may decline as uses of handheld computer tablets and computers by field workers and superintendents on the construction site increase, thereby allowing access to the greater and more detailed information contained in the BIM 3D depictions for the project.

24.06 FABRICATION/3D PRINTING BIM APPLICATIONS

Another interesting evolution of BIM has been to generate model data repurposed by yet other software that allows 3D printers to sinter the model data and create physical building components and systems, and even whole buildings.

Figure 24.7
Gantry Arm System[52]

---

52. Example of 3D model data repurposed by a 3D printer. Drs. Richard Buswell and Simon Austin, Gantry Arm System.

Computer-assisted modifications to develop multiple design iterations of a single design while editing geometries in real time, and use of robotic assembly using algorithmic 2D templates for fabrication, are two primary deliverables that already can be generated from BIM models. CNC (computer numerical control) fabrication also can be extrapolated directly from model data to create custom-shaped design features like a decorative wall section, ceiling tiles, or other architectural details.

3D printers can also use BIM data to construct parts of a structure by printing them on site, which typically involve track and gantry arm systems that must be constructed before printing of building foundation and walls occurs (Figure 24.7 and 24.8).

Figure 24.8

On-site Structure Construction and Printed Parts[53]

Robotic construction from BIM model data is on the increase (e.g., SAM Semi-Automatic Mason™, Fastbrick™ Robotics[54]), including 3D printing drones with laser finders. Construction sites (including sites under oceans and on other planets) may one day be filled with robotic equipment aware of the

---

53. Contour Crafting, http://contourcrafting.com/.
54. SAM Semi-Automatic Mason™, https://www.construction-robotics.com/sam100/; Fastbrick™ Robotics, https://www.fbr.com.au/.

Figure 24.9
MIT/Stratasys Lab©

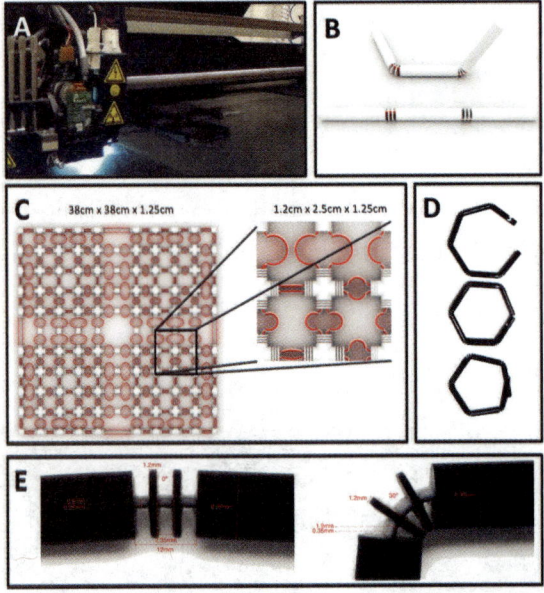

spatial limitations around them and adapting operation based on them, as the Internet of Things[55] expands.

The materials being printed on 3D printers using BIM data can be composites—concrete reinforced with plastic fibers, metallic-impregnated glass, two or more metals, carbon-fiber epoxies, and recycled materials repurposed into new 3D-printed shapes. Typically, strength is the core goal of these hybrid materials. The undesirable byproduct of using these materials, however, is that building codes presume use of more traditional materials like concrete, steel beams, and lumber. Accordingly, demonstrating the structural sufficiency of 3D-printed materials and component parts may be necessary, to the extent permitting officials are willing to explore their use.

Materials printed on 3D printers may also contain programming that allows them to be responsive to the environment, for example, hydrophilic 3D-printed materials that bend, twist, and deflect in the presence of water and can return to a static state when water is no longer present (Figure 24.9). Expect to see yet other materials developed to respond to other environmental conditions, such as heat and light.

---

55. The internetworking of physical devices, vehicles (connecting our smart devices), buildings and other items, embedded with electronics, software, sensors, actuators, and network connectivity that enable these objects to collect and exchange data.

BIM modeling using these new 3D-printed materials will require several layers of interactive contracting to be successfully implemented. At a minimum, these will include contracts for the initial design modeling, for licensed use of 3D printer technology and for the proprietary materials that are generated from the printing process.

24.07 CONCLUSION

BIM is well on its way to making 2D CAD obsolete. BIM is simply more powerful and does things that CAD cannot do at all. BIM allows for critical collaboration to refine designs in an early, richly interactive way; aids in undertaking construction costing, schedule and sustainability analysis; and permits computer-assisted facility maintenance of a completed structure. The cost-efficiencies of these processes, viewed on a life cycle basis, will continue to popularize this technology in the construction industry.[56]

As fabrication and 3D printing change the process by which project components and systems are delivered, expect contract model deliverable requirements for projects using BIM will become more detailed and focused on scalable model content that can be readily adapted for direct fabrication from the project model.

Expect human-computer interfaces in BIM to continue to refine and optimize design solutions to address owner programing requirements in an increasingly efficient and intuitive way. Also expect that BIM will be delivered as virtual reality—allowing for the appearance that one is within a model itself and experiencing the evolving design in augmented virtual environment or mixed reality.

For legal counsel assisting with BIM contract terms or disputes arising from BIM use, it will be important to learn about the specific BIM technology employed for the specific construction project. Counsel must explore how the technology will be used to generate meaningful contract terms, allowing the parties to extract best value from BIM and related 3D applications. Fully articulating PxP development steps in the parties' contracts also will be critical to aiding project success using BIM, along with clearly assigning specific responsibilities for model development to the parties creating and analyzing models needed for the project.

---

56. To learn more about BIM processes and procurement methods, see K. Johnson, P. O'Connor, & B. Clifford, *Building Information Modeling*, in MORE STICKS AND BRICKS: A LAYWERS GUIDE TO ADVANCED CONSTRUCTION SYSTEMS AND TECHNIQUES 49–80 (S. McSorley, B. Bacon, & L. Barrett, eds., American Bar Association, 2018).

QUESTIONS

1. In what three critical ways is 3D BIM different than 2D CAD development of designs?
2. What is meant by calling BIM a "life cycle tool"?
3. What is the role of a BIM Manager in developing models needed for a project?
4. How is a BIM Execution Plan created, and which parties should interact with lawyers who will draft contract terms about the creation of a PxP for a specific project?
5. If 3D-printed building components will be developed from BIM data, what additional contract terms should be added to a BIM Addendum?
6. What is an IFC and why would reference be made to use of IFCs in a BIM Addendum?
7. If you were retained by the project owner to prepare a BIM Addendum, and the designers expressed concern during negotiations that they were taking on unreasonable risk by allowing access to their model data to be reused for developing a fabrication model, to what provisions of that contract could you direct them to address their concerns? How would your arguments change if you were representing the designer in this situation? Would they change if you represented the general contractor?

Table of Cases

2-J Corp. v. Tice, 126 F.3d 539 (3d Cir. 1997), 692 n.106
3D Imaging Services, LLC v. McLaren, Inc., No. 333100, 2017 WL 3397478 (Mich. Ct. App. Aug. 8, 2017), 811 n.1
42 E., LLC v. D.R. Horton, Inc., 722 S.E.2d 1 (N.C. Ct. App. 2012), 219 n.54
1000 Virginia Ltd. Partnership v. Vertecs, 146 P.3d 423 (Wash. 2006), 643–645
2314 Lincoln Park West Condominium Ass'n v. Mann, Gin, Ebel & Frazier, Ltd., 555 N.E.2d 346 (Ill. 1990), 702–704, 713 n.157

Aas v. Superior Court, 12 P.3d 1125, 101 Cal. Rptr. 2d 718, 24 Cal. 4th 627 (2000), 662 n.43, 664 n.52, 701 n.128
Abbruzzese v. Miller, 1996 Ohio App. LEXIS 4304 (1996), 460 n.6
A & B Constr., Inc. v. Atlas Roofing & Skylight Co., 867 F. Supp. 100 (D.R.I. 1994), 422 n.74
Ace Constructors, Inc. v. United States, 70 Fed. Cl. 253 (2006), 440 n.50, 450 n.93, 470 n.36
Action Concrete Contractors, Inc. v. Chappelear, 745 S.E.2d 77 (S.C. 2013), 541 n.64
Adams v. Dreyfus Interstate Dev. Corp., 352 So. 2d 76 (Fla. 4th Dist. Ct. App. 1977), 519 n.24
Adarand Constructors, Inc. v. Mineta, 534 U.S. 103, 122 S. Ct. 511 (2001), 245 n.121
Adarand Constructors, Inc. v. Pena, 115 S. Ct. 2097 (1995), 245–247, 288
Adarand Constructors, Inc. v. Pena, 515 U.S. 200 (1995), 796 n.26
Adarand Constructors v. Skinner, 790 F. Supp. 240 (D. Colo. 1992), 245 n.121
Adarand Constructors v. Slater, 228 F.3d 1147 (10th Cir. 2000), 245 n.121
Advanced Materials, Inc. v. Perry, 108 F.3d 307 (Fed. Cir. 1997), 267 n.16
Adver. & Policy Comm. of the Avis Rent-A-Car Sys. v. Avis Rent-A-Car Sys., 780 S.W.2d 391 (Tex. App. Houston [14th Dist.] 1989, writ granted), *judgment vacated,* 796 S.W.2d 707 (Tex. 1990), 126
Aetna Bridge Co. v. State Dep't of Transp., 795 A.2d 517 (R.I. 2002), 313 n.93
AFM Corp. v. S. Bell Tel. & Tel. Co., 515 So. 2d 180 (Fla. 1987), 667 n.65
A.H.A. General Constr., Inc. v. New York City Hous. Auth., 699 N.E.2d 368 (N.Y. Ct. App. 1998), 436 n.36, 437 n.44, 450 n.90
Aircraft Gear Corp. v. Kaman Aerospace Corp., 856 F. Supp. 446 (N.D. Ill. 1994), 635 n.45

A.J. Tenwood Associates v. Orange Senior Citizens Hous. Co., 491 A.2d 1280 (N.J. App. Div. 1985), *cert. denied*, 501 A.2d 976 (N.J. 1985), 640 n.59

Albion Coll. v. Stockade Bldgs. Inc., 2016 WL 2908262 (Mich. App. 2016), 166 n.48

Aleutian Constructors v. United States, 24 Cl. Ct. 372 (1991), 167 n.51, 655 n.5

Al Johnson Constr. Co. v. United States, 854 F.2d 467 (Fed. Cir. 1988), 633

All Clean, Inc. v. Timberline Properties, 264 P.3d 244 (Utah Ct. App. 2011), 538, 543 n.74

Allied Chem. Corp. v. Am. Indep. Oil Co., 623 S.W.2d 760 (Tex. App. Houston [1st Dist.] 1981, writ ref'd n.r.e.), 133

Allied Chem. Corp. v. Van Buren Sch. Dist. No. 42, 575 S.W.2d 445 (Ark. 1979), 747 n.71

Allied Contractors, Inc. v. United States, 381 F.2d 995 (Ct. Cl. 1967), 50 n.49

Allied Fire & Safety Equipment Co. v. Dick Enterprises, Inc., 886 F. Supp. 491 (E.D. Pa. 1995), 298

Allied Properties v. John A. Blume & Assocs., 25 Cal. App. 3d 848, 102 Cal. Rptr. 259 (1972), 166

Al Munford Halls, Inc. v. United States, 34 Fed. Cl. 62 (Fed. Cl. 1995), *vacated in part on other grounds*, 86 F.3d 1178 (C.A. Fed. 1996), 388–389

Alpha Painting & Constr. Co. Inc. v. Delaware River Port Auth. of Pa. and N.J., 853 F.3d 671 (3d Cir. 2017), 237 n.55

Alstom Power, Inc. v. Balcke-Durr, Inc., 849 A.2d 804 (Conn. 2004), 125 n.31, 126 n.39, 127 n.40

Altrutech, Inc. v. Hooper Holmes, Inc., 6 F. Supp. 2d 1269 (D. Kan. 1998), 125 n.29

Am. Drilling Serv. Co. v. City of Springfield, 614 S.W.2d 266 (Mo. Ct. App. 1981), 304 n.68

Amelco Elec. v. City of Thousand Oaks, 38 P.3d 1120 (Cal. 2002), 448 n.86

American Can Co. v. United States, 69 Ct. Cl. 1 (1929), 450 n.94

American Civil Constr., LLC v. Fort Myer Constr. Corp., 296 F. Supp. 3d 198 (D.D.C. 2018), 518 n.19

American Demolition, Inc. v. Hapeville Hotel Ltd., 413 S.E.2d 749 (Ga. App. 1991), 460–461

American Imaging Servs., Inc., B-246124.2, 92-1 CPD para. 188 (Feb. 13, 1992), 799

American Motors Inns of Fla., Inc. v. Bell Elec. Co., 260 So. 2d 276 (Fla. 4th DCA 1972), 346

American Pipe & Steel Corp. v. Firestone Co., 292 F.2d 640 (9th Cir. 1961), 763 n.12

American Towers Owners Ass'n, Inc. v. CCI Mechanical, Inc., 930 P.2d 1182 (Utah 1996), 690 n.101, 706 n.134

Amfac Dist. Corp. v. J.B. Contractors, Inc., 703 P.2d 566 (Ariz. Ct. App. 1985), 552 n.120

Am. Ins. Co. v. Ohio Bureau of Workers' Compensation, 577 N.E.2d 756 (Ohio App. 1991), 579 n.10

Am. Mach. & Tool v. Strite-Anderson Mfg., 353 N.W.2d 592 (Minn. App. 1934), 132 n.79

Amp-Rite Electric Co. v. Wheaton Sanitary Dist., 220 Ill. App. 3d 130, 580 N.E.2d 622 (2d Dist. 1991), 37 n.3

Am. Ship Bldg. Co. v. United States, 654 F.2d 75 (Ct. Cl. 1981), 51 n.55

Appeal of _____. *See Name of party*

Aquilino v. United States, 10 N.Y.2d 271 (1961), 534 n.23
Aragona Constr. Co. v. United States, 165 Ct. Cl. 382 (1964), 447 n.81
Archon Constr. Co., Inc. v. U.S. Shelter, L.L.C., 78 N.E.3d 1067, 413 Ill. Dec. 791, 2017 Ill. App (1st) 153409 (Ill. Ct. App. 2017), 426 n.5
Arcon Constr. Co. v. State, By and Through Dep't of Transp., 314 N.W.2d 303 (S.D. 1982), 244 n.112
Argonaut Ins. Co. v. Commercial Standard Ins. Co., 380 So. 2d 1066 (Fla. App. 1980), 579 n.10
Argonaut Ins. Co. v. Town of Cloverdale, Ind., 699 F.2d 417 (7th Cir. 1983), 377 n.66
Armenteros v. Baptist Hosp. of Miami, Inc., 714 So. 2d 518 (Fla. Dist. Ct. App. 1998), 406–408
A. R. Moyer, Inc. v. Graham, 285 So. 2d 397 (Fla. 1973), 708 n.141
Arnell Constr. Corp. v. Bd. of Educ. of the City of New York, 598 N.Y.S.2d 1 (N.Y. App. Div. 1993), 443 n.61
A. Servidone/B. Anthony Constr. Corp., J.V. v. State, No. 2016-05238, 2019 N.Y. slip op. 00082, 2019 WL 138601 (N.Y. App. Div. 2019), 124 n.19, 127 n.44
ASI Constructors, Inc. v. United States, 129 Fed. Cl. 707 (2016), 464 n.23
A.S. McGaughan Co. v. Barram, 113 F.3d 1256 (Fed. Cir. 1997), 442 n.57
Asphalt Roads & Materials Co. v. Virginia Dept. of Transp., 512 S.E.2d 804 (Va. 1999), 488–489
Associated Gen. Contractors of Cal. v. City and Co. of S.F., 748 F. Supp. 1443 (N.D. Cal. 1990), aff'd, 950 F.2d 1401 (9th Cir. 1991), 247 n.133
Atherton Condo. Apartment-Owners Ass'n Bd. of Directors v. Blume Dev. Co., 799 P.2d 250 (Wash. 1990), 706 n.134
Atlantic Mutual Ins. Co. v. Metron Eng'g and Constr. Co., 83 F.3d 897 (7th Cir. 1996), 122 n.15
Atl. Dredging Co., United States v., 253 U.S. 1 (1920), 462 n.12, 710 n.150
Audit Services, Inc. v. Francis Tindall Constr., 600 P.2d 811 (Mont. 1979), 434 n.28
AUI Const. Group, LLC v. Vaessen, 2016 Ill. App. (2d) 160009 (Ill. App. Ct. 2016), 544 n.84
Austin Co. v. Vaughn Bldg. Corp., 643 S.W.2d 113 (Tex. 1982), 130
Avatar Dev. v. DePani Constr., Inc., 834 So. 2d 873 (Fla. 4th Dist. Ct. App. 2004), 522 n.34
A.W. Wendell & Sons, Inc. v. Qazi, 626 N.E.2d 280 (Ill. App. Ct. 1993), 126 n.33

Badger Sheet Metal Works of Green Bay, Inc. v. Process Partners, Inc., 2017 WL 2559982 (E.D. Wis. 2017), 273 n.22
Bagwell Coatings, Inc. v. Middle S. Energy, Inc., 797 F.2d 1298 (5th Cir. 1986), 709 n.144
Bajakajian, United States v., 524 U.S. 321, 118 S. Ct. 2028, 141 L. Ed. 2d 314 (1998), 769
Baker Marine Corp. v. Weatherby Eng'g. Co., 710 S.W.2d 690 (Tex. App. 1986), 333 n.12
Baldi Bros. Constructors v. U.S., 50 Fed. Cl. 74 (2001), 738–741, 742 n.53, 757
In re Baldwin Builders, 232 B.R. 406 (9th Cir. BAP 1999), 554
Balfour Beatty Infrastructure, Inc. v. Rummel Klepper & Kahl, LLP, 451 Md. 600, 155 A.3d 445 (2017), 33, 629 n.34, 659 n.26, 667 n.64, 675 n.86, 708 n.141, 711 n.152
Balfour Beatty Rail, Inc. v. Kansas City S. Ry. Co., 173 F. Supp. 3d 363 (N.D. Tex. 2016), 742 n.52

Ballou v. Basic Construction Company, 407 F.2d 1137 (4th Cir. 1969), 220

Baltimore Neighborhoods, Inc. v. Rommel Builders, Inc., 3 F. Supp. 2d 661 (D. Md. 1998), 155 n.16

Barsotti's, Inc. v. Consol. Edison Co. of New York, 680 N.Y.S.2d 88 (N.Y. App. Div. 1998), 437 n.47

Basic Modular Facilities, Inc. v. Ehsanipour, 70 Cal. App. 4th 1480 (1999), 541 n.63

Bates County Redi-Mix, Inc. v. Windler, 162 S.W.3d 98 (Mo. Ct. App., Western Dist. 2005), *reh'g denied* (2005), 539

Bat Masonry Co., Inc. v. Pike-Paschen Joint Venture III, 842 F. Supp. 174 (D. Maryland 1993), 297

Bayshore Dev. Co. v. Bonfoey, 75 Fla. 455, 78 So. 507 (1918), 163 n.33

Bay State-Spray & Provincetown S.S., Inc. v. Caterpillar Tractor Co., 404 Mass. 103, 533 N.E.2d 1350 (Mass. 1989), 668 n.72

Bd. of Educ. of Hudson City Sch. Dist. v. Sargent, Webster, Crenshaw & Folley, 539 N.Y.S.2d 814 (N.Y. App. Div. 1989), 199 n.4, 203 n.17, 210–213, 214 n.31, 218 n.48

Bd. of Educ. v. URS Co., No. 64496, 1994 WL 520862 (Ohio Ct. App. Sept. 22, 1994), *aff'd in part and rev'd in part*, 648 N.E.2d 811 (Ohio 1995), 214 n.33

Bd. of Regents of Univ. of Texas v. S & G Constr. Co., 529 S.W.2d 90 (Tex. Civ. App. 1975), *overruled on other grounds by* Fed. Sign v. Texas Southern Univ., 951 S.W.2d 401, 121 Ed. Law Rep. 394, 40 Tex. Sup. Ct. J. 676 (1997), 130, 131 n.71, 373 n.51

Bd. of Trustees of Santa Fe Cmty. Coll. v. Caudill Rowlett Scott, Inc., 461 So. 2d 239 (Fla. Dist. Ct. App. 1984), 613 n.4

Beachwalk Villas Condo. Ass'n v. Martin, 305 S.C. 144, 406 S.E.2d 372 (1991), 165 n.44

Beacon Constr. Co. v. United States, 314 F.2d 501 (1963), 50 n.51

Beacon Residential Cmty. Assn. v. Skidmore, Owings & Merrill LLP, 59 Cal. 4th 568, 327 P.3d 850 (2014), 657 n.12, 658 n.16, 667, 668 n.77, 669, 684 n.97, 707–708 n.140

Beaufort Builders, Inc. v. White Plains Church Ministries, Inc., 783 S.E.2d 35 (N.C. Ct. App. 2016), 665–666, 707 n.137

Bebo Constr. Co. v. Mattox & O'Brien, P.C., 990 P.2d 78 (Colo. 1999), 700

Becho, Inc. v. United States, 47 Fed. Cl. 595 (2000), 446 n.78, 447 n.80

Beebe, United States v., 180 U.S. 343, 21 S. Ct. 371, 45 L. Ed. 563 (1901), 793

Bell v. Tollefsen, 189 Okla. 149 (1989), 546 n.89

Bentley Const. Dev. & Eng. Inc. v. All Phase Elec. & Maintenance, Inc., 562 So. 2d 800 (Fla. Dist. Ct. App. 1990), 386 n.109

Bentley v. State, 73 Wis. 416, 41 N.W. 338 (1889), 46

Berkel & Co. Contractors v. Christman Co., 533 N.W.2d 838 (Mich. Ct. App. 1995), 304 n.69

Berkley Insurance Company v. Hawthorn Bank, 2018 WL 1516885 (W.D. Mo. 2018), 379 n.71

Berlangieri v. Running Elk Corp., 2003-nMSC-024, 134 N.M. 341, 76 P.3d 1098 (2003), 752

Berry v. Blackard Constr. Co., 13 Ill. App. 3d 768, 300 N.E.2d 627 (4th Dist. 1973), 56 n.75

Berschauer/Phillips Constr. Co. v. Seattle Sch. Dist. No. 1, 881 P.2d 986 (Wash. 1994), 706 n.136, 711–712

Bethlehem Steel Co., United States v., 205 U.S. 105 (1907), 754 n.83

Big Chief Drilling Co. v. U.S., 26 Ct. Cl. 1276, 1992 U.S. Cl. Ct. Lexis 454 (1992), 47 n.39

Bignold v. King Cnty., 399 P.2d 611 (Wash. 1965), 216 n.41

Bilt-Rite Contractors, Inc. v. The Architectural Studio, 581 Pa. 454, 866 A.2d 270 (2005), 710 n.149, 712 n.155

Bituminous Const., Inc. v. Rucker Enterprises, Inc., 816 F.2d 965 (4th Cir. 1987), 376 n.62

Black + Vernooy Architects v. Smith, 346 S.W.3d 877 (Tex. App.—Austin 2011), 417 n.61

Blagg v. Fred Hunt Co., 612 S.W.2d 321 (Ark. 1981), 690 n.101

Blair v. Dunham, 134 F.2d 729 (6th Cir. 1943), 404 n.32

Blake Constr. Co., Inc. v. C.G. Coakley Co., Inc., 431 A.2d 569 (D.C. 1981), 14 n.37, 500 n.4

Blake Constr. Co. Inc. v. Alley, 353 S.E.2d 724 (Va. 1987), 707 n.137

Blake Constr. Co. v. United States, 987 F.2d 743 (Fed. Cir. 1993), 167 n.51, 635 n.48

Bloomsburg Mills, Inc. v. Sordoni Constr. Co., 401 Pa. 358, 164 A.2d 201 (1960), 165 n.44

Blount Bros. Constr. v. United States, 172 Ct. Cl. 1, 348 F.2d 471 (1965), 312

BMW of N. Am., Inc. v. Gore, 517 U.S. 559, 116 S. Ct. 1589, 134 L. Ed. 2d 809 (1996), 769

Bonebrake v. Cox, 499 F.2d 951 (8th Cir. 1974), 285 n.8

Border Brook Terrace Condo. Ass'n v. Gladstone, 622 A.2d 1248 (N.H. 1993), 706 n.134

Borg-Warner Acceptance Corp. v. Tascosa Nat'l Bank, 784 S.W.2d 129 (Tex. App. Amarillo, 1990, writ denied), 130 n.64

Borough of Lansdowne, Pa. v. Sevenson Envt. Serv., Inc., 2000 WL 1886578 (E.D. Pa. Dec. 12, 2000), 663 n.48, 714–715

Bourgeois v. Arrow Fence Co., Inc., 592 So. 2d 445 (La. Ct. App. 1991), 722 n.9

Bovee v. Gravel, No. 2001-347, 2002 WL 1940968 (Vt. Aug. 13, 2002), 658 n.22

Bovis Lend Lease LMB, Inc. v. GCT Venture, Inc., 728 N.Y.S.2d 25 (N.Y. App. 2001), 313

Bowen Eng'g Corp. v. W.P.M. Inc., 557 N.E.2d 1358 (Ind. Ct. App. 1990), 238 n.66

Bowman v. Walnut Mountain Prop. Owners Ass'n, 251 Ga. App. 91, 553 S.E.2d 389 (2001), 39 n.10

Boyajian v. United States, 423 F.2d 1231 (Ct. Cl. 1970), 743

Bradford Sec. Processing Services, Inc. v. Plaza Bank & Trust, 653 P.2d 188 (Okla. 1982), 658 n.22

Bradley Woodcraft, Inc. v. Bodden, 795 S.E.2d 253 (N.C. Ct. App. 2016), 689 n.100

Brady Brick & Supply Co. v. Lotito, 43 Ill. App. 3d 69 (1976), 534 n.27

Brady Brick & Supply Co. v. Lotito, 356 N.E.2d 1126 (Ill. App. Ct. 1976), 373 n.47

Brainard v. Am. Skandia Life Assurance Corp., 432 F.3d 655 (6th Cir. 2005), 793

Branch Banking and Trust Co. v. Creasy, 269 S.E.2d 117 (N.C. 1980), 378 n.68

Branstetter v. Cox, 496 P.2d 1345 (Kan. 1972), 126 n.39

Brewer v. Custom Builders Corp., 356 N.E.2d 565 (Ill. App. Ct. 1976), 617 n.15

Bridgeport Restoration Co., Inc. v. A. Petrucci Constr. Co., 211 Conn. 230, 557 A.2d 1263 (1989), 289 n.23
Brody v. Bock, 897 P.2d 769 (Colo. 1995), 700
Bronster, State *ex rel.*, v. United States Steel Corp., 919 P.2d 294 (Haw. 1996), 715 n.165
Brooks-Callaway Co., United States v., 318 U.S. 120, 63 S. Ct. 474, 87 L. Ed. 653, 1943 U.S. LEXIS 1282 (1943), 336–339
Brooks v. Holsombach, 525 So. 2d 910 (Fla. 4th Dist. Ct. App. 1988), 519 n.24
Broomfield Senior Living Owner, LLC v. R.G. Brinkmann Co., 413 P.3d 219 (Colo. App. 2017), 613 n.3
Broom v. Douglass, 175 Ala. 268, 57 So. 860 (1912), 221
Browning v. Maurice B. Levien & Co., 262 S.E.2d 355 (N.C. Ct. App. 1980), *disc. rev. denied*, 267 S.E.2d 673 (N.C. 1980), 368 n.25
Brown v. Fowler, 279 N.W.2d 907 (S.D. 1979), 701 n.126
Brown v. Royal Maccabees Life Ins. Co., 137 F.3d 1236 (10th Cir. 1998), 125 n.26
Broyles v. Brown Eng'g Co., 275 Ala. 35, 151 So. 2d 767 (1963), 165 n.44
Brushton-Moira Cent. Sch. Dist. v. Alliance Wall Corp., 600 N.Y.S.2d 511 (1993), 681 n.93
Bryan Co., The, United States v., No. 3:11-CV-302-CWR-LRA, 2012 WL 2051861 (S.D. Miss. June 6, 2012), 155 n.16
Bryant Elec. Co. v. City of Fredericksburg, 762 F.2d 1192 (4th Cir. 1985), 707 n.137
Buckley Co. v. City of New York, 505 N.Y.S.2d 140 (N.Y. App. Div. 1986), 426 n.3
Buckner Constr. Co., State v., 704 S.W.2d 837 (Tex. App. 1985), 443 n.63
Buffalo City Sch. Dist., City of, v. LPCiminelli, No. 1287, 17-00176, 73 N.Y.S.3d 836, 2018 N.Y. slip op. 01832, 2018 WL 1357529 (N.Y. App. Div. 2018), 281 n.29
Burling Builders, Inc. v. CMO, 2017 Ill. App. (1st) 170818-U, 2017 WL 4340440 (Ill. Ct. App. 2017), 234 n.36
Burns v. Black & Veatch Architects, Inc., 854 S.W.2d 450 (Mo. Ct. App. 1993), 444 n.65
Burran v. Dambold, 422 F.2d 133 (1970), 163 n.34
Bush Constr. Machinery, Inc. v. Kansas City Factory Outlets, L.L.C., 81 S.W.3d 121 (2002), 543 n.78
Bush v. Jones, 144 F. 942 (3d Cir. 1906), 55 n.73
Butler v. Bd. of Supervisors for Hinds Cnty., 659 So. 2d 578 (Miss. 1995), 433 n.22

Caddell Constr. Co., Inc. v. United States, 78 Fed. Cl. 406 (2007), 50–51
Cadral Corp. v. Solomon, Cordwell, Buenz & Assoc., Inc., 147 Ill. App. 3d 466, 497 N.E.2d 1285 (1st Dist. 1986), 44
Caldwell v. Bechtel, 631 F.2d 989 (D.C. Cir. 1980), 665 n.55
Calloway v. City of Reno, 993 P.2d 1259 (Nev. 2000), 662 n.43, 664 n.53, 690 n.101, 697 n.124
Camden Nat'l Bank v. Crest Constr., Inc., 952 A.2d 213 (Me. 2008), 199 n.4
Camosy, Inc. v. River Steel, Inc., 624 N.E.2d 894 (Ill. App. 1993), 290 n.28
Camp v. Leonard, 133 N.C. App. 554, 515 S.E.2d 909 (1999), 390 n.129
Canape v. Petersen, 897 P.2d 762 (Colo. 1995), 401
Capitol Steel Fabricators, Inc. v. Mega Constr. Co., 68 Cal. Rptr. 2d 672 (Cal. 1998), 304 n.70
Carabetta Enters., Inc. v. United States, 482 F.3d 1360 (Fed. Cir. 2007), 783

Cardinal Chem. Co. v. Morton Int'l, Inc., 508 U.S. 83, 113 S. Ct. 1967, 124 L. Ed. 2d 1 (1993), 775–776
Cardinal Dev. Co. v. Stanley Constr. Co., 497 S.E.2d 847 (Va. 1998), 437 n.42
Carlson T.V. v. City of Marble, 612 F. Supp. 669 (D. Minn. 1985), 241 n.87
Carson v. Roediger, 513 N.W.2d 713 (Iowa 1994), 535 n.28
Carter Steel & Fabricating Co. v. Ohio Dep't of Transp., 721 N.E.2d 1115 (Ohio Ct. App. 1999), 358
Carter v. Deitz, 556 So. 2d 842 (La. Ct. App. 4th Cir. 1990), *writ denied*, 566 So. 2d 992 (La. 1990), 159 n.25
Carvalho v. Toll Bros. & Developers, 675 A.2d 209 (N.J. 1996), 417 n.60
Casa Clara Condo. Ass'n, Inc. v. Charley Toppino & Sons, Inc., 620 So. 2d 1244 (Fla. 1993), 663 n.48, 690 n.101
Casa Linda Tile & Marble Installers, Inc. v. Highlands Place 1981, Ltd., 642 So. 2d 766 (Fla. Dist. Ct. App. 1994), 380 n.82
Casey v. Overhead Door Corp., 74 Cal. App. 4th 112 (1999), 661 n.36
Casitas Municipal Water District v. United States, 72 Fed. Cl. 746 (2006), *aff'd in part*, 543 F.3d 1276 (Fed. Cir. 2008), 784
Cath-dr/Balti Joint Venture, ASBCA Nos. 53581, 54239, 05-2 BCA ¶ 33046 (Aug. 17, 2005), 786
Cave Hill Corp. v. Hiers, 570 S.E.2d 790 (Va. 2002), 126 n.35
CCI, Inc., ASBCA No. 57316, 14-1 BCA ¶ 35,546 (2014), 484 n.91
CEMS, Inc. v. United States, 59 Fed. Cl. 168 (2003), 482 n.89, 743
Centex Corp. v. United States, 395 F.3d 1283 (Fed. Cir. 2005), 783
Cent. Ohio Joint Vocational Sch. Bd. Dist. of Educ. v. Peterson Constr. Co., 129 Ohio App. 3d 58 (1998), 49 n.47
Central Parking System of Missouri, LLC v. Tucker Parking Holdings, LLC, 519 S.W.3d 485 (Mo. Ct. App. 2017), 612 n.1
Certified Power Systems, Inc. v. Dominium Energy Brayton Point, LLC, 2012 WL 384600 (Mass. Super. Ct. 2012), 13 n.34
CFTC v. Sidoti, 178 F.3d 1132 (11th Cir. 1999), 332, 333
CGM Constr. v. Sydor, No. 521885, 42 N.Y.S.3d 407, 2016 N.Y. Slip Op. 07895, 2016 WL 6883897 (N.Y. App. Div. 2016), 56 n.81
CH2M Hill, Inc. v. Herman, 192 F.3d 711 (7th Cir. 1999), 397 n.17
CH2M Hill Southeast, Inc. v. Pinellas Cnty., 698 So. 2d 1238 (1997), 165 n.40
Chamberlain Mfg. Corp., ASBCA 18103, 74-1 BCA ¶ 10,368 (1973), 762 n.8
Champion Cos. of Wis., Inc. v. Stafford Dev., Ltd. Liab. Co., 794 N.W.2d 916 (Wis. Ct. App. 2010), 719 n.2
Chaney Bldg. Co. v. City of Tucson, 716 P.2d 28 (Ariz. 1986), 159 n.25
Charles H. Sells, Inc. v. Chance Hills Joint Venture, 163 Misc. 2d 814, 622 N.Y.S.2d 422 (1995), 537–538
Charles T. Parker Construction Co. v. United States, 433 F.2d 771 (Ct. Cl. 1970), 475 n.60
Chemimetals Processing, Inc. v. Schrimsher, 535 S.E.2d 594 (N.C. Ct. App. 2000), 374 n.56
Chen-Cheng Wang *ex rel.* United States v. FMC Corp., 975 F.2d 1412 (9th Cir. 1992), 389
Cheswold Volunteer Fire Co. v. Lambertson Constr. Co., 489 A.2d 413 (Del. 1984), 649 n.80, 651 n.84

Chevron Oil Co. v. E.D. Walton Constr. Co., 517 F.2d 1119 (5th Cir. 1975), 129 n.62
Chicago Heights Venture v. Dynamit Nobel of Am., 782 F.2d 723 (7th Cir. 1986), 690 n.101
Chicago R.I. & P. Ry. Co. v. Md. Cas. Co., 75 F.2d 596 (8th Cir. 1935), 135 n.97
Christie v. United States, 237 U.S. 234 (1915), 46, 462 n.14, 463 n.16, 710 n.150
Christopher B. Burke Engineering, Ltd. v. Heritage Bank of Central Illinois, 43 N.E.3d 963 (Ill. 2015), 537
Cienega Gardens v. United States, 331 F.3d 1319 (Fed. Cir. 2003), 783
Citadel Corp. v. Sun Chem. Corp., 443 S.E.2d 489 (Ga. Ct. App. 1994), 452 n.100
City Express, Inc. v. Express Partners 87 Hawaii 466, 959 P.2d 836 (Hawaii 1998), 681–683, 711 n.153
City Line Joint Venture v. United States, 503 F.3d 1319 (Fed. Cir. 2007), 783
City of ____ v. *See Name of party*
Clark Constr. Co. v. Pena, 930 F. Supp. 1470 (M.D. Ala. 1996), 242 n.99, 243 n.104
Clark-Fitzpatrick, Inc./Frankl Found. Co. v. Gill, 652 A.2d 440 (R.I. 1994), 436 n.41
Clarkson Construction Co. v. Occupational Safety and Health Review Comm'n, 531 F.2d 451 (10th Cir. 1976), 396
Clark Trucking of Hope Mills, Inc. v. Lee, 109 N.C. 71, 426 S.E.2d 288 (N.C. App. 1993), 291 n.33
Clemens v. Benzinger, 207 N.Y.S. 539 (1925), 424 n.77
C. Norman Peterson Co. v. Container Corp. of America, 218 Cal. Rptr. 592 (1985), 446 n.77
Cnty. of Dauphin v. Fidelity & Deposit Co. of Md., 770 F. Supp. 248 (M.D. Pa. 1991), *aff'd*, 937 F.2d 596 (3d Cir. 1991), 754 n.78
Cnty. of Maricopa v. Walsh & Oberg Architects, Inc., 494 P.2d 44 (Ariz. Ct. App. 1972), 746
Cnty. Redevelopment and Hous. Auth. v. W. M. Schlosser Co., Inc., 41 Va. Cir. 118 (1996), 489 n.114
Coastal Marine Construction, AGBCA No. 89-190-3, 90-2 BCA ¶ 22,895 (1990), 478 n.69
C.O.B.A.D. Constr. Corp. v. Sch. Bd. of Broward Cnty., 765 So. 2d 844 (Fla. Dist. Ct. App. 2000), 453 n.107
Cobb v. Pasadena City Bd. of Ed., 134 Cal. App. 2d 93, 285 P.2d 41 (Cal. Dist. Ct. App. 1955), 228 n.12
C.O. Falter Constr. Corp. v. City of Binghamton, 684 N.Y.S.2d 86 (1999), 754 n.82
Cogefar-Impresit, U.S.A., Inc., DOTBCA No. 2721, 97-2 BCA (CCH) ¶ 29,188 (1997), 355 n.52
Coghlin Elec. Contractors, Inc. v. Gilbane Bldg. Co., et al., 2015 WL 5123135 (Sept. 2, 2015), 472 Mass. 549 (2015), 104–105
College of Notre Dame of Maryland, Inc. v. Morabito Consultants, Inc., 752 A.2d 265 (Md. Ct. Spec. App. 2000), 640 n.59
College Savings Bank v. Florida Prepaid Postsecondary Education Expense Board, 131 F.3d 353 (3d Cir. 1997), *aff'd*, 527 U.S. 666, 119 S. Ct. 2219, 144 L. Ed. 2d 605 (1999), 774, 775, 776, 777
College Savings Bank v. Florida Prepaid Postsecondary Education Expense Board, 148 F.3d 1343 (Fed. Cir. 1998), 776
Collins v. Reynard, 607 N.E.2d 1185 (Ill. 1992), 704 n.132

Columbia Gas Transmission Corp. v. New Ulm Gas, Ltd., 940 S.W.2d 587 (Tex. 1996), 127–128 n.46

Columbus, City of, v. Barngrower, 250 Ga. App. 589, 552 S.E.2d 536 (2001), 38 n.8

Commercial Contractors, Inc. v. United States, 154 F.3d 1357 (Fed. Cir. 1998), 766, 769, 770

Commercial Union Ins. Co. v. Martinez, 635 S.W.2d 611 (Tex. App. Dallas, 1982, writ ref'd n.r.e.), 127 n.41

Comptech Int'l. Inc. v. Milam Commerce Park, Ltd., 753 So. 2d 1219 (Fla. 1999), 691 n.104, 702 n.129

Concrete Gen., Inc. v. Washington Suburban Sanitary Comm'n, 779 F. Supp. 370 (D. Md. 1991), 245 n.123

Concrete Works of Colo., Inc. v. City & Co. of Denver, 321 F.3d 950 (10th Cir. 2003), *cert. denied*, 540 U.S. 1028, 124 S. Ct. 556 (2003), 246 n.129

Condon-Johnson & Assoc., Inc. v. Sacramento Mun. Util. Dist., 149 Cal. App. 4th 1384 (2007), 493

Conforti & Eisele, Inc. v. John C. Morris Assoc., 418 A.2d 1290 (N.J. Super. 1980), 709 n.144

Congregation of the Passion, Holy Cross Province v. Touche Ross & Co., 636 N.E.2d 503 (1994), 704 n.131

Connelly v. Paul, 731 S.W.2d 657 (Tex. App. Houston [1st Dist.] 1987, writ ref'd n.r.e.), 131 n.77

Conner Bros. Constr. Co., Inc. v. Pete Green, Sec'y of the Army, No. 2008-1188, 550 F.3d 1368 (Dec. 31, 2008), 778–785

Conner Bros. Constr. Co., Inc. v. United States, 65 Fed. Cl. 657 (2005), 51 n.56, 636 n.50

Connolly Dev., Inc. v. Superior Court, 17 Cal. 3d 803 (1976), 530 n.5, 531 n.7, 532 n.14

Conrad Bros., Inc., Appeal of, 1996 WL 675811 (B.C.A. 1996), *aff'd*, 135 F.3d 778 (Fed. Cir. 1998), 49 n.45

In re Consol. Contracting & Eng'g, 1996 WL 639911 (Comp. Gen. Nov. 6, 1996), 237 n.57

Consol. Hardwoods, Inc. v. Alexander Concrete Constr., Inc., 811 P.2d 440 (Colo. App. 1991), 697 n.125

Consolidated Engineering Company, No. 43159, 98 C. Cls. 256 (Feb. 1, 1943), 310–311

Consumer Power Co. v. Mississippi Valley Structural Steel Co., 636 F. Supp. 1100 (E.D. Mich. 1986), 684 n.98

Continental Ins. Co. v. City of Virginia Beach, 908 F. Supp. 341 (E.D. Va. 1995), 378 n.69

Contra Costa Constr. Corp. v. Daly City, 192 P. 178 (Cal. 1920), 433 n.22

Contractors Ass'n of E. Pa. v. City of Phila., 91 F.3d 586 (3d Cir. 1996), 245 n.123, 246 n.126

Cook v. Carlson, 364 F. Supp. 24 (D.S.D. 1973), 531

Coombs v. Beede, 89 Me. 187, 36 A. 104 (1896), 160

Copenhaver v. Rogers, 384 S.E.2d 593 (Va. 1998), 707 n.137

Coppola Constr. Co., Inc. v. Hoffman Enterprises Ltd. P'ship, 309 Conn. 342, 71 A.3d 480 (Conn. 2013), 434 n.27

Corpus Christi Bank & Trust v. Smith, 525 S.W.2d 501 (Tex. 1975), 134 n.93

Council of Co-Owners Atlantis Condo., Inc. v. Whiting-Turner Contracting Co., 308 Md. 18 (Md. 1986), 715 n.162

Council of Co-Owners Atlantis Condo., Inc. v. Whiting-Turner Contracting Co., 517 A.2d 336 (Md. 1986), 692–695

Covington, City of, v. Heard, 428 So. 2d 1135 (La. Ct. App. 1983), 635

Craftique, Inc. v. Stevens & Co., 364 S.E.2d 129 (N.C. 1988), 379 n.73

Craft v. Stevenson Lumber Yard, Inc., 179 N.J. 56, 843 A.2d 1076 (2004), 540 n.62

Craig v. Everett M. Brooks Co., 222 N.E.2d 752 (Mass. 1967), 708 n.141

Craviolini v. Scholer & Fuller Associated Architects, 89 Ariz. 24, 357 P.2d 611 (1961), 220

Crest Constr. Corp. v. Shelby Cnty. Bd. of Educ., 612 So. 2d 425 (Ala. 1992), 240 n.79

Cross Constr. Co., ENG BCA No. 3676, 79-1 BCA ¶ 13,707 (1979), 472 n.42

Curry v. Thornsberry, 98 S.W.3d 477 (Ark. App. 2003), *aff'd*, 128 S.W.3d 438 (Ark. 2003), 649 n.82, 651 n.86

Cuspide Properties, Ltd. v. Earl Mechanical Servs., 53 N.E.3d 818, 2015 Ohio 5019 (Ohio Ct. App. 2015), 546 n.90

Daanen & Janssen, Inc. v. Cedarapids, Inc., 405 N.W.2d 842 (1998), 670, 671, 672, 673

D. A. Elia Constr. Corp. v. N.Y. State Thruway Auth., 734 N.Y.S.2d 295 (App. Div. 2001), 715 n.161

Daewoo Eng'g & Const. Co. v. United States, 73 Fed. Cl. 547 (2006), 764–770

Daewoo Eng'g & Constr. Co., Ltd. v. United States, No. 2007-5129, 557 F.3d 1332 (Feb. 20, 2009), *reh'g and reh'g en banc denied* (Apr. 27, 2009), 764–770

Dakota Gasification Co. v. Pascoe Bldg. Sys., 91 F.3d 1094 (8th Cir. 1996), 690 n.101

Dalton v. Cessna Aircraft Co., 98 F.3d 1298 (Fed. Cir. 1996), 459 n.3

Daubert v. Merrell Dow Pharm., Inc., 509 U.S. 579 (1993), 350, 351

Dave Kolb Grading, Inc. v. Terra Venture Bridgeton Project Joint Venture, 85 F.3d 351 (8th Cir. 1996), 426 n.3

David L. Threlkeld & Co., Inc. v. Metallgesellschaft Ltd. (London), 923 F.2d 245 (2d Cir. 1991), 605 n.19

Davidson & Jones, Inc. v. New Hanover Cnty., 255 S.E.2d 580 (N.C. App. 1979), 665 n.55

Davies Mach. Co. v. Pine Mountain Club, Inc., 39 Cal. App. 3d 18 (1974), 544 n.81

Davis & Associates, Inc. v. Midcon, Inc., 127 N.M. 134, 978 P.2d 341 (Ct. App. 1999), 243 n.103

Davis v. La Crosse Hospital Ass'n, 121 Wis. 579, 99 N.W. 351 (1904), 553 n.124

Dawco Constr., Inc. v. United States, 930 F.2d 872 (Fed. Cir. 1991), *rev'd on other grounds,* Reflectone, Inc. v. Dalton, 60 F.3d 1572 (Fed. Cir. 1995), 743

Daymar, Inc., DOTBCA No. 77-13, 78-1 BCA ¶ 12,903 (1977), 476 n.61

Day v. City of Beatrice, 169 Neb. 858 (1960), 241 n.86

Day v. United States, 245 U.S. 159 (1917), 45

D&D Underground Utilities, Inc. v. Walter Martin Excavating, Inc., 2015 WL 13427765 (E.D. Ky. 2015), 319 n.1, 320 n.2

Dean v. Ruscon Corp., 468 S.E.2d 645 (S.C. 1996), 645 n.69

DeAtley Constr., Inc. v. United States, 71 Fed. Cl. 370 (2006), 444 n.64

Dehnert v. Arrow Sprinklers, Inc., 705 P.2d 846 (Wyo. 1985), 220, 223

De Leon v. Saldana, 745 S.W.2d 55 (Tex. App. San Antonio 1987), *writ denied* (July 13, 1988), 111 n.13

Demetriades v. Kaufmann, 680 F. Supp. 658 (S.D.N.Y. 1988), 176
Deming v. United States, 1 Ct. Cl. 190 (1865), 780, 781
Dep't of Transp. v. Idol, 440 S.E.2d 863 (N.C. Ct. App. 1994), 375 n.57
Dermott v. Jones, 69 U.S. 1, 17 L. Ed. 762 (1864), 5 n.10, 46
Detroit Edison Co. v. NABCO, Inc., 35 F.3d 236 (6th Cir. 1994), 690 n.101
Devaney v. New Haven Bd. of Zoning Appeals, 132 Conn. 537, 45 A.2d 828 (1946), 39 n.12
DeVito v. United States, 413 F.2d 1147 (Ct. Cl. 1969), 334 n.14
D. Federico Co. v. New Bedford Redevelopment Auth., 723 F.2d 122 (1st Cir. 1983), 710 n.149
D.H. Dave & Gerben Contracting Co., 1962 BCA ¶ 3,493, 1962 WL 939, 740
Dillon Co. Sch. Dist. Two v. Lewis Sheet Metal, 332 S.E.2d 555 (S.C. Ct. App. 1985), 646 n.71
DiMaria Construction, Inc. v. Interarch, 799 A.2d 555 (N.J. Super. Ct. App. Div. 2001), 220, 223
Dinsmore v. Lake Elec. Co., Inc., 719 N.E.2d 1282 (Ind. Ct. App. 1999), 544 n.82
Diocese of Rochester v. R-Monde Contractors, Inc., 562 N.Y.S.2d 593 (N.Y. Sup. Ct. 1989), 629 n.33
Di Sciullo v. Griggs & Co. Homes, Inc., 2015 WL 6393813 (E.D.N.C. 2015), 266 n.15, 363 n.6
Dist. Intown Properties Ltd. P'ship v. D.C., 198 F.3d 874 (D.C. Cir. 1999), 159 n.24
D.M.K., Inc. v. Town of Pittsfield, 290 Wis. 2d 474, 711 N.W.2d 672 (Wis. Ct. App. 2006), 239 n.68
D & N Electric, Inc. v. Underground Festival, Inc., 202 Ga. App. 435, 414 S.E.2d 891 (1992), 546 n.88
Donald C. Winter v. Cath-dr/Balti Joint Venture, No. 2006-1359 (Aug. 17, 2007), *reh'g and reh'g en banc denied* (Nov. 21, 2007), 786–795
Donald Frederick Evans v. Continental Homes, Inc., 785 F.2d 897 (11th Cir. 1986), 176
Donnelly Constr. Co. v. Oberg/Hunt/Gilleland, 677 P.2d 1292 (Ariz. 1984), 709 n.144
Donovan v. City of Deadwood, 538 N.W.2d 790 (S.D. 1995), 159 n.23
Don's Bldg. Supply, Inc. v. OneBeacon Ins. Co., 267 S.W.3d 20 (Tex. Sup. Ct. 2008), 566 n.3
Doornbos Heating & Air Conditioning, Inc. v. James D. Schlenker, M.D., S.C., 403 Ill. App. 3d 468 (2010), 536 n.35
Dorchester Dev. Corp. v. Safeco Ins. Co., 737 S.W.2d 380 (Tex. App.-Dallas 1987, no writ), 563
Douglas Corp., 58-1 BCA Par. 1727, 1958 WL 266 (ASBCA 1958), 339 n.18
Drennan v. Star Paving Co., 333 P.2d 757 (Cal. 1958), 290 n.25, 290 n.27, 290 n.29, 291 n.30
Drennon Constr. & Consulting, Inc. v. Dep't of the Interior, CBCA No. 2391, 13-1 BCA ¶ 35,213 (2013), 480 n.76, 484
Drews Co., Inc. v. Ledwith-Wolfe Assocs., 371 S.E.2d 532 (S.C. 1988), 333 n.13
Drilling Serv. Co. v. Baebler, 484 S.W.2d 1 (Mo. 1972), 541 n.63
Dufficy & Sons, Inc. v. BRW, Inc., 74 P.3d 380 (Colo. App. 2002), *rev'd*, 99 P.3d 66 (Colo. 2004), 709 n.145
Dugan & Meyer Constr. Co., Inc. v. Ohio Dep't of Admin. Services, 113 Ohio St. 3d 226, 864 N.E.2d 68 (2007), 47–49

Duncan, Fox, & Co. v. North & South Wales Bank, 6 App. Cas. 1 (H.L. 1880), 582 n.12
Duncan v. Mo. Bd. for Architects, Prof'l Eng'rs & Land Surveyors, 744 S.W.2d 524 (Mo. Ct. App. 1988), 209 n.24, 395 n.6
Duquesne Light Co. v. Westinghouse Elec. Corp., 66 F.3d 604 (3d Cir. 1995), 711 n.153
D.W. Wilburn, Inc. v. K. Norman Berry Associates, Architects, PLLC, 2016 WL 7405774 (Ky. Ct. App. 2016), 203 n.17

Eades v. Capitol Material Co., Inc., 121 F.2d 72 (D.C. 1941), 404 n.31
Eagle Supply & Mfg., L.P. v. Bechtel Jacobs Co., LLC, 868 F.3d 423 (6th Cir. 2017), 737 n.51
East Coast Repair & Fabrication, LLC v. United States, 199 F. Supp. 3d 1006 (E.D. Va. 2016), 743 n.55
Eastover Corp. v. Martin Builders, 543 So. 2d 1358 (La. Ct. App. 1989), 382–383
Eastover Ridge, LLC v. Metric Constructors, Inc., 138 N.C. App. 360, 533 S.E.2d 827 (2000), 363 n.7
East River S.S. Corp. v. Transamerica Delaval, Inc., 476 U.S. 858 (1986), 659 n.28, 661 n.40, 664 n.53, 705
E.B. Roberts Constr. Co. v. Concrete Contractors, Inc., 704 P.2d 859 (Colo. 1985), 541 n.68
E. C. Ernst, Inc. v. Curtis T. Bedwell & Sons, Inc., U.S. *ex rel.*, 506 F. Supp. 1324 (D.C. Pa. 1981), 373 n.47
E. C. Ernst, Inc. v. Manhattan Constr. Co., 387 F. Supp. 1001 (S.D. Ala. 1974), 14 n.35
E. C. Ernst, Inc. v. Manhattan Construction Co. of Texas, 551 F.2d 1026 (5th Cir. 1977), 221, 709 n.144
Econ. Forms Corp. v. Williams Bros. Constr. Co., 754 S.W.2d 451 (Tex. App. Houston [14th Dist.] 1988), 134 n.93
Edinger & Son v. City of Louisville, 802 F.2d 213 (6th Cir. 1986), 245 n.123
Edward M. Crough, Inc. v. Dist. of Columbia Dep't of Gen. Servs., 572 A.2d 457 (D.C. 1990), 358
Edwin R. Marden Corp. v. United States, 442 F.2d 364 (Ct. Cl. 1971), 446 n.76
EH Constr. LLC v. Delor Design Grp., Inc., No. 1998-CA-001476-NR, 2000 WL 339939 (Ky. Ct. App. Mar. 31, 2000), 658 n.21
Eichleay Corp., ASCBA No. 5183, 60-2 BCA ¶ 2688, 1960 WL 538 (July 29, 1960), *aff'd on reconsider.*, 61-1 BCA ¶ 2894, 1960 WL 684 (1960), 732, 733
Elec. Supply Co. of Durham, Inc. v. Swain Elec. Co., Inc., 403 S.E.2d 291 (N.C. 1991), 384 n.100
Elec-Trol, Inc. v. C. J. Kern Contractors, Inc., 284 S.E.2d 119 (N.C. Ct. App. 1981), 218 n.51
Elger Mfg., Inc. v. Liberty Mut. Ins. Co., 972 F.2d 805 (7th Cir. 1992), 696 n.114
Elk and Jacobs Drywall v. Town Contractors, Inc., 229 S.E.2d 260 (S.C. 1976), 386 n.109
Ell-Dorer Contracting Co. v. State of New Jersey, 197 N.J. Super. 175 (App. Div. 1984), 487
Ellerbe Becket, Inc., United States v., 976 F. Supp. 1262 (D. Minn. 1997), 155 n.14
Ellis-Don Constr., Inc. v. HKS, Inc., 353 F. Supp. 2d 603 (M.D.N.C. 2004), 702, 704–705
Elmira, City of, v. Larry Walter, Inc., 76 N.Y.2d 912, 563 N.Y.S.2d 45, 564 N.E.2d 655 (1990), 754 n.84

El Paso Field Servs. v. MasTec North America, Inc., 389 S.W.3d 802 (Tex. 2012), 633 n.39
Emberton v. State Farm Mut. Auto. Ins. Co., 373 N.E.2d 1348 (Ill. 1978), 413 n.57
Embree Construction Group, Inc. v. Rafcor, Inc., 330 N.C. 487, 411 S.E.2d 916 (1992), 390
Eng'g Contractors Ass'n of S. Fla. v. Metro. Dade Co., 122 F.3d 895 (11th Cir. 1997), 245 n.123, 245 n.124, 246 n.125
England v. Contel Advanced Sys., Inc., 384 F.3d 1372 (2004), 771 n.25
Ensley Branch, NAACP v. Seibels, 31 F.3d 1548 (11th Cir. 1994), 245 n.124
Equal Rights Center v. Archstone Smith Trust, 603 F. Supp. 2d 814 (D. Md. 2009), 155–156 n.16
E. & R. Constr. Co., U.S. *ex rel.*, v. Guy H. James Constr. Co., 390 F. Supp. 1193 (M.D. Tenn. 1972), *aff'd*, 489 F.2d 756 (6th Cir. 1974), 437 n.43
Erie Railroad Co. v. Tompkins, 304 U.S. 64 (1938), 649 n.80, 651 n.84
Erlich v. Menezes, 21 Cal. 4th 543, 87 Cal. Rptr. 2d 886, 981 P.2d 978 (1999), 10–11 n.28
Ernst v. Ohio Dep't of Adm. Serv., 69 Ohio App. 3d 330 (1990), 373 n.47
ESI Montgomery Cnty., Inc. v. Montenay Int'l Corp., 899 F. Supp. 1061 (S.D.N.Y. 1995), 649 n.81, 651 n.85
ES-KO, Inc. v. United States, 44 Fed. Cl. 429 (Fed. Cl. 1999), 242 n.101
Estate of _____. *See Name of party*
Everett Plywood Corp. v. United States, 227 Ct. Cl. 415, 651 F.2d 723 (Ct. Cl. 1981), 783
Excavation Technologies, Inc. v. Columbia Gas Co. of Pa., 604 Pa. 50, 985 A.2d 840 (2009), 712 n.155
Exch. Nat'l Bank of Chi. v. City of Des Plaines, 336 N.E.2d 8, 32 Ill. App. 3d 722 (Ill. App. 1 Dist. 1964), 39 n.10

Fabe v. WVP Corp., 760 S.W.2d 490 (Mo. Ct. App. 1988), 215–216
Farabaugh v. Penn. Turnpike Comm'n, 911 A.2d 1264 (Pa. 2006), 444 n.66
Farmer Constr. Ltd. v. Washington, 98 Wash. 2d 600, 656 P.2d 1086 (Wash. 1983), 237 n.58
Farmers Group, Inc. v. Trimble, 691 P.2d 1138 (Colo. 1984), 700
F.B. Reynolds v. Texarkana Constr. Co., 374 S.W.2d 818 (Ark. 1964), 291 n.31
F. Craig Stuart v. Coldwell Banker Commercial Group, Inc., 745 P.2d 1284 (Wash. 1987), 677–679
Federal Crop Ins. Corp. v. Merrill, 332 U.S. 380 (1947), 433
Federal Ins. Co. v. I. Kruger, Inc., 829 So. 2d 732 (Ala. 2002), 304 n.67
Federal Sign v. Tex. So. Univ., 951 S.W.2d 401 (Tex. 1997), 130 n.69, 130 n.70, 131 n.71
Fed. Sign v. Texas Southern Univ., 951 S.W.2d 401, 121 Ed. Law Rep. 394, 40 Tex. Sup. Ct. J. 676 (1997), 373 n.51
Felhaber Corp. v. State, 410 N.Y.S.2d 920 (N.Y. App. Div. 1978), 441 n.53
Ferentchak v. Village of Frankfort, 105 Ill. 2d 474, 923 N.E.2d 808 (1984), 55 n.71
F.H. Paschen, S.N. Nielsen & Associates, LLC v. Southeastern Commercial Masonry, Inc., 2015 WL 7015389 (E.D. La. 2015), 218 n.51
Fid. & Deposit Co. of Md. v. Hartford Cas. Ins. Co., 215 F. Supp. 2d 1171 (D. Kan. 2002), 564

Fidelity and Deposit Co. v. City of Sheboygan Falls, 713 F.2d 1261 (7th Cir. 1983), 49 n.42
Fieldstone Co. v. Briggs Plumbing Products, Inc., 54 Cal. App. 4th 357 (1997), 659 n.30
Filbert v. City of Philadelphia, 181 Pa. 530, 37 A. 545 (Pa. 1897), 46
Filippi v. Filippi, 818 A.2d 608 (R.I. 2003), 126 n.36
Fireman's Fund Ins. Co. v. SEC Donohue, Inc., 679 N.E.2d 1197, 223 Ill. Dec. 424, 176 Ill. 2d 160 (1997), 706 n.134, 713 n.157
Fireman's Fund Ins. Co. v. United States, 92 Fed. Cl. 598 (2010), 730 n.25
Fireman's Fund Ins. Co. v. United States, 909 F.2d 495 (Fed. Cir. 1990), 369 n.30, 370, 377 n.67
First Interstate Bank of Denver v. Central Bank & Trust Co., 937 P.2d 855 (Colo. App. 1997), 649 n.81, 651 n.85
First Union Nat'l Bank of North Carolina v. King, 306 S.E.2d 508 (N.C. Ct. App. 1983), 378 n.68
First Union Nat'l Bank v. RPB 2, LLC, 674 N.W.2d 1 (N.D. 2004), 552 n.120
Fischbach & Moore Int'l Corp. v. Christopher, 987 F.2d 759 (Fed. Cir. 1993), 768–769
Fisher v. Coghlan, 778 N.Y.S.2d 812 (N.Y. App. Div. 2004), 199 n.4
Fisher v. Katz, 266 F. Supp. 180 (S.D.N.Y. 1976), 658 n.23
Flagstaff Affordable Hous. Ltd. P'ship v. Design All., Inc., 223 Ariz. 320, 223 P.3d 664 (2010), 660 n.31, 667 n.64, 681 n.93
Flatiron-Lane v. Case Atlantic Co., 2015 WL 777686 (M.D.N.C. 2015), 742 n.52
Fleischer v. Hellmuth, Obata and Kassabaum, Inc., 870 S.W.2d 832 (Mo. App. 1993), 706 n.135
Fleming v. Borden, 37 S.E. 219 (N.C. 1900), 378 n.68
Flippin Materials Co. v. United States, 160 Ct. Cl. 357 (1963), 465 n.26
Floor Craft Floor Covering, Inc. v. Parma Cmty. Gen. Hosp. Ass'n, 560 N.E.2d 206 (Ohio 1990), 706 n.134
Florida Department of State v. Treasure Salvors, Inc., 458 U.S. 670, 102 S. Ct. 3304, 73 L. Ed. 2d 1057 (1982), 775
Florida Prepaid Postsecondary Education Expense Board v. College Savings Bank, 527 U.S. 627, 119 S. Ct. 2199, 144 L. Ed. 2d 575 (1999), 774, 776
Fluor Intercont'l, Inc. v. Dep't of State, CBCA No. 1559, 13 BCA ¶ 35,334 (2013), 484 n.92
FNB Mortg. Corp. v. Pac. Gen. Grp., 76 Cal. App. 4th 1116 (3d Dist. 1999), 649 n.83, 651 n.86
Foley Co. v. U.S., 11 F.3d 1032 (Fed. Cir. 1993), 270 n.19, 481 n.82
Folk Construction Co. v. United States, 2 Cl. Ct. 681 (1983), 313
In re Fordson Eng'g Corp., 25 B.R. 506 (Bankr. D. Mich. 1982), 501 n.9
Forsgren Associates, Inc. v. Pacific Golf Community Development, LLC, 182 Cal. App. 4th 135, 105 Cal. Rptr. 654 (2010), 546–547
Forte Bros., Inc. v. Nat'l Amusements, Inc., et al., 525 A.2d 1301 (R.I. 1987), 630
Fortec Constructors, Inc. v. United States, 8 Cl. Ct. 490 (1985), *aff'd*, 804 F.2d 141 (Fed. Cir. 1986), 351–352, 472 n.41
Fortec Constructors v. United States, 760 F.2d 1288 (1985), 478 n.70
Fort Knox Self Storage, Inc. v. Western Technologies, Inc., 140 N.M. 233, 142 P.3d 1 (N.M. Ct. App. 2006), 750–752

Foster Construction C.A. & Williams Bros. Co. v. United States, 435 F.2d 873 (Ct. Cl. 1970), 467–468, 471 n.40, 476, 477 n.64, 485, 487
Four Star Enters. Equip., Inc. v. Emps. Mut. Cas. Co., 451 S.W.3d 776 (Mo. Ct. App. 2014), 550 n.107
Foxcroft Townhome Owners Ass'n v. Hoffman Rosner Corp., 449 N.E.2d 125 (Ill. 1983), 690 n.101
Fox v. Mountain West Elect., Inc., 52 P.3d 848 (Idaho 2002), 426 n.4
Frank Sullivan Co. v. Midwest Sheet Metal Works, 335 F.2d 33 (8th Cir. 1964), 434 n.26
Fraya S.E., ASBCA No. 5222, 02-2 BCA (CCH) ¶ 31,975 (2002), 351
Fred Howland, Inc. v. Gore, 152 Fla. 781, 13 So. 2d 303 (1942), 346
Fretwell v. Prot. Alarm Co., 764 P.2d 149 (Okla. 1988), 300 n.55
Fru-Con Corp. and Granite Constr., JV v. Illinois, 50 Ill. Ct. Cl. 50 (1996), 491–492
Fuller Co. v. Brown Minneapolis Tank & Fabricating Co., 678 F. Supp. 506 (E.D. Pa. 1987), 448 n.86
Fullilove v. Klutznick, 448 U.S. 448, 100 S. Ct. 2758 (1980), 244 n.115

G4S Tech., LLC v. Mass. Tech. Park Corp., 479 Mass. 721, 99 N.E.3d 728 (Mass. 2018), 501 n.9
GAF Corp. v. United States, 19 Cl. Ct. 490 (1990), 635 n.45
Gagne v. Bertram, 43 Cal. 2d 481, 275 P.2d 15 (1954), 166
Garaman, Inc. v. Williams, 912 P.2d 1121 (Wyo. 1996), 161–163
Garden City Floral Co. v. Hunt, 255 P.2d 352 (Mont. 1953), 188
Gardner-Zenkes Co. v. State, 109 N.E.2d 729, 790 P.2d 1010 (1990), 50 n.50
Gehan Homes, Ltd. v. Employers Mutual Casualty Co., 146 S.W.3d 833 (Tex. App.-Dallas 2004), 565–566
G.E.I. Recycling, Inc. v. Atl. Envtl., Inc., 821 So. 2d 431 (Fla. Dist. Ct. App. 2002), 304 n.68
Gen. Constr. Co. v. Pub. Util. Dist. No. 2 of Grant Cnty., 380 P.3d 636, 195 Wash. App. 698 (Wash. Ct. App. 2016), 201 n.13
Gen. Corrosion Servs. Corp. v. K Way Equip. Co., 631 S.W.2d 578 (Tex. App. Tyler, 1982, no writ), 131 n.73
General Contracting & Constr. Co. v. United States, 84 Ct. Cl. 570 (1937), 447 n.82
General Contracting Corp. v. United States, 96 Ct. Cl. 255 (1942), 474 n.52
General Eng'g & Machine Works v. O'Keefe, 991 F.2d 775 (Fed. Cir. 1993), 762 n.8
General Motors Acceptance Corp. v. Daniels, 492 A.2d 1306 (Md. 1985), 377 n.65
George Hyman Constr. Co. v. Washington Metro. Transit Auth., 816 F.2d 753 (D.C. Cir. 1987), 731 n.27
George Sollitt Constr. Co. v. United States, 64 Fed. Cl. 229 (2005), 636 n.49, 730 n.25
Georgetown Township High School v. Hardy, 38 Ill. App. 3d 722, 349 N.E.2d 88 (1976), 55 n.74
George v. El Paso Cnty. Water Control & Imp. Dist. No. 1, 332 S.W.2d 144 (Tex. Civ. App. El Paso, 1960), 125 n.25, 132 n.84
George Washington Bridge Bus Station Development Venture, LLC v. Associated Specialty Contracting, No. 150549/16, 3731N, 52 N.Y.S.3d 321, 2017 N.Y. slip op. 02913, 2017 WL 1348160 (N.Y. App. Div. 2017), 545 n.87, 550 n.107
Gesco, Inc. v. Edward L. Nezelek, Inc., 414 So. 2d 535 (Fla. Dist. Ct. App. 1982), 332

Getzschman v. Miller Chem. Co., Inc., 232 Neb. 885, 443 N.W.2d 260 (1989), 183 n.77
Gherna v. Ford Motor Co., 246 Cal. App. 2d 639 (1966), 691 n.105
Gilbane Bldg. Co. v. Brisk Waterproofing Co., 585 A.2d 248 (1991), 304 n.69
Gilbane Bldg. Co. v. Nemours Found., 606 F. Supp. 995 (D. Del. 1985), 690 n.102
Gilbert Pac. Corp. v. Oregon, 822 P.2d 729 (Or. Ct. App. 1991), 309
Giles & Ransome, Inc. v. First Nat'l Realty Corp., 238 Md. 203, 108 A.2d 582 (1965), 543 n.78, 544 n.80
Gill Constr., Inc. v. 18th & Vine Auth., 157 S.W.3d 699 (Mo. App. 2004), 447 n.85
Gillum v. Republic Health Corp., 778 S.W.2d 558 (Tex. App. Dallas 1989), 110 n.7
G.L. Christian & Associates v. United States, 160 Ct. Cl. 1, 312 F.2d 418, *reh'g denied*, 160 Ct. Cl. 58, 320 F.2d 345, *cert. denied*, 375 U.S. 954 (1963), 762
Glen-Gery Corp. v. Warfle Constr. Co., 734 A.2d 926 (Pa. Super. Ct. 1999), 376 n.62
Gogo v. L.A. etc. Flood Control Dist., 114 P.2d 65 (Cal. Ct. App. 1941), 492
Golomore Associates v. New Jersey State Highway Auth., 173 N.J. Super. 55 (App. Div. 1980), 487
Gonnert v. Victor At W. 53, LLC, No. 40690/04, 2006 N.Y. slip op. 50284(U) (N.Y. slip op. Mar. 3, 2006), 404 n.30
Gostovich v. City of W. Richland, 75 Wash. 2d 583, 452 P.2d 737 (1969), 237 n.53
Gould, Inc. v. United States, 935 F.2d 1271 (Fed. Cir. 1991), 269
Grady v. S. E. Gustafson Constr. Co., 103 N.W.2d 737 (1960), 304 n.71
Graham Constr. Co., Inc. v. Earl, 362 Ark. 220, 2005 WL 1041149 (2005), 50 n.49
Gramm v. Ins. Unlimited, 378 P.2d 662 (Mont. 1963), 372 n.43
Granite Constr. Co. v. United States, 24 Cl. Ct. 735 (1991), 234 n.41, 464
Granite Constr. Co. v. United States, 962 F.2d 998 (Fed. Cir. 1992), 444 n.64
Gravely v. Providence P'ship, 549 F.2d 958 (4th Cir. 1977), 166 n.48
Graves Lumber Co. v. Croft, 20 N.E.3d 412 (Ohio Ct. App. 9th Dist. Summit County 2014), 534 n.25
Great Lakes Construction Co. v. United States, 95 C. Cls. 479 (1942), 310
Great N. Life Ins. Co. v. Read, 322 U.S. 47, 64 S. Ct. 873, 88 L. Ed. 1121 (1944), 775
Greenberg v. Perkins, 845 P.2d 530 (Colo. 1993), 700
Greenbriar, Ltd. v. City of Alabaster, 881 F.2d 1570 (11th Cir. 1989), 330 n.2
Green Constr. Co. v. Kansas Power & Light Co., 1 F.3d 1005 (10th Cir. 1993), 51 n.58
Greystone Homes, Inc. v. Midtec, Inc., 168 Cal. App. 4th 1194, 86 Cal. Rptr. 3d 196 (2008), 660 n.30, 668 n.75
Grochal v. Ocean Technical Services Corp. (*In re* Baltimore Marine Indus., Inc.), 476 F.3d 238 (4th Cir. 2007), 371
Grossman Holdings Ltd. v. Hourihan, 414 So. 2d 1037 (Fla. 1982), 748
Grossman v. Sea Air Towers, Ltd., 513 So. 2d 686 (Fla. App. 1987), *rev. denied*, 520 So. 2d 584 (Fla. 1988), 747 n.69
Gross v. Sweet, 49 N.Y.2d 102 (N.Y. 1979), 212
Guardian Constr. v. Tetra Tech, Inc., 583 A.2d 1378 (Del. Super. 1990), 715 n.164
Guerini Stone Co. v. P.J. Carlin Const. Co., 248 U.S. 334, 39 S. Ct. 102 (1919), 361 n.1, 371 n.42, 372 n.46
Gulf Constr. Co. v. Self, 676 S.W.2d 624 (Tex. App. Corpus Christi, 1984), 129 n.62
Gulf Constr. Group, Inc., ENG BCA No. 5958, 93-3 BCA ¶ 26,174 (1993), 481 n.83
Guy F. Atkinson Co., ENG BCA No. 4693, 87-3 BCA ¶ 19,971 (1987), 475 n.60

Hadley v. Baxendale, 156 Eng. Rep. 145 (Ex. 1854), 658 n.15
Hagerman Constr. Corp. v. Long Elec. Co., 741 N.E.2d 390 (Ind. Ct. App. 2000), 418–420
Halcrow, Inc. v. Dist. Ct., 302 P.2d 1148 (Nev. 2013), 47 n.38
Hall Street Assoc., L.L.C. v. Mattel, Inc., 552 U.S. 576, 128 S. Ct. 1396 (2008), 609
Hamel v. Am. Cont'l Corp., 713 P.2d 1152 (Wyo. 1986), 555 n.132
Hamp's Constr., L.L.C. v. City of New Orleans, 924 So. 2d 104 (La. 2006), 238 n.59
Hampton v. Phipps, 108 U.S. 260, 2 S. Ct. 622, 27 L. Ed. 719 (1883), 582 n.12
Harbert/Lummus Agrifuels Projects v. United States, 142 F.3d 1429 (Fed. Cir. 1998), 793
Harco Energy, Inc. v. Re-Entry People, Inc., 23 S.W.3d 389 (Tex. App. Amarillo 2000), 108 n.2
Hardeman-Monier-Hutcherson, A Joint Venture, 68-2 BCA ¶ 7,220, 1968 WL 633, 740
Hardeman-Monier-Hutcherson v. United States, 458 F.2d 1364 (1972), 463 n.20
Harmony Constr., Inc. v. State Dep't of Transp., 668 A.2d 746 (Del. Ch. 1995), 239 n.74
Harper v. O'Charley's, LLC, 2017 WL 5598815 (S.D. Ala. 2017), 649 n.81
Harrison v. Facade, Inc., 355 S.W.2d 543 (Tex. Civ. App. Dallas, 1962, no writ), 132 n.81
Harrison v. Williams Dental Group, P.C., 140 S.W.3d 912 (Tex. App. Dallas 2004), 109 n.4
Hathaway v. Gen. Mills, Inc., 711 S.W.2d 227 (Tex. 1986), 126 n.34
Havens v. Safeway Stores, 678 P.2d 625 (Kan. 1984), 373 n.48
Haws & Garrett General Contractors, Inc. v. Gorbett Bros. Welding Co., 480 S.W.2d 607 (Tex. 1972), 110 n.6, 111
Held v. Mitsubishi Aircraft Int'l, Inc., 672 F. Supp. 369 (D. Minn. 1987), 661 n.38
Helene Curtis Indus., Inc. v. United States, 312 F.2d 774, 160 Ct. Cl. 437 (1963), 234 n.36, 463 n.20
Henningsen v. United States Fid. & Guar. Co., 208 U.S. 404 (1908), 582, 583
Hensel Phelps Constr. Co., ASBCA No. 49270, 99-2 B.C.A. ¶ 30,531 (1999), 326 n.7
Hercules, Inc. v. United States, 24 F.3d 188 (Fed. Cir. 1994), 234 n.39
Hercules, Inc. v. United States, 516 U.S. 417 (1996), 632 n.38
Hernandez v. Home Depot, U.S.A., No. 05 C 5963, 2007 WL 2298408 (N.D. Ill. Aug. 3, 2007), 135 n.97
Hewett-Kier Constr., Inc. v. Lemuel Ramos and Assoc., Inc., 775 So. 2d 373 (Fla. App. 2002), 709 n.144
Hicks v. Smith, 330 S.W.2d 641 (Tex. Civ. App. Fort Worth, 1959, writ ref'd n.r.e.), 124 n.24
Hilliard & Bartko Joint Venture v. Fedco Sys., Inc., 522 A.2d 961 (Md. 1987), 643 n.67
Hill v. Polar Pantries, 219 S.C. 263, 64 S.E.2d 885 (1951), 165
Himmel Corp. v. Stade, 52 Ill. App. 3d 294, 367 N.E.2d 411 (1977), 163 n.36
H. Landau & Co. v. United States, 886 F.2d 322 (Fed. Cir. 1989), 792
Hoel-Steffen Constr. Co. v. United States, 197 Ct. Cl. 561 (1972), 480 n.76
Hoel-Steffen Constr. Co. v. United States, 456 F.2d 760 (Ct. Cl. 1972), 436 n.38
Hoffman Constr. Co. of Oregon v. United States, 40 Fed. Cl. 184 (Fed. Cl. 1998), *aff'd in part, rev'd in part on other grounds*, 178 F.2d 131 (Fed. Cir. 1999), 326 n.5
Hollerbach v. United States, 233 U.S. 165 (1914), 46, 462 n.14, 463 n.16, 710 n.150

Home Elec. Co. of Lenoir, Inc. v. Hall, etc., 358 S.E.2d 539 (N.C. 1987), 291 n.32
Horovitz v. Levine, 755 So. 2d 687 (Fla. Dist. Ct. App. 1999), 332
Horowitz v. United States, 267 U.S. 458, 45 S. Ct. 344, 69 L. Ed. 736 (1925), 780, 781, 782
Hosp. Mortg. Grp. v. First Prudential Dev. Corp., 411 So. 2d 181 (Fla. 1982), 518 n.20
Hous. Auth. of the City of Texarkana v. Johnson Constr. Co., 264 Ark. 523, 573 S.W.2d 316 (1978), 50 n.49
Houston, City of, v. R.F. Ball Constr. Co., 570 S.W.2d 75 (Tex. Civ. App. 1978), 375 n.58
Hous. Vt. v. Goldsmith & Morris, 165 Vt. 428, 685 A.2d 1086 (1996), 182 n.77
Howard S. Wright Constr. Co. v. Superior Court, 106 Cal. App. 4th 314 (2003), 545 n.85, 546 n.89
H.R. Johnson Constr. Co. v. Bd. of Educ., 16 Ohio Misc. 99, 241 N.E.2d 403 (Ohio Com. Pl. Ct. 1968), 242 n.100
Hubbard v. Shankle, 138 S.W.3d 474 (Tex. App. Fort Worth 2004), 108 n.3
Hubert v. Aitken, 2 NYS 711, *order adhered to on rearg*, 5 NYS 839, *aff'd*, 123 N.Y. 655 (N.Y. 1890), 213
Hubert v. Aitken, 2 N.Y.S. 711 (C.P. 1888), *aff'd*, 25 N.E. 954 (N.Y. 1890), 655 n.3
Hughes Commc'ns Galaxy, Inc. v. United States, 998 F.2d 953 (Fed. Cir. 1993), 780
In re Hunters Run Ltd. Partnership, 875 F.2d 1425 (9th Cir. 1989), 554
Hunt v. Ellisor & Tanner, Inc., 739 S.W.2d 933 (Tex. App. 1987), 212, 213, 628–629

Iannuccillo v. Material Sand & Stone Co., 713 A.2d 1234 (R.I. 1998), 341 n.22
IES Commercial, Inc. v. Manhattan Torcon A Joint Venture, 2018 WL 4616029 (D. Md. 2018), 446 n.75
Inc. Town of Bono v. Universal Tank & Iron Works, Inc., 395 S.W.2d 330 (Ark. 1965), 201
Indian River Constr. Co. v. City of Jacksonville, 390 So. 2d 1139 (Fla. Dist. App. 1977), 436 n.41
Indus. Asphalt, Inc. v. Garret Corp., 180 Cal. App. 3d 1001 (1986), 530 n.1
In re _____. *See Name of party*
Ins. Co. of N. Am. v. Town of Manchester, 17 F. Supp. 2d 81 (D. Conn. 1998), 707 n.139
Inst. Sci. & Tech. Inst., Inc. v. United States, 53 Fed. Cl. 798 (2002), 267 n.16
Interstate Contracting Corp. v. City of Dallas, Texas, 407 F.3d 708 (5th Cir. 2005), 426 n.1
Interwest Constr. v. Brown, 29 F.3d 611 (C.A. Fed. 1994), 56 n.79
Itek Corp. v. First Nat'l Bank of Boston, 730 F.2d 19 (1st Cir. 1984), 768

Jackson Constr. Co. v. United States, 62 Fed. Cl. 84 (2004), 732 n.28
Jacobs Engineering Group v. Conagra Foods, Inc., 301 Neb. 38, 917 N.W.2d 435 (Neb. 2018), 423
Ja Din, Inc. v. L-J, Inc., 898 F. Supp. 894 (E.D. Fla. 1995), 434 n.25
Jaeger v. Henningson, Durham & Richardson, Inc., 714 F.2d 773 (8th Cir. 1983), 209 n.24
J. A. Jones Constr. Co. v. Lehrer McGovern Bovis, Inc., 89 P.3d 1009 (Nev. 2004), 447 n.83
James Cape & Sons Co. v. Mulcahy, 285 Wis. 2d 200, 700 N.W.2d 243 (Wis. 2005), 243 n.107, 244 n.111
Jankoviak v. Butcher, 159 N.E.2d 377 (Ill. App. Ct. 1959), 553 n.123

Jardel Enterprises, Inc. v. Triconsultants, Inc., 770 P.2d 1301 (Colo. App. 1988), 697 n.124

J.B. Service Court v. Wharton, 632 P.2d 943 (Wyo. 1981), 575

J.D. Construction v. IBEX Int'l Group, 126 Nev. 366 (Nev. 2010), 260 n.8

Jefferson Constr. Co. v. United States, 176 Ct. Cl. 1363 (1966), 478 n.70

Jewish Board of Guardians v. Grumman Allied, 96 A.D.2d 465, aff'd, 62 N.Y.2d 684 (N.Y. App. Div. 1983), 212

J.F. Shea Co. v. United States, 4 Cl. Ct. 46 (1983), 234 n.40

Jimenez, Inc., VABCA No. 6351, et al., 02-2 BCA (CCH) ¶ 32019 (2002), 351

Jimenez v. Superior Court, 58 P.3d 450 (Cal. 2002), 662 n.44, 691 n.104

J. J. Brown Co. v. J. L. Simmons Co., 118 N.E.2d 781 (Ill. App. Ct. 1954), 333 n.13

J. Lawson Jones Constr. Co., Inc., ENG BCA No. 4363, 86-1 BCA ¶ 18,719 (1986), 473 n.47

J.L. Simmons Co. v. United States, 412 F.2d 1360, 188 Ct. Cl. 684 (1969), 167 n.50, 634 n.45, 635 n.48

J. M. Beeson Company v. Ernesto Sartori, 553 So. 2d 180, Nos. 87-1953, 87-2415 and 87-2693 (1989), 344–347

Jo-Bar Mfg. Corp. v. United States, 535 F.2d 62 (Ct. Cl. 1976), 436 n.40

Johanson v. Huizenga Holdings, Inc., 963 F. Supp. 1175 (S.D. Fla. 1997), 155 n.14

John B. Pike & Son, Inc. v. State of New York, 647 N.Y.S.2d 654 (N.Y. Cl. 1996), 311

John Driggs Co., Inc., ENGBCA No. 4926, 87-2 B.C.A. (CCH) ¶ 19,833 (1987), 343 n.27

John E. Green Plumbing & Heating Co., Inc. v. Turner Constr. Co., 500 F. Supp. 910 (E.D. Mich. 1980), aff'd, 742 F.2d 965 (7th Cir. 2004), 755 n.87

John Martin Co. v. Morse/Diesel, Inc., 819 S.W.2d 428 (Tenn. 1991), 715 n.163

John Massman Contracting Co. v. United States, 23 Cl. Ct. 24 (1991), 168 n.52

Johnson v. Bd. of Cnty. Comm'rs, 913 P.2d 119 (Kan. 1996), 300 n.55

Johnson v. Jones, 921 F. Supp. 1573 (E.D. Mich. 1996), 177

Johnson v. Salem Title Co., 246 Or. 409, 425 P.2d 519 (1967), 152–154, 655 n.5

Jones v. J.H. Hiser Constr. Co., 60 Md. App. 671, 484 A.2d 302 (1984), 363 n.6

Jones v. United States, 1 Ct. Cl. 383 (1865), 780, 781, 782

Jordan v. Bd. of Educ. of Taylor's Falls, 39 Minn. 298, 39 N.W. 801 (1888), 6 n.12

Joseph F. Egan, Inc. v. City of New York, 215 N.E.2d 490 (N.Y. Ct. App. 1966), 437 n.42

Joseph Sternberg, Inc. v. Walber 36th Street Assoc., 594 N.Y.S.2d 144 (N.Y. App. Div. 1993), 426 n.4

J.R. Sinnott Carpentry, Inc. v. Phillips, 443 N.E.2d 597 (Ill. App. Ct. 1982), 617 n.15

J. R. Youngdale Constr. Co., Inc. v. United States, 23 Cl. Ct. 460, 1991 WL 130539 (Cl. Ct. 1991), aff'd, 956 F.2d 1172 (Fed. Cir. 1992), 327 n.10

J. S. Sweet Co. v. White County Bridge Comm'n, 714 N.E.2d 219 (Ind. Ct. App. 1999), 440 n.48

Juliano v. Gaston, 455 A.2d 523 (N.J. 1982), 697 n.125

Julian Speer Co. v. Ohio State Univ., 680 N.E.2d 254 (Ohio Ct. Cl. 1997), 442 n.59

Kahn v. Terry, 628 So. 2d 390 (1993), 182–184

Kaiser Indus. Corp. v. United States, 169 Ct. Cl. 310 (1965), 472 n.46, 473 n.47

Kaiser Indus. Corp. v. United States, 340 F.2d 322 (Ct. Cl. 1965), 478 n.72

Kalisch-Jarcho, Inc. v. City of New York, 533 N.E.2d 258 (N.Y. 1988), 446 n.72
K-Con, Inc. v. Secretary of Army, 908 F.3d 719 (Fed. Cir. 2018), 50 n.51, 761 n.6
K-Con Bldg. Sys. v. United States, 107 Fed. Cl. 571 (2012), 731 n.26
Keang Nam Enter. Ltd., ASBCA No. 13747, 69-1 BCA ¶ 7,705 (1969), 472 n.43
Kecko Piping Company, Inc. v. Town of Monroe, 172 Conn. 197, 374 A.2d 179 (1977), 220
Keck v. Dryvit Sys., Inc., 830 So. 2d 1 (Ala. 2002), 662 n.43, 684 n.96
Keller v. A. O. Smith Harvestore Prods., Inc., 819 P.2d 69 (Colo. 1991), 700
Kelley v. Widener Concrete Constr., LLC, 401 S.W.3d 531 (Mo. Ct. App. 2013), 721–722
Kemper Architects, P.C. v. McFall, Konkel & Kimball Consulting Engineers, Inc., 843 P.2d 1178 (Wyo. 1992), 162
Kemp v. United States, 38 F. Supp. 568 (D. Md. 1941), 243 n.110
Kennedy v. Columbia Lumber & Mfg. Co., 299 S.C. 335, 384 S.E.2d 730 (1989), 675 n.88, 695 n.112, 701 n.127
Kenny Constr. Co. of Illinois v. Metro. Sanitary Dist. of Greater Chicago, 288 N.E.2d 1 (Ill. 1971), 490–491
Kensington Corp. v. State, 253 N.W.2d 781 (Mich. Ct. App. 1997), 309 n.85
Kent Sand & Gravel, LLC v. Jacksonville Machine & Repair, Inc., 403 Md. 173, 941 A.2d 468 (2008), 545 n.86
Kern v. City of Lawrenceburg, 625 N.E.2d 1326 (Ind. Ct. App. 1993), 375 n.60
Key Int'l Mfg. v. Morse/Diesel, Inc., 142 A.D.2d 448 (N.Y. App. 1988), 681 n.93
Khoury Construction Co., Inc. v. Earhart, 382 S.E.2d 392 (Ga. Ct. App. 1989), 382
Kiewit Infrastructure West Co. v. United States, 137 Fed. Cl. 689 (Fed. Cl. 2018), 249 n.143
Kincaid v. Landing Dev. Corp., 344 S.E.2d 869 (S.C. App. 1986), 163 n.34
Kinetic Builders, Inc., ASBCA No. 32627, 88-2 BCA ¶ 20,657 (1988), 473 n.48
Kingdomware Technologies, Inc. v. U.S., 136 S. Ct. 1969 (2016), 804
Kingery Constr. Co. v. Scherbarth Welding, Inc., 185 N.W.2d 857 (Neb. 1971), 319 n.1
King Fisher Marine Serv., Inc. v. United States, 16 Cl. Ct. 231 (1989), 451 n.96
Kingston Constructors, Inc. v. Washington Metro. Area Transit Auth., 930 F. Supp. 651 (D.D.C. 1996), 754 n.80
Kinsey Contracting Co., Inc. v. City of Fayetteville, 106 N.C. App. 383, 416 S.E.2d 607 (N.C. Ct. App. 1992), 239
Klose v. Sequoia Union High Sch. Dist., 258 P.2d 515 (Cal. App. 1953), 292 n.35
Knutton v. Cofield, 160 S.E.2d 29 (N.C. 1968), 385 n.104
In re Estate of Koch, 912 N.W.2d 205, 322 Mich. App. 383 (Mich. Ct. App. 2017), 129 n.63
Kokomo, F. & W. Traction Co. v. Kokomo Trust Co., 193 Ind. 219, 137 N.E. 763 (1923), 553 n.125
Koontz v. Thomas, 333 S.C. 702, 511 S.E.2d 407 (S.C. App. 1999), 182 n.77
Kostohryz v. McGuire, 298 Minn. 513, 212 N.W.2d 850 (1973), 182 n.77
Kritikos v. Andersen, 125 So. 3d 885 (Fla. 4th DCA 2013), 748
Kroger Co. v. L.G. Barcus & Sons, Inc., 13 So. 3d 1232 (La. App. 2d Cir. 6/17/09), 640–641
Krygoski Constr. Co. v. United States, 94 F.3d 1537 (Fed. Cir. 1996), 522 n.32
KSLA-TV, Inc. v. Radio Corp. of America, 732 F.2d 441 (5th Cir. 1984), 649 n.82
Kubrick, United States v., 444 U.S. 111 (1979), 639 n.56
Kumho Tire Co. v. Carmichael, 526 U.S. 137 (1997), 350

Laconco, Inc., State v., 430 So. 2d 1376 (La. Ct. App. 1983), 381
La Crosse, City of, v. Schubert, Schroeder & Assoc., 240 N.W.2d 124 (Wis. 1976), 691 n.104
Lafayette Steel Erectors, Inc. v. Roy Anderson Corp., 71 F. Supp. 582 (S.D. Miss. 1997), 304 n.68
Lamb v. Georgia-Pacific Corp., 392 S.E.2d 307 (Ga. App. 1990), 691 n.104
LAN/STV v. Martin K. Eby Constr. Co., Inc., 435 S.W.3d 234 (Tex. 2014), 659 n.25, 659 n.26, 675 n.87, 696 n.116, 696 n.119, 710 n.150
Lassiter v. Bank of North Carolina, 146 N.C. App. 264, 551 S.E.2d 920 (2001), 389–390
Lawrence v. General Panel Corp., 2019 WL 100382 (S.C. 2019), 347 n.29
Lee Lewis Constr., Inc. v. Harrison, 70 S.W.3d 778 (Tex. 2001), 410–412
Lee R. Smith, ASBCA No. 11135, 66-2 BCA ¶ 5,857 (1966), 473 n.47
Legacy Builders, LLC v. Andrews, 335 P.3d 1063 (Wy. 2014), 745 n.62, 746 n.63
Leis Family Ltd. P'ship v. Silversword Eng'g, 126 Haw. 532, 273 P.3d 1218 (Ct. App. 2012), 706 n.134
Lennar Corp. v. Great American Ins. Co., 2006 WL 406609 (Tex. App.-Houston [14th Dist.] 2006, pet. filed), 564, 565, 566
Levering & Garrigues Co. v. United States, 73 Ct. Cl. 566 (1932), 462 n.14, 463, 463 n.17
Levernier Constr., Inc. v. U.S., 947 F.2d 497 (1991), 771 n.25
Lewis Elec. Co. v. Miller, 791 N.W.2d 691 (Iowa 2010), 536 n.36
L. G. Everist, Inc. v. United States, 231 Ct. Cl. 1013 (1982), 472 n.45
Lidderdale's Executors v. Robinson's Executor, 12 Wheat. 594, 6 L. Ed. 740 (1827), 582 n.12
Linda Newman Constr. Co. v. United States, 48 Fed. Cl. 231 (2000), 452 n.104, 453 n.105
Linde Enterprises, Inc. v. Hazelton City Auth., 412 Pa. Super. 67, 602 A.2d 897 (1992), 710 n.149
Lion Raisins, Inc. v. United States, 51 Fed. Cl. 238 (2001), 239 n.69
In re Liquidation of Lumbermens Mutual Cas. Co., 2018 IL App (1st) 171613, 2018 WL 6173580 (Ill. Ct. App. 2018), 440 n.48
Litton Systems, Inc. v. Frigitemp Corp., 613 F. Supp. 1377 (S.D. Miss. 1985), 447 n.85
L. L. Hall Constr. Co. v. United States, 379 F.2d 559 (Ct. Cl. 1966), 441 n.54, 441 n.55
Lloyd Wood Coal Co. v. Clark Equip. Co., 543 So. 2d 671 (Ala. 1989), 691 n.105
Local Joint Executive Bd. v. Stern, 651 P.2d 637 (Nev. 1982), 711 n.151
Logan Equipment Corp. v. Profile Const. Co., Inc., 585 A.2d 73 (R.I. 1991), 543 n.78
Lonberg v. Sanborn Theaters, Inc., 259 F.3d 1029 (9th Cir. 2001), 155 n.15
Lonergan v. San Antonio Loan & Trust Co., 104 S.W. 1061 (Tex. 1907), 632–633 n.39
Los Angeles Testing Lab., United States ex rel., v. Rogers & Rogers, 161 F. Supp. 132 (S.D. Cal. 1958), 665 n.55, 709 n.143
Lott v. Brown, 2018 WL 6191301 (Tex. App. 2018), 111 n.12
Lovering-Johnson, Inc. v. City of Prior Lake, 558 N.W.2d 499 (Minn. Ct. App. 1997), 242 n.98
Lundgren v. Freeman, 307 F.2d 104 (9th Cir. 1962), 220
Luria Bros. & Co. v. United States, 369 F.2d 701 (Ct. Cl. 1966), 444 n.67
L.W. Blinn Lumber Co. v. Pioneer Drainage Dist., 50 Cal. App. 364 (1920), 539 n.54
In re Lynch III Props. Corp., 125 B.R. 857 (Bkrtcy. E.D.N.Y. 1991), 369 n.28

MacKnight Flintic Stone Co. v. The Mayor, 160 N.Y. 72 (1899), 46
MacPherson v. Buick Motor Co., 217 N.Y. 382, 111 N.E. 1050 (1916), 657, 678
Macri v. U.S. for Use of John H. Maxwell & Co., 353 F.2d 804 (9th Cir. 1965), 372 n.44
Magnolia Constr. Co. v. Mississippi Gulf S. Eng'rs, Inc., 518 So. 2d 1194 (Miss. 1988), 214 n.31, 709 n.145
Magnum Constr. Mgmt. Corp. v. City of Miami Beach, 209 So. 3d 51 (Fla. Ct. App. 2016), 748 n.72
Magnus Pacific Corp. v. United States, 133 Fed. Cl. 640 (Fed. Cl. 2017), 234 n.36, 462 n.13
Main Elec., Ltd. v. Printz Servs. Corp., 980 P.2d 522 (Colo. 1999), 304 n.67
Malarchick v. Pierce, 264 N.W.2d 478 (N.D. 1978), 384 n.102
Mall v. Pawelski, 626 So. 2d 291 (Fla. Dist. Ct. App. 1993), 747 n.71
M. A. Mortenson Co. v. United States, 843 F.2d 1360 (Fed. Cir. 1988), 327 n.10
Mann v. Clowser, 59 S.E.2d 78 (Va. 1950), 50 n.49
Manzo v. Ford, 731 S.W.2d 673 (Tex. App. Houston [14th Dist.] 1987, no writ), 129 n.57, 129 n.59, 131 n.73
Mark V, Inc. v. Mellekas, 845 P.2d 1232 (N.M. 1993), 124 n.18
Marrick Homes LLC v. Rutkowski, 232 Md. App. 689, 161 A.3d 53 (2017), 152 n.7, 661 n.37
Martin K. Eby Constr. Co., Inc. v. Jacksonville Transp. Auth., 436 F. Supp. 2d 1276 (M.D. Fla. 2005), 47 n.38, 49 n.42
Maryland Cas. Co. v. King, 381 P.2d 153 (Okla. 1963), 579 n.10
Mateyka v. Schroeder, 504 N.E.2d 1289 (Ill. 1987), 434 n.29
Maverick Diversified, Inc., ASBCA Nos. 19838, 19955, and 20091, 76-2 BCA ¶ 12,104 (1976), 473 n.47
Mayor and City Council of Columbus v. Clark-Dietz & Assocs. Eng'rs, Inc., 550 F. Supp. 610 (N.D. Miss. 1982), 709 n.145
McClintic-Marshall Co. v. Ford Motor Co., 236 N.W. 792 (Mich. 1931), 547 n.95
McConnell v. Corona City Water Co., 149 Cal. 60, 85 P. 929 (1906), 49 n.46
McConnell v. Servinsky Eng'g, PLLC, 22 F. Supp. 3d 610 (W.D. Va. 2014), 660 n.33, 665 n.54, 666, 696 n.118, 706–707 n.137
McDevitt & Street Co. v. Marriott Corp., 713 F. Supp. 906 (E.D. Va. 1989), *aff'd in part, rev'd in part*, 911 F.2d 723 (4th Cir. 1990), *on remand*, 754 F. Supp. 513 (E.D. Va. 1991), 434 n.30, 710 n.149
McDonough v. Whalen, 313 N.E.2d 435 (Mass. 1974), 702 n.130
McDowell v. Perry, 9 Cal. App. 2d 555 (1935), 536 nn.33–36
MCI Constructors, Inc. v. Hazen & Sawyer, P.C., 401 F. Supp. 2d 504 (M.D.N.C. 2005), 219 n.54
McJunkin Corp. v. City of Orangeburg, 238 F.2d 528 (4th Cir. 1956), 128 n.47
McKee By & Through McKee v. City of Pleasanton, 242 Kan. 649, 750 P.2d 1007 (1988), 161 n.30
McKinley v. Brandt Constr., Inc., 859 N.E.2d 572 (Ohio Ct. App. 2006), 618 n.19
McKnight v. Lange Mfg. Co., 155 S.W. 977 (Tex. App. 1913), 377 n.66
McNeal v. Marco Bay Assocs., 492 So. 2d 778 (Fla. Dist. Ct. App. 1986), 332
McQuagge v. United States, 197 F. Supp. 460 (W.D. La. 1961), 432 n.18
MCS Portable Restroom Service, March 28, 2007, B-299291, 2007 CPD P 55, 2007 WL 926295 (Comp. Gen.), 797–803

Mega Constr. Co. v. United States, 29 Fed. Cl. 396 (Fed. Cl. 1993), 326 n.5

Memphis & L.R.R. Co. v. Dow, 120 U.S. 287, 7 S. Ct. 482, 30 L. Ed. 595 (1887), 582 n.11

Mennonite Deaconess Home and Hosp., Inc. v. Gates Eng'g Co., 219 Neb. 303, 363 N.W.2d 155 (1985), 285 n.7

Menorah Nursing Home, Inc. v. Zukov, 548 N.Y.S.2d 702 (N.Y. App. Div. 1989), 579 n.10

MEP Construction, LLC v. Truco MP, LLC, 2018 Ill. App. (1st) 180539-U, 2018 WL 6920124 (Ill. App. 1 Dist. 2018), 541 n.67

Merchs. Envtl. Indus., Inc. v. SLT Realty Ltd. P'ship, 731 N.E.2d 394 (Ill. App. Ct. 2000), 552 n.119

Meridian Eng'g Co. v. United States, 130 Fed. Cl. 147 (2016), 440 n.51

Meridian Eng'g Co. v. United States, 885 F.3d 1351 (Fed. Cir. 2018), 763 n.14, 804 n.31

Merrill Stevens Dry Dock Co. v. M/V Yeocomico II, 329 F.3d 809 (11th Cir. 2003), 332

Metcalf Constr. Co. v. United States, 742 F.3d 984 (Fed. Cir. 2014), 484–485

Metric Constr., Inc. v. Nat'l Aeronautics & Space Admin., 169 F.3d 747 (Fed. Cir. 1999), 442 n.58

Metric Constr. Co. v. United States, 81 Fed. Cl. 804 (2008), 441 n.56

Metropolitan Atlanta Rapid Transit Authority v. Green International, Inc., 509 S.E.2d 674 (Ga. Ct. App. 1999), 203, 214 n.33

Metro. Steel Indus., Inc. v. Perini Corp., 828 N.Y.S.2d 395 (N.Y. App. Div. 2007), 450 n.95

M. Glosser & Sons, Inc. v. Micco, 309 A.2d 602 (Pa. Commw. Ct. 1973), 373 n.50

M & G Services, Inc. v. Buffalo Lake Advanced Biofuels, LLC, 895 N.W.2d 277 (Minn. App. 2017), 532 n.12

Micro-King Co., United States *ex rel.,* v. Cmty. Science Tech., Inc., 574 F.2d 1292 (5th Cir. 1978), 372 n.44

Mid Continent Aircraft Corp. v. Curry Cnty. Spraying Serv., Inc., 572 S.W.2d 308 (Tex. 1978), 669 n.82

Mike Bldg. & Constr., Inc. v. Just Homes, LLC, 2010 NY slip op. 20041, 901 N.Y.S.2d 458 (Sup. Ct.), 727 n.19

Mike McGarry & Sons, Inc. v. Construction Resources One, LLC, 107 N.E.3d 91 (Ohio Ct. App. 2018), 531 n.10

Mike M. Johnson, Inc. v. Cnty. of Spokane, 78 P.3d 161 (Wash. 2003), 453 n.106

Miller Elevator Co. v. United States, 30 Fed. Cl. 662 (Fed. Cl. 1994), 426 n.3, 433 n.23, 480 n.77

Miller v. Big River Concrete, LLC, 14 S.W.3d 129 (Mo. App. 2000), 706 n.135

Miller v. Bourgoin, 613 A.2d 292 (Conn. App. Ct. 1992), 380 n.82

Miller v. DeWitt, 37 Ill. 2d 273, 226 N.E.2d 630 (1967), 187–188, 413 n.56

Miller v. United States Steel Corp., 902 F.2d 573 (7th Cir. 1990), 695 n.113

Millgard Corp. v. McKee/Mays, 831 F.2d 88 (5th Cir. 1987), 646 n.70

Milton Constr. Co. v. Alabama Highway Dep't, 568 So. 2d 784 (Ala. 1990), 755 n.85

Mingus Constructors, Inc. v. U.S., 812 F.2d 1387 (Fed. Cir. 1987), 383 n.98, 436 n.39

Missler v. Anne Arundel Cnty., 314 A.2d 451 (Md. 1974), 127 n.44, 127 n.45

Mojave Enters. v. United States, 3 Cl. Ct. 353 (1983), 234 n.36

Money v. Fort Hayes State Univ. Endowment Ass'n, 64 P.3d 458 (Kan. App. 2003), 126 n.37

TABLE OF CASES

Monson v. Paramount Homes, Inc., 515 S.E.2d 445 (N.C. App. 1999), 650 n.83, 651 n.86
Mont. Fair Hous. v. Am. Capital Dev., 81 F. Supp. 2d 1057 (D. Mont. 1999), 155 n.16
Montgomery Indus. Int'l., Inc. v. Thomas Constr. Co., 620 F.2d 91 (5th Cir. 1980), 290 n.27
Montgomery Ward & Co., Inc. v. Dalton, 665 S.W.2d 507 (Tex. App. El Paso, 1983, no writ), 133–134
Montrose Contracting Co. v. Cnty. of Westchester, 80 F.2d 841 (2d Cir. 1936), 49 n.46
Moore Bros. Co. v. Brown & Root, Inc., 207 F.3d 717 (4th Cir. 2000), 386 n.108, 386 n.112, 387 n.113
Moorman Mfg. Co. v. Nat'l Tank Co., 435 N.E.2d 443 (Ill. 1982), 308 n.80, 713 n.156
Moransais v. Heathman, 744 So. 2d 973 (Fla. 1999), 663 n.47, 665 n.56, 709 n.144
Morgillo v. Empire Paving, Inc., 118 A.3d 760 (Conn. App. Ct. 2015), 719 n.4
Morrison-Knudsen Co. v. United States, 184 Ct. Cl. 661, 397 F.2d 826 (1968), 478 n.72, 482
Morris v. Osmose Wood Preserving, Inc., 667 A.2d 624 (Md. 1995), 662 n.41
Morse/Diesel, Inc. v. Trinity Indus., Inc., 655 F. Supp. 346 (S.D.N.Y. 1987), 657 n.13
Moses H. Cone Memorial Hosp. v. Mercury Constr. Corp., 460 U.S. 1, 103 S. Ct. 927, 74 L. Ed. 2d 765 (1983), 9 n.26
Mounds View, City of, v. Walijarvi, 263 N.W.2d 420 (Minn. 1978), 161 n.29
Moundsview Ind. S.D. No. 621 v. Buetow Assoc., 253 N.W.2d 836 (Minn. 1977), 212, 213, 626–628, 629 n.33
MTB Group, Inc. v. United States, 65 Fed. Cl. 516 (2005), 252
Muchisky v. Frederic Roofing Co., 838 S.W.2d 74 (Mo. Ct. App. 1992), 656 n.8
Mudgett v. Marshall, 574 A.2d 867 (Me. 1990), 655 n.5
Mullane v. Central Hanover Bank & Trust Co., 339 U.S. 306, 70 S. Ct. 652, 94 L. Ed. 865 (1950), 159
Mullen v. Town of Louisburg, 225 N.C. 53, 33 S.E.2d 484 (1945), 239 n.73
Munilla Constr. Mgmt., LLC v. United States, 130 Fed. Cl. 635 (Fed. Cl. 2017), 271 n.20
Munsey Trust Co., United States v., 332 U.S. 234 (1947), 581, 582
Murphy Dev., LLC, United States v., No. 3:08-0960, 2009 WL 3614829 (M.D. Tenn. Oct. 27, 2009), 156 n.16
Murphy v. City of Springfield, 738 S.W.2d 521 (Mo. Ct. App. 1987), 308 n.81
Murphy v. E.R. Squibb & Sons, Inc., 710 P.2d 247 (Cal. 1985), 660 n.30
Mustang Pipeline Company, Inc. v. Driver Pipeline Company, Inc., 134 S.W.3d 195 (Texas 2004), 501–505
MW Builders, Inc. v. United States, 134 Fed. Cl. 469 (Fed. Cl. 2017), 342 n.26
MW Builders, Inc. v. United States, 136 Fed. Cl. 584 (Fed. Cl. 2018), 384 n.100, 443 n.62
Myers & Chapman, Inc. v. Thomas G. Evans, Inc., 323 N.C. 559, 374 S.E.2d 385 (1988), 367 n.21
Myrtle Beach Pipeline Corp. v. Emerson Elec. Co., 843 F. Supp. 1027 (D.S.C. 1993), 674

N. Am. Mech., Inc. v. Walsh Constr. Co. II, LLC, 132 F. Supp. 3d 1064 (E.D. Wis. 2015), 737 n.50, 811 n.1
Nastri v. Wood Bros. Homes, Inc., 690 P.2d 158 (Ariz. App. 1984), 697 n.124

Natelli, United States v., 527 F.2d 311 (2d Cir. 1975), *cert. denied,* 425 U.S. 934 (1976), 658 n.23
Nat'l Am. Ins. Co. v. Certain Underwriters at Lloyd's London, 93 F.3d 529 (9th Cir. 1996), 436 n.37
Nat'l Glass, Inc. v. J.C. Penney Props., Inc., 336 Md. 606, 650 A.2d 246 (1994), 553 n.126
Nat'l Presto Indus., Inc. v. United States, 338 F.2d 99 (Ct. Cl. 1964), 465 n.25
Nat'l Union Fire Ins. Co. of Pittsburgh, PA v. CBI Indus., Inc., 907 S.W.2d 517 (Tex. 1995), 127
Nat'l Union Fire Ins. Co. v. Pratt & Whitney Canada, Inc., 107 Nev. 535, 815 P.2d 601 (1991), 661 n.40, 690 n.103
Nat'l Union Indem. Co. v. G. E. Bass & Co., 369 F.2d 75 (5th Cir. 1966), 369 n.28, 377 n.66
N. Contracting, Inc. v. Illinois, 2004 WL 422704 (N.D. Ill. Mar. 3, 2004), 247 n.135
Neal & Co. Inc. v. United States, 36 Fed. Cl. 600 (1996), 473 n.48
Neal R. Gross & Co., Inc., B-2940924.2, Jan. 17, 1991, 91-1 CPD para. 53, 799
Neece v. AAA. Realty Co., 322 S.W.2d 597 (1959), 124 n.24
In re Nelson Co., 959 F.2d 1260 (3d Cir. 1992), 124 n.21
Nelson v. Commw., 368 S.E.2d 239 (N.E. 1988), 159 n.25
Netherlands Ins. Co. v. BSHM Architects, Inc., 111 N.E.3d 1229, 2018 Ohio 3736 (Ohio Ct. App. 2018), 618 n.19
Netherland v. Wittner, 662 S.W.2d 786 (Tex. App. Houston [14th Dist.] 1983, writ ref'd n.r.e.), 129 n.62
Nether Providence Twp. Sch. Auth. v. Thomas M. Durkin & Sons, Inc., 476 A.2d 904 (Pa. 1984), 433 n.22
New Albany Historic Preservation Comm'n v. Bradford Realty, Inc., 965 N.E.2d 79 (2012), 159
Newell Recycling of Atlanta, Inc. v. Jordan Jones and Goulding, Inc., 703 S.E.2d 323 (Ga. 2010), 641–642
Newfield House, Inc. v. Massachusetts Department of Public Welfare, 651 F.2d 32 (1st Cir. 1981), 775
NewMech Companies, Inc. v. Independent School Dist. No. 206, 558 N.W.2d 22 (Minn. Ct. App. 1997), 242 n.102
New Pueblo Constructors, Inc. v. State, 144 Ariz. 95, 696 P.2d 185 (1985), 742 n.54
New SD, Inc. v. Rockwell Inter. Corp., 79 F.3d 953 (9th Cir. 1996), 763 n.12
Newsom v. United States, 676 F.2d 647 (Ct. Cl. 1982), 443 n.61
New York, City of, v. Aetna Cas. & Surety Co., 1997 WL 379704 (S.D.N.Y. 1997), 579 n.10
Nolte v. Hudson Nav. Co., 16 F.2d 182 (2d Cir. 1926), 131 n.74, 131 n.77
Northern Corp. v. Chugach Elec. Ass'n, 518 P.2d 76 (Alaska 1974), 341 n.23
Northern Montana Hosp. v. Knight, 811 P.2d 1276 (Mont. 1991), 649 n.82, 651 n.86
Northridge Co. v. W. R. Grace and Co., 471 N.W.2d 179 (Wis. 1991), 691 n.104
Northrop Grumman Corp. v. United States, 47 Fed. Cl. 20 (2000), 465 n.25
North Slope Tech. Ltd., Inc. v. United States, 14 Cl. Ct. 242 (1988), 233 n.35, 234–235, 477 n.64
Nortz v. United States, 294 U.S. 317 (1935), 310
Nota Constr. Corp. v. Keyes Assoc., Inc., 694 N.E.2d 401 (Mass. App. 1998), 715 n.164

Nova Group, Inc., ASBCA No. 55408, 10-2 BCA ¶ 34,533 (2010), 484 n.92
Nowicki v. Cannon Steel Erection Co., 711 N.E.2d 536 (Ind. Ct. App. 1999), 404 n.30
Nystrom v. Servus Robots, L.L.C., LF-1517-3, 2000 WL 249246 (Va. Cir. Ct. Mar. 2, 2000), 697 n.122

Ocean Ridge Development Corp. v. Quality Plastering, Inc., 247 So. 2d 72 (Fla. 4th DCA 1971), 345
Ohio Crane Co. v. Hicks, 110 Ohio St. 168, 143 N.E. 388 (1924), 48
Old Dominion Elec. Coop. v. Ragnar Benson, Inc., 2006 U.S Dist. LEXIS 56145 (E. Dist. Va. 2006), 354 n.49, 356 n.55
Olympic Products Co. v. Roof Sys., Inc., 363 S.E.2d 367 (N.C. App. 1988), 701 n.126
Olympus Corp. v. United States, 98 F.3d 1314 (Fed. Cir. 1996), 472 n.44
One North McDowell Assoc. v. McDowell Dev. Co., 389 S.E.2d 834 (N.C. App. 1990), 649 n.81, 651 n.85
Orshoski v. Krieger, No. OT-01-009, 2001 WL 1388037 (Ohio Ct. App. Nov. 9, 2001), *appeal denied*, 763 N.E.2d 1185 (Ohio 2002), 658 n.22
Ossining Union Free Sch. Dist. v. Anderson LaRocca Anderson, 539 N.E.2d 91 (N.Y. 1989), 713 n.159
Otinger v. Water Works & Sanitary Sewer Bd., 177 So. 2d 320 (Ala. 1965), 341 n.24
Owens-Corning Fiberglas Corp. v. United States, 419 F.2d 439, 190 Ct. Cl. 211 (1969), 311–312

Pac. Alaska Contractors, Inc. v. United States, 436 F.2d 461 (Ct. Cl. 1971), 471 n.40
Pacific Sash & Door Co. v. Bumiller, 162 Cal. 664 (1912), 539 n.54
Pa. Dep't of Transp. v. Jones D. Morrisey, Inc., 682 A.2d 9 (Pa. Commw. Ct. 1996), 47 n.38
Paine v. Spottiswoode, 612 A.2d 235 (Me. 1992), 47 n.38
Palmer v. Brown, 273 P.2d 306 (Cal. Dist. Ct. App. 1954), 368 n.26
Palmetto Linen Serv., Inc. v. U.N.X., Inc., 205 F.3d 126 (4th Cir. 2000), 675 n.88, 685 n.99, 701 n.127
Paralyzed Veterans of Am. v. Ellerbe Becket Architects & Eng'rs, 945 F. Supp. 1 (D.D.C. 1996), 155 n.15
Parker v. Panama City, 151 So. 2d 469 (Fla. Dist. Ct. App. 1963), 228 n.11
Parsons Evergreene, LLC, Appeal of, ASBCA LEXIS 258 (A.S.B.C.A. Sept. 5, 2018), 470 n.37
Pathman Construction Co., ASBCA No. 23392, 85-2 B.C.A. ¶ 18,096 (1985), 326 n.7
Patriot Contracting, LLC v. Star Ins. Co., 2017 WL 713677 (E.D. La. 2017), 386 n.108
Paul Hardeman, Inc. v. Arkansas Power & Light Co., 380 F. Supp. 298 (E.D. Ark. 1974), 12 n.32
Paul M. Spillman v. American Homes of Mocksville, Inc., 422 S.E.2d 740 (N.C. App. 1992), 676
Paul N. Howard Co. v. Puerto Rico Aqueduct Sewer Authority, 744 F.2d 880 (1st Cir. 1984), 775
Pavel v. A. S. Johnson, 674 A.2d 521 (Md. App. 1996), 291 n.30
PBS&J Constructors, Inc., ASBCA Nos. 57814, 57964, 14-1 BCA ¶ 35,680 (2014), 486
PCL Constr. Services, Inc. v. United States, 47 Fed. Cl. 745 (2000), 49 n.47, 50 n.49

Pearlman v. Reliance Ins. Co., 371 U.S. 132, 83 S. Ct. 232, 9 L. Ed. 2d 190 (1962), 370–371, 580–583, 586
Peck v. Horrocks Eng'rs, Inc., 106 F.3d 949 (10th Cir. 1997), 414–416
Peerless Ins. Co. v. Cerny & Assocs., Inc., 199 F. Supp. 951 (D. Minn. 1961), 378 n.70
Penn Cent. Transp. Co. v. City of New York, 438 U.S. 104, 98 S. Ct. 2646 (1978), 159 n.24
Pennhurst State Sch. & Hosp. v. Halderman, 465 U.S. 89, 104 S. Ct. 900, 79 L. Ed. 2d 67 (1984), 775
Penzel Constr. Co., Inc. v. Jackson R-2 Sch. Dist., 544 S.W.3d 214 (Mo. Ct. App. 2017), 47 n.38, 742 n.52
Pepi Corp. v. Galliford, 254 S.W.3d 457 (Tex. Ct. App. 2007), 718 n.1
Perini Corp. v. United States, 180 Ct. Cl. 768 (1967), 481–482
Perkins v. Northeastern Log Homes, 808 S.W.2d 809 (Ky. 1991), 648 n.79
Peru Associates, Inc. v. State, 70 Misc. 2d 775, 334 N.Y.S.2d 772 (Ct. Cl. 1971), *aff'd*, 39 A.D.2d 1018, 335 N.Y.S.2d 373 (1972), 519 n.24
Peter Kiewit & Sons Co., ENG BCA No. 4861, 4967 and 4973, 85-2 BCA ¶ 18,082 (1985), 472 n.46
Peter Kiewit Sons' Co. v. Summit Constr. Co., 422 F.2d 242 (8th Cir. 1969), 447 n.80, 448 n.87
Peterson v. Ramsey Cnty., 563 N.W.2d 103 (N.D. 1997), 384 n.101
PetroChem Services, Inc. v. United States, 837 F.2d 1076 (Fed. Cir. 1988), 235 n.44
Petrus Family Trust Dated May 1, 1991 v. Kirk, 163 Idaho 490 (Idaho 2018), 697 n.123
Pfeifer v. City of Bellingham, 772 P.2d 1018 (Wash. 1989), 649 n.82, 651 n.86
Phoenix Bridge Co. v. United States, 211 U.S. 188 (1908), 45
Pilgrim Enters., Inc. v. Maryland Cas. Co., 24 S.W.3d 488 (Tex. App.-Houston [1st Dist.] 2000), 563
Pincelli v. Ohio Bridge Corp., 213 N.E.2d 356 (Ohio 1966), 243 n.104
Pioneer Constr., Inc. v. Global Inv. Corp., 202 Cal. App. 4th 161 (2011), 554
Pipeline, Inc. v. Bond Safeguard Ins. Co., 223 Cal. App. 4th 438 (2014), 551
P.J. Maffei Bldg. Wrecking Corp. v. United States, 732 F.2d 913 (Fed. Cir. 1984), 479 n.74
Plaquemine, City of, v. N. Am. Constructors, 832 So. 2d 447 (La. App. 2002), 747 n.70
Port of Houston Auth. of Harris Cnty. v. Zachry Constr. Corp., 513 S.W.3d 543 (Tex. App.-Hous. (14 Dist.) 2016), 434 n.25
Ports Authority v. Roofing Co., 294 N.C. 73, 240 S.E.2d 345 (1978), 676
Post Bros. Constr. Co. v. Yoder, 569 P.2d 133 (Cal. 1977), 376 n.63
P & P Oil Service Co., Inc. v. Bethlehem Steel Corp., 643 N.E.2d 9 (Ind. Ct. App. 1994), 539 n.56, 544 n.81
Prairie State Nat'l Bank v. United States, 164 U.S. 227, 17 S. Ct. 142, 41 L. Ed. 412 (1896), 370 n.37, 378 n.71, 582, 583
P.R. Contractors, Inc. v. United States, 76 Fed. Cl. 621 (2007), 270 n.19
Preload Tech. v. A.B. & J. Constr. Co., 696 F.2d 1080 (5th Cir. 1983), 290 n.27, 291 n.32
Prestige Ford v. Ford Dealer Computer Services, 324 F.3d 391 (5th Cir. 2003), 608 n.25
Price Trucking Corp. v. Norampac Industries, Inc., 748 F.3d 75 (2d Cir. 2014), 534 n.25
Priebe & Sons v. United States, 332 U.S. 407 (1947), 754 n.79
Pritchard Bros., Inc. v. Grady Co., 428 N.W.2d 391 (Minn. 1988), 709 n.144
Private Mortgage Inv. Servs., Inc. v. Hotel & Club Assocs., Inc., 296 F.3d 308 (4th Cir. 2002), 658 n.19

Providence Washington Ins. Co. v. Beck, 255 N.E.2d 600 (Mass. 1970), 373 n.52

Prudential Ins. Co. v. Stratton, 685 S.W.2d 818 (Ark. Ct. App. 1985), *supplemented*, 690 S.W.2d 750 (1985), 348 n.34

P.T.&L. Construction Co., Inc. v. State of New Jersey, 531 A.2d 1330 (N.J. 1987), 487–488

Pulte Home Corp. v. Osmose Wood Preserving, Inc., 60 F.3d 734 (11th Cir. 1995), 662 n.41, 685–689, 691

Pulte Home Corp. v. Parex, Inc., 579 S.E.2d 188, 2003 WL 1903424 (Va. Apr. 17, 2003), 707 n.137

PYCA Indus., Inc. v. Harrison County Waste Water Mgmt. Dist., 177 F.3d 351 (5th Cir. 1999), 437 n.46

Quern v. Jordan, 440 U.S. 332, 99 S. Ct. 1139, 59 L. Ed. 2d 358 (1979), 777

Questar Builders, Inc. v. CB Flooring, LLC, 978 A.2d 651 (Md. App. 2009), 522 n.33

RaDec Constr., Inc. v. Sch. Dist., No. 17 of Douglas County, 535 N.W.2d 408 (Neb. 1995), 440 n.48

Ralph M. Parsons Co., ASBCA No. 24347, 85-1 BCA ¶ 17,787, *aff'd on reconsid.*, 85-2 BCA ¶ 18,112, 634

Ramada Development Co. v. Rauch, 644 F.2d 1097 (5th Cir. 1981), 345

Randa/Madison Joint Venture III v. Dahlberg, 239 F.3d 1264 (Fed. Cir. 2001), 473 n.50, 474 n.51

Raymond v. Baehr, 163 N.W.2d 51 (Minn. 1968), 163 n.34

Raynor Steel Erection v. York Constr. Co., 351 S.E.2d 136 (N.C. 1986), 701 n.126

Raytheon Co. v. White, 305 F.3d 1354 (Fed. Cir. 2002), 742, 743

R. B. Wright Constr. Co. Through Rembrant, Inc. v. United States, 919 F.2d 1569 (Fed. Cir. 1990), 51 n.56

RDP Royal Palm Hotel, L.P. v. Clark Constr. Group, Inc., 168 Fed. Appx. 348, 2006 U.S. App. LEXIS 3815 (2006), 328–333

Record Steel and Construction v. United States, 62 Fed. Cl. 508 (2004), 486

Reflectone, Inc. v. Dalton, 60 F.3d 1572 (Fed. Cir. 1995), 743

R. E. Gaddie, Inc. v. Price, 528 S.W.2d 708 (Ky. 1975), 404 n.31

Reich v. Simpson, Gumpertz & Heger, Inc., 3 F.3d 1 (1st Cir. 1993), 397 n.16

Reilly v. Rangers Mgmt., Inc., 727 S.W.2d 527 (Tex. 1987), 124

Reliance Ins. Co. v. Utah Dep't of Transp., 858 P.2d 1363 (Utah 1993), 358

R. H. Macy & Co. v. Williams Tile & Terrazzo Co., Inc., 585 F. Supp. 175 (N.D. Ga. 1984), 708 n.141

Rhone Poulenc Rorer Pharm., Inc. v. Newman Glass Works, 112 F.3d 695 (3d Cir. 1997), 49 n.44, 51, 636–638

Richard Hoffman Corp. v. Integrated Bldg. Systems, 581 F. Supp. 367 (N.D. Ill. 1984), 57 n.82

Richards v. Powercraft Homes, Inc., 678 P.2d 427 (Ariz. 1984), 612 n.1

Richmond v. J. A. Croson Co., 488 U.S. 469, 109 S. Ct. 706, 102 L. Ed. 2d 854 (1989), 244–247, 796 n.26

Ridge Heating, Air Conditioning & Plumbing, Inc. v. Brennen, 135 Md. App. 247, 762 A.2d 161 (2000), *aff'd*, 366 Md. 336, 738 A.2d 691 (2001), 535 n.28

Rissler & McMurray Co. v. Sheridan Area Water Supply Joint Powers Bd., 929 P.2d 1228 (Wyo. 1996), 706 n.135

Ritchies Food Distrib., Inc. v. Refrigerated Constr. Serv., 2004 WL 957659 (Ohio Ct. App. 2004), 122 n.15
R.L. Harris, Inc. v. Cincinnati, N.O. & T. P. Ry. Co., 198 Tenn. 339, 280 S.W.2d 800 (1955), 543 n.78
R & L Supply, Ltd. v. Evangelical Lutheran Good Samaritan Society, 462 N.W.2d 515 (S.D. S. Ct. 1990), 541 n.68
RMA Engineering S.A.R.L. v. United States, 140 Fed. Cl. 191 (Fed. Cl. 2018), 442 n.60
RMGS, Inc. v. United States, 140 Fed. Cl. 728 (Fed. Cl. 2018), 241 n.84
Robert R. Jones Assocs. v. Nino Homes, 858 F.2d 274 (6th Cir. 1988), 176
Robert W. Carlstrom Co., Inc. v. German Evangelical Lutheran, 662 N.W.2d 168 (Minn. Ct. App. 2003), 480
Robinson's Inc. v. Short, 146 So. 2d 108, *cert. denied*, 152 So. 2d 170 (Fla. Ct. App. 1962), 55 n.72
Rochester Optical Mfg. Co., B-292247, B-292247.2, 2003 CPD para. 138 (Aug. 6, 2003), 800
Rocky Mountain Fire & Cas. Co. v. Biddulph Oldsmobile, 640 P.2d 851 (Ariz. 1982), 691 n.105
Roger H. Proulx & Co. v. Crest Liners, Inc., 98 Cal. App. 4th 182 (2002), 696 n.114
Rogers & Rogers, United States v., 161 F. Supp. 132 (S.D. Cal. 1958), 203 n.17
Rolf Jensen & Associates, Inc. v. Eighth Judicial District Ct. of the State of Nevada, 282 P.3d 743 (Nev. 2012), 155 n.15
Ron Medlin Constr. v. Harris, 704 S.E.2d 486 (N.C. 2010), 727 n.18
Roscoe-Ajax Constr. Co., Inc. & Knickerbocker Constr. Corp. v. United States, 458 F.2d 55 (Ct. Cl. 1972), 473 n.49, 474 n.52
Rosell v. Silver Crest Enterprises, 7 Ariz. App. 137, 436 P.2d 915 (1968), 56 n.80
Rosenstein v. Standard & Poor's Corp., 636 N.E.2d 665 (Ill. App. 1993), 704 n.133, 713 n.158
Rosen v. Bureau of Professional and Occupational Affairs, 763 A.2d 962 (Pa. Commw. Ct. 2000), 147 n.3
Ross Eng'g. Co. v. United States, 92 Ct. Cl. 253, 1940 WL 4077 (Ct. Cl. 1940), 327 n.8, 327 n.9
Rozny v. Marnul, 250 N.E.2d 656 (Ill. 1969), 658 n.22, 713 n.156
R & P Enters. v. LaGuarta, Gavrel & Kirk, Inc., 596 S.W.2d 517 (Tex. 1980), 124 n.20, 125 n.26, 129 n.60
RPR & Assocs. v. O'Brien/Atkins Assocs., P.A., 921 F. Supp. 1457 (M.D.N.C. 1995), 214 n.34, 221–222
Rudolph v. First Southern Fed. Sav. & Loan Ass'n, 414 So. 2d 64 (Ala. 1982), 390 n.129
Runnells v. Quinn, 890 A.2d 713 (Me. 2006), 728 n.21
Ryan v. Morgan Spear Assocs., Inc., 546 S.W.2d 678 (Texas Civ. App. Corpus Christi 1977, writ refused n.f.e., June 1, 1977), 166 n.48, 368 n.27

Sabco Corp. v. Marquise Const. Corp., No. 13512/10, 2014-00739, 25 N.Y.S.3d 628, 2016 N.Y. slip op. 01313, 2016 WL 716909 (N.Y. App. Div. 2016), 259 n.7
Sacramento Reg'l Transit Dist. v. Grumman Flexible, 158 Cal. App. 3d 289 (1984), 669 n.81
Saddler v. United States, 152 Ct. Cl. 557, 287 F.2d 411 (1961), 447 n.82
Safeco Credit v. United States, 44 Fed. Cl. 406 (1999), 451 n.97

Sandarac Ass'n, Inc. v. W.R. Frizzell Architects, 609 So. 2d 1349 (Fla. Dist. Ct. App. 1992), *overruled by* Moransais v. Heathman, 744 So. 2d 973 (Fla. 1999), 663 n.47

Sanders Co. Plumbing & Heating, Inc. v. City of Independence, 694 S.W.2d 841 (Mo. Ct. App. 1985), 710 n.149, 715 n.161

Santa Fe, Inc., VABCA No. 1983, 84-3 BCA ¶ 17,538 (1984), 480 n.76

Santa Fe Engineers, Inc., ASBCA Nos. 24,578, et al., 94-2 B.C.A. (CCH) ¶ 26,872 (1994), 322–323

Santa Fe Eng'rs, Inc. v. United States, 801 F.2d 379 (Fed. Cir. 1986), 452 n.104

Saratoga Fishing Co. v. J. M. Martinac & Co., 520 U.S. 875 (1997), 691 n.104

Sasso Contracting Co., Inc. v. State of New Jersey, 173 N.J. Super. 486 (App. Div. 1980), *cert. denied*, 85 N.J. 101 (1980), 487

Saturn Constr. Co. v. Conn. Dep't of Pub. Works, 1994 WL 590604 (Conn. Super. Ct. 1994), 754 n.81

Save the Prairie Society v. Greene Development Group, Inc., 323 Ill. App. 3d 862, 256 Ill. Dec. 643, 752 N.E.2d 523 (1st Dist. 2001), 39 n.10

Sch. Bd. of Broward Cnty. v. Pierce Goodwin, Alexander, & Linville, 137 So. 3d 1059 (Fla. Dist. Ct. App. 2014), 165 n.40, 746 n.68

Schofield v. Gerda, 2017 WL 2180708 (Tex. Ct. App. 2017), 228 n.12

Schultz v. King, 68 Nev. 207, 228 P.2d 401 (1951), 540 n.58, 540 n.59

Schwartz v. Kuhn, 71 Misc. 149, 126 N.Y.S. 568 (1911), 213

Scott & Fetzer Co. v. Montgomery Ward & Co., 493 N.E.2d 1022 (Ill. 1986), 692

Scott v. Matlack, Inc., 39 P.3d 1160 (Col. 2002), 398–401, 404 n.31

Scribante v. Edwards, 181 P. 75 (Cal. Ct. App. 1919), 201 n.11

Scully v. Otis Elevator Co., 275 N.E.2d 905 (Ill. App. Ct. 1971), 404 n.32

S & D Mechanical Contractors v. Enting Water Conditioning Systems, Inc., 71 Ohio App. 3d 228, 593 N.E.2d 354 (1991), 55 n.73, 56 n.77

Sears, Roebuck & Co. v. Enco Associates, Inc., 43 N.Y.2d 389 (N.Y. 1977), 213

Secord v. Willow Ridge Stables, Inc., 690 N.Y.S.2d 375 (N.Y. App. Div. 1999, mem. op.), 413 n.55

Seely v. White Motor Co., 63 Cal. 2d 9, 45 Cal. Rptr. 17, 403 P.2d 145 (1965), 659 n.28, 659 n.30, 660–661, 662 n.42, 667 n.69, 669, 678, 705

Segari v. Uchello, 44 So. 2d 722 (La. Ct. App. 1950), 125 n.30

Semida v. Rice, 863 F.2d 1156 (4th Cir. 1988), 658 n.23

Seminole Tribe of Florida v. Florida, 517 U.S. 44, 116 S. Ct. 1114, 134 L. Ed. 2d 252 (1996), 776

Sensenbrenner v. Rust, Orling & Neale Architects, Inc., 374 S.E.2d 55 (Va. 1988), 697 n.122

Servidone Constr. Corp. v. United States, 19 Cl. Ct. 346, *aff'd*, 931 F.2d 860 (Fed. Cir. 1991), 473 n.47, 475 n.59, 478 n.66, 739

7 World Trade Co. v. Westinghouse Elec. Corp., 682 N.Y.S.2d 385 (1998), 661 n.38

Severin v. United States, 99 Ct. Cl. 435 (1943), 308 n.83, 309–311, 312

Seward Housing Corp. v. Conroy Bros. Co., 573 N.W.2d 364 (1998), 302 n.63

Shafer Elec. & Constr. v. Mantia, 96 A.3d 989 (Pa. 2014), 719 n.3

Sharon Steel Corp. v. Workers Compensation Appeal Bd., 670 A.2d 1194 (Pa. Commw. 1996), 649 n.83, 651 n.86

Sharp v. Coopers & Lybrand, 83 F.R.D. 343 (E.D. Pa. 1974), 658 n.23

Sheetz, Aiken & Aiken, Inc. v. Spann, Hall, Ritchie, Inc., 512 So. 2d 99 (Ala. 1987), 215 n.37

Shepard v. City of Palatka, 414 So. 2d 1077 (Fla. 5th DCA 1981), 212

Sherman R. Smoot Corp., ASBCA No. 52261, 03-1 BCA (CCH) ¶ 32,197 (2003), 350 n.41

Sherman R. Smoot Co. v. Ohio Dep't of Adm. Serv., 136 Ohio App. 3d 166 (2000), 47 n.38, 51

Shine v. Childs, 382 F. Supp. 2d 602 (S.D.N.Y. 2005), 177–179

Shively v. Belleville Twp. High Sch. Dist. No. 201, 329 Ill. App. 3d 1156, 769 N.E.2d 1062 (2002), 67 n.10

Shoffner Indus., Inc. v. W. B. Lloyd Constr. Co., 257 S.E.2d 50 (N.C. App. 1979), 709 n.144

Showplace Square Loft Co. v. Primecore Mortgage Trust, Inc., 289 B.R. 403 (Bankr. N.D. Cal. 2003), 554 n.130

S & H Riggers & Erectors, Inc. v. Occupational Safety & Health Comm'n, 659 F.2d 1273 (5th Cir. 1981), 401 n.21

Sienna Court Condo. Ass'n v. Champion Aluminum Corp., 2017 IL App (1st) 143364, 75 N.E.3d 260 (2017), *rev'd on other grounds*, 2018 IL 122022, ___ N.E.3d ___ (2018), 166 n.48

Sierra v. Garcia, 106 N.M. 573, 746 P.2d 1105 (1987), 751

Silliman Co. v. S. Ippolito & Sons, Inc., 467 A.2d 1249 (Conn. App. Ct. 1983), 371 n.42

Sime v. Tvenge Assocs. Architects & Planners, P.C., 488 N.W.2d 606 (N.D. 1992), 160

Simon v. Drake Constr. Co., 87 Ohio App. 3d 23, 621 N.E.2d 837 (8th Dist. Cuyahoga Cnty. 1993), 163–164

Simpson v. United States, 172 U.S. 372 (1899), 46, 460

Sims v. Lewis, 374 So. 2d 298 (Ala. 1979), 618 n.23

Sipco Servs. Marine, Inc. v. Wyatt Field Serv. Co., 857 S.W.2d 602 (Tex. App. 1993), 290 n.29, 291 n.32

Sirrah Enterprises, LLC v. Wunderlich, 399 P.3d 89, 242 Ariz. 542 (Ariz. 2017), 656 n.7

S.J. Amoroso Constr. Co. v. United States, 981 F.2d 1073 (9th Cir. 1992), 237 n.58, 238 n.61

Skidmore, Owings & Merrill, 5 BNA OSHC 1762 (OSHRC 1977), 397 n.16

Skidmore, Owings & Merrill v. Intrawest I Ltd. Pshp., NO. 35195-8-I, 1997 Wash. App. LEXIS 1505 (Ct. App. Sept. 8, 1997), 84 n.28

Skyland Developers, Inc. v. Sky Harbor Assocs., 586 S.W.2d 564 (Tex. Civ. App. Corpus Christi, 1979, no writ), 129 n.57

Slippery Rock Area Sch. Dist. v. Tremco, Inc., 2016 WL 3198122 (W.D. Pa. 2016), 57 n.83

S & M Constructors, Inc. v. Columbus, 70 Ohio St. 2d 69, 434 N.E.2d 1349 (1982), 48–49

Smith, United States v., 256 U.S. 11 (1921), 462 n.14, 463 n.17

Smith v. Goff, 325 P.2d 1061 (Okla. 1958), 205

Smith v. Seaboard Coast Line R.R. Co., 639 F.2d 1235 (5th Cir. 1981), 301 n.61

S. & M/Traylor Bros. (JV), ENG BCA Nos. 3878, 3904, 3943, 82-1 BCA ¶ 15,484 (1981), 479 n.73

Solartech Renewables, LLC v. Techcity Properties, No. 526774, 2018 N.Y. slip op. 08739, 2018 WL 6683171 (N.Y. App. Div. 2018), 110 n.8

Soletanche Rodio Nicholson (JV), ENG BCA Nos. 5796 and 5891, 94-1 BCA ¶ 26,472 (1993), 475 n.60

In re South Bay Expressway, L.P. v. Otay River Constructors, 434 B.R. 589 (2010), 551 nn.113–116, 552 n.117

Southern Green Builders, LP v. Cleveland, 558 S.W.3d 251 (Tex. App. 2018), 125 n.27

Southland Corp. v. Keating, 465 U.S. 1 (1984), 604 n.17

Southland Enterprises, Inc. v. United States, 24 Cl. Ct. 596 (1991), 452 n.103

Souza & McCue Constr. Co., Inc. v. Superior Court of San Benito County, 370 P.2d 338 (Cal. 1962), 462 n.15, 463 n.17

Sowders v. M.W. Kellogg Co., 663 S.W.2d 644 (Tex. Ct. App. 1983), 647 n.74

Spearin, United States v., 248 U.S. 132, 39 S. Ct. 59 (1918), 45–51, 55 n.74, 104, 105, 165, 459 n.2, 461–462, 484, 630–638, 810, 811

SPE GO Holdings, Inc. v. W & O Constr., Inc., 2018 WL 6181645 (6th Cir. 2018), 135 n.94

Spring Motors Distrib. v. Ford Motor Co., 489 A.2d 660 (N.J. 1985), 684 n.96

Stabler Constr., Inc. v. Comm. of Pennsylvania, 692 A.2d 1150 (Pa. 1997), 49

Standard Constrs., Inc. v. Chevron Chem. Co., 101 S.W.3d 619 (Tex. App. Houston [1st Dist.] 2003, petition denied), 128, 129 n.58

Star Development Group, LLC v. Constructure Management, Inc., 2018 WL 1525703 (D. Md. 2018), 333 n.12

State Contracting & Eng'g Corp. and State Paving Corp. v. State of Florida, et al., No. 00-1434, 258 F.3d 1329 (Jul. 20, 2001), *reh'g and reh'g en banc denied* (Sep. 6, 2001), 772–777

State Contracting & Eng'g Corp. v. Florida, No. 97-7014-CIV-DIMITROULEAS (S.D. Fla. Mar. 2, 2000), 772

State Contracting & Eng'g Corp. v. Florida, No. 99-1236, 1999 WL 717798 (Fed. Cir. Sept. 2, 1999), 774

State *ex rel.* _____ v. *See Name of party*

State Farm & Cas. Co. v. Rodriguez, 88 S.W.3d 313 (Tex. App.-San Antonio 2002, pet. denied), 563

State Mechanical Contractors, Inc. v. Vill. of Pleasant Hill, 132 Ill. App. 3d 1027, 87 Ill. Dec. 532, 477 N.E.2d 509 (Ill. App. 1985), 242 n.99

State Ready Mix, Inc. v. Moffatt & Nichol, 232 Cal. App. 4th 1227, 181 Cal. Rptr. 3d 921 (2015), 665 n.54, 707–708 n.140

State Road Department of Florida v. Tharp, 146 Fla. 745, 1 So. 2d 868 (1941), 775

State v. _____. *See Name of party*

Stearman v. Centex Homes, 78 Cal. App. 4th 611 (2000), 659 n.30, 691 n.104

Sterling Millwrights, Inc. v. United States, 26 Cl. Ct. 49 (1992), 168 n.53

Stevens Const. Corp. v. Carolina Corp., 63 Wis. 2d 342, 217 N.W.2d 291 (1974), 56 n.76, 382 n.88, 382 n.91

Stitt v. Royal Park Fashions, Inc., 546 S.W.2d 924 (Tex. Civ. App. Dallas, 1977, writ ref'd n.r.e.), 129 n.57

St. Joseph Hosp. v. Corbetta Constr. Co., Inc., 21 Ill. App. 3d 925, 316 N.E.2d 51 (1974), 163, 622–625, 747 n.70

Stock & Grove, Inc. v. United States, 204 Ct. Cl. 103 (1974), 471 n.39, 472 n.45

Stoeckert v. United States, 391 F.2d 639 (Ct. Cl. 1968), 445 n.71

Stone's Throw Condominium Ass'n, Inc. v. Sand Cove Apartments, Inc., 749 So. 2d 520 (Fla. App. 1999), 709 n.144

Stone & Webster Eng'g Corp. v. Duquesne Light Co., 79 F. Supp. 2d 1 (D. Mass. 2000), 649 n.80, 651 n.84

Stoney v. Franklin, 44 UCC Rep. Serv. 2d 1211 (Va. Cir. Ct. 2001), 684 n.96

Storm v. St. Clair Corp., 153 S.W.3d 360 (Mo. Ct. App. 2005), 746 n.64

Stout, Hall & Bangs v. United States, 27 C. Cls. 385 (1892), 310–311

Stovall v. Reliance Ins. Co., 107 P.3d 1219 (Kan. 2005), 746 n.65, 746 n.66

St. Paul Fire & Marine Ins. Co. v. City of Green River, Wyo., 93 F. Supp. 2d 1170 (D. Wyo. 2000), *aff'd*, 6 Fed. Appx. 828 (10th Cir. 2001), 518 n.21, 572–577

St. Paul Fire & Marine Ins. Co. v. Pearson Constr. Co., 547 N.E.2d 853 (Ind. 4th Dist. 1989), 49 n.48

St. Paul Fire & Marine Ins. Co. v. United States, 370 F.2d 870 (5th Cir. 1967), 579 n.10

Strand Hunt Constr. v. West, No. 96-1323, 1997 U.S. App. LEXIS 5424 (Fed. Cir. Mar. 21, 1997), 771 n.25

Stricker, P.E. v. H.H. Taylor, 158 Or. App. 608, 975 P.2d 930 (1999), 541 n.68

Strickland Tower Maintenance, Inc. v. AT&T Communications, Inc., 128 F.3d 1422 (10th Cir. 1997), 452 n.102

Strouss v. Simmons, 66 Haw. 32, 657 P.2d 1004 (1982), 549 n.103

Sturdza v. United Arab Emirates, 11 A.3d 251 (D.C. 2011), 148–151

Stuyvesant Dredging Co. v. United States, 834 F.2d 1576 (Fed. Cir. 1987), 167, 636 n.49

Subsurfco, Inc. v. B-Y Water Dist., 337 N.W.2d 448 (S.D. 1983), 349 n.36

Suit-Kote Corp. v. City of Binghamton Bd. of Contract & Supply, 628 N.Y.S.2d 861, 216 A.D.2d 831 (N.Y. App. Div. 1995), 240 n.75

Sulem v. B.T.R. East Greenbush, Inc., 589 N.Y.S.2d 969 (N.Y. App. Div. 1992), 404 n.30

Sullivan Indus., Inc. v. Double Seal Glass Co., Inc., 480 N.W.2d 623 (Mich. App. 1991), 684 n.98

Sulzer Bingham Pumps, Inc. v. Lockheed Missiles & Space Co., Inc., 947 F.2d 1362 (9th Cir. 1991), 761 n.2, 763 n.10

Summit Custom Homes, Inc. v. Great Am. Lloyds Ins. Co., 202 S.W.3d 823 (Tex. Civ. App. 2006), 562–566

Sundstrom v. New York, 159 App. Div. 241 (N.Y. App. Div. 1913), 46

Sunnyslope Grading, Inc. v. Bradford, Miller, & Risberg, Inc., 437 N.W.2d 213 (Wis. 1989), 669 n.81

Sun Valley Water Beds v. Herm Hughes & Son, Inc., 782 P.2d 188 (Utah 1989), 639 n.57

Superior Site Work, Inc. v. NASDI, LLC, 2018 WL 3716891 (E.D.N.Y. 2018), 452 n.99

Superior Steel, Inc. v. Ascent at Roebling's Bridge, LLC, 540 S.W.3d 770 (Ky. 2017), 386 n.108

Sutton Siding & Remodeling, Inc. v. Baker, 2017 Ill. App. (4th) 150956-U, 2017 WL 1065758 (Ill. Ct. App. 2017), 532 n.12

SV v. RV, 933 S.W.2d 1 (Tex. 1996), 643 n.65

SW. Bell Tel. v. PUC, 467 F.3d 418 (5th Cir. 2006), 124 n.22

SWR, Inc., B-294266, 2004 CPD para. 219 (Oct. 6, 2004), 800

Sylvan Crest Sand & Gravel Co. v. United States, 150 F.2d 642 (2d Cir. 1945), 522 n.34

Synaptek, Inc. v. United States, 141 Fed. Cl. 443 (Fed. Cl. 2018), 239 n.69

Tabasso Homes, Inc., State v., 42 Del. 110 (1942), 534 n.24, 534 n.26
Taylor & Polk Constr., Inc., United States *ex rel.*, v. Mill Valley Constr., Inc., 29 F.3d 154 (4th Cir. 1994), 339 n.18
TDC Management Corp., United States v., 24 F.3d 292 (D.C. Cir. 1994), 388, 389
Temple Beth Sholom & Jewish Ctr., Inc. v. Thyne Constr. Corp., 399 So. 2d 525 (Fla. 2d DCA 1981), 748
Temple-Eastex Inc. v. Addison Bank, 672 S.W.2d 793 (Tex. 1984), 130, 132
Terracon Consultants W., Inc. v. Mandalay Resort Grp., 125 Nev. 66, 206 P.3d 81 (2009), 681 n.93
Tharp v. Keeter/Schaefer Investments, L.P., 943 S.W.2d 811 (Mo. Ct. App. 1997), 375 n.59
ThermoCor, Inc. v. United States, 35 Fed. Cl. 480 (1996), 482 n.89
The _____ v. *See Name of party*
Thompson Thrift Construction v. Lynn, 89 N.E.3d 249, 2017 Ohio 1530 (Ohio Ct. App. 2017), 375 n.59
Thompson v. Gordon, 241 Ill. 2d 428, 349 Ill. Dec. 936, 948 N.E.2d 39 (2011), 55 n.71
Thompson v. Waters, 526 S.E.2d 650 (N.C. 2000), 658 n.20
Three Affiliated Tribes of the Fort Berthold Reservation v. Wold Eng'g, P.E., 419 N.W.2d 920 (N.D. 1988), 159 n.25
Tiara Condo. Ass'n, Inc. v. Marsh & McLennan Companies, Inc., 110 So. 3d 399 (Fla. 2013), 659 n.26, 660 n.31, 660 n.33, 662 n.42, 663 n.46, 666–667, 669, 691 n.104
Tishman Constr. Corp., Inc. v. City of New York, 228 A.D.2d 292, 643 N.Y.S.2d 589 (1st Dep't 1996), 526–527
Titan Pac. Constr. Corp. v. United States, 17 Cl. Ct. 630, 1989 WL 78828 (1989), *aff'd*, 899 F.2d 1227 (Fed. Cir. 1990), 340 n.21
Tolan and Son, Inc. v. KLLM Architects, Inc., 719 N.E.2d 288 (Ill. App. 1999), 713 n.157
Tommy L. Griffin Plumbing & Heating Co. v. Jordan, Jones & Goulding, Inc., 320 S.C. 49, 463 S.E.2d 85 (1995), 165 n.44, 699, 709 n.144
Topco, Inc. v. State of Montana, 912 P.2d 805 (Mont. 1996), 308
Top Line Builders, Inc. v. Bovenkamp, 320 P.3d 130 (Wash. Ct. App. 2014), 540 n.61
Tourist Vill. Motel, Inc. v. Massachusetts Eng'g Co., 801 F. Supp. 903 (D.N.H. 1992), 674 n.84
Town Ctr. Office Plaza Ass'n, Inc. v. Carlson Real Estate Ventures, LLC, 2017 WL 1375304 (Minn. App. 2017), 646 n.70
Town of Alma v. AZCO Constr., Inc., 10 P.3d 1256 (Colo. 2000), 698–701
Trauma Serv. Group v. United States, 104 F.3d 1321 (Fed. Cir. 1997), 790
Travelers Cas. & Sur. Co. of America v. Sweet's Contracting, Inc., 450 S.W.3d 229, 2014 Ark. 484 (Ark. 2014), 387 n.113
Trax-Fax, Inc. v. Hobba, 627 S.E.2d 90 (Ga. App. 2006), 649 n.80, 651 n.84
Triad Elec. & Controls, Inc. v. Power Sys. Eng'g, Inc., 117 F.3d 180 (5th Cir. 1997), 128 n.54
Triangle Constr. Co., Inc. v. Fouche and Associates, Inc., 218 So. 3d 1180 (Miss. App. 2017), 124 n.21
Trinity River Auth. v. URS Consultants, 889 S.W.2d 259 (Tex. 1994), 648 n.79
Truitt v. Diggs, 611 P.2d 633 (Okla. 1980), 205
Trustees of Indiana University v. United States, 618 F.2d 736 (Ct. Cl. 1980), 802

Tucci & Sons, Inc. v. Dep't of Transp., CBCA No. 4779, 17-1 BCA ¶ 36,599 (2016), 464 n.21
Tufano Contracting Corp. v. State, 269 N.Y.S.2d 564 (N.Y. App. Div. 1966), 447 n.84
Turner Constr. Co. v. Scales, 752 P.2d 467 (Alaska 1988), 648 n.79
Turnkey Enterprises, Inc. v. United States, 597 F.2d 750 (Ct. Cl. 1979), 472 n.41
Tuttle/White Constructors, Inc. v. Montgomery Elevator Co., 385 So. 2d 98 (Fla. Dist. Ct. App. 1980), 332, 385 n.105
Twist Architecture & Design, Inc. v. Or. Bd. of Architect Examiners, 361 Or. 507, 395 P.3d 574 (Or. 2017), 151 n.5
Tyger Constr. Co. v. United States, 31 Fed. Cl. 177 (1994), 49 n.46

Ullmann v. May, 147 Ohio St. 468, 72 N.E.2d 63 (1947), 48
Ultimate Concrete, LLC v. United States, 2019 WL 156933 (Fed. Cl. 2019), 442 n.57, 804 n.32
UMC Electronics Co. v. United States, 249 F.3d 1337 (Fed. Cir. 2001), 766, 770
Umpqua River Navigation Co. v. Crescent City Harbor Dist., 618 F.2d 588 (9th Cir. 1980), 710 n.149
Unadilla Silo Co., Inc. v. Hess Bros., Inc., 123 N.J. 268, 586 A.2d 226 (1991), 543 n.76
Underground Construction Co., Inc. v. City of Oakland, 2013 WL 1998909 (Cal. App. 2013), 281 n.30
United Air Lines, Inc. v. CEI Indus. of Illinois, Inc., 499 N.E.2d 558 (Ill. App. 1986), 691 n.104
United Contractors v. United States, 177 Ct. Cl. 151 (1966), 482 n.89
United States ex rel. _____ v. See Name of party
United States v. _____. See Name of party
Urban Pathfinders, Inc., ASBCA No. 23134 79-1 BCA ¶ 13,709 (1979), 790
Urban Plumbing & Heating Co. v. United States, 187 Ct. Cl. 15, 408 F.2d 382 (Ct. Cl. 1969), 785
USA Fabrics, Inc., B–295737, B–295737.2, 2005 CPD para. 82 (Apr. 19, 2005), 800
U.S. for Use and Benefit of Aucoin Elec. Supply Co. v. Safeco Ins. Co. of America, 555 F.2d 535 (5th Cir. 1977), 373 n.49
U.S. for Use and Benefit of Ken's Carpets Unlimited, Inc. v. Interstate Landscaping Co., Inc., 37 F.3d 1500 (6th Cir. 1994), 727 n.20
U.S. Specialty Ins. Co. v. Strategic Planning Associates, LLC, 2019 WL 296864 (E.D. La. 2019), 519 n.25
Utah, Nevada and California Stage Co., United States v., 199 U.S. 414, 26 S. Ct. 69, 50 L. Ed. 251 (1905), 46, 234
Utility Contractors, Inc. v. United States, 8 Cl. Ct. 42 (1985), 167 n.51
Utley-James, Inc., GSBCA No. 5370, 85-1 B.C.A. (CCH) ¶ 17,816 (1984), 323–324

Valhal Corp. v. Sullivan Associates, Inc., 44 F.3d 195 (3d Cir. 1995), 189–193, 51–752
Value Group, Inc. v. Mendham Lake Estates, L.P., 800 F. Supp. 1228 (D.N.J. 1992), 177
Vann v. United States, 190 Ct. Cl. 546 (1970), 478 n.67
Victory Constr. Co. & Paul Krummel (JV) v. United States, 206 Ct. Cl. 274 (Ct. Cl. 1975), 481 n.82
Village of Cross Keys, Inc. v. U.S. Gypsum Co., 556 A.2d 1126 (Md. App. 1989), 715 n.165

Village of Pawnee v. Azzarelli Constr. Co., 539 N.E.2d 895 (Ill. App. Ct. 1989), 349 n.36, 383 n.94
Vincent, Missouri *ex rel.*, v. Schneider, 194 S.W.3d 853 (Mo. 2006), 127 n.42
Vintage Constr., Inc. v. State Dep't of Transp., 713 P.2d 1213 (Alaska 1986), 243 n.109
Virginia Sch. of Arts, Inc. v. Eichelbaum, 493 S.E.2d 510 (Va. 1997), 290 n.26
Vulcan Painters, Inc. v. MCI Contractors, Inc., 41 F.3d 1457 (11th Cir. 1995), 452 n.102

Waggoner v. W & W Steel Co., 657 P.2d 147 (Okla. 1982), 204–209
Walker & Co. v. Harrison, 347 Mich. 630, 81 N.W.2d 352 (1957), 518 n.19
Walker v. Chancey, 117 So. 705 (Fla. 1928), 386 n.110
Walpert, Smullian & Blumenthal, P.A. v. Katz, 361 Md. 645, 762 A.2d 582 (Md. 2000), 33 n.42, 658 n.23
Walters Beach Condo. Ass'n v. Home-Owners Ins. Co., 2017 WL 5503789 (Mich. App. 2017), 612 n.1
Ward Petroleum Corp. v. Fed. Deposit Ins. Corp., 903 F.2d 1297 (10th Cir. 1990), 768
Ward v. Ernst & Young, 435 S.E.2d 628 (Va. 1993), 707 n.137
Wargo Builders, Inc. v. Douglas L. Cox Plumbing & Heating, Inc., 268 N.E.2d 597 (Ohio App. 1971), 290 n.27
Wash. Constr. Co. v. Spinella, 84 A.2d 617 (N.J. 1951), 124 n.23
Waterview Site Services, Inc. v. Pay Day, Inc., 125 Conn. App. 561, 11 A.3d 692 (2010), 546 n.88
Watson, Watson, Rutland/Architects, Inc. v. Montgomery Cnty. Bd. of Educ., 559 So. 2d 168 (Ala. 1990), 629 n.33
Wausau Tile, Inc. v. County Concrete Corp., 593 N.W.2d 445 (Wis. 1999), 670–673, 696 n.117
W.C. English, Inc. v. Rummel, Klepper & Kahl, LLP, 2017 WL 2123878 (W.D. Va. 2017), 380 n.81
Weber v. Pascarella Mason St., LLC, 930 A.2d 779 (Conn. App. Ct. 2007), 125 n.31, 126 n.32, 126 n.39, 127 n.40
Weekley v. Weekley, 27 S.E.2d 591 (W. Va. 1943), 124 n.20
Weeks Construction, Inc. v. Oglala Sioux Hous. Auth., 797 F.2d 668 (8th Cir. 1986), 547 n.96
Weeks Dredging & Contracting v. United States, 13 Cl. Ct. 193 (1987), *aff'd*, 861 F.2d 728 (Fed. Cir. 1988), 470 n.36, 473 n.50, 474–475, 478 n.68
Wegroup PC/Architects and Planners v. State, 885 P.2d 709 (Or. 1994), 436 n.41
Weill Constr. Co., Inc. v. Thibodeaux, 491 So. 2d 166 (La. Ct. App. 1985), 745 n.61
Wellons, Inc. v. Eagle Valley Clean Energy, LLC, Civil Action No. 15-cv-01252-RBJ, 2017 U.S. Dist. LEXIS 160889 (D. Colo. Sept. 29, 2017), 532 n.11
Westerhold v. United States, 28 Fed. Cl. 172 (1993), 452 n.98
WestFair Elec. Contractors v. Aetna Cas. & Surety Co., 661 N.E.2d 967 (N.Y. 1995), 304 n.70
Westgate Planet Hollywood Las Vegas, LLC v. Tutor-Saliba Corp., 421 P.3d 280 (Nev. 2017), 264 n.12
Westinghouse Elec. Corp. v. N.Y.C. Transit Auth., 623 N.E.2d 531 (N.Y. 1993), 219 n.54
Westminister, City of, v. Brannan Sand & Gravel Co., Inc., 940 P.2d 393 (Colo. 1997), 550 n.107

Westminster, City of, v. Centric-Jones Constructors, 100 P.3d 472 (Colo. App. 2003), 746 n.68
W.F. Magann v. Diamond Mfg. Co., Inc., 580 F. Supp. 1299, *rev'd in part on other grounds* (D.C.S.C. 1984), 234 n.38
W.G. Glenney Co. v. Bianco, 27 Conn. App. 199, 604 A.2d 1345 (1992), 555 n.132
Whitaker v. W. Vill. Ltd. P'ship, No. CIV.A. 3:03-CV-0411P, 2004 WL 1778963 (N.D. Tex. Aug. 4, 2004), 155 n.15
White v. Mitchell, 123 Wash. 630, 213 Pac. 10 (1923), 166 n.44
Widett v. U.S. Fidelity & Guar. Co., 815 F.2d 885 (2d Cir. 1987), 706 n.134
Wilko v. Swan, 346 U.S. 427, 74 S. Ct. 182 (1953), 609 n.29
Willamette Crushing Co. v. Arizona *ex rel.* Dep't of Transp., 188 Ariz. 79, 932 P.2d 1350 (App. 1997), 168 n.52, 328 n.11
William R. Clarke Corp. v. Safeco Ins. Co. of Am., 938 P.2d 372 (Cal. 1997), 304 n.70
Williams & Sons Erectors, Inc. v. South Carolina Steel Corp., 983 F.2d 1176 (2d Cir. 1993), 452 n.103
Williams v. United States, 127 F. Supp. 617 (Ct. Cl. 1955), 435 n.32
Willmschen v. Trinity Lakes Improvement, 840 N.E.2d 1275, 362 Ill. App. 3d 546 (2d Dist. 2005), 38 n.9
Willms Trucking Co. v. J. W. Constr. Co., 442 S.E.2d 197 (S.C. Ct. App. 1994), 452 n.102
Wills v. Black & West, Architects, 344 P.2d 581 (Okla. 1959), 205
Wilson v. Dryvit Sys., Inc., 206 F. Supp. 2d 749 (E.D.N.C. 2002), 662 n.44, 695 n.111
Wilson v. United States, 11 Ct. Cl. 513 (1875), 781, 785
Winstar Corp., United States v., 518 U.S. 839, 116 S. Ct. 2432, 135 L. Ed. 2d 964 (1996), 780, 782, 783, 784, 785 n.1
Winter v. FloorPro, Inc., 570 F.3d 1367 (Fed. Cir. 2009), 777
Wisch & Vaughan Constr. Co. v. Melrose Properties, 21 S.W.3d 36 (Mo. App. S.D. 2000), 426 n.2
W. Oil Fields, Inc. v. Pennzoil United, Inc., 421 F.2d 387 (5th Cir. 1970), 133 n.85
Womack v. United States, 182 Ct. Cl. 399 (1968), 481 n.86
Woodson v. Martin, 663 So. 2d 1327 (Fla. 2d Dist. Ct. App. 1995), *rev'd*, 685 So. 2d 1240 (Fla. 1996), 663 n.49
WRB Corp. v. United States, 183 Ct. Cl. 409 (U.S. 1968), 434 n.24, 743
Wunderlich Contracting Co. v. United States, 351 F.2d 956 (Ct. Cl. 1965), 447 n.79
Wunderlich v. California, 423 P.2d 545 (Cal. 1967), 492–493
W.V. Nelson Constr. Co. v. City of Lindstrom, 565 N.W.2d 434 (Minn. Ct. App. 1997), 229 n.14
W.W. Harris v. Phillips Pipe Line Co., 517 S.W.2d 361 (Tex. Civ. App. Austin, 1974, writ ref'd n.r.e.), 129 n.62
W & W Steel, LLC v. BSC Steel, Inc., 944 F. Supp. 2d 1066 (D. Kan. 2013), 725 n.14, 726 n.16
Wygant v. Jackson Bd. of Educ., 476 U.S. 267, 106 S. Ct. 1842 (1986), 245 n.120
Wyman v. Ayer Properties, LLC, 469 Mass. 64, 11 N.E.3d 1074 (2014), 665 n.54, 666 n.61, 667–668, 669, 697 n.121

XPO Logistics Worldwide Gov't Servs., LLC v. United States, 133 Fed. Cl. 162 (Fed. Cl. 2017), 271 n.21

Yankee Atomic Elec. Co. v. United States, 112 F.3d 1569 (Fed. Cir. 1997), 783, 784
Yankee Candle Co. v. New England Candle Co., 14 F. Supp. 2d 154 (D. Mass. 1998), *vacated pursuant to settlement*, 29 F. Supp. 2d 44 (D. Mass. 1998), 175–177
Youngdale & Sons Constr. Co. v. United States, 27 Fed. Cl. 516 (1993), 466 n.27, 473 n.47, 475 n.59
Young-Montenay, Inc. v. United States, 15 F.3d 1040 (Fed. Cir. 1994), 770
Young v. Oak Leaf Builders, Inc., 626 S.E.2d 240 (Ga. Ct. App. 2006), 618 n.20

Zenda Grain & Supply Co. v. Farmland Indus., Inc., 894 P.2d 881 (Kan. App. 1995), 301 n.56

Index

Acceptance of work, 382–383
Access, site, 36–38
Accessibility, and Americans with Disabilities Act, 155
Accident compensation, 403–417
  active negligence and, 404–405
  architects in, 413–417
  engineers in, 413–417
  and liability based on control of workplace, 405
  owners and, 405–409
  prime contractors in, 409–413
  tort liability and, 404–405
  workers' compensation in, 403
  See also Safety
Accident prevention, 394–402. *See also* Safety
Accord, changes and, 450–453
Acts of God, 334–335
Actual authority, public construction contracting and, 760, 786–795
ADA. *See* Americans with Disabilities Act (ADA)
Added first benefit, damages and, 746–748
Added value, damages and, 746–748
Addenda, to bid package, 232
Additional work, defined, 426
Adjacencies, access to, 36–38
Adjudication, in dispute resolution, 602
Advertising, in public procurement, 231
Advisory opinions, in dispute resolution, 601–602
Affirmative action, 244–247

AGC. *See* Associated General Contractors of America (AGC)
Agency construction management, 78–81
Agency law, in contract administration, 200–201
AIA. *See* American Institute of Architects (AIA)
Alabama
  economic loss rule in, 662n43
  mechanic's lien in, 537
Alaska, archaeological/historic sites in, 41
Allowances
  in bid package, 232
  in contract pricing, 278
Ambiguity, in contracts, 127–128, 129–131, 132
American Institute of Architects (AIA), 4–5
  Building Information Modeling contract forms, 830–832
  forms from, 114–118, 123–124
  insurance requirements, 558–561
  site conditions clauses from, 468
  on termination for convenience, 522–524
  termination of contract forms from, 507–511
Americans with Disabilities Act (ADA), as building code, 155
Ancient world, construction in, 1–3
Anti-indemnity statutes, 301–302
Apparent authority, 434
Applications for payment, 366–368

INDEX

Arbitration, 9
  attacking, 607
  award modification in, 607–608
  basis in statute of, 604–606
  binding, 602
  confirmation of award in, by court, 608–609
  contractual nature of remedy in, 605–607
  non-binding, 602
  principles of, 604–609
  vacation of award in, by court, 608–609
Archaeologic sites, 41–42
Architect
  accident compensation and, 413–417
  authority of, 200–201
  in claims process, 218–220
  in contract administration, 198–201
  in contractor termination, 219–220
  in design team, 20–21
  in dispute resolution, 218–219
  economic loss rule and role of, 655
  immunity of, in quasi-judicial functions, 221–222
  overpayment and, 378
  owner liability for acts of, 201
  as owner's agent, 199
  as owner's representative, 199–200
  in termination of contract, 511
Architect certification, 367–368
Architectural consultants, in design team, 146
Architectural Works Copyright Protection Act (AWCPA), 176–177
Asbestos, 43
Associated General Contractors of America (AGC), 5–6, 118–119, 468
At-Risk Construction Management, 81–85, 104–105
Audit rights, and contract pricing, 280–281
AWCPA. *See* Architectural Works Copyright Protection Act (AWCPA)

Bankruptcies
  and mechanic's lien, 553–555
  in public-private partnerships, 94n37

BEES. *See* Building for Environmental and Economic Sustainability (BEES)
Best value analysis, 816, 816n10
"Best value" awards, in public sector, 249–251
Betterment, damages and, 746–748
Bidder
  lowest, duty to award to, 236
  responsible, 238–240
Bidding, subcontractor
  and enforcement of bid by subcontractor, 291–292
  and prime contractor enforcement of bid, 289–291
  process, 288–289
Bidding, unbalanced, 270–271
Bidding irregularities, waiver of, 236–238
Bidding mistakes, 243–244
Bidding phase, 172
Bid document escrow, 595
Bid package, 231–235
Bid preparation, 235–236
Bid protests, 240–243
Bid responsiveness, 236–238
Bid security, 243–244
BIM. *See* Building Information Modeling (BIM)
Bonds
  payment, 578–579
  payment and performance, 28
  surety, 568–570
Breach, material, in termination of contract, 499, 501–506
Budget
  and contract pricing, 280
  and design agreement, 181–184
  project, in owner's program, 53–54
Builder credits, in contract pricing, 280
Builder rebates, in contract pricing, 280
Builders risk insurance, 566–567
Building codes
  design professional and, 151–159
  socioeconomic, 154–159
  traditional, 154
  variations from, 163–164
Building for Environmental and Economic Sustainability (BEES), 824

Building Information Modeling (BIM), 314–316
  3D printing and, 840–843
  4D analysis in, 821
  5D analysis in, 821–822
  after completion of construction, 836–837
  archiving with, 829
  building performance simulation, 826
  clashes, 819
  code check programs with, 820
  collaboration with, 810–811
  comparison with computer-assisted design (CAD), 814–816
  computer-assisted design vs., 813–816, 820
  conflict resolution and, 811
  ConsensusDocs forms for, 832–833
  construction phase, 827–828
  contract forms, 829–833
  contracting, 829–837
  contract risk assessment with, 834–837
  data transfer with, 818, 834–835
  defined, 812–813, 813n5
  deliverables schedule with, 834
  design coordination and analysis in, 816–820
  emergence of, 810
  end purposes in, 834
  energy analysis of model, 826
  execution planning, 837–840
  fabrication with, 840–843
  facility management, 828
  goals, 838
  granularity in, 819–820
  information exchanges with, 836–837, 838–839
  Information Foundation Classes in, 818
  Level of Development (LOD), 830–832
  life cycle process, 816–829
  mechanics of, 813–829
  process maps in, 838
  Project Execution Plan, 837–840
  proprietary software in, 818
  reliance on, 835–836
  risk mitigation with, 827
  safety planning with, 827–828
  Spearin doctrine and, 810–811
  supporting infrastructure in, 839
  sustainability analysis in, 822–827
Building site
  access to, 36–38
  adjacencies, 36–38
  archaeological concerns with, 41–42
  easement agreements for, 37–38
  environmental concerns with, 42–43
  historical concerns with, 41–42
  in owner responsibilities, 36–43
  right to use, 38
buildingSMARTalliance, 812
Business Roundtable and Construction Industry Institute, 589
"But for" analysis, 356–357
Buy American Act, 761, 796–797

CAD. *See* Computer-assisted design (CAD)
Caesar Augustus, 2–3
California
  claims of defective design professional services, 708–709
  differing site conditions in, 492–493
  economic loss rule in, 667
  implied warranty in, 166
  mechanic's lien in, 530–531, 532–533, 546, 550–551, 554
  pay-if-paid clauses in, 304
Cardinal change, 446–448
CDA. *See* Contract Disputes Act (CDA)
CERCLA. *See* Comprehensive Environmental Response Compensation and Liability Act (CERCLA)
Certificate of occupancy, completion and, 347
CFR. *See* Code of Federal Regulations (CFR)
CGL. *See* Comprehensive general liability (CGL) insurance
Changed conditions, defined, 457–458. *See also* Differing site conditions (DSCs); Site conditions
Change order(s)
  completion date and, 438–441
  as contract, 451
  in contract administration, 216–217

Change order(s), *continued*
   contract pricing and, 438–441
   defined, 425, 428–429
   drawings and, 442–443
   in Federal Acquisition Regulation, 429
   mixed pricing contracts and, 271–272
   process for, 428–431
   requests, responding to, 216–217
   reservation of rights with, 452–453
   specifications and, 442–443
   time and material pricing and, 438–441
   unit pricing and, 439
Changes
   accord and, 450–453
   additional work as, 426
   administration of, 448–450
   apparent authority and, 434
   authority to issue, 432–435
   cardinal, 446–448
   clause, 426–428
   constructive, 427, 441–444
   deleted work as, 426
   duty to perform, 444–446
   express, 427
   extra work as, 426
   forms of, 426
   inevitability of, 425–426
   notice requirements for claims for, 435–438
   payment and, 379
   pricing and, 431
   in public vs. private projects, 433
   quantum meruit and, 426
   ratification and, 434–435
   releases and, 450–453
   satisfaction and, 450–453
   and scope of work, 442
   sources of, 425–426
Chicanery, 8
Christian doctrine, 761–762
Civil construction projects, design team contracting in, 146–147
Civil False Claims Act, 763, 764–770
Civil litigation, Occupational Health and Safety Act in, 397–401
Claims
   for changes, notice for, 435–438
   defined, 388
   differing site conditions, federal, 469–476
   and False Claims Act, 388–389
   waiver of, 382–383
Claims, subcontractor
   barriers to, 307–308
   and liquidating agreements, 312–313
   pass-through system and, 308–312
   problem of, 306–307
Claims process, architect role in, 218–220
Clean Water Act, 43
CMAA. *See* Construction Managers Association of America (CMAA)
CMAR. *See* At-Risk Construction Management
COBie. *See* Construction-Operations Building Information Exchange (COBie)
Code of Federal Regulations (CFR), 761
Code of Hammurabi, 2
Codes. *See* Building codes
Collaborative contracting
   and computerized communications, 314–317
   privity system and, 313–314
Collapsed as-built analysis, 356–357
Collateral assignment to lender, in contract, 135
Colorado, economic loss rule in, 699
Commencement, time of, 326–328
Commercial General Liability insurance, 559–560
Commercial impracticability, 340–341
Commissioning, 250
Common law
   mechanic's lien and, 530
   site conditions in, 459–465
   termination of contract in, 498–506
Common law standard of care, 160–164
Compensable delays, 334–341
Competition in Contracting Act, 761
Competitive bidding laws, 8
Completion
   and certificate of occupancy, 347
   certification of, 217–218
   final, 348–350

substantial, 343–348
time for, 326–328
Comprehensive Environmental Response Compensation and Liability Act (CERCLA), 42–43
Comprehensive general liability (CGL) insurance, 561–566
Computer-assisted design (CAD), 809, 813–816, 820, 843
Concealment, of site conditions, 463–464
Concession agreement, 94
Concurrent delay, 341–343
Conflicting warranties, defective construction and, 630–638
ConsensusDocs, 468, 511–515, 813n5, 832–833
Consequential damages waiver, in design agreement, 189–193
Construction documents phase, 172
Construction loan, 57–60
Construction management
  agency, 78–81
  at-risk, 81–85
  defined, 66
  overview of, 77–78
  in public sector, 248–249
  risk factors in, 80–81
Construction Managers Association of America (CMAA), 119
Construction manager's damages, 722–723
Construction-Operations Building Information Exchange (COBie), 828
Construction phase, 173
Construction team
  in construction process, 22–25
  contractor in, 22–23
  subcontractors in, 24–25
Consultants, in design team, 21–22
Contextual contract theory, 6–8
Contingencies, in contract pricing, 278–280
Contract administration
  agency law in, 200–201
  architect as owner's agent in, 199
  architect as owner's representative, 199–200

  architect role in, 198–201
  change orders in, 216–217
  completion certification in, 217–218
  contractor termination and, 219–220
  coordination in, 214–215
  defective construction claims and, 702–709
  economic loss rule and, 679–683, 702–709
  emerging roles in, 222
  overview of, 198–200
  performance certification in, 217–218
  progress payment approval in, 215–216
  quality control and, 203–214
  requests for information in, 202–203
  work rejection in, 216
  work stoppage in, 216
Contract Disputes Act (CDA), 771, 804
Contractor
  acceptance of payment by, 383–384
  in construction team, 22–23
  in contract, 134
  damages, 723–724
  defective construction claims against, by owner, 616–620
  defective construction claims by, against design professional, 629–630
  overpayment and, 378
  termination of contract by, 507–509
Contractor certification, 367
Contractor selection
  advertising in, 231
  affirmative action and, 244–247
  bidding mistakes in, 243–244
  bid package in, 231–235
  bid preparation in, 235–236
  bid protests in, 240–243
  bid responsiveness in, 236–238
  bid security in, 243–244
  criteria, 236–252
  and duty to award to lowest bidder, 236
  hiring preferences and, 244–247
  overview of, 225
  private procurement principles in, 226–227
  project delivery systems and, 226

Contractor selection, *continued*
  public procurement principles in, 227–252
  responsible bidder in, 238–240
  reverse online bidding in, 251–252
  waiver of bidding irregularities in, 236–238
Contractor's equipment, in cost-plus contracts, 262–263
Contractor termination, architect role in, 219–220
Contract pricing
  allowances in, 278
  audit rights and, 280–281
  budget and, 280
  builder credits in, 280
  builder rebates in, 280
  change orders and, 438–441
  changes and, 277, 431
  contingencies in, 278–280
  and "cost of work" definition, 277
  cost-plus contracts in, 260–267
  cost-plus with guaranteed maximum in, 267–268
  default pricing through dispute resolution in, 274
  default pricing through third party in, 274
  index pricing in, 272
  interim payment clauses in, 275–276
  material price escalation clauses in, 274–275
  mechanisms, 256–272
  mixed pricing contracts in, 271–272
  and scope of work, 276–277
  and self-performed work, 278
  and sharing of savings, 277
  site conditions and, 458–459
  stipulated-sum contracts in, 256–260
  terms in, 272–276
  time and material pricing in, 273
  unbalanced bidding and, 270–271
  unit-price contracts in, 268–271, 439
  and Variations in Estimated Quantities clauses, 269–270

Contracts and contracting
  ambiguity in, 127–128, 129–131, 132
  from American Institute of Architects, 114–118, 123–124
  from Associated General Contractors of America, 118–119
  Building Information Modeling, 829–837
  changes clause in, 426–428
  collateral assignment to lender in, 135
  commencement of services prior to, 109–110
  consequential damages in, 743–744
  construction by owner in, 140
  from Construction Managers Association of America, 119
  contractor in, 134
  course of performance of, in interpretation, 131–132
  creation of, 110–111
  custom, 113–114
  customs and usages in, 132
  damages and breach of, 719–728
  defined, 108
  for design agreements, 107–108, 120
  from Design-Build Institute of America, 119
  design professional service description in, 136
  documents, 120–121
  early start letters and, 109–110
  from Engineers Joint Contract Documents Committee, 119
  enumeration of documents in, 122
  formation of, 107–111
  form selection, 112–114
  implied, 110–111
  incorporation by reference in, 122
  inferable standard in, 138
  integration clause in, 121–122
  intent of parties in, 127–128
  internal conflicts within, 122–124
  interpretation of, 124–134
  logical interpretation of, 128–129
  manuscript documents in, advantages and disadvantages of, 113–114
  in mechanic's lien, 535–536

oral, 109
owner-furnished items in, 139–140
owner in, 134
parol evidence rule in, 125–127
parties to, 134–136
price lock-in and, 109–110
prior dealings in interpretation of, 131–132
in public-private partnership, 94, 96
quasi, 110–111
reasonable interpretation of, 128–129
references to other parties in, 135–136
rules of construction of, 124–125
safety programs in, 402
scope of, 136–140
site indications clause in, 459–461
Spearin doctrine and, 47–49
specific vs. general terms in, 133–134
standard industry forms for, 112–113, 114–119
terminology of, in interpretation, 133–134
third-party beneficiaries in, 134–135
work description in, 136–139
written over printed terms in, 133–134
See also Design team contracting
Contract theory, contextual, 6–8
Contractual insurance requirements, 558–561
Contributory negligence, 421–422
Coordination
  avoiding obligation of, 298
  in contract administration, 214–215
  duty of, 296
  of subcontract work, 296–298
Copyright Act, 176
Cost of work, defined, 277
Cost-plus contracts
  in contract pricing, 260–267
  cost of work in, 261–265
  equipment in, 262–263
  estimates and, 266–267
  with guaranteed maximum, 267–268
  labor in, 264–265
  limitations in, 261–265
  necessity of costs in, 265
  overhead in, 265–266

  payment in, 363
  profit in, 265–266
  reasonableness of costs in, 265
  self-performed work in, 263–264
  small tool allowance in, 263
  subcontracted work in, 261–262
CPM. *See* Critical path method (CPM) schedules
Criminal False Claims Act, 764
Criminal law, public construction contracting and, 760, 763–771
Critical path method (CPM) analysis, 350–352
Critical path method (CPM) schedules, 320–324. *See also* Schedule and scheduling
Custom, in contracts, 132

Damages
  and added first benefit, 746–748
  and added value, 746–748
  betterment and, 746–748
  breach of contract, 719–728
  in builders risk insurance, 567
  calculation of, 728–745
  and cause of action, 718
  compensatory, 728–745
  consequential, in construction contracts, 743–744
  consequential, waiver of, 753
  consequential, waiver of, in design agreement, 189–193
  construction manager, 722–723
  contractor, 723–724
  design professionals, 722–723
  and economic loss rule, 660–661
  and economic waste, 745–746
  estimation of actual, 734–736
  expectation interest and, 719–724
  and home office overhead, 731–733
  and idle equipment, 730–731
  industry standards in estimation of, 735–736
  jury verdict method in estimation of, 742–743
  liquidated, 384–385
  liquidated, for delay, 753–755

Damages, *continued*
   and lost profits, 733–734
   measured mile approach with, 734–735
   measures of, general, 719–728
   measures of, vs. cause of action, 718
   mitigation of, 745–748
   and no-damages-for-delay clause, 755–756
   overview of, 717–718
   owner's, 719–722
   and price increases, 730
   and promissory estoppel, 724–726
   proof of, 728–745
   and proof of actual costs, 729–734
   punitive, 744
   and quantum meruit, 727–728
   recordkeeping and, 744–745
   and reliance interest, 724–726
   and restitution interest, 726–727
   should-cost estimates with, 736
   and termination of contract, 516–517
   time and motion studies in estimation of, 736
   and tort claims, 728
   total cost method with, 736–741
   and unjust enrichment, 726–727
   See also Liability
Damage to other property test, 689–690
Davis Bacon Act, 797
DBEs. *See* Disadvantaged business enterprises (DBEs)
DBOM. *See* Design-build, operate, and maintain (DBOM)
DEAR. *See* Department of Energy Acquisition Regulation (DEAR)
Deaths, construction, 393. *See also* Safety
Default pricing through dispute resolution, 274
Default pricing through third party, 274
Defective construction
   accrual date and, 642–643
   causes of action and, 640
   conflicting warranties and, 630–638
   contract administration and, 702–709
   contract claims in, 616–619, 621–622
   defectiveness in, 612–613
   deficiency in, 612–613
   design professional claims in, 620–630, 702–709
   drawings in, defective, 622–625
   drawings in, failure to comply with, 616–617
   and economic loss rule, 619, 624, 669–674, 684–695, 696–702
   express warranty breach in, 617
   implied warrant and, 631–634
   implied warranty breach in, 618–619
   and legal analysis of defects, 611–615
   manifestations of, vs. defects, 613–614
   notice requirements with, 620
   and observation of construction, 625–629
   owner claims in, against contractors, 616–620
   performance specifications and, 635–636
   responsibility for, 614–615
   Spearin doctrine and, 630–638
   specifications in, defective, 622–625
   specifications in, failure to comply with, 616–617
   statutes of limitations and, 638–647
   statutes of repose and, 647–649
   statutory claims in, 619–620
   time-based defenses in, 638–649
   tolling and, 645–646
   tort claims in, 619, 621–622
Defense Federal Acquisition Regulatory Supplement (DFARS), 761
Delaware, mechanic's lien in, 533
Delays
   analysis methods with, 352–357
   "but for" analysis with, 356–357
   causes of, 335
   collapsed as-built analysis with, 356–357
   compensable, 334–341
   concurrent, 341–343
   contract law and, 340–341
   Critical Path Method analysis and, 350–352
   excusable, 334–341
   and financial inability, 339

impacted as-planned analysis of, 354–355
and no-damages-for-delay clause, 755–756
pacing and, 342–343
proof of claims for, 350–352
time impact analysis with, 355
unforeseeability and, 336–339
weather in, 340
windows analysis with, 356

Deleted work
contractual mechanism for, 427–428
defined, 426

Department of Energy Acquisition Regulation (DEAR), 761

Design agreements, 107–108, 120. *See also* Contracts and contracting

Design-Bid-Build, 8, 64
architect in, 71
claim difficulty with, 74–75
contractor in, 71–72
defined, 66
and Multiple Prime approach, 76
overview of, 70–71
risk factors in, 73–75
selection factors in, 72–73
variations of, 76–77

Design-Build
challenges of, 88–89
common variations with, 90–91
defined, 66
and differing site conditions, 483–486
insurance and, 89–90
overview of, 85–86
performance criteria in, 88
preferred providers in, 89
procurement with, 88–89
in public sector, 247–248
risk factors in, 87–90
selection factors in, 86–87

Design-build, operate, and maintain (DBOM), 93

Design-Build Institute of America (DBIA), 119

Design development phase, 171–172

Design documents, ownership of, 175–180

Design process phases, 169–173

Design professionals
construction observation by, 625–629
contractor claims against, in defective construction, 629–630
damages, 722–723
defective construction claims against, 620–630, 702–709
and Economic Loss Rule, 679–683
and Occupational Health and Safety Act, 397
in public procurement, 228–230
statutes barring indemnity of, 301

Design specifications
in design team contracting, 166–168
in owner's program, 55
performance specifications vs., 166–168

Design team
architect in, 20–21
building codes and, 151–159
in construction process, 20–22
consultants in, 21–22
engineers in, 21–22
licensure of, 147–151
regulation of, 147–151

Design team contracting
Americans with Disabilities Act and, 155
applicable legal principles in, 175–179
architectural consultants in, 146
basic services in, vs. supplemental/additional services, 173–174
budget and, 181–184
in civil construction projects, 146–147
consequential damages waiver in, 189–193
disclaimers in, 186–188
engineering consultants in, 146
exculpatory provisions in, 186–188
Fair Housing Act and, 155
green codes and, 156–158
historic preservation and, 158–159
implied warranties in, 165–166
insurance in, 186
landmark preservation and, 158–159
liability limitations in, 186–193
overview of, 144

Design team contracting, *continued*
owner in, 145
owner responsibilities in, 174–175
and ownership of design documents, 175–180
payment in, 185
performance specifications vs. design specifications in, 166–168
quantum meruit in, 148–151
scope of services in, 168–174
standard of care in, 159–166
strict liability and, 159–160
termination in, 193–194
DFARS. *See* Defense Federal Acquisition Regulatory Supplement (DFARS)
Differing site conditions (DSCs)
allocation of risk of, 458
in California, 492–493
and causation of increased costs, 474–475
claim, federal, 469–476
in commercial agreements, 468–469
in common law, 459–465
defined, 457–458
in Design-Build contracts, 483–486
disclaimers and, 478–479
and duty to investigate, 476–478
exculpatory language with, 478–479
in Federal Acquisition Regulation, 466–468
in Illinois, 490–492
indications and, 461–465
limitations on claims for, 476–483
materially different than indicated, 470–475
in New Jersey, 486–488
notice of, 479–480
pricing and, 458–459
reasonableness with, 472–473
reasonably unforeseeable, 473–474
regulatory frameworks for, 465–469
representations and, 461–465
in state courts, 486–493
of unusual nature, 475–476
and variation in estimated quantities clauses, 480–482
in Virginia, 488–490

Disadvantaged business enterprises (DBEs), 287–288
Disclaimer, of *Spearin* warranty, 51
Disclaimers
in design agreement, 186–188
with site conditions, 478–479
Discrepancies, in bid package, 233
Dispute resolution, 11–15
adjudication in, 602
advisory opinions in, 601–602
arbitration in, 602, 604–609
architect in, 218–219
bid document escrow in, 595
binding resolution stage in, 590, 591
boards, 596–599
control stage in, 590, 591, 594–599
cooperation incentives in, 592
cooperation stage in, 590, 592–594
early, 594–599
geotechnical baseline summary report in, 595
historical development of, 588–589
importance of, 587–589
independent decision maker in, 600–601
mediation in, 600
minitrial in, 601
negotiation in, 590
non-binding resolution stage in, 590, 591, 600–602
notice provisions in, 594
open communications in, 594
partnering in, 593–594
prevention in, 590, 592–594
risk allocation in, 592
spectrum of, 589–591
standing neutrals in, 596–599
step chart, 589–590
step negotiations in, 594–595
system design, 603–604
unique needs in, of construction, 587
Disputes, public construction contracting and, 760, 804–806
Doctrine of Conditions, 365
Doctrine of Sanctity of Contract, 5–6
Drawings
defective, 622–625

deficient, requests for information and, 202–203
failure to comply with, 616–617
latent ambiguities in, 443
patent ambiguities in, 443
Spearin doctrine and, 49–51
DSCs. *See* Differing site conditions (DSCs)
Duty of coordination, 296
Duty to award to lowest bidder, 236
Duty to investigate site conditions, 476–478
Duty to mitigate damages, 745
Duty to perform changes, 444–446
Dynamo, 817n12

Early start letters, 109–110
Easement agreements, 37–38
Economic Loss Rule
  in Alabama, 662n43
  and architect authority, 201
  and architect role, 655
  in California, 667
  and contract administration, 679–683, 702–709
  damages in, 660–661
  and damage to other property test, 689–690
  and defective construction, 619, 624, 669–674, 684–695, 696–702
  defined, 659–660
  and Design-Bid-Build approach, 75
  and design professional services, 679–683
  in Florida, 665–666
  in Illinois, 704, 712–713
  and improper furnishing of materials, 674–679, 696–702
  limitation of, 668–669
  in Maryland, 692, 695
  in Massachusetts, 666, 667
  negligence and, 658
  negligent misrepresentation and, 709–715
  and privity of contract, 657, 665–666, 669–683
  proper application of, 661
  purpose of, 661–669
  scope of, 661–669
  and specialization, 655–656
  and subcontractor claims, 307–308
  and testing services, 679–683
  theory behind, 33
  tort law and, 657–659
  as umbrella term of doctrines, 664–665
  without privity of contract, 683–709
  workmanship and, 674–679, 696–702
Economic waste, 745–746
Eichleay formula, 732
EJCDC. *See* Engineers' Joint Contract Documents Committee (EJCDC)
Energy analysis using Building Information Modeling, 826
Engineer
  in accident compensation, 413–417
  as lead design professional, 146–147
Engineering consultants, in design team, 146
Engineer-Procure-Construct (EPC), 91, 103
Engineers, in design team, 21–22
Engineers' Joint Contract Documents Committee (EJCDC), 468, 515–516
Engineers' Joint Contract Documents Committee (EJCDC) forms, 119
Environmental analysis, 822
Environmental concerns, with building site, 42–43
EPC. *See* Engineer-Procure-Construct (EPC)
Equipment
  in cost-plus contracts, 262–263
  idle, damages and, 730–731
Equipment suppliers, mechanic's lien and, 543–544
Escrow, of bid documents, 595
Estimates, and cost-plus contracts, 266–267
Estoppel, promissory, 290, 724–726
Evidence of financing, 59–60
Exculpatory provisions
  in design agreement, 186–188
  with site conditions, 478–479
Excusable delays, 334–341

Expectation interest, 719–724
Express authority, 790–792
Extra work, defined, 426

FAA. *See* Federal Arbitration Act (FAA)
Facility management using Building Information Modeling, 828
Failure to perform, in termination of contract, 499
Fair Housing Act (FHA), accessibility and, 155
False Claims Act, 388–389, 763, 764–770
False Statements Act, 763, 771
FAR. *See* Federal Acquisition Regulation (FAR)
"Fatal four," 393
Federal Acquisition Regulation (FAR), 269, 429, 436, 439–440, 450, 459, 466–468, 761, 796–797
Federal Arbitration Act (FAA), 9, 604
Federal Disputes Clause, 805–806
Federal enclave doctrine, 762n9
Federal Tort Claims Act, 771
FHA. *See* Fair Housing Act (FHA)
Final completion, 348–350, 381–385
Financing, 57–59
Financing evidence, 59–60
Float, in scheduling, 321–322
Florida
  Americans with Disabilities Act compliance in, 155
  bid protests in, 241
  economic loss rule in, 666
Flow-down obligations and rights, 292–295
Flow-up provisions, 293–294
Fraud, public construction contracting and, 760, 763–771
Front loading, 364–365

GAI. *See* General agreement of indemnity (GAI)
Gantry Arm System, 840
General agreement of indemnity (GAI), 378
General Conditions of the Contract for Construction, 115

General liability insurance, 561–566
Georgia, mechanic's lien in, 549
Geotechnical information
  in owner role, 44–45
  in site conditions, 471
Gilgamesh, 2
Government. *See entries at* Public
Gramm-Leach-Bliley legislation, 558
Great San Francisco Earthquake of 1906, 8
Green codes, 156–158
Greenfield project, 40
Green Globes, 825
Guaranteed cost savings contracts, 250

Hammurabi's Code, 2
Handwritten portions of contract, 133–134
Hawaii, mechanic's lien in, 549
Heard Act, 6
Heat-loss analysis using Building Information Modeling, 822
Historically underutilized business zone (HUBZone), 796
Historic preservation, 158–159
Historic sites, 41–42
History of construction, 1–11
Hold harmless clause, 749
Holmes, Oliver Wendell, Jr., 12
Home office overhead, damages and, 731–733
HUBZone. *See* Historically underutilized business zone (HUBZone)
Hudson formula, 732–733

Idaho, mechanic's lien in, 549
Idle equipment, damages and, 730–731
IDM. *See* Initial Decision Maker (IDM)
Illinois
  archaeological/historic sites in, 41
  bid protests in, 241
  differing site conditions in, 490–492
  economic loss rule in, 704, 712–713
  mechanic's lien in, 533, 547–548
Immunity, of architect, in quasi-judicial functions, 221–222
Impacted as-planned, 354–355
Implied authority, 792–793

Implied contracts, 110–111
Implied warranty
   breach of, in defective construction, 618–619
   and defective construction, 631–634
   in design team contracting, 165–166
   to supply accurate information, 45–51
Improvement concept, in mechanic's lien, 536–540
Indemnification clauses, and liability limitations, 748–752
Indemnity
   risk allocation and, 418–421
   workers' compensation and, 422–423
Indemnity agreements, subcontractor, 299–301
Indemnity obligations, subcontractor, 299–302
Index pricing, 272
Indiana, mechanic's lien in, 539
Inferable standard, in contract, 138
Information Foundation Classes (IFCs), 818
Initial Decision Maker (IDM), 600–601
Inspections, in quality control, 209–214
Insurance
   American Institute of Architects requirements, 558–561
   builders risk, 566–567
   causes of loss in, 560
   commercial general liability, 559–560
   comprehensive general liability, 561–566
   contractual requirements for, 558–561
   in design agreement, 186
   Design-Build and, 89–90
   failure to secure, in termination of contract, 500
   general liability, 561–566
   in Owner Controlled Insurance Program, 558
   professional liability, 568
   property, 560
   regulation, 558
   risk allocation and, 417–418
   role of, 557–558
   subcontractor default, 585
   title, 29
   types of, 558
   waivers of subrogation with, 560–561, 567–568
   workers' compensation, 567
Insurance companies, 27–28
Insured, defined, 557
Insurer, defined, 557
Integrated Project Delivery (IPD), 96–99, 315–316, 810–811
Integration clause, 121–122
Interest, payment and, 379
Interim payment clauses, 275–276
IPD. *See* Integrated Project Delivery (IPD)

Jesus of Nazareth, 3n5, 3n6
Johnson, Samuel, 7n18
Joint checks, 375–377
Judicial indemnity authority, 299
Jury verdict method, in damages estimation, 742–743

Kansas, bidding process in, 230

Labor, in cost-plus contracts, 264–265
Labor price increases, 730
Landmark preservation, 158–159
Latent ambiguity, patent for, 443
LBC. *See* Living Building Challenge (LBC)
Lender, collateral assignment to, in contract, 135
Lender liability, 389–390
Lenders, construction, 25–27
Lender's mortgage, subordination of lien rights to, 58
Letters of credit, 584–585
Liability
   in design agreement, limitation of, 186–193
   in flow-down provisions, 294–295
   hold harmless clause and, 749
   indemnification clauses and, 748–752
   lender, 389–390
   limitation clause, 749
   limitations on, 748–756
   strict, inapplicability of, 159–160
   See also Damages

Liability insurance, 561–566, 568
Licensure, of design professionals, 147–151
Lien
　stop notice and, 374
　waivers, 374–375
　See also Mechanic's lien
Lien rights, subordination of, to lender's mortgage, 58
Life cycle costing, 250
Limitation of liability clause, 749
Liquidated damages, 384–385, 753–755
Liquidating agreements, 312–313
Living Building Challenge (LBC), 825, 826
Loan, construction, 57–60
Lowest bidder, duty to award to, 236

Manifestations of defective construction, defects vs., 613–614
Manufacturers approval, in quality control, 204
Manufacturers objection, in quality control, 204
Maryland
　Americans with Disabilities Act compliance in, 155
　bid protests in, 241
　design procurement in, 230
　economic loss rule in, 692, 695
Massachusetts, economic loss rule in, 666, 667
Material breach, in termination of contract, 499, 501–506
Material price escalation clauses, 274–275
Material price increases, damages and, 730
McNamara-O'Hara Service Contract Act, 797
Measured mile approach, 734–735
Mechanic's lien, 373–374
　in Alabama, 537
　amount of, 540–543
　bankruptcy and, 553–555
　in California, 530–531, 532–533, 546, 550–551, 554
　categories, 534–535
　and common law, 530
　contract in requirements for, 535–536
　in Delaware, 533
　derivative, 534
　entitlement to, 542–544
　equipment suppliers and, 543–544
　in Georgia, 549
　in Hawaii, 549
　hybrid, 534–535
　in Idaho, 549
　in Illinois, 533, 547–548
　improvement concept in, 536–540
　incorrect calculation of amount of, 541–542
　independent, 534
　in Indiana, 539
　interests in, 532
　interests subject to, 545–547
　lienability with, 544–545
　in Montana, 536
　in New Jersey, 537
　in New York, 533
　in Oklahoma, 535
　in Oregon, 533
　origin of, 529–531
　in Pennsylvania, 530, 534–535
　perfecting, 547–548
　priorities in, 549
　with public projects, 550–552
　release, 552–553
　requirements for, 535–544
　secondary expenses in, 541
　statutory framework for, 531–534
　in Texas, 535, 542
　title and, 530
　in Utah, 538
　waiver, 552–553
　in Washington, 543
Mediation, in dispute resolution, 600
Miller Act, 6
Minitrial, in dispute resolution, 601
Minnesota
　Americans with Disabilities Act compliance in, 667
　differing site conditions in, 480
　standard of care in, 161
Minority and Women Business Enterprises (MWBE), 244–247, 287–288

Misrepresentation
  economic loss rule and, 709–715
  of site conditions, 462–463
Mississippi
  Americans with Disabilities Act
    compliance in, 155
  notice of changes in, 437
Mistake, mutual, with site conditions,
    464–465
Mitigation, of damages, 745–748
Mixed pricing contracts, 271–272
Montana, mechanic's lien in, 536
Multiple Prime approach, 76, 78
Mutual mistake, with site conditions,
    464–465
MWBE. See Minority and Women
    Business Enterprises (MWBE)

National Association of Builders, 5–6, 9
National Building Information Model
    Standard Project Committee, 812
National Historic Preservation Act
    (NHPA), 42
National Institute of Building
    Sciences, 812
Nebraska, bid protests in, 241
Negligence
  active, and accident compensation,
    404–405
  contributory, 421–422
  economic loss rule and, 658
  and Occupational Health and Safety
    Act, 399–401
Negligence laws, 301
Negligent misrepresentation, economic
    loss rule and, 709–715
Negotiation phase, 172
Neutrals, in dispute resolution,
    596–599
Nevada, Americans with Disabilities Act
    compliance in, 241
New Jersey
  bid protests in, 241
  differing site conditions in, 486–488
  mechanic's lien in, 537
New York
  historic/landmark preservation in, 159

  indemnity and safety negligence
    in, 421
  mechanic's lien in, 533, 534,
    537–538, 540
  notice of changes in, 437
NHPA. See National Historic Preservation
    Act (NHPA)
19th century, 4–11
North Carolina
  bidding in, 249
  liens in, 371
North Dakota, standard of care in, 160

Observation of construction, by design
    professionals, defective construction
    claims and, 625–629
Occupational Health and Safety Act
    (OSHA)
  in civil litigation, 397–401
  design professionals and, 397
  employer/employee relationship
    in, 396
  negligence and, 399–401
  safety and, 395–397
OCIP. See Owner Controlled Insurance
    Program (OCIP)
Ohio, bid protests in, 242
Oklahoma
  design professional selection in, 230
  mechanic's lien in, 535
Oral contract, 109. See also Contracts
    and contracting
Oregon, mechanic's liens in, 533
OSHA. See Occupational Health and
    Safety Act (OSHA)
Overhead
  in cost-plus contracts, 265–266
  fixed fee for, 265
  percentage of contract for, 265–266
Overpayment, 377–378
Owner
  acceptance of work by, 382–383
  accident compensation and, 405–409
  archaeological sites and, 41–42
  building site in role of, 36–43
  conditional assignment of subcontract
    to, 295

Owner, *continued*
  construction by, in contract, 140
  in construction process, 18–19
  in contract, 134
  defective construction claims by, against contractor, 616–620
  in design team contracting, 145, 174–175
  environmental concerns in role of, 42–43
  geotechnical information in role of, 44–45
  historic sites and, 41–42
  implied warranty of, to supply accurate information, 45–51
  liability of, for architect's acts, 201
  overpayment and, 377–378
  payment in role of, 57–60
  payment obligations of, 371–378
  private, 19
  project delivery system selection and capability of, 102–103
  public, 18–19
  right of, to site, 38
  in subcontractor selection, 285–286
  in supplier selection, 285–286
  surveys in role of, 44
  termination of contract by, 509–511
  title in role of, 38–39
  utility availability in role of, 40–41
  zoning in role of, 39–40
Owner-contractor agreement, 115, 120
Owner Controlled Insurance Program (OCIP), 27n38, 558
Owner-furnished items, in contract, 139–140
Owner's damages, in breach of contract, 719–722
Ownership of design documents, 175–180
Owner's program
  design specifications in, 55
  overview of, 52–53
  performance specifications in, 56
  project budget in, 53–54
  proprietary specifications in, 57
  reference standard specifications in, 55–56
  schedule in, 53–54
  specifications in, 54–57

Pacing, 342–343
Parol evidence rule, 125–127
Partial negligence statutes, 301
Partnering, in dispute resolution, 593–594
Pass-through system, and subcontractor claims, 308–312
Patent ambiguity, latent vs., 443
Pay-if-paid clauses, 304, 385–387
Payment
  acceptance of work and, 382–383
  applications for, 366–368
  and architect certification, 367–368
  basis for, 362–365
  changes and, 379
  contractor acceptance of, 383–384
  and contractor certification, 367
  in cost-plus contract, 363
  in design agreement, 185
  and Doctrine of Conditions, 365
  and False Claims Act, 388–389
  final, 381–385
  final completion and, 381–385
  front loading and, 364–365
  interest and, 379
  joint checks in, 375–377
  lender liability and, 389–390
  liquidated damages and, 384–385
  mechanic's lien and, 373–375
  method of securing subcontractor, 305–306
  overpayment, 377–378
  overview of, 361–362
  owner's obligation in, 371–378
  percentage of completion, 259–260
  periodic progress, 364
  process, 302–303, 365–381
  progress, in contract administration, 215–216
  and Prompt Payment Act, 387–388
  provisions, risk of, 304–305
  retainage and, 369–371
  risk of owner failure in, 303
  and schedule of values, 364–365
  in stipulated-sum contracts, 259–260

stop work and, 372–373
to subcontractors, 302–306
substantial completion and, 347–348, 379–381
substantial performance and, 379–381
to suppliers, 302–306
and termination of contract, 500–501
three-party arrangement in, 302–303
timing of, 371–373
in unit-price contract, 362
See also Mechanic's lien
Payment bonds, 578–579
Pay when paid, 385–387
Pennsylvania
mechanic's lien in, 530, 534–535
Spearin doctrine in, 49
Percentage of completion payments, in stipulated-sum contracts, 259–260
Performance, time and, 319–320
Performance bond surety obligations, 571–577
Performance certification, in contract administration, 217–218
Performance criteria, in Design-Build, 88
Performance specifications
defective construction and, 635–636
design specifications vs., 166–168
in design team contracting, 166–168
in owner's program, 56
Periodic progress payment, 364
PFI. *See* Private finance initiative (PFI)
Practical impossibility, 340–341
Pre-bid conference, 232–233
Prevailing wages, 796–797
Price increases, damages and, 730
Pricing. *See* Contract pricing
Prime contractor, accident compensation and, 409–413
Private finance initiative (PFI), 92
Private procurement, in contractor selection, 226–227
Privatization, 250
Privity system, 313–314
Professional liability insurance, 568
Profit
in cost-plus contracts, 265–266
fixed fee for, 265

lost, damages and, 733–734
percentage of contract for, 265–266
Progress payments, approval of, in contract administration, 215–216
Project budget, in owner's program, 53–54
Project delivery systems
commercial importance of, 67–69
compensation mechanisms and, 101–102
construction procurement and, 101
contractor selection and, 226
cost in, 67–68
design quality in, 68–69
evolution of, 64–67
and industry sector customs, 103
innovative approaches in, 66, 91–99
legal importance of, 104–105
nomenclature for, 65–66
overview of, 63–64
owner capability and, 102–103
and reduction in claims, 69
selection constraints with, 101–103
selection of, 69–70, 100
time in, 68
Project Execution Plan (PxP), 837–840
Project site. *See* Building site
Project team, 30–33
Promissory estoppel, 290, 724–726
Prompt Payment Act, 387–388
Property insurance, 560
Proprietary specifications, in owner's program, 57
Protests, public construction contracting and, 760, 804–806
Public construction contracting
actual authority and, 760, 786–795
Christian doctrine and, 761–762
criminal law and, 760, 763–771
disputes and, 760, 804–806
fraud and, 760, 763–771
private vs., 760
protests and, 760, 804–806
regulatory requirements with, 760, 761–763
socioeconomic requirements with, 760, 795–804
sovereign acts and, 760, 778–785

Public construction contracting, *continued*
  sovereign immunity and, 760, 771–777
  statutory requirements with, 760, 761–763
Public owners, 18–19
Public-Private Partnership, 92–96
  bankruptcies in, 94n37
  common variations in, 96
  concession agreement in, 94
  contract in, 94, 96
  risk factors in, 95–96
  selection factors in, 95
Public procurement
  advertising in, 231
  "best value" awards in, 249–251
  bid package in, 231–235
  bid protests in, 240–243
  construction management in, 248–249
  in contractor selection, 227–252
  Design-Build in, 247–248
  design professionals in, 228–230
  and mechanic's lien, 550–552
  private vs., 227–228
Punitive damages, 744
PxP. *See* Project Execution Plan (PxP)

Qualifications-based selection, 250
Quality control
  aesthetic effects and, 209
  contract administration and, 203–214
  inspections in, 209–214
  manufacturers approval in, 204
  manufacturers objection in, 204
  review and approval procedures in, 203
  shop drawings in, 204–209
  site visits in, 209–214
  subcontractor approval in, 204
  subcontractor objection in, 204
  substitutions in, 204–209
  suppliers approval in, 204
  suppliers objection in, 204
Quantum meruit, 111, 148–151, 426, 727–728
Quasi-contracts, 110–111
Qui tam, 763

Ratification, changes and, 434–435
RCRA. *See* Resource Conservation and Recovery Act (RCRA)
Recordkeeping, damages and, 744–745
Reference standard specifications, in owner's program, 55–56
Regenerative buildings, 825
Regulation, of design professionals, 147–151
Rejection of work
  in contract administration, 216
  improper, as change, 443–444
Release, of mechanic's lien, 552–553
Reliance interest, 724–726
"Repeatedly" requirement, in termination of contract, 510–511
Requests for information (RFIs), 202–203
Resource Conservation and Recovery Act (RCRA), 43
Responsibility, for defective construction, 614–615
Restitution interest, 726–727
Retainage, 369–371
Reverse online bidding, 251–252
RFIs. *See* Requests for information (RFIs)
RhinoBIM, 816n10
Right to cure, and termination of contract, 514–515
Risk
  allocation, 417–423, 459–461, 592
  assessment, in Building Information Modeling, 834–837
  assumption of, 421–422
  mitigation, with Building Information Modeling, 827
  of owner's failure to pay, 303
  safety and, 417–423
  in stipulated-sum contracts, 257–258
  transfer, 417–423
Risk of payment provisions, 304–305
Roman law, 2–3

Safety
  accident prevention in, 394–402
  and compensation for accidents, 403–417

contractual responsibility for, 402
"fatal four" in, 393
insurance and, 417–418
Occupational Safety and Health Act in, 395–397
and risk allocation/transfer, 417–423
state legislation in, 394–395
and workers' compensation, 403
See also Accident compensation
Safety planning, with Building Information Modeling, 827–828
San Francisco Earthquake of 1906, 8
Satisfaction, changes and, 450–453
Schedule and scheduling
critical path method, 320–324
float in, 321–322
legal significance of, 325–326
in owner's program, 53–54
updates, 325
See also Delays
Schedule of values, 364–365
Schematic design phase, 170–171
Scholarship, construction law, 15–16
Scope of work, and contract pricing, 276–277
SDBs. *See* Small disadvantaged businesses (SDBs)
Sealed bid, 8
Self-performed work
and contract pricing, 278
in cost-plus contracts, 263–264
Sermon on the Mount, 3n5
Sharing-of-savings clause, 277
Should-cost estimates, 736
Site. *See* Building site
Site conditions
allocation of risk of, 458
bid package and, 233–234
in commercial agreements, 468–469
in common law, 459–465
concealment of, 463–464
contracts with clause for, 459–461
in Design-Build contracts, 483–486
disclaimers with, 478–479
duty to investigate, 476–478
exculpatory language with, 478–479

in Federal Acquisition Regulation, 466–468
indications of, 461–465, 470–472
misrepresentation of, 462–463
mutual mistake with, 464–465
notice with, 479–480
physical, 471–472
pricing and, 458–459
regulatory frameworks for, 465–469
representations of, 461–465
superior knowledge of, 463–464
of unusual nature, 475–476
and variation in estimated quantities clauses, 480–482
and warranty of specifications, 461–462
See also Differing site conditions
Site indications clause, 459–461
Site visits, in quality control, 209–214
SketchUp, 816n10, 817
Small disadvantaged businesses (SDBs), 287
Small tool allowance, in cost-plus contracts, 263
Socioeconomic "codes," 154–159
Socioeconomic requirements, with public construction contracting, 760, 795–804
Soil mechanics, 8–9
Solar analysis, 823
Sole negligence laws, 301
South Carolina, bid protests in, 155
Sovereign acts, public construction contracting and, 760, 778–785
Sovereign immunity, public construction contracting and, 760, 771–777
Spearin doctrine, 45–51, 630–638, 810–811
Specialization, economic loss rule and, 655–656
Specifications
change orders and, 442–443
defective, 622–625
failure to comply with, 616–617
in owner's program, 54–57
Spearin doctrine and, 49–51, 634–635
warranty of, site conditions and, 461–462

Standard of care
  common law, 160–164
  contractual, 164–165
  in design team contracting, 159–166
  general statement of, 160–161
  nature of, 159–160
  proof of, 161–163
  strict liability and, 159–160
  violation of, 161–163
Standing neutrals, in dispute resolution, 596–599
State courts, differing site conditions treatment in, 486–493
State legislation, in accident prevention, 394–395
Statutes of limitations, defective construction claims and, 638–647
Statutes of repose, defective construction claims and, 647–649
Stipulated-sum contracts
  abuse of, 259–260
  in contract pricing, 256–260
  percentage of completion payments in, 259–260
  risks in, 257–258
  scope limitations in, 257–259
Stop notice, 374
Stop work, payment and, 372–373
Strict liability, inapplicability of, 159–160
Subcontracted work
  avoiding obligation of, 298
  coordination of, 296–298
  in cost-plus contracts, 261–262
Subcontractor approval, in quality control, 204
Subcontractor bidding
  and enforcement of bid by subcontractor, 291–292
  and prime contractor enforcement of bid, 289–291
  process, 288–289
Subcontractor claims
  barriers to, 307–308
  and liquidating agreements, 312–313
  pass-through system and, 308–312
  problem of, 306–307
Subcontractor default insurance, 585

Subcontractor indemnity agreements, 299–301
Subcontractor indemnity obligations, 299–302
Subcontractor objection, in quality control, 204
Subcontractors
  flow-down and, 292–295
  owner in selection of, 285–286
  payment to, 302–306
  restrictions on selection of, 286–287
  selection of, 285–288
  socioeconomic considerations in selection of, 287–288
  suppliers vs., 283–285
Subcontractors, in construction team, 24–25
Substantial completion, 343–348, 379–381
Substantial performance, 379–381
Superior knowledge, of site conditions, 463–464
Suppliers
  flow-down and, 292–295
  owner in selection of, 285–286
  payment to, 302–306
  restrictions on selection of, 286–287
  selection of, 285–288
  socioeconomic considerations in selection of, 287–288
  subcontractors vs., 283–285
  in Uniform Commercial Code, 284
Suppliers approval, in quality control, 204
Suppliers objection, in quality control, 204
Supremacy Clause, 604
Sureties, 28, 377, 517–518, 579–583
Surety bond obligations, 571–577
Surety bonds, 568–570
Surveys, in owner role, 44
Sustainability analysis, in Building Information Modeling, 822–827
Sustainability Certification, 158
Sustainability Documentation, 158
Sustainable design, 250

Team assembly, 30–32
Tennessee, Americans with Disabilities Act compliance in, 155

Termination, contractor, architect role in, 219–220
Termination, in design agreement, 193–194
Termination of contract
  American Institute of Architects forms in, 507–511
  architect in, 511
  catchall with, 511
  ConsensusDocs forms in, 511–515
  by contractor, 507–509
  for convenience, 521–527
  damages and, 516–517
  Engineers' Joint Contract Documents Committee forms in, 515–516
  failure to perform in, 499
  insurance and, 500
  material breach in, 499, 501–506
  by owner, 509–511
  payment disputes and, 500–501
  post-termination issues with, 516–521
  "repeatedly" requirement in, 510–511
  responsibilities after, 516
  right to, under common law, 498–506
  right to, under commonly used forms, 506–516
  and right to cure, 514–515
  specified breach in, 514
  surety and, 517–518
  and survival, 515
  wrongful, 518–521
Terminology, in contract interpretation, 133–134
Terzaghi, Carl, 8, 8n23
Texas
  Americans with Disabilities Act compliance in, 155
  implied warranty in, 632n39
  indemnity in, 421
  mechanic's lien in, 535, 542
Third-party beneficiaries, in contract, 134–135
3D printing, and Building Information Modeling, 840–843
Time and material pricing, 273
  and change administration, 448–449
  change orders and, 438–441

Time and motion studies, 736
Time and timeliness
  of commencement, 326–328
  for completion, 326–328
  for completion, extension of, 334–341
  for completion, waiver of, 328–334
  float and, 321–322
  performance and, 319–320
  in project delivery systems, 68
  scheduling and, 319–320
  See also Delays
Time impact analysis, 355
Title
  mechanic's lien and, 530
  in owner role, 38–39
Title insurance, 29
Tolling, and defective construction, 645–646
Tool allowance, in cost-plus contracts, 263
Tort claims
  damages and, 728
  in defective construction, 619
Tort liability, accident compensation and, 404–405
Total cost method, in damages estimation, 736–741
Trade Agreements Act, 797
Transaction structure, 30–32
Truthful Cost or Pricing Data Act, 761
Turnkey, 91

UCC. *See* Uniform Commercial Code (UCC)
Unbalanced bidding, 270–271
Unified Soil Classification System, 9
Uniform Arbitration Act, 9
Uniform Commercial Code (UCC), 131–132, 284, 584
Uniform Contract of the American Institute of Architects, 9
Unit-price contracts, 268–271, 362, 439
Unjust enrichment, 726–727
Uruk, 2
Usage, in contracts, 132
Utah, mechanic's lien in, 538
Utilities, availability of, 40–41

Value-based contracting, 250–251
Variation in Estimated Quantities (VEQ) clauses, 269–270, 480–482
VEQ. *See* Variation in Estimated Quantities (VEQ) clauses
Virginia, differing site conditions in, 488–490
Vitruvius, 3n6

Waiver
  of bidding irregularities, 236–238
  of claims, 382–383
  consequential damages, 753
  consequential damages, in design agreement, 189–193
  lien, 374–375
  of mechanic's lien, 552–553
  of subrogation, 560–561, 567–568
  of time for completion, 328–334
Warranty, conflicting, and defective construction, 630–638
Warranty, express, breach of, in defective construction, 617
Warranty, implied
  breach of, in defective construction, 618–619
  in design team contracting, 165–166
  and site conditions, 461–462
  to supply accurate information, 45–51
Washington, mechanic's lien, 543
Waste, economic, 745–746
Weather, in delay, 340
West Virginia, differing site conditions in, 486n101
Wetlands, 43
Windows analysis, 356
WMBE, 796
Workers' compensation, 403, 422–423
Workers' compensation insurance, 567
Work rejection, in contract administration, 216
Work stop, in contract administration, 216
Wrongful termination of contract, 518–521

Zoning, as owner responsibility, 39–40